Organizational Behavior

NINTH EDITION

Organizational Behavior

NINTH EDITION

Don Hellriegel
Texas A&M University

John W. Slocum, Jr.
Southern Methodist University

Richard W. Woodman
Texas A&M University

South-Western College Publishing
Thomson Learning™

Australia • Canada • Denmark • Japan • Mexico • New Zealand • Philippines
Puerto Rico • Singapore • South Africa • Spain • United Kingdom • United States

Organizational Behavior, 9/e, by Hellriegel, Slocum, and Woodman

Vice President/Publisher: Jack W. Calhoun
Executive Editor: John Szilagyi
Developmental Editor: Judith O'Neill
Marketing Manager: Rob Bloom
Production Editor: Sandra Gangelhoff
Manufacturing Coordinator: Sandee Milewski
Media Technology Editor: Kurt Gerdenich
Media Developmental Editor: Vicky True
Media Production Editor: Kristen Meere
Internal Design: Rokusek Design
Cover Design: Rokusek Design
Cover Illustration: John Rokusek
Production House: Pre-Press Company, Inc.
Compositor: Pre-Press Company, Inc.
Printer: Von Hoffmann Press, Inc.

Printed in the United States of America
1 2 3 4 5 03 02 01 00

For more information contact South-Western College Publishing, 5101 Madison Road, Cincinnati, Ohio, 45227 or find us on the Internet at http://www.swcollege.com

For permission to use material from this text or product, contact us by
• telephone: 1-800-730-2214
• fax: 1-800-730-2215
• web: http://www.thomsonrights.com

Library of Congress Cataloging-in-Publication Data

Hellriegel, Don.
Organizational behavior / Don Hellriegel, John W. Slocum, Jr., Richard W. Woodman.—9th ed.
p. cm.
Includes bibliographical references and index.
ISBN 0-324-06956-1 (package)
ISBN 0-324-00977-1 (text only)
ISBN 0-324-06776-3 (CD-ROM only)
1. Organizational behavior. I. Slocum, John W. II. Woodman, Richard W. III. Title.

HD58.7 .H44 2000

158.7—dc21 00-038745

This book is printed on acid-free paper.

To Jill, Kim, and Lori (DH)
Christopher, Bradley, and Jonathan (JWS)
David and Anna (RWW)

Brief Contents

Preface *xxiii*

Chapter 1 Introduction to Organizational Behavior 2

Part 1: Individual Processes 35

Chapter 2 Personality and Attitudes 36
Chapter 3 Perception and Attribution 66
Chapter 4 Learning and Reinforcement 98
Chapter 5 Motivation in the Work Setting 128
Chapter 6 Motivating Performance: Goal Setting and Reward Systems 162
Chapter 7 Work Stress 190

Part 2: Group and Interpersonal Processes 221

Chapter 8 Group and Team Behavior 222
Chapter 9 Power and Political Behavior 264
Chapter 10 Conflict and Negotiation 292
Chapter 11 Leadership: Foundations 322
Chapter 12 Leadership: Contemporary Developments 354
Chapter 13 Interpersonal Communication 376

Part 3: Organizational Processes 413

Chapter 14 Decision Making in Organizations 414
Chapter 15 Job Design 444
Chapter 16 Organization Design 472
Chapter 17 Organizational Culture 510
Chapter 18 Organizational Change 542

Appendix: Tools and Techniques for Studying Organizational Behavior 581

Integrating Cases C-1

Author Index I-1

Subject and Organizational Index I-11

Internet Organization Index I-27

CONTENTS

Preface xxiii

Chapter 1 **Introduction to Organizational Behavior 2**

Preview Case: Cynthia Danaher 3

THE MANAGING SELF COMPETENCY 6

Core Components 6

- ***Competency: Managing Self****—Ford's Competency Program*

Career Management 7

THE MANAGING COMMUNICATION COMPETENCY 8

Core Components 8

Relationship to Managerial Roles 9

- ***Competency: Managing Communication****—The Microcommunication*

THE MANAGING DIVERSITY COMPETENCY 10

Core Components 11

Categories of Diversity 11

- ***Competency: Managing Diversity****—Boundaryless Behavior*

Changing Workforce and Customers 14

Gender 14

Race and Ethnicity 15

Age 16

THE MANAGING ETHICS COMPETENCY 16

Core Components 16

Ethical Dilemmas 17

- ***Competency: Managing Ethics****—Michael Roth at MONY Group*

THE MANAGING ACROSS CULTURES COMPETENCY 17

Core Components 18

Individualism–Collectivism 19

- ***Competency: Managing Across Cultures****—China's Collectivism*

THE MANAGING TEAMS COMPETENCY 20

Core Components 20

Individualism and Teams 22

THE MANAGING CHANGE COMPETENCY 23

Core Components 23

Technological Forces 24

- ***Competency: Managing Change****—Embracing Speed*

LEARNING FRAMEWORK 24

Environmental Forces 25

Individual Processes 25

Team and Interpersonal Processes 27

Organizational Processes 28

CHAPTER SUMMARY 28

Key Terms and Concepts 30

Discussion Questions 30

DEVELOPING COMPETENCIES 31

- ***Competency: Managing Diversity****—Attitudes Toward Diversity*
- ***Competency: Managing Communication****—James Halpin of CompUSA*

Part 1: Individual Processes 35

Chapter 2

Personality and Attitudes 36

Preview Case: Omigosh! Individual Differences! 37
SOURCES OF PERSONALITY DIFFERENCES 38
Heredity 39
Environment 39
PERSONALITY STRUCTURE 41
PERSONALITY AND BEHAVIOR 42
- ***Competency: Managing Across Cultures****—A Letter from the Swedish Sales Force*

Self-Esteem 42
Locus of Control 44
Goal Orientation 45
Introversion and Extroversion 47
Dogmatism and Authoritarianism 47
Organizational Implications 48
- ***Competency: Managing Teams****—Personality and Teams at Hewlett-Packard*

The Person and the Situation 49
ATTITUDES AND BEHAVIOR 49
Components of Attitudes 49
Links to Behavior 50
Behavioral Intentions Model 50
WORK ATTITUDES 51
Job Satisfaction 51
- ***Competency: Managing Communication****—A Happy Staff Leads to Happy Customers*

Organizational Commitment 54
- ***Competency: Managing Self****—Winning Mother's Loyalty and Commitment*

INDIVIDUAL DIFFERENCES AND ETHICAL BEHAVIOR 54
Types of Management Ethics 56
- ***Competency: Managing Ethics****—Who's Your Phone Company?*

Establishing Ethical Attitudes 57
CHAPTER SUMMARY 58
Key Terms and Concepts 59
Discussion Questions 59
DEVELOPING COMPETENCIES 60
- ***Competency: Managing Self****—Assessing the Big Five*
- ***Competency: Managing Self****—Emotional IQ*

Chapter 3

Perception and Attribution 66

Preview Case: Your World Is Not My World 67
THE PERCEPTUAL PROCESS 68
- ***Competency: Managing Communication****—Subtle Signals Sent by Office Design*

PERCEPTUAL SELECTION 71
External Factors 71
Internal Factors 72
- ***Competency: Managing Across Cultures****—Time Perception*

PERCEPTUAL ORGANIZATION 75
PERSON PERCEPTION 76
The Person Perceived 77
The Perceiver 77
The Situation 78
Impression Management 78
- ***Competency: Managing Self****—Alan Page at Mott's*

PERCEPTUAL ERRORS 80
Accuracy of Judgment 80
Perceptual Defense 81
Stereotyping 81
• ***Competency: Managing Diversity****—Stereotypes of Women at Work*
Halo Effect 83
Projection 83
Expectancy Effects 83
ATTRIBUTIONS: PERCEIVING THE CAUSES OF BEHAVIOR 84
The Attribution Process 85
Internal Versus External Causes of Behavior 86
Attributions of Success and Failure 88
• ***Competency: Managing Self****—You're Fired!*
CHAPTER SUMMARY 90
Key Terms and Concepts 90
Discussion Questions 91
DEVELOPING COMPETENCIES 91
• ***Competency: Managing Diversity****—Measuring Perceptions of Women as Managers*
• ***Competency: Managing Ethics****—The Foundation for New Era Philanthropy*

Chapter 4 Learning and Reinforcement 98
Preview Case: *Dialing for Dollars 99*
TYPES OF LEARNING 100
Classical Conditioning 100
Operant Conditioning 102
Social Cognitive Theory 102
• ***Competency: Managing Teams****—Steelcase Incorporated*
• ***Competency: Managing Self****—The Challenge Course*
CONTINGENCIES OF REINFORCEMENT 106
Positive Reinforcement 107
• ***Competency: Managing Change****—Columbia Medical Center of Plano*
Organizational Rewards 110
• ***Competency: Managing Across Cultures****—Amway in Hungary*
Negative Reinforcement 111
Omission 112
Punishment 112
Using Contingencies of Reinforcement 115
SCHEDULES OF REINFORCEMENT 116
Continuous and Intermittent Reinforcement 116
Fixed Interval Schedule 116
Variable Interval Schedule 116
Fixed Ratio Schedule 117
Variable Ratio Schedule 117
Comparison of Intermittent Reinforcement Schedules 117
BEHAVIORAL MODIFICATION 118
Pinpointing Relevant Behaviors 118
Charting Behavior 119
Choosing a Contingency of Reinforcement 120
Problem Solved? 120
• ***Competency: Managing Communication****—Manufacturing in Eastern Europe*
Behavioral Modification Issues 121
CHAPTER SUMMARY 123
Key Terms and Concepts 124
Discussion Questions 124

DEVELOPING COMPETENCIES 125
- *Competency: Managing Self—What Is Your Self-Efficacy?*
- *Competency: Managing Ethics—Medical Incentives*
- *Competency: Managing Change—Westinghouse*

Chapter 5 Motivation in the Work Setting 128
Preview Case: How Starbucks Motivates Employees 129
THE BASIC MOTIVATIONAL PROCESS 130
Core Phases of the Process 132
Motivational Challenges 133
CONTENT MODELS OF MOTIVATION 134
Needs Hierarchy Model 134
ERG Model 136
- *Competency: Managing Across Cultures—A Tale of Two Plants in Romania*
Achievement Motivation Model 139
- *Competency: Managing Self—John Schnatter of Papa John's Pizza*
Motivator-Hygiene Model 142
Comparisons Among Content Models 145
PROCESS MODELS OF MOTIVATION 146
Expectancy Model 146
- *Competency: Managing Communication—The Walt Disney Company*
Equity Model 150
- *Competency: Managing Ethics—To Steal or Not: That's the Question*
Comparisons Among Process Models 156
CHAPTER SUMMARY 156
Key Terms and Concepts 157
Discussion Questions 158
DEVELOPING COMPETENCIES 158
- *Competency: Managing Self—What Do You Want from Your Job?*
- *Competency: Managing Teams—SEI Investments*

Chapter 6 Motivating Performance: Goal Setting and Reward Systems 162
Preview Case: Marriott Hotels 163
BASICS OF GOAL SETTING 164
Importance of Goal Setting 164
Importance of Stakeholders 165
Customer Service Goals 166
- *Competency: Managing Communication—Fruit of the Loom*
MODEL OF GOAL SETTING AND PERFORMANCE 167
Challenge 168
- *Competency: Managing Teams—NASCAR Racing*
Moderators 169
Mediators 171
Performance 172
- *Competency: Managing Ethics—Sundstrand*
Rewards 172
Satisfaction 174
Significance in Practice 174
MANAGEMENT BY OBJECTIVES 174
Goal Setting 175
Diversity and Goal Setting 176
Participation and Implementation 177
Performance Appraisal and Feedback 177
Significance in Practice 178

REWARD SYSTEMS IN HIGH-PERFORMANCE WORK SYSTEMS 178
Gain-Sharing and Profit-Sharing Plans 179
Flexible Benefit Plans 180
Banking Time Off 181
Skill-Based Pay 181
Significance in Practice 182
• *Competency: Managing Across Cultures—Reward Practices in Different Countries*
CHAPTER SUMMARY 184
Key Terms and Concepts 185
Discussion Questions 185
DEVELOPING COMPETENCIES 185
• *Competency: Managing Self—Goal-Setting Questionnaire*
• *Competency: Managing Change—Improving Safety*

Chapter 7 Work Stress 190
Preview Case: Stress on the Job 191
NATURE OF STRESS 192
Fight-or-Flight Response 192
The Stress Experience 193
SOURCES OF STRESS 194
• *Competency: Managing Across Cultures—Siesta Sunset*
Work Stressors 194
• *Competency: Managing Change—How About Creating Saner Workloads?*
• *Competency: Managing Self—Technology Workers and Stress*
Life Stressors 200
EFFECTS OF STRESS 201
Stress and Health 202
Stress and Performance 202
• *Competency: Managing Self—"Just Enough but Not Too Much"*
Stress and Job Burnout 205
• *Competency: Managing Communication—Management Myths That Lead to Burnout*
PERSONALITY AND STRESS 206
The Type A Personality 209
The Hardy Personality 209
STRESS MANAGEMENT 210
Individual Methods 210
Organizational Methods 211
• *Competency: Managing Self—Employees Who Value Time*
Wellness Programs 213
CHAPTER SUMMARY 215
Key Terms and Concepts 216
Discussion Questions 216
DEVELOPING COMPETENCIES 217
• *Competency: Managing Self—Assessing Your Stress Level*
• *Competency: Managing Change—Stress Management at Metropolitan Hospital*

Part 2: Group and Interpersonal Processes 221

Chapter 8 Group and Team Behavior 222
Preview Case: CRI's Team System 223
TYPES OF GROUPS AND TEAMS 224
Basic Types of Groups 224

- ***Competency: Managing Diversity**—Informal Practices and Black Managers*

Basic Types of Teams 226

- ***Competency: Managing Teams**—Whole Foods Markets' Self-Managed Teams*

VIRTUAL TEAMS 229

Core Features 231

Technology Links 231

- ***Competency: Managing Across Cultures**—Global Virtual Teams*

DEVELOPMENTAL STAGES OF TEAMS 232

Forming Stage 233

Storming Stage 234

Norming Stage 235

Performing Stage 235

Adjourning Stage 235

INFLUENCES ON TEAM EFFECTIVENESS 236

Content 236

Goals 237

Team Size 238

Team Member Roles and Diversity 238

- ***Competency: Managing Change**—IBM's Planned Diversity Initiatives*

Norms 242

Cohesiveness 243

Leadership 245

- ***Competency: Managing Self**—Joan McCoy Learns Team Leadership*

TEAM DECISION MAKING 246

Self-Managing Team Decision-Making Model 248

Assessment of Model 250

GUIDING TEAM CREATIVITY 252

Nominal Group Technique 252

Traditional Brainstorming 253

Electronic Brainstorming 253

- ***Competency: Managing Communication**—FedEx Brainstorms Electronically*

CHAPTER SUMMARY 255

Key Terms and Concepts 256

Discussion Questions 256

DEVELOPING COMPETENCIES 257

- ***Competency: Managing Teams**—Team Assessment*
- ***Competency: Managing Teams**—Artisan Industries Team*

Chapter 9 **Power and Political Behavior 264**

***Preview Case:** Ronald Szoc Learns About Power and Politics* 265

POWER 266

- ***Competency: Managing Change**—Revenge of the Nerds*

INTERPERSONAL SOURCES OF POWER 267

Reward Power 268

Coercive Power 268

Legitimate Power 269

Expert Power 270

Referent Power 270

Relationships Among Power Sources 270

STRUCTURAL SOURCES OF POWER 271

Knowledge as Power 272

- ***Competency: Managing Across Cultures**—Workplace Democracy in Africa*

Resources as Power 273

Decision Making as Power 273

Networks as Power 274
Lower Level Employee Power 275
• ***Competency: Managing Diversity**—Bilingual Employees Acquire Power*
THE EFFECTIVE USE OF POWER 277
POLITICAL BEHAVIOR 279
• ***Competency: Managing Change**—The Politics of Innovation*
Organizational Politics 279
Forces Creating Political Behavior 281
• ***Competency: Managing Ethics**—The Politics of Employee Appraisal*
PERSONALITY AND POLITICAL BEHAVIOR 284
Need for Power 284
Machiavellianism 284
Locus of Control 285
Risk-Seeking Propensity 285
• ***Competency: Managing Across Cultures**—Comparing Chinese and American Risk Preferences*
CHAPTER SUMMARY 286
Key Terms and Concepts 287
Discussion Questions 287
DEVELOPING COMPETENCIES 287
• ***Competency: Managing Self**—How Much Power Do You Have in Your Group?*
• ***Competency: Managing Change**—The Art of Persuasion*

Chapter 10 Conflict and Negotiation 292
***Preview Case:** Terry Peters 293*
CONFLICT MANAGEMENT 294
Varieties of Conflict 294
Attitudes Toward Conflict 295
• ***Competency: Managing Change**—Motorola's Dilemma with Retailers*
LEVELS OF CONFLICT 297
Intrapersonal Conflict 297
Interpersonal Conflict 299
• ***Competency: Managing Self**—Personalities That Create Conflict in the Office*
Intragroup Conflict 300
Intergroup Conflict 301
• ***Competency: Managing Diversity**—Gender Issues in CPA Firms*
INTERPERSONAL CONFLICT HANDLING STYLES 302
Avoiding Style 303
Forcing Style 304
• ***Competency: Managing Ethics**—Whistle-Blowers as Objects of the Forcing Style*
Accommodating Style 306
Collaborating Style 306
Compromising Style 307
Effectiveness of the Styles 307
NEGOTIATION IN CONFLICT MANAGEMENT 308
Types of Negotiations 308
• ***Competency: Managing Self**—Negotiating Nice*
Negotiator's Dilemma 310
Negotiating Across Cultures 311
• ***Competency: Managing Across Cultures**—The Chinese Approach to Negotiation*
Mediation 313
CHAPTER SUMMARY 314
Key Terms and Concepts 315
Discussion Questions 315

DEVELOPING COMPETENCIES 316
- *Competency: Managing Self—Conflict Handling Styles*
- *Competency: Managing Self—Intervening in Employee Disputes*

Chapter 11 Leadership: Foundations 322
Preview Case: Carly Fiorina Leads HP 323
ESSENTIALS OF LEADERSHIP 324
Leadership and Management 324
Power and Follower Behavior 326
- *Competency: Managing Self—Lloyd Ward Leads Maytag*

BASIC LEADERSHIP MODELS 329
Traits Model of Leadership 329
Behavioral Model of Leadership 330
- *Competency: Managing Communication—Douglas McKenna on Leadership*

Contrasts with Contingency Models 331
FIEDLER'S CONTINGENCY MODEL 333
Group Atmosphere 334
Task Structure 334
Position Power 334
Leadership Style 334
Implications and Limitations 335
- *Competency: Managing Ethics—Stephen Hardis's Leadership in Ethics*

HERSEY AND BLANCHARD'S SITUATIONAL MODEL 336
Leadership Styles and Followers 337
Implications and Limitations 339
- *Competency: Managing Across Cultures—Ferdinand Piëch's Leadership of VW*

VROOM-JAGO LEADERSHIP MODEL 339
Leadership Styles 339
Situational Variables 341
Main Features of the Model 342
- *Competency: Managing Change—Brooke McCurdy's Leadership*

Implications and Limitations 344
DIFFERENCES IN THE THREE CONTINGENCY MODELS 345
Leader Behaviors 345
Contingency Variables 346
Leadership Effectiveness 346
CHAPTER SUMMARY 346
Key Terms and Concepts 347
Discussion Questions 348
DEVELOPING COMPETENCIES 348
- *Competency: Managing Self—What's Your Leadership Style?*
- *Competency: Managing Communication—Richard Branson's Leadership*

Chapter 12 Leadership: Contemporary Developments 354
Preview Case: Gordon Bethune on Teams and Leadership 355
ATTRIBUTION MODEL OF LEADERSHIP 356
Attributions by Leaders 356
Attributions by Employees 357
Significance for Leaders 357
- *Competency: Managing Across Cultures—Peter Job on International Managers*

TRANSACTIONAL AND CHARISMATIC LEADERSHIP MODELS 359
Transactional Leadership Model 359
- *Competency: Managing Change—Robert Shapiro's Leadership of Monsanto*

Charismatic Leadership Model 359

- ***Competency: Managing Communication****—Herb Kelleher of Southwest Airlines*
  Significance for Leaders

TRANSFORMATIONAL LEADERSHIP MODEL 362

Inspirational Motivation 364
Intellectual Stimulation 365
- ***Competency: Managing Self****—Alan Naumann of Calico Technologies*

Idealized Influence 366
- ***Competency: Managing Teams****—Laurie Tucker of FedEx*

Individualized Consideration 366
Significance for Leaders 367

DO LEADERS MATTER? 368

Irrelevance of Leaders 368
Substitutes for Leaders 369

CHAPTER SUMMARY 370

Key Terms and Concepts 370
Discussion Questions 371

DEVELOPING COMPETENCIES 371

- ***Competency: Managing Self****—Transformational Leadership*
- ***Competency: Managing Communication****—Managing for the Future*

Chapter 13 Interpersonal Communication 376

Preview Case: *Karen Leary 377*

ESSENTIALS OF INTERPERSONAL COMMUNICATION 378

Sender and Receiver 378
Transmitters and Receptors 379
Messages and Channels 380
Meaning, Encoding, Decoding, and Feedback 381
Interpersonal Challenges 381
- ***Competency: Managing Diversity****—Texaco's Discrimination Case*

Cultural Challenges 385
- ***Competency: Managing Across Cultures****—Godiva Chocolates*

INTERPERSONAL NETWORKS 388

Types of Networks 388
Effects of Networks 389
Importance of Networks 390
- ***Competency: Managing Teams****—Lisa Guedea Carreño's Team*

INFORMATION TECHNOLOGIES 393

- ***Competency: Managing Ethics****—Putting Your Résumé Online*

FOSTERING DIALOGUE 396

Communication Openness 396
Constructive Feedback 398
Appropriate Self-Disclosure 399
- ***Competency: Managing Self****—How Self-Aware Are You?*

Active Listening 399

NONVERBAL COMMUNICATION 401

Types of Nonverbal Cues 401
Cultural Differences 402
Status Differences 403
Gender Differences 403

CHAPTER SUMMARY 404

Key Terms and Concepts 405
Discussion Questions 406

DEVELOPING COMPETENCIES 406

- ***Competency: Managing Self****—Interpersonal Communication Practices*
- ***Competency: Managing Across Cultures****—Juan Perillo and Jean Moore*

Part 3: Organizational Processes 413

Chapter 14 **Decision Making in Organizations 414**
Preview Case: Cassandra Matthews's Tough Decision 415
ETHICAL FOUNDATIONS 416
Ethical Intensity 416
- ***Competency: Managing Ethics****—A Bottom-Line Issue*

Ethical Principles and Rules 419
Concern for Others 421
Benefits and Costs 421
Assessment of Rights 422
- ***Competency: Managing Across Cultures****—Business Ethics in Russia and the United States*

MODELS OF MANAGERIAL DECISION MAKING 424
Rational Model 424
- ***Competency: Managing Self****—Ben Franklin on Making Trade-Offs*

Bounded Rationality Model 425
- ***Competency: Managing Communication****—Knowledge Management at Renaissance, Inc.*

Political Model 428
STAGES OF MANAGERIAL DECISION MAKING 430
Recognition Stage 430
Interpretation Stage 431
- ***Competency: Managing Diversity****—Barriers to Advancement*

Focus Stage 433
Choice Stage 434
Consequences Stage 435
- ***Competency: Managing Communication****—Decision Making at Alteon WebSystems*

FOSTERING ORGANIZATIONAL CREATIVITY 435
Lateral Thinking Method 436
Devil's Advocate Method 438
CHAPTER SUMMARY 439
Key Terms and Concepts 439
Discussion Questions 440
DEVELOPING COMPETENCIES 440
- ***Competency: Managing Self****—Living Ethics*
- ***Competency: Managing Change****—Is Opportunity Knocking?*

Chapter 15 **Job Design 444**
Preview Case: Texas Nameplate Company 445
COMMON JOB DESIGN APPROACHES 446
Comparative Framework 446
Job Rotation 447
Job Engineering 447
- ***Competency: Managing Change****—Westinghouse Air Brake*

Job Enlargement 448
Job Enrichment 450
Sociotechnical Systems 450
- ***Competency: Managing Diversity****—Benteler Automotive Corporation*

Ergonomics 450
JOB DESIGN AND TECHNOLOGY 451
Role of Workflow Uncertainty 452
Role of Task Uncertainty 452

Combined Effects of Workflow and Task Uncertainty 452
Role of Task Interdependence 453
• ***Competency: Managing Communication***—*David Berdish Fosters Dialogue*
Interrelationships Among Job Design and Technology Concepts 454
JOB CHARACTERISTICS ENRICHMENT MODEL 454
Framework 454
Job Characteristics 456
Individual Differences 457
Job Diagnosis 458
Implementation Approaches 459
Job Characteristics and Technology 461
Social Information Processing 461
• ***Competency: Managing Across Cultures***—*Job Design in the Malaysian Nursing Context*
SOCIOTECHNICAL SYSTEMS MODEL 462
Social Systems 463
Technological Systems 464
Moderators 464
Core Concepts 465
• ***Competency: Managing Teams***—*Consolidated Diesel's Engine Plant*
Implementation Issues 465
CHAPTER SUMMARY 467
Key Terms and Concepts 468
Discussion Questions 468
DEVELOPING COMPETENCIES 468
• ***Competency: Managing Change***—*Data Entry Operators*
• ***Competency: Managing Teams***—*GE's Aircraft-Engine Assembly Facility*

Chapter 16 Organization Design 472
Preview Case: *Procter & Gamble 473*
KEY FACTORS IN ORGANIZATION DESIGN 475
Environmental Factors 475
Strategic Courses 478
Technological Factors 480
• ***Competency: Managing Communication***—*U.S. West*
Comparative Framework 482
MECHANISTIC AND ORGANIC SYSTEMS 483
Hierarchy of Authority 484
Division of Labor 485
Rules and Procedures 485
Impersonality 486
Chain of Command 486
Span of Control 486
• ***Competency: Managing Change***—*Cisco Systems, Inc.*
TYPES OF ORGANIZATION DESIGNS 487
Functional Design 487
Place Design 489
Product Design 490
Multidivisional Design 491
• ***Competency: Managing Communication***—*Johnson & Johnson's Multidivisional Design*
Integration Issues 493
ORGANIZATIONS OF THE FUTURE 495
Matrix Design 495

Multinational Design 497
• ***Competency: Managing Across Cultures****—Electrolux*
Network Design 498
Virtual Organization 502
• ***Competency: Managing Teams****—British Petroleum's Virtual Organization*
CHAPTER SUMMARY 504
Key Terms and Concepts 505
Discussion Questions 505
DEVELOPING COMPETENCIES 506
• ***Competency: Managing Self****—Inventory of Effective Design*
• ***Competency: Managing Change****—Salomon*

Chapter 17 Organizational Culture 510
Preview Case: *DaimlerChrysler's Diverse Cultures* 511
DYNAMICS OF ORGANIZATIONAL CULTURE 512
• ***Competency: Managing Self****—Gene Veno Finds a Cultural Fit*
Developing Organizational Culture 514
• ***Competency: Managing Across Cultures****—Pharmacia & Upjohn*
Maintaining Organizational Culture 517
Changing Organizational Culture 521
• ***Competency: Managing Change****—Harley-Davidson: Learning Organization*
TYPES OF CORPORATE CULTURES 523
Bureaucratic Culture 524
Clan Culture 525
Entrepreneurial Culture 525
Market Culture 526
• ***Competency: Managing Teams****—Conflict at Andersen Worldwide*
Organizational Implications 527
PERFORMANCE AND ORGANIZATIONAL CULTURE 528
Strong Cultures 528
Cautionary Notes 528
ETHICAL BEHAVIOR AND ORGANIZATIONAL CULTURE 529
Impact of Culture 530
Whistle-Blowing 530
MANAGING CULTURAL DIVERSITY 531
Significant Challenges 532
• ***Competency: Managing Communication****—Marriott Marquis*
Some Guidelines 533
ORGANIZATIONAL SOCIALIZATION 534
Socialization Process 534
Socialization Outcomes 534
CHAPTER SUMMARY 536
Key Terms and Concepts 537
Discussion Questions 537
DEVELOPING COMPETENCIES 538
• ***Competency: Managing Ethics****—Assessing a Culture's Ethical Behaviors*
• ***Competency: Managing Teams****—Southwest Airlines' Team Culture*

Chapter 18 Organizational Change 542
Preview Case: *What Horse's Rear Designed That?* 543
THE CHALLENGE OF CHANGE 544
Pressures for Change 544
• ***Competency: Managing Change****—The Challenge for J.C. Penney*
Characteristics of Effective Change Programs 548
Organizational Diagnosis 551

- *Competency: Managing Communication—The Chairman's Rice Pudding*

RESISTANCE TO CHANGE 553

- *Competency: Managing Change—St. Louis Mall Declares War on E-Commerce*

Individual Resistance 554
Organizational Resistance 556
Overcoming Resistance 558

- *Competency: Managing Teams—Overcoming Resistance at Nucor*

ORGANIZATION DEVELOPMENT 559
Action Research 561
Appreciative Inquiry 561
CHANGE MANAGEMENT 562
Changing Behavior 562
Changing Culture 564

- *Competency: Managing Across Cultures—An Interview with Ford's Jacques Nasser*

Changing Task and Technology 566
Changing Organization Design 569

- *Competency: Managing Change—Dumbsizing*

Changing Strategy 572
ETHICAL ISSUES IN ORGANIZATIONAL CHANGE 573
CHAPTER SUMMARY 573
Key Terms and Concepts 575
Discussion Questions 575
DEVELOPING COMPETENCIES 575

- *Competency: Managing Self—Measuring Support for Change*
- *Competency: Managing Ethics—Kindred Todd and the Ethics of OD*

Appendix: Tools and Techniques for Studying Organizational Behavior 581

THE SCIENTIFIC APPROACH 581
PREPARATION OF RESEARCH DESIGNS 582
Purposes of Research Designs 582
Hypothesis 582
Experimental Design 583
TYPES OF RESEARCH DESIGN 584
Case Study 585
Field Survey 585
Laboratory Experiment 586
Field Experiment 587
COMPARISON OF RESEARCH DESIGNS 587
Realism 588
Scope 588
Precision 588
Control 588
Cost 588
DATA COLLECTION METHODS 588
Interviews 589
Questionnaires 589
Observation 591
Nonreactive Measures 591
Qualitative Methods 591
CRITERIA FOR DATA COLLECTION 592
Reliability 592
Validity 592
Practicality 592

ETHICS IN RESEARCH 593
Misrepresentation and Misuse of Data 593
Manipulation 594
Value and Goal Conflicts 594
SUMMARY 594
Key Terms and Concepts 595
REFERENCES 595

Integrating Cases C-1
ROBERT PRINCETON AT FALLS VIDEO C-1
Background on Falls Video C-1
Princeton Joins the Team C-1
The Final Days C-2
THE RICHMOND POLICE DEPARTMENT: CHANGE AND REORGANIZATION C-3
Background Information C-3
The Situation C-3
Organization Design C-3
Employee Relations C-4
Community Issues C-4
Chief's Leadership Style C-4
IT'S MY BIKE C-5
IS TECHNICAL COMPETENCE ENOUGH? C-7
Background C-7
Settling In on the Job C-7
Working with Spinner C-8
Discussion About Spinner C-8
FRIENDS OR FOES? C-9
The Incident C-10
Mike Russo's Reprimand C-11
Continuing Performance Problems C-11
BUD THORNTON'S BRUSH WITH DEATH C-11
Bud Thornton, the Person C-11
The Company and the Union C-12
The Situation C-12
BOB KNOWLTON C-14
NORDSTROM, INC. C-18
WHAT DO WE DO WITH HOWARD? C-20
Howard Lineberry, Lead Surveyor C-20
Mel Cutler, Surveyor's Helper C-23
Tad Pierson, Project Engineer C-24

Author Index I-1

Subject and Organizational Index I-11

Internet Organization Index I-27

PREFACE

This, our ninth edition of *Organizational Behavior*, continues a commitment that has shaped each successive edition. The impulse behind this book, and the challenge that we respond to, is to reflect the latest thinking and practices for use in foundation organizational behavior courses. Another goal, equally motivating and equally challenging, is to fully involve students who have no prior formal training in the topics, issues, and concepts central to organizational behavior in the usefulness of its ideas.

Students will really like the ninth edition. It's current and will grab their interest through a variety of methods, including cases, self-assessment questionnaires, a graceful internal design, and sophisticated graphics. Because they are so richly detailed, the examples will not only make discussion in and out of the classroom lively, but will also spark independent exploration. Students need to be challenged to go beyond their readings to actively engage organizational behavior issues and concepts. This edition will encourage students to do just that. Written in lively and engaging language, it will help students take more away from the course than just a new vocabulary and a new set of concepts. The text requires students to take an active part in their own learning by approaching issues and problems intelligently through the use of self-insights to assess their responses and to make appropriate action plans.

Our ultimate goal in this edition is to help students develop the competencies and knowledge that they will need to be effective professionals, managers, and leaders. Now, more than ever, the keys to an organization's effectiveness and competitiveness are, very simply, its employees. Technology, financial capital, physical assets, and access to proprietary information are increasingly recognized as being little more than short-term sources of competitive advantage. Long-term competitive advantage comes from another source: the rich array of individual and team-based competencies capable of being put into action by an organization's employees, managers, and leaders.

DEVELOPING LEADERS

Organizational behavior—the study of human behavior, attitudes, and performance in organizations—provides value-added knowledge for individuals and teams at all organizational levels. This knowledge is crucial to the development of tomorrow's leaders in organizations of all types and sizes.

COMPETENCIES: THE FOUNDATION

We promote the development of competencies throughout the book, building themes and solutions around a core of seven crucial and fundamental capabilities. It is an orientation that we carefully frame at the outset and connect to frequently. In particular, we substantially revised Chapter 1 to set the stage for the continuous weaving of these seven foundation competencies into our discussions and the applications that support them. They are identified and described as follows:

- The *managing self competency* involves the ability to assess your own strengths and weaknesses; set and pursue professional and personal goals; balance work and personal life; and engage in new learning—including new or changed skills, behaviors, and attitudes.
- The *managing communication competency* involves the ability to transmit, receive, and understand information, ideas, thoughts, and feelings—nonverbally, verbally, in electronic and written form, by listening, and other methods.

- The *managing diversity competency* involves the ability to value unique individual and group characteristics, embrace such characteristics as potential sources of organizational strength, and respect the uniqueness of each individual.
- The *managing ethics competency* involves the ability to incorporate values and principles that distinguish right from wrong in decision making and behavior.
- The *managing across cultures competency* involves the ability to recognize and embrace similarities and differences among nations and cultures and then to approach key organizational and strategic issues with an open and curious mind.
- The *managing teams competency* involves the ability to develop, support, facilitate, and/or lead groups to achieve organizational goals.
- The *managing change competency* involves the ability to recognize and implement needed adaptations or entirely new transformations in the people, tasks, strategies, structures, or technologies in the person's area of responsibility.

Competencies: The Features That Drive Their Development

Competencies could be learned through casual practice and random feedback—in other words, by chance—but our choice is not to let chance drive competency development. Instead, we provide structure and consistent opportunity for students to expand their base of knowledge and to increase their skills. We put the bits and pieces together, integrating skills, behaviors, attitudes, and knowledge through targeted self-assessments matched to specific competencies. The payoff for students is that we clarify, define, and provide benchmarks for them not only to gauge their competencies independently but to compare their competency levels with those of other students and practicing managers as well. Students, first, must be able to assess accurately their levels of proficiency in each of the seven foundation competencies and then begin to develop action plans for improving their potential as effective professionals, managers, and leaders. In this book we provide specially designed features to assist students in their journey.

In-Chapter Competency Boxes

Each chapter includes four to six boxed inserts that mirror one of the seven competencies, providing insights, examples, and applications to assist students' competency development. These boxed inserts harmonize with the chapter's theories and topics, illustrating how organizations—such as Ford, Disney, and Coca-Cola—use organizational behavior theories to achieve high levels of performance reliably and credibly. The following are a few examples.

- *Competency: Managing Self*—Ford's Competency Program (Chapter 1) showcases Ford Motor Company's reliance on measures of fundamental competence and evaluations of the *potential* for achieving higher levels of competence when recruiting, selecting, and promoting employees.
- *Competency: Managing Communication*—The Walt Disney Company (Chapter 5) details the strengths of Disney's commitment to its values and traditions and the steps it takes to convey those values and traditions to newly hired employees.
- *Competency: Managing Diversity*—Stereotypes of Women at Work (Chapter 3) takes a look at how current research in gender roles among expatriate workers is forcing a reassessment of the conventional wisdom regarding who chooses overseas assignments and who succeeds in them.
- *Competency: Managing Ethics*—The Politics of Employee Appraisal (Chapter 9) takes a hard look at the biases that can creep into employee evaluations.
- *Competency: Managing Across Cultures*—Peter Job on International Managers (Chapter 12) captures the commonsense wisdom of Reuters CEO, Peter Job,

about conducting business in a variety of markets throughout the world, complementing solidly the way we define this competency.

- *Competency: Managing Teams*—Consolidated Diesel's Engine Plant (Chapter 15) illustrates how the application of the sociotechnical systems model at Consolidated Diesel plays a particularly significant role in how teams create value and virtually guarantees that contributions to organizational effectiveness reach down through all levels of the organization.
- *Competency: Managing Change*—Harley-Davidson: Learning Organization (Chapter 17) provides an instructive example of how a company changed its culture and thereby brought its business back from the brink of bankruptcy.

End-of-Chapter *Developing Competencies* Exercises, Questionnaires, and Cases

In addition to the boxed competency features within each chapter, we end each chapter with two *Developing Competencies* exercises, questionnaires, or cases—36 in all. Each one focuses on the development of one of the seven foundation competencies, and over 50 percent of them are new to this edition. They provide an additional means for actively engaging students in the development of their own professional competencies and to deepen their understanding of the many facets of each competency.

Student CD-ROM

The CD-ROM packaged with every copy of the book provides a self-assessment tool for students to use and to reuse as their competencies mature. Individual ratings can be compared with those of practicing professionals as well as with those of other students, leading to additional insights and the spurring of targeted development. Video, glossaries, and links to online resources complete this collection of technology-based tools and content.

Self-Assessment Instruments

Today's successful professionals and managers know that self-awareness is a crucial vantage point from which to improve individual and organizational effectiveness. This self-identification of strengths and needed improvements is an important first step in the process of learning to manage oneself and others effectively. Our inclusion of many self-assessment instruments, at strategic points throughout the text, helps students identify their capabilities and thereby make needed adjustments. Although these self-assessment instruments assess each student's level of proficiency, their real focus is on suggesting ways for students to further sharpen their strengths, competencies, and related abilities for becoming effective professionals, managers, and leaders. Examples of these self-assessment instruments presented in each chapter and in the end-of-chapter *Developing Competencies* section include the following.

- Attitudes Toward Diversity (Chapter 1)
- Measuring Perceptions of Women as Managers (Chapter 2)
- The Big Five Personality Questionnaire (Chapter 3)
- What Is Your Self-Efficacy? (Chapter 4)
- What Do You Want from Your Job? (Chapter 5)
- Goal-Setting Questionnaire (Chapter 6)
- Assessing Your Stress Level (Chapter 7)
- Team Assessment (Chapter 8)
- How Much Power Do You Have in Your Group? (Chapter 9)

- Conflict-Handling Styles (Chapter 10)
- What is Your Leadership Style? (Chapter 11)
- Managing for the Future (Chapter 12)
- Interpersonal Communication Practices (Chapter 13)
- Assessment of Ethical Intensity (Chapter 14)
- Job Characteristics Inventory (Chapter 15)
- Inventory of Effective Design (Chapter 16)
- Assessing an Organization's Ethical Behaviors (Chapter 17)
- Measuring Support for Change (Chapter 18)

Product Support Web Site

A rich Web site at http://hellriegel.swcollege.com complements the text, providing many extras for students and instructors. Resources include a tutorial on how to find things on the Internet; interactive quizzes; downloadable ancillaries, and links to useful sites, online publications, and databases.

End-of Book Integrating Cases

Of the nine *Integrating Cases* at the end of the book, six are new to this edition. Each case requires students to develop their ability to draw from a variety of concepts, techniques, and competencies to address the questions posed. The cases can be used in a variety of learning formats and have been specifically selected and shaped to assist in the development of the abilities key to effective professional, managerial, and leadership roles.

Chapter-Opening Preview Cases

Each chapter opens with a *Preview Case*. It sets the stage for the topics discussed in the chapter and serves either to introduce one or more of the foundation competencies or to provide a new slant on them. Frequent flashbacks to the Preview Case refresh particular concepts, issues, and competencies to ensure that students make the all-important connections between theory and practice.

End-of-Chapter Discussion Questions

We continue to provide *Discussion Questions*, typically 8 to 12 in number, at the end of each chapter. Most are new to this edition and are designed to prompt students to relate concepts, models, and competencies to their own experiences or to the competency features presented in the chapter. Many also trigger self-insight and reflection, thus promoting, on yet another level, the internalization of chapter content.

ORGANIZATION

Our experience, and that of our readers, suggested that the framework and organization of the book work well. All of the chapters were thoroughly revised and updated, with new issues and topics woven into the text throughout. For example, we expanded our presentation of the relationships between new information technologies and various organizational behavior concepts and issues.

After the introductory chapter, the book is divided into three main parts.

- Part I (Individual Processes) contains chapters on personality and attitudes, perception and attribution, learning and reinforcement, two chapters on motivation, and a chapter on work stress.
- Part II (Group and Interpersonal Processes) consists of chapters on group and team behavior, power and political behavior, conflict and negotiation, two chapters on leadership, and a chapter on interpersonal communication.

- Part III (Organizational Processes) contains chapters on decision making, job design, organization design, organizational culture, and organizational change.

Our approach to introducing students to organizational behavior is to move from the individual to the group to the organizational level. However, the chapters are written to stand alone, which allows material to be covered in any order desired by the instructor.

Immediately following the last chapter are an appendix on research methods, the integrating cases, and indexes, including the usual author and subject indexes. In addition, we provide an index of the Internet addresses for the organizations featured in the book. By visiting these Web sites, students can develop a deeper understanding of the challenges now facing organizations in a highly competitive, global economy .

SUPPLEMENTS

A full array of teaching and learning supplements is available for use with the ninth edition of *Organizational Behavior*:

Instructor's Manual (ISBN 0-324-00978-X)

Written by Michael K. McCuddy, of Valparaiso University, the Instructor's Manual contains comprehensive resource materials for lectures, including enrichment modules for enhancing and extending relevant chapter concepts; suggested answers for all end-of-chapter discussion questions; notes on using end-of-chapter *Developing Competencies* exercises, questionnaires, and cases, including suggested answers to case questions; teaching notes for the integrating cases; and a guide to the videos available for use with the text.

Test Bank (ISBN 0-324-00981-X)

Written by David M. Leuser, of Plymouth State College, the Test Bank contains over 3,900 questions from which to choose. A selection of true/false, multiple choice, short essay, and critical-thinking essay questions are provided for each chapter. Questions are categorized by difficulty level, by learning objective, and according to Bloom's taxonomy. Cross-references to material in the textbook, where answers can be found, are also included. Explanations are provided for why statements are false in the true/false sections.

A computerized version of the Test Bank is available upon request. **ExamView® Pro (ISBN 0-324-00986-0),** a very easy-to-use test-generating program, enables instructors to quickly create printed tests, Internet tests, and online (LAN-based) tests. Instructors can enter their own questions using the word processor provided as well as customize the appearance of the tests they create. The QuickTest wizard permits test generators to use an existing bank of questions to create a test in minutes, using a step-by-step selection process.

Study Guide (ISBN 0-324-00980-1)

Written by Roger D. Roderick, of Arkansas State University, the Study Guide contains learning objectives, chapter outlines with ample room for student note taking, practice questions (both directed and applied), and answers to all practice questions.

Video

A new video library is available to users of the ninth edition to show how real organizations and leaders deal with real organizational behavior issues. A tape of *Video Examples* (ISBN 0-324-00984-4), featuring such companies as Ben & Jerry's, Valassis Communications, and Enforcement Technology Inc. (ETEC), examines a range of issues. Critical-thinking questions appear at appropriate intervals in the 10 to 15-

minute programs to concentrate viewers' observations on key decisions and actions. A new *Video Cohesion Case* (ISBN 0-324-00985-2) features Horizons Companies, a provider of multimedia, video, Web development, branding, and marketing services, with three locations (Columbus, Ohio, San Diego, and Nashville) and eight divisions, including its own record label. A comprehensive video guide appears in the *Instructor's Manual*, with supporting case material and notes for each video segment.

PowerPoint™ Presentation Slides (ISBN 0-324-00979-8)

Developed by Michael K. McCuddy, of Valparaiso University, and prepared in conjunction with the Instructor's Manual, over 225 PowerPoint slides are available to supplement course content, adding structure and visual dimension to lectures.

Transparency Acetates (ISBN 0-324-00982-8)

Acetates for each chapter are provided free to adopters. The package includes many exhibits from the text, as well as specially constructed diagrams and lists to add emphasis and interest to lectures.

Instructor's Resource CD-ROM (ISBN 0-324-06777-1)

Key instructor ancillaries (Instructor's Manual, Test Bank, and PowerPoint slides) are provided on CD-ROM, giving instructors the ultimate tool for customizing lectures and presentations.

Organizational Behavior: Experiences and Cases (ISBN 0-324-04850-5)

A new edition of *Organizational Behavior: Experiences and Cases*, by Dorothy Marcic, Joseph Seltzer, and Peter Vaill, is available to add practical applications to go along with the text's theoretical frameworks.

Experiencing Organizational Behavior (ISBN 0-324-07352-6)

An innovative new product, *Experiencing Organizational Behavior* is a totally online collection of Web-based modules that uses the latest Flash technology in its animated scenarios, graphs, and models. Designed to reinforce key organizational behavior principles in a dynamic learning environment, *Experiencing Organizational Behavior* maintains high motivation through the use of challenging problems. Try it by visiting http://www.experiencingob.com.

All of these supplements are available from South-Western College Publishing or from your Thomson Learning representative.

ACKNOWLEDGEMENTS

We express our grateful appreciation to the following individuals who provided thoughtful reviews and useful suggestions for improving this edition of our book.

Roger Volkema
American University

Ron A. DiBattista
Bryant College

David R. Hannah
The University of Texas at Austin

Dong I. Jung
San Diego State University

Kathi J. Lovelace
Western Washington University

John B. Washbush
University of Wisconsin, Whitewater

In addition, we thank our editor, John Szylagyi, our production editor, Sandy Gangelhoff, our copy editor, Jerrold Moore, and our development editor, Judy O'Neill, for their superb professional contributions at various stages in the creation of this book. We extend special thanks to Argie Butler at Texas A&M University and Billie Boyd at Southern Methodist University for their outstanding support with manuscript preparation.

John Slocum acknowledges his SMU colleagues, David Lei and Don VandeWalle, Bill Joyce at Tuck, and Mick McGill at the Associates First Capital Corporation for their constructive reviews of his work. His recent sabbatical leave at Dartmouth's Tuck School gave him time to reflect, gain new perspectives, and unlearn some old writing habits. Al Neimi, Dean of the Cox School, gave him a renewed interest in scholarship by providing the emotional and intellectual support for this project. For rearranging tee-times, John's golfing friends at Stonebriar Country Club—Bill Detwiler, Howard Johnson, David Norwood, Ralph Sorrentino, and Jon Wheeler—need thanks. Believe it or not, it's hard to say **no** to playing golf on a beautiful Friday afternoon to spend time revising a chapter, going to the library, or simply "reflecting." However, he still needs strokes! Finally, John wants to thank Don Hellriegel. It's hard to believe that we have known each other for almost 40 years, written nine editions of this book, eight editions of our management book, been present when our children were born, seen our children graduate from college, get married, raise their own children, argue about everything from A&M and SMU sports to a chapter's content. Through all these years, we have remained great friends. It's hard to imagine a better friend.

Don Hellriegel and Dick Woodman express appreciation to their colleagues at Texas A&M University who collectively create a work environment that nurtures their continued learning and professional development. In particular, the learning environment fostered by A. Benton Cocanougher, Dean, and Ricky W. Griffin, Head of the Department of Management, is gratefully acknowledged. Finally, Don would like to echo the sentiments expressed by John Slocum regarding their almost 40 years of friendship and professional working relationships.

Don Hellriegel, Texas A&M University

John W. Slocum, Jr., Southern Methodist University

Richard W. Woodman, Texas A&M University

About the Authors

DON HELLRIEGEL

Don Hellriegel is Professor of Management and holds the Bennett Chair in Business within the Lowry Mays College and Graduate School of Business at Texas A&M University. He received his B.S. and M.B.A. from Kent State University and his Ph.D. from the University of Washington. Dr. Hellriegel has been a member of the faculty at Texas A&M since 1975 and has served on the faculties of the Pennsylvania State University and the University of Colorado.

His research interests include interorganizational relationships, corporate venturing, effect of organizational environments, managerial cognitive styles, and organizational innovation and strategic management processes. His research has been published in a number of leading journals.

Professor Hellriegel served as Vice President and Program Chair of the Academy of Management (1986), President Elect (1987), President (1988), and Past President (1989). In September 1999, he was elected to a three-year term as Dean of the Fellows Group of the Academy of Management. He served a term as Editor of the Academy of Management Review and served as a member of the Board of Governors of the Academy of Management (1979–1981); (1982–1989). Dr. Hellriegel has occupied many other leadership roles, among which include President, Eastern Academy of Management; Division Chair, Organization and Management Theory Division; President, Brazos County United Way; Co-Consulting Editor, West Series in Management; Head (1976–1980 and 1989–1994), Department of Management (TAMU); Interim Dean, College of Business Administration (TAMU); and Interim Executive Vice Chancellor (TAMUS).

He has consulted with a variety of groups and organizations, including—among others—3DI, Sun Ship Building, Penn Mutual Life Insurance, Texas A&M University System, Ministry of Industry and Commerce (Nation of Kuwait), Ministry of Agriculture (Nation of Dominican Republic), American Assembly of Collegiate Schools of Business, and Texas Innovation Group.

JOHN W. SLOCUM, JR.

John Slocum holds the O. Paul Corley Professorship in Organizational Behavior at the Edwin L. Cox School of Business, Southern Methodist University. He has also taught on the faculties of the University of Washington, the Ohio State University, the Pennsylvania State University, the International University of Japan, and Dartmouth's Amos Tuck School. He holds a B.B.A. from Westminster College, an M.B.A. from Kent State University, and a Ph.D. in organizational behavior from the University of Washington.

Professor Slocum has held a number of positions in professional societies. He was elected as a Fellow to the Academy of Management in 1976 for his outstanding contributions to the profession of management and as a Fellow to the Decision Sciences Institute in 1984 for his research in behavioral decision theory. He was awarded the Alumni Citation for Professional Accomplishment by Westminster College and both the Nicolas Salgo and the Rotunda Outstanding Teaching awards from SMU. He served as President of the Eastern Academy of Management in 1973. From 1975–1986, he served as a member of the Board of Governors, Academy of Management. From 1979–1981, he served as Editor of the Academy of Management Journal. In 1983–1984, he served as 39th President of the 8,500-member Academy and as

Chairman of the Board of Governors of that organization. Currently, he serves as Associate Editor of *Organizational Dynamics* and Co-Editor of the *Journal of World Business.*

Professor Slocum has served as a consultant to such organizations as Mellon National Bank, ARAMARK, Corning Glass Works, Fort Worth Museum of Science and History, Pier 1, Henry C. Beck Company, Kodak, Price Waterhouse, Hershey Foods, Mack Trucks, Celanese, General Telephone and Electric, NASA, Southland Corporation, Transnational Trucks, and Brooklyn Union.

RICHARD W. WOODMAN

Richard W. Woodman is Anderson Clayton & Co. and Clayton Fund Professor of Management at Texas A&M University, where he teaches organizational behavior, organization development, and research methodology in the Lowry Mays College and Graduate School of Business. He received his B.S. and M.B.A. degrees from Oklahoma State University and his Ph.D. from Purdue University. From 1993–1997, he served as department head and he is currently the coordinator of the Ph.D. program in the Department of Management.

His research interests focus on organizational change and organizational creativity. His published work can be found in the *Academy of Management Journal, Academy of Management Review, Group & Organization Management, Journal of Applied Behavioral Science, Journal of Applied Psychology, Journal of Creative Behavior, Journal of Management, Journal of Organizational Change Management, Organization Development Journal, Organizational Dynamics, Psychological Bulletin,* and the *Strategic Management Journal,* among others. Dr. Woodman is Co-Editor of the JAI Press annual series, *Research in Organizational Change and Development.* He is currently on the editorial boards of the *Academy of Management Journal, Applied Behavioral Science Review,* and the *Journal of Organizational Change Management* and previously served on the boards of the *Academy of Management Review* and the *Journal of Management.*

He has also served as national Program Chair and Division Chair of the Organization Development and Change division of the Academy of Management. In a previous life, Dr.Woodman was a military intelligence officer in the U.S. Army, worked in both the petroleum and banking industries, and served for several years as vice-president of a financial institution.

CHAPTER 1

Introduction to Organizational Behavior

LEARNING OBJECTIVES

When you have finished studying this chapter, you should be able to:

1. Explain the managing self competency.
2. Explain the managing communication competency.
3. Explain the managing diversity competency.
4. Explain the managing ethics competency.
5. Explain the managing across cultures competency.
6. Explain the managing teams competency.
7. Explain the managing change competency.
8. Outline the framework for learning about organizational behavior.

Preview Case: *Cynthia Danaher*

THE MANAGING SELF COMPETENCY
- Core Components
- ***Competency: Managing Self***—*Ford's Competency Program*
- Career Management

THE MANAGING COMMUNICATION COMPETENCY
- Core Components
- Relationship to Managerial Roles
- ***Competency: Managing Communication***—*The Microcommunication*

THE MANAGING DIVERSITY COMPETENCY
- Core Components
- Categories of Diversity
- ***Competency: Managing Diversity***—*Boundaryless Behavior*
- Changing Workforce and Customers
- Gender
- Race and Ethnicity
- Age

THE MANAGING ETHICS COMPETENCY
- Core Components
- Ethical Dilemmas

THE MANAGING ACROSS CULTURES COMPETENCY
- ***Competency: Managing Ethics***—*Michael Roth at MONY Group*
- Core Components
- Individualism–Collectivism

THE MANAGING TEAMS COMPETENCY
- Core Components
- ***Competency: Managing Across Cultures***—*China's Collectivism*
- Individualism and Teams

THE MANAGING CHANGE COMPETENCY
- Core Components
- Technological Forces

LEARNING FRAMEWORK
- ***Competency: Managing Change***—*Embracing Speed*
- Environmental Forces
- Individual Processes
- Team and Interpersonal Processes
- Organizational Processes

CHAPTER SUMMARY
- Key Terms and Concepts
- Discussion Questions

DEVELOPING COMPETENCIES
- ***Competency: Managing Diversity***—*Attitudes Toward Diversity*
- ***Competency: Managing Communication***—*James Halpin of CompUSA*

PREVIEW CASE

CYNTHIA DANAHER

Cynthia Danaher was named vice president and general manager of Hewlett-Packard Company's Medical Products Group several years ago. At the time, she told the 5,300 employees in the group: "I want to do this job, but it's scary and I need your help." She also stated that they finally had a boss who "knows how to make coffee." Three years after making this statement, Danaher indicated that this approach was a mistake. If she held the meeting today, she wouldn't state that she was scared and wouldn't mention her coffee-making ability. Instead, she would propose some of the growth goals for the business and challenge employees to think about what *they* needed to do to in order for the company to achieve them.

Danaher has altered her leadership style as she has been promoted. She now thinks that, when a manager is in charge of thousands of employees, the ability to set direction and delegate is more crucial than team building and coaching. Danaher acknowledges that at times she found the transition to senior management so difficult that she considered quitting her job. "I felt a lot of grief letting go of who I'd been." In her previous job, as head of the Medical Products Group's ultrasound-imaging business, Danaher was very close to the 500 employees in that division. She knew many of them by name and was involved in virtually all decisions, from product development to sales and advertising. Moving to that post from her prior job of marketing manager of ultrasound imaging was like "going from sixth grade into junior high. I knew all the customers, I knew the product line, and I knew all the staff," Danaher stated.

She noted that her promotion to general manager was "like going from eighth grade to college." She spent her first months scrambling to learn aspects of the business that she hadn't managed before while trying to maintain her style as a hands-on, involved-with-employees leader. "Whether it was product pricing or someone's parent going to a nursing home, I wanted to help people solve their problems," she says.

But overseeing 10 times the number of people she had previously supervised, plus half a dozen major businesses, that style "nearly killed me. I needed distance to get my new job done." Initially, Danaher resisted letting go of the details. Eager to foster teamwork, she held an off-site retreat with her top managers. She asked questions like "How can we trust one another?" But she did most of the talking, while her managers, who compete with each other for resources while running their distinct businesses, remained hesitant to share problems.

For more information on the Medical Products Group at Hewlett-Packard, visit the group's home page at ***www.healthcare.agilent.com/mpg.***

At first, she blamed herself for their lack of cooperation. Later, she concluded, "It isn't my job to bring them together." Instead, she encouraged them to promote teamwork in their own units. Becoming more independent and tougher-minded has been especially hard. She says. "I was brought up to believe that if I did what was best for everyone else, and made others comfortable, I was a good person." She says. "I don't think men are raised that way."

Danaher has learned to say no and delegate more. When one manager asked her to help interview candidates for a lower level managerial job, she declined, saying the choice was his to make. She relies heavily on her administrative assistant to keep her on a schedule and screen her from constant interruptions by employees seeking her counsel. But she hasn't entirely shed her sympathetic style. "If an employee has a sick child and needs to get to the hospital, I'm on the phone trying to help," she says. "I still get involved, but I choose where more carefully, and it's not out of obligation, but wanting to."[1]

Hewlett-Packard (HP) Company's Medical Products Group (MPG), based in Andover, Massachusetts, provides a combination of clinical measurements and information management solutions for clients. The group markets more than 400 medical products and services, including patient-monitoring systems, point-of-care diagnostics systems, clinical-information systems, ultrasound-imaging technologies, defibrillators, electrocardiographs, and some 800 medical-supply products. Clearly, Cynthia Danaher heads a major business group that is large, complex, high tech, and continually introducing new products. She learned that being a manager isn't easy and that the demands of her role changed with her promotions up the corporate ladder. These changes created the need for different mixtures of managerial competencies. A **competency** is an interrelated set of skills, behaviors, attitudes, and knowledge needed by an individual to be effective in most professional and managerial positions. A number of competencies can be identified in most organizations.[2] One of our themes in this book is to weave into the text seven foundation competencies that affect behavior in organizations. These seven competencies are increasingly important to the effectiveness of most professionals, not simply those in managerial and leadership roles, as in the case of Cynthia Danaher. We discuss some of these foundation competencies in considerable depth in specific chapters. For example, most of Chapter 13, Interpersonal Communication, focuses on developing the managing communication competency. In addition, in other chapters we present competencies that build on our foundation competencies and address specific issues. For example, in Chapters 11 and 12 we discuss the importance of the foundation competencies and other competencies needed to be an effective leader.

As Figure 1.1 suggests, our goal is to assist you in further developing the seven foundation competencies. The double-headed arrows indicate that the competencies needed for achieving effectiveness are highly interrelated and that drawing rigid boundaries between them isn't feasible. The following are definitions and brief examples of the seven foundation competencies.

- The **managing self competency** involves the ability to assess your own strengths and weaknesses; set and pursue professional and personal goals; balance work and personal life; and engage in new learning—including new or changed skills, behaviors, and attitudes. Cynthia Danaher demonstrated competency in *managing self* by assessing her comments to the employees upon being named vice president and general manager of HP's Medical Products Group. Reread the opening of the Preview Case to review what Danaher indicated she would have said if the meeting were held today.
- The **managing communication competency** involves the ability to transmit, receive, and understand ideas, thoughts, and feelings—nonverbal, verbal, written, listening, electronic, and the like—for transferring and exchanging information and emotions. Recall Danaher's reflection on her initial approach to *managing communication* in the first off-site retreat with her top managers after being promoted. Danaher did most of the talking, but her managers, who compete with each other while running distinct businesses, remained hesitant to share their problems.
- The **managing diversity competency** involves the ability to value unique individual and group characteristics, embrace such characteristics as potential sources of organizational strength, and respect the uniqueness of each individual. This competency also involves the ability to help people work effectively together even though their interests and backgrounds may be quite diverse. Cynthia Danaher reflected on the diversity that she brought to her top-management role as a woman. Danaher noted that becoming more autonomous and tougher minded has been especially hard for her.
- The **managing ethics competency** involves the ability to incorporate values and principles that distinguish right from wrong in decision making and behavior. Although Danaher has learned to say no and delegate more, she has retained a sense of ethical obligation to her employees. Recall her comment: "If an employee has a sick child and

Figure 1.1 **Foundation Competencies for Individual and Managerial Effectiveness**

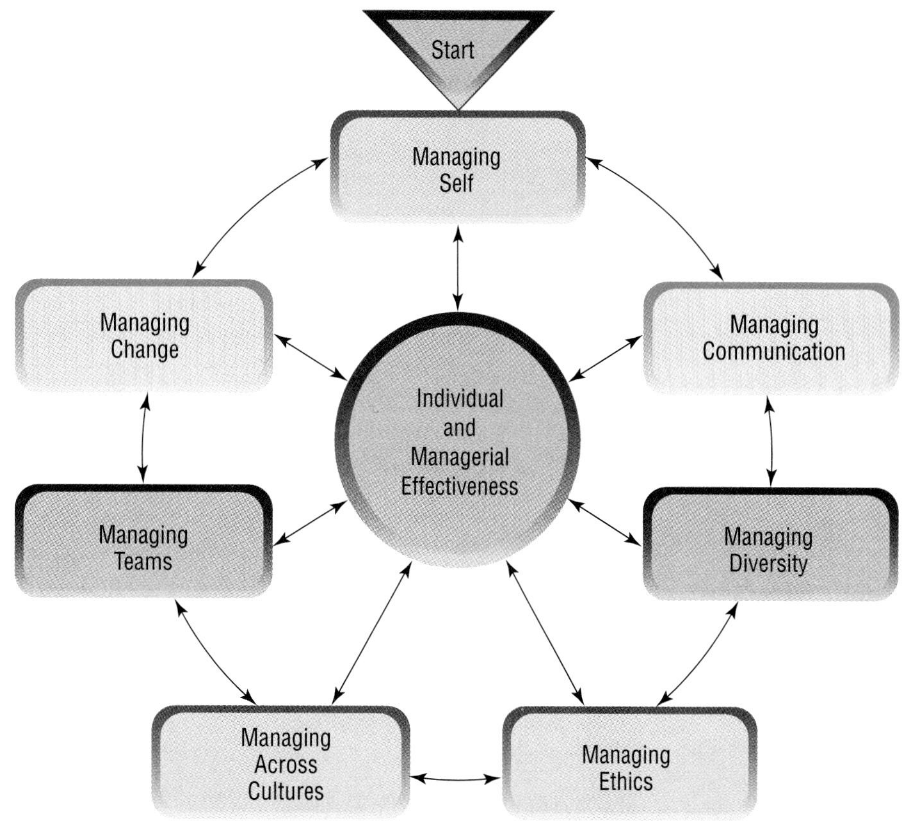

needs to get to the hospital, I'm on the phone trying to help. I still get involved, but I choose where more carefully, and it's not out of obligation, but wanting to."

- The **managing across cultures competency** involves the ability to recognize and embrace similarities and differences among nations and cultures and then to approach key organizational and strategic issues with an open and curious mind. The 5,300 employees in Danaher's Medical Products Group operate worldwide. Danaher recognizes the need for the group to adjust some marketing, distribution, communication, human resource, and control processes to differences among nations and cultures.
- The **managing teams competency** involves the ability to develop, support, facilitate, or lead groups to achieve organizational goals. Prior to being named vice president and general manager, Danaher effectively used her managing teams competency in other positions. However, she now recognizes that once a manager has been put in charge of thousands of employees, setting direction and delegating is more vital than team building and coaching for all her employees.
- The **managing change competency** involves the ability to recognize and implement needed adaptations or entirely new transformations in the people, tasks, strategies, structures, or technologies in the person's area of responsibility. Danaher changed the top-management team, structure, and strategy of the Medical Products Group. It moved out of slow-growth businesses to focus on more profitable clinical equipment. Some of the employees she considered friends avoided her and told her she was ruining the group. She stated: "I didn't used to be able to tolerate that, and I'd try to explain over and over why change had to occur. Change is painful."

The seven foundation competencies for improving your effectiveness comprise one of three main themes of this book. The second theme of this book is that there are no easy or complete answers as to why people and organizations fail to function smoothly. However, your study of organizational behavior should give you the basic ability to look at and understand the behavior of people in organizations to help you address organizational and behavioral issues and develop solutions to them. **Organizational behavior** is the study of human behavior, attitudes, and performance in organizations. It is interdisciplinary—drawing concepts from social and clinical psychology, sociology, cultural anthropology, industrial engineering, and organizational psychology.

The third theme of this book is the importance of organizational behavior to you. Most of you are or will be employees in organizations and many will eventually become team leaders or managers. Studying organizational behavior should help you attain the competencies needed to be an effective employee, team leader, and/or manager. The knowledge and competencies you acquire should help you diagnose, understand, explain, and act on what is happening around you in your job.

In the remainder of this chapter, we describe each of the seven foundation competencies and then conclude by presenting the framework for the entire book.

Learning Objective:

1. Explain the managing self competency.

THE MANAGING SELF COMPETENCY

The *managing self competency* involves the ability to assess your own strengths and weaknesses, set and pursue professional and personal goals, balance work and personal life, and engage in new learning—including new or changed skills, behaviors, and attitudes.[3]

Core Components

The core components of the managing self competency include the following abilities.

- To understand your own and others' personality and attitudes (see especially Chapter 2, Personality and Attitudes).
- To perceive, appraise, and interpret accurately yourself, others, and the immediate environment (see especially Chapter 3, Perception and Attribution).
- To understand and act on your own and others' work-related motivations and emotions (see especially Chapter 5, Motivation and the Work Setting).
- To assess and establish your own developmental, personal (life-related) and work-related goals (see especially Chapter 6, Motivating Performance: Goal Setting and Reward Systems).
- To take responsibility for managing yourself and your career over time and through stressful circumstances (see especially Chapter 7, Work Stress).

In our view, managing self is the most fundamental of the seven foundation competencies. The achievement of this competency creates the underlying personal attributes needed for successfully developing the other six competencies. For example, you cannot develop the managing diversity competency if you are unable to perceive, appraise, and interpret accurately your own values, reactions, and behaviors with respect to cultural beliefs, practices, and behaviors that differ from your own.

Managing self is a key competency for everyone in an organization. No longer can anyone realistically think that an organization can meet all of a person's developmental, training, and career needs. The following Managing Self Competency feature relates the highlights of how the Ford Motor Company changed its recruitment practices on campuses to emphasize competency-based selection of college graduates.

COMPETENCY: MANAGING SELF

FORD'S COMPETENCY PROGRAM

At the center of Ford Motor Company's recruitment and selection processes are the Ford Leadership Criteria. These criteria are an agreed-upon set of knowledge, experiences, skills, abilities, values, and personal characteristics that the company believes people must possess to be successful and help the company achieve its goals. Taken together, the six criteria provide a road map that guides all stages of the recruitment and selection processes.

These criteria also provide the foundation on which all the company's human resources systems—not just selection—are based. In addition to having a strong educational background and functional experience, the *personal characteristics* being sought in a college-level candidate include the ability and willingness to

- take reasoned risks;
- demonstrate independent judgment and self-confidence, even in stressful situations;
- stay the course to achieve agreed-upon goals, even in ambiguous and complex situations;
- maintain focus, intensity, and persistence, even under adversity;
- apply lessons learned from successes as well as failures to improve future results; and
- seek out alternatives and new ways of doing business.

Consequently, Ford redesigned its selection process to measure a candidate's potential in this and other areas in campus interviews. Recruiters use a variety of approaches and sources of information to assess candidates in terms of the four main categories of personal characteristics: knowledge, experience, skills, and values.[4]

For more information on careers at the Ford Motor Company, visit its Careers home page at: ***www.ford.com.***

CAREER MANAGEMENT

A **career** is a sequence of work-related positions occupied by a person during a lifetime.[5] It embraces attitudes and behaviors that are part of ongoing work-related tasks and experiences. The popular view of a career usually is restricted to the idea of moving up the ladder in an organization. This opportunity no longer is available to many people because of downsizing, mergers, and the increasing tendency of management to place the responsibility on employees to develop their own competencies. A person may remain at the same level, acquiring and developing new competencies, and have a successful career without ever being promoted. A person also can build a career by moving among various jobs in different fields, such as accounting, management information systems, and marketing, or among organizations such as Hewlett-Packard, Dell, and McDonald's. Thus a career encompasses not only traditional work experiences but also the opportunity of career alternatives, individual choices, and individual experiences. Let's briefly consider five aspects of a career.

- The nature of a career in itself doesn't imply success or failure or fast or slow advancement. Career success or failure is best determined by the individual, rather than by others.
- No absolute standards exist for evaluating a career. Career success or failure is related to a person's self-concept, goals, and abilities. Individuals should evaluate their own career goals and progress in terms of what is personally meaningful and satisfying.

- An individual should examine a career both subjectively and objectively. Subjective elements of a career include values, attitudes, personality, and motivations, which may change over time. Objective elements of a career include job choices, positions held, and specific skills developed.
- **Career development** involves making decisions about an occupation and engaging in activities to attain career goals. The central idea in the career development process is time. The shape and direction of a person's career over time are influenced by many factors (e.g., the economy, availability of jobs, skill acquisition, personal characteristics, family status, and job history).
- Cultural factors play a role in careers. Cultural norms in countries such as Japan, the Philippines, and Mexico also influence the direction of a person's career. By U.S. standards, women are discriminated against as managers in these cultures. In India and South Korea, social status and educational background largely determine career paths.

Ralph Waldo Emerson's classic essay "Self-reliance" offers good advice for a person's career: "Trust thyself." To be successful, people need to commit themselves to a lifetime of learning, including the development of a career plan. A **career plan** is the individual's choice of occupation, organization, and career path. For example, Cynthia Danaher has gone through a series of positions with increasing responsibility since joining Hewlett-Packard in 1984 to work in sales development for ultrasound imaging. Before that, she was a sales representative with the General Electric Company Medical Systems Division.

Learning Objective:

2. Explain the managing communication competency.

THE MANAGING COMMUNICATION COMPETENCY

The *managing communication competency* involves the ability to use all the modes of transmitting, understanding, and receiving ideas, thoughts, and feelings—verbal, listening, nonverbal, written, electronic, and the like—for accurately transferring and exchanging information and emotions.[6] This competency may be thought of as the *circulatory system* that nourishes the other competencies. Just as arteries and veins provide for the movement of blood in a person, communication allows the exchange of information, thoughts, ideas, and feelings.

CORE COMPONENTS

The core components of the managing communication competency include the following abilities.

- To convey information, ideas, and emotions to others in such a way that they are received as intended. This ability is strongly influenced by the **describing skill**—identifying concrete, specific examples of behavior and its effects. This skill also includes recognizing that too often individuals don't realize that they are not being clear and accurate in what they say, resulting from a tendency to jump quickly to generalizations and judgments (see especially Chapter 13, Interpersonal Communication).
- To provide constructive feedback to others (see especially Chapters 10, Conflict and Negotiations, and 13, Interpersonal Communication).
- To engage in **active listening**—the process of integrating informational and emotional inputs in a search for shared meaning and understanding. Active listening requires the use of the **questioning skill**—the ability to ask for information and opinions in a way that gets relevant, honest, and appropriate responses. This skill helps to bring relevant information and emotions into the dialogue and reduce misunderstandings, regardless of whether the parties agree. (See especially Chapters 10 and 13).

- To use and interpret **nonverbal communication** effectively—human actions and the meanings that are attached to them. Facial expressions, body movements, and physical contact are often used to send nonverbal messages. The **empathizing skill** is especially important in nonverbal communication and active listening. It refers to detecting and understanding another person's values, motives, and emotions. The empathizing skill helps to reduce tension and increase trust and sharing (see especially Chapter 13).
- To engage in **verbal communication** effectively—presenting ideas, information and emotions to others, either one-to-one or in groups. We provide the opportunity for you to apply this skill in the Developing Competencies section at the end of several chapters and in the Integrating Cases section at the end of the book.
- To engage in **written communication** effectively—the ability to transfer data, information, ideas, and emotions by means of reports, letters, memos, notes, e-mail messages, and the like.
- To use effectively a variety of computer-based (electronic) resources, such as e-mail and the Internet. The **Internet** is a worldwide collection of interconnected computer networks. Through an array of computer-based information technologies, the Internet directly links organizations and their employees to customers, suppliers, information sources, the public, and millions of individuals worldwide. We help you develop this skill throughout the book by presenting numerous Internet addresses and encouraging you to learn more about the organizations, issues, and people discussed.

Relationship to Managerial Roles

The managing communication competency is linked to effective performance in four managerial roles.[7]

The **liaison role** is concerned with the development of information sources, both inside and outside an organization. Managers establish, maintain, and extend a network of personal contacts that can feed information to them. They spend time with other managers and government officials to build a network of contacts through which they learn of trends or impending legislation that can affect their organizations. Keith Hughes, chief executive officer (CEO) of The Associates, maintains close contact with members of the Federal Reserve Board. Doing so enables him to monitor possible changes in interest rates that will affect The Associates' customers in the manufactured housing and home improvement loan businesses. Within an organization, the ability to generate unsolicited information and ideas keeps managers informed about operations. The liaison role helps the manager build an information system and is closely related to the information role of monitor.

In the **monitor role,** managers seek and receive information. Managers are like radar systems, scanning the environment for information that may affect their departments or organizations. Managers need current information because they must react quickly to events taking place around them. Therefore much of the information they receive is verbal.

What do managers do with the information received? In the **disseminator role,** managers share and distribute information to others in an organization. Sometimes it is passed along as privileged information, meaning that, unless a manager passed it along, other managers and employees wouldn't have access to it. Information sharing goes on all the time, but adequately informing subordinates may be difficult and time-consuming. Managers must sort through the information they have received—most of it verbally—and decide whom to share it with and how best to do so. Managers must then convey the information to others verbally or in writing, both of which take time to do.

Managers' role in the information system doesn't end with being a disseminator. They also must pass along information to those outside the organization. In

COMPETENCY: MANAGING COMMUNICATION

THE MICROCOMMUNICATION

The president (name is confidential) of an aeronautics manufacturing company thought that the maintenance costs and turnaround time of the company's U.S. competitors were much better than its own. He thought that the company was going to lose customers and profits and wanted to communicate his fear and urgent desire for change to the firm's senior managers. One afternoon, he called them into the boardroom. Projected on a screen was the image of a smiling man flying an old-fashioned biplane with his scarf blowing in the wind. The right half of the transparency was covered. The president explained that he felt as this pilot did, given the company's recent good fortune. The organization had just finished its most successful year in history. Then with a deep sigh, he announced that this happiness was quickly vanishing. As the president lifted the covering sheet, the pilot was shown flying directly into a wall. The president stated in a stern voice, "This is what I see happening to us." He claimed that the company was headed for a crash if people didn't take action fast. He lectured the senior managers about the steps needed to counter this threat.

The reaction from the team was immediate and negative. Directly after the meeting, the senior managers gathered in small clusters in the hallways to talk about the president's "scare tactics." They resented what they perceived to be the president's overstatement of the case. As the senior managers saw it, they had exerted enormous effort that year to break the company's records in sales and profitability. They were proud of their achievements. In fact, they had entered the meeting expecting recognition of their achievements. But, to their absolute surprise, they had been scolded.[8]

the **spokesperson role,** managers make official statements to outsiders through speeches, reports, television commercials (e.g., Dave Thomas, CEO and founder of Wendy's Old Fashioned Hamburgers), and other media. In this case, if the manager says it, the organization says it.

The feature above illustrates the importance of emotion in a miscommunication by a top-level manager.

Let's consider the president's mistakes. First, he should have engaged in playing the *monitor* role with a few members of his senior team to determine its emotional state. From that, he would have learned that they were in need of thanks and recognition. Second, he could have engaged in the *disseminator* role by holding a separate session devoted simply to praising the team's accomplishments. Later, in a second meeting, he could have shared his own anxieties about the coming year. And rather than blame the team for ignoring the future, he could have calmly described what he saw as developing threats to the company. Third, he could have asked his management team to help him develop new initiatives by engaging in the *liaison* role.[9]

Learning Objective:

3. Explain the managing diversity competency.

THE MANAGING DIVERSITY COMPETENCY

The *managing diversity competency* involves the ability to value unique individual and group characteristics, embrace such characteristics as potential sources of organizational strength, and appreciate the uniqueness of each individual.[10]

Core Components

The core components of the managing diversity competency include the following abilities.

- To foster an environment of inclusion with those who possess characteristics different from your own (see especially Chapter 3, Perception and Attribution).
- To learn from those with different characteristics, experiences, perspectives, and backgrounds. Diversity of thought and behavior is vital to stimulating creativity and innovation (see especially Chapters 14, Decision Making in Organizations, and 18, Organizational Change).
- To embrace and develop personal tendencies—such as *intellectual openness* and attitudes that demonstrate respect for people of other cultures and races—that support diversity in the workplace and elsewhere (see especially Chapter 2, Personality and Attitudes).
- To communicate and personally practice a commitment to work with individuals and team members because of their talents and contributions, regardless of their personal attributes (see especially Chapter 8, Teams and Group Behavior).
- To provide leadership—*walk the talk*—in confronting obvious bias, promoting inclusion, and seeking win–win or compromise solutions to power struggles and conflicts that appear to be based on diversity issues (see especially Chapters 9, Power and Political Behavior, and 10, Conflict and Negotiation).
- To apply governmental laws and regulations as well as organizational policies and regulations concerning diversity as they relate to a person's position.

The case for the managing diversity competency is well stated by Elizabeth Pathy Salett, president of the National Multicultural Institute. She comments:

> As our nation becomes more culturally diverse, we are presented with a series of opportunities and challenges for the future. Can we capitalize on the strength that begins from our differences? Can we create a work environment that draws upon the talents of all our workers? Can we attract a diverse market, serving a variety of tastes and interests? Our ability to meet these challenges will have an enormous impact on worker productivity, management strategies, and organizational success.[11]

Categories of Diversity

ABC, CBS, NBC, CNN, and other media usually focus on race, gender, and ethnicity when mentioning *diversity*. As suggested in Figure 1.2, however, diversity includes these characteristics and many more. Even a single aspect of diversity, such as physical abilities and qualities, contains various characteristics that may affect individual or team behaviors. One challenge for managers is to determine whether those effects deny opportunity and are wasteful and counterproductive, simply reflect a tolerance of differences, or lead to embracing diversity as a value-added organizational resource.[12] A second challenge is to assist in developing individual, team, and organizational competencies—including learning new knowledge, attitudes, skills, and methods of intervention—to value and embrace diversity as a source of creativity and strength.

Figure 1.2 identifies the more common categories of diversity dealt with in organizations. They are subdivided into *primary categories*—genetic characteristics that affect a person's self-image and socialization—and *secondary categories*—learned characteristics that a person acquires and modifies throughout life. As suggested by the arrows, these categories aren't independent. For example, a woman (gender) with children (parental status) is likely to be directly affected by an organization with *family-friendly* or *family-unfriendly* policies and attitudes. An example of a family-unfriendly attitude would be: Your job must always come first if you are to get ahead in this organization.

Figure 1.2 **Selected Categories of Diversity**

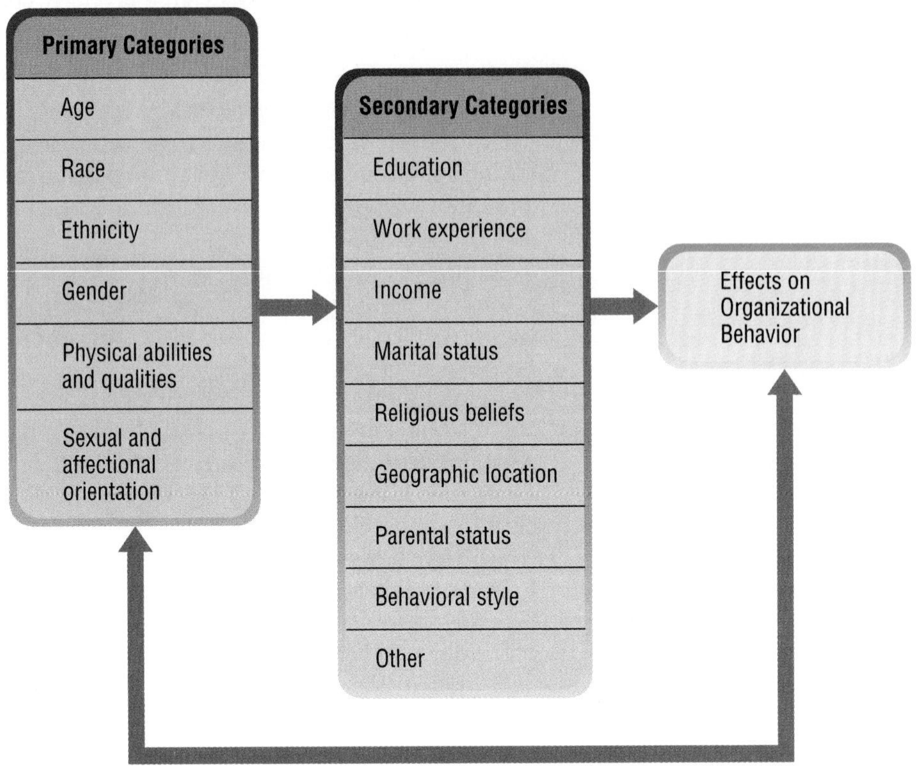

Source: Adapted from Bradford, S. Fourteen dimensions of diversity: Understanding and appreciating differences in the workplace. In J. W. Pfeiffer (ed.), *1996 Annual: Volume 2, Consulting*. San Diego: Pfeiffer and Associates, 1996, 9–17.

The following are brief explanations of the primary categories of diversity. Individuals have relatively little influence over these characteristics.

- *Age:* the number of years a person has been alive and the generation in which she or he was born (e.g., depression era, baby boomers, or generation X in the United States).
- *Race:* the biological groupings within humankind, representing superficial physical differences, such as eye form and skin color. Race accounts for less than 1 percent of the difference in a person's genetic heredity.
- *Ethnicity:* identification with a cultural group that has shared traditions and heritage, including national origin, language, religion, food, and customs. Some people identify strongly with these cultural roots; others do not.
- *Gender:* biological sex as determined by XX (female) or XY (male) chromosomes.
- *Physical abilities and qualities:* a variety of characteristics, including body type, physical size, facial features, specific abilities or disabilities, and visible and invisible physical and mental talents or limitations.
- *Sexual orientation:* feelings of sexual attraction toward members of the same or opposite gender, such as heterosexual, homosexual, or bisexual.

The following are brief explanations of the secondary categories of diversity. Individuals have relatively more influence over them during their lifetimes by making choices.

- *Education:* the individual's formal and informal learning and training.
- *Work experience:* the employment and volunteer positions the person has held and the variety of organizations for which the person has worked.

- *Income:* the economic conditions in which the person grew up and his or her current economic status.
- *Marital status:* the person's situation as never married, married, widowed, or divorced.
- *Religious beliefs:* fundamental teachings received about deities and values acquired from formal or informal religious practices.
- *Geographic location:* the location(s) in which the person was raised or spent a significant part of her or his life, including types of communities and urban areas versus rural areas.
- *Parental status:* having or not having children and the circumstances in which the children are raised, such as single parenting and two-adult parenting.
- *Personal style:* tendency of the individual to think, feel, or act in a particular way.[13]

We discuss many of these categories of diversity throughout the book. In addition, many of the chapters contain a Managing Diversity Competency feature that relates one or more categories of diversity to a specific organizational topic. One such feature is the following presentation of how the General Electric (GE) Corporation is attempting to embrace the many aspects of diversity through the theme of boundaryless behavior.

COMPETENCY: MANAGING DIVERSITY

BOUNDARYLESS BEHAVIOR

Recognizing that differences often create barriers to productivity in an organization, GE's CEO Jack Welch calls for a company with boundaryless behavior. He states, "Boundaryless behavior is the soul of today's GE. Simply put, people seem compelled to build layers and walls between themselves and others, and that human tendency tends to be magnified in large, old institutions. . . . These walls cramp people, inhibit creativity, waste time, restrict vision, smother dreams, and above all, slow things down."

To help implement the *boundaryless behavior* concept, GE established a self-assessment program with several key diversity practices:

- top management commitment and involvement in diversity initiatives;
- recruitment goals for diversity;
- support of work-life programs;
- communication of diversity strategy;
- reward and recognition of those who walk-the-talk; and
- integrate diversity into business strategy.

Dr. Gene Andrews, GE manager of workforce diversity, states:

> At GE, we recognize that we are increasingly relying on teams and that our teams are increasingly diverse. Because of this, it just makes sense for us to put emphasis on ensuring that all of our team members feel and experience a real sense of inclusion and that they are afforded the opportunity to ramp up the learning curve as quickly as possible. We do this through practices such as a buddy system to assist new employees with their transition to GE, a high-impact and business-focused employee orientation, and a mentoring program to help all employees with career and personal development issues. We expect that these practices will also contribute to the bottom line in terms of both individual and team productivity and reduced turnover costs resulting from an anticipated increase in employee retention.[14]

*For more information on General Electric, visit the company's home page at **www.ge.com.***

In the remainder of this section, we present a brief overview of the organizational implications for some of the primary categories of diversity. As you consider them, think about their potential impact on your career.

Changing Workforce and Customers

The makeup of the workforce and customer base in the United States, Canada, and other countries will continue to change. The majority of new employees will continue to be women, members of non-Caucasian races, and from ethnically diverse groups (virtually every country in the world is represented in the U.S. population). In addition, an increasing number of global organizations, such as Coca-Cola and IBM, have many employees, customers, and suppliers in locations around the world. Workforces in Asia, Western Europe, Latin America, and North America are growing more complex and diverse. Managers and employees need to recognize and embrace differences resulting from this diversity, particularly in terms of what employees want from their jobs. Let's consider three of the challenges that organizations face with a diverse workforce.[15]

First, there are language differences. Unless employees can understand each other, communication is difficult or even impossible. Employees can't train each other or work together if they can't communicate. Translators may be used for hiring, but—for the day-to-day communication that fosters a friendly, informal, and productive work setting—language barriers pose real and often serious problems. Such problems may lead to misunderstandings regarding performance goals, work methods, safety measures, and other essential working conditions.

Second, natural ethnic groupings within an organization may develop. Such tendencies need to be constructively managed. Employees, especially if they don't speak English, may seek out others of the same ethnic group for assistance. At the Marriott's Quorum Hotel in Addison, Texas, a large percentage of its housekeeping staff is from Vietnam. With English as a second language, these employees often seek out other Vietnamese rather than a supervisor for help. They don't want to embarrass themselves because they are not able to speak English fluently. Although natural ethnic groupings may create a strong sense of togetherness within ethnic groups, it may not promote working with others who don't share the same language and cultural heritage. At J.C. Penney's corporate headquarters in Plano, Texas, once a month the cafeteria staff prepares meals, hangs flags, and displays other items from countries in which the company does business. This type of observance is one way for employees to get some feeling for living and working in different cultures.

Third, attitudes and cultural differences are another possible challenge. Most people have developed attitudes and beliefs about others by the time they seek a job. However, some attitudes and beliefs create frustration, anger, and bitterness in those at whom they're aimed. Managers and others who want to foster employee tolerance recognize that major changes are required. In some organizations, women and minorities are bypassed when important, formal decisions are made. Informally, these people often are left out when others go to lunch or a sporting event. These informal get-togethers often give older employees a chance to counsel younger employees about coping with problems. Unfortunately, most managers and employees usually accept change only if the potential benefits are clear and worthwhile.

To create an environment in which everyone can contribute to the organization's goals, attitudes usually must change. What are your attitudes toward diversity? Before reading further, please complete the Attitudes Toward Diversity Questionnaire in the Developing Competence section at the end of this chapter. How did you score?

Gender

Women now represent nearly half (47 percent) of the workforce in the United States. They also account for about 11 percent of officers at large corporations, up from about 8.5 percent in 1995.[16]

Consider a few results from a survey of randomly selected female and male top and middle managers who subscribe to *Fortune* magazine.[17] These results are representative of those obtained in other such surveys. In *Fortune*'s survey, respondents were provided with a list of 18 attitudes or situations that could potentially erect barriers to women's professional success. The existence of a male-dominated corporate culture was cited by 91 percent of the women and 75 percent of the men as the number one barrier to the advancement of women. Women also felt that the existence of a glass ceiling (88 percent), their exclusion from informal network communication (86 percent), management's attitude that women are less career-oriented than men (84 percent), and the lack of female mentors (78 percent) were among the top five barriers to their advancement.

The **glass ceiling** refers to a barrier so subtle that it is transparent, yet so strong that it prevents women and minorities from moving up in management. There appear to be three primary causes of the glass ceiling. First, managers and executives are not held accountable for results in the areas of equal employment opportunity and affirmative action. Second, women and minorities are not encouraged to apply for or even made aware of job openings at higher levels. Third, these groups lack training and development opportunities that would allow them to improve their competencies and chances for promotion.

Let's consider one of the programs at Aetna—the global provider of health, retirement, and financial services products—designed to help shatter the glass ceiling. The Aetna Emerging Leaders Program is designed to groom the next generation of leaders by guiding participants through a rigorous multiyear development plan. One of the goals is to build wide-ranging diversity into Aetna's talent base. Candidates must have 5 to 7 years of work experience either within Aetna or outside the company. The program guides participants through a series of 12- to 24-month assignments in different areas of the business. According to Orlene Weyland, program director, this program is different because it's highly individualized, and it reaches people early in their careers. Each candidate receives coaching, education, mentoring, and a career path guidance.[18]

Many women with children hold full-time jobs and still bear primary responsibility for family care. An estimated 75 percent of working women are in their childbearing years. Dupont, Deloitte & Touche, Eli Lilly, Hewlett-Packard, Marriott International, and Motorola are among the firms having family-friendly policies and strategies. Such firms often offer child care, flextime (ability to arrive and leave work at varied hours), job-sharing (two individuals, often women, who want to work part-time and share a job), telecommuting (opportunity for certain groups of employees to work at home some or most of the time), and flexibility in accommodating employees with urgent family needs.[19]

Race and Ethnicity

Each year, one-third of the newcomers to the U.S. workforce are minority group members. The U.S. workforce has approximately 16.5 million African Americans, up almost 20 percent from 1988. Hispanics, Asians, and other minorities comprise 14 percent of the workforce, up 4 percent from 1988.[20] In addition to the glass ceiling, minority group members also face **racism,** the notion that a person's genetic group is superior to all others. Racism takes three interrelated basic forms: (1) *individual racism*—the extent to which a person holds attitudes, values, feelings, and/or engages in behaviors that promote the person's own racial group as superior; (2) *cultural racism*—the arrogant elevation of the cultural features and achievements of one race as superior while actively ignoring or denigrating those of other races; and (3) *institutional racism*—organizational and/or social rules, regulations, laws, policies, and customs that serve to maintain the dominant status of and control by one racial group. Each form of racism may operate openly or secretly and intentionally or unintentionally.[21]

Fannie Mae, formally known as the Federal National Mortgage Association, has established explicit programs to root out all forms of racism. This organization is the largest source of home mortgage funds for low- to middle-income households in the United States. Of the company's 3,700 employees, 23 percent of its top managers are minorities. In 1999, Franklin Rains assumed the position of CEO, making him the first African American to lead a Fortune 500 company.

Fannie Mae's diversity effort began with mandatory diversity awareness training for all managers and employees. Since then, all employees have attended daylong seminars to help them understand the importance of diversity to the business of reviewing mortgage applications and deciding which ones qualify. Other diversity efforts include minority recruitment, mentoring, employee support groups, and special programs to heighten awareness of black and Hispanic history. The organization also has started doing more business with women- and minority-owned financial services firms. Fannie Mae's commitment to diversity is further evidenced by making diversity a corporate goal and core value that is reviewed quarterly. In addition, diversity is part of the performance goals and rewards for all company officers, directors, and managers—including bonuses, merit increases, and promotions.[22]

Age

The U.S. and Canadian workforces are aging along with the baby boomers. From 1990 to 2000, the number of people aged 35 to 47 increased by 38 percent, whereas the number between 48 and 53 increased by 67 percent.[23] The increase in the number of middle-aged employees has collided with the efforts of many companies, such as Kodak, Sanyo Electric, and British Petroleum, to reduce layers of middle management in order to remain competitive. Over time, the competencies that many of these employees have gained are valuable only to the firms they work for. Displaced, older employees who lose their jobs often have great difficulty matching previous levels of responsibility and salaries, even when they are able to find new jobs. Moreover, older workers often are less likely than younger workers to relocate or train for new occupations.

The need to manage a career or careers over a lifetime—not just in the early years—is now an imperative rather than an option. Most individuals can no longer count on progressing along a single career path in one organization as they age. One of the main reasons is that the traditional view that loyalty between the organization and the employee increases with years of service—and thus age—is no longer valid in most U.S. and Canadian organizations.[24]

Learning Objective:

4. Explain the managing ethics competency.

THE MANAGING ETHICS COMPETENCY

The *managing ethics competency* involves the ability to incorporate values and principles that distinguish right from wrong in making decisions and choosing behaviors.[25] **Ethics** are the values and principles that distinguish right from wrong.

Core Components

The core components of the managing ethics competency include the following abilities.

- To identify and describe the principles of ethical decision making and behavior (see especially Chapter 14, Decision Making in Organizations).
- To assess the importance of ethical issues in considering alternative courses of action. The decision to shop at Wal-Mart versus Kmart is not related to any ethical issue of consequence.
- To apply governmental laws and regulations, as well as the employer's rules of conduct, in making decisions and taking action within a person's level of responsibilities and authority. In general, the greater a person's level of responsi-

bilities and authority, the more the person is likely to face increasingly complex and ambiguous ethical issues and dilemmas. For example, decisions having ethical demands and importance are likely to be far less for an associate at a Home Depot store than for the store manager (see especially Chapter 11, Leadership Foundations).

- To demonstrate dignity and respect for others in working relationships—such as taking action against discriminatory practices as individually feasible and in terms of a person's position. The manager at a Sears store is more able to stop an employee from showing disrespect to members of a minority group than is a checkout associate in the store (see especially Chapter 12, Leadership: Contemporary Developments).
- To demonstrate honesty and openness in communication, limited only by legal, privacy, and competitive considerations (i.e., Do what you say and say what you do). (See especially Chapters 10, Conflict and Negotiations, and 13, Interpersonal Communication.)

Ethical Dilemmas

The ethical issues facing managers and other employees have grown in significance in recent years, fueled by public concern about how business is conducted. Ethical behavior sometimes is difficult to define, especially in a global economy with its varied beliefs and practices. Although ethical behavior in business clearly has a legal component, absolutes in one country aren't always applicable in another country.

Managers and employees alike face situations in which there are no clear right or wrong answers. The burden is on individuals to make ethical decisions. An **ethical dilemma** occurs when an individual or team must make a decision that involves multiple values. An ethical dilemma doesn't simply involve choosing right over wrong because there may be several competing values. Some ethical dilemmas arise from competitive and time pressures, among other factors.[26] Consider the following incident. The minister of a foreign government asks you to pay a special consulting fee of $200,000 to him. In return, the official promises special assistance in obtaining a $100 million contract for your firm that would produce at least a $5 million profit. The contract will be awarded to a foreign competitor if not awarded to your company. Your choice is to pay the fee or not to pay the fee. What would you do? In a survey of *Harvard Business Review* readers, 42 percent said that they would refuse to pay; 22 percent said that they would pay but consider it unethical; 36 percent said that they would pay and consider it ethical in the foreign context.[27]

Top-management leadership, policies and rules, and the prevailing organizational culture can do much to reduce, guide, and assist the individual regarding ethical dilemmas. The Managing Ethics Competency feature on page 18 demonstrates the leadership by Michael Roth, chairman and CEO of the MONY Group, a major provider of life insurance, annuities, mutual funds, and other financial services. In it he notes some of the company's policies for reducing ethical dilemmas that might otherwise be experienced by its employees and for basing their decisions on ethical considerations.

Learning Objective:

5. Explain the managing across cultures competency.

THE MANAGING ACROSS CULTURES COMPETENCY

The *managing across cultures competency* involves the ability to recognize and embrace similarities and differences among nations and cultures and then approach key organizational and strategic issues with an open and curious mind.

Competency: Managing Ethics

Michael Roth at MONY Group

We have a simple method of determining what constitutes good business ethics at MONY, and that is, What's the right thing? You have to ask yourself, "Am I doing the right thing? And if I were on the other side of the table, how would I expect to be treated? How would I expect a loved one to be treated?" However you answer those questions, that's the way we expect you to deal with our policyholders and our customers. What we're trying to get across with our ethics initiatives is that the product is the last issue you talk about with your policyholder and customer. First, you want to establish a relationship that is based on trust. We're looking to meet a need of our customer as opposed to selling him or her a product.

We've had a code of ethics for many years. The first part of our code says we want to make sure everyone is well trained in ethical practices. Therefore, we have a requirement that everyone, including the executives at the home office, take an ethics course, which is basically the Life Underwriters Training Course (LUTC) on ethics. What's interesting about that is that LUTC has chosen our company to put its course on CD-ROM for the entire industry to use, so we must be doing it right.

I personally meet with all our new agents at our campus school. I indicate to them that professionalism breeds good sales ethics. If you know what you're doing and you're well trained, and if you're looking at this as a long-term career, then doing the right thing is the way to succeed. It just makes good business sense. If you're in it for the quick buck, there's no place for you here. Go find a job elsewhere. I think it's good business for our sales force and our employees to practice a high level of ethical behavior. What we want to do is have Mutual of New York be known in the marketplace, and in the industry, as a company that does the right thing. And, frankly, we ultimately hope to distinguish ourselves from the rest of the industry as a company that not only talks a good game, but, in fact, acts that way.

That has to come from the top. Not just from me, but from all the senior officers in our organization. Frankly, I don't give a speech that doesn't include a section on good ethical practices: why we have to stand for doing the right thing and that we won't accept anything less. And in dealing with our sales force, if there are any deviations from the rules, we deal with them swiftly.

I think the question that we continually ask ourselves is whether we're actually walking the walk as well as talking the talk. We hold ourselves up as standing for doing the right thing: we can't say it and not make it a consistent theme within our organization.[28]

*For more information on the MONY Group, Inc., visit the organization's home page at **www.mony.com/AboutMONY/Ethics/**.*

Core Components

The core components of the managing across cultures competency include the following abilities.

- To understand, appreciate, and use the factors that make a particular culture unique and recognize the characteristics of a culture that are likely to influence a person's behaviors. **Culture** is the pattern of living, thinking, and believing that is developed and transmitted by a group of human beings, consciously or unconsciously, to subsequent generations.[29] Consider the following five core concepts identified for the Japanese culture and how they may differ from your own culture.
  1. *Wa:* means that harmony and peace come from loyalty, obedience, and cooperation with other people, including family, peers, and work associates. It is a sacred state that must be maintained.

2. *Amae:* describes (a) the indulgent, dependent love that exists between parents and children, and (b) the total trust between people who are bound by the same obligations—for example, an employee and manager in a work setting. This particular relationship can exist only between two Japanese, never with foreigners (*enryo*).
3. *Tate Shakai:* refers to a vertical society. In Japanese society, everything is *ranked* and all important relationships are *vertical* rather than *horizontal.* This ranking extends to seniority and titles in a company, to schools and universities (Tokyo University is considered the highest), and to roles in a family.
4. *Giri:* comprise the universal obligations a person acquires at birth. These obligations extend to ancestors, parents, and the nation; they define a role that individuals must fulfill during their lifetimes.
5. *On:* the specific, reciprocal obligations that a person incurs throughout life—for example, obligations to teachers and superiors at work.[30]

- To identify and understand how work-related values, such as individualism and collectivism, influence the preferences of individuals and groups in their decisions and organizational practices.[31]
- To understand and motivate employees with different values and attitudes. These may range from the more individualistic, Western style of work, to paternalistic, non-Western attitudes, to the extreme "the state-will-take-care-of-me" collectivist mindset.[32]
- To communicate in the language of the country with which the individual has working relationships. This ability is crucial for employees that have ongoing communication with those who have a different native language. The tensions and "finger pointing" when language insensitivity exists between the home country headquarters and employees in a foreign country are illustrated in the following incident. Kone is a Finnish multinational elevator company with subsidiaries around the world. In a study of the company's language practices, one of its Spanish middle managers commented:

  > We should receive this [corporate] information in Spanish, so that it could be used here. I have a lot of information about maintenance here in these folders, but I don't have time to translate it into Spanish. At present, I can't read it, nor understand it, or use it.[33]

  The manager not only ignored the information received from Finland but also placed the blame for the situation on Kone's corporate headquarters. Assigning blame to someone else served to justify in his own mind his inaction.
- To deal with extreme conditions, especially for those with assignments in foreign countries. This need applies even if the assignment is short term or the person has international responsibilities from the home office. Some extreme conditions include economic instability, political unrest, cultural conflicts, governmental bureaucratic obstacles, lack of laws or constantly shifting laws governing and protecting business interests, public anger or resentment of outsiders, armed insurrections or even full-blown military coups, and so on.[34] Conditions in Russia were difficult, extreme, and uncertain for domestic and foreign firms alike during the 1990s. Some firms, such as Caterpillar and Chase Manhattan Bank, have forged ahead with their long-term plans and investments in Russia despite these difficulties.[35]
- To address managerial and other issues through a **global mindset.** Such a mindset means scanning the environment with a worldwide perspective, always looking for unexpected trends that may create threats or opportunities for a unit or an entire organization. Some call this the ability to *think globally, act locally.*[36]

INDIVIDUALISM–COLLECTIVISM

Individualism and collectivism are two of the fundamental work-related values that must be thoroughly understood and used to develop the *managing across cultures competency.*[37]

We address the impacts of these and other values throughout the book. **Individualism** is the tendency of people to look after themselves and their immediate families, which implies a loosely integrated society. The individual is emotionally independent from organizations and institutions. The culture emphasizes individual initiative, decision making, and achievement. Everybody is believed to have the right to privacy and personal freedom of expression. Countries characterized by an emphasis on individualism include the United States, New Zealand, the United Kingdom, and Australia.

In contrast, **collectivism** is the tendency of people to emphasize their belonging to groups and to look after each other in exchange for loyalty. The social framework tends to be tight, and in-groups (relatives, clans, and organizations) focus on their common welfare and distinguish themselves from out-groups. Collectivism usually involves emotional dependence of the individual on groups, organizations, and institutions. The sense of belonging and "we" versus "I" in relationships is fundamental. Individuals' private lives are open to the groups and organizations to which they belong. In-group goals are generally thought to be more important than the individual's personal goals. When conflict arises between individual goals and in-group goals, the general expectation is that in-group goals and decision making should prevail. Countries characterized by an emphasis on collectivism include Japan, China, Venezuela, and Indonesia.

Harmony is another feature of cultures that emphasize collectivism. People in the same group are supposed to have similar views. Also, face-saving is important in this culture. Individuals in China, Japan, Taiwan, and Korea care about whether their behavior would be considered shameful by the other members of their in-groups. They also avoid pointing out other people's mistakes in public so that the others won't lose face. Because individuals are so tightly integrated into their in-groups, they feel that they have a common fate and thus are highly interdependent.

In contrast, those people in countries that emphasize individualism, such as Canada, the United States, and the United Kingdom, do form in-groups. However, individuals in these countries generally do not think that they have a common fate with their in-groups. They view themselves as independent, unique, and special. Thus they are less likely to conform to the expectations of others. When group goals conflict with personal goals, individuals commonly pursue their own goals. In addition, seeking personal identity is highly valued in individualistic cultures. Confrontation with others within an in-group is acceptable. Personal achievement, pleasure, and competition are all highly valued.[38]

The Managing Across Cultures Competency feature on page 21 focuses on some managerial implications of the Chinese emphasis on collectivism.

Learning Objective:

6. Explain the managing teams competency.

THE MANAGING TEAMS COMPETENCY

The *managing teams competency* involves the ability to develop, support, facilitate, and lead groups to achieve organizational goals.[39] The components of this competency are developed in several chapters, especially Chapters 8, Group and Team Behavior; 10, Conflict and Negotiations; 12, Leadership: Contemporary Development; and 18, Organizational Change. In addition, the other competencies reviewed in this chapter contribute to the variety of abilities needed to be effective as a team member or leader (as suggested previously in Figure 1.1).

CORE COMPONENTS

The core components of the managing teams competency include the following abilities.

- To determine the circumstances in which a team approach is appropriate and, if using it is appropriate, the type of team to use.
- To participate in and/or lead the process of setting clear performance goals for the team.

COMPETENCY: MANAGING ACROSS CULTURES

CHINA'S COLLECTIVISM

Individual rights are a foreign concept to traditional Chinese. Unity is essential when they are confronted with many hardships. Living up to Confucian obligations to others, especially family, is a person's first duty. "Looking out for number one" at the expense of the group is unimaginable.

Buddhism suppresses individual identity, and individual competitiveness is seen as selfishness. The terms *individual* and *freedom* have no direct translation into Chinese. The same is true for the notion of privacy, which is likened to discomfort: The more prolonged it is, the more intolerable it becomes. The imperative to conform to group norms makes shame a more effective control technique than guilt, which is diminished in importance by the unique ethics of a particular group.

Related to collectivism is the emphasis on harmony. Order is the highest social ideal in China. The entire social structure of *guanxi* (defined as relationships, ritual behavior (*li*), and avoiding loss of face) is directed toward preventing potential conflict that could jeopardize harmony. Guanxi includes friendships with implications for the continued exchange of favors—the oil that lubricates social relationships. A very personal communication style and humility are by-products of the search for harmony, compared to the direct, assertive, open communication style, self-promotion, and ambition common in the West. So is their reluctance to do business with strangers. Westerners may find it difficult to grasp or imitate Chinese subtlety and modesty. Criticism of others must be very carefully crafted, and even praise should be moderate. The customary use of introductions, go-betweens, and referrals has more to do with avoiding situations that may be disharmonious (say, encountering a foreigner likely to be ignorant of *li*) than with favoritism or cronyism.

Westerners encounter the issue of harmony most directly in negotiating with their Chinese counterparts. They must not show anger, impatience, or any form of disharmony and unpleasantness when frustrated; persistence is a much more effective reaction. Avoiding personal questions, other than inquiries regarding the welfare of children, is essential. Touching, off-color humor, and topics such as politics and religion are taboo. Simply bringing up such a topic will arouse anxiety, even though nothing offensive has been said, because it creates the potential for or expectation of disharmony. A smile or laugh that seems a bit nervous or oddly out of place—a common Chinese reaction to stressful situations—is a signal of potential disharmony.[40]

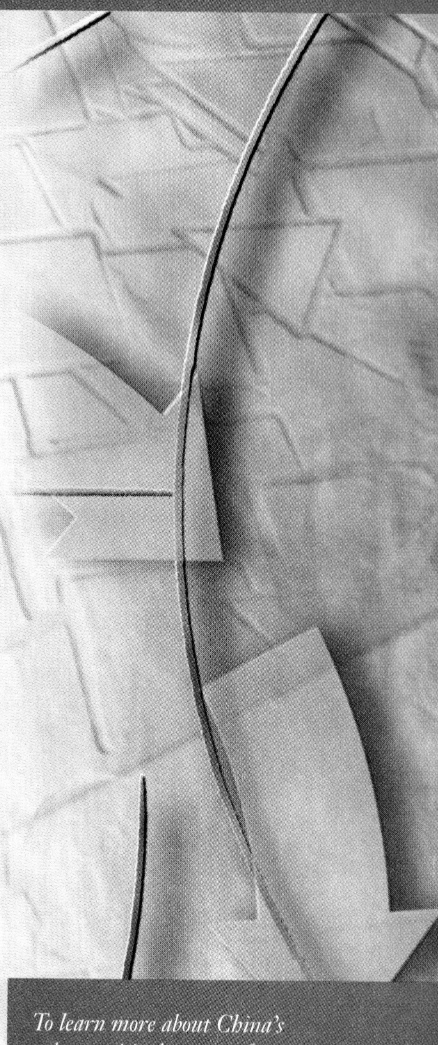

To learn more about China's culture, visit the nonprofit Chinese Culture Online Library *at **www.librarycatalog.com/ccol/index.***

- To participate in and/or provide the leadership in defining responsibilities and tasks for the team as a whole, as well as its individual members.
- To demonstrate a sense of mutual and personal accountability for the achievement of team goals, not just an individual's own goals. That is, the individual doesn't approach problems and issues with a mindset of "that's not my responsibility or concern."
- To use and apply decision-making methods that are appropriate to the goals, issues, and tasks confronting the team.
- To deal with personal and task-related conflicts among team members before they become too disruptive.
- The ability to assess a person's own performance and that of the team in relation to goals, including the ability to take corrective action as needed.

Individualism and Teams

As indicated previously, in some countries, people strongly believe in the importance and centrality of the individual. In the United States, the United Kingdom, and Canada, educational, governmental, and business institutions frequently state that they exist to serve individual goals. Two cultural values that strongly affect decisions about whether to use teams and groups in organizations are individualism and collectivism (discussed in the preceding section).

The cultural belief in individualism creates uneasiness over the influence that teams or groups have in organizations. Recall that individualism means being distinct and separate from the group, emphasizing personal goals, and showing less concern and emotional attachment to groups, especially in work organizations. Employees in individualistic cultures are expected to act on the basis of their personal goals and self-interests.

The cultural belief in collectivism in countries such as China and Japan seems to have the opposite effect in organizations. The use of teams is a natural extension of their nations' cultural values. Their uneasiness revolves around the relative influence and assertiveness of the individual in teams. As we suggested in the preceding section, collectivism means being an integral part of the group, subordinating personal goals to group goals, showing deep concern for the welfare of the group, and feeling emotional ties to the group.[41] Thus we might characterize the basic difference as "fitting into the team" versus "standing out from the team." Even in societies that value individualism, the actual use of teams and groups is substantial in such firms as Hewlett-Packard, Ford, General Electric, and MONY.

The potential for teams and individuals to have incompatible goals clearly exists, but these goals need not always conflict and in fact often are compatible. The potential for conflict and commonality is suggested by the following observations.

- Groups do exist, and all employees need to take them into account.
- Groups mobilize powerful forces that create important effects for individuals.
- Groups may create both good and bad results.
- Groups can be managed to increase the benefits from them.[42]

The free rider concept is one example of conflicting team and individual goals. A **free rider** is a team member who obtains benefits from membership but doesn't bear a proportional share of the responsibility for generating the benefit.[43] Students sometimes experience the free-rider problem when a faculty member assigns a team project for which all the members receive the same (team) grade. Let's assume that seven students are in a team and that two members make little or no contribution. The non-contributing members obtain the benefit of the team grade but didn't bear a proportional share of the work in earning the team grade. Free riders are likely to be highly individualistic people who believe that they can minimize their contribution to a team effort so long as they are not held accountable individually.

Free riding is repulsive to most team and group members for three reasons. First, free riding violates an equity standard: Team members don't want others to receive the same rewards for less effort. Second, it violates a standard social responsibility: Everyone should do his or her fair share. Third, it violates the standard of reciprocity or exchange.[44] A team may do poorly if too many of its members are free riders who contribute little or nothing to the task.

The circumstances under which teams should be used versus the individual approach—that is, a single employee or manager taking primary control and personal accountability for performing a task, resolving an issue, or solving a problem—should be assessed continually. Levi Straus, one of the world's most successful brands, has faced difficult times in recent years. Some people have suggested that the excessive and ineffective use of teams and groups by Robert (Bob) Haas, the CEO, contributed to these problems. Critical comments by former top executives about Haas include:

He's not the sort of manager who says, "Here's what you did wrong." Instead, he sits down, looks you in the eye, and asks, "What do you think you did wrong?" . . . I love Bob to death, but he has a tendency to want to involve everybody in decision making. He's compassionate to a fault! . . . Everything had to go into a corporate process, so nothing ever got resolved. . . . Almost half my time was spent in meetings that were absolutely senseless. If you asked [Levi's executives] for the time, they would build you a clock, and still not be able to tell you the time.[45]

Learning Objective:

7. Explain the managing change competency.

THE MANAGING CHANGE COMPETENCY

The *managing change competency* involves the ability to recognize and implement needed adaptations or entirely new transformations in the people, tasks, strategies, structures, or technologies in a person's area of responsibility.

CORE COMPONENTS

The core components of the managing change competency include the following abilities.

- To apply the six previously discussed competencies in the diagnosis, development, and implementation of needed changes.
- To provide leadership in the process of planned change (see especially Chapters 11, Leadership: Foundations, and 12, Leadership: Contemporary Developments). As we describe them in those chapters, leadership styles and approaches may need to vary under conditions of crisis and the need for major changes. Consider the case of Jack Welch, GE's CEO. At one time, he was nicknamed "Neutron Jack" because of his autocratic approach and style of leadership. He was faced with the need to make transformational and difficult decisions, including the elimination of tens of thousands of employees, entire levels of management, and several divisions. After completing this overhaul, Welch shifted his leadership approach and made it known that there was no place for autocrats at GE. Not many leaders can change their behaviors as dramatically as Welch. In many instances, the directive autocrat needs to be replaced by a more democratic or permissive leader when a crisis has passed.[46]
- To diagnose pressures for and resistances to change in specific situations. These pressures may be internal—such as the organizational culture—or external—such as new technologies or competitors (see especially Chapters 17, Organizational Culture, and 18, Organizational Change).
- To apply the systems model of change and other processes to introduce and achieve organizational change. Most chapters of the book provide insights for developing this ability (see especially Chapter 18, Organizational Change). The basis of the systems model of change is **conceptualization,** or the ability to combine information from a number of sources, to integrate information into more general situations and contexts, and to apply information in new or broader ways. Individuals with this skill are able to identify key issues and diagnose them by examining the basic questions of *who, what, why, when, where,* and *how.* We focus on this ability throughout the book.
- To seek out, learn, share, and apply new knowledge in the pursuit of constant improvement, creativity, and entirely new approaches or goals. These behaviors require **risk taking,** or the willingness to take reasonable chances by recognizing and capitalizing on opportunities while also recognizing their potential negative outcomes and monitoring progress toward goals.

Technological Forces

Technology, especially computer-based information technologies, continue to revolutionize how

1. customers are served;
2. employees communicate and network with one another and external stakeholders, such as customers, suppliers, competitors, and governmental agencies;
3. tasks are performed;
4. organizations are structured;
5. human resources are led and managed;
6. planning and control systems operate;
7. individuals and organizations learn to innovate and adapt; and
8. many other tasks are performed.[47]

Technological change may have positive effects, including products of higher quality and services at lower costs. But it also may have negative effects, including erosion of personal privacy, work-related stress, and health problems (e.g., eyestrain, carpal tunnel syndrome, and exposure to toxic substances).

New technologies are increasing the need for constant learning, adaptation, and innovation by individuals, groups, and entire organizations. In *Blur: The Speed of Change in the Connected Economy*, Davis and Meyer proposed a formula to represent the rapidly accelerating rate of technological and other changes:

Speed × Connectivity × Intangibles = Blur

Speed:	Every aspect of organizations operate and change in real time.
Connectivity:	Everything is becoming electronically connected to everything else: products, people, companies, countries—everything.
Intangibles:	Every offer has both tangible and intangible economic value. The intangible is growing faster, which is the growing role of personal services for many organizations and the economy as a whole.
Blur:	The New World in which we will come to live and work.[48]

The revolution in technologies is a driving force in creating the state of *blur* and the need to actively manage change. Throughout this book, we discuss topics that are related to the introduction and use of technology and which, in turn, are affected by it.

The rise of the Internet is the most obvious expression of an economy and a culture that have become focused on speed. The Internet is a technology that seems to bring the entire world to a person's desktop instantaneously and to satisfy quickly any query or curiosity. The ever-expanding online World Wide Web is but the most recent indication of a trend over the past few decades that has brought businesses, customers, and others continually closer in real time. Technologies ranging from PCs to television to automated teller machines to 1-hour photo processing have intensified expectations about acceptable time frames for seeing results.

The Managing Change Competency feature on page 25 reveals how Drew Santin and his firm, Santin Engineering, Inc., of Peabody, Massachusetts, increased speed to meet the needs of their clients.

Learning Objective:

8. Outline the framework for learning about organizational behavior.

LEARNING FRAMEWORK

The framework for learning about organizational behavior and improving the competencies of employees in organizations consists of four basic components: (1) environmental influences; (2) individual processes; (3) group and interpersonal processes; and (4) organizational processes. Figure 1.3 shows the relationships among these components, as well as the principal aspects of each. These relationships are much too dynamic—in

Competency: Managing Change

Embracing Speed

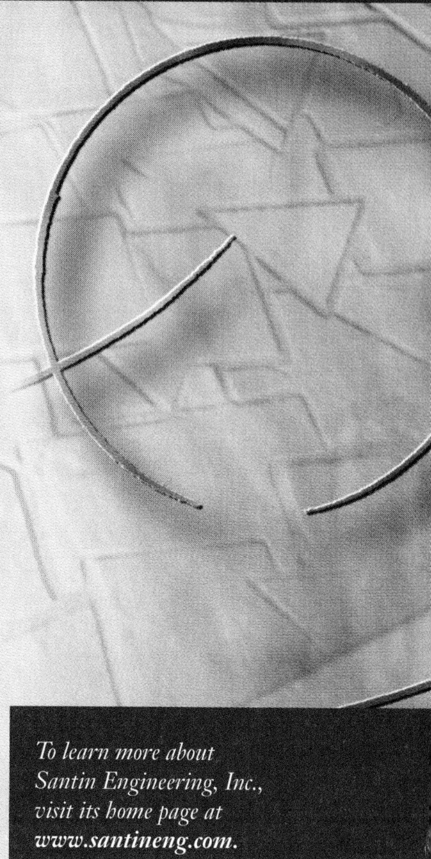

Drew Santin's company, Santin Engineering, Inc., makes quick prototypes for manufacturers who want to see how their newest products will look, feel, and perform—and they want to know now, not tomorrow. Compounding the pressure is the fact that Santin's biggest markets—computer-component manufacturers and makers of clothing accessories and costume jewelry—are among the most demanding. His customers count on him to help them cope with their own ever-accelerating customer demands for quick turnaround.

Santin states, "I'm dealing with an industry, in PC components, where the two-year time frame for developing a new product, which was the case not long ago, now has become six months or less. And in some cases, we have to be able to help our customers turn around in a window that may be as short as a month. The fashion industry is the same way: They can see things get knocked off by competitors even before they go to market. So our ability to get a customized solution in front of the customer is crucial. The pressure is constant to reduce their time frames and to help them get a performing product in the shortest possible period of time." Instead of carrying around the need for speed like an albatross, he and his 60 employees are embracing it—and making Santin Engineering a speed merchant. Employees routinely work nights and weekends to help customers trim precious hours and days from the development process.

Santin cross-trains its employees to ensure maximum flexibility for customers. With computer-based software, engineers can produce quick plastic representations of production components on the spot—even while a meeting with a client is taking place.[49]

To learn more about Santin Engineering, Inc., visit its home page at ***www.santineng.com.***

terms of variety and change—to define them as laws or rules. As we preview each component, the dynamics and complexities of organizational behavior will become clear.

Environmental Forces

Organizations are fundamentally *open systems*, which means that their long-term effectiveness is determined by their ability to anticipate, manage, and respond to changes in the environment. The external stakeholders and forces that create pressures, demands, and expectations for organizations are numerous—and changing more rapidly than ever. External forces and stakeholders include shareholders, customers, competitors, suppliers, labor force (including current and prospective employees), creditors, governmental agencies and regulations, the natural environment, the economy, and cultures.

The competencies that we have previewed embrace the interplay between environmental forces and the actions of managers and employees. Throughout this book, therefore, we discuss the relationships among various environmental influences, competencies, and organizational behavior in general.

Individual Processes

People make assumptions about those with whom they work or spend time in leisure activities. To some extent, these assumptions influence a person's behavior toward others. Effective employees understand what affects their own behaviors before

Figure 1.3 **Framework for Learning**

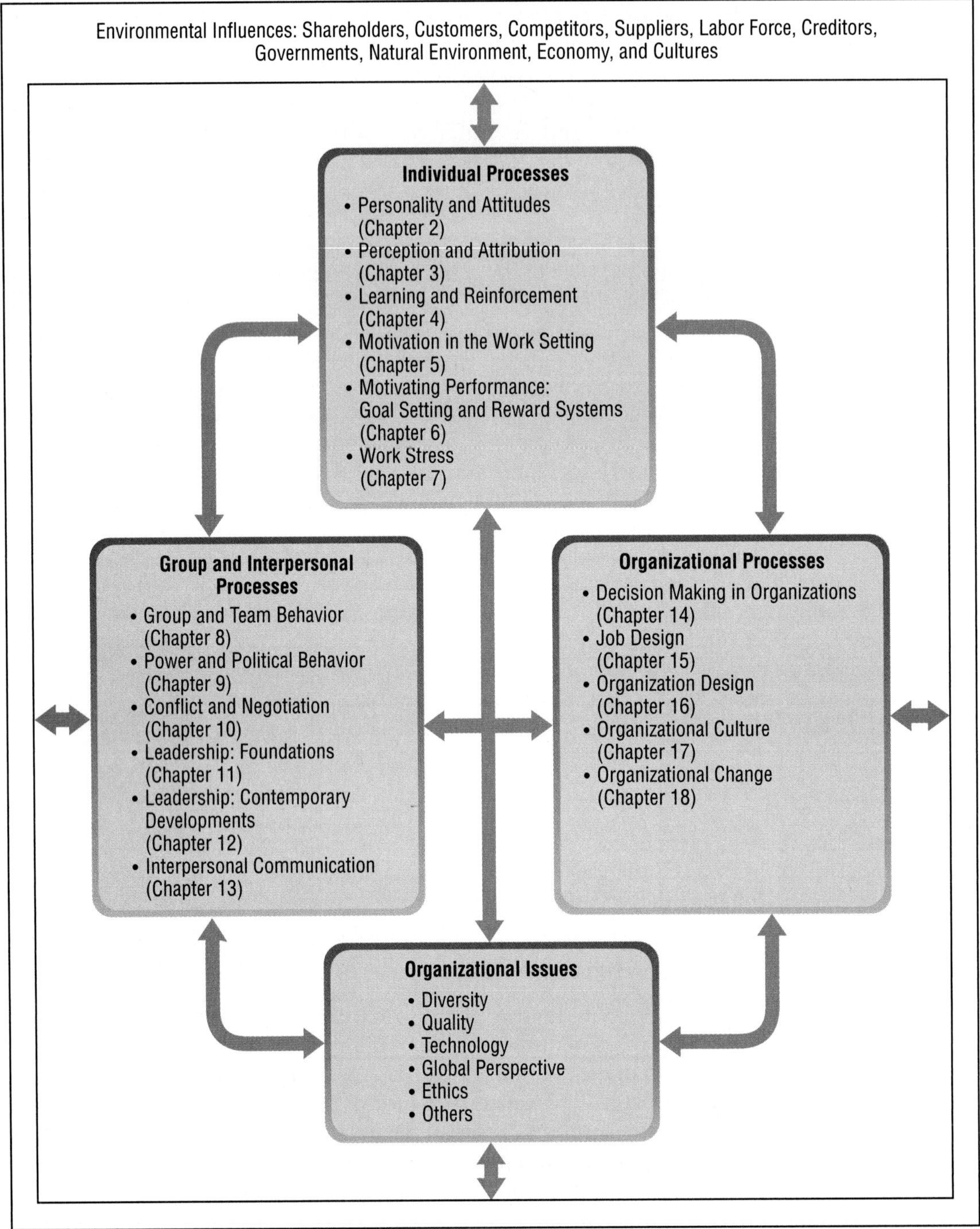

attempting to influence the behaviors of others. (In Part I, Chapters 2–7, we focus on the behavior of individuals.)

Individual behavior is the foundation of organizational performance. Understanding individual behavior, therefore, is crucial for effective management, as illustrated by Cynthia Danaher in the Preview Case. Each person is a physiological system composed of various subsystems—digestive, nervous, circulatory, and reproductive—and a psychological system composed of various subsystems—attitudes, perceptions, learning capabilities, personality, needs, feelings, and values. In Part I, we concentrate on the individual's psychological system. Both internal and external factors shape a person's behavior on the job. Internal factors include learning ability, motivation, perception, attitudes, personality, and values.

In Chapter 2 we examine how personality and attitudes can affect an individual's behavior at work. In Chapter 3, we discuss perceptions and attributions on the job. Different individuals give their own meaning to situations and so may view the same situation differently. To verify this assertion, compare your score on the Attitudes Toward Diversity Questionnaire in the Developing Competencies section with the scores of others. How similar or dissimilar are they? Think about the reasons for these differences and discuss them with your classmates. In Chapter 4, we identify principles of learning and ways that rewards can be used to communicate decisions and encourage or inhibit employee behaviors. In Chapter 5, we explain how to stimulate, sustain, and stop certain behaviors in organizations. We explore various motivators and the importance of motivation in terms of performance. In Chapter 6, we examine how goal-setting and performance enhancement techniques have been used successfully. In Chapter 7 we focus on work-related stress and how employees at all levels are attempting to cope with it, including the use of organizationally sponsored wellness activities.

Among the external factors that affect a person's behavior are the organization's reward system, organizational politics, group behavior, managerial leadership styles, and the organization's design. We examine these factors in Parts II and III of this book.

Team and Interpersonal Processes

Being inherently social, people generally don't choose to live or work alone. Most of their time is spent interacting with others: People are born into a family group, worship in groups, work in teams, and play in groups. Much of a person's identity is based on the ways that other individuals and groups perceive and treat that person. For these reasons—and because many managers and employees spend considerable amounts of time interacting with other people—competencies in communication, interpersonal, and team dynamics are vital to everyone in an organization.

Many organizational goals can be achieved only with the cooperation of others. The histories of organizations such as Motorola, Sony, San Diego Zoo, and MONY provide examples of the creative use of teams to improve the quality of life and to satisfy the needs of their employees and customers. The productivity generated by effective team action makes the development of team competencies an essential aspect of professional and managerial development. Furthermore, membership in productive and cohesive teams and groups is indispensable to maintaining psychological health throughout a person's life.

Being an effective team member requires an understanding of the dynamics within and between teams and other types of groups. Team members must be skillful in eliminating barriers to achieving their goals, solving problems, maintaining productive interaction among team members, and overcoming obstacles to team effectiveness. In Chapter 8, we present methods of increasing team or group effectiveness. However, not all behaviors are aimed at improving performance. As Cynthia Danaher discovered, power and political behavior, the topics that we address in Chapter 9, are realities of organizational life. Employees and managers use power to accomplish goals and, in may cases, to strengthen their own positions. A person's success or failure in using or reacting to power is largely determined by understanding power, knowing how and when to use it, and being able to predict its probable effects on others. In Chapter 10, we explain why conflict arises and how managers, teams, and employees can effectively resolve conflict, including the process of negotiation.

Organizations need leaders who can integrate customer, employee, and organizational goals. The ability of organizations to achieve their goals depends on the degree to which leadership abilities and styles enable managers and team leaders to control, influence, and act effectively. In Chapters 11 and 12, we examine how leaders influence others and how individuals can develop leadership competencies. Effective leadership involves management of conflict, which may arise over any number of issues. How employees communicate with superiors, peers, subordinates, and others can help make them effective team members or lead to low morale and lack of commitment. For that reason and because most managers and professionals spend considerable amounts of time dealing with others, we stress interpersonal communication in Chapter 13.

Organizational Processes

Decision making in organizations isn't particularly orderly or totally within the control of the decision makers. In Chapter 14 we consider the factors, both internal and external, that influence individual, team, and organizational decisions. We identify and explore the phases of decision making and some ethical concepts and dilemmas encountered.

To work effectively, all employees must clearly understand their jobs and the organization's design. In Chapter 15, we describe the process of designing jobs, work methods, and relationships among employees at various levels. The technology utilized has a tremendous impact on job design and employee behavior. As we present it in Chapter 16, organization design addresses the features and structure of the organization. An organization chart presents a simplified view of organizational authority, responsibility, and functions. However, organization design is far more complex than can be depicted on such a chart. We identify factors that influence organization design and present some typical organization designs.

Individuals enter organizations to work, earn money, and pursue career goals. In Chapter 17, we discuss how employees learn what is expected of them. Basically, they do so by exposure to the organization's culture. It is the set of shared assumptions and understandings about how things really work—that is, which policies, practices, and norms are important—in the organization. Newcomers have to understand the organization's culture in order to be accepted and become productive. Some organizations use formal introductory programs for new employees; others simply rely on coworkers, and still others use a combination of these methods to teach the newcomer what to do and what not to do on the job.

The management of change involves adapting an organization to the demands of the environment and modifying the actual behaviors of employees. If employees don't learn new behaviors, the organization can't change. Many things must be considered when an organization undertakes significant change, including the types of pressure being exerted for change, the types of resistance to change that are likely to be encountered, and who should implement change. In Chapter 18, we explore the dynamics of organizational change and present several basic strategies for achieving change.

CHAPTER SUMMARY

1. Explain the managing self competency.

The *managing self competency* involves the ability to assess a person's own strengths and weaknesses; set and pursue professional and personal goals; balance work and personal life; and engage in new learning—including new or changed skills, behaviors, and attitudes. This competency underlies the other six foundation competencies. Five components of this competency were noted. It requires a lifelong process of learning and career management.

2. Explain the managing communication competency.

The *managing communication competency* involves the ability to transmit, receive, and understand data, information, thoughts, and emotions—nonverbal, verbal, written, listening, electronic, and the like. We presented seven components of this competency: describing, active listening, questioning, nonverbal communication, empathizing, verbal communication, and written communication. This competency is like a *circulatory system* that nourishes and carries the other competencies.

3. Explain the managing diversity competency.

The *managing diversity competency* involves the ability to value unique individual and group characteristics, embrace such characteristics as potential sources of organizational strength, and respect the uniqueness of each individual. We identified six components of this competency and presented a framework of six primary categories of diversity: age, race, ethnicity, gender, physical abilities and qualities, and sexual orientation. We also identified eight secondary categories of diversity, including education, work background, and religious beliefs. We highlighted how several types of diversity—changing workforce and customers, gender, race and ethnicity, and age—affect most employees, managers, teams, departments, and organizations. These types of diversity are important because they often reflect differences in perspectives, life-styles, attitudes, values, and behaviors. How employees embrace and respond to diversity greatly influence an organization's effectiveness.

4. Explain the managing ethics competency.

The *managing ethics competency* involves the ability to incorporate values and principles that distinguish right from wrong into decision making and behaviors. We highlighted five components of this competency. Ethics are the values and principles that distinguish right from wrong. Managers and employees often experience ethical dilemmas—situations in which the individual or team must make a decision that involves multiple values.

5. Explain the managing across cultures competency.

The *managing across cultures competency* involves the ability to recognize and embrace similarities and differences among nations and cultures—even within the same organization—and then to approach key organizational and strategic issues with an open and inquisitive mind. We briefly discussed five components of this competency. Individualism and collectivism are two of the fundamental work-related values that need to be understood in order to develop this competency. These and other values affect people's perceptions, communication, decisions, and behaviors.

6. Explain the managing teams competency.

The *managing teams competency* involves the ability to develop, support, facilitate, or lead groups to achieve organizational goals. We identified nine core components of this competency and the potential for individual and team differences and commonalities in goals. We discussed the problems caused by the free rider, or a team member who benefits from team membership but doesn't bear a proportional share of responsibility for completing team tasks.

7. Explain the managing change competency.

The *managing change competency* involves the ability to recognize and implement needed adaptations or entirely new transformations in the people, tasks, strategies, structures, or technologies in a person's area of responsibility. We presented five components of this competency and identified technological forces as one of the primary sources of change. The ever-increasing pace of change, *blur*, was defined as a function of *speed* times *connectivity* times *intangibles*. The Internet is one of the primary enablers of increasing speed and the state of *blur*.

8. Outline the framework for learning about organizational behavior.

The final goal of this chapter was to consider organizational behavior from an open systems perspective. This perspective involves the dynamic interplay among environmental influence, individual processes, group and interpersonal processes, and organizational processes. The competencies that we introduced are developed and addressed through the dynamic interplay among these components.

KEY TERMS AND CONCEPTS

Active listening
Blur
Career
Career development
Career plan
Collectivism
Competency
Conceptualization
Connectivity
Culture
Describing skill
Disseminator role
Empathizing skill
Ethical dilemma
Ethics
Free rider
Glass ceiling
Global mindset
Individualism
Intangibles
Internet
Liaison role
Managing across cultures competency
Managing change competency
Managing communication competency
Managing diversity competency
Managing ethics competency
Managing self competency
Managing teams competency
Monitor role
Nonverbal communication
Organizational behavior
Questioning skill
Racism
Risk taking
Speed
Spokesperson role
Verbal communication
Written communication

DISCUSSION QUESTIONS

1. Identify two strengths and two weaknesses in your own competencies. What specific steps might you take over the next 2 years to reduce the weaknesses?
2. Refer to the list of the six personal characteristics being sought in college-level candidates by the Ford Motor Company (see Competency: Managing Self—Ford's Competency Program). How would you assess yourself in terms of these personal characteristics? Which two of the personal characteristics need the greatest personal development in your case?
3. Develop an outline of the actions needed to improve your managing communication competency. What are you currently doing to further develop it? What do you plan to do over the next 2 years?
4. How would someone who knows you well describe your ability to engage in active listening?
5. Identify three categories of diversity that represent significant issues in an organization or team of which you are currently a member. How is this organization or team—and its members—addressing these issues?
6. The most successful organizations and teams will be those that recognize the challenge and opportunity of embracing a diverse workforce. What obstacles stand in the way of embracing or creating such a workforce in an organization or team of which you are or have been a member? Select a different organization or team than you used to respond to Question 5.
7. Identify two ethical dilemmas that you have faced during the past year. How did you resolve them?
8. How would you describe and compare your societal culture with the five core concepts of the Japanese culture?
9. What is your dominant personal value orientation—individualism or collectivism? What is the basis for your answer?
10. Think of a team in which you are currently or have been a member. How would you evaluate the members of this team—in general—with respect to the core components of the managing teams competency? Which members stand out, either especially strong or especially weak,

in terms of these components? Briefly describe their characteristics.

11. For the most challenging job you now have or have had in the past, list the technologies used to assist in performing your tasks. How would your performance of these tasks change if any two of the technologies were no longer available?

12. What aspect of your life or role that you play reflects some or all of the variables that go into creating the state of *blur*? Explain.

DEVELOPING COMPETENCIES

Competency: Managing Diversity—Attitudes Toward Diversity

Respond to the following statements. Use a scale of 5 to 1 to indicate how strongly you agree with the statements.

SA = Strongly Agree (5)
A = Agree (4)
N = Neutral (3)
D = Disagree (2)
SD = Strongly Disagree (1)

	SA	A	N	D	SD
1. I make a conscious effort to not think stereotypically.	5	4	3	2	1
2. I listen with interest to the ideas of people who don't think like I do.	5	4	3	2	1
3. I respect other people's opinions, even though I may disagree.	5	4	3	2	1
4. If I were at a social event with people who differed ethnically from me, I would make every effort to talk to them.	5	4	3	2	1
5. I have a number of friends who are not my age, race, or gender, or of the same economic status and education.	5	4	3	2	1
6. I recognize the influence that my upbringing has had on my values and beliefs and that my way isn't the only way.	5	4	3	2	1
7. I like to hear both sides of an issue before making a decision.	5	4	3	2	1
8. I don't care how the job gets done, as long as it is done ethically and I see results.	5	4	3	2	1
9. I don't get uptight when I don't understand everything going on around me.	5	4	3	2	1
10. I adapt well to change and new situations.	5	4	3	2	1
11. I enjoy traveling, seeing new places, eating different foods, and experiencing different cultures.	5	4	3	2	1
12. I enjoy people-watching and trying to understand the dynamics of human interactions.	5	4	3	2	1
13. I have learned from my mistakes.	5	4	3	2	1
14. When I am in unfamiliar surroundings, I watch and listen before acting.	5	4	3	2	1
15. When I get lost, I don't try to figure it out for myself but ask for directions.	5	4	3	2	1
16. When I don't understand what someone is telling me, I ask questions.	5	4	3	2	1
17. I really try not to offend or hurt others.	5	4	3	2	1
18. People are generally good, and I accept them as they are.	5	4	3	2	1
19. I watch for people's reactions whenever I'm speaking to them.	5	4	3	2	1
20. I try not to assume anything.	5	4	3	2	1

Scoring

Total your answers. If your score is 80 or above, you probably value diversity and can adapt easily to a multicultural work environment. Continue to look for areas of improvement. If you scored below 50, you probably need to work on understanding the need to value diversity.[50]

Competency: Managing Communication

James Halpin of CompUSA

CompUSA is the largest retailer and seller of personal computer-related products and services in the United States. The company's mission is to market goods and services of high value to help customers manage information to improve their personal and organizational lives. CompUSA currently operates more than 200 computer superstores in major metropolitan markets throughout the United States, serving retail, corporate, governmental, and educational customers, and has more than 20,000 employees. James Halpin joined CompUSA in 1993 as president and chief operating officer (COO) and became CEO later that year. The following excerpts are from a recent in-depth interview of Halpin. They focus on communication within the company, including some aspects of the values and ethics expected of its employees.

We are a very verbal company. We don't write many letters. If you go through my files, the only thing you'll see is things like letters of congratulations I send to employees when I get letters from customers saying somebody did a great job. These are the only letters you'll see, because everything else we do quickly in oral form. If you have an idea, you just walk into somebody's office and say, "OK, what do you think about this?" So we do a lot of brainstorming instead of letter writing. A lot of companies are very much into writing things. We once had a guy from another company who was going to give a presentation using a hundred slides. One of our employees cautioned him: "But Jim, our CEO, has the patience of a gnat. So pick out two." "I can't do it in two," he said. "Then cancel the presentation," my staff member told him, "because after slide five, Jim is going to get antsy." The point of the story is that we try to do things quickly and mostly orally.

We have E-mail, but typically we just walk into each other's offices. Verbal is so much better. We've also got video conferencing, which is great, but you can't get the same intensity of emotion through a TV set as you can eyeball-to-eyeball. I also have coffee and donuts on Friday mornings with our team members in the office and out in the stores. For a while employees were intimidated, but then they would just start talking about everything and anything. They feel like they know us because they see us all the time on video. Every quarter we bring everyone in the home offices together to talk about the results—good, bad, and ugly. We broadcast results to the stores, and anybody can call in with questions and get answers. I've learned a lot of things about our company I would never have known otherwise. For example, I didn't realize we paid everyone once a month. I assumed I got paid once a month because I was an executive. But then I found out we were paying hourly employees once a month too. Now, how would I ever have known that unless they told me? So you find out things like that and you take care of them.

Companies get unions because management stops listening. For instance, an employee asks for a microwave for the break room, and management says, "Yeah, sure," but does nothing about it. Then, all of a sudden the union guy says, "Microwave? I'll get you a microwave." Next thing you know, he gets a microwave for the staff, and you've got a union. So the important thing is we have to continue to listen to our people and communicate down the organization as far as we can. Companies get in trouble through politics because it involves lying. You would get fired at CompUSA for lying. It is well known that if you lie, it's your last day. Just tell the truth. That's why employees don't have to worry about somebody going over their head. For instance, once a merchant was having an argument with the COO and said: "Well, I want to talk to Jim about it. Do you mind?" The COO asked him: "Can you tell the truth?" The merchant said he could, and so he came to see me. As long as you tell the truth, it makes everything so simple.

There is no middle ground. You are either honest or you're not. You can be stupid and get away with it. Because stupid is stupid. But if you lie, it's because you mean to lie. We talk very straight. We don't believe in lying. If something's great, we say so. If it's bad, that's exactly what we call it.[51]

For more information on CompUSA, visit the firm's Web site at ***www.compusa.com.***

Questions

1. What are the similarities and differences in the communication process and practices of higher level management in an organization that you have worked for compared to CompUSA?
2. What do you like best about Halpin's approach to communication? Why? What do you like least? Why?
3. See the core components of the managing communication competency. Which of these components can you identify in Halpin's comments?
4. How are potential ethical dilemmas handled at CompUSA? Do you agree with Halpin's view? Why?

REFERENCES

1. Adapted from Hymowitz, C. How Cynthia Danaher learned to stop sharing and start leading. *Wall Street Journal,* March 16, 1999, B1. Medical Products Group Team; http://interactive.medical.hp.com, March 31, 1999.
2. Wood, R. *Competency-Based Recruitment and Selection.* West Sussex, England: John Wiley & Sons, 1998; Morgan, G. *Riding the Waves of Change: Developing Managerial Competencies for a Turbulent World.* San Francisco: Jossey-Bass, 1998.
3. The section draws from: Weisinger, H. *Emotional Intelligence at Work.* San Francisco: Jossey-Bass, 1998; Evers, F. T., and Rush, J. C. The bases of competence: Skill development during transition from university to work. *Management Learning,* 1996, 27, 275–300; Rigano, D., and

Edwards, J. Incorporating reflection into work practice. *Management Learning,* 1998, 29, 431–446; Whetten, D. A., and Cameron, K. S. *Developing Management Skills,* 4th ed. Reading, Mass.: Addison-Wesley, 1998; Bazerman, M. H., Tenbrunsel, A. E., and Wade-Benzoni, K. Negotiating with yourself and losing: Making decisions with competing internal preferences. *Academy of Management Review,* 1998, 23, 225–241.

4. Adapted from *Ford 2000 Leadership Criteria.* Dearborn, Mich.: Ford Motor Company, 1996; and *Ford HR Competencies.* Dearborn, Mich.: Ford Motor Company, 1999.
5. Hall, D. T., and Associates. *The Career is Dead—Long Live the Career: A Relational Approach.* San Francisco: Jossey-Bass, 1996; Schein, E. H. Career anchors revisited: Implications for career development in the 21st century. *Academy of Management Executive,* 1996, 10(4) 89–103; Drucker, P. F. Managing oneself. *Harvard Business Review,* March–April 1999, 65–74; Roberts Callister, R., Kramer, M. W., and Turban, D. B. Feedback seeking following career transitions. *Academy of Management Journal,* 1999, 42, 429–438.
6. This section draws from Ellinor, L., and Gerard, G. *Dialogue: Rediscover the Transforming Power of Conversations.* New York: John Wiley & Sons, 1998; Musson, G., and Cohen, L. Understanding language processes: A neglected skill in the management curriculum. *Management Learning,* 1999, 30, 27–42; Van Every, E. J., and Taylor, J. R. Modeling the Organization as a system of communication activity. *Management Communication Quarterly,* 1998, 12, 128–147; McLagan, P., and Krembs, P. *On-The-Level: Performance Communication That Works.* San Francisco: Berrett-Kohler, 1995; Wood, J. T. *Communication Mosaics: A New Introduction to the Field of Communication.* Belmont, Calif.: Wadsworth, 1998; Yankelovich, D. *The Magic of Dialogue: Transforming Conflict into Cooperation.* New York: Simon & Schuster, 1999.
7. Mintzberg, H. *The Nature of Managerial Work.* New York: Harper & Row, 1973; Bartlett, C. A., and Ghoshal, S. The myth of the generic manager: New personal competencies for new management roles. *California Management Review,* Fall 1997, 92–116.
8. Adapted from Conger, J. A. The necessary art of persuasion. *Harvard Business Review,* May–June 1998, 84–95.
9. Conger, 1998.
10. This section draws from Gallos, J. V., Ramsey, V. J., and Associates. *Teaching Diversity: Listening to the Soul, Speaking from the Heart.* San Francisco: Jossey-Bass, 1997; Kossek, E. E., and Lobel, S. A. (eds.). *Managing Diversity: Human Resource Strategies for Transforming the Workplace.* Cambridge, Mass.: Blackwell, 1996; Rosenzweig, P. Managing the new global workforce. Fostering diversity and forging consistency. *European Management Journal,* 1998, 16, 644–652; Bowen, W. G., Bok, D., and Burkhart, G. A report card on diversity: Lessons for business from higher education. *Harvard Business Review,* January–February 1999, 139–149.
11. Wheeler, M. L. Capitalizing on diversity: Navigating the sea of the multicultural workforce and workplace. *Business Week,* December 14, 1998. Unpaginated insert.
12. Powell, G. N. The simultaneous pursuit of person–organization fit and diversity. *Organizational Dynamics,* Winter 1998, 50–61.
13. Loden, M., and Rosener, J. *Workforce America.* Burr Ridge, Ill.: Irwin, 1991; Butler, T., and Waldroop, J. Job sculpting: The art of retaining your best people. *Harvard Business Review,* September–October 1999, 144–152.
14. Adapted from Wheeler, M. L. Diversity: Making the business case. *Business Week,* December 1996 (unpaginated special section); Ashkenas, R., Ulrich, D., Jick, T., and Kerr, S. *The Boundaryless Organization.* San Francisco: Jossey-Bass, 1995.
15. Jackson, S. E., and Ruderman, M. N. *Diversity in Work Teams.* Washington, D.C.: American Psychological Association, 1996; Lau, D. C., and Murnighan, J. K. Demographic diversity and faultlines: The compositional dynamics of organizational groups. *Academy of Management Review,* 1998, 23, 325–340.
16. Hammonds, K. H. You've come a short way, baby. *Business Week,* November 23, 1998, 82–83.
17. Worton, B. Women at work. *Fortune,* March 4, 1996 (unpaginated special section).
18. Diversity—Part I: Building a competitive workforce. *Forbes,* May 13, 1999 (special insert), 1–31; Morrison, A. M. *The New Leaders: Guidelines on Leadership Diversity in America.* San Francisco: Jossey-Bass, 1992; to learn more about Aetna, visit its home page at www.aetna.com/aindex.htm.
19. Catalyst. *Advancing Women in Business: The Catalyst Guide.* San Francisco: Jossey-Bass, 1998.
20. Gardenswartz, L., and Rowe, A. *Managing Diversity: A Complete Reference and Planning Guide.* New York, McGraw-Hill, 1998.
21. Gallos, J. V., Ramsey, V. J., and Associates. *Teaching Diversity.* San Francisco: Jossey-Bass, 1996; Johnson, R. S. The 50 best companies for Asians, blacks & Hispanics. *Fortune,* August 3, 1998, 94–122.
22. Adapted from Caudron, S. Diversity watch. *Black Enterprise.* September 1998, 91–94; Fannie Mae's home page @ www.fanniemae.com.
23. Wentling, R. M., and Palma-Rivas, N. *Diversity in the Workforce: A Literature Review.* Berkeley, Calif.: National Center for Research in Vocational Education, University of California at Berkeley, 1998.
24. Hall, D. T., and Moss, J. E. The new protean contract: Helping organizations and employees adapt. *Organizational Dynamics.* Winter 1998, 22–30.
25. This section draws from Donaldson, T., and Werhane, P. (eds.). *Ethical Issues in Business: A Philosophical Approach.* Tappan, N.J.: Prentice Hall 1999; Werhane, P., and Freeman, R. E. *Blackwell Encyclopedic Dictionary of Business Ethics.* Cambridge, Mass.: Blackwell 1999; Solomon, R. C. *A Better Way to Think About Business: How Values Become Virtues.* New York: Oxford University Press, 1999; Badaracco, Jr., J. L. *Defining Moments: When Managers Must Choose between Right and Right.* Boston: Harvard Business School Press, 1997.
26. Brass, D. J., Butterfield, K. D., and Skaggs, B. C. Relationships and unethical behavior: A social network perspective. *Academy of Management Review,* 1998, 23, 14–31; Treviño, L. K., Weaver, G. R., Gibson, D. G., and Toffer, B. L. Managing ethics and legal compliance: What works and what hurts. *California Management Review,* Winter 1999, 131–151; Swanson, D. L. Toward an integrative

theory of business and society: A research strategy for corporate social performance. *Academy of Management Review*, 1999, 24, 506–521.

27. Brenner, S. N., and Mollander, E. A. Is the ethics of business changing? *Harvard Business Review*, January–February 1977, 57.
28. Adapted from Ethics from the top: An interview with Michael I. Roth. *Leaders*, April–June, 1997, 188–189.
29. Harris, P. R., and Moran, R. T. *Managing Cultural Differences*, 4th ed. Houston: Gulf, 1996; Mead, R. *International Management: Cross-Cultural Dimensions*. Cambridge, Mass.: Blackwell, 1998; Rosen, R. H. *Global Literacies: National Cultures and Business Leadership*. New York: Free Press, 2000.
30. Catlin, L. B., and White, T. F. *International Business: Cultural Sourcebook and Case Studies*. Cincinnati: South-Western, 1994; Donahue, R. T. *Japanese Culture and Communication: Critical Cultural Analysis*. Lanham, N.Y.: University Press of America, 1998.
31. Hoftede, G. *Cultures and Organizations: Software of the Mind*, rev. ed. Blacklick, Ohio: McGraw-Hill College, 1997; Cray, D., and Mallory, G. R. *Making Sense of Managing Culture*. London: International Thomson Business Press, 1998.
32. Farid, E., and Harris, P. R. *Multicultural Management 2000: Essential Cultural Insights for Global Business Success*. Houston: Gulf, 1998.
33. Marschan, R., Welch, D., and Welch, L. Language: The forgotten factor in multinational management. *European Management Journal*, 15, 1997, 591–597.
34. Bersticker, A. C. Competing successfully in a global economy. *Thunderbird International Business Review*, 40, 1998; Adler, N.J. *International Dimensions of Organizational Behavior*. Cincinnati: South-Western, 1996.
35. Puffer, S. M., McCarthy, D. J., and Zhuplev, A. V. Doing business in Russia: Lessons from early entrants. *Thunderbird International Business Review*, 1998, 40, 461–484; Puffer, S. M. *Management Across Cultures: Insights from Fiction and Practice*. Cambridge, Mass.: Blackwell, 1996.
36. Early, P. C., and Erez, M. *The Transplanted Executive: Why You Need to Understand How Workers in Other Countries See the World Differently*. New York: Oxford University Press, 1997.
37. Hofstede, G. *Cultures Consequences: International Differences in Work-Related Values*. Thousand Oaks, Calif.: Sage, 1984; Triandis, H. C. *Individualism and Collectivism*. Westview Press, 1995; Cavanagh, G. F., Fisher, C. T., and Cavanagh, G. E. *American Business Values: With International Perspectives*, 4th ed. Old Tappan, N.J.: Prentice-Hall, 1998.
38. Lin, R. Y. How individualism–collectivism influences Asian and U.S. managers in choosing their career goals and tactics. *Journal of Asian Business*, 1995, 2, 97–116.
39. This section draws from McIntyre, M. G. *The Management Team Handbook: Five Key Strategies for Maximizing Group Performance*. San Francisco: Jossey-Bass, 1998; Albers Mohrman, S., Mohrman, A. M., Mohrman, A. M. Jr., *Designing and Leading Team-Based Organizations: A Leaders/Facilitators Guide*. San Francisco: Jossey-Bass, 1997; Korine, H. The new team organization: Learning to manage arbitrariness. *European Management Journal*, 1999, 17, 1–7.
40. Adapted from Scarborough, J. Comparing Chinese and Western cultural roots: Why "east is east and . . . ." *Business Horizons*, November–December 1998, 15–33; Seligman, S. D. *Chinese Business Etiquette: A Guide to Protocol, Manners, and Culture in the People's Republic of China*. New York: Warner Books, 1999; Tsang, E. N. Can guanxi be a source of sustained competitive advantage for doing business in China? *Academy of Management Executive*, 1998, 12(2) 64–73.
41. Usunier, J. *International and Cross-Cultural Management Research*. Thousand Oaks, Calif.: Sage, 1998.
42. Sherriton, J. C., and Stern, J. L. *Corporate Culture Team Culture: Removing the Hidden Barriers to Team Success*. New York: AMACOM, 1997; Forrester, R., and Drexler, A. B. A model for team-based performance. *Academy of Management Executive*, August 1999, 36–49.
43. Albanese, R., and Van Fleet, D. D. Rational behavior in groups: The free-riding tendency. *Academy of Management Review*, 1985, 10, 244–255.
44. Schnake, M. E. Equity in effort: The "sucker effect" in co-acting groups. *Journal of Management*, 1991, 17, 41–55.
45. Munk, N. How Levi's trashed a great American brand. *Fortune*, April 12, 1999, 83–90.
46. Muczyk, J. P., and Steel, R. P. Leadership style and the turnaround executive. *Business Horizons*, March–April 1998, 39–46.
47. Wind, J. Y., and Main, J. *Driving Change: How the Best Companies Are Preparing for the 21st Century*. New York: Free Press, 1998.
48. Davis, S., and Meyer, C. *Blur: The Speed of Change in the Connected Economy*. Reading, Mass.: Addison-Wesley, 1998, 5.
49. Adapted from Buss, D. D. Embracing speed. *Nation's Business*, June 1999, 12–17.
50. Adapted from Hill-Storks, H. Diversity Self-Assessment Questionnaire, 1994. Used with permission.
51. Adapted from Puffer, S. M. CompUSA's CEO James Halpin on technology rewards and commitment. *Academy of Management Executive*, May 1999, 29–36.

PART 1

Individual Processes

Chapter 2 Personality and Attitudes

Chapter 3 Perception and Attribution

Chapter 4 Learning and Reinforcement

Chapter 5 Motivation in the Work Setting

Chapter 6 Motivating Performance: Goal Setting and Reward Systems

Chapter 7 Work Stress

CHAPTER

2

Personality and Attitudes

LEARNING OBJECTIVES

When you have finished studying this chapter, you should be able to:

1. Explain the basic sources of personality differences among people.
2. Describe the "Big Five" personality factors and identify your own profile in terms of these factors.
3. Identify some examples of specific personality traits that have important relationships to work behavior.
4. Define the concept of attitudes and explain the general relationship between attitudes and behavior.
5. Explain the importance of job satisfaction and organizational commitment in organizational behavior.
6. Describe the relationship between individual differences and ethical behavior.

Preview Case: *Omigosh! Individual Differences!*

SOURCES OF PERSONALITY DIFFERENCES

Heredity

Environment

PERSONALITY STRUCTURE

PERSONALITY AND BEHAVIOR

Self-Esteem

Competency: Managing Across Cultures*—A Letter from the Swedish Sales Force*

Locus of Control

Goal Orientation

Introversion and Extroversion

Dogmatism and Authoritarianism

Organizational Implications

Competency: Managing Teams*—Personality and Teams at Hewlett-Packard*

The Person and the Situation

ATTITUDES AND BEHAVIOR

Components of Attitudes

Links to Behavior

Behavioral Intentions Model

WORK ATTITUDES

Job Satisfaction

Competency: Managing Communication*—A Happy Staff Leads to Happy Customers*

Organizational Commitment

INDIVIDUAL DIFFERENCES AND ETHICAL BEHAVIOR

Competency: Managing Self*—Winning Mother's Loyalty and Commitment*

Types of Management Ethics

Competency: Managing Ethics*—Who's Your Phone Company?*

Establishing Ethical Attitudes

CHAPTER SUMMARY

Key Terms and Concepts

Discussion Questions

DEVELOPING COMPETENCIES

Competency: Managing Self*—Assessing the Big Five*

Competency: Managing Self*—Emotional IQ*

PREVIEW CASE

OMIGOSH! INDIVIDUAL DIFFERENCES!

David and Anna have been friends since high school. Now, only several years after receiving their university degrees, both are well on the way to successful careers. After a couple of years with Arthur Andersen, David started his own CPA firm and has more business than he can handle. Anna followed a similar path—after 18 months as an interior designer with a well-known architectural firm, she left to establish her own design business. Now, they have an opportunity to work together again, for David has hired Anna's firm to design the new offices that he will be moving his small organization into early next year. Like a lot of successful professionals, both David and Anna have had to learn how to manage others as well as their own careers now that they have started their own businesses.

David and Anna are going over the latest design for David's new offices. They have finished reviewing the design changes, and, because they are old friends, their conversation has drifted to comparing notes about the challenges of managing their own firms. As we join them, Anna is speaking.

"It happened again today. Amy lost her temper and threatened to quit for probably the fourth time this week. Ever since I reorganized the design teams, she has been impossible to live with. But, here's another puzzle. Reilly's work was quite marginal on the last job, but she is fast becoming a real star on your project. She tells me that she really likes the way we have restructured the work. I guess the puzzle for me is that both Amy and Reilly have similar backgrounds; they're both very talented people and seem to enjoy the same types of design work, yet they have reacted in very different ways to our new team structure."

"I know what you mean," responded David. "You may remember meeting Terry and Kate last week just before they left for our audit of Air Designs, Inc. Both are very competent accountants and, in general, are working out very well. However, I created a new approach for the Air Design audit because I was concerned that we didn't have much experience with that type of business. Kate has responded very well to the changed procedures, but Terry has been very unhappy about them. In just a short time, he's gone from being one of my most pleasant employees to being very difficult to get along with."

Anna sighed. "Some of the more subtle aspects of managing people seem to be escaping me. We can have employees faced with exactly the same set of circumstances and yet get such very different reactions. I simply don't understand why there are such differences in behavior among these folks."

As the Preview Case indicates, people often react very differently to organizational change. Some 2,000 years ago, the Greek philosopher Theophrastus asked, "Why is it that while all Greece lies under the same sky and all Greeks are educated alike, it has befallen us to have characters variously constituted?"[1] This question—Why are people different?—is as important for understanding human behavior today as it was in ancient Greece. Managers and employees alike must comprehend and appreciate individual differences in order to understand the behavior of people in complex social settings, such as the job setting in organizations.[2]

In Part I of this book we cover individual processes in organizations. We focus first on the individual to help you begin to develop an understanding of organizational behavior. The term **individual differences** refers to the fact that people vary in many ways. In this chapter, we discuss the individual differences of personality and attitudes. We begin by addressing the concept of personality. Later in the chapter, we explore the role of attitudes in organizational behavior.

Learning Objective:

1. Explain the basic sources of personality differences among people.

SOURCES OF PERSONALITY DIFFERENCES

Behavior always involves a complex interaction of the person and the situation. Events in the surrounding environment (including the presence and behavior of others) strongly influence the way people behave at any particular time; yet people always bring something of themselves to the situation. This "something," which represents the unique qualities of the individual, is *personality*.[3] No single definition of personality is accepted universally.[4] However, one key idea is that personality represents personal characteristics that lead to consistent patterns of behavior. People quite naturally seek to understand these behavioral patterns in interactions with others. A well-known personality theorist, Salvatore Maddi, proposed the following definition of **personality:**

> Personality is a stable set of characteristics and tendencies that determine those commonalities and differences in the psychological behavior (thoughts, feelings, and actions) of people that have continuity in time and that may not be easily understood as the sole result of the social and biological pressures of the moment.[5]

This definition contains three important ideas. First, the definition doesn't limit the influence of personality only to certain behaviors, certain situations, or certain people. Rather, personality theory is a **general theory of behavior**—an attempt to understand or describe all behaviors all the time. In fact, attempting to define the concept of personality means trying to explain the very essence of being human.

Second, the phrase "commonalities and differences" suggests an important aspect of human beings. In certain respects, every person is like

- all other people;
- some other people; and
- no other person.[6]

Theories of personality often describe what people have in common and what sets them apart. To understand the personality of an individual, then, is to understand both what that individual has in common with others and what makes that particular individual unique. Thus each employee in an organization is unique and may or may not respond as others do in a particular situation, as indicated in the Preview Case. This complexity makes managing and working with people extremely challenging.

Finally, Maddi's definition refers to personality as being "stable" and having "continuity in time." Most people intuitively recognize this stability. If your entire personality could change suddenly and dramatically, your family and friends would confront a stranger. Although significant changes normally don't occur suddenly, an individual's personality may change over time. Personality development occurs to a certain extent throughout life, but the greatest changes occur in early childhood.[7]

How is an individual's personality determined? This question has no simple answer because too many variables contribute to the development of each individual's personality. As Figure 2.1 shows, two primary sources shape personality differences: heredity and environment, or nature and nurture. Examining these sources helps us to understand why individuals are different.

HEREDITY

Deeply ingrained in many people's notions of personality is a belief in its genetic basis. Expressions such as "She is just like her father," and "He gets those irritating qualities from your side of the family, dear," reflect such beliefs. Historically, the **nature–nurture controversy** in personality theory was a sharp disagreement about the extent to which genetic factors influence personality. Those holding the extreme nature position argued that personality is inherited. Those adhering to the extreme nurture position argued that a person's experiences determine personality. Current thinking is more balanced—both heredity (genes) and environment (experiences) are important, although some personality characteristics may be influenced more by one factor than the other.[8] That is, some personality traits seem to have a strong genetic component, whereas other traits seem to be largely learned (based on experiences).

Some personality experts argue that heredity sets limits on the range of development of characteristics and that within this range environmental forces determine personality characteristics. However, recent research on the personalities of twins who have been raised apart indicates that genetic determinants may play a larger role than many experts had believed. Some studies of twins suggest that as much as 50 to 55 percent of personality traits may be inherited. Further, inherited personality traits seem to explain about 50 percent of the variance in occupational choice. In other words, you probably inherited some traits that will influence your career choices.[9]

ENVIRONMENT

Many behavioral experts still believe that the environment plays a larger role in shaping personality than do inherited characteristics. Aspects of the environment that influence personality formation include culture, family, group membership, and life experiences.

Figure 2.1 **Sources of Personality Differences**

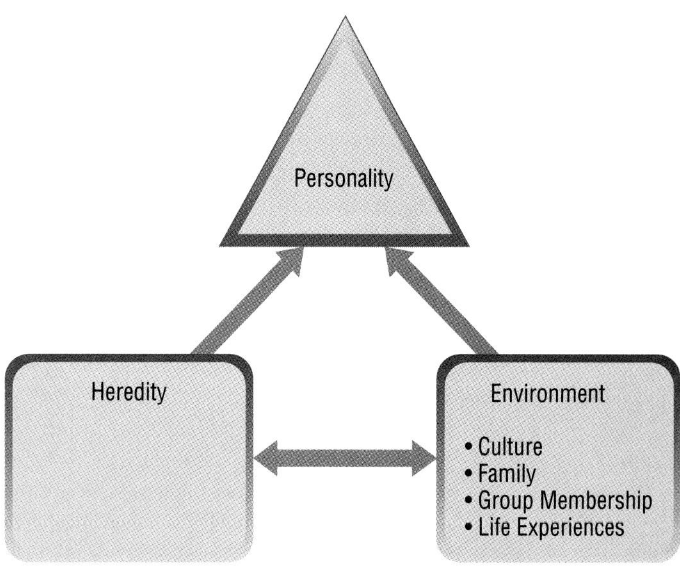

Culture. The term **culture** refers to the distinctive ways that different human populations or societies organize their lives. Anthropologists working within different cultures have clearly demonstrated the important role that culture plays in personality development.[10] Individuals born into a particular culture are exposed to family and societal values and to norms of acceptable behavior. Culture also defines how the different roles in that society are to be performed. For example, U.S. culture generally rewards people for being independent and competitive, whereas Japanese culture generally rewards individuals for being cooperative and group oriented.

Culture helps determine broad patterns of behavioral similarity among people, but differences in behavior—which at times can be extreme—usually exist among individuals within a culture. Most cultures aren't homogeneous (although some cultures are more homogeneous than others). For example, the work ethic (hard work is valued; an unwillingness to work is sinful) usually is associated with Western cultures. But this value doesn't influence everyone within Western cultures to the same degree. Thus, although culture has an impact on the development of employees' personalities, not all individuals respond to cultural influences equally. Indeed, one of the most serious errors that managers can make is to assume that their subordinates are just like themselves in terms of societal values, personality, or any other individual difference.

Family. The primary vehicle for socializing an individual into a particular culture is the person's immediate family. Both parents and siblings play important roles in the personality development of most individuals. Members of an extended family—grandparents, aunts, uncles, and cousins—also can influence personality formation. In particular, parents (or a single parent) influence their children's development in three important ways.

- Through their own behaviors, they present situations that bring out certain behaviors in children.
- They serve as role models with which children often strongly identify.
- They selectively reward and punish certain behaviors.[11]

The family's situation also is an important source of personality differences. Situational influences include the family's size, socioeconomic level, race, religion, and geographic location; birth order within the family; parents' educational level; and so on. For example, a person raised in a poor family simply has different experiences and opportunities than does a person raised in a wealthy family. Being an only child is different in some important respects from being raised with several brothers and sisters.

Group Membership. The first group to which most individuals belong is the family. People also participate in various groups during their lives, beginning with their childhood playmates and continuing through teenaged schoolmates, sports teams, and social groups to adult work and social groups. The numerous roles and experiences that people have as members of groups represent another important source of personality differences. Although playmates and school groups early in life may have the strongest influences on personality formation, social and group experiences in later life continue to influence and shape personality. Understanding someone's personality requires understanding the groups to which that person belongs or has belonged in the past.

Life Experiences. Each person's life also is unique in terms of specific events and experiences, which can serve as important determinants of personality. For example, the development of self-esteem (a personality dimension that we discuss shortly) depends on a series of experiences that include the opportunity to achieve goals and meet expectations, evidence of the ability to influence others, and a clear sense of being valued by others. Thus a complex series of events and interactions with other people helps shape the adult's level of self-esteem.

Learning Objective:

2. Describe the "Big Five" personality factors and identify your own profile in terms of these factors.

PERSONALITY STRUCTURE

The number and variety of specific personality traits or dimensions are bewildering. The term, **personality trait,** typically refers to the basic components of personality. Researchers of personality have identified, named, and examined literally *thousands* of traits over the years. Trait names simply represent the terms that people use to describe each other. However, a list containing hundreds or thousands of terms isn't very useful either in understanding the structure of personality in a scientific sense or in describing individual differences in a practical sense. To be useful, these terms need to be organized into a small set of concepts or descriptions. Recent research has done just that, identifying several general factors that can be used to describe an individual's personality.

Five main factors summarize personality structure.[12] These **"Big Five" personality factors,** as they often are referred to, describe the individual's adjustment, sociability, conscientiousness, agreeableness, and intellectual openness. As shown in Figure 2.2, each factor includes a potentially large number and range of specific traits or

Figure 2.2 **The "Big Five" Personality Factors**

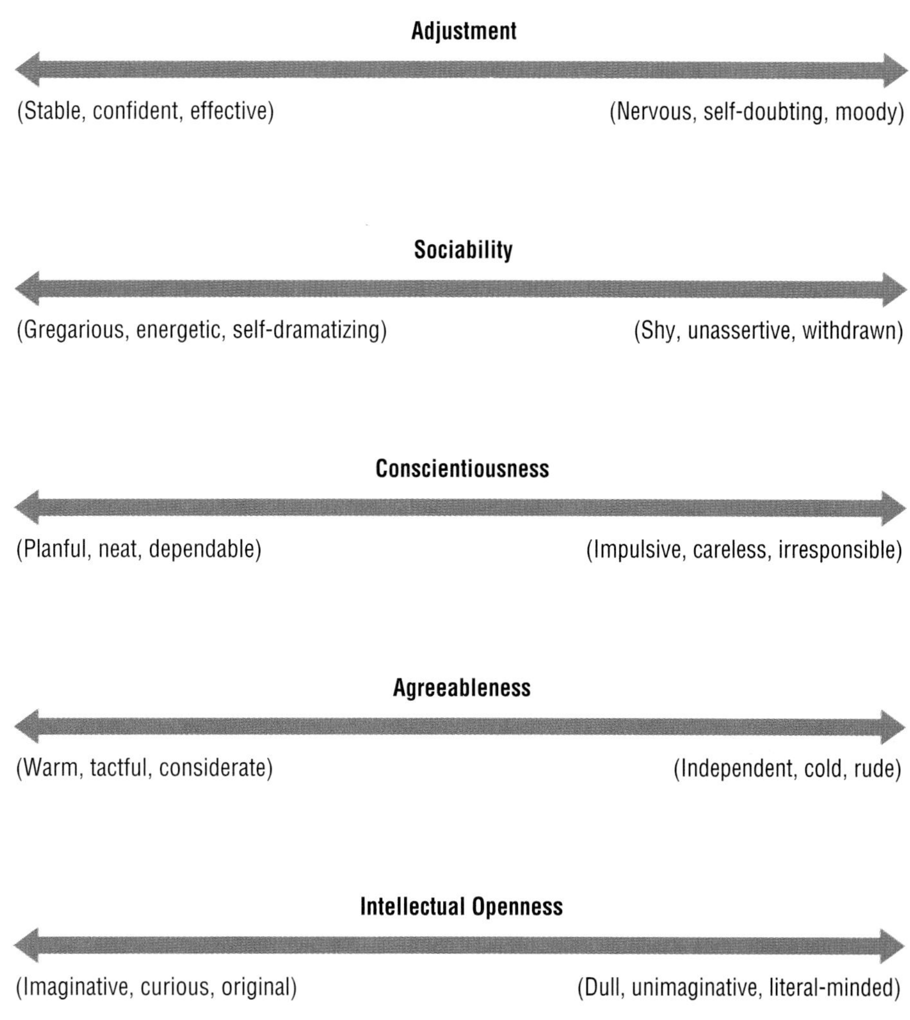

Source: Developed from Hogan, R. T. Personality and personality measurement. In M. D. Dunnette and L. M. Hough (eds.), *Handbook of Industrial and Organizational Psychology,* vol. 2, 2nd ed. Palo Alto, Calif.: Consulting Psychologists Press, 1991, 878–879; McCrae, R. R., and Costa, P. T. A five-factor theory of personality. In L. A. Pervin and O. P. John (eds.), *Handbook of Personality,* 2nd ed. New York: Guilford, 1999, 139–153.

dimensions. That is, each factor is both a collection of related traits and a continuum. For example, an individual with a personality at one extreme of the *agreeableness* factor might be described as warm and considerate. But with a personality at this factor's other extreme, the person would be considered cold or rude. The Developing Competencies section at the end of this chapter contains a questionnaire that you can use to assess yourself in terms of these five personality factors.

Learning Objective:

3. Identify some examples of specific personality traits that have important relationships to work behavior.

PERSONALITY AND BEHAVIOR

The main reason that we are interested in individual personality in the study of organizational behavior is the linkage between personality and behavior. For example, researchers have extensively investigated the relationships between the Big Five personality factors and job performance.[13] Their findings indicate that employees who are responsible, dependable, persistent, and achievement oriented (the *conscientiousness* factor in Figure 2.2), perform better than those who lack these traits.

Although each personality factor represents a collection of related traits, the link between personality and specific behaviors often is most clear when we focus on a single trait rather than one of the five factors. We examine several *specific* personality traits that are particularly important for understanding aspects of organizational behavior. Then, throughout the book, we explain additional personality traits as they relate to topics under discussion—for example, in relation to perception (Chapter 3), work stress (Chapter 7), political behavior (Chapter 9), and leadership (Chapter 11).

As we weave an understanding of personality and other individual differences into our exploration of a variety of topics in organizational behavior, we hope that you come to understand the crucial role that personality plays in explaining behavior. People clearly pay a great deal of attention to attributes of the personalities of the coworkers with whom they interact. The Managing Across Cultures Competency feature on the next page shows how Peter Jones, a vice president of Computex, was faced with serious problems created by one of his managers who apparently had a less than perfectly pleasant personality.

SELF-ESTEEM

Self-esteem is the result of an individual's continuing evaluation of himself or herself. In other words, people develop, hold, and sometimes modify opinions of their own behaviors, abilities, appearance, and worth. These general assessments reflect responses to people and situations, successes and failures, and the opinions of others. Such evaluations are sufficiently accurate and stable to be widely regarded as a basic personality trait or dimension. In terms of the Big Five personality factors, self-esteem most likely would be part of the *adjustment* factor (see Figure 2.2).

Self-esteem affects behavior in organizations and other social settings in several important ways. Self-esteem is related to initial vocational choice. For example, individuals with high self-esteem take risks in job selection, are attracted to high-status occupations (e.g., medicine or law), and are more likely to choose unconventional or nontraditional jobs (such as forest ranger or jet pilot) than are individuals with low self-esteem. A study of college students looking for a job reported that those with high self-esteem (1) received more favorable evaluations from recruiters, (2) were more satisfied with the job search, (3) received more job offers, and (4) were more likely to accept jobs before graduation than were students with low self-esteem.[14]

Self-esteem is also related to numerous social and work behaviors. For example, employees with low self-esteem are more easily influenced by the opinions of other workers than are employees with high self-esteem. Employees with low self-esteem set lower goals for themselves than do employees with high self-esteem. Further, employees with high self-esteem place more value on actually attaining those goals than do employees with low self-esteem. Employees with low self-esteem are more

COMPETENCY: MANAGING ACROSS CULTURES

A LETTER FROM THE SWEDISH SALES FORCE

Peter Jones, vice president–Europe, for Computex Corporation, opened a letter at his San Francisco office early one morning. He was dismayed at the letter's contents (some portions of which have been edited out).

Dear Mr. Jones:

The writers of this letter represent the sales force from Computex Sweden with the exception of our sales manager. We have decided to bring to your attention a rather serious matter, which if left unresolved, will result in resignations from the majority of us in the near future. We don't want to be in this situation, and we recognize that we are going outside of the chain-of-command with this letter, but we are approaching you in an attempt to save our sales team for the benefit of ourselves and Computex Corporation.

We consider ourselves to be an experienced, professional, and competent group of people. We have always been proud to work for Computex. We are well known in many areas of business in Sweden—many of our customers are friends and they view us as representatives of Computex. It is our feeling that the business will be significantly harmed if most of us were to leave. We provide this background because none of us have ever personally met you.

Our problems seem, to us, fairly straightforward. They arise solely as the result of the personality, character traits, and behavior of our general manager, Mr. Miller. He loses his temper almost daily, and most of these outbursts are an overreaction to small things. His mood and opinions seem to change almost on an hourly basis. He treats us with disrespect, and seldom delivers on his promises to "value our opinions" and "involve us more deeply in the business." Most of the fine slogans that he states publicly in meetings and individual discussions have proven to be only words. Interpersonal relationships between Mr. Miller and us have deteriorated to the point where most of us spend as little time as possible in the office. None of us have ever before experienced working with an individual who has such a mercurial personality and treats the people around him in such a fashion.

If this sales team was not composed of mature individuals who continue to be interested in working for Computex, most of us would have left by now. As it is, so far only one salesperson has left the company because of Mr. Miller. However, we are not willing to put up with this situation indefinitely. As we stated earlier, unless some positive changes are made, most of us will soon be working for your competitors.

It is not our objective to cost Mr. Miller his job. We recognize that he has done some good things in terms of generating new business. He presents himself well to the outside world. The problem, rather, is internal to our office and our day-to-day working relationships with him, which have become intolerable. If he could control his mood, treat us with more respect, and deliver on his promises, we think the office could succeed under his leadership.

We are fully aware of the seriousness of contacting you in this way. However, we believe that one person is ruining the entire organization and immediate action is required. Because the problem is so personal, we don't see how it can be resolved without some sort of action from you.

We are hoping for a positive solution.

Signed: "nine of your sales representatives in Sweden"

Jones sighed heavily as he finished reading the letter. "What do I do now?" he wondered. He was unsure whether this was strictly a "personality" conflict or a "cross-cultural" problem. He didn't particularly like Miller personally and thought that he had a rather abrasive personality, but nothing like this had ever happened in his previous assignments, one of which had been international. He began to wish that he had not sent Miller to Sweden in the first place. I wish I'd sent Gonzalez or Taylor, he thought to himself. What to do? What to do? Jones knew that this problem would be a real test of his management skills.[15]

For more information on Computex Corporation, visit the organization's home page at www.computexas.com.

susceptible than employees with high self-esteem to adverse job conditions such as stress, conflict, ambiguity, poor supervision, poor working conditions, and the like. In a general sense, self-esteem is positively related to achievement and a willingness to expend effort to accomplish tasks. Clearly, self-esteem is an important individual difference in terms of effective work behavior.[16]

Locus of Control

Locus of control refers to the extent to which individuals believe that they can control events affecting them. On the one hand, individuals who have a high **internal locus of control** (internals) believe that their own behavior and actions primarily, but not necessarily totally, determine many of the events in their lives. On the other hand, individuals who have a high **external locus of control** (externals) believe that chance, fate, or other people primarily determine what happens to them. Locus of control typically is considered to be a part of the *conscientiousness* factor (see Figure 2.2). Table 2.1 contains a locus of control measure that you can use to assess your own locus of control beliefs.

Many differences between internals and externals are significant in explaining aspects of behavior in organizations and other social settings.[17] Evidence indicates that internals control their own behavior better, are more active politically and socially, and seek information about their situations more actively than do externals.

Table 2.1

A Locus of Control Measure

For each of these 10 questions, indicate the extent to which you agree or disagree, using the following scale.

1 = strongly disagree
2 = disagree
3 = slightly disagree
4 = neither disagree nor agree
5 = slightly agree
6 = agree
7 = strongly agree

_____ 1. When I get what I want it's usually because I worked hard for it.
_____ 2. When I make plans I am almost certain to make them work.
_____ 3. I prefer games involving some luck over games requiring pure skill.
_____ 4. I can learn almost anything if I set my mind to it.
_____ 5. My major accomplishments are entirely due to my hard work and ability.
_____ 6. I usually don't set goals, because I have a hard time following through on them.
_____ 7. Competition discourages excellence.
_____ 8. Often people get ahead just by being lucky.
_____ 9. On any sort of exam or competition I like to know how well I do relative to everyone else.
_____10. It's pointless to keep working on something that's too difficult for me.

To determine your score, reverse the values you selected for questions 3, 6, 7, 8, and 10 (1 = 7, 2 = 6, 3 = 5, 4 = 4, 5 = 3, 6 = 2, 7 = 1). For example, if you strongly disagreed with the statement in question 3, you would have given it a value of "1." Change this value to a "7." Reverse the scores in a similar manner for questions 6, 7, 8, and 10. Now add the 10 point values together.

Your score: _____

A study of college students found a mean of 51.8 for men and 52.2 for women using this questionnaire. The higher your score, the higher your internal locus of control. Low scores are associated with external locus of control.

Source: Adapted from Burger, J. M. *Personality: Theory and Research.* Belmont, Calif.: Wadsworth, 1986, pp. 400–401.

Compared to externals, internals are more likely to try to influence or persuade others and are less likely to be influenced by others. Internals often are more achievement oriented than externals. Compared to internals, externals appear to prefer a more structured, directive style of supervision. As pointed out in Chapter 1, the ability to manage effectively in the global environment is an important competency. Interestingly, a study showed that managers with a high internal locus of control adjusted more readily to international transfers than did managers with a high external locus of control.[18] The letter from the sales force of Computex Sweden may reflect an internal locus of control orientation and an effort, by attempting to influence Peter Jones, to gain greater control over the events in their working lives.

Recall that we are particularly interested in the relationship between these personality dimensions and specific behaviors. Figure 2.3 shows some of the important relationships between locus of control and job performance.

Goal Orientation

Another individual difference of importance for behavior in work settings is *goal orientation* or the preference for one type of goal versus another. Specifically, two orientations are considered important in terms of understanding some aspects of individual job performance. A **learning goal orientation** is a predisposition to develop competence by acquiring new skills and mastering new situations. A **performance goal orientation** is a predisposition to demonstrate and validate competence by seeking favorable judgments from others (e.g., a supervisor) and avoiding negative judgments.[19] Table 2.2 contains a questionnaire that you can use to assess your own learning and performance goal orientations with regard to your academic studies.

Figure 2.3 **The Effects of Locus of Control on Performance**

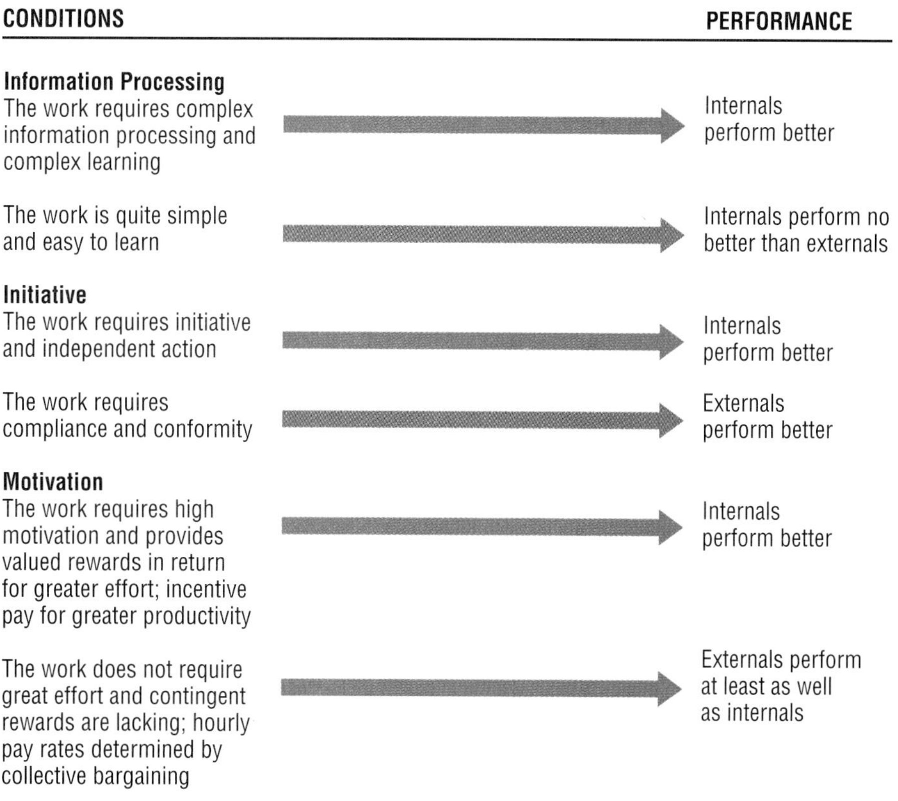

Source: Miner, J. B. *Industrial–Organizational Psychology.* New York: McGraw-Hill, 1992, 151. Reprinted with permission of McGraw-Hill.

Table 2.2 **Academic Goal Orientation**

Instructions: People have different ideas about the purpose of college. Read each statement below and select an answer from the following scale that reflects how much you agree or disagree with the statement.

1 = Strongly agree	5 = Sort of disagree
2 = Agree	6 = Disagree
3 = Sort of agree	7 = Strongly disagree
4 = Neither agree nor disagree	

Learning Goal Orientation Scale

_____ 1. I prefer challenging and difficult classes so that I'll learn a great deal.
_____ 2. I truly enjoy learning for the sake of learning.
_____ 3. I like classes that really force me to think hard.
_____ 4. I'm willing to enroll in a difficult course if I can learn a lot from taking it.
_____ Total score for learning goal orientation (sum the response to questions 1–4).

Performance Goal Orientation Scale

_____ 5. I think that it's important to get good grades to show how intelligent you are.
_____ 6. I would rather drop a difficult class than earn a low grade.
_____ 7. To be honest, I really like to prove my ability to others.
_____ 8. I prefer to avoid situations in classes where I could risk performing poorly.
_____ Total score for performance goal orientation (sum the responses to questions 5–8).

The scales measure your learning and performance goal orientations in an academic setting. Comparing your scores on the two scales may indicate your tendency toward either a learning or a performance goal orientation.

Source: Adapted from VandeWalle, D., Cron, W., and Slocum, J. W. Individual differences in goal orientation in an academic setting. Unpublished manuscript, Cox School of Business, Southern Methodist University, September 1999.

The implications of these goal orientations for work behavior are dramatic. A performance goal orientation can lead to a "helpless" response pattern in behavior. That is, employees with a strong performance goal orientation may avoid challenges at work and perform poorly when they encounter obstacles that are difficult to overcome. When faced with failure, such individuals are likely to become unhappy and dissatisfied and seek to withdraw from the situations in which they find themselves. By contrast, individuals with a strong learning goal orientation are more likely to exhibit "mastery-oriented" responses to work challenges. That is, employees with a strong learning goal orientation strive to overcome failure and setbacks by increasing their efforts and seeking new solutions to the problem. They treat failure as a form of useful feedback, typically maintain their composure when challenged, and sustain or increase performance even when they face obstacles that are difficult to overcome. Although an individual's goal orientation can vary somewhat in different situations, there is strong evidence that a significant amount of goal orientation can be considered to be an aspect of the individual's personality.[20] A strong learning goal orientation may be summed up by the slogan often placed by coaches on the walls of locker rooms: When the going gets tough, the tough get going. In the Preview Case, Reilly exhibited a possible learning goal orientation when she welcomed the formation of the new design teams.

Recently, the relationship between goal orientation and job performance was investigated in a study of salespeople employed by a medical supplies distributor. As expected, superior sales performance was associated with a learning goal orientation. The researchers concluded that simply "wanting to look good" (a performance goal orientation) would not allow salespeople to succeed. These salespeople needed to have the desire to develop the skills needed for success (a learning goal orientation). One recommendation to the organization was to seek evidence of a learning goal orientation when selecting new employees for their sales force.[21]

Introversion and Extroversion

In everyday usage, the words *introvert* and *extrovert* describe a person's congeniality: An introvert is shy and retiring, whereas an extrovert is socially gregarious and outgoing. The terms have similar meanings when used to refer to a personality dimension. **Introversion** is a tendency to be directed inward and have a greater affinity for abstract ideas and sensitivity to personal feelings. Introverts are quiet, introspective, and emotionally unexpressive. **Extroversion** is an orientation toward other people, events, and objects. Extroverts are sociable, lively, impulsive, and emotionally expressive. Introversion and extroversion are part of the collection of traits that comprise the *sociability* factor (see Figure 2.2).

Although some people exhibit the extremes of introversion and extroversion, most are only moderately introverted or extroverted, or are even relatively balanced between the extremes. Introverts and extroverts appear in all educational, gender, and occupational groups. As might be expected, extroverts are well represented in managerial occupations because the manager's role often involves working with others and influencing them to attain organizational goals. Research even suggests that some extroversion may be essential to managerial success. However, either extreme extroversion or extreme introversion can interfere with an individual's effectiveness in an organization.

One of the most striking implications of the introversion–extroversion personality dimension involves task performance in different environments. The evidence suggests that introverts perform better alone and in a quiet environment, whereas extroverts perform better in an environment with greater sensory stimulation, such as a noisy office with many people and a high level of activity.

Recall our discussion of the sources of personality differences among people (nature versus nurture). Interestingly, many experts consider introversion and extroversion to be a personality dimension with a relatively high genetically determined component.[22]

Dogmatism and Authoritarianism

Dogmatism refers to the rigidity of a person's beliefs. The highly dogmatic individual perceives the world as a threatening place, often regards legitimate authority as absolute, and accepts or rejects other people on the basis of their agreement or disagreement with accepted authority or doctrine. In short, the high-dogmatic (HD) individual is close-minded, and the low-dogmatic (LD) person is open-minded. As a result, HDs appear to depend more on authority figures in the organization for guidance and direction and are more easily influenced by them than are LDs. Some relationship between the degree of dogmatism and interpersonal and group behavior also seems to exist. For example, HDs typically need more group structure than do LDs to work effectively with others. Hence the performance of HDs assigned to task forces and committees may vary somewhat, depending on how the group goes about its work. A high degree of dogmatism is related to a limited search for information in decision-making situations, which sometimes leads to poor managerial performance.

Authoritarianism is closely related to dogmatism but is narrower in scope. The events of World War II spurred the original research on authoritarianism. That research was designed to identify personalities susceptible to fascist or other antidemocratic appeals. Over time, however, the concept broadened. The *authoritarian personality* now describes someone who adheres to conventional values, obeys recognized authority, exhibits a negative view of society, respects power and toughness, and opposes the expression of personal feelings. In organizations, the authoritarian personality probably is subservient to authority figures and may even prefer superiors who have a highly directive, structured leadership style. Both dogmatism and authoritarianism are related to the *intellectual openness* factor (see Figure 2.2).

Organizational Implications

It should be evident by now that the personality dimensions discussed, and the specific relationships for each, have important implications for organizational behavior. However, managers or groups should not try to change or otherwise directly control employee personality; to do so is generally impossible anyway. Even if such control were possible, it would be highly unethical. Rather, the challenge for managers and employees is to understand the crucial role played by personality in explaining some aspects of human behavior in the workplace. Knowledge of important individual differences provides managers, employees, and students of organizational behavior with valuable insights and a framework that they can use to diagnose events and situations. The following Managing Teams Competency feature describes such a situation—an attempt at Hewlett-Packard to create effective work teams.

Competency: Managing Teams

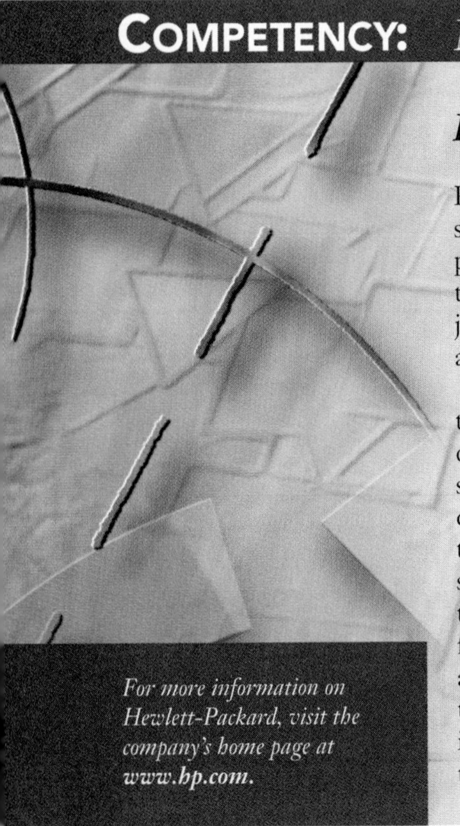

For more information on Hewlett-Packard, visit the company's home page at ***www.hp.com.***

Personality and Teams at Hewlett-Packard

Reed Breland became a team facilitator at Hewlett-Packard's 180-person financial services center in Colorado Springs 2 years ago. After several months in his new position, Breland noticed that members of one of his teams were having a difficult time working together. "It was a classic case of personality conflict," he says. "They just didn't like each other. But when two people on an eight-person team don't get along, believe me, it's disruptive."

Breland gave the team time to try to work things out. "Of course, I spoke to them about the problems, but I was mainly interested in making sure they understood that the work had to get done, regardless of how they got along," he says. However, after 9 months the team was still not working well together. Productivity was inadequate and morale was poor. "I knew I had to do something then, because it had affected their work," explains Breland. He then simply dissolved the team and had its members placed elsewhere rather than trying to determine who was right and wrong. Breland says the team members are doing fine in their other assignments. He compares their team dynamics with those of a sports team: "If the chemistry isn't right, it doesn't matter how good or bad the players are. It's not going to work. As a team leader you have to know when it's reached that point. It's more of an art than a science, but that's what makes the job so interesting.[23]

The Person and the Situation

Although understanding differences in personality is important, behavior always involves an interaction of the person and the situation. Sometimes the demands of the situation may be so overwhelming that individual differences are relatively unimportant. For example, if an office building is burning, everyone in it will try to flee. However, the fact that all employees behaved the same way says nothing about the personalities of those individuals. In other cases, individual differences may explain more about behavior. In the Preview Case, Amy and Reilly faced the same situation, but reacted very differently because of their individual differences.

The relative importance of situational versus dispositional (personal) determinants of behavior continues to be debated, but considerable evidence exists for roles by both. Taking an **interactionist perspective,** that is, considering both the person and the situation, helps in understanding behavior in organizations. For that reason, our perspective is consistently interactionist throughout this book. You will discover that many of the topics covered, such as leadership, political behavior, power differences, stress, and resistance to change, examine both *personal and situational causes* for the organizational behavior discussed. Both *interact* to determine behavior.

Learning Objective:

4. Define the concept of attitudes and explain the general relationship between attitudes and behavior.

ATTITUDES AND BEHAVIOR

Attitudes are another type of *individual difference* that affects behavior. **Attitudes** are relatively lasting feelings, beliefs, and behavioral tendencies directed toward specific people, groups, ideas, issues, or objects.[24] Attitudes reflect an individual's background and experiences. As with personality development, significant people in a person's life—parents, friends, and members of social and work groups—strongly influence attitude formation. Also, some evidence points to genetic influences on the attitudes that people develop.[25]

Components of Attitudes

People often think of attitudes as a simple concept, but in reality attitudes and their effects on behavior can be extremely complex. An attitude consists of three components:

- an *affective* component—the feelings, sentiments, moods, and emotions about some person, idea, event, or object;
- a *cognitive* component—the beliefs, opinions, knowledge, or information held by the individual; and
- a *behavioral* component—the predisposition to act on a favorable or unfavorable evaluation of something.[26]

These components don't exist or function separately. An attitude represents the *interplay* of a person's affective, cognitive, and behavioral tendencies with regard to something—another person or group, an event, or an issue. For example, suppose that an individual holds a strong, negative attitude about the use of nuclear power. During a job interview with the representative of a large corporation, he discovers that the company is a major supplier of nuclear power generation equipment. He might feel a sudden intense dislike for the company's interviewer (the affective component). He might form a negative opinion of the interviewer based on beliefs and opinions about the type of person who would work for such a company (the cognitive component). He might be tempted to make an unkind remark to the interviewer or suddenly terminate the interview (the behavioral component). However, the person's *actual* behavior may or may not be easy to predict and will depend on several factors that we discuss shortly.

Links to Behavior

To what extent do attitudes predict or cause behavior? Behavioral scientists used to contend that individuals' behaviors were consistent with their attitudes. However, they now accept the notion that a simple, direct link between attitudes and behavior frequently doesn't exist. In the interview example just presented, the person being interviewed might have the negative feelings, opinions, and behavioral predisposition described and yet choose not to behave negatively toward the interviewer. The interviewee might not act on his attitude because (1) he desperately needs a job; (2) the norms of courteous behavior outweigh his desire to express his negative attitude; (3) he decides that the interviewer is an inappropriate target for negative behavior; and/or (4) he acknowledges the possibility of having incomplete information.

Pollsters and others often measure attitudes and attempt to predict subsequent behavior. Doing so often is difficult; however, observing three principles can improve the accuracy of predicting behavior from attitudes.

- General attitudes best predict general behaviors.
- Specific attitudes best predict specific behaviors.
- The less time that elapses between attitude measurement and behavior, the more consistent will be the relationship between attitude and behavior.[27]

For example, attitudes toward women in management in general aren't as good a predictor of whether someone will work well for a female manager as are specific attitudes toward a particular manager. General attitudes toward religion aren't good predictors of specific behavior, such as giving to a certain church-related charity or observing a specific religious holiday. However, these general attitudes may accurately predict general religious behavior, such as the overall level of involvement in church activities. Moreover, attitudes may change over time. Generally, the longer the elapsed time between the measurement of an attitude and a behavior, the less likely it is that the relationship between them will be strong. This third principle is well known to political pollsters (after some earlier embarrassments), and they typically are careful not to predict voting behavior too far ahead of an actual election. (Or they may be careful to add certain qualifiers to published polls, such as: If the election were held today . . .)

Behavioral Intentions Model

The **behavioral intentions model** is an attempt to explain the relationships between attitudes and behavior. The model suggests that focusing on a person's specific *intention* to behave in a certain way makes behavior more predictable and the relationship between the attitude and behavior more understandable than if intention is not considered.[28] Figure 2.4 illustrates the model and shows that intentions depend on both attitudes and norms regarding the behavior. **Norms** are rules of behavior, or proper ways of acting, that members of a group or a society have accepted as appropriate. Norms thus impose social pressures to behave or not to behave in certain ways. (We explore the concept of norms in Chapter 8.) If both attitudes and norms are positive with regard to a behavior, an individual's intention to behave in a certain way will be strong. If attitudes and norms conflict, their relative strengths may determine an individual's intention and actual behavior.

According to the behavioral intentions model, an individual's beliefs regarding specific behaviors affect both attitudes and norms. In the case of attitudes, beliefs concern the relationship between the behavior and its consequences (outcomes). Beliefs regarding norms reflect an individual's perceptions of how others expect that person to act. This model helps explain why the relationship between attitudes and behavior sometimes is strong and at other times is weak.

The behavioral intentions model also indicates another possible explanation of behavior: Real or perceived situational or internal obstacles may prevent a person

Figure 2.4 **Behavioral Intentions Model**

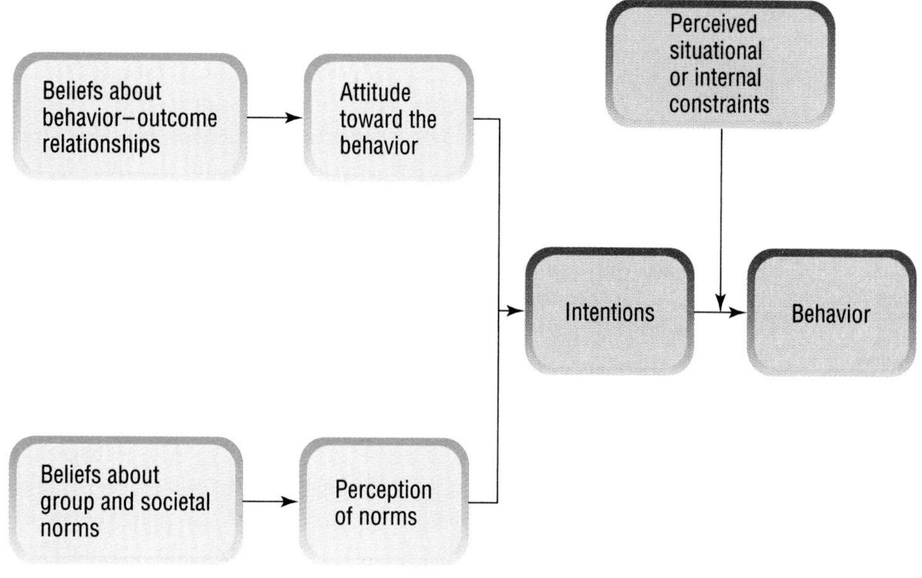

Source: Adapted from Ajzen, I., and Fishbein, M. *Understanding Attitudes and Predicting Social Behavior.* Englewood Cliffs, N.J.: Prentice-Hall, 1980, 8.

from behaving in an intended manner. For example, someone might fully intend to perform a task quickly and efficiently but lack the competency to do so. Moreover, the perception or belief that she lacks the necessary competencies might prevent a person from performing the task (having the same effect as the actual lack of skill).

Over the years, behavioral scientists have proposed various models to explain attitude–behavior relationships. However, the simple model shown in Figure 2.4 predicts behavior about as well as more complex explanations do.[29] This model seems particularly useful for predicting certain specific behaviors, such as turnover in organizations. That is, if a person intends to quit, he or she usually does so eventually. Thus attitude–behavior relationships are important for understanding certain aspects of organizational behavior.

Learning Objective:

5. Explain the importance of job satisfaction and organizational commitment in organizational behavior.

WORK ATTITUDES

The importance of attitude–behavior relationships can best be demonstrated by examining two key work attitudes—job satisfaction and organizational commitment. Of interest also are the complex relationships between job satisfaction and job performance.

Job Satisfaction

In organizational behavior, perhaps the attitude of greatest interest is the general attitude of employees toward work or toward a job, often called **job satisfaction.**[30] The sources of job satisfaction are of particular interest because they often suggest corrective actions that can be taken.

Sources of Job Satisfaction. Job satisfaction is sometimes regarded as a single concept; that is, a person is satisfied or not satisfied with the job. However, it actually is a collection of specific job attitudes that can be related to various aspects of the job. For example, a popular measure of job satisfaction—the job descriptive index (JDI)—measures satisfaction in terms of five specific aspects of a person's job: pay, promotion, supervision, the work itself, and coworkers.[31] Obviously, an employee may be satisfied with some aspects of the job and, at the same time, be dissatisfied with others.

The sources of job satisfaction and dissatisfaction vary from person to person. Sources important for many employees include the challenge of the job, the degree of interest that the work holds for the person, the extent of required physical activity, the characteristics of working conditions (e.g., temperature, humidity, proximity to others, and so on), the types of rewards available from the organization (e.g., the level of pay), the nature of coworkers, and the like. Table 2.3 lists work factors that often are related to levels of employee job satisfaction. An important implication of the relationships suggested is that job satisfaction perhaps should be considered primarily as an outcome of the individual's work experience. Thus high levels of dissatisfaction might indicate to managers that problems exist, say, with working conditions, the reward system, or the employee's role in the organization.

Relation to Job Behavior. Of special interest to managers and employees are the possible relationships between job satisfaction and various job behaviors and other outcomes in the workplace. A commonsense notion is that job satisfaction leads directly to effective task performance. (A happy worker is a good worker.) Yet, numerous studies have shown that a simple, direct linkage between job satisfaction and job performance often doesn't exist.[32] The difficulty of relating attitudes to behavior is pertinent here. Earlier, we noted that general attitudes best predict general behaviors and that specific attitudes are related most strongly to specific behaviors. These principles

Table 2.3 Effects of Various Work Factors on Job Satisfaction

WORK FACTORS	EFFECTS
Work itself	
Challenge	Mentally challenging work that the individual can successfully accomplish is satisfying.
Physical demands	Tiring work is dissatisfying.
Personal Interest	Personally interesting work is satisfying.
Reward structure	Rewards that are equitable and that provide accurate feedback for performance are satisfying.
Working conditions	
Physical	Satisfaction depends on the match between working conditions and physical needs.
Goal attainment	Working conditions that promote goal attainment are satisfying.
Self	High self-esteem is conducive to job satisfaction.
Others in the organization	Individuals will be satisfied with supervisors, coworkers, or subordinates who help them attain rewards. Also, individuals will be more satisfied with colleagues who see things the same way they do.
Organization and management	Individuals will be satisfied with organizations that have policies and procedures designed to help them attain rewards. Individuals will be dissatisfied with conflicting roles and/or ambiguous roles imposed by the organization.
Fringe benefits	Benefits do not have a strong influence on job satisfaction for most workers.

Source: Adapted from Landy, F. J. *Psychology of Work Behavior,* 4th ed. Pacific Grove, Calif.: Brooks/Cole, 1989, 470.

COMPETENCY: MANAGING COMMUNICATION

A HAPPY STAFF LEADS TO HAPPY CUSTOMERS

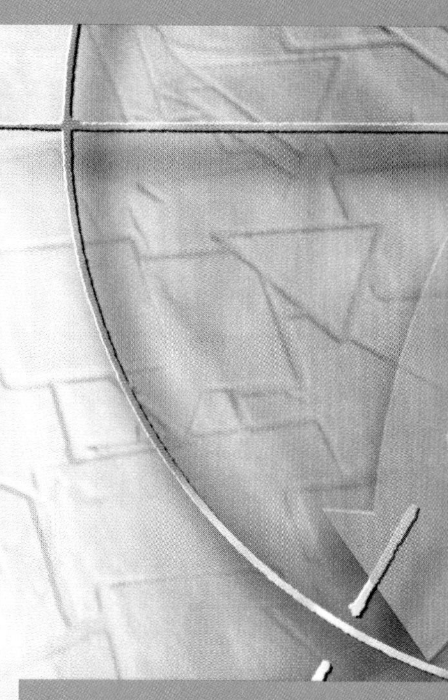

Many companies are beginning to pay a lot more attention to nonfinancial factors that contribute to profits. For example, employee satisfaction, customer satisfaction, and financial results seem to be linked when employee commitment and customer loyalty are important (which would seem to be most of the time). The following are some examples from the corporate world.

AC-Nielsen began tying manager's bonuses partly to employee-satisfaction scores on a wide range of issues when their studies showed that the quality of employees' lives on the job had a direct and powerful effect on the quality of their family relationships. In another initiative, Nielsen added personal benefits such as adoption and infertility aid after workers reported dissatisfaction with family support. After 3 years of linking employee and customer satisfaction data, Nielsen found that when employee satisfaction rises, financial results also improve.

Sun Microsystems polls its employees monthly, using an e-mail questionnaire, about "performance inhibitors" that have gotten in their way in the past month. Results are compiled into an "employee quality index" that is a broad indicator of levels of job satisfaction. Among other things, Sun has found strong links among job satisfaction, the likelihood that employees will recommend Sun as a place to work, and the likelihood that customers will recommend it as a place to do business.

Dick Clark (his real name), leader of the financial services unit at Monsanto, recently conducted surveys of customer and employee satisfaction. He found that employees' satisfaction with their work–personal life balance was one of the two strongest predictors of customer satisfaction. The other factor was employees' general satisfaction with their jobs. Clark says, "It's common sense. When people feel great about the place where they work, they provide better customer service."[33]

*For more information on AC-Nielsen, Sun Microsystems, and Monsanto, visit these organizations' home pages at **www.acnielsen.com; www.sun.com; and www.monsanto.com.***

explain, at least in part, why the expected relationships often don't exist. Overall job satisfaction, as a collection of numerous attitudes toward various aspects of the job, represents a general attitude. Performance of a specific task, such as preparing a particular monthly report, can't necessarily be predicted on the basis of a general attitude. Even though tight linkages between satisfaction and specific task performance cannot always be drawn, job satisfaction is often important in terms of organizational effectiveness. For example, studies have shown that levels of job satisfaction in the workforce and organizational performance are linked. That is, organizations with satisfied employees tend to be more effective than organizations with unsatisfied employees.[34] Further, many organizations appreciate the linkage between customer satisfaction and the satisfaction of employees who interact with their customers. Examples of this linkage are apparent in the Managing Communication Competency feature above.

Job satisfaction is important for many reasons in addition to those mentioned. Because satisfaction represents an outcome of the work experience, high levels of dissatisfaction help to identify organizational problems that need attention. In addition, job dissatisfaction is strongly linked to absenteeism, turnover, and physical and mental health problems.[35] For example, research clearly shows that highly dissatisfied employees are more likely to be absent from work than are satisfied employees. Further, dissatisfied employees are more likely to leave a job for other employment. High levels of absenteeism and turnover are costly for organizations. According to Steve Watson, a partner at Heidrick & Struggles, it typically costs firms about 20 percent of a person's salary to recruit a replacement. Thus, when Arthur Andersen loses a $50,000 per year staff accountant, the firm may spend $10,000 to hire a comparable employee.

Many management experts suggest that the strong relationship between dissatisfaction and absenteeism and turnover is a compelling reason for paying careful attention to employee job satisfaction.

Organizational Commitment

Another important work attitude that has a bearing on organizational behavior is commitment to the organization. **Organizational commitment** refers to the strength of an employee's involvement in the organization and identification with it. Strong organizational commitment is characterized by

- a belief in and acceptance of the organization's goals and values;
- a willingness to exert considerable effort on behalf of the organization; and
- a desire to remain with the organization.[36]

Organizational commitment goes beyond loyalty to include an active contribution to accomplishing organizational goals. The concept of organizational commitment represents a broader work attitude than job satisfaction because it applies to the entire organization rather than just to the job. Further, commitment typically is more stable than satisfaction because day-to-day events are less likely to change it.

Sources of Commitment. As with job satisfaction, the sources of organizational commitment may vary from person to person. Employees' initial commitment to an organization is determined largely by their individual characteristics (e.g., personality and values) and how well their early job experiences match their expectations. Later, organizational commitment continues to be influenced by job experiences, with many of the same factors that lead to job satisfaction also contributing to organizational commitment or lack of commitment: pay, relationships with supervisors and coworkers, working conditions, opportunities for advancement, and so on. Over time, organizational commitment tends to become stronger because (1) individuals develop deeper ties to the organization and their coworkers as they spend more time with them; (2) seniority often brings advantages that tend to develop more positive work attitudes; and (3) opportunities in the job market may decrease with age, causing workers to become more strongly attached to their current job.[37]

Relation to Job Behavior. Managers are very interested in the relationships between organizational commitment and job behavior.[38] The relationship between organizational commitment and turnover is one of the most important.[39] Simply stated, the stronger an employee's commitment is to the organization, the less likely the person is to quit. Strong commitment also is often correlated with low absenteeism and relatively high productivity. Attendance at work (being on time and taking little time off) is usually higher for employees with strong organizational commitment. Further, committed individuals tend to be more goal directed and waste less time while at work, which has a positive impact on typical productivity measures. Effective management can foster increased commitment and loyalty to the organization as the Managing Self Competency feature on page 55 indicates.

Learning Objective:

6. Describe the relationship between individual differences and ethical behavior.

INDIVIDUAL DIFFERENCES AND ETHICAL BEHAVIOR

Ethical behavior in organizations has, appropriately, received great attention in recent years. Part of this attention focuses on the influence that individual differences might have on ethical behavior. For example, one study suggested that locus of control and cognitive moral development are important in helping explain whether people will behave ethically or unethically.[40] **Cognitive moral development** refers to an

COMPETENCY: MANAGING SELF

WINNING MOTHER'S LOYALTY AND COMMITMENT

Diane Hook was hit by a crime that is every parent's nightmare. She and her husband did their best to hire a good nanny for their baby daughter. They used an agency that did criminal and background checks. She personally checked references and had friends actually help interview candidates to get multiple opinions. The person they hired had glowing references, which spoke of their newly hired nanny "as if she was Mother Teresa," Hook recalls.

Yet, despite their care in the hiring process, the new nanny seriously abused their baby. A secretly installed videotape actually caught her slapping the 9-month old baby, twisting the baby's leg, and angrily stuffing a blanket into her mouth. Diane Hook and her husband were afraid of the public exposure that prosecuting the nanny would bring, but they filed charges anyway in order to protect other parents from having to go through the same experience.

The case dragged on for 2 years before the nanny agreed to a plea bargain that put her in prison for 4 years. The experience was extremely trying for the Hooks as it included difficult publicity, threatening phone calls, and a great deal of expense. However, crucial support emerged from an unlikely source: Diane Hook's employer, Merck-Medco.

Shortly after the videotaping, Hook walked into the office of her manager, Margie McGlynn, prepared to resign. At the time, she felt like she could never again entrust her child to anyone but family. Instead of allowing her to quit, however, McGlynn said, "Now isn't the time to make a decision that has such a tremendous bearing on your life." McGlynn urged her to take time off to heal her family. She offered to keep Hook on the payroll and allow her to work from home as she felt able to. Per Lofberg, the president of Merck-Medco, approved the arrangement.

Fortunately, the baby suffered no lasting harm. Diane Hook believes that the respite from job worries speeded her own recovery from the ordeal. For a time, she worked only when the baby slept or when her husband stayed home from work one day a week to watch the child. Now, she is back at work on a permanent part-time schedule. The baby (now 3 years old) stays with a trusted friend, and a second child is in a high-quality child care center.

Needless to say, Diane Hook is deeply committed to Merck-Medco. Recently, when a distressed coworker decided to quit after her child was diagnosed with developmental difficulties, Hook told her "exactly what Margie said to me—now is not the time." Hook strongly believes that all firms should provide the same kinds of support that she received from her employer. She holds that "employers who help their employees work through significant personal traumas end up being better for it."[41]

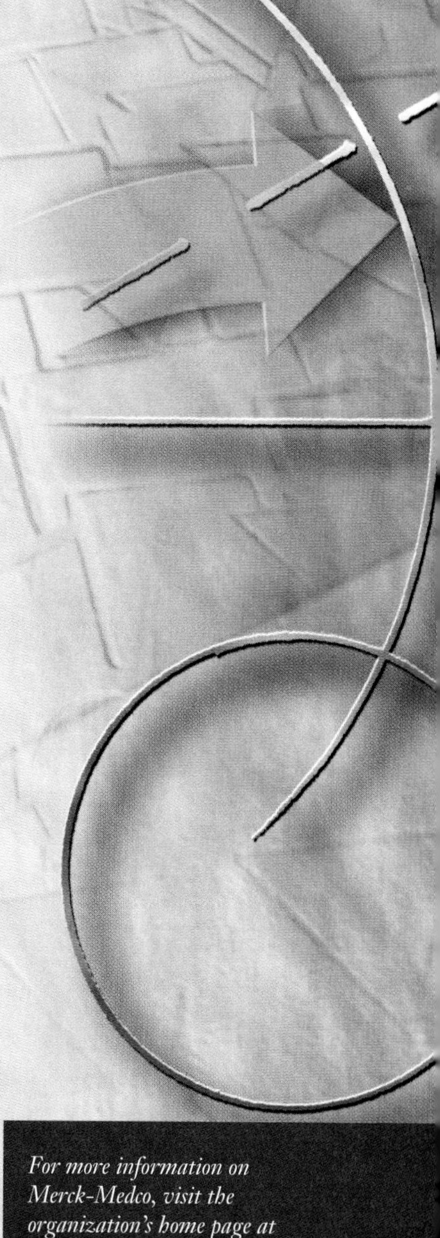

For more information on Merck-Medco, visit the organization's home page at ***www.merck-medco.com.***

individual's level of moral judgment. People seem to pass through stages of moral reasoning and judgment as they mature. Judgment with regard to right and wrong becomes less dependent on outside influences (e.g., parents) and less self-centered (It's right because it's right for me.). At higher levels of cognitive moral development, individuals develop a deeper understanding of the principles of justice, ethical behavior, and balancing individual and social rights.

Research has demonstrated that individuals with high internal locus of control exhibit more ethical behavior when making organizational decisions than do individuals with high external locus of control. Further, individuals with higher levels of cognitive moral development are more likely to behave ethically than are others.

Types of Management Ethics

The terms *immoral*, *amoral*, and *moral* management identify important ethical differences among managers.[42]

Immoral Management. Managerial behaviors devoid of any ethical principles represent **immoral management.** Those practicing immoral management believe in the maximum exploitation of opportunities for corporate or personal gain to the exclusion of other considerations. Any corner will be cut if doing so appears useful. Even legal standards are barriers to be overcome rather than guidelines for appropriate behavior.

The Frigitemp Corporation provides an example of immoral management at the highest levels of the firm. According to testimony provided during federal investigations and criminal trials, corporate officials (including the chairman of the board of directors and the president) admitted making illegal payoffs of millions of dollars. In addition, corporate officers embezzled funds, exaggerated earnings in reports to shareholders, took kickbacks from suppliers, and even provided prostitutes for customers. Frigitemp eventually went bankrupt because of the misconduct of some of its top-level managers.

Moral Management. The opposite extreme from immoral management is **moral management.** That is, managerial and employee behaviors focus on and follow ethical norms, professional standards of conduct, and compliance with applicable regulations and laws. Moral management doesn't mean lack of interest in profits. However, the moral manager will not pursue profits outside the boundaries of the law and sound ethical principles.

McCulloch Corporation, a manufacturer of chain saws, provides a good example of moral management. Chain saws can be dangerous to use, and studies have consistently shown large numbers of injuries from saws not equipped with chain brakes and other safety features. The Chain Saw Manufacturers Association fought hard against mandatory federal safety standards, preferring to rely on voluntary standards even in the face of evidence that voluntary standards were neither high enough nor working. However, McCulloch consistently supported and practiced higher safety standards; in fact, chain brakes have been standard on McCulloch saws since 1975. McCulloch made numerous attempts to persuade the Chain Saw Manufacturers Association to adopt higher standards when research results indicated that they could greatly reduce injuries. When McCulloch failed to persuade the association to support these higher standards, it withdrew from the association.

Amoral Management. Managerial behaviors that are indifferent to ethical considerations—as though different standards of conduct apply to business than to other aspects of life—characterize **amoral management.** Amoral managers and employees seem to lack awareness of ethical or moral issues and act with no thought for the impact that their actions might have on others.

An example of amoral management was Nestlé's decision to market infant formula in Third World countries. Nestlé received massive amounts of negative publicity for this marketing strategy, and governments in several countries launched investigations. These investigations indicated that the company apparently gave no thought to the possible disastrous health consequences of selling the formula to illiterate and impoverished people in areas where it would likely be mixed with impure, disease-ridden water. The following Managing Ethics Competency feature, while amusing, presents another example of amoral management.

COMPETENCY: MANAGING ETHICS

WHO'S YOUR PHONE COMPANY?

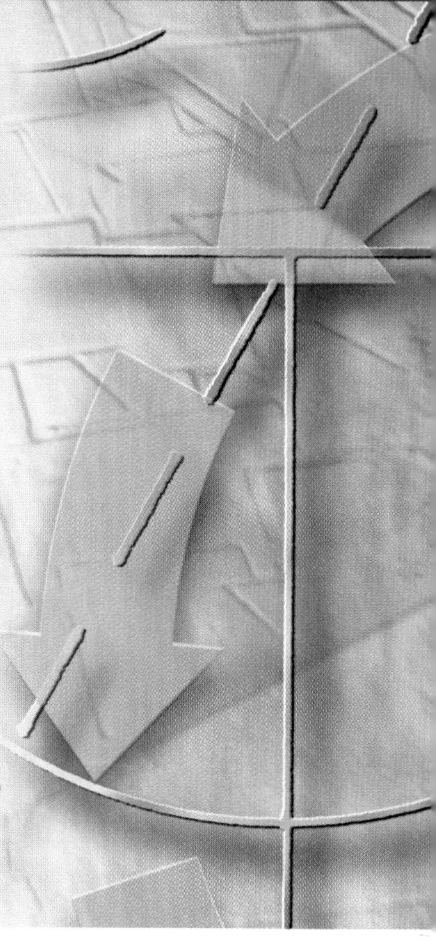

Imagine that you're in Houston and you need assistance calling a relative in Dallas. The local telephone operator asks you to pick a long-distance company for the call. If your answer is, "I don't know," "I don't care," "It doesn't matter," or "Whoever," you may have to pay extra for the call. A company in the Fort Worth suburb of Kennedale has registered those phrases as names of Texas long-distance carriers whose rates for operator-assisted calls are about twice those of the major phone companies.

"It's not deceptive at all," said Dennis Dees, president of KTNT Communications, Inc., the holding company for the oddly named subsidiaries. Dees also claims that the KTNT company name is only coincidentally similar to that of phone giant AT&T. When questioned about the prices his company charges and the way it attracts customers, Dees declared: "There's nothing to be defensive about. I'm charging a fair price compared to the market price for my product. I've come up with names that are pretty creative and it's successful for us. There's no reason to be embarrassed."

The Texas Public Utility Commission said that it is aware of Dees' companies, which are properly registered with the state. Officials apparently can do nothing but warn consumers to be careful. The head of the Fort Worth Better Business Bureau is of the opinion that Dees' companies do not meet the BBB standard for advertising. "It doesn't give everybody all the information they need to make an informed decision," he says. An editorial in the local paper concluded that what Dees was doing was legal, but "it sure as hell seems wrong." "We're not trying to be anything we're not," countered Dees. "We are, 'I Don't Care.' That is our company, and if that's what you want, we're your phone company."[43]

ESTABLISHING ETHICAL ATTITUDES

A story is often told about President Calvin Coolidge, who was famous for being a "man of few words." One Sunday, President Coolidge had attended church without his wife. Later in the day, Mrs. Coolidge inquired as to the subject of the minister's sermon. "Sin," replied Coolidge. "What did he say about it?" his wife persisted. "He was against it," answered Coolidge. Unfortunately, to simply be *against* unethical behavior in organizations isn't enough. Managers and employees need a framework of ethical beliefs and behavior in order to diagnose and address ethical problems in the workplace. Throughout this book, we explore ethical issues involved in a variety of aspects of organizational behavior.

Of course, an organization cannot directly manage personality dimensions (e.g., locus of control) or cognitive individual differences (e.g., cognitive moral development). Still, managers can take steps such as the following to instill moral management by fostering ethical attitudes in the workforce.

- Identify ethical attitudes crucial for the organization's operations. For example, a security firm might stress honesty, whereas a drug manufacturer may identify responsibility as most important to ensure product quality. After identifying important ethical attitudes, training programs can focus on developing such attitudes among employees.
- Select employees with desired attitudes. The organization might develop and use standard interview questions that assess an applicant's ethical values.

- Incorporate ethics in the performance evaluation process. Criteria that individuals are evaluated on will have an important influence on work-related attitudes that they develop. Organizations should make ethical concerns part of the job description and evaluation.
- Establish a work culture that reinforces ethical attitudes. Managers and organizations can take many actions to influence organizational culture. This culture, in turn, has a major influence on ethical behavior in the organization.[44]

Citicorp, the huge, multinational financial services organization, stresses development of ethical attitudes and behaviors among its employees. Its concerns about ethical behavior resulted in the development and use of an ethics game, or exercise, entitled "The Work Ethic—An Exercise in Integrity."[45] The game can be played by individuals in a small group or by large groups divided into several teams. Individuals or teams are presented with ethical dilemmas based on the company's actual experiences. Employees can compare their proposed solutions to what Citicorp management considers to be the correct, ethical course of action. Managers use the game in training programs, staff meetings, and departmental retreats and to orient new employees. The goals of the game are to help employees recognize ethical dilemmas in decision making, to teach employees how Citicorp responds to misconduct, and to increase understanding of its rules and policies regarding ethical behavior. The ethics game isn't the only ethics training that Citicorp uses, but it is an excellent example of how an organization can foster ethical attitudes and behaviors among managers and employees.

CHAPTER SUMMARY

1. Explain the basic sources of personality differences among people.

Personality is a person's set of relatively stable characteristics and traits that account for consistent patterns of behavior in various situations. Each individual in some ways is like other people and in some ways is unique. An individual's personality is the product both of inherited traits or tendencies and experiences. These experiences occur within the framework of the individual's biological, physical, and social environment—all of which are modified by the culture, family, and other groups to which the person belongs.

2. Describe the "Big Five" personality factors and identify your own profile in terms of these factors.

An individual's personality may be described by a set of factors known as the Big Five. Specifically, these personality factors describe an individual's degree of adjustment, sociability, conscientiousness, agreeableness, and intellectual openness. Remember, you can assess your own profile in terms of the Big Five by using the questionnaire at the end of this chapter.

3. Identify some examples of specific personality traits that have important relationships to work behavior.

In the study of organizational behavior, we are particularly interested in the linkage between personality and behavior in the work setting. Many specific personality dimensions, including self-esteem, locus of control, goal orientation, introversion/extroversion, dogmatism, and authoritarianism have been shown to have important relationships to work behavior and outcomes. In addition, an understanding of interactions between the person and the situation is important for comprehending organizational behavior.

4. Define the concept of attitudes and explain the general relationship between attitudes and behavior.

Attitudes are patterns of feelings, beliefs, and behavioral tendencies directed toward specific people, groups, ideas, issues, or objects. Attitudes have affective (feelings, emotions), cognitive (beliefs, knowledge), and behavioral (a predisposition to act in a particular way) components. The relationship between attitudes and behavior isn't always clear, although important relationships exist. We can improve the prediction of behavior from attitudes by remembering that general attitudes best predict general behaviors and that specific attitudes most accurately predict specific behaviors. In addition, the attitude–behavior relationship may become clearer when an individual's intentions to behave in a certain way are known and the specific attitudes and norms that might be related to the behavior are understood.

5. Explain the importance of job satisfaction and organizational commitment in organizational behavior.

Job satisfaction—the general collection of attitudes that an employee holds toward the job—is of great interest in understanding organizational behavior. The simple notion that job satisfaction directly causes an individual to perform well on all tasks all the time doesn't stand up to careful scrutiny. Nevertheless, levels of satisfaction among employees do have an important relationship to the overall effectiveness of the organization. Among other things, dissatisfied employees are more likely to be absent, more likely to quit, more likely to treat customers poorly, and so on.

Another work attitude of interest is commitment to the organization. As an attitude, organizational commitment represents the strength of an employee's involvement in an organization and identification with it. As does satisfaction, commitment has a strong relationship to turnover. High levels of organizational commitment among a workforce are associated with many positive outcomes, including strong loyalty, high productivity, and low absenteeism.

6. Describe the relationship between individual differences and ethical behavior.

Individual differences such as locus of control and cognitive moral development are related to ethical behavior. Further, important ethical differences among managers are captured by the terms immoral management, moral management, and amoral management. Organizations can and should take constructive steps to foster ethical attitudes and moral management among their managers and employees.

KEY TERMS AND CONCEPTS

Amoral management
Attitudes
Authoritarianism
Behavioral intentions model
"Big Five" personality factors
Cognitive moral development
Culture
Dogmatism
Emotional intelligence
External locus of control
Extroversion
General theory of behavior
Immoral management
Individual differences
Interactionist perspective
Internal locus of control
Introversion
Job satisfaction
Learning goal orientation
Locus of control
Moral management
Nature–nurture controversy
Norms
Organizational commitment
Performance goal orientation
Personality
Personality trait
Self-esteem

DISCUSSION QUESTIONS

1. Explain why personality theory is considered to be a general theory of behavior.
2. Using the categories identified in the chapter, describe the basic sources of personality differences between yourself and a person you know well.
3. Explain the opposing positions in the nature–nurture controversy. What influences on personality formation seem most important to you. Why?
4. Using the Big Five personality factors, describe your perceptions of (a) a close family member and (b) a person for whom you have worked.
5. From those discussed in the chapter, identify a specific personality dimension that seems particularly important or interesting to you. Provide an example from your own work or other experience of an instance when this dimension seemed strongly related to someone's behavior.

6. Describe the basic components of attitudes. Select a strong attitude that you hold and describe it in terms of these components.
7. Using the behavioral intentions model, explain why attitude–behavior relationships may sometimes appear to be strong and at other times appear to be weak.
8. Describe the levels of (a) job satisfaction and (b) organizational commitment that seemed to exist in some organization with which you have first-hand experience.
9. From the popular business press (e.g., *Wall Street Journal, Fortune, Forbes,* or *Business Week*) or similar publications find and describe examples of immoral management, moral management, and amoral management.
10. How important is it for organizations to actively encourage ethical behavior by managers and employees? Defend your answer.

DEVELOPING COMPETENCIES

Competency: Managing Self—Assessing the Big Five

The Big Five Locator Questionnaire[46]

Instructions: On each numerical scale that follows, indicate which point is generally more descriptive of you. If the two terms are equally descriptive, mark the midpoint.

1.	Eager	5 4 3 2 1	Calm
2.	Prefer Being with Other People	5 4 3 2 1	Prefer Being Alone
3.	A Dreamer	5 4 3 2 1	No-Nonsense
4.	Courteous	5 4 3 2 1	Abrupt
5.	Neat	5 4 3 2 1	Messy
6.	Cautious	5 4 3 2 1	Confident
7.	Optimistic	5 4 3 2 1	Pessimistic
8.	Theoretical	5 4 3 2 1	Practical
9.	Generous	5 4 3 2 1	Selfish
10.	Decisive	5 4 3 2 1	Open-Ended
11.	Discouraged	5 4 3 2 1	Upbeat
12.	Exhibitionist	5 4 3 2 1	Private
13.	Follow Imagination	5 4 3 2 1	Follow Authority
14.	Warm	5 4 3 2 1	Cold
15.	Stay Focused	5 4 3 2 1	Easily Distracted
16.	Easily Embarrassed	5 4 3 2 1	Don't Give a Darn
17.	Outgoing	5 4 3 2 1	Cool
18.	Seek Novelty	5 4 3 2 1	Seek Routine
19.	Team Player	5 4 3 2 1	Independent
20.	A Preference for Order	5 4 3 2 1	Comfortable with Chaos
21.	Distractible	5 4 3 2 1	Unflappable
22.	Conversational	5 4 3 2 1	Thoughtful
23.	Comfortable with Ambiguity	5 4 3 2 1	Prefer Things Clear-Cut
24.	Trusting	5 4 3 2 1	Skeptical
25.	On Time	5 4 3 2 1	Procrastinate

Big Five Locator Score Conversion Sheet

Norm Score	Adjustment	Sociability	Openness	Agreeableness	Conscientiousness	Norm Score
80						80
79			25			79
78						78
77	22					77
76			24			76
75						75
74						74
73	21		23			73
72		25				72
71				25		71
70	20	24	22			70

Norm Score	Adjustment	Sociability	Openness	Agreeableness	Conscientiousness	Norm Score
69					25	69
68				24		68
67		23	21		24	67
66	19					66
65		22		23	23	65
64			20			64
63					22	63
62	18	21	19	22		62
61					21	61
60		20				60
59	17		18	21	20	59
58						58
57		19				57
56			17			56
55	16	18		20	19	55
54			16	19		54
53						53
52		17			18	52
51	15					51
50		16	15	18	17	50
49						49
48	14	15			16	48
47			14	17		47
46		14			15	46
45			13			45
44	13			16	14	44
43		13				43
42			12			42
41				15	13	41
40	12	12	11			40
39						39
38				14	12	38
37		11	10			37
36	11					36
35		10		13	11	35
34			9			34
33	10	9			10	33
32				12		32
31			8			31
30		8			9	30
29	9			11		29
28		7	7		8	28
27				10		27
26		6			7	26
25	8		6			25
24				9	6	24
23						23
22			5		22	22
21	7	5				21
20				8		20
Enter Norm Scores Here	Adj =	S =	O =	A =	C =	

Instructions:

1. Find the sum of the circled numbers on the *first* row of each of the five-line groupings (Row 1 + Row 6 + Row 11 + Row 16 + Row 21 = _____). This is your raw score for "adjustment." Circle the number in the ADJUSTMENT column of the Score Conversion Sheet that corresponds to this raw score.
2. Find the sum of the circled numbers on the *second* row of each of the five-line groupings (Row 2 + Row 7 + Row 12 + Row 17 + Row 22 = _____). This is your raw score for "sociability." Circle the number in the SOCIABILITY column of the Score Conversion Sheet that corresponds to this raw score.
3. Find the sum of the circled numbers on the *third* row of each of the five-line groupings (Row 3 + Row 8 + Row 13 + Row 18 + Row 23 = _____). This is your raw score for "openness." Circle the number in the OPENNESS column of the Score Conversion Sheet that corresponds to this raw score.
4. Find the sum of the circled numbers on the *fourth* row of each of the five-line groupings (Row 4 + Row 9 + Row 14 + Row 19 + Row 24 = _____). This is your raw score for "agreeableness." Circle the number in the AGREEABLENESS column of the Score Conversion Sheet that corresponds to this raw score.
5. Find the sum of the circled numbers on the *fifth* row of each of the five-line groupings (Row 5 + Row 10 + Row 15 + Row 20 + Row 25 = _____). This is your raw score for "conscientiousness." Circle the number in the CONSCIENTIOUSNESS column of the Score Conversion Sheet that corresponds to this raw score.
6. Find the number in the far right or far left column that is parallel to your circled raw score. Enter this norm score in the box at the bottom of the appropriate column.
7. Transfer your norm score to the appropriate scale on the Big Five Locator Interpretation Sheet.

Big Five Locator Interpretation Sheet

STRONG ADJUSTMENT: secure, unflappable, rational, unresponsive, guilt free	Resilient — Responsive — Reactive 35 45 55 65	WEAK ADJUSTMENT: excitable, worrying, reactive, high-strung, alert
LOW SOCIABILITY: private, independent, works alone, reserved, hard to read	Introvert — Ambivert — Extrovert 35 45 55 65	HIGH SOCIABILITY: assertive, sociable, warm, optimistic, talkative
LOW OPENNESS: practical, conservative, depth of knowledge, efficient, expert	Preserver — Moderate — Explorer 35 45 55 65	HIGH OPENNESS: broad interests, curious, liberal, impractical, likes novelty
LOW AGREEABLENESS: skeptical, questioning, tough, aggressive, self-interest	Challenger — Negotiator — Adapter 35 45 55 65	HIGH AGREEABLENESS: trusting, humble, altruistic, team player, conflict averse, frank
LOW CONSCIENTIOUSNESS: spontaneous, fun loving, experimental, unorganized	Flexible — Balanced — Focused 35 45 55 65	HIGH CONSCIENTIOUSNESS: dependable, organized, disciplined, cautious, stubborn

Note: The Big Five Locator is intended for use only as a quick assessment for teaching purposes.

Competency: Managing Self—Emotional IQ

An individual difference that has recently received a great deal of interest is the notion of *emotional intelligence*. According to psychologist Daniel Goleman, emotional intelligence (EQ) is actually more crucial than general intelligence (IQ) in terms of career success. **Emotional intelligence** refers to how well an individual handles herself and others rather than how smart she is or how capable she is in terms of technical skills. Emotional intelligence includes the attributes of self-awareness, impulse control, persistence, confidence, self-motivation, empathy, and social deftness. We can think of EQ as being the social equivalent of IQ. In organizations undergoing rapid change, emotional intelligence may determine who gets promoted and who gets passed over; or who gets laid off, and who stays, according to Goleman. Studies have consistently shown, for example, that the competencies associated with emotional intelligence (e.g., the ability to persuade others, the ability to understand others, and so on) are twice as important for career success than are raw intelligence (IQ) or technical competencies. You can assess your EQ by using the following scale.

Instructions: Using a scale of 1 through 4, where 1 = strongly disagree, 2 = somewhat disagree, 3 = somewhat agree, and 4 = strongly agree, respond to the ten statements below.

_____ 1. I usually stay composed, positive, and unflappable even in trying moments.
_____ 2. I am able to admit my own mistakes.
_____ 3. I hold myself accountable for meeting my goals.
_____ 4. I regularly seek out fresh ideas from a wide variety of sources.
_____ 5. I'm good at generating new ideas.
_____ 6. I can smoothly handle multiple demands and changing priorities.
_____ 7. I pursue goals beyond what's required or expected of me in my current job.
_____ 8. Obstacles and setbacks may delay me a little, but they don't stop me.
_____ 9. My impulses or distressing emotions don't often get the best of me at work.
_____ 10. I operate from an expectation of success rather than a fear of failure.
_____ Total points (Add the point values given to items 1 through 10.)

A score below 70 percent (28 of the 40 possible points) may indicate a problem. However, don't despair if your score is lower than you would like. EQ can be learned. In fact, Goleman says, "We are building emotional intelligence throughout life—it's sometimes called maturity."[47]

REFERENCES

1. Quoted in Eysenck, H. J. *Personality, Genetics, and Behavior.* New York: Prager, 1982, 1.
2. Barrick, M. R., Stewart, G. L., Neubert, M. J., and Mount, M. K. Relating member ability and personality to work-team processes and team effectiveness. *Journal of Applied Psychology,* 1998, 83, 377–391; George, J. M. The role of personality in organizational life: Issues and evidence. *Journal of Management,* 1992, 18, 185–213; Sackett, P. R., Gruys, M. L., and Ellingson, J. E. Ability–personality interactions when predicting job performance. *Journal of Applied Psychology,* 1998, 83, 545–556.
3. Pervin, L. A., and John, O. P. *Handbook of Personality,* 2nd ed. New York: Guilford, 1999.
4. See, for example, Mischel, W., and Shoda, Y. Reconciling processing dynamics and personality dispositions. *Annual Review of Psychology,* 1998, 49, 229–258.
5. Maddi, S. R. *Personality Theories: A Comparative Analysis,* 5th ed. Homewood, Ill.: Dorsey, 1989, 10.
6. See, for example, Revelle, W. Personality processes. *Annual Review of Psychology,* 1995, 46, 295–328.
7. Caspi, A., and Roberts, B. W. Personality continuity and change across the life course. In L. A. Pervin and O. P. John (eds.), *Handbook of Personality,* 2nd ed. New York: Guilford, 1999, 300–326; Lewis, M. On the development of personality. In L. A. Pervin and O. P. John (eds.), *Handbook of Personality,* 2nd ed. New York: Guilford, 1999, 327–346.
8. Turkheimer, E. Heritability and biological explanation. *Psychological Review,* 1998, 105, 782–791; Plomin, R., and Caspi, A. Behavioral genetics and personality. In L.A. Pervin and O. P. John (eds.), *Handbook of Personality,* 2nd ed. New York: Guilford, 1999, 251–276.
9. Bouchard, T. J. Genes, environment, and personality. *Science,* 1994, 264, 1700–1701; Lykken, D. T., Bouchard, T. J., McGue, M., and Tellegen, A. Heritability of interests. *Journal of Applied Psychology,* 1993, 78, 649–661; Rose, R. J. Genes and human behavior. *Annual Review of Psychology,* 1995, 46, 625–654.
10. Cooper, C. R., and Denner, J. Theories linking culture and psychology: Universal and community-specific processes. *Annual Review of Psychology,* 1998, 49, 559–584; Cross, S. E., and Markus, H. R. The cultural constitution of personality. In L. A. Pervin and O. P. John (eds.), *Handbook of Personality,* 2nd ed. New York: Guilford, 1999, 378–396; Miller, J. G. Cultural psychology: Implications for basic psychological theory. *Psychological Science,* 1999, 10, 85–91.
11. Pervin, L. A. *Personality: Theory and Research,* 4th ed. New York: John Wiley & Sons, 1984, 10.
12. Hogan, R. T. Personality and personality measurement. In M. D. Dunnette and L. M. Hough (eds.), *Handbook of Industrial & Organizational Psychology,* vol. 2, 2nd ed. Palo Alto, Calif.: Consulting Psychologists Press, 1991, 873–919; John, O. P., and Srivastava, S. The big five trait taxonomy: History, measurement, and theoretical perspectives. In L. A. Pervin and O. P. John (eds.), *Handbook of Personality,* 2nd ed. New York: Guilford, 1999, 102–138; McCrae, R. R., and Costa, P. T. A five-factor theory of personality. In L. A. Pervin and O. P. John (eds.), *Handbook of Personality,* 2nd ed. New York: Guilford, 1999, 139–153.
13. Barrick, M. R., and Mount, M. K. Autonomy as a moderator of the relationships between the big five personality dimensions and job performance. *Journal of Applied Psychology,* 1993, 78, 111–118; Barrick, M. R., and Mount, M. K. The big five personality dimensions and job performance: A meta-analysis. *Personnel Psychology,* 1991, 44, 1–26; Seibert, S. E., Crant, J. M., and Kraimer, M. L. Proactive personality and career success. *Journal of Applied Psychology,* 1999, 84, 416–427.
14. Ellis, R. A., and Taylor, M. S. Role of self-esteem within the job search process. *Journal of Applied Psychology,* 1983, 68, 632–640.

15. Adapted from Hilb, M. Computex Corporation. In G. Oddou and M. Mendenhall (eds.), *Cases in International Organizational Behavior.* Oxford: Blackwell, 1999, 55–57.
16. Gardner, D. G., and Pierce, J. L. Self-esteem and self-efficacy within the organizational context. *Group & Organization Management*, 1998, 23, 48–70; Leary, M. R. Making sense of self-esteem. *Current Directions in Psychological Science*, 1999, 8, 32–35; Renn, R. W., and Prien, K. O. Employee responses to performance feedback from the task: A field study of the moderating effects of global self-esteem. *Group & Organization Management*, 1995, 20, 337–354.
17. Lefcourt, H. M. Curability and impact of the locus of control construct. *Psychological Bulletin*, 1992, 112, 411–414; Lefcourt, H. M. *Locus of Control: Current Trends in Theory and Research*, 2nd ed. Hillsdale, N.J.: Lawrence Erlbaum Associates, 1982.
18. Black, J. S. Locus of control, social support, stress, and adjustment in international transfer. *Asia Pacific Journal of Management*, April 1990, 1–30.
19. Dweck, C. S. Motivational processes affecting learning. *American Psychologist*, 1986, 41, 1040–1048; Dweck, C. S., and Leggett, E. L. A social-cognitive approach to motivation and personality. *Psychological Review*, 1988, 95, 256–273.
20. Button, S. B., Mathieu, J. E., and Zajac, D. M. Goal orientation in organizational research: A conceptual and empirical foundation. *Organizational Behavior and Human Decision Processes*, 1996, 26–48.
21. VandeWalle, D., Brown, S. P., Cron, W. L., and Slocum, J. W., Jr. The influence of goal orientation and self-regulation tactics on sales performance: A longitudinal field test. *Journal of Applied Psychology*, 1999, 84, 249–259.
22. Engler, B. *Personality Theories*, 3rd ed. Boston: Houghton Mifflin, 1991, 329–334; Eysenck, H. J. *Personality, Genetics, and Behavior.* New York: Prager, 1982, 161–197.
23. Adapted from Caminti, S. What team leaders need to know. *Fortune*, February 20, 1995, 94, 98.
24. Myers, D. G. *Social Psychology*, 4th ed. New York: McGraw-Hill, 1993, 112
25. Baumeister, R. F. On the interface between personality and social psychology. In L. A. Pervin and O. P. John (eds.), *Handbook of Personality*, 2nd ed. New York: Guilford, 1999, 367–377; Tesser, A. The importance of heritability in psychological research: The case of attitudes. *Psychological Review*, 1993, 100, 129–142; Weiss, H. M., and Cropanzano, P. Affective events theory: A theoretical discussion of the structure, causes, and consequences of affective experiences at work. In B. M. Staw and L. L. Cummings (eds.), *Research in Organizational Behavior*, vol. 18. Greenwich, Conn.: JAI Press, 1996, 1–74.
26. Breckler, S. J. Empirical validation of affect, behavior, and cognition as distinct components of attitude. *Journal of Personality and Social Psychology*, 1984, 47, 1191–1205; Eagly, A. H., and Chaiken, S. *The Psychology of Attitudes.* San Diego: Harcourt, Brace, Jovanovich, 1992; Petty, R. E., Wegener, D. T., and Fabrigar, L. R. Attitudes and attitude change. *Annual Review of Psychology*, 1997, 48, 609–647.
27. Cote, S. Affect and performance in organizational settings. *Current Directions in Psychological Science*, 1999, 8, 65–68; Penrod, S. *Social Psychology*. Englewood Cliffs, N.J.: Prentice-Hall, 1983, 345–347.
28. Ajzen, I., and Fishbein, M. *Understanding Attitudes and Predicting Social Behavior.* Englewood Cliffs, N.J.: Prentice-Hall, 1980; Hulin, C. Adaptation, persistence, and commitment in organizations. In M. D. Dunnette and L. M. Hough (eds.), *Handbook of Industrial & Organizational Psychology*, vol. 2, 2nd ed. Palo Alto, Calif.: Consulting Psychologists Press, 1991, 469–471.
29. Ajzen, I. The theory of planned behavior. *Organizational Behavior and Human Decision Processes*, 1991, 50, 1–33; Petty, R. E., Wegener, D. T., and Fabrigar, L. R. Attitudes and attitude change. *Annual Review of Psychology*, 1997, 48, 609–647.
30. See, for example, Ganzach, Y. Intelligence and job satisfaction. *Academy of Management Journal*, 1998, 41, 526–539; Judge, T. A., Locke, E. A., Durham, C. C., and Kluger, A. N. Dispositional effects on job and life satisfaction: The role of core evaluations. *Journal of Applied Psychology*, 1998, 83, 17–34; Kossek, E. E., and Ozeki, C. Work–family conflict, policies, and the job—life satisfaction relationship: A review and directions for organizational behavior—human resources research. *Journal of Applied Psychology*, 1998, 83, 139–149; Robie, C., Ryan, A. M., Schmieder, R. A., Parra, L. F., and Smith, P. C. The relation between job level and job satisfaction. *Group & Organization Management*, 1998, 23, 470–495.
31. Hanisch, K. A. The job description index revisited. *Journal of Applied Psychology*, 1992, 77, 377–382; Smith, P. C., Kendall, L. M., and Hulin, C. L. *The Measurement of Satisfaction in Work and Retirement.* Chicago: Rand McNally, 1969.
32. Cote, S. Affect and performance in organizational settings. *Current Directions in Psychological Science*, 1999, 8, 65–68; Iaffaldano, M.T., and Muchinsky, P. M. Job satisfaction and job performance: A meta-analysis. *Psychological Bulletin*, 1985, 97, 251–273.
33. Adapted from Shellenbarger, S. More managers find a happy staff leads to happy customers. *Wall Street Journal*, December 23, 1998, B1.
34. Ostroff, C. The relationship between satisfaction, attitudes, and performance: An organizational level analysis. *Journal of Applied Psychology*, 1992, 77, 963–974.
35. Duffy, M. K., Ganster, D. C., and Shaw, J. D. Positive affectivity and negative outcomes: The role of tenure and job satisfaction. *Journal of Applied Psychology*, 1998, 83, 950–959; Miner, J. B. *Industrial—Organizational Psychology.* New York: McGraw-Hill, 1992, 119–124; Muchinsky, P. M. *Psychology Applied to Work*, 3rd ed. Pacific Grove, Calif.: Brooks/Cole, 1990, 327–337.
36. Mowday, R. T., Porter, L. W., and Steers, R. M. *Employee—Organization Linkages: The Psychology of Commitment, Absenteeism, and Turnover.* New York: Academic Press, 1982, 27; see also, Brown, S. P. A meta-analysis and review of organizational research on job involvement. *Psychological Bulletin*, 1996, 120, 235–255; Mathieu, J. E., and Zajac, D. M. A review and meta-analysis of the antecedents, correlates, and consequences of organizational commitment. *Psychological Bulletin*, 1990, 108, 171–194.

37. Miner, J. B. *Industrial–Organizational Psychology.* New York: McGraw-Hill, 1992, 124–128.
38. See, for example, Baruch, Y. The rise and fall of organizational commitment. *Human Systems Management,* 1998, 17, 135–143; Becker, T. E., Billings, R. S., Eveleth, D. M., and Gilbert, N. L. Foci and bases of employee commitment: Implications for job performance. *Academy of Management Journal,* 1996, 39, 464–482; Ellemers, N., de Gilder, D., and van den Heuvel, H. Career-oriented versus team-oriented commitment and behavior at work. *Journal of Applied Psychology,* 1998, 83, 717–730.
39. Cohen, A. Organizational commitment and turnover: A meta-analysis. *Academy of Management Journal,* 1993, 36, 1140–1157; Dessler, G. How to earn your employees' commitment. *Academy of Management Executive,* May 1999, 58–67.
40. Trevino, L. K., and Youngblood, S. A. Bad apples in bad barrels: A causal analysis of ethical decision making behavior. *Journal of Applied Psychology,* 1990, 75, 378–385.
41. Adapted from Shellenbarger, S. An employer's support in nanny-abuse case wins mother's loyalty. *Wall Street Journal,* September 30, 1998, B1.
42. The following examples are from Carroll, A. B. In search of the moral manager. *Business Horizons,* March/April, 1987, 2–6; see also, Mitroff, I. I. On the fundamental importance of ethical management. *Journal of Management Inquiry,* 1998, 7, 68–79.
43. Adapted from Drago, M. Don't care now? You may when telephone bill arrives. *Bryan–College Station Eagle,* July 12, 1996, A1, A5.
44. Goddard, R. W. Are you an ethical manager? *Personnel Journal,* March 1988, 38–47.
45. Trevino, L. K. A cultural perspective on changing and developing organizational ethics. In W. A. Pasmore and R. W. Woodman (eds.), *Research in Organizational Change and Development,* vol. 4. Greenwich, Conn.: JAI Press, 1990, 195–230.
46. Reprinted with permission from Howard, P. J., Medina, P. L., and Howard, J. M. The big five locator: A quick assessment tool for consultants and trainers. In J. W. Pfeiffer (ed.), *The 1996 Annual: Volume 1, Training.* San Diego, Pfeiffer & Company, 1996, 119–122. Copyright © 1996 Pfeiffer, an imprint of Jossey-Bass, Inc., Publishers. All rights reserved.
47. Adapted from Fisher, A. Success secret: A high emotional IQ. *Fortune,* October 26, 1998, 293–298

CHAPTER

3 Perception and Attribution

LEARNING OBJECTIVES

When you have finished studying this chapter, you should be able to:

1. Define *perception* and describe the major elements in the perceptual process.
2. Explain perceptual selection and identify the major factors that influence what individuals selectively perceive.
3. Describe the concept of perceptual organization.
4. Identify the factors that determine how one person perceives another.
5. Describe the major errors in perception that people make.
6. Explain how attributions influence behavior and identify important attributions that people make in the work setting.

Preview Case: *Your World Is Not My World*

THE PERCEPTUAL PROCESS

Competency: Managing Communication—*Subtle Signals Sent by Office Design*

PERCEPTUAL SELECTION

External Factors

Internal Factors

Competency: Managing Across Cultures—*Time Perception*

PERCEPTUAL ORGANIZATION

PERSON PERCEPTION

The Person Perceived

The Perceiver

The Situation

Impression Management

Competency: Managing Self—*Alan Page at Mott's*

PERCEPTUAL ERRORS

Accuracy of Judgment

Perceptual Defense

Stereotyping

Competency: Managing Diversity—*Stereotypes of Women at Work*

Halo Effect

Projection

Expectancy Effects

ATTRIBUTIONS: PERCEIVING THE CAUSES OF BEHAVIOR

The Attribution Process

Internal Versus External Causes of Behavior

Attributions of Success and Failure

Competency: Managing Self—*You're Fired!*

CHAPTER SUMMARY

Key Terms and Concepts

Discussion Questions

DEVELOPING COMPETENCIES

Competency: Managing Diversity—*Measuring Perceptions of Women as Managers*

Competency: Managing Ethics—*The Foundation for New Era Philanthropy*

PREVIEW CASE

YOUR WORLD IS NOT MY WORLD

You met David and Anna in the Chapter 2 Preview Case. Recall that David has a small CPA firm and that Anna has her own interior design business. They have been good friends for a long time and now have the chance to work together again as Anna's firm is providing the interior design work for David's new offices. One result of this recent opportunity to work together is an increasing reliance on each other as a "sounding board" for the managerial problems they each grapple with.

They are relaxing with a cup of coffee after having finally settled on the final office design. As we join them, Anna is speaking: "I had the strangest thing happen last week. Just about the time I start to feel reasonably competent as a manager—("I'm a terrific designer," she said in a quick aside. They both laughed.)—something like this seems to occur." "Well, what happened?" David inquired.

"My two newest designers, Hannah and Caleb, are both coming off the six-month probationary period that I use for new hires," Anna explained. "So I guess they are a little anxious about feedback on their performance and their future with us. I didn't really understand how anxious they were, however, until I gave each of them a new assignment. I was very busy and gave this assignment to them in writing by leaving an e-mail message on each of their computers one evening after I had worked late. This impersonal approach turns out to have been a big mistake, at least where Caleb was concerned." Really intrigued now, David urged her to continue.

"Anyway," said Anna, "Within an hour of arriving at the office the next day, each of them was in my office. And, the first conversation, with Hannah, was a lot more pleasant than the next one, with Caleb. Hannah apparently was thrilled with the new assignment and came by to thank me profusely. Hannah had correctly perceived the new assignment as a reward for her performance to that point and a vote of confidence in her future with the firm. But Caleb came storming into my office. He was really shook up by the reassignment and after calming down somewhat quietly asked me if I wanted him to resign. I was absolutely floored by his response to my e-mail."

"I would have been surprised as well," said David. "What did you do next?" "Well," Anna said, "I immediately assured him that we didn't want him to resign and tried to explain why we needed him to move on to the new assignment at this time. Indeed, I told him that we were quite pleased with his performance and weren't trying to signal anything other than complete confidence in him when we changed his assignment." "How in the world did Caleb arrive at such a different interpretation of your e-mail than what you intended?" David wondered. "We spent some time discussing that," said Anna. "It turns out that Caleb was worried about his performance. In addition, he was particularly concerned about one aspect of the design he was working on that he considered inadequate and didn't really feel like he had done everything with it that he could. Then, when he got the reassignment, he sort of flipped out. He interpreted it as confirming his worst fears—we were displeased with his performance and were pulling him off the project."

"Wow," said David. "Really," said Anna. "Of course, Hannah's interpretation of the new assignment is the one I wanted, and I felt badly that Caleb had misperceived the situation in such a negative fashion. I think I learned an important lesson. I would never have believed that two people's perceptions of the same event could be so different."

The Preview Case illustrates the importance of perceptions in organizational behavior. In a very real sense, people live in their own perceptual worlds. People base their behaviors on what they *perceive* reality to be, not necessarily on what reality *is*, and no two people will necessarily perceive a situation in exactly the same way. Recognizing the difference between the perceptual worlds of employees and managers and the reality of the organization is important in understanding organizational behavior.

In this chapter, we explore *individual differences* in terms of the important processes of *perception* and *attribution*. First, we describe the perceptual process. Then, we examine the external and internal factors that influence perception, the ways that people organize perceptions, the process of *person perception*, and various errors in the perceptual process. We then explore the attributions that people make to explain the behaviors of themselves and others.

Learning Objective:

1. Define *perception* and describe the major elements in the perceptual process.

THE PERCEPTUAL PROCESS

Perception is the selection and organization of environmental stimuli to provide meaningful experiences for the perceiver. Perception involves searching for, obtaining, and processing information in the mind. It represents the psychological process whereby people take information from the environment and make sense of their worlds.[1]

The key words in the definition of perception are *selection* and *organization*. Different people often perceive a situation differently, both in terms of what they selectively perceive and how they organize and interpret the things perceived. Figure 3.1 summarizes the basic elements in the perceptual process from initial observation to final response.

People receive stimuli from the environment through their five senses: taste, smell, hearing, sight, and touch. Everyone selectively pays attention to some aspects of the environment and selectively ignores other aspects of it at any particular time. For example, an apartment dweller may listen expectantly for a friend's footsteps in the hall but ignore sounds of the people upstairs. In an office, a secretary may ignore the bell announcing arrival of the elevator but jump at the sound of the fax machine. A person's selection process involves both external and internal factors, filtering sensory perceptions and determining which will receive the most attention. In other words, a complex set of factors, some internal to the person and some in the external environment, combine to determine what is perceived by the mind. We discuss this important process in more detail shortly.

The individual then organizes the stimuli selected into meaningful patterns. How people interpret what they perceive also varies considerably. A wave of the hand may be interpreted as a friendly gesture or as a threat, depending on the circumstances and the state of mind of those involved. As indicated in the Preview Case, perceptions are very important in understanding organizational behavior because an individual's behavior, at any particular time, is based in part on perceptions of the situation. Certainly, in organizations managers and employees need to recognize that perceptions of events and behaviors may (1) vary among individuals and (2) be inaccurate.

As shown in Figure 3.1, a person's interpretation of sensory stimuli will lead to a response—overt (actions), covert (motivation, attitudes, and feelings), or both. As each person selects and organizes sensory stimuli differently and thus may have different interpretations and responses, perceptual differences help explain why people behave differently in the same situation. In other words, people often perceive the same things in different ways, and their behavioral responses depend, in part, on their perceptions.

The ways that individuals select, organize, and interpret their perceptions to make sense of their worlds are not something that managers and organizations can

Figure 3.1 **Basic Elements in the Perceptual Process**

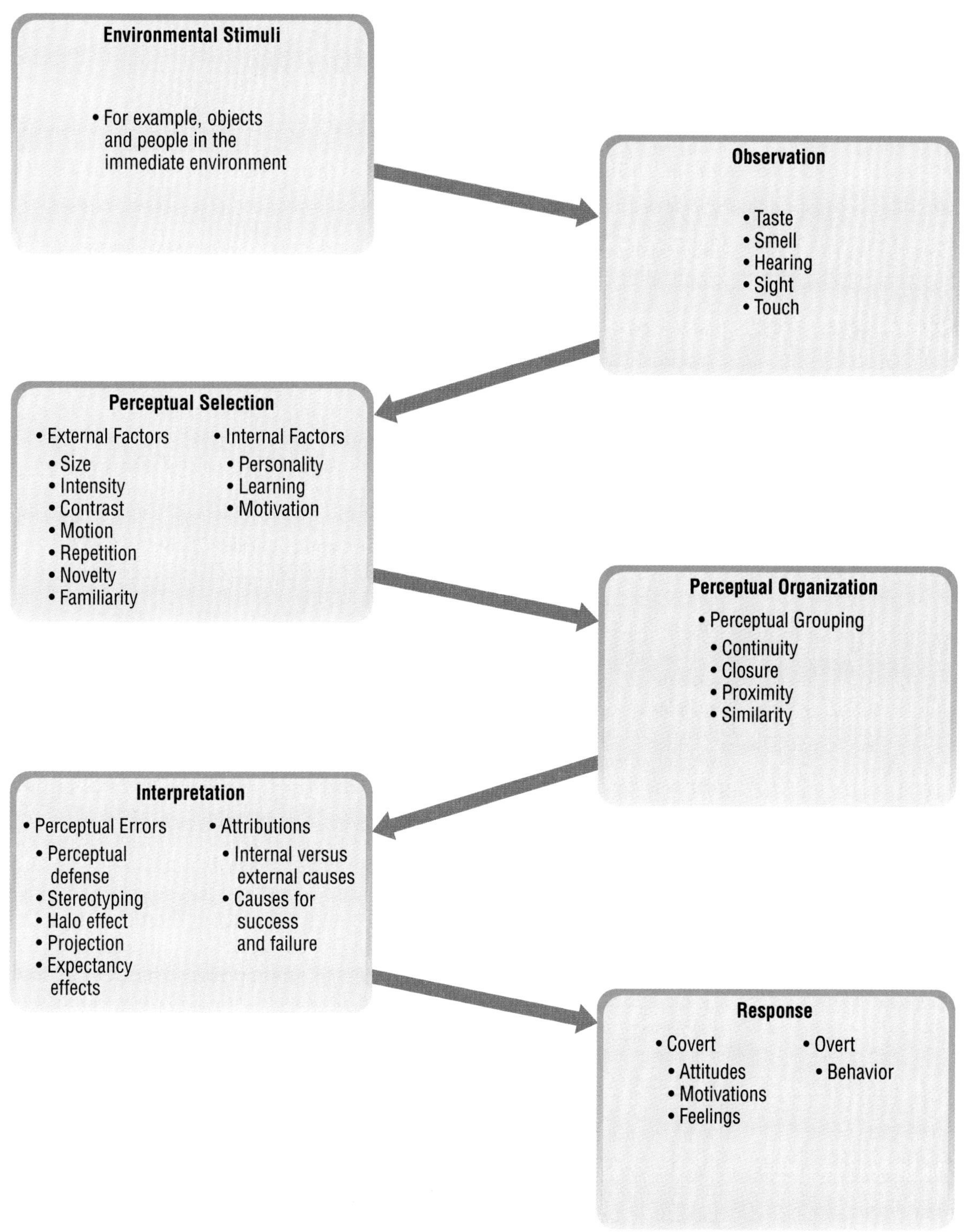

safely ignore. The following Managing Communication Competency feature explores the impact that office design, layout, and décor can have on perceptions of both customers and employees. What is being communicated may be subtle, yet of great importance.

COMPETENCY: MANAGING COMMUNICATION

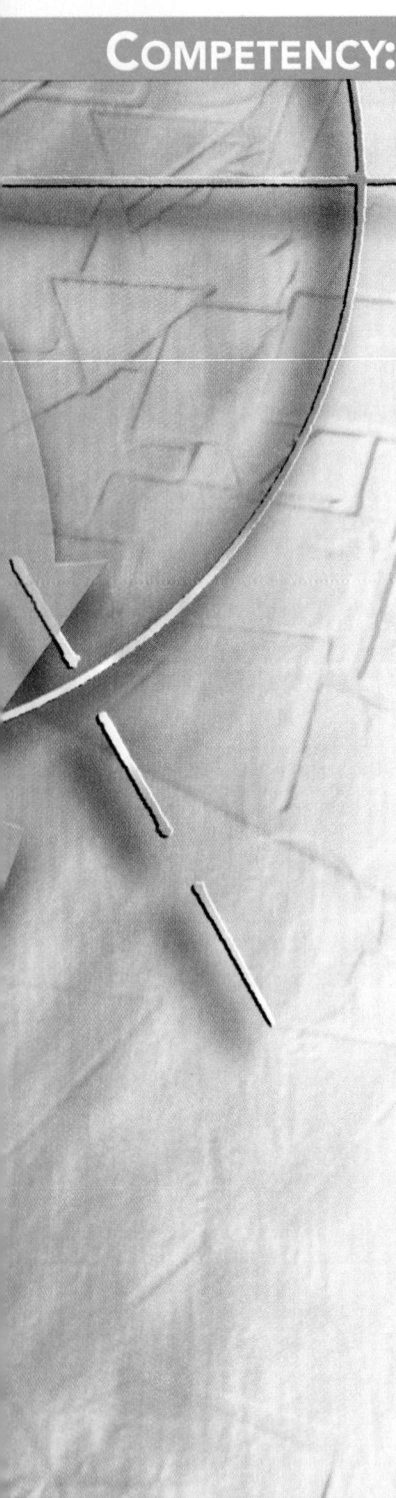

SUBTLE SIGNALS SENT BY OFFICE DESIGN

Office design—lighting, colors, and arrangement of furnishings and other physical objects—influences the perceptions of customers, suppliers, prospective employees, and visitors. Moreover, the design of their offices may affect employees' behavior in various ways.

Office layout—who is located next to whom—influences perceptions of which individuals and functions the organization values most. For example, offices arranged by rank, whereby the highest level managers occupy the top floors, the most desirable office space, and so on, convey the message that the organization highly values status. Even the arrangement of furniture influences perceptions of a firm. For example, one study showed that visitors had very different impressions of an organization, depending on whether the chairs in the reception area faced one another or were at right angles to one another. Organizations that placed chairs facing one another were perceived as more "rigid," "tense," and "deliberate" than organizations using the right-angle layout for visitor seating. Further, executives visiting the firms where seating was arranged at right angles perceived these organizations as "warmer," "friendlier," and more "comfortable." Visitors strongly preferred to do business with the "warmer and friendlier" firms.

In organizations, people perceive that items such as flags, corporate logos, and pictures of company officers indicate a highly structured organization in which employees have limited autonomy. People are likely to perceive an organization that displays certificates of achievement, plaques, and trophies as one that values and rewards good performance. Workplace studies consistently show that flowers and plants increase perceptions of warmth and friendliness. Artwork, though, is likely to be tricky. Having art on the walls is generally perceived positively, but the content of some pictures might have the opposite effect. For example, one firm that was having trouble recruiting women discovered that pictures of men on horseback displayed prominently throughout the building gave prospective women employees the impression that the firm was cold, hostile, and generally unfriendly.

Trinity Communications of Boston provides an excellent example of an organization that is very aware of the relationships between office design and employee perceptions and behaviors. Trinity was the 1999 winner of the Best Office Design contest sponsored by *Buildings* magazine. When Trinity Communications, a communications/public relations firm, was spun off from its parent company, it needed a fresh appearance for its new office space. Management's desire was to redesign the offices to reflect the firm's creative spirit and nonhierarchical structure while at the same time not alienating its clients, many of whom were quite traditional in outlook.

Trinity Communications rejected the notion of traditional private offices in favor of an open office with low workstation walls. They created oases—intimate brainstorming areas where each space is unique and features comfortable couches and chairs, residential-style light fixtures, and small conference tables. In addition, the center of the offices contains a cappuccino bar that provides another comfortable gathering space and work area. Clever use of bright, yet comfortable colors and distinctive lighting throughout the offices also provide a sense of fun and high energy.

Trinity believes that its newly designed space serves as a tool both to attract new clients and to foster collaboration and creativity among employees. Visitors to the office often comment favorably on the overall look and friendly attitudes that permeate the office. According to the old adage, you only get one chance to make a good first impression. Managers and employees at Trinity believe that they have created a space that does exactly that.[2]

*For more information on Trinity Communications, visit the organization's home page at **www.trinity-communications.com/home.htm**.*

Learning Objective:

2. Explain perceptual selection and identify the major factors that influence what individuals selectively perceive.

PERCEPTUAL SELECTION

The phone is ringing, your TV is blaring, a dog is barking outside, your PC is making a strange noise, and you smell coffee brewing. Which of these stimuli will you ignore? Which will you pay attention to? Can we predict or explain your selection of stimuli that grab your attention at a particular time?

Perceptual selection is the process by which people filter out most stimuli so that they can deal with the most important ones. Perceptual selection depends on several factors, some of which are in the external environment and some of which are internal to the perceiver.[3]

EXTERNAL FACTORS

External perception factors are characteristics that influence whether the stimuli will be noticed. The following external factors may be stated as *principles* of perception. In each case we present an example to illustrate the principle.

- *Size.* The larger an external factor, the more likely it is to be perceived. A hiker is far more likely to notice a fully grown fir tree than a seedling.
- *Intensity.* The more intense an external factor (bright lights, loud noises, and the like), the more likely it is to be perceived. The language in an e-mail message from a manager to an employee can reflect the intensity principle. For example, an e-mail that reads, "Please stop by my office at your convenience," wouldn't fill you with the same sense of urgency as an e-mail that reads, "Report to my office immediately!"
- *Contrast.* External factors that stand out against the background or that aren't what people expect are the most likely to be noticed. In addition, the contrast of objects with others or with their backgrounds may influence how they are perceived. Figure 3.2 illustrates this aspect of the contrast principle. Which of the solid center circles is larger? The one on the right appears to be larger, but it isn't: The two circles are the same size. The solid circle on the right appears to be larger because its background, or frame of reference, is composed of much smaller circles. The solid circle on the left appears to be smaller because its background consists of larger surrounding circles.
- *Motion.* A moving factor is more likely to be perceived than a stationary factor. Soldiers in combat learn this principle very quickly. Video games also demonstrate that motion is quickly detected.
- *Repetition.* A repeated factor is more likely to be noticed than a single factor. Marketing managers use this principle in trying to get the attention of prospective customers. An advertisement may repeat key ideas, and the ad itself may be presented many times for greater effectiveness. Marketing managers at Nike have developed the Nike "swoosh" symbol which is consistently used worldwide on all its products.
- *Novelty and familiarity.* Either a familiar or a novel factor in the environment can attract attention, depending on the circumstances. People would quickly notice

Figure 3.2 **Contrast Principle of Perception**

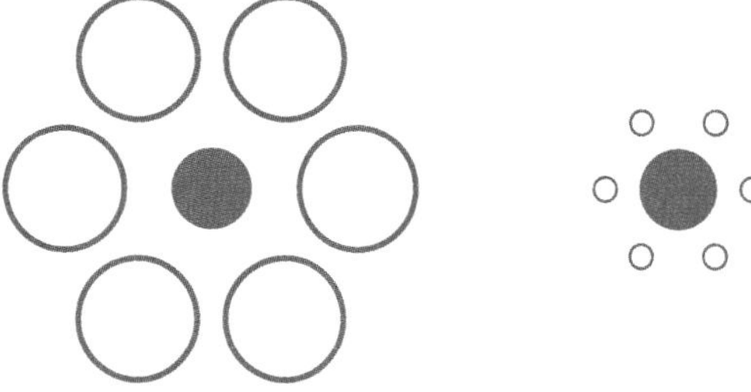

an elephant walking along a city street. (Both novelty and size increase the probability of perception.) Someone is likely to notice the face of a close friend first among a group of approaching people.[4]

A combination of these or similar factors may be operating at any time to affect perception. Along with a person's internal factors, they determine whether any particular stimulus is more or less likely to be noticed.

INTERNAL FACTORS

Internal perception factors are aspects of the perceiver that influence perceptual selection. The powerful role that internal factors play in perception manifests itself in many ways. Some of the more important internal factors include personality (Chapter 2), learning (Chapter 4), and motivation (Chapters 5 and 6).

Personality. Personality has an interesting influence on what and how people perceive. Any of the several personality dimensions that we discussed in Chapter 2, along with numerous other traits, may influence the perceptual process.[5] Under many circumstances, personality appears to strongly affect how an individual perceives other people—the process of *person perception*, which we discuss shortly.

An aspect of the personality called **field dependence/independence** provides a good example of the relationship between personality and perception. A field-dependent person tends to pay more attention to external environmental cues, whereas a field-independent person relies mostly on bodily sensations. In a test where a subject has to decide whether an object is vertically upright, a field-dependent individual will rely on cues from the environment, such as the corners of rooms, windows, and doors. A field-independent individual will rely mostly on bodily cues, such as the pull of gravity, to make the same judgment. A field-dependent person needs more time to find hidden figures embedded in complex geometric designs than does a field-independent person. A field-dependent person is influenced more by the background or surrounding design than is a field-independent person.

As a personality trait, field dependence/independence has some implications for organizational behavior. For example, compared to a field-dependent employee, a field-independent employee interacts more independently with others. That is, a field-independent employee relies less on cues from others (e.g., a team leader or supervisor) to identify appropriate interpersonal behavior. In addition, a field-independent employee seems to be more aware of important differences in others' roles, status, and needs.[6]

Recognizing personality differences, such as field dependence/independence, can play an important role when a manager is being assigned to an overseas position. Managers who accept an assignment in Asia must recognize that many Asian cultures emphasize harmony with nature, of which *feng shui*, literally "wind water," is a good example. Thus many Asians believe that artificial aspects of the environment must exist in harmony with nature; the orientation and layout of buildings, such as homes and offices, affect the lives of those who live and work in them. When Larry Henderson, plant manager for Celanese Chemical's operation in Singapore, was sent to build a new plant, he called in a *feng shui* expert to help assess the location. Singaporeans believe that when *feng shui* is good, business will prosper. Henderson's ability to be adaptable and to understand the local culture provides an example of field independence.

Learning. Another internal factor affecting perceptual selection is learning. Among other things, learning determines the development of perceptual sets. A **perceptual set** is an expectation of a particular interpretation based on past experience with the same or similar stimuli. What do you see in Figure 3.3? If you see an attractive, elegantly dressed woman, your perception concurs with the majority of first-time viewers.

Figure 3.3 **Test of Perceptual Set**

However, you may agree with a sizable minority and see an ugly, old woman. The woman you first see depends, in large part, on your perceptual set.

In organizations, managers' and employees' past experiences and learning strongly influence their perceptions. For example, studies have indicated that business executives and other decision makers are influenced by their functional backgrounds when making decisions. Thus, under some circumstances, they are likely to frame problems in terms of their own experiences and values. For example, they might perceive their own areas of expertise as being the most important to consider when solving certain types of problems. Conversely, studies have also indicated that decision makers can "rise above" their own experiences and limitations, accurately recognizing and effectively solving problems in areas other than those with which they are most familiar.[7] Indeed, critical decision-making skills include the ability to recognize what types of knowledge and expertise are needed with regard to a particular problem and to avoid framing issues only in terms of the person's own expertise.

The effects of learning on perception have important implications for organizational behavior. First, managers should avoid overly simplistic assumptions about the abilities of people to process information and make decisions. Internal factors clearly influence and even bias which information managers and employees might pay the most attention to. At the same time, through education and experience, people can overcome perceptual biases. Second, the existence of these biases presents yet another diversity management challenge. That is, employees from different areas of the organization may have trouble working together on task forces and teams because each will tend to see problems and issues from the perspectives of their own departments or functions. Thus, in order to be effective, managers and employees must learn how to deal with this type of diversity.

The culture into which a person is born determines many life experiences, and learned cultural differences influence the perceptual process. For example, a study demonstrated differences in perceptions of punctuality among managers in Japan, Mexico, Taiwan, and the United States.[8] On average, U.S. managers would consider a colleague late for an important business meeting after about 7 minutes. Managers in the other three countries are somewhat more tolerant of tardiness and would perceive a colleague as late only after about 10 or 11 minutes. The following Managing Across Cultures Competency feature examines some other interesting differences in the perception of time in different cultures.

COMPETENCY: MANAGING ACROSS CULTURES

TIME PERCEPTION

For the traveler or the person attempting to live in another culture, the adjustment to a different perception of time may be quite difficult. An investigation of culture shock among U.S. Peace Corps volunteers revealed that two of the three greatest sources of adjustment difficulties related to perceptions of time: the general pace of life and the punctuality of people.

The general pace at which people live their lives in various cultures has been investigated. One study compared the pace of life in six countries: England, Japan, Indonesia, Italy, Taiwan, and the United States. In each country, researchers collected data from its largest city and one medium-sized city on three measures of the pace or tempo of life.

- *The accuracy of bank clocks.* The researchers checked 15 clocks in each downtown area and compared the times they showed to a verifiable correct time.
- *The speed at which pedestrians walk.* The researchers timed 100 pedestrians, walking alone, for 100 feet.
- *The length of time needed to purchase a stamp.* The researchers measured the response time to a written request to purchase a commonly used denomination of postage stamp.

Figure 3.4 shows the results of this study. Japanese cities rated the highest on all three measures: They had the most accurate bank clocks, the fastest pedestrians, and the quickest postal clerks. U.S. cities were second in two of the three categories. Indonesian cities had the least accurate clocks and the slowest pedestrians. Italian cities had the slowest postal clerks.

Research thus suggests that a city and a culture have a pace of life that influences people's behaviors. It varies from culture to culture and can be important for understanding the perceptions of time in these cultures. Adjusting to a new pace of life is one of the challenges facing employees and managers of multinational corporations when they are transferred from their home countries to foreign assignments.[9]

Figure 3.4 **The Pace of Life in Six Countries**

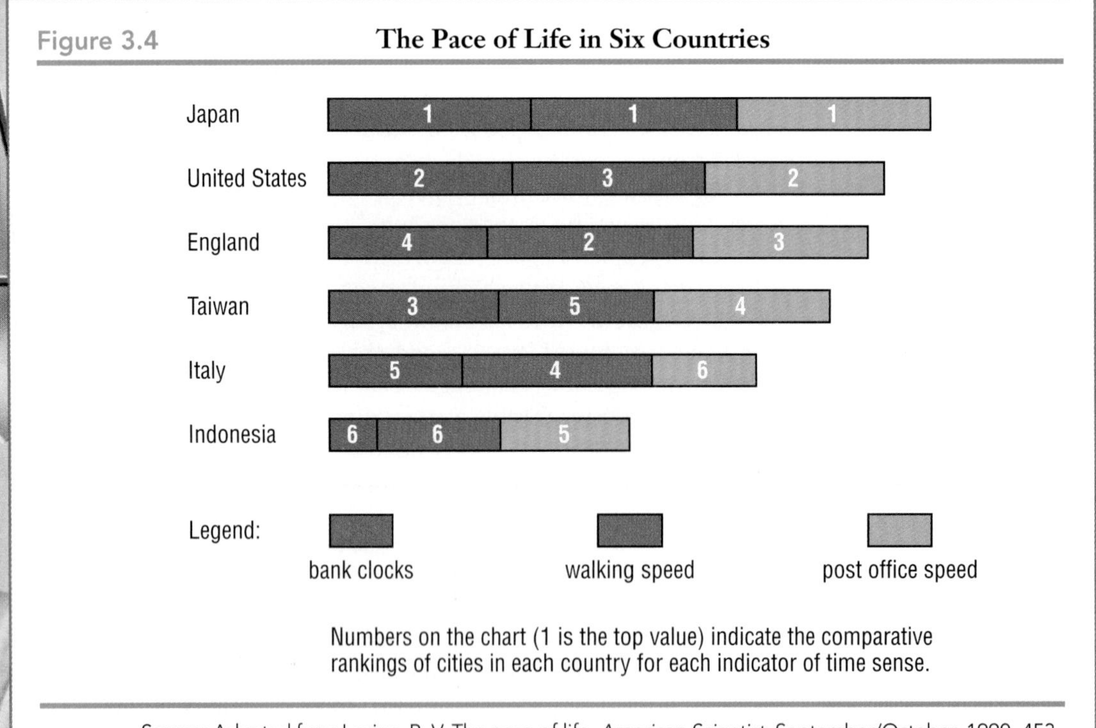

Source: Adapted from Levine, R. V. The pace of life. *American Scientist*, September/October, 1990, 453.

Motivation. Motivation also plays an important role in determining what a person perceives. A person's most urgent needs and desires at any particular time can influence perception.

For example, imagine that while taking a shower you faintly hear what sounds like the telephone ringing. Do you get out of the shower, dripping wet, to answer it? Or do you conclude that it is only your imagination? Your behavior in this situation may depend on factors other than the loudness of the ringing. If you are expecting an important call, you're likely to leap from the shower. If you aren't expecting a call, you're more likely to attribute the ringing sound to shower noises. Your decision, then, has been influenced by your expectations and motivations.

This example illustrates a significant aspect of perception: Internal factors such as motivation influence the interpretation of sensory information. An employee at Tyco, a firm that has just announced a layoff of 2,600 workers, is more sensitive to help-wanted advertisements than is an employee at Dell Computer whose job is not threatened.

In general, people perceive things that promise to help satisfy their needs and that they have found rewarding in the past. They tend to ignore mildly disturbing events (a barking dog) but will react to dangerous ones (the house being on fire). Summarizing an important aspect of the relationship between motivation and perception is the **Pollyanna principle,** which states that people process pleasant stimuli more efficiently and accurately than they do unpleasant stimuli. For example, an employee who receives both positive and negative feedback during a performance appraisal session may more easily and clearly remember the positive statements than the negative statements.

Learning Objective:

3. Describe the concept of perceptual organization.

PERCEPTUAL ORGANIZATION

Perceptual organization is the process by which people group environmental stimuli into recognizable patterns. That is, selection gives way to organization, and the stimuli selected for attention now appear as a whole. For example, most people have a mental picture of an object made of wood and having four legs, a seat, a back, and armrests: an image of a chair. Then, when people actually see an object having these attributes, they are able to organize the incoming information into a meaningful whole and recognize the object as a "chair."

Much remains to be learned about how the human mind assembles, organizes, and categorizes information.[10] However, certain factors in perceptual organization, such as perceptual grouping, are helpful in understanding perceptual organization. **Perceptual grouping** is the tendency to form individual stimuli into a meaningful pattern by continuity, closure, proximity, and similarity.

Continuity is the tendency to perceive objects as continuous patterns. Continuity is a useful organizing principle, but it may also have negative aspects. For example, the tendency to perceive continuous patterns may result in an inability to perceive uniqueness and detect change. In economic or business forecasting, a common continuity error is to assume that the future will simply reflect current events and trends.

Closure is the tendency to complete an object and perceive it as a constant, overall form. In other words, it is the ability to perceive a whole object, even though only part of the object is evident. Most people somehow perceive the odd-shaped inkblots in Figure 3.5 as a Dalmatian dog walking toward a tree. Someone who had never seen a Dalmatian wouldn't be able to make that closure. People can also organize their perceptions in terms of the closure principle when dealing with ideas and information. For example, a manager facing a complex decision may be able to develop a fairly accurate understanding of the issues even though some information is lacking.

Figure 3.5 **An Example of Closure**

Source: Reproduced by permission from Sekuler, R., and Blake, R. *Perception,* 2nd ed. New York: McGraw-Hill, 1990, 129.

Based on experience and imagination, the manager can fill in the missing pieces needed to make a decision.

The notion of **proximity** suggests that a group of objects may be perceived as related because of their nearness to each other. Employees often perceive other employees working together in a department as a team or unit because of their physical proximity. Sharon Moore, a senior vice president of The Associates, noticed that five people on the third floor of her building had quit their jobs. Even if they did so for completely unrelated reasons, Moore may perceive the resignations as a problem on the third floor and examine morale, pay, and working conditions there in an attempt to determine what's wrong. We can see the organizing principle of proximity at play in terms of time as well. For example, three events occurring in a work setting at about the same time may be perceived as related even if they are not.

The concept of **similarity** holds that the more alike objects (or ideas) are, the greater is the tendency to perceive them as a common group. Similarity is very important in most team sports—thus the use of different colors of uniforms by opposing teams. In football, for example, the quarterback must be able to spot an open receiver without a moment's hesitation, which would be extremely difficult (if not impossible) if both teams wore uniforms of the same color. Lucent Technologies in Dallas, Texas, uses color codes for different departments to partition and define separate functions and responsibilities visually. A company might require visitors to its plant to wear yellow hard hats and employees to wear white hard hats. Employees can then easily identify people who are unfamiliar with everyday safety precautions and routines when they are in work areas. Although the principle of similarity obviously is useful in helping people make sense of their worlds, a negative aspect of this organizing principle is found in the perceptual error of stereotyping, which we address shortly.

Learning Objective:

4. Identify the factors that determine how one person perceives another.

PERSON PERCEPTION

Of particular interest in organizational behavior is the process of person or social perception.[11] **Person perception** is the process by which individuals attribute characteristics or traits to other people. It is closely related to the attribution process, which we discuss later in this chapter.

The person perception process is the same as the general process of perception shown in Figure 3.1. That is, the process follows the same sequence of observation, selection, organization, interpretation, and response. However, the object being perceived in the environment is another person. Perceptions of situations, events, and objects are important, but individual differences in perceptions of other people are crucial to understanding behavior in work settings. For example, suppose that you meet a new employee. In order to get acquainted and to make him feel at ease, you invite him to lunch. During lunch, he begins to tell you his life history and focuses on his accomplishments. Because he talks only about himself (he asks you no questions about yourself), you may form the impression that he is very self-centered. Later, you may come to see other aspects of his personality, but your perceptions may always be strongly affected by this first impression, called the **primacy effect.**

In general, the factors influencing person perception are the same as those that influence perceptual selection: Both external and internal factors affect person perception. However, we may usefully categorize factors that influence how a person perceives another as

- characteristics of the person being perceived,
- characteristics of the perceiver, and
- the situation or context within which the perception takes place.

THE PERSON PERCEIVED

In perceiving someone else, an individual processes a variety of cues about that person: facial expressions, general appearance, skin color, posture, age, gender, voice quality, personality traits, behaviors, and the like. Some cues may contain important information about the person, but many do not. People seem to have **implicit personality theories** about the relationships among physical characteristics, personality traits, and specific behaviors.[12] Table 3.1 illustrates implicit personality theory in action. People often seem to believe that some voice-quality characteristics indicate that the speaker has certain personality traits. However, you should realize that the relationships presented in Table 3.1 have no real basis. Think about your first contact with someone over the telephone. Later, upon meeting, did that person look and act as you expected?

THE PERCEIVER

Listening to an employee describe the personality of a coworker may tell you as much about the employee's personality as it does about that of the person being described. Does this surprise you? It shouldn't if you recall that factors internal to the perceiver,

Table 3.1

Personality Judgments on the Basis of Voice Quality

VOICE QUALITY: HIGH IN	MALE VOICE	FEMALE VOICE
Breathiness	Younger, artistic	Feminine, pretty, petite, shallow
Flatness	Similar results for both sexes:	Masculine, cold, withdrawn
Nasality	Similar results for both sexes: characteristics	Having many socially undesirable
Tenseness	Cantankerous (old, unyielding)	Young, emotional, high-strung, not highly intelligent

Source: Adapted from Hinton, P. R. *The Psychology of Interpersonal Perception,* London: Routledge, 1993, 16.

including personality, learning, and motivation, influence perception. Internal factors are particularly important in person perception. A person's own personality traits, values, attitudes, current mood, past experiences, and so on, determine, in part, how that person perceives someone else.

Accurately perceiving the personality of an individual raised in another culture often is difficult.[13] For example, Japanese managers in the United States and U.S. managers in Japan may face disorienting experiences as they try to learn how to deal with business associates from the other culture. One reason is that the perceiver interprets perceptions of the other person's traits and behavior in light of his or her own cultural experiences, attitudes, and values. Often these factors are inadequate for making accurate judgments about the personality and behavior of people from a different culture.

The Situation

The situation or setting also influences how one person perceives another. The situation may be particularly important in understanding first impressions or primacy effects. For example, if you meet someone for the first time and she is with another person that you respect and admire, that association may positively influence your assessment of the new acquaintance. But, if she is with someone you dislike intensely, you may form a negative first impression. Of course, these initial perceptions may change over time if you continue to interact with her and get to know her better. Nevertheless, the first impression may continue to color your later perception of the individual.

Thus, in understanding the process of person perception, you have yet another use for the interactionist perspective introduced in Chapter 2. That is, both person and situation interact to determine how you perceive others.

Impression Management

The use of **impression management** by an individual is an attempt to manipulate or control the impressions that others form about the person.[14]

> We all put on a show at times, by using our nonverbal communication to create a deliberate impression. The clothes we choose to wear for an interview or a date, wearing sunglasses even when it's cloudy as it looks "cool," having our hair cut in a certain style, putting on a "telephone voice," feigning interest in a boring lecture given by our instructor, behaving nicely when grandparents come to visit; these are all ways of managing impressions.[15]

Impression management has two distinct facets, as Figure 3.6 (on page 80) shows.[16] The first facet, **impression motivation,** concerns the degree to which an individual actively manages the impression that he or she makes. Sometimes impression management might be strongly motivated; at other times little or no motivation may exist. For example, someone dressing for a job interview might be acutely conscious of trying to make a favorable impression on an interviewer. But, when meeting old friends, the same person might be far less concerned about the clothing worn.

A second facet in impression management, **impression construction,** refers to an individual's consciously choosing (1) an image to convey and (2) how to go about doing that. For example, a woman applying for a job as a bank manager might choose to convey stability and conservatism. When interviewing for this position, she probably would wear a conservative business suit. Further, she may rewrite her résumé to emphasize job tenure (to appear stable and dependable) and to omit her skydiving hobby (to not appear reckless).

Impression management provides another example of an *individual difference.* Some people seem preoccupied with impression management; others are less concerned about how they might be perceived. In sum, however, impression management is an important part of understanding person perception. Almost everyone cares about the impression that he or she makes on others, at least part of the time. Certainly, in organizations the impressions made on others may have significant implications for an employee's career. An example of that consideration is illustrated in the Managing Self Competency feature below.

COMPETENCY: MANAGING SELF

ALAN PAGE AT MOTT'S

Alan Page loved electronics as far back as he can remember. As a child, he was more interested in how the Christmas tree lights worked than he was in opening presents. He took his first course in computer programming in the seventh grade. Looking back, he figures that it was inevitable that he would become an electronic "techie" of one type or another.

In his first job, he repaired computer systems. Then, he got a position designing databases for a consumer-research company. Finally, he landed a position at Mott's, Inc., the Stamford, Connecticut, food company, as a database analyst. He hoped that his new position would carry him beyond simply performing technological "fix-up" projects, as the purpose of his new position was to find ways to use technology to advance the business. What he discovered, however, was that he had to manage the impressions that others had of his role.

Page explained: "I had to learn the business, navigate tricky office politics, and figure out how to influence nontechnical people who were sometimes suspicious of a techie. Most of all, I had to transform my image from that of a support person to that of a strategic thinker. This took time."

At first, it was an uphill battle for Page. By default, he often became the technological fix-it person on projects because of his background. Page says that sometimes he was his own worst enemy. "I would drift back to fixing things, because I was comfortable with that," he says. "I thought, 'if I fix this, that person will be happy.'"

So, Page honed his business skills by attending marketing presentations and strategic planning meetings. He learned how his colleagues made assumptions to project sales, revenues, costs, and profits. He studied the data the company uses to track their business. As he developed more business know-how, he still had to learn how to communicate with nontechnical people. At first, Page had the typical techie's certainty that his way was the right way. "There were meetings where I'd say, 'this is how it is and this is what we should do,'" he says. "That ruffled some feathers."

However, he soon developed a more effective approach. He learned to seek the viewpoints of others and to work with colleagues to develop an understanding of what they wanted to accomplish. He learned how to compromise and how to listen. He developed the capacity to see the bigger picture and to avoid quick-fix "techie" solutions that ignored the people side of the business. As a result, he was able to begin designing solutions and systems to move the business forward.

Page believes that his colleagues' perceptions of him have changed dramatically for the better. "Now I'm not just seen as someone who can fix tech problems; they see me as someone who can help solve *business* problems." For Alan Page, this change in his image has stirred hopes of advancement. "You can't go anywhere in this company if you're just seen as the techie guy."[17]

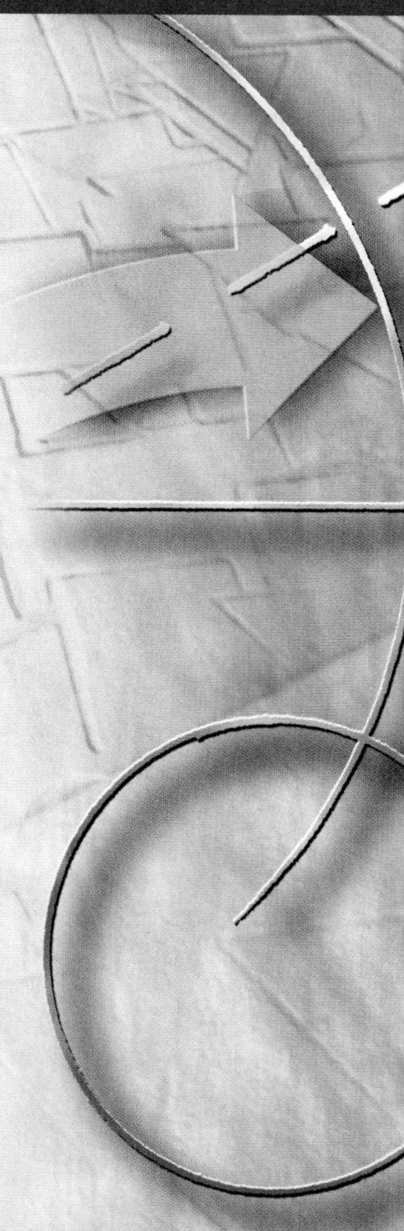

For more information on Mott's, Inc., visit the company's home page at ***www.motts.com/home.htm.***

Figure 3.6 **The Facets of Impression Management**

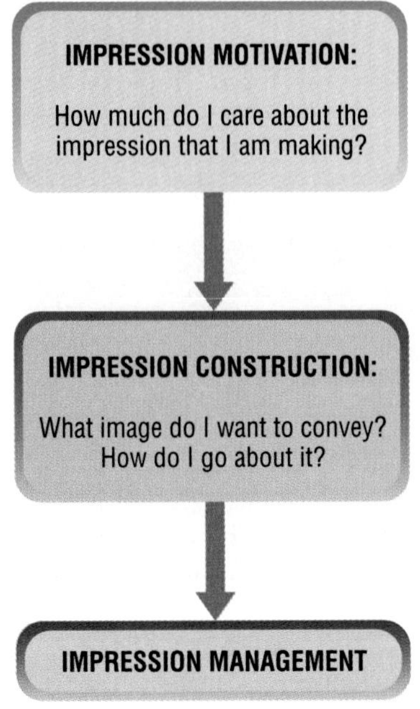

Learning Objective:

5. Describe the major errors in perception that people make.

PERCEPTUAL ERRORS

Unfortunately, the perceptual process may result in errors in judgment or understanding. An important part of understanding individual differences in perception is understanding the source of these errors. First, we examine the notion of accuracy of judgment in person perception. Then, we explore five of the most common types of perceptual errors: perceptual defense, stereotyping, the halo effect, projection, and expectancy effects.

ACCURACY OF JUDGMENT

How accurate are people in their perceptions of others? This question is important in organizational behavior.[18] For example, misjudging the characteristics, abilities, or behaviors of an employee during a performance appraisal review could result in an inaccurate assessment of the employee's current and future value to the firm. Another example of the importance of accurate person perception comes from the employment interview. Considerable evidence suggests that interviewers can easily make errors in judgment and perceptions when basing employment decisions on information gathered in face-to-face interviews. The following types of interview errors are the most common.

- *Similarity error.* Interviewers are positively predisposed toward job candidates who are similar to them (in terms of background, interests, hobbies, and the like) and negatively biased against job candidates who are unlike them.
- *Contrast error.* Interviewers have a tendency to compare job candidates to other candidates interviewed at about the same time, rather than to some absolute standard. For example, an average candidate might be rated too highly if preceded by several mediocre candidates; a candidate might be scored too low if preceded by an outstanding applicant.
- *Overweighting of negative information.* Interviewers tend to overreact to negative information as though looking for an excuse to disqualify a job candidate.

- *Race, sex, and age bias.* Interviewers may be more or less positive about a candidate on the basis of the candidate's race, gender, or age.
- *First-impression error.* The primacy effect previously discussed may play a role in the job interview, as some interviewers are quick to form impressions that are resistant to change.[19]

There are no easy answers to the general problems of accuracy in person perception. We do know that accuracy in person perception represents another important *individual difference.* Some people are quite accurate in judging and assessing others, and some people are extremely inept in doing so. However, people can learn to make more accurate judgments in person perception. Perceptions of others will be more accurate if the perceiver can avoid (1) generalizing from a single trait to many traits, (2) assuming that a single behavior will show itself in all situations, and (3) placing too much reliance on physical appearance. In addition, as person perception is influenced by characteristics of both the perceiver and the situation, accuracy in person perception can be improved when the perceiver understands these potential biases. Unfortunately, the errors that individuals make in person perception (and in other aspects of the perceptual process) are so common that names have been given to some of them. We now turn our attention to several of these specific perceptual errors.

Perceptual Defense

Perceptual defense is the tendency for people to protect themselves against ideas, objects, or situations that are threatening. A well-known folk song suggests that people "hear what they want to hear and disregard the rest." Once established, an individual's way of viewing the world may become highly resistant to change. Sometimes this perceptual defense may have negative consequences in the work setting. For example, there is evidence that this perceptual error can result in a failure to perceive the need to be creative in finding a way to solve problems. As a result of perceptual defense, the individual simply proceeds in the customary fashion even in the face of evidence that "business as usual" is not accomplishing anything.[20]

In the discussion of perceptual selection we noted that people tend to perceive things that are supportive and satisfying and ignore disturbing things. Avoiding unpleasant stimuli often is more than escapism; it may be a sensible defensive device. People can become psychologically deaf or blind to disturbing parts of the environment. Thus employees who really enjoy their work and are satisfied with their pay, like most of their colleagues, might simply ignore some negative aspect of the work experience (e.g., an irritating coworker).

Stereotyping

Stereotyping is the tendency to assign attributes to someone solely on the basis of a category of people of which that person is a member.[21] People generally expect someone identified as a doctor, president of a company, or minister to have certain positive attributes, even if they have met some who didn't have those attributes. A person categorized as a dropout, ex-convict, or alcoholic is automatically perceived negatively. Even identifying an employee by such broad categories as Hispanic, older worker, or female can lead to misperceptions. The perceiver may dwell on certain characteristics expected of everyone in that category and fail to recognize the characteristics that distinguish the person as an individual. For example, disabled workers frequently must overcome stereotypes in order to receive fair consideration for promotion or even to be hired in the first place.[22]

Stereotypes of women continue to hamper their advancement in many organizations. This issue is explored in the Managing Diversity Competency feature on page 82. In addition, a questionnaire that you can use to assess your own perceptions with regard to women as managers is presented at the end of the chapter.

COMPETENCY: MANAGING DIVERSITY

STEREOTYPES OF WOMEN AT WORK

In *My Fair Lady*, Professor Henry Higgins asks: "Why can't a woman be more like a man?" Are most organizations still asking this question, or does it only seem that way? Consider the following.

The authors of a recent report concluded that women have a big problem when it comes to overseas assignments: They can't get them. Although women comprise almost half the global workforce, they account for less than 12 percent of the expatriate population. Why is this happening (or failing to happen, as the case may be)? The study on which the report was based showed that many male managers still believe that women aren't interested in overseas jobs or won't be effective in them. These managers typically cite dual career issues, a presumed heightened risk of sexual harassment, and gender prejudices in many countries, as reasons why their female employees are often not seriously considered for international assignments. In contrast, a recent survey of female expatriates and their supervisors revealed that women, on average, are just as interested in foreign assignments and every bit as effective once there. Indeed, some of the traits considered crucial for success overseas—such as knowing when to keep your mouth shut, being a strong team player, and soliciting a variety of opinions and perspectives when solving problems—are more often associated with women's management styles than with men's.

For organizations struggling to balance gender issues, changes in work cultures, and increased global competition, few issues are more important than fully utilizing the talents of all the organization's employees. Women have played an increasingly bigger role in the workplace in many countries for more than a generation. In the United States, for example, women between the ages of 25 and 35 have more education than their male counterparts. Women are currently starting new businesses at twice the rate of men. Women are also joining the workforce in record numbers, and the participation rate for women between the ages of 25 and 54 is now over 75 percent. Although the male participation rate for the same age group is slightly over 90 percent, the labor force participation rates for women and men are converging. Women seem destined to play an even bigger role in organizational life than they have in the past.

As a result, here's an interesting challenge for organizations: Are women managers essentially like their male counterparts? If so, then gender differences are a marginal concern. However, a major debate is going on in scientific circles around the world with regard to gender differences in thought, emotions, and information processing styles. Some evidence from this type of research is beginning to suggest that women are, on average, superior to men in many organizational roles. Examples cited include roles where the manager needs to interact closely with customers or clients and roles where the manager needs to facilitate discussion and smooth conflicts. As an example of the latter, one study indicated that female project team leaders were more effective, on average, than males in leading cross-functional teams designed to foster high rates of innovation.

For many years, conventional wisdom seemed to be that, in order to be successful, the female manager needed to become more like the typical male manager. However, now the question seems to be: Will tomorrow's businesswomen succeed by becoming more like men or less like them? The jury is still out, but the evidence indicates that gender differences are real, and, importantly for many organizational roles in the years ahead, women will have a competitive advantage.[23]

Halo Effect

Evaluation of another person solely on the basis of one attribute, either favorable or unfavorable, is called the **halo effect.** In other words, a halo blinds the perceiver to other attributes that also should be evaluated to obtain a complete, accurate impression of the other person. Managers have to guard against the halo effect in rating employee performance. A manager may single out one trait and use it as the basis for judging all other performance measures. For example, an excellent attendance record may produce judgments of high productivity, quality work, and industriousness, whether they are accurate or not.

Projection

Projection is the tendency for people to see their own traits in other people. That is, they project their own feelings, personality characteristics, attitudes, or motives onto others. For example, employees frightened by rumors of impending organizational changes may not only judge others to be more frightened than they are but may also assess various policy decisions as more threatening than warranted. Projection may be especially strong for undesirable traits that perceivers possess but fail to recognize in themselves. People whose personality traits include stinginess, obstinacy, and disorderliness tend to rate others higher on these traits than do people who don't have these personality traits.

Expectancy Effects

Expectancy effects in the perceptual process are the extent to which prior expectations bias perceptions of events, objects, and people.[24] Sometimes people simply perceive what they anticipate perceiving as indicated in the following dialogue from Shakespeare's *Hamlet.*

Polonius: My lord, the Queen would speak with you, and presently.
Hamlet: Do you see yonder cloud that's almost in the shape of a camel?
Polonius: By th' mass, and 'tis like a camel indeed.
Hamlet: Methinks it is like a weasel.
Polonius: It is back'd like a weasel.
Hamlet: Or like a whale?
Polonius: Very like a whale.

(Act III, scene ii)

Of course, Shakespeare was making a joke about an individual (Polonius) who seemingly would agree with anything to curry favor with the Prince of Denmark (Hamlet). Faced with an ambiguous stimulus (in this case, a cloud), however, many individuals could be led to expect to see a particular object, and this expectation would color their perceptions.

Expectancy effects may also bias perception even in less ambiguous situations. For example, your perception of a team to which you have been assigned recently may be positive if your supervisor told you that the team's work is important and that it will be staffed by talented people from several departments. However, your perception may be negative if she told you that the team exists solely for political reasons and contains some real "deadwood" from other departments. You might also perceive identical behavior by other members of the team quite differently under each set of expectations.

Earlier we noted that past experiences and learning are important to the perceptual process. As a result, people often approach situations expecting certain things to happen or other people to have certain attributes. These expectations may strongly influence their perceptions of reality.

Another aspect of expectancy effects is the **self-fulfilling prophecy.** Expecting certain things to happen shapes the behavior of the perceiver in such a way that the expected is more likely to happen. For example, a team leader who has been led to believe that a new employee has great potential might do two things: (1) she might assess the employee's performance as being better than it really is (an expectancy effect); and (2) she might behave toward the new employee in such a way (e.g., by providing encouragement or additional training) that the new employee's performance is, in fact, very good (a self-fulfilling prophecy).

Learning Objective:

6. Explain how attributions influence behavior and identify important attributions that people make in the work setting.

ATTRIBUTIONS: PERCEIVING THE CAUSES OF BEHAVIOR

The **attribution process** refers to the ways in which people come to understand the causes of their own and others' behaviors.[25] Attributions play an important role in the process of person perception. Attributions made about the reasons for someone's behavior may affect judgments about that individual's fundamental characteristics or traits (what he or she is really like).

The attributions that employees and managers make concerning the causes of behavior are important in understanding organizational behavior. For example, managers who attribute poor performance directly to their subordinates tend to behave more punitively than do managers who attribute poor performance to circumstances beyond their subordinates' control. A manager who believes that an employee failed to perform a task correctly because he lacked proper training might be understanding and give the employee better instructions or more training. The same manager might be quite angry if he believes that the subordinate made mistakes simply because he didn't try very hard.

Behavioral reactions to the same outcome can be dramatically different, depending on perceptions of the situation and the attributions made. For example, Table 3.2 lists some of the possible differences in managerial behavior when employees are perceived positively versus when they are perceived negatively. The possible relationships between attributions and behavior will become clearer as we examine the attribution process.

Table 3.2 Possible Results Stemming from Differences in Perceptions of Performance

BOSS'S BEHAVIOR TOWARD PERCEIVED STRONG PERFORMERS	BOSS'S BEHAVIOR TOWARD PERCEIVED WEAK PERFORMERS
Discusses project objectives. Gives subordinate the freedom to choose own approach to solving problems or reaching goals.	Gives specific directives when discussing tasks and goals.
Treats mistakes or incorrect judgments as learning opportunities.	Pays close attention to mistakes and incorrect judgments. Quick to emphasize what subordinate is doing wrong.
Is open to subordinate's suggestions. Solicits opinions from subordinate.	Pays little attention to subordinate's suggestions. Rarely asks subordinate for input.
Gives subordinate interesting and challenging assignments.	Gives subordinate routine assignments.
May frequently defer to subordinate's opinions in disagreements.	Usually imposes own views in disagreements.

The Attribution Process

People make attributions in an attempt to understand the behavior of other people and to make better sense of their environments. Individuals don't consciously make attributions in all circumstances (although they may do so unconsciously much of the time).[26] However, under certain circumstances, people are likely to make causal attributions consciously. For example, causal attributions are common in the following situations.

- The perceiver has been asked an explicit question about another's behavior. (Why did Christie do that?)
- An unexpected event occurs. (I've never seen Stephen behave that way. I wonder what's going on.)
- The perceiver depends on another person for a desired outcome. (I wonder why my boss made that comment about my expense account.)
- The perceiver experiences feelings of failure or loss of control. (I can't believe I failed my midterm exam!)

Figure 3.7 presents a basic model of the attribution process. People infer "causes" to behaviors that they observe in others, and these interpretations often largely determine their reactions to those behaviors. The perceived causes of behavior reflect several antecedents: (1) the amount of information the perceiver has about the people and the situation and how that information is organized by the perceiver; (2) the perceiver's beliefs (implicit personality theories, what other people might do in a similar situation, and so on); and (3) the motivation of the perceiver (e.g., the importance to the perceiver of making an accurate assessment). Recall our discussion of internal factors that influence perception—learning, personality, and motivation. These same internal factors influence the attribution process. The perceiver's information and beliefs depend on previous experience and are influenced by the perceiver's personality.

Based on information, beliefs, and motives, the perceiver often distinguishes between internal and external causes of behavior; that is, whether people did something because of a real desire or because of the pressure of circumstances. The assigned cause of the behavior—whether internal or external—helps the perceiver attach meaning to the event and is important for understanding the subsequent

Figure 3.7 **The Attribution Process**

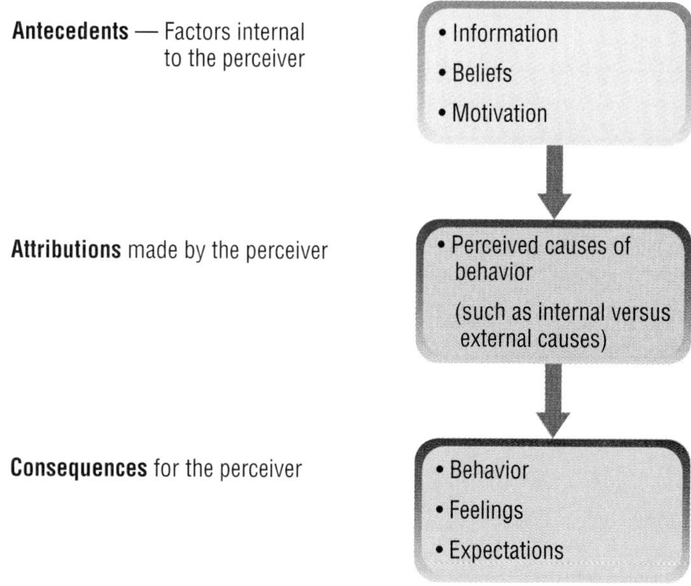

consequences for the perceiver. Among the consequences of this attribution process are the subsequent behavior of the perceiver in response to the behavior of others, the impact on feelings or emotions (how the perceiver now feels about events, people, and circumstances), and the effects on the perceiver's expectations of future events or behavior.

Internal Versus External Causes of Behavior

Imagine the following scene in a busy department. Christie Lopez, the office manager, and Stephen Smith, a section head for accounts receivable, are arguing loudly in Christie's private office. Even though they had closed the door before starting their discussion, their voices have gotten louder until everyone else in the office has stopped working and is staring in discomfort and embarrassment at the closed door. After several minutes, Stephen jerks open the door, yells a final, unflattering remark at Christie, slams the door, and stomps out of the department.

Anyone observing this scene is likely to wonder about what is going on and make certain attributions about why Stephen behaved the way he did. On the one hand, attributions regarding his behavior could focus on internal causes: He gets mad easily because he has a bad temper; he behaves this way because he is immature and doesn't handle pressure well; or he isn't getting his work done, and Christie called him on the carpet for it. On the other hand, attributions could focus on external causes: He behaves this way because Christie provoked him; or both their behaviors are the result of unreasonable workloads imposed on the department by top management. Some of those who witnessed the events may perceive more than a single cause in such an interaction. Also, as should be clear by now, different individuals in the department are likely to interpret the events they witnessed differently.

A central question in the attribution process concerns how perceivers determine whether the behavior of another person stems from internal causes (personality traits, emotions, motives, or ability) or external causes (other people, the situation, or chance). A widely accepted model proposed by Harold Kelley attempts to explain how people determine why others behave as they do.[27] This explanation states that in making attributions, people focus on three major factors:

- *consistency*—the extent to which the person perceived behaves in the same manner on other occasions when faced with the same situation;
- *distinctiveness*—the extent to which the person perceived acts in the same manner in different situations; and
- *consensus*—the extent to which others, faced with the same situation, behave in a manner similar to the person perceived.[28]

As Figure 3.8 suggests, under conditions of high consistency, high distinctiveness, and high consensus, the perceiver will tend to attribute the behavior of the person perceived to external causes. When distinctiveness and consensus are low, the perceiver will tend to attribute the behavior of the person to internal causes. Of course, other combinations of high and low consistency, distinctiveness, and consensus are possible. Some combinations, however, may not provide the perceiver with a clear choice between internal and external causes.

Note that consistency is high under both attribution outcomes. When consistency is low, the perceiver may attribute the behavior to either internal or external causes, or both. For example, imagine that a candidate running for the U.S. Senate gives a speech in favor of gun control while campaigning in his home state and then speaks in opposition to gun control when addressing a convention of the National Rifle Association in another state. In this case, an observer might make either internal attributions (e.g., a character flaw "causes" the politician to tell these people what he thinks they want to hear) or external attributions (e.g., the audience "causes" the politician to change his speech), or both.

Figure 3.8 **Kelley's Theory of Causal Attributions**

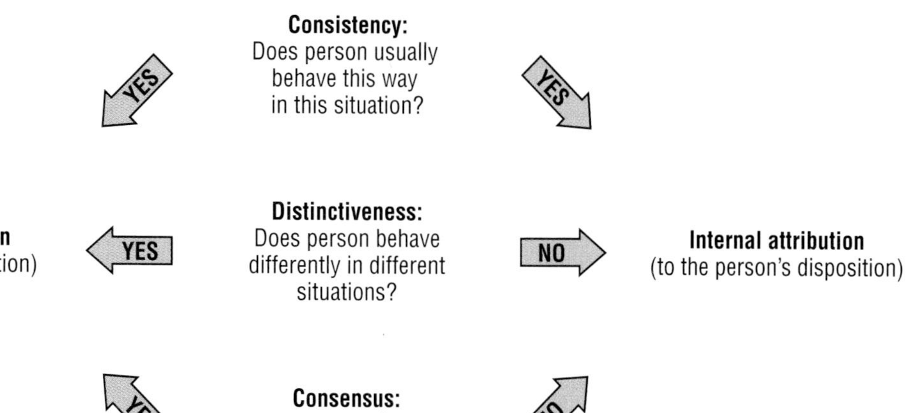

Source: Myers, D. G. *Social Psychology,* 4th ed. New York: McGraw-Hill, 1993, 77. Reprinted with permission from McGraw-Hill.

In the example of the argument between Christie and Stephen, an observer would likely attribute causation to Stephen if others typically do not have similar arguments with Christie (low consensus) and Stephen often has similar arguments with others in various work situations (low distinctiveness). But, if other individuals frequently have run-ins with Christie (high consensus) and Stephen seldom has arguments in other situations with his fellow employees (high distinctiveness), observers may attribute his behavior to external causes (in this case, Christie). You may want to reread this paragraph while examining Figure 3.8 to be sure that you understand the differences that lead to either internal or external attributions of behavior.

With regard to internal versus external causes of behavior, observers often make what is known as the **fundamental attribution error.** This type of error is the tendency to underestimate the impact of situational or external causes of behavior and to overestimate the impact of personal or internal causes of behavior when seeking to understand why people behave the way they do. In organizations, employees often tend to assign blame for conflict (Chapter 10), political behavior (Chapter 9), or resistance to change (Chapter 18) to the individuals involved and fail to recognize the effect of the dynamics of the situation. For example, a CEO might attribute a high level of political behavior on the part of her vice presidents to aspects of their personalities, not recognizing that competition for scarce resources is causing much of the political behavior.

Some cultural differences exist in the fundamental attribution error. For example, in North America, this type of error would be as just described (underestimating external causes and overestimating internal causes). In India, however, the more common attribution error is for people to overestimate situational or external causes for the observed behavior.[29] This difference in attributions may reflect the way that people view personal responsibility or perhaps differences in "average" locus of control beliefs in the different societies.

The fundamental attribution error isn't the only bias that can influence judgments concerning internal versus external causes of behavior. A study of supervisors showed that they were more likely to attribute effective performance to internal causes for high-status employees and less likely to attribute success to internal causes for low-status employees. Similarly, supervisors were more likely to attribute ineffective performance to internal causes for low-status employees and less likely to attribute failure to internal causes for high-status employees.[30]

Attributions of Success and Failure

The attributions that employees and managers make regarding success or failure in task performance are very important. Managers may base decisions about rewards and punishments on their perceptions of why subordinates have succeeded or failed at some task. In general, individuals often attribute their own and others' success or failure to four causal factors: ability, effort, task difficulty, and luck.

- I succeeded (or failed) because I had the competencies to do the job (or because I did not have the competencies to do the job). Such statements are ability attributions.
- I succeeded (or failed) because I worked hard (or because I did not work hard). Such statements are effort attributions.
- I succeeded (or failed) because it was easy (or because it was too hard). Such statements are attributions about task difficulty.
- I succeeded (or failed) because I was lucky (or unlucky). Such statements are attributions about luck or the circumstances surrounding the task.[31]

Causal attributions of ability and effort are internal, and causal attributions of task difficulty and luck are external. These attributions about success or failure reflect differences in self-esteem and locus of control—personality dimensions discussed in Chapter 2. For example, individuals with high self-esteem and high internal locus of control are likely to assess their own performance positively and to attribute their good performance to internal causes.[32]

The organizational importance of these success and failure attributions is demonstrated by research in hospitals that examined the feedback provided to nurses by their managers.[33] When the managers perceived that poor performance was the result of lack of effort, their feedback messages to nurses tended to be punitive or negative in tone. Their attributions also affected the specific content of the feedback. When the managers inferred that poor performance reflected lack of ability, their messages to nurses focused on instructions for doing the job better. When they thought that poor performance meant lack of effort, their messages to nurses tended to stress orders to be followed. Thus the managers' attributions about the reasons for performance failures by staff nurses influenced their communication behaviors, as suggested by the model of the attribution process previously shown in Figure 3.7.

Not surprisingly, many people tend to attribute their successes to internal factors (ability or effort) and attribute their failures to external factors (task difficulty or luck). This tendency is known as a **self-serving bias.** The tendency of employees to accept responsibility for good performance but to deny responsibility for poor performance often presents a serious challenge for managers during performance appraisals. A self-serving bias may also create other types of problems. For example, it prevents individuals from accurately assessing their own performance and abilities and makes more difficult determining why a course of action has failed. The general tendency to blame others for a person's own failures often is associated with poor performance and an inability to establish satisfying interpersonal relationships at work and in other social settings.[34] In general, a version of the self-serving bias seems to operate when people are asked to compare themselves to others in the work setting. That is, managers and employees often view themselves to be more ethical, more effective, better performing, and so on, than the "average" other person.

One of the more traumatic events that can occur to anyone is being fired from a job. The attributions that an individual in such a circumstance might make may well be crucial in terms of his or her future success, as the Managing Self Competency feature on page 89 demonstrates.

COMPETENCY: MANAGING SELF

YOU'RE FIRED!

In an era of downsizing and other massive layoffs, losing a job doesn't carry the stigma in our society that it once did. But—it still hurts! Inevitably you ask yourself: What went wrong? What could I have done differently? And, perhaps most important: What am I going to do now?

For most people, undertaking a job search at any time is always stressful. It has been described as a combination of the worst aspects of a blind date and a fraternity rush party. Undertaking a job search *after* suffering the psychological blow of being fired can be a formidable challenge for anyone. However, you can do certain things to increase your chances of success and even to end up with a more satisfying job. Constructive suggestions include the following.

1. *Work through the firing psychologically.* Emotionally, people often feel like hiding out or taking a sabbatical. But, experts suggest that beginning the search for a new job immediately is crucial. The first contact or two may be hard, but the sooner you get started and the more people you talk to, the quicker you will find another position. Of course, reestablishing your normal good spirits may be either a long or slow process, depending on your ability to bounce back. Maintaining a sense of humor helps. Hal Lancaster, of the *Wall Street Journal*, suggests that "getting fired is nature's way of telling you that you had the wrong job in the first place."
2. *Figure out what went wrong.* This step is an important part of coming to grips, psychologically, with the situation. Experts suggest that if you do not understand what you contributed to the firing, you are likely to repeat the same mistakes. Further, they suggest that you need to talk to your former bosses, coworkers, and friends and seek honest feedback to help you understand your strengths and weaknesses. Of course, doing so may be difficult, as many firms' human resource professionals prefer to say as little as possible at the time of dismissal in order to minimize lawsuits. If you can't get insights from your former employer, experts suggest utilizing a career counselor to help you make the same evaluation.
3. *Work with your former employer to develop an exit statement.* Experts almost always recommend that you have something in writing from your former employer that will be an asset in your job search. Specific suggestions include having a paragraph that describes what you accomplished in your former job followed by a paragraph that explains why you are no longer with the firm. There are lots of "socially acceptable" reasons that can be given in such a document: a change in management style, a change in strategy, the desire to pursue interests that no longer fit what the employer wants, and so on. Surprisingly, the fired employee can often get a former boss or other officials to sign such a document. People often want to be helpful, and if such a request is approached in a constructive, problem-solving manner, many times the former employer is willing to help create a letter or other document that condemns neither the company nor yourself. This approach has the advantage of creating a situation where prospective future employers hear the same "story" from both the former employer and the job applicant.
4. *Avoid negative attributions as part of your explanation.* Experts say that you should never say anything bad about your former employer. Don't make excuses; don't trash the people you used to work for; and don't blame everything on other people. Focus on the positive aspects of any written understanding that you have obtained. Accept responsibility for both your failures and successes. Quickly move the discussion to the future, stressing what you've learned from previous jobs and focus on what you can do for a new employer.

Few people have heard of Arthur Blank and Bernard Marcus who were managers at Handy Dan, a California retailer, before being summarily fired as a result of personality clashes with the chain's owner. However, most people have heard of the extremely successful business they started after they were fired: Home Depot. Blank and Marcus say that their success might never have occurred if Handy Dan hadn't sacked them. So, suggestion No. 5 is: *Look for the silver lining.*[35]

For more information on Home Depot, visit the firm's home page at ***www.homedepot.com/.***

CHAPTER SUMMARY

1. Define *perception* and describe the major elements in the perceptual process.

Perception is the psychological process whereby people select information from the environment and organize it to make sense of their worlds. Environmental stimuli are observed, selected, organized, interpreted, and responded to as a result of the perceptual process. Understanding the two major components of this process—selection and organization—is particularly important.

2. Explain perceptual selection and identify the major factors that influence what individuals selectively perceive.

People use perceptual selection to filter out less important information in order to focus on more important environmental cues. Both external factors in the environment and factors internal to the perceiver influence perceptual selection. External factors can be thought of as characteristics of the object perceived that influence whether it is likely to be noticed. Internal factors include personality, learning, and motivation.

3. Describe the concept of perceptual organization.

Perceptual organization represents the process by which people assemble, organize, and categorize information from the environment. This process groups environmental stimuli into recognizable patterns (wholes) that allow people to interpret what they perceive.

4. Identify the factors that determine how one person perceives another.

How people perceive each other is particularly important for organizational behavior. Person perception is a function of the characteristics of the person perceived, the characteristics of the perceiver, and the situation within which the perception takes place. People may go to great lengths to manage the impressions that others form about them. Understanding the dynamics of impression management is also useful for understanding the behavior of people at work.

5. Describe the major errors in perception that people make.

Unfortunately, the perceptual process may result in errors of judgment or understanding in many ways. The more important and common perceptual errors include perceptual defense, stereotyping, halo effect, projection, and expectancy effects. However, through training and experience, individuals can learn to judge or perceive others more accurately.

6. Explain how attributions influence behavior and identify important attributions that people make in the work setting.

Attribution deals with the perceived causes of behavior. People infer causes for the behavior of others, and their perceptions of why certain behaviors occur influence their own subsequent behavioral responses and feelings. Whether behavior is internally caused by the nature of the person or is externally caused by circumstances is an important attribution that people make about the behaviors of others. Individuals also make attributions concerning task success and failure, which have important implications for organizational behavior.

KEY TERMS AND CONCEPTS

Attribution process
Closure
Continuity
Expectancy effects
Field dependence/independence
Fundamental attribution error
Halo effect
Implicit personality theories
Impression construction
Impression management
Impression motivation
Perception
Perceptual defense
Perceptual grouping
Perceptual organization
Perceptual selection
Perceptual set
Person perception
Pollyanna principle
Primacy effect

Projection
Proximity
Self-fulfilling prophecy
Self-serving bias
Similarity
Stereotyping

DISCUSSION QUESTIONS

1. Provide an example from your own experience of people seeming to interpret the same situation differently. Explain why you think that this happened.
2. Explain the process of person perception. What factors determine how one person perceives another?
3. From your own experience, describe a time when the *situation,* or context, played a key role in someone's perception of another person. How might that perception have been different if the situation had been different?
4. Provide two examples of impression management based on your own experience. (One description should be your own attempt at impression management, and the other description should be another person's attempt.) Were these attempts at impression management successful? Why or why not?
5. From your own experience, provide three examples of perceptual errors. Discuss the outcomes of each instance.
6. What perceptual errors seem particularly important in the work setting? Explain why these types of errors seem important to you.
7. Provide an example of an occasion when you felt that it was particularly important to make an accurate judgment about whether someone's behavior represented what he or she was really like or simply reflected the circumstances of the situation. Using Kelley's model of causal attributions (Figure 3.8), explain how you made this judgment.
8. Provide an example—either from your own experience or from something you've read—of an observer apparently making the fundamental attribution error.
9. Describe an important task at which you failed. Describe a second important task at which you succeeded. In each case, identify the attributions that you made to explain your success or failure.
10. Provide two real examples of the occurrence of a self-serving bias.

DEVELOPING COMPETENCIES

Competency: Managing Diversity—Measuring Perceptions of Women as Managers[36]

Gender role stereotypes limit the opportunity for women to advance to managerial positions in many firms. Although these stereotypes are slowly changing, widely held attitudes about the inadequacies of women as managers represent a barrier to greater career opportunities for many women.

Because specific attitudes and stereotypes can be pervasive and powerful influences on behavior, considering their role in the treatment—by both men and women—of women in managerial positions is important. Attitudes about the managerial abilities of women may affect how a manager or executive judges a woman's performance in a managerial role. In addition, such attitudes may influence the granting or withholding of developmental opportunities. The following questionnaire is designed to help you explore your attitudes toward women as managers.

Instructions: From each set (of three) statements, select the one with which you *most agree* and place an M (for "most agree") in the blank to the right of that statement. For each set, also select the statement with which you *least agree* and place an L (for "least agree") in the blank to the right of that statement. Note that one statement in each set will not be chosen.

1. A. Men are more concerned with the cars they drive than with the clothes their wives wear. ____
   B. Any man worth his salt should not be blamed for putting his career above his family. ____
   C. A person's job is the best single indicator of the sort of person he is. ____
2. A. Parental authority and responsibility for discipline of the children should be divided equally between the husband and the wife. ____
   B. It is less desirable for women than for men to have jobs that require responsibility. ____
   C. Men should not continue to show courtesies to women, such as holding doors open for them and helping them with their coats. ____
3. A. It is acceptable for women to assume leadership roles as often as men. ____

B. In a demanding situation, a female manager would be no more likely to break down than would a male manager. _____

C. Some professions and types of businesses are more suitable for men than for women. _____

4\. A. Recognition for a job well done is less important to women than it is to men. _____

B. A woman should demand money for household and personal expenses as a right rather than a gift. _____

C. Women are temperamentally fit for leadership positions. _____

5\. A. Women tend to allow their emotions to influence their managerial behavior more than men do. _____

B. The husband and the wife should be equal partners in planning the family budget. _____

C. If both husband and wife agree that sexual fidelity is not important, there is no reason why both should not have extramarital affairs. _____

6\. A. A man's first responsibility is to his wife, not to his mother. _____

B. A man who is able and willing to work hard has a good chance of succeeding in whatever he wants to do. _____

C. Only after a man has achieved what he wants from life should he concern himself with the injustices in the world. _____

7\. A. A wife should make every effort to minimize irritations and inconveniences for the male head of the household. _____

B. Women can cope with stressful situations as effectively as men can. _____

C. Women should be encouraged not to become sexually intimate with anyone, even their fiancés, before marriage. _____

8\. A. The "obey" clause in the marriage service is insulting to women. _____

B. Divorced men should help to support their children but should not be required to pay alimony if their former wives are capable of working. _____

C. Women have the capacity to acquire the necessary skills to be successful managers. _____

9\. A. Women can be aggressive in business situations that demand it. _____

B. Women have an obligation to be faithful to their husbands. _____

C. It is childish for a woman to assert herself by retaining her maiden name after marriage. _____

10\. A. Men should continue to show courtesies to women, such as holding doors open for them or helping them with their coats. _____

B. In job appointments and promotions, women should be given equal consideration with men. _____

C. It is all right for a wife to have an occasional casual, extramarital affair. _____

11\. A. The satisfaction of her husband's sexual desires is a fundamental obligation of every wife. _____

B. Most women should not want the kind of support that men traditionally have given them. _____

C. Women possess the dominance to be successful leaders. _____

12\. A. Most women need and want the kind of protection and support that men traditionally have given them. _____

B. Women are capable of separating their emotions from their ideas. _____

C. A husband has no obligation to inform his wife of his financial plans. _____

Score your responses by using the form and following the instructions given. Your total score indicates your feelings about women managers. The higher your score, the more prone you are to hold negative gender role stereotypes about women in management. Possible total scores range from 10 to 70; a "neutral" score (one that indicates neither positive nor negative attitudes about women as managers) is in the range of 30 to 40.

Instructions:

1. Record your response for the indicated items in the spaces provided.
2. On the basis of the information provided, determine the points for each item and enter these points in the space provided to the right. For example, if in item 3, you chose alternative A as the one with which you *most agree* and alternative B as the one with which you *least agree*, you should receive three points for item 3. Note that items 1 and 6 are "buffer items" and are not scored.
3. When you have scored all 10 scorable items, add the points and record the total at the bottom of this page in the space provided. That is your total score.

POINTS PER ITEM RESPONSE*								
Your Response	Item No.	1	3		5		7	Points
	1	Not Scored						
M ____ L ____	2	C(M) B(L)	A(M) B(L)	C(M) A(L)	A(M) C(L)	B(M) A(L)	B(M) C(L)	
M ____ L ____	3	A(M) C(L)	A(M) B(L)	B(M) C(L)	C(M) B(L)	B(M) A(L)	C(M) A(L)	
M ____ L ____	4	C(M) B(L)	C(M) A(L)	A(M) B(L)	B(M) A(L)	A(M) C(L)	B(M) C(L)	
M ____ L ____	5	C(M) A(L)	C(M) B(L)	B(M) A(L)	A(M) B(L)	B(M) C(L)	A(M) C(L)	
M ____ L ____	6	Not Scored						
M ____ L ____	7	B(M) A(L)	B(M) C(L)	C(M) A(L)	A(M) C(L)	C(M) B(L)	A(M) B(L)	
M ____ L ____	8	C(M) B(L)	C(M) A(L)	A(M) B(L)	B(M) A(L)	A(M) C(L)	B(M) C(L)	
M ____ L ____	9	A(M) B(L)	A(M) C(L)	C(M) B(L)	B(M) C(L)	C(M) A(L)	B(M) A(L)	
M ____ L ____	10	B(M) A(L)	B(M) C(L)	C(M) A(L)	A(M) C(L)	C(M) B(L)	A(M) B(L)	
M ____ L ____	11	C(M) A(L)	C(M) B(L)	B(M) A(L)	A(M) B(L)	B(M) C(L)	A(M) C(L)	
M ____ L ____	12	B(M) A(L)	B(M) C(L)	C(M) A(L)	A(M) C(L)	C(M) B(L)	A(M) B(L)	
								Total ____

*M indicates item chosen as "most"; L indicates item chosen as "least."

Competency: Managing Ethics—The Foundation for New Era Philanthropy

In the practice of impression management, creating the desired impression can be greatly aided if others strongly desire to see what you want them to see. The story of the Foundation for New Era Philanthropy provides a classic example of this dynamic.

John G. Bennett Jr. was the founder of what appeared to be a forward-thinking charitable foundation. New Era proposed to pool money from a variety of other charities and wealthy individuals and, through astute investing, fund-raising, and money management, promised to leverage these funds in ways that would allow generous people and charities to dramatically increase their ability to do good works. Specifically, Bennett promised to do the following.

1. Double within 6 months any money contributed to the foundation by selected charities and individuals and return the total to the original charities for distribution. Supposedly New Era had a group of wealthy "anonymous donors" too busy to find their own charities to give to, and it would use this money to double the amount of contributions solicited.
2. Double within 6 months new money that the charities and individuals approached had to promise to raise and return the total to the original charities for distribution.

This sounds too good to be true. Unfortunately, it was.

The beginning of the end came when Prudential Securities was doing a routine audit of $60 million in treasury bills held by New Era. They discovered that the foundation had borrowed $52 million against these bills, but had repaid only $7 million of the loan. Prudential gave New Era 24 hours to come up with the missing money, which it was unable to do. Ensuing events revealed that that there were no "anonymous donors" and that New Era had about $100 million in net liabilities. Basically, New Era was running a classic Ponzi scheme, whereby money from new investors is used to pay off previous investors. Many well-intentioned, supposedly well-informed, sophisticated investors and charities had been taken in by New Era's plan. How could this have happened?

The dynamics of impression management and impression formation coupled with Bennett's personal history seem to offer the best explanation. Bennett was an expansive, likable person who was described as an "incurable optimist." People wanted to believe in him and what he was proposing to do. He had a track record in a business that provided training to nonprofit foundation managers and fund-raisers. As a result he had become well known to the people who managed and contributed to various charities.

Contributing to this positive image was the fact that many of the initial beneficiaries of Bennett's fund-raising were churches and other religious organizations. Bennett himself served on the boards of directors of several Christian groups and was a regular attendant at Philadelphia-area prayer breakfasts. Many of his staunchest supporters were very rich and well connected to the highest levels of government, prestigious universities, investment firms, and the like. Why were so many smart, successful people taken in by this scheme?

One simple explanation, consistent with the notions of impression management, was that "the rich and well connected prefer to believe that they are so because they are smart and enterprising. What worked for Bennett was that these smart and enterprising people are likely to put their faith in other smart and enterprising people. Once Bennett succeeded in developing the *impression* that he was one of them—smart and enterprising—he had it made."[37]

Questions

1. Using the notions of impression management discussed in the chapter, describe Bennett's *impression motivation.*
2. Again, using ideas from the discussion of impression management, speculate about Bennett's *impression construction.*
3. Identify and explain the perceptual errors that may have occurred in this situation.
4. Imagine that you are the managing director of a charity that lost a great deal of money with New Era. Describe the likely attributions that you might make to explain this failure in judgment. Be imaginative and have some fun with this question.

REFERENCES

1. Bertenthal, B. I. Origins and early development of perception, action, and representation. *Annual Review of Psychology*, 1996, 47, 431–459; Goldstone, R. L. Perceptual learning. *Annual Review of Psychology*, 1998, 49, 585–612; Sekular, R., and Blake, R. *Perception*, 2nd ed. New York: McGraw-Hill, 1990.
2. Based on Ornstein, S. The hidden influences of office design. *Academy of Management Executive*, 1989, 3, 144–147; Ornstein, S. Impression management through office design. In R. A. Giacalone and T. Rosenfeld (eds.), *Impression Management in the Organization.* Hillsdale, N.J.: Lawrence Erlbaum, 1989, 411–426; Raiford, R. First impressions. *Buildings*, July 1999, 93.
3. Henderson, J. M., and Hollingworth, A. High-level scene perception. *Annual Review of Psychology*, 1999, 50, 243–271; Kinchla, R. A. Attention. *Annual Review of Psychology*, 1992, 43, 711–742; Milliken, B., Joordens, S., Merikle, P. M., and Seiffert, A. E. Selective attention: A reevaluation of the implications of negative priming. *Psychological Review*, 1998, 105, 203–229.
4. Farah, M. J., Wilson, K. D., Drain, M., and Tanaka, J. N. What is "special" about face perception? *Psychological Review*, 1998, 105, 482–498.
5. Hogan, R. T. Personality and personality measurement. In M. D. Dunnette, and L. M. Hough (eds.), *Handbook of Industrial and Organizational Psychology*, vol. 2, 2nd ed. Palo Alto, Calif.: Consulting Psychologists Press, 1991, 886–891; Weiner, B., and Graham, S. Attribution in personality psychology. In L. A. Pervin and O. P. John (eds.), *Handbook of Personality*, 2nd ed. New York: Guilford, 1999, 605–628.
6. McBurney, D. H., and Collings, V. B. *Introduction to Sensation/Perception*, 2nd ed. Englewood Cliffs, N.J.: Prentice-Hall, 1984, 327–345.
7. Chattopadhyau, P., Glick, W. H., Miller, C. C., and Huber, G. P. Determinants of executive beliefs: Comparing functional conditioning and social influence. *Strategic Management Journal*, 1999, 20, 763–788; Dearborn, D., and Simon, H. A. Selective perception: A note on the departmental identifications of executives. *Sociometry*, 1958, 21, 140–144; Waller, M. J., Huber, G. P, and Glick, W. H. Functional background as a determinant of executive's selective perception. *Academy of Management Journal*, 1995, 38, 943–974.
8. Dorfman, P. W. et al. Perceptions of punctuality: Cultural differences and the impact of time perceptions on job satisfaction and organizational commitment. Paper presented at the Pan Pacific conference, Beijing, China, June 8–10, 1993.
9. Based on Levine, R. V. The pace of life. *American Scientist*, September/October 1990, 450–459; Levine, R. V., and Wolff, E. Social time: The heartbeat of culture. *Psychology Today*, March 1985, 28–35.
10. Archambault, A., O'Donnell, C., and Schyns, P. G. Blind to object changes: When learning the same object at different levels of categorization modifies its perception. *Psychological Science*, 1999, 10, 249–255; Kingstone, A., and Bishof, W. F. Perceptual grouping and motion coherence in visual search. *Psychological Science*, 1999, 10, 151–156; Roitblat, H. L., and von Fersen, L. Comparative cognition: Representations and processes in learning and memory. *Annual Review of Psychology*, 1992, 43, 671–710;

Squire, L. R., Knowlton, B., and Musen, G. The structure and organization of memory. *Annual Review of Psychology*, 1993, 44, 453–495.

11. Ashforth, B. E., and Humphrey, R. H. Labeling processes in the organization: Constructing the individual. In L. L. Cummings and B. M. Staw (eds.), *Research in Organizational Behavior*, vol. 17. Greenwich, Conn.: JAI Press, 1995, 413–461; Fiske, S. T. Social cognition and social perception. *Annual Review of Psychology*, 1993, 44, 155–194; Hamilton, D. L., and Sherman, S. J. Perceiving persons and groups. *Psychological Review*, 1996, 103, 336–355.
12. Baron, R. M., Graziano, W. G., and Stangor, C. *Social Psychology*. Fort Worth: Holt, Rinehart, and Winston, 1991, 122–123.
13. Bond, M. H., and Smith, P. B. Cross-cultural social and organizational psychology. *Annual Review of Psychology*, 1996, 47, 205–235; Caligiuri, P. M., and Cascio, W. F. Can we send her there? Maximizing the success of Western women on global assignments. *Journal of World Business*, 1998, 33, 394–416; Linowes, R. G. The Japanese manager's traumatic entry into the United States: Understanding the American–Japanese cultural divide. *Academy of Management Executive*, November 1993, 21–40; Thomas, D. C., and Ravlin, E. C. Responses of employees to cultural adaptation by a foreign manager. *Journal of Applied Psychology*, 1995, 80, 133–146.
14. Bolino, M. C. Citizenship and impression management: Good soldiers or good actors? *Academy of Management Review*, 1999, 24, 82–98; Frink, D. D., and Ferris, G. R. Accountability, impression management, and goal setting in the performance evaluation process. *Human Relations*, 1998, 51, 1259–1274; Schlenker, B. R., and Weigold, M. F. Interpersonal processes involving impression regulation and management. *Annual Review of Psychology*, 1992, 43, 133–168; Stevens, C. K., and Kristof, A. L. Making the right impression: A field study of applicant impression management during job interviews. *Journal of Applied Psychology*, 1995, 80, 587–606; Wayne, S. J., and Liden, R. C. Effects of impression management on performance ratings: A longitudinal study. *Academy of Management Journal*, 1995, 38, 232–260.
15. Hinton, P. R. *The Psychology of Interpersonal Perception*. London: Routledge, 1993, 23.
16. Bolino, M. C., and Turnley, W. H. Measuring impression management in organizations: a scale development based on the Jones and Pittman Taxonomy. *Organizational Research Methods*, 1999, 2, 187–206; Leary, M. R., and Kowalski, R. M. Impression management: A literature review and two-component model. *Psychological Bulletin*, 1990, 107, 34–47.
17. Adapted from Lancaster, H. Making the switch from a Mr. fix-it to a problem-solver. *Wall Street Journal*, March 23, 1999, B1.
18. Funder, D. C. On the accuracy of personality judgment: A realistic approach. *Psychological Review*, 1995, 102, 652–670; Kenny, D. A., and DePaulo, B. M. Do people know how others view them? An empirical and theoretical account. *Psychological Bulletin*, 1993, 114, 145–161; Kruglanski, A. W. The psychology of being right: The problem of accuracy in social perception and cognition. *Psychological Bulletin*, 1989, 106, 395–409.
19. Cable, D. M., and Gilovich, T. Looked over or overlooked? Prescreening decisions and post-interview evaluations. *Journal of Applied Psychology*, 1998, 83, 501–508; Fisher, C. D., Schoenfeldt, L. F., and Shaw, J. B. *Human Resource Management*, 3rd ed. Boston: Houghton Mifflin, 1996, 326–327; Huffcutt, A. I., and Roth, P. L. Racial group differences in employment interview evaluations. *Journal of Applied Psychology*, 1998, 83, 179–189.
20. Kilbourne, L. M., and Woodman, R. W. Barriers to organizational creativity. In R. E. Purser and A. Montuori (eds.), *Social Creativity*, vol. 2. Cresskill, N.J.: Hampton Press, 1999, 125–150.
21. Hilton, J. L., and von Hippel, W. Stereotypes. *Annual Review of Psychology*, 1996, 47, 237–271; Paul, A. M. Where bias begins: The truth about stereotypes. *Psychology Today*, May–June 1998, 52–57; Shih, M., Pittinsky, T. L., and Ambady, N. Stereotype susceptibility: Identity salience and shifts in quantitative performance. *Psychological Science*, 1999, 10, 80–83.
22. Colella, A., DeNisi, A. S., and Varma, A. The impact of ratee's disability on performance judgments and choice as partner: The role of disability–job fit stereotypes and interdependence of rewards. *Journal of Applied Psychology*, 1998, 83, 102–111; Stone, D. L., and Colella, A. A model of factors affecting the treatment of disabled individuals in organizations. *Academy of Management Review*, 1996, 21, 352–401.
23. Farrell, C. Women in the workplace: Is parity finally in sight? *Business Week*, August 9, 1999, 35; Lancaster, H. To get shipped abroad, women must overcome prejudice at home. *Wall Street Journal*, June 29, 1999, B1; Schrage, M. Why can't a woman be more like a man? *Fortune*, August 16, 1999, 184.
24. Snyder, M., and Stukas, A. A. Interpersonal processes: The interplay of cognitive, motivational, and behavioral activities in social interaction. *Annual Review of Psychology*, 1999, 50, 273–303.
25. Baron, R. A., and Byrne, D. *Social Psychology: Understanding Human Interaction*, 6th ed. Boston: Allyn & Bacon, 1991, 55–83; Harvey, J. H., and Wells, G. (eds.), *Attribution: Basic Issues and Applications*. New York: Academic Press, 1988; Myers, D. G. *Social Psychology*, 4th ed. New York: McGraw-Hill, 1993, 74–108.
26. Azar, B. Influences from the mind's inner layers. *The APA Monitor*, February 1996, 1, 25.
27. Kelley, H. H. The process of causal attribution. *American Psychologist*, 1973, 28, 107–128.
28. Hinton, P. R. *The Psychology of Interpersonal Perception*. London: Routledge, 1993, 143–146; Kasof, J. Attribution and creativity. In M. A. Runco and S. R. Pritzker (eds.), *Encyclopedia of Creativity*, vol. 1. San Diego: Academic Press, 1999, 147.
29. Miller, J. G. Culture and the development of everyday causal explanation. *Journal of Personality and Social Psychology*, 1984, 46, 961–978.
30. Heneman, R. L., Greenberger, D. B., and Anonyus, C. Attributions and exchanges: The effects of interpersonal factors on the diagnosis of employee performance. *Academy of Management Journal*, 1989, 32, 466–476; see also, Elkins, T. J., and Phillips, J. S. Evaluating sex discrimination

claims: The mediating role of attributions. *Journal of Applied Psychology*, 1999, 84, 186–199; Manzoni, J. F., and Barsoux, J. L. The set-up-to-fail syndrome. *Harvard Business Review*, March–April, 1998, 101–113.

31. Babladelis, G. *The Study of Personality.* New York: Holt, Rinehart, and Winston, 1984, 76.
32. Levy, P. E. Self-appraisal and attributions: A test of a model. *Journal of Management*, 1993, 19, 51–62.
33. Kim, Y. Y., and Miller, K. I. The effects of attributions and feedback goals on the generation of supervisory feedback message strategies. *Management Communication Quarterly*, 1990, 4, 6–29.
34. Tennen, H., and Affleck, G. Blaming others for threatening events. *Psychological Bulletin*, 1990, 108, 209–232.
35. Faircloth, A. How to recover from a firing. *Fortune*, December 7, 1998, 239–240; Lancaster, H. You're fired! It's time to regain your cool and pick up the pieces. *Wall Street Journal*, April 13, 1999, B1.
36. Adapted from Yost, E. B., and Herbert, T. T. Attitudes toward women as managers. In L. D. Goodstein and J. W. Pfeiffer (eds.), *The 1985 Annual: Developing Human Resources.* San Diego: University Associates, 1985, 117–127. Reprinted with permission.
37. Adapted from Ritti, R. R. *The Ropes to Skip and the Ropes to Know: Studies in Organizational Behavior*, 5th ed. New York: John Wiley & Sons, 1998, 30–31.

CHAPTER

4 Learning and Reinforcement

LEARNING OBJECTIVES

When you have finished studying this chapter, you should be able to:

1. Explain the differences between classical, operant, and social cognitive theory.
2. Describe the contingencies of reinforcement.
3. List the four schedules of reinforcement and explain when each is effective.
4. Describe the processes and principles of behavioral modification.

Preview Case: *Dialing for Dollars*

TYPES OF LEARNING
- Classical Conditioning
- Operant Conditioning
- Social Cognitive Theory
- ***Competency: Managing Teams***—*Steelcase Incorporated*
- ***Competency: Managing Self***—*The Challenge Course*

CONTINGENCIES OF REINFORCEMENT
- Positive Reinforcement
- ***Competency: Managing Change***—*Columbia Medical Center of Plano*
- Organizational Rewards
- ***Competency: Managing Across Cultures***—*Amway in Hungary*
- Negative Reinforcement
- Omission
- Punishment
- Using Contingencies of Reinforcement

SCHEDULES OF REINFORCEMENT
- Continuous and Intermittent Reinforcement
- Fixed Interval Schedule
- Variable Interval Schedule
- Fixed Ratio Schedule
- Variable Ratio Schedule
- Comparison of Intermittent Reinforcement Schedules

BEHAVIORAL MODIFICATION
- Pinpointing Relevant Behaviors
- Charting Behavior
- Choosing a Contingency of Reinforcement
- Problem Solved?
- Behavioral Modification Issues
- ***Competency: Managing Communication***—*Manufacturing in Eastern Europe*

CHAPTER SUMMARY
- Key Terms and Concepts
- Discussion Questions

DEVELOPING COMPETENCIES
- ***Competency: Managing Self***—*What Is Your Self-Efficacy?*
- ***Competency: Managing Ethics***—*Medical Incentives*
- ***Competency: Managing Change***—*Westinghouse*

PREVIEW CASE

DIALING FOR DOLLARS

As President of Great North American, Joe Salatino gauges his success by the amount of money he pays his employees. The firm's salespeople will sell more than $20 million in office, promotional, arts-and-crafts, and computer supplies to more than 60,000 businesses around the country this year. The head of the Dallas-based telemarketing company believes that spending money on commissions and bonuses is necessary to keep his 95-person sales force motivated. Great North American annually sells more than 7 million yards of packaging tape, 8 million paper clips, and 11 million BIC and Papermate pens and pencils bearing customer logos, along with about 12,000 other products.

The company's salesroom features all kinds of motivational devices. On a recent Friday morning, rotating blue lights, like those at Kmart, signal that a special deal on pens is on. For the next hour, customers can get two for one on stars and stripes promotional pens. When the blue-light special is off, they're back up to 39 cents apiece. When the light goes off, a manager draws a large snowball on one of the large dry-erase boards to indicate another sale. The noise and pace is fast and furious.

Many of Salatino's salespeople earn more than $60,000 a year, and the top producers earn more than $100,000. Gary Gieb, aka Jack Johnson because it's easier to spell and sounds all-American over the phone, earned more than $100,000 last year. During a typical day, he makes some 20 to 25 calls an hour. If a customer places an order, the entire transaction takes just under 5 minutes. He earns a commission of between 5 and 12 percent on list price, depending on the merchandise. A salesperson usually needs about a year to build an account base, and many employees who can't handle the self-starting selling intensity and bedlam usually leave within the first month. To establish loyal customers, many top-selling salespeople subscribe to the customer's hometown newspaper so that they can chat with the customer about local issues, such as who had a baby and who won the high school football game. Peggy Gordon topped $70,000 last year selling educational supplies that police and sheriff's departments take on visits to schools.[1]

Great North American's motivational tactics are based on specific principles drawn from an area of psychology called learning theory. The **learning theory** approach stresses the assessment of behavior in objective, measurable (countable) terms.[2] Behavior must be publicly observable, which deemphasizes unobservable, inner, cognitive behavior. In this chapter, we explore the development, maintenance, and change of employee work behaviors, using principles derived from learning theory.

Desirable work behaviors contribute to achieving organizational goals; conversely, undesirable work behaviors hinder achieving these goals. Labeling behavior as *desirable* or *undesirable* is entirely subjective and depends on the value system of the person making the assessment. For example, a team member at Pfizer Pharmaceuticals' assembly line who returns late from a coffee break exhibits undesirable behavior from the manager's viewpoint, desirable behavior from the viewpoint of friends with whom the worker chats during the break, and desirable behavior from the worker's viewpoint because of the satisfaction of social needs.

The work setting and organizational norms are objective bases for determining whether a behavior is desirable or undesirable. The more a behavior deviates from organizational norms, the more undesirable it is. At American Airlines, undesirable behavior includes anything that results in lost baggage and late departures and arrivals. However, norms vary considerably from one organization to another. For example, at Microsoft's research and development laboratory, engineers and scientists are encouraged to question top-management's directives because professional judgment is crucial to the organization's success in the telecommunications market. In contrast, in a military unit such questioning may be considered insubordination and justification for severe disciplinary action.

Effective managers do not try to change employees' personalities or basic beliefs. Rather, they focus on identifying observable employee behaviors and the environmental conditions that affect these behaviors. They then attempt to control external events in order to guide employee behavior. As we discussed in Chapters 2 and 3, an individual's personality and attitudes influence behavior. Directly influencing these characteristics in employees often is difficult. Focusing on behaviors that others can observe therefore may be a starting point.

Learning Objective:

1. Explain the differences among classical, operant, and social cognitive theory.

TYPES OF LEARNING

Learning is a relatively permanent change in the frequency of occurrence of a specific individual behavior.[3] In an organization, employees need to learn and practice productive work behaviors. To a great extent, learning new work behaviors depends on environmental factors. The manager's goal, then, is to provide learning experiences in an environment that will promote employee behaviors desired by the organization. In the work setting, learning can take place in one of three ways: classical conditioning, operant conditioning, and according to social cognitive theory. Of the three, operant conditioning and social cognitive theory are most helpful in understanding the behaviors of others.

CLASSICAL CONDITIONING

Classical conditioning is the process by which individuals learn to link the information value from a neutral stimulus to a stimulus that would not naturally cause a response. This learned response may not be under an individual's conscious control.[4] Examples of stimuli and responses, or **reflexive behavior,** are shown in Table 4.1. In the classical conditioning process, an unconditioned stimulus (environmental event) brings out a natural response. Then a neutral environmental event, called a conditioned stimulus, is paired with the unconditioned stimulus that brings out the behavior. Eventually, the conditioned stimulus alone brings out the behavior, which is called a conditional response.

Table 4.1 **Examples of Reflexive Behavior**

STIMULUS (S)	RESPONSE (R)
The Individual	
• is stuck by a pin and	flinches.
• is shocked by an electric current and	jumps or screams.
• has something in an eye and	blinks.
• hits an elbow on the corner of a desk and	flexes arm.

The name most frequently associated with classical conditioning is Ivan Pavlov, the Russian physiologist whose experiments with dogs led to the early formulations of classical conditioning theory. In Pavlov's famous experiment, the sound of a metronome (the conditioned stimulus) was paired with food (the unconditioned stimulus). The dogs eventually exhibited a salivation response (conditioned response) to the sound of the metronome alone. The classical conditioning process is shown in Figure 4.1.

The process of classical conditioning can help you understand a variety of behaviors that occur in everyday organizational life. At Presbyterian Hospital's emergency room, special lights in the hallway indicate that a patient who needs treatment has just arrived. Nurses and other hospital staff report that they feel nervous when the lights go on. In contrast, at a recent luncheon in the dining room at Stonebriar Country Club, Ralph Sorrentino, manager of technology at Deloitte & Touche, was thanked by his friend David Norwood for introducing a new work system. Now, whenever Sorrentino sees the dining room, he feels good.

Organizations spend billions of dollars on advertising campaigns designed to link the information value of a stimulus to customer purchase behavior. In a TV ad, Taco Bell has successfully created a link between its food and a dog, Dinky. The Chihuahua is the unconditioned stimulus, and its food is the conditioned stimulus. The positive feelings that buyers have toward the dog are associated with the food, which Taco Bell hopes will lead people to buy its products. Similarly, Budweiser has linked its frog, ferret, and two lizards (Frank and Louie) in an award winning TV beer ad. When people see the frog, ferret, and lizards (unconditioned stimulus) in the swamp, they associate them with Budweiser (the conditioned stimulus). Associating the upbeat mood created by these creatures with Bud is intended to lead customers to drink its beer. Both organizations have successfully used the concepts of classical conditioning to increase sales of their products.

Figure 4.1 **Classical Conditioning**

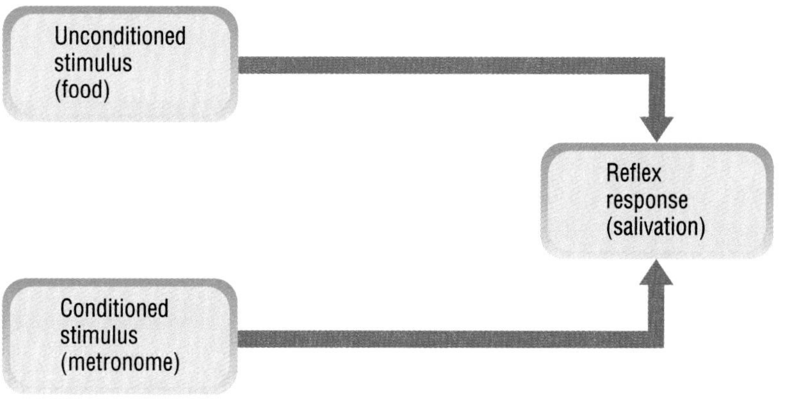

Classical conditioning is probably relatively unused in work settings. The reason is that desired employee behaviors usually don't include responses that can be changed with classical conditioning techniques. There is greater interest in the voluntary behaviors of employees and how they can be changed through operant conditioning.

Operant Conditioning

The person most closely linked with this type of learning is B. F. Skinner.[5] He coined the term **operant conditioning** to refer to a process by which individuals learn voluntary behavior. Voluntary behaviors are called *operants* because they operate, or have some influence, on the environment. Learning occurs from the consequences of behaviors, and many employee work behaviors are operant behaviors. In fact, most behaviors in everyday life (e.g., talking, walking, reading, or working) are forms of operant behavior. Table 4.2 shows some examples of operant behaviors and their consequences.

Managers are interested in operant behaviors because they can influence the results of such behaviors. For example, the frequency of an employee behavior can be increased or decreased by changing the results of that behavior. The crucial aspect of operant conditioning is what happens as a consequence of the behavior. The strength and frequency of apparently conditioned behaviors are determined mainly by consequences. Thus managers and team members must understand the effects of different types of consequences on the task behaviors of employees.

Social Cognitive Theory

Albert Bandura and others have extended and expanded Skinner's work by demonstrating that people can learn new behavior by watching others in a social situation and then imitating their behavior.[6] According to the **social cognitive theory,** learning is viewed as knowledge acquisition through cognitive processing of information. In other words, the social part acknowledges that individuals learn by being part of a society and the cognitive part recognizes that individuals use thought processes to make decisions. Much of the work that goes on in organizations occurs because of the knowledge and behavior generated by people in that organization. Recall the Preview Case on Great North American. Prospective employees walk into the firm and see phone banks, salespeople with head sets on, and flashing lights advertising new promotional items. By watching others they develop mental pictures of what working there would be like. Based on these observations, they decide whether to join the organization. Bandura suggested that observers often learn faster than those who do not observe the behaviors of others because they don't need to unlearn behaviors and can avoid needless and costly errors.

Social cognitive theory has five dimensions—symbolizing, forethought, vicarious learning, self-control, and self-efficacy—as shown in Figure 4.2. These five dimensions can help you understand why different employees may behave differently when facing the same situation.

Table 4.2 Examples of Operant Behaviors and Their Consequences

BEHAVIORS	CONSEQUENCES
The Individual	
• works and	is paid.
• is late to work and	is docked pay.
• enters a restaurant and	eats.
• enters a football stadium and	watches a football game.
• enters a grocery store and	buys food.

Figure 4.2 **Five Dimensions of Social Cognitive Theory**

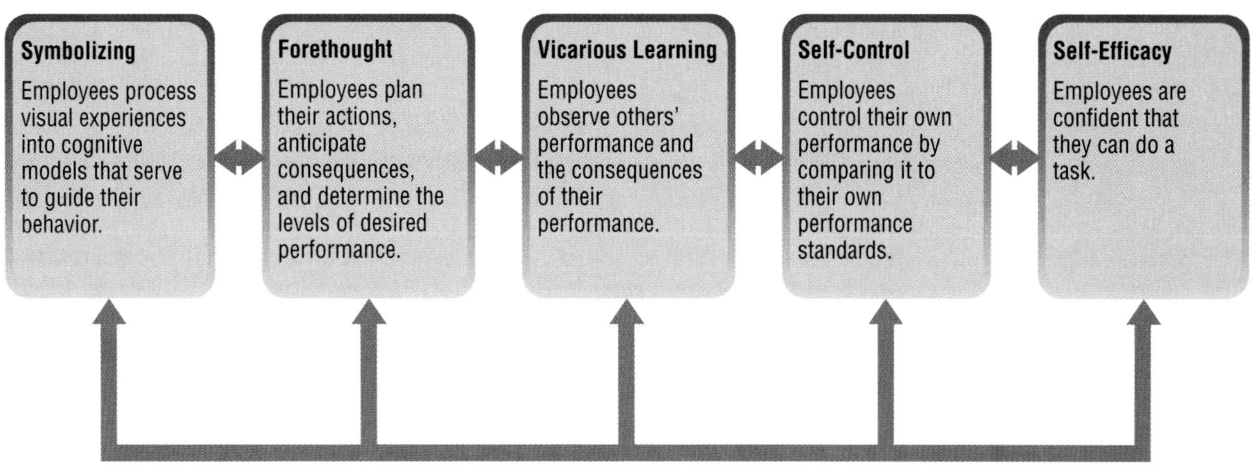

Source: Adapted from Stajkovic, A. D., and Luthans, F. Social cognitive theory and self-efficacy. *Organizational Dynamics,* Spring 1998, 65.

Individuals have an ability to use *symbols* that enable them to react to their environment. By using symbols, people process visual experiences into models that serve to guide their behavior. At Great North American, the rotating blue light is a symbol. It alerts salespeople to the fact that a special offering is taking place and that they should "plug" that item to customers. People use *forethought* to anticipate, plan, and guide their behaviors and actions. For example, when noticing the rotating blue light, Jack Johnson immediately calls a customer who has traditionally purchased that particular item during past specials. Almost all forms of learning can occur *vicariously* by observing the behavior of others and the consequences of that behavior. Employees' capacity to learn by observation enables them to obtain accurate information without having to perform these behaviors through trial and error. All self-help videos rely on vicarious learning. People who enter the telemarketing room at Great North American can quickly imagine themselves performing telemarketing tasks. For **vicarious learning** to occur, several conditions must be met.

- The learner must observe the model when the behavior is being performed.
- The learner must accurately perceive the model's behavior.
- The learner must remember the behavior.
- The learner must have the skills and abilities necessary to perform the behavior.
- The learner must observe that the model receives rewards for the behavior.[7]

Joe Salatino knows that not all people are cut out to work as telemarketers. After job applicants see the operation, many never apply for a job because what they see isn't consistent with their own ideas of the type of job they want. **Self-control learning** occurs when a new behavior is learned even though there is no external pressure to do so. Billie Boyd, an administrative assistant at Southern Methodist University, had a new software package for graphics on her desk for a month. She knew that she had to learn how to use it even though her supervisor hadn't put any pressure on her to do so. She worked Saturdays on her own to learn this new technique. Boyd's goal was to learn to use the software to produce figures for this book. Her approach exhibited self-control.

Most people engage in self-control to learn behaviors on and off the job. Both mundane tasks, such as learning how to use e-mail, and more complex tasks, such as preparing to give a subordinate a performance appraisal, can be learned. When an employee learns through self-control, managers don't need to be controlling because the employee takes responsibility for learning and performing the desired behaviors. In fact, if a manager exercises control, it may well be redundant and counterproductive.

In recent years, the concept of teams has taken the business world by storm. Unfortunately, in many cases, management continues to exert control over teams, whose members have few opportunities to apply self-control to their tasks. For teams to be effective, managers must empower their members to make decisions. **Empowerment** means giving employees the authority, skills, and freedom to perform their tasks.[8] The Managing Teams Competency feature below highlights how Steelcase Incorporated, a Minnesota manufacturer of business furniture, empowers teams to improve productivity.

The fifth aspect of social cognitive theory is the concept of self-efficacy. **Self-efficacy** refers to the individual's estimate of his or her own ability to perform a specific task in a particular situation.[9] The greater the perceived ability to perform the task, the higher the employee's self-efficacy will be. Employees with high self-efficacy believe that (1) they have the ability needed, (2) they are capable of the effort required, and (3) no outside events will keep them from performing at a high level. If employees have low self-efficacy, they believe that no matter how hard they try, something will happen to prevent them from reaching the desired level of performance. Self-efficacy influences people's choices of tasks and how long they will spend trying to reach their goals.[10] For example, a novice golfer who has taken only a few lessons might shoot a good round. Under such circumstances, the golfer might attribute the score to "beginner's luck" and not to ability. But, after many lessons and hours of practice, a person with low self-efficacy who still can't break 100 may decide that the demands of the game are too great to justify spending any more time on it. However, a high self-efficacy individual will try even harder to improve his or her game. This effort might include taking more lessons, watching videotapes of the individual's own swing, and practicing even harder and longer.

Self-efficacy affects learning in three ways.

- *Self-efficacy influences the activities and goals that individuals choose for themselves.* In a sales contest at Great North American, telemarketers with low self-efficacy

COMPETENCY: MANAGING TEAMS

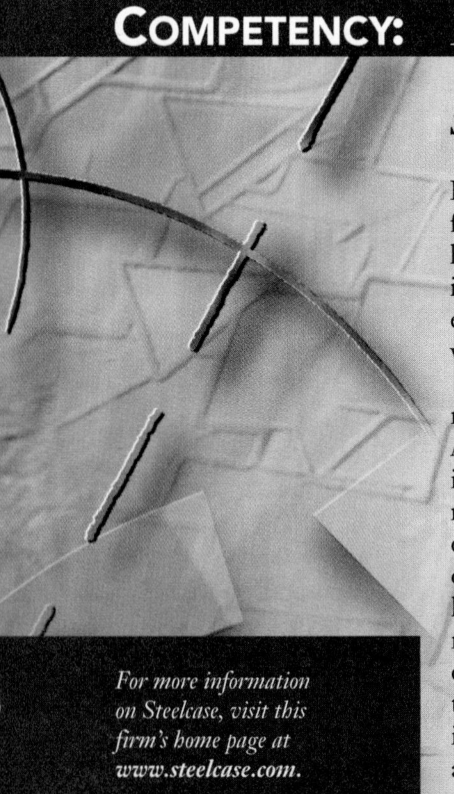

*For more information on Steelcase, visit this firm's home page at **www.steelcase.com**.*

STEELCASE INCORPORATED

For 18 years, Jerry Hammond had been a spot welder, making parts of business furniture without even knowing the people in nearby departments by name. Now, he knows his fellow workers because they are a team that is responsible for deciding how to manufacture a part and for running as many as six different pieces of equipment. Team members are cross-trained, as time permits, during regular working hours.

When Steelcase's management decided to create teams and empower them, it realized that barriers between workers and managers would have to be removed. As a result, only customers now have reserved parking spaces, a common cafeteria is provided, and only a few walls remain in the plant. Whenever new equipment is needed, a team of employees who will be responsible for operating it makes the decision about what to buy and how it should be positioned on the shop floor. Forty-one self-directed production teams and four support teams tackle day-to-day problems, such as safety, scrap and waste, paint quality, shipping, and the like. As a result, Steelcase has only one supervisor for every 33 workers, compared to its competitors' ratio of 1 to 12. Steelcase's workers are 45 percent more productive than its competitors', turning a customer's order into a finished product in 3 days instead of 3 weeks and slashing costs. Teams of employees working with suppliers also have been able to cut raw material inventory by half.[11]

didn't set challenging, or "stretch" goals. These people weren't lazy; they simply thought that they would fail to achieve a lofty goal. The high self-efficacy telemarketers thought that they were capable of achieving high-performance goals—and did so.

- *Self-efficacy influences the effort that individuals exert on the job.* Individuals with high self-efficacy work hard to learn new tasks and are confident that their efforts will be rewarded. Low self-efficacy individuals lack confidence in their ability to succeed and see their extra effort as futile because they are likely to fail anyway.
- *Self-efficacy affects the persistence with which a person stays with a complex task.* Because high self-efficacy people are confident that they will perform well, they are likely to persist in spite of obstacles or in the face of temporary setbacks. At IBM, low-performing employees were more likely than high-performing employees to dwell on obstacles hindering their ability to do assigned tasks. When people believe that they aren't capable of doing the required work, their motivation to do a task will be low.

Managers or fellow team members can use several sources of self-efficacy to help employees learn to believe in themselves. Past experience is the most powerful influence on self-efficacy. At work, the challenge is to create situations in which the employee may respond successfully to the task(s) required. A manager's expectations for a subordinate's performance—as well as the expectations of peers—also can affect a person's self-efficacy. If a manager holds high expectations for the employee and provides proper training and suggestions, the person's self-efficacy is likely to increase. Small successes boost self-efficacy and lead to more substantial accomplishments later. If a manager holds low expectations for the employee and gives little constructive advice, the employee is likely to form an impression that he or she cannot achieve the goal and, as a result, perform poorly.

Guidelines for using social cognitive theory to improve behavior in organizations are just starting to emerge.[12] They include the following.

- Identify the behaviors that will lead to improved performance.
- Select the appropriate model for employees to observe.
- Be sure that employees are capable of meeting the technical skill requirements of the required new behaviors.
- Structure a positive learning situation to increase the likelihood that employees will learn the new behaviors and act accordingly.
- Provide positive consequences (praise, raises, or bonuses) to employees who perform as expected.
- Develop organizational practices that maintain these newly learned behaviors.

During the past decade, the concept of building a training program around physically and psychologically challenging outdoor experiences has been adopted by many human resource trainers and offered to organizations as a way to instill team spirit, develop leadership skills, and improve a person's self-efficacy. These challenging courses help employees uncover leadership competencies, resolve conflict, encourage individual risk taking, and build confidence. Employees are scaling cliffs, shooting river rapids, and negotiating tricky "ropes courses" to improve their competencies. The Managing Self Competency feature on page 106 highlights how Wade Bibbee, Director of The Challenge, a Dallas-based management training firm that works with Chili's restaurants, uses the guidelines just mentioned to improve job performance.

In the next section, we return to operant conditioning, or the idea that behavior is influenced by its consequences. It is the most widely used theory of learning and has organizational implications for designing effective reward systems. To understand this theory fully requires a review of its basic elements.

COMPETENCY: MANAGING SELF

THE CHALLENGE COURSE

When participants arrive at the "ropes" course, they meet Wade Bibbee and his team of trainers. People gather in a circle for the next 15 to 20 minutes while Bibbee outlines the safety measures that everyone must follow. He briefly describes the challenges that everyone will face during the 8-hour day and stresses that if a person doesn't want to participate in an activity, the group should not pressure the individual to do so. The course is divided into a series of four segments: icebreakers, by which people get comfortable with each other; initiatives, which are unique problems designed to create communication among participants; lower elements, in which the group communicates and solves problems; and upper elements, which are designed to challenge people by testing their responses to risky situations. Sixteen activities—ranging from crossing a log 6 inches off the ground to leaping off a 25-foot-high telephone pole to scaling a 15-foot wall—are related to these four segments.

The first activity is designed to build trust. One person at a time attempts to walk across a 32-foot-long log suspended 6 inches off the ground and held there by wires attached to nearby trees. Bibbee quickly jumps on the log and walks across it with the help of his assistants who prevent him from falling off by bracing him as necessary. Walking the entire length of the log without the help of others is impossible because of its swinging motion. When he finishes, he thanks his helpers for their help. Participants quickly line up to walk the log. When all have finished, the group discusses the purpose of the task, which is to help improve a person's performance by relying on others.

The telephone pole activity requires each participant to scale a tapered pole about 25 feet high, using a ladder and wooden rungs. The idea is to climb the pole, pull yourself up onto a revolving wooden dish the size of a dinner dish, execute an about-face, leap toward a bellpull about 12 feet away, and ring the bell. After one of Bibbee's employees demonstrates the activity, a participant slips into a harnesslike piece of equipment that is securely attached by lines to overhead lines and belaying cables. After the person has leaped and either grabbed or missed the bellpull the other group members pull the lines tight and slowly lower the person to the ground. As the person comes down, participants cheer and clap their hands. Once safely on the ground, fellow participants hug and congratulate the person.[13]

Learning Objective:

2. Describe the contingencies of reinforcement.

CONTINGENCIES OF REINFORCEMENT

A **contingency of reinforcement** is the relationship between a behavior and the preceding and following environmental events that influence that behavior. A contingency of reinforcement consists of an antecedent, a behavior, and a consequence.[14]

An **antecedent** precedes and is a stimulus to a behavior. Presenting or withdrawing a particular antecedent can increase the probability that a particular behavior will occur. At Great North American, each telemarketer prepares a daily "to do" list containing the items being promoted and whom to call. As an antecedent, this list helps the telemarketers organize their tasks and focus their attention on the specific behaviors required.

A **consequence** is the result of a behavior, which can be either positive or negative in terms of goal or task accomplishment. A manager's response to an employee is contingent on the consequence of the behavior (and sometimes on the behavior itself, regardless of consequence). The consequence for the telemarketers is meeting their goals and those of the organization.

Figure 4.3 **Example of Contingent Reinforcement**

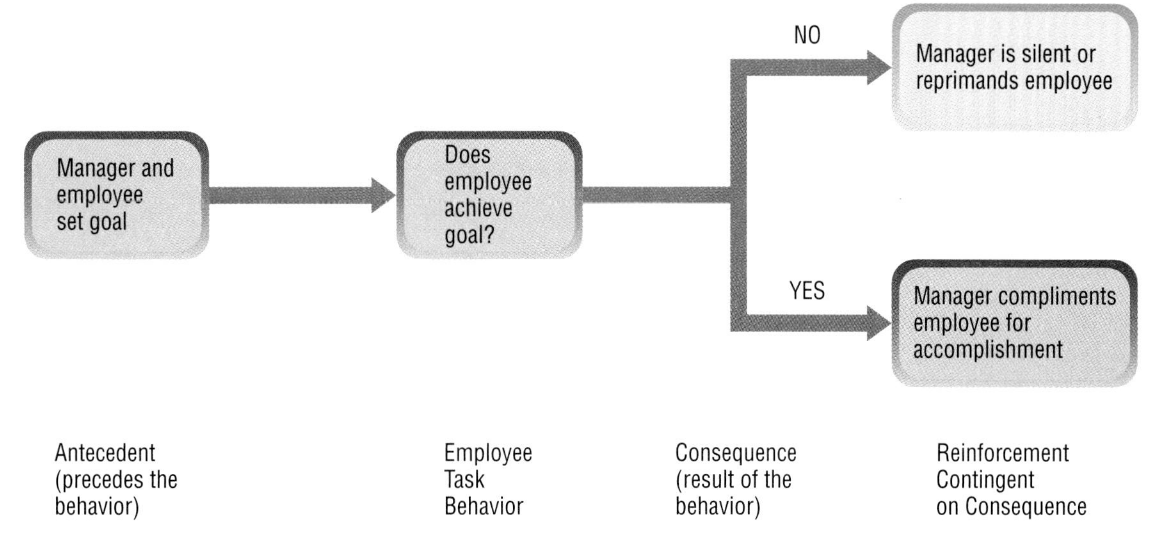

Figure 4.3 shows an example of contingent reinforcement. First, the employee and manager jointly set a goal (say, selling $100,000 worth of equipment next month). Next, the employee performs tasks to achieve this goal (e.g., calling on four new customers a week, having regular lunches with current buyers, and attending a 2-day training program on new methods of selling). If the employee reaches the sales goal, the manager praises the employee—an action contingent on achievement of the goal. If the employee fails to reach the goal, the manager doesn't say anything or reprimands the employee.

The contingency of reinforcement concept involves three main types of contingency. First, an event can be presented (applied) or withdrawn (removed), contingent on employee behavior. The event also may be positive or aversive. **Positive events** are desirable or pleasing to the employee. **Aversive events** are undesirable, or displeasing, to the employee. Figure 4.4 shows how these events can be combined to produce four types of contingencies of reinforcement. It shows whether a particular type of contingency is likely to increase or decrease the frequency of the behavior. It also is the basis for the following discussion of contingencies of reinforcement. **Reinforcement** is a behavioral contingency that increases the frequency of a particular behavior that it follows. On the one hand, reinforcement, whether positive or negative, always increases the frequency of the employee behavior. On the other hand, omission and punishment always decrease the frequency of the employee behavior.

Positive Reinforcement

Positive reinforcement entails presenting a pleasant consequence after the occurrence of a desired behavior. That is, a manager rewards an employee's behavior that is desirable in terms of achieving the organization's goals.

Reinforcement Versus Reward. The terms *reinforcement* and *reward* are often confused in everyday usage. A **reward** is an event that a person finds desirable or pleasing. Thus whether a reward acts as a reinforcer is subjective to the individual. A manager who singled out and praised an employee in front of coworkers for finding an error in the team's report believed that she was reinforcing the desired behavior. Later, however, she learned that the employee was given the silent treatment by other team members and had stopped looking for errors.

Figure 4.4 **Types of Contingencies of Reinforcement**

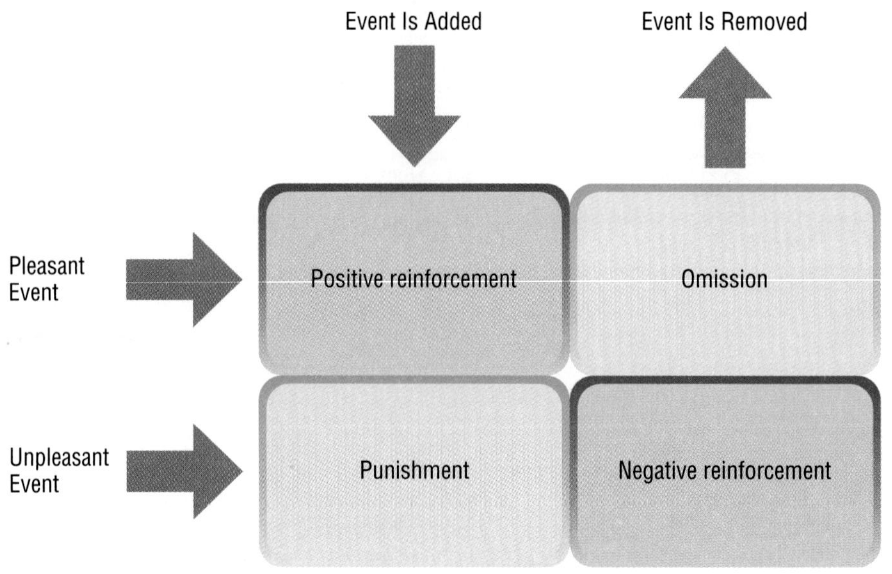

Thus, to qualify as a reinforcer, a reward must increase the frequency of the behavior it follows. Recall that, at Great North American, telemarketers earn commissions only if they reach their sales goals. Money can be regarded as a positive reinforcer for a particular individual only if the frequency of desired behavior (in this case, high performance) increases. A reward doesn't act as a reinforcer if the frequency of the behavior decreases or remains unchanged.

Primary and Secondary Reinforcers. A **primary reinforcer** is an event for which the individual already knows the value. Food, shelter, and water are primary reinforcers. However, primary reinforcers don't always reinforce. For example, food may not be a reinforcer to someone who has just completed a five-course meal.

Most behaviors in organizations are influenced by secondary reinforcers. A **secondary reinforcer** is an event that once had neutral value but has taken on some value (positive or negative) for an individual because of past experience. Money is an obvious example of a secondary reinforcer. Although it can't directly satisfy a basic human need, money has value because an individual can use it to purchase both necessities and discretionary items. Calvert, a Bethesda, Maryland, financial firm, groups its secondary reinforcers into three categories: *core benefits*, such as life insurance, sick leave, holiday pay, and a retirement savings plan; *optional benefits*, such as dental and eye-care coverage, and spending accounts for health and dependent care; and *other benefits*, such as tuition reimbursement, car pooling, and career planning.[15]

The Managing Change Competency feature on page 109 highlights the use of secondary reinforcers by Columbia Medical Center of Plano (Texas) to improve the attendance and cut down turnover of its housekeeping employees.

Principles of Positive Reinforcement. Several factors influence the effectiveness of positive reinforcement. These factors can be thought of loosely as principles because they help explain optimum reinforcement conditions.[16]

The **principle of contingent reinforcement** states that the reinforcer must be administered only if the desired behavior is performed. A reinforcer administered when the desired behavior has not been performed is ineffective. At Columbia Medical Center of Plano, the housekeeping employees received the $100 only if their performance was at 92 percent or greater and they had perfect attendance for a month.

COMPETENCY: MANAGING CHANGE

COLUMBIA MEDICAL CENTER OF PLANO

One of the main problems facing many hospitals is the high turnover rate of its housekeeping staff, which leads to patient dissatisfaction. Because patient satisfaction helps determine a hospital's overall performance, reducing housekeeping staff turnover is extremely important. At the Columbia Medical Center of Plano (Texas), employee turnover among the hospital's 130 housekeeping personnel during the past year averaged 12 percent each month. These employees make up 1,316 patients' beds a month or 15,792 a year, clean 1,474 restrooms every day, and distribute 20,410 nursing and medical uniforms a year. The cost of hiring a new housekeeping employee was $424, and replacing the people who left was costing the hospital $79,368 a year. Jack Gustin, the chief operating officer (COO), designed an attendance program to cut down employee turnover.

With unemployment levels low in Plano, the hospital's housekeeping employees have many alternative job opportunities, such as McDonald's, Home Depot, and Burger King, that pay a wage just above the minimum of $5.25 per hour. Gustin knew that, in order to improve the hospital's profitability, he had to lower housekeeping staff turnover to 40 percent per year from 144 percent.

He designed a reinforcement system that paid the 130 housekeeping employees a bonus of $100 for every month that they had perfect attendance and had a performance rating of 92 percent or better. The director of housekeeping and selected employees determined that 23 specific housekeeping tasks, such as vacuuming, dusting, and changing sheets, needed to be performed. The housekeeping staff was capable of performing all these tasks, and supervisors could observe employee behaviors while they were performing the tasks. The employees were notified that the new system would be started the next month and that employees should direct any questions about the system to Gustin.

By the end of the first month, monthly turnover was down to 8 percent, and by the end of the sixth month, it had leveled off at 3 percent. The decline in turnover not only saved the hospital money, but it also greatly improved the housekeeping staff's performance and immediately increased patient satisfaction.[17]

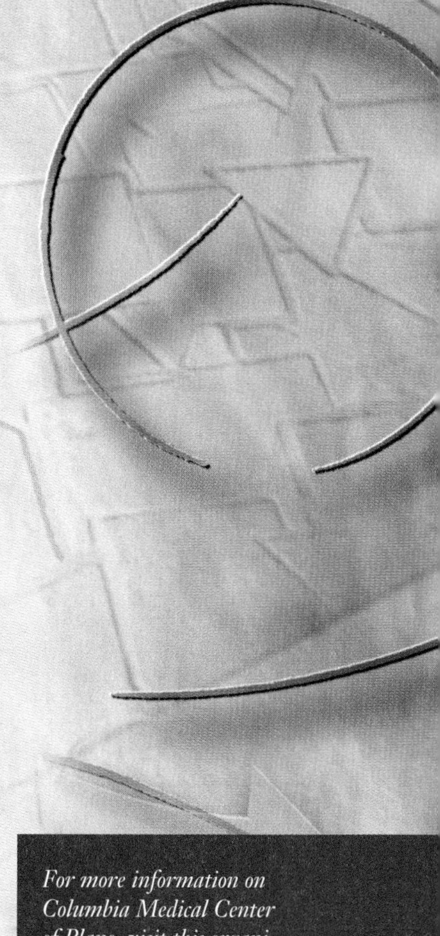

*For more information on Columbia Medical Center of Plano, visit this organization's home page at **www.columbia-hca.com.***

The **principle of immediate reinforcement** states that the reinforcer will be most effective if administered immediately after the desired behavior has occurred. The more time that elapses after the behavior occurs, the less effective the reinforcer will be. At Columbia Medical Center of Plano, the reinforcer ($100) was paid monthly.

The **principle of reinforcement size** states that the larger the amount of reinforcer delivered after the desired behavior, the more effect the reinforcer will have on the frequency of the desired behavior. The amount, or size, of the reinforcer is relative. A reinforcer that may be significant to one person may be insignificant to another person. Thus the size of the reinforcer must be determined in relation both to the behavior and the individual. For housekeepers at Columbia Medical Center of Plano, the $100 was a significant amount of money.

The **principle of reinforcement deprivation** states that the more a person is deprived of the reinforcer, the greater effect it will have on the future occurrence of the desired behavior. However, if an individual recently has had enough of a reinforcer and is satisfied, the reinforcer will have less effect.

Organizational Rewards

Although the material rewards—salary, bonuses, fringe benefits, and so on—that organizations commonly use are obvious, most organizations also offer a wide range of other rewards, many of which aren't immediately apparent. They include verbal approval, assignment to desired tasks, improved working conditions, and extra time off. At Toyota's Camry assembly plant in Georgetown, Kentucky, management rewards employees for *kaizens*. A **kaizen** is a suggestion that results in safety, cost, or quality improvements.[18] The awards are distributed equally among all members of a team. The awards are not cash payments; rather, they are gift certificates redeemable at local retail stores. Toyota learned that an award that could be shared by the employees' families was valued more than extra money in the paycheck. These awards instill pride and encourage other employees to scramble for new ideas and products in the hope that they, too, will receive them. In addition, self-administered rewards are important. For example, self-congratulation for accomplishing a particularly difficult assignment can be an important personal reinforcer. Table 4.3 contains an extensive list of organizational rewards. Remember, however, that such rewards will act as reinforcers only if the individuals receiving them find them desirable or pleasing.

The pressure to do business globally has forced organizations to develop reward systems that appeal to employees in various countries. As the Managing Across Cultures Competency feature on page 111 indicates, the success of Amway in Hungary rests on the enthusiasm of its employees to become part of a market economy to improve their standard of living.

Table 4.3

Rewards Used by Organizations

MATERIAL REWARDS	SUPPLEMENTAL BENEFITS	STATUS SYMBOLS
Pay	Company automobiles	Corner offices
Pay raises	Health insurance plans	Offices with windows
Stock options	Pension contributions	Carpeting
Profit sharing	Vacation and sick leave	Drapes
Deferred compensation	Recreation facilities	Paintings
Bonuses/bonus plans	Child-care support	Watches
Incentive plans	Club privileges	Rings
Expense accounts	Parental leave	Private restrooms

SOCIAL/ INTERPERSONAL REWARDS	REWARDS FROM THE TASK	SELF-ADMINISTERED REWARDS
Praise	Sense of Achievement	Self-congratulation
Developmental feedback	Jobs with more responsibility	Self-recognition
Smiles, pats on the back, and other nonverbal signals	Job autonomy/self-direction	Self-praise
Requests for suggestions	Performing important tasks	Self-development through expanded knowledge/skills
Invitations to coffee or lunch		Greater sense of self-worth
Wall plaques		

COMPETENCY: MANAGING ACROSS CULTURES

AMWAY IN HUNGARY

The person transferred from Atlanta, Georgia, by Coca-Cola to Budapest, Hungary, need not feel deprived of favorite products from U.S.-based firms. Avon Products and Mary Kay have set up shops to sell cosmetics, Herbalife International to sell vitamins, and Tupperware to sell Tupperware products. These firms sell products to distributors, who not only sell the products but also recruit people to sell them. The distributors in Amway's structure receive benefits not only from their own sales, but also from the sales of those people they recruit, who in turn can recruit more people.

Amway has more than 95,000 sales promoters, close to 1 percent of Hungary's population, who sold more than $40 million worth of merchandise, including soap, toiletries, knives, pots, and cosmetics. They're tenacious and take their jobs very seriously. They attend Amway conventions and seminars, listen to Amway motivational tapes, watch Amway sales videos, and attend Amway's leadership training.

Amway's incentives for high sales are a key to its success. Where a top factory worker once was rewarded with her name in a socialist newsletter, a plaque, and a holiday at one of the state's resorts, a top Amway sales promoter is now rewarded with her name in *Anagram*, Amway's monthly magazine, a handsome plaque, and a holiday at one of the company's convention sites, such as London, Paris, or Rome. Of course, a big check comes with the perks. The top 325 sales promoters in Hungary make at least $500 per month. With average Hungarian salaries at $200 per month, many people want to join Amway.[19]

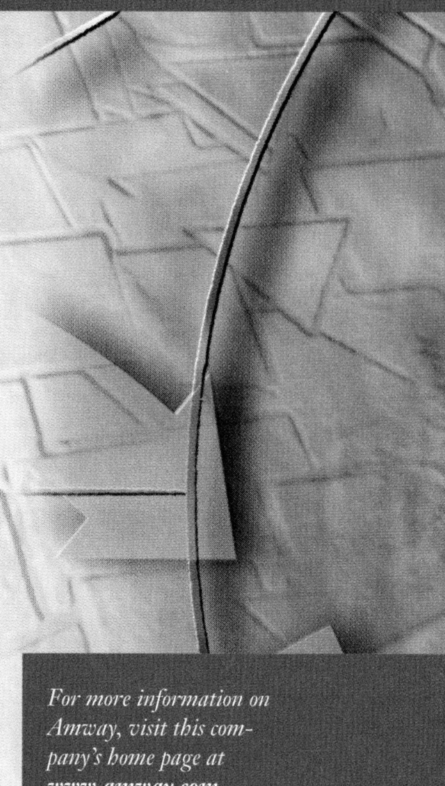

For more information on Amway, visit this company's home page at www.amway.com.

NEGATIVE REINFORCEMENT

In **negative reinforcement** (see Figure 4.4), an unpleasant event that precedes the employee behavior is removed when the desired behavior occurs. This procedure increases the likelihood that the desired behavior will occur. Negative reinforcement is sometimes confused with punishment because both use unpleasant events to influence behavior. However, negative reinforcement is used to increase the frequency of a desired behavior, whereas punishment is used to decrease the frequency of an undesired behavior.

Managers and team members frequently use negative reinforcement when an employee hasn't done something that is necessary or desired. For example, air-traffic controllers want the capability to activate a blinking light and a loud buzzer in the cockpits of planes that come too close to each other. The air-traffic controllers wouldn't shut these devices off until the planes moved farther apart. This type of procedure is called **escape learning** because the pilots begin to move their planes away from each other in order to escape the light and buzzer. In escape learning, an unpleasant event occurs until an employee performs a behavior, or escape response, to terminate it.

Avoidance is closely related to escape. In **avoidance learning,** a person prevents an unpleasant event from occurring by completing the proper behavior. For example, after several frustrating encounters with a computer program, you will learn the commands needed to avoid the computer's error messages. Escape and avoidance are both types of negative reinforcement that increase desired behaviors and remove unpleasant events.

Omission

Omission is the removal of all reinforcing events. Whereas reinforcement increases the frequency of a desirable behavior, omission decreases the frequency and eventually extinguishes an undesirable behavior (see Figure 4.4). Managers use omission to reduce undesirable employee behaviors that prevent achievement of organizational goals. The omission procedure consists of three steps:

1. identifying the behavior to be reduced or eliminated,
2. identifying the reinforcer that maintains the behavior, and
3. stopping the reinforcer.

Omission is a useful technique for reducing and eventually eliminating behaviors that disrupt normal workflow. For example, a team reinforces the disruptive behavior of a member by laughing at the behavior. When the team stops laughing (the reinforcer), the disruptive behavior will diminish and ultimately stop.

Omission can also be regarded as a failure to reinforce a behavior positively. In this regard, the omission of behaviors may be accidental. If managers fail to reinforce desirable behaviors, they may be using omission without recognizing it. As a result, the frequency of desirable behaviors may inadvertently decrease.

Omission may effectively decrease undesirable employee behavior, but it doesn't automatically replace the undesirable behavior with desirable behavior. Often when omission is stopped, the undesirable behavior will return if alternative behaviors haven't been developed. Therefore, when omission is used, it should be combined with other methods of reinforcement to develop the desired behaviors.

Punishment

Punishment (see Figure 4.4) is an unpleasant event that follows a behavior and decreases its frequency. As in positive reinforcement, a punishment may include a specific antecedent that cues the employee that a consequence (punisher) will follow a specific behavior. Whereas a positive contingency of reinforcement encourages the frequency of a desired behavior, a contingency of punishment decreases the frequency of an undesired behavior.

To qualify as a punisher, an event must decrease the undesirable behavior. Just because an event is thought of as unpleasant, it isn't necessarily a punisher. The event must actually reduce or stop the undesired behavior before it can be defined as a punisher.

Organizations typically use several types of unpleasant events to punish individuals. Material consequences for failure to perform adequately include a cut in pay, a disciplinary suspension without pay, a demotion, or a transfer to a dead-end job. The final punishment is the firing of an employee for failure to perform. In general, organizations reserve the use of unpleasant material events for cases of serious behavior problems.

Interpersonal punishers are used extensively. They include a manager's oral reprimand of an employee for unacceptable behavior and nonverbal punishers such as frowns, grunts, and aggressive body language. Certain tasks themselves can be unpleasant. The fatigue that follows hard physical labor can be considered a punisher, as can harsh or dirty working conditions. However, care must be exercised in labeling a punisher. In some fields and to some employees, harsh or dirty working conditions may be considered as just something that goes with the job.

The principles of positive reinforcement discussed earlier have equivalents in punishment. For maximum effectiveness, a punisher should be directly linked to the undesirable behavior (principle of contingent punishment); the punisher should be administered immediately (principle of immediate punishment); and, in general, the greater the size of the punisher, the stronger will be the effect on the undesirable behavior (principle of punishment size).

Negative Effects of Punishment. An argument against the use of punishment is the chance that it will have negative effects, especially over long or sustained periods of time. Even though punishment may stop an undesirable employee behavior, the potential negative consequences may be greater than the original undesirable behavior. Figure 4.5 illustrates some potential negative effects of punishment.

Punishment may cause undesirable emotional reactions.[20] An employee who has been reprimanded for staying on break too long may react with anger toward the manager and the organization. Such reactions may lead to behavior detrimental to the organization. Sabotage, for example, typically is a result of a punishment-oriented management system.

Punishment frequently leads only to short-term suppression of the undesirable behavior, rather than to its elimination. Thus suppression of an undesirable behavior over a long period of time usually requires continued and, perhaps, increasingly severe punishment. Another problem is that control of the undesirable behavior becomes contingent on the manager's presence. When the manager isn't around, the undesirable employee behavior is likely to recur.

In addition, the punished individual may try to avoid or escape the situation. From an organizational viewpoint, this reaction may be unacceptable if an employee avoids a particular, essential task. High absenteeism is a form of avoidance that is likely to occur when punishment is used frequently. Quitting is the employee's final form of escape, and organizations that depend on punishment are likely to have high rates of employee turnover. Some turnover is desirable, but excessive turnover is damaging to an organization. Recruitment and training are costly, and competent, high-performing employees are more likely to become frustrated and leave.

Figure 4.5 **Potential Negative Effects of Punishment**

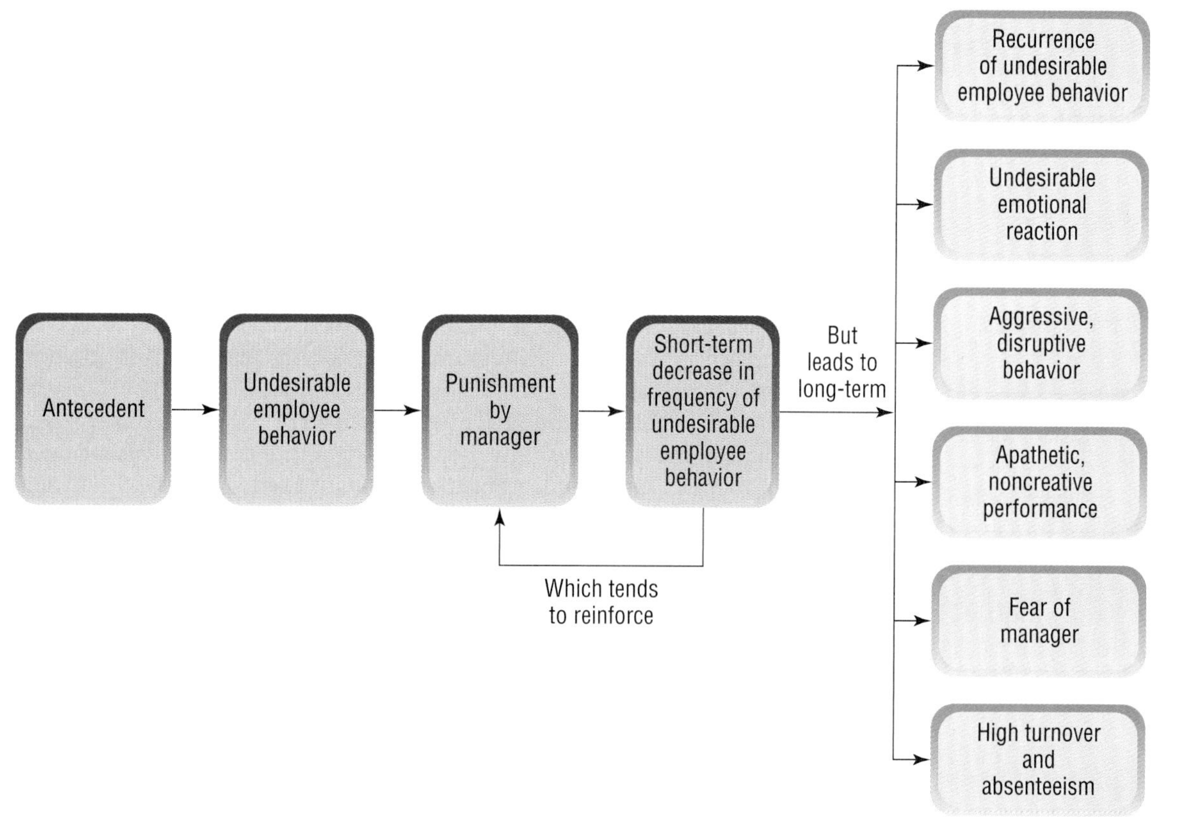

Punishment suppresses employee initiative and flexibility. Reacting to punishment, many an employee has said, I'm going to do just what I'm told and nothing more. Such an attitude is undesirable because organizations depend on the personal initiative and creativity that individual employees bring to their jobs. Overusing punishment produces apathetic employees, who are not an asset to an organization. Sustained punishment can also lead to low self-esteem. Low self-esteem, in turn, undermines the employee's self-confidence, which is necessary for performing most jobs (see Chapter 2).

Punishment produces a conditioned fear of management. That is, employees develop a general fear of punishment-oriented managers. Such managers become an environmental cue, indicating to employees the probability that an aversive event will occur. If operations require frequent, normal, and positive interaction between employee and manager, the situation can quickly become intolerable. Responses to fear, such as "hiding" or reluctance to communicate with a manager, may well hinder employee performance.

A manager may rely on punishment because it often produces fast results in the short run. In essence, the manager is reinforced for using punishment because the approach produces an immediate change in an employee's behavior. That may cause the manager to ignore punishment's long-term detrimental effects, which can be cumulative. Although a few incidents of punishment may not produce negative effects, its long-term, sustained use most often results in negative outcomes for the organization.

Effective Use of Punishment. Positive reinforcement is more effective than punishment over the long run. Effectively used, however, punishment does have an appropriate place in management. The most common form of punishment in organizations is the oral reprimand. It is intended to diminish or stop an undesirable employee behavior. An old rule of thumb is: Praise in public; punish in private. Private punishment establishes a different type of contingency of reinforcement than public punishment. In general, a private reprimand can be constructive and informative. A public reprimand is likely to have negative effects because the person has been embarrassed in front of his or her peers.

Oral reprimands should never be given about behavior in general and especially never about a so-called bad attitude. An effective reprimand pinpoints and specifically describes the undesirable behavior to be avoided in the future. It focuses on the target behavior and avoids threatening the employee's self-image. The effective reprimand punishes specific undesirable behavior, not the person. Behavior is easier to change than the person.

Punishment (by definition) trains a person in what not to do, not in what to do. Therefore a manager must specify an alternative behavior to the employee. When the employee performs the desired alternative behavior, the manager must then reinforce that behavior positively.

Finally, managers should strike an appropriate balance between the use of pleasant and unpleasant events. The absolute number of unpleasant events isn't important, but the ratio of pleasant to unpleasant events is. When a manager uses positive reinforcement frequently, an occasional deserved punishment can be quite effective. However, if a manager never uses positive reinforcement and relies entirely on punishment, the long-run negative effects are likely to counteract any short-term benefits. Positive management procedures should dominate in any well-run organization.

John Huberman, a Canadian psychologist, began promoting the idea of positive discipline in the mid 1960s, but it wasn't until the 1970s when Richard Grote introduced positive discipline at Frito-Lay that the idea became widespread. Grote began searching for a better management technique after a customer discovered a vulgar message written by a disgruntled employee on a corn chip. Grote gave the employee a day off with pay and called it "positive discipline." **Positive discipline** emphasizes changing employee behaviors by reasoning rather than by imposing increasingly severe punishments.[21] Management's primary duty is to help all employees understand that the needs of the organization require certain standards of behavior and performance. A manager's task is to coach employees, issuing oral and then written reminders only when they fail to maintain behavioral and performance standards. It is the employee's responsibility to exercise self-discipline in achieving those standards. More than 200 companies, including AT&T, General Electric, New England General Electric, and Union Carbide, have used positive discipline to deal with problem employees and change undesirable employee behaviors. On the face of it, this approach sounds like a contradiction in terms. However, according to Richard Grote, positive discipline places the responsibility for behavioral change with the one person who can best change that behavior—the employee.

New England General Electric's program works as follows. An employee who comes to work late, does a sloppy job, or mistreats another employee gets an oral reminder about the behavior rather than a written reprimand. If the undesirable behavior persists, the employee is issued a written reminder. If the behavior still persists, the employee is then suspended with pay for a day, called a "decision-making day." The purpose of the day is for the employee to decide whether to conform to the standards.

This procedure accomplishes several things. First, it communicates to the employee that the organization is serious about the matter. Second, it sends a signal to other employees who have been flirting with the idea of challenging the standards that the organization doesn't put up with unacceptable behavior. Finally, the suspension provides tangible evidence that the employee's job is at risk.

New England General Electric's approach has been very successful. More than 85 percent of the employees going through the positive discipline program have changed their behaviors and stayed with the organization. Employees that don't change their behaviors are fired.[22]

Using Contingencies of Reinforcement

For a positive reinforcer to cause an employee to repeat a desired behavior, it must have value to that employee. If the employee is consistently on time, the manager or team leader positively reinforces this behavior by complimenting the employee. But, if the employee has been reprimanded in the past for coming to work late and then reports to work on time, the manager or team leader uses negative reinforcement and refrains from saying anything to embarrass the employee. The employee is expected to learn to avoid these unpleasant comments by coming to work on time.

If the employee continues to come to work late, the manager or team leader can use either omission or punishment to try to stop this undesirable behavior. The team leader who chooses omission doesn't praise the tardy employee but simply ignores the employee. The use of punishment may include reprimanding, fining, or suspending—and ultimately firing—the employee if the behavior persists.

The following guidelines are recommended for using contingencies of reinforcement in the work setting.

- Do not reward all employees in the same way.
- Carefully examine the consequences of nonactions as well as actions.
- Let employees know which behaviors will be reinforced.
- Let employees know what they are doing wrong.
- Don't punish employees in front of others.
- Make the response equal to the behavior by not cheating workers out of their just rewards.[23]

Learning Objective:

3. List the four schedules of reinforcement and explain when each is effective.

SCHEDULES OF REINFORCEMENT

Schedules of reinforcement determine when reinforcers are applied. Deliberately or not, reinforcement is always delivered according to some schedule.[24]

CONTINUOUS AND INTERMITTENT REINFORCEMENT

Continuous reinforcement means that the behavior is reinforced each time it occurs and is the simplest schedule of reinforcement. An example of continuous reinforcement is dropping coins in a soft-drink vending machine. The behavior of inserting coins is reinforced (on a continuous schedule) by the machine delivering a can of soda (most of the time!). Verbal recognition and material rewards generally are not delivered on a continuous schedule in organizations. In organizations such as Mary Kay Cosmetics, Tupperware, and Amway, salespeople are paid a commission for each sale, usually earning commissions of 25 to 50 percent of sales. Although the reinforcer (money) is not paid immediately, people track their sales immediately and quickly convert sales into amounts owed to them by the organization. However, most managers who supervise employees other than salespeople seldom have the opportunity to deliver a reinforcer every time their employees demonstrate a desired behavior. Therefore behavior typically is reinforced intermittently.

Intermittent reinforcement refers to a reinforcer being delivered after some, but not every, occurrence of the desired behavior. Intermittent reinforcement can be subdivided into (1) interval and ratio schedules and (2) fixed and variable schedules. In an **interval schedule,** reinforcers are delivered after a certain amount of time has passed. In a **ratio schedule,** reinforcers are delivered after a certain number of behaviors have been performed. These two schedules can be further subdivided into fixed (not changing) or variable (constantly changing) schedules. Thus there are four primary types of intermittent schedules: fixed interval, variable interval, fixed ratio, and variable ratio.[25]

FIXED INTERVAL SCHEDULE

In a **fixed interval schedule,** a constant amount of time must pass before a reinforcer is provided. The first desired behavior to occur after the interval has elapsed is reinforced. For example, in a fixed interval, 1-hour schedule, the first desired behavior that occurs after an hour has elapsed is reinforced.

Administering rewards according to this type of schedule tends to produce an uneven pattern of behavior. Prior to the reinforcement, the behavior is frequent and energetic. Immediately following the reinforcement, the behavior becomes less frequent and energetic. Why? Because the individual rather quickly figures out that another reward won't immediately follow the last one until a certain amount of time has passed. A common example of administering rewards on a fixed interval schedule is the payment of employees weekly, biweekly, or monthly. That is, monetary reinforcement comes regularly at the end of a specific period of time. Such time intervals, unfortunately, are generally too long to be an effective form of reinforcement for newly acquired work-related behavior.

VARIABLE INTERVAL SCHEDULE

A **variable interval schedule** represents changes in the amount of time between reinforcers. Jack Gustin, COO for the Columbia Medical Center of Plano (see the Managing Change Competency feature) used a variable interval schedule to observe the behaviors of housekeeping personnel. A person would receive $100 for a perfect attendance and a score above 92 percent on 23 performance indicators. To observe their behavior, Gustin announced to all housekeeping people that, during the month, he would make seven inspections at random times. During the first week, he observed and recorded the performance of employees on Tuesday between 3:00 and 4:00 P.M.

and Wednesday from 6:00 to 7:30 A.M. The following week, he made no observations. During the third week, he observed employees on Monday between 10:00 and 11:00 A.M. and then Friday from 12:00 to 1:45 P.M. During the fourth week, he observed employees on Monday between 8:00 and 9:00 P.M. and from 11:00 P.M. to 12:00 A.M., and Thursday from 2:00 to 3:30 P.M. If he didn't change his schedule, the employees would anticipate his tours and adjust their behaviors to get a reward.

Fixed Ratio Schedule

In a **fixed ratio schedule,** the desired behavior must occur a specified number of times before it is reinforced. Administering rewards under a fixed ratio schedule tends to produce a high response rate when the reinforcement is close, followed by periods of steady behavior. The employee soon determines that reinforcement is based on the number of responses and performs the responses as quickly as possible in order to receive the reward. The individual piece-rate system used in many manufacturing plants is an example of such a schedule. Great North American, Answer First, and other telemarketers use this schedule of reinforcement.

Variable Ratio Schedule

In a **variable ratio schedule,** a certain number of desired behaviors must occur before the reinforcer is delivered, but the number of behaviors varies around some average. Managers frequently use a variable ratio schedule with praise and recognition. For example, team leaders at Sprint vary the frequency of reinforcement when they give employees verbal approval for desired behaviors. Gambling casinos, such as Bally's and Harrah's, among others, and state lotteries use this schedule of reinforcement to lure patrons to shoot craps, play poker, feed slot machines, and buy lottery tickets. Patrons win, but not on any regular basis.

Comparison of Intermittent Reinforcement Schedules

Table 4.4 summarizes the four types of intermittent reinforcement schedules. Which is superior? The ratio schedules—fixed or variable—usually lead to better performance than do interval schedules. The reason is that ratio schedules are more closely related to the occurrence of desired behaviors than are interval schedules, which are based on the passage of time.[26]

Table 4.4

Comparison of Schedules of Reinforcement

SCHEDULE	FORM OF REWARD AND EXAMPLE	INFLUENCE ON PERFORMANCE	EFFECTS ON BEHAVIOR
Fixed interval	Reward on fixed time basis: weekly or monthly paycheck	Leads to average and irregular performance	Fast extinction of behavior
Fixed ratio	Reward tied to specific number of responses: piece-rate pay system	Leads quickly to very high and stable performance	Moderately fast extinction of behavior
Variable interval	Reward given after varying periods of time: unannounced inspections or appraisals and rewards given randomly each month	Leads to moderately high and stable performance	Slow extinction of behavior
Variable ratio	Reward given for some behaviors: sales bonus tied to selling X accounts but X constantly changing around some mean	Leads to very high performance	Very slow extinction of behavior

Learning Objective:

4. Describe the processes and principles of behavioral modification.

BEHAVIORAL MODIFICATION

Behavioral modification refers to processes and principles that are based on operant conditioning. Figure 4.6 illustrates the processes of behavioral modification.[27]

Pinpointing Relevant Behaviors

Not all employee behaviors are desirable or undesirable from a managerial viewpoint. In fact, many behaviors are neutral; they neither add to nor detract from the achievement of organizational goals. Thus the first and most important step in applying behavioral modification principles is to identify the behaviors that have a significant impact on an employee's overall performance. The manager should then concentrate on them, trying to increase desirable behaviors and decrease undesirable behaviors. Pinpointing relevant behaviors consists of three activities:

Figure 4.6 **Behavioral Modification Processes and Principles**

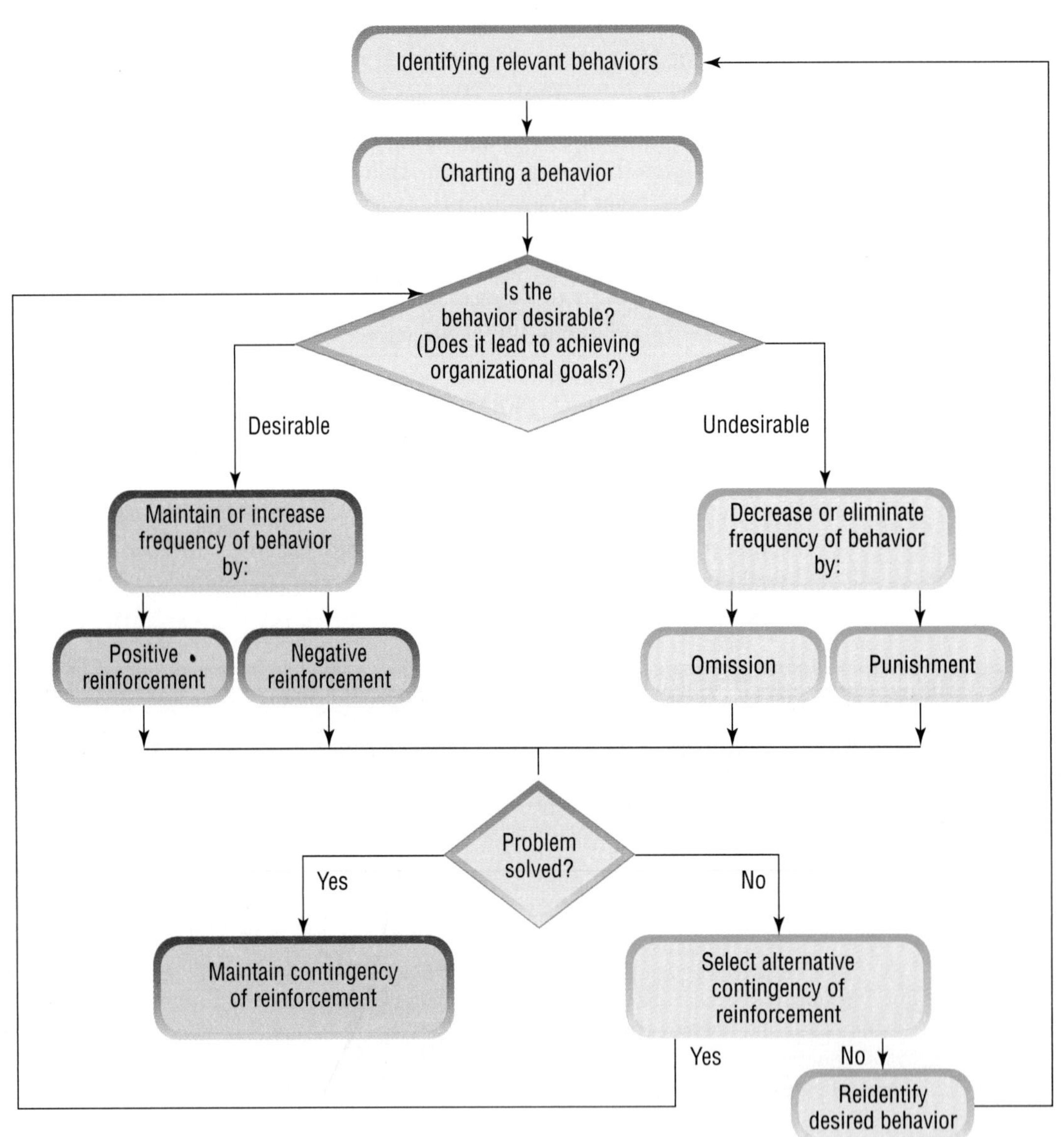

1. observing the behaviors,
2. measuring the behaviors, and
3. describing the situation in which the behaviors occur.

Training is often necessary to enable managers to pinpoint behaviors. Frequently, the untrained manager confuses employee attitudes, feelings, and values with behaviors.

Charting Behavior

One of the ways managers track employee behaviors is by **charting** or measuring them over time. Figure 4.7 shows how Veronica Wiredu, Minister of Mines and Energy at Accra, Ghana, charts employee lateness. The horizontal axis reflects time in months. The vertical axis represents the number of employees who are late. Each bar on the chart represents the measurement of the employee's lateness during a 1-month period.

An employee behavior chart usually is divided into at least two periods: the baseline period and the intervention period. During the baseline period behavior is measured before any attempt is made to change it. In this case, the baseline period covers the months of June through September. Observations are made by an individual without the employee's knowledge in order to get an accurate measurement.

During the intervention period, the employee's behavior is measured after one or more contingencies of reinforcement—positive reinforcement, negative reinforcement, omission, or punishment—is used. In this case, Wiredu used a positive reinforcement (praise) and an intervention period of October through March. During this time the individual might be shown the chart, providing a type of feedback. Sometimes feedback by itself is enough to cause a change in behavior. However, a reward or penalty frequently accompanies feedback and may have a greater effect on the behavior. As shown in Figure 4.7, positive reinforcement reduced the amount of lateness significantly during the period October through March.

Figure 4.7 **Employee Behavior Chart**

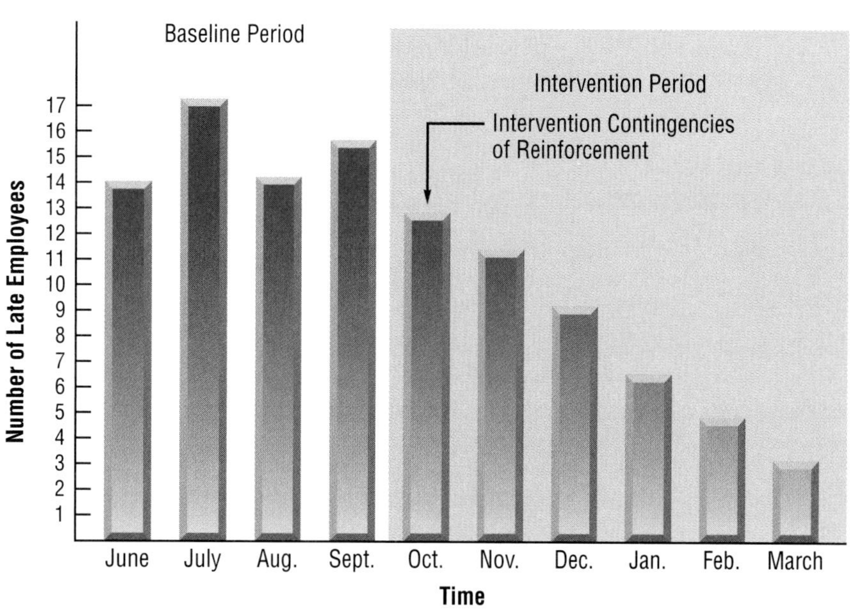

Source: Interview with V. Wiredu, Minister of Mines and Energy, Accra, Ghana. Pennsylvania State University Program for Strategic Leadership, October 1998.

Charting has two main features. First, observations during the baseline period show the frequency of certain behaviors. Sometimes charting a behavior reveals that the behavior isn't as much of a problem as originally thought. Second, by charting through the intervention period, the manager can determine whether the intervention strategy is working. Charting then becomes an evaluation method. Sometimes a chart reveals no change in behavior, which means that the intervention wasn't successful.

Choosing a Contingency of Reinforcement

After a behavior has been identified and charted for a baseline period, a contingency of reinforcement aimed at changing the behavior should be selected. The manager must decide which type of reward is most likely to have the desired effect on the employee's behavior. Rewards should be used to increase or maintain desirable behaviors. Obviously, positive reinforcement is the first alternative to consider. The other alternative is to apply negative reinforcement. Wiredu used negative reinforcement by lecturing a person each time he or she was late. As shown in Figure 4.7, this contingency of reinforcement was successful in decreasing lateness.

If the behavior is undesirable, the manager's goal will be to reduce or eliminate it. Either punishment or omission would be appropriate. A combination of reinforcement contingencies to extinguish undesirable behaviors while reinforcing (increasing) other, desirable behaviors also might be used.

Problem Solved?

Experience gives the effective manager a valuable tool in choosing contingencies of reinforcement in attempting to modify employee behaviors. The ability to generalize from similar past situations or from similar incidents with the same employee is essential. If the manager is successful in affecting the target behavior, the contingency of reinforcement must be maintained for lasting results.

There is no guarantee that a chosen contingency of reinforcement will be effective. Every manager or team leader encounters situations in which the first intervention tactic fails. Then a different contingency of reinforcement should be tried or the desired behavior should be redefined. In either case, she must again go through the various steps of the procedure. However, an evaluation of the previous effort can simplify this procedure. She may conclude that a different form of positive reinforcement is needed and use it in an attempt to increase the desired behavior. She might also try a different contingency of reinforcement—for instance, a change from positive to negative reinforcement. Or she might try a combination of contingencies of reinforcement.

Changing behavior may be extremely difficult because people often resist change. An excellent example of the difficulties involved in changing behavior comes from the phenomenon of dieting. Over the past decade, millions of people have tried various weight-loss programs, making dieting a $40 billion per year industry.[28] Obesity is on the rise, and more than 55 percent of all adults in the United States are estimated to be overweight, up from 25 percent in 1980. Although the big three—Weight Watchers, Nutri/System, and Jenny Craig—have reported losses in sales to Susan Powter Centers and supermarkets, which now stock their shelves with low-calorie cuisine, it is still a huge business. Most diet centers use principles of behavioral modification to change their customers' eating behaviors and, as a result, help them to lose weight. Unfortunately, government studies indicate that most dieters regain two-thirds of the weight lost within a year and that 95 percent of the people who go to a diet center fail to maintain their lower weight. *Consumer Reports* asked more than 19,000 readers who had joined a diet program to rate their satisfaction with it. Based on the responses received, the magazine concluded that people generally were dissatisfied with weight-loss programs. Respondents protested that the programs cost more than they were led to believe and that consultants pressured them to buy their products and to keep coming back.

Using the principles of behavioral modification illustrated in Figure 4.6, a weight-loss center weighs and measures the dieter before the dieter starts the program. The dieter and a counselor jointly establish weight-loss goals. Usually, two or more pounds drop off the first week because early losses are water, not fat. This quick loss gives the dieter positive reinforcement that the diet is working. The dieter normally buys food substitute products from the center, which typically accounts for 85 percent of the center's revenues. At Jenny Craig the typical female dieter wants to lose 30 pounds. At a rate of 1.5 to 2 pounds a week, the food substitute bill would be more than $900. As the dieter loses additional weight, she receives counseling on types of food to eat, attends exercise sessions, and receives motivational reinforcements, including water bottles, T-shirts, and gym bags, among others. The positive reinforcement received from the loss of weight and the counselor encourages the dieter to buy additional food substitutes and enroll in other activities sponsored by the diet center. The diet center's counselor charts progress and celebrates every ounce and inch lost with the dieter.

Internationally, after more than a decade, organizations in the Commonwealth of Independent States and Eastern Europe continue to struggle to become more effective competitors in the global marketplace. Many such organizations have tried various tactics, including use of the principles of behavioral modification, to improve performance. The Managing Communication Competency feature on page 122 highlights how organizations have changed their communication channels to improve their performance.

Behavioral Modification Issues

Three issues are involved in the use of behavioral modification processes and principles: individual differences, group norms, and ethical considerations.[29]

Individual Differences. Behavioral modification often ignores individual differences in needs, values, abilities, and desires. What is reinforcing to one person may not be to another, but effective managers or team leaders can account for individual differences in two ways. First, they can try to select and hire employees who value the rewards offered by the organization, as Joe Salatino does at Great North American. Proper employee selection can lead to hiring people whose needs most closely match the reinforcers provided by the organization. Although not easy to do, this approach can be an effective way for managers to take individual differences into account.

Second, managers or team leaders can allow employees to participate in determining their rewards. Thus, if the present contingencies of reinforcement are ineffective, employees can be asked to state what they would do to correct the situation. This method allows employees to have a greater voice in designing their work environment and should lead to greater employee involvement. However, if this method is used simply to exploit employees, they will look for ways to get around it.

Group Norms. When employees believe that management is trying to exploit them, group norms emerge to control the degree of cooperation with management. This control typically takes the form of restricting output. When this situation arises, implementation of a program (particularly one that relies on praise and other nonmaterial rewards) is likely to meet with stiff resistance from the work group. Group members will feel little need to cooperate with management because this behavior will likely lead to pressure to increase productivity, without a corresponding increase in pay or other rewards.

The power of group norms can reduce the effectiveness of most reward systems. When employees and managers have a history of distrust, the principles covered in this chapter probably won't help. First, trust must be forged between employee and manager. Once that has been done, these principles have a better chance of succeeding.

COMPETENCY: MANAGING COMMUNICATION

MANUFACTURING IN EASTERN EUROPE

A team of researchers from the University of Nebraska has been working with textile managers from Albania, Macedonia, and Russia, using principles of behavioral modification for the past decade. The team found that in many countries, once an acceptable wage has been achieved, social reinforcers are as effective as monetary reinforcers. Using the principles of behavioral modification, the researchers identified conditions that needed to be changed in the production of clothing, including loom downtime, poor fabric quality, scrap, and absenteeism. Each of the behaviors causing these conditions was carefully charted over many months and the consequences, such as lost productivity and increased unit costs, were recorded. Three types of intervention were used. One group was given monetary reinforcers when its performance improved; a second group was given social reinforcers, such as attention and recognition by management; and the third group received a combination of the first two reinforcers. Although monetary reinforcers had a greater positive impact on behavior than did nonmonetary reinforcers, the greatest change in behavior occurred when monetary reinforcers were used along with attention and recognition. The social reinforcer was not insincere praise (a pat on the back, or a "thanks for coming to work on time") or the old communist approach of pinning medals on workers' chests, but rather communicating praise for specific behaviors. During the former communist regime, little attention was paid to employee suggestions, and political repercussions against employees who offered suggestions often followed. As a result, managers needed to be trained in how to deliver social rewards. Attention and recognition were given one-on-one by a manager who had actually observed the behavior. Praise included comments such as: "I noticed that you were the only one who made it to work on time during the bad snowstorm"; or "I saw how you handled that customer's problem. She has a big account with us"; or "I saw that you stayed after quitting time to finish that vital report that I gave you at the last minute. That really helped me out with my boss the next morning." When managers deliberately and systematically communicated attention and recognition as responses contingent on key performance behaviors, worker performance improved. As a result, communicating praise to workers who have performed well is now widely used to improve employee productivity.[30]

Ethical Considerations. Behavioral modification has stirred some controversy in terms of ethics, with criticisms centering on a person's freedom and dignity. According to proponents of behavioral modification, the way to manage people effectively is to establish control systems that shape their behaviors. The proponents recognize that behaviors are shaped by their consequences and that managers should administer rewards in ways that promote desirable behaviors from the organization's point of view. They don't worry too much about individuals' freedom to choose which behaviors to engage in to satisfy their own desires and wants.

Others argue the ethics of someone deciding what is good or beneficial for other people and having enough power to manipulate or impose that decision. They question what manipulation does to a person's sense of self-worth. Promising employees a reward for doing a task they already enjoy doing can lead them to see the reward as the motivation for performing the task, thus undermining their enjoyment of the task. A person may think, If I have to be bribed or forced into doing this, then I must not enjoy doing the task for its own sake. In essence, is it better for an individual to enjoy a task than for managers to manipulate employees into performing it? Furthermore, instead of the widespread use of punishment, wouldn't the use of positive reinforcers be more humanitarian?

Managers have some other problems to consider as well. Employees may engage in only those behaviors that are being rewarded or measured and ignore those that aren't being rewarded or measured. For example, managers may reward the quantity of work produced and overlook its quality. Or they may rely on measuring employee tardiness or absenteeism, both of which can easily be measured, rather than try to evaluate their ideas and other contributions to the work being done, which often is difficult to do. Under such conditions, employees will show up on time for work but the quality of their work probably will suffer.

Many managers feel societal pressures to reinforce behaviors that they really don't desire themselves. This emphasis may lead employees to engage in behaviors, such as participating in recycling campaigns or carpools, even though such behaviors may interfere with the employees' effectiveness.

CHAPTER SUMMARY

1. Explain the differences between classical, operant, and social cognitive theory.

Classical conditioning began with Pavlov's work. He started a metronome (conditioning stimulus) at the same time food was placed in the dog's mouth (unconditioned stimulus). Quickly the sound of the metronome alone evoked salivation. Operant conditioning learning focuses on the effects of reinforcement on desirable and undesirable behaviors. Changes in behavior result from the consequences of previous behavior. People tend to repeat a behavior that leads to a pleasant result and not to repeat a behavior that leads to an unpleasant result. In short, when a behavior is reinforced, it is repeated; when it is punished or not reinforced, it is not repeated. Social cognitive theory focuses on people learning new behaviors by observing others and then modeling their own behaviors on those observed. The five factors emphasized in social cognitive theory are symbolizing, forethought, vicarious learning, self-control, and self-efficacy.

2. Describe the contingencies of reinforcement.

There are two types of reinforcement: (1) positive reinforcement, which increases a desirable behavior because the person is provided with a pleasurable outcome after the behavior has occurred; and (2) negative reinforcement, which also maintains the desirable behavior by presenting an unpleasant event before the behavior occurs and stopping the event when the behavior occurs. Both positive and negative reinforcement increase the frequency of a desirable behavior. Conversely, omission and punishment reduce the frequency of an undesirable behavior. Omission involves stopping everything that reinforces the behavior. A punisher is an unpleasant event that follows the behavior and reduces the probability that the behavior will be repeated.

3. List the four schedules of reinforcement and explain when each is effective.

There are four schedules of reinforcement. In the fixed interval schedule, the reward is given on a fixed time basis (e.g., a weekly or monthly paycheck). It is effective for maintaining a level of behavior. In the variable interval schedule, the reward is given around some average time during a specific period of time (e.g., the plant manager walking through the plant an average of five times every week). This schedule of reinforcement can maintain a high level of performance because employees do not know when the reinforcer will be delivered. The fixed ratio schedule ties rewards to certain outputs (e.g., a piece-rate system). This schedule maintains a steady level of behavior once the person has earned the reinforcer. In the variable ratio schedule, the reward is given around some mean, but the number of behaviors varies (as does a payoff from a slot machine). This schedule is the most powerful because both the number of desired behaviors and their rate change.

4. Describe the processes and principles of behavioral modification.

The processes and principles of behavior modification include pinpointing behaviors, charting these behaviors, and choosing a contingency of reinforcement to obtain desirable behaviors and stop undesirable behaviors. After a behavior has been identified and charted for a baseline period, a contingency of reinforcement aimed at changing the behavior is selected. Rewards should be used to increase desired behaviors and withheld to stop undesirable behaviors. Three issues surround the use of behavioral modification processes: individual differences, group norms, and ethical considerations.

KEY TERMS AND CONCEPTS

Antecedent
Aversive events
Avoidance learning
Behavioral modification
Charting
Classical conditioning
Consequence
Contingency of reinforcement
Continuous reinforcement
Empowerment
Escape learning
Fixed interval schedule
Fixed ratio schedule
Intermittent reinforcement
Interval schedule
Kaizen
Learning
Learning theory
Negative reinforcement
Omission
Operant conditioning
Positive discipline
Positive events
Positive reinforcement
Primary reinforcer
Principle of contingent reinforcement
Principle of immediate reinforcement
Principle of reinforcement deprivation
Principle of reinforcement size
Punishment
Ratio schedule
Reflexive behavior
Reinforcement
Reward
Secondary reinforcer
Self-control learning
Self-efficacy
Social cognitive theory
Variable interval schedule
Variable ratio schedule
Vicarious learning

DISCUSSION QUESTIONS

1. What principles of reinforcement did Great North American use?
2. Describe the basic differences between classical conditioning, the social cognitive theory, and the operant conditioning theory. Which type is most important for managers? Why?
3. How do producers of self-help videos use social cognitive theory to change a person's behavior?
4. How can a manager or a team raise an employee's level of self-efficacy?
5. Visit either a local health club or diet center and schedule an interview with the manager. What types of rewards does it give its members who achieve targeted goals? Does it use punishment?
6. Steven Kerr, vice president for executive education at General Electric, wrote an article entitled "On the Folly of Rewarding A While Hoping for B." The essence of the article is that organizations often unintentionally reward behaviors that they don't want to occur. Using this premise, what behavior(s) does Great North American reward that may have a negative impact on cooperation among its telemarketers?
7. How can a team leader use punishment effectively?
8. What ethical considerations should be addressed before management introduces a behavioral modification program in the workplace?

DEVELOPING COMPETENCIES

Competency: Managing Self —What Is Your Self-Efficacy?

The following questionnaire gives you a chance to gain insights into your self-efficacy in terms of achieving academic excellence. Please answer the following seven questions in the spaces provided, using the following 5-point scale. An interpretation of your score follows.

5 = Strongly agree 2 = Disagree
4 = Agree 1 = Strongly disagree
3 = Moderate

1. I am a good student. 5 4 3 2 1
2. It is difficult to maintain a study schedule. 5 4 3 2 1
3. I know the right things to do to improve my academic performance. 5 4 3 2 1
4. I find it difficult to convince my friends who have different viewpoints on studying than mine. 5 4 3 2 1
5. My temperament is not well suited to studying. 5 4 3 2 1
6. I am good at finding out what teachers want. 5 4 3 2 1
7. It is easy for me to get others to see my point of view. 5 4 3 2 1

Add your scores to questions 1, 3, 6, and 7. Enter that score here _____. For questions, 2, 4, and 5, reverse the scoring key. That is, if you answered question 2 as strongly agree, give yourself 1 point, agree is worth 2 points, and so on. Enter your score here for questions 2, 4, and 5 _____. Enter your combined score here _____. This is your *self-efficacy* score for academic achievement. If you scored between 28 and 35, you believe that you can achieve academic excellence. Scores lower than 18 indicate that you believe no matter how hard you try to achieve academic excellence, something may prevent you from reaching your desired level of performance. Scores between 19 and 27 indicate a moderate degree of self-efficacy. Your self-efficacy may vary with the course you are taking. In courses in your major, you may have greater self-efficacy than in those outside of your major.[31]

Competency: Managing Ethics—Medical Incentives

Members of Harris Methodist Health Plan, a 310,000 member health maintenance organization (HMO) in Dallas, Texas, sued the HMO because it fined primary care doctors (general practitioners, pediatricians, and internists) who wrote more prescriptions than their contracts allowed. Texas regulators found that most of Harris's compensation arrangement with physicians violated the law. Under Harris's contracts, the insurer pays its physicians a set percentage (ranging from 10 to 12.8 percent) of each member's monthly premium to cover all services that a person might need. Doctors who can keep their patients healthy and out of the office can make a profit. Like most HMOs, Harris offers bonuses to doctors who meet a predetermined budget for hospitalizations and referrals to specialists. Harris had a policy of firing physicians who wrote more prescriptions than their contracts allowed. In 1997, doctors spent $4.5 million over the limit, resulting in a loss to the HMO of $1.5 million. As a result, physicians stopped referring patients to a specialist and dropped writing prescriptions that had to be filled at the Harris pharmacy in order not to be fined and/or fired.

Richard Hubner, a primary care physician, sued the HMO because it withheld more than $8,000 from him because of deficits in his pharmacy budget. He contended that his patients needed drugs to return to their health and that he shouldn't be fined for helping patients. Kent Clay, an attorney for patients, is also suing the HMO for not referring patients to specialists because it is affecting the primary care physician's pocketbook. The HMO is accused of not providing quality care because this level of care affects the HMO's profitability and its profits are shared with all primary care physicians.[32]

Questions

1. What contingencies of reinforcement did Harris HMO adopt to pay its primary care physicians? How have these methods affected patient care?
2. What are some of the ethical dilemmas facing Harris HMO?
3. If you were the chief administrator of Harris HMO, what would you do to correct the problem?
4. What elements of the Managing Ethics Competency are represented in this case (see Chapter1)?

Competency: Managing Change—Westinghouse

At the Westinghouse plant in College Station, Texas, management was committed to develop a high-commitment culture that would motivate employees to feel a sense of responsibility for the electronic parts they were making. Employees worked in 8- to 12-person teams and tracked and monitored their own performance. All employees were on salary, and raises were based on performance. Thus workers who showed proficiency in various jobs could boost their pay significantly.

When the plant first opened, management's attendance goal was 98 percent. After approximately 18 months of operation, this attendance goal was not being achieved, although management didn't have a system in place to track attendance specifically. Managers believed that attendance was somewhere around 93 percent, with the industry average between 93 and 97 percent. Westinghouse management estimated that each 1 percentage-point drop in attendance cost the company an additional $80,000. Management believed that this figure, based solely on hiring temporary workers for the day, was conservative and didn't account for lower team productivity, increased scrap costs, lost customer orders, and the like.

A task force of managers and employees was formed to design and implement a process to monitor attendance and make suggestions for improvement. The group designed a program that its members hoped would motivate employees to meet or exceed a 97 percent attendance rate. Attendance performance was categorized as follows.

Level 1: Perfect (100%), with no make-up time.
Level 2: Good to excellent (97–100%), including make-up time.
Level 3: Needing improvement (95–96.9%), including make-up time.
Level 4: Unacceptable (below 95%).

Positive reinforcement was used at Levels 1 and 2. Perfect attendance for 1 month was rewarded by listing employee names in the Westinghouse newsletter; perfect attendance for the entire team led to its being mentioned in the local newspaper. Perfect attendance for 6 months brought a letter of commendation from the plant manager, a paid luncheon, and reserved parking privileges. Perfect attendance for a year brought a $100 gift certificate, letters of commendation from headquarters, listing the employee's name on plaques displayed in the plant, and reserved parking. For Level 2 attendance, longer amounts of time were needed to earn rewards. It took 3 months for an individual to have his or her name mentioned in the Westinghouse newspaper, 6 months for an employee to get a paid luncheon, and 1 year for an employee to receive a commendation from the department manager and receive a gift certificate for $50.

At Level 3, employees were verbally warned by their manager to improve their attendance. Steps to increase their attendance were discussed with the team leader and department manager. Employees in Level 3 had to develop an action plan to improve their attendance. A follow-up meeting at the end of 2 months was scheduled to evaluate their performance and/or revise their action plans.

At Level 4, additional verbal warnings were given; a formal document was prepared by the team leader and department manager and forwarded to the plant manager; and a person's pay was docked. Termination was discussed unless attendance improved to 97 percent within the next month.[33]

Questions

1. What contingencies of reinforcement did the task force recommend to improve attendance? What schedule(s) of reinforcement did it recommend?
2. Given these rewards, would you improve your attendance? If so, why? If not, why?
3. What do you think happened at the plant? Did attendance improve?
4. Using the concepts outlined in this chapter, support your answer.

REFERENCES

1. Adapted from Narum, B. Office supplier encourages employees with open style. *Dallas-Fort Worth Business Journal,* March 9, 1997, 14–15; Hall, C. High-intensity telemarketer turns up the volume. *Dallas Morning News,* November 16, 1997, 16–17.
2. Weiss, H. M. Learning theory and industrial and organizational psychology. In M. D. Dunnette and L. M. Hough (eds.), *Handbook of Industrial & Organizational Psychology,* 2nd ed. Palo Alto, Calif.: Consulting Psychologist Press, 1990, 170–221.
3. Kanfer, R. Motivation theory and industrial and organizational psychology. In M. D. Dunnette and L. M. Hough (eds.), *Handbook of Industrial & Organizational Psychology,* 2nd ed. Palo Alto, Calif.: Consulting Psychologist Press, 1990, 75–169.
4. Shimp, T. A., Stuart, E. W., and Engle, R. W. A program of classical conditioning experiments testing variations in the conditioned stimulus and context. *Journal of Consumer Research,* 1991, 18, 1–10.
5. Skinner, B. F. *About Behaviorism.* New York: Knopf, 1974; Martinko, M. J., and Fadil, P. Operant technologies: A theoretical foundation for organizational change and development. *Leadership & Organization Development Journal,* 1994, 15(5), 16–21.
6. For excellent overviews, see Bandura, A. *Social Learning Theory.* Englewood Cliffs, N.J.: Prentice-Hall, 1977; Bandura, A. *Social Foundations of Thought and Action.* Englewood Cliffs, N.J.: Prentice-Hall, 1986; Bandura, A. *Self-efficacy: The exercise of control.* Salt Lake City, Utah: W. H. Freeman, 1997.
7. Stajkovic, A. D., and Luthans, F. Social cognitive theory and self-efficacy: Going beyond traditional motivational and behavioral approaches. *Organizational Dynamics,* Spring 1998, 62–74; Stajkovic, A. D., and Luthans, F. Self-efficacy and work-related performance: A meta-analysis. *Psychological Bulletin,* 1998, 124, 240–261.
8. Spreitzer, G. M. Psychological empowerment in the workplace: Dimensions, measurement, and validation. *Academy of Management Journal,* 1995, 38, 1442–1465.
9. Stajkovic, A. D., and Luthans, F. Social cognitive theory and self-efficacy. *Psychological Bulletin,* 1998, 124, 240–262; O'Neill, B. S., and Mone, M. A. Investigating equity sensitivity as a moderator of relations between

self-efficacy and workplace attitudes. *Journal of Applied Psychology*, 1998, 83, 805–813.

10. Stajkovic, A. D., and Summer, S. Self-efficacy and causal attributions: Direct and reciprocal links. *Journal of Applied Social Psychology*, in press; Applebaum, S. H. Self-efficacy as a mediator of goal setting performance: Some human resource applications. *Journal of Managerial Psychology*, 1996, 11, 33–48.
11. Adapted from Kinni, T. B. *America's Best: Industry Week's Guide to World-Class Manufacturing Plants.* New York: John Wiley & Sons, 1996, 313–314; Cohen, J. The cost of wellness. *Management Review*, 1994, 83, 29–33.
12. Bandura, A. *Self-efficacy in changing societies.* New York: Cambridge University Press, 1997; Jex, S. M., and Bliese, P. D. Efficacy beliefs as a moderator of the impact of work-related stressors: A multilevel study. *Journal of Applied Psychology*, 1999, 84, 349–361; Parker, S. K. Enhancing role breadth self-efficacy: The roles of job enrichment and other organizational interventions. *Journal of Applied Psychology*, 1998, 83, 835–852.
13. Adapted from personal experiences at The Challenge course, September 1999. Also see Padilla, C. Team leaders show employees the ropes. *Plano Star Courier*, December 6, 1998, 10B.
14. Bandura, A. *Social Learning Theory.* Englewood Cliffs, N.J.: Prentice-Hall, 1977.
15. Anfuso, D. Creating a culture of caring pays off. *Personnel Journal*, August 1995, 70–77.
16. Latham, G. P., and Huber, V. L. Schedules of reinforcement: Lessons from the past and issues for the future. *Journal of Organizational Behavior Management*, 1992, 12, 125–149; Komaki, J. L. *Leadership from an Operant Perspective.* New York: Routledge, 1998.
17. Adapted from conversations with J. Gustin, formerly chief operating officer, Columbia Medical Center of Plano, Plano, Texas, September 1999.
18. Besser, T. L. Rewards and organizational goal achievement: A case study of Toyota Motor manufacturing in Kentucky. *Journal of Management Studies*, 1995, 32, 383–400.
19. Adapted from Murakin, R. Workers of Hungary Unite in Amway. *Washington Post*, August 6, 1994, D1.
20. Butterfield, K. D., Trevino, L. K., and Ball, G. A. Punishment from the manager's perspective: A grounded investigation and inductive model. *Academy of Management Journal*, 1996, 39, 479–512; Dunegan, K. J. Fines, frames, and images: Examining formulation effects on punishment decisions. *Organizational Behavior & Human Decision Processes.* 1996, 68, 58–68.
21. Grote, D. *Discipline Without Punishment.* New York: AMACOM, 1995.
22. Adapted from Grote, 1995, 164–168.
23. Kerr, S. Organizational rewards: Practical, cost-neutral alternatives that you may know, but don't practice. *Organizational Dynamics*, Summer 1999, 61–70; Greve, H. R. Performance, aspirations, and risky organizational change. *Administrative Science Quarterly*, 1998, 43, 58–87.
24. Bandura, A. *Principles of Behavior Modification.* New York: Holt, Rinehart and Winston, 1969.
25. Latham, G. P., and Huber, V. L. Schedules of reinforcement: Lessons from the past and issues for the future. *Journal of Organizational Behavior Management*, 1992, 12, 125–150.
26. Hendry, C. Understanding and creating whole organizational change through learning theory. *Human Relations*, 1996, 49, 621–642.
27. Stajkovic, A. D., and Luthans, F. A meta-analysis of the effects of organizational behavior modification on task performance. *Academy of Management Journal*, 1997, 40, 1122–1149.
28. Lopez, S., and Park, P. The bulge and the beautiful. *American Scene*, September 21, 1998, 1ff.; Vrania, S., Deogun, N., and Beatty, S. Jenny's list slims down. *Wall Street Journal*, July 8, 1998, B8.
29. Stajkovic, A. D., and Luthans, F., 1997; Whitener, E. M., Brodt, S. E., Korsgard, M. A., and Werner, J. M. Managers as initiators of trust: An exchange relationship framework for understanding managerial trustworthy behavior. *Academy of Management Review*, 1998, 23, 513–530.
30. Adapted from Luthans, F., Stajkovic, A. D., Luthans, B. C., and Luthans, K. W. Applying behavioral management in Eastern Europe. *European Management Journal*, 1998, 16, 466–475; Welsh, D. H. B., Luthans, F., and Sommer, S. M. Managing Russian factory workers: The impact of U.S.-based behavioral and participative techniques. *Academy of Management Journal*, 1993, 36, 58–79.
31. Brown, S., Cron, W. L., and Slocum, J. W., Jr. Effects of goal-directed emotions on salesperson volitions, behavior, and performance: A longitudinal study. *Journal of Marketing*, 1997, 61, 39–50; Lee, C., and Bobko, P. Self-efficacy beliefs: Comparison of five measures. *Journal of Applied Psychology*, 1994, 79, 364–370; Maurer, T. J., and Pierce, H. R. A comparison of Likert scale and traditional measures of self-efficacy. *Journal of Applied Psychology*, 1998, 83, 324–330.
32. Adapted from Fuquay, J. Texas health plan doctors settle lawsuit. *Forth Worth Star-Telegram*, September 27, 1997, 1ff; Ornstein, C. Members sue Harris Methodist Plan, Dallas area's largest HMO. *Knight-Ridder/Tribune News*, May 14, 1998, 1ff; Ornstein, C. Arlington, Texas-based HMO to pay $1.1 million to settle doctors' lawsuit. *Dallas Morning News*, September 3, 1998, 1ff. For additional information, visit the Dallas Morning News Web site at http://www.dallasnews.com.
33. Adapted from Beard, J. W., Woodman, R. W., and Moesel, D. Using behavioral modification to change attendance patterns in the high-performance, high-commitment environment. In R. W. Woodman and W. A. Pasmore (eds.), *Research in Organizational Change and Development*, vol. 11. Stamford, Conn.: JAI Press, 1998, 183–224. For additional information, visit the Westinghouse Web site at http://www.westinghouse.com.

CHAPTER

5

Motivation in the Work Setting

LEARNING OBJECTIVES

When you have finished studying this chapter, you should be able to:

1. Define motivation and describe the motivation process.
2. Describe and apply four content models of motivation.
3. Describe and apply two process models of motivation.

Preview Case: *How Starbucks Motivates Employees*

THE BASIC MOTIVATIONAL PROCESS

Core Phases of the Process

Motivational Challenges

CONTENT MODELS OF MOTIVATION

Needs Hierarchy Model

ERG Model

Competency: Managing Across Cultures— *A Tale of Two Plants in Romania*

Achievement Motivation Model

Competency: Managing Self— *John Schnatter of Papa John's Pizza*

Motivator-Hygiene Model

Comparisons Among Content Models

PROCESS MODELS OF MOTIVATION

Expectancy Model

Equity Model

Competency: Managing Communication— *The Walt Disney Company*

Competency: Managing Ethics— *To Steal or Not: That's the Question*

Comparisons Among Process Models

CHAPTER SUMMARY

Key Terms and Concepts

Discussion Questions

DEVELOPING COMPETENCIES

Competency: Managing Self— *What Do You Want from Your Job?*

Competency: Managing Teams— *SEI Investments*

PREVIEW CASE

HOW STARBUCKS MOTIVATES EMPLOYEES

The Starbucks Support Center is located at Starbucks Coffee Company's headquarters in Seattle. There's energy here—not induced by a caffeine rush—but from associates drinking up a robust blend of teamwork, sense of mission, and challenge. As one of *Fortune* magazine's "100 Best Companies to Work for in America," not to mention one of the world's fastest growing purveyors of indulgence, Starbucks has been giving its employees a daily lift since 1971.

Woven into the company's mission statement is the objective to "Provide a great work environment and treat each other with respect and dignity." It takes more than company declarations to motivate and inspire people. So how does a young, developing company on an aggressive growth track motivate more than 27,000 people and inspire balance and a team spirit?

The answer is what Starbucks refers to as "a special blend of employee benefits" and a work/life program that focuses on the physical, mental, emotional, and creative aspects of each person. Starbucks developed an innovative work/life program to brew a committed coffee culture—and a long-term partnership. In fact employees at Starbucks are called partners.

Joan Moffat, the Starbucks manager of partner relations and work/life, is responsible for the company's work/life program. It includes on-site fitness services, referral and educational support for child-care and elder-care issues, an Info-line for convenient information, and the Partner Connection—a program that links employees with shared interests and hobbies. Starbucks has comparatively low health-care costs, low absenteeism, and one of the strongest retention rates in the industry. "Our turnover rate is 60 percent, which is excellent as compared to the restaurant and retail industry," says Moffat. Moreover, employees reap the benefits of the company's ongoing success.

Starbucks is committed to providing an atmosphere that breeds respect and values the contributions that people make each day, regardless of who or where they are within the company. All partners who work a minimum 20 hours a week receive full medical and dental coverage, vacation days, and stock options as part of Starbucks Bean Stock program. Eligible partners can choose health coverage from two managed care plans or a catastrophic plan. They also can select between two dental plans and a vision plan. Because of the young, healthy workforce, Starbucks has low health-benefit costs. According to Annette King, the human resources (HR) benefits manager, the company's health-care costs are approximately 20 percent lower than the national average.

The company also provides disability and life insurance, a discounted stock purchase plan, and a retirement savings plan with company matching contributions. These benefits provide a powerful incentive for partners, particularly part-timers, to stay with the company, thus reducing Starbucks' recruiting and training costs. "We have historically had low turnover, most of which can be attributed to the culture and a sense of community," says Moffat.

Three years ago, HR began examining how it could become more attuned to employees. For instance, some employees who started with the company when they were in college are now buying homes and dealing with the realities of child care and elder care. Starbucks responded by providing flexible work schedules as part of its work/life program. "Our environment lends itself to meet multiple life demands. By virtue of our strong sales and accelerated growth, flex schedules have not hurt productivity in the least," says Moffat. "Flexibility is particularly inherent in our stores because of our extended hours of operation and the diversity of our workforce—from students to parents—who need to work alternative hours."

*For more information on Starbucks, visit this firm's home page at **www.starbucks.com**.*

Recent studies have shown that 60 percent of U.S. workers have child- or elder-care responsibilities. Starbucks recognized—as many other companies have—that partners less encumbered by personal stress and obligations are more innovative and productive. Starbucks implemented several programs that specifically address the life stages and personal needs of its workforce. To help deal with the fast-paced and demanding environment at Starbucks, it also provides referral services for partners and eligible dependents enrolled in the medical plan. It connects them with information that helps make extraordinary life issues more manageable. Moffat recently put the program to use when she needed elder-care advice for her grandmother. In another case, a partner needed emergency child care for his ill son. Starbuck's Working Solutions program made prompt arrangements for a certified in-home caretaker, no work was missed, and Starbucks covered half of the cost.[1]

Howard Schultz, chairman and CEO of Starbucks, says that his greatest challenge is to attract, develop, and manage a worldwide workforce. He believes that Starbucks must provide motivational systems that will cut costs while maintaining high quality. Permitting employees to participate in the incentive programs described in the Preview Case, among others, has led to greater productivity. Since going public in 1992, the company's stock has risen by more than 800 percent; its retail sales exceeded $2 billion in 2000. Starbucks can be found in restaurants, hotels, offices, airlines, and in more than 1,700 stores in the United States and United Kingdom.[2]

Learning Objective:

1. Define motivation and describe the motivation process.

THE BASIC MOTIVATIONAL PROCESS

Motivation represents the forces acting on or within a person that cause the person to behave in a specific, goal-directed manner. Because the work motives of employees affect their productivity, one of management's jobs is to channel employee motivation effectively toward achieving organizational goals. Particularly important is motivating people who come from widely different backgrounds. Table 5.1 highlights some of the factors that managers must address when dealing with multicultural workforce motivation. Note the diversity in what employees want. As an effective motivator, a manager must be able to identify and understand these differences and help employees satisfy their wants and needs through the organization.

Managers are not always sure which rewards their employees value. According to Robert Reich, former U.S. Secretary of Labor, four trends are currently affecting employee motivation. First, organizations are hiring fewer permanent employees and contracting out (outsourcing) a variety of services. Contract workers—such as engineers, accountants, computer programmers, food preparers, and many other types—are paid fees for completing specific projects. They have to purchase their own dental, health, and life insurance coverage; they have no paid sick leave, holidays, or vacations; and many work at home (called *telecommuters*). Managing telecommuters requires managers who excel in communication, ethics, and change competencies. Managers don't see these employees every day, so it is especially important for such employees to become committed to the vision of the organization and that their behaviors be consistent with its goals.

Second, employees may work for five or six organizations during their careers. Previously, organizations had their choice of employees. Now, employees have many choices and ask organizations: Why should I join you? Loyalty can no longer be taken for granted—by the employer or the employee. Organizations therefore have to develop and implement effective strategies to recruit and retain people from whom they want a commitment. For many U.S. companies the trend of downsizing and outsourcing work in order to lower costs is likely to continue for some time. Thus individuals, particularly managers and other professionals, should be willing to explore job opportunities with firms around the world.

Understanding how to lead and motivate workers from different cultures will become increasingly important in the years ahead and will require people to learn foreign languages and customs. For example, when John Lichtenthal, a human resource manager for Celanese Chemical, was assigned to Celanese's new $125 million plant in Singapore, he was confronted with a dilemma. The plant was completed and ready to open by July 10, but according to local custom, plants should only be opened on "lucky days." The next "lucky day" was September 3. Lichtenthal had a difficult time convincing executives at Celanese's Dallas headquarters to delay the plant opening. After many heated telephone conversations, the president of Celanese agreed to open the plant on September 3.

Third, people should be prepared to work in a team or on their own. Increasingly, employees are being asked to work in teams to produce goods and services, as on the assembly lines at Taco Bell, Saturn, and Nissan. Thus more and more man-

Table 5.1 **Diversity in the Workforce: What Do People Want?**

Able-Bodied People Want

To develop more ease in dealing with physically disabled people
To give honest feedback and appropriate support without being patronizing or overprotective

Younger and Older Employees Want

To have more respect for their life experiences
To be taken seriously
To be challenged by their organizations, not patronized

Disabled People Want

To have greater acknowledgment of and focus on abilities, rather than on disabilities
To be challenged by colleagues and organizations to be the best
To be included, not isolated

Heterosexuals Want

To become more aware of lesbian and gay issues
To have a better understanding of the legal consequences of being gay in America
To increase dialogue about personal issues with lesbians and gay men

Gay Men and Lesbians Want

To be recognized as whole human beings, not just sexual beings
To have equal employment protection
To have increased awareness among people regarding the impact of heterosexism in the workplace

Women Want

To be recognized as equal contributors
To have active support of male colleagues
To have work and family issues actively addressed by organizations

Men Want

To have the same freedom to grow/feel that women have
To be perceived as allies, not the enemy
To bridge the gap with women at home and at work

People of Color Want

To be valued as unique individuals, as members of ethnically diverse groups, as people of different races, and as equal contributors
To establish more open, honest, working relationships with people of other races and ethnic groups
To have the active support of white people in fighting racism

White People Want

To have their ethnicity acknowledged
To reduce discomfort, confusion, and dishonesty in dealing with people of color
To build relationships with people of color based on common goals, concerns, and mutual respect for differences

Source: Adapted from Vincola, A. Work & life: In search of the missing links. *HR Focus,* August 1998, 75, S3–5; Bond, M. A., and Pyle, J. L. The ecology of diversity in organizational settings: Lessons from a case study. *Human Relations,* 1998, 51, 589–624; Powell, G. N. Reinforcing and extending today's organizations: The simultaneous pursuit of person–organization fit and diversity. *Organizational Dynamics,* Winter 1998, 50–62.

agers are looking for employees who have developed multiple talents and good communication competency.

Fourth, employees must continually upgrade their competencies to keep up with rapidly changing technology and workplace requirements. Becoming proficient at the seven competencies discussed in this book is a good starting place.[3]

Experts might not agree about everything that motivates employees—and the effects of working conditions on their careers—but they do agree that an organization must

- attract people to the organization and encourage them to remain with it,
- allow people to perform the tasks for which they were hired, and
- stimulate people to go beyond routine performance and become creative and innovative in their work.

Thus, for an organization to be effective, it must tackle the motivational challenges involved in arousing people's desires to be productive members of the organization.

Core Phases of the Process

A key motivational principle states that performance is based on a person's level of ability and motivation. This principle is often expressed by the formula

$$\text{Performance} = f(\text{ability} \times \text{motivation}).$$

According to this principle, no task can be performed successfully unless the person who is to carry it out has the ability to do so. **Ability** is the person's talent for performing goal-related tasks. However, regardless of a person's competence, ability alone isn't enough to ensure performance at a high level. The person must also want to achieve a high level of performance. Thus discussions of motivation generally are concerned with (1) what drives behavior, (2) what direction behavior takes, and (3) how to maintain that behavior.

The motivational process begins with identifying a person's needs, shown as phase 1 in Figure 5.1. **Needs** are deficiencies that a person experiences at a particular time. These deficiencies may be psychological (e.g., the need for recognition), physiological

Figure 5.1 **Core Phases of the Motivational Process**

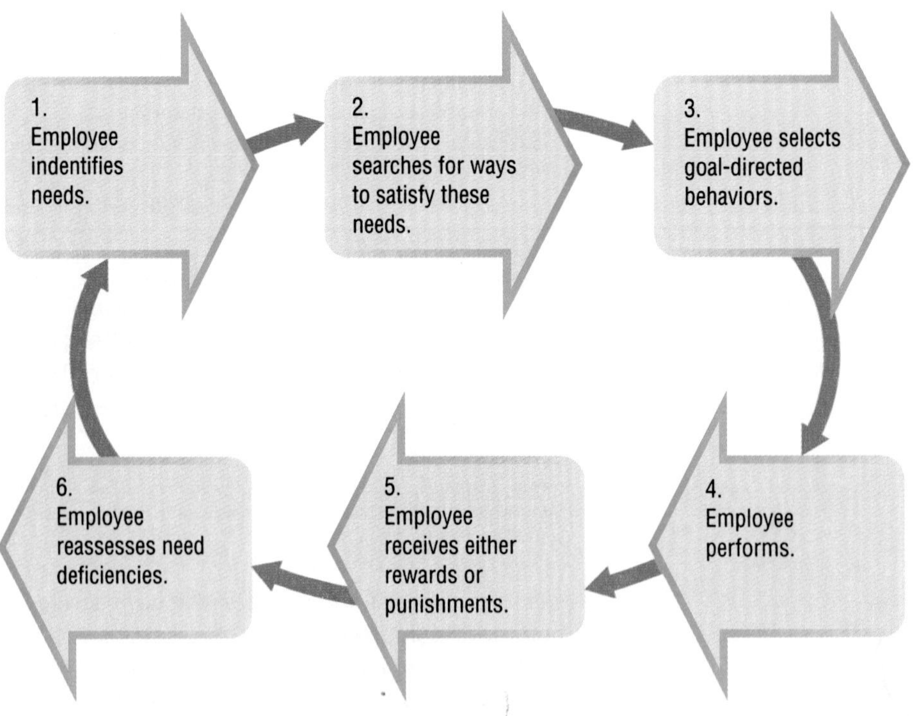

(e.g., the need for water, air, or food), or social (e.g., the need for friendship). Needs often act as energizers. That is, needs create tensions within the individual, who finds them uncomfortable and therefore is likely to make an effort (phase 2) to reduce or eliminate them.

Motivation is goal directed (phase 3). A **goal** is a specific result that an individual wants to achieve.[4] An employee's goals often are driving forces, and accomplishing those goals can significantly reduce needs. For example, some employees have strong drives for advancement and expectations that working long hours on highly visible projects will lead to promotions, raises, and greater influence. Such needs and expectations often create uncomfortable tension within these individuals. Believing that certain specific behaviors can overcome this tension, these employees act to reduce it. Employees striving to advance may seek to work on major problems facing the organization in order to gain visibility and influence with senior managers (phase 4). Promotions and raises are two of the ways that organizations attempt to maintain desirable behaviors. They are signals (feedback) to employees that their needs for advancement and recognition and their behaviors are appropriate (phase 5). Once the employees have received either rewards or punishments, they reassess their needs (phase 6).

Motivational Challenges

In concept the basic motivational process just described is simple and straightforward. In the real world, of course, the process isn't so clear-cut. The first challenge is that motives can only be inferred; they cannot be seen. James Taylor, manager of campus dining services for ARAMARK, observed two employees in his department who were debugging software programs that estimate the number of meals served in residence halls. He knows that both employees are responsible for the same type of work, have similar competencies, and have been with the organization for about 5 years. One employee is able to spot problems more easily and faster than the other. He knows that both employees have similar competencies and training, so the difference in their output strongly suggests that they have different motivations. Taylor recognized that he would have to investigate further to determine what motivates each person.

A second challenge centers on the dynamic nature of needs. As pointed out in the Preview Case, Starbucks has developed numerous programs in its attempt to meet employee needs. Doing so is always difficult because, at any one time, everyone has various needs, desires, and expectations. Moreover, these factors change over time and may also conflict with each other. Employees who put in many extra hours at work to fulfill their needs for accomplishment may find that these extra work hours conflict directly with needs for affiliation and their desires to be with their families.

A third challenge involves the considerable differences in people's motivations and in the energy with which people respond to them. Just as different organizations produce a variety of products and offer a variety of services, different people have a variety of motivations. Gary Brown knew that he wanted to open a restaurant after visiting his brother one weekend in San Francisco. Working 70 hours a week didn't bother him. Once he had developed and perfected his idea, he created his own recipes and opened his first restaurant in Dallas. His Routh Street Brewery soon employed more than 25 people, and Brown began looking for another location to open a second restaurant. He was motivated to be his own boss and operator of an upscale restaurant in Dallas. In contrast, Paul Ginn, a sales manager for Telstra in Australia, took a 1-year job assignment in his firm's Hong Kong office. Ginn joined a group of Australian managers there so that he could satisfy his needs to belong to such a group and to learn quickly about Chinese business customs. Ginn learned that Chinese managers are taught to be indirect in conversation, carefully editing remarks to reflect both good manners and the status of their listeners. He also discovered that many Chinese managers think that Australians are impatient, noisy, disruptive, and confrontational, often saying things that are better left unsaid.[5]

There is no shortage of models, strategies, and tactics for motivating employees. As a result, organizations constantly experiment with new motivational programs and practices. For discussion purposes it is useful to group motivational models into two general categories: content and process.

Learning Objective:

2. Describe and apply four content models of motivation.

CONTENT MODELS OF MOTIVATION

Content models of motivation focus on the specific factors that energize, direct, and inhibit a person's behavior. An attractive salary, good working conditions and friendly coworkers are important to most people. Hunger (the need for food) or a desire for a steady job (the need for job security) are also factors that arouse people and may cause them to set specific goals (earning money to buy food or working in a financially stable industry). Four widely recognized content models of motivation are Maslow's needs hierarchy, Alderfer's ERG model, McClelland's achievement motivation model, and Herzberg's two-factor model.

Needs Hierarchy Model

The most widely recognized model of motivation is the **needs hierarchy model.** Abraham H. Maslow suggested that people have a complex set of exceptionally strong needs, which can be arranged in a hierarchy.[6] Underlying this hierarchy are the following basic assumptions.

- Once a need has been satisfied, its motivational role declines in importance. However, as one need is satisfied, another need gradually emerges to take its place, so people are always striving to satisfy some need.
- The needs network for most people is very complex, with several needs affecting behavior at any one time. Clearly, when someone faces an emergency, such as desperate thirst, that need dominates until it is gratified.
- Lower level needs must be satisfied, in general, before higher level needs are activated sufficiently to drive behavior.
- There are more ways of satisfying higher level than lower level needs.

This model states that a person has five types of needs: physiological, security, affiliation, esteem, and self-actualization. Figure 5.2 shows these five needs categories, arranged in Maslow's hierarchy.

Physiological Needs. The needs for food, water, air, and shelter are all **physiological needs** and are the lowest level in Maslow's hierarchy. People concentrate on satisfying these needs before turning to higher order needs. Managers should understand that, to the extent that employees are motivated by physiological needs, their concerns do not center on the work they are doing. They will accept any job that meets those needs. Managers who focus on physiological needs in trying to motivate subordinates assume that people work primarily for money and are mainly concerned with comfort, avoidance of fatigue, and the like.

Security Needs. The needs for safety, stability, and absence of pain, threat, or illness are all **security needs.** Like physiological needs, unsatisfied security needs cause people to be preoccupied with satisfying them. People who are motivated primarily by security needs value their jobs mainly as defenses against the loss of basic needs satisfaction. Managers who feel that security needs are most important focus on them by emphasizing rules, job security, and fringe benefits. Managers who think that subordinates are primarily interested in security neither encourage innovation nor reward risk taking. Their employees, in turn, will strictly follow the rules set for them.

Figure 5.2 **Maslow's Needs Hierarchy**

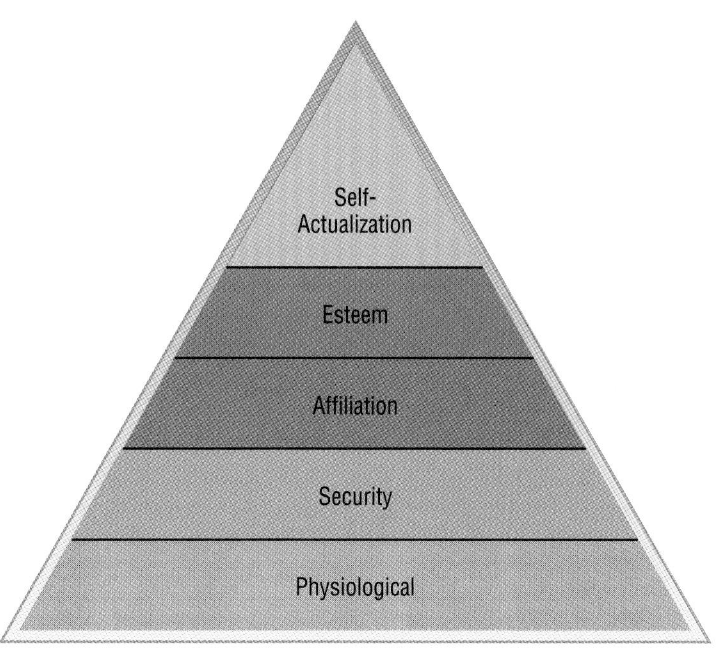

Affiliation Needs. The needs for friendship, love, and a feeling of belonging are all **affiliation needs.** When physiological and security needs have been satisfied, affiliation needs emerge. Managers should realize that, when affiliation needs are the primary source of motivation, people value their work as an opportunity for finding and establishing warm and friendly interpersonal relationships. To help satisfy their affiliation needs while stationed in Singapore for Celanese Chemical, John Lichtenthal and his wife, Mica, joined a group of U.S. managers and their spouses. This group attended plays, toured other countries, celebrated U.S. holidays, enjoyed each other's friendship, and helped each other cope with the trials and enjoy the adventures of living in a foreign country. Managers and team leaders who believe that employees are striving primarily to satisfy these needs are likely to act supportively. They emphasize employee acceptance by coworkers, extracurricular activities (e.g., organized sports programs, cultural events, and company celebrations), and team-based norms.

Esteem Needs. Personal feelings of achievement and self-worth and recognition or respect from others meet **esteem needs.** People with esteem needs want others to accept them for what they are and to perceive them as competent and able. Managers who focus on esteem needs try to motivate employees with public rewards and recognition for achievements. These managers may use lapel pins, articles in the company paper, achievement lists on the bulletin board, and the like to foster employees' pride in their work. They also recognize that some people don't like public recognition, preferring to be told in private that they are performing well.

Self-Actualization Needs. Self-fulfillment comes from meeting **self-actualization needs.** People who strive for self-actualization seek to increase their problem-solving abilities. Managers who emphasize self-actualization may involve employees in designing jobs, make special assignments that capitalize on employees' unique skills, or give employee teams leeway in planning and implementing their work. The self-employed often have strong self-actualization needs. When Gary Brown opened his first Routh Street Brewery, he fulfilled many of his self-actualization needs.

In Practice. Maslow's needs hierarchy model also suggests the types of behaviors that will help fulfill various needs. The three lowest needs—physiological, safety, and social—are also known as **deficiency needs.** According to Maslow, unless these needs are satisfied, an individual will fail to develop into a healthy person, both physically and psychologically. In contrast, esteem and self-actualization needs are known as **growth needs.** Satisfaction of these needs helps a person grow and develop as a human being.

This model provides incomplete information about the origin of needs. However, it implies that higher level needs are present in most people, even if they don't recognize or act to meet those needs. These higher level needs will motivate most people if nothing occurs to block their emergence.

The needs hierarchy is based on U.S. cultural values. In cultures that value uncertainty avoidance, such as Japan and Greece, job security and lifelong employment are stronger motivators than self-actualization. Moreover, in Denmark, Sweden, and Norway the value and rewards of a high quality of life are more important than productivity. Thus social needs are stronger than self-actualization and self-esteem needs. In countries such as China, Japan, and Korea that value collectivist and community practices over individual achievements, belonging and security are considerably more important than meeting growth needs. Therefore, although the needs that Maslow identified may be universal, the logic or sequence of the hierarchy differs from culture to culture.[7]

Maslow's work has received much attention from managers, as well as psychologists.[8] Research has found that top managers are better able to satisfy their esteem and self-actualization needs than are lower level managers; part of the reason is that top managers have more challenging jobs and opportunities for self-actualization. Employees who work on a team have been able to satisfy their higher level needs by making decisions that affect their team and company. For example, at Lockheed Martin's Camden, Arkansas plant, employees are trained to perform multiple tasks, including hiring and training team members—and even firing those who fail to perform adequately. As team members learn new tasks, they start satisfying their higher level needs. Employees who have little or no control over their work (e.g., assembly-line workers) may not even experience higher level needs in relation to their jobs. Studies have also shown that the fulfillment of needs differs according to the job a person performs, a person's age and background, and the size of the company.

ERG Model

Clay Alderfer agrees with Maslow that individuals have a hierarchy of needs. However, instead of the five categories of needs suggested by Maslow, Alderfer's **ERG model** holds that the individual has three sets of basic needs: existence, relatedness, and growth.[9] Alderfer describes them in the following way.

- **Existence needs,** or material needs, are satisfied by food, air, water, pay, fringe benefits, and working conditions.
- **Relatedness needs** are met by establishing and maintaining interpersonal relationships with coworkers, superiors, subordinates, friends, and family.
- **Growth needs** are expressed by an individual's attempt to find opportunities for unique personal development by making creative or productive contributions at work.

Alderfer's arrangement of these categories of needs is similar to Maslow's. Existence needs generally correspond to Maslow's physiological and safety needs; relatedness needs generally correspond to Maslow's affiliation needs; and growth needs generally correspond to Maslow's esteem and self-actualization needs.

However, the two models differ in their views of how people attempt to satisfy different sets of needs. Maslow states that unfilled needs are motivators and that the next higher level need isn't activated until the preceding lower level need is satisfied. Thus a person progresses up the needs hierarchy as each set of lower level needs is satisfied. In contrast, the ERG model suggests that, in addition to this **fulfillment–progression process,** a *frustration–regression process* is at work. That is, if a person is continually frustrated in attempts to satisfy growth needs, relatedness needs will reemerge as a motivating force. The individual will return to satisfying this lower level need instead of attempting to satisfy growth needs, and frustration will lead to regression.

Figure 5.3 illustrates these relationships. A solid arrow indicates a direct relationship between needs, desires, and needs satisfaction. A dashed arrow represents what happens when a set of needs is frustrated. For example, if a person's growth needs are frustrated on the job because of the lack of challenging assignments, the importance of relatedness needs, usually satisfied by their coworkers, increases. The same behavior (performing routine tasks) that had led to the frustration of growth needs now becomes the means for the person to satisfy relatedness needs. Often, when attempts to satisfy relatedness needs have been frustrated, people seek refuge in food and alcohol or drugs to satisfy their existence needs. The frustration–regression idea is based on the assumption that existence, relatedness, and growth needs vary along a continuum of concreteness, with existence being the most concrete and growth being the least concrete. Alderfer further proposes that when lesser concrete needs are not met, more concrete needs fulfillment is sought. (Note that the direction of the dashed lines in Figure 5.3 is downward from needs frustration to needs strength.)

In Practice. Because the ERG model holds that individuals are motivated to engage in behavior to satisfy one of three sets of needs, it provides an important insight for managers. What should a manager do if a subordinate's growth needs are blocked, perhaps because the job doesn't permit satisfaction of these needs or there are no resources to satisfy them? The answer is that the manager should try to redirect the employee's behavior toward satisfying relatedness or existence needs.[10]

Few research studies have tested the ERG model of motivation. However, several studies do support its three sets of needs, rather than the five categories of needs in Maslow's hierarchy. Some managers question the model's universality, finding that it doesn't help them understand what motivates employees in their organizations.

Figure 5.3 **ERG Model**

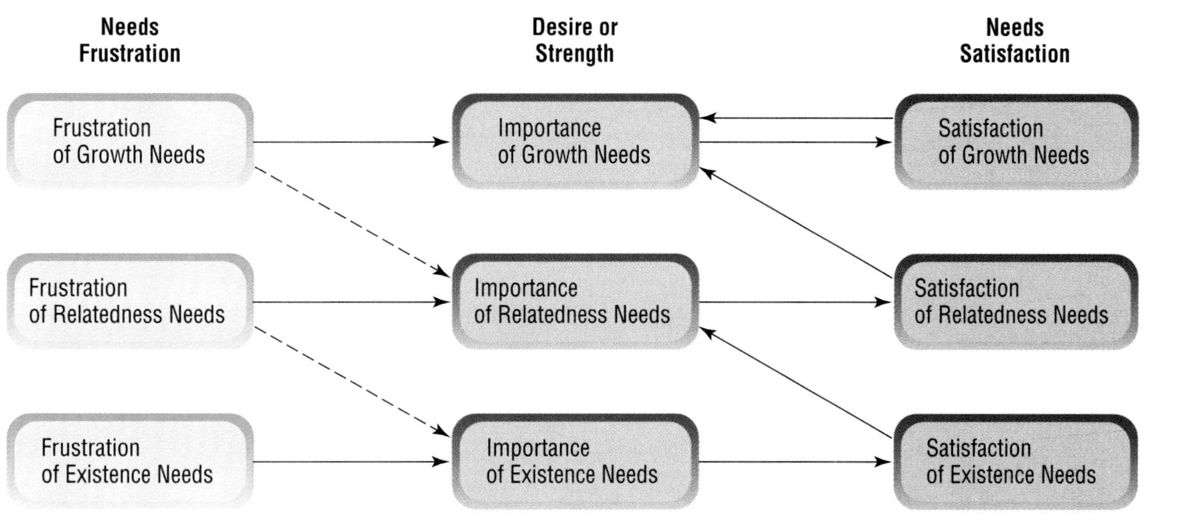

Source: From *Psychology of Work Behavior,* by F. Landy. Copyright ©1989, 1985, 1980, 1976 by Brooks/Cole Publishing Company, Pacific Grove, CA 93950, a division of International Thomson Publishing, Inc. By permission of the publisher.

We believe that Maslow's needs hierarchy and Alderfer's ERG models both offer useful ways of thinking about employee motivation. The fact that there is disagreement over the exact number of categories of needs should be noted, but both models hold that satisfying needs is an important part of motivation.

The following Managing Across Cultures Competency feature indicates how these needs-based models can be used to understand the behavior of factory workers

Competency: Managing Across Cultures

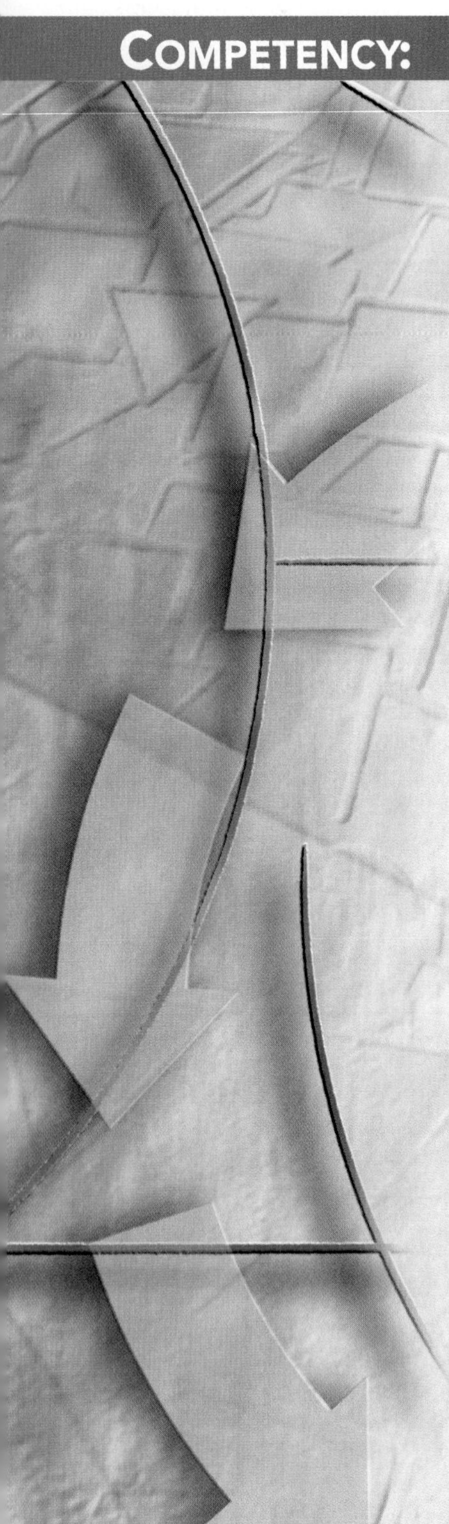

A Tale of Two Plants in Romania

Perla Hargita is a mineral water bottling firm in the Transylvania Alps of northwestern Romania. It is a family-owned company that has been in business for more than two generations. Its two plants employee 285 people, 60 percent of whom live in the town. The two plants combined bottle a minimum of 30,000 liters of water a day, which increases to 45,000 liters in the summer. The water is shipped all over Romania and exported to other Eastern European countries, as well as to Canada and Australia.

In the glass-bottling plant, most of the equipment is antiquated. The oldest equipment was manufactured in Germany and is very reliable, but the newer equipment made in Romania has frequent breakdowns. The Romanian equipment can't be replaced because all firms are now required to "buy Romanian." Safety standards in the factory are virtually nonexistent. Steam rises in clouds from the open bottle washer as hot water splashes on the concrete floor. The machinery screeches and grinds as bottles progress through the system. Recycled glass bottles are washed, filled, capped, and labeled on an open conveyor belt line. One group of workers, mainly young women, visually inspects the empty bottles for defects, while others make certain that the bottles are filled to the proper level. Bottle caps frequently blow off the filled bottles, sounding like shotgun blasts. There are no safety guards to keep workers' fingers from being caught in the conveyor and no yellow lines to mark off safe areas for walking, and the lighting in many areas of the plant is poor. Accidents are frequent, but workers don't report them to the plant manager for fear of being dismissed. The machinery makes such a deafening noise that the workers can't talk to each other without shouting. The workers are not provided with ear plugs or eye protection. Micu Korton, the plant manager, acknowledges that most workers suffer severe hearing loss but states that it is just an occupational hazard.

The plastic-bottling plant is modern, all white, brightly lit, clean, dry, and quiet enough for workers to talk with each other in a normal voice. Three white-coated technicians monitor digital control panels. Only a soft hum can be heard from the computerized machinery. The bottling line is completely enclosed in a clear acrylic tunnel that provides a safe, sanitary, and efficient environment for the operation. In a seamless process, heated plastic pellets are formed into bottles. The bottles are filled with water, capped, labeled, and banded into 12-packs for boxing and shipping.

During the summer, workers in both plants eagerly work 4 hours overtime a day. They make at least 10 percent more than they could by farming potatoes or working in the declining textile industry. Wages at Perla Hargita average 1,235,537 lieu, or about $124, per month. In the summer, this increases to $186 for a 12-hour workday. In addition, both plants provide bottled water, beer, and other bottled drinks to all employees at a discount. Workers at both plants get several paid holidays per year and a small bonus at Christmas. Women make up most of the workforce in the glass-bottling plant, whereas men are employed in the plastic-bottling plant. In Romania, women typically earn 25 percent less than men.[11]

in Romania. After reading this selection, make a prediction about turnover and productivity at the two plants described. What opportunities do workers in each plant have to satisfy their needs?

Achievement Motivation Model

David McClelland proposed a learned needs model of motivation that he believed to be rooted in culture.[12] He argued that everyone has three particularly important needs: for achievement, affiliation, and power. Individuals who possess a *strong power motive* take action that affects the behaviors of others and has a strong emotional appeal. These individuals are concerned with providing status rewards to their followers. Individuals who have a *strong affiliation motive* tend to establish, maintain, and restore close personal relationships with others. Individuals who have a *strong achievement motive* compete against some standard of excellence or unique contribution against which they judge their behaviors and achievements.

McClelland has studied achievement motivation extensively, especially with regard to entrepreneurship. His **achievement motivation model** states that people are motivated according to the strength of their desire either to perform in terms of a standard of excellence or to succeed in competitive situations. According to McClelland, almost all people believe that they have an "achievement motive," but probably only about 10 percent of the U.S. population are strongly motivated to achieve. The amount of achievement motivation that people have depends on their childhood, their personal and occupational experiences, and the type of organization for which they work. Table 5.2 shows an application of McClelland's model to presidents of the United States. Presidents' motives can be documented by the legislation they have proposed and the policies they have pursued during their tenures.

According to McClelland's model, motives are "stored" in the preconscious mind just below the level of full awareness. They lie between the conscious and the unconscious, in the area of daydreams, where people talk to themselves without quite being aware of it. A basic premise of the model is that the pattern of these daydreams can be tested and that people can be taught to change their motivation by changing these daydreams.

Measuring Achievement Motivation. McClelland measured the strength of a person's achievement motivation with the **Thematic Apperception Test (TAT).** The TAT uses unstructured pictures that may arouse many kinds of reactions in the person being tested. Examples include an inkblot that a person can perceive as many

Table 5.2 Presidents' Needs for Power, Achievement, and Affiliation

	NEEDS		
PRESIDENT	Power	Achievement	Affiliation
Clinton, B.	Moderate	High	High
Bush, G.	Moderate	Moderate	Low
Reagan, R.	High	Moderate	Low
Kennedy, J. F.	High	Low	High
Roosevelt, F. D.	High	Moderate	Low
Lincoln, A.	Moderate	Low	Moderate
Washington, G.	Low	Low	Moderate

Source: Adapted from House, R. J., Spangler, W. D., and Woycke, J. Personality and charisma in the U.S. president: A psychological theory of leader effectiveness. *Administrative Science Quarterly,* 1992, 36, 395.

Figure 5.4

Source: PhotoDisc®

different objects or a picture that can generate a variety of stories. There are no right or wrong answers, and the person isn't given a limited set of alternatives from which to choose. A major goal of the TAT is to obtain the individual's own perception of the world. The TAT is called a projective method because it emphasizes individual perceptions of stimuli, the meaning each individual gives to them, and how each individual organizes them (recall the discussion of perception in Chapter 3).

One projective test involves looking at the picture shown in Figure 5.4 for 10 to 15 seconds and then writing a short story about it that answers the following questions.

- What is going on in this picture?
- What is the woman thinking?
- What has led up to this situation?

Write your own story about the picture. Then compare it with the following story written by a manager exhibiting strong achievement motivation, who McClelland would describe as a high achiever.

> The individual is an officer in a small entrepreneurial organization that wants to get a contract for her company. She knows that the competition will be tough, because all the big firms are bidding on this contract. She is taking a moment to think how happy she will be if her company is awarded the large contract. It will mean stability for the company and probably a large raise for her. She is satisfied because she has just thought of a way to manufacture a critical part that will enable her company to bring in a low bid and complete the job with time to spare.

What motivational profile did you identify? Does it match the executive's?

Characteristics of High Achievers. Self-motivated high achievers have three main characteristics.[13] First, they like to set their own *goals*. Seldom content to drift aimlessly and let life happen to them, they nearly always are trying to accomplish something. High achievers seek the challenge of making tough decisions. They are selective about the goals to which they commit themselves. Hence they are unlikely to automatically accept goals that other people, including their superiors, attempt to select for them. They exercise self-control over their behaviors, especially the ways they pursue the goals they select. They tend to seek advice or help only from experts who can provide needed knowledge or skills. High achievers prefer to be as fully responsible for attaining their goals as possible. If they win, they want the credit; if they lose, they accept the blame. For example, assume that you are given a choice between rolling dice with one chance in three of winning or working on a problem with one chance in three of solving the problem in the time allotted. Which would you choose? A high achiever would choose to work on the problem, even though rolling the dice is obviously less work and the odds of winning are the same. High achievers prefer to work at a problem rather than leave the outcome to chance or to other people.

Second, high achievers avoid selecting extremely difficult goals. They prefer *moderate goals* that are neither so easy that attaining them provides no satisfaction nor so difficult that attaining them is more a matter of luck than ability. They gauge what is possible and then select as difficult a goal as they think they can attain. The game of ringtoss illustrates this point. Most carnivals have ringtoss games that require participants to throw rings over a peg from some minimum distance but specify no maximum distance. Imagine the same game but with people allowed to stand at any distance they want from the peg. Some will throw more or less randomly, standing close and then far away. Those with high-achievement motivation will seem to calculate carefully where they should stand to have the greatest chance of winning a prize and still feel challenged. These individuals seem to stand at a distance that isn't so close as to make the task ridiculously easy and isn't so far away as to make it impossible. They set a distance moderately far away from which they can potentially ring a peg. Thus they set personal challenges and enjoy tasks that will stretch their abilities.

Third, high achievers prefer tasks that provide *immediate feedback.* Because of the goal's importance to them, they like to know how well they're doing. That's one reason why the high achiever often chooses a professional career, a sales career, or entrepreneurial activities. Golf appeals to most high achievers: Golfers can compare their scores to par for the course, to their own previous performance on the course, and to their opponents' score; performance is related to both feedback (score) and goal (par).

Financial Incentives. Money has a complex effect on high achievers. They usually value highly their services and place a high price tag on them. High achievers are usually self-confident. They are aware of their abilities and limitations and thus are confident when they choose to do a particular job. They are unlikely to remain very long in an organization that doesn't pay them well. Whether an incentive plan actually increases their performance is an open question because they normally work at peak efficiency. They value money as a strong symbol of their achievement and adequacy. A financial incentive may create dissatisfaction if they feel that it inadequately reflects their contributions.

When achievement motivation is operating, outstanding performance on a challenging task is likely. However, achievement motivation doesn't operate when high achievers are performing routine or boring tasks or when there is no competition against goals. John Schnatter's drive to become No. 1 in the pizza industry has made Papa John's a major competitor in this $40 billion a year industry. While holding just under a 5 percent share of the take-out pizza market, Schnatter's goal is to take market share away from Pizza Hut (which has about 22 percent) by having better ingredients and making a better pizza. How he has achieved these remarkable results are highlighted in the following Managing Self Competency feature. After reading this material, you should be able to relate McClelland's three learned needs to Schnatter's motivations and how he motivated others.

COMPETENCY: MANAGING SELF

JOHN SCHNATTER OF PAPA JOHN'S PIZZA

Since graduating from Ball State University in Muncie, Indiana, in 1983, John Schnatter has built Papa John's into a billion dollar company. He is personally worth more than $245 million. To achieve such results, he is singularly obsessive about high quality and performance. He preaches to his employees about pizza in near biblical terms. He requires all employees to memorize the company's Six Core Values, including stay focused, customer satisfaction must be superior, and people are priority No. 1 *always*—and calls on employees during meetings to stand up and shout them out. He created a Ten Point Perfect Pizza Scale that measures the quality of pizzas. For example, pieces of the toppings should not touch, there should be no "peaks or valleys" along the pizza's border, all mushrooms should be sliced to 0.25 inch, and no splotchy coloring should appear on the crust. The employee newsletter carries articles such as "The Papa John's Black Olive Story" or "The Papa John's Tomato Story." Such articles inform employees about how special ingredients are used to make Papa John's pizza.

At headquarters in Louisville, Kentucky, most employees (including Schnatter) wear Papa John's teal-blue polo shirts, with Pizza Wars embroidered across them. Employees even have their own clothing embroidered with Papa John's logo. Papa John's employees are not soldiers in a battle; they're crusaders in a holy war. By 2003, Schnatter wants Papa John's to be the No.1 pizza brand in the world and by 2008, the leader in sales.[14]

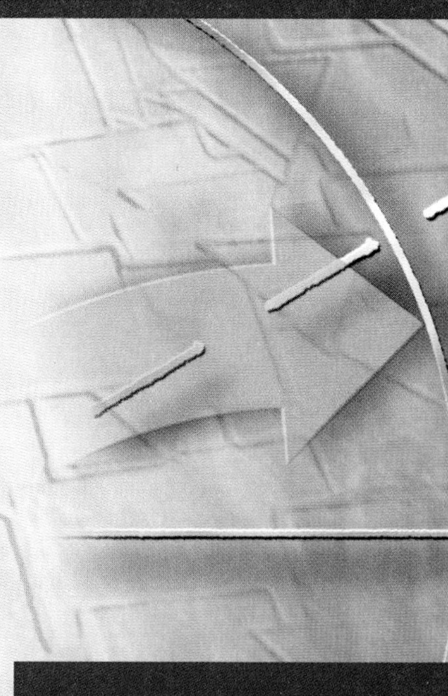

For more information on Papa John's, visit the organization's home page at ***www.papajohns.com.***

In Practice. McClelland and his associates at McBer and Company have conducted most of the research supporting the achievement motivation model. Based on this research, they recommend the following approach.

- Arrange tasks so that employees receive periodic feedback on their performance. Feedback enables employees to modify their behaviors as necessary.
- Provide good role models of achievement. Employees should be encouraged to have heroes to emulate.
- Help employees modify their self-images. High-achievement individuals accept themselves and seek job challenges and responsibilities.
- Guide employee aspirations. Employees should think about setting realistic goals and the ways that they can attain them.
- Make it known that managers who have been successful are those that are higher in power motivation than in affiliation motivation.

One of the main problems with the achievement motivation model is also its greatest strength.[15] The TAT method is valuable because it allows the researcher to tap the preconscious motives of people. This method has some advantages over questionnaires, but the interpretation of a story is more of an art than a science. As a result, the method's reliability is open to question. The permanency of the model's three needs has also been questioned. Further research is needed to explore the model's validity.

Motivator-Hygiene Model

The **motivator-hygiene model** is one of the most controversial models of motivation, probably because of two unique features. First, it stresses that some job factors lead to satisfaction, whereas others can prevent dissatisfaction but not be sources of satisfaction. Second, it states that job satisfaction and dissatisfaction do not exist on a single continuum.

Frederick Herzberg and his associates examined the relationship between job satisfaction and productivity in a group of accountants and engineers. Through the use of semistructured interviews, they accumulated data on various factors that these professionals said had an effect on their feelings about their jobs. Two different sets of factors emerged: motivators and hygienes.[16]

Motivator Factors. The first set of factors, **motivator factors,** includes the work itself, recognition, advancement, and responsibility. These factors are related to an individual's positive feelings about the job and to the content of the job itself. These positive feelings, in turn, are associated with the individual's experiences of achievement, recognition, and responsibility. They reflect lasting rather than temporary achievement in the work setting. In other words, motivators are **intrinsic factors,** which are directly related to the job and are largely internal to the individual. The organization's policies may have only an indirect impact on them. But, by defining exceptional performance, for example, an organization may enable individuals to feel that they have performed their tasks exceptionally well. Can you identify some motivators used at Perla Hargita, the Romanian water bottling company, to motivate its employees?

Hygiene Factors. The second set of factors, **hygiene factors,** includes company policy and administration, technical supervision, salary, fringe benefits, working conditions, and interpersonal relations. These factors are associated with an individual's negative feelings about the job and are related to the environment in which the job is performed. Hygienes are **extrinsic factors,** or factors external to the job. They serve as rewards for high performance only if the organization recognizes high performance. Can you identify the hygiene factors used by Starbucks (see the Preview Case) to attract new employees?

Cultural Influences. One of the important themes of this book is recognizing and addressing cultural diversity in the workforce. As U.S. organizations continue to expand overseas and foreign organizations establish manufacturing operations in Canada, Mexico, and the United States, managers must be aware of cultural differences and how these differences can affect the motivation of employees.[17] Herzberg believes that, despite cultural differences, motivators and hygienes affect workers similarly around the world. The data in Table 5.3 support this view. It shows that for U.S. workers about 80 percent of the factors that lead to job satisfaction can be traced to motivators. For workers in the other countries listed, motivators accounted for 60 to 90 percent of the reason for job satisfaction. Hygienes accounted for most of the reasons that workers were dissatisfied with their jobs. In Finland, 80 percent of the workers indicated that hygiene factors contributed mainly to job dissatisfaction, whereas only 10 percent said that hygiene factors contributed to their job satisfaction.

With the passage of the North American Free Trade Agreement (NAFTA), managers and employees in North America will be working more closely with others who don't necessarily share similar work motivation. It doesn't take U.S. managers very long to realize that employees in Mexico have different attitudes toward work. In the United States workers generally favor taking the initiative, having individual responsibility, and taking failure personally. They are competitive, have high goals, and live for the future. Workers are comfortable operating in a group, with the group sharing both success and failure. They tend to be cooperative, flexible, and enjoy life as it is now.[18]

In Mexico, employees' priorities are family, religion, and work. During the year, plant managers host family dinners to celebrate anniversaries of employees who have worked there 5, 10, 15, and 20 years. Employees may use the company clubhouse for weddings, baptisms, anniversary parties, and other family celebrations. Organizations also host a family day during which employees' families can tour the plant, enjoy entertainment and food, and participate in sports.

Table 5.3 Motivators and Hygienes Across Cultures

MOTIVATORS	SATISFYING JOB EVENTS	DISSATISFYING JOB EVENTS
United States	80%	20%
Japan	82%	40%
Finland	90%	18%
Hungary	78%	30%
Italy	60%	35%
HYGIENES		
United States	20%	75%
Japan	10%	65%
Finland	10%	80%
Hungary	22%	78%
Italy	30%	70%

Source: Adapted from Roberts, K., Kossek, E. E., and Ozeki, C. Managing the global workforce: Challenges and strategies. *Academy of Management Executive*, 1998, 12(4), 98–106; Snell, S. A., Snow, C. C., Canney Davidson, S., and Hambrick, D. C. Designing and supporting transnational teams: The human resource agenda. *Human Resource Management*, 1998, 37, 147–158. Herzberg, F. Worker's needs: The same around the world. *Industry Week*, September 21, 1987, 29–32.

The typical workday in Mexico is 8 A.M. to 5:30 P.M. Employees are picked up by the company bus at various locations throughout the city. Employees like to eat their main meal in the middle of the day, the cost of which is heavily subsidized (as much as 70 percent) by the company. Interestingly, managers serve the employees this meal.[19]

Because the motivator-hygiene model states that satisfaction and dissatisfaction do not form a single continuum, a person can be both satisfied and dissatisfied at the same time. The separate and distinct continuums specified in the model are indicated in Figure 5.5.

In Practice. The research designed to test the motivator-hygiene model hasn't provided clear-cut evidence that either supports or rejects it. One aspect of the model that appeals to managers is the use of common terms to explain how to motivate people. They don't have to translate psychological terms into everyday language. However, because hygiene factors are easy to identify, they have become targets for shareholder complaints when the value of a company's stock drops.

Despite its attractive features, several significant criticisms have been leveled at the motivator-hygiene model.[20] One is that Herzberg used a method-bound procedure; that is, the method he used to measure the factors determined the results. He asked two key questions: "Can you describe, in detail, when you felt exceptionally good about your job?" and "Can you describe, in detail, when you felt exceptionally bad about your job?" In response to such questions, people tend to give socially desirable answers, that is, answers they think the researcher wants to hear or that sound "reasonable." Also, people tend to attribute good job results to their own efforts and to attribute reasons for poor results to others (recall the discussion of the self-serving bias attribution in Chapter 3).

Another serious question about the motivator-hygiene model is whether satisfaction and dissatisfaction really are two separate dimensions, as Figure 5.5 indicates. Research results are mixed. Some researchers have found factors that can contribute to both satisfaction and dissatisfaction, whereas others have found that motivator factors can contribute to dissatisfaction and hygiene factors can contribute to satisfaction. For example, at Starbucks, employees reported that hygiene factors are strongly related to their job satisfactions. These findings, however, haven't disproved the concept that satisfaction and dissatisfaction are two different continuums.

Some evidence, though not strong, links experiences such as increasing job responsibility, challenge, and advancement opportunities to high performance. Unfortunately, researchers have paid little attention to constructing a model that explains

Figure 5.5 **Motivator-Hygiene Situations**

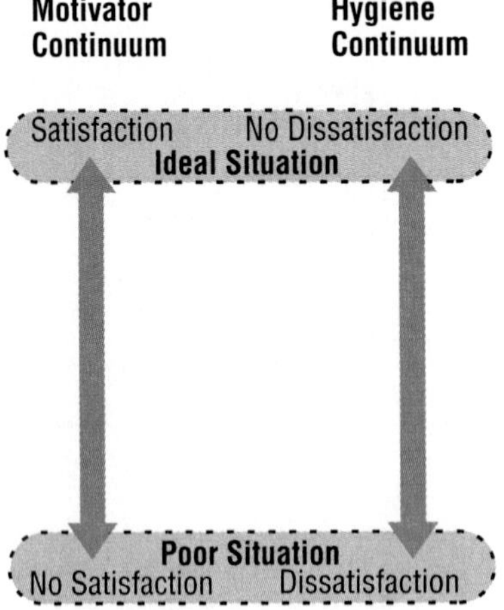

why certain job factors affect performance positively or negatively. Similarly, few attempts have been made using content models to explain why certain outcomes are attractive to employees or why they choose one type of behavior over another to obtain a desired outcome.

Comparisons Among Content Models

The four content models emphasize the basic motivational concepts of needs, achievement motivation, and motivators-hygienes. Figure 5.6 highlights the relationships among these four models. The needs hierarchy model served as the basis for the ERG model. Therefore there are some important similarities between the two: Self-actualization and esteem needs make up growth needs; affiliation needs are similar to relatedness needs; and security and physiological needs are the building blocks of existence needs. A major difference between these two models is that the hierarchy of needs model offers a static needs system based on fulfillment–progression, whereas the ERG model presents a flexible three-needs classification system based on frustration–regression.

The motivator-hygiene model draws on both of the needs models. That is, if hygiene factors are present, security and physiological needs (needs hierarchy) are likely to be met. Similarly, if hygiene factors are present, satisfaction of relatedness and existence needs (ERG model) isn't likely to be frustrated. Motivator factors focus on the job itself and the opportunity for the person to satisfy higher order needs, or growth needs (ERG model).

The achievement motivation model doesn't recognize lower order needs. The need for affiliation can be satisfied if a person meets hygiene factors on the job. If the job itself is challenging and provides an opportunity for a person to make meaningful decisions, it is motivating. These conditions go a long way toward satisfying the need for achievement.

The content models provide an understanding of the particular work-related factors that start the motivational process. These models, however, promote little understanding of why people choose a particular behavior to accomplish task-related goals. This aspect of choice is the primary focus of process models of motivation.

Figure 5.6 **Matching Content Models**

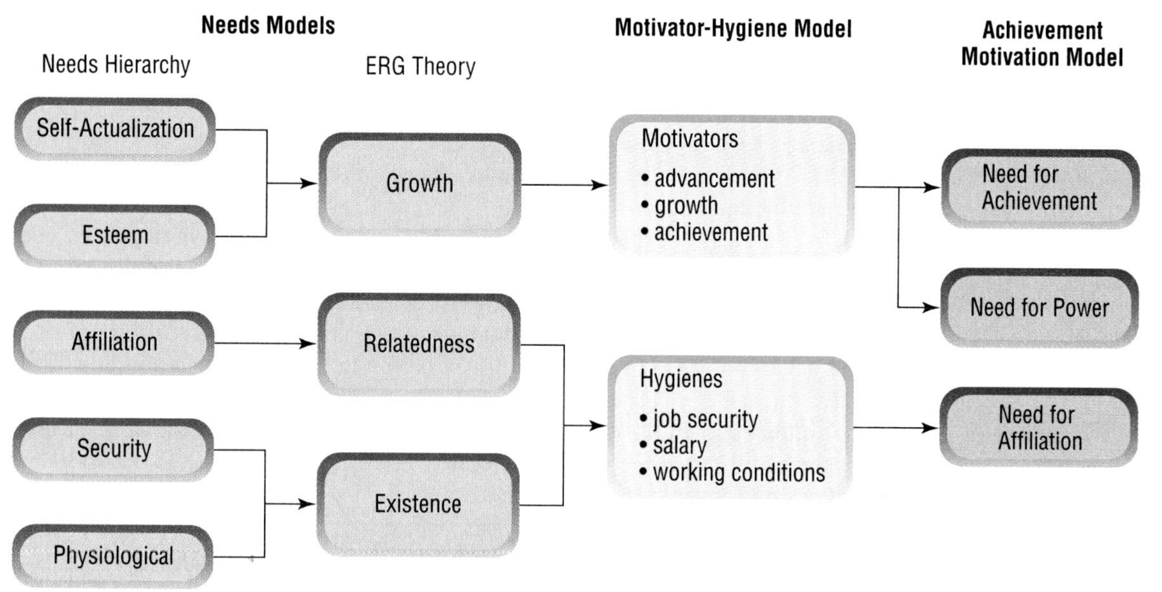

Learning Objective:

3. Describe and apply two process models of motivation.

PROCESS MODELS OF MOTIVATION

Process models are used to describe and analyze how personal factors (internal to the person) interact and influence each other to produce certain kinds of behavior. An example would be that individuals exert more effort to obtain rewards that satisfy important needs than to obtain rewards that do not. The four best known process models of motivation are expectancy, reinforcement, equity, and goal setting. In this section, we cover the expectancy and equity models of motivation. In Chapter 4, we discussed the reinforcement model, and in Chapter 6 we present the goal-setting model.

EXPECTANCY MODEL

The expectancy model differs markedly from the content models just discussed. Instead of focusing on factors in the work environment that contribute to job satisfaction or dissatisfaction, the expectancy model covers the entire work environment.[21] The **expectancy model** states that people are motivated to work when they expect to achieve things they want from their jobs. These things might include satisfaction of safety needs, the excitement of doing a challenging task, or the ability to set and achieve difficult goals. A basic premise of the expectancy model is that employees are rational people. They think about what they have to do to be rewarded and how much the rewards mean to them before they perform their jobs. Four assumptions about the causes of behavior in organizations provide the basis for this model.

First, a combination of forces in the individual and the environment determines behavior (recall the discussion of the interactionist perspective in Chapter 2). Neither the individual nor the environment alone determines behavior. People join organizations with expectations about their jobs that are based on their needs, motivations, and past experiences. These factors all influence how people respond to an organization, but they can and do change over time.

Second, individuals decide their own behaviors in organizations, even though many constraints are placed on individual behavior (e.g., through rules, technology, and work-group norms). Most individuals make two kinds of conscious decisions: (1) decisions about coming to work, staying with the same organization, and joining other organizations (membership decisions); and (2) decisions about how much to produce, how hard to work, and the quality of workmanship (job-performance decisions).

Third, different individuals have different needs and goals. As we showed in Table 5.1, employees want different rewards from their work, depending on their gender, race, age, and other characteristics. Of the many rewards that Starbucks offers to its employees, which one(s) do you find attractive? Why? In 5 years, are these same rewards likely to be attractive to you?

Fourth, individuals decide among alternatives based on their perceptions of whether a specific behavior will lead to a desired outcome. Individuals do what they perceive will lead to desired outcomes and avoid doing what they perceive will lead to undesirable outcomes.[22]

In general, the expectancy model holds that individuals have their own needs and ideas about what they desire from their work (rewards). They act on these needs and ideas when making decisions about what organization to join and how hard to work. The model also holds that individuals are not inherently motivated or unmotivated, rather that motivation depends on the situation facing individuals and how it fits their needs.

To help you understand the expectancy model, we must define its most important variables and explain how they operate. They are first-level and second-level outcomes, expectancy, valence, and instrumentality.

First-Level and Second-Level Outcomes. The results of behaviors associated with doing the job itself are called **first-level outcomes.** They include level of performance, amount of absenteeism, and quality of work. **Second-level outcomes** are the rewards (either positive or negative) that first-level outcomes are likely to produce. They include a pay increase, promotion, acceptance by coworkers, and job security.

Expectancy. The belief that a particular level of effort will be followed by a particular level of performance is called **expectancy.** It can vary from the belief that there is absolutely no relationship between effort and performance to the certainty that a given level of effort will result in a corresponding level of performance. Expectancy has a value ranging from 0, indicating no chance that a first-level outcome will occur after the behavior, to +1, indicating certainty that a particular first-level outcome will follow a behavior. For example, if you believe that you have no chance of getting a good grade on the next exam by studying this chapter, your expectancy value would be 0. Having this expectancy, you shouldn't study this chapter.

Instrumentality. The relationship between first-level outcomes and second-level outcomes is called **instrumentality.** It can have values ranging from –1 to +1. A –1 indicates that attainment of a second-level outcome is inversely related to the achievement of a first-level outcome. For example, Tammy Stebbins wants to be accepted as a member of her work group, but it has a norm for an acceptable level of performance. If Stebbins violates this norm, she won't be accepted by her work group. Therefore Stebbins limits her performance so as not to violate the group's norm. A +1 indicates that the first-level outcome is positively related to the second-level outcome. For example, if you received an A on all your exams, the probability that you would achieve your desired second-level outcome (passing this course) approaches +1. If there were no relationship between your performance on a test and either passing or failing this course, your instrumentality would be 0.

Valence. An individual's preference for a particular second-level outcome is called **valence.** Outcomes having a positive valence include being respected by friends and coworkers, performing meaningful work, having job security, and earning enough money to support yourself and a family. Outcomes having a negative valence are things that you want to avoid, such as being laid off, being passed over for a promotion, or being discharged for sexual harassment. An outcome is positive when it is preferred and negative when it is not preferred or is to be avoided. An outcome has a valence of 0 when the individual is indifferent about receiving it.

Putting It Together. In brief, the expectancy model holds that work motivation is determined by individual beliefs regarding effort–performance relationships and the desirability of various work outcomes associated with different performance levels. Simply put, you can remember the model's important features by the saying:

> People exert work effort to achieve performance that leads to valued work-related outcomes.

Expectancy Model in Action. The five key variables just defined and discussed lead to a general expectancy model of motivation, as shown in Figure 5.7. Motivation is the force that causes individuals to expend effort, but effort alone is not enough. Unless an individual believes that effort will lead to some desired performance level (first-level outcome), he or she won't make much of an effort. The effort–performance relationship is based on a perception of the difficulty of achieving a particular behavior (say, working for an A in this course) and the probability of achieving that behavior. On the one hand, you may have a high expectancy that, if you attend class, study the book, take good notes, and prepare for exams, you can achieve an A in this class. That expectancy is likely to translate into making the effort required on those activities to get an A. On the other hand, you may believe that, even if you attend class, study the book, take good notes, and prepare for exams, your chances of getting an A are only 20 percent. That expectancy is likely to keep you from expending the effort required on these activities to achieve an A.

Figure 5.7 **Expectancy Model in Action**

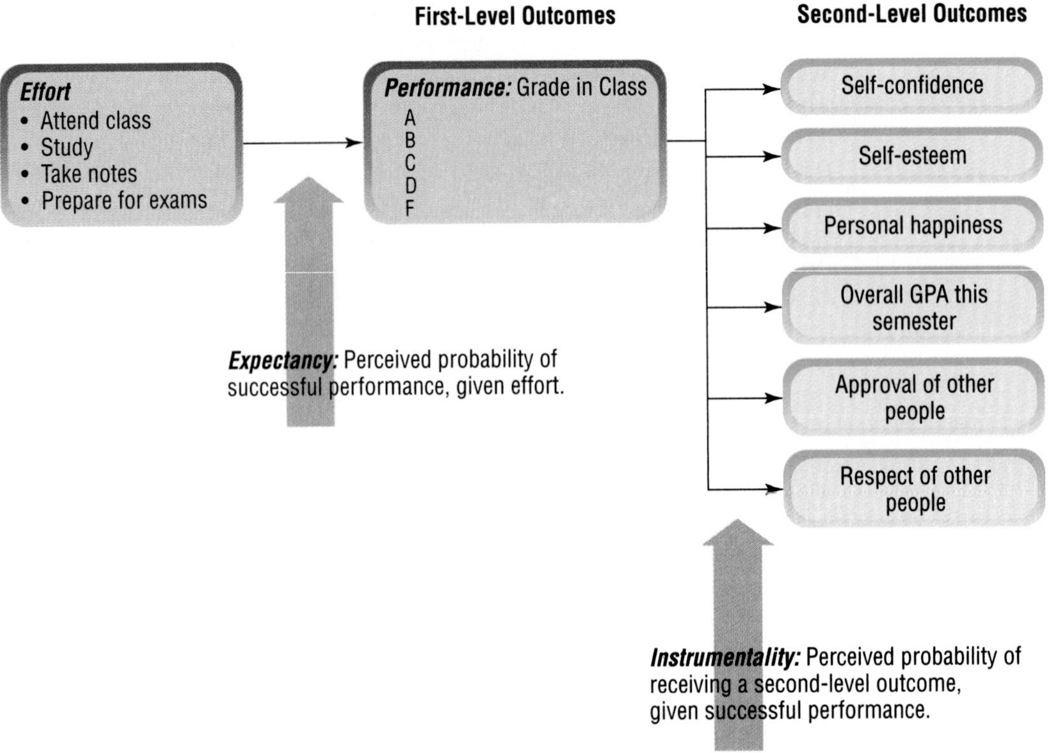

Source: Cron, W. L., Slocum, J. W., and VandeWalle, D. Goal orientations: A longitudinal study of academic performance. Unpublished manuscript, Cox School of Business, SMU, Dallas, Texas, 2000.

Performance level is important in obtaining desired second-level outcomes. Figure 5.7 shows six desirable second-level outcomes: self-confidence, self-esteem, personal happiness, overall GPA this semester, approval of other people, and respect of other people. In general, if you believe that a particular level of performance (A, B, C, D, or F) will lead to these desired outcomes, you are more likely to try to perform at that level. If you really desire these six second-level outcomes and you can achieve them only if you get an A in this course, the instrumentality between receiving an A and these six outcomes will be positive. But, if you believe that getting an A in this course means that you will not gain personal happiness and the approval and respect of other people, the instrumentality between an A and these outcomes will be negative. That is, if the higher the grade, the less likely you are to experience personal happiness, you might choose not to get an A in this course. Once you have made this choice, you will lessen your effort and start cutting class, not studying for exams, and so on.

Research Findings. Researchers are still working on ways to test this model, which has presented some problems. First, the model tries to predict choice or the amount of effort an individual will expend on one or more tasks. However, there is little agreement about what constitutes choice or effort for different individuals. Therefore this important variable is difficult to measure accurately. Second, the expectancy model doesn't specify which second-level outcomes are important to a particular individual in a given situation. Although researchers are expected to address this issue, comparison of the limited results to date is often difficult because each study is unique. Take another look at the second-level outcomes in Figure 5.7. Would you choose them? What others might you choose? Third, the model contains an implicit assumption that motivation is a conscious choice process. That is, the individual consciously calculates the pain or pleasure that he or she expects to attain or avoid when making a choice. The expectancy model says nothing about unconscious motivation or personality characteristics. In fact, people often do not make conscious choices about which outcomes to seek. Can you recall going through this process concerning your grade while taking this course? Finally, expectancy theory works best in cultures that emphasize internal attribution. When people in a culture believe that they can control their work environment and their own behavior, such as in the United States, Canada, and the United Kingdom, expectancy theory can explain behavior. In cultures where people believe the work environment and their own behavior are not completely under their control, such as in Brazil, Saudi Arabia, Iran, Japan, and China, the assumptions of the model might not be valid. For example, a Canadian manager in Japan decided to promote one of her young female Japanese sales representatives to manager (a status and monetary reward). To her surprise, the promotion diminished the new Japanese manager's performance. Why? Japanese have a high need for harmony—to fit in with their colleagues. The promotion, an individualistic reward, separated the new manager from her colleagues, embarrassed her, and therefore diminished her work motivation.[23]

In Practice. Although some research problems remain, the expectancy model has some important implications for motivating employees. These implications can be grouped into seven suggestions for action.[24]

- Managers should try to determine the outcomes that each employee values. Two ways of doing so are observing employee reactions to different rewards and asking employees about the types of rewards they want from their jobs. However, managers must recognize that employees can and do change their minds about desired outcomes over time.
- Managers should define good, adequate, and poor performance in terms that are observable and measurable. Employees need to understand what is expected of them and how these expectations affect performance. When the Baxter Pharmaceutical Company announced a new examination table for doctors, its salespeople wanted to know what behaviors, such as cold-calling on new accounts or trying to sell the new tables to their existing accounts, would lead to more sales. To the extent that Baxter was able to train its salespeople in selling its new product, it was able to link salespeople's efforts with performance.
- Managers should be sure that desired levels of performance set for employees can be attained. If employees feel that the level of performance necessary to get a reward is higher than they can reasonably achieve, their motivation to perform will be low. For example, Nordstrom tells its employees: "Respond to Unreasonable Customer Requests." Employees are urged to keep scrapbooks with "heroic" acts, such as hand delivering items purchased by phone to the airport for a customer leaving on a last-minute business trip, changing a customer's flat tire, or paying a customer's parking ticket when in-store gift wrapping has taken longer than expected. It is hardly surprising that Nordstrom pays its employees much more than they could earn at a rival's store. For those who love to sell and can meet its demanding standards, Nordstrom is nirvana.[25]
- Managers should directly link the specific performance they desire to the outcomes desired by employees. Recall the discussion in Chapter 4 of how operant conditioning principles can be applied to improve performance. If an employee has achieved the desired level of performance for a promotion, the employee should be promoted as soon as possible. If a high level of motivation is to be created and maintained, it is extremely important for employees to see clearly and quickly the reward process at work. Concrete acts must accompany statements of intent in linking performance to rewards.
- Managers should never forget that perceptions, not reality, determine motivation. Too often, managers misunderstand the behavior of employees because they tend to rely on their own perceptions of the situation and forget that employees' perceptions may be different.

- Managers should analyze situations for conflicts. Having set up positive expectancies for employees, managers must look at an entire situation to determine whether other factors conflict with the desired behaviors (e.g., the informal work group or the organization's formal reward system). Motivation will be high only when employees perceive many rewards and few negative outcomes associated with good performance.
- Managers should be sure that changes in outcomes or rewards are large enough to motivate significant efforts. Trivial rewards may result in minimal efforts, if any, to improve performance. Rewards must be large enough to motivate individuals to make the effort required to substantially change performance.

Managers at The Walt Disney Company have relied on these practices to create highly successful theme parks that excel at satisfying the customer. The company has been able to build customer loyalty by doing little extra things—point-of-contact excellence—for customers and making sure that customers get exactly what they want. Point-of-contact excellence is referred to as a "magic moment." Disney's carefully screened employees or "cast members" are taught how to make each interaction with an individual customer an incident of lasting impression. Each employee strives for 60 such magic moments during an eight-hour shift. The following Managing Communication Competency feature highlights how Disney communicates its motivational expectations to its 45,000 cast members at Disney World in Orlando, Florida. What model(s) of motivation does Disney rely on to motivate its cast members?

Equity Model

Feelings of unfairness were among the most frequent sources of job dissatisfaction reported to Herzberg and his associates. Some researchers have made this desire for fairness, justice, or equity a central focus of their models. Assume that you just received a 7 percent raise. Will this raise lead to higher performance, lower performance, or no change in performance? Are you satisfied with this increase? Would your satisfaction with this pay increase vary with the consumer price index, with what you expected to get, or with what others in the organization performing the same job and at the same performance level received?

The **equity model** focuses on an individual's feelings of how fairly he or she is treated in comparison with others.[26] It contains two major assumptions. The first is that individuals evaluate their interpersonal relationships just as they would evaluate the buying or selling of a home, shares of stock, or a car. The model views relationships as exchange processes in which individuals make contributions and expect certain results.

The second assumption is that individuals don't operate in a vacuum. They compare their situations to those of others to determine the equity of an exchange. In other words, what happens to the individual is important in terms of what happens to the others involved (e.g., coworkers, relatives, and neighbors).

General Equity Model. The equity model is based on the comparison of two variables: inputs and outcomes. **Inputs** represent what an individual contributes to an exchange; **outcomes** are what an individual receives from the exchange. Some typical inputs and outcomes are shown in Table 5.4 on page 152. A word of caution: The items in the two lists aren't paired and don't represent specific exchanges.

According to the equity model, individuals assign weights to various inputs and outcomes according to their perceptions of the situation. Because most situations involve multiple inputs and outcomes, the weighting process isn't precise. However, people generally can distinguish between important and less important inputs and outcomes. After they arrive at a ratio of inputs and outcomes for themselves, they compare it with their perceived ratios of inputs and outcomes of others who are in the same or a similar situation. These relevant others become the objects of comparison for individuals in determining whether they feel equitably treated.[27]

COMPETENCY: MANAGING COMMUNICATION

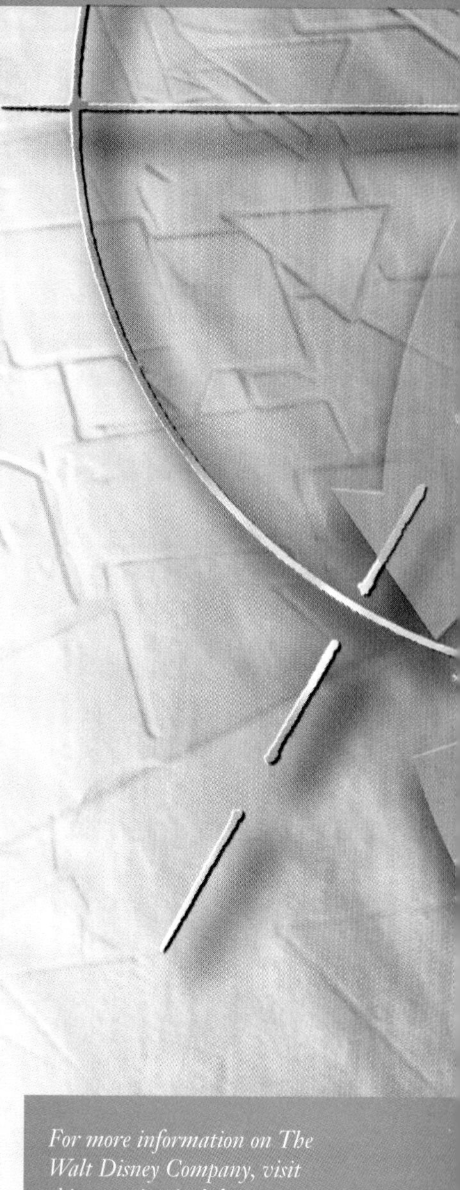

THE WALT DISNEY COMPANY

To become a Disney employee, each person has to begin thinking of himself or herself as a member of a team—actually, a cast member. To accomplish this, managers from the Disney human resource department conduct thorough 45-minute interviews of all prospective employees. They try to discover whether applicants really care about people, whether they have high standards for themselves, what their personal values are, and whether they like hard work. Applicants passing this screening are ushered into a building called "Central Casting." Turning a handle resembling the Doorknob character from *Alice in Wonderland*, they enter a hallway lined with statuettes and paintings of Disney characters. Next they watch a 10-minute video that informs them about the schedule (open 365 days a year), strict guidelines for employees' appearance, and the need to provide for their own transportation. After the interview and video, about 20 percent decide not to fill out an application for a job at Disney.

Once hired, new employees start a two-day initiation process known as "Disney Traditions." Vice presidents, housekeepers, popcorn poppers, and others all go through the same process in classes of 40. Disney pays no attention to job title. All students wear name tags with only their first names because only guests are afforded special status. Split into smaller groups, these new employees go into the Magic Kingdom to observe veteran cast members as they greet guests.

During this two-day process, newly hired cast members learn Disney's four cardinal principles of guest relations—safety, courtesy, show, and efficiency. Everything that a guest can hear, touch, feel, or smell is considered part of the "show," including clean streets, piano music, the smell of popcorn, and special effects. Disney bans newspapers in its parks for two reasons: (1) cast members don't have to pick up discarded newspapers, and (2) without outside distractions, guests can enjoy the Disney experience more.

After this two-day orientation, new hires are assigned to specific locations. They meet their supervisor and their Disney qualified trainer, who is a veteran at the same job and is always available to answer questions. With an outline and checklist, new employees start training programs of varying lengths. Their trainer helps them look at the emotions, needs, and expectations of guests. For example, more than 20,000 people lock keys in their cars each year. To solve this problem, cast members roam parking lots, offering assistance with free key making. When guests forget where they parked their cars, they need only tell the cast member approximately when they arrived at the park for the cast member to find their cars.[28]

For more information on The Walt Disney Company, visit this organization's home page at www.disney.com.

Equity exists whenever the ratio of a person's outcomes to inputs equals the ratio of outcomes to inputs for relevant others. For example, an individual may feel properly paid in terms of what he or she puts into a job compared to what other workers are getting for their inputs. Inequity exists when the ratios of outcomes to inputs are unequal. Laura Maier, a manager of technical systems for NASA at the Kennedy Space Center, works harder than her coworkers, completes all her tasks on time while others don't, and puts in longer hours than others, but receives the same pay raise as the others. What happens? Maier believes that her inputs are greater than those of her coworkers and therefore should merit a greater pay raise. Inequity can also occur when people are overpaid. In this case, the overpaid employees might be motivated by guilt or social pressure to work harder to reduce the imbalance between their inputs and outcomes and those of their coworkers.

Table 5.4

Examples of Inputs and Outcomes in Organizations

INPUTS	OUTCOMES
Age	Challenging job assignments
Attendance	Fringe benefits
Interpersonal skills, communication skills	Job perquisites (parking space or office location)
Job effort (long hours)	Job security
Level of education	Monotony
Past experience	Promotion
Performance	Recognition
Personal appearance	Responsibility
Seniority	Salary
Social status	Seniority benefits
Technical skills	Status symbols
Training	Working conditions

Consequences of Inequity. **Inequity** causes tension within an individual and among individuals. Tension is not pleasurable, so a person is motivated to reduce it to a tolerable level. To reduce a perceived inequity and the corresponding level of tension, the person may choose to act in one or more of the following ways. This tension-reduction process is illustrated in Figure 5.8.

- People may either increase or decrease their inputs to what they feel to be an equitable level. For example, underpaid people may reduce the quantity of their production, work shorter hours, be absent more frequently, and so on. Figure 5.9 shows these relationships graphically.
- People may change their outcomes to restore equity. Many union organizers try to attract nonmembers by pledging to improve working conditions, hours, and pay without an increase in employee effort (input).
- People may distort their own inputs and outcomes. As opposed to actually changing inputs or outcomes, people may mentally distort them to achieve a more favorable balance. For example, people who feel inequitably treated may distort how hard they work (This job is a piece of cake.) or attempt to increase the importance of the job to the organization (This is really an important job!).
- People may leave the organization or request a transfer to another department. In doing so, they hope to find a more favorable balance.
- People may shift to a new reference group to reduce the source of the inequity. The star high school athlete who doesn't get a scholarship to a major university might decide that a smaller school has more advantages, thereby justifying a need to look at smaller schools when making a selection.

Figure 5.8 **Inequity as a Motivational Process**

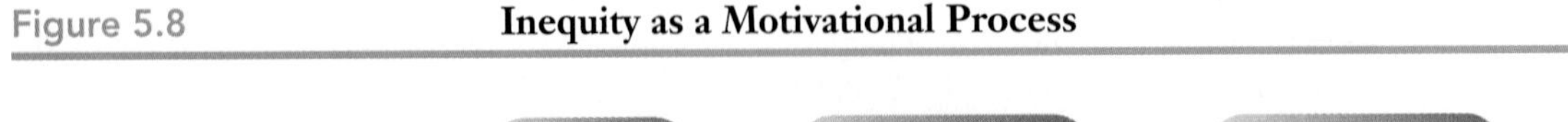

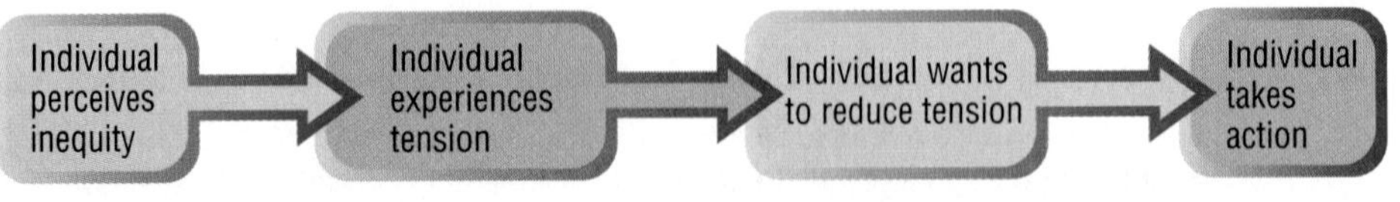

Figure 5.9 **Performance Levels for Underpaid and Overpaid Employees**

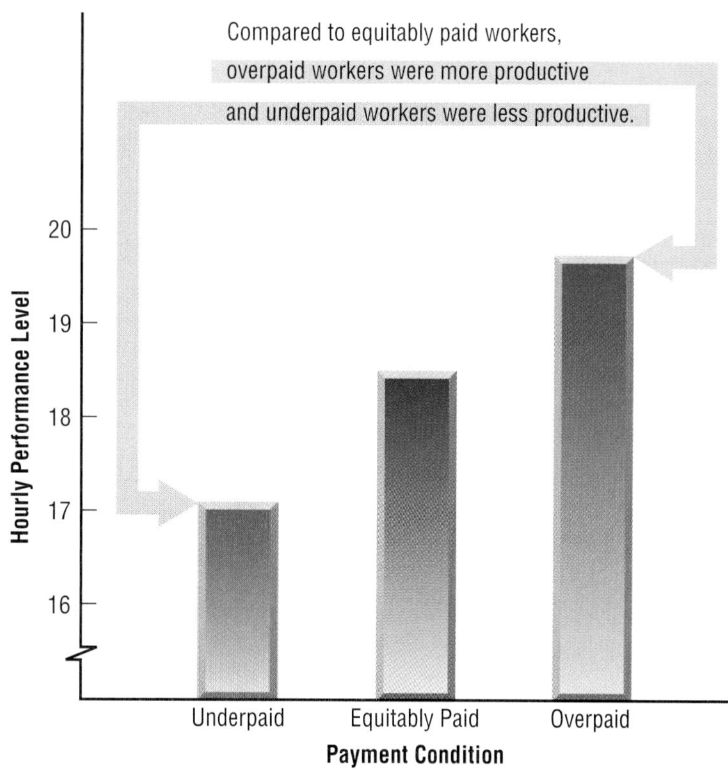

- People may distort the inputs or outcomes of others. People may come to believe that others in a comparison group actually work harder than they do and therefore deserve greater rewards.

Keeping these six actions in mind, let's take a look at employee theft as a reaction to inequity. Employee theft is one of the most serious problems facing organizations. Each day companies lose an average of \$9 per employee. One of every 28 employees is stealing from his or her company. The typical male thief annually steals about \$185,000; the female thief, about \$48,000. The American Management Association estimates that employee theft costs U.S. organizations more than \$400 billion a year. Of that amount, about \$250 billion is stolen from retail department stores and over the Internet. Theft is up almost 22.2 percent a year for the past 5 years.[29] After reading both accounts in the following Managing Ethics Competency feature, decide which you think was associated with greater employee theft.

Procedural Justice. In contrast to equity theory, which emphasizes the *outcome* of the decision, the procedural justice theory examines the impact of the *process* used to make a decision. The perceived fairness of rules and procedures is referred to as **procedural justice.**[30] The procedural justice theory holds that employees are going to be more motivated to perform at a high level when they perceive as fair the procedures used to make decisions about the distribution of outcomes. Employees are motivated to attain fairness in how decisions are made, as well as in the decisions themselves.

Research has shown that reactions to pay raises, for example, are greatly affected by employees' perceptions about the fairness of the raises.[31] If in the minds of the employees the pay raises were administered fairly, the employees were more satisfied with their increases than if the employees judged the procedures used to make these

COMPETENCY: MANAGING ETHICS

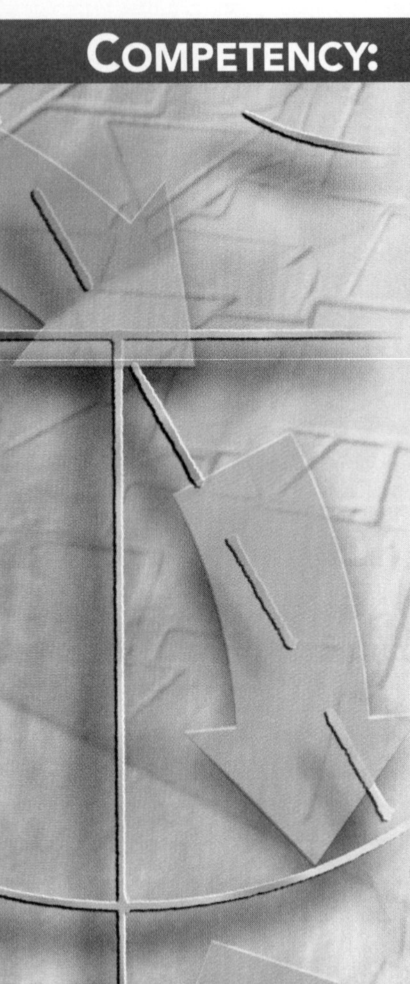

To Steal or Not: That's the Question

The organization reduced its payroll by 15 percent for 10 weeks at each of two plants instead of laying people off. Management drafted two accounts concerning the reduction in pay but read only one account at each plant. Before announcing the reduction in pay, overall theft was running about 3 percent annually.

Account A

The reason why I'm sharing this information with you is that I want you to understand what's happening here. As you probably know, we've lost our key contract, which will make things pretty lean around there. Starting Monday, each one of us will take a 15 percent cut in pay. This applies to you, to me, to everyone. Fringe benefits won't be touched. I don't expect this cut to last more than ten weeks. We hope to be stronger than ever after this trying time. I want to thank each and every one of you personally for gutting it out with us.

Account B

It is inevitable in a business like ours that cost-cutting measures are needed. Unfortunately, the time has come for us to take such measures. I know that it won't be easy for anyone, but the president has decided that a 15 percent cut across the board will be instituted starting Monday. All employees, including the president, will share in this effort to save our company. We're pretty sure that the cuts will last only ten weeks. I'll answer a few questions, but then I have to catch a plane for another meeting.

The Outcome

Theft by employees who heard account B increased by more than 250 percent. Why? Employees who heard account B believed that they weren't hearing the entire story. They reduced perceived inequities by acts of theft. To be effective, equity explanations must be perceived to be honest, genuine, and not manipulative.[32]

increases to be unfair. The perceived fairness of the procedures used to allocate pay raises is a better predictor of satisfaction than the absolute amount of pay received. Similarly, students base their faculty member evaluations on perceptions of fair grading decisions.

In both the pay and evaluation situations, the individual can't directly control the decision but can react to the procedures used to make it. Even when a particular decision has negative outcomes for the individual, fair procedures help ensure that the individual feels that his or her interests are being protected.

Employees' assessments of procedural justice have also been related to their trust in management, intention to leave the organization, evaluation of their supervisor, employee theft, and job satisfaction. Consider some of the relatively trivial day-to-day issues in an organization that are affected by procedural justice: decisions about who will cover the phones during lunch while others are away from their desks, the choice of the site of the company picnic, or who gets the latest software for a personal computer.

Procedural justice has also been found to affect the attitudes of workers who survive a layoff. When workers are laid off, survivors (those who remain on the job) are often in a good position to judge the fairness of the layoff in terms of how it was handled. When a layoff is handled fairly, survivors feel more committed to the organization than when they believe that the laid-off workers were unfairly treated.[33]

Organizational Citizenship Behavior. In many organizations, employees perform tasks that are voluntary or not formally required.[34] **Organizational citizenship behavior** exceeds formal job duties but is necessary for the organization's survival or important to its image and acceptance. Examples of organizational citizenship behavior include helping coworkers solve problems, making constructive suggestions, volunteering to perform community service work (e.g., blood drives, United Way campaigns, and charity work). Although not formally required by employers, these behaviors are important in all organizations. Helping coworkers is an especially important form of organizational citizenship behavior when it comes to computers. Every organization has some computer gurus, but often it's the secretary who doesn't go to lunch who can fix a problem easier and without putting down the struggling user. Managers often underestimate the amount of this informal helping that takes place in organizations.

Employees have considerable discretion over whether to engage in organizational citizenship behaviors. Employees who have been treated fairly and are satisfied are more likely to do so than employees who feel unfairly treated. Fairly treated employees engage in citizenship behaviors because they want to give something back to the organization. Most people desire to have fair exchanges with coworkers and others in their organization.

Ray Hertz, a marketing consultant for the Internet & New Media division of EDS, developed a simple yet innovative method to acknowledge organizational citizenship behaviors at his Dallas office. At the beginning of the year, Hertz gives each of his 10 employees a jar containing 12 marbles. Throughout the year, employees may give marbles to others who have helped them in some way or who have provided an extraordinary service. Employees are recognized throughout the year and are proud of the number of marbles they accumulate, even though they receive no monetary reward from Hertz.

Equity Model Findings. Most of the research on the equity model focuses on pay and other compensation issues.[35] A review of these studies indicates some shortcomings. First, the comparison group is always known. But what happens if the comparison group changes or the situation changes in other respects?

Second, the research focuses mainly on short-term comparisons. Are pay cuts, temporary assignments, longer working hours, and the like such that a person believes that inputs or outcomes are likely to remain the same? That is, do perceptions of inequity or equity increase, decrease, or stabilize over time? In the preceding Managing Ethics Competency feature, what is likely to happen to the rate of theft after the 10-week period if salaries aren't restored to their previous levels? Would you expect theft to increase in group A? Answers to these types of questions would help give insight into the dynamic character of equity and inequity.

Third, the equity model doesn't specify the type of action (from among the actions listed) that a person would choose in order to reduce the perceived inequity in a particular situation. That is, is one strategy used primarily when pay is involved, another when theft or absenteeism is involved, and yet another when productivity is involved?

In Practice. Despite these questions, managers often use the equity model in making a variety of decisions, such as taking disciplinary actions, giving pay raises, allocating office and parking space, and dispensing other perks. The equity model leads to two primary conclusions. First, employees should be treated fairly. When individuals believe that they are not being treated fairly, they will try to correct the situation and reduce tension by means of one or more of the types of actions identified previously in this section. A sizable inequity increases the probability that individuals will choose more than one type of action to reduce it. For example, individuals may partially withdraw from the organization by being absent more often, arriving at work late, not completing assignments on time, or stealing. The organization may try to reduce the inputs of such employees by assigning them to monotonous jobs, taking away some perquisites, and giving them only small pay increases.

Second, people make decisions concerning equity only after they compare their inputs and outcomes with those of comparable employees.[36] These relevant others may be employees of the same organization or of other organizations. The latter present a major problem for managers, who cannot control what other organizations pay their employees. For example, Rand Hammond, a partner at Ernst & Young, hired a recent business school undergraduate for $42,500, the maximum the company could pay for the job. The new employee thought that this salary was very good until she compared it to the $45,250 that fellow graduates were getting at GTE, MCI, and Sprint. She felt that she was being underpaid in comparison with her former classmates, causing an inequity problem for her (and the company).[37]

The idea that fairness in organizations is determined by more than just money has received a great deal of attention from managers. Organizational fairness is influenced by how rules and procedures are used and how much employees are consulted in decisions that affect them.

Comparisons Among Process Models

The expectancy and equity models emphasize different aspects of motivation. The expectancy model holds that employees are rational and evaluate how much the reward means to them before they perform their jobs. How well employees will perform depends, in part, on what they believe is expected of them. Once their manager has communicated these expectations, employees assign probabilities that their efforts will lead to desired first-level outcomes (e.g., performance, quality, and absenteeism). These outcomes are linked to valued rewards (e.g., high pay or job security) they desire from their jobs. It is the manager's job to make the desired rewards attainable by clearly linking rewards to performance. Allowing employees to choose among rewards, such as improved insurance, child-care and elder-care facilities for family members, and additional vacation days, is important because of different employee preferences. **Cafeteria-style benefit plans**—reward systems that permit employees to select their fringe benefits from a menu of alternatives—have become very popular. Because benefits represent about 35 percent of payroll costs in many organizations, letting employees choose the ones they prefer and linking them to performance is important to retaining valued employees and controlling costs.[38]

In contrast to the expectancy model, where employees make judgments about the value of rewards, the equity model holds that employees comparing themselves to others in similar situations determine equity. According to the equity model, people are motivated to escape inequitable situations but to remain on the job and perform at high levels in equitable situations. Because perceptions of fairness often vary among employees, different employees may react differently in various situations.

Both models emphasize the role of rewards and an individual's decision-making processes. These models suggest that managers concerned about improving employee performance should actively create proper work environments, match employees to jobs, and establish clear performance–reward systems. Motivation for high performance won't exist unless managers recognize such performance when it occurs and reward it quickly.

CHAPTER SUMMARY

1. Define motivation and describe the motivation process.

We described a six-stage motivational model, indicating that individuals behave in certain ways to satisfy their needs. We also presented three motivational challenges—motives can only be inferred, needs are dynamic, and there are considerable differences in people's motivations. To help you understand these challenges, we examined two major classes of models of motivation: content and process. Content models focus on the factors within the person that drive, sustain, or inhibit behavior and describe the specific needs that motivate people. Process models provide a description and analysis of how behavior is driven, sustained, or stopped.

2. Describe and apply four content models of motivation.

We presented four widely recognized content models of motivation. Maslow proposed that people have five types of needs: physiological, security, affiliation, esteem, and self-actualization and that when a need is satisfied it no longer motivates a person. Alderfer agreed with Maslow that needs motivate people but claimed that people have only three types of needs: existence, relatedness, and growth. If a person's growth need can't be satisfied, the person focuses on satisfying relatedness needs. McClelland believed that people have three learned needs (achievement, affiliation, and power) that are rooted in the culture of a society. We focused on the role of the achievement need and indicated the characteristics associated with high achievers. The final content model discussed was Herzberg's. He claimed that two types of factors affect a person's motivation: motivators and hygienes. Motivators, such as job challenge, lead to job satisfaction but not to job dissatisfaction. Hygiene factors, such as working conditions, prevent job dissatisfaction but can't lead to job satisfaction.

3. Describe and apply two process models of motivation.

We reviewed two process models of motivation. The expectancy model holds that individuals know what they desire from work. They choose activities only after they decide that the activities will satisfy their needs. The primary components of this model are first- and second-level outcomes, expectancy, instrumentality, and valence. An individual must believe that effort expended will lead (expectancy) to some desired level of performance (first-level outcome) and that this level of performance will lead (instrumentality) to desired rewards (second-level outcomes and valences). Otherwise, the individual won't be motivated to expend the effort necessary to perform at the desired level. The equity model focuses on the individual's perception of how fairly he or she is treated in comparison with others in similar situations. To make this judgment, an individual compares his or her inputs (experience, age) and outcomes (salary) with those of relevant others. If equity exists, the person isn't motivated to act. If inequity exists, the person may engage in any one of six behaviors to reduce this inequity. Both procedural justice and organizational citizenship behavior are based on the equity model and have significant implications for employees' perceptions of equity.

KEY TERMS AND CONCEPTS

Ability
Achievement motivation model
Affiliation needs
Cafeteria-style benefit plans
Content models
Deficiency needs
Equity model
ERG model
Esteem needs
Existence needs
Expectancy
Expectancy model
Extrinsic factors
First-level outcomes
Fulfillment-progression process
Goal
Growth needs
Hygiene factors
Inequity
Inputs
Instrumentality
Intrinsic factors
Motivation
Motivator factors
Motivator-hygiene model
Needs
Needs hierarchy model
Organizational citizenship behavior
Outcomes
Physiological needs
Procedural justice
Process models
Relatedness needs
Second-level outcomes
Security needs
Self-actualization needs
Thematic Apperception Test (TAT)
Valence

DISCUSSION QUESTIONS

1. Think about the worst job you have had. What motivational approach was used in that organization? Now think about the best job you have had. What motivational approach was used in that organization?
2. Identify the hygiene factors in the Starbucks Preview Case. According to Herzberg, what role do they play? Are they consistent with the theory?
3. How would the expectancy model explain the behaviors of employees who stole from their company after it a nnounced that all employees would have to take a 10 percent pay cut for the next 5 weeks?
4. Why is job satisfaction not strongly related to job performance?
5. How could someone like John Schnatter, CEO of Papa John's, apply the ERG model to motivate employees?
6. Why might an employee with a low level of motivation be a top performer?
7. Would you like to work at Disney? What aspect(s) of Disney's recruiting process did you find appealing? What are the motivations behind your answer?
8. Imagine that you have just been selected to become a new sales manager for Dell Computers in Romania. What would you do to motivate employees to join your firm? To be high producers?
9. What steps can an organization take to encourage procedural justice by its managers?
10. How can an organization use inequity to motivate employees?

DEVELOPING COMPETENCIES

Competency: Managing Self—What Do You Want from Your Job?

We have listed the 16 most often mentioned characteristics that employees want from their jobs in random order.[39] Please rank them in order of both their importance to you and then in terms of satisfaction for you. Rank these characteristics 1 (most important), 2 (next most important), 3 (next most important), and so on, through 16 (least important). Use the same procedure to rank satisfaction. Then compare your answers to those of managers working in a wide variety of jobs and industries provided at the end of this exercise.

Job Characteristics	Importance Rank	Satisfaction Rank
1. Working independently	_____	_____
2. Chances for promotion	_____	_____
3. Contact with people	_____	_____
4. Flexible hours	_____	_____
5. Health insurance and other benefits	_____	_____
6. Interesting work	_____	_____
7. Work important to society	_____	_____
8. Job security	_____	_____
9. Opportunity to learn new skills	_____	_____
10. High income	_____	_____
11. Recognition from team members	_____	_____
12. Vacation time	_____	_____
13. Regular hours	_____	_____
14. Working close to home	_____	_____
15. Little job stress	_____	_____
16. A job in which I can help others	_____	_____

Answers

For job importance, the rank order of characteristics is 1–6; 2–14; 3–15; 4–16; 5–1; 6–2; 7–13; 8–3; 9–4; 10–11; 12–5; 13–8; 14–12; 15–10; 16–9.

For job satisfaction, the rank order of characteristics is 1–3; 2–14; 3–2; 4–6; 5–13; 6–4; 7–9; 8–7; 9–11; 10–12; 11–15; 12–8; 13–5; 14–1; 15–16; 16–10.

Questions

1. Choose any model of motivation and think about your answers. What situational factors (such as being in school, looking for a new job, desiring more responsibility, desiring to work for a foreign organization, and the like) influenced your ranking of importance?
2. What characteristics gave most of the respondents their greatest job satisfaction? What model of motivation helps you understand these rankings?

Competency: Managing Teams—SEI Investments

The first sign that there's something unusual about SEI Investments, a $456 million financial company, is the design of its headquarters building in Oaks, Pennsylvania. On the outside, it looks like a Playskool version of a farm. On the inside, it looks like a beehive. All the furniture is on wheels so that employees can create their own work areas. Colorful cables spiral down from the ceiling, carrying electricity, Internet access, and telephone cords. So many people move their desks around so often that SEI has created software to map everyone's location. There are no secretaries, walls, or organizational charts. Tasks are distributed among 140 self-managed teams. Some are permanent, designed to serve big customers, but many are temporary. People come together to solve a problem and disband when the work is finished. Different people work on different parts of a problem until it is completed.

When SEI moved into its new headquarters in 1996, the company's president declared that each employee could only bring two boxes of possessions from the old office to Oaks. And as there were no prearranged offices or floor plans, it was up to the teams to arrange things as they saw fit. Teams could have as few as 2 or as many as 30 members. Most employees belong to one "base" team and to three or four ad-hoc teams. The only power a person has is persuasion. No bureaucracy provides resources, and no senior managers issue orders. The ability to motivate others is exhibited through communication and team competencies.

All employees know the goals that matter most: earnings per share and assets under management. SEI establishes corporate-level goals and translates these into goals for the team. According to Henry Greer, SEI's president, "Our goals are passed out to the teams and they figure out what they have to do to hit them. Once the team understands its goal(s), everyone on that team drives toward that goal. Greer and his assistants do not care how many vacation days people take, so long as they hit their goals.

To motivate people to work together in teams, Greer and his staff follow four principles.

- Top leaders look for ways to expand SEI's Internet and interactive media capabilities. This means recruiting and retaining high-potential individuals. Typically, they look for people who have confidence in their ideas, can articulate and sell these ideas to others, have respect for others, and have a drive to succeed.
- Team leaders must have a sixth sense for trouble. Teams at SEI have maximum freedom to experiment but a clear responsibility to disclose when an experiment fails. Team leaders must read people's expressions and listen to hall talk to understand when a team is not making progress.
- Even self-managed teams need leaders. People must demonstrate competencies to be chosen by their fellow employees to be team leaders. Team leaders need communication and change management competencies that enable them to use a "soft" hand to guide the team. It's up to the team leader to describe the project in an enthusiastic manner so that others will want to join the team. Once the team leader has assembled the team, all its members work together to reach the goal.
- SEI's commitment to teamwork is a major part of an employee's pay. SEI uses incentive compensation whereby employees can earn anywhere from 10 to 100 percent of their base pay. "Each team gets a pot of money," says Greer, "and decides how to distribute it." Some teams have members vote on each other's bonuses, while other teams defer to the team leader.[40]

For more information on SEI, visit the organization's home page at www.seic.com.

Questions

1. Choose a content theory of motivation and describe how SEI uses this theory's concepts to motivate its employees.
2. Choose a process theory of motivation and describe how SEI uses this theory's concepts to motivate its employees.
3. Would you like to work for this firm? If so, why?

REFERENCES

1. Adapted from Weiss, N. How Starbucks impassions workers to drive growth. *Workforce*, 1998, 77, 60–65; Lardner, J. OK, here are your options. *U.S. News & World Report*, March 1, 1999, 44–45; Schultz, H., and Jones-Yang, D. *Pour Your Heart into It: How Starbucks Built a Company One Cup at a Time.* Westport, Conn.: Hyperion Press, 1997.
2. For additional information, visit the company's home page at www.starbucks.com.
3. Reich, R. B. The company of the future. *Fast Company*, November 1998, 124–150; Personal communication with J. Lichtenthal, director of human resources, Celanese Chemical Corporation, November 1998.
4. Locke, E. A., and Latham, G. P. *A Model of Goal Setting and Task Performance.* Princeton, N.J.: Prentice-Hall, 1990, 6–8; Brown, S. P., Cron, W. L., and Slocum, J. W. Effects of trait competitiveness and perceived intraorganizational competition on salesperson goal setting and performance. *Journal of Marketing*, 1998, 62(4), 88–98.
5. For an excellent overview of motivation models, see Ambrose, M. L., and Kulik, C. T. Old friends, new faces: Motivation research in the 1990s. *Journal of Management*, 1999, 25, 231–237.
6. Maslow, A. H. *Motivation and Personality.* New York: Harper & Row, 1970.
7. Adler, N. J. *International Dimensions of Organizational Behavior*, 3rd. ed. Cincinnati: South-Western, 1997, 158–166.

8. Maslow, A. H., and Kaplan, A. R. *Maslow on Management.* New York: John Wiley & Sons, 1998.
9. Alderfer, C. P. *Existence, Relatedness and Growth: Human Needs in Organizational Settings.* New York: Free Press, 1972.
10. Winer, B. *Human Motivation.* New York: Holt, Rinehart and Winston, 1980; Landy, F. L., and Becker, W. S. Motivation Model Reconsidered. In L. L. Cummings and B. M. Staw (eds.), *Research in Organizational Behavior,* vol. 9. Greenwich, Conn.: JAI Press, 1987, 1–38.
11. Adapted from Kriska, P. Motivating employees in Romania. Unpublished manuscript, Cox School of Business, Southern Methodist University, Dallas, Texas, 1999.
12. McClelland, D. C. *Motivational Trends in Society.* Morristown, N.J.: General Learning Press, 1971.
13. McClelland, D. C., and Burnham, D. Power is the great motivator. *Harvard Business Review,* March–April, 1976, 100–111; Payne, D. K. *Training Resources Group.* Boston: McBer & Company, 1998; Sagie, A., Elizur, D., and Yamauchi, H. The structure and strength of achievement motivation: A cross-cultural comparison. *Journal of Organizational Behavior,* 1996, 17, 431–445.
14. Adapted from Routh, D. This isn't no pizza party. *Fortune,* November 9, 1998, 158–167; www.papajohns.com.
15. Hansemark, O. C. Objective versus projective measurement of need for achievement: The relation between TAT and CMPS. *Journal of Managerial Psychology,* 1997, 12, 280–290; Phillips, J. M., and Gully, S. M. Role of goal orientation, ability, need for achievement, and locus of control in self-efficacy and goal-setting process. *Journal of Applied Psychology,* 1997, 82, 792–803.
16. Herzberg, F. I., Mausner, B., and Snyderman, B. B. *The Motivation to Work.* New York: John Wiley & Sons, 1959.
17. Stroh, L. K., and Caligiuri, P. M. Increasing global competitiveness through effective people management. *Journal of World Business,* 1998, 33,1–16; Puffer, S. M., McCarthy, D. J., and Naumov, A. I. Russian managers' beliefs about work: Beyond the stereotypes. *Journal of World Business,* 1997, 32, 258–276; Tietjen, M. A., and Myers, R. M. Motivation and job satisfaction. *Management Decision,* 1998, 36, 226–232.
18. Schuler, R. S., Jackson, S. E., Jackofsky, E. F., and Slocum, J. W., Jr. Managing human resources in Mexico: A cultural understanding. *Business Horizons,* May–June 1996, 55–61.
19. Greer, C. R., and Stephens, G. K. Employee relations issues for U.S. companies in Mexico. *California Management Review,* 1996, 38(3), 121–145.
20. Villanova, P. Predictive validity of situational constraints in general versus specific performance domains. *Journal of Applied Psychology,* 1996, 81, 532–548.
21. Vroom, V. H. *Work and Motivation.* New York: John Wiley & Sons, 1964.
22. Tubbs, M. E., Boehme, D. M., and Dahl, J. G. Expectancy, valence, and motivational force functions in goal-setting research: An empirical test. *Journal of Applied Psychology,* 1993, 78, 361–373.
23. Lynd-Stevenson, R. M. Expectancy theory and predicting future employment status in the young unemployed. *Journal of Occupational and Organizational Psychology,* 1999, 72, 101–106.
24. McFadyen, R. G., and Thomas, J. P. Economic and psychological models of job search behaviors of the unemployed. *Human Relations,* 1997, 50, 1461–1485; Allen, R. E., Lucero, M. A., and Van Norman, K. L. An examination of the individual's decision to participate in an employee involvement program. *Group & Organization Management,* 1997, 22, 117–144; Fudge, R. S., and Schlacter, J. L. Motivating employees to act ethically: An expectancy theory approach. *Journal of Business Ethics,* 1999, 18, 295–296.
25. Hellriegel, D., Slocum, J. W., Jr., and Woodman, R. W. *Organizational Behavior,* 8th ed. Cincinnati: South-Western, 1998, C10–12.
26. Adams, J. S. Toward an Understanding of Inequity. *Journal of Abnormal and Social Psychology,* 1963, 67, 422–436.
27. Korsgaad, M. A., Roberson, L., and Rymph, R. D. What motivates fairness? The role of subordinate assertive behavior on managers' interactional fairness. *Journal of Applied Psychology,* 1998, 83, 731–744; Lind, E. A., Kray, L., and Thompson, L. The social construction of justice: Fairness judgments in response to own and others' unfair treatment by authorities. *Organizational Behavior & Human Decision Processes,* 1998, 75(1), 1–22; Chen, C. C., Meindl, J. R., and Hui, H. Deciding on equity or parity: A test of situational, cultural, and individual factors. *Journal of Organizational Behavior,* 1998, 19, 115–129.
28. Adapted from Hiebeler, R., Kelly, T. B., and Ketteman, C. *Best Practices: Building Your Business with Customer-Focused Solutions.* New York: Simon & Schuster, 1998, 185–186, 193–199; www.disney.com.
29. Wells, J. T. A fistful of dollars. *Security Management,* 1999, 43(8), 70–75; Pedone, R. Business' $400 billion theft problem. *Long Island Business News,* July 6, 1998, 1–3B; Employee theft rising. *Chain Store Age Executive with Shopping Center Age,* October 1, 1998, 54–55.
30. Moorman, R. H., Blakeley, G. L., and Niehoff, B. P. Does perceived organizational support mediate the relationship between procedural justice and organizational citizenship behavior? *Academy of Management Journal,* 1998, 41, 351–358.
31. Tomer, J. F. Organizational capital and joining-up: Linking the individual to the organization and society. *Human Relations,* 1998, 51, 825–847; Shore, L. M., Barksdale, K., and Shore, T. H. Managerial perceptions of employee commitment to the organization. *Academy of Management Journal,* 1995, 38, 1593–1611.
32. Adapted from Greenberg, J. Employee theft as a reaction to underpayment inequity: The hidden costs of pay cuts. *Journal of Applied Psychology,* 1990, 75, 561–568; Wahn, J. Organizational dependence and the likelihood of complying with organizational pressures to behave unethically. *Journal of Business Ethics,* 1993, 12, 245–251.
33. van Dierendonck, D., Schaufeli, W. B., and Buunk, B. P. The evaluation of an individual burnout intervention program: The role of inequity and social support. *Journal of Applied Psychology,* 1998, 83, 392–408; Brockner, J., Wiesenfeld, B. M., and Martin, C. L. Decision frame, procedural justice and survivors' reactions to job layoffs. *Organizational Behavior & Human Decision Processes,* 1995, 63, 59–69.

34. Deckrop, J. R., Mangel, R., and Cirka, C. C. Getting more than you pay for: Organizational citizenship behavior and pay-for-performance plans. *Academy of Management Journal,* 1999, 42, 420–428; Chattopadhyau, P. Beyond direct and symmetrical effects: The influence of demographic dissimilarity on organizational citizenship behavior. *Academy of Management Journal,* 1999, 42, 273–288; Bolino, M. C. Citizenship and impression management: Good soldiers or good actors? *Academy of Management Review,* 1999, 24, 82–98.
35. Allen, T. D., and Rush, M. C. The effects of organizational citizenship behavior on performance judgments: A field study and a laboratory experiment. *Journal of Applied Psychology,* 1998, 83, 247–261; Organ, D. W., and Ryan, K. A meta-analytic review of attitudinal and dispositional predictors of organizational citizenship behavior. *Personnel Psychology,* 1995, 48, 775–803.
36. Kidwell, R. E., Mossholder, K. W., and Bennett, N. Cohesiveness and organizational citizenship behavior: A multilevel analysis using work groups and individuals. *Journal of Management,* 1997, 23, 775–794; Van Dyne, L., and Ang, S. Organizational citizenship behavior of contingent workers in Singapore. *Academy of Management Journal,* 1998, 41, 692–703.
37. Personal communication with R. Hammond, partner, Ernst & Young, Dallas, Texas, August 1999.
38. Personal communication with D. Norwood, executive vice president, Holmes Murphy, Dallas, Texas, August 1999.
39. Adapted from a survey of employees conducted by Seglin, J. L. The happiest workers in the world. *Inc.,* May 1996, 62–76.
40. Adapted from Kirsner, S. Every day it is a new place. *Fast Company,* April–May, 1998, 130–134; personal communication with H. Macy, former SEI employee, September 1999.

CHAPTER

Motivating Performance: Goal Setting and Reward Systems

LEARNING OBJECTIVES

When you have finished studying this chapter, you should be able to:

1. State the basics of goal setting, including the role of customers, suppliers, and others.
2. Explain how performance is affected by goal setting.
3. Assess management by objectives (MBO) as a management philosophy and system.
4. Describe reward systems in high-performance work systems.

Preview Case: *Marriott Hotels*

BASICS OF GOAL SETTING

Importance of Goal Setting
Importance of Stakeholders
Customer Service Goals
Competency: Managing Communication—*Fruit of the Loom*

MODEL OF GOAL SETTING AND PERFORMANCE

Challenge
Moderators
Competency: Managing Teams—*NASCAR Racing*
Mediators
Performance
Rewards
Competency: Managing Ethics—*Sundstrand*
Satisfaction
Significance in Practice

MANAGEMENT BY OBJECTIVES

Goal Setting
Diversity and Goal Setting
Participation and Implementation
Performance Appraisal and Feedback
Significance in Practice

REWARD SYSTEMS IN HIGH-PERFORMANCE WORK SYSTEMS

Gain-Sharing and Profit-Sharing Plans
Flexible Benefit Plans
Banking Time Off
Skill-Based Pay
Significance in Practice
Competency: Managing Across Cultures—*Reward Practices in Different Countries*

CHAPTER SUMMARY

Key Terms and Concepts
Discussion Questions

DEVELOPING COMPETENCIES

Competency: Managing Self—*Goal-Setting Questionnaire*
Competency: Managing Change—*Improving Safety*

PREVIEW CASE

MARRIOTT HOTELS

When Aileen Nikitiades walked down the aisle to shake the hand of J. W. Marriott at Marriott's hotel in Washington, D.C., employees were standing and cheering. Nikitiades was one of 102 employees invited to have dinner with J. W. Marriott, chairman of the company, at his home. This dinner was the final step in recognition under the Golden Circle program—the chairman's circle—which rewards top performers for exceeding their quarterly goals by more than 15 percent for the entire year. All winners had their pictures taken with Marriott during dinner. Nikitiades proudly displays hers in her office.

In a recent year, Marriott rewarded all salespeople who met their goals with a bronze personalized plaque and a letter from the senior vice president of sales, Richard Hanks. Surpassing goals by 15 percent in a quarter earned them a silver plaque, and another letter from Hanks. Those who reached the gold level earned $500 in catalog merchandise, a gold plaque, and a letter from Hanks. Those who topped the 15 percent target for the entire year made it to the final stage—the chairman's circle. They received the award's logo embossed on special stationery and business cards, as well as a trip to Washington with a guest to attend the chairman's dinner. Thirty-five percent of the sales force achieved the bronze level in 1998, but only 3.5 percent made it to the chairman's circle.

*For more information on Marriott, visit this firm's home page at **www.marriott.com.***

Each January, Marriott sends its salespeople a 20-page brochure that describes the rewards and outlines goals in such areas as cross-selling (e.g., scheduling the catering of a major event also leads to suggestions for room reservations), room booking revenue, food and beverage revenue, calls per hour, client satisfaction indices, and occupancy rates. With her supervisor, each salesperson sets goals to achieve during each quarter of the year.[1]

To survive in today's global competitive market, setting challenging goals that take into account time and quality and provide feedback to employees is no longer an option. It must happen!

IBM recently launched a Web site for its 9,000 salespeople. The initial prompt asks a salesperson for his or her title, job description, and base salary. Following the representative's response, another screen opens, showing information on that person's progress toward meeting goals that had been set. Getting such personalized information to each salesperson was a complex and challenging task. Now that the task has been accomplished, each salesperson can use the data to calculate the difference between hitting, say, 105 percent and 115 percent of a quota. IBM spends millions annually on incentives, so employees are anxious to know how their performance at any particular time compares to their goals. The advantages of receiving timely and accurate feedback are reflected by the more than 3,500 people who regularly check their personal data. The Web site averages 500 hits a day and usually peaks when a quarter ends.[2]

The motivational concepts that cut across the achievements in both the Marriott and IBM examples are setting goals, developing feedback systems, and providing reward systems that get individuals to strive to reach those goals. In this chapter, we first outline the role played by customers, suppliers, and other stakeholders of an organization and how they affect goal setting. Then we present a model of goal setting and performance based on the individual. This model sets the stage for the discussion of management by objectives as a philosophy and system of integrating goal setting into organizational life. In the final section we return to reward systems, which we described in Chapters 4 and 5. Here, we consider the types of reward systems being used by high-performance work systems to reinforce desired behaviors of employees.

Learning Objective:

1. State the basics of goal setting, including the role of customers, suppliers, and others.

BASICS OF GOAL SETTING

Goal setting is a process intended to increase efficiency and effectiveness by specifying the desired outcomes toward which individuals, teams, departments, and organizations should work. **Goals** are the future outcomes (results) that individuals and groups desire and strive to achieve.[3] An example of an individual goal is: I am planning to graduate with a 3.0 grade point average by the end of the spring semester, 2004.

IMPORTANCE OF GOAL SETTING

The process of goal setting is no easy task, but the effort is worthwhile. The most important reasons for having goals include the following.

- Goals guide and direct behavior. They increase role clarity by focusing effort and attention in specific directions, thereby reducing uncertainty in day-to-day decision making.
- Goals provide challenges and indicators against which individual, team, departmental, or organizational performance can be assessed.
- Goals justify the performance of various tasks and the use of resources to pursue them.
- Goals define the basis for the organization's design. They determine, in part, communication patterns, authority relationships, power relationships, and division of labor.
- Goals serve an organizing function.
- Goals reflect what the employees and managers consider important and thus provide a framework for planning and control activities.[4]

IMPORTANCE OF STAKEHOLDERS

Disagreement and conflict, as we discuss in Chapter 10, are often stimulated through the process of setting goals. Because diverse groups have a stake in organizational decisions, managers are faced with the continuing need to develop, modify, and discard goals. **Stakeholders** are groups having potential or real power to influence an organization's decisions, such as the choice of goals and actions. Stakeholders commonly include customers or clients, employees, suppliers, shareholders, governmental agencies, unions, public interest groups, and lenders, among others.

Table 6.1 shows some of the organizational goals that are of particular interest to five stakeholder groups. Note that all these groups have different goals. Because of these varied concerns, some of the goals of a particular group may be incompatible with those of other groups. Therefore, creating a unified and logical system of goal setting for an organization is difficult when

- each stakeholder group has substantial power in relation to the organization;
- each stakeholder group pushes to maximize its own interests and perceives the interests of some or all other groups to be incompatible with its own;
- the stakeholders keep changing what they expect (want) from the organization; and/or
- the management team itself is divided into competing groups within the organization.[5]

Taken together, these situations present a worst-case scenario. Thus, if some of the goals listed are pushed to extremes by powerful stakeholders, executives will have to use keen negotiating skills to balance or resolve the resulting conflicts. The 191-day lockout of NBA players by NBA owners in 1998–1999 cost players more than $500 million in lost salaries. Detroit, Seattle, and other NBA cities reported losing more than $500,000 a game in tax-related revenues from concession stands and parking. The City of Philadelphia and its businesses estimated that they lost more than

Table 6.1 Goals of Typical Stakeholders

Customers
- Good service
- Competitive prices
- Product quality
- Product variety
- Product satisfaction guaranteed

Employees
- Good compensation and job security
- Opportunity to learn
- Opportunities for fun on the job
- Sense of meaning or purpose in the job
- Opportunities for advancement
- Opportunities for personal development
- Good management of diversity issues

Shareholders
- Growth in dividend payments
- Increase in stock price
- Growth in market share
- Ethical behavior of employees

Bankers
- Financial strength of the organization
- Maintenance of assets that serve as collateral on loans
- Improvements in productivity to keep costs competitive
- Repayment schedule

Suppliers
- Timely debt payment
- Repeat customers
- Prompt service
- Business growth

$9 million in revenue when the NBA All-Star game was canceled. Not until David Stern, NBA Commissioner, and Billy Hunter, union representative for the NBA players, engaged in marathon bargaining sessions was a settlement reached. Fortunately, managers and employees usually aren't confronted with such diverse and incompatible demands.

The most important stakeholders for any organization are its customers or clients. Their goals need to be reflected in the goals of the organization as a whole, as well as in the goals of individual employees and teams within the organization. This perspective was certainly reflected in Marriott's goal-setting process and IBM's goal of providing accurate and timely feedback to its employees.

Customer Service Goals

Two main issues need to be addressed in setting goals for quality in customer service. The first is that customers or clients are the sole judge of service quality. They assess it by comparing the service they receive to the service they desire. Organizations such as Southwest Airlines, State Farm Insurance Company, Lexus, Merck, and Ritz Carlton Hotels can maintain their strong reputations for quality service only by consistently meeting or exceeding customer service expectations. Second, organizations tend to ignore service quality when competitors start vying for their business.[6]

Customer service goals may be stated in terms of five overall criteria. In the following list, each criterion is defined and a sample comment from a dissatisfied customer is presented.

- *Reliability:* The ability to perform the promised service dependably and accurately. Car leasing customer: "Too often they take care of your problems too fast. They fix your car and two days later you have to take it back for the same problem. They could be a little more attentive and fix the problem permanently."
- *Tangibles:* The appearance of physical facilities, equipment, personnel, and communication materials. Hotel customer: "They get you real pumped up with the beautiful ad. When you go in, you expect bells and whistles to go off. Usually, they don't."
- *Responsiveness:* The willingness to help customers and to provide prompt service. Business equipment repair customer: "You put in a service call and wait. No one calls back; there is no communication."
- *Assurance:* The knowledge and courtesy of employees and their ability to convey trust and confidence. Life insurance customer: "I quote pages out of my policy and my agent cannot interpret what it means to me in language that I can understand."
- *Empathy:* The provision of caring, individualized attention to customers or clients. Airline customer: "They'll out-and-out lie to you about how delayed a flight will be so that you won't try to get a flight on another airline."

Fruit of the Loom, a manufacturer of T-shirts, fleecewear, knit sports shirts, and undergarments, used these five service criteria and decided that it wasn't providing good service. Its managers realized that the company needed to create a communication system that would enable it to respond quickly and creatively to customers, lower its distribution costs, and improve customer service. The Activewear division sells T-shirts and other garments to 50 distributors, who in turn sell them to more than 30,000 decorators who print regional and personalized logos, names, pictures, and designs on clothing and sell it themselves. Following the lead of Dell Computers and Amazon.com, Fruit of the Loom spent more than $3.5 million to create a Web site and communication system that permits customers to customize their products. The following Managing Communication Competency feature highlights how Fruit of the Loom achieved its goal of creating better business-to-business relationships and customer service.

COMPETENCY: MANAGING COMMUNICATION

FRUIT OF THE LOOM

The company asked its customers what they wanted on a Web site. Customers indicated that they wanted an electronic catalog with text and graphics, product news, a feedback form, a glossary of frequently used terms, and links to other related Fruit of the Loom divisional sites. Based on these responses, Fruit of the Loom created a Web site loaded with catalogs, inventory-management software, and order-processing software. Fruit of the Loom now can create customized electronic catalogs, provide customers with real-time information on product availability and special offers, and round-the-clock ordering.

This communication system has resulted in a $4 million dollar sales increase for the company. Some customers have reported sales increases of as much as 25 percent. How were such results achieved? First, it used to take 3 to 5 days to process a customer's order. The new system allows customers to search the electronic catalogs and place orders within 5 minutes, 24 hours a day, 7 days a week. Second, customers using the Web site save themselves $20 in processing costs for each order placed. Third, each customer (e.g., Wal-Mart, Sears, and J.C. Penney) provides Fruit of the Loom with daily sales forecasts, inventory balances, and other market information. These data allow the company to lower its inventory levels, reduce cycle time for replenishing items, and reduce out-of-stock items. Fourth, like American Airline's Sabre reservation system, Fruit of the Loom's Web site lets customers view competing products. If a competitor's product is unavailable, a Fruit of the Loom product is shown on the Web site for the customer to order.[7]

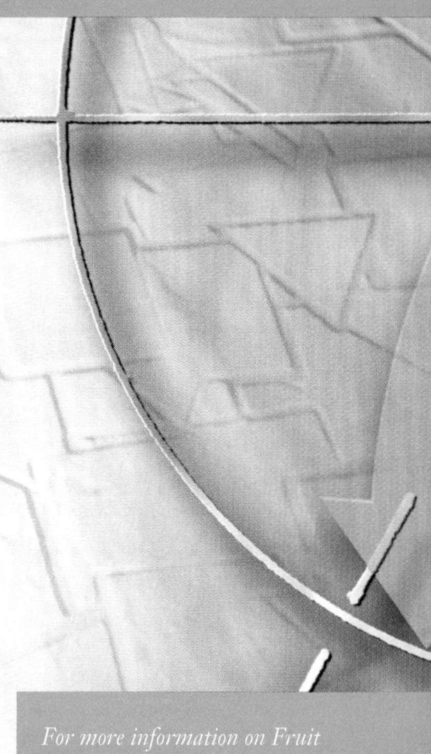

*For more information on Fruit of the Loom, visit this firm's home page at **www.fruit.com**.*

Learning Objective:

2. Explain how performance is affected by goal setting.

MODEL OF GOAL SETTING AND PERFORMANCE

Just as organizations strive to achieve certain goals, individuals also are motivated to strive for and attain goals. In fact, the goal-setting process is one of the most important motivational tools for affecting the performance of employees in organizations. In this section we consider one of the most widely accepted theories of goal setting and indicate how goal-setting techniques can be applied to motivate individuals and teams.

Ed Locke and Gary Latham developed a sophisticated model of individual goal setting and performance. Figure 6.1 presents a simplified version of their model.[8] It shows the key variables and the general relationships that can lead to high individual performance, some of which we have discussed in previous chapters. The basic idea behind this model is that a goal serves as a motivator because it allows people to compare their present performance with that required to achieve the goal. To the extent that people believe they will fall short of a goal, they will feel dissatisfied and will work harder to attain the goal so long as they believe that it can be achieved. Having a goal also may improve performance because the goal makes clear the type and level of performance expected. As we showed in Chapter 5, John Schnatter's goals for Papa John's were very clear: Expand the business by 10 percent a year, hire drivers who maintain safe-driving records, and deliver a hot pizza to every customer within 30 minutes. Such goals clearly communicate performance expectations to all employees of the company. By reviewing performance against the goals each year, Schnatter also provides information on how well employees are doing in terms of these agreed upon targets. With these general ideas in mind, let's review the basic features of the Locke–Latham goal-setting model.

Figure 6.1 **Model of Goal Setting**

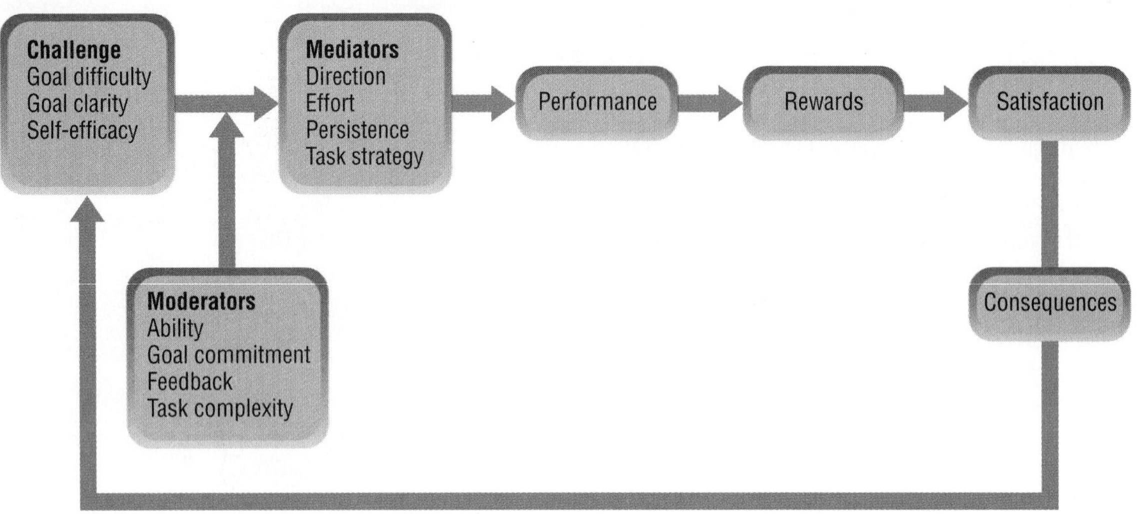

Source: Adapted from Locke, E. A., and Latham, G. P. *A Theory of Goal Setting and Task Performance*. Englewood Cliffs, N.J.: Prentice-Hall, 1990, 253.

CHALLENGE

Goal setting is the process of developing, negotiating, and establishing targets that challenge the individual. Employees with unclear goals or no goals are prone to work slowly, perform poorly, exhibit a lack of interest, and accomplish less than employees whose goals are clear and challenging. In addition, employees with clearly defined goals appear to be more energetic and productive. They get things done on time and then move on to other activities (and goals).

Goals may be implicit or explicit, vague or clearly defined, and self-imposed or externally imposed. Whatever their form, goals serve to structure the individual's time and effort. Two key attributes of goals are particularly important.

- **Goal difficulty.** A goal should be challenging, but not impossible to achieve. If it is too easy, the individual may delay or approach the goal lackadaisically. If a goal is too difficult, the individual may not really accept it and thus not try to meet it.
- **Goal clarity.** A goal must be clear and specific if it is to be useful in directing effort. The individual thus will know what is expected and not have to guess.

Clear and challenging goals lead to higher performance than do vague or general goals. Texas Industries of Dallas sells more than $1.2 billion worth of concrete, steel, and dirt a year. Robert Rogers, TXI's president, installed a goal-setting program that pays employees as much as 20 percent of their salaries if their product innovations are implemented. Barnett Reese, a TXI sales manager in Houston, developed a way to mix red clay and slag. This mixture absorbs wetness and is now used in the infields at many major league baseball parks. Selling for more than $100 a ton, or 10 times what the ingredients are worth, Reese's innovation is extremely profitable and he was well rewarded for it. Rogers and his top management team have set a company goal of earning 15 percent of the company's total revenues from innovative products each year. Rogers believes that setting the goal at a specific amount (e.g., 15 percent) is better than setting a goal of "trying to be innovative" or "doing your best." [9] Goals that are difficult but not impossible lead to higher performance than do easy goals. However, unrealistically high goals may not be accepted or may lead to high performance only in the short run. Individuals eventually get discouraged and stop trying, as predicted by expectancy theory (see Chapter 5).

Along with goal difficulty and clarity, a third key factor that influences the establishment of challenging goals is self-efficacy. In Chapter 4, we defined *self-efficacy* as the individual's belief that he or she can perform at a certain level in a given situation. As might be expected, individuals who set high goals perform at a high level when they also have high self-efficacy. A person's self-efficacy is dependent on the task. For example, a golfer with a low handicap has high self-efficacy on the golf course. But the same person might have low self-efficacy when meeting sales quotas for a new piece of equipment that her company has just introduced.[10]

With clear and challenging goals, employee behaviors are more likely to be focused on job-related tasks, high levels of performance, and goal achievement. Table 6.2 provides a summary of the key links between goal setting and individual performance.

The following Managing Teams Competency feature on page 170 illustrates how people in teams use the basic concepts of goal challenge, goal clarity, and self-efficacy to instill teamwork. In NASCAR racing, it is often how well the pit crew performs that determines whether the driver wins the race.

Moderators

Figure 6.1 also shows four of the factors that moderate the strength of the relationship between goals and performance. We start with *ability* because it limits an individual's capacity to respond to a challenge. The relation of goal difficulty to performance is curvilinear, not linear. That is, performance levels off as the limits of a person's ability are approached. In Chapter 2, we discussed a person's goal orientation and indicated that there are two types of goal orientation—performance and learning—which can affect a person's ability to perform. Individuals with a *learning goal orientation* believe that they have the ability to acquire new competencies and master new situations. They seek challenging new assignments that open their eyes to new ways of doing tasks. Those with a *performance goal orientation* believe that their ability to complete a task is relatively stable and avoid placing themselves in a situation in which they might receive a negative evaluation.[11]

The second factor, **goal commitment,** refers to an individual's determination to reach a goal, regardless of whether the goal was set by that person or someone else.[12] What is your goal commitment in this class? Take a minute and complete the questionnaire in Table 6.3 on page 171. Your commitment to a goal is likely to be stronger if you

Table 6.2

Impact of Goals on Performance

WHEN GOALS ARE	PERFORMANCE WILL TEND TO BE
Specific and clear	Higher
Vague	Lower
Difficult and challenging	Higher
Easy and boring	Lower
Set participatively	Higher
Set by management (top down)	Lower
Accepted by employees	Higher
Rejected by employees	Lower
Accompanied by rewards	Higher
Unrelated to rewards	Lower

COMPETENCY: MANAGING TEAMS

NASCAR RACING

Ray Evernham is considered by many NASCAR people to be a premier crew chief. Over the past 5 years, he and Jeff Gordon have won more races than any other NASCAR team. Evernham and Gordon give much of the credit to their pit crew, known as the Rainbow Warriors, because crew members wear rainbow-striped jumpsuits.

When the Rainbow Warriors crew was assembled more than 5 years ago, they decided to do things differently. In the past, mechanics who worked on a race car all week also suited up on Sunday to work as the pit crew. The car was the number one priority. The crew relied on horsepower and the driver to win the race. Pit crews didn't practice and set goals. Evernham and Gordon knew that all drivers have essentially the same equipment. Thus the ingredient that would separate winning from losing drivers was their ability to create a team. They decided to have two crews: The first crew was responsible for the mechanics of the car (e.g., engine and suspension components); the second—the pit crew—was responsible for the car during the race. Under Evernham and Gordon's leadership, the Rainbow Warriors hired a coach to develop specifically the teamwork competency of the pit crew. The training included rope climbing, scaling walls, wind sprints, guys carrying each other on their backs, and the like. All members of the pit crew also needed to be trained on all tasks so that members could rotate tasks among themselves, depending on race conditions. From analyzing other NASCAR drivers, Evernham determined that if Gordon's car could leave 1 second faster than the competition, Gordon would gain 300 feet on the competition (a car going 200 mph travels nearly 300 feet a second). The pit crew set a goal of having the car exit the pit in 17 seconds or less. During a race, all team members hear each other on their scanners. They use special code words to signal whether they are changing two or four tires when Gordon pulls into the pit. The crew also determines whether to gas the car fully or just to put in enough gas to finish the race. Evernham and his crew also determine when Gordon should come in for a pit stop. Before the race, all the Rainbow Warriors sit in a circle to discuss race strategy. The circle symbolizes that the team is stronger than any one individual. When Gordon wins a race, signs a personal services contact, or is paid to sign autographs, all the members of both teams receive a percentage of that money.[13]

For more information on NASCAR, visit this organization's home page at www.nascar.com.

make a public commitment to achieve it, if you have a strong need for achievement, and if you believe that you can control the activities that will help you reach that goal.

The effect of participation on goal commitment is complex. Positive goal commitment is more likely if employees participate in setting their goals, which often leads to a sense of ownership. Not expecting or wanting to be involved in goal setting reduces the importance of employee participation in terms of goal commitment. Even when a manager has to assign goals without employee participation, doing so leads to more focused efforts and better performance than if no goals were set.

The expected rewards for achieving goals play an important role in the degree of goal commitment. The greater the extent to which employees believe that positive rewards (merit pay raises, bonuses, promotions, opportunities to perform interesting tasks, and the like) are contingent on achieving goals, the greater is their commitment to the goals. These notions are similar to the ideas contained in the expectancy theory of motivation. Similarly, if employees expect to be punished for not achieving goals, the probability of goal commitment also is higher.[14] However, recall that pun-

Table 6.3

Goal Commitment Questionnaire

ITEM	Strongly Agree	Agree	Undecided	Disagree	Strongly Disagree
	RESPONSE CATEGORY				
1. I am strongly committed to achieving a grade of _____.	_____	_____	_____	_____	_____
2. I am willing to expend the effort needed to achieve this goal.	_____	_____	_____	_____	_____
3. I really care about achieving this grade.	_____	_____	_____	_____	_____
4. Much personal satisfaction can be gained if I achieve this grade.	_____	_____	_____	_____	_____
5. Revising my goal, depending on how other classes go, isn't likely.	_____	_____	_____	_____	_____
6. A lot would have to happen to abandon my grade goal.	_____	_____	_____	_____	_____
7. Expecting to reach my grade goal in this class is realistic for me.	_____	_____	_____	_____	_____

Scoring: Give yourself 5 points for each Strongly Agree response; 4 points for each Agree response; 3 points for each Undecided response; 2 points for each Disagree response; and 1 point for each Strongly Disagree response. The higher your total score, the greater is your commitment to achieve your grade goal in this class.

Source: Adapted from VandeWalle, D., Cron, W. L., and Slocum, J. W., Jr. Effects of feedback on goal setting. Unpublished paper, SMU, Cox School of Business, Dallas, Texas, 2000; Hollenbeck, J. R., Williams, C. R., and Klein, H. J. An empirical examination of the antecedents of commitment to goals. *Journal of Applied Psychology,* 1989, 74, 18–23.

ishment and the fear of punishment as the primary means of guiding behavior may create long-term problems (see Chapter 4).

Employees compare expected rewards against rewards actually received. If received rewards are consistent with expected rewards, the reward system is likely to continue to support goal commitment. If employees think that the rewards they receive are much less than the rewards they expected, they may perceive inequity. If perceived or actual inequity exists, employees eventually lessen their goal commitment. Teamwork and peer pressures are other factors that affect a person's commitment to a goal.[15]

Feedback makes goal setting and individual responses to goal achievement (performance) a dynamic process. It provides information to the employee and others about outcomes and the degree of employee performance.[16] Feedback enables the individual to relate received rewards to those expected in terms of actual performance. This comparison, in turn, can influence changes in the degree of goal commitment.

Task complexity is the last moderator of the strength of the relationship between goals and performance that we consider. For simple tasks (e.g., answering telephones at Marriott's reservation center), the effort encouraged by challenging goals leads directly to high task performance. For more complex tasks (e.g., studying to achieve a high grade), effort doesn't lead directly to effective performance. The individual must also decide where and how to allocate effort. We consider various issues associated with simple and complex jobs in Chapter 15 when we discuss job design.

MEDIATORS

Let's assume that an individual has challenging goals and that the moderating factors support achievement of these goals. How do the four mediators—direction, effort, persistence, and task strategy—affect performance? *Direction* of attention focuses behaviors on activities expected to result in goal achievement and steers the individual away from activities irrelevant to the goals. The *effort* a person exerts usually depends on the difficulty of the goal. That is, the greater the challenge, the greater will be the effort expended, assuming that the person is committed to reaching the goal. *Persistence* involves a person's willingness to work at the task over an extended period of time until the results are achieved. Most sports require participants to practice long and hard to hone their competencies and maintain them at a high level. Finally, *task strategy* is the way in which an individual—often through experience and instruction—decides to tackle a task.

PERFORMANCE

Performance is likely to be high when (1) challenging goals are present, (2) the moderators (ability, goal commitment, feedback, and task complexity) are present, and (3) the mediators (direction, effort, persistence, and task strategy) are operating. Alan Rosskamm, president of Jo-Ann Stores, a 12-store retail chain that sells fabrics, home décor items, and craft supplies, has used these three guidelines to set goals for his stores. In an industry where inventory turns over less than twice a year, his goals are to have inventory turn over five times a year, maintaining 8 percent margins compared to the industry's standard of 5 to 6 percent, and sell about $120 dollars of merchandise per square foot versus the $85 per square foot average in the industry. To achieve these goals, Rosskamm asked customers to develop a dream store. As a result of listening to customers, he has designed his stores like Home Depot, except much smaller. He wants to give customers confidence to do crafts on their own after they have been properly trained. To help them do so, Jo-Ann Stores regularly schedules classes on faux marble painting, quilting, upholstering, stenciling, ceramics, and floral arrangements. There are also craft-oriented day-care centers for children while their parents shop.[17]

Three basic types of quantitative indicators can be used to assess performance: units of production or quality (amount produced or number of errors); dollars (profits, costs, income, or sales); and time (attendance and promptness in meeting deadlines). When such measures are unavailable or inappropriate, qualitative goals and indicators may be used. In addition, many organizations have developed a **code of ethics** to support employees in setting ethical goals and making ethical decisions. Creating ethics guidelines has several advantages that Boeing, GTE, and Johnson & Johnson, among others, consider important. Some of the advantages for setting ethical goals are

- to help employees identify what their organization recognizes as acceptable business practices;
- to legitimize the consideration of ethics as part of decision making;
- to avoid uncertainties among employees about what is right and wrong; and
- to avoid inconsistencies in decision making caused by an organizational reward system that appears to reward unethical behavior.[18]

What happens if a company's code of ethics isn't enforced and employees behave unethically? The following Managing Ethics Competency feature illustrates how Sundstrand Corporation, a Fortune 500 company located in Rockford, Illinois, changed the goals and behaviors of employees after it paid a $227 million fine for unethical behaviors. The company's stock fell from $64 to $48 a share, and the U.S. Department of Defense, Sundstrand's biggest customer, cut its orders by 38 percent. One thing that the firm began to do was to encourage whistleblowers. **Whistleblowers** are employees who expose wrongdoing by their organizations.

REWARDS

We discussed rewards at length in Chapters 4 and 5, so we merely summarize them here. When an employee attains a high level of performance, rewards can become important inducements to continue to perform at that level. Rewards can be external

COMPETENCY: MANAGING ETHICS

SUNDSTRAND

Sundstrand is a large defense contractor that was prosecuted for unethical behavior by Pentagon officials. It decided to embark on a program to emphasize ethical behavior, including encouragement of internal whistleblowing by its employees so that any illegal or unethical activities could be detected and corrected early. As a result, employees guilty of unethical behavior now suffer harsh consequences, such as suspension, dismissal, unappealing work assignments, and social ostracism by fellow workers.

To create an ethical climate, Sundstrand's management took several actions. First, it created the position of corporate director, business and ethics, and had that position report directly to the president. Second, it selected for that position a person who had worked 45 years in the company and was nearing retirement. He had gained a reputation for being highly ethical during his career, and his career stage made him more likely to be immune to internal politics. Third, it required all employees to attend an orientation session during which they each were given a book. In each book was a card for the employees to sign, indicating that they had read the book, understood it, and realized their obligation to follow the ethical guidelines presented in it. As a condition of their employment, they were asked to sign and return the card. After another 50 to 90 days, all employees were required to participate in 4-hour training sessions on ethics. Fourth, the corporate director and his staff wrote a manual detailing the kinds of ethical dilemmas that occurred most frequently in the defense industry. Covered were legal interpretations for contract pricing, receipt and payment of gratuities, and conflicts of interest; a hotline number was also included. Working with groups of 50 employees, the director held sessions lasting 35 to 40 minutes with all 8,000 employees. That meant holding sessions at 2:30 A.M. with employees in San Diego and at 7:30 P.M. with employees in Rockford. He personally wanted to assure all employees that appropriate action would be taken when ethical violations are substantiated and that whistleblowers would be protected.

To evaluate the success of this program, the director's office monitored the

1. total number of calls received each year,
2. total number of self-conduct checks by employees wondering about the ethics of a behavior,
3. number of hotline callers, and
4. number of reports of ethical violations that the director and his staff investigated.

The whistleblowing program has been instrumental in shaping ethical behaviors at Sundstrand. Seventy-four percent of the reported cases identified valid company concerns, whereas 26 percent were groundless. Of the valid cases, 50 percent involved human resource issues and 24 percent involved legitimate ethical violations. Six percent of the violators were terminated, 7 percent attended additional ethical training, and 11 percent received a reprimand.[19]

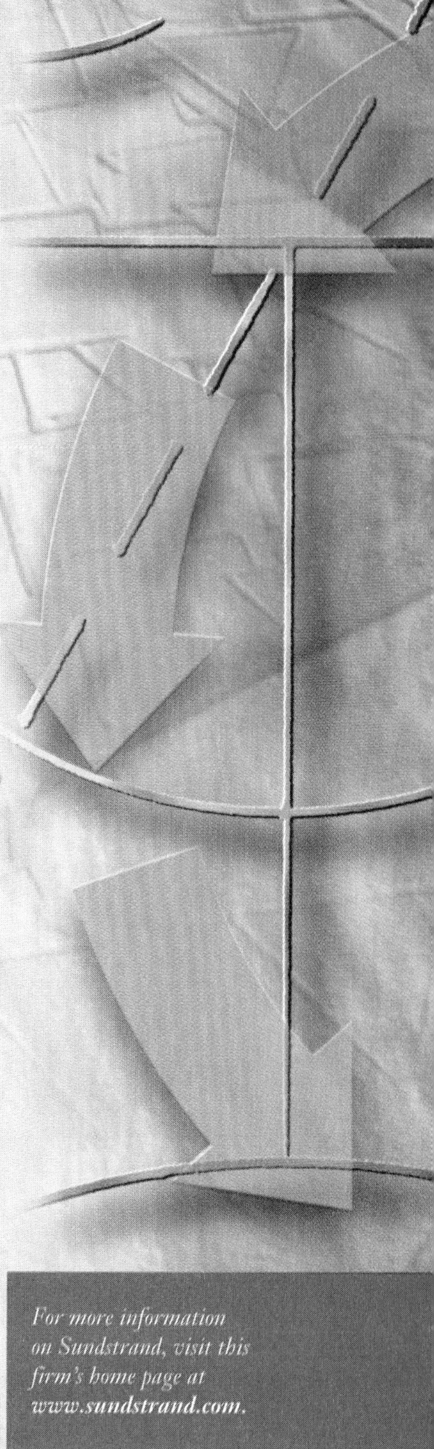

For more information on Sundstrand, visit this firm's home page at www.sundstrand.com.

(bonuses, paid vacations, and the like) or internal (a sense of achievement, pride in accomplishment, and feelings of success). Marriott, IBM, and Gordon's NASCAR organization all reward people for high performance. However, what is viewed as a reward in one culture may not be viewed as a reward in another. For example, doing business in Vietnam requires the exchange of gifts during the first day of a business meeting. Although the gifts may be small and relatively inexpensive, gifts with a company logo are highly valued. The gifts should be wrapped, but white or black paper should not be used because these colors are associated with death. In contrast, exchanging gifts at a business meeting in the United States is generally not expected. Praising an individual in public for achievement in Vietnam will cause the individual to be embarrassed; rewards are not to be given in public. Conversely, public acclaim for achievement in the United States is highly valued.[20]

Satisfaction

Many factors—including challenging work, interesting coworkers, salary, the opportunity to learn, and good working conditions—influence a person's satisfaction with the job (see Chapter 2). However, in the Locke–Latham model, the primary focus is on the employee's degree of satisfaction with performance. Employees who set extremely high, difficult goals may experience less job satisfaction than employees who set lower, more easily achievable goals. Difficult goals are less frequently achieved, and satisfaction with performance is associated with success. Thus some compromise on goal difficulty may be necessary in order to maximize both satisfaction and performance. However, some level of satisfaction is associated with simply striving for difficult goals, such as responding to a challenge, making some progress toward reaching the goals, and the belief that benefits may still be derived from the experience regardless of the outcome.

Significance in Practice

Individuals who are both satisfied with and committed to an organization are more likely to stay with it and to accept the challenges that it presents than are individuals who are less satisfied and committed. Turnover and absenteeism rates for satisfied individuals are low. This link brings us full circle to the beginning of the Locke–Latham goal-setting model. What might happen if things go badly and an individual who had been satisfied becomes dissatisfied? Individual responses fall into at least six possible categories: (1) job avoidance (quitting); (2) work avoidance (absenteeism, arriving late, and leaving early); (3) psychological defenses (alcohol and/or drug abuse); (4) constructive protest (complaining); (5) defiance (refusing to do what is asked); and (6) aggression (theft or assault). Quitting is the most common outcome of severe dissatisfaction.[21]

The goal-setting model has important implications for employees, managers, and teams alike. First, it provides an excellent framework to assist the manager or team in diagnosing the potential problems with low- or average-performing employees. Several diagnostic questions might be: (1) How were the goals set? (2) Are the goals challenging? (3) What is affecting goal commitment? and (4) Does the employee know when he or she has done a good job? Second, it provides concrete advice to the manager on how to create a high-performance work environment. Third, it portrays the system of relationships and interplay among key factors, such as goal difficulty, goal commitment, feedback, and rewards, to achieve high performance.

Learning Objective:

3. Assess management by objectives (MBO) as a management philosophy and system.

MANAGEMENT BY OBJECTIVES

Management by objectives (MBO) is a philosophy and system of management that serves as both a planning aid and a way of life in the workplace. This widely used management approach reflects a positive philosophy about people and a participative management style. Management by objectives involves managers and employees in jointly setting goals for work performance and personal development, periodically evaluating the employee's progress toward achieving these goals, and integrating individual, team, departmental, and organizational goals. American Airlines, Bristol-Myers Squibb, and Intel are among the organizations that use MBO successfully.

Although many people have contributed to the development of MBO, Peter Drucker coined the term *management by objectives* in about 1950.[22] The MBO model contains the four basic components shown in Figure 6.2: goal setting, subordinate participation, implementation, and performance appraisal and feedback. The arrows indicate the strong interrelationship among the components and that an effective MBO process requires all the components to operate simultaneously.

Goal Setting

Managers and employees define and focus on job goals rather than rules, activities, and procedures. In this discussion, we use the terms *goals, objectives, outputs, quotas, results, ends,* and *performance standards* synonymously. The goal-setting process includes identifying specific areas of job responsibility, developing performance standards in each area, and (possibly) formulating a work plan for achieving the goals. Vantive Corporation, a Santa Clara, California–based provider of customer service software, pays current employees $2,500 for each new salesperson they recruit. If a new employee stays at least 3 months, the person who did the recruiting earns an additional $2,500. Employees who recruited a person who remains with the company for a year become eligible to enter a contest that sends the winner to any destination in the world. Jannifer Grech, a telerepresentative for Vantive, set and achieved her goal of $7,500 last year and used that money for a down payment on a house.[23]

What happens when employees don't make their goals? When employees are under extreme pressure to meet goals, they may resort to cutting corners, overcharging customers, or falsifying research results. Reliance on a numerically based reward system often produces unintended behaviors that hurt productivity and harm customers.

Rod Rodin, is the CEO of Marshall Industries, a billion dollar electronics distributor in Los Angeles that serves more than 30,000 customers who order more than 700,000 parts a month. He quickly recognized that the company's reward system was encouraging behaviors that led to poor service, dissatisfied customers, and, ultimately, lower profits. Rodin found that more than 20 percent of each month's sales were shipped to clients during the last three days of the month. Managers were hiding customer returns or opening bad credit accounts just to make their monthly sales goals. Divisions were hiding products from each other or saying that products had been shipped and that they really had none on hand. Salespeople fought over how to split commissions on revenue from a customer who did design work in Boston but made purchases in Dallas.

Figure 6.2 **Management by Objectives Process**

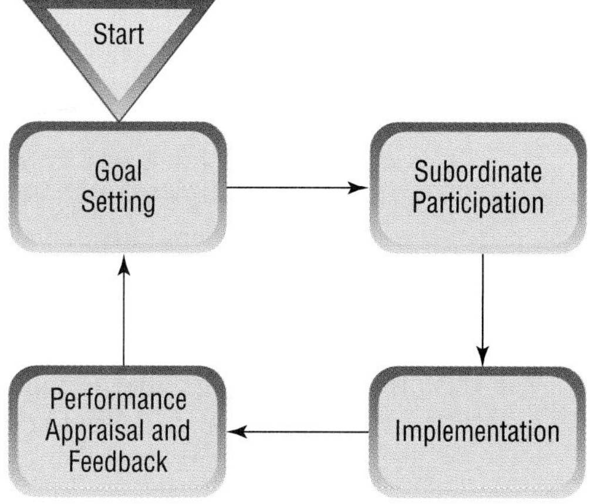

Employee and team performance was reviewed and ranked on the basis of numerical criteria, such as receivables outstanding, gross sales dollars, and the like. Rodin's solution was to scrap the incentive compensation system. He declared that there would be no more contests, prizes, or bonuses for individual achievements. Everyone at Marshall was put on a salary and shared in a companywide bonus pool if the organization as a whole met its goals. Since that decision in 1991, the company's annual sales have grown from $582 million to just over $1.2 billion, and the value of its stock has soared from $9 to $57.[24]

Particular job responsibilities usually change less dramatically and less frequently over time than does the specific goal associated with each area of responsibility. However, specific sales volumes can vary greatly because of general economic conditions, changed market acceptance, more or fewer opportunities in a sales territory, and so on. Auto Nation, a nationwide franchise operation that specializes in selling preowned cars at its 43 locations, recently eliminated daily quotas because its management discovered that salespeople were becoming too aggressive with customers. Quotas have been replaced with a monthly goal for each franchise: to sell 400 cars.

Various guidelines have been offered to managers and team leaders on how to set goals. The following are some examples.

- State what must be done. A job description may be helpful in setting goals with a subordinate. It should list the tasks to be performed, the outcomes expected, coordination required with other jobs, equipment to be used, any supervisory duties involved, and so on. Competencies on which job success depends can further clarify what the job entails.
- Specify how performance will be measured. Often time, money, or physical units can be measured. Sometimes, though, success is more subjective and difficult to measure. If so, specifying behaviors or actions that will lead to success can be used as indicators of performance.
- Specify the performance standard. A readily accepted approach is to start goal setting by letting previous performance set the standard. Most employees consider their average previous performance, or that of their team, to be a fair goal. Performance in some jobs, though, can't be measured so precisely. The job may be unique or so new that no previous performance measures are available. If so, goal setting becomes a matter of judgment.
- Set deadlines to reach goals. Some goals lend themselves to daily or weekly accomplishment. Others can be accomplished only monthly, quarterly, or annually.
- Rank goals in order of importance and difficulty. A clear understanding of priorities helps employees focus on what is most important at the time. Also, people work best when they have compelling goals.[25]

Diversity and Goal Setting

Managers at The Associates, Exxon, Texaco, and Lockheed Martin, among others, have also used such guidelines to confront diversity issues in their organizations. Workforce diversity is now a fact of organizational life that influences recruitment, retention, motivation, and performance of employees. Although many tools for changing the behaviors of employees exist, setting goals is a key. **Affirmative action programs** are supposed to involve a good-faith effort on the part of an organization to seek out, recruit, and encourage minority applicants for jobs. Yet in many organizations, that simply means placing the words "We are an equal opportunity employer" at the bottom of advertisements, and running those ads in selected "minority publications." Such efforts certainly do not discourage minority applicants, but they do very little to encourage them. Monica Powell, vice president of human resources at The Associates decided to take some actions that went beyond a good-faith program.

Powell and her staff established goals for the number of minority employees by division (e.g., consumer lending and credit card operations). To achieve these goals, the company sent recruiters from human resources and other departments to colleges that tended to enroll higher proportions of minority students. Specialists examined standardized test scores to determine possible racial or gender bias. Recruiters contacted minority faculty and staff to identify deserving students. Once they had identified such students, recruiters helped them with basic tools such as résumé writing, preparing for an interview, and job hunting.

To help identify talent further, managers at The Associates developed two programs. First, the company began a summer program for minority students following their junior year that was designed to qualify them for first-level management jobs after graduation. A manager was assigned to coach a student, but, before the coaching started, both coach and student were required to attend a half-day seminar on diversity issues. During the summer, senior managers were introduced to all the students through workshops, recreational events, and other activities. More than half the participating students were offered jobs upon graduation from college.[26]

Participation and Implementation

A moderate to high level of participation by subordinates in the goal-setting process is an essential component of MBO. However, before subordinates can participate effectively, they must have some autonomy in their jobs rather than merely doing what they are told. The reason is that MBO requires subordinates to plan and control their own tasks to a large extent. Thus highly routine and programmed jobs should be redesigned before they become part of the MBO process.

Implementation of MBO requires translating the outcomes from the goal-setting process into actions that ultimately will lead to the attainment of the desired goals. Action planning, which indicates how goals are to be achieved, often accompanies the implementation phase. During implementation, managers must give greater latitude and choice to employees, perhaps by discontinuing day-to-day oversight of their activities. But managers must be available to coach and counsel employees to help them reach their goals—playing a greater helping or facilitating role and a less judgmental role. Managers should hold periodic meetings during the year with employees to review progress, discuss assistance needed, and make any necessary changes in goals, which should be modified as necessary. This approach allows employees to perceive MBO as a flexible system and encourages them to address new problems or changes as they occur.

Performance Appraisal and Feedback

Performance appraisal under MBO involves (1) identifying measurement factors or goals against which to evaluate performance; (2) measuring performance against those goals; (3) reviewing performance with the employee; and (4) developing ways to improve future performance. Employees develop a clear understanding of their progress through performance appraisal and feedback. Feedback is a key element of MBO because it identifies the extent to which employees have attained their goals. The knowledge of results is essential to improved job performance and personal development in terms of new skills, attitudes, and motivation. Performance may be recognized and rewarded in many different ways. Ultimately, however, the satisfaction gained from achieving goals becomes one of the most cherished rewards.[27]

Management by objectives encourages self-evaluation of performance. Honest self-evaluation by employees provides insight into their own performance and the possible need to modify their behaviors to achieve their goals. When people are self-motivated and capable of managing many of their own tasks, managers can turn their attention to other issues that must be resolved and other problems that must be solved.

Alamco, a $12 million Clarksburg, West Virginia, oil and gas company, recently won a Wellness Council of America award for using MBO to encourage healthful lifestyles among its 96 employees. Yearly cash incentives for six healthful behaviors or conditions were jointly set by all employees: not smoking or chewing tobacco ($100); wearing a seat belt ($25); a cholesterol level below 150 ($100); blood pressure below 135/85 ($50); a waist-to-hip ratio of 0.8 or less for women and 0.95 or less for men ($50); and getting 30 minutes of exercise three times a week ($25). In addition, spouses earn half the incentive amounts. Last year, Alamco distributed $19,000 and saved more than 65 percent on its health insurance premiums. Absenteeism is down and camaraderie is up.[28]

Significance in Practice

Critics have attacked MBO, particularly with respect to ways that organizations apply it. These criticisms relate mainly to how managers actually use the process, rather than to how it is supposed to be used. Among the criticisms are the following.

- Too much emphasis is placed on reward–punishment psychology (i.e., people are rewarded for accomplishing goals and punished for not doing so).
- An excessive amount of paperwork and red tape develops—the very things that MBO is supposed to reduce.
- The process is controlled and imposed from the top, allowing little opportunity for real employee participation.
- The process turns into a zero-sum (win–lose) game between manager and employee.
- Aspects of jobs that can be objectively rather than subjectively measured receive the most emphasis.
- Too much emphasis on individual goals and performance drives out recognition of the need for collaborative teamwork and group goals. Individuals may satisfy their own goals to the detriment of overall goals.[29]

Learning Objective:

4. Describe reward systems in high-performance work systems.

REWARD SYSTEMS IN HIGH-PERFORMANCE WORK SYSTEMS

In Chapters 4 and 5 we discussed types of rewards that organizations make available to employees. From the concepts discussed in these chapters, along with those presented so far in this chapter, you should by now recognize that one of the basic goals of all managers is to motivate employees to perform at their highest levels. The term **high-performance work system** is often used to describe the integration of well-established theories of motivation with new technologies that link pay and performance. Managers agree that tying pay to job performance is essential. However, the actual implementation of programs designed to bring about such a relationship is often quite difficult. Questions that arise include: Should pay increases be tied to the performance of an individual or team? Recall that Rod Rodin, CEO of Marshall Industries, found that rewarding individuals created unhealthy competition among employees and destroyed morale. Deciding to reward all employees in the organization raises another question: Should the reward be based on cost savings and distributed annually or on profits and distributed when people retire or leave the organization? The accounting procedures required by cost savings plans are enormous and complex, but they allow rewards to be distributed relatively quickly. Also, many employees view fringe benefits, salaries, opportunities to engage in challenging assignments, and the achievement of difficult goals as rewards. In this section, we discuss four popular reward systems that organizations use to motivate employees: gain-sharing, flexible benefit plans, banking time off, and skill-based pay.[30] Their strengths and limitations are summarized in Table 6.4.

Table 6.4

Reward Systems in High-Performance Work Settings

REWARD SYSTEM	STRENGTHS	LIMITATIONS
Gain sharing	Rewards employees who reach specified production levels and control costs.	Formula can be complex; employees must trust management.
Profit sharing	Rewards organizational performance.	Difficult for individuals and teams to have an impact on overall organizational performance.
Flexible benefits	Tailored to fit individual needs.	Administrative costs high and difficult to use with teams.
Banking time off	Additional time off is contingent on employee performance.	Training costs to improve employee skills and competencies are high.
Skill-based pay	After acquiring new skills, employee is paid more.	Labor costs increase as employees master more skills. Employee can "top out" at the highest wage rate.

Gain-Sharing and Profit-Sharing Plans

Through **gain-sharing plans,** regular cash bonuses are provided to employees for increasing productivity, reducing costs, or improving quality.[31] According to Towers Perrin, a compensation consulting organization, over 50 percent of all U.S. companies had some type of gain-sharing pay plan for their employees. The average payout for employees was 7.6 percent, up from 5.9 percent just a few years ago. Many organizations, such as Continental Airlines, Wal-Mart, and Pizza Hut, are discovering that, when designed correctly, gain-sharing plans can contribute to employee motivation and involvement. Specific formulas tailor-made for each organization are used to calculate both performance contributions and gain-sharing awards. Many gain-sharing plans encourage employees to become involved in making decisions that will affect their rewards. Gain-sharing plans are tied to a plant, division, or department's improvement.

A popular version of gain-sharing is the Scanlon plan, named after Joe Scanlon, a union leader in the 1930s.[32] The **Scanlon plan** is a system of rewards for improvements in productivity. This plan is designed to save labor costs, and incentives are calculated as a function of labor costs relative to the sales value of production. Working together, employees and managers develop a formula that bases the distribution of rewards on a ratio of total labor costs to total sales volume. If actual labor costs are less than expected, the surplus goes into a bonus pool. For example, Baltimore County workers calculated that they needed $100,000 worth of labor to generate $500,000 worth of services to residents of that county. In the following year, the same services were provided for $80,000 worth of labor. Forty percent of the $20,000 saved was then distributed to the employees, with the county keeping the balance. Employee bonuses were based on a percentage of their salaries.[33] In many cases, the bonus pool is equally split between organization and employees.

Although gain-sharing plans sound good, they have had mixed success. The Fleet Financial Group recently abandoned its gain-sharing program. As a part of a two-year cost-cutting effort, management had created a gain-sharing program tied to the company's ratio of expenses to revenue and its stock prices. The more costs were cut and the higher the stock rose, the more employees were supposed to be rewarded. But when Fleet's stock price remained depressed even after cost cutting, workers got the minimum payout—averaging $615 per employee. Many employees stated that, considering the blood, sweat, and tears that went into getting the bonus, it turned out to be meaningless. What further enraged employees was that top management received big bonuses that weren't tied to the same measures.[34]

In contrast, **profit-sharing plans** give employees a portion of the company's profits.[35] As the name suggests, profit-sharing plans distribute profits to all employees. Average profit-sharing figures are difficult to calculate, but according to some experts they typically range between 4 and 6 percent of a person's salary. In a recent year, The Associates paid its 33,400 employees an average of 3.45 percent of their salaries into their retirement accounts, costing the company more than $22 million. According to Towers Perrin, profit sharing may have a limited impact because employees may feel that they can do little to influence the organization's overall profitability. That is, company profits are influenced by many factors, such as competitor's products, state of the economy, and the inflation rate of the economy that are well beyond the employees' control. Profit-sharing plans are very popular in Japan. For example, at Seiko Instruments many managers and workers receive bonuses twice a year that equal 4 or 5 months' salary. These bonuses are based on the company's overall performance.[36]

Flexible Benefit Plans

Flexible benefit plans allow employees to choose the benefits they want, rather than having management choose for them. According to David Norwood, vice president of Holmes and Murphy, a compensation consulting firm, a typical corporation's benefits plan currently is about 37 percent of its total employee compensation package.[37] That represents a huge cost, considering that only 5 percent or less is set aside for merit pay increases in most organizations. Under flexible benefit plans, employees decide—beyond a base program—how they want to receive additional benefit amounts, tailoring the benefits package to their needs. The idea is that employees can make important and intelligent decisions about their benefits. Some employees take all their discretionary benefits in cash; others choose additional life insurance, child or elder care, dental insurance, or retirement plans. Extensive benefits options may be highly attractive to an employee with a spouse and family at home. However, many benefits might be only minimally attractive to a young, single employee. Older employees value retirement plans more than younger employees and are willing to put more money into them. Employees with elderly parents may desire financial assistance in providing care for them. At Traveler's Insurance Company employees can choose benefits of up to $5,000 a year for the care of dependent elderly parents.

Thousands of organizations now offer flexible benefits plans. They have become very popular because they offer three distinct advantages. First, they allow employees to make important decisions about their personal finances and to match employees' needs with their benefits plans. Second, such plans help organizations control their costs, especially for health care. Employers can set the maximum amount of benefit dollars they will spend on employees' benefits and avoid automatically absorbing cost increases. Third, such plans highlight the economic value of many benefits to employees. Most employees have little idea of the cost of benefits because the organization is willing to pay for them even though employees might not want some of them or might prefer alternatives.

Moreover, the changing workforce is causing employers to consider flexible benefits as a tool to recruit and retain employees. Starbucks Coffee Company believes that its use of flexible benefits plans have cut employee turnover from 150 to 60 percent (see chapter 5). Starbucks calculates that hiring an employee costs $550. If so, a competitor with 300 percent turnover would have to hire three people at a cost of 3 × $550 =

\$1,650 per job per year, whereas Starbucks would need to spend only $0.6 \times \$550 = \$330$ per job per year.

Some limitations are associated with flexible benefits plans. First, because different employees choose different benefits packages, record keeping becomes more complicated. Sophisticated computer systems are essential for keeping straight the details of employees' records. Second, accurately predicting the number of employees that might choose each benefit is difficult. That may affect the firm's group rates for life and medical insurance, as the costs of such plans are based on the number of employees covered.

Banking Time Off

Time off from work with pay is attractive to some people. Typically, the length of vacations and scheduling them are based on the number of years that employees have worked for an organization. An extension of such a system is basing time off on performance. That is, employees can earn time-off credit by high performance and bank it for future use. At Silicon Graphics, all high-performing employees are eligible for a 6-week sabbatical every 4 years. If employees don't use their time, they can roll the credit over to a savings investment plan. In setting up such programs, organizations should be aware of some potential problems. For example, an employee who wants to use banked time during a busy time for the organization may negatively affect productivity. In addition the organization may incur increased costs because of having to pay overtime or bring in a temporary employee to cover for an employee taking extended time off.

Sabbaticals are becoming increasingly popular as a way for high-performing employees to learn new competencies. According to Marita Wesley-Clough, creative strategy director at Hallmark Cards, a person in accounting may take a job in artistic development. After joining this department, the person spends 4 months exploring new skills, such as stitchery, papermaking, glassblowing, or ceramics. The accountant would leave his or her office and relocate full time to Hallmark's 180,000 square-foot innovation center. Alternatively, the same person may decide to spend 6 months on an intensive mission learning about specific cultural beliefs and practices, such as spirituality in tribes. For example, Jan Bryan-Hunt developed a new line of jewelry, Symbolic Notions, during her 6-week sabbatical. Hallmark is now testing the concept in more than 40 of its stores.[38]

Skill-Based Pay

Paying people according to their value in the labor market makes a great deal of sense. After all, employees who develop multiple skills are valuable assets to the organization. As we have emphasized earlier, competencies, such as communication, are often based on mastering a number of individual skills, such as verbal, written, and media presentations. **Skill-based pay** depends on the number and level of job-related skills that an employee has learned.[39] At Toyota, for example, workers not only are expected to operate machines, but also to take responsibility for maintenance and troubleshooting, quality control, and even modifying computer programs. About 40 percent of large U.S. organizations, including TRW, Honeywell, and Westinghouse, use skill-based pay for at least some of their production workers.

Skill-based pay is easiest to describe in terms of a production team in a manufacturing plant. Typically, management can fairly easily identify all the skills needed to perform various tasks and the skills that employees need to learn. Employees' pay is based on their skill levels. At General Electric's plant in Bayamon, Puerto Rico, there are 172 hourly workers, 15 advisors, and the plant manager. The workers are divided into teams. Each team is responsible for one of the plant's operations, such as receiving, assembly, or shipping. The advisors assist the teams only when they need help.

General Electric agreed to provide the hourly employees with the skills and knowledge needed to perform multiple jobs. It also designed a pay structure to reward employees who learn and use these skills. Hourly workers change jobs every 6 months so that they can learn each job and how it affects other plant operations. In return, employees are rewarded with a "triple-scoop" compensation plan that pays for skills, knowledge, and business performance. Workers receive a $0.25 per hour pay increase the first time they go through each of the four 6-month rotations. In addition, they can almost double their pay by "declaring a major" and becoming an expert in an area such as maintenance or quality control. Further pay increases can be earned by completing courses in English, business practices, and other subjects. By meeting goals for plant performance and individual attendance, bonuses of more than $200 per quarter also are possible. The Bayamon workforce now is 20 percent more productive than the workforce in a similar plant.[40]

The most obvious advantage of skill-based pay in a production situation is flexibility. When employees can perform multiple tasks, managers gain tremendous flexibility in workforce utilization. Largely as a result of the Tylenol poisoning tragedy in 1982, Johnson & Johnson decided to completely redo its packaging of Tylenol to add greater safety. Because of the firm's skill-based pay system, employees understood the technology involved and were able to introduce quickly the new packaging changes. Johnson & Johnson also found that skill-based pay can increase productivity while decreasing supervisory costs. Employees are motivated to gain and use new skills because the organization equitably rewards them for doing so.

However, skill-based pay does have some disadvantages. The most obvious one has to do with the high pay rates that the plan tends to produce. By its very nature, the plan encourages individuals to become more valuable to the organization and, as a result, to be paid more. Designed to increase opportunities to learn multiple skills, skill-based pay plans require a large investment in training and lost production time as employees learn new skills. Thus the organization sometimes has inexperienced and overpaid employees doing the work, at least in the short run. A worst-case scenario for the organization is that many employees know how to do every job but that all jobs are being done by employees who aren't highly proficient. Finally, employees can be frustrated when no job openings are available in areas for which they have learned new skills. Most skill-based programs require employees to perform skills regularly in order to be paid for them. Thus effectively managing skill-based pay systems is a challenge for many organizations.

Significance in Practice

Management must make certain trade-offs when choosing among these four reward systems. Figure 6.3 provides some guidance for choosing a suitable reward system. It shows you under what circumstances an individual or team plan is appropriate and under what situations specific individual or team plans are most effective. If you answer the first five diagnostic questions *yes*, reward systems that permit individuals to calculate their own rewards might be of value. If you answer the first five diagnostic questions *no*, team, department, or organizationwide reward systems might be more appropriate. If you want to reward individuals' performance, you should then ask three additional questions. If the answers to all these questions are *yes*, a skilled-based or gain-sharing system is appropriate. Similarly, if a group or team reward system seems appropriate, you should ask three additional questions. If the answers to all these questions are *yes*, profit-sharing and flexible benefit programs are appropriate.

There is ample evidence that organizations in various countries utilize different reward systems. Cultural values learned in childhood are passed down from one generation to the next and serve to differentiate one country from another. The following Managing Across Cultures Competency feature highlights how reward practices differ by country.

Figure 6.3 **Deciding Among Alternative Reward Systems**

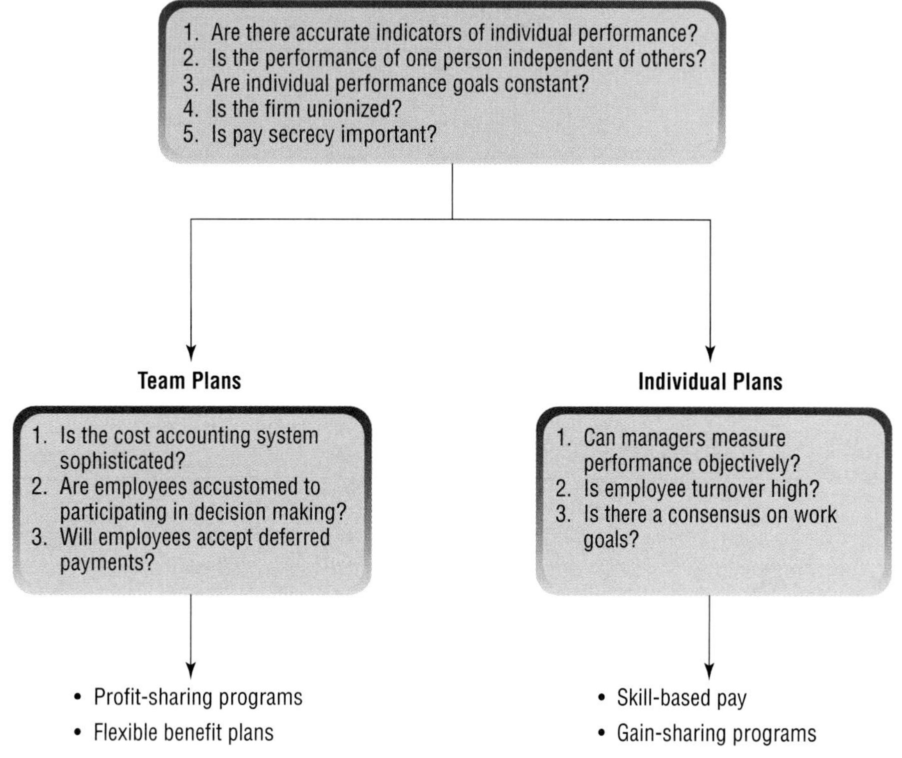

Source: Adapted from Wagner, J. A., and Hollenbeck, J. R. *Organizational Behavior,* 3rd ed. Englewood Cliffs, N.J.: Simon and Schuster, 1998, 100.

COMPETENCY: MANAGING ACROSS CULTURES

REWARD PRACTICES IN DIFFERENT COUNTRIES

The information displayed in Table 6.5 was taken from a large international study. Using data gathered from IBM, Towers Perrin, and Price Waterhouse, the researchers examined the pay and fringe benefit practices of companies in 24 countries. We have used 3 countries as examples for each reward system. In societies where unpredictability and risky situations are to be avoided, basing pay on seniority was used frequently because seniority provides an objective guideline. People can easily understand what seniority is and can calculate their own without much help from others. This method takes the uncertainty out of pay decisions.

Pay based on individual performance was used extensively in countries that value the individual more highly than the team. Individualistic cultures believe that people should take care of themselves, and hence individual responsibility for results is important. In countries that place a high value on the quality of life and caring for others, extensive fringe benefits (e.g., workplace child-care programs, maternity-leave programs, and sabbatical leaves) were stressed. Finally, companies operating in cultures that value linking pay to performance—either individual or team performance—favored stock options. These results are supported by the fact that, in the United States, most companies used either a profit-sharing or a gain-sharing program to reward high-performing individuals. In South Korea, Japan, and other countries where "fitting in" is important, such reward systems do not advance and support the culture's values. Gain-sharing and skill-based pay systems reward individuals, sometimes at the expense of the team or department.[41]

Table 6.5 Reward Practices in Different Countries

TYPE OF REWARD PRACTICE	COUNTRY
Pay based on seniority	Greece, Portugal, Belgium
Pay based on individual/team performance	Australia, United Kingdom, United States
Extensive fringe-benefit plans	Sweden, Norway, the Netherlands
Stock options and bonus plans linked to individual/team/firm performance	Austria, United Kingdom, United States

Source: Adapted from Schuler, R. S., and Rogovsky, N. Understanding compensation practices variation across firms: The impact of national culture. *Journal of International Business Studies,* 1998, 29, 159–177.

CHAPTER SUMMARY

1. State the basics of goal setting, including the role of customers, suppliers, and others.

Goal setting is a process intended to increase efficiency and effectiveness by specifying the desired outcomes toward which individuals, departments, teams, and organizations should work. Goal setting doesn't take place in a vacuum. Stakeholders such as customers, shareholders, and employees influence the selection of organizational goals. On a day-to-day basis, customers or clients are probably the driving force in the selection of goals that are most crucial to organizational and employee performance. Quality goals in customer service include reliability, tangibility, responsiveness, assurance, and empathy.

2. Explain how performance is affected by goal setting.

A goal-setting model developed by Locke and Latham was presented. Goal setting is the process of developing, negotiating, and establishing targets that challenge the individual. The model emphasizes the challenges provided for the individual: goal difficulty, goal clarity, and self-efficacy. Setting difficult but clear goals for individuals who believe that they have the ability to complete the task leads to high performance. Four moderating factors—ability, goal commitment, feedback, and task complexity—influence the strength of the relationship between challenging goals and performance. If the individual has the ability, is committed to the goal, is given feedback on progress toward achievement of the goal, and if the task is complex, high performance will result. All four must be present to motivate a person to achieve his or her goal. Four mediators—direction, effort, persistence, and task strategy—facilitate goal attainment. That is, these four characteristics channel or focus the person's motivational efforts. Performance, rewards, satisfaction, and consequences complete the model.

3. Assess management by objectives (MBO) as a management philosophy and system.

Management by objectives (MBO) is both a philosophy and a management system. It encourages setting general organizational goals and increasingly more specific goals for departments, teams, and individual employees. The four basic components of the model are goal setting, subordinate participation, implementation, and performance appraisal and feedback.

4. Describe reward systems in high-performance work systems.

Reward systems represent a powerful means for motivating high levels of individual and team performance. Four reward systems, in particular, are designed to enhance performance: gain sharing, flexible benefits, banking time off, and skill-based pay plans. Gain-sharing programs are regular cash bonuses for employees who increase their productivity, reduce costs, or improve quality. A version of these plans is profit sharing, which gives employees a portion of the organization's profits. Flexible benefit plans allow employees to choose the benefits that are important to them. Banking time off and sabbaticals are ways for high-performing employees to learn new competencies while taking time off from their regular duties. Skill-based pay systems pay a person according to the number and level of job-related skills that the employee masters. The value of these skills is determined by the labor market.

KEY TERMS AND CONCEPTS

Affirmative action programs
Code of ethics
Flexible benefit plans
Gain-sharing plans
Goal clarity
Goal commitment
Goal difficulty
Goal setting
Goals
High-performance work system
Management by objectives (MBO)
Profit-sharing plans
Scanlon plan
Skill-based pay
Stakeholders
Whistleblowers

DISCUSSION QUESTIONS

1. Explain Marriott Hotel's program according to the concepts presented in the goal-setting model.
2. Think of an organization for which you currently work or have worked. How does this organization and its employees measure up in terms of the five service-quality goals stated in the chapter?
3. List your five most important personal goals. Evaluate the difficulty and clarity of each goal. What are the implications, if any, of this assessment for your future?
4. Think of this course. Evaluate your level of goal commitment. What factors do you think influenced your level of goal commitment? Did your level of commitment influence your performance? Explain.
5. Using the MBO model, why was Gordon's NASCAR team effective?
6. Why do people sometimes falsify records to achieve goals?
7. Keith Hughes, CEO of The Associates, said: "If you cannot define it and measure it, you are not going to get it." What implications does this statement have for setting goals? For measuring them?
8. What are the similarities and differences between gain-sharing and profit-sharing plans? Which system would motivate you to achieve greater performance? Why?
9. What are some problems that employees might face in an organization that has adopted a skill-based pay program?
10. Can a flexible benefits plan be tied to employee performance? If so, what are the advantages of doing so? The disadvantages?
11. How does a country's culture affect the type of rewards that high-performing employees are offered?

DEVELOPING COMPETENCIES

Competency: Managing Self—Goal-Setting Questionnaire

Instructions: The following statements refer to a job you currently hold or have held. Read each statement and then select a response from the following scale that best describes your view. You may want to use a separate sheet of paper to record your responses and compare them with the responses of others.

Scale

Almost Never 1 2 3 4 5 Almost Always

_____ 1. I understand exactly what I am supposed to do on my job.
_____ 2. I have specific, clear goals to aim for on my job.
_____ 3. The goals I have on this job are challenging.
_____ 4. I understand how my performance is measured on this job.
_____ 5. I have deadlines for accomplishing my goals on this job.
_____ 6. If I have more than one goal to accomplish, I know which are most important and which are least important.
_____ 7. My goals require my full effort.
_____ 8. My manager tells me the reasons for giving me the goals I have.
_____ 9. My manager is supportive with respect to encouraging me to reach my goals.

_____10. My manager lets me participate in the setting of my goals.

_____11. My manager lets me have some say in deciding how I will go about implementing my goals.

_____12. If I reach my goals, I know that my manager will be pleased.

_____13. I get credit and recognition when I attain my goals.

_____14. Trying for goals makes my job more fun than it would be without goals.

_____15. I feel proud when I get feedback indicating that I have reached my goals.

_____16. The other people I work with encourage me to attain my goals.

_____17. I sometimes compete with my coworkers to see who can do the best job in reaching our goals.

_____18. If I reach my goals, my job security will be improved.

_____19. If I reach my goals, my chances for a pay raise are increased.

_____20. If I reach my goals, my chances for a promotion are increased.

_____21. I usually feel that I have a suitable action plan(s) for reaching my goals.

_____22. I get regular feedback indicating how I am performing in relation to my goals.

_____23. I feel that my training was good enough so that I am capable of reaching my goals.

_____24. Organization policies help rather than hurt goal attainment.

_____25. Teams work together in this company to attain goals.

_____26. This organization provides sufficient resources (e.g., time, money, and equipment) to make goal setting effective.

_____27. In performance appraisal sessions, my supervisor stresses problem solving rather than criticism.

_____28. Goals in this organization are used more to help you do your job well rather than punish you.

_____29. The pressure to achieve goals here fosters honesty as opposed to cheating and dishonesty.

_____30. If my manager makes a mistake that affects my ability to attain my goals, he or she admits it.

Scoring and Interpretation

Add the points shown for items 1 through 30. Scores of 120 to 150 may indicate a high-performing, highly satisfying work situation. Your goals are challenging and you are committed to reaching them. When you achieve your goals, you are rewarded for your accomplishments. Scores of 80 to 119 may suggest a highly varied work situation with some motivating and satisfying features and some frustrating and dissatisfying features. Scores of 30 to 79 may suggest a low-performing, dissatisfying work situation.[42]

Competency: Managing Change—Improving Safety

Safety issues continue to be of great concern to employees and managers. Since the passage of the Occupational Safety and Health Act (OSHA) in 1970, managers have been particularly alert to the need for reducing injury-related accidents at work and ways of doing so. In a certain farm machinery company, three departments had particularly troublesome safety records: final assembly, parts, and raw material preparation. Although management had posted safety warnings, safety violations were still occurring too frequently.

The company hired four consultants who developed a checklist based on the company's safety manual. The consultants then randomly observed workers in the three departments to determine whether they followed the company's safety rules (e.g., did employees wear safety glasses with shields on both sides when working underneath equipment and did they wear leather gloves?). These observations were made two to four times a week in full view of the employees. A total of 167 observations were made during the study. After each observation session, the safety performance of each of the three departments was computed by dividing the number of employees working safely by the total number of departmental employees observed and multiplying by 100. Weekly departmental safety performance was determined by averaging the results of the observations during that week. The results were posted so that all employees knew their department's safety performance score. The average safety record for the raw material department was 72 percent, for the final assembly department it was 53 percent, and for the parts department it was 48 percent.

The consultants designed a training program to improve safety in these departments. All employees attended a 30-minute meeting during which management told them that the safety goal would be related to their department's weekly safety performance. Management also said that 100 percent weekly safety performance was unrealistically high and therefore not expected. The employees were told further that, if 90 percent of the employees performed their jobs safely, not only would the goal be attained, but the frequency of injuries also would decline.[43]

Questions

1. Design a goal-setting program for achieving a 90 percent accident-free environment in the three departments. You may choose to work through the goal-setting model presented in the text as a start.
2. What type of reward system would you design to achieve a high-performance work system? State your reasons.

REFERENCES

1. Adapted from Kaydo, C. Marriott's incentives strike gold. *Sales & Marketing,* November 1998, 97.
2. Adapted from Marchetti, M. Helping reps count every penny. *Sales & Marketing,* July 1998, 77.
3. Locke, E. A., and Latham, G. P. *A Theory of Goal Setting & Task Performance.* Englewood Cliffs, N.J.: Prentice-Hall, 1990, 7.
4. Locke, E. A., and Kristof, A. L. Volitional choices in the goal achievement process. In P. Gollwitzer and J. A. Bargh (eds.), *The Psychology of Action: Linking Cognition and Motivation to Behavior.* New York: Guilford, 1996, 365–384.
5. Pitts, R. A., and Lei, D. *Strategic Management: Building and Sustaining Competitive Advantage,* rev. ed. Cincinnati: South-Western, 2000; Kumar, K., and Subramanian, R. Meeting the expectations of stakeholders. *SAM Advanced Management Journal,* 1998, 63(2), 31–41; Buck, T., Filatotchev, I., and Wright, M. Agents, stakeholders and corporate governance in Russian firms. *Journal of Management Studies,* 1998, 35(1), 81–105.
6. Berry, L. L., and Seiders, K. Service fairness: What it is and why it matters. *Academy of Management Executive,* 1998, 12(2), 8–21; Tax, S. S., Brown, S. W., and Chandrashekaran, M. Customer evaluations of service complaint experiences. *Journal of Marketing,* 1998, 62(2), 60–77.
7. Adapted from Cusack, L., and Enslow, B. Mission imprintable. *Sales & Marketing,* September 1998, 20–22.
8. Locke and Latham, 252–267; see also Latham, G. P., and Seijts, G. H. The effects of proximal and distal goals on performance on a moderately difficult complex task. *Journal of Organizational Behavior,* 1999, 20, 421–450.
9. Adapted from Waxler, C. The million-dollar suggestion box. *Forbes,* September 7, 1998, 171–172.
10. Stajkovic, A. D., and Luthans, F. Social cognitive theory and self-efficacy. *Organizational Dynamics,* Spring 1998, 62–75; Durham, C. C., Locke, E. A., and Knight, D. Effects of leader role, team set goal difficulty, self-efficacy and tactics on team effectiveness. *Organizational Behavior and Human Decision Processes,* 1997, 72, 203–221.
11. VandeWalle, D., Brown, S. P., Cron, W. L., and Slocum, J. W., Jr. The influence of goal orientation and self-regulation tactics on sales performance: A longitudinal field test. *Journal of Applied Psychology,* 1999, 84, 249–259; Wright, P. M., O'Leary-Kelly, A. M., Cortina, J. M., Klein, H. J., and Hollenbeck, J. R. On the meaning and measurement of goal commitment. *Journal of Applied Psychology,* 1994, 79, 795–808.
12. Donovan, J. J., and Rodosevich, D. J. The moderating role of goal commitment on the goal–difficulty performance relationship: A meta-analytical review and critical analysis. *Journal of Applied Psychology,* 1998, 83, 308–316; Klein, H. J., and Kim, J. S. A field study of the influence on situations constraints, leader–member exchange and goal-commitment on performance. *Academy of Management Journal,* 1998, 41, 88–96; Podsakoff, P. M., MacKenzie, S. B., and Adhearne, M. Moderating effects of goal acceptance on the relationship between group cohesiveness and productivity. *Journal of Applied Psychology,* 1997, 82, 974–984.
13. Adapted from Salter, C. Life in the fast lane. *Fast Company,* October 1998, 172–178.
14. Becker, T. E., Billings, R. S., Eveleth, D. M., and Gilbert, N. L. Foci and bases of employee commitment: Implications for job performance. *Academy of Management Journal,* 1996, 39, 464–482.
15. Brown, S. P., Cron, W. L., and Slocum, J. W., Jr. Effects of goal-directed emotions on salesperson volitions, behavior and performance: A longitudinal study. *Journal of Marketing,* 1997, 61, 39–50.
16. VandeWalle, D., and Cummings, L. L. A test of the influence of goal orientation on the feedback seeking process. *Journal of Applied Psychology,* 1997, 82, 390–400; Austin, J. T., and Klein, H. J. Work motivation and goal striving. In K. Murphy (ed.), *Individual Differences and Behavior in Organizations,* San Francisco: Jossey-Bass, 1996, 209–257.
17. Adapted from Schifrin, M. Bop while you shop. *Forbes,* July 6, 1998, 69–70.
18. Kaptein, M., and Wempe, J. Twelve gordian knots when developing an organizational code of ethics. *Journal of Business Ethics,* 1998, 19, 853–870.
19. Adapted from Benson, J. A., and Ross, D. L. Sundstrand: A case in transformation of cultural ethics. *Journal of Business Ethics,* 1998, 7, 1517–1527.
20. Smith, E. D., Jr., and Pham, C. Doing business in Vietnam: A cultural guide. *Business Horizons,* May–June 1996, 47–51; Von Glinow, M. A., and Clarke, L. Vietnam: Tiger or Kitten? *Academy of Management Executive,* 1995, 9(4), 35–48.
21. Cohen, A. Nonwork influences on withdrawal cognitions. *Human Relations,* 1997, 50, 1511–1537
22. Greenwood, R. G. Management by objectives: As developed by Peter Drucker, assisted by Harold Smidy. *Academy of Management Review,* 1981, 6, 225–230.
23. Marchetti, M. Selling in Silicon Valley. *Sales and Marketing,* September 1998, 46–54.
24. Adapted from Dess, G. P., and Picken, J. C. *Beyond Productivity.* New York: American Management Association, 1999, 164–167.
25. Fenton-O'Creevy, M. Employee involvement and the middle manager. *Journal of Organizational Behavior,* 1998(1), 67–84.
26. Personal conversations with M. McGill., D. Hamblin, and M. Powell, The Associates, Dallas, Texas, August, 1999.
27. Frink, D. D., and Ferris, G. R. Accountability, impression management, and goal-setting in the performance evaluation process. *Human Relations,* 1998, 51, 1259–1284.
28. Fenn, D. Healthful habits pay off. *Inc.,* April, 1996, 111.
29. Shalley, C. A. Effects of coaction, expected evaluation, and goal-setting on creativity and productivity. *Academy of Management Journal,* 1995, 38, 483–503; Latham, G. P. *Increasing Productivity Through Performance Appraisal.* Reading, Mass.: Addison-Wesley, 1992.

30. Lawler, E. E. III. *Strategic Pay: Aligning Organizational Strategies and Pay Systems.* San Francisco: Jossey-Bass, 1990.
31. Personal conversation with J. Joyce, compensation specialist, Tower Perrin, July 1999, New York; Welbourne, T. M., and Gomez-Mejia, L. R. Gainsharing: A critical review and a future research agenda. *Journal of Management,* 1995, 21, 559–609.
32. Schuler, R. S. and Jackson, S. E. *Human Resource Management,* 6th ed. Cincinnati: South-Western, 2000; Tyler, L. S., and Fisher, B. The Scanlon concept: A philosophy as much as a system. *Personnel Administrator,* July 1983, 33–37.
33. Fox, J., and Lawson, B. Gainsharing program lifts Baltimore employees' morale. *American City and County,* September 1997, 112(10), 93–94.
34. McCartney, S. Back on course. *Wall Street Journal,* May 15, 1996, A1.
35. Gomez-Mejia, L. R., and Balkin, D. B. *Compensation, Organizational Strategy, and Firm Performance.* Cincinnati: South-Western, 1992; Kim, D., and Voos, P. B. Unionization, union involvement and the performance of gainsharing plans. *Industrial Relations,* 1997, 52, 304–333.
36. Personal conversation with M. McGill, executive vice president, human resources, The Associates, Dallas, Texas, September 1999.
37. Personal conversation with D. Norwood, executive vice president, Holmes and Murphy, Dallas, Texas, September 1999; see also McBain, R. Pay, performance, and motivation. *Journal of General Management,* Autumn 1998, 20–32.
38. Dess, G. G., and Picken, J. C. *Beyond Productivity.* New York: American Management Association, 1999.
39. Besser, T. L. Rewards and organizational goal achievement: A case study of Toyota Motor Manufacturing in Kentucky. *Journal of Management Studies,* 1995, 32, 383–399; Murray, B., and Gerhart, B. An empirical analysis of skill-based pay programs and plant performance outcomes. *Academy of Management Journal,* 1998, 41, 68–79.
40. McGill, M. E., and Slocum, J. W., Jr. *The Smarter Organization.* New York: John Wiley & Sons, 1994.
41. Schuler, R. S., and Rogovsky, N. Understanding compensation practice variations across firms: The impact of national culture. *Journal of International Business Studies,* 1998, 21, 159–177.
42. Adapted from Locke and Latham, 355–358.
43. Adapted from Reber, R. A., Wallin, J. A., and Chhokar, J. S. Improving safety performance with goal setting and feedback. *Human Performance,* 1990, 3(1), 51–61.

CHAPTER 7

Work Stress

LEARNING OBJECTIVES

When you have finished studying this chapter, you should be able to:

1. Explain the concepts of stress and stressors and describe the general nature of the body's stress response.
2. Diagnose the sources of stress in organizations.
3. Describe the effects of stress on health and job performance.
4. Explain the relationship between personality and stress.
5. Identify several individual and organizational methods for coping with stress.

Preview Case: *Stress on the Job*

NATURE OF STRESS

Fight-or-Flight Response

The Stress Experience

SOURCES OF STRESS

Work Stressors

Competency: Managing Across Cultures—*Siesta Sunset*

Competency: Managing Change—*How About Creating Saner Workloads?*

Competency: Managing Self—*Technology Workers and Stress*

Life Stressors

EFFECTS OF STRESS

Stress and Health

Stress and Performance

Competency: Managing Self—*"Just Enough but Not Too Much"*

Stress and Job Burnout

PERSONALITY AND STRESS

Competency: Managing Communication—*Management Myths That Lead to Burnout*

The Type A Personality

The Hardy Personality

STRESS MANAGEMENT

Individual Methods

Organizational Methods

Competency: Managing Self—*Employees Who Value Time*

Wellness Programs

CHAPTER SUMMARY

Key Terms and Concepts

Discussion Questions

DEVELOPING COMPETENCIES

Competency: Managing Self—*Assessing Your Stress Level*

Competency: Managing Change—*Stress Management at Metropolitan Hospital*

PREVIEW CASE

STRESS ON THE JOB

Organizations have continued to grapple with questions concerning the seriousness of stress in the workplace and the appropriate organizational response. One traditional school of thought is summed up by the notion that companies should basically ignore stress. We might call this the "stop whining and get back to work" approach. Another school of thought suggests that companies should avoid offering stress management programs to employees for fear of increasing lawsuits. The logic is that raising the issue of workplace stress simply calls attention to problems that cannot be effectively dealt with, so that the only real impact is to increase the probability that employees experiencing stress will be more likely to sue. However, studies of work stress suggest that it is far from being a trivial concern. Further, organizations that ignore the impact of stress on employees and productivity run far greater risks than organizations that attempt to manage stress effectively. Consider the following examples of the dramatic impact of job stress gleaned from the business press.

- Weatherford Enterra's stock dropped *more than 10 percent* when the company revealed that Chief Executive Philip Burguieres was going to take time off for "stress-related health reasons."
- The downsizing phenomenon has clearly placed employees who lose their jobs under considerable stress. However, that is not the only stress-related effect. Studies have shown that the *anticipation* of layoffs among employees can produce a significant increase in anxiety and major decreases in performance. Further, the survivors of downsizing often face increased workloads, suffer from the personal loss of close friends and colleagues, and experience fear as a result of the possibility of future cuts in the workforce. All of these dynamics can dramatically increase stress.
- A 60-year-old vice president of a paper company in Texas with 30 years' experience was moved to an entry-level supervisor position when the firm decided that it needed "new ideas" and a "fresh perspective" from executives. In his new position, the former vice president reported to a manager in his twenties. The older manager sued, and won, on the basis of emotional distress and age discrimination. Interestingly, he won the largest amount not for the discrimination charges but for the punitive damages associated with emotional distress.
- An insurance claims adjuster in Iowa was faced with major changes in his job that resulted in an increased workload and 12-hour workdays, and subjected him to close supervision, which he found stressful. He successfully sued, arguing that these job conditions led to a major depression.[1]

Examples such as those reported in the Preview Case suggest that stress in the workplace is one of the major issues that managers and organizations must cope with. Organizations that ignore stress management, or assign it a low priority, are likely to suffer lower productivity, poor morale, and increased legal costs. The negative consequences of stress are so dramatic that managers need to (1) work hard to reduce excessive stress in the workplace and (2) help employees develop stress-coping skills.

A great many people experience unacceptable levels of stress. It can stem from events in their personal lives or at work. Although small amounts of stress can have positive effects by energizing people to achieve goals, excessive stress may seriously and negatively affect a person's health and job performance.

Because many organizations subject their employees to excessive stress, you need to understand the effects of work stress, the relationship between stress and performance, and the sources of stress in organizations. Everyone should understand the relationships between stress and health. In this chapter, we examine the nature of stress, the sources of stress at work, and the effects of stress. People can effectively handle varying amounts of stress, and we explore some of these individual differences. Finally, we examine ways that employees and organizations can cope with stress.

Learning Objective:

1. Explain the concepts of stress and stressors and describe the general nature of the body's stress response.

NATURE OF STRESS

Stress is a consequence of or a general response to an action or situation that places special physical or psychological demands, or both, on a person.[2] As such, stress involves an interaction of the person and the environment. The physical or psychological demands from the environment that cause stress are called **stressors**. Stressors can take various forms, but all stressors have one thing in common: They create stress or the potential for stress when an individual perceives them as representing a demand that may exceed that person's ability to respond.

FIGHT-OR-FLIGHT RESPONSE

Numerous changes occur in the human body during a stress reaction. Breathing and heart rates alter so that the body can operate with maximum capacity for physical action. Brain wave activity goes up to allow the brain to function maximally. Hearing and sight become momentarily more acute. Muscles ready themselves for action. These biochemical and bodily changes represent a natural reaction to an environmental stressor: the **fight-or-flight response**.[3] An animal attacked by a predator in the wild basically has two choices: to fight or to flee. The animal's bodily responses to the stressor (the predator) increase its chances of survival. Similarly, our cave-dwelling ancestors benefited from this biological response mechanism. People gathering food away from their caves would have experienced a great deal of stress upon meeting a saber-toothed tiger. In dealing with the tiger, they could have run away or stayed and fought. The biochemical changes in their bodies prepared them for either alternative and contributed to their ability to survive.[4]

The human nervous system still responds the same way to environmental stressors. This response continues to have survival value in a true emergency. However, for most people most of the time, the "tigers" are imaginary rather than real. In work situations, for example, a fight-or-flight response usually isn't appropriate. If an employee receives an unpleasant work assignment from a manager, physically assaulting the manager or storming angrily out of the office obviously is inappropriate. Instead, the employee is expected to accept the assignment calmly and do the best job possible. Remaining calm and performing effectively may be especially difficult when the employee perceives an assignment as threatening and the body is prepared to act accordingly.

Medical researcher Hans Selye first used the word *stress* to describe the body's biological response mechanisms. Selye considered stress to be the nonspecific response of the human body to any demand made on it.[5] However, the body has only a limited capacity to respond to stressors. The workplace makes a variety of demands on people, and too much stress over too long a period of time will exhaust their ability to cope with those stressors.

The Stress Experience

Several factors determine whether an individual experiences stress at work or in other situations. Figure 7.1 identifies four of the primary factors: (1) the person's perception of the situation, (2) the person's past experience, (3) the presence or absence of social support, and (4) individual differences with regard to stress reactions.

Perception. In Chapter 3 we defined *perception* as a key psychological process whereby a person selects and organizes environmental information into a concept of reality. Employee perceptions of a situation can influence how (or whether) they experience stress. For example, two DaimlerChrysler employees have their job duties substantially changed—a situation likely to be stressful for many people. The first employee views the new duties as an opportunity to learn new competencies and thinks that the change is a vote of confidence from management in her ability to be flexible and take on new challenges. In contrast, the second employee perceives the same situation to be extremely threatening and concludes that management is unhappy with his performance.

Past Experience. A person may perceive a situation as more or less stressful, depending on how familiar that person is with the situation and prior experience with the particular stressors involved. Past practice or training may allow some employees in an organization to deal calmly and competently with stressors that would greatly intimidate less experienced or inadequately trained employees. The relationship between experience and stress is based on reinforcement (see Chapter 4). Positive reinforcement or previous success in a similar situation can reduce the level of stress that a person experiences under certain circumstances; punishment or past failure under similar conditions can increase stress under the same circumstances.

Social Support. The presence or absence of other people influences how individuals in the workplace experience stress and respond to stressors.[6] The presence of coworkers may increase an individual's confidence, allowing that person to cope more

Figure 7.1 **The Relationship Between Stressors and Stress**

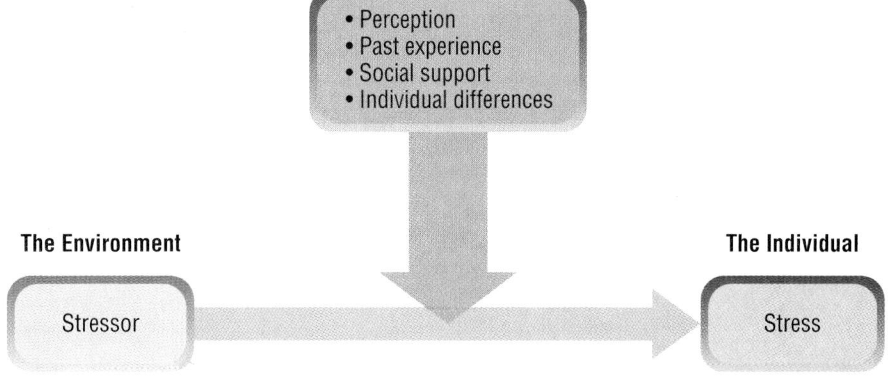

effectively with stress. For example, working alongside someone who performs confidently and competently in a stressful situation may help an employee behave similarly. Conversely, the presence of fellow workers may irritate some people or make them anxious, reducing their ability to cope with stress.

Individual Differences. Individual differences in motivation, attitudes, personality, and abilities also influence whether employees experience work stress and, if they do, how they respond to it.[7] Simply stated, people are different, as we pointed out in Chapters 2 and 3. What one person considers a major source of stress, another may hardly notice. Personality characteristics, in particular, may explain some of the differences in the ways that employees experience and respond to stress. For example, the Big Five personality factor that we labeled *adjustment* in Chapter 2 seems to be important in individual responses to various stressors in the work setting. Individuals at one extreme of adjustment (described as stable and confident) are more likely to cope well with a wide variety of work stressors; individuals at the other extreme (described as nervous and self-doubting) typically have greater difficulty in coping with the same stressors.

The story is told of a Harvard University undergraduate who had to drop out of college because of serious psychological problems brought on by stress from the demands of school. Eventually, this individual enlisted in the U.S. Navy and became a pilot. He was based on an aircraft carrier much of the time. Military pilots usually consider taking off and landing on carriers to be particularly stressful and dangerous. Despite the danger, this particular pilot served with distinction for a number of years and felt psychologically well during the entire time. When he retired from the Navy, he again enrolled in Harvard. As before, he experienced psychological difficulties, which became so severe that he had to be hospitalized.[8] This story dramatically illustrates the role of individual differences in stress reactions. Most people would find flying a plane from an aircraft carrier to be extremely stressful, whereas being a student would be far less stressful. Yet, for this Navy pilot, the opposite was the case. We further discuss relationships between personality and stress later in this chapter.

Learning Objective:

2. Diagnose the sources of stress in organizations.

SOURCES OF STRESS

Individuals commonly experience stress in both their personal and work lives. Understanding these sources of stress and their possible interaction is important. To consider either source in isolation may give an incomplete picture of the stress that a person is experiencing. Note the combined effects of work stress and stress from other aspects of life on the residents of Mexico City, as described in the following Managing Across Cultures Competency feature on page 195.

WORK STRESSORS

As indicated in the Preview Case, stress in the workplace is a problem of considerable significance. In the United States, nationwide surveys typically show that about 25 percent of all employees suffer from a variety of stress-induced problems. A survey of more than 400,000 employees conducted by International Survey Research of Chicago reported that about 40 percent of these people say that their workloads are excessive and that they have too much "pressure" at work.[9] A recent study by The National Institute of Occupational Safety and Health identified the following categories of stressors as representing the primary sources of stress for employees: (1) excessive workload and pace, (2) rigid or otherwise undesirable work schedules, (3) role stressors (conflict and ambiguity), (4) concerns about career security,

COMPETENCY: MANAGING ACROSS CULTURES

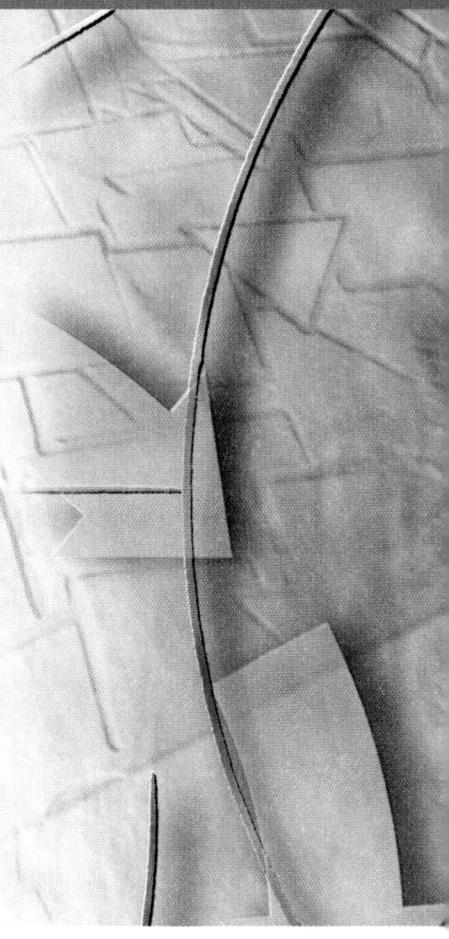

SIESTA SUNSET

Mexicans, particularly residents of Mexico City, are gulping stress medication in record amounts. Mañana-land isn't supposed to be like this—what's going on?

There are signs that Mexico's breakneck pace to urbanize and modernize has brought both opportunities and stress to Mexican workers. During the past few years, Mexican doctors have reported increases in cigarette smoking, drinking, and drug abuse. (However, drug abuse is at a relatively low level compared to that in the United States.) Claudio Garcia Barriga, chief of the outpatient department of a large psychiatric hospital in Mexico City, observed, "In the past five years, there's been a very important increase in the problem of stress, and we continue to see a steady increase in stress crises." Garcia reports that some 15 percent of the hospital's patients show stress symptoms.

Mexico City has more than 20 million residents, and problems associated with overcrowding were blamed for most stress in past years. Recently, however, Mexico's changing economy has been the source of much stress. Industrial changes stemming from the North American Free Trade Agreement (NAFTA) between Canada, Mexico, and the United States is feeding job insecurity fears among Mexican workers just as it has north of the border. The fears seem to be well founded. As Mexico has opened itself to private investment, hundreds of thousands of workers have lost jobs to cost cutting, downsizing, and closing of businesses in the face of increased competition. Time-honored work rules also are changing. For example, many firms no longer tolerate traditional on-the-job siestas. In addition, wage controls and inflation have squeezed workers' buying power. These economic uncertainties, coupled with the pollution and traffic that are overwhelming Mexico City, have sent stress levels soaring.[10]

(5) poor interpersonal relationships at work, and (6) unpleasant job conditions.[11] We more fully explore these stressors shortly.

Work stress is certainly not limited to North America. For example, during a worldwide comparative study of work stress, researchers gathered information from 1,065 managers in 10 countries on five continents: Brazil, the United Kingdom, Egypt, Germany, Japan, Nigeria, Singapore, South Africa, Sweden, and the United States. Fifty-five percent of all respondents mentioned time pressures and deadlines as stressors, followed closely by work overload, mentioned by almost 52 percent. Other frequently identified stressors included inadequately trained subordinates, long working hours, attending meetings, and conflicts arising from work versus family demands.[12]

Work stressors can, of course, take a variety of forms. Thus managers and employees need a framework for thinking about and diagnosing sources of work stress. Figure 7.2 presents such a framework, identifying seven principal sources of work stress. Note that these categories closely match those used by the National Institute of Occupational Safety and Health mentioned previously. Figure 7.2 also shows that internal factors influence the ways in which individuals experience these stressors.

Workload. For many people, having too much work to do and not enough time or resources to do it can be stressful. **Role overload** exists when demands exceed the capacity of a manager or employee to meet all of them adequately. Many stressful jobs

Figure 7.2 **Sources of Work Stress**

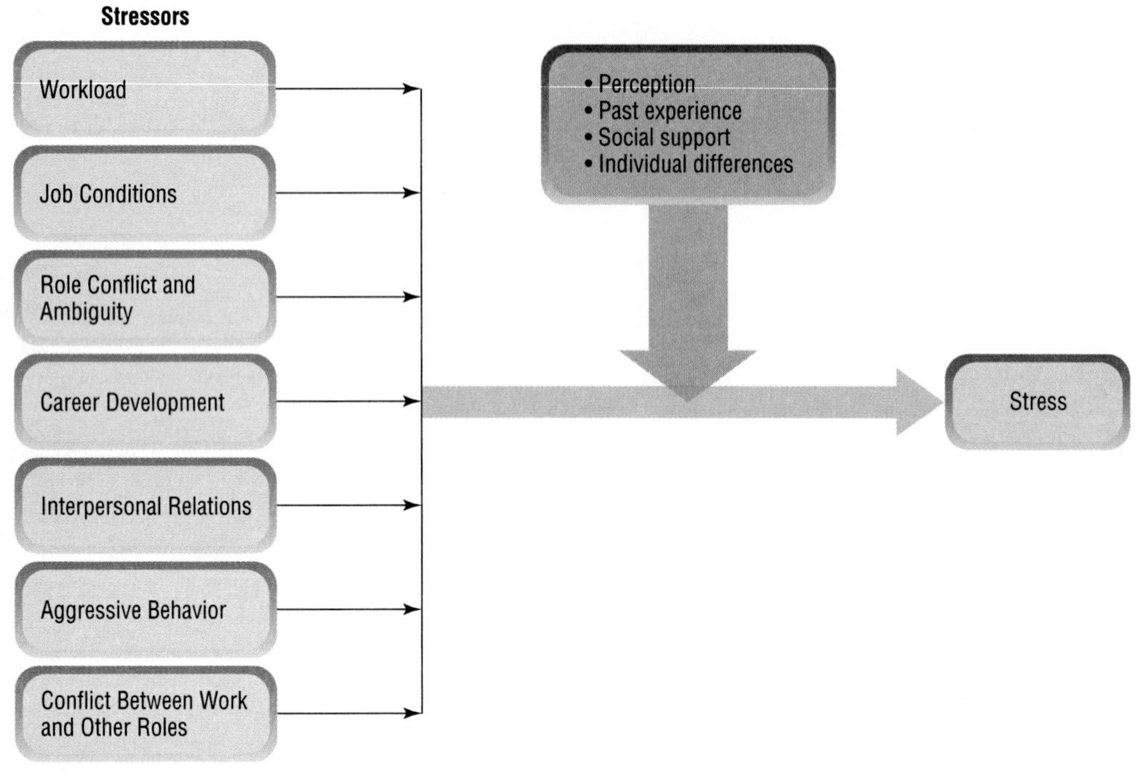

may be in a continuous condition of role overload. Surveys commonly identify work overload or "having to work too hard" as a major source of stress. The negative impact of excessive workload on absenteeism and other job outcomes is illustrated in the Managing Change Competency feature on the next page.

Having too little work to do also may create stress.[13] Have you ever had a job with so little to do that the workday seemed never to end? If so, you can understand why many people find an *underload* situation stressful. Managers sometimes are guilty of trying to do their subordinates' work, or *micromanage*, when their jobs aren't challenging enough. Micromanaging might reduce the manager's stress caused by boredom, but it is likely to increase subordinates' stress as the boss constantly watches them or second-guesses their decisions.

Job Conditions. Poor working conditions represent another important set of job stressors. Temperature extremes, loud noise, too much or too little lighting, radiation, and air pollution are but a few examples of working conditions that can cause stress in employees. Job performance deteriorates, sometimes markedly, when these environmental stressors are present. Moreover, their effects are cumulative over time. Heavy travel demands or long-distance commuting are other aspects of jobs that employees may find stressful. Poor working conditions, excessive travel, and long hours all add up to increased stress and decreased performance. In addition, cutting-edge technology, while clearly of great benefit to society in general and many individuals in particular, nevertheless has created job conditions that may be quite stressful. The impact of this observation is made clear in the Managing Self Competency feature on page 198 that addresses the relationship of technology to stress.

COMPETENCY: MANAGING CHANGE

HOW ABOUT CREATING SANER WORKLOADS?

Absenteeism as a response to stress is increasing at many companies. Consider the example of a product manager for a New Jersey manufacturer. Like many employees, this manager is working 10 hours a day on average, often for 7 days a week. His responsibilities have doubled to cover for laid-off coworkers. He states: "We run lean—a little too lean. I feel like I am working at 110 percent of capacity, yet no matter how hard I work, it piles up on my desk. I could work 20 hours a day and still wouldn't be done."

What is his response? Every so often, he takes an unscheduled day off. The product manager, who asked to remain anonymous because he fears management's reaction, explained: "You look at the piles on your desk and say, it doesn't matter if I'm here or not, I'm never going to get done anyway." So he sometimes calls in that he will be absent (usually not giving a reason) and stays home to "cool off," exercise, or run errands.

Art Powell, a strategic planner for a financial services firm, often works 70 hours a week. His weekends are devoted to family concerns, leaving him little time when he is not confronted by responsibilities of one type or another. He openly admits that he occasionally takes an unscheduled day off to run errands, make repairs on his home, or just to relax. He says, "Sometimes I just go to Home Depot and walk the aisles, even if I don't buy anything."

CCH, Inc., a Riverwoods, Illinois, human resource information firm, surveyed 401 companies and reported that unscheduled absences rose 25 percent during a recent year. Aon Consulting of Chicago surveyed 1,800 workers and found an 11 percent rise over a 3-year period in time lost because of unscheduled absences. In both surveys, stress and needing time for "personal matters" were the fastest growing causes of these absences.

Organizations are starting to discover that if employees are going to take time off anyway, it may be better to build it into the system. CCH reports that some large corporations reported declines of as much as 7 percent in unscheduled absences by introducing progressive programs to deal with excessive workloads and the stress that accompanies them. Policies that allow the use of paid-time-off banks, alternative work arrangements, backup child-care services, and more work at home are helping employees address their needs for more control over their schedules. In addition, experts agree that organizations need to spend more time trying to figure out whether current workload levels make sense. More effective ways of designing work and allocating duties might go a long way toward reducing the stress and increasing the job commitment and satisfaction of Art Powell and the New Jersey product manager mentioned at the beginning of this feature.[14]

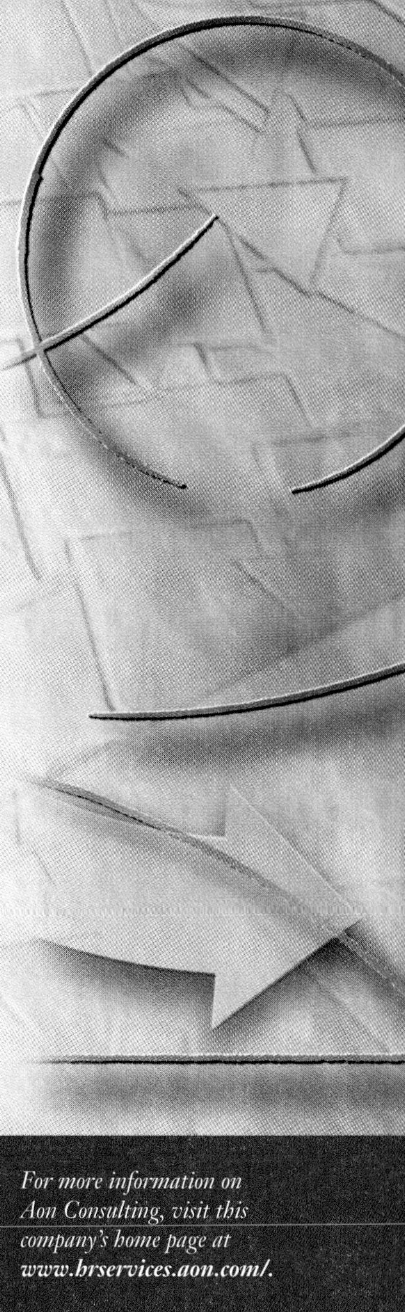

For more information on Aon Consulting, visit this company's home page at ***www.hrservices.aon.com/.***

Role Conflict and Ambiguity. Differing expectations of or demands on a person at work produce **role conflict.** (We discuss role conflict in detail in Chapter 10.) **Role ambiguity** occurs when an employee is uncertain about assigned job duties and responsibilities. Role conflict and role ambiguity are particularly significant sources of job-related stress.[15] Many employees suffer from role conflict and ambiguity, but conflicting expectations and uncertainty particularly affect managers. Having responsibility for the behavior of others and a lack of opportunity to participate in important decisions affecting their job are other aspects of employees' roles that may be stressful.

COMPETENCY: MANAGING SELF

TECHNOLOGY WORKERS AND STRESS

Many technology-assisted jobs of the modern age have both maximum flexibility and maximum stress. Computers have lowered the entry barriers for many high-stress jobs, from accounting to programming, by making it possible to perform them anytime, anywhere. Abigal Roitman, an electronic day-trader of stocks, provides a good example of the maximum flexibility–maximum stress combination that often comes with high-tech occupations. Roitman's job gives her the flexibility needed to cut her hours short, to be home during the day if she chooses (she can trade stocks either from home or her office in Manhattan), or to take time off with family. However, the job also gives her the opportunity to work and to stay stressed-out around the clock. She is trying to survive as both a stock trader and a devoted mother, but doing so requires her to draw mental boundaries between work and home. Often that is difficult, as work and home can be the same place.

The stresses of trading can be ceaseless because markets are always open somewhere in the world. Sometimes, Roitman stays up long after her family has gone to bed, checking international exchanges and studying price patterns on stocks from the previous day. Roitman has successfully made a living at day-trading for almost 4 years, although most day-traders wash out quickly, in part due to high stress. Despite her obvious success, she says, "It's easy to take it very, very seriously and get stressed-out."

A somewhat less glamorous example of stress and technology can be found with the estimated 3 to 4 million telephone sales representatives in the United States. The computer has both improved these jobs and made them more stressful. For example, let's observe Bev DeMille as she is having a bad night. The 51-year-old telemarketer is on her fourteenth phone call of the shift, but so far she has sold just one magazine renewal. "Come on computer, move it," she says, waiting for the next beep in her headset and the next name to flash on her screen. Around her, coworkers tethered to their desks by telephone cords gesture as they speak and signal supervisors to listen to the confirmation of a sale. A supervisor half DeMille's age reprimands her: "You're low girl—1 in 14." DeMille glares at her video screen. "I don't know where he gets off saying that," she says. But she knows that pressure goes with the job. Working for nine other employers in her 10 years in telemarketing, she has seen coworkers take tranquilizers to relieve stress. She has seen people fired for missing sales targets. When confronted once on a previous job for leaving her desk to go to the ladies' room without permission, she retorted: "My bladder couldn't see you."

Sometimes called *new-collar* workers, telemarketers, other similar salespeople, and data processors comprise about 40 percent of the workforce born after 1945. Working primarily with computers and telephones, in a sense they perform blue-collar work in a white-collar world. In terms of stress, lack of variety in their work, limited opportunity for advancement, and heavy performance pressure, the new-collar worker has been described as similar to "turn-of-the-century factory workers except that they are more educated and use high technology."[16]

Career Development. Major stressors related to career planning and development involve job security, promotions, transfers, and developmental opportunities. An employee can feel stress by underpromotion (failure to advance as rapidly as desired) or overpromotion (promotion to a job that exceeds the individual's competencies).

The current wave of reorganization and downsizing may seriously threaten careers and cause stress as indicated in the Preview Case. When jobs, teams, departments, or entire organizations are restructured, employees often have numerous career-related concerns: Can I perform competently in the new situation? Can I advance? Is my new job secure? Typically, employees find these concerns stressful.

Interpersonal Relations. Groups and teams have a major impact on the behavior of people in organizations. (We explore these dynamics in Chapter 8.) Good working relationships and interactions with peers, subordinates, and superiors are crucial aspects of organizational life, helping people achieve personal and organizational goals. When relationships are poor, they can become sources of stress. For example, a study of clerical employees indicated that intrusions by others—interruptions from noisy coworkers, ringing telephones, and other people walking into and around their workstations—were principal sources of stress.[17] A high level of political behavior, or "office politics," also may create stress for managers and employees (see Chapter 9). The nature of relationships with coworkers may influence how employees react to other stressors. In other words, interpersonal relationships can be either a source of stress or the social support that helps employees cope with stressors.

Aggressive Behavior. A frightening category of work stressors is overly aggressive behavior in the workplace, often taking the form of violence or sexual harassment. Aggressive behavior that causes actual physical or psychological harm to an employee is classified as **workplace violence.** An American Management Association survey found that almost 25 percent of responding organizations reported that an employee had been physically attacked or killed in the workplace. Homicide is second only to transportation accidents as the most common cause of workplace fatalities. Although homicide is the most extreme example of workplace violence, several million employees a year are subjected to violence of one form or another, ranging from actual physical assaults to threats or other forms of unwanted harassment. Individuals subject to violence or the threat of violence in the workplace are more likely to experience negative stress reactions, including lower productivity and higher absenteeism. Lost productivity and legal expenses related to workplace violence cost employers more than $4 billion annually.[18] The current level of violence in organizations is a major source of work stress that needs to be understood and managed.

A second form of overly aggressive behavior in the workplace is sexual harassment. **Sexual harassment** is unwanted contact or communication of a sexual nature.[19] In a *New York Times/CBS News* poll, fully 30 percent of female employees reported that they had been the object of unwanted sexual advances, propositions, or discussions at work. As with workplace violence, this problem seems to be growing. Management clearly has a strong responsibility to do everything in its power to prevent sexual harassment from occurring. When it does occur, it needs to be dealt with firmly. Some practical suggestions for managers who have to deal with this disruptive issue include the following.

- Take all complaints about sexual harassment seriously.
- Publish a policy strongly condemning sexual harassment.
- Inform all employees of their rights and responsibilities under the policy.
- Develop a proactive complaint procedure that provides alternative means for filing a complaint.
- Immediately respond to any complaint and investigate it with objectivity, confidentiality, and due process.
- Discipline managers and employees involved in sexual harassment.
- Keep thorough records of complaints, investigations, and actions taken.

- Frequently hold training sessions to educate managers and employees about sexual harassment issues and individuals' responsibilities. Republish the sexual harassment policy periodically.
- Conduct exit interviews to uncover any evidence that sexual harassment might exist.[20]

Organizations need to have policies that clearly identify what constitutes sexual harassment, procedures for dealing with it, and penalties for engaging in this unacceptable behavior. Policies are not sufficient, however, if managers don't back them up with serious and prompt action.

Conflict Between Work and Other Roles. A person has many roles in life (e.g., breadwinner, family member, little league coach, and/or church volunteer, to name a few), only one of which is typically associated with work (although some individuals may hold more than one job at a time). These roles may present conflicting demands that become sources of stress. Furthermore, work typically meets only some of a person's goals and needs. Other goals and needs may conflict with career goals, presenting an additional source of stress. For example, employees' personal desires to spend time with their families may conflict with the extra hours they must work to advance their careers. Current demographic trends, such as the increasingly large numbers of dual-career couples, have brought work and family role conflicts into sharp focus.

Life Stressors

The distinction between work and nonwork stressors isn't always clear, although it is clear that a major source of stress for many people is conflict between work and family demands.[21] As Figure 7.3 illustrates, both work and family stressors may contribute to work–family conflict because stress in one area can reduce a person's ability to cope with stress in the other. This conflict represents a further source of stress, which in turn can lead to serious problems, such as depression.

Much of the stress felt by managers and employees may stem from stressors in their personal lives, or **life stressors.** People must cope with a variety of life stressors,

Figure 7.3 **Stressors and Work–Family Conflict**

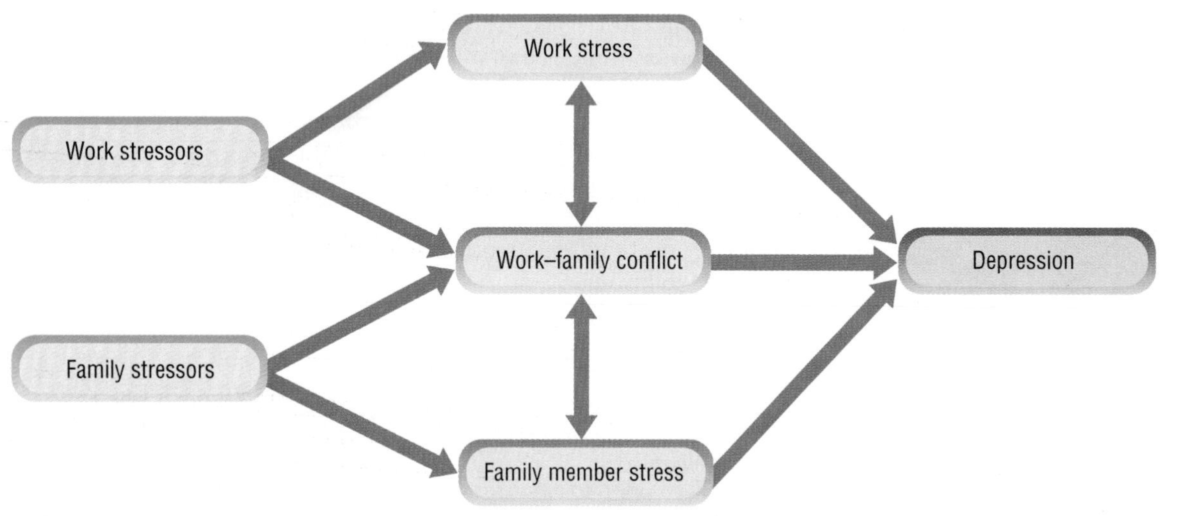

Source: Adapted from Frone, M. R., Russell, M., and Cooper, M. L. Antecedents and outcomes of work–family conflict: Testing a model of the work–family interface. *Journal of Applied Psychology,* 1992, 77, 66.

and individuals deal with these stressors differently because of their personality, age, gender, experience, and other characteristics. Events that cause stress for one person may not do so for another person. However, life stressors that affect almost everyone are those caused by significant changes: divorce, marriage, death of a family member, and the like. As mentioned previously, the human body has a limited capacity to respond to stressors. Too much change too quickly can exhaust the body's ability to respond, with negative consequences for a person's physical and mental health.

Table 7.1 contains some stressful events that college students typically face. These events are rated on a 100-point scale, with 1 indicating the least stressful event and 100 the most stressful. Events labeled "high levels of stress" might be assigned 71 to 100 points, depending on the specific circumstances of the student being evaluated. "Moderate levels of stress" might be scored from 31 to 70 points, and "low levels of stress" assigned scores from 1 to 30 points. During the course of a year, if a student faces events that total 150 points or more, the student has a 50–50 chance of getting sick as a result of excessive stress.[22]

Recall that stress is the body's general response to any demand made on it. Note that the list of stressful events in Table 7.1 contains both unpleasant events, such as failing a course, and pleasant events, such as finding a new love interest. This dual nature of life stressors demonstrates that they involve both negative and positive experiences. For example, vacations and holidays actually may be quite stressful for some people but very relaxing and refreshing for others. In addition, viewing unpleasant life events as having only negative effects is incorrect. People often can both cope with and grow from experiencing unpleasant events. They can also enjoy the positive effects and stimulation of pleasurable events, such as significant accomplishments, vacations, or gaining a new family member.

Learning Objective:

3. Describe the effects of stress on health and job performance.

EFFECTS OF STRESS

As previously noted, all forms of stress, including stress at work, can have both positive and negative effects. Our concern with work stress, however, focuses on its negative effects because of their relationship to productivity and organizational effectiveness.

Table 7.1

Stressful Events for College Students

Events Having High Levels of Stress
- Death of parent
- Death of spouse
- Divorce
- Flunking out
- Unwed pregnancy

Events Having Moderate Levels of Stress
- Academic probation
- Change of major
- Death of close friend
- Failing important course
- Finding a new love interest
- Loss of financial aid
- Major injury or illness
- Parents' divorce
- Serious arguments with romantic partner
- Outstanding achievement

Events Having Relatively Low Levels of Stress
- Change in eating habits
- Change in sleeping habits
- Change in social activities
- Conflict with instructor
- Lower grades than expected

Source: Adapted from Baron, R. A., and Byrne, D. *Social Psychology: Understanding Human Interaction*, 6th ed. Boston: Allyn & Bacon, 1991, 573.

The American Institute of Stress estimates the cost to the U.S. economy from stress-related medical problems and lost productivity at $300 billion per year. These costs include lost productivity, mistakes, and medical treatment.

The effects of work stress occur in three main areas: physiological, emotional, and behavioral. Examples of the effects of excessive stress in these areas are as follows.

- **Physiological effects of stress** include increased blood pressure, increased heart rate, sweating, hot and cold spells, breathing difficulties, muscular tension, and increased gastrointestinal disorders.
- **Emotional effects of stress** include anger, anxiety, depression, lowered self-esteem, poorer intellectual functioning (including an inability to concentrate and make decisions), nervousness, irritability, resentment of supervision, and job dissatisfaction.
- **Behavioral effects of stress** include decreased performance, absenteeism, higher accident rates, higher turnover rates, higher alcohol and other drug abuses, impulsive behavior, and difficulties in communication.

These effects of work stress have important implications for organizational behavior and organizational effectiveness. We examine some of these effects in terms of health and performance, including job burnout.

Stress and Health

Stress and coronary heart disease are strongly linked. Other serious health problems commonly associated with stress include back pain, headaches, stomach and intestinal problems, upper respiratory infections, and various mental problems. Medical researchers recently have discovered possible links between stress and cancer. Although determining the precise role that stress plays in individual cases is difficult, many illnesses appear to be stress-related.[23]

Stress-related illnesses place a considerable burden on people and organizations. The costs to individuals seem more obvious than the costs to organizations. However, we are able to identify at least some of the organizational costs associated with stress-related disease. First, costs to employers include increased premiums for health insurance as well as lost workdays from serious illnesses (e.g., heart disease) and less-serious illnesses (e.g., headaches). Estimates are that each employee who suffers from a stress-related illness loses an average of 16 days of work a year. Second, over three-fourths of all industrial accidents are caused by a worker's inability to cope with emotional problems worsened by stress. Third, legal problems for employers are growing, as indicated in the Preview Case. The number of stress-related worker compensation claims is increasing. The link between the levels of stress in the workplace and worker compensation claims is clear. When employees experience higher amounts of stress, more worker compensation claims will be filed. Studies have shown similar patterns of results across many different industries, as indicated by the data in Table 7.2.

Courts are beginning to recognize **post-traumatic stress disorder** as a condition that may justify a damage claim against an employer. We normally think of post-traumatic stress disorder as a psychological disorder brought on, for example, by horrible experiences in combat during wartime. However, employees have successfully claimed suffering from this stress disorder as a result of sexual harassment, violence, and other unpleasant circumstances in the workplace. Awards of damages in the millions of dollars have resulted from court cases involving workplace post-traumatic stress disorder claims.[24]

Stress and Performance

The positive and negative effects of stress are most apparent in the relationship between stress and performance. Figure 7.4 depicts the general stress–performance

Table 7.2 **Relationship Between Job Stress and Workers' Compensation Claims**

TYPE OF BUSINESS	LEVEL OF STRESS	FREQUENCY OF CLAIMS PER 100 EMPLOYEES
Plastics manufacturer	Low	0.6
	High	4.2
Copy machine distributor	Low	1.9
	High	15.5
Furniture manufacturer	Low	13.2
	High	31.8
Cable TV company	Low	15.7
	High	39.0

Source: Adapted from DeFrank, R. S., and Ivancevich, J. M. Stress on the job: An executive update. *Academy of Management Executive*, August 1998, 59.

relationship. At low levels of stress, employees may not be sufficiently alert, challenged, or involved to perform at their best. As the curve indicates, increasing a low amount of stress may improve performance—but only up to a point. An optimal level of stress probably exists for most tasks. Beyond that point, performance begins to deteriorate.[25] At excessive levels of stress, employees are too agitated, aroused, or threatened to perform at their best. The following Managing Self Competency feature provides an example of the curvilinear relationship between stress and performance.

Figure 7.4 **Typical Relationship Between Performance and Stress**

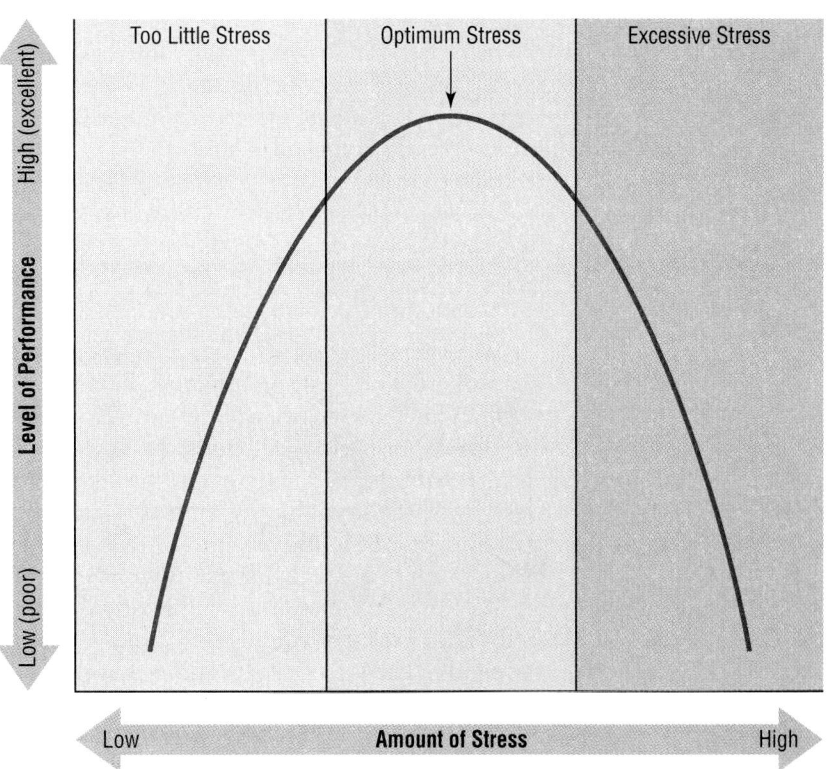

COMPETENCY: MANAGING SELF

"JUST ENOUGH BUT NOT TOO MUCH"

Linda Herring was puzzled. During the past several months, she had presented three important reports to the firm's board of directors. The first had been a catastrophe. She had been so nervous that she could actually remember little that had gone on. Herring did know, however, that she had somehow gotten through her formal presentation—which seemed to go okay—before disaster struck. It came in the form of a series of questions, each more confusing than the last. The board members eventually took pity on her and stopped the questioning. They thanked her for her efforts and turned their attention to other matters. Later, Mary Shockley—her boss and the firm's president—helped Herring analyze her performance. They determined that, with one or two exceptions, Herring actually knew the answers to the questions asked. What seemed to happen, they decided, was that she had been far too agitated to think clearly. Indeed, Herring had been so upset that she even had trouble focusing on what was being asked. Several times she had asked that questions be repeated. Shockley's advice was preparation and practice. In addition, "You have to make stress work for you—but you can't be so stressed out that you can't think straight."

Herring didn't fully understand the implications of Shockley's last comment, but she carefully prepared for her next presentation. Like a highly trained athlete before the big game, she was actually looking forward to the presentation. Although "keyed up" when the time came, Herring made a superb presentation, full of energy and enthusiasm, and fielded the board members' questions with confidence. The board members were effusive in their praise (and probably a little relieved because the first presentation had gone so badly).

Now Herring had just come from her third presentation to the board. Even though well prepared, today she had been "flat." She hadn't been nervous. In fact, she had been working on another project right up until the time she went into the boardroom. Although her presentation certainly went better than the first one, she knew without being told that it hadn't measured up to the peak performance of last time. "What's going on?" she wondered. With Shockley's help, she again attempted to diagnose her performance. After some discussion, they finally decided that, whereas Herring had felt too much stress during her first presentation, this time she had, ironically, probably not felt enough.

Managers often want to know the optimum stress points for both themselves and their subordinates. This information, however, is difficult to pin down accurately. For example, an employee may be absent from work frequently because of boredom (too little stress) or because of overwork (excessive stress). Also, the curve in Figure 7.4 changes with the situation; that is, the curve varies for different people and different tasks. Too little stress for one employee may be just right for another on a particular task. Similarly, the optimum amount of stress for a specific individual for one task may be too much or too little for that person's effective performance of other tasks.

As a practical matter, managers should be more concerned about the excessive stress side of the curve in Figure 7.4 than with how to add to employee stress. Motivating individuals to perform better is always important, but attempting to do so by increasing the level of stress is shortsighted.

The downsizing of many organizations yields good examples of the effects of excessive stress on performance. A survey of 531 large companies indicated that 85 percent expected their restructuring to raise profits. Yet, only 46 percent of these companies actually had increased earnings after downsizing. An examination of the experiences of Jostens Learning Corporation, the largest U.S. maker of educational software, is illustrative of some reasons for these disappointing results. Although layoffs lowered direct labor costs, these lower costs were more than offset by declines in productivity owing to increased stress and lowered morale among the surviving employees.[26]

Studies of the stress–performance relationship in organizations often show a strong negative correlation between the amount of stress in a team or department and its overall performance. This is, the greater the stress that employees are experiencing, the lower will be their productivity. This negative relationship indicates that these work settings are operating on the right-hand side (excessive stress) of the curve in Figure 7.4. Managers and employees in these situations need to find ways to reduce the number and magnitude of stressors.

Stress and Job Burnout

Job burnout refers to the adverse effects of working conditions where stressors seem unavoidable and sources of job satisfaction and relief from stress seem unavailable. The burnout phenomenon typically contains three components:

- a state of emotional exhaustion;
- depersonalization of individuals; and
- feelings of low personal accomplishment.[27]

Depersonalization refers to the treatment of people as objects. For example, a nurse might refer to the "broken knee" in room 107, rather than use the patient's name.

Most job burnout research has focused on the human services sector of the economy—sometimes called the "helping professions." Burnout is thought to be most prevalent in occupations characterized by continuous direct contact with people in need of aid. Figure 7.5 suggests that the highest probability of burnout occurs among those individuals who have both a high frequency and a high intensity of interpersonal contact. This level of interpersonal contact may lead to emotional exhaustion, a key component of job burnout.[28]

Figure 7.5 **Predicted Level of Job Burnout Based on Frequency and Intensity of Interpersonal Contact**

Frequency of Interpersonal Contact	Intensity of Interpersonal Contact: Low	Intensity of Interpersonal Contact: High
High	Receptionist Sales representative Librarian Benefits representative **(Moderate burnout)**	Social worker Customer service representative Schoolteacher Nurse **(High burnout)**
Low	Research physicist Forest ranger Oil refinery operator Laboratory technician **(Low burnout)**	Paramedic Public defender Fire fighter Police detective **(Moderate burnout)**

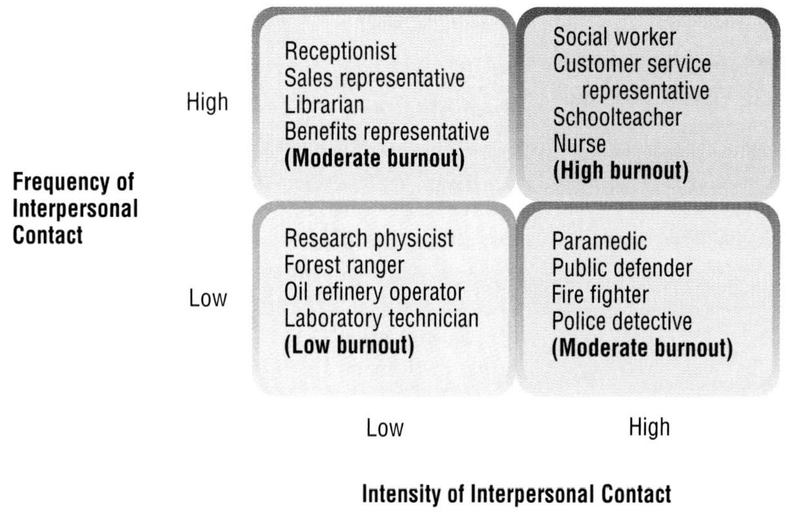

Source: Cordes, C. L., and Dougherty, T. W. A Review and integration of research on job burnout. *Academy of Management Review*, 1993, 18, 643. Reprinted with permission.

The individuals who may be most vulnerable to job burnout include social workers, nurses, physicians, police officers, air traffic controllers, teachers, and lawyers. Burnout also may affect managers, shopowners, or professionals who constantly face stressors with little or no relief. Evidence suggests that women, on average, are somewhat more likely to face burnout than are men. Surveys have indicated that 11 percent more women than men report that high stress has affected their health. A Northwestern Life Insurance study found that the job burnout rate was 36 percent for women versus 28 percent for men. Note also that the "high burnout" cell in Figure 7.5 contains occupations that have traditionally attracted more women than men.

Individuals who experience job burnout seem to have some common characteristics. Three characteristics in particular are associated with a high probability of burnout.

- Burnout candidates experience a great deal of stress as a result of job-related stressors.
- Burnout candidates tend to be idealistic and self-motivating achievers.
- Burnout candidates often seek unattainable goals.[29]

Job burnout thus represents a combination of certain individual characteristics and job situations. Individuals who suffer from burnout often have unrealistic expectations concerning their work and their ability to accomplish desired goals because of the nature of the situation in which they find themselves. Unrelieved stressful working conditions, coupled with an individual's unrealistic expectations or ambitions, may lead to physical, mental, and emotional exhaustion. In burnout, the individual can no longer cope with job demands, and the willingness even to try drops dramatically.

Job burnout is a significant problem for organizations and their employees. Traditionally, some managers in certain occupations treated the potential for burnout as an "acceptable" risk that goes along with serving clients or customers. However, more organizations are recognizing just how counterproductive overwork and burnout can be. The steps being taken by some organizations to dispel the management "myths" that lead to burnout are reported in the Managing Communication Competency feature on the next page.

Learning Objective:

4. Explain the relationship between personality and stress.

PERSONALITY AND STRESS

The problems caused by stress depend substantially on the type of person involved. Personality influences (1) how individuals are likely to perceive situations and stressors and (2) how they will react to these stressors.

Many personality dimensions or traits are related to stress, including self-esteem and locus of control (personality traits discussed in Chapter 2). A personality trait may affect the likelihood that someone will perceive a situation or an event as a stressor.[30] For example, an individual with low self-esteem is more likely to experience stress in demanding work situations than is a person with high self-esteem. The reason may be that individuals high in self-esteem typically have more confidence in their ability to meet job demands. Employees with high internal locus of control may take more effective action, more quickly, in coping with a sudden emergency (a stressor) than might employees with high external locus of control. Individuals high in internal locus of control are likely to believe that they can moderate the stressful situation.

Before reading further, respond to the statements in Table 7.3. This self-assessment exercise is related to the discussion that follows.

COMPETENCY: MANAGING COMMUNICATION

MANAGEMENT MYTHS THAT LEAD TO BURNOUT

Sue Shellenbarger, of the *Wall Street Journal*, interviewed dozens of managers in an attempt to understand managerial behavior that seems to push employees over the edge into job burnout. In the process, she identified three myths that organizations need to dispel if they are to reduce incidents of burnout among their staff.

Myth One: When a client says jump, the only answer is "how high?"
Lawyers, accountants, and management consultants are particularly vulnerable to believing in this myth even when it appears to result in high levels of burnout and turnover on their staffs. However, Shellenbarger reports that a few professional firms are taking steps to integrate personal needs and concerns with the work lives of their employees. For example, Deloitte & Touche has implemented a policy that limits their employees' travel time. It is no longer company policy for employees to spend all 5 working days of the week at clients' offices. At a maximum, employees are to spend only 3 nights (4 working days) away from home and work the fifth day in their own offices each week, even when on lengthy assignments. Malva Rabinowitz, a Deloitte managing director, states, "most clients recognize that this policy is a good thing." Among other things, it also limits the amount of time that clients' employees have to be involved with the work that Deloitte is doing for them, thus allowing better control of their own schedules.

Myth Two: Reining in employees' workloads will turn them into slackers.
Managers often behave as though a reduction in work overload will cause productivity to drop. Yet, studies often show the opposite result. Ernst & Young has a committee that monitors its staff accountants' workloads to head off burnout situations. The company says that its policies are raising retention rates and improving client service. Jeff Calvello, a senior manager at Ernst, observes that employees typically won't admit to burning out; thus having some compassionate, objective overview is useful. "About the only time we would find out that someone was suffering from job burnout was during the exit interview, and then it was too late."

Myth Three: If employees are working themselves into the ground, it's their own fault.
Although this attribution may sometimes be true for some people, it is far from true for most. At the International Food Policy Research Institute, a nonprofit research organization in Washington, D.C., consultants discovered that a "crisis mentality" was driving scientists and support staff to work incredibly long hours. Management of the institute assumed that either (a) employees wanted to work these hours or (b) employees were managing their time poorly. Neither of these assumptions were valid. Rather, a shift in research focus coupled with an increased emphasis on using research teams allied with groups from other agencies and organizations had created an inefficient pattern of work for many people. Meetings, phone calls, and other forms of coordinated activity were eating up the workday, driving more productive research and writing into the evening hours. Once the Institute's management became aware of the inefficient patterns of work behavior, major changes were made in workplace routine. The redesign of activities reduced the amount of time people were having to work, which in turn reduced stress and increased productivity. In this case, management initially viewed the time problems as failures of individuals when, in fact, it was a failure of the organization.[31]

For more information on Deloitte & Touche, Ernst & Young, and the International Food Policy Institute, visit these organizations' home pages at ***www.us.deloitte.com/***, ***www.ey.com/***, *and* ***www.ifpri.org/***.

Table 7.3

A Self-Assessment of Type A Personality

Choose from the following responses to answer the questions below:

A. Almost always true
B. Usually true
C. Seldom true
D. Never true

_____ 1. I do not like to wait for other people to complete their work before I can proceed with my own.
_____ 2. I hate to wait in most lines.
_____ 3. People tell me that I tend to get irritated too easily.
_____ 4. Whenever possible, I try to make activities competitive.
_____ 5. I have a tendency to rush into work that needs to be done before knowing the procedure I will use to complete the job.
_____ 6. Even when I go on vacation, I usually take some work along.
_____ 7. Even when I make a mistake, it is usually due to the fact that I have rushed into the job before completely planning it through.
_____ 8. I feel guilty for taking time off from work.
_____ 9. People tell me I have a bad temper when it comes to competitive situations.
_____ 10. I tend to lose my temper when I am under a lot of pressure at work.
_____ 11. Whenever possible, I will attempt to complete two or more tasks at once.
_____ 12. I tend to race against the clock.
_____ 13. I have no patience for lateness.
_____ 14. I catch myself rushing when there is no need.

Score your responses according to the following key:

- *An intense sense of time urgency* is a tendency to race against the clock, even when there is little reason to. The person feels a need to hurry for hurry's sake alone, and this tendency has appropriately been called "hurry sickness." Time urgency is measured by items 1, 2, 8, 12, 13, and 14. Every A or B answer to these six questions scores one point.

  Your score = _____

- *Inappropriate aggression and hostility* reveals itself in a person who is excessively competitive and who cannot do anything for fun. This inappropriately aggressive behavior easily evolves into frequent displays of hostility, usually at the slightest provocation or frustration. Competitiveness and hostility is measured by items 3, 4, 9, and 10. Every A or B answer scores one point.

  Your score = _____

- *Polyphasic behavior* refers to the tendency to undertake two or more tasks simultaneously at inappropriate times. It usually results in wasted time due to an inability to complete the tasks. This behavior is measured by items 6 and 11. Every A or B answer scores one point.

  Your score = _____

- *Goal directedness without proper planning* refers to the tendency of an individual to rush into work without really knowing how to accomplish the desired result. This usually results in incomplete work or work with many errors, which in turn leads to wasted time, energy, and money. Lack of planning is measured by items 5 and 7. Every A or B response scores one point.

  Your score = _____

TOTAL SCORE = _____

If your score is 5 or greater, you may possess some basic components of the Type A personality.

Source: Reproduced with permission of the Robert J. Brady Co., Bowie, Maryland, 20715, from its copyrighted work *The Stress Mess Solution: The Causes and Cures of Stress on the Job*, by G. S. Everly and D. A. Girdano, 1980, 55.

THE TYPE A PERSONALITY

People with a **Type A personality** are involved in a never-ending struggle to achieve more and more in less and less time. Characteristics of this personality type include

- a chronic sense of urgency about time;
- an extremely competitive, almost hostile orientation;
- an aversion to idleness; and
- an impatience with barriers to task accomplishment.

Two medical researchers first identified the Type A personality when they noticed a recurrent personality pattern in their patients who suffered from premature heart disease.[32] In addition to the characteristics just listed, *extreme* Type A individuals often speak rapidly, are preoccupied with themselves, and are dissatisfied with life.

The questionnaire in Table 7.3 measures four sets of behaviors and tendencies associated with the Type A personality: (1) time urgency, (2) competitiveness and hostility, (3) polyphasic behavior (trying to do several things at once), and (4) a lack of planning. Medical researchers have discovered that these behaviors and tendencies often relate to life and work stress. They tend to cause stress or make stressful situations worse than they otherwise might be.

Evidence links Type A behavior with a vulnerability to heart attacks. Current research, however, suggests that the Type A personality description is too broad to predict coronary heart disease accurately. Rather, research indicates that only certain aspects of the Type A personality—particularly anger, hostility, and aggression—are strongly related to stress reactions and heart disease.[33] For years, the conventional wisdom among medical researchers was that Type A individuals were two to three times more likely to develop heart disease than were Type B individuals. Type B individuals tend to be more easygoing and relaxed, less concerned about time pressures, and less likely to overreact to situations in hostile or aggressive ways. In sum, the **Type B personality** is considered to be the opposite of the *Type A personality*.

THE HARDY PERSONALITY

A great deal of interest has emerged in identifying aspects of the personality that might buffer or protect individuals from the negative health consequences of stress. Personality traits that seem to counter the effects of stress are known collectively as the **hardy personality**. As a personality type, **hardiness** is defined as "a cluster of characteristics that includes feeling a sense of commitment, responding to each difficulty as representing a challenge and an opportunity, and perceiving that one has control over one's own life."[34] The hardy personality is characterized by

- a sense of positive involvement with others in social situations;
- a tendency to attribute one's own behavior to internal causes (recall the discussion of attribution in Chapter 3); and
- a tendency to perceive or welcome significant changes in life with interest, curiosity, and optimism.[35] (Recall our earlier discussion in this chapter of change as a significant life stressor.)

A high degree of hardiness reduces the negative effects of stressful events. Hardiness seems to reduce stress by altering the way that people perceive stressors. The concept of the hardy personality provides a useful insight into the role of individual differences in reactions to environmental stressors. An individual having a low level of hardiness perceives many events as stressful; an individual having a high level of hardiness perceives fewer events as stressful. A person with a high level of hardiness isn't overwhelmed by challenging or difficult situations. Rather, faced with a stressor, the hardy personality copes or responds constructively by trying to find a solution—to control or influence events. This behavioral response typically reduces stress reactions, lowers blood pressure, and reduces the probability of illness.

Learning Objective:

5. Identify several individual and organizational methods for coping with stress.

STRESS MANAGEMENT

Organizational and individual programs to help managers and employees cope with stress have become increasingly popular as the toll taken by stress has become more widely known. Methods are available to individuals and organizations for managing stress and reducing its harmful effects. **Stress management** refers to any program that reduces stress by helping people understand the stress response, recognize stressors, and use coping techniques to minimize the negative impact of stress.[36]

INDIVIDUAL METHODS

Stress management by individuals includes activities and behaviors designed to (1) eliminate or control the sources of stress and (2) make the individual more resistant to or better able to cope with stress. The first step in individual stress management involves recognizing the stressors that are affecting the person's life. Next, the individual needs to decide what to do about them. Figure 7.6 shows how personal goals and values, coupled with practical stress management skills, can help individuals cope with stressors and reduce negative stress reactions.

Figure 7.6 **Individual Strategy for Stress Management**

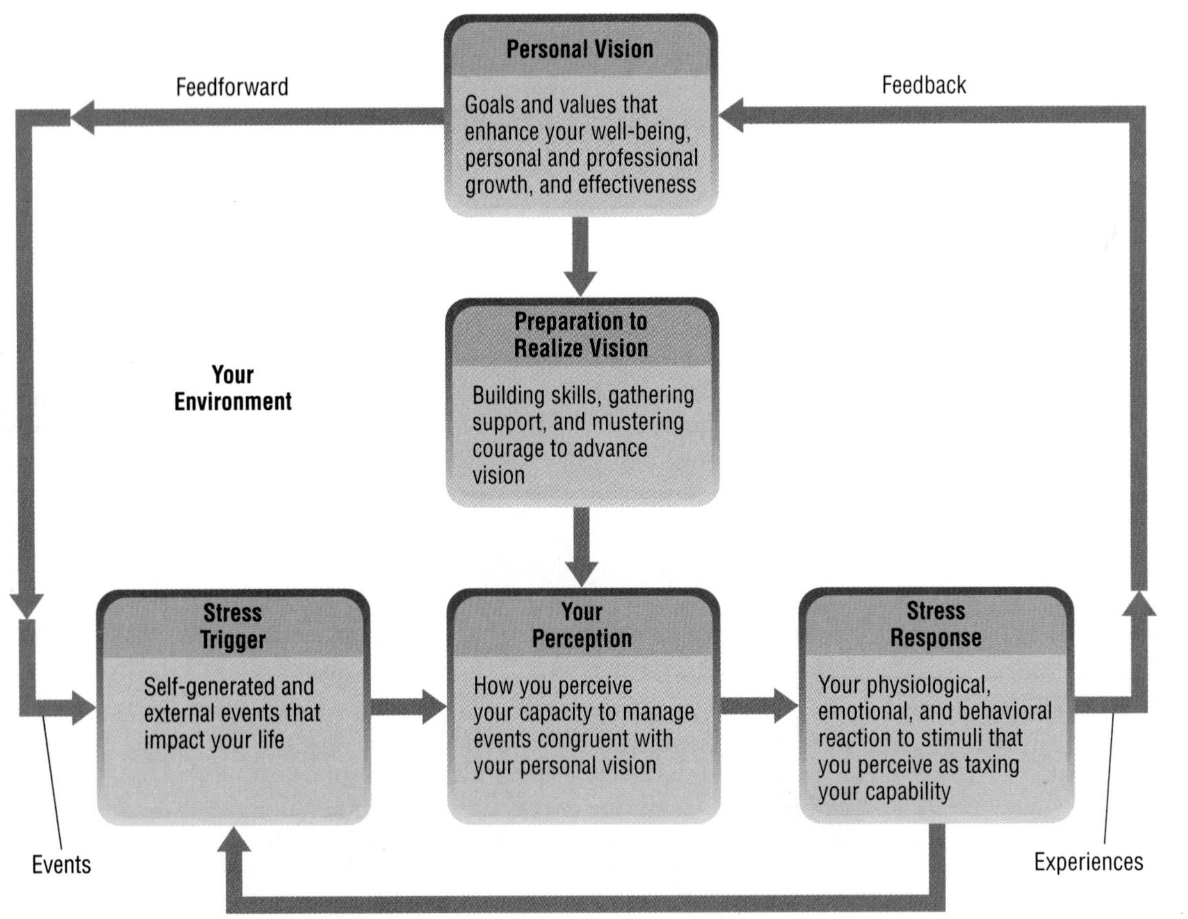

Source: Kindler, H. S., and Ginsburg, M. *Stress Training for Life*. Nichols Publishing Company. Reprinted with permission.

Practical suggestions for individual stress management include the following.

- Plan ahead and practice good time management.[37]
- Get plenty of exercise, eat a balanced diet, get adequate rest, and generally take care of yourself.
- Develop a sound philosophy of life and maintain a positive attitude.
- Concentrate on balancing your work and personal life. Always take the time to have fun.
- Learn a relaxation technique.

Among the advantages of relaxation techniques are that individuals can use them during the workday to cope with job demands. For example, a common "relaxation response" to stress is to (1) choose a comfortable position, (2) close your eyes, (3) relax your muscles, (4) become aware of your breathing, (5) maintain a passive attitude when thoughts surface, and (6) continue for a set period of time (e.g., 20 minutes).[38]

An in-depth study of six successful top executives revealed that they used remarkably similar methods of coping with stress.[39] These executives came from a variety of industries and included the president of an oilfield service company, the founder of a residential real estate firm, the CEO of a large commercial bank, and a navy admiral. First, they worked hard at balancing work and family concerns. Work was central to their lives, but it wasn't their sole focus. These executives also made effective use of leisure time to reduce stress. In addition, they were skilled time managers and goal setters. Important components of their effective use of time were identifying crucial goals and constructively planning for their attainment. Finally, these executives cited the essential role of social support in coping with stress. They didn't operate as loners; rather they received emotional support and important information from a diverse network of family, friends, coworkers, and industry colleagues. Additionally, these executives worked hard at maintaining fair exchanges in these relationships. That is, they both received support from others and gave support to others in their networks.

Organizational Methods

After a major layoff, Phillips Petroleum Company formed a team to respond to problems created by stress among its current and former employees. Further, Phillips paid for outside help to supplement the counseling available within the organization. Ford Motor Company offers stress management classes and free counseling services for workers who feel overloaded. Chevron Corporation conducts workshops to help employees deal with stress.[40] A large percentage of organizations have adopted or are developing stress management programs.

As Figure 7.7 shows, stress management by organizations is designed to reduce the harmful effects of stress in three ways: (1) identify and then modify or eliminate work stressors, (2) help employees modify their perception and understanding of work stress, and (3) help employees cope more effectively with the consequences of stress.[41]

Stress management programs aimed at eliminating or modifying work stressors often include

- improvements in the physical work environment;
- job redesign to eliminate stressors;
- changes in workloads and deadlines;
- structural reorganization;
- changes in work schedules, more flexible hours, and sabbaticals;
- management by objectives or other goal-setting programs;
- greater levels of employee participation, particularly in planning changes that affect them; and
- workshops dealing with role clarity and role analysis.

Figure 7.7 **Targets of Organizational Stress Management Programs**

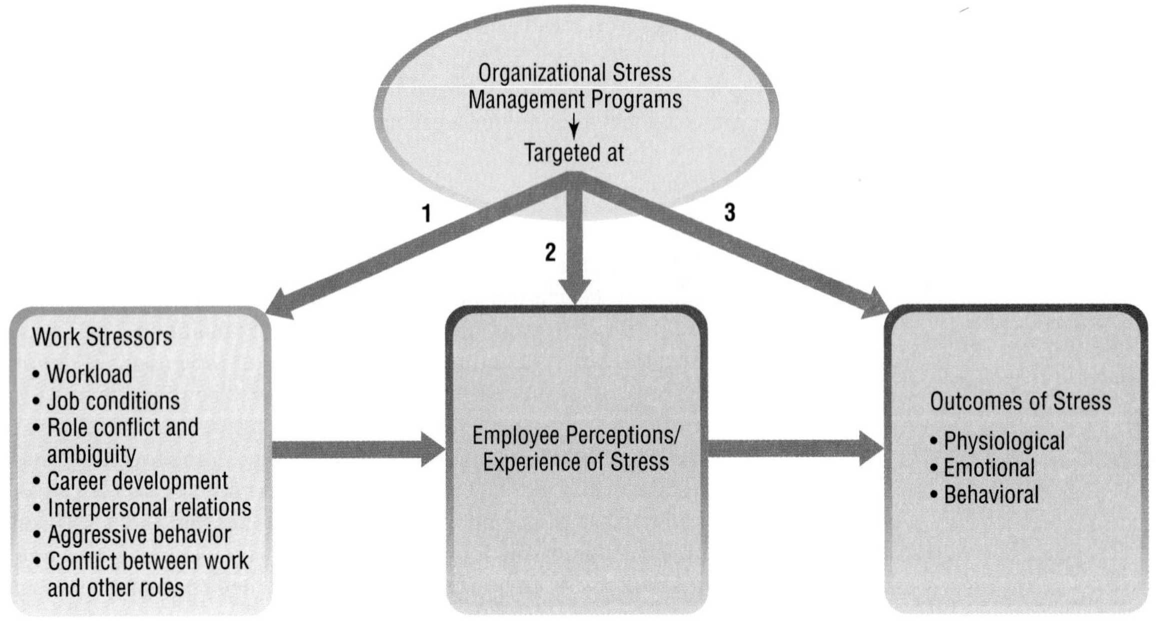

Source: Adapted from Ivancevich, J. M., Matteson, M. T., Freedman, S. M., and Phillips, J. S. Worksite stress management interventions. *American Psychologist*, 1990, 45, 253.

Programs that promote role clarity and role analysis can be particularly useful in removing or reducing role ambiguity and role conflict—two main sources of stress. When diagnosing stressors in the workplace, managers should be particularly aware of the large amount of research showing that uncertainty and perceived lack of control heighten stress. For example, Figure 7.8 shows the relationships commonly observed between work stressors and an individual's control over his or her work. Note that the greatest stress occurs when jobs are high in stressors and low in controllability. Thus involvement of employees in organizational change efforts that will affect them, work redesign that reduces uncertainty and increases control over the pace of work, and improved clarity and understanding of roles all should help reduce work stress. An important way to provide employees with more control and less stress is to give individuals more control over their *time*. The value of this approach is emphasized in the Managing Self Competency feature on page 213.

Programs of stress management targeted at perceptions and experiences of stress and outcomes of stress (see Figure 7.7, arrows 2 and 3) include

- team building;
- behavior modification;
- career counseling and other employee assistance programs;
- workshops on time management;
- workshops on job burnout to help employees understand its nature and symptoms;
- training in relaxation techniques; and
- physical fitness or "wellness" programs.

Dividing stress management programs into these categories doesn't mean that they are necessarily unrelated in practice. In addition, programs that appear in the list might overlap in terms of their impact on the three target areas shown in Figure 7.7. For example, a workshop dealing with role problems might clarify job descriptions and duties, reducing the magnitude of these potential stressors. At the same time,

COMPETENCY: MANAGING SELF

EMPLOYEES WHO VALUE TIME

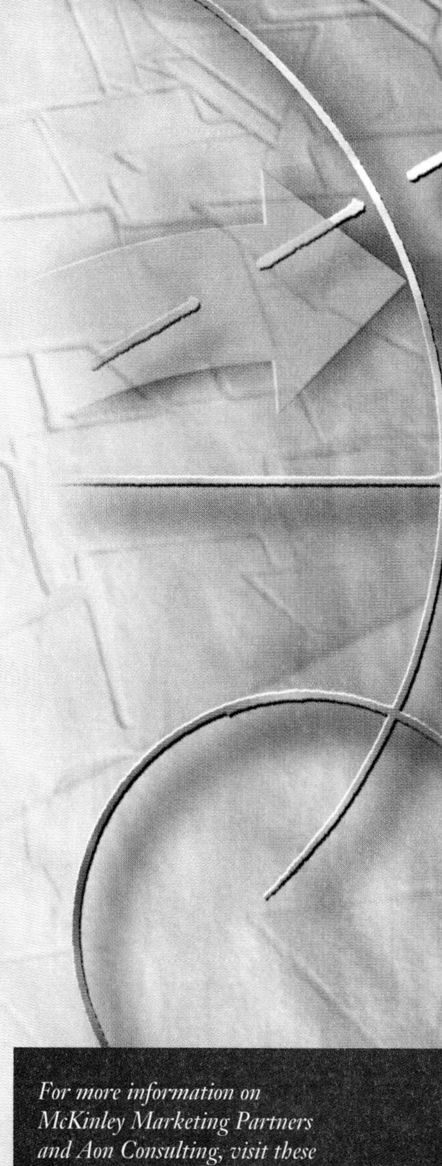

Brock Holmes appeared to have it all. He had a challenging job, high pay with stock options, and coworkers that he liked a lot. However Holmes, who was director of marketing for a Baby Bell, badly wanted something he didn't have: time.

His work schedule was impossible. Some days he worked only a somewhat normal 8-to-10-hour day, but many other days he worked from 7 A.M. till midnight. His schedule was dominated by one crisis after another, leaving little time for his wife and daughter. He also longed for time to pursue his passions of composing and playing music. His lack of control over his time finally drove him to abandon his stock options and high pay. Holmes is now an independent contractor with McKinley Marketing Partners, a placement firm in Alexandria, Virginia. He works intensely—usually for about 14 hours a day on Monday, Tuesday, and Wednesday. Thursdays and Fridays he spends at home, coaching his daughter's soccer team and composing music. He has both published his music and given concerts since leaving his former job. About his earlier work experience, Holmes says, "Those paying your salary assume that they can ask you to be wherever they want, whenever they want." Now, however, "most of my stress over time is gone."

The way many people experience and value their time seems to be changing. As people feel rushed to get more things done at work and at home, they place more value on blocks of time that they can control. Employers, in turn, are beginning to recognize that the value placed on time is influencing people's decisions about what jobs they are willing to accept. In addition, giving employees more control over their time seems to work as a retention tool.

A recent survey by Aon Consulting found that employees ranked paid vacation time and holidays as the fourth-most important benefit, up from tenth in a previous survey. A survey of 352 companies by the American Management Association indicated that employers reported more success in reducing turnover when they gave employees more control over their time. "Giving them a life" ranked as more successful than did offering more cash in terms of dealing with turnover problems.

Sam Noble, a health-care analyst who works for Value Management Group in Dallas, perhaps typifies the type of employee who attaches high importance to time. Noble says, "There's a point where money doesn't matter anymore after I have a certain amount of disposable income. It's more important to have reduced stress, a relaxed work style, and the time I need to be with my children and family." He was attracted to join Value Management by its avowed corporate philosophy: "Make sure you get the job done and done well. Then, take what time you need as long as you don't abuse it."[42]

For more information on McKinley Marketing Partners and Aon Consulting, visit these companies' home pages at ***www.mckinleyinc.com/*** *and* ***www.hrservices.aon.com/.***

through greater knowledge and insight into roles and role problems, employees might be able to cope more effectively with this source of stress. Similarly, career counseling might reduce career concerns as a source of stress while improving the ability of employees to cope with career problems.

WELLNESS PROGRAMS

Wellness programs are activities that organizations sponsor to promote good health habits or to identify and correct health problems.[43] More than 50,000 U.S. firms provide some type of company-sponsored health promotion program. Each year the Health Project (a nonprofit group composed of business executives, labor leaders,

Figure 7.8

Impacts of Employee Control and Amount of Work Stressors

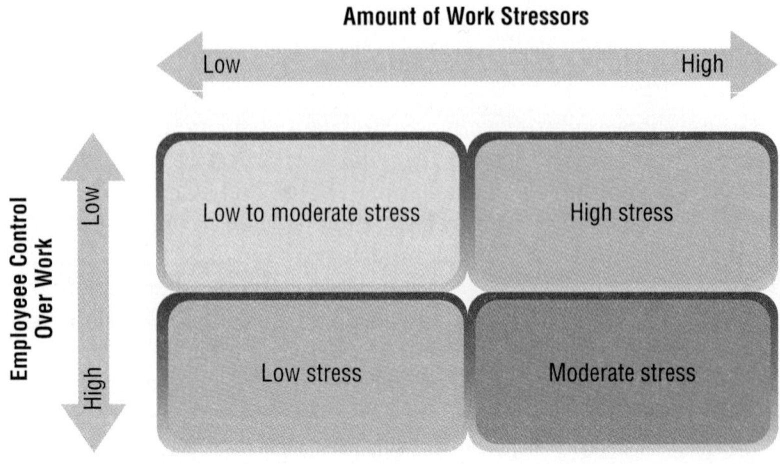

Source: Adapted from Fox, M. L., Dwyer, D. J., and Ganster, D. C. Effects of stressful job demands and control on physiological and attitudinal outcomes in a hospital setting. *Academy of Management Journal*, 1993, 36, 291.

professors, and government officials) award the C. Everett Koop National Health Award to companies having the most successful wellness programs. Some former winners of this award are shown in Table 7.4.

There are three main types of wellness programs.[44] The first are programs aimed at raising awareness and providing information. These programs may or may not directly improve health; rather they are designed to inform employees about the consequences of unhealthy behavior. For example, Sara Lee provides female employees with a series of workshops on prenatal care, nutrition, and strategies for preventing disease. Johnson & Johnson has lunch-hour seminars on stress-coping techniques. Companies often use these programs to generate interest in more active exercise and lifestyle change programs.

A second type of wellness program involves employees in ongoing efforts to modify their lifestyles. Such efforts might involve physical fitness programs (e.g., jogging or walking), smoking cessation programs, weight control programs, and the like. For example, L.L. Bean has a running club for employees and programs that offer lessons in ballroom dancing and cross-country skiing. Bonne Bell encourages employees to ride bicycles to work and has arranged for its employees to purchase bikes at cost. The company also provides an extensive series of exercise programs for employees and has built tennis and volleyball courts, a running track, and shower and locker-room facilities. Employees may use all these facilities at no cost and even get an extra 30 minutes for lunch if they want to exercise. The firm sells running suits and shoes at discount prices and offers $250 bonuses for employees who exercise at least 4 days a week.

A third variety of wellness program has as its goal the creation of an environment that will help employees maintain the healthy lifestyle developed in the other programs. AT&T employees formed support groups to help each other maintain their healthy lifestyle changes as a result of AT&T's Total Life Concept wellness program. The exercise facilities provided free of charge by Bonne Bell are another example. At Safeway, employees built their own fitness center on company property. The firm provides a full-time fitness director to oversee the exercise programs and activities.

Wellness programs can provide substantial benefits to both individuals and organizations. AT&T has obtained dramatic health benefits in terms of reduced blood pressure and cholesterol levels from its Total Life Concept program. Safeway estimates that its wellness program has almost completely eliminated workplace accidents and

Table 7.4 Winning Health Care Programs

COMPANY	WINNING WELLNESS PROGRAM
Aetna	Aetna boasts five state-of-the-art health clubs with 7,600 enrollees. Exercise machines cost $282 less per year than is needed to insure couch potatoes.
L.L. Bean	L.L. Bean pays up to $200 to employees whose families quit smoking or take prenatal classes. Its annual health insurance premiums are $2,000 per employee, half the national average.
Champion	Champion's 18,000 mill workers pay no deductible on preventive exams and immunizations. This creates big savings from early detection of cancer and diabetes.
Coors	Coors pays bonuses for healthy habits. Employees can use the award of $500 per family to buy extra holidays or pay for financial planning.
Dow	Dow's Backs in Action encourages exercise and dieting. On-the-job strains and sprains have decreased by 90%.
DuPont	DuPont budgets $20 million per year on tests and checkups for employees. Free treatment includes frequent mammographies and flu shots.
First Chicago	First Chicago pays for 800 births each year in its female workforce. Educational programs have reduced C-sections and underweight babies.
Johnson & Johnson	Johnson & Johnson employees receive free checkups six times annually for their infants. Prevention saves $13 million a year.
Quaker	Quaker grants $500 bonuses for exercise, not smoking, and using seat belts.
Steelcase	Steelcase tests 4,000 employees for health problems and safety awareness. Estimated savings from promoting healthy lifestyles are $20 million over 10 years.
Tenneco	Among other things, Tenneco promotes healthy eating habits for 1,500 pipeline workers. Health costs are shrinking along with waistlines.
Union Pacific	U P motivates employees to focus on healthy lifestyles. A $1.2 million per year investment in wellness programs generates a 3-to-1 return.

Source: Adapted from Tully, S. America's healthiest companies. *Fortune*, June 12, 1995, 19.

reduced tardiness and absenteeism by more than 60 percent. At Johnson & Johnson locations that used the wellness program, hospital costs during the first 5 years increased by only one-third as much as they did at company locations that didn't use the program. The company wellness program also reduced absenteeism by 18 percent.

CHAPTER SUMMARY

1. Explain the concepts of stress and stressors and describe the general nature of the body's stress response.

Stress is a consequence of or a response to a situation that places either physical or psychological demands on a person. The body's general biological response to stressors prepares the individual to fight or flee—behaviors generally inappropriate in the workplace. Many factors determine how employees experience work stress, including their perception of the situation, past experiences, the presence or absence of other employees, and a variety of individual differences.

2. Diagnose the sources of stress in organizations.

Stressors at work stem from many sources, including (1) workload, (2) job conditions, (3) role conflict and ambiguity, (4) career development, (5) interpersonal relations, (6) aggressive behavior, including violence and sexual harassment, and (7) conflict between work and other roles. In addition, significant changes or other events in an individual's personal life may also be sources of stress.

3. Describe the effects of stress on health and job performance.

Stress affects people physiologically, emotionally, and behaviorally. Researchers have linked stress to several serious health problems, particularly coronary heart disease. An inverted U-shaped relationship exists between stress and performance. An optimal level of stress probably exists for any particular task, and less or more stress than that level may lead to reduced performance. Job burnout is a major result of unrelieved job-related stress.

4. Explain the relationship between personality and stress.

Several personality dimensions are related to stress. Individuals having a Type A personality are prone to stress and have an increased chance of heart disease. Some specific dimensions of the Type A personality, such as hostility, are particularly important in terms of stress-related illness. In contrast, the collection of personality traits known as hardiness seems to reduce the effects of stress.

5. Identify several individual and organizational methods for coping with stress.

Stress is a crucial issue for both individuals and organizations. Fortunately, various techniques and programs can help people manage stress in the workplace. These programs often focus on identifying and removing workplace stressors as well as helping employees cope with stress. Wellness programs are particularly promising in helping employees cope with stress.

KEY TERMS AND CONCEPTS

Behavioral effects of stress
Depersonalization
Emotional effects of stress
Fight-or-flight response
Hardiness
Hardy personality
Job burnout
Life stressors
Physiological effects of stress
Post-traumatic stress disorder
Role ambiguity
Role conflict
Role overload
Sexual harassment
Stress
Stress management
Stressors
Type A personality
Type B personality
Wellness programs
Workplace violence

DISCUSSION QUESTIONS

1. Based on your own experience, describe a work situation that you found stressful. Use Figures 7.1 and 7.2 to identify the factors causing the stress and explain their impact.
2. Give examples of times when the fight-or-flight response seemed particularly inappropriate for (a) your own behavior and (b) the behavior of another person.
3. Explain the role of individual differences (e.g., age, gender, past experience, and personality) in experiencing stress.
4. Identify and list some of the stressors in a job that you have held. Which were the most difficult to deal with? Why?
5. Provide an example from your own experience (at work, in sports activities, etc.) that illustrates the inverted U-shaped relationship between stress and performance.
6. Either from your own experience or from something you have read in the business press, describe a real-world example of job burnout.
7. How would you describe yourself in comparison to (a) the Type A personality, (b) the hardy personality?
8. Describe a situation in which you coped well with stress. Describe another situation when you did not cope well with stress. Describe the differences in how you perceived the two situations.

9. Describe the techniques, approaches, and competencies that you use in your own life to cope with stress.

10. Identify and describe the three most important initiatives that you would include in a stress management program for an organization. Why would they be your highest priority?

DEVELOPING COMPETENCIES

Competency: Managing Self—Assessing Your Stress Level

The following questionnaire has been widely used to measure stress levels.[45] As you answer the questions, think only of the past month. After selecting an answer for each question, add your points to obtain a total.

_____ 1. How often have you been upset because of something that happened unexpectedly?

0 = never 1 = almost never 2 = sometimes 3 = fairly often 4 = very often

_____ 2. How often have you felt that you were unable to control the important things in your life?

0 = never 1 = almost never 2 = sometimes 3 = fairly often 4 = very often

_____ 3. How often have you felt nervous and "stressed"?

0 = never 1 = almost never 2 = sometimes 3 = fairly often 4 = very often

_____ 4. How often have you felt confident about your ability to handle your personal problems?

4 = never 3 = almost never 2 = sometimes 1 = fairly often 0 = very often

_____ 5. How often have you felt that things were going your way?

4 = never 3 = almost never 2 = sometimes 1 = fairly often 0 = very often

_____ 6. How often have you been able to control irritations in your life?

4 = never 3 = almost never 2 = sometimes 1 = fairly often 0 = very often

_____ 7. How often have you found that you could not cope with all the things that you had to do?

0 = never 1 = almost never 2 = sometimes 3 = fairly often 4 = very often

_____ 8. How often have you felt that you were on top of things?

4 = never 3 = almost never 2 = sometimes 1 = fairly often 0 = very often

_____ 9. How often have you been angered because of things that were outside your control?

0 = never 1 = almost never 2 = sometimes 3 = fairly often 4 = very often

_____ 10. How often have you felt difficulties were piling up so high that you could not overcome them?

0 = never 1 = almost never 2 = sometimes 3 = fairly often 4 = very often

_____ Total

Stress levels vary among individuals. Compare your total score to the following averages.

AGE	GENDER	MARITAL STATUS
18–29 . . . . . . 14.2	Men 12.1	Widowed 12.6
30–44. . . . . . . 13.0	Women. . . 13.7	Married or living with. . . . 12.4
45–54. . . . . . . 12.6		Single or never wed 14.1
55–64 . . . . . . .11.9		Divorced. 14.7
65 and over . . 12.0		Separated 16.6

Competency: Managing Change—Stress Management at Metropolitan Hospital

This stress management program was carried out over a 2-year period at Metropolitan Hospital. The initial impetus for the project was widespread complaints from middle managers about feeling stress, overworked, and subject to unexpected changes in policies and procedures. Top administrators sought help in dealing with these problems from external organization development (OD) consultants with skills and experience in stress management.

The initial stage of the project consisted of diagnosing the causes and consequences of experienced stress at the hospital. Understanding the sources of stress was seen as a necessary prelude to developing an appropriate plan for managing stress. The consultants developed a questionnaire to collect data from the 45 middle managers responsible for almost every phase of operation of the hospital. The design of the questionnaire was guided by a conceptual model of stress similar to that shown in Figure 7.2. The questionnaire included items about various organizational stressors, including ongoing, recurrent stressors as well as those associated with recent changes. It also included questions about the managers' use of stress management techniques, such as exercise, nutritional awareness, and the creation of support systems. The questionnaire ended with items about possible immediate stress effects (e.g., irritability, sleep difficulty, and changes in eating and drinking patterns) and longer term impacts (e.g., reduced general health, job dissatisfaction, and poor work performance).

Analysis of the data showed that many of the organizational change events and ongoing working conditions were significantly related to the managers' levels of perceived stress. Among the most stressful organizational change events were major and frequent changes in instructions, policies, and procedures; numerous unexpected crises and deadlines; and sudden increases in the activity level or pace of work. The ongoing working conditions contributing most to stress included work overload, feedback only when performance was unsatisfactory, lack of confidence in management, and role conflict and ambiguity. The managers reported little use of stress management techniques to help them cope with these stressors. Only 20 percent engaged in regular physical exercise, and, surprisingly, 60 percent had marginally or poorly balanced diets. Among the most commonly reported health problems were tension headaches, diarrhea or constipation, common colds, and backaches.

Based on the data, senior management with the help of the consultants implemented several organizational improvements. To reduce work overload and role ambiguity, each managerial position was analyzed in terms of work distribution, job requirements, and performance standards. Actions based on this analysis resulted in more balanced workloads across the jobs and in clearer job descriptions. Hospital administrators also began working with department managers to define job descriptions and expectations and to provide ongoing performance feedback. The managers were given training in time management, how to organize their workloads better, and in general how to delegate work to subordinates more effectively.

The "fire-fighting" climate at the hospital had caused many managers to focus on their own departments while neglecting important lateral relations with other units. Monthly cross-departmental meetings were implemented to improve lateral relations among department heads and supervisors. Efforts were also made to provide an organizational culture that encouraged the building of peer-support groups.

To reduce uncertainty about organizational changes, senior managers spent more time informing and educating middle managers about forthcoming changes. Top management also held quarterly information meetings with first-line supervisors in order to clear up misunderstandings, misinterpretations, and rumors.

In addition to the changes aimed at reducing organizational stressors, measures were taken to help managers identify and cope with stress more effectively. The hospital instituted yearly physical examinations to detect stress-related problems. It also trained managers to identify stress symptoms and problems both in themselves and subordinates. The hospital developed an exercise club and various sports activities and offered weekly yoga classes. It also created a training program combining nutritional awareness with techniques for coping with tension headaches and backaches. Fresh fruit was made available as an alternative to doughnuts in all meetings and training sessions.

Initial reactions to the stress management program were positive, and the hospital's management is assessing the longer term effects. Measures of stressors and experienced stress will be taken every 12 to 18 months to monitor the program so that further changes can be made as necessary.[46]

Questions

1. Identify the primary ideas and concepts from the chapter that appear in this case in one form or another.
2. Using Figure 7.2, diagnose the work stressors at Metropolitan Hospital.
3. Using Figure 7.7, analyze Metropolitan Hospital's stress management program.

REFERENCES

1. Adapted from DeFrank, R. S. and Ivancevich, J. M. Stress on the job: An executive update. *Academy of Management Executive*, August 1998, 55–66.
2. Jex, S. M. *Stress and Job Performance*. Thousand Oaks, Calif.: Sage, 1998, 1–8; Kahn, R. L., and Byosiere, P. Stress in organizations. In M. D. Dunnette and L. M. Hough (eds.), *Handbook of Industrial and Organizational Psychology*, vol. 3, 2nd ed. Palo Alto, Calif.: Consulting Psychologists Press, 1992, 571–650.
3. Carpi, J. Stress—It's worse than you think. *Psychology Today*, January–February 1996, 34–40; Contrada, R., Baum, A. S., Glass, D., and Friend, R. The social psychology of health. In R. M. Baron, W. G. Graziano, and C. Stangor (eds.), *Social Psychology*. Fort Worth: Holt, Rinehart, and Winston, 1991, 620–624.
4. This example is based on Matteson, M. T., and Ivancevich, J. M. *Controlling Work Stress: Effective Human Resource and Management Strategies*. San Francisco: Jossey-Bass, 1987, 12–14; also see Widmaier, E. P. So you think this is the age of stress? *Psychology Today*, January–February 1996, 41–44.
5. Selye, H. History and present status of the stress concept. In L. Goldberger and S. Breznitz (eds.), *Handbook of Stress*. New York: Free Press, 1982, 7–17; Selye, H. *The Stress of Life*, rev. ed. New York: McGraw-Hill, 1976, 1.
6. McGuigan, F. J. *Encyclopedia of Stress*. Old Tappan, N.J.: Prentice-Hall, 1999; Manning, M. R., Jackson, C. N., and Fusilier, M. R. Occupational stress, social support, and the costs of health care. *Academy of Management Journal*, 1996, 39, 738–750; Uchino, B. N., Uno, D., and Holt-Lunstad, J. Social support, physiological processes, and health. *Current Directions in Psychological Science*, 1999, 8, 145–148.
7. Jex, S. M., Bliese, P. D. Efficacy beliefs as a moderator of the impact of work-related stressors: A multilevel study. *Journal of Applied Psychology*, 1999, 84, 349–361; Lazarus, R. S. From psychological stress to the emotions: A history of changing outlooks. *Annual Review of Psychology*, 1993, 44, 1–21; Schaubroeck, J., Ganster, D. C., and Fox, M. L. Dispositional affect and work-related stress. *Journal of Applied Psychology*, 1992, 77, 322–335.
8. This story is attributed to Henry Murray, as described by Pervin, L. A. Persons, situations, interactions: The history

of a controversy and a discussion of theoretical models. *Academy of Management Review*, 1989, 14, 350–360.
9. Shellenbarger, S. Are saner workloads the unexpected key to more productivity? *Wall Street Journal*, March 10, 1999, B1.
10. Adapted from Ellison, K. Siesta sunset: Stress invades mañana-land. *Houston Chronicle*, July 28, 1992, 7A.
11. Jex, *Stress and Job Performance*, 10.
12. Cooper, C. L., and Arbose, J. Executive stress goes global. *International Management*, May 1984, 42–48; also see Peterson, M. F., et al. Role conflict, ambiguity, and overload: A 21-nation study. *Academy of Management Journal*, 1995, 38, 429–452.
13. Melamed, S., Ben-Avi, I., Luz, J., and Green, M. S. Objective and subjective work monotony: Effects on job satisfaction, psychological distress, and absenteeism in blue-collar workers. *Journal of Applied Psychology*, 1995, 80, 29–42.
14. Shellenbarger, S. Future work policies may focus on teens, trimming workloads. *Wall Street Journal*, December 30, 1998, B1; Shellenbarger, S. Overloaded staffers are starting to take more time off work. *Wall Street Journal*, September 23, 1998, B1.
15. See, for example, Leigh, J. H., Lucas, G. H., and Woodman, R. W. Effects of perceived organizational factors on role stress–job attitude relationships. *Journal of Management*, 1988, 14, 41–58; Miner, J. B. *Industrial-Organizational Psychology*. New York: McGraw-Hill, 1992, 158–159; Peterson, et al., *Academy of Management Journal*, 429–452.
16. Milbank, D. "New-collar" work: Telephone sales reps do unrewarding jobs that few can abide. *Wall Street Journal*, September 9, 1993, B1; Shellenbarger, S. Technology affords this trader freedom, but also adds binds. *Wall Street Journal*, September 9, 1998, B1.
17. Sutton, R. I., and Rafaeli, A. Characteristics of work stations as potential occupational stressors. *Academy of Management Journal*, 1987, 30, 260–276.
18. Statistics in this section are drawn from O'Leary-Kelly, A. M., Griffin, R. W., and Glew, D. J. Organization-motivated aggression: A research framework. *Academy of Management Journal*, 1996, 21, 225–253; also see Allen, R. E., and Lucero, M. A. Beyond resentment: Exploring organizationally targeted insider murder. *Journal of Management Inquiry*, 1996, 5, 86–103.
19. Hollway, W., and Jefferson, T. PC or not PC: Sexual harassment and the question of ambivalence. *Human Relations*, 1996, 49, 373–394; Lengnick-Hall, M. L. Sexual harassment research: A methodological critique. *Personnel Psychology*, 1995, 48, 841–865.
20. Oliver, J. E., Ellerbee, S. B., and Ostapski, S. A. The sexual harassment survey: Exploring gender differences. In E. Biech (ed.), *The 2000 Annual: Volume 1—Training*. San Francisco: Jossey-Bass/Pfeiffer, 2000, 135–152.
21. Kossek, E. E., and Ozeki, C. Work–family conflict, policies, and the job–life satisfaction relationship: A review and directions for organizational behavior–human resources research. *Journal of Applied Psychology*, 1998, 83, 139–149.
22. Baron, R. A., and Byrne, D. *Social Psychology: Understanding Human Interaction*, 6th ed. Boston: Allyn & Bacon, 1991, 571–573; the type of rating scale shown in Table 7.1 is based on the work of Holmes, T. H., and Rahe, R. H. The social readjustment rating scale. *Journal of Psychosomatic Medicine*, 1967, 11, 213–218.
23. Adler, J. Stress. *Newsweek*, June 14, 1999, 56–63; Cohen, S. Psychological stress, immunity, and upper respiratory infections. *Current Directions in Psychological Science*, 1996, 5, 86–90; Cohen, S., and Williamson, G. M. Stress and infectious disease in humans. *Psychological Bulletin*, 1991, 109, 5–24.
24. McMorris, F. A. Can post-traumatic stress arise from office battles? *Wall Street Journal*, February 5, 1996, B1, B10.
25. Jex, *Stress and Job Performance*, 25–67; Xie, J. L, and Johns, G. Job scope and stress: Can job scope be too high? *Academy of Management Journal*, 1995, 38, 1288–1309.
26. Cascio, W. F. Downsizing: What do we know? What have we learned? *Academy of Management Executive*, February 1993, 95–104; Lublin, J. A. Walking wounded: Survivors of layoffs battle angst, anger, hurting productivity. *Wall Street Journal*, December 6, 1993, A1.
27. Lee, R. T., and Ashforth, B. E. A meta-analytic examination of the correlates of the three dimensions of job burnout. *Journal of Applied Psychology*, 1996, 81, 123–133; Lee, R. T., and Ashforth, B. E. On the meaning of Maslach's three dimensions of burnout. *Journal of Applied Psychology*, 1990, 75, 743–747; van Dierendonck, D., Schaufeli, W. B., and Buunk, B. P. The evaluation of an individual burnout intervention program: The role of inequity and social support. *Journal of Applied Psychology*, 1998, 83, 392–407.
28. Wright, T. A., and Cropanzano, R. Emotional exhaustion as a predictor of job performance and voluntary turnover. *Journal of Applied Psychology*, 1998, 83, 486–493.
29. Niehouse, O. I. Controlling burnout: A leadership guide for managers. *Business Horizons*, July–August, 1984, 81–82; also see Etzion, D., Eden, D., and Lapidot, Y. Relief from job stressors and burnout: Reserve service as a respite. *Journal of Applied Psychology*, 1998, 83, 577–585; Levinson, H. When executives burn out. *Harvard Business Review*, July–August 1996, 152–163.
30. Jex, *Stress and Job Performance*, 78–84.
31. Shallenbarger, S. Three myths that make managers push staff to the edge of burnout. *Wall Street Journal*, March 17, 1999, B1.
32. Friedman, M., and Rosenman, R. *Type A Behavior and Your Heart*. New York: Knopf, 1974.
33. Friedman, H. S., and Booth-Kewley, S. Personality, type A behavior and coronary heart disease: The role of emotional expression. *Journal of Personality and Social Psychology*, 1987, 53, 783–792; Lee, C., Jamieson, L. F., and Earley, P. C. Beliefs and fears and Type A behavior: Implications for academic performance and psychiatric health disorder symptoms. *Journal of Organizational Behavior*, 1996, 17, 151–168; Sotile, W., and Sotile, M. High powered couples. *Psychology Today*, July–August 1996, 50–55.
34. Baron, R. A., and Byrne, D. *Social Psychology: Understanding Human Interaction*, 6th ed. Boston: Allyn & Bacon, 1991, 606.
35. Contrada, R., Baum, A. S., Glass, D., and Friend, R. The social psychology of health. In R. M. Baron, W. G.

Graziano, and C. Stangor (eds.), *Social Psychology.* Fort Worth: Holt, Rinehart and Winston, 1991, 626–627.

36. Brehm, B. A. *Stress management: Increasing your stress resistance.* Reading, Mass.: Addison-Wesley, 1999; Byrum-Robinson, B. Stress-management training for the nineties. In J. W. Pfeiffer (ed.), *The 1993 Annual: Developing Human Resources.* San Diego: Pfeiffer & Company, 1993, 264; Neufeld, R. W. J. Dynamic differentials of stress and coping. *Psychological Review,* 1999, 106, 385–397.
37. Robinson, B., and De Diemar, L. Time management for those who hate it. *The 1999 Annual: Volume 1—Training.* San Francisco: Jossey Bass/Pfeiffer, 1999, 151–168.
38. Carpi, J. A smorgasbord of stress-stoppers. *Psychology Today,* January–February 1996, 35–37.
39. Nelson, D. L., Quick, J. C., and Quick, J. D. Corporate warfare: Preventing combat stress and battle fatigue. *Organizational Dynamics,* Summer 1989, 65–79; also see Delbecq, A. L., and Friedlander, F. Strategies for personal and family renewal: How a high survivor group of executives cope with stress and avoid burnout. *Journal of Management Inquiry,* 1995, 4, 262–269.
40. Trost, C. Workplace stress. *Wall Street Journal,* December 1, 1992, A1.
41. Ivancevich, J. M., Matteson, M. T., Freedman, S. M., and Phillips, J. S. Worksite stress management interventions. *American Psychologist,* 1990, 45, 252–261.
42. Adapted from Shellenbarger, S. Employees who value time as much as money now get their reward. *Wall Street Journal,* September 22, 1999, B1; Shellenbarger, S. What job candidates really want to know: Will I have a life? *Wall Street Journal,* November 17, 1999, B1.
43. Gebhardt, D. L., and Crump, C. E. Employee fitness and wellness programs in the workplace. *American Psychologist,* 1990, 45, 262–272.
44. Company examples in this section are drawn from Jeffrey, N. A. Wellness plans try to target the not-so-well. *Wall Street Journal,* June 20, 1996, B1, B2; Roberts, M., and Harris, T. J. Wellness at work. *Psychology Today,* May 1989, 54–58.
45. Adapted from a questionnaire developed by Sheldon Cohen contained in Adler, J. Stress. *Newsweek,* June 14, 1999, 63.
46. Adapted from Cummings, T. G., and Worley, C. G. *Organization Development and Change,* 6th ed. Copyright 1997. By permission of South-Western College Publishing, a division of International Thomson Publishing Inc., Cincinnati, OH 45227.

PART 2

Group and Interpersonal Processes

Chapter 8 Group and Team Behavior

Chapter 9 Power and Political Behavior

Chapter 10 Conflict and Negotiation

Chapter 11 Leadership: Foundations

Chapter 12 Leadership: Contemporary Developments

Chapter 13 Interpersonal Communication

CHAPTER

8 Group and Team Behavior

LEARNING OBJECTIVES

When you have finished studying the chapter, you should be able to:

1 Describe the most common types of groups and teams in organizations.
2. Identify the unique features of virtual teams.
3. Explain the five-stage model of team development.
4. Describe seven of the key influences on team effectiveness.
5. Explain the self-managing team decision-making model.
6. Guide team creativity through the use of the nominal group technique, traditional brainstorming, and electronic brainstorming.

Preview Case: *CRI's Team System*

TYPES OF GROUPS AND TEAMS

Basic Types of Groups

Competency: Managing Diversity—*Informal Practices and Black Managers*

Basic Types of Teams

VIRTUAL TEAMS

Competency: Managing Teams—*Whole Foods Markets' Self-Managed Teams*

Core Features

Technology Links

DEVELOPMENTAL STAGES OF TEAMS

Competency: Managing Across Cultures—*Global Virtual Teams*

Forming Stage

Storming Stage

Norming Stage

Performing Stage

Adjourning Stage

INFLUENCES ON TEAM EFFECTIVENESS

Context

Goals

Team Size

Team Member Roles and Diversity

Competency: Managing Change—*IBM's Planned Diversity Initiatives*

Norms

Cohesiveness

Leadership

TEAM DECISION MAKING

Competency: Managing Self—*Joan McCoy Learns Team Leadership*

Self-Managing Team Decision-Making Model

Assessment of Model

GUIDING TEAM CREATIVITY

Nominal Group Technique

Traditional Brainstorming

Electronic Brainstorming

CHAPTER SUMMARY

Competency: Managing Communication—*FedEx Brainstorms Electronically*

Key Terms and Concepts

Discussion Questions

DEVELOPING COMPETENCIES

Competency: Managing Teams—*Team Assessment*

Competency: Managing Teams—*Artisan Industries' Team*

PREVIEW CASE

CRI'S TEAM SYSTEM

Custom Research, Inc. (CRI), provides marketing research, customer satisfaction, and database analysis services worldwide. The company is headquartered in Minneapolis and has branch offices in New York and San Francisco. Recently, the firm won the Malcolm Baldrige National Quality Award. With just 100 full-time employees at that time, CRI was the smallest company—and the first professional services firm of any size—to win the award. CRI now has 130 employees.

The cofounders of CRI—Judy Corson and Jeff Pope—attribute a large part of their firm's success to adoption of a team system. The foundation of this system is the use of cross-functional teams, which bring together the knowledge and skills of people from various specialties to solve mutual problems and achieve specific goals.

CRI has nine cross-functional teams, with five to nine members in each team. Each team handles the functions necessary to complete a research study and serve specific clients' needs. The teams have separate profit and loss statements and client satisfaction, productivity, and performance goals. "They are running their own little business," says Judy Corson. The teams have in-depth knowledge about their clients' needs and preferences because of the continuity of services provided. They seek client feedback regularly and maintain "client books." When a team's clients visit the office, all team members meet with them.

Teams and their clients are increasingly linked electronically, including electronic distribution of completed research reports. Some clients send requests for research proposals to CRI's electronic mailbox. The company responds electronically, and a proposal may be accepted with few conversations between CRI and the client. However, the electronic connections do not substitute for personal service. Team members also wear pagers, and clients can always reach someone on the team in an emergency. In effect, CRI team members are an extension of a client's staff.

*For more information on CRI, visit this organization's home page at **www.cresearch.com.***

Team members take pride in their accountability to clients and to one another. They demonstrate a sense of ownership of their team, clients, and CRI. The following team member comments illustrate this feeling.

- Stephanie Parent: "I like being on the team. You feel like you belong. Everyone knows what's going on."
- Christine Sharratt: "You don't feel like you've handed something off to another department and it will come back eventually. There are no black holes."
- Lisa Gudding: "There are no slugs. Everyone pulls their weight."
- Jeanne Wichterman: "When a client needs something in an hour, we work together to solve the problem."[1]

The Preview Case illustrates two key points regarding many outstanding organizations: (1) they make use of teams; and (2) they are high touch *and* high tech, not one or the other. Jeff Pope, one of the cofounders of CRI comments: "Our technology investments key our responsiveness to clients and cycle-time reductions. Teams and technology have helped us become one of the most productive and financially successful firms in our industry."[2]

In this chapter we focus on one of the seven core competencies introduced in Chapter 1. Recall that *the managing teams competency* involves the ability to develop, support, facilitate, and lead groups to achieve organizational goals. The managers and employees of CRI score high on the managing teams competency.

We present ways to understand formal teams and informal groups and—based on that understanding—ways to increase their effectiveness. We emphasize (1) the varieties of groups and teams found in organizations, (2) the ways in which team members develop and learn, (3) the principal factors that influence team effectiveness, (4) the ways in which members of effective teams make decisions, and (5) the methods that managers and team leaders can use to encourage team creativity. As we noted in Chapter 1, all the other core competencies contribute to the variety of abilities needed to be effective as a team leader or member.

Recall from Chapter 1 our discussion of the potential impacts of the cultural values of *individualism* and *collectivism* in the use of teams. CRI attempts to integrate and balance these values in its use of teams, through its broader organizational culture and by communicating the following expectations:

> Whether you are managing an account, working on a project team, or supporting a team, CRI expects you to use your own ideas and initiative. Open access to people and resources throughout the company helps you do your job better.
>
> All employees have a personalized annual development plan that includes technical training and general business education. CRI is organized around Account Teams, so employees get experience in building and running a Team's business while enjoying the partnership of working on a team.[3]

Learning Objective:

1. Describe the most common types of groups and teams in organizations.

TYPES OF GROUPS AND TEAMS

In this chapter, we focus on small groups and teams. We don't consider large groups such as political parties, ethnic groups, or occupational groups.

BASIC TYPES OF GROUPS

For our purposes, a **group** is any number of people who share goals, often communicate with one another over a period of time, and are few enough so that each individual may communicate with all the others, person-to-person.[4]

Many Classifications. Most individuals belong to various types of groups, which can be classified in many ways. For example, a person concerned with obtaining membership in a group or gaining acceptance as a group member might classify groups as open or closed to new members. A person evaluating groups in an organization according to their primary goals might classify them as friendship groups or task groups. A **friendship group** evolves informally to meet its members' personal security, esteem, and belonging needs. A **task group** is created by management to accomplish certain organizational goals. However, a single group in an organization may serve both friendship and task purposes. The primary focus of this chapter is on types of task groups, commonly known today as teams.

Informal Groups. An **informal group** is one that develops out of the day-to-day activities, interactions, and sentiments of the members for the purpose of meeting their social needs. A friendship group is one of the most common types of informal groups in or out of organizations.

The purposes of informal groups are not necessarily related to formal organizational goals. The formal organization, however, often has considerable influence on the development of informal groups through the physical layout of work, the leadership practices of superiors, and the type of technology used.[5] For example, moving certain people from one building to another is likely to have an impact on the membership of informal groups. The distance between them may make face-to-face communication difficult and cause groups to wither or re-form. In contrast, a new manager taking over a department and telling its employees to "shape up or ship out" may cause an informal group to form, with its members uniting against the manager. Some managers believe that close-knit informal groups have undesirable effects on an organization. Such managers often view groups as a potential source of anti-establishment power, as a way of holding back information when the group doesn't identify with organizational goals, or as a means of pressuring individuals to slow production.

Informal groups can provide their members with desirable benefits (e.g., security and protection). Some informal groups set production limits for their members, fearing that management might use an outstanding worker as a standard for output and that increased production might lead to some workers being laid off. An informal group can provide positive feedback to other members. The all-too-common belief that higher productivity will work against the interests of workers is kept alive and enforced by some informal groups within organizations.[6]

Informal groups can also exercise undesirable power over individual members. Such powers usually fall into two categories. First, a group may be able to manipulate rewards and punishments and thus pressure members to conform to its standards of behavior. Second, a group may restrict a member's freedom and the ways by which the social needs of its members can be satisfied on the job. Informal groups have been known to ridicule certain members or give them the silent treatment for not conforming to group standards of "acceptable" production. Such treatment may threaten the individual's safety, social, and esteem needs. Managers probably should try to minimize the undesirable effects of informal groups rather than try to eliminate them.[7]

Informal groups in organizations can't always be classified simply as positive or negative because many exhibit both characteristics from time to time, depending on the circumstances or issues facing the organization. CRI designed its team system to capture, insofar as possible, the positive peer influence that often occurs through informal groups.

The Managing Diversity Competency feature on the next page illustrates the potential negative impacts of informal groups and practices on the progress and roles of African-American managers in organizations with predominantly white, male managers. These incidents reflect what can happen when the core components of the managing diversity competency are inadequate in the eyes of black managers.

Effective Groups. In much of this chapter we focus on making groups, especially teams, more effective. First, you need to know how to recognize effective or ineffective groups. In brief, an effective group has the following basic characteristics.

- Its members know why the group exists; they have shared goals.
- Its members support agreed upon guidelines or procedures for making decisions.
- Its members communicate freely among themselves.
- Its members have learned to receive help from one another and to give help to one another.
- Its members have learned to deal with conflict within the group.
- Its members have learned to diagnose individual and group processes and improve their own and the group's functioning.[8]

The degree to which a group lacks one or more of these characteristics determines whether—and to what extent—it is ineffective. These basic characteristics apply both to formal groups (e.g., the cross-functional teams at CRI discussed in the Preview

Competency: Managing Diversity

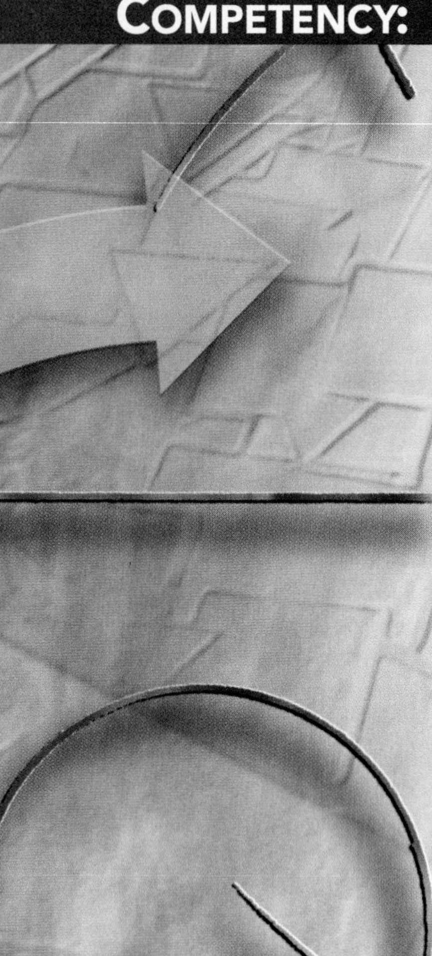

Informal Practices and Black Managers

Bob Tassie, an African American and former vice president of communications for CBS Sports, comments on this situation: A group of managers—all white—go out regularly once a week for refreshments after work and blacks aren't invited. "If you don't reach out, you'll never be a part of that group," says Tassie, now president of Unity Media, a media buying company. "And the chitchat that goes on there is as important as what goes on at work. Once you're part of the informal group, colleagues will start seeing you not as an icon, but as someone who pays a mortgage, has children in school, just like them."

Black managers often walk a fine line between accommodating the white corporate culture and maintaining their identity. "Maybe that means displaying African-American art in my office," says Robert Phillips, director of affirmative action for the City of Portland and Multnomah County, Oregon. But, he adds, "I can't come in wearing dashikis and beads or the organization will push me to the side."

Black managers sometimes have to contend with the informal group view that they got there because of being black. Jim Kennedy, president of Management Team Consultants of San Rafael, California, advises companies on how to hire a diverse workforce. He recommends a staff meeting to discuss the criteria used to fill the position and the qualifications of the new black manager. Kennedy suggests that management acknowledge that adding a minority candidate may have been a consideration but that if the person isn't competent, he'll be fired in a few weeks and management will be embarrassed. The meeting may not change minds, but it at least brings the issue into the open. Phillips contends: "In organizations where there were only white managers for a long time, the best thing is to put it on the table up front. If you don't, you get an undercurrent of people talking."[9]

Case) and to informal groups (e.g., the white managers who go out for refreshments once a week noted in the Managing Diversity Competency feature). Beginning with the discussion of basic types of teams, and continuing throughout the rest of the chapter, our use of the word *team* encompasses the word *group* unless we specifically use *group* for a particular reason.

Basic Types of Teams

A **team** is a small number of employees with complementary competencies (abilities, skills, and knowledge) who are committed to common performance goals and working relationships for which they hold themselves mutually accountable.[10] The heart of any team is a shared commitment by its members for their joint performance. Team goals could be as basic as responding to all customers within 24 hours, or as large-scale as reducing defects by 20 percent over the next 6 months. The key point is that these goals can't be achieved without the cooperation and communication of team members. When a team is formed, its members must have (or quickly develop) the right mix of complementary competencies to achieve the team's goals. Also, its members need to be able to influence how they will work together to accomplish those goals.[11] Of the many basic types of teams, we consider four of the most common: functional teams, problem-solving teams, cross-functional teams, and self-managed teams. First, we need to discuss briefly team empowerment, which may vary widely for any type of team.

Team Empowerment. The term **team empowerment** refers to the degree to which its members perceive the group as (1) capable of being effective (potency),

(2) performing important and valuable tasks (meaningfulness), (3) having independence and discretion (autonomy) in performing the work, and (4) experiencing a sense of importance and significance (impact) in the work performed and goals achieved.[12] You may relate the key dimensions of empowerment—*potency*, *meaningfulness*, *autonomy*, and *impact*—to your own experience with an important task-related team by responding to the brief questionnaire in Table 8.1. To obtain your team empowerment score follow the directions in the table. Scores may range from 20 to 100. Scores of 20 through 45 suggest low team empowerment. Scores of 46 through 74 indicate moderate levels of team empowerment. Scores of 75 through 100 reveal a state of significant to very high team empowerment.

Table 8.1 Questionnaire for Assessing Team Empowerment

Instructions: Think of a team that you have been (or are) a member of in a work setting. Respond to each statement below by indicating the degree to which you agree or disagree with it in terms of the team identified. The scale is as follows.

5	4	3	2	1
Strongly Agree	Agree	Undecided/ Neutral	Disagree	Strongly Disagree

Place the appropriate number value next to each item.

Potency Items

_____ 1. The team had confidence in itself.
_____ 2. The team believed that it could be very good at producing high-quality work.
_____ 3. The team expected to be seen by others as high performing.
_____ 4. The team was confident that it could solve its own problems.
_____ 5. The team viewed no job as too tough.

Meaningfulness Items

_____ 6. The team cared about what it did.
_____ 7. The team thought that its work was valuable.
_____ 8. The team viewed its group goals as important.
_____ 9. The team believed that its projects were significant.
_____ 10. The team considered its group tasks to be worthwhile.

Autonomy Items

_____ 11. The team could select different ways to do its work.
_____ 12. The team determined how things were done.
_____ 13. The team had a lot of choice in what it did without being told by management.
_____ 14. The team had significant influence in setting its goals.
_____ 15. The team could rotate tasks and assignments among team members.

Impact Item

_____ 16. The team assessed the extent to which it made progress on projects.
_____ 17. The team had a positive impact on other employees.
_____ 18. The team had a positive impact on customers.
_____ 19. The team accomplished its goals.
_____ 20. The team made a difference in the organization.

_____ **Total:** Add points for items 1 through 20. This total is your perceived team empowerment score.

Source: Adapted from Kirkman, B. I., and Rosen, B. Beyond self-management: Antecedents and consequences of team empowerment. *Academy of Management Journal*, 1999, 42, 58–74; Guzzo, R. A., Campbell, R. J., and Shea, G. P. Potency in groups: Articulating a construct. *British Journal of Social Psychology*, 1993, 32, 87–106; Thomas, K. W., and Tymon, W. G., Jr. *Empowerment Inventory.* Tuxedo, N.Y.: Xicom, 1993.

Merrily Mazza, vice president of editing, design, and production for the McGraw-Hill Higher Education Group, comments: "In theory, it is easy to use the word 'team' to describe groups in your workplace but creating true empowered teams is not as easily carried out."[13] For McGraw-Hill, the need to create empowered teams grew out of the company's situation—an increased workload without an increased workforce. Mazza states: "Managers could not keep tight controls and still meet the deadlines. It seemed only logical to turn over some of that control to those who actually did the work. Since they had more direct familiarity with the processes, they could control production between themselves better and quicker."[14] Implementation of empowered teams at McGraw-Hill increased productivity and reduced costs within the first several years; the number of textbooks produced each year has nearly doubled. Mazza notes: "For the customized production of our company's product, teams have been incredibly valuable and are a bottom line for companies no matter how you look at it."[15]

Let's now consider the attributes of four basic types of teams.

Functional Teams. **Functional teams** usually represent individuals who work together daily on a cluster of ongoing and interdependent tasks. Functional teams often exist within functional departments—marketing, production, finance, auditing, human resources, and the like. Within the human resources department, one or more functional teams could operate within the recruiting, compensation, benefits, safety, training and development, affirmative action, industrial relations, and similar functions. Several years ago, Macy's implemented a team system at its Herald Square flagship store in New York City. Macy's team system included functional teams for receiving and delivery, placement, fill-in, recovery, and administration. The administrative team handles all damaged goods, merchandise returns to vendors, markdowns and other price changes, and hanger and security tag pickup at the cash register and wrapping areas.[16]

Problem-Solving Teams. **Problem-solving teams** focus on specific issues in their areas of responsibility, develop potential solutions, and often are empowered to take action within defined limits.[17] Such teams frequently address quality or cost problems. Their members usually are employees from a specific department who meet at least once or twice a week for an hour or two. Teams may have the authority to implement their own solutions if they don't require major procedural changes that might adversely affect other operations or require substantial new resources. Problem-solving teams do not fundamentally reorganize work or change the role of managers. In effect, managers delegate certain problems and decision-making responsibilities to a team. This approach contrasts with delegating specific tasks and authority to individuals.

Consider the case of a consultant who was called in to help resolve interpersonal problems among a small group of employees and mold them into an effective problem-solving team. Darrel Ray is a consultant who specializes in work-team development. He recalls working with one particularly memorable group: a "team" of five black men and five white women charged with processing credit card insurance claims for a financial services company. "Sparks were flying the moment they got together," says Ray, who is president of Managers Consulting Services in Shawnee Mission, Kansas. Expected to manage themselves, team members found it impossible to work together. Resentment, backstabbing, and unresponsiveness on both sides were rampant. Cooperation and communication—the hallmarks of successful teamwork—were nonexistent.

Ray, the problem-solving team facilitator—a black male—intervened over a period of a month and got the members to air their differences. In one 3-hour session "there was a lot of yelling and crying," says Ray. But once they had expressed the fears, stereotypes, and assumptions they had about one another, they were able to get on with the business at hand. After a month, and several special team meetings, productivity had jumped markedly and some of the team members were even socializing after work. As the interpersonal climate improved, Ray's interventions no longer were needed and were discontinued.[18]

Cross-Functional Teams. **Cross-functional teams** bring together the knowledge and skills of people from various work areas to identify and solve mutual problems. Cross-functional teams draw members from several specialties or functions and deal with problems that cut across departmental and functional lines to achieve their goals. Some cross-functional teams operate on a continuing basis, as is the case with the nine cross-functional teams at CRI. Other cross-functional teams may be disbanded after the problems they addressed have been solved and their goals achieved.

Cross-functional teams are often most effective in situations that require adaptability, speed, and a focus on responding to customer needs.[19] They may design and introduce quality improvement programs and new technology, meet with customers and suppliers to improve inputs or outputs, and link separate functions (e.g., marketing, finance, manufacturing, and human resources) to increase product or service innovations. The development of Boeing's 777 jetliner involved the extensive use of cross-functional teams. Previously, design engineers worked independently of the production and operations people who actually built the planes. The traditional approach was for the designers to say, "Here are the plans, go build it." For production of the Boeing 777, hundreds of integrated design–build teams were formed. Their members were drawn from diverse functional areas, including marketing, finance, engineering, and information systems. Each design–build team focused on a specific plane component—tail section, wings, electrical systems, and so on. Integration teams that included higher levels of management coordinated these teams.[20]

Self-Managed Teams. **Self-managed teams** normally consist of employees who must work together effectively daily to manufacture an entire product (or major identifiable component) or service. These teams perform a variety of managerial tasks, such as (1) scheduling work and vacations by members, (2) rotating tasks and assignments among members, (3) ordering materials, (4) deciding on team leadership (which can rotate among team members), (5) setting key team goals, (6) budgeting, (7) hiring replacements for departing team members, and (8) sometimes even evaluating one another's performance.[21] Each member may even learn all the jobs that have to be performed by the team.

The impact of self-managed teams may be enormous. They have raised productivity 30 percent or more and have substantially raised quality in organizations that have used them. They fundamentally change how work is organized and higher level leadership is practiced.[22] A sense of high-level team empowerment is often created through self-managed teams (see Table 8.1). The introduction of self-managed teams typically eliminates one or more managerial levels, thereby creating a flatter organization. We discuss additional aspects of self-managed teams throughout this chapter, including a model of decision making and collaboration for self-managed teams.

The Whole Foods Markets natural foods grocery store chain, with more than 1,400 employees and 90 stores, is very successful. Its key organizing approach and management philosophy is the use of empowered self-managing teams, as clearly illustrated in the Managing Teams Competency feature on the next page.

Learning Objective:

2. Identify the unique features of virtual teams.

VIRTUAL TEAMS

Functional, problem-solving, cross-functional, and even self-managed teams are increasingly able to operate as virtual teams. A **virtual team** is a group of individuals who collaborate through various information technologies on one or more projects while being at two or more locations.[23] The team members may be from one organization or multiple organizations. Recall the example of the extensive use of cross-functional teams by Boeing in developing the 777 jetliner. A number of these teams functioned as virtual teams for most of their collaborations and often included team members from suppliers (e.g., GE) and customers (e.g., American Airlines). Unlike

COMPETENCY: MANAGING TEAMS

WHOLE FOODS MARKETS' SELF-MANAGED TEAMS

The Whole Foods Markets culture is premised on decentralized teamwork. "The team," not the hierarchy, is the defining unit of activity. Each of the stores is a profit center that typically has 10 self-managed teams—produce, grocery, prepared foods, and so on—with designated leaders and clear performance targets. The team leaders in each store are a team, store leaders in each region are a team, and the company's six regional presidents are a team.

The Whole Foods culture features a strong sense of community with a fierce commitment to productivity. Employee participation reinforces individual attention to performance and profits, and solid financial results give people more freedom to innovate. Three principles define how the company operates.

The first principle is *all work is teamwork*. Everyone who joins Whole Foods quickly grasps the primacy of teamwork. That's because teams—and only teams—have the power to approve new hires for full-time jobs. Store leaders screen candidates and recommend them for a job on a specific team. But it takes a two-thirds vote of the team, after what is usually a 30-day trial period, for the candidate to become a full-time employee. Team members are tough on new hires for another reason: money. The company's gain-sharing program ties bonuses directly to team performance—specifically, to sales per labor hour, the most important productivity measurement at Whole Foods. Democracy reinforces discipline: Vote for someone who doesn't perform, and your bonus may vanish within months. The first requirement of effective teamwork is trust. At Whole Foods, building trust starts with the hiring vote. Another element involves salaries. Trust (both among team members and between members and leaders) is promoted by eliminating a major source of distrust—misinformed conjecture about who makes what. Every Whole Foods store has a book that lists the previous year's salary and bonus for all employees—by name.

The second principle is *anything worth doing is worth measuring*. Whole Foods takes that simple principle to extremes—and then shares what it measures with everyone in the company. John Mackey, the CEO, calls it a "no-secrets" management philosophy. He states, "In most companies, management controls information and therefore controls people. By sharing information, we stay aligned to the vision of shared fate." For example, each previous day's sales are posted by team and compared with the same day last year. Once a month, stores get detailed information on profitability. The report analyzes sales, product costs, wages and salaries, and operating profits for all stores. Because the data are so sensitive, they are not posted publicly. But they are freely available to anyone in the company who wants to see them. And store managers routinely review the data with their team leaders. The reports are indispensable to the teams, which make the decisions about labor spending, ordering, and pricing—the factors that determine profitability.

The third principle is *be your own toughest competitor.* "All-for-one" doesn't imply complacency. Whole Foods is serious about accountability. Teams are expected to set ambitious goals and achieve them. But accountability doesn't imply bureaucratic oversight. At Whole Foods, pressure for performance comes from peers rather than from headquarters, and it comes in the form of internal competition. Teams compete against their own goals for sales, growth, and productivity; they also compete against different teams in their store and against similar teams in different stores and regions. This competition is a major reason why performance information is so available. It becomes the gauge by which every team can measure itself against every other team.[24]

*For more information on Whole Foods Markets, visit this firm's home page at **www.wholefoods.com**.*

teams that primarily operate through person-to-person meetings by members of the same organization, virtual teams primarily work across distance (any place), across time (any time), and increasingly across organizational boundaries (members from two or more organizations).

Core Features

The core features of a virtual team are goals, people, and links.[25] Goals are important to any team, but especially so to a virtual team. Clear, precise, and mutually agreed upon goals are the glue that holds a virtual team together. The roles of hierarchy, including the ability to hire and fire by a superior, and bureaucracy, including the use of many rules and regulations to guide outcomes, are minimized in effective virtual teams.

As in all teams, people are at the core of effective virtual teams, but there are some unique twists. Everyone in a virtual team needs to be autonomous and self-reliant while simultaneously working collaboratively with others. This dichotomy requires a foundation of trust among team members. The most apparent feature of a virtual team is in the array of technology-based links used to connect members and carry out its tasks. Virtual teams are increasingly common because of rapid advances in computer and telecommunications technologies.

Technology Links

Three broad categories of technologies are often used in the operation of virtual teams: desktop videoconferencing systems, collaborative software systems, and Internet/intranet systems.[26] Virtual teams can function with only simple e-mail and telephone systems. However, desktop video conferencing systems (DVCSs) re-create some of the aspects of face-to-face interactions of conventional teams. This technology makes possible more complex levels of communication among team members. The DVCS is a relatively simple system for users to operate. A small camera mounted atop a computer monitor provides the video feed to the system; voice transmissions operate through an earpiece–microphone combination or speakerphone. Connection to other team members is managed through software on the user's computer. DVCSs create the potential for two primary types of team communication.

- All team members are connected in a session. With present technology, as many as 16 team members can videoconference simultaneously. Thus each participant can see and hear as many as 15 other team members on his or her computer monitor.
- A group meeting around a conference table can interact with one or more non-present team members or outside resources. The same DVCSs used for individual interaction also permits a conference of team members to have a traditional teleconference with one or more outside parties.

In addition to providing video and audio connections, most DVCSs enable users to share information and applications while they are interconnected. For example, users can simultaneously work on documents, analyze data, or sketch out ideas on a shared whiteboard. A *whiteboard* is a computer program that enables multiple network users to watch on-screen as one person works on an application. Whiteboards are the equivalent of chalk and blackboards.

Collaborative software systems (group support systems) comprise the second category of technologies that enable the use of virtual teams. Effective collaboration requires team members to work both interactively and independently. Collaborative software is designed to augment both types of activity and to foster teamwork. For example, Lotus Notes, a dominant collaborative software product, is designed specifically for asynchronous teamwork (e.g., communication and data sharing where team members are working either at different times or independently). It combines scheduling, electronic messaging, and document and data sharing. Although Lotus Notes and other such software may be used to support teamwork in a traditional work environment, they are vital to the operation of empowered virtual teams.[27]

Internet and intranet technologies represent the third major enabler of virtual teams. Recall that intranets give organizations the advantage of using Internet technology to disseminate organizational information and enhance interemployee communication while maintaining system security. They allow virtual teams to archive text, visual, audio, and numerical data in a user-friendly format. The Internet and intranets also allow virtual teams to keep other organizational members and important external stakeholders, such as suppliers and customers, up-to-date on a team's progress.[28]

The following Managing Across Cultures Competency feature provides three examples of the successful use of virtual teams across national boundaries. These examples illustrate the ability to address specific issues through a *global mind-set.* Recall that this means the ability to scan the environment with a worldwide perspective so as to *think globally, act locally.*

Learning Objective:

3. Explain the five-stage model of team development.

DEVELOPMENTAL STAGES OF TEAMS

The formation of effective teams is not automatic. Various conditions for failure or progress occur throughout a team's development. To provide a sense of these conditions, we present a basic five-stage developmental sequence that teams may go through: forming, storming, norming, performing, and adjourning.[29] The types of work-related and socially related behaviors that may be observed differ from stage to stage. Figure 8.1 shows the five stages on the horizontal axis and the level of team maturity on the vertical axis. It also indicates that a team can fail and disband during

COMPETENCY: MANAGING ACROSS CULTURES

GLOBAL VIRTUAL TEAMS

Eastman Kodak used a virtual team to develop a single-use camera for the European market. Although the camera's functional features were similar to those marketed worldwide, Kodak wanted to adapt the product's appearance and supporting features so that it would appeal specifically to European buyers. Two German engineers worked with the design team, first in Rochester, New York, and later through computer and telecommunications links from Germany. By creating a virtual team that could function independently of time and space, Kodak was able to respond rapidly to a regional market opportunity.

Tandem Computers, which became the Tandem Division of Compaq in 1999, employed a virtual design for an urgent project involving information systems developers from London, Tokyo, and several U.S. cities. A plan for passing work from one time zone to the next was devised so that program code was written by developers in London, tested in the United States, and debugged in Tokyo. By the time the London developers came to work the next day, another cycle was ready to begin. This approach allowed the project to receive attention around the clock. Quite literally, the sun never set on Tandem's global virtual team.

Intel has used virtual teams for numerous projects: formulating and delivering sales strategies for specific products, developing new products, and manufacturing microprocessor elements. With members from company locations in the United States, Ireland, Israel, England, France, and Asia, the teams quickly come together electronically, do their work, and then disband. Members regroup in a variety of other teams as new projects surface.[30]

*For more information on these companies, visit their home pages at Eastman Kodak—**www.kodak.com**; Tandem Division—**ww.tandem.com**; and Intel—**www.intel.com**.*

Figure 8.1 **Stages of Team Development**

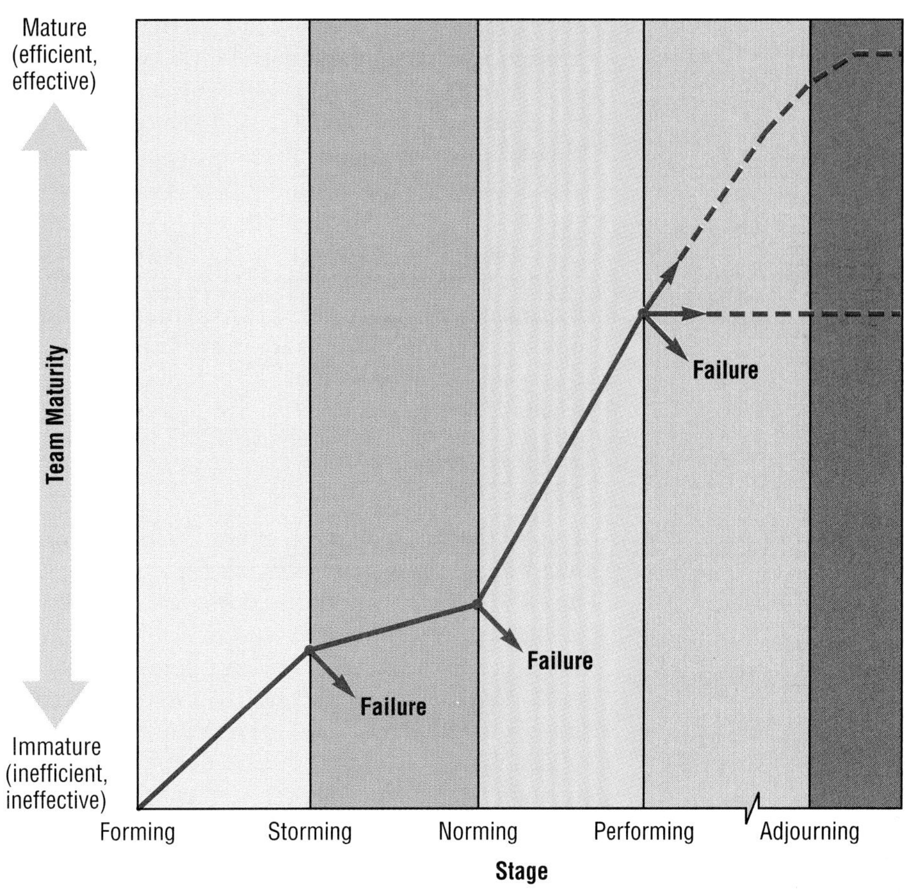

Source: Adapted from Tuckman, B. W., and Jensen, M. A. C. Stages of small-group development revisited. *Groups and Organization Studies,* 1977, 2, 419–442; Kormanski, C. Team interventions: Moving the team forward. In J. W. Pfeiffer (ed.). *The 1996 Annual: Volume 2 Consulting.* San Diego: Pfeiffer and Company, 1996, 19–26.

a stage or when moving from one stage to another. Pinpointing the developmental stage of a team at any specific time is difficult. Nevertheless, managers and team members need to understand these developmental stages because each can influence a team's effectiveness. In the following discussion we describe behaviors that might occur at each stage. Of course, teams and groups do not necessarily develop in the straightforward manner depicted in this model.[31] Team members with high levels of the seven core competencies presented throughout this book are likely to speed up and alter the stages of development presented here.

Forming Stage

In the forming stage, team members often focus on defining or understanding goals and developing procedures for performing their tasks. Team development in this stage involves getting acquainted and understanding leadership and other member roles. In terms of social behaviors, it should also deal with members' feelings and the tendency of most members to depend too much on one or two of the team's members. Otherwise, individual members might (1) keep feelings to themselves until they know the situation, (2) act more secure than they actually feel, (3) experience confusion and uncertainty about what is expected of them, (4) be nice and polite, or at least certainly not hostile, and (5) try to size up the personal benefits relative to the personal costs of being involved with the team or group.[32]

Caouette and O'Connor investigated the impact of a collaborative software system on the development and performance of two corporate teams.[33] Their model's stages of development provided the lens through which they viewed the team-building process. One strength of their study was their investigation of actual corporate teams solving real problems. They were fortunate in having access to an organization whose top managers were as interested in the results of the study as they were. This interest allowed the investigators to study the two teams in detail, using meeting transcripts and individual interviews, unhindered. One team studied had used a collaborative software system from the start, whereas the second team used the system only after the team had already matured to an extent. The investigators' findings indicated that the two teams developed and performed quite differently. The team that started with the collaborative system improved faster than the other team at each stage of development, but most noticeably at the storming stage. Caouette and O'Connor found that a collaborative software system can help a group get started (forming), but only when the group considers that use of the system is important to doing the task at hand.

Storming Stage

During the storming stage, conflicts emerge over work behaviors, relative priorities of goals, who is to be responsible for what, and the task-related guidance and direction of the leader. Social behaviors are a mixture of expressions of hostility and strong feelings. Competition over the leadership role and conflict over goals may dominate this stage. Some members may withdraw or try to isolate themselves from the emotional tension generated. The key is to manage conflict during this stage, not to suppress it or withdraw from it. The team can't effectively evolve into the third stage if its members go to either extreme. Suppressing conflict will likely create bitterness and resentment, which will last long after team members attempt to express their differences and emotions. Withdrawal may cause the team to fail.

This stage may be shortened or mostly avoided if the members use a team-building process from the beginning. This process involves the development of decision-making, interpersonal, and technical competencies when they are lacking. Team-building facilitators can help team members work through the inevitable conflicts that will surface during this and the other stages.[34]

Levi Strauss & Company implemented a team system in its factories several years ago and abandoned the individually-based piecework incentive system for a team-based incentive system. In the new system, teams of 10 to 35 employees were formed. The team members rotated in performing the tasks needed to make pairs of jeans or slacks. The pay of team members was based on team outputs. For some teams with members of comparable skills and motivation, the team approach seemed to work. But, in most cases, the teams seemed to become stuck in the storming stage. The more skilled employees on many of the teams pitted themselves against slower team members, which damaged morale and triggered infighting. Threats and insults became common. Longtime friendships dissolved as faster workers tried to banish slower ones. "You heard so much shouting, lots of times you didn't even look up from your work," recalls seamstress Mary Farmer. Adds Deborah Mulvaney, a former team coach at the Dockers plant in Powell, Tennessee: "My girls were getting into it every day of the week." Moreover, in a number of cases, efficiency—defined as the quantity of quality pants produced per hour worked—initially went down to 77 percent of the preteam level and after several years returned only to 93 percent of the preteam individual piecework level.[35]

In the previously cited study by Caouette and O'Connor, they were concerned initially that extensive use of the collaborative software system might increase the amount of conflict among team members. However, their findings were just the opposite: Use of this technology reduced the number of times team members were in conflict and the amount of time required to resolve conflict, especially at the storming stage.

Norming Stage

Work behaviors at the norming stage evolve into a sharing of information, acceptance of different options, and positive attempts to make decisions that may require compromise. During this stage, team members set the rules by which the team will operate. Social behaviors focus on empathy, concern, and positive expressions of feelings that lead to a sense of cohesion. Cooperation and a sense of shared responsibility develop among team members.

Rich Claiborne is a vice president of APAC Teleservices, a sales and service company headquartered in Cedar Raids, Iowa. He recounts the negative norm of not speaking out at meetings for fear of killing a person's career. He comments: "Speaking either wasn't valued or it was quickly tabled and you got the feeling it was considered stupid. So the tendency becomes not to say anything at all." He recalls wasting hours in meetings about a new contract because the team leader didn't want to raise issues that might kill the deal. Claiborne states: "In the past, it was really easy to hide out at meetings for me. When anyone asked if there were any problems, I would say no."[36]

The Caouette and O'Connor study concluded that use of the collaborative software system from the beginning helped the team keep on track. Team members spent a significant amount of time ensuring that all of them were acting together to perform the task (norming).

Performing Stage

During the performing stage, team members show how effectively and efficiently they can achieve results together. The roles of individual members are accepted and understood. The members have learned when they should work independently and when they should help each other. The two dashed lines in Figure 8.1 suggest that teams may differ after the performing stage. Some teams continue to learn and develop from their experiences, becoming more efficient and effective. Other teams—especially those that developed norms not fully supportive of efficiency and effectiveness—may perform only at the level needed for their survival. Excessive self-oriented behaviors, development of norms that inhibit effective and efficient task completion, poor leadership, or other factors may hurt productivity.[37] In contrast, the self-managed teams at Whole Foods Markets are designed to have norms, members, leaders, information systems, and reward mechanisms that strongly support the performing stage.

The Caouette and O'Connor study showed that the team that began initially to use collaborative software systems found that the improvements in the first stages of team development paid off later in greater productivity. They concluded that when a team gets off to a good start, it tends to perform better; good work begets more good work (performing).

Adjourning Stage

The termination of work behaviors and disengagement from social behaviors occurs during the adjourning stage. Some teams, such as a problem-solving team or a cross-functional team created to investigate and report on a specific issue within 6 months, have well-defined points of adjournment. Recall the virtual teams at Eastman Kodak, Tandem Computers, and Intel that we described in the previous Managing Across Cultures Competency feature: All had specific points of adjournment. Other teams, such as the cross-functional teams at CRI and the self-managed teams at Whole Foods Markets, may go on indefinitely. These teams will "adjourn" if top management decides to revise the current team system. In terms of relations-oriented behaviors, some degree of adjourning occurs when team members resign or are reassigned.

The Caouette and O'Connor study concluded that initial use of the collaborative system software even smoothed the way for a more satisfying conclusion to the task. The technology appeared to help the team disband because closure (adjourning) on the task was more apparent. Their study acknowledges that collaborative system software cannot make a poor team with hostile interpersonal relations function well. However, it can make a satisfactory or good team function even better.

The developmental stages of teams—regardless of the framework used to describe and explain them—are not easy to traverse.[38] Failure can occur at any point in the sequence, as indicated in Figure 8.1. Several primary factors influence team behaviors and effectiveness. These influences help explain variations in outcomes between teams and within a specific team over time.

Learning Objective:

4. Describe seven of the key influences on team effectiveness.

INFLUENCES ON TEAM EFFECTIVENESS

The influences on team and group effectiveness, as you might expect, are interrelated. Figure 8.2 identifies seven of these factors. They should be analyzed both separately and in relation to each other. This approach is necessary to gain an understanding of team dynamics and effectiveness—and to develop the competencies needed to be an effective team member and leader.

CONTEXT

The **context** (external environment) can directly affect each of the six other factors because it comprises the conditions that affect a team. The team's context might include technology, value orientations of members, physical working conditions, management practices, formal organizational rules, strategies developed by higher management, and organizational rewards and punishments. Our discussion of virtual teams, as well as the potential impacts of computer-based collaborative software systems on nonvirtual teams, illustrated the contextual influence of technology. Also, we noted the contextual influence of higher management's decision at Levi Strauss to change from an individual piecework incentive system to a team-based incentive compensation system. In that case, the influence was negative and certainly not anticipated.

If the members of a team or organization tend to be oriented much more to *individualism* than *collectivism* (contextual factor), perhaps the compensation system should be tailored so that individuals can see that their own interests are being served by being strong team contributors. This notion is based on three assumptions:

- Motivation primarily comes from the individual, not the team.
- The development of competencies and the application of behaviors are individual undertakings.
- Fairness in dealing with teams does not mean equal pay for all.[39]

Introduction of the team system at Levi Strauss seemingly did not adequately consider these assumptions, which appeared to be valid for many of its factory employees. In contrast, Kendall-Futuro Inc., (K-F), of Newport, Kentucky, has had a great deal of success with teams and contends that credit is due to its compensation program. The company uses gain sharing, in which team members are financially rewarded for gains in productivity. It no longer bases pay on a salary plus piecework combination but rather on a salary plus team performance combination. Gain sharing has been around for decades, but increasingly is being used to reward team performance. Gain sharing measures performance against a standard, and a bonus is awarded for meeting it. In gain sharing, team members normally are not penalized for failing to meet the standard. Each team member receives a basic salary and, in addition, a gain-sharing bonus when it has been earned.[40]

Kendall-Futuro's approach is one way to compensate teamwork, but it's not for everyone. There are few hard-and-fast rules for encouraging team performance, but there are several general guidelines. For example, companies that use teams most effectively in the United States generally still base a substantial portion of pay on the

Figure 8.2 **Some Influences on Team Effectiveness**

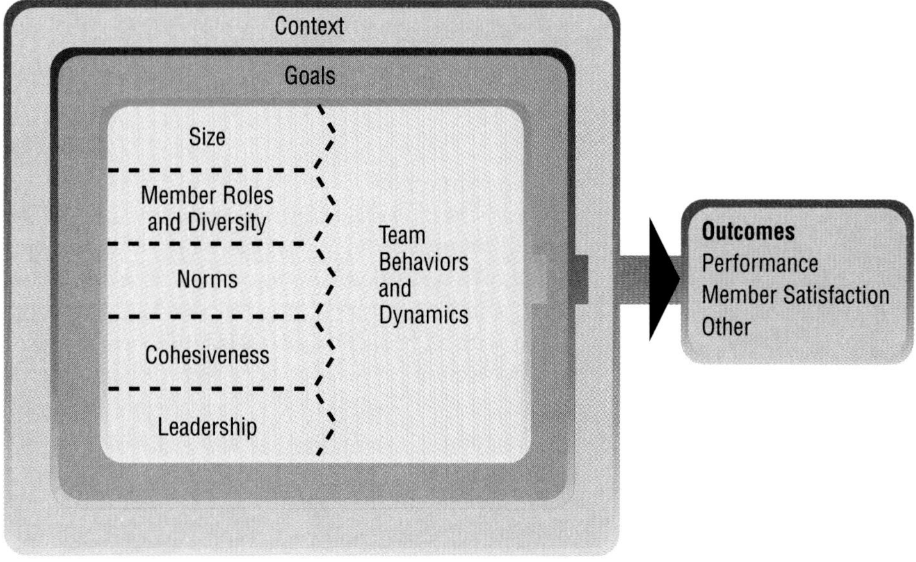

individual's contributions but with a significant difference. They make teamwork and the ability to work with others a key factor in an individual's annual performance pay.[41]

Goals

We discussed many aspects of goals in Chapter 6. Throughout the book, we return repeatedly to the concept that goals influence individual, team, and organizational effectiveness. Obviously, individual and organizational goals are likely to influence team goals and behaviors in pursuit of these goals. **Team goals** are the outcomes desired for the team as a whole, not just the individual goals of the individual members.

Both compatible and conflicting goals often exist within a team. Moreover, teams typically have both relations-oriented and task-oriented goals. Effective teams spend two-thirds or more of their time on task-oriented issues and roughly one-third or less of their time on relations-oriented issues. The pursuit of only one or the other type of goal over the long run can hurt performance, increase conflicts, and cause a team to disband. The influence of goals on group dynamics and outcomes becomes even more complex when the possible compatibilities and conflicts among member goals, broader team goals, and even broader organizational goals are considered.[42]

One mechanism for dealing with these issues is **superordinate goals,** which two or more individuals, teams, or groups might pursue but can't be achieved without their interaction and cooperation. Such goals do not replace or eliminate individual or team goals and may be qualitative or quantitative. An example of a qualitative goal is: We need to pull together for the good of the team. An example of a quantitative goal is: We need to work together if we are to reach the team goal of launching a new line within 9 months. Superordinate goals are likely to have a more powerful effect on the willingness of individuals or teams to cooperate if they are accompanied by superordinate rewards. Such rewards are given to the interacting and cooperating individuals or team members and are determined by the results of their joint efforts. Kendall-Futuro's gain-sharing compensation system is designed to link an individual's goals (higher individual pay and good merit reviews) with team goals (working together to earn bonuses awarded for meeting standards), which represent superordinate goals for each team member.

Team Size

The effective size of a team can range from 2 members to a normal upper limit of about 16 members. However, collaborative software systems and the Internet are enabling larger teams to work effectively on some tasks. Twelve members probably is the largest size that allows each member to interact easily with every other member face to face.[43] Table 8.2 shows six dimensions of teams in terms of leader behaviors, member behaviors, and team process. The likely effects of team size on each dimension are highlighted. Note that members of teams of 7 or less interact differently than do members of teams or groups of 13 to 16. A 16-member board of directors will operate differently from a 7-member board. Large boards of directors often form committees of 5 to 7 members to consider specific matters in greater depth than can the entire board.

As with all influences on teams, the effects identified in Table 8.2 need to be qualified. For example, adequate time and sufficient member commitment to a team's goals and tasks might lead to better results from a team of 9 or more members than from a hurried and less committed team of a smaller size. If a team's primary task is to tap the knowledge of the members and arrive at decisions based primarily on expertise rather than judgment, a larger team won't necessarily reflect the effects identified in Table 8.2.

In one recent survey of companies, the typical upper limit on team size was 15 members. Larger teams usually were associated with the performance of simpler tasks. Wilson Sporting Goods' surlyn cover injection golf-ball manufacturing teams, with 12 to 15 members each, are examples of simple work teams. Here, injection mold operators place golf ball cores in a mold having the appropriate dimple pattern. The surlyn cover material is injected around each core. Production of thousands of golf balls each day requires the effective functioning of a team of operators, all doing similar tasks. For problem-solving teams, the survey found that the size used most often was generally 10 or less members. As a team becomes larger, the emotional identification and sense of deeply shared commitment becomes more difficult to establish and maintain.[44]

Team Member Roles and Diversity

Similarities and differences among members and their roles influence team behavior, dynamics, and outcomes. Obviously, managers can't alter the basic personalities or attributes of team members (see Chapters 2 and 3). Therefore attempts to influence their behavioral roles in a team or group are more useful.[45] These roles may be for-

Table 8.2 Typical Effects of Size on Teams

	TEAM SIZE		
DIMENSION	2–7 Members	8–12 Members	13–16 Members
1. Demands on leader	Low	Moderate	High
2. Direction by leader	Low	Moderate	Moderate to high
3. Member tolerance of direction by leader	Low to moderate	Moderate	High
4. Member inhibition	Low	Moderate	High
5. Use of rules and procedures	Low	Moderate	Moderate to high
6. Time taken to reach a decision	Low	Moderate	High

mally classified as task-oriented, relations-oriented, and self-oriented. Each member has the potential for performing each of these roles over time.

Task-Oriented Role. The **task-oriented role** of a team member involves facilitating and coordinating work-related decision making. This role may include

- *initiating* new ideas or different ways of considering team problems or goals and suggesting solutions to difficulties, including modification of team procedures;
- *seeking information* to clarify suggestions and obtain key facts;
- *giving information* that is relevant to the team's problem, issue, or task;
- *coordinating* and clarifying relationships among ideas and suggestions, pulling ideas and suggestions together, and coordinating members' activities; and
- *evaluating* the team's effectiveness, including questioning the logic, facts, or practicality of other members' suggestions.

Relations-Oriented Role. The **relations-oriented role** of a team member involves building team-centered feelings and social interactions. This role may include

- *encouraging* members through praise and acceptance of their ideas, as well as indicating warmth and solidarity;
- *harmonizing* and mediating intrateam conflicts and tensions;
- *encouraging* participation of others by saying, "Let's hear from Megan," or "Why not limit the length of contributions so all can react to the problem?" or "Rahul, do you agree?"
- *expressing* standards for the team to achieve or apply in evaluating the quality of team processes, raising questions about team goals, and assessing team progress in light of these goals; and
- *following* by going along passively or constructively and serving as a friendly member.

Self-Oriented Role. The **self-oriented role** of a team member involves the person's self-centered behaviors that are at the expense of the team or group. This role may include

- *blocking progress* by being negative, stubborn, and unreasoningly resistant—for example, the person may repeatedly try to bring back an issue that the team had considered carefully and rejected;
- *seeking recognition* by calling attention to oneself, including boasting, reporting on personal achievements, and in various ways avoiding being placed in a presumed inferior position;
- *dominating* by asserting authority, manipulating the team or certain individuals, using flattery or proclaiming superiority to gain attention, and interrupting the contributions of others; and
- *avoiding* involvement by maintaining distance from others and remaining insulated from interaction.

Effective teams often are composed of members who play both task-oriented and relations-oriented roles over time. A particularly adept individual who reveals behaviors valued by the team probably has relatively high *status*—the relative rank of an individual in a team. A team dominated by individuals who are performing mainly self-oriented behaviors is likely to be ineffective because the individuals do not adequately address team goals and needed collaboration.

Table 8.3 provides a questionnaire for evaluating some of your task-oriented, relations-oriented, and self-oriented behaviors as a team member. The questionnaire asks you to assess your tendency to engage in each role, on a scale of 1 to 5 (or almost never to almost always). Member composition and roles greatly influence team or group behaviors. Either too much or too little of certain member behaviors can adversely affect team performance and member satisfaction.[46] Scores of 20–25 on task

Table 8.3

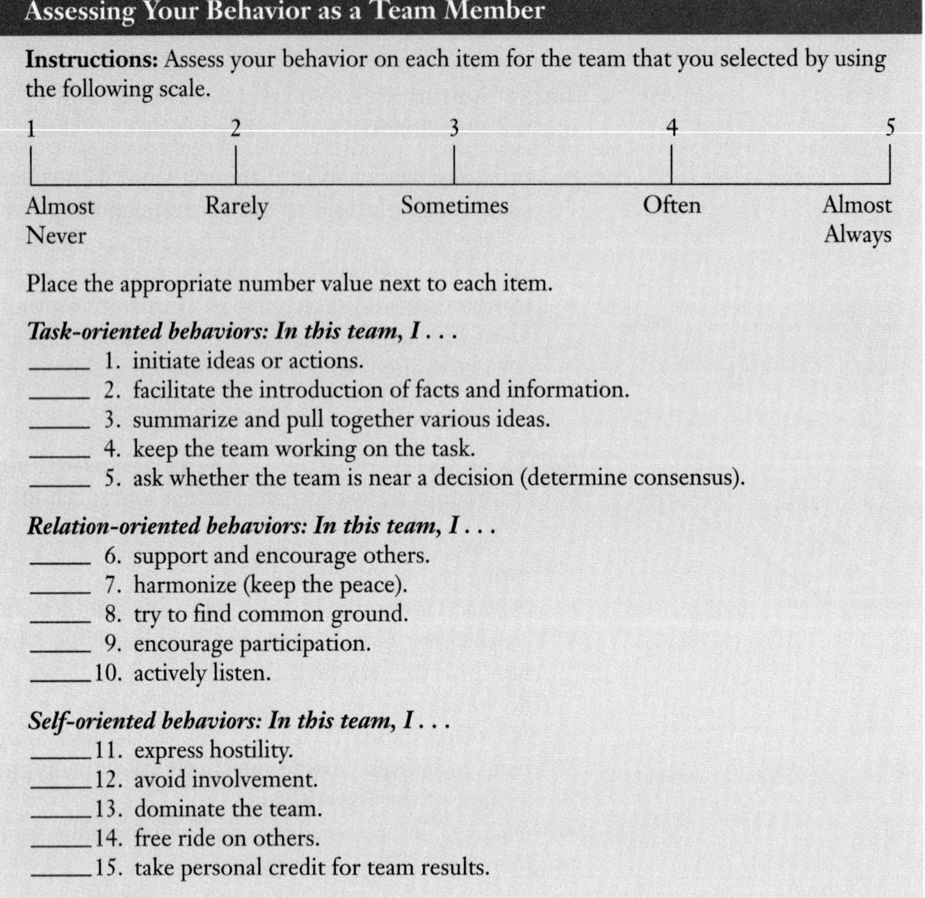

Assessing Your Behavior as a Team Member

Instructions: Assess your behavior on each item for the team that you selected by using the following scale.

1	2	3	4	5
Almost Never	Rarely	Sometimes	Often	Almost Always

Place the appropriate number value next to each item.

Task-oriented behaviors: In this team, I . . .

_____ 1. initiate ideas or actions.
_____ 2. facilitate the introduction of facts and information.
_____ 3. summarize and pull together various ideas.
_____ 4. keep the team working on the task.
_____ 5. ask whether the team is near a decision (determine consensus).

Relation-oriented behaviors: In this team, I . . .

_____ 6. support and encourage others.
_____ 7. harmonize (keep the peace).
_____ 8. try to find common ground.
_____ 9. encourage participation.
_____ 10. actively listen.

Self-oriented behaviors: In this team, I . . .

_____ 11. express hostility.
_____ 12. avoid involvement.
_____ 13. dominate the team.
_____ 14. free ride on others.
_____ 15. take personal credit for team results.

oriented behaviors, 20–25 on relations-oriented behaviors, and 5–10 on self-oriented behaviors by each member probably would indicate an effectively functioning team.

Team Diversity. The growing diversity of the workforce adds complexity—beyond individual differences in personality and behavioral roles in teams—to understanding team behavior and processes.[47] As discussed in previous chapters, the composition of the workforce is undergoing continued change in terms of age, gender, race, cultural values, physical well-being, lifestyle preferences, ethnicity, educational background, religious preference, occupational background, and the like. Team effectiveness will be hampered if members hold false stereotypes about each other in terms of such differences.[48]

Although attitudes are changing, diversity too often is viewed more negatively than positively. This negative reaction may be due, in large part, to six underlying attitudes involving stereotypical false assumptions.

1. Otherness is a deficiency.
2. Diversity poses a threat to the organization's effective functioning.
3. Expressed discomfort with the dominant group's values is perceived as oversensitivity by minority groups.
4. Members of all groups want to become and should be more like the dominant group.
5. Equal treatment means the same treatment.
6. Managing diversity simply requires changing the people, not the organizational culture.

The goal of achieving diversity creates unique challenges in making it work for rather than against the long-term interests of individuals, teams, and organizations. Once a we–they distinction is perceived, people tend to discriminate against others who are different. Moreover, they tend to perceive these others as inferior, adversarial, and competitive.[49]

The attitude expressed throughout this book about diversity is that of **positive multiculturalism.** This condition allows an individual to acquire new competencies, perspectives, and attitudes that improve the person's ability to relate effectively to others within the same or other teams regardless of their backgrounds and characteristics. Positive multiculturalism is additive; that is, individuals can maintain their self-defining attributes while adding competencies and positive attitudes to help them form and maintain sound working relationships with others. Thus a person can become bilingual by learning English but retaining a native language.[50]

IBM has embraced diversity and positive multiculturalism as an imperative that requires managed change. Top-level leadership is being provided in this process of planned change, which grew out of a comprehensive diagnosis of the pressure for and resistance to positive multiculturalism. The following Managing Change Competency feature shows that IBM is making extensive use of various types of teams and groups in this effort.

COMPETENCY: MANAGING CHANGE

IBM's Planned Diversity Initiatives

Addressing diversity on a global level is crucial at IBM, where the global diversity theme is "none of us is as strong as all of us." Diversity at IBM is being fostered worldwide through a system of diversity councils and teams. These groups help ensure that everyone at IBM can be a part of the dialogue around diversity, says Ted Childs, IBM's vice president for global workforce diversity.

IBM's 48 diversity councils operate in geographic areas worldwide, including Latin America, Asia Pacific, Europe, and several U.S. sites. Their purpose is to advise management in their regions about diversity issues, says Childs, who cochairs the company's Global Diversity Council with IBM's highest-ranking woman in Japan.

Achieving a balance between work and personal life is one of six global workforce challenges being addressed by the council. The other challenges are the global marketplace, cultural awareness and acceptance, diversity of the management team, advancement of women, and integration of people with disabilities. "Each IBM geographic region is executing strategies to address these challenges," says Childs.

Eight formal executive-level diversity teams organized by constituent groups report to senior management on the issues relevant to their respective constituencies—women, African Americans, Hispanics, Native Americans, Asian Americans, gays and lesbians, the disabled, and white men. At the local level, 64 volunteer Diversity Network Teams, also organized by constituency and completely employee driven, are active. "It's our hope that all of the groups will help us maintain or sustain an ongoing dialogue about issues so that if things emerge that are of interest, we talk about them," says Childs.

"Looking at the company through the lens of their constituency," continues Childs, "the task forces were asked to focus on three key questions: First, what's required for your group to feel welcomed and valued at IBM? Second, what can we do in partnership with you to maximize the productivity of your group? And what actions can the company take in the pursuit of market share to influence the buying decisions of your constituency?"

Taken together, these questions illustrate IBM's strong focus on diversity as an issue that links employees and customers. Childs concludes: "Workforce diversity is the bridge between the workplace and the marketplace."[51]

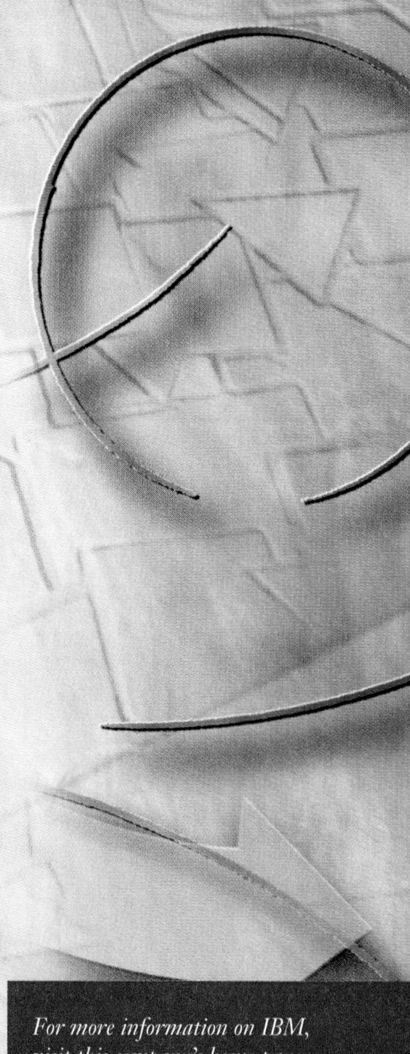

For more information on IBM, visit this company's home page at www.IBM.com.

NORMS

Norms are the rules and patterns of behavior that are accepted and expected by members of a team.[52] They help define the behaviors that members believe to be necessary to help them reach their goals. Over time, every team establishes norms and enforces them on its members. (Norms often are more rigidly defined and enforced in informal groups—by peer pressure—than in formally organized teams.) Such norms may further or inhibit achievement of organizational goals.

Norms Versus Organizational Rules. Norms differ from organizational rules. Managers may write and distribute formal organizational rules to employees in the form of manuals and memoranda. At times, employees refuse to accept such rules and ignore them. In contrast, norms are informal, often unwritten expectations that are enforced by team members. If a member consistently and excessively violates these norms, the other members sanction the individual in some way. Sanctions may range from physical abuse to threats to ostracism to positive inducements (rewards) for compliance. Those who consistently adhere to the team's norms typically receive praise, recognition, and acceptance from the other members.

Team members may be only vaguely aware of some of the norms that are operating, but they should be made aware of these norms for at least two reasons. First, awareness increases the potential for individual and team freedom and maturity. Second, norms can positively or negatively influence the effectiveness of individuals, teams, and organizations.[53] For example, team norms of minimizing and correcting defects are likely to reinforce an organization's formal quality standards.

Relation to Goals. Teams often adopt norms to help them attain their goals.[54] Moreover, some organizational development efforts are aimed at helping members evaluate whether their team's norms are consistent with, neutral with respect to, or conflict with organizational goals. (See Chapter 18 for a discussion of organizational development.) For example, a team may claim that one of its goals is to become more efficient to help it meet organizational goals. However, the team members' behaviors might be inconsistent with this stated goal; that is, the team's norms might actually inhibit production and attempts to make changes.

Even if team members are aware of such norms, they may rationalize them as being necessary in order to achieve their own goals. Members may claim that producing more than the norm will "burn them out" or reduce product or service quality, resulting in lower long-term effectiveness. If a team's goals include minimizing managerial influence and increasing the opportunity for social interaction, its members could perceive norms restricting employee output as desirable.

Enforcing Norms. Teams don't establish norms for every conceivable situation. They generally form and enforce norms with respect to behaviors that they believe to be particularly important. Members are most likely to enforce norms under one or more of the following conditions.[55]

- Norms aid in team survival and provide benefits. For instance a team might develop a norm not to discuss individual salaries with other members in the organization to avoid calling attention to pay inequities.
- Norms simplify or make predictable the behaviors expected of members. When coworkers go out for lunch together, there can be some awkwardness about how to split the bill at the end of the meal. A group may develop a norm that results in some highly predictable way of behaving—split the bill evenly, take turns picking up the tab, or individually pay for what each ordered.
- Norms help avoid embarrassing interpersonal situations. Norms might develop about not discussing romantic involvements in or out of the office (so that differences in moral values don't become too obvious) or about not getting together

socially in members' homes (so that differences in taste or income don't become too obvious).

Norms express the central values and goals of the team and clarify what is distinctive about its identity. Employees of an advertising agency may wear unconventional but stylish clothing. Other professionals may view their doing so as deviant behavior. However, the advertising agency personnel may say, "We think of ourselves, personally and professionally, as trendsetters, and being fashionably dressed conveys that to our clients and the public."

Conforming to Norms. Conformity may result from the pressures to adhere to norms.[56] The two basic types of conformity are compliance and personal acceptance. **Compliance conformity** occurs when a person's behavior reflects the team's desired behavior because of real or imagined pressure. In fact, some individuals may conform for a variety of reasons, even though they don't personally agree with the norms. They may think that the appearance of a united front is necessary for success in accomplishing team goals. On a more personal level, someone may comply in order to be liked and accepted by others. Meeting this need may apply especially to members of lower status in relation to those of higher status, such as a subordinate and a superior. Finally, someone may comply because the costs of conformity are much less than the costs of nonconformity, which could threaten the personal relationships in the team.

The second type of conformity is based on positive personal support of the norms. In **personal acceptance conformity,** the individual's behavior and attitudes are consistent with the team's norms and goals. This type of conformity is much stronger than compliance conformity because the person truly believes in the goals and norms. At its Camry assembly plant in Georgetown, Kentucky, Toyota makes explicit use of teams to develop norms and peer pressure in support of organizational goals. Management makes extensive use of *community of fate* as a superordinate goal at all levels—that is, we're all in this together—as a means of achieving personal acceptance conformity.[57]

All of the preceding helps explain why some members of highly conforming teams may easily change their behavior (compliance type of conformity), whereas others may oppose changes and find them highly stressful (personal acceptance type of conformity). Without norms and reasonable conformity to them, teams would be chaotic and few tasks could be accomplished. Conversely, excessive and blind conformity may threaten expressions of individualism and a team's ability to change and learn.

Cohesiveness

Cohesiveness is the strength of the members' desire to remain in a team and their commitment to it. Cohesiveness is influenced by the degree of compatibility between team goals and individual members' goals. Members who have a strong desire to remain in a team and personally accept its goals form a highly cohesive team.

This relationship between cohesiveness and conformity isn't a simple one. Low cohesiveness usually is associated with low conformity. However, high cohesiveness doesn't exist only in the presence of high conformity. High-performing teams may have high member commitment and a desire to stick together while simultaneously respecting and encouraging individual differences. This situation is more likely to develop when cohesiveness arises from trusting relationships and a common commitment to performance goals.

In confronting problems, members of a cohesive team are likely to encourage and support nonconformity.[58] For example, a **hot group** performs extremely well and is dedicated; it usually is small, and its members are turned on by an exciting and challenging goal. Hot groups completely engage their members, capturing their attention to the exclusion of almost everything else. For its members, the characteristics of a hot group are the same: vital, absorbing, full of debate and laughter, and very hard working.[59] They may arise from the need for dealing with major challenges and changes, innovation, complex projects, or crises. For example, the development of the Boeing 777 jetliner spawned several hot groups.

Relation to Groupthink. When decision-making teams are both conforming and cohesive, a phenomenon called groupthink can emerge. **Groupthink** is an agreement-at-any-cost mentality that results in ineffective team decision making and poor decisions. Irving L. Janis, who coined the term, focused his research on high-level government policy teams faced with difficult problems in a complex and dynamic environment. Team decision making is common in all types of organizations, so the possibility of groupthink exists in both private-sector and public-sector organizations. Figure 8.3 outlines the initial conditions that are likely to lead to groupthink, its characteristics, and the types of defective decision making that result from it.

The characteristics of groupthink include the following.

- An *illusion of invulnerability* is shared by most or all team members, which creates excessive optimism and encourages taking extreme risks. Statements such as "No one can stop us now," or "The other group has a bunch of jerks," often are made by members suffering from an illusion of invulnerability.
- *Collective rationalization* discounts warnings that might lead team members to reconsider their assumptions before committing themselves to major policy decisions. In the early 1970s, U.S. auto executives made statements such as: "We are confident that only a small segment of auto buyers are willing to buy Japanese-made autos."
- An *unquestioned belief* in the team's inherent morality leads members to ignore the ethical or moral consequences of their decisions.
- *Stereotypical views* of rivals and adversaries (other groups) picture them as too evil to warrant genuine attempts to negotiate or too weak or stupid to counter whatever attempts are made to defeat their purpose.
- *Direct pressure* is exerted on any member who expresses strong arguments against any of the team's illusions, stereotypes, or commitments, making clear that such dissent is contrary to what is expected of all loyal members. The leader might say, "What's the matter? Aren't you a team member anymore?"

Figure 8.3 **The Groupthink Process**

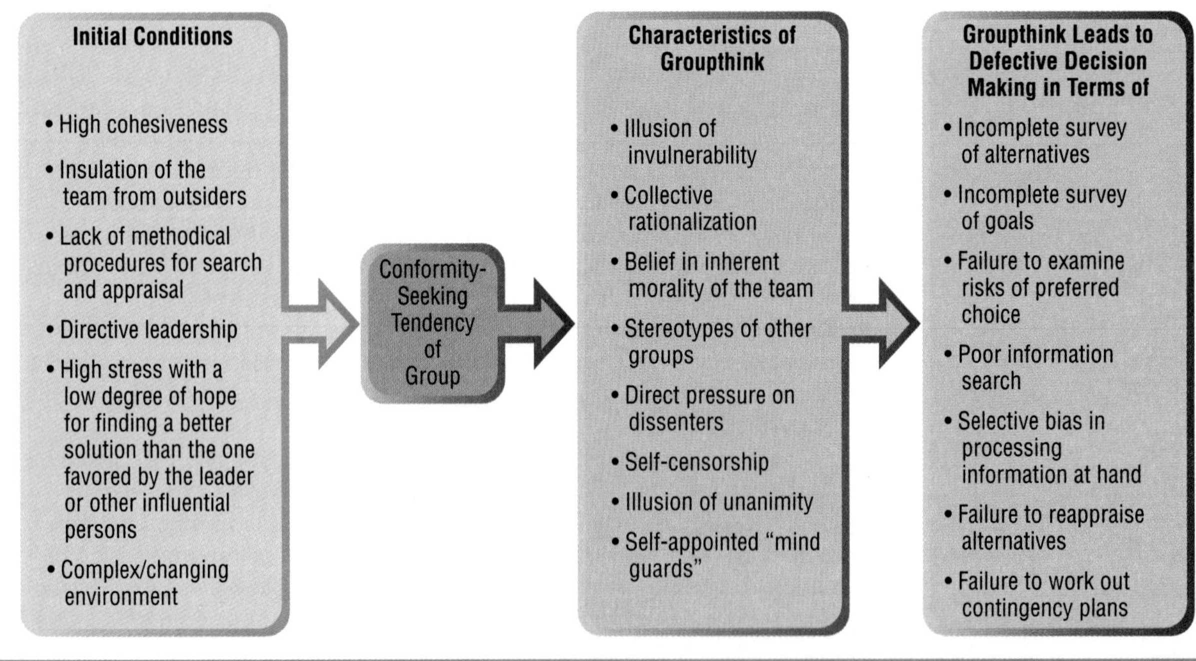

- *Self-censorship* of deviations from any apparent team consensus reflects the inclination of members to minimize the importance of their doubts and not present counterarguments. A member might think: If everyone feels that way, my feelings must be wrong.
- A *shared illusion of unanimity* results, in part, from self-censorship and is reinforced by the false assumption that silence implies consent.
- The emergence of *self-appointed "mind-guard"* members serves to protect the team from adverse information that might shatter the shared complacency about the effectiveness and morality of their decision.[60]

In a recent study of 23 top-management teams, the CEOs of 6 expressed concern about groupthink in their organizations' teams. The CEOs of a large financial retailing company and a global financial services firm commented:

- We're all too much on the same wavelength. We were all part of a management buyout four years ago. We've been through some tough battles together, and now we share a lot of common views. But in this industry you have to be fresh and experimental. If we all agree on everything, how new or exciting can our ideas be?
- There's a lack of genuine debate. Sometimes there's a half-hearted "devil's advocate" gesture, but they really don't confront each other or me on the big issues. We're too comfortable, too self-congratulatory. It's gotten obvious to me in the past few months. I have to find a way to shake things up.[61]

Groupthink isn't inevitable, and several steps can be taken to avoid it. For example, a leader should try to remain neutral and encourage dialogue and new ideas. Small subgroups or outside consultants can be used to introduce new viewpoints. People holding diverse views can be encouraged to present them.

Impact on Outcomes. Team performance and productivity can be affected by cohesiveness. **Productivity** is the relationship between the inputs consumed (labor hours, raw materials, money, machines, and the like) and the outputs created (quantity and quality of goods and services). Cohesiveness and productivity can be related, particularly for teams having high performance goals. If the team is successful in reaching those goals, the positive feedback of its successes may heighten member commitment and satisfaction. For example, a winning basketball team is more likely to be cohesive than one with a poor record, everything else being equal. Also, a cohesive basketball team may be more likely to win games. Conversely, low cohesiveness may interfere with a team's ability to win games. The reason is that members aren't as likely to communicate and cooperate to the extent necessary to reach the team's goals. High team cohesiveness actually may be associated with low efficiency if team goals conflict with organizational goals. Team members might think that the boss holds them accountable rather than that they hold themselves accountable to achieve results. Therefore the relationships among cohesiveness, productivity, and performance can't be anticipated or understood unless the team's goals and norms are also known.

Leadership

Studies of teams in organizations emphasize the importance of emergent, or informal, leadership in accomplishing goals. An **informal leader** is an individual whose influence in a team grows over time and usually reflects a unique ability to help the team reach its goals.

Multiple Leaders. Team leadership is often thought of in terms of one person. The CRI and Whole Foods Markets teams had different leaders over time and for different tasks. Moreover, because a team often has both relations-oriented and task-oriented goals, it may have two or more leaders. These two types of goals may require different skills and leadership styles, creating a total set of demands that one person may have difficulty satisfying. Informal leaders of teams aren't likely to emerge unless the formal leader ignores task-related responsibilities or lacks the necessary skills to carry them out.[62] In contrast, relations-oriented leaders of teams are likely to emerge informally.

Effective Team Leaders. Leaders greatly influence virtually all aspects of team composition and behaviors (e.g., size, members and roles, norms, goals, and context). A leader often assumes a key role in the relations between the team and external groups, such as customers or suppliers, and often influences the selection of new members. Even when the team participates in the selection process, the team leader may screen potential members, thereby limiting the number and range of candidates, as at Whole Foods Markets.

Recall the Managing Teams Competency feature on Whole Foods Markets. Top management, especially John Mackey (founder and current CEO) established and emphasizes a set of core values and principles to reflect what is truly important to the organization as a whole. Four of its core values and principles focus on the central role of teams.

- Our success is dependent upon the collective energy and intelligence of all our Team Members. We strive to create a work environment where motivated Team Members can flourish and succeed to their highest potential. We appreciate effort and reward results.
- The fundamental work unit of the company is the self-directed Team. Teams meet regularly to discuss issues, solve problems, and appreciate each other's contributions. Every Team Member belongs to a Team.
- We believe knowledge is power and we support our Team Members' right to access information that impacts their jobs. Our books are open to our Team Members, including our annual individual compensation report. We also recognize everyone's right to be listened to and heard regardless of their point of view.
- Our company continually improves through unleashing the collective creativity and intelligence of all our Team Members. We recognize that everyone has a contribution to make. We keep getting better at what we do.[63]

The seven key influences on team behaviors and dynamics discussed so far (see Figure 8.2) make the creation and maintenance of effective teams no easy leadership task. We discuss leadership and the qualities and characteristics of effective leaders in detail in Chapters 11 and 12. For now, we contrast the team leadership abilities of John Mackey at Whole Foods Markets with those of Joan McCoy at ARCO Alaska prior to her learning the importance of team leadership abilities. As demonstrated in the Managing Self Competency feature on the next page, McCoy did assess and accept her weaknesses in team leadership, set new professional development goals, and adopted new behaviors and attitudes.

Learning Objective:

5. Explain the self-managing team decision-making model.

TEAM DECISION MAKING

The many different types of goals, problems, and tasks confronting an organization require varying degrees of interdependency among individuals, teams, and external groups. They require both individual and team decision making. Organizations can incur excessive costs if either individual or team decision-making approaches are used improperly. The unnecessary use of team decision making is wasteful because the participants' time could have been used more effectively on other tasks; it creates boredom, resulting in a feeling that time is being squandered, and reduces motivation. Conversely, the improper use of individual decision making can result in poor coordi-

COMPETENCY: MANAGING SELF

JOAN MCCOY LEARNS TEAM LEADERSHIP

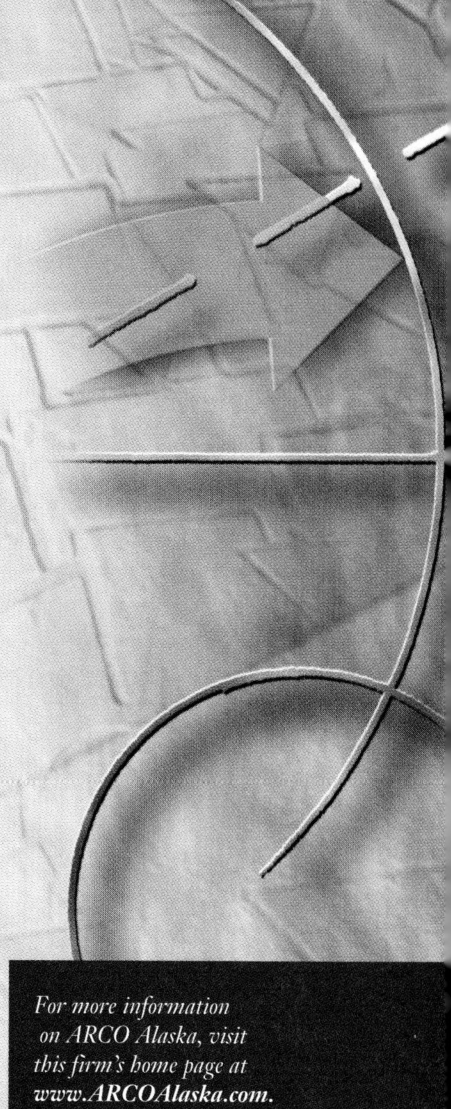

Joan McCoy, director of community relations at ARCO Alaska, was devastated. She had been passed over for a promotion that she thought she had earned. She was sitting in her office after receiving the bad news, "feeling like someone had knocked the air out of me," she recalls. "I was angry and confused, and I guess I sulked for a while. Then I went into my manager's office and asked her what I needed to do to get promoted. She told me to get leadership-development training."

That advice surprised McCoy, who had never imagined that her leadership skills needed improving. She had handled a delicate (and potentially perilous) job for one of the largest oil companies in the United States. She had accepted her responsibilities and performed in the field with care and commitment.

But when dealing with her colleagues at work, McCoy failed to use the interpersonal skills that had made her so successful with public groups. To her peers, her zeal to succeed made her seem cold, aloof, and standoffish. She was so afraid of doing less-than-perfect work that she would delegate only the most minor assignments to her staff. This frustrated McCoy's team and gave her a crushing workload.

"I thought I would be rewarded if I kept my nose to the grindstone," she says. "I never worried about my relationships with coworkers. And so I was oblivious to problems that were all around me."

Several sessions with Lois Frankel, a senior partner at Corporate Coaching International based in Los Angeles, helped open her eyes. Frankel surveyed McCoy's coworkers, superiors, and subordinates about her performance. Their consensus: McCoy had failed to build a team; she didn't listen; and she didn't offer constructive feedback.

Ironically, her isolation had caused her to get little recognition for her accomplishments. "I figured that people knew I was doing a good job. But according to the feedback I got, they actually didn't know. So I began using e-mail to promote my team. I've also been trying to visit a few key executives in the company each week. Overall, I'm becoming more visible."

When dealing with her staff, McCoy reminds herself to be inclusive. Before, she simply bulldozed ahead without consulting anyone; now she asks for input from staffers. "I still like to be in control, and sometimes it's hard to let go. But I'm learning that when you share the workload, you also get to share the worry."[64]

*For more information on ARCO Alaska, visit this firm's home page at **www.ARCOAlaska.com.***

nation, little creativity, and numerous errors. In brief, team decision making is likely to be superior to individual decision making when

1. the greater diversity of information, experience, and approaches to be found in a team is important to the task at hand;
2. acceptance of the decisions arrived at is crucial for effective implementation by team members;
3. participation is important for reinforcing the values of representation versus authoritarianism and demonstrating respect for individual members through team processes; and
4. the team members rely on each other in performing their jobs.

The teams that we have commented on at CRI, McGraw-Hill Higher Education Group, Macy's, Boeing, Whole Foods Markets, Eastman Kodak, Tandem Computers, Intel, Kendall-Futuro, IBM, and Toyota appear to meet these criteria for the use of team decision making.

SELF-MANAGING TEAM DECISION-MAKING MODEL

Figure 8.4 shows one model for effective self-managing team decision making when a team is operating with a high degree of empowerment.[65] Its use may improve decision making for all types of empowered teams—from a class project team to the cross-functional teams at CRI to the self-managed teams at Whole Foods Markets. This model is based on the assumption that the team has achieved the performing stage of development (see Figure 8.1). In general, self-managed teams are empowered to engage regularly in all phases of decision making, as depicted in the model.

Phase I: Problem Definition. In *phase I*, a self-managing team should fully explore, clarify, and define the problem. Team members may assume that they know what the problem is in a situation, but they may be wrong. They could be looking at only a symptom or a part of the problem. Even when it has correctly identified the problem, the team may need to collect more detailed information and define it more sharply. Thus a key part of problem definition is the generation and collection of information. Problem definition also requires that the team identify or recognize the goals that it is trying to achieve by solving the problem. When team members are clear about goals, which in itself may be a major problem area, they can determine better whether the problem really exists and, if it does, the relative priority that should be assigned to solving it. If members can respond *yes* to questions such as the following, the team dynamics involved in phase I probably were effective.

- Was everyone who might have relevant data present or represented at the team meeting?
- Were those most directly involved in defining the problem encouraged by the leader and other team members to give information?
- Did the team members take the information relating to the problem and consider how it all fits together?
- Was everyone asked whether he or she agrees with the final problem statement as written?

Phase II: Idea Generation. *Phase II* prolongs the idea-generating process and discourages premature conclusions. If a self-managing team is more solution-oriented than problem-oriented it may choose the first or one of the first solutions suggested. An eventual solution can be much better if the team considers many ideas and several alternative solutions. The more ideas generated and creativity encouraged, the more likely the team is to come up with good potential solutions. The team dynamics involved in phase II probably were effective if members can respond *yes* to questions such as the following.

Figure 8.4 **Self-Managing Team Model**

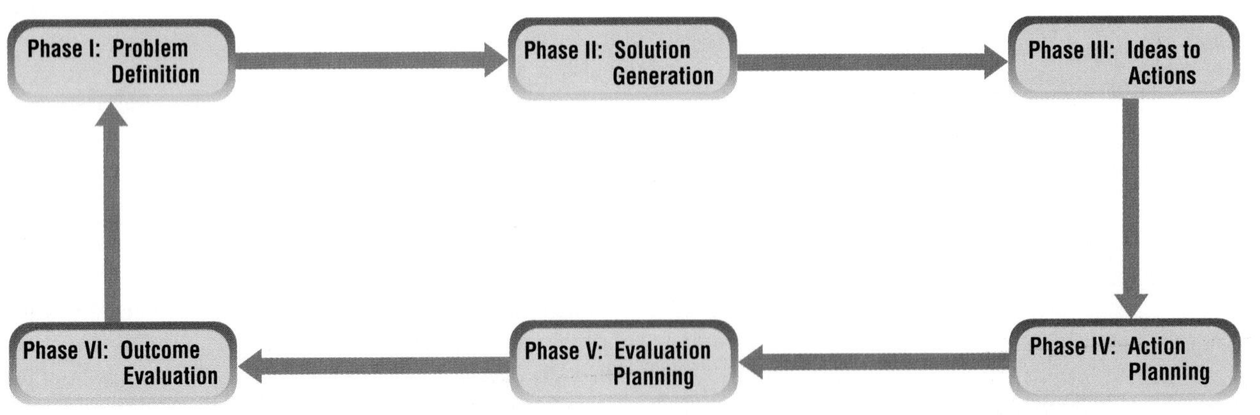

- Have all the resources of the team been used to generate ideas?
- Did the leader and other team members take time to encourage those who might be slower at expressing ideas, pausing and asking for more ideas when necessary?
- Did the team members take time to examine all the ideas and combine them into sets of alternatives?
- Was criticism tactfully discouraged and evaluative comments postponed (e.g., asking for another alternative instead of giving criticism)?

Phase III: Idea Evaluation. *Phase III* focuses on the team's evaluation of ideas and alternatives leading to a likely solution. Even though one alternative may not work alone, it could provide a useful part of the solution. Thus the members of a self-managing team should take time to combine the best parts of alternative solutions and then carefully evaluate each possibility. Rather than weeding out poor alternatives (and making those who suggested them feel defensive), team members should select the best ones and concentrate on them until everyone can agree on a solution or recognize the need to move on. A *yes* to questions such as the following suggests that team dynamics were on target in phase III.

- Did team members examine the alternatives in terms of human, financial, and other costs associated with each and in terms of new problems that might arise?
- Were the team members able to evaluate ideas critically without attacking those who proposed or supported various ideas?
- Is the chosen solution related to the problem statement and goals developed earlier?
- Was final consensus reached on a trial solution? If not, was the extent of agreement among team members clearly established?

Phase IV: Action Planning. *Phase IV* involves deciding on the actions needed to make the plan work smoothly. Members of a self-managing team should anticipate implementation problems, make plans to involve those whose support will be needed, and assign and accept responsibilities for taking action. Only if the team members determine who is to do what and when, can the agreed upon solution get a fair test. Key questions requiring a *yes* response in phase IV include the following.

- Did team members identify the various forces that might help or hinder the actions being planned?
- Were all team members involved in the discussion, particularly in giving information needed to define actions and ensure that essential steps weren't left out?
- Were all the needed resources (material as well as human, including people not present) for taking each of the actions clearly identified?
- Did each person who accepted responsibility for a task make a clear commitment to carry out that responsibility?

Phase V: Evaluation Learning. *Phase V* offers the greatest potential for team development in decision making. To take advantage of this opportunity, team members must determine the type of information needed, who will obtain it, and when it must be collected. Sometimes teams stop at phase IV, losing the chance to learn from experience. Even if a solution is a tremendous success, team members benefit from knowing what made the solution work so that it can be applied, when appropriate, to the solution of other problems. If a solution is a total disaster, team members may feel like hiding the fact that they had anything to do with it. However, members of a self-managing team who know what went wrong can avoid making the same mistakes in the future. In real life, solutions generally work moderately well; most are neither great successes nor great failures. By keeping track of what is happening, team members can make minor improvements or adjustments that will help significantly in other team problem-solving efforts. Diagnosis should not be based on guesswork but on hard, accurate information about the effect of actions. Questions requiring a *yes* response for effective team dynamics in phase V include the following.

- Have the team members reviewed the desired outcomes and developed measures to indicate the degree of success achieved in attaining the outcomes?
- Were any differences among team members regarding definitions and measures of success openly discussed, explored, and resolved?
- Were contingency plans outlined for critical steps so that the overall plan could continue with modification but without major interruption?
- Was a timetable developed for step-by-step interim evaluation learning (monitoring of effects as actions were taken)?

Phase VI: Outcome Evaluation Learning. When enough information has been collected to determine how well the solution worked, a self-managing team should move to *phase VI* and comprehensively evaluate the outcome. The outcome demonstrates whether the problem was solved. If the problem or some part of it remains, the team can recycle it by looking at the information, perhaps even redefining the problem, and coming up with new ideas or trying a previously rejected alternative. This phase also involves a review and evaluation of how well the team members worked together. As we suggested in the discussion of team development stages, mature teams and groups can openly and constructively learn from outcomes. A response of *yes* to each of the following questions indicates effective team dynamics during phase VI.

- Were team members able to compare, in detail, the outcomes with the goals set earlier?
- Were all team members involved in influencing both what the team did and how the team operated?
- Did team members determine whether any new problems were created and, if so, then make plans to deal with them?
- Did team members learn to solve problems in accordance with this decision-making model (Figure 8.4)?

An increasing number of organizations that make use of teams are incorporating their versions of the recommended phases of team decision making presented here. For example, Table 8.4 presents Ford Motor Company's 8D team problem-solving process. Included is each step number, the name of the corresponding process in the step, and what should be done within that step. We added a fourth column to indicate the phase of decision making in the team model that most directly corresponds to Ford's prescribed problem-solving step for its teams.

Assessment of Model

Team decision making rarely proceeds as neatly or systematically as suggested in the descriptions of these six phases.[66] Self-managing and other types of empowered teams may jump around or skip phases because of the nature of the problem being solved or the team's diversity. However, this self-managing team decision-making model provides a solid foundation for improving the decision-making process of most teams. It stresses the need for competence and a norm of full participation by team members. Teams—even if operating properly—probably are more effective in phase III (ideas to actions) through phase V (evaluation planning) than in phases I, II, and VI. Phase I (problem definition) and phase II (solution generation) benefit from processes different from the usual face-to-face interactions of individuals. As indicated in Table 8.4, Ford Motor's 8D team problem-solving process provides an explicit guide for increasing the likelihood that its teams will address most of the questions and issues presented for all the phases.

In addition to those suggested here, various other processes and procedures have been developed for improving the effectiveness of decision-making teams. For example, in the next section, we consider aids especially designed to improve team effectiveness in phases I and II.

Table 8.4

Ford Motor's 8D Team Problem-Solving Process

STEP NO.	PROCESS STEP	WHAT TO DO	PHASES IN SELF-MANAGING TEAM MODEL
1	Become aware of the problem.	Make each problem-solving team member aware of bad parts, processes, nonconformances, and customer concerns.	Phase I
2	Use team approach.	Establish a small group of people with the process or product knowledge, allocated time, authority, and skill in the technical discipline to solve the problem and implement corrective actions. This team is to have a designated leader.	Assumes that team already is established
3	Describe the problem.	Specify the customer problem by identifying in specific terms the who, what, when, where, why, how, and how many of the problem. • Analyze existing data. • Establish operational definition.	Phases I and II
4	Implement and verify interim (containment) actions.	Define and implement containment actions to isolate the problem from any customer until permanent corrective action is available. Verify effectiveness of actions.	Phases II, IV, and V Quick fix and process
5	Define and verify root cause.	Check team composition and process. Identify potential causes. • Review and improve the problem description. • Evaluate each potential cause by comparison to the problem description. Select likely causes. • Test each potential cause through experimentation and statistical analysis. • Identify alternative corrective actions to eliminate root cause.	Phases II, III, and IV
6	Choose and verify corrective actions.	Check team composition and process. Evaluate solutions for improved interim actions. Evaluate the degree of problem reduction or elimination using preproduction tests.	Phase V
7	Implement permanent corrective actions.	Check team composition and process. Identify prevention and protection actions. Monitor effectiveness of problem reduction or elimination.	Phases IV and V
8	Prevent recurrence.	Modify the management systems, operating systems, practices, and procedures to prevent recurrence of this and all similar problems.	Phase VI
9	Congratulate the team.	Use various recognition and reward techniques.	Not considered

Source: Adapted from Chaudhry, A. M. To be a problem solver, be a classicist. *Quality Progress,* June 1999, 47–51.

Learning Objective:

6. Guide team creativity through the use of the nominal group technique, traditional brainstorming, and electronic brainstorming.

GUIDING TEAM CREATIVITY

We now turn to a discussion of three of the many approaches for guiding and stimulating team and group creativity—nominal group technique, traditional brainstorming, and electronic brainstorming. These approaches can assist team members with the problem definition (phase I), solution generation (phase II), and the initial part of the ideas to action (phase III) phases in the self-managing decision-making model (see Figure 8.4).

NOMINAL GROUP TECHNIQUE

The **nominal group technique** (NGT) is a structured process designed to guide and stimulate creative team decision making where agreement is lacking or team members have incomplete knowledge about the nature of the problem. This technique has a special purpose: to make individual judgments the essential inputs in arriving at a team decision. Team members must pool their judgments in order to solve the problem and determine a satisfactory course of action.

The NGT is most beneficial for (1) identifying the crucial variables in a specific situation; (2) identifying key elements of a plan designed to implement a particular solution to some problem; or (3) establishing priorities with regard to the problem to be addressed and goals to be attained. The NGT isn't particularly well suited for routine team meetings that focus primarily on task coordination or information exchange. Nor is it usually appropriate for the negotiating that takes place between incompatible groups (e.g., a union and management committee). The NGT consists of four distinct stages: generating ideas, recording ideas, clarifying ideas, and voting on ideas.[67] Various suggestions have been made for modifying or tailoring these stages to specific situations. Collaborative software technology is now available to aid in the performance of the tasks in these stages.

Generating Ideas. The first stage in the process is to have team members generate ideas. Each participant separately writes down ideas in response to a statement of the problem, a question, or some other central focus of the team. A question could be something as simple as "What problems do you think we should consider over the next year?" followed by "Take 5 minutes to write down some of your own ideas on a piece of paper." The generation of ideas or solutions privately by team members avoids the direct pressures of status differences or competition among members to be heard. Yet it retains some of the peer and creative tension in the individual generated by the presence of others. This stage and the subsequent stages provide time for thinking and reflection to avoid premature choices among ideas.[68]

Recording Ideas. The second stage is to record one idea (generated in the first stage) from each group member in turn on a flip chart, white board, or other device visible to all team members. A variation is to have members submit their ideas anonymously on index cards. The process continues until the team members are satisfied that the list reflects all the ideas individually generated. This round-robin approach emphasizes equal participation by team members and avoids losing ideas that individuals consider significant. Listing them for everyone to see depersonalizes the ideas and reduces the potential for unnecessary conflict. Team members often are impressed and pleased with the list of ideas presented, which provides momentum and enthusiasm for continuing the process.

Clarifying Ideas. Team members then discuss in turn each idea on the list during the third stage. The purpose of this discussion is to clarify the meaning of each idea and allow team members to agree or disagree with any item. The intent is to present the logic behind the ideas and minimize misunderstanding, not to win arguments concerning the relative merits of the ideas. Differences of opinion aren't resolved at this stage, but rather by the voting procedure in the fourth stage.

Voting on Ideas. Using the list developed, which may contain 15 to 30 or more ideas, the team may proceed in one of several ways. Perhaps the most common voting procedure is to have team members individually select a specific number (say, 5) of the ideas that they believe are the most important. Each person writes these 5 ideas on index cards. The team leader then asks the members to rank their items from most to least important. The index cards are collected and the votes tabulated to produce a priority list. An alternative to this single vote is to feed back the results of a first vote, allow time for discussion of the results, and then vote again. Feedback and discussion are likely to result in a final decision that most closely reflects the members' actual preferences.

Regardless of format, the voting procedure determines the outcome of the meeting: a team decision that incorporates the individual judgments of the participants. The procedure is designed to document the collective decision and provide a sense of accomplishment and closure.

Assessment of the Nominal Group Technique. The advantages of the NGT over traditional team discussion include greater emphasis and attention to idea generation, increased attention to each idea, and greater likelihood of balanced participation by each member. Nominal groups may not be superior when people are aware of existing problems and willing to communicate them. The approach may be most effective when certain blockages or problems exist in a team, such as domination by a few team members.[69]

Traditional Brainstorming

Usually done with five to twelve people, **traditional brainstorming** is a process whereby individuals state as many ideas as possible during a 20- to 60-minute period. Guidelines for brainstorming include (1) the wilder the ideas the better, (2) don't be critical of any ideas, and (3) hitchhike on or combine previously stated ideas. The group setting for traditional brainstorming was supposed to generate many more and better ideas than if the same number of individuals worked alone.[70] However, research indicates that brainstorming isn't nearly as effective as once thought. In fact, the nominal group technique has proved to be much more effective than traditional brainstorming as an aid for generating ideas.[71]

To brainstorm effectively is to think of an idea, express it, and get on with thinking of and expressing more new ideas. In face-to-face brainstorming, however, people may be prevented from doing so because someone else is talking. As a result, team members may get bogged down waiting for other people to finish talking. Team members also may be anxious about how others will view them if they express their ideas. This problem may be particularly acute when ideas can be interpreted as critical of current practice or when superiors or others who may affect team members' futures are present. Withholding ideas for these reasons defeats the purpose of brainstorming.

Electronic Brainstorming

In **electronic brainstorming,** collaborative software technology is used to enter and automatically disseminate ideas in real time to all team members, each of whom may be stimulated to generate other ideas. For example, Ventana Corporation, headquartered in Tucson, Arizona, is one of the leading providers of collaborative software technology, including electronic brainstorming software. For this approach to work, each team member must have a computer terminal that is connected to all other members' terminals. The software allows individuals to enter their ideas as they think of them. Every time an individual enters an idea, a random set of the team's ideas is presented on each person's screen. The individual can continue to see new random sets of ideas by pressing the appropriate key.[72]

Research on electronic brainstorming is encouraging. It tends to produce significantly more novel ideas than traditional brainstorming. It also removes the main barrier of traditional brainstorming: members seeing and hearing which ideas are whose; that is, it permits anonymity and thus lets team members contribute more freely to idea generation. They need not fear "sounding like a fool" to other employees and managers when spontaneously generating ideas. These advantages appear to be greater for teams of seven or more people.[73] Jay Nunamaker, CEO of Ventana Corporation and a professor at the University of Arizona's Karl Eller Graduate School of Management, is a leading expert on electronic meetings. He says, "Ventana initially added anonymity to its software to meet the needs of the U.S. military. Admirals can really dampen interaction at a meeting. But we didn't realize the impact it would have in corporate settings. Even with people who work together all the time, anonymity changes the social protocols. People say things differently."[74]

The following Managing Communication Competency feature reveals how electronic brainstorming stimulated creativity and improved communication in meetings at FedEx. These sessions fostered the ability to convey information, ideas, and emotions to others so that they are received as intended. It aided in the ability to provide constructive feedback to others, especially to higher level managers, participating in the electronic brainstorming session. The computers ran GroupSystems V software from Ventana Corporation. Note that the brainstorming software used incorporated elements of the nominal group technique along with an opportunity for some discussion.

COMPETENCY: MANAGING COMMUNICATION

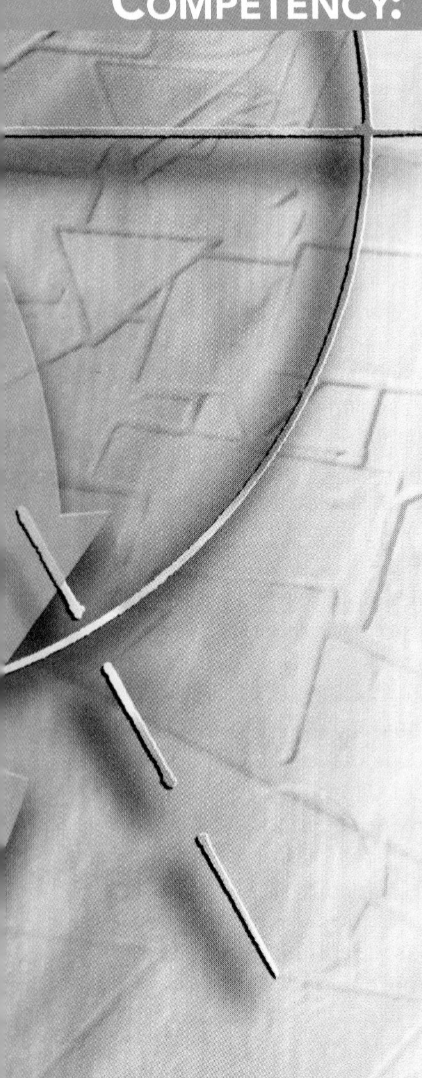

FEDEX BRAINSTORMS ELECTRONICALLY

In a conference room at a university campus about 10 miles from downtown Memphis, Tennessee, 25 FedEx executives engaged in a meeting dedicated to how to have better meetings. The mood was not upbeat. Richard Collard, senior manager of network operations commented, "We just seem to meet and meet and meet and we never seem to do anything." Susan Baker, a colleague of Collard's, seconds those sentiments, saying that "meetings are our middle name. The least productive ones are when there are too many people, especially when there are dominant personalities."

But this meeting is intended to be different. It certainly *feels* different. For one thing, the room is specifically designed for technology-enabled meetings. Facilitator Jana Markowitz is the founder of The Collective Mind, a consulting firm that specializes in collaborative meeting design. She sits at the front of the room at a computer workstation beneath a big screen. Additional workstations, connected over a local area network, are spaced around a large U-shaped table where the meeting participants sit.

The meeting is carefully scripted; Markowitz takes the agenda very seriously. It's also quiet, a big reason why things stay on schedule. Thanks to the software, there are few distractions, digressions, or arguments. Markowitz poses an agenda item, asks for debate, and the participants begin typing.

The meeting begins with an electronic check-in. The software's "mood meter" allows everyone to rate, on a scale from 1 to 10, whether FedEx has too many meetings. The results aren't projected onto the screen until everyone has voted, perhaps to avoid the bandwagon effect. Not surprisingly, though, a bandwagon forms. Meetings aren't very popular in Memphis; an awful lot of 10s appear on the screen.

Next comes brainstorming. Markowitz asks the group to identify reasons why meetings go bad. People simply enter their ideas into the computer; instantly, each idea appears on both the big screen and everyone's monitors. The participants can also enter explanations and elaborations, which remain hidden until the facilitator highlights a specific item. This brainstorming process lasts all of about 5 minutes and generates 35 reasonably interesting ideas about what's wrong with meetings. Ten minutes of live discussion help collapse the list into 22 final items.

Then it's time to vote. Markowitz asks the group to rank each of the 22 items on a 1 to 10 scale, where 1 means "irritating, but not an impediment to work" and 10 stands for "complete impediment to getting work done." Some people vote faster than others. The voting proves to be a rich source of follow-up discussion. The runaway winner—"poorly defined agendas"—registers an overall score of 86, or a mean rating of 7.82 (on the 1 to 10 scale). The software allows the group to sort any of the 22 problems by these and other variables. It also allows each participant to see how his or her rankings differ from the group consensus. Forty minutes into this electronic meeting, Markowitz is making converts. "It would take my group three meetings to do this!" exclaims one participant.

And so it goes for another 50 minutes. Lots of ideas and electronic input, limited but focused discussions. A genuine sense of accomplishment prevails. "The telephone didn't eliminate the need for face-to-face communication," Markowitz concludes, "and technology won't get rid of meetings. But it can make them more effective."[75]

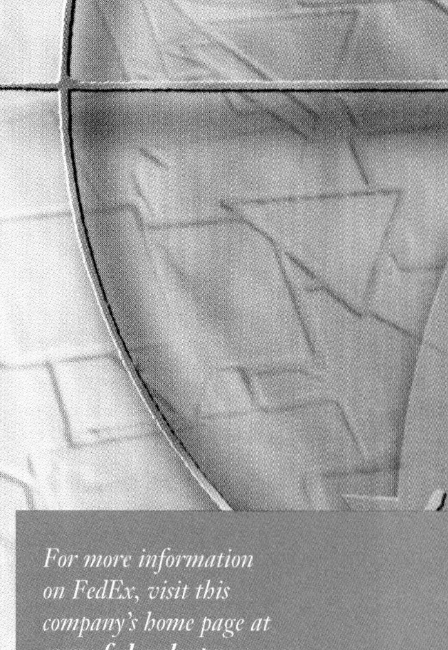

*For more information on FedEx, visit this company's home page at **www.federalexpress.com**.*

CHAPTER SUMMARY

1. Describe the most common types of groups and teams in organizations.

In this chapter we focused on developing the *managing teams competency*—the ability to develop, support, facilitate, and lead groups to achieve team and organizational goals. Groups and teams are classified in numerous ways. In organizations, a basic classification is by the group's primary purpose, including informal groups and task groups (now commonly called *teams*). The four types of task groups discussed were functional teams, problem-solving teams, cross-functional teams, and self-managed teams. We noted the basic characteristics of effective teams and the attributes of team empowerment.

2. Identify the unique features of virtual teams.

Any type of task group could function somewhat or primarily as a virtual team. The core features of effective virtual teams typically include (1) clear, precise, and mutually accepted goals; (2) an array of computer and telecommunication technologies (e.g., desktop videoconferencing systems, collaborative software systems, and Internet and/or intranet systems; and (3) people with strong team management competencies and the other core competencies developed throughout this book.

3. Explain the five-stage model of team development.

The five-stage developmental model focuses on forming, storming, norming, performing, and adjourning. The issues and challenges a team faces change with each stage. Of course, there are several other models for understanding the developmental sequence of teams. Teams do not necessarily develop in the straightforward manner presented in the five-stage developmental model, especially when the members possess strong team management and related competencies.

4. Describe seven of the key influences on team effectiveness.

Team dynamics and effectiveness are influenced by the interplay of context, goals, size, member roles, norms, cohesiveness, and leadership. One type of changing contextual influence on how teams work, interact, and network with other teams is that of information technology, especially the rapid developments in collaborative software systems. Other contextual influences are the nature of the organization's reward system and how it fits the basic value orientations of team members, especially in terms of individualism and collectivism. Team members need to clearly understand and accept team goals as outcomes desired by each member for the team as a whole. Team size can substantially affect the dynamics among the members and the ability to create a sense of mutual accountability. Teams of about 16 or more members typically break down into smaller task groups. Member roles may be task-oriented, relations-oriented, or self-oriented. Norms differ from rules in important ways and can have a positive or negative impact on performance. The pressures to adhere to norms may result in either compliance conformity or personal acceptance conformity. Another factor having an impact on the effectiveness of teams is cohesiveness, which is related to conformity, groupthink, and productivity. Team leaders may be selected formally or emerge informally.

5. Explain the self-managing team decision-making model.

Team decision making is likely superior to individual decision making when certain conditions exist: the need to bring diverse perspectives and expertise to bear on an issue or when acceptance by team members of a decision is important to its implementation. One useful model for effective self-managing team decision making involves six phases: (1) problem definition, (2) idea generation, (3) idea evaluation, (4) action planning, (5) evaluation learning, and (6) outcome evaluation learning.

6. Guide team creativity through the use of the nominal group technique, traditional brainstorming, and electronic brainstorming.

The nominal group technique (NGT) consists of four distinct stages: (1) generating ideas, (2) recording ideas, (3) clarifying ideas, and (4) voting on ideas. It is especially useful when agreement is lacking or team members have incomplete knowledge as to the nature of a problem. Traditional brainstorming involves using a set of guidelines for a face-to-face session in which the individuals state as many ideas as possible during a 20- to 60-minute period. Electronic brainstorming involves the use of collaborative software technology by each team member to enter into a computer and automatically disseminate ideas to all other members. Research suggests that electronic brainstorming typically generates more and better ideas than does traditional brainstorming.

KEY TERMS AND CONCEPTS

Cohesiveness
Compliance conformity
Context
Cross-functional teams
Electronic brainstorming
Friendship group
Functional teams
Group
Groupthink
Hot group
Informal group
Informal leader
Nominal group technique
Norms
Personal acceptance conformity
Positive multiculturalism
Problem-solving teams
Productivity
Relations-oriented role
Self-managed teams
Self-oriented role
Superordinate goals
Task group
Task-oriented role
Team
Team empowerment
Team goals
Traditional brainstorming
Virtual team

DISCUSSION QUESTIONS

1. Think of four informal and task groups of which you are or have been a member during the past 3 years. In terms of the types of groups and teams presented in this chapter, how would you classify each of them? Did any of them appear to be of more than one type? Explain.
2. For one of the groups you identified in Question 1, how would you evaluate it in terms of the six basic characteristics of effective groups?
3. Based on your completion of Table 8.1, what actions are needed to increase the degree of empowerment for this team? Are those actions feasible?
4. If you were employed at Whole Foods Markets, what do you think you would like or dislike about its team system?
5. Assume that you had to complete a class project as a member of a virtual team that could only meet twice face-to-face. Identify at least four of the special

challenges that your virtual team would face in undertaking the project.

6. Think of a new team or group in which you participated during the past 3 years. Describe and explain the degree to which the development of this team or group matched the five-stage model of team development.
7. For a team or group of which you have been a member, describe its environment (context) in terms of technology, organizational rules, influence of higher level management, and organizational rewards and punishments. In what ways did the context appear to affect the team's or group's dynamics and effectiveness?
8. What were the formal and informal goals of the team or group you identified in Question 7? Were the informal goals consistent and supportive of the formal goals? Explain.
9. How would you describe the team or group you identified in Question 7 as a whole in terms of task-oriented behaviors, relations-oriented behaviors, and self-oriented behaviors? Which of these types of behaviors seemed to contribute the most to its performance? The least?
10. Reread the Managing Self Competency feature "Joan McCoy Learns Team Leadership." Assume that a similar feature was being written about your team leadership competency. What would it say?
11. The self-managing decision-making model depicted in Figure 8.4 presents a phased sequence that empowered teams can follow. How may the factors identified in Figure 8.2 work for or against the use of this model?
12. What are the similarities and differences between the nominal group technique (NGT) and electronic brainstorming?

DEVELOPING COMPETENCIES

Competency: Managing Teams—Team Assessment[76]

Instructions: Think of a student or work-related team in which you have been a member and that was formed to achieve one or more goals. This team could be associated with a specific course, student organization, or job.

1. Evaluate the *success* of your team on each *item* in this instrument. Use the following scale and assign a value from 1 to 5 to each item. Record the number next to each numbered item. How successful do you think your team was on each of the items?

1	2	3	4	5
Not at all successful (well below expectations)	Somewhat successful (though below expectations)	Moderately successful (meets expectations)	Fairly high level of success (exceeds expectations)	Very high level of success (far exceeds expectations)

2. Based on the item assessments and any other related dimensions for each factor, evaluate the *overall success* of your team on each of the seven summary *factors*. Sum the item scores for each factor. Divide the sum (total) by the number of items in that factor.

I. Goals Factor

_____ 1. Team members understood the goals and scope of the team.

_____ 2. Team members were committed to the team goals, and took ownership of them.

[ ] ***Overall Goals Factor:*** Add the scores for items 1 and 2 and divide by 2 = _____.

II. Team Performance Management Factor

_____ 3. Individual roles, responsibilities, goals, and performance expectations were specific, challenging, and accepted by team members.

_____ 4. Team goals and performance expectations were specific, challenging, and accepted by team members.

_____ 5. The workload of the team was shared more or less equally among team members.

_____ 6. Everyone on my team did his or her fair share of the work.

_____ 7. No one on my team depended on other team members to do his or her work.

_____ 8. Nearly all the members on my team contributed equally to the work.

[ ] ***Overall Team Performance Management Factor:*** Add the scores for items 3 through 8 and divide by 6 = _____.

III. Team Basics Factor

_____ 9. My team had enough members to handle the tasks assigned (i.e., small enough to meet and communicate frequently and easily, and yet not too small for the work required of the team).

_____ 10. The team as a whole possessed the competency levels required to achieve its goals.

_____ 11. The team members possessed the complementary competencies required to achieve the team's goals.

[ ] ***Overall Team Basics Factor:*** Add the scores for items 9 through 11 and divide by 3 = _____.

IV. Team Processes Factor

_____ 12. My team was able to solve problems and make decisions.
_____ 13. My team was able to encourage desirable but to discourage undesirable team conflict.
_____ 14. My team members were able to communicate, listen, and give constructive feedback.
_____ 15. Team meetings were conducted effectively.
_____ 16. Members of my team were very willing to share information with other team members about our work.
_____ 17. Members of my team cooperated to get the work done.
_____ 18. Being on my team gave me the opportunity to work on a team and to provide support for other team members.
_____ 19. My team increased my opportunities for positive social interaction.
_____ 20. Members of my team helped each other when necessary.

☐ ***Overall Team Processes Factor:*** Add the scores for items 12 through 20 and divide by 9 = _____.

V. Team Spirit Factor

_____ 21. Members of my team had great confidence that the team could perform effectively.
_____ 22. My team took on the tasks assigned and completed them.
_____ 23. My team had a lot of team enthusiasm.
_____ 24. My team had high morale.
_____ 25. The team developed norms (i.e., expectations concerning team member behavior) that contributed to effective team functioning and performance.
_____ 26. Team members invested energy intensely on behalf of the team.

☐ ***Overall Team Spirit Factor:*** Add the scores for items 21 through 26 and divide by 6 = _____.

VI. Team Outcomes Factor

_____ 27. The team attained measurable results (if objective or quantifiable measures were available).
_____ 28. The product or service delivered by the team met or exceeded the expectations of those receiving it.
_____ 29. My team carried out its work in such a way as to maintain or enhance its ability to work together on future team tasks.
_____ 30. Generally, the team experience served to satisfy, rather than frustrate, the personal needs of team members.

☐ ***Overall Team Outcomes Factor:*** Add the scores for items 27 through 30 and divide by 4 = _____.

VII. Team Learning Factor

_____ 31. We took time to figure out ways to improve team processes.
_____ 32. Team members often spoke up to test assumptions about issues under discussion.
_____ 33. Team members got all the information they needed from others.
_____ 34. Someone always made sure that we stopped to reflect on the team's processes.
_____ 35. The team as a whole asked for feedback from others as it progressed.
_____ 36. The team actively reviewed its own progress and performance.

☐ ***Overall Team Learning Factor:*** Add the scores for items 31 through 36 and divide by 6 = _____.

Interpretation

Overall scores of 4 or 5 on a factor suggests considerable success (exceeding expectations and success). A score of 3 on a factor suggests a satisfactory level of success and a feeling of just "okay." Overall scores of 1 or 2 on a factor suggests that the team processes needed considerable improvement. You might consider all seven factors as a whole to arrive at a final summary assessment. Insights for action steps are likely to be learned through each factor and the specific items that are in it.

Competency: Managing Teams—Artisan Industries' Team[77]

Part I

In mid October, 29-year-old Bill Meister, president of Artisan Industries, had to meet with his management team to consider increasing prices. A year before, he had taken over the failing $13-million-a-year wooden gift manufacturing company from his father. It had been a hectic year, but he had stopped the company's slide toward bankruptcy. However, much work remained to be done to improve almost every area of the company.

The following team members met in his office at 11:00 A.M. one morning.

1. Bob was the 30-year-old vice president of finance. He had been with the company 3 years, coming from the staff of a major accounting firm. He headed accounting and the office staff in general.
2. Cal was 35 years old and had been with the company 8 years. Although he had a bachelor's degree in accounting,

he had held many jobs in the company. Currently, he was installing a small computer system and reported directly to Bob.

3. Edith was Bill Meister's 40-year-old sister and manager of routine sales from the home office. The external sales force that called on firms was made up of independent sales representatives. Only clerical people reported to Edith. She had no college training.
4. Consultant: A 40-year-old woman with bachelors and MBA degrees. She had 10 years experience in consulting.

Bill called the meeting to order in the presence of a management consultant who happened to be visiting to discuss other plans for improvement.

Bill: OK, we've been discussing the need for a price increase for some time now. Bob recommends increasing prices 16 percent right away. I'd like to get all of your thoughts on this. Bob?

Bob: My analysis of profit statements to date indicates that a 16 percent increase is necessary right now if we are to have any profit this year. My best estimate is that we're losing money on every order we take. We haven't raised prices in over a year and have no choice but to do so now.

Cal: I agree. What's the sense in taking orders on which we lose money?

Bob: Exactly. If we raise prices across the board immediately, we can have a profit of about $500,000 at year end.

Cal: It would've been better to have increased prices with our price list last May or June, rather than doing it on each order here in the middle of our sales season, but we really have no choice now.

Bob: There's just no way we can put it off.

Bill (pausing, looking around the room): So, you all recommend a price increase at this time?

Cal and **Bob:** Yes.

Bob: We can't wait to increase prices as new orders are written in the field or through a new price list. Right now, we already have enough of a backlog of orders accepted at the old prices and orders awaiting our acknowledgement to fill the plant until the holiday season ends in six to eight weeks. We must accept orders only at the new prices.

Cal: If we acknowledge all the orders we have now, like that 30-page one Edith has for $321,000, then the price change won't even be felt this year.

Bob: No, we should acknowledge any orders at the old prices. I would hold the orders and send each customer a printed letter telling them of the price increase and asking them to reconfirm their orders with an enclosed mailer if they still want them.

Cal: Orders already acknowledged would keep the plant busy until they responded.

Bill: So, is this the best thing to do?

Bob: We're in business to make money; we'd be crazy not to raise prices!

Bill: Edith, you look unhappy. What do you think?

Edith (shrugging): I don't know.

Bob (visibly impatient): We're losing money on every order.

Edith: I'm just worried about trying to raise prices right in the middle of the season.

Cal: Well, if we wait, we might as well forget it.

Bob: Just what would you suggest we do, Edith?

Edith: I don't know. (Pause.) This order (picking up the 30-page order) took the salesman a month to work up with the customer. There are over 175 items on it, and the items must be redistributed to the customer's nine retail outlets in time for the holidays. I'm worried about it.

Bob: It's worthless to us as it is.

Cal: Look, in our letter, we can mention inflation and that this is our first increase in a long while. Most customers will understand this. We've got to try. It's worth the risk, isn't it, Edith?
(Edith shrugs.)

Bill: What do you suggest, Edith?

Edith: I don't know. We need the increase, but it bothers me.

Bob: Business is made of tough decisions; managers are paid to make 'em.
(All become quiet, look around the room, and finally look at Bill.)

Questions for Part I

1. Explain what happened at this meeting: What was each person's role? What was each person doing and trying to do? Was it a good meeting? Why or why not?
2. What is the decision going to be? Give all the specifics of the decision.
3. What do you think of the decision? Can you think of ways to improve on it?
4. What would you do if you were there?

Part II

Consultant (calmly): I think Edith has raised a good point. *You are* considering making a big move right in the middle of your busy season. It will cause problems. If you can't avoid the increase, then what can you do to avoid or minimize the problems?

Bob (hostile and obviously disgusted): It would be ridiculous to put off the price increase.

Consultant (calmly): That may be true, but is it being done in the best way? There are always alternatives to consider. I don't think you are doing a good job of problem solving here. (Pause.) Even with the basic idea of an increase, it can be done poorly or done well. There is room for more thought. How can it be done with the least penalty? (All are quiet as the consultant looks around the team, waiting for anyone to add comments. Hearing none, she continues.) For example, by the time you mail them a letter and they think about it and mail it back, two or three weeks may pass. The price increase wouldn't take effect until the season is almost over. How can you get the increase to make money right away? And though you are bound to lose some orders, what can you do to minimize these losses? (She pauses to allow comments).

Edith: Yes, that's what I meant.

Consultant: On this order, for example (picking up the $321,000 order), we could call them right now and explain the situation and possibly be shipping at the higher prices this afternoon.

Bob: (with no hostility and with apparent positive attitude): OK. I will call them as soon as we leave here.

Cal: We have a pile of orders awaiting acknowledgement...

Bob: Right, we can get some help and pick out the bigger orders and start calling them this afternoon.

Consultant: How about involving the sales force? Some could lose their commissions because clients cancel their orders.

Edith: Yes, the salespeople know the customers best. We should call them to contact the customer. They got the order and know the customer's needs. But we will have to convince the salespeople of the necessity for the increase. I can start getting in touch with them by phone right away.

Bob: OK, we can handle the bigger orders personally by phone and use a letter for the small ones.

Consultant: Why not make it so that no action keeps the order? Tell them that we are saving their place in our shipping schedule and will go ahead and ship if they don't contact you in 5 to 7 days. Is it best to put the control in their hands?

Edith: That bothered me. Increasing the price is serious, and we need to handle it carefully if it's to work. I think most people will go ahead and accept the merchandise.

Bob: Edith and I can get together this afternoon on the letter. (All become silent again.)

Bill: OK, can you all get started after lunch? Let's meet in the morning to see how it's going.

Questions for Part II

1. What do you think of the decision now? Is it better than the first one? Why might you call the first decision *suboptimal*?
2. Would the team have made the new decision without the help of the consultant? Why or why not?
3. Initially, the team was not involved in problem solving. Why wasn't it?
4. What does this incident say about empowerment of the management team and the work environment at Artisan? Using the items in Table 8.1, evaluate this team's empowerment.
5. What does this case illustrate about team problem solving? About communication?

REFERENCES

1. Adapted from Berry, L. L. *Discovering the Soul of Service.* New York: Free Press, 1999, 187–190; Greco, S. Loose or lose. *Inc. Online*, December 1998, unpaged: www.inc.com/incmagazine/archives/12980571, July 11, 1999; www.cresearch.com, July 11, 1999.
2. Berry, 189.
3. What we offer employees—Build your career with a winner. www.cresearch.com/wh/wh03, July 7, 1999.
4. Homans, G. C. *The Human Group.* New York: Harcourt, Brace and World, 1959, 2; also see Miller, J. Living systems: The group. *Behavioral Science*, 1971, 16, 302–398.
5. Parks, C. D., and Sanna, L. J. *Group Performance and Interaction.* Boulder, Colo.: Westview Press, 1999.
6. Ackroyd, S., and Thompson, P. *Organizational Misbehavior.* Thousand Oaks, Calif.: Sage, 1999.
7. Turniansky, B., and Hare, A. P. *Individuals and Groups in Organizations.* Thousand Oaks, Calif.: Sage, 1999.
8. Napier, R. W., and Gershenfeld, M. K. *Groups: Theory and Experience*, 6th. ed. Boston: Houghton Mifflin College, 1999.
9. Adapted from Lancaster, H. Black managers often must emphasize building relationships. *Wall Street Journal*, March 4, 1997, B1; Mehra, A., Kilduff, M., and Brass, D. J. At the margins: A distinctiveness approach to the social identity and social networks of underrepresented groups. *Academy of Management Journal*, 1998, 441–452.
10. Henry, J. E. *Lessons from Team Leaders: A Team Fitness Companion.* Milwaukee: ASQ Quality Press, 1998.
11. Syer, J. *How Teamwork Works: The Dynamics of Effective Team Development.* Blacklick, Ohio: McGraw-Hill College, 1997.
12. Kirkman, B. I., and Rosen, B. Beyond self-management: Antecedents and consequences of team empowerment. *Academy of Management Journal*, 1999, 42, 58–74; Wetlaufer, S. Organizing for empowerment: An interview with AES's Roger Sant and Dennis Bakke. *Harvard Business Review*, January–February 1999, 110–123.
13. Adapted from Calder, N., and Douglas, P. C. Empowered employee teams: The new key to improving corporate success. *Quality Digest*, March 1999, 26–30.
14. Calder and Douglas, 28.
15. Calder and Douglas, 28.
16. Adapted from New system keeps the goods flowing. *Chain Store Age*, September 1996, 42–48; Munk, N. Shopping at Macy's. *Forbes*, February 12, 1996, 37–38.
17. Rose, E., and Buckley, S. *50 Ways to Teach Your Learner: Activities and Interventions for Building High-Performance Teams.* San Francisco: Jossey-Bass, 1999.
18. Adapted from Hayes, C. The new spin on corporate work teams. *Black Enterprise*, June 1995, 22–29.
19. Michalski, W. J., and King, D. G. (eds.). *40 Tools for Cross-Functional Teams: Building Synergy for Breakthrough Creativity.* Portland, Ore.: Productivity Press, 1998.

20. Lubove, S. Destroying the old hierarchies. *Forbes*, June 3, 1996, 62–71; Labich, K. Boeing finally hatches a plan. *Fortune*, March 1, 1999, 101–106.
21. Purser, R., and Cabana, S. *The Self-Managing Organization: How Leading Companies Are Transforming the Work of Teams for Real Impact.* New York: Free Press, 1999.
22. Kraft, R. *Utilizing Self-Managing Teams: Effective Behavior of Team Leaders.* Hamden, Conn.: Garland, 1999.
23. Duarte, D. L., and Tennant Snyder, N. *Mastering Virtual Teams: Strategies, Tools, and Techniques That Succeed.* San Francisco: Jossey-Bass, 1999.
24. Adapted from Fishman, C. Whole Foods is all teams. *Fast Company*, April 1996, 103–106; Bates, E. Whole food fight. *Metro Canta Cruz*, September 3–9, 1998, 1–3; About Whole Foods Markets, www.wholefoods.com/company, July 11, 1999.
25. Lipnack, J., and Stamps, J. Virtual teams: The new way to work. *Strategy and Leadership*, January/February 1999, 14–19; Carmel, E. *Global Software Teams: Collaborating Across Borders and Time Zones.* Upper Saddle River, N.J.: Prentice Hall PTR, 1999.
26. This presentation is based primarily on Townsend, D. M., DeMarie, S. M., and Hendrickson, A. R. Virtual teams: Technology and the workplace of the future. *Academy of Management Executive*, August 1998, 17–29.
27. Davenport, T. H., and Pearlson, K. Two cheers for the virtual office. *Sloan Management Review*, Summer 1998, 51–65.
28. Lipnack, J., and Stamps, J. *Virtual Teams: Reaching Across Space, Time, and Organizations.* Somerset, N.J.: John Wiley & Sons, 1997.
29. Adapted from Boudreau, M., Loch, K. D., Robey, D., and Straud, D. Going global: Using information technology to advance the competitiveness of the virtual organization. *Academy of Management Executive*, November 1998, 120–128.
30. Tuckman, B. W. Development sequence in small groups. *Psychological Bulletin*, 1965, 62, 384–399; Tuckman, B. W., and Jensen, M. A. C. Stages of small group development revisited. *Group & Organization Studies*, 1977, 2, 419–427; Obert, S. L. Developmental patterns of organizational task groups: A preliminary study. *Human Relations*, 1983, 36, 37–52.
31. Gersick, C. J. Time and transition in work teams: Toward a new model of group development. *Academy of Management Journal*, 1988, 31, 9–41.
32. Montebello, A. R. *Work Teams That Work.* Minneapolis: Best Sellers, 1994.
33. Caouette, M., and O'Connor, B. The impact of group support systems on corporate teams' stages of development. *Journal of Organizational Computing and Electronic Commerce*, 1998, 8, 57–81.
34. Herbelin, S., and Guiney, P. (eds.). *The Do's and Don'ts of Work Team Coaching.* Riverbank, Calif.: Herbelin, 1998.
35. King, R. T., Jr. Levi's factory workers are assigned to teams, and morale takes a hit. *Wall Street Journal*, May 20, 1998, A1, A6.
36. Lancaster, H. Learning some ways to make meetings less stressful. *Wall Street Journal*, May 26, 1998, B1.
37. Cannon-Bowers, J. A., and Salas, E. (eds.). *Making Decisions Under Stress: Implications for Individual and Team Training.* Hyattsville, Md.: American Psychological Association, 1999.
38. Jones, G. R., and George, J. M. The experience and evolution of trust: Implications for cooperation and teamwork. *Academy of Management Review*, 1998, 23, 531–546.
39. Pascarella, P. Compensating teams. *Across the Board*, February 1997, 16–18.
40. Denton, D. K. How a team can grow. *Quality Progress*, June 1999, 53–58.
41. Milkovich, G. T., and Newman, J. M. *Compensation.* Blacklick, Ohio: McGraw-Hill College, 1999.
42. Gibson, C. B. Do they do what they believe they can? Group efficacy and group effectiveness across tasks and cultures. *Academy of Management Journal*, 1999, 42, 138–152.
43. Berelson, B., and Steiner, G. A. *Human Behavior: An Inventory of Scientific Finding.* New York: Harcourt, Brace and World, 1964, 356–360.
44. Ratcliff, R. L., Beckstead, S. M., and Hanks, S. H. The use and management of teams: A how-to guide. *Quality Progress*, June 1999, 31–38.
45. Kelly, S., and Allison, M. A. *The Complexity Advantage.* New York: McGraw-Hill, 1999.
46. Bales, R. E. *Personality and Interpersonal Behavior.* New York: Holt, Rinehart and Winston, 1970; Lustig, M. W. Bales' interpersonal rating forms: Reliability and dimensionality. *Small Group Behavior*, 1987, 18, 99–107.
47. Murphy, K. R. (ed.) *Individual Differences and Behavior in Organizations.* San Francisco: Jossey-Bass, 1996.
48. Lau, D. C., and Murnighan, J. K. Demographic diversity and fault lines: The compositional dynamics of organizational groups. *Academy of Management*, 1998, 23, 325–340.
49. Barry, B., and Bateman, T. S. A social trap analysis of the management of diversity. *Academy of Management Review*, 1996, 21, 757–740.
50. Triandis, H. C., Kurowski, L. L., and Gelfand, M. J. Workplace diversity. In H. C. Triandis, M. D. Dunnette, and L. M. Hough (eds.), *Handbook of Industrial and Organizational Psychology*, vol. 4, 2nd ed. Palo Alto, Calif.: Consulting Psychologists Press, 1994, 796–827.
51. Adapted from Scheinholtz, D. (Ed.). Diversity—The bottom line: Building a competitive workforce. *Forbes*, May 3, 1999, special insert, 1–31.
52. Ezzamel, M., and Willmott, H. Accounting for teamwork: A critical study of group-based systems of organizational control. *Administrative Science Quarterly*, 1998, 43, 358–396.
53. Brass, D. J., Butterfield, K. D., and Skaggs, B. C. Relationships and unethical behavior: A social network perspective. *Academy of Management Review*, 1998, 23, 14–31.
54. Roethlisberger, F. J., and Dickson, W. J. *Management and the Worker: Technical versus Social Organization in an Industrial Plant.* Cambridge, Mass.: Harvard University Press, 1939.
55. Feldman, D. C. The development and enforcement of group norms. *Academy of Management Review*, 1984, 9, 47–53; also see Spich, R. S., and Keleman, R. S. Explicit norm structuring process: A strategy for increasing task-group effectiveness. *Group and Organization Studies*, 1985, 10, 37–59.
56. Hackman, J. R. Group influences on individuals. In M. D. Dunnette, and L. M. Hough (eds.), *Handbook of Industrial*

and Organizational Psychology, vol. 3, 2nd ed. Palo Alto: Calif.: Consulting Psychologists Press, 1992, 199–267.
57. Besser, T. L. *Team Toyota*. Ithaca: State University of New York Press, 1996.
58. Edmondson, A. Psychological safety and learning behaviors in work teams. *Administrative Science Quarterly*, 1999, 44, 358–383; Harrison, D. A., Price, K. H., and Bell, M. P. Beyond relational demography: Time and the effects of surface- and deep-level diversity on work group cohesion. *Academy of Management Journal*, 1998, 41, 96–108.
59. Lipman-Blumen, J., and Leavitt, H. J. *Hot Groups: Seeding Them, Feeding Them, and Using Them to Ignite Your Organization*. New York: Oxford University Press, 1999.
60. Janis, L. L. *Groupthink*, 2nd ed. Boston: Houghton Mifflin, 1982; Whyte, G. Groupthink reconsidered. *Academy of Management Review*, 1989, 14, 40–56; Sims, R. R. Linking groupthink to unethical behavior in organizations. *Journal of Business Ethics*, September 1992, 651–652.
61. Hambrick, D. C. Fragmentation and the other problems CEOs have with their top management teams. *California Management Review*, Spring 1995, 110–127.
62. Kraft, R. *Utilizing Self-Managing Teams: Effective Behavior of Team Leaders*. Hamden, Conn.: Garland, 1999.
63. Adapted from Whole Foods Markets: Our Core values. www.wholefoods.com/company/ about/body/values, July 11, 1999.
64. Adapted from Kalplan, M. How to overcome your strengths. *Fast Company*, May 1999, 225–230; Frankel, L. P. *Jump-Start Your Career: How the "Strengths" That Got You Where You Are Today Can Hold You Back Tomorrow*. Pittsburgh: Three Rivers Press, 1998.
65. Morris, W. C., and Sashkin, M. *Organization Behavior in Action: Skill Building Experiences*. St. Paul: West, 1976; Vroom, V. H., and Jago, A. G. *The New Leadership: Managing Participation in Organizations*. Old Tappan, N.J.: Prentice Hall, 1998.
66. Schminke, M., and Wells, O. Group process and performance and their effects on individuals' ethical frameworks. *Journal of Business Ethics*, 1999, 18, 367–381; Lewicki, R. J., McAllister, D. J., and Bies, R. J. Trust and distrust: New relationships and realities. *Academy of Management Review*, 1998, 23, 438–458.
67. Major portions of this discussion for the nominal group technique were excerpted from Woodman, R. W. Use of the nominal group technique for idea generation and decision making. *Texas Business Executive*, Spring 1981, 50–53; Delbecq, A. L., Van de Ven, A. H., and Gustafson, D. H. *Group Techniques for Program Planning: A Guide to Nominal and Delphi Processes*. Middleton, Wisc.: Green Briar Press, 1986.
68. Fisher, M. *The IdeaFisher*. Princeton, N.J.: Peterson's/ Pacesetter's Books, 1996.
69. Chapman, R. J. The effectiveness of working group risk identification and assessment techniques. *International Journal of Project Management*, 1998, 16, 333–343; McManus, K. Tools @ work: A project management system for innovation. *Journal for Quality & Participation*, September/October 1998, 60–61.
70. Osborn, A. F. *Applied Imagination*, rev. ed. New York: Scribner, 1957.
71. Mullen, B., Johnson, C., and Salas, E. Productivity loss in brainstorming groups: A meta-analytical integration. *Basic and Applied Social Psychology*, 12, 1991, 3–23.
72. For a description of the wide array of collaborative software products and services offered by the Ventana Corporation, visit this company's home page at www.ventana.com.
73. Dennis, A. R., Heninger, W. G., and Walker, E. D. Structuring time and tasks in electronic brainstorming. *MIS Quarterly*, 1999, 23, 95–108; Pendergast, M., and Haynes, S. Groupware and social networks: Will life ever be the same again. *Information and Software Technology*, 1999, 41, 311–318.
74. Blitt, B. The seven sins of deadly meetings. In *Handbook of the Business Revolution*. Boston: Fast Company, 1997, 27–31.
75. Adapted from Blitt, 27–31.
76. Adapted from *The Student Team Audit Instrument*. Developed by Jon M. Werner, a faculty member in the Department of Management at the University of Wisconsin-Whitewater; Edmondson, A. Psychological safety and learning behavior in work teams. *Administrative Science Quarterly*, 1999, 44, 350–383.
77. Prepared by and adapted with permission from Barnes, F. C., University of North Carolina at Charlotte.

CHAPTER

9 POWER AND POLITICAL BEHAVIOR

LEARNING OBJECTIVES

When you have finished studying this chapter, you should be able to:

1. Explain the concept and dynamics of organizational power.
2. Describe the interpersonal sources of power.
3. Discuss the main categories of structural sources of power.
4. Discuss effective and ineffective uses of power.
5. Explain the concept of organizational politics and diagnose personal and situational factors that contribute to political behavior.
6. Describe some personality dimensions that are related to political behavior.

Preview Case: *Ronald Szoc Learns About Power and Politics*

POWER

INTERPERSONAL SOURCES OF POWER

Competency: Managing Change—*Revenge of the Nerds*

Reward Power

Coercive Power

Legitimate Power

Expert Power

Referent Power

Relationships Among Power Sources

STRUCTURAL SOURCES OF POWER

Knowledge as Power

Competency: Managing Across Cultures—*Workplace Democracy in Africa*

Resources as Power

Decision Making as Power

Networks as Power

Lower Level Employee Power

Competency: Managing Diversity—*Bilingual Employees Acquire Power*

THE EFFECTIVE USE OF POWER

POLITICAL BEHAVIOR

Organizational Politics

Competency: Managing Change—*The Politics of Innovation*

Forces Creating Political Behavior

Competency: Managing Ethics—*The Politics of Employee Appraisal*

PERSONALITY AND POLITICAL BEHAVIOR

Need for Power

Machiavellianism

Locus of Control

Risk-Seeking Propensity

CHAPTER SUMMARY

Competency: Managing Across Cultures—*Comparing Chinese and American Risk Preferences*

Key Terms and Concepts

Discussion Questions

DEVELOPING COMPETENCIES

Competency: Managing Self—*How Much Power Do You Have in Your Group?*

Competency: Managing Change—*The Art of Persuasion*

PREVIEW CASE

RONALD SZOC LEARNS ABOUT POWER AND POLITICS

Ronald Szoc is senior vice president at Ruesch International, Inc., a Washington-based currency trading firm. He can still remember his first, important lesson in office politics—which he learned the hard way.

His lesson in power and political behavior came while he was part of a small consulting group at Westinghouse Electric Corporation. The consulting group consisted of the director and just six employees. Szoc remembers that the six of them all felt that the director was doing a poor job. The group planned a "coup" to bring this fact to the attention of the director's superiors and have him replaced with someone more to their liking. As luck would have it, word of their planning reached corporate headquarters prematurely. Three management representatives from headquarters flew to Evanston, Illinois, where the consulting arm was located and asked to meet with the six employees at a local hotel.

Szoc recalls, "Discussions were brief. We were told in no uncertain terms: We don't care how you feel. We don't care whether or not you think the director is doing a bad job. He's critical to the operations of your group because of his background, experience, and reputation. Without him, there is no group. Do you understand what we are telling you? Do you have any questions?"

For more information on Ruesch International, Inc., and Westinghouse Electric Corporation, visit their home pages at ***www.ruesch.com*** *and* ***www.westinghouse.com.***

Szoc remembers the experience as an epiphany. "For the first time, I understood something very important about organizations. I thought: This is not about questions of truth or efficiency or productivity. I realized that there was a political dimension to organizational life."[1]

In this chapter, we focus on power and political behavior in organizations. People often are uncomfortable discussing the concepts of power and organizational politics. Both terms carry emotional, often negative, implications. We argue that this should not be the case; these labels are simply descriptive terms that apply to certain aspects of the behavior of people in organizations. Managers and employees need to be aware of power and political behavior in order to understand organizational behavior fully.[2]

Certainly, people can use power in unfair or harmful ways. Likewise, political behavior can be unproductive for an organization. Managers and employees must try to avoid such outcomes, but they cannot change reality by refusing to accept the existence of power differences or political behavior. In this chapter, we discuss the nature of power, the sources of power in organizations, and the effective and ineffective uses of power. We also explore political behavior in organizations, including the relationships between personality and political behavior.

Learning Objective:

1. Explain the concept and dynamics of organizational power.

POWER

Power is the capacity to influence the behavior of others.[3] The term *power* may be applied to individuals, groups, teams, departments, organizations, and countries. For example, a certain team within an organization might be labeled as powerful, which suggests that it has the ability to influence the behavior of individuals in other teams or departments. This influence may affect resource allocations, space assignments, goals, hiring decisions, and many other outcomes and behaviors in an organization. At Lockheed Martin, engineering departments are powerful; at Microsoft, software designers are powerful; at 3M, research and development people are powerful; and at Mary Kay, marketing people are powerful. We explore the reasons for power differences in organizations shortly.

People continually attempt to influence the behavior of others in the normal course of everyday living. For example, people quite naturally attempt to reinforce the pleasing or satisfying behaviors of family members and friends. Also, people often attempt to punish undesirable behavior (perhaps in very subtle ways) so that it will not be repeated. The behaviors of people at work are no different in this respect than the behaviors of people in general.

Power is a social term; that is, an individual has power in relation to other people, a team has power in relation to other groups, and so on. Thus the concept of power characterizes interactions among people—more than one person must be involved for the concept to have meaning. Further, power is never absolute or unchanging. It is a dynamic relationship that changes as situations and individuals change. For example, a manager may strongly influence the behavior of one subordinate but, at the same time, only marginally influence another. Managers may be powerful with respect to their own subordinates, yet be unable to influence the behaviors of employees in other departments. In addition, relationships change with time. Last month's successful influence attempt may fail tomorrow, even though the same people are involved in both situations.

Power relationships are the medium within which business is conducted. People often take these relationships for granted, but when they shift, everything changes. Some of the most basic power relationships in our society are changing.[4] Several of these power shifts may be described as follows.

- *From employers to employees.* The notion that employers are in charge of the employment relationship is one of our most deeply rooted assumptions about work. People "apply" for a job. If lucky, they are "granted" an interview. Prospective employees "receive an offer." These and other common expressions imply that employers, not employees, have the power. But for a great many organizations, it just isn't that way anymore. Employees in many fields are increasingly calling the shots. When managers and executives are asked what they're worried about, attracting top talent is typically near the top of the list. Companies are desperate for good people. In some industries, including computer firms and design firms, students are being offered signing bonuses and recruited much earlier in their college careers than was previously the case. Observers have described this behavior on the part of employers as quite similar to that exhibited by professional sports teams as they attempt to recruit top athletes who are free agents.

- *From large companies to medium-sized companies.* Some experts think that the advantages of size are fading and that giant companies will eventually be regarded as a historical phenomenon. Large companies, such as Wal-Mart or General Motors, can take advantage of economies of scale. However, in an economy based on information rather than on tangible products, economies of scale in manufacturing are less valuable than they used to be. With the costs of computing power and telecommunications rapidly falling, vast networks of human beings also are less of an advantage. For many sectors of the economy, particularly those based on information, medium-sized companies will be more competitive than huge firms, as they can make and act on decisions much more quickly.
- *From big government to the private sector.* Huge governments, like huge corporations, may be a historical phenomenon as well. Observers argue that private enterprise has regained the initiatives and power that had previously been shifted to governments around the world. A worldwide wave of privatization and deregulation has transformed societies in Eastern Europe and the former Soviet Union. Somewhat less dramatically, and also less noticed, deregulation has also been significant in countries such as Britain, Chile, Sweden, and the United States.
- *From management to shareholders.* With regard to the practical exercise of power, CEOs have been in control for decades because stock ownership of firms has been too widely dispersed for shareholders to wield much power. However, share ownership is increasingly concentrated in the hands of institutions (investment firms, mutual funds, and the like). These institutions expect and demand increases in shareholder value. CEOs who fail to deliver are seeing members of their boards of directors being replaced, their stock options being voted down, and themselves being fired.

The Managing Change Competency feature on page 268 further illustrates the dynamic, changing nature of power in corporate America.

The terms *power* and *authority*, although closely related, do not mean the same thing. **Authority** is power legitimated by (1) being formally granted by the organization and (2) being accepted by employees as being right and proper.[5] The most obvious organizational example is the superior–subordinate relationship. An organization has a formal authority structure with individuals, teams, departments, and divisions being charged with responsibility for certain activities and functions. When individuals join an organization, they generally recognize the authority structure as legitimate; that is, employees accept the manager's right to set policy and give direction. So long as directives are reasonable and related to the job, employees generally obey them. Authority is narrower in scope than power and applies to fewer behaviors in an organization.

In addition to exercising authority, an individual or team may be able to influence the behavior of other people in an organization for many other reasons. In general, power sources in an organization may be categorized as (1) interpersonal and (2) structural, as shown in Figure 9.1.

Learning Objective:

2. Describe the interpersonal sources of power.

INTERPERSONAL SOURCES OF POWER

Power issues in organizations often focus on interpersonal relationships between managers and subordinates, or leaders and followers. French and Raven identified five interpersonal sources of power: reward power, coercive power, legitimate power, expert power, and referent power.[6]

COMPETENCY: MANAGING CHANGE

REVENGE OF THE NERDS

Until recently, employers typically didn't consider that middle managers had much real power in organizations. Middle managers have been described as the "dray horses of business, yoked up to companies for the long haul." Their duties were often considered relatively easy to perform—conveying information up and down the hierarchy, monitoring subordinates and the environment, and controlling routine tasks and operations.

In the early 1990s, there was a "middle-management recession" in the United States. Many companies decided that their excess baggage was not production workers, but rather middle managers and, as a consequence, millions of them lost their jobs. Some employers also concluded that the information revolution coupled with new forms of organization meant that many middle managers wouldn't be needed in the future. Things had never looked more dismal for the middle manager—powerless, unwanted, and unneeded.

Amazingly enough, this power relationship between employers and middle managers has undergone a dramatic reversal in a very short time. Alan Schonberg, president of Management Recruiters International, a Cleveland search firm says, "There is higher demand for middle managers today than I have seen in my 33 years in the business. There are more middle-management job openings than there are people to fill them. The middle-manager job candidate has so many options that he has power over the employer."

How did this shift in power come to be? The answer, in part, is that many organizations overdid middle management cuts. Organizations typically make two mistakes during downsizing: (1) They wait too long to act so that the numbers of people let go are larger than they would be if they had acted earlier; and (2) regardless of timing, they tend to overreact and reduce employment further than they should. Now, many firms have far fewer middle managers than they need and are frantically having to rehire them in large numbers.

In addition, the strong trend toward organizing work around teams and projects has increased, rather than decreased, the opportunities for middle managers to play key roles in organizations. Not all middle managers can adapt to the new roles, which in some respects seem very different from the traditional middle-management job. However, the work experience of many middle managers has prepared them well for the cross-functional and across boundary aspects of team leadership in the organization of the future. And, to their chagrin, many organizations have discovered that managers who can effectively play these roles are in short supply.[7]

For more information on Management Recruiters International, visit this organization's home page at ***www.BrilliantPeople.com.***

REWARD POWER

Reward power is an individual's ability to influence others' behaviors by rewarding their desirable behaviors. For example, to the extent that subordinates value rewards that the manager can give—praise, promotions, money, time off, and so on—they may comply with requests and directives. A manager who controls the allocation of merit pay raises in a department has reward power over the employees in that department. Accordingly, employees may comply with some attempts by managers to influence their behaviors because they expect to be rewarded for their compliance.

COERCIVE POWER

Coercive power is an individual's ability to influence others' behaviors by punishing their undesirable behaviors. For example, subordinates may comply because they

Figure 9.1 **Sources of Power in Organizations**

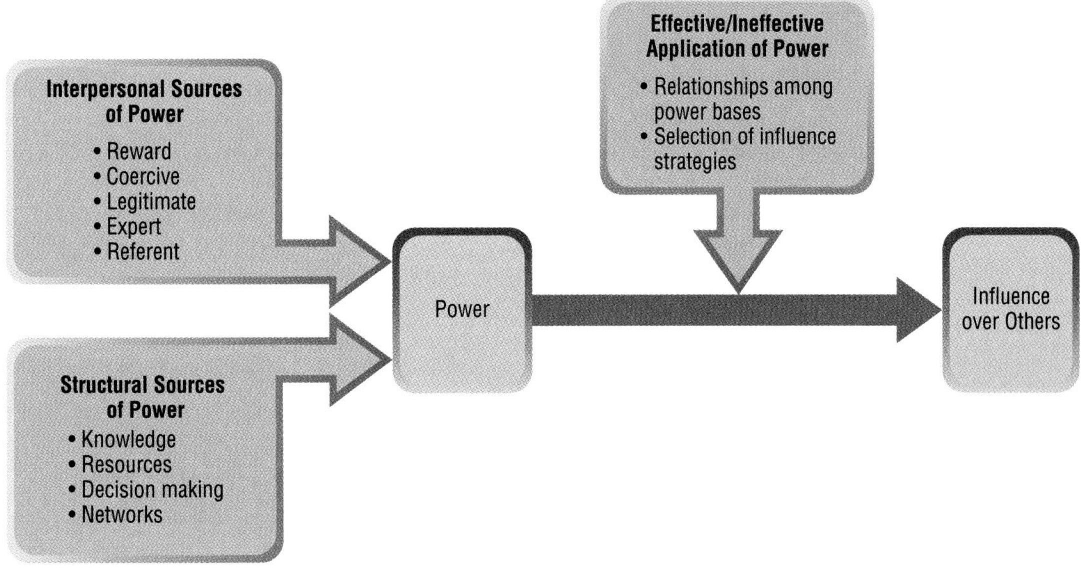

expect to be punished for failure to respond favorably to managerial directives. Punishment may take the form of reprimands, undesirable work assignments, closer supervision, tighter enforcement of work rules, suspension without pay, and the like. The organization's ultimate punishment is to fire the employee.

Recall, however, that punishment can have undesirable side effects (see Chapter 4). For example, the employee who receives an official reprimand for shoddy work may find ways (other than the obvious one the organization wants) to avoid the punishment, such as by refusing to perform the task, falsifying performance reports, or being absent frequently.

Legitimate Power

Legitimate power most often refers to a manager's ability to influence subordinates' behaviors because of the manager's formal position in the organization. Subordinates may respond to such influence because they acknowledge the manager's legitimate right to prescribe certain behaviors. Sometimes nonmanagerial employees possess legitimate power. For example, a safety inspector at Lockheed Martin Vought's plant in Camden, Arkansas, has the legitimate power to shut down production if there is a safety violation, even if the plant manager objects.

Legitimate power is an important organizational concept. Typically, a manager is empowered to make decisions within a specific area of responsibility, such as customer service, quality control, marketing, or accounting. This area of responsibility, in effect, defines the activities for which the manager (and sometimes other employees) can expect to exercise legitimate power to influence behavior. The farther that managers get from their specific areas of responsibility, the weaker their legitimate power becomes. Employees have a **zone of indifference** with respect to the exercise of managerial power.[8] Within the zone of indifference, employees will accept certain directives without questioning the manager's power, and the manager may have considerable legitimate power to influence subordinates' behavior. Outside that zone, however, legitimate power disappears rapidly. For example, a secretary will type letters, answer the phone, open the mail, and do similar tasks for a manager without question. However, if the manager asks the secretary to go out for a drink after work, the secretary may refuse.

The manager's request clearly falls outside the secretary's zone of indifference. The manager has no legitimate right to expect the secretary to comply.

Expert Power

Expert power is an individual's ability to influence others' behaviors because of recognized competencies, talents, or specialized knowledge. To the extent that managers can demonstrate competence in implementing, analyzing, evaluating, and controlling the tasks of subordinates, they will acquire expert power. Expert power often is relatively narrow in scope. For example, a team member at Overhead Door Company might carefully follow the advice of her team leader about how to program a numerically controlled lathe, yet ignore advice from the team leader regarding which of three company health plans she should choose. In this instance, the team member is recognizing expertise in one area while resisting influence in another. A lack of expert power often plagues new managers and employees. Even though a young accountant might possess a great deal of knowledge about accounting theory and procedures, that expertise must be demonstrated and applied over time to be recognized and accepted. Similarly, employees or managers from underrepresented groups may have difficulty getting their expertise recognized by others, as illustrated by the following incident.

> The head of a large division of a multinational corporation was running a meeting devoted to performance assessment. Each senior manager stood up, reviewed the individuals in his group, and evaluated them for promotion. Although there were women in every group, not one of them made the cut. One after another, each manager declared, in effect, that every woman in his group didn't have the self-confidence needed to be promoted. The division head began to doubt his ears. How could it be that all the talented women in the division suffered from a lack of self-confidence?[9]

An assessment indicated that the firm, in fact, had many promotable women. The managers conducting the performance appraisal sessions had failed to recognize the knowledge and potential of their female subordinates. The reason, in part, involved lack of appreciation for differences in men's and women's interpersonal and communication styles, approaches to problem solving, and the like.

Referent Power

Referent power is an individual's ability to influence others' behaviors as a result of being respected, admired, or liked. For example, subordinates' identification with a manager often forms the basis for referent power. This identification may include the desire of subordinates to emulate the manager. (See Chapter 12 for an explanation of how this source of power is related to charismatic leadership.) A young manager may copy the leadership style of an older, admired, and more experienced manager. The older manager thus has some ability—some referent power—to influence the behavior of the younger manager. Referent power usually is associated with individuals who possess admired personality characteristics, charisma, or a good reputation. Thus it often is associated with political leaders, movie stars, sports figures, or other well-known individuals (hence their use in advertising to influence consumer behavior). However, managers and employees also may have considerable referent power because of the strength of their personalities. Meg Whitman, CEO of eBay, and Herb Kelleher, CEO of Southwest Airlines, use their referent power to motivate employees to achieve their organization's goals.

Relationships Among Power Sources

Managers and employees alike possess varying amounts of interpersonal sources of power. As implied by Figure 9.1, these sources don't operate independently. A study conducted in two paper mills provides an example of how power sources are related.[10] One of the mills dropped an incentive pay plan based on performance in favor of a pay plan based strictly on seniority. Compared to the second plant, which retained the performance system, subordinates' perceptions of the use of various sources of power by supervisors in the first plant changed noticeably. Discontinuing the incentive plan lowered the perceived reward power of supervisors, as might be expected, but other results were more complex. Perceptions of supervisors' use of punishment increased (attributable perhaps to less control over rewards). The perceived use of referent and legitimate power decreased, but expert power appeared to be unaffected. These findings suggest that the interpersonal sources of power that influence behavior are complex and interrelated.

The ways in which managers and employees use one type of power can either enhance or limit the effectiveness of power from another source. For example, managers who administer rewards to subordinates also tend to be well liked and seem to have greater referent power than managers who don't give out rewards. However, the use of coercive power can reduce referent power. The threatened or actual use of punishment appears to reduce liking or admiration, leading to a reduction in referent power. Further, employees often view managers who possess knowledge valuable to them as having greater legitimate power in addition to having expert power.

These five sources of interpersonal power may be divided into two broad categories: organizational and personal. Reward power, coercive power, and legitimate power have organizational bases; that is, top managers can give to or take away from lower level managers or others the right to administer rewards and punishments. The organization can change employees' legitimate power by changing their positions in the authority hierarchy or by changing job descriptions, rules, and procedures. Referent power and expert power, however, depend much more on personal characteristics—personality, leadership style, and knowledge—brought to the job. In the long run, the organization may influence expert power by, for example, making additional training available. But the individuals determine how they use that training, that is, the extent to which they apply the new knowledge. Workplace studies often show that personal sources of power (expert and referent power) are more important than organizational sources (legitimate, reward, and coercive power). We do not argue that these organizational sources are unimportant; however, we do believe that careful selection and proper training are important to supervisory and managerial effectiveness.

Learning Objective:

3. Discuss the main categories of structural sources of power.

STRUCTURAL SOURCES OF POWER

Certainly, much of the interest in organizational power tends to focus on the power of managers over subordinates. However, an additional crucial perspective is that the characteristics of a situation also affect or determine power. Situational characteristics include the design of the organization, the type of departmental structure, the *opportunity* to influence, access to powerful individuals and critical resources, the nature of the position an individual holds, and so on.[11] For example, the power associated with a particular position or job is affected by its visibility to upper management and its importance or relevance with respect to the organization's goals or priorities. Table 9.1 contains some examples of position characteristics that determine relative power within an organization. Note that, whereas the legitimate power previously discussed applies primarily to managerial positions, the characteristics described in Table 9.1 are relevant for both managerial and nonmanagerial positions.

Structural and situational sources of power reflect the division of labor and position in different teams and departments. Work assignments, locations, and roles naturally result in unequal access to information, resources, decision making, and other people. Any of an almost infinite variety of specific situational factors could become a source of power in an organization. Important structural sources of power include knowledge, resources, decision making, and networks.

Table 9.1 Position Characteristics Associated with Power

CHARACTERISTIC	DEFINITION	EXAMPLE
Centrality	Relationship among positions in a communication network	More-central positions will have greater power.
Criticality	Relationships among tasks performed in a workflow process	Positions responsible for the most critical tasks will have more power.
Flexibility	Amount of discretion in decision making, work assignments, and so on	More-autonomous positions will have more power.
Visibility	Degree to which task performance is seen by higher management in the organization	More-visible positions will have more power.
Relevance	Relationship between tasks and high-priority organizational goals	Positions most closely related to important goals will have more power.

Source: Adapted from Whetten, D. A., and Cameron, K. S. *Developing Managerial Skills*, 4th ed. Reading, Mass.: Addison-Wesley, 1998, 238.

Knowledge as Power

Organizations are information processors that must use knowledge to produce goods and services. The concept of **knowledge as power** means that individuals, teams, or departments that possess knowledge crucial to attaining the organization's goals have power. Those in a position to control information about current operations, develop information about alternatives, or acquire knowledge about future events and plans have enormous power to influence the behaviors of others. Thus certain staff and support activities—a data processing center, for example—sometimes seem to have influence disproportionate to their relationship to the organization's goals and main activities.

Personal computers and computerized workstations are having a dramatic impact on the access to and use of information—and thus on power relationships—in many organizations. Information is now widely available to many more employees than in the past. Greater access to information tends to flatten the hierarchy and make hoarding information by individuals and departments more difficult. Further, computer networks provide employees with information that previously was available only to management. Information sharing has important implications for the quality of decision making and other aspects of performance. The extensive use of computer networks is spreading and presenting management with both opportunities and challenges. An example of such changes is presented in the Managing Across Cultures competency feature on the next page.

Some experts now claim that intellectual capital is corporate America's most valuable asset. **Intellectual capital** represents the knowledge, know-how, and skill that exists in an organization.[12] This intellectual capital can provide an organization with a competitive edge in the marketplace. However, perhaps because knowledge is power, sharing of information doesn't come easily at some firms. A study at Price Waterhouse found that some junior employees wouldn't share information on the computer network because of the firm's intensely competitive culture.[13] Computer networks can create a flatter, more democratic organization as they are doing in Africa. But that will happen only if such organizational changes are supported by top management and a compatible organizational culture.

COMPETENCY: MANAGING ACROSS CULTURES

WORKPLACE DEMOCRACY IN AFRICA

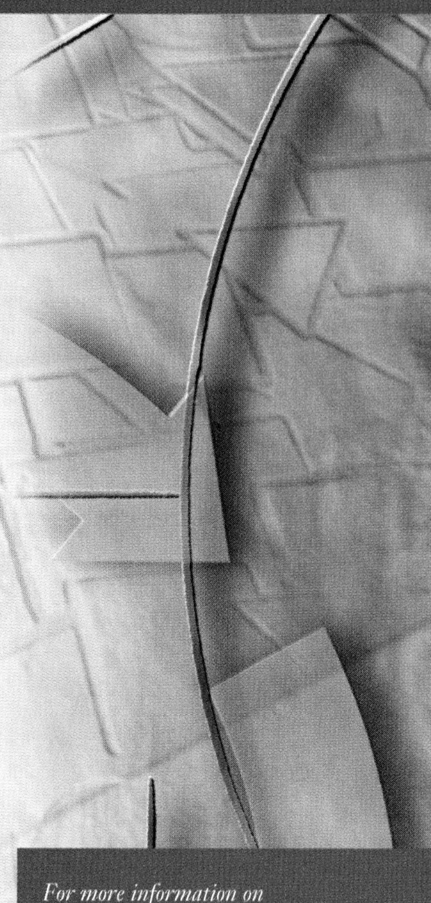

In African firms there has long been a very traditional view concerning access to information. Historically, information was shared only with those deemed trustworthy who could be counted on not to misuse the information. For example, salary information and the differential benefits available to management and labor have been jealously guarded secrets. The gap, in terms of education and skill level, between management and other employees in African firms has been the widest in the world. This gap probably contributed to the widespread notion in African firms that only managers (and sometimes just the highest level managers) could be entrusted with meaningful information about the organization.

However, the very nature of the employment relationship is changing within African organizations, according to Patrick Deale, a partner with SPA Consultants in South Africa. There has been a shift from authoritarianism and paternalism to greater employee participation and consensus-oriented management. This shift is being fueled by two developments: (1) the transformation to political democracy in many African countries is leading to a greater emphasis on "workplace democracy"; and (2) as in more advanced economies, the increased use of sophisticated information technologies is making information available to "rank-and-file" employees in Africa as well.

Eskom, Africa's largest producer of electricity, provides a good example of an organization in which information sharing with employees has begun. As a matter of corporate philosophy, Eskom is seeking to introduce a work culture characterized by maximum information sharing and meaningful participation in decision making by all employees to the extent practicable. Eskom's goal is to provide employees at the lowest levels of the organization with the skills, access to information, and time to participate fully in decisions that affect their work. Computer networks, as well as expanded training opportunities, will be essential if Eskom is to achieve its vision of information sharing and workplace democracy.[14]

For more information on Eskom, visit this organization's home page at www.eskom.co.za.

RESOURCES AS POWER

Organizations need a variety of resources, including human resources, money, equipment, materials, supplies, and customers, to survive. The importance of specific resources to a firm's success and the difficulty of obtaining them vary. The concept of **resources as power** suggests that individuals, teams, or departments who can provide essential or difficult-to-obtain resources acquire power in the organization. Which resources are the most important depends on the situation, the organization's goals, the economic climate, and the goods or services being produced. The old saying that "he who has the gold makes the rules" sums up the idea that resources are power.

DECISION MAKING AS POWER

Decisions in organizations often are made sequentially, with many individuals, groups, or teams participating (see Chapter 14). The decision-making process creates additional power differences. The concept of **decision making as power** recognizes that individuals, teams, or departments acquire power to the extent that they can affect the decision-making process. They might influence the goals being developed, premises being used in evaluating an issue, alternatives being considered, outcomes being projected, and so on. For example, Southern California Edison uses a technique known as *scenario planning* to develop strategic plans for the future of the electric utility. Scenario planners might look ahead 10 years and develop a dozen possible versions of the future—another Middle East oil crisis, heightened environmental concerns, an economic boom in southern California, a major recession, and so on. Each scenario has implications for needed capacity, investment funds, human resources, and the like. The individuals and departments involved in scenario planning at Edison wield considerable influence, regardless of whether they make the final decisions about resource allocations.

The ability to influence the decision-making process is a subtle and often overlooked source of power. Decision-making power doesn't necessarily reside with the final decision maker in an organization. A powerful machine politician in New York City once reportedly said, "I don't care who does the electing, as long as I have the power to do the nominating."

Networks as Power

The existence of structural and situational power depends not only on access to information, resources, and decision making, but also on the ability to get cooperation in carrying out tasks. Managers and departments that have connecting links with other individuals and departments in the organization will be more powerful than those who don't. Certainly, traditional superior–subordinate vertical relationships are important aspects of power, but these linkages don't begin to tell the whole story. Horizontal linkages provided by both internal and external networks help explain a lot of power differences. The concept of **networks as power** implies that various affiliations, channels of information, and coalitions, both inside and outside the organization, represent sources of power.

As examples of the concept of networks as power, consider the following connecting links. Note that each example relates to a factor already discussed that creates power differences.

- *Information links.* To be effective, managers and employees must be "in the know," both formally and informally. (Knowledge is power.)
- *Supply links.* Outside links provide managers with the opportunity to bring materials, money, or other resources into their organizations, departments, or teams. (Resources are power.)
- *Support links.* A manager's job must allow for decision-making discretion—the exercise of judgment. Managers must know that they can make decisions and pursue innovative, risk-taking ventures without each decision or action having to go through a stifling, multilayered approval process. Managers need the backing of important people in the organization, whose support becomes another resource they bring to their own work. (Participation in decision making is power and an important indicator of support links.)[15]

A further example of the importance of networks and connecting links is shown in Table 9.2. It contains Kanter's analysis of the root causes of powerlessness for supervisors, staff professionals, and top executives.

Understanding internal networks is the key to understanding how work gets done in an organization. To identify and determine how they work together, managers and employees can undertake a **network analysis**, whereby they attempt to diagram important relationship networks within the organization. For example, the *advice network* reveals employees that others depend on to solve problems and provide technical information. The *trust network* shows which employees share delicate political information with each other. The *communication network* (see Chapter 13) indicates who talks to whom on a regular basis. By understanding these and other networks, managers can diagnose the informal organization and understand more about how work actually gets done (or fails to get done) in the organization, as well as identify power differences among individuals, teams, and departments.[16]

Table 9.2 **Sources of Powerlessness**

POSITION	LACK OF POWER DUE TO:
First-line supervisors	Routine jobs characterized by rigid rules Limited access to information Limited advancement possibilities
Staff professionals	Tasks viewed as peripheral to the "real work" of the organization Blocked careers Easy replacement by outside experts
Top executives	Limited or blocked lines of information from lower levels of organization Lack of control of lines of supply Reduced lines of support due to political challenges from special-interest groups or other members of the public

Source: Kanter, R. M. *Rosabeth Moss Kanter on the Frontiers of Management*. Boston: Harvard Business Review Books, 1997, 153.

Lower Level Employee Power

Although we commonly think of power as something that managers have, lower level employees also may wield considerable power. Some sources of interpersonal power—expert power, in particular—may allow subordinates to influence their managers. For example, the staff assistant who can set up and use a Windows 98 spreadsheet has the power to influence a manager if the manager is unable to use the spreadsheet and must rely on the staff assistant's expertise.

Although lower level employees may have some interpersonal power, their ability to influence others' behaviors more likely stems from structural or situational sources. Figure 9.2 suggests that their power is a result of their positions in the organization.

Figure 9.2 **Model of Lower Level Employee Power**

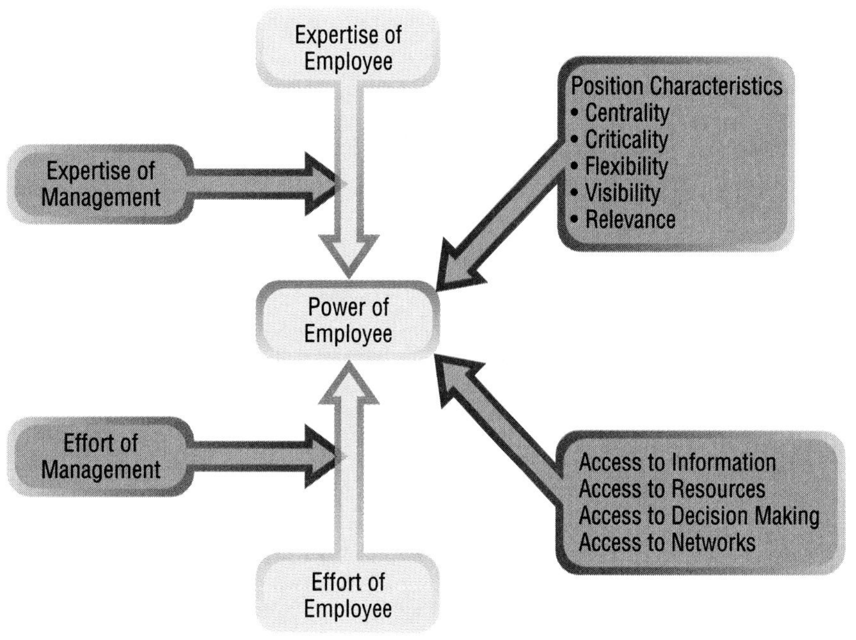

Take another look at Table 9.1 to remind yourself of the important position characteristics related to power. In addition to these characteristics, lower level employees may be able to control access to information or resources and important aspects of the decision-making process. Networks or affiliations with powerful individuals or groups may be yet another source of their power. Further, the expertise of employees and the amount of effort expended also influence the extent of their power. As Figure 9.2 illustrates, whether expertise and effort increase employees' power depends, in part, on their superior's expertise and effort. Employees can acquire power by expending effort in areas where management puts little effort. If an employee's manager has little knowledge about a certain task and the employee has considerable knowledge about it, the relative power of the employee increases. For example, language skills can increase the relative power of bilingual employees, as demonstrated in the following Managing Diversity Competency feature.

COMPETENCY: MANAGING DIVERSITY

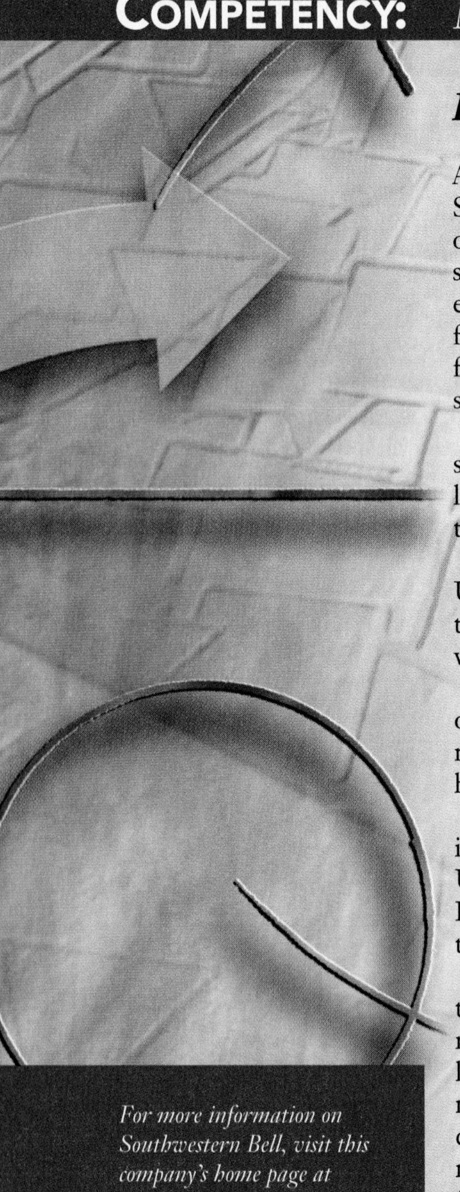

*For more information on Southwestern Bell, visit this company's home page at **www.swbell.com**.*

BILINGUAL EMPLOYEES ACQUIRE POWER

At the first hint of Spanish, Southwestern Bell directory-assistance operators in San Antonio, a heavily Hispanic city, push a button to route callers to a bilingual operator such as Maggie Morales. Morales and other workers state that this new system, while effective, has made their jobs a lot tougher. Sifting through differences in language and culture means that she can't always meet the company's goal for getting off the phone in 21.5 seconds or less. "In Spanish, it can take a while to figure out that 'eternity general' isn't a hospital, but the attorney general's office," she says.

Maggie Morales doesn't mind the extra work. But like many of her colleagues, she wants the company to pay her more for her language skills. "The more computer languages you know, the more you make," says fellow operator Lillian Stevens, who taught herself Spanish. "Why shouldn't that be the same for languages?"

That question is being asked by bilingual employees in many organizations. As U.S. companies expand overseas and reach out to more non-English-speaking customers at home, demand for workers with language skills is rising fast. These workers' pay expectations are rising fast as well.

But the debate is complex. Many other workers believe it unfair to pay someone extra for a skill that may come as naturally as talking. Employers who want to reward workers for their second languages are finding that it isn't easy to figure out how to do so in a way that will be perceived as equitable.

Still, workers at companies from AT&T to the U.S. Postal Service are pressing their demands with greater insistence. Early in 1996, about 2,500 bilingual U.S. Customs Service inspectors threatened to slow down international travel in Florida, New York, and California by refusing to speak a foreign language unless the Treasury Department paid them more.

The bilingual issue has moved to center stage because of business and social trends. Corporate recruitment of bilingual workers has increased dramatically in recent years. Companies are more aggressively marketing to the estimated 20 million U.S. residents for whom English is a second language. Accompanying the marketing shift is a big change in the way foreign languages are perceived. As recently as the early 1980s, Southwestern Bell operators in Texas could be reprimanded for speaking Spanish on the job. Today, the company advertises extensively for bilingual workers.[17]

Learning Objective:

4. Discuss effective and ineffective uses of power.

THE EFFECTIVE USE OF POWER

When managers, employees, or teams face a situation in which they want to influence the behaviors of others, they must choose a strategy. **Influence strategies** are the methods by which individuals or groups attempt to exert power or influence others' behaviors. Table 9.3 lists various influence strategies used in the workplace.

We are interested in identifying effective influence strategies and understanding the situations in which each might be used. For the influence strategies shown in Table 9.3, research indicates that rational persuasion, inspirational appeal, and consultation often are the most effective in a variety of circumstances. The least effective strategies seem to be pressure, coalition, and legitimating. However, to assume that certain strategies will always work or that others will always fail is a mistake. Differences in effectiveness occur when attempts to influence are downward rather than upward in the organizational hierarchy. Likewise, differences in effectiveness appear when various strategies are used in combination rather than independently. This process is complex, and to understand fully the effectiveness of various influence strategies requires an understanding of the power sources available, the direction of attempts to influence (i.e., upward, downward, or laterally), and the goals being sought.[18]

Having the *capacity* (power) to influence the behaviors of others and effectively using this capacity (power) aren't the same thing. Managers who believe that they can always effectively influence the behaviors of others by acquiring enough power simply to order other people around generally are ineffective. The ineffective use of power has many negative implications, both for the individual and the organization. For example, a study examined the consequences of an overreliance on assertiveness and persistence as an influence strategy (the *pressure* strategy in Table 9.3). Managers who were aggressive and persistent with others—characterized by a refusal to take no for an answer, reliance on repeated reminders, frequent use of face-to-face confrontations, and the like—suffered negative consequences. Compared to other managers studied, these aggressive managers (1) received the lowest performance evaluations, (2) earned less money, and (3) experienced the highest levels of job tension and stress.[19]

Table 9.3 Influence Strategies

INFLUENCE STRATEGY	DEFINITION
Rational persuasion	Use logical arguments and factual evidence.
Inspirational appeal	Appeal to values, ideals, or aspirations to arouse enthusiasm.
Consultation	Seek participation in planning a strategy, activity, or change.
Ingratiation	Attempt to create a favorable mood before making request.
Exchange	Offer an exchange of favors, share of benefits, or promise to reciprocate at later time.
Personal appeal	Appeal to feelings of loyalty or friendship.
Coalition	Seek aid or support of others for some initiative or activity.
Legitimating	Seek to establish legitimacy of a request by claiming authority or by verifying consistency with policies, practices, or traditions.
Pressure	Use demands, threats, or persistent reminders.

Source: Adapted from Yukl, G., Guinan, P. J., and Sottolano, D. Influence tactics used for different objectives with subordinates, peers, and superiors. *Group & Organization Management*, 1995, 20, 275; Buchanan, D., and Badham, R. *Power, Politics and Organizational Change*. London: Sage, 1999, 64.

Effective influence in organizations also depends on an exchange process somewhat related to the *exchange* influence strategy in Table 9.3. The **exchange process** in power relationships is based on the law of reciprocity—the almost universal belief that people should be compensated in some way for what they do.[20] Imagine that an employee is asked by her manager to work through the weekend on an important project. The employee does so but receives no recognition, no extra time off, no extra pay—not even a "thank you." The employee later discovers that her manager took sole credit for the project, which was quite successful. This employee, and most observers, would agree that the manager violated an important aspect of a good working relationship: giving recognition or other rewards in exchange for the employee's contributions.

The expectation of reciprocal actions, or exchange, occurs repeatedly in organizations. In part, because people expect to be compensated, or otherwise have "favors" returned, influence becomes possible in many situations. The exchange process is particularly important with peers or colleagues because formal authority to ensure compliance is absent. Power in the exchange process stems from the ability to offer something that others need. The metaphor of currencies provides a useful way to understand how the exchange process influences behavior. Table 9.4 provides some interesting examples of the many types of currencies "traded" in organizations. Note the similarities between these currencies and the sources of power previously discussed.

The effective use of power is a difficult challenge for managers and employees alike. The goal is to influence the behaviors of others in ways that are consistent with both the needs of the organization and its employees. If the use of power isn't carefully managed, powerful individuals may exploit those with less power and substitute their self-interests for the legitimate interests of the organization. Managers and employees who use power effectively often possess five characteristics.[21]

First, they understand both the interpersonal and the structural sources of power and the most effective methods of using them to influence people. For example, professionals (e.g., R&D scientists, engineers, lawyers, or professors) tend to be more readily influenced by expertise than by other interpersonal sources of power. Effective managers and employees often recognize the structural and situational problems that exist in a power relationship and modify their own behaviors to fit the actual situation. As a result, they tend to develop and use a wide variety of power sources and influence strategies. Some ineffective managers rely too much on one or a few power bases or influence strategies.

Table 9.4 Organizational Currencies Traded in the Exchange Process

CURRENCY	EXAMPLE
Resources	Lending or giving money, budget increases, personnel, space
Assistance	Helping with existing projects or undertaking unwanted tasks
Cooperation	Giving task support, providing quicker response time, approving a project, or aiding implementation
Information	Providing organizational or technical knowledge
Advancement	Giving a task or assignment that can aid in promotion
Recognition	Acknowledging effort, accomplishment, or abilities
Network/contracts	Providing opportunities for linking with others
Personal support	Giving personal and emotional backing

Source: Adapted from Cohen, A. R., and Bradford, D. L. Influence without authority: The use of alliances, reciprocity, and exchanges to accomplish work. *Organizational Dynamics*, Winter 1989, 11; also see Ulrich, D., Zenger, J., and Smallwood, N. *Results-Based Leadership*. Boston: Harvard Business School Press, 1999.

Second, they understand the nature of the exchange process underlying many successful attempts to influence others. They recognize that, over time, unless reciprocal exchanges are roughly equivalent and fair, hard feelings will result and their ability to influence others will decline.

Third, they know what is and what is not legitimate behavior in acquiring and using power. The misuse or lack of understanding of a source of power can destroy its effectiveness. For example, individuals erode expert power if they attempt to demonstrate expertise in areas where they lack the required knowledge. Individuals may lose referent power by behaving in ways that are inconsistent with characteristics or traits that are attractive to others.

Fourth, they tend to seek positions that allow the development and use of power. In other words, they choose jobs that involve the crucial issues and concerns of an organization. These jobs provide opportunities for and, indeed, demand influencing the behavior of others. Successful performance in these positions, in turn, allows individuals to acquire power.

Finally, they use maturity and self-control in applying their power. They recognize that their actions influence the behaviors and lives of others. Although they are not necessarily reluctant or afraid to use their power—recognizing that influencing the behaviors of employees is a legitimate and necessary part of the manager's role—they nevertheless exercise power carefully. They do so in ways that are principled and fair and that are consistent with organizational needs and goals.

Learning Objective:

5. Explain the concept of organizational politics and diagnose personal and situational factors that contribute to political behavior.

POLITICAL BEHAVIOR

Political behavior involves attempts by some to influence the behaviors of others and the course of events in the organization in order to protect their self-interests, meet their own needs, and advance their own goals.[22] Described in this way, almost all behavior may be regarded as political. Labeling behavior as political, however, usually implies a judgment that certain people are gaining something at the expense of others or the organization as a whole. However, a balanced understanding of political behavior and its consequences is needed. People often are self-centered and biased when labeling actions as political behavior. Employees may justify their own political behavior as defending legitimate rights or interests, yet call similar behavior by others "playing politics." In any event, the Managing Change Competency feature on page 280 dramatically illustrates outcomes typically perceived as negative that can stem from unchecked political behavior by powerful people.

ORGANIZATIONAL POLITICS

Organizational politics involves actions by individuals, teams, or departments to acquire, develop, and use power and other resources in order to obtain preferred outcomes when uncertainty or disagreement about choices exists.[23] When people share power but differ about what must be done, many decisions and actions quite naturally will be the result of a political process.

Employees are often concerned about office politics.[24] Typically, they also believe that an ideal work setting would be free from political behavior. Negative attitudes about political behavior and organizational politics can block understanding of this crucial aspect of organizational behavior. Examples of behaviors often seen as political are shown in Table 9.5. People tend to assume that political behavior doesn't yield the best organizational decisions or outcomes—that somehow, by pushing for their own positions, they cause inferior actions or decisions to be produced. Although this result can occur, political behavior isn't always detrimental to an organization. For example, a study involving managers in 30 organizations indicated that they were able to identify beneficial, as well as harmful, effects of political behavior.[25] Beneficial effects

COMPETENCY: MANAGING CHANGE

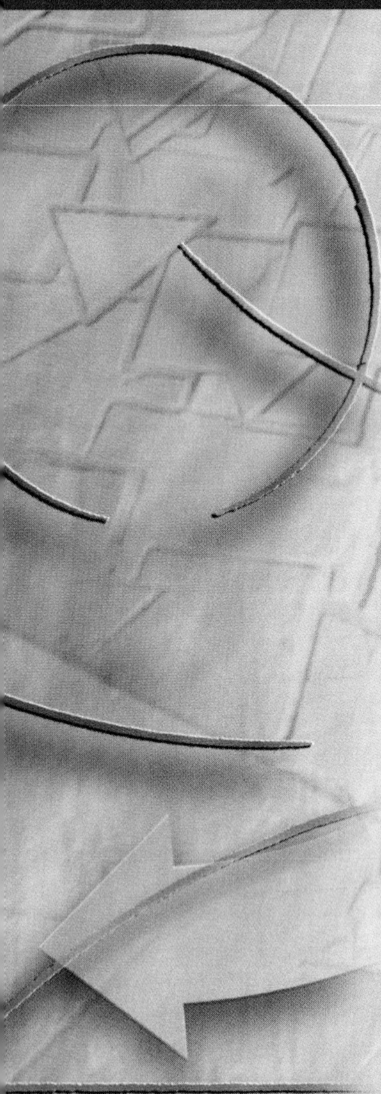

THE POLITICS OF INNOVATION

In 1873, Christopher Sholes invented the typewriter. Well over a century later, this same typewriter keyboard is still the principal tool that most people use to communicate via the computer. What is unknown to most people, though, is that the particular configuration of keys (referred to as the QWERTY keyboard) was purposely engineered to *slow down* typists in order to accommodate the limitations of the original typewriter. It relied on gravity to return struck keys to their resting positions and could jam if keys were struck in quick succession. Thus the keyboard was designed to prevent typists from striking keys too rapidly, particularly keys located next to each other, so keys containing letters used frequently were separated by space on the keyboard. With modern typewriters, this mechanical problem no longer exists, nor is it a problem with PC keyboards.

Surprisingly, a keyboard with a significantly improved configuration of keys has been in existence since 1932. The Dvorak simplified keyboard (DSK) has repeatedly been shown to be faster and more accurate than the standard keyboard in use, yet this innovation has never been adopted. Why?

The story of the DSK keyboard pits a solitary inventor against large organizations with a stake in maintaining the status quo. For some 30 years, Dr. August Dvorak fought to have his keyboard adopted as the standard. Dvorak and his associates conducted time and motion studies, participated in international typing contests, and even arranged for trial tests to be conducted by the federal government. Studies and tests showed the DSK keyboard improved productivity by 35 to 100 percent, with approximately 50 percent fewer mistakes. From 1934 to 1941, DSK-trained typists won the World Typewriting Championships. Dvorak failed to gain a government contract for his typewriters despite government tests that showed an average 74 percent gain in productivity. Both the U.S. Navy and the General Services Administration rejected converting to the DSK keyboard because of the costs of replacing equipment and retraining typists. The U.S. Navy assigned a security classification to test results of the DSK, thereby ensuring that few people would be aware of them.

Dvorak also faced active resistance from typewriter manufacturers. Manufacturers sponsored most of the typing contests and routinely attempted to prevent DSK typists from competing. Results of typing contests typically failed to list the machines that typists used when DSK typists won. Even instances of sabotage of Dvorak's machines were documented.

Adoption of the DSK was defeated by political resistance on the part of typewriter manufacturers who had little incentive to use the improved keyboard. The increased productivity from the new keyboard could have reduced sales of typewriters, as an office would need fewer machines if each typist could produce more. Further, manufacturers would have been required to pay royalties on the DSK, which was a patented invention.

Today, of course, the QWERTY keyboard is still with us in PC use. Cynthia Crossen, a *Wall Street Journal* reporter, states, "Take a good look at your computer keyboard, and behold one of the worst-designed, least-friendly tools in the workplace today." Crossen points out that the computer keyboard contains a number of keys, such Print Scrn, Scroll Lock, and Pause, that were developed during the earliest days of personal computers (primarily for the early DOS operating system) and have little or no use in current software. Even the function keys across the top of the keyboard are unneeded for programs involving the use of a "mouse." Although some companies, such as Apple, have experimented with different keyboard layouts, computer makers in general have little desire to redesign them. In addition to believing that people need to have a layout that matches their typing training, computer makers cite the tremendous cost of making a change because most current software is written for the standard keyboard. Sound familiar?[26]

For more information on the Wall Street Journal *and Apple Computer, visit these companies' home pages at* ***www.wsj.com*** *and* ***www.apple.com.***

Table 9.5

Common Political Tactics	
Taking counsel	The individual exercises great caution in seeking or giving advice.
Maneuverability	The individual maintains flexibility and never completely commits himself to any one position or program.
Communication	The individual never communicates everything she knows. Instead she withholds information and/or times its release carefully.
Compromising	The individual accepts compromise only as a short-term tactic while continuing to press ahead with his own agenda.
Confidence	Once the individual has made a decision, he must always give the impression of knowing what he is doing, even when he does not.
Always the boss	An atmosphere of social friendship limits the power of the manager, thus the manager always maintains a sense of distance and separation with his subordinates.

Source: Buchanan, D., and Badham, R. *Power, Politics, and Organizational Change*. London: Sage, 1999, 193.

included career advancement, recognition and status for individuals looking after their legitimate interests, and achievement of organizational goals—getting the job done—as a result of the normal political process in the organization. Harmful effects included demotions and loss of jobs for "losers" in the political process, a misuse of resources, and creation of an ineffective organizational culture. The effect on culture may be among the most undesirable consequences of continual political behavior. Organizational politics may arouse anxieties that cause employees to withdraw emotionally from the organization. The withdrawal, in turn, makes creating an organizational culture characterized by high performance and high commitment very difficult.

Political behavior, then, can meet appropriate and legitimate individual and organizational needs, or it can result in negative outcomes. In any event, managers and employees must understand political behavior because it definitely will occur. Eliminating political behavior isn't possible—it can only be managed.

Forces Creating Political Behavior

The probability of political behavior typically increases in proportion to disagreements over goals, unclear goals, different ideas about the organization and its problems, different information about the situation, the need to allocate scarce resources, and so on.[27] If these forces didn't exist, perhaps political behavior wouldn't exist either. However, outcomes are never certain, resources are never infinite, and people must make difficult choices between competing goals and methods to attain them. Thus political behavior will naturally occur as individuals, teams, and departments attempt to obtain their preferred outcomes. Managers shouldn't try to prevent the inevitable, but rather should try to ensure that these activities do not have negative consequences for the organization and its employees.

Managers and employees are more likely to act politically when (1) decision-making procedures and performance measures are uncertain and complex, and (2) competition for scarce resources is strong. Conversely, in more stable and less complex environments where decision-making processes are clear and competitive behavior is less, excessive political behavior is unlikely. Figure 9.3 illustrates these conclusions.

Even though personality and other individual differences may contribute to political behavior, such behavior is typically more strongly influenced by aspects of the situation. Organizations make engaging in political behavior easier when they provide few rules or policies. Ambiguous circumstances allow individuals to define situations in ways that satisfy their own needs and desires. Further, when employees want more of a resource (e.g., equipment or office space) than is available, political behavior is likely to occur.

FIGURE 9.3 **Probability of Political Behavior in Organizations**

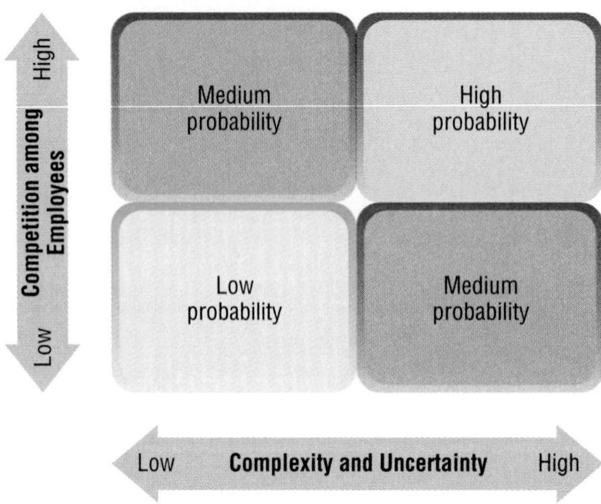

Source: Adapted from Beeman, D. R., and Sharkey, T. W. The use and abuse of corporate politics. *Business Horizons*, March–April 1987, 27.

In addition to the dimensions shown in Figure 9.3, political behavior is higher in organizations that reward it. A reward system may focus solely on individual accomplishment and minimize team contributions. When that's the case, individuals may be tempted to behave politically to ensure that they receive some of the rewards. If their political actions result in rewards, employees may be even more likely to engage in such actions in the future. Similarly, individuals who had avoided political behavior, may start behaving politically when they observe such behavior being rewarded. In sum, the organizational reward system can be a significant factor in the occurrence of political behavior.

Decisions can be made less political by increasing the resources available (thus reducing conflict over scarce resources) or by making decisions seem less important than they really are. However, strategies to reduce the political behavior associated with decision making may have some unintended consequences that translate into real costs for an organization. Table 9.6 shows several examples of

TABLE 9.6 **Strategies for Avoiding the Use of Political Behavior in Decision Making and Their Possible Costs**

STRATEGY	COSTS
Slack or excess resources, including additional administrative positions	Inventory, excess capacity, extra personnel, and salary
Strong-culture—similarity in beliefs, values, and goals produced through recruitment, socialization, and use of rewards and punishments	Fewer points of view, less diverse information represented in decision making, and potentially lower quality decisions
Making decisions appear less important	Decision avoided; critical analysis not done; important information not uncovered
Reducing system complexity and uncertainty	Creation of rigid rules and procedures; reduction of capacity for change

Source: Adapted from Pfeffer, J. *Power in Organizations.* Marshfield, Mass.: Pitman, 1981, 93; Pfeffer, J. *Managing with Power: Politics and Influence in Organizations.* Boston: Harvard Business School Press, 1993.

strategies used to avoid organizational politics and the potential costs associated with each strategy.

The performance appraisal process provides a good example of a situation in organizations that may create political behavior. Performance for many employees isn't easily measured, and the process results in the allocation of scarce resources (pay, bonuses, benefits, etc.) based on complex criteria. The following Managing Ethics Competency feature describes political behavior in the performance appraisal process.

Many organizations ignore the existence of politics in the appraisal process or may assume that use of quantitative performance appraisal forms will minimize it. However, as described in the Managing Ethics Competency feature below, political behavior may be a fact of life in many appraisal processes. In particular, because of the ambiguous nature of managerial work, appraisals of managers are susceptible to

COMPETENCY: MANAGING ETHICS

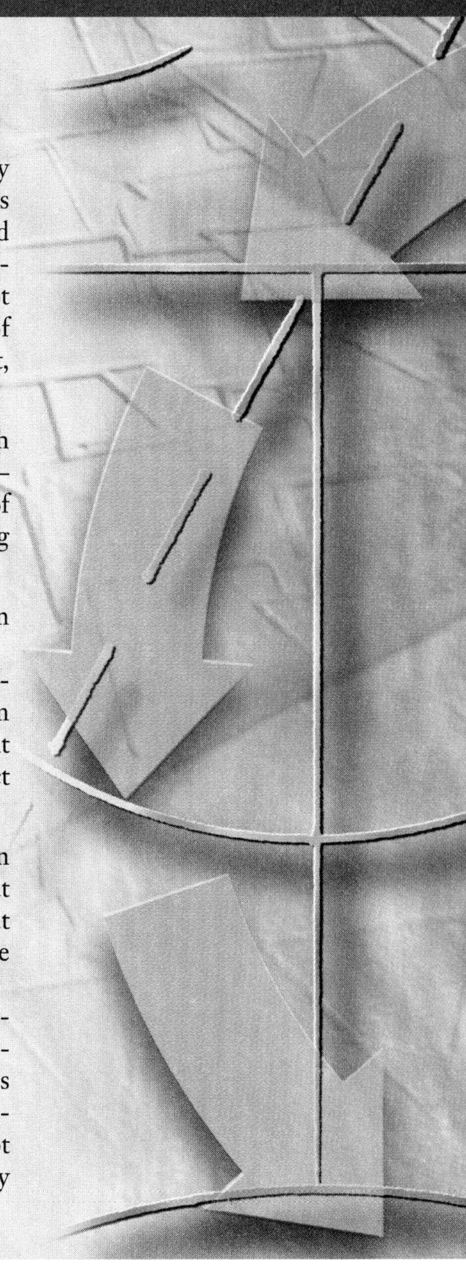

THE POLITICS OF EMPLOYEE APPRAISAL

> There is really no getting around the fact that whenever I evaluate one of my people, I stop and think about the impact—the ramifications of my decisions on my relationship with the employee and his or her future here. I'd be stupid not to. Call it being politically minded, or using managerial discretion, or fine-tuning the ratings, but in the end, I've got to live with him or her, and I'm not going to rate a person without thinking about the fallout. There are a lot of games played in the rating process, and whether we (managers) admit it or not, we are all guilty of playing them at our discretion.

That statement comes from one of 60 executives who participated in in-depth interviews concerning their performance appraisal processes. These executives—from seven large corporations—had performance appraisal experience in a total of 197 different companies. An analysis of these interviews resulted in the following conclusions.

- Political considerations were nearly always part of the performance evaluation process.
- Politics played a role in the performance appraisal process because (1) executives took into consideration the daily interpersonal dynamics between them and their subordinates; (2) the formal appraisal process results in a permanent written document; and (3) the formal appraisal can have considerable impact on the subordinate's career and advancement.

In addition, these executives believed that there usually is a justifiable reason for generating appraisal ratings that were less than accurate. Overall, they felt that it was within their managerial discretion to do so. Thus the findings suggest that the formal appraisal process is indeed a political process and that few ratings are determined without some political consideration.

Perhaps the most interesting finding from the study (because it debunks a popular belief) is that accuracy is not the primary concern of these executives when appraising subordinates. Their main concern is how best to use the appraisal process to motivate and reward subordinates. Hence managerial discretion and effectiveness, not accuracy, are the real goals. Managers made it clear that they would not allow excessively inaccurate ratings to cause problems for themselves and that they attempted to use the appraisal process to their own advantage.[28]

political manipulation. What is the risk, ethical or otherwise, of using performance appraisal as a political tool? Among other things, political performance appraisals can

- undermine organizational goals and performance;
- compromise the link between performance and rewards (see Chapters 5 and 6);
- increase political behavior in other organizational processes and decisions; and
- expose the organization to litigation if managers are terminated.[29]

Some experts who have studied political behavior in the appraisal process suggest that organizations adopt the following guidelines to help cope with the problem.

- Articulate goals and standards as clearly and specifically as possible.
- Link specific actions and performance results to rewards.
- Conduct structured, professional reviews, including specific examples of observed performance and explanations for ratings given.
- Offer performance feedback on an ongoing basis, rather than once a year.
- Acknowledge that appraisal politics exists and make this topic a focus of ongoing discussions throughout the organization.[30]

Learning Objective:

6. Describe some personality dimensions that are related to political behavior.

PERSONALITY AND POLITICAL BEHAVIOR

In this chapter, we have focused primarily on the situational and structural determinants of political behavior. However, just as power has both personal and situational sources, political behavior can stem from each source as well; some individuals are more likely to engage in political behavior than others. In particular, several personality traits are related to a willingness to use power and engage in political behavior. We discuss four of them: the need for power, Machiavellianism, locus of control, and risk-seeking propensity.

Need for Power

The **need for power** is a motive or basic desire to influence and lead others and to control a person's own environment. As a result, individuals with a high need for power are likely to engage in political behavior in organizations. Successful managers often have strong needs for power. The desire to have an impact, to control events, and to influence others often is associated with effective managerial behavior, equitable treatment of subordinates, and even higher morale among subordinates.

However, some aspects of strong needs for power may not be particularly useful for effective management. The need for power may take two different forms: personal power and institutional power.[31] Managers who emphasize personal power strive to dominate others; they want loyalty to themselves, rather than to the organization. When this type of manager leaves the organization, his or her subordinates may no longer be able to function effectively, at least in the short run. Managers who emphasize institutional power, however, demonstrate a more socially acceptable need for power. They create a good climate or culture for effective work, and their subordinates develop an understanding of and loyalty to the organization. Interestingly, some research indicates that female managers often demonstrate greater needs for institutional power and lesser needs for personal power than do their male counterparts.[32]

Machiavellianism

Niccolo Machiavelli was a sixteenth-century Italian philosopher and statesman whose best-known writings include a set of suggestions for obtaining and holding governmental power. Over the centuries, Machiavelli has come to be associated with the use of deceit and opportunism in interpersonal relations. Thus **Machiavellians** are people who view and manipulate others for their own purposes.

As a personal style of behavior toward others, **Machiavellianism** is characterized by (1) the use of guile and deceit in interpersonal relationships, (2) a cynical view of the nature of other people, and (3) a lack of concern with conventional morality.[33] A person who scores high on a test to measure Machiavellianism probably agrees with the following statements.

- The best way to handle people is to tell them what they want to hear.
- Anyone who completely trusts anyone else is asking for trouble.
- Never tell anyone the real reason you did something unless it is useful to do so.
- It is wise to flatter important people.

Machiavellians are likely to be effective manipulators of other people. They often are able to influence others, particularly in face-to-face contacts, and tend to initiate and control social interactions. As a result, Machiavellianism can be associated with a tendency to engage in political behavior. For example, a study that examined the relationship between a propensity to engage in political behavior in organizations and a variety of individual differences reported that Machiavellianism was the strongest correlate of political behavior among the variables investigated.[34] The study concluded that Machiavellianism may be a good predictor of political behavior in many organizational situations.

Locus of Control

Recall that **locus of control** refers to the extent to which individuals believe that they can control events that affect them (see Chapter 2).[35] Individuals with a high internal locus of control believe that events result primarily from their own behavior. Those with a high external locus of control believe that powerful others, fate, or chance primarily determine events that affect their lives. Internals tend to exhibit more political behavior than externals and are more likely to attempt to influence other people. Further, they are more likely to assume that their efforts will be successful. The study of relationships between political behavior and individual differences, referred to in the preceding section, also supported the notion that the propensity to engage in political behavior is stronger for individuals who have a high internal locus of control than for those who have a high external locus of control.

Risk-Seeking Propensity

Individuals differ (sometimes markedly) in their willingness to take risks, or in their **risk-seeking propensity.** Some people are risk avoiders, and others can be described as risk seekers.[36] Negative outcomes (e.g., low performance ratings, demotions, and loss of influence) are possible for individuals and groups who engage in political behavior in organizations. In other words, engaging in political activity isn't risk free; to advocate a position and to seek support for it is to risk being perceived as opposing some other position. In many situations, risk seekers are more willing to engage in political behavior, whereas risk avoiders tend to avoid such behavior because of its possible negative consequences. Some differences in risk-seeking or risk-avoiding behavior may be related to culture. The Managing Across Cultures Competency feature on page 286 provides an example of this cultural effect.

COMPETENCY: MANAGING ACROSS CULTURES

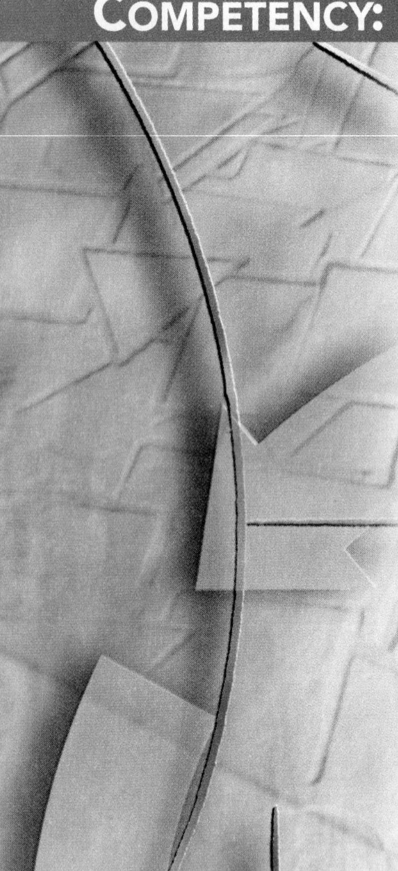

COMPARING CHINESE AND AMERICAN RISK PREFERENCES

Who do you think is the more likely to take risks in business ventures, an American or a Chinese? Most people (at least in North America) would pick the American businessman or businesswoman. However, there is some evidence that they (and you if you chose the American) would be wrong.

In a research study, Chinese and American participants were given questionnaires that asked them to choose between options with a certain payoff (e.g., winning $400) or options with a probabilistic payoff (e.g., winning either $2,000 or nothing depending on the toss of a coin). Faced with this scenario, the Chinese participants made the riskier choice more often than did the American subjects. In addition, both the Chinese participants and the American participants were asked to predict which of them would choose the probabilistic option. Interestingly, both groups of people predicted that the Americans would take more risks.

It appears that our stereotype of Chinese culture, suggesting that Chinese will be more cautious when faced with a choice between a risky or a safe option, may not be correct. (Note that even the Chinese thought that it would be so!) An explanation advanced for these surprising results is called the *cushion hypothesis*. Individuals in a collectivist society, such as China's, may in fact be more willing to take risks under some circumstances because they can rely on their social network to help them with the negative consequences that may ensue. The same results may or may not always occur in organizational settings, but at the very least, these findings should suggest some caution in terms of making predictions about risk-seeking behavior based on cultural stereotypes.[37]

CHAPTER SUMMARY

1. Explain the concept and dynamics of organizational power.

Power is the capacity to influence the behaviors of others. Power is a social term; that is, individuals have power in relation to others. Power also involves a dynamic relationship among people that can change over time.

2. Describe the interpersonal sources of power.

Sources of power stem from both interpersonal and structural factors in an organization. Interpersonal power sources can be categorized as reward power, coercive power, legitimate power, expert power, and reference power. These power sources may complement or detract from one another.

3. Discuss the main categories of structural sources of power.

Structural power differences stem from unequal access to information, resources, decision making, and networks with others. Lower level employees, despite their positions in the organizational hierarchy, may have considerable power to influence events and behavior.

4. Discuss effective and ineffective uses of power.

Individuals who can effectively influence others' behaviors usually understand clearly the sources of power—and its appropriate and fair uses. Such individuals also usually understand the important role that the exchange process plays in the ability to influence the behaviors of others.

5. Explain the concept of organizational politics and diagnose personal and situational factors that contribute to political behavior.

Organizational politics involves the use of power and other resources by individuals, teams, or departments to obtain their own preferred outcomes. Political behavior is inevitable, owing to naturally occurring disagreements and uncertainty about choices and actions. Political behavior can have both positive and negative consequences; it may or may not result in optimal decisions, and some real costs are associated with avoiding political behavior. Political behavior is more likely to occur when resources are scarce or rules and procedures are unclear. The performance appraisal process often invites political behavior, sometimes with negative results.

6. Describe some personality dimensions that are related to political behavior.

Certain personality traits predispose some people to engage in political behavior. Specifically, the probability that individuals will do so increases if they have (1) a strong need for power, (2) a Machiavellian interpersonal style, (3) a high internal locus of control, and (4) a preference for risk taking.

KEY TERMS AND CONCEPTS

Authority
Coercive power
Decision making as power
Exchange process
Expert power
Influence strategies
Intellectual capital
Knowledge as power
Legitimate power
Locus of control
Machiavellianism
Machiavellians
Need for power
Network analysis
Networks as power
Organizational politics
Political behavior
Power
Referent power
Resources as power
Reward power
Risk-seeking propensity
Zone of indifference

DISCUSSION QUESTIONS

1. Explain why the sources of power in organizations provide another good example of the value of an interactionist approach to understanding organizational behavior.
2. Describe situations when (a) you had the power to influence the behavior of another person, and (b) another person had the power to influence you. In each case, explain the sources of power that applied to the circumstances.
3. Make some suggestions for the effective use of power. What competencies might allow you to use power effectively?
4. In terms of the exchange process, give three examples of "currencies" that are commonly exchanged in an organization with which you are familiar.
5. Based on your own experiences, give examples of both effective and ineffective uses of power and their outcomes. Explain why each outcome occurred.
6. Based on your own organizational experiences, describe a situation when a lower level employee had the power to influence others. Use Figure 9.2 to help you explain the sources of that person's power.
7. Use the position characteristics associated with power shown in Table 9.1 to analyze a position that you have held in an organization in terms of its power (or lack of power).
8. Why is the performance appraisal process prone to political abuse? How can the probability of political behavior be minimized in performance appraisal?
9. Based on your own experience, describe a situation in which political behavior seemed to be excessive. Why was this so?
10. Assess your own personality in terms of (a) need for power, (b) Machiavellianism, (c) locus of control, and (d) preference for risk taking.
11. Assess the personality of a person well known to you in terms of (a) need for power, (b) Machiavellianism, (c) locus of control, and (d) preference for risk taking.

DEVELOPING COMPETENCIES

Competency: Managing Self—How Much Power Do You Have in Your Group?

Instructions: Think of a group of which you are a member. For example, It could be a team at work, a committee, or a group working on project at your school. Use the scale shown to respond to the following statements.

1 = Strongly disagree
2 = Disagree
3 = Slightly disagree
4 = Neither agree nor disagree
5 = Slightly agree
6 = Agree
7 = Strongly agree

_____ 1. I am one of the more vocal members of the group.
_____ 2. People in the group listen to what I have to say.
_____ 3. I often volunteer to lead the group.
_____ 4. I am able to influence group decisions.
_____ 5. I often find myself on "center stage" in group activities or discussions.
_____ 6. Members of the group seek me out for advice.
_____ 7. I take the initiative in the group for my ideas and contributions.
_____ 8. I receive recognition in the group for my ideas and contributions.
_____ 9. I would rather lead the group than be a participant.
_____ 10. My opinion is held in high regard by group members.
_____ 11. I volunteer my thoughts and ideas without hesitation.
_____ 12. My ideas often are implemented.
_____ 13. I ask questions in meetings just to have something to say.
_____ 14. Group members often ask for my opinions and input.
_____ 15. I often play the role of scribe, secretary, or note taker during meetings.
_____ 16. Group members usually consult me about important matters before they make a decision.
_____ 17. I clown around with other group members.
_____ 18. I have noticed that group members often look at me, even when not talking directly to me.
_____ 19. I jump right into whatever conflict the group members are dealing with.
_____ 20. I am very influential in the group.

Figure 9.4 **Visibility/Influence Matrix**

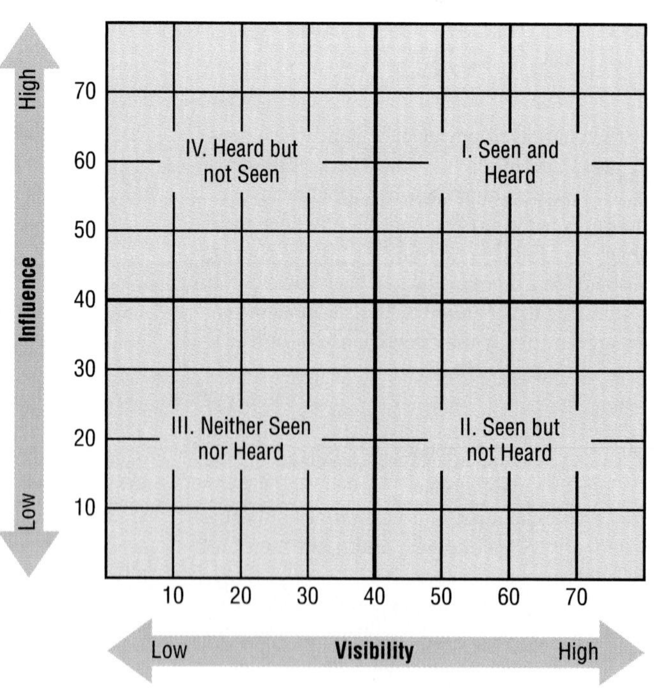

Source: Adapted from Reddy, W. B., and Williams, G. The visibility/credibility inventory: Measuring power and influence. In J. W. Pfeiffer (ed.), *The 1988 Annual: Developing Human Resources.* San Diego: University Associates, 1988, 124.

Scoring

Visibility		Influence	
Item	Your Score	Item	Your Score
1.	_____	2.	_____
3.	_____	4.	_____
5.	_____	6.	_____
7.	_____	8.	_____
9.	_____	10.	_____
11.	_____	12.	_____
13.	_____	14.	_____
15.	_____	16.	_____
17.	_____	18.	_____
19.	_____	20.	_____
Total	_____	Total	_____

Use the scores calculated and mark your position on the visibility/influence matrix shown in Figure 9.4. The combinations of visibility and influence shown are described as follows.

1. *High visibility/high influence.* Group members in quadrant I exhibit behaviors that bring high visibility and allow them to exert influence on others. In organizations, these people may be upwardly mobile or on the "fast track."
2. *High visibility/low influence.* Group members in quadrant II are highly visible but have little real influence. This condition could reflect their personal characteristics but also could indicate that formal power resides elsewhere in the organization. Often these people may hold staff, rather than line, positions that give them visibility but that lack "clout" to get things done.
3. *Low visibility/low influence.* Group members in quadrant III, for whatever reason, are neither seen nor heard. Individuals in this category may have difficulty advancing in the organization.
4. *Low visibility/high influence.* Group members in quadrant IV are "behind the scenes" influencers. These individuals often are opinion leaders and "sages" who wield influence but are content to stay out of the limelight. [38]

Competency: Managing Change—The Art of Persuasion

Robert Marcell was head of Chrysler's small-car design team in the early 1990s. The company had not had a new subcompact design since 1978 and eagerly sought to develop one. However, senior management at Chrysler was convinced that a small car should be developed in alliance with a foreign manufacturer in order to acquire a better design and to share development costs.

Marcell did not agree with this position. He was convinced that Chrysler should design and produce the new car by itself. Marcell knew that persuading senior management to change their minds would be very difficult. In addition, morale was poor on his design team, some of whom believed that the opportunity to design subcompacts was forever lost to their foreign competition. In effect, Marcell had two audiences that he had to persuade to accept his point of view—senior management and his own design team. He decided that his persuasion strategy would be to use emotional themes that his colleagues and senior management could relate to.

Marcell first spent a lot of time talking to people throughout Chrysler to learn their views, including their hopes and fears for the future. He became convinced that many individuals shared his viewpoint that to surrender the design to a foreign manufacturer was to surrender the company's soul. In addition, Marcell discovered that many Chrysler employees were hungry for a challenge and a chance to restore their self-esteem and pride. Armed with a deep understanding of his audience and the needs of the firm, Marcell was now ready to make his move. He prepared a short talk built around slides of his hometown of Iron River in upper Michigan with plans to present his ideas both to his team and senior management. Iron River was a defunct mining town that had lost most of its business to foreign competition. During his presentation, Marcell showed slides of his boarded-up high school, run-down homes of his childhood friends, closed churches, an abandoned railroad yard, and the crumbling ruins of the town's ironworks. After each picture, he intoned, "We couldn't compete." He argued, persuasively, that Detroit and the U.S. automobile industry faced a similar future unless the design and production of small cars was brought back to the United States.

Marcell ended his slide show on a positive note. He spoke movingly of his pride in his design team and challenged his designers and senior management to build a "made-in-America" subcompact that would prove that they could still compete. The speech, which echoed the sentiments held by many members of his design team, rekindled their fighting spirit. Shortly after hearing this talk, his team began drafting ideas for a new car. In the presentation to senior management, Marcell ended with, "If we dare to be different, we could be the reason the U.S. auto industry survives. We could be the reason our kids and grandkids don't end up working at fast-food chains." Chrysler chairman Lee Iacocca was so touched that he stayed for 2 hours after Marcell's presentation talking about preliminary design ideas. Shortly after these presentations, Iacocca reversed the previous decision made by senior management and gave Marcell's group approval to develop a new small car, which became the Neon.[39]

For more information on Chrysler, visit this company's home page at ***www.chryslercars.com.***

Questions

1. It has been suggested that many people in business do not really understand the concept of persuasion. They seem to regard this influence strategy as "convincing and selling." However, experts argue that persuasion is really "learning and negotiating." Was Marcell's approach to persuading others to accept his point of view convincing and selling or was it learning and negotiating? Explain your conclusion.
2. In addition to the general notion of using the "art of persuasion," which influence strategies from Table 9.3 did Marcell use? Defend your choices.
3. Describe occasions when you (a) successfully persuaded others to accept your point of view, and (b) failed to persuade others. What accounted for the differences in your success or failure?
4. Describe occasions when you observed another individual (a) successfully persuade people, and (b) fail to persuade others. What accounted for the differences in these two circumstances?

REFERENCES

1. Adapted from Sherman, E. Mastering politics. *Computerworld*, October 11, 1999, 58–59.
2. Buchanan, D., and Bodham, R. *Power, Politics, and Organizational Change.* London: Sage, 1999; Kramer, R. M., and Neale, M. A. (eds.). *Power and Influence in Organizations.* Thousand Oaks, Calif.: Sage, 1998.
3. Hollander, E. P. Power. In C. L. Cooper and C. Argyris (eds.), *The Concise Blackwell Encyclopedia of Management.* Oxford: Blackwell, 1998, 501–503; Pfeffer, J. *Managing with Power: Politics and Influence in Organizations.* Boston: Harvard Business School Press, 1993.
4. Descriptions of the shifts in power relationships are drawn from Colvin, G. Naked power: The scoreboard. *Fortune*, April 27, 1998, 449–451; Smith, E.A. Views of the 21st century organization. In E. Bieck (ed.), *The 2000 Annual: Volume 2—Consulting.* San Francisco: Jossey Bass/Pfeiffer, 2000, 293–307.
5. Elenkov, D. S. Can American management concepts work in Russia? A cross-cultural comparative study. *California Management Review*, Summer 1998, 133–156; French, J. R. P., and Raven, B. The bases of social power. In D. Cartwright (ed.), *Studies in Social Power.* Ann Arbor: University of Michigan Institute for Social Research, 1959, 150–167; Podsakoff, P. M., and Schrieshiem, C. A. Field studies of French and Raven's bases of power: Critique, reanalysis, and suggestions for future research. *Psychological Bulletin*, 1985, 97, 387–411.
6. Adapted from Colvin, G. Revenge of the Nerds. *Fortune*, March 2, 1998, 223–224.
7. Pfeffer, J. *Power in Organizations.* Marshfield, Mass.: Pitman, 1981, 4–6; Tyler, T. R. The psychology of authority relations. In R. M. Kramer and M. A. Neale (eds.), *Power and Influence in Organizations.* Thousand Oaks, Calif.: Sage, 1998, 251–260.
8. See, for example, the classic work by Barnard, C. I. *The Functions of the Executive.* Cambridge, Mass.: Harvard University Press, 1938, 110.
9. Tannen, D. The power of talk: Who gets heard and why. *Harvard Business Review*, September–October 1995, 138; also see Martin, J., and Meyerson, D. Women and power. In R. M. Kramer and M. A. Neale (eds.), *Power and Influence in Organizations.* Thousand Oaks, Calif.: Sage, 1998, 311–348.
10. Greene, C. N., and Podsakoff, P. M. Effects of withdrawal of a performance-contingent reward on supervisory influence and power. *Academy of Management Journal*, 1981, 24, 527–542.
11. Atwater, L. E. The relationship between supervisory power and organizational characteristics. *Group & Organization Management*, 1995, 20, 460–485; Brass, D. J., and Burkhardt, M. E. Potential power and power use: An investigation of structure and behavior. *Academy of Management Journal*, 1993, 36, 441–470; Hayward, M. L. A., and Boeker, W. Power and conflicts of interest in professional firms: Evidence from investment banking. *Administrative Science Quarterly*, 1998, 43, 1–22; Hultin, M., and Szulkin, R. Wages and unequal access to organizational power: An empirical test of gender discrimination. *Administrative Science Quarterly*, 1999, 44, 453–472.
12. Tobin, D. R. *The Knowledge-enabled Organization.* New York: AMACOM, 1998.
13. Wilke, J. R. Computer links erode hierarchical nature of workplace culture. *Wall Street Journal*, December 9, 1993, A1, A7.
14. Adapted from Booth, P. Workplace democracy in Africa. *IHRIM Journal*, June 1999, 62–63.
15. Kanter, R. M. Power failure in management circuits. *Harvard Business Review*, July–August 1979, 66; also see Ibarra, H., and Andrews, S. B. Power, social influence, and sense making: Effects of network centrality and proximity on employee perceptions. *Administrative Science Quarterly*, 1993, 38, 277–303.
16. Krackhardt, D., and Hanson, J. R. Informal networks: The company behind the chart. *Harvard Business Review*, July–August 1993, 104–111; Mintzberg, H., and Van der Heyden, L. Organigraphs: Drawing how companies really work. *Harvard Business Review*, September–October 1999, 87–94.
17. Adapted from Fritsch, P. Bilingual employees are seeking more pay and many now get it. *Wall Street Journal*, November 13, 1996, A1, A6.
18. Dulebohn, J. H., and Ferris, G. R. The role of influence tactics in perceptions of performance evaluations' fairness. *Academy of Management Journal*, 1999, 42, 288–303; Falbe, C. M., and Yukl, G. Consequences of managers using single influence tactics and combinations of tactics. *Academy of Management Journal*, 1992, 35, 638–652; Kramer, R. M., and Hanna, B. A. Under the influence? Organizational paranoia and the misperception of others' influence behavior. In R. M. Kramer and M. A. Neale (eds.), *Power and Influence in Organizations.* Thousand Oaks, Calif.: Sage, 1998, 145–179; Maslyn, J. M., Farmer, S. M., and Fedor, D. B. Failed upward influence attempts. *Group & Organization Management*, 1996, 21, 461–480; Pfeffer, J., and Cialdini, R. B. Illusions of influence. In R. M. Kramer and M. A. Neale (eds.) *Power and Influence in Organizations.* Thousand Oaks, Calif.: Sage, 1998, 1–20; Thacker, R. A., and Wayne, S. J. An examination of upward influence tactics and assessments of promotability. *Journal of Management*, 1995, 21, 739–756; Yukl, G., Kim, H., and Falbe, C. M. Antecedents of influence outcomes. *Journal of Applied Psychology*, 1996, 81, 309–317.
19. Schmidt, S. M., and Kipnis, D. The perils of persistence. *Psychology Today*, November 1987, 32–34; also see Judge, T. A., and Bretz, R. D. Political influence behavior and career success. *Journal of Management*, 1994, 20, 43–65.
20. Cohen, A. R., and Bradford, D. L. Influence without authority: The use of alliances, reciprocity, and exchange to accomplish work. *Organizational Dynamics*, Winter 1989, 5–17.
21. These characteristics of managerial effectiveness are based, in part, on Kotter, J. P. Power, dependence, and effective management. *Harvard Business Review*, April 1977,

1125–1136; also see Wageman, R., and Mannix, E. A. Uses and misuses of power in task-performing teams. In R. M. Kramer and M. A. Neale (eds.), *Power and Influence in Organizations.* Thousand Oaks, Calif.: Sage, 1998, 261–285.

22. Bacharach, S. B., and Lawler, E. J. Political alignments in organizations. In R. M. Kramer and M. A. Neale (eds.), *Power and Influence in Organizations.* Thousand Oaks, Calif.: Sage, 1998, 68–73.
23. Buchanan, D., and Badham, R. *Power, Politics, and Organizational Change.* London: Sage, 1999, 60; Rogers, D. Politics. In C. L. Cooper and C. Argyris (eds.), *The Concise Blackwell Encyclopedia of Management.* Oxford: Blackwell, 1998, 491–493.
24. Ferris, G. R., Frink, D. D., Bhawak, D. P. S., Zhou, J., and Gilmore, D. C. Reactions of diverse groups to politics in the workplace. *Journal of Management*, 1996, 22, 23–44; Maslyn, J. M., and Fedor, D. B. Perceptions of politics: Does measuring different foci matter? *Journal of Applied Psychology*, 1998, 84, 645–653; Parker, C. P., Dipboye, R. L., and Jackson, S. L. Perceptions of organizational politics: An investigation of antecedents and consequences. *Journal of Management*, 1995, 21, 891–912.
25. Madison, D. L., Allen, R. W., Porter, L. W., Renwick, P. A., and Mayes, B. T. Organizational politics: An exploration of managers' perceptions. *Human Relations*, 1980, 33, 79–100.
26. Adapted from Crosson, C. Print scrn, numlock and other mysteries of the keyboard. *Wall Street Journal*, October 22, 1996, B1, B8; Frost, P. J., and Ergi, C. P. The political process of innovation. In L. L. Cummings and B. M. Staw (eds.), *Research in Organizational Behavior*, vol. 13. Greenwich, Conn.: JAI Press, 1991, 230, 251–252.
27. Beemon, D. R., and Sharkey, T. W. The use and abuse of corporate politics. *Business Horizons*, July–August 1987, 26–30; Kacmar, D. M., and Ferris, G. R. Politics at work: Sharpening the focus of political behavior in organizations. *Business Horizons*, July–August 1993, 70–74; Witt, L. A. Enhancing organizational goal congruence: A solution to organizational politics. *Journal of Applied Psychology*, 1998, 83, 666–674.
28. Excerpted with permission from Longenecker, C. O., Sims, H. P., and Gioia, D. A. Behind the mask: The politics of employee appraisal. *Academy of Management Executive*, August 1987, 183–193; also see Dulebohn, J. H., and Ferris, G. R. The role of influence tactics in perceptions of performance evaluations' fairness. *Academy of Management Journal*, 1999, 42, 288–303.
29. Gioia, D. A., and Longenecker, C. O. Delving into the dark side: The politics of executive appraisal. *Organizational Dynamics*, Winter 1994, 54.
30. Longenecker, Sims, and Gioia, 56.
31. Greenberg, J., and Baron, R. A. *Behavior in Organizations*, 7th ed. Upper Saddle River, N.J.: Prentice-Hall, 2000, 409–410; McClelland, D. C. *Human Motivation.* Glenview, Ill.: Scott, Foresman, 1985; Sankowsky, D. Understanding the abuse of power. *Organizational Dynamics*, Spring 1995, 57–71.
32. Ragins, B. R., and Sundstrom, E. Gender and power in organizations: A longitudinal perspective. *Psychological Bulletin*, 1989, 105, 70; also see Martin and Meyerson, 311–348.
33. Christie, R., and Geis, F. L. *Studies in Machiavellianism.* New York: Academic Press, 1970; Wilson, D. S., Near, D., and Miller, R. R. Machiavellianism: A synthesis of the evolutionary and psychological literatures. *Psychological Bulletin*, 1996, 119, 285–299.
34. Woodman, R. W., Wayne, S. J., and Rubinstein, D. Personality correlates of a propensity to engage in political behavior in organizations. *Proceedings of the Southwest Academy of Management*, 1985, 131–135.
35. Spector, P. E. Locus of control. In C. L. Cooper and C. Argyris (eds.), *The Concise Blackwell Encyclopedia of Management.* Oxford: Blackwell, 1998, 369.
36. Sitkin, S. B., and Pablo, A. L. Reconceptualizing the determinants of risk behavior. *Academy of Management Review*, 1992, 17, 9–38.
37. Adapted from Fung, S. Risky business. *Across the Board*, July–August 1999, 10–11.
38. Adapted from Reddy, W. B., and Williams, G. The visibility/credibility inventory: Measuring power and influence. In J. W. Pfeiffer (ed.), *The 1988 Annual: Developing Human Resources.* San Diego: University Associates, 1988, 115–124.
39. Adapted from Conger, J. A. The necessary art of persuasion. *Harvard Business Review*, May–June 1998, 84–95.

CHAPTER

10

Conflict and Negotiation

LEARNING OBJECTIVES

When you have finished studying this chapter, you should be able to:

1. Explain the four basic varieties of conflict and describe three differing attitudes toward organizational conflict.
2. Identify the four primary levels of conflict within organizations.
3. Use five interpersonal conflict handling styles.
4. Discuss the basic types of negotiations and describe several negotiation strategies.

Preview Case: *Terry Peters*

CONFLICT MANAGEMENT

- Varieties of Conflict
- Attitudes toward Conflict
- ***Competency: Managing Change***—*Motorola's Dilemma with Retailers*

LEVELS OF CONFLICT

- Intrapersonal Conflict
- Interpersonal Conflict
- Intragroup Conflict
- ***Competency: Managing Self***—*Personalities That Create Conflict in the Office*
- Intergroup Conflict

INTERPERSONAL CONFLICT HANDLING STYLES

- ***Competency: Managing Diversity***—*Gender Issues in CPA Firms*
- Avoiding Style
- Forcing Style
- ***Competency: Managing Ethics***—*Whistle-Blowers as Objects of the Forcing Style*
- Accommodating Style
- Collaborating Style
- Compromising Style
- Effectiveness of the Styles

NEGOTIATION IN CONFLICT MANAGEMENT

- Types of Negotiations
- ***Competency: Managing Self***—*Negotiating Nice*
- Negotiator's Dilemma
- Negotiating Across Cultures
- Mediation
- ***Competency: Managing Across Cultures***—*The Chinese Approach to Negotiation*

CHAPTER SUMMARY

- Key Terms and Concepts
- Discussion Questions

DEVELOPING COMPETENCIES

- ***Competency: Managing Self***—*Conflict Handling Styles*
- ***Competency: Managing Self***—*Intervening in Employee Disputes*

PREVIEW CASE

TERRY PETERS

Terry Peters is a senior majoring in management at a large state university. She had just completed a final round of interviewing at a major consulting firm. She thought that the final office visit, with its intensive interview, had gone quite well. Subsequently, she was delighted to receive a phone call from the human resources department of the consulting firm the following morning offering her a position.

Peters was so relieved and excited to get the offer that she stated, without really thinking about it, "Oh, that's wonderful. I would love to work for your company." When the recruiter remarked, "I'm delighted that we don't have any competition to worry about," Peters realized that she had made a mistake.

She tried to regain her composure while the recruiter described the basic offer: a salary of $40,000, 2 weeks' vacation, some profit-sharing options, and the standard health benefits. "Any questions?" asked the recruiter. Peters stammered, "Can the salary be increased?" "What did you have in mind?" the recruiter quickly asked. Peters hesitated and then suggested $42,000. The recruiter said, "Sure, we can do that. I'll write up a final contract and put it in overnight mail. I'll also tell everyone here that you have accepted the offer."

After exchanging some pleasantries, Peters hung up the phone, feeling a mixture of excitement and regret. She knew that she hadn't really played her cards very well. Further, she felt conflicted by the fact that she had three other job offers, one for more money, and hadn't really even stopped to weigh her options carefully. She was genuinely excited by the offer from the consulting firm but had allowed herself to be caught up in the moment, affected perhaps by her recent visit with the firm. It had been several weeks since she had visited the other companies, and she wondered if perhaps the timing caused her to overvalue the last visit. She also wondered, somewhat too late she thought to herself, if consulting was really the best place to start. She had offers from a bank and two large retailers to join their management training programs. She also suddenly realized that the recruiter had very quickly accepted her counteroffer that was only $2,000 a year more than the original. "Rats," she said out loud, "I'll bet I could have gotten more." At the same time, she was very uncertain about how assertive a new graduate should be in attempting to negotiate a salary with a prospective employer. She certainly wouldn't want to do anything that would get the working relationship off on the wrong foot. Belatedly, Terry Peters was coming to realize that she really hadn't been prepared to deal with this situation and wondered how she should have handled herself.[1]

The need to manage conflict occurs every day in organizations. **Conflict** refers to a process in which one party (person or group) perceives that its interests are being opposed or negatively affected by another party.[2] This definition implies incompatible concerns among the people involved and includes a variety of conflict issues and events.

In this chapter we examine conflict and negotiation from several viewpoints. First, we present the basic forms of conflict and examine three attitudes about it. Second, we identify four levels of conflict found in organizations. Third, we discuss five interpersonal styles in conflict management and the conditions under which each style may be appropriate. Fourth, we address the types of negotiation, basic negotiation strategies, and some of the complexities involved in negotiations when the parties are from different cultures. We conclude with some highlights of third-party mediation in the negotiation process.

Learning Objective:

1. Explain the four basic varieties of conflict and describe three differing attitudes toward organizational conflict.

CONFLICT MANAGEMENT

Conflict management consists of diagnostic processes, interpersonal styles, negotiation strategies, and other interventions that are designed to avoid unnecessary conflict and reduce or resolve excessive conflict.[3] The ability to understand and correctly diagnose conflict is essential to managing it.[4]

VARIETIES OF CONFLICT

Table 10.1 suggests that there are four basic varieties of conflict. Regardless of the form it takes, the essence of conflict is incompatibility.

Goal conflict stems from incompatible preferred or expected outcomes. In the Preview Case, Terry Peters felt conflicted because her goals with regard to the type of job she wanted were unclear. Goal conflict also includes inconsistencies between the individual's or group's values and norms (e.g., standards of behavior) and the demands or goals assigned by higher level managers in the organization.

A common type of goal conflict occurs when an individual or group is assigned or selects incompatible goals. For example, a student may set goals of earning $150 a week and achieving a 3.25 grade point average (on a 4.0-point system) while being enrolled full-time during the coming semester. A month into the semester, the student may realize that there aren't enough hours in the week to achieve both goals. **Goal incompatibility** refers to the extent to which an individual's or group's goals are at odds with the capacity to achieve the goals. Thus, even without the goal of earning $150 per week, the student could face inner conflict because of the difficulty in achieving a 3.25 grade point average.

Cognitive conflict occurs when ideas and thoughts within an individual or between individuals are incompatible. **Affective conflict** occurs when feelings and emotions within an individual or between individuals are incompatible. In the Preview Case, Terry Peters experienced both conflicted thoughts and emotions as she responded to the job offer from the consulting firm.

Table 10.1 Basic Varieties of Conflict

VARIETY	CORE MEANING
Goal conflict	Incompatible preferences
Cognitive conflict	Incompatible thoughts
Affective conflict	Incompatible feelings
Procedural conflict	Incompatible views on process

Procedural conflict refers to individuals differing over the process to use for resolving issues. Union–management negotiations often involve procedural conflicts before negotiations actually begin. The parties may have procedural conflicts over who will be involved in the negotiations, where they will take place, and when sessions will be held (and how long they will last). After negotiations have been concluded, different interpretations about how a grievance system is to operate provide another example of procedural conflict.

Attitudes toward Conflict

The presence of the four basic varieties of conflict need not necessarily harm an organization or keep its members from being effective. In fact, of the three attitudes toward conflict that we discuss—positive, negative, and balanced—only one—negative—is concerned with conflict's harmful aspects.

Positive Attitude. Conflict in organizations can be a positive force. The creation and/or resolution of conflict may lead to constructive problem solving. The need to resolve conflict can lead people to search for ways of changing how they do things. The conflict resolution process can stimulate innovation and positive change, as well as make change more acceptable. A study of managers demonstrated this view. The positive effects they noted generally fell into three main categories: beneficial effects on productivity ("Our work productivity went up" and "We produced quality products on time"), relationship outcomes ("Sensitivity to others was increased" and "Better communication methods were developed"), and constructive organizational change ("We adopted more effective controls" and "Better job descriptions and expectations were drawn up").[5]

The intentional introduction of conflict into the decision-making process may even be beneficial. In team decision making, a problem may arise when a cohesive team's desire for agreement interferes with its ability to consider alternative solutions. A team may encounter groupthink (see Chapter 8), which it can reduce by introducing conflict in the form of one or more dissenting opinions. Finally, individuals may come to quite different conclusions about what is fair and ethical in specific situations. A positive attitude toward conflict encourages people to work out their differences, participate in developing an ethical and fair organization, and deal directly with injustices.

Negative Attitude. Conflict also may have serious negative effects, diverting efforts from goal attainment, and depleting resources, especially time and money. Conflict also may negatively affect the psychological well-being of employees and cause stress (see Chapter 7). If they are severe, conflicting thoughts, ideas, and beliefs may lead to resentment, tension, and anxiety. These feelings appear to result from the threat that conflict poses to important personal goals and beliefs. Over an extended period of time, conflict may make the creation and maintenance of supportive and trusting relationships difficult.

When cooperation is required, severe conflict and competition typically hurt performance. Pressure for results tends to emphasize immediate and measurable goals—such as reducing sales costs—at the expense of longer range and more important goals—such as product quality. When high product quality is a primary organizational goal, conflict based on competition between coworkers is often ill-advised. Deep and lasting conflicts that aren't addressed may even trigger violence among employees or between employees and others.[6]

Balanced Attitude. Our attitude is that conflict may sometimes be desirable and at other times destructive. Although some conflicts can be avoided and reduced, others have to be resolved and properly managed. The balanced attitude is sensitive to the consequences of conflict, ranging from negative outcomes (loss of skilled employees, sabotage, low quality of work, stress, and even violence) to positive outcomes (creative alternatives, increased motivation and commitment, high quality of work, and personal satisfaction).

The balanced attitude recognizes that conflict occurs in organizations whenever interests collide. Sometimes, employees will think differently, want to act differently, and seek to pursue different goals. When these differences divide interdependent individuals, they must be managed constructively.[7] How easily or effectively conflict can be managed depends on various factors, such as how important the issue is to the people involved and whether or not strong leadership is available. Table 10.2 identifies some of the factors that distinguish between conflicts that are difficult to resolve and conflicts that are easier to resolve.

The following Managing Change Competency feature describes the cognitive, affective, and even procedural conflicts that Motorola triggered by issuing new

COMPETENCY: MANAGING CHANGE

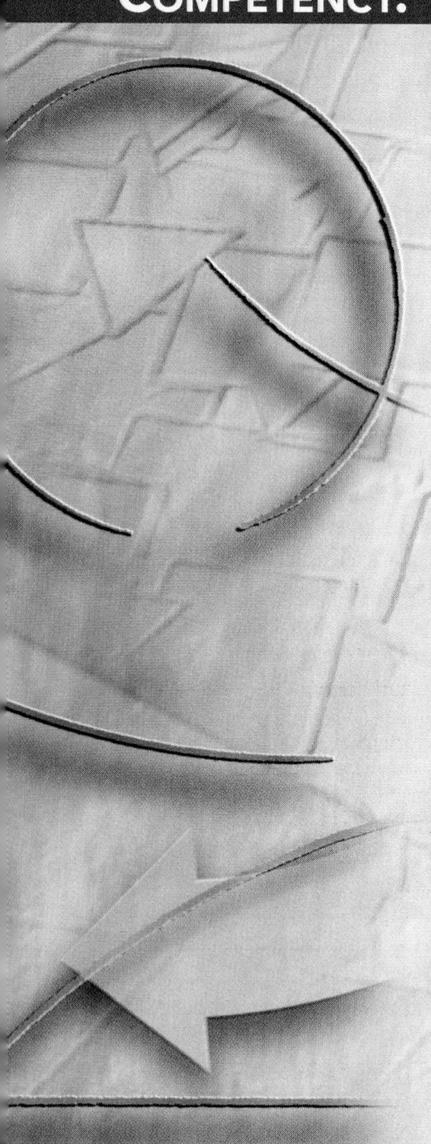

MOTOROLA'S DILEMMA WITH RETAILERS

Headquartered in Schaumburg, Illinois, Motorola is a worldwide leader in wireless communications. The firm manufactures cellular telephones, pagers, two-way radios, semiconductors, and other electronic items.

When Motorola executives asked Robert Qureshi to meet in a side room at a Dallas, Texas, cellular telephone conference, he thought they wanted his opinion on a new distribution policy. Instead, they told him that, as a Signature retailer, at least three-quarters of the cellular phones he carried in his 50 stores must be made by Motorola. If he didn't meet that quota, Motorola wouldn't supply him with its new products, including StarTac, the sleek model that's wowing customers as the world's smallest cellular phone. "I thought they were crazy," said Qureshi, president of Cellular Concepts, a cellular phone retailer. "This is going to drive Motorola's market share into the toilet."

Qureshi was not the only one concerned. Other retailers bristled at what they called Motorola's strong-arm tactics as it tried to boost its slumping market share. They say the strategy is backfiring, tempting vendors to turn to competitors, further eroding Motorola's position as the world's No. 1 cell phone maker.

Motorola said that it doesn't plan to change the policy because it makes good business sense. "We want a say in how our products are displayed and promoted," said Jim Caile, vice president of marketing for Motorola's General Systems Division. Motorola said that it wants retailers to carry a full line of its products, not just pick their favorites. It asks retailers whether they want to be Signature retailers. "There is supposed to be a choice in whether or not they (retailers) want to be a Signature retailer," Caile said.

Retailers and carriers contend that there is no real choice. Increasing the array of Motorola phones would mean pushing rivals' models off the shelf. At the same time, not having StarTac could mean turning customers away. No other major cell phone company is trying to tie up its retailers with anything like Motorola's approach.

Retailers and carriers are in conflict with Motorola over the policy. "I want to have a good relationship with all my vendors, but I refuse to distribute under Motorola's current terms," said Cynthia White, chief operating officer of Bell Atlantic Nynex Mobile, the nation's No. 3 cellular phone provider.

On balance, this policy has proved to be a disaster. By 1998 (the last full year for which figures are available), Motorola's share of the cellular phone market had dropped to 41 percent from a high of 54 percent. Recently, Motorola laid off 15,000 employees.[8]

*For more information on Motorola, visit the company's home page at **www.mot.com**.*

Table 10.2 **Effects of Various Dimensions of Conflict**

DIMENSION	DIFFICULT TO RESOLVE	EASY TO RESOLVE
The issue itself	A matter of principle	Simply dividing up something
Size of the stakes	Large	Small
Continuity of interaction	Single transaction	Long-term relationship
Characteristics of participants' "groups"	Disorganized, with weak leadership	Cohesive, with strong leadership
Involvement of third parties	No neutral third party available	Trusted, prestigious, neutral third party available

Source: Adapted from Greenhalgh, L. Managing conflict. In R. J. Lewicki, D. M. Saunders, and J. W. Minton (eds.), *Negotiation*, 3rd ed. Boston: Irwin/McGraw-Hill, 1999, 7.

requirements for dealers who handled its cellular phones. Motorola issued new rules that required Signature retailers to carry its full line of cellular phones. Some conflict probably was inevitable, but Motorola's action triggered more and deeper forms of conflict than the company had anticipated.

Learning Objective:

2. Identify the four primary levels of conflict within organizations.

LEVELS OF CONFLICT

Four primary levels of conflict may be present in organizations: intrapersonal (within an individual), interpersonal (between individuals), intragroup (within a group), and intergroup (between groups). Figure 10.1 suggests these levels of conflict are often cumulative and interrelated. For example, an employee struggling with whether to stay on a certain career path may show hostility toward coworkers, thus triggering interpersonal conflicts.

INTRAPERSONAL CONFLICT

Intrapersonal conflict occurs within an individual and usually involves some form of goal, cognitive, or affective conflict. It is triggered when a person's behavior will result in outcomes that are mutually exclusive.[9] Inner tensions and frustrations commonly result. For example, a graduating senior, such as Terry Peters in the Preview Case, may have to decide between jobs that offer different challenges, pay, security, and locations. Trying to make such a decision may create one (or more) of three basic types of intrapersonal goal conflict.

Figure 10.1 **Levels of Conflict in Organizations**

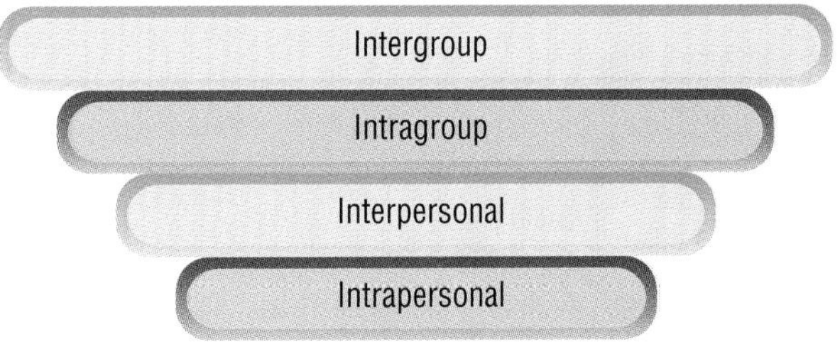

- **Approach–approach conflict** means that an individual must choose between two or more alternatives, each of which is expected to have a positive outcome (e.g., a choice between two jobs that appear to be equally attractive). The multiple job offers that Terry Peters received provide a good example of approach–approach conflict.
- **Avoidance–avoidance conflict** means that an individual must choose between two or more alternatives, each of which is expected to have a negative outcome (e.g., relatively low pay or extensive out-of-town traveling).
- **Approach–avoidance conflict** means that an individual must decide whether to do something that is expected to have both positive and negative outcomes (e.g., accepting an offer of a good job in a bad location).

Many decisions involve the resolution of intrapersonal goal conflict. The intensity of intrapersonal conflict generally increases under one or more of the following conditions: (1) several realistic alternative courses of action are available for handling the conflict; (2) the positive and negative consequences of the alternative courses of action are roughly equal; or (3) the source of conflict is important to the individual.

Cognitive Dissonance. Intrapersonal conflict may also be a consequence of **cognitive dissonance,** which occurs when individuals recognize inconsistencies in their own thoughts and/or behaviors.[10] Such inconsistencies are usually stressful and uncomfortable, leading to intrapersonal conflict. A sufficient level of discomfort usually motivates a person to reduce the dissonance and achieve balance. Balance is often achieved by (1) changing thoughts and/or behaviors or (2) obtaining more information about the issue that is causing the dissonance. Both goal conflict and cognitive conflict accompany many important personal decisions. The greater the goal conflict before the decision, the greater the cognitive dissonance is likely to be after the decision. Individuals experience dissonance because they know that the alternative accepted has negative (avoidance) outcomes and that the alternative rejected has positive (approach) outcomes. The more difficulty individuals have in arriving at the original decision, the greater is their need to justify the decision afterward. Some cognitive dissonance is inevitable. In the Preview Case, Terry Peters seems to be suffering from some cognitive dissonance.

Neurotic Tendencies. **Neurotic tendencies** are irrational personality mechanisms that an individual uses—often unconsciously—that create inner conflict. In turn, inner conflict often results in behaviors that lead to conflict with other people.[11] Although the psychological sources of neurotic tendencies are beyond the scope of this book, we briefly describe several ways that those with strong neurotic tendencies may think and act in the workplace. Neurotic managers make excessive use of tight organizational controls (e.g., budgets, rules and regulations, and monitoring systems) because they distrust people. They often are fearful of uncertainty and risk, not just distrustful of others. Neurotic managers often are driven to plan and standardize every detail of their departments' operations by emphasizing rules and procedures. Still others are excessively bold and impulsive in their actions. They rely on hunches and impressions rather than available facts and advice. Such managers usually don't use participation and consultation in their decision making unless required to do so by some higher authority.

Individuals with strong neurotic tendencies struggle unsuccessfully with intrapersonal conflict, unable to resolve their own problems. Their excessive distrust and need to control triggers conflict with others, especially subordinates who come to feel micromanaged and distrusted. A common reaction to leaders with neurotic tendencies is either overt (open) or covert (hidden) aggression and hostility. Subordinates often try to even the score and protect themselves from further abuse. These actions give the manager an even stronger sense of employee worthlessness. The manager's hostility and attempts to control and punish become ever more vigorous.

Workplace Violence. Severe unresolved intrapersonal conflict within employees, customers, or others may trigger violent interpersonal conflict. Much violence in the workplace has its source in severe intrapersonal conflict.[12] We discussed workplace violence as a major source of work stress in Chapter 7. As we pointed out there, the problem seems to be getting worse. In fact, during 1998, almost 9 percent of all homicides in the United States were committed by workers against their coworkers.[13] This percentage, equaling that in 1995, is the highest ever recorded. Most workplace violence does not, of course, result in death. Nevertheless these grim statistics emphasize the potentially dire consequences of not adequately diagnosing and managing the forms, levels, and sources of intense conflict in the workplace.

Interpersonal Conflict

Interpersonal conflict occurs when two or more individuals perceive that their attitudes, behaviors, or preferred goals are in opposition. As with intrapersonal conflict, much interpersonal conflict is based on some type of role conflict or role ambiguity.

Role Conflict. In the work setting, a **role** is the cluster of tasks and behaviors that others expect a person to perform while doing a job.[14] Figure 10.2 presents a role episode model, which involves role senders and a focal person. Role senders are individuals who have expectations of how the focal person should behave. A role episode begins before a message is sent because role senders have expectations, perceptions, and evaluations of the focal person's behaviors. These attributions, in turn, influence the actual role messages that the senders transmit. The focal person's perceptions of these messages and pressures may then lead to role conflict. **Role conflict** occurs when a focal person perceives incompatible messages and pressures from role senders. The focal person responds with coping behaviors that serve as inputs to the role senders' attribution process. A **role set** is the group of role senders that directly affect the focal person. A role set might include the employee's manager, other team members, close friends, immediate family members, and important clients or customers.

Four types of role conflict may occur as a result of incompatible messages and pressures from the role set.[15]

- **Intrasender role conflict** may occur when different messages and pressures from a single member of the role set are incompatible.
- **Intersender role conflict** may occur when the messages and pressures from one role sender oppose messages and pressures from one or more other senders.

Figure 10.2 **Role Episode Model**

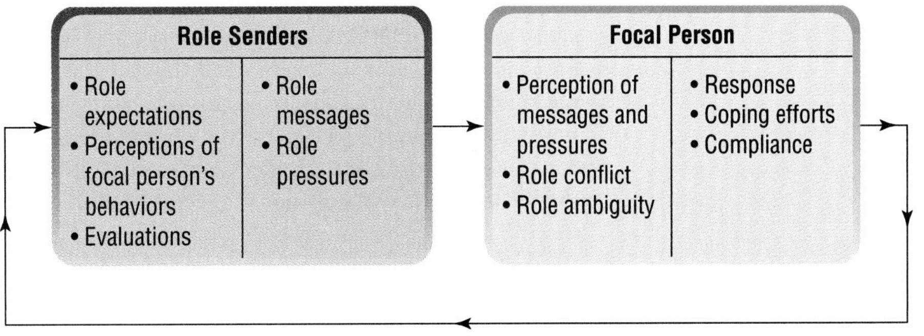

Source: Based on Kahn, R. L., et al. *Organizational Stress: Studies in Role Conflict and Ambiguity.* New York: John Wiley & Sons, 1964, 26.

- **Interrole conflict** may occur when role pressures associated with membership in one group are incompatible with pressures stemming from membership in other groups.
- **Person–role conflict** may occur when role requirements are incompatible with the focal person's own attitudes, values, or views of acceptable behavior. Intrapersonal conflict typically accompanies this type of role conflict.

Role Ambiguity. **Role ambiguity** is the uncertainty and lack of clarity surrounding expectations about a single role.[16] Like role conflict, severe role ambiguity causes stress and triggers subsequent coping behaviors. These coping behaviors often include (1) aggressive action (e.g., verbal abuse, theft, and violence) and hostile communication, (2) withdrawal, or (3) approaching the role sender or senders to attempt joint problem solving. Research findings suggest that high levels of role conflict and role ambiguity have numerous dramatic effects, including stress reactions, aggression, hostility, and withdrawal behaviors (turnover and absenteeism).[17] Stress is a common reaction to severe role conflict and role ambiguity (see Chapter 7). However, effective managers and professionals possess the ability to cope with the many ambiguities inherent in their roles.

Personality Differences. In addition to role conflict and role ambiguity as sources of conflict, some people are just harder to get along with than others. The *interactionist* perspective suggests the importance of understanding both situational and personality causes of interpersonal conflict. The Managing Self Competency feature on the next page provides a good example of the interpersonal conflict that can be created by personality differences.

Intragroup Conflict

Intragroup conflict refers to disputes among some or all of a group's members, which often affect the group's dynamics and effectiveness. Family-run businesses can be especially prone to severe intragroup and other types of conflicts.[18] These conflicts typically become more intense when an owner–founder approaches retirement, actually retires, or dies.

Only 3 in 10 family-run businesses make it to the second generation, and only 1 in 10 survives into the third generation. The biggest obstacles to succession are the relationships among the family members who own the business and bear responsibility for keeping it alive for another generation. What determines whether a family business soars or nosedives? It depends, in large part, on the respect that family members give each other in the workplace, their willingness to take on roles at work different from those they have at home, and their ability to manage conflict. Randall Carlock, a consultant on family business and founder of the Audio King electronic stores chain, comments, "Families don't express their needs and wants clearly and don't deal with conflict very well. When that moves into their place of business, that spells real trouble. Take the way most parents negotiate with their kids in the business. They basically tell them what they're going to do, or they threaten them, or they tell them, 'You're lucky to have this job.' That's not how you handle an employee, and that's not how you develop a future leader."[19]

Although the consequences of excessive intragroup conflict are typically negative, the balanced view of conflict suggests that some conflict within teams or departments may be useful. For example, Michael Eisner, CEO and chairman of Disney, describes the conflict within groups at Walt Disney Company in positive terms. He credits the existence of "supportive conflict" with sparking much of the fabled creativity at Disney. Eisner stated, "This whole business starts with ideas, and we're convinced that ideas come out of an environment of supportive conflict, which is synonymous with appropriate friction. We create a very loose environment where people are not afraid to speak their minds or be irreverent. They say what they think, and they are urged to

COMPETENCY: MANAGING SELF

PERSONALITIES THAT CREATE CONFLICT IN THE OFFICE

Jean Holland is the founder and CEO of the Growth & Leadership Center (GLC), which is located in the Silicon Valley of California. An executive coaching firm, GLC is dedicated to helping executives and other professionals who seem unable or unwilling to get along with others to salvage their careers. As a result of her work, Holland has identified several personality types that create inordinate amounts of conflict in their firms.

For example, she describes Nick Kepler, the director of technology development at Advanced Micro Devices as a classic *controller.* Kepler was great at working with his own people, but he created conflict when he had to work with others. He had a strong tendency to be territorial and defensive. In addition, he had an overbearing emotionless demeanor that tended to intimidate people and destroy rapport with them. Holland's coaching helped him realize that he had to change and learn how to work effectively with others outside his own group. Unless he did, he had no hope of being successful and continuing to advance in the firm.

Holland describes the *intimidator* as an individual who stifles creativity in his or her staff, inhibits open communication among coworkers, and generally scares the hell out of peers. Kepler, who is now an avid supporter of Holland's work, also had some intimidator symptoms. The *withholder* is characterized as an individual who omits sharing important information, tends to leave people "out of the loop," and is particularly ineffective at building a team. The *techno-bound* focuses on technical issues and considers "people problems" to be an illogical waste of time. The *stressor* is someone who often prevents others from taking needed action, is quick to shift blame to others, and generally wastes coworkers' time.

Despite using the language of personality, Holland sees these "types" as consisting mainly of ineffective and conflicted behaviors that can be changed. The key, she asserts, is for individuals to learn to develop greater insight into how their behaviors affect the people around them. By using the concepts described here, Holland has successfully helped her clients learn how to diagnose their own behaviors and reduce the levels of interpersonal conflict that stem from those behaviors.[20]

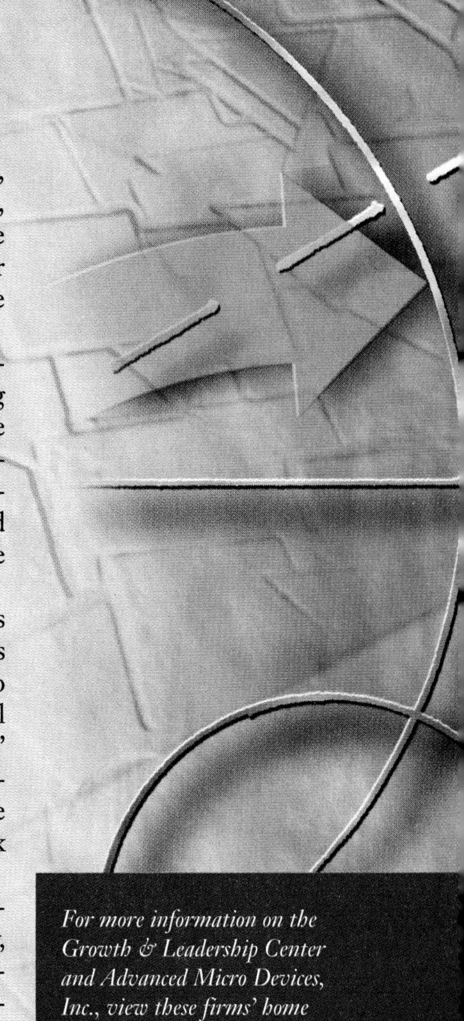

For more information on the Growth & Leadership Center and Advanced Micro Devices, Inc., view these firms' home pages at ***www.glc-corp.com*** *and* ***www.amd.com.***

advocate strongly for ideas. That can be hard and somewhat uncomfortable at times as people say a lot of challenging, provocative things. However, this gets a lot of ideas out there so that we can take a look at them."[21]

INTERGROUP CONFLICT

Intergroup conflict refers to opposition, disagreements, and disputes between groups or teams. It often occurs in union–management relations, as in the dispute between American Airlines and the pilots' union. This dispute lasted for several years, eventually ending up in court following a pilot "sickout" that forced American to cancel hundreds of flights during the Presidents' Day Weekend in 1999.[22] Such conflicts may be highly intense, drawn out, and costly to those involved. The pilots' union, for example, was fined $45.5 million for not promptly obeying a court order to return to work. Under high levels of competition and conflict, the parties develop attitudes toward each other that are characterized by distrust, rigidity, a focus only on self-interest, failure to listen, and the like. We briefly consider four categories of intergroup conflicts within organizations: vertical, horizontal, line–staff, and diversity.

Vertical Conflict. Disputes between employees at different levels in an organization are called **vertical conflict.** It often occurs when superiors attempt to control subordinates too tightly and the subordinates resist. Subordinates may resist because they believe that the controls infringe too much on their freedom to do their jobs appropriately and effectively. Vertical conflicts also may arise because of inadequate communication, goal conflict, or a lack of agreement concerning information and values (cognitive conflict).

Horizontal Conflict. Disputes between groups of employees at the same hierarchical level in an organization are called **horizontal conflict.** It can occur when each department or team strives only for its own goals, disregarding the goals of other departments and teams, especially if those goals are incompatible. Contrasting attitudes of employees in different departments and teams may also lead to conflict.

Line–Staff Conflict. Disputes over authority relationships often involve **line–staff conflict.** Most organizations have staff departments (e.g., human resources, legal, and accounting) to assist line departments. Line managers normally are responsible for some process that creates part or all of the firm's goods or services. Staff personnel often serve in an advisory or control role that requires specialized professional or technical knowledge.[23] They also may specify the methods and partially control the resources used by line managers. For example, in many manufacturing organizations, staff engineers specify how each product is to be made and what materials are to be used. At the same time, line managers are held responsible for results (e.g., downtime, rework, and labor costs per unit). Thus line managers may feel that staff personnel are encroaching on their areas of legitimate authority and actually directing production tasks. Line managers often think that staff personnel reduce their authority over workers while their responsibility for the results remains unchanged. That is, they perceive that their authority is less than their actual responsibility because of staff involvement.

Diversity-Based Conflict. We discussed in previous chapters how serious intergroup conflicts may arise from workforce diversity. The most difficult diversity-based conflicts to resolve in organizations appear to relate to issues of race, gender, ethnicity, and religion. They may encompass all four levels of conflict within the organization—intrapersonal, interpersonal, intragroup, and intergroup.[24]

The Managing Diversity Competency feature on page 303 presents highlights of the pressures and conflicts experienced by some public accounting firms stemming from gender differences.

Learning Objective:

3. Use five interpersonal conflict handling styles.

INTERPERSONAL CONFLICT HANDLING STYLES

Individuals handle interpersonal conflict in various ways.[25] Figure 10.3 presents a model for understanding and comparing five interpersonal conflict handling styles. The styles are identified by their locations on two dimensions: *concern for self* and *concern for others.* The desire to satisfy your own concerns depends on the extent to which you are *assertive* or *unassertive* in pursuing personal goals. Your desire to satisfy the concerns of others depends on the extent to which you are *cooperative* or *uncooperative.* The five interpersonal conflict handling styles thus represent different combinations of assertiveness and cooperativeness. Although you may have a natural tendency toward one or two of the styles, you may use all of them as the context and people involved change. For example, the style you use in working through a conflict with a good friend may be quite different from that you utilize with a stranger after a minor auto accident. The Developing Competencies section at the end of this chapter contains a questionnaire that you can use to assess your own styles for handling conflict.

COMPETENCY: MANAGING DIVERSITY

GENDER ISSUES IN CPA FIRMS

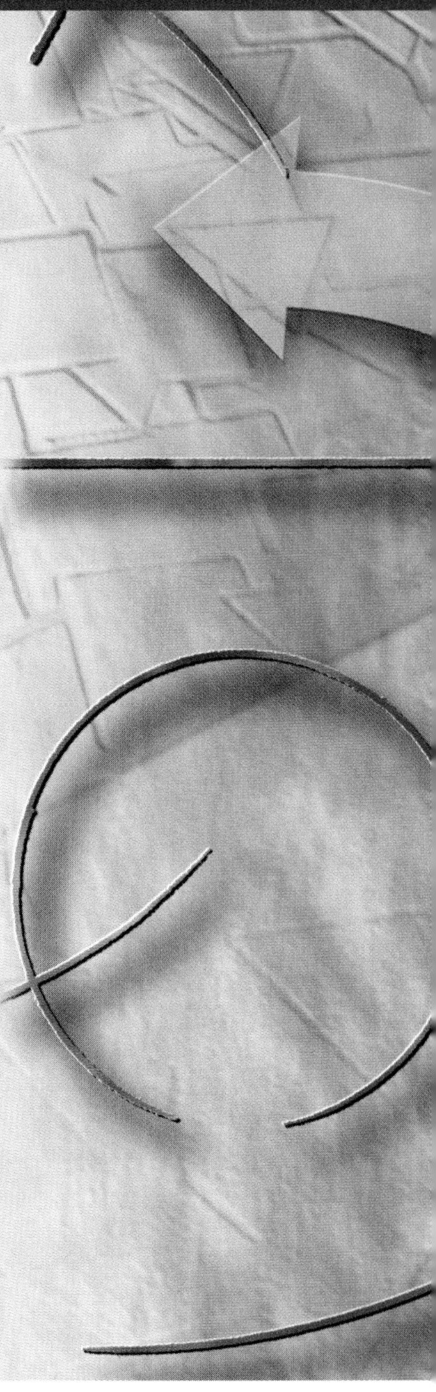

Public accounting firms have long struggled with high levels of conflict experienced by women certified public accountants (CPAs). Historically, turnover among women working in public accounting has been greater than turnover among men. CPA firms had attempted to treat all professionals alike, regardless of gender. Although this approach clearly is appropriate much of the time, it created an unusual circumstance with regard to family. Women who wanted to have children often faced having their careers derailed. As a result, large CPA firms historically had few women as senior managers and partners.

A series of surveys among CPAs during the 1990s highlighted the higher levels of conflict and stress experienced by women CPAs. Further, data gathered from these surveys indicated that many accounting managers assumed that their firms were doing everything possible to further women employees' careers. Often managers seemed to believe that the high turnover rates for women CPAs simply reflected personal choices and preferences and thus were not part of their firms' responsibility. In addition, many managers indicated that there was little they could do to improve the situation.

Information about high levels of conflict and unhelpful attitudes opened a lot of eyes at CPA firms. Many organizations began to take steps to help women CPAs reduce their experienced conflict between family and professional aspirations. Among the more successful programs have been the use of flexible work arrangements (part-time work, flexible hours, telecommuting, and the like), more realistic and flexible career paths (reducing the "up or out" syndrome prevalent at many firms), and more "family-friendly" policies that are emphasized and enforced by higher management. In addition, CPA firms have begun to hire more experienced people, getting away somewhat from the notion that new accountants should only be added to the organization directly out of colleges and universities. A viable labor market for more experienced individuals, in turn, creates more opportunities for women to return to the profession after, for example, staying home with young children for several years.

As a result of these types of improvements, by 1999 the situation in North American CPA firms had improved substantially. One indication of this improved environment is that turnover rates among women and men CPAs are now virtually identical. Less positive, however, is the finding that women still comprise only about one-third of senior managers and less than 25 percent of the promotions to partner. These percentages are expected to continue to improve under the considerable pressure on CPA firms to do a better job of retaining talented employees. As the percentages of women staying with these organizations improves, so should the gender balance in managerial and executive ranks.[26]

AVOIDING STYLE

The **avoiding style** refers to unassertive and uncooperative behaviors. A person uses this style to stay away from conflict, ignore disagreements, or remain neutral. The avoidance approach reflects an aversion to tension and frustration and may involve a decision to let a conflict work itself out. Because ignoring important issues often frustrates others, the consistent use of the avoidance style usually results in unfavorable evaluations by others.[27] This style is illustrated by the following statements.

Figure 10.3 **Interpersonal Conflict Handling Styles**

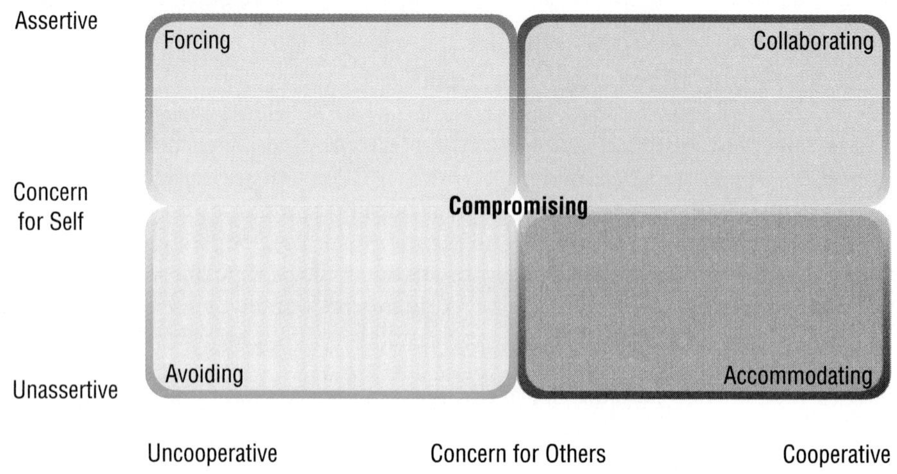

Source: Adapted with permission from Thomas, K. W. Conflict and conflict management. In M. D. Dunnett (ed.), *Handbook of Industrial and Organizational Psychology.* Chicago: Rand McNally, 1976, 900.

- If there are rules that apply, I cite them. If there aren't, I leave the other person free to make his or her own decision.
- I usually don't take positions that will create controversy.
- I shy away from topics that are sources of disputes with my friends.
- That's okay. It wasn't important anyway. Let's leave well enough alone.

When unresolved conflicts affect goal accomplishment, the avoiding style will lead to negative results for the organization. This style may be desirable under some situations, as when (1) the issue is minor or only of passing importance and thus not worth the individual's time or energy to confront the conflict; (2) the individual doesn't have enough information to deal effectively with the conflict at that time; (3) the individual's power is so low relative to the other person's that there's little chance of causing change (e.g., disagreement with a new strategy approved by top management); and (4) others can resolve the conflict more effectively.

Forcing Style

The **forcing style** refers to assertive and uncooperative behaviors and represents a win–lose approach to interpersonal conflict. Those who use the forcing approach try to achieve their own goals without concern for others. This style includes aspects of coercive power and dominance.[28] It may help a person achieve individual goals, but like avoidance, forcing tends to result in unfavorable evaluations by others. The forcing style is illustrated by the following statements.

- I like to put it plainly: Like it or not, what I say goes, and maybe when others have had the experience I have, they will remember this and think better of it.
- I convince the other person of the logic and benefits of my position.
- I insist that my position be accepted during a disagreement.
- I usually hold onto my solution to a problem after the controversy starts.

Forcing-prone individuals assume that conflict resolution means that one person must win and the other must lose. When dealing with conflict between subordinates or departments, forcing-style managers may threaten or actually use demotion, dismissal, negative performance evaluations, or other punishments to gain compliance. When conflict occurs between peers, an employee using the forcing style might try to get his or her own way by appealing to the manager. This approach represents an attempt to use the manager to force the decision on the opposing individual.

Overreliance on forcing by a manager lessens employees' work motivation because their interests haven't been considered. Relevant information and other possible alternatives usually are ignored. In some situations the forcing style may be necessary, as when (1) emergencies require quick action, (2) unpopular courses of action must be taken for long-term organizational effectiveness and survival (e.g., cost-cutting and dismissal of employees for unsatisfactory performance), and (3) the person needs to take action for self-protection and to stop others from taking advantage of him or her.

As we have discussed elsewhere, **whistle-blowing** is the disclosure by current or former organizational members of illegal, immoral, or illegitimate organizational practices in an attempt to change those practices. All too often top management believes that whistle-blowers are creating negative rather than positive conflict. As a result, role senders, especially from within the organization, commonly use the forcing style of conflict handling on whistle-blowers. The following Managing Ethics Competency feature contains some examples of the coercive pressures, including the threat of, or actual, dismissal experienced by two whistle-blowers in their efforts to be ethical.

COMPETENCY: MANAGING ETHICS

WHISTLE-BLOWERS AS OBJECTS OF THE FORCING STYLE

"Think back to when you were a kid," stated Ohio State University business professor Marcia Micelli, who has studied whistle-blowers for 22 years. "Nobody likes someone who tattles."

Consider the experience of George Galatis, an engineer at Northeast Utilities, which operates five nuclear plants in New England. After repeated, unsuccessful efforts over 2 years to have safety concerns and violations addressed, he went directly to the U.S. Nuclear Regulatory Commission (NRC). Galatis told his manager and a vice president that he was going to the NRC. He experienced what he calls "subtle forms of harassment, retaliation, and intimidation." His performance evaluation was downgraded, and his personnel file was forwarded to Northeast's lawyers. His manager "offered" to move him out of the nuclear group. He would walk into a meeting, and the room suddenly would go silent.

A senior vice president issued a memo warning employees that "experienced antinuclear activists" had "the intention of shutting the station down and eliminating 2,500 jobs." The memo stirred up some of Galatis's colleagues. "You're taking food out of my girl's mouth," one of them told him. "If I had it to do over again," says Galatis, "I wouldn't." He believes that his nuclear career is over. Though still employed by Northeast, he feels that whistle-blowers are routinely shut out by the industry.

Consider the experience of Robert Manley. He had been president of Valencia National Bank in Valencia, California, since he helped found it in 1987. He was fired in 1995, ostensibly for poor performance. But in pending suits in state and federal courts, he claims that the firing stemmed from the controversy he created by exposing bad loans to bank directors. The bank later conceded that two directors defaulted on loans totaling $300,000. It maintains that Manley's firing was unrelated.

Manley was out of work for 2 months, and his next job was temporary. His current position, as first vice president of correspondent banking for Community Bank in Pasadena, pays considerably less than he made at Valencia. A long commute has forced him to withdraw from many community activities in his hometown of Santa Clarita.[29]

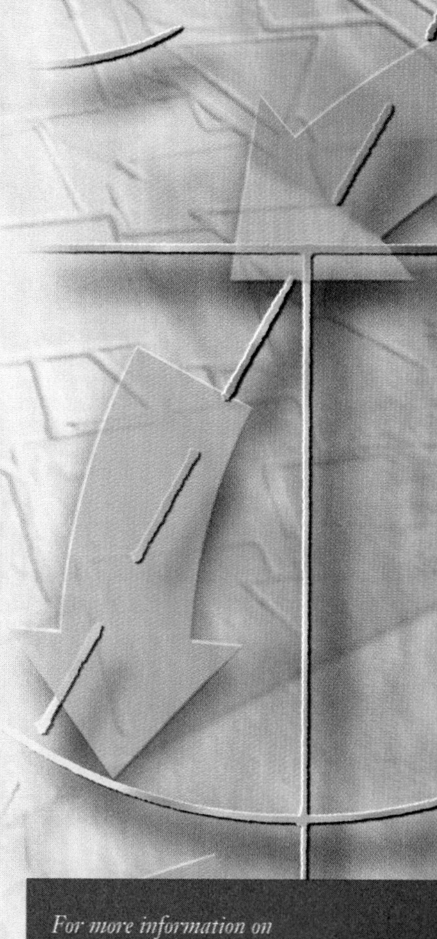

For more information on Northeast Utilities and the Nuclear Regulatory Commission, visit these organizations' home pages at www.nu.com and www.nrc.gov.

Accommodating Style

The **accommodating style** refers to cooperative and unassertive behaviors. Accommodation may represent an unselfish act, a long-term strategy to encourage cooperation by others, or a submission to the wishes of others. Individuals using the accommodating style are typically evaluated favorably by others, but they may also be perceived as weak and submissive. An accommodating style is suggested by the following statements.

- Conflict is best managed through the suspension of my personal goals to maintain good relationships with those whom I value.
- If it makes other people happy, I am all for it.
- I like to smooth over disagreements by making them appear less important.
- I ease conflict by suggesting that our differences are trivial and then show goodwill by blending my ideas into those of the other person.

When using the accommodating style, an individual may act as though the conflict will go away in time and appeal for cooperation. The person will try to reduce tensions and stress by reassurance and support. This style shows concern about the emotional aspects of conflict but little interest in working on its substantive issues. The accommodating style simply results in the individual covering up or glossing over personal feelings. It is generally ineffective if used as a dominant style.[30] The accommodating style may be effective in the short run when (1) the individual is in a potentially explosive emotional conflict situation, and smoothing is used to defuse it; (2) maintaining harmony and avoiding disruption are especially important in the short run; and (3) the conflicts are based primarily on the personalities of the individuals and cannot be easily resolved.

Collaborating Style

The **collaborating style** refers to strong cooperative and assertive behaviors. It is the win–win approach to interpersonal conflict handling. The person using collaboration desires to maximize joint results. An individual who uses this style tends to (1) see conflict as natural, helpful, and even leading to a more creative solution if handled properly; (2) exhibit trust in and candor with others; and (3) recognize that when conflict is resolved to the satisfaction of all, commitment to the solution is likely. An individual who uses the collaborating style is often seen as dynamic and evaluated favorably by others. Statements consistent with this style include the following.

- I first try to overcome any distrust that might exist between us. Then I try to get at the feelings that we mutually have about the topics. I stress that nothing we decide is cast in stone and suggest that we find a position that we can give a trial run.
- I tell the others my ideas, actively seek out their ideas, and search for a mutually beneficial solution.
- I like to suggest new solutions and build on a variety of viewpoints that may have been expressed.
- I try to dig into an issue to find a solution good for all of us.

With this style, conflict is recognized openly and evaluated by all concerned. Sharing, examining, and assessing the reasons for the conflict should lead to development of an alternative that effectively resolves it and is fully acceptable to everyone involved.[31] Collaboration is most practical when there is (1) sufficient required interdependence to justify expending the extra time and energy needed to make working through individual differences worthwhile; (2) sufficient parity in power among individuals so that they feel free to interact candidly, regardless of their formal superior–subordinate status; (3) the potential for mutual benefits, especially over the long run, for resolving the dispute through a win–win process; and (4) sufficient organizational support for investing the necessary time and energy in resolving disputes in this manner. The norms, rewards, and punishments of the organization—especially those set by top management—provide the framework for encouraging or discouraging collaboration.

Compromising Style

The **compromising style** refers to behaviors at an intermediate level of cooperation and assertiveness. The individual using this style engages in give and take and may make a series of concessions. Compromising is commonly used and widely accepted as a means of resolving conflict. The compromising style is illustrated by the following statements.

- I want to know how and what others feel. When the timing is right, I explain how I feel and try to show them where they are wrong. Of course, it's often necessary to settle on some middle ground.
- After failing to get my way, I usually find it necessary to seek a fair combination of gains and losses for all of us.
- I give in to others if they are willing to meet me halfway.
- As the old saying goes, half a loaf is better than nothing. Let's split the difference.

An individual who compromises with others tends to be evaluated favorably. Various explanations are suggested for the favorable evaluation of the compromising style, including: (1) it is seen primarily as a cooperative "holding back;" (2) it reflects a pragmatic way for dealing with conflicts; and (3) it helps maintain good relations for the future.

The compromising style shouldn't be used early in the conflict resolution process for several reasons. First, the people involved are likely to compromise on the stated issues rather than on the real issues. The first issues raised in a conflict often aren't the real ones, so premature compromise will prevent full diagnosis or exploration of the real issues. For example, students telling professors that their courses are tough and challenging may simply be trying to negotiate an easier grading system. Second, accepting an initial position is easier than searching for alternatives that are more acceptable to everyone involved. Third, compromise is inappropriate to all or part of the situation when it isn't the best decision available. Further discussion may reveal a better way of resolving the conflict.

Compared to the collaborating style, the compromising style doesn't maximize mutual satisfaction. Compromise achieves moderate, but only partial, satisfaction for each person. This style is likely to be appropriate when (1) agreement enables each person to be better off, or at least not worse off than if no agreement were reached; (2) achieving a total win–win agreement simply isn't possible; and (3) conflicting goals or opposing interests block agreement on one person's proposal.

Effectiveness of the Styles

Studies conducted on the use of different interpersonal conflict handling styles indicate that collaboration tends to be characteristic of (1) more successful rather than less successful individuals and (2) high-performing rather than medium- and low-performing organizations. People tend to perceive collaboration in terms of the constructive use of conflict. The use of collaboration seems to result in positive feelings in others, as well as favorable self-evaluations of performance and abilities.

In contrast to collaboration, forcing and avoiding often have negative effects. These styles tend to be associated with a less constructive use of conflict, negative feelings from others, and unfavorable evaluations of performance and abilities. The effects of accommodation and compromise appear to be mixed. The use of accommodation sometimes results in positive feelings from others. But these individuals do not form favorable evaluations of the performance and abilities of those using the accommodating style. The use of the compromising style generally is followed by positive feelings from others.[32]

Learning Objective:

4. Discuss the basic types of negotiations and describe several negotiation strategies.

NEGOTIATION IN CONFLICT MANAGEMENT

Negotiation is a process in which two or more individuals or groups, having both common and conflicting goals, state and discuss proposals for specific terms of a possible agreement.[33] Negotiation includes a combination of compromise, collaboration, and possibly some forcing on vital issues. A negotiation situation is one in which

- two or more individuals must make a decision about their interdependent goals and objectives,
- the individuals are committed to peaceful means for resolving their dispute, and
- there is no clear or established method or procedure for making the decision.[34]

Types of Negotiations

The four basic types of negotiations are distributive, integrative, attitudinal structuring, and intraorganizational.[35]

Distributive Negotiations. Traditional win–lose, fixed-amount situations—wherein one party's gain is the other party's loss—characterize **distributive negotiations.** They often occur over economic issues, and the interaction patterns may include guarded communication, limited expressions of trust, use of threats, and dis- torted statements and demands. In short, the parties are engaged in intense, emotion-laden conflict. The forcing and compromise conflict handling styles are dominant in distributive negotiations.

Some individuals and groups still believe in extreme distributive (win–lose) negotiations, and negotiators have to be prepared to counter them. Awareness and understanding probably are the most important means for dealing with win–lose negotiation ploys by the other party. Four of the most common win–lose strategies that you might face as a negotiator are the following.[36]

- *I want it all.* By making an extreme offer and then granting concessions grudgingly, if at all, the other party hopes to wear down your resolve. You will know that you have met such a negotiator when you encounter the following tactics: (1) the other party's first offer is extreme; (2) minor concessions are made grudgingly; (3) you are pressured to make significant concessions; and (4) the other party refuses to reciprocate.
- *Time warp.* Time can be used as a powerful weapon by the win–lose negotiator. When any of the following techniques are used, you should refuse to be forced into an unfavorable position: (1) the offer is valid only for a limited time; (2) you are pressured to accept arbitrary deadlines; (3) the other party stalls or delays the progress of the negotiation; and (4) the other party increases pressure on you to settle quickly.
- *Good cop, bad cop.* Negotiators using this strategy hope to sway you to their side by alternating sympathetic with threatening behavior. You should be on your guard when you are confronted with the following tactics: (1) the other party becomes irrational or abusive; (2) the other party walks out of a negotiation; and (3) irrational behavior is followed by reasonable, sympathetic behavior.
- *Ultimatums.* This strategy is designed to try to force you to submit to the will of the other party. You should be wary when the other party tries any of the following: (1) you are presented with a take-it-or-leave-it offer; (2) the other party overtly tries to force you to accept its demands; (3) the other party is unwilling to make concessions; and (4) you are expected to make all the concessions.

Integrative Negotiations. Joint problem solving to achieve results benefiting both parties is called **integrative negotiations.** The parties identify mutual problems, identify and assess alternatives, openly express preferences, and jointly reach a mutually acceptable solution. Rarely perceived as equally acceptable, the solution is simply advantageous to both sides. Those involved are strongly motivated to solve problems, exhibit flexibility and trust, and explore new ideas. The collaborative and compromise conflict handling styles are dominant in integrative negotiations.

In the best-seller, *Getting to Yes*, R. Fisher and W. Ury outline four key principles for integrative (win–win) negotiations. These principles provide a foundation for an integrative negotiation strategy, which they call "principled negotiation," or "negotiation on the merits."[37]

- *Separate the people from the problem.* The first principle in reaching a mutually agreeable solution is to disentangle the substantive issues of the negotiation from the interpersonal relationship issues between the parties and deal with each set of issues separately. Negotiators should see themselves as working side by side, dealing with the substantive issues or problems instead of attacking each other.
- *Focus on interests, not positions.* People's egos tend to become identified with their negotiation positions. Furthermore, focusing only on stated positions often obscures what the participants really need or want. Rather than focusing only on the positions taken by each negotiator, a much more effective strategy is to focus on the underlying human needs and interests that had caused them to adopt those positions.
- *Invent options for mutual gain.* Designing optimal solutions under pressure in the presence of an adversary tends to narrow people's thinking. Searching for the one right solution inhibits creativity, particularly when the stakes are high. These blinders can be offset by establishing a forum in which a variety of possibilities are generated before decisions are made about which action to take.
- *Insist on using objective criteria.* The parties should discuss the conditions of the negotiation in terms of some fair standard, such as market value, expert opinion, custom, or law. This principle steers the focus away from what the parties are willing or unwilling to do. By using objective criteria, neither party has to give in to the other, and both parties may defer to a fair solution.

Leigh Steinberg and Ron Shapiro provide good examples of individuals who emphasize integrative negotiations. Note the emphasis on the collaborative and compromising approaches in the Managing Self Competency feature on page 310.

Attitudinal Structuring. **Attitudinal structuring** is the process by which the parties seek to establish desired attitudes and relationships. Throughout any negotiations, the parties reveal certain attitudes (e.g., hostility or friendliness and competitiveness or cooperativeness) that influence their interactions.

At one time, hostile and competitive attitudes prevailed between the major San Francisco hotels and the members of Culinary Local 2. One element in their attitudinal restructuring was the use of La Vonne Ritter as a third-party mediator. She spent several days with union and hotel leadership developing a training program for problem-solving teams composed of hotel management and union representatives and creating a mission statement for their new working relationships. The following elements of the mission statement focus on attitudinal structuring.

- It shall be the mission of the San Francisco Hotels Multi-Employer Group and the unions to create a new partnership in labor relations.
- We are committed to jointly creating world-class models in the hotel industry demonstrating that union–employer partnerships can achieve a truly successful competitive edge.
- Acknowledging that joint ownership of the process is necessary to ensure success of the parties, we will share all relevant information to foster better communication.
- To accomplish this mission, we commit ourselves to openness, human dignity, courtesy, mutual respect, and an ever increasing level of trust.[38]

COMPETENCY: MANAGING SELF

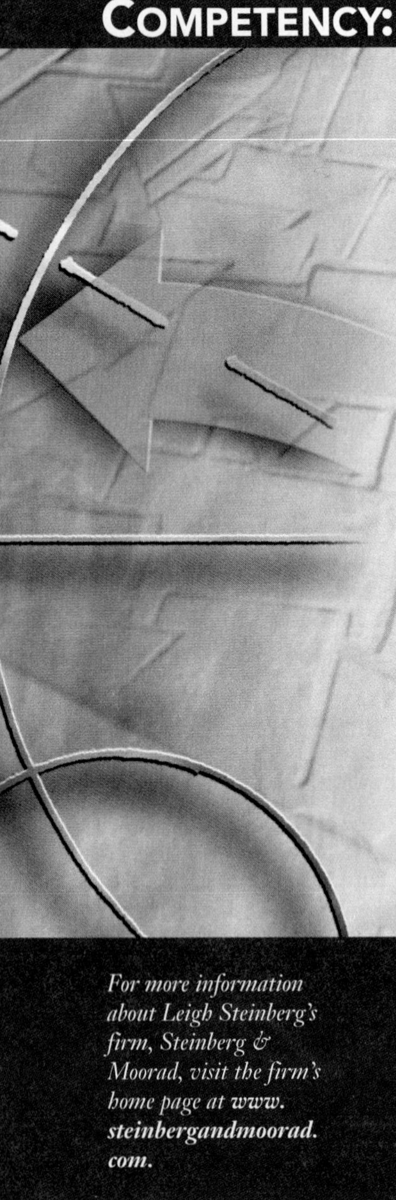

For more information about Leigh Steinberg's firm, Steinberg & Moorad, visit the firm's home page at ***www.steinbergandmoorad.com.***

NEGOTIATING NICE

Ron Shapiro and Leigh Steinberg are legends in the world of high-stakes negotiations. Shapiro is the agent for baseball stars such as Cal Ripkin, Jr., and Dante Bichette. Steinberg is well known as the agent for a number of high-profile NFL quarterbacks such as Troy Aikman, Warren Moon, and Steve Young. Both are, no doubt, formidable opposition at the negotiation table. Yet each, in his own way, also has a reputation for "negotiating nice."

Shapiro, at one time, represented Oprah Winfrey before she became really famous. He lost her as a client when another agent lured her away with promises of getting her more money for her TV contract. Against his better judgment, Shapiro's firm ended up suing Oprah because she still owed them some commissions. Shapiro won, and got his money but today recognizes the court victory as a short-term gain that cost him a lot of long-term goodwill. Shapiro says, "My relationship with Oprah is a good example of how not to negotiate. I derived a career-long lesson from that experience: Don't negotiate as if you'll never again do business with the person across the table."

Shapiro now argues that "the power of nice" is the path to successful negotiations. "Forget about winners and losers. Forget about conquerors and victims. Negotiation is not war. It isn't about getting the other side to wave a flag and surrender. Don't think hurt. Think help. Don't demand. Listen. The best way to get most of what you want is to help the other side get some of what it wants."

Steinberg calls his negotiation strategy "winning with integrity." Like Shapiro, Steinberg uses an integrative approach to the negotiation process. His negotiating "rules" can be described as follows.

- Align yourself with people who share your values.
- Learn all you can about the other party.
- Establish a climate of cooperation, not conflict.
- In the face of intimidation, show no fear.
- Learn to listen; be comfortable with silence.
- Avoid playing split-the-difference.
- Never push a losing argument to the end.
- Develop relationships, not conquests.[39]

Intraorganizational Negotiations. Groups often negotiate through representatives. However, these representatives first may have to obtain the agreement of their respective groups before they can agree with each other. In **intraorganizational negotiations,** each set of negotiators tries to build consensus for agreement and resolve intragroup conflict before dealing with the other group's negotiators. For example, the members of the federation of San Francisco hotels had to spend a considerable amount of time negotiating among themselves the new concepts, attitudes, and practices that were necessary to reach satisfactory agreement with the members of Culinary Local 2.

NEGOTIATOR'S DILEMMA

Negotiators increasingly realize the importance of cooperatively creating value by means of integrative negotiations. However, they must also acknowledge the fact that both sides may eventually seek gain through the distributive process. The **negotiator's**

dilemma means that the tactics of self-gain tend to repel moves to create greater mutual gain. An optimal solution normally results when both parties openly discuss the problem, respect each other's substantive and relationship needs, and creatively seek to satisfy each other's interests. However, such behavior doesn't always occur.[40]

Win–win negotiators are vulnerable to the tactics of win–lose negotiators. As a result, negotiators often develop an uneasiness about the use of integrative strategies because they expect the other party to use distributive strategies. This mutual suspicion often causes negotiators to leave joint gains on the table. Moreover, after a win–win negotiator has been stung in several encounters with experienced win–lose strategists, the pull toward self-gain tactics becomes insidious. Win–win strategists soon "learn" to become win–lose strategists. Finally, if both negotiators use distributive strategies, the probability of achieving great mutual benefits is virtually eliminated. The negotiations will likely result in both parties receiving only minimal benefits.

Graphically, the integrative and distributive negotiation strategies may be placed on vertical and horizontal axes, representing the two negotiating parties. Then, a matrix of possible outcomes emerging from the negotiation process can be developed to illustrate the negotiator's dilemma, as shown in Figure 10.4 for person A and person B.

Negotiating Across Cultures

The numerous issues and complexities relevant to all negotiations are increased, sometimes dramatically, when negotiators are from different cultures.[41] Table 10.3 provides examples of some of the differences in negotiators from different cultures. These examples are based on a study of more than 300 negotiators in 12 countries. As previously discussed, two fundamental approaches to negotiation are win–win versus win–lose. Note that 100 percent of the respondents from Japan emphasized win–win in their negotiation approach. In contrast, only 37 percent of the Spanish negotiators utilized a win–win approach. The table also compares negotiators from these countries in terms of the degree of formality in their negotiations, whether their communication tends to be direct or indirect, and whether they emphasize attaining general agreement or detailed understandings or contracts.

The degree of formality refers to a negotiator's style. For example, a negotiator with a very formal style might insist on addressing individuals by their titles, avoid the use of personal stories and anecdotes, and avoid any mention of private or family life.

Figure 10.4 **Matrix of Negotiated Outcomes**

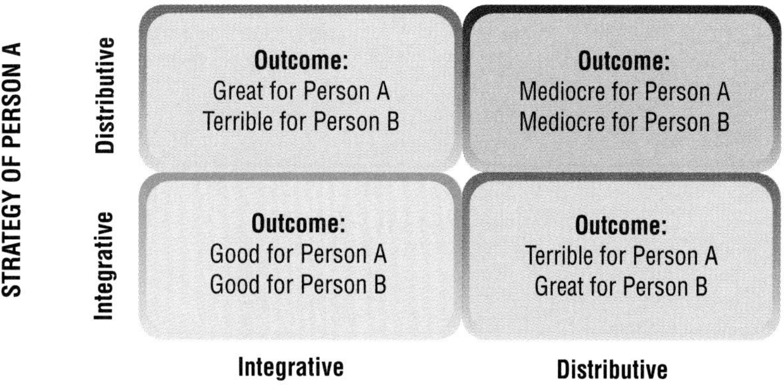

Source: Adapted from Anderson, T. Step into my parlor: A survey of strategies and techniques for effective negotiation. *Business Horizons*, May–June 1992, 75.

A negotiator with an informal style, in contrast, might use first names as a form of address, strive to develop a personal relationship with other parties, and purposefully dress more casually. The contrast between direct and indirect communications has to do primarily with how straightforward and to the point communications typically are during the negotiations. Indirect communications consist of heavy use of nonverbal communication (see Chapter 13) and many vague or oblique references and statements. German and U.S. negotiators are typically viewed as very direct in their negotiations; French and Japanese negotiators are viewed as more indirect.

The traditional assumptions and generalizations may not always apply to negotiation and conflict resolution between the parties when long-term and insider relationships have been established. This situation applies particularly to negotiations by the Japanese with those whom they view as insiders. Almost by definition, Japanese

Table 10.3 Cultural Effects on Negotiating Style

NEGOTIATING ATTITUDE: WIN–WIN OR WIN–LOSE?

	Japan	China	Argentina	France	India	USA	UK	Mexico	Germany	Nigeria	Brazil	Spain
Win–Win (%):	100	82	81	80	78	71	59	50	55	47	44	37

PERSONAL STYLE: FORMAL OR INFORMAL?

	Nigeria	Spain	China	Mexico	UK	Argentina	Germany	Japan	India	Brazil	France	USA
Formal (%):	53	47	46	42	35	35	27	27	22	22	20	17

COMMUNICATION STYLE: DIRECT OR INDIRECT?

	Japan	France	China	UK	Brazil	India	Germany	USA	Argentina	Spain	Mexico	Nigeria
Indirect (%):	27	20	18	12	11	11	9	5	4	0	0	0

AGREEMENT FORM: GENERAL OR SPECIFIC?

	Japan	Germany	India	France	China	Argentina	Brazil	USA	Nigeria	Mexico	Spain	UK
General (%):	46	45	44	30	27	27	22	22	20	17	16	11

Source: Adapted from Salacuse, J. W. Ten ways that culture affects negotiating style: Some survey results. *Negotiation Journal*, July 1998, 221–240.

businesspeople consider Westerners to be outsiders. Thus Westerners often incorrectly assume that the Japanese never use direct or confrontational approaches to conflict resolution and negotiations. In fact, they often are very direct in resolving differences of opinion with *insiders.* They explicitly state the principal differences among group members and state demands, rejections, and counteroffers directly.[42]

Similar to the Japanese, the Chinese often consider Westerners to be outsiders. In the West, people typically think of win–win and win–lose approaches as polar opposites. However, to the Chinese, these are subtly intertwined as illustrated in the Managing Across Cultures Competency feature below.

MEDIATION

Mediation is a process by which a third party helps two or more other parties resolve one or more conflicts. Most of the actual negotiations occur directly between the involved individuals. But, when the parties appear likely to become locked in win–lose conflict, a mediator, acting as a neutral party, may be able to help them resolve their differences.[43]

COMPETENCY: MANAGING ACROSS CULTURES

THE CHINESE APPROACH TO NEGOTIATION

Negotiations between individuals from Western countries and the Chinese have increased substantially in recent years. Unfortunately, both parties frequently find these negotiations unsatisfactory. Guy Faure, a professor at the Sorbonne University in Paris, has studied many failed negotiations for the past 5 years. Faure suggests that the lack of negotiation success is due to a fundamentally different conception of negotiations in China and the West. In particular, he suggests two metaphors, "mobile warfare" and "joint quest," that would help Westerners understand the Chinese approach to negotiations. These two metaphors represent two very different types of activity that need to be understood.

Mobil warfare represents a conflict-based form of negotiation. The negotiation activity is conceived as a fight between conflicting interests. The negotiation partner is defined as an adversary and, thus, making negative value judgments about the adversary is acceptable. As a consequence, the Chinese party is allowed great freedom of action in dealing with this "adversary." Even though this approach seems to be quite negative, the final goal of the negotiation isn't really to destroy the other side— just to score more points. Each party can be allowed to achieve some gains from the negotiation, but the Chinese side feels justified in getting more.

The *joint quest* approach is more collaborative in that the objective is to develop a common approach to exploring issues. The joint quest approach is conceived of as a long and exacting task in order to find common ground, common meaning, and a common vision of what might be jointly attained. The long, drawn out nature of these negotiations runs counter to the expectations of most Westerners, who typically are quite impatient with this approach.

In sum, the Chinese approach to negotiation borrows from the Taoist concept of balanced dynamics built on elements that are both contradictory and complementary. Negotiations are, at the same time, a focus on tactics (mobile warfare) and a quest toward a common goal (joint quest). If the Westerner responds only to the mobile warfare tactics and fails to recognize the subtle joint quest activities, the negotiation is doomed to end in conflict. However, a richer understanding can avoid this outcome, and negotiations between Chinese and Westerners do not have to fail.[44]

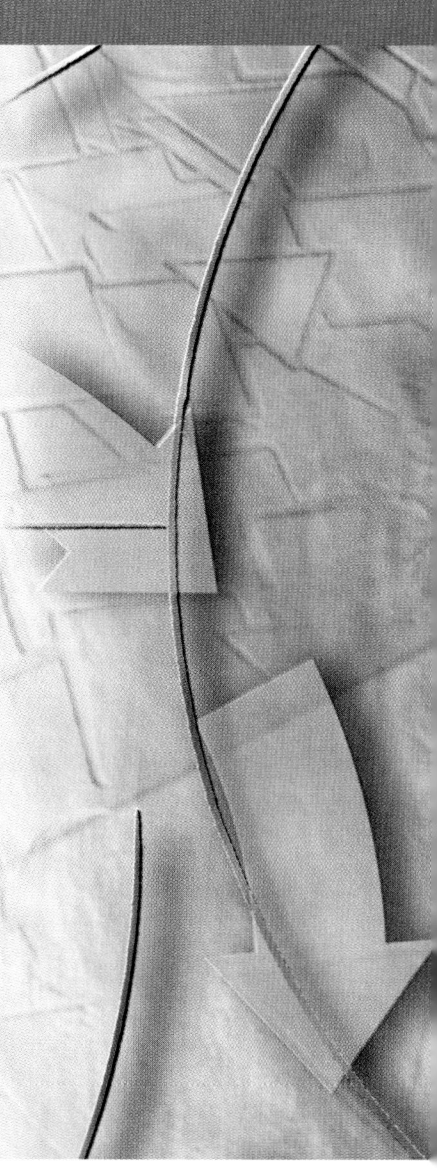

Competencies and Tasks. Mediators need special competencies. They must (1) be able to diagnose the conflict, (2) be skilled at breaking deadlocks and facilitating discussions at the right time, (3) show mutual acceptance, and (4) have the ability to provide emotional support and reassurance. In brief, an effective mediator must instill confidence in and acceptance by the parties in conflict.

Key tasks in the mediator's role include the following.

- *Ensure mutual motivation.* Each party should have incentives for resolving the conflict.
- *Achieve a balance in situational power.* If the situational power of the individuals isn't equal, establishing trust and maintaining open lines of communication may be difficult.
- *Coordinate confrontation efforts.* One party's positive moves must be coordinated with the other party's readiness to do likewise. A failure to coordinate positive initiatives and readiness to respond can undermine future efforts to work out differences.
- *Promote openness in dialogue.* The mediator can help establish norms of openness, provide reassurance and support, and decrease the risks associated with openness.
- *Maintain an optimum level of tension.* If the threat and tension are too low, the incentive for change or finding a solution is minimal. However, if the threat and tension are too high, the individuals involved may be unable to process information and envision creative alternatives. They may begin to polarize and take rigid positions.[45]

Intergroup Dialogue Technique. A mediator usually tries to assist negotiations without setting down a specific set of procedures for the parties to follow. Occasionally, however, a structured approach is useful to ensure that the negotiators concentrate on the real issues and direct their efforts toward resolving them. One example of such an approach is the **intergroup dialogue technique,** which refers to the following process.[46]

- Each group meets in a separate room and develops two lists. On one list, the members indicate how they perceive themselves as a group, particularly in their relationship with the other group. On the second list, they indicate how they view the other group.
- The two groups come together and share perceptions. The mediator helps them clarify their views and come to a better understanding of themselves and the other group.
- The groups return to their separate rooms to look at the issues further, diagnose the current problem, and determine what each group contributes to the conflict.
- The groups meet again to share their new insights. The mediator urges them to identify common issues and plan the next stages for seeking solutions.

The intergroup dialogue technique doesn't guarantee successful conflict resolution. Instead, it provides a process for the parties in conflict to explore and work through their differences. A competent mediator uses the technique to move the individuals toward a resolution of issues.

CHAPTER SUMMARY

1. Explain the four basic varieties of conflict and describe three differing attitudes toward organizational conflict.

Conflict is a part of organizational life. Four basic varieties of conflict are goal conflict, cognitive conflict, affective conflict, and procedural conflict. Conflict need not have destructive outcomes for individuals or an organization. Through effective conflict management, its negative effects may be minimized and its positive effects maximized, resulting in a balanced attitude toward conflict. Effective conflict management requires an understanding of the different ways in which conflict develops and can be resolved.

2. Identify the four primary levels of conflict within organizations.

Conflict occurs at four different levels within organizations: intrapersonal, interpersonal, intragroup, and intergroup. Intrapersonal conflict occurs *within* the individual. Interpersonal conflict occurs when someone's wishes or desires are perceived to be in opposition to another's. Intragroup conflict occurs between or among group members. Intergroup conflict occurs between groups or teams.

3. Use five interpersonal conflict handling styles.

The five styles for handling interpersonal conflict are avoiding, forcing, accommodating, collaborating, and compromising. An individual may have a natural preference for one or two of these styles but is likely to use all of them over time when dealing with various interpersonal conflict situations. As a reminder, an instrument for measuring your own conflict handling style is presented at the end of this chapter.

4. Discuss the basic types of negotiations and describe several negotiation strategies.

Negotiation is an important process in conflict management. The four basic types of negotiations are distributive, integrative, attitudinal structuring, and intraorganizational. The two basic approaches to negotiation tactics and behaviors are the win–win and win–lose processes. Negotiations involving individuals from different cultures are even more complex than negotiations involving only individuals from the same culture. Mediation can be helpful when the negotiating parties anticipate or experience difficulties in reaching agreement.

KEY TERMS AND CONCEPTS

Accommodating style
Affective conflict
Approach–approach conflict
Approach–avoidance conflict
Attitudinal structuring
Avoidance–avoidance conflict
Avoiding style
Cognitive conflict
Cognitive dissonance
Collaborating style
Compromising style
Conflict
Conflict management
Distributive negotiations
Forcing style
Goal conflict
Goal incompatibility
Horizontal conflict
Integrative negotiations
Intergroup conflict
Intergroup dialogue technique
Interpersonal conflict
Interrole conflict
Intersender role conflict
Intragroup conflict
Intraorganizational negotiations
Intrapersonal conflict
Intrasender role conflict
Line–staff conflict
Mediation
Negotiation
Negotiator's dilemma
Neurotic tendencies
Person–role conflict
Procedural conflict
Role
Role ambiguity
Role conflict
Role set
Vertical conflict
Whistle-blowing

DISCUSSION QUESTIONS

1. Describe your personal attitudes toward conflict. Are they positive, negative, or balanced?
2. Provide three examples from personal experience that illustrate your attitudes toward conflict.
3. Based on your own work or school experience, provide examples of (a) goal conflict, (b) cognitive conflict, (c) affective conflict, and (d) procedural conflict. Such conflict can be your own or that which you observed in others.

4. Give personal examples of (a) approach–approach conflict, (b) avoidance–avoidance conflict, and (c) approach–avoidance conflict.
5. Provide examples of (a) intrasender role conflict, (b) intersender role conflict, (c) interrole conflict, and (d) person–role conflict that you have experienced.
6. Based on your own experiences at work or at school, provide two examples of intragroup conflict. One example should illustrate positive consequences of such conflict, and the other example should demonstrate negative consequences.
7. Have you been involved in negotiations when the other party used win–lose tactics? Describe the situation. What did you do in response to these tactics? How did you feel? What was the outcome?
8. Reread the Managing Self Competency feature about Ron Shapiro and Leigh Steinberg. Can their approaches accurately be described as win–win? Why or why not?
9. Based on your personal experience, describe a situation when an integrative negotiation approach (win–win) seemed to work. Why was it successful?
10. Will integrative negotiations (win–win) always work? Why or why not? Describe some of the difficulties that an individual might encounter while attempting integrative negotiations.

DEVELOPING COMPETENCIES

Competency: Managing Self—Conflict Handling Styles[47]

Instructions: Each numbered item contains two statements that describe how people deal with conflict. Distribute 5 points between each pair of statements. The statement that more accurately reflects your likely response should receive the highest number of points. For example, if response (a) strongly describes your behavior, then record

__5__ a.
__0__ b.

However, if (a) and (b) are both characteristic, but (b) is slightly more characteristic of your behavior than (a), then record

__2__ a.
__3__ b.

1. ____ a. I am most comfortable letting others take responsibility for solving a problem.
   ____ b. Rather than negotiate differences, I stress those points for which agreement is obvious.
2. ____ a. I pride myself in finding compromise solutions.
   ____ b. I examine all the issues involved in any disagreement.
3. ____ a. I usually persist in pursuing my side of an issue.
   ____ b. I prefer to soothe others' feelings and preserve relationships.
4. ____ a. I pride myself in finding compromise solutions.
   ____ b. I usually sacrifice my wishes for the wishes of a peer.
5. ____ a. I consistently seek a peer's help in finding solutions.
   ____ b. I do whatever is necessary to avoid tension.
6. ____ a. As a rule, I avoid dealing with conflict.
   ____ b. I defend my position and push my view.
7. ____ a. I postpone dealing with conflict until I have had some time to think it over.
   ____ b. I am willing to give up some points if others give up some too.
8. ____ a. I use my influence to have my views accepted.
   ____ b. I attempt to get all concerns and issues immediately out in the open.
9. ____ a. I feel that most differences are not worth worrying about.
   ____ b. I make a strong effort to get my way on issues I care about.
10. ____ a. Occasionally I use my authority or technical knowledge to get my way.
    ____ b. I prefer compromise solutions to problems.
11. ____ a. I believe that a team can reach a better solution than any one person can working independently.
    ____ b. I often defer to the wishes of others.
12. ____ a. I usually avoid taking positions that would create controversy.
    ____ b. I'm willing to give a little if a peer will give a little, too.
13. ____ a. I generally propose the middle ground as a solution.
    ____ b. I consistently press to "sell" my viewpoint.
14. ____ a. I prefer to hear everyone's side of an issue before making judgments.
    ____ b. I demonstrate the logic and benefits of my position.
15. ____ a. I would rather give in than argue about trivialities.
    ____ b. I avoid being "put on the spot."
16. ____ a. I refuse to hurt a peer's feelings.
    ____ b. I will defend my rights as a team member.
17. ____ a. I am usually firm in pursuing my point of view.
    ____ b. I'll walk away from disagreements before someone gets hurt.
18. ____ a. If it makes peers happy, I will agree with them.
    ____ b. I believe that give-and-take is the best way to resolve any disagreement.

19. ______ a. I prefer to have everyone involved in a conflict generate alternatives together.
______ b. When the team is discussing a serious problem, I usually keep quiet.

20. ______ a. I would rather openly resolve conflict than conceal differences.
______ b. I seek ways to balance gains and losses for equitable solutions.

21. ______ a. In problem solving, I am usually considerate of peers' viewpoints.
______ b. I prefer a direct and objective discussion of any disagreement.

22. ______ a. I seek solutions that meet some of everyone's needs.
______ b. I will argue as long as necessary to get my position heard.

23. ______ a. I like to assess the problem and identify a mutually agreeable solution.
______ b. When people challenge my position, I simply ignore them.

24. ______ a. If peers feel strongly about a position, I defer to it even if I don't agree.
______ b. I am willing to settle for a compromise solution.

25. ______ a. I am very persuasive when I have to be to win in a conflict situation.
______ b. I believe in the saying, "Kill your enemies with kindness."

26. ______ a. I will bargain with peers in an effort to manage disagreement.
______ b. I listen attentively before expressing my views.

27. ______ a. I avoid taking controversial positions.
______ b. I'm willing to give up my position for the benefit of the group.

28. ______ a. I enjoy competitive situations and "play" hard to win.
______ b. Whenever possible, I seek out knowledgeable peers to help resolve disagreements.

29. ______ a. I will surrender some of my demands, but I have to get something in return.
______ b. I don't like to air differences and usually keep my concerns to myself.

30. ______ a. I generally avoid hurting a peer's feelings.
______ b. When a peer and I disagree, I prefer to bring the issue out into the open so we can discuss it.

Scoring

Record your responses (number of points) in the space next to each statement number and then sum the points in each column.

Column 1	Column 2	Column 3	Column 4	Column 5
3 (a) ______	2 (a) ______	1 (a) ______	1 (b) ______	2 (b) ______
6 (b) ______	4 (a) ______	5 (b) ______	3 (b) ______	5 (a) ______
8 (a) ______	7 (b) ______	6 (a) ______	4 (b) ______	8 (b) ______
9 (b) ______	10 (b) ______	7 (a) ______	11 (b) ______	11 (a) ______
10 (a) ______	12 (b) ______	9 (a) ______	15 (a) ______	14 (a) ______
13 (b) ______	13 (a) ______	12 (a) ______	16 (a) ______	19 (a) ______
14 (b) ______	18 (b) ______	15 (b) ______	18 (a) ______	20 (a) ______
16 (b) ______	20 (b) ______	17 (b) ______	21 (a) ______	21 (b) ______
17 (a) ______	22 (a) ______	19 (b) ______	24 (a) ______	23 (a) ______
22 (b) ______	24 (b) ______	23 (b) ______	25 (b) ______	26 (b) ______
25 (a) ______	26 (a) ______	27 (a) ______	27 (b) ______	28 (b) ______
28 (a) ______	29 (a) ______	29 (b) ______	30 (a) ______	30 (b) ______
Total ______	Total ______	Total ______	Total ______	Total ______

Next carry over the totals from the column totals and then plot your total scores on the following chart to show the profile of your conflict handling styles. A total score of 36 to 45 for a style may indicate a strong preference and use of that style. A total score of 0 to 18 for a style may indicate little preference and use of that style. A total score of 19 to 35 for a style may indicate a moderate preference and use of that style.

	Total	0	10	20	30	40	50	60
Column 1 (Forcing)	____		•	•	•	•	•	•
Column 2 (Compromising)	____		•	•	•	•	•	•
Column 3 (Avoiding)	____		•	•	•	•	•	•
(Column 4 (Accommodating)	____		•	•	•	•	•	•
Column 5 (Collaborating)	____		•	•	•	•	•	•
		0	10	20	30	40	50	60

Interpretation

When used appropriately, each of these styles can be an effective approach to conflict handling. Any one style or a mixture of the five can be used during the course of a dispute. Are you satisfied with this profile? Why or why not? Is this profile truly representative of your natural and primary conflict handling styles?

Competency: Managing Self—Intervening in Employee Disputes

Imagine yourself in the following two situations in an organization.

Scenario A: Two days before major contract work was to begin at the worksite of an important client, a dispute had erupted between the project director and the controller of a small emission-testing (pollution control) company with regard to hiring temporary workers. The project director argued that the extra workers were necessary for a timely completion of the work and, further, that she had the authority to hire temporary workers as well as do anything else necessary to complete the contract successfully. The controller strongly disagreed, arguing that company policy and regulations allowed the project director to purchase equipment and materials *only*. Adding employees to payroll, in the opinion of the controller, required the approval of both the human resources and finance departments. The dispute was brought to the president of the firm for resolution.

Scenario B: The marketing manager and the production manager of a manufacturing company were in sharp disagreement over some design changes. The production manager was upset about current procedures, which allowed marketing to make changes to product design in order to satisfy customers. Frequently, such changes were made right before production runs were scheduled to start, often resulting in delays that affected the manufacture of other products. Each change typically took 3 days of work to alter the specifications of the components, caused a loss of production line time that had already been reserved for manufacturing other products, and, in general, lowered cost-effectiveness. The production manager wanted to limit design changes to a minimum of 2 weeks before production was scheduled to begin. In other words, the deadline for the final design would be 2 weeks prior to production. The marketing manager was outraged by this suggestion and argued that last-minute design changes were often necessary to meet customer demands and keep the business. They had to cope with their competitor's willingness to make last-minute changes, as well as some disorganization from their customers who often seemed to come up with ideas (some of which were quite good) at the last moment. The marketing manager pointed out that they were having a tough enough time as it was maintaining market share in the global environment and it was crazy to do anything to reduce market share. The conflict had escalated to an extent that coordination and cooperation between marketing and production was suffering and morale was adversely affected. Finally, the president had to step in.[48]

Questions

1. Imagine that you are the president of the firm in these two situations. How would you intervene in the disputes? Would you attempt to facilitate a discussion between the disputants but leave the final solution in their hands? Would you listen carefully to their positions, analyze the situation, and then mandate a solution? Or would you stay aloof from the disputes, emphasizing to the individuals involved that they needed to learn how to handle such conflicts on their own? Select a strategy to resolve these conflicts. Using material from this chapter, explain and defend your decisions.
2. Based on your own experience (at work or school), describe a situation in which you had to decide whether to intervene in a dispute between two individuals. What did you do? Would you now do anything differently, and if so, what?

REFERENCES

1. Adapted from Thomson, L. *The Mind and Heart of the Negotiator.* Upper Saddle River, N.J.: Prentice Hall, 1998, 30.
2. Brown, L. D., and Clarkson, A. E. Conflict. In C. L. Cooper and C. Argyris (eds.), *The Concise Blackwell Encyclopedia of Management.* Oxford, England: Blackwell, 1998, 105–107; Walls, J. A., Jr. Conflict and its management. *Journal of Management,* 1995, 21, 515–558.
3. Greenhalgh, L. Managing conflict. In F. J. Lewicki, D. M. Saunders, and J. W. Minton (eds.), *Negotiation,* 3rd ed. Boston: Irwin/McGraw-Hill, 1999, 6–13; Kottler, J. *Beyond Blame: A New Way of Resolving Conflicts in Relationships.* San Francisco: Jossey-Bass, 1994.
4. Kramer, R. M. Trust and distrust in organizations: Emerging perspectives, enduring questions. *Annual Review of Psychology,* 1999, 50, 569–598; Watkins, M. Negotiating in a complex world. *Negotiation Journal,* July 1999, 245–270.
5. Baron, R. A. Positive effects of conflict: A cognitive perspective. *Employee Responsibilities and Rights Journal,* 1991, 4, 25–35; Mescon Group. *Managing Conflict in Teams.* Cincinnati: South-Western, 1996.
6. Conlon, D. E., and Sullivan, D. P. Examining the actions of organizations in conflict: Evidence from the Delaware Court of Chancery. *Academy of Management Journal,* 1999, 42, 319–329; Labig, C. E. *Preventing Violence in the Workplace.* New York: AMACOM, 1995.
7. Costantino, C. A., and Merchant, C. S. *Designing Conflict Management Systems.* San Francisco: Jossey-Bass, 1996; Cropanzano, R., Agunis, H., Schminke, M., and Denham, D. L. Disputant reactions to managerial conflict resolution tactics. *Group & Organization Management,* 1999, 24, 124–154.
8. Adapted from Motorola may have blundered by strong-arming some retailers. *Houston Chronicle,* September 8, 1996, 10E; Alleven, M. Motorola Inc.'s. new Signature retail program has upset dealers. *Wireless Week,* September 16, 1996, 1; Roth, D. Burying Motorola: From poster boy to whipping boy. *Fortune,* July 6, 1998, 28–29.
9. Locke, E. A., Smith, K. G., Erez, M., Chah, D., and Schaeffer, A. The effects of intra-individual goal conflict on performance. *Journal of Management,* 1994, 20, 67–91.
10. Festinger, L. A. *A Theory of Cognitive Dissonance.* Evanston, Ill.: Row, Peterson, 1967; Lewis, B. Cognitive dissonance. In C. L. Cooper and C. Argyris (eds.), *The Concise Blackwell Encyclopedia of Management.* Oxford, England: Blackwell, 1998, 83.
11. Czander, W. H. *The Psychodynamics of Work and Organizations: Theory and Applications.* New York: Guilford, 1993; Maccoby, M. Narcissistic leaders: The incredible pros, the inevitable cons. *Harvard Business Review,* January–February 2000, 69–77.
12. Braverman, M. *Preventing Workplace Violence.* Thousand Oaks, Calif.: Sage, 1999; O'Leary-Kelly, A. M., Griffin, R. W., and Glew, D. J. Organization-motivated aggression: A research framework. *Academy of Management Review,* 1996, 21, 225–253.
13. A '90s Crime. *Newsweek,* November 15, 1999, 6.
14. Polzer, J. T. Role. In C. L. Cooper and C. Argyris (eds.), *The Concise Blackwell Encyclopedia of Management.* Oxford, England: Blackwell, 1998, 574–575.
15. Kahan, R. L., Wolfe, D. M., Quinn, R. P., Snoek, J. D., and Rosenthal, R. A. *Occupational Stress: Studies in Role Conflict and Ambiguity.* New York: John Wiley & Sons, 1964; Polzer, J. T. Role conflict. In C. L. Cooper and C. Argyris (eds.), *The Concise Blackwell Encyclopedia of Management.* Oxford, England: Blackwell, 1998, 575–576.
16. Polzer, J. T. Role ambiguity. In C. L. Cooper and C. Argyris (eds.), *The Concise Blackwell Encyclopedia of Management.* Oxford, England: Blackwell, 1998, 575.
17. Peterson, M. F., and Associates. Role conflict, ambiguity and overload: A 21 nation study. *Academy of Management Journal,* 1995, 38, 429–452.
18. Allvesson, M. *Communication Power and Organization.* New York: Water D. deGruyter, 1996.
19. Kahn, A. Taking on a family business can call for greater expertise. *Bryan–College Station Eagle,* March 20, 1994, C6; Lenzner, R., and Upbin, B. Brother vs. brother vs. mother vs. cousin. *Forbes,* June 17, 1996, 44–46.
20. Adapted from Conlin, M. Tough love for techie souls. *Business Week,* November 29, 1999, 164–170.
21. Wetlaufer, S. Common sense and conflict: An interview with Disney's Michael Eisner. *Harvard Business Review,* January–February 2000, 116.
22. Field, D. Airlines battle unions in court. *USA Today,* January 10, 2000, 1B.
23. March, S., and Simon, H. *Organizations,* 2nd ed. Cambridge, Mass.: Blackwell, 1993.
24. Jehn, K. A., Northcraft, G. B., and Neale, M. A. Why differences make a difference: A field study of diversity, conflict, and performance in workgroups. *Administrative Science Quarterly,* 1999, 44, 741–763; Simons, T., Pelled, L. H., and Smith, K. A. Making use of difference: Diversity, debate, and decision comprehensiveness in top management teams. *Academy of Management Journal,* 1999, 42, 662–673.
25. Thomas, K. W. Conflict and negotiation processes in organizations. In M. D. Dunnette and L. M. Hough (eds.), *Handbook of Industrial and Organizational Psychology,* 2nd ed., vol. 3. Palo Alto, Calif.: Consulting Psychologists Press, 1992, 651–717; Thomas, K. W. The conflict handling modes: Toward more precise theory. *Management Communication Quarterly,* 1988, 1, 430–436.
26. Adapted from Doucet, M. S., and Hooks, K. L. Toward an equal future. *Journal of Accountancy,* June 1999, 71–80.
27. Sorenson, P. W., Hawkins, K., and Sorenson, R. L. Gender, psychological type and conflict style preference. *Management Communication Quarterly,* 1995, 9, 115–126.
28. Dana, D. Retaliatory cycle: Introducing the elements of conflict. In E. Bieck (ed.), *The 2000 Annual: Volume 2—Consulting.* San Francisco: Jossey-Bass/Pfeiffer, 2000, 45–49; Weider-Hatfield, D., and Hatfield, J. D. Superiors' conflict management strategies and subordinate outcomes. *Management Communication Quarterly,* 1996, 10, 189–208.

29. Adapted from Lancaster, H. Workers who blow the whistle on bosses often pay a high price. *Wall Street Journal*, July 8, 1995, B1; Pooley, E. Nuclear warriors. *Time*, March 4, 1996, 46–54; Weber, C. E. *Stories of Virtue in Business.* Lanham, Md.: University Press of America, 1995.
30. Martocchio, J. J., and Judge, T. A. When we don't see eye to eye: Discrepancies between supervisors and subordinates in absence disciplinary decisions. *Journal of Management*, 1995, 21, 251–278.
31. Blanchard, K., and O'Connor, M. *Managing by Values.* San Francisco: Berrett-Kohler, 1997.
32. Rahim, M. A. *Managing Conflict in Organizations*, 2nd ed. New York: Praeger, 1992; Susskind, L., McKearnan, S., and Thomas-Larmer, J. *The Consensus-Building Handbook.* Thousand Oaks, Calif.: Sage, 1999.
33. Brett, J. F., Northcraft, G. B., and Pinkley, R. L. Stairways to heaven: An interlocking self-regulation model of negotiation. *Academy of Management Review*, 1999, 224, 435–451; Lewicki, R. J. *Essentials of Negotiation.* Burr Ridge, Ill.: Irwin, 1996.
34. Lewicki, R. J., Saunders, D. M., and Minton, J. W. (eds.). *Negotiation*, 3rd ed. Boston: Irwin/McGraw-Hill, 1999, 1.
35. Polzer, J. T. Negotiation tactics. In C. L. Cooper and C. Argyris (eds.), *The Concise Blackwell Encyclopedia of Management.* Oxford, England: Blackwell, 1998, 429; Walton, R. E., and McKersie, R. B. *A Behavioral Theory of Labor Negotiations.* New York: McGraw-Hill, 1965.
36. Brett, J. M., Shapiro, D. L., and Lytle, A. L. Breaking the bonds of reciprocity in negotiations. *Academy of Management Journal*, 1998, 41, 410–424; Mayer, R. *Power Plays: How to Negotiate, Persuade, and Finesse Your Way to Success in Any Situation.* New York: Times Books, 1996.
37. Anderson, T. Step into my parlor: A survey of strategies and techniques for effective negotiations. *Business Horizons*, May–June 1992, 71–76; Fisher, R. *Getting Ready to Negotiate: The Getting to Yes Workbook.* New York: Viking Penguin, 1995; Fisher, R., and Ury, W. *Getting to Yes: Negotiating Agreement Without Giving In.* New York: Penguin Books, 1981.
38. Korshak, S. R. Negotiating trust in the San Francisco hotel industry. *California Management Review*, Fall 1995, 117–137.
39. Adapted from Powers of persuasion. *Fortune*, October 12, 1998, 160–164; Shapiro, R., and Jankowski, M. *The Power of Nice.* New York: John Wiley & Sons, 1998; Steinberg, L. *Winning With Integrity.* New York: Villard, 1998.
40. Friedman, R. A. *Front Stage Backstage: The Dynamic Structure of Labor Negotiations.* Cambridge, Mass.: MIT Press, 1994.
41. Fang, T. *Chinese Business Negotiating Style.* Thousand Oaks, Calif.: Sage, 1998; Ghauri, P. N., and Usunier, J. C. *International Business Negotiations.* New York: Elsevier Science, 1996; Salacuse, J. W. Ten ways that culture affects negotiating style: Some survey results. *Negotiation Journal*, July 1998, 221–240; Tinsley, C. Models of conflict resolution in Japanese, German, and American cultures. *Journal of Applied Psychology*, 1998, 83, 316–323.
42. Black, J. S., and Mendenhall, M. Resolving conflicts with the Japanese: Mission impossible. *Sloan Management Review*, Spring 1993, 49–59; Brett, J. M. and Ukumura, T. Inter- and intracultural negotiation: U.S. and Japanese negotiators. *Academy of Management Journal*, 1998, 41, 495–510.
43. Arnold, J. A., and O'Connor, K. M. Ombudspersons or peers? The effect of third-party expertise and recommendations on negotiation. *Journal of Applied Psychology*, 1999, 84, 776–785; Slaikeu, K. L. *When Push Comes to Shove: A Practical Guide to Mediating Disputes.* San Francisco: Jossey-Bass, 1995; Weiss, D. S. *Beyond the Walls of Conflict: Mutual Gains Negotiating in Unions & Management.* Burr Ridge, Ill.: Irwin, 1996.
44. Adapted from Faure, G. O. Negotiation: The Chinese concept. *Negotiation Journal*, April 1998, 137–148.
45. Moore, C. W. *The Mediation Process: Practical Strategies for Resolving Conflict.* San Francisco: Jossey-Bass, 1996; Pinkley, R. L., and Northcraft, G. B. Cognitive interpretations of conflict: Implications for dispute processes and outcomes. *Academy of Management Journal*, 1994, 37, 193–205.
46. Blake, R. R., Shepard, H. A., and Mouton, J. S. *Managing Intergroup Conflict in Industry.* Houston: Gulf, 1964; Bush, R. A., and Folger, J. P. *The Promise of Mediation: Responding to Conflict Through Empowerment and Recognition.* San Francisco: Jossey-Bass, 1994; Gelfand, M. J., and Realo, A. Individualism–collectivism and accountability in intergroup negotiations. *Journal of Applied Psychology*, 1999, 84, 721–736.
47. Adapted from Baskerville, D. M. How do you manage conflict? *Black Enterprise*, May 1993, 63–66; Thomas, K. W., and Kilmann, R. H. *The Thomas–Kilmann Conflict Mode Instrument.* Tuxedo, N.Y.: Xicom, 1974; Rahim, M.A. A measure of styles of handling interpersonal conflict. *Academy of Management Journal*, 1983, 26, 368–376.
48. Adapted from Elangovan, A. R. Deciding how to intervene in employee disputes. In R. J. Lewicki, D. M. Saunders, and J. W. Minton (eds.), *Negotiation*, 3rd ed. Boston: Irwin/McGraw-Hill, 1999, 458–469.

CHAPTER

11 Leadership: Foundations

LEARNING OBJECTIVES

When you have finished studying this chapter, you should be able to:

1. Outline the essentials of leadership.
2. Explain two basic models of leadership—traits and behavioral.
3. Describe Fiedler's contingency model of leadership.
4. Explain Hersey and Blanchard's situational model of leadership.
5. Discuss the Vroom–Jago time-driven leadership model.
6. State the differences in the three contingency models of leadership.

Preview Case: *Carly Fiorina Leads HP*

ESSENTIALS OF LEADERSHIP

Leadership and Management

Power and Follower Behavior

Competency: Managing Self—*Lloyd Ward Leads Maytag*

BASIC LEADERSHIP MODELS

Traits Model of Leadership

Behavioral Model of Leadership

Contrasts with Contingency Models

Competency: Managing Communication—*Douglas McKenna on Leadership*

FIEDLER'S CONTINGENCY MODEL

Group Atmosphere

Task Structure

Position Power

Leadership Style

Implications and Limitations

Competency: Managing Ethics—*Stephen Hardis's Leadership in Ethics*

HERSEY AND BLANCHARD'S SITUATIONAL MODEL

Leadership Styles and Followers

Implications and Limitations

VROOM–JAGO LEADERSHIP MODEL

Leadership Styles

Competency: Managing Across Cultures—*Ferdinand Piëch's Leadership of VW*

Situational Variables

Main Features of the Model

Competency: Managing Change—*Brooke McCurdy's Leadership*

Implications and Limitations

DIFFERENCES IN THE THREE CONTINGENCY MODELS

Leader Behaviors

Contingency Variables

Leadership Effectiveness

CHAPTER SUMMARY

Key Terms and Concepts

Discussion Questions

DEVELOPING COMPETENCIES

Competency: Managing Self—*What's Your Leadership Style?*

Competency: Managing Communication—*Richard Branson's Leadership*

PREVIEW CASE

CARLY FIORINA LEADS HP

Carla (Carly) S. Fiorina, at age 44, became the first woman to lead a top 20 U.S. industrial corporation when she was appointed CEO of Hewlett-Packard (HP) in 1999. Fiorina was the first person from outside the company chosen to lead HP.

Before joining HP, Fiorina was a star executive at Lucent Technologies. She played a key role in the successful spin-off of Lucent from AT&T in 1996. She helped transform Lucent from a maker of phone equipment to a provider of the equipment needed by any company using the Internet. The HP search committee members contend that Fiorina is an ideal match for the top leadership needed. They came by their decision after each one detailed 20 competencies they would like to see in the new CEO. Then they reduced the list to four essential competencies, which played to Fiorina's strengths: (1) the ability to conceptualize and communicate sweeping strategies, (2) the operations ability to deliver on quarterly financial goals, (3) the power to bring urgency to an organization, and (4) the management competencies to foster an Internet vision throughout the company. The committee had looked at 300 potential candidates before selecting Fiorina.

Upon her appointment, Fiorina announced a set of priorities. The first priority was to craft a vision of HP as an Internet company that can weave together a vast range of products—from $25 inkjet cartridges to $1 million supercomputers—for any customer that has to compete both online and offline. She stated, "Customers need a sense of how HP's broad product portfolio translates into real advantages for them. We haven't given them that yet." The second priority was to increase HP's rate of innovation. "It's not rocket science that we need to be innovating at a rapid rate," Fiorina says. The third priority was to adapt HP's consensus-style culture to deal with the challenges of *blur* (see Chapter 1). Fiorina believes that "disposing of the bad habits while retaining the good shouldn't be a problem. Our people are very proud and smart. So, first, you reinforce the things that work and then appeal to their brains to address what doesn't."

As a leader, Fiorina has a personal touch that inspires loyalty. She's known for giving balloons and flowers to employees who land big contracts. When Lucent was spun off from AT&T in early 1996, Fiorina stayed up all night with Comptroller Jim Lusk and other employees to ensure that the prospectus for the stock offering was perfect. And it's not just business: When the wife of a senior Lucent executive fell ill, Fiorina helped make sure that she got medical advice, treatment, and emotional support. "I think the world of Carly. She's a great leader," says Nina Aversano, North American president of Lucent's global service-provider business.

For more information on Hewlett-Packard, visit this company's home page at www.hp.com.

Fiorina brought leadership and outstanding marketing abilities to HP. Her service commitment to customers at Lucent is legendary. For example, Bell Atlantic Corporation wanted to cut down the amount of time it took to order telephone equipment. The process used to take 9 months, but Fiorina motivated her staff and reduced the time for critical orders to 3 months. "She stepped in and made sure it got done," says Paul A. Lacouture, group president for network services at Bell Atlantic.[1]

Carly Fiorina has established a pattern of outstanding leadership in a remarkable career that has brought her positions of increasing responsibility and authority. With her appointment as CEO of HP, she has embarked on a new set of leadership challenges. We explore various aspects of Fiorina's leadership in this chapter.

As you will see in this chapter and Chapter 12, the topic of leadership is like that of a prism—something new and different appears each time you look at it from a new angle. Our purpose is to identify and describe for you the diverse issues, ideas, and approaches to leadership. In doing so we present various leadership perspectives and models and suggest some of their strengths, limitations, and applications. These chapters also are intended to facilitate personal insights into your own leadership competencies and the need for their further development. Our assumption is simple: Leadership can be learned, but not taught. Learning leadership means that an individual is actively seeking to make the personal changes required to become a leader.

Learning Objective:

1. Outline the essentials of leadership.

ESSENTIALS OF LEADERSHIP

Leadership will always be important to organizations. The need for effective leadership and the difficulty of providing it have increased rapidly because of the accelerating complexity and change experienced by organizations such as HP.

LEADERSHIP AND MANAGEMENT

Effective leadership and management encompasses the seven foundation competencies developed throughout this book: *managing self*, *managing communication*, *managing diversity*, *managing ethics*, *managing across cultures*, *managing teams*, and *managing change*. Although leadership embraces these important foundation competencies, it also goes beyond them.

Leadership is the process of developing ideas and a vision, living by values that support those ideas and vision, influencing others to embrace them in their own behaviors, and making hard decisions about people and other resources.[2] Noel Tichy, who has studied many outstanding business leaders, describes leadership in these words:

> Leadership is accomplishing something through other people that wouldn't have happened if you weren't there. And in today's world, that's less and less through command and control, and more and more through changing people's mindsets and hence altering the way they behave. Today, leadership is being able to mobilize ideas and values that energize other people.[3]

A **leader** is the person who reflects the key attributes of leadership—ideas, vision, values, influencing others, and making tough decisions. In contrast, a **manager** directs the work of others and is responsible for results. Effective managers bring a degree of order and consistency to the work setting for their employees.

As noted in the Preview Case, Carly Fiorina at HP has a long history of being a leader. She had the idea and vision of transforming Lucent Technologies when it broke off from AT&T from serving as a provider of phone equipment to a provider for Internet users. One of her first priorities upon becoming the CEO at HP was to craft a vision of HP as an Internet company that can create a seamless array of products and services for customers. Her ability to influence others is demonstrated by the intense loyalty she inspires. Fiorina's rapid rise is due in part to her ability to make hard decisions such as those needed to reduce the time required to fill telephone equipment orders at Lucent Technologies. Her sense of people, their value, and their desire to contribute is reflected in her respect for HP's culture while honestly communicating the need for adapting it to the rapidly changing environment in which HP competes.

Table 11.1 provides an overview of the contrasts between the essentials of management and leadership in terms of five major categories: primary thinking process, typical pattern of direction setting, approach to employee relations, orientation to mode of operation, and relative emphasis placed on methods and tools used to meet responsibilities. The pairs of attributes within each category are presented as the far ends of a continuum. We recognize that most leaders and managers don't function at the extremes. However, patterns that tend toward leadership or management are likely to emerge as leaders and managers develop and utilize their competencies. As you review Table 11.1, mark the point on each continuum that reflects the relative emphasis on leadership or management by a person that you have worked for to help you define your own personal leadership traits. Individuals may lean more heavily toward either the leadership or the management profile at various times as they confront different types of issues and problems. However, most tend to operate primarily in terms of either the leadership or the management profile.[4] Carly Fiorina clearly fits the leadership profile.

Table 11.1 Comparisons between Management and Leadership

CATEGORY	MANAGEMENT		LEADERSHIP
Thinking Process	• Initiates	└┴┴┴┴┴┘	Originates
	• Focuses on things	└┴┴┴┴┴┘	Focuses on people
	• Looks inward	└┴┴┴┴┴┘	Looks outward
	• Accepts reality	└┴┴┴┴┴┘	Investigates reality
Direction Setting	• Operational plans	└┴┴┴┴┴┘	Vision
	• Improve the present	└┴┴┴┴┴┘	Create the future
	• Immediate financials	└┴┴┴┴┴┘	New markets
	• Sees trees	└┴┴┴┴┴┘	Sees forest
Employee Relations	• Tight control	└┴┴┴┴┴┘	Empower
	• Subordinates	└┴┴┴┴┴┘	Associates
	• Instructs	└┴┴┴┴┴┘	Learns
	• Directs and coordinates	└┴┴┴┴┴┘	Trusts and develops
Mode of Operating	• Efficiency (do things right)	└┴┴┴┴┴┘	Effectiveness (do the right things)
	• Asks "how" and "when"	└┴┴┴┴┴┘	Asks "what" and "why"
	• Deals with complexity	└┴┴┴┴┴┘	Embraces complexity
	• Manages change	└┴┴┴┴┴┘	Creates change
Decision Methods	• Policies, rules, and procedures	└┴┴┴┴┴┘	Values and principles
	• Relies on process and system	└┴┴┴┴┴┘	Relies on ideas and people
	• Achieves what's expected	└┴┴┴┴┴┘	Strives to excel
	• Serves top managers	└┴┴┴┴┴┘	Serves clients and customers

Adapted from Bolton, B. More than ever, IS needs leaders. *Computerworld: Leadership Series,* May 19, 1997, 1–11; Robinson, G. Leadership versus management. *British Journal of Administrative Management,* January/February 1999, 20–21; Parachin, V. M. Ten essential leadership skills. *Supervision,* February 1999, 13–15; Bennis, W., and Goldsmith, J. *Learning to Lead: A Workbook on Becoming a Leader.* Reading, Mass.: Perseus, 1997.

The essentials of leadership are captured in the following quotes of two leaders:[5]

> No leader can possibly have all the answers. . . . The actual solutions about how best to meet the challenges of the moment have to be made by the people closest to the action. . . . The leader has to find the way to empower these frontline people, to challenge them, to provide them with the resources they need, and then to hold them accountable. As they struggle with . . . this challenge, the leader becomes their coach, teacher, and facilitator. Change how you define leadership, and you change how you run a company.
>
> Steve Miller
> Group Managing Director
> Royal Dutch/Shell

> The first responsibility of a leader is to define reality. The last is to say thank you. In between, the leader is a servant.
>
> Max De Pree
> CEO, Herman Miller

Power and Follower Behavior

Leaders and managers use many sources of power to influence followers by appealing to one or more of their needs. Effective leadership depends as much on the acceptance of influence by the follower as on the leader's providing it. Power and influence are central to a leader's or manager's role. In Chapter 9, we described the sources of a manager's power as legitimate, reward, coercive, referent, and expert. It's useful to think of a leader's power in the same way. Let's review those sources of power in relation to the leader and follower roles.

Legitimate Power. Followers may do something because the leader has the right to request them to do it and they have an obligation to comply. This legitimate power comes from the leader's position in the organization. Consider these examples of the exercise of legitimate power.

- Mike Ferrette at IBM trusted us to do our jobs and held us accountable for the aggressive deliverable dates we set for ourselves. He was rewarded with a production level from his development staff that I have yet to see anywhere else.
- My boss is Piero Di Matteo at Los Angeles Air Force Base. He believes that if you carry out your assignments on time, there will be no problems. If you get stuck, he's there to guide you.[6]

Reward Power. Followers may do something to get rewards that the leader influences (e.g., promotions, pay raises, bonuses, developmental opportunities, and the like). Thus reward power comes from the leader's ability to provide something positively desired by followers in return for their behaviors that the leader expected and wanted. Consider these examples of the exercise of reward power.

- Bill Weingart at First Data Merchant Services Corporation in Hagerstown, Maryland, realizes the importance of recognizing and rewarding employees and encourages education and self-improvement. He is a mentor to all who have the opportunity to work with or for him. I expect never to encounter anyone like him again in my entire working career.
- Soon after coming to work for Miley Ainsworth, a staff director at FDX Corporation (FedEx's parent company in Memphis, Tennessee), my mother went into intensive care. Miley let me work odd hours and come and go often to fit the short visiting time periods at the intensive care unit. That was almost 10 years ago, and I am still with him.[7]

Coercive Power. Followers may behave in ways to avoid punishments that the leader controls (e.g., demotions, reprimands, no pay raises, and termination). Coercive power is the potential to influence others through the use of sanctions or punishment. Unfortunately, coercive power doesn't necessarily encourage desired behavior, but it may stop or reduce undesirable behaviors. Consider these examples of the application of coercive power:

- The boss looked at me and shouted, "I don't care what your [expletive] job title is or what they [expletive] told you when you were hired. You'll do what I [expletive] tell you to do, the [expletive] way I tell you to do it, and if you don't like it, there's the [expletive] door." I had my résumé out the very next day.
- The project manager began a meeting on an important project by saying, "There are going to be some dead bodies before this is over."[8]

At times, leaders do need to exercise coercive power, which comes from their legitimate power, by demoting or dismissing followers for poor performance, unacceptable behavior (e.g., sexual harassment), and lack of integrity—lying, deceitful conduct, and the like.

Referent Power. Followers may engage in behaviors because they admire the leader, want to be like the leader, and want to receive the leader's approval. Referent power usually is associated with individuals who possess admired personal characteristics, such as humility, integrity, and courage. Consider these two examples of the use of referent power.

- Rudy Gragnani, a manager of the Coca-Cola Company bottler in Richmond, Virginia, displayed true leadership for me. A customer, an expressive New Yorker, and I were loudly discussing a problem when Rudy walked by. Later, he chewed me out for yelling at my customer. But at the next management meeting, the New Yorker expressed his thanks to me. Rudy understood that what he saw as an argument was just New York style. He apologized to me for misreading the situation and forwarded the thanks from the accounting area for my efforts.
- Tim Jensen at Syntel, Inc., USA, in New Castle, Delaware, believes that employees should be given choices and freedom to grow into the roles they love. He is one in a million.[9]

Expert Power. Followers may engage in behaviors because they believe that the leader has special knowledge and knows what is needed to accomplish a goal or solve a problem. Expert power has a narrow scope: Followers are influenced by a leader only within that leader's area of expertise. Consider this example of the exercise of expert power.

- I went to work for a manager who was one of the sharpest people I had ever worked for. And the applications we worked on were some of the most intelligently constructed, flexible, reusable, modular applications I had ever seen. And it was a fantastic environment for me to learn in.[10]

An effective organizational leader—whether a first-line manager or top-level executive like Carly Fiorina—uses all these sources of power.[11] For successful organizations, the pattern in the use of the sources of power is shifting toward greater reliance on reward, referent, and expert power, with less reliance on coercive and legitimate power. This new pattern is influenced by changing technologies, increasing abilities of employees and teams to make decisions, flattening of organizational hierarchies, and changing work and personal life expectations of employees.

The following Managing Self Competency feature illustrates the interplay of various sources of power used by Lloyd Ward during his career until his recent appointment as CEO of Maytag. Ward, an African American, has made a remarkable journey from the depths of poverty to the key leadership role of a major corporation.

COMPETENCY: MANAGING SELF

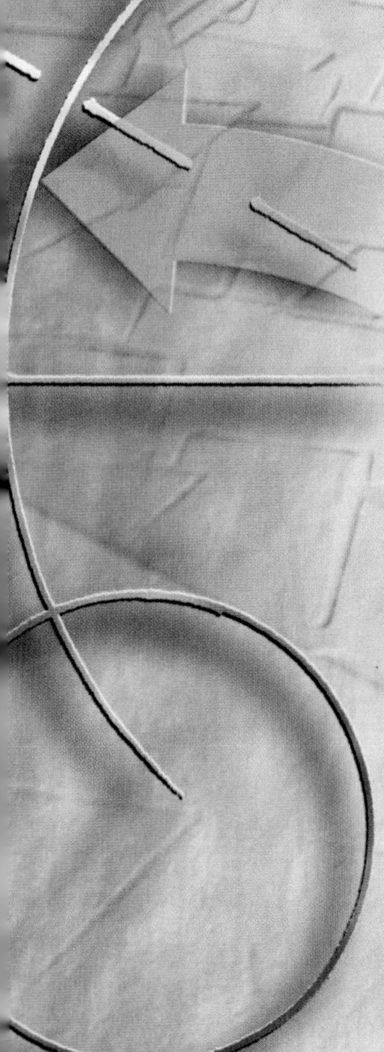

LLOYD WARD LEADS MAYTAG

Lloyd David Ward is a study in ambition, intelligence, and resilience. When he assumed the top job at Maytag Corporation in 1999, Ward, 50, had made a longer journey than any other executive in corporate America. He defeated the combination of poverty and prejudice and did so at some of the world's best-known companies, from Procter & Gamble to Ford to PepsiCo. Working with former Maytag CEO Leonard A. Hadley, Ward played a key role in reinventing the appliance company during the period 1996–1999.

A master motivator who listens as well as he speaks, Ward convinced Maytag veterans that change was both necessary and possible. Colleagues laud his ability to challenge people's beliefs without criticizing them personally, to seize issues that give people a common ground, and then to exploit positively their newfound understanding (referent power). "He is a good thinker," says PepsiCo, Inc., CEO Roger A. Enrico, "but he is an exceptional leader."

Ward's engaging ways seem always on display. He greets people with a firm handshake, pulling himself closer to them, putting a palm on the back of an elbow, and quickly asking questions about their own lives, even when he has never before met them. "Were you born here?" "What's your husband's name?" "How long have you worked here?"

During a tour of a Sears, Roebuck & Company store in Des Moines, Iowa, for example, Ward met a longtime salesman who had persuaded a woman to buy Maytag's top-of-the-line Neptune washer sight unseen over the phone. Ward went up to him with a grin: "I'm Lloyd Ward with Maytag." "I know who you are," the salesman said. "I read about you in the newspaper." Ward's attention-deflecting response was quick: "You're the one whose picture should be in the paper if you sold a Neptune over the phone!" (reward power).

In 1987, Ward left Procter & Gamble and joined Frito-Lay, a division of PepsiCo. He was constantly in the field trying to motivate people, even showing up at the loading docks to give an informal pep talk to workers there (referent and reward power). Through it all, Ward's competitiveness and motivational tactics helped increase his division's overall market share in the region from 50 percent to 56 percent. People in that division had decided that you couldn't grow market share because it was already so high," says Steven S. Reinemund, chairman of Frito-Lay. "Lloyd didn't accept that. He went on a personal crusade" (legitimate power).

Ward left a promising career at PepsiCo and joined Maytag, headquartered in Newton, Iowa, to head the firm's Appliance Division because of the opportunity it provided to become CEO later. It was a big risk for him. It was also a big risk for Maytag leaders, who typically promoted carefully groomed insiders. Hadley, for example, had been at the company for 40 years. This time, however, he instructed the board that his successor should be an outsider. The company needed "an extroverted marketing man," he says. "Brand management is very delicate. It's one of the things I drooled over when I had only seen [Ward's] résumé" (expert power).

Ward set about reinvigorating the company's unsophisticated marketing culture. He sped up the pace of product introductions: Maytag launched 20 new products in 1999, up from only a few in the mid 1990s. He attracted more than a dozen executives, mostly from PepsiCo and P&G to join him at Maytag (legitimate power). He developed new consumer-research methods by sending Maytag employees into people's homes to watch them cook and clean, rather than simply asking them to fill out surveys. One result was a new $400 washer to help Maytag compete for the lower end of the business it had long shunned. "Ward has been able to almost reinvent Maytag," says Mike London, a senior vice president at Best Buy Company, a major client (legitimate and referent power).[12]

For more information on Maytag, visit this company's home page at www.maytag.com.

Learning Objective:

2. Explain two basic models of leadership—traits and behavioral.

BASIC LEADERSHIP MODELS

The traits and behavioral models are probably the most basic, popular, and oldest of the leadership models. The more recent, more complex leadership models often draw on elements of these two models.

TRAITS MODEL OF LEADERSHIP

The **traits model of leadership** is based on observed characteristics of many leaders—both successful and unsuccessful—to predict leadership effectiveness. The resulting lists of traits are then compared to those of potential leaders to assess their likelihood of success or failure. There is support for the notion that successful leaders have interests and abilities and, perhaps, even personality traits that are different from those of less effective leaders.

Key Traits. Some evidence suggests that four traits are shared by most (but not all) successful leaders.

- *Intelligence.* Successful leaders tend to have somewhat higher intelligence than their subordinates.
- *Maturity and breadth.* Successful leaders tend to be emotionally mature and have a broad range of interests.
- *Inner motivation and achievement drive.* Successful leaders are results oriented; when they achieve one goal, they seek another. They do not depend primarily on employees for their motivation to achieve goals.
- *Honesty.* Successful leaders have integrity. When individuals in leadership positions state one set of values but practice another set, followers quickly see them as untrustworthy. Many surveys show that honesty is the most important characteristic when employees are asked to rank and comment on various traits of successful and unsuccessful leaders. The critical characteristic of trust translates into the degree of willingness by employees to follow leaders. Confusion over the leader's thinking and values creates negative stress, indecision, and personal politics.[13]

Limitations. The traits model of leadership is inadequate for successfully predicting actual leadership effectiveness for at least three reasons.[14] First, in terms of personality traits, there are no consistent patterns between specific traits or sets of traits and leadership effectiveness. More than 100 different personality traits of successful leaders in various leadership positions have been identified. For example, the traits pattern of successful leaders of salespeople includes optimism, enthusiasm, and dominance. The traits pattern of successful production leaders usually includes being progressive, introverted, and cooperative. These descriptions are simply generalities. Many successful leaders of salespeople and production employees do not have all, or even some, of these characteristics. There also is often disagreement over which traits are the most important for an effective leader.

The second limitation of the traits model is that it often attempts to relate physical characteristics—such as height, weight, appearance, physique, energy, and health—to effective leadership. Most of these factors are related to situational factors that can have a significant impact on a leader's effectiveness. For example, people in the military or law enforcement must be a particular minimum height and weight in order to perform certain tasks well. Although these characteristics may help an individual rise to a leadership position in such organizations, neither height nor weight correlates highly with effective leadership. In business and other organizations, height and weight generally play no role in performance and thus are not requirements for a leadership position.

The third limitation of the traits model is that leadership itself is complex. A relationship between personality and a person's interest in particular types of jobs could well exist, which a study relating personality and effectiveness might not identify. For example, one study found that high earners (a measure of success) in small firms were more ambitious, were more open-minded, and described themselves as more considerate than low earners.

Behavioral Model of Leadership

To predict effectiveness the **behavioral model of leadership** focuses on what leaders actually *do* and *how* they do it. There are several versions of this model, but the one presented here suggests that effective leaders help individuals and teams achieve their goals in two ways. First, they build task-centered relations with employees that focus on the quality and quantity of work accomplished. Second, they are considerate and supportive of employees' attempts to achieve personal goals (e.g., work satisfaction, promotions, and recognition) and work hard at settling disputes, keeping people happy, providing encouragement, and giving positive reinforcement.

The greatest number of studies of leader behavior have come from the Ohio State University leadership studies program, which began in the late 1940s under the direction of Ralph Stogdill. This research was aimed at identifying leader behaviors that are important for attaining team and organizational goals. These efforts resulted in the identification of two main dimensions of leader behavior: consideration and initiating structure.[15] Our review of the behavioral model is based on that leadership studies program.

Consideration. **Consideration** is the extent to which leaders have job relationships characterized by mutual trust, two-way communication, respect for employees' ideas, and empathy for their feelings. Leaders with this style emphasize the satisfaction of employee needs. They typically find time to listen, are willing to make changes, look out for the personal welfare of employees, and are friendly and approachable. A high degree of consideration indicates psychological closeness between leader and subordinates; a low degree shows greater psychological distance and a more impersonal leader.

When is consideration effective? The most positive effects of leader consideration on productivity and job satisfaction occur when (1) the task is routine and denies employees little, if any, job satisfaction; (2) followers are predisposed toward participative leadership; (3) team members must learn something new; (4) employees feel that their involvement in the decision-making process is legitimate and affects their job performance; and (5) employees feel that strong status differences should not exist between them and their leader. Carly Fiorina and Lloyd Ward clearly demonstrate consideration in their leadership roles.

Initiating Structure. **Initiating structure** is the extent to which leaders define and prescribe their roles and those of employees in order to set and accomplish the goals in their areas of responsibility. Leaders with this style emphasize the direction of team or individual employee activities through planning, communicating, scheduling, assigning tasks, emphasizing deadlines, and giving orders. They maintain definite standards of performance and expect subordinates to achieve them. In short, leaders with a high degree of initiating structure concern themselves with accomplishing tasks by setting performance goals, giving directions, and expecting them to be followed.

When is initiating structure effective? The most positive effects of leader initiating structure on productivity and job satisfaction occur when (1) a high degree of pressure for output is imposed by someone other than the leader; (2) the task satisfies employees; (3) employees depend on the leader for information and direction on how to complete the task; (4) employees are psychologically predisposed toward being instructed in what to do and how to do it; and (5) more than 12 employees report to the leader.

Limitations. Some studies suggest that a leader who emphasizes initiating structure generally improves productivity, at least in the short run. However, leaders who rank high on initiating structure and low on consideration generally have large numbers of grievances, absenteeism, and high turnover rates among employees. The view now widely accepted is that effective leaders, such as Carly Fiorina and Lloyd Ward, can have high consideration and initiating structure at the same time.

Researchers initially assumed that leader behavior was related to indirect measures of performance—such as absenteeism, grievances, and turnover—as well as direct measures of performance—such as the number of units produced, defects in quality, and cost per unit. Later studies by others have failed to show a significant relationship between leadership behaviors and group performance. This failure indicates that individual and team productivity is largely influenced by other factors, including (1) the employee's social status within the group; (2) the technology used; (3) employee expectations of a certain style of leadership; and (4) employee views of the leader's referent, reward, and legitimate power.

Perhaps the main limitation of the behavioral model was the lack of attention it gave to the effects of the situation on effective leadership style. It focused on relationships between leaders and employees but gave little consideration to the situation in which the relationships occurred. As you know from our discussion of the *interactionist perspective* in Chapter 2, a better understanding of behavior usually results when both the person and the situation are examined.

Interpersonal communication is the vehicle used by leaders to implement consideration and initiating structure. The Managing Communication Competency feature on page 332 conveys how a pattern of high consideration and high initiating structure may be communicated by a leader. This feature is based on an interview of Douglas McKenna, the general manager of leadership development for Microsoft Corporation. In this interview, McKenna revealed how he communicates—through information, ideas, emotions, active listening, and oral communication—his leadership style. McKenna's remarks focused on his role as a human resources leader.

Contrasts with Contingency Models

The traits and behavioral models sought to find characteristics that apply in most leadership situations. In contrast, contingency leadership models identify variables that permit certain leadership characteristics and behaviors to be effective in given situations.

Four variables frequently cited as having an influence on a leader's behavior are (1) a leader's personal characteristics; (2) the employees' personal characteristics; (3) the team's characteristics; and (4) the structure and tasks of the team, department, or organization. These contingency variables, shown in Figure 11.1, don't act independently but interact to influence the effectiveness of a leader's style of behavior. Thus

Figure 11.1 **Contingency Variables That Affect Leader Behavior**

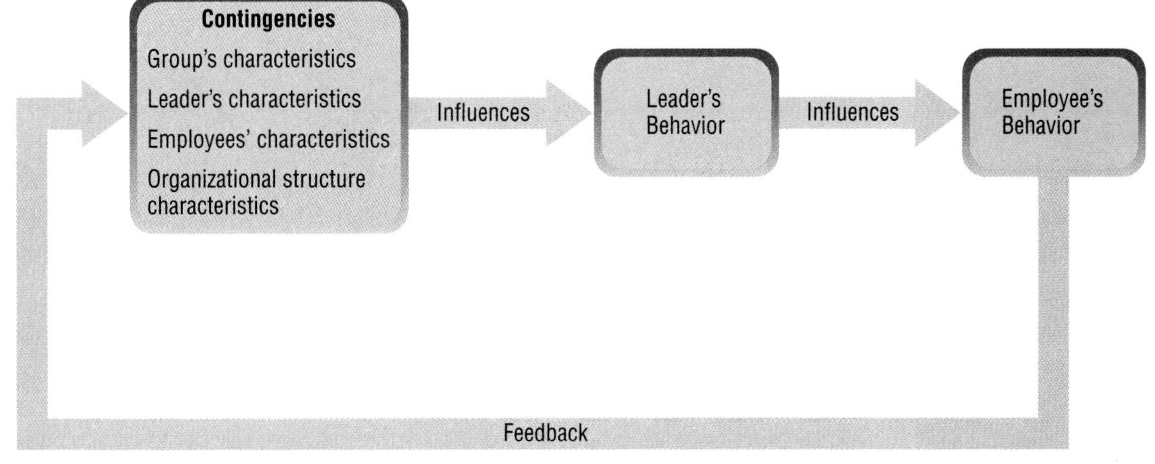

COMPETENCY: MANAGING COMMUNICATION

DOUGLAS MCKENNA ON LEADERSHIP

A great human resources leader brings an independent, courageous, intellectually honest perspective to an organization's leadership group. A great human resources leader is constantly putting information in front of executives that mirrors the state of the organization's people. A great human resources leader takes tough stands, makes hard decisions, and is willing to be unpopular on behalf of the company's people assets. A great human resources leader is a credible, connected partner with key business and technical leaders throughout the organization. The problem is that most human resources "leaders" get caught up in trying to make sure they're valued by line executives. So rather than taking stands for themselves, they're constantly trying to do what everyone else wants them to do. Unfortunately, this is a sure path to being undervalued and underutilized [reflects both high consideration and initiating structure].

I focus on making sure I have clear convictions and strong connections. Clear convictions means that people in my organization know what I care about, what principles and values are nonnegotiable to me and what results we must contribute to justify our place in the business. Strong connections means making sure that everyone in the organization knows our direction, goals and strategy. It also means we have relationships that can withstand strong, heated disagreement and continue to work constructively together [reflects both high consideration and initiating structure].

Looking back on the past six years, I think I've been least successful when I got caught up in worrying about the reactions of others to things that I thought needed to be done for the good of the company. This overreactiveness to others led me astray in two different ways. One way was to anticipate that I would have to fight or sell hard to get the "right" thing done. Another way was to try to polish off all the rough edges in my ideas or plans so that no one would disagree so vigorously that things wouldn't progress. More and more, I find that I'm successful when I simply listen hard to others, think through to my own convictions, and then take a stand. I try to worry less about how others will react and worry more about really determining what I believe. It's not a matter of fighting, selling, or polishing. It's a matter of letting others know what you think and believe and inviting them to do the same for themselves [reflects high consideration and initiating structure].

At the end of a particularly rough day, I really believe that who you are as a leader is more important than what you do. Character and maturity are more fundamental to a leader's effectiveness than technique. There are thousands of management books that will teach you good techniques. But good technique and step-by-step approaches break down quickly under real-time pressure from customers, bosses, employees, peers, and even family members. To be a great leader in tough times, you have to pay the painful personal price it takes to grow up as a person—to set your own course, respect the courses of others, and form adult partnerships with others to pursue a vision. Books and mentors can help, but insight has to be put into action to produce growth[16] [reflects importance of the managing self competency].

For more information on the Microsoft Corporation, visit the company's home page at www.microsoft.com.

the leadership process is complex, and simple prescriptions (e.g., democratic leaders always have more satisfied employees than autocratic leaders) just aren't valid.

In the next three sections, we present three specific contingency models of leadership: Fiedler's contingency model, Hersey and Blanchard's situational leadership model, and the Vroom–Jago model. Each model focuses primarily on one of the four contingency variables.

Learning Objective:

3. Describe Fiedler's contingency model of leadership.

FIEDLER'S CONTINGENCY MODEL

Fred Fiedler and his associates developed the first contingency model of the leadership process.[17] **Fiedler's contingency model** specifies that performance is contingent upon both the leader's motivational system and the degree to which the leader controls and influences the situation. The model's three contingency variables—group atmosphere, task structure, and the leader's position power—are shown in Figure 11.2. In combination, the three contingency variables create eight situations, as shown in Figure 11.3, which comprise Fiedler's basic contingency model.

GROUP ATMOSPHERE

A leader's degree of acceptance by the team is called **group atmosphere.** A leader who is accepted by and inspires loyalty in employees needs few signs of rank to get them to commit themselves to a task. When leader and employees get along well together, there is little friction. In groups that reject the leader, the leader's basic problem is to keep from having employees bypass the leader or sabotage the task.

TASK STRUCTURE

Task structure is the extent to which a task performed by employees is routine or nonroutine. A routine task is likely to have clearly defined goals, to consist of only a few steps or procedures, to be verifiable, and to have a correct solution. At the other extreme is the task that is completely nonroutine. In this situation, the leader may no more know how to perform the task than the employees do. Such a task is likely to have unclear or changing goals and multiple paths to accomplishment; the task cannot be done "by the numbers."

For the most part, the managers and other professionals who work directly with leaders such as Carly Fiorina, Lloyd Ward, and Douglas McKenna probably have unstructured tasks. However, many employees in those same organizations—technicians, assembly workers, custodial employees, clerical staff, and others—probably have relatively structured tasks to perform on a daily basis.

POSITION POWER

The extent to which a leader has reward, coercive, and legitimate power is known as **position power.** In most businesses, leaders such as Carly Fiorina, Lloyd Ward, and

Figure 11.2 **Variables in Fiedler's Contingency Model**

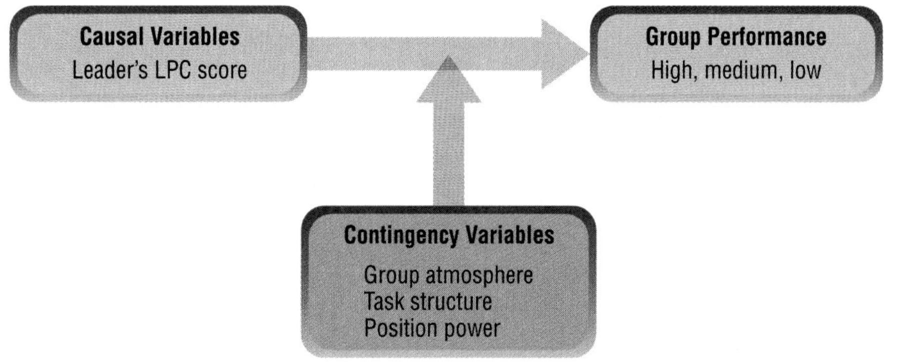

Source: Adapted from Yukl, G. A. *Leadership in Organizations.* Englewood Cliffs, N.J.: Prentice-Hall, 1989, 196.

Figure 11.3 **Fiedler's Basic Contingency Model**

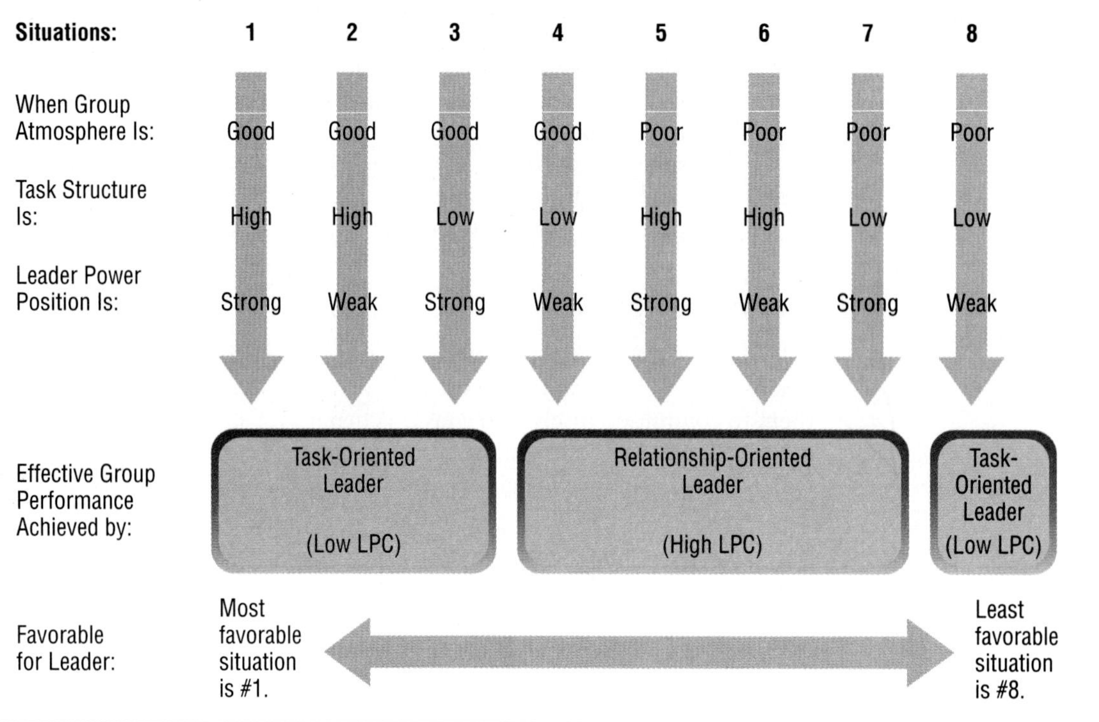

Source: Adapted from Fiedler, F. E. *Leadership Experience and Leadership Performance.* Alexandria, Va.: U.S. Army Research Institute, 1994.

Douglas McKenna have high position power. They have the authority to hire, reward, discipline, and fire employees. In most nonprofit, social, and voluntary organizations, boards, and committees, leaders tend to have low position power.

Leadership Style

The **least preferred coworker (LPC)** scale is used to measure a person's leadership style. Scores are obtained by asking employees first to think about all the people with whom they have worked and then to identify the individual with whom they have worked least well. The person then rates this least preferred coworker on a set of 18 scales, 5 of which are as follows.

Pleasant	8	7	6	5	4	3	2	1	Unpleasant
Friendly	8	7	6	5	4	3	2	1	Unfriendly
Accepting	8	7	6	5	4	3	2	1	Rejecting
Relaxed	8	7	6	5	4	3	2	1	Tense
Close	8	7	6	5	4	3	2	1	Distant

Low-LPC leaders describe their least preferred coworker in negative terms. Low-LPC leaders are primarily motivated by the task and gain satisfaction from accomplishing it. If assigned tasks are being accomplished satisfactorily by their subordinates, low-LPC leaders will try to form and maintain relationships with their subordinates. Thus low-LPC leaders focus on improving relationships with their subordinates *after* they have been assured that the assigned tasks are being completed. *High-LPC* leaders give a more positive description of their least preferred coworker and are sensitive to others. They are primarily motivated by establishing and maintaining close interpersonal relationships. If high-LPC leaders have established good relationships with their subordinates, *then* they will focus on task accomplishment.

IMPLICATIONS AND LIMITATIONS

Let's return to Figure 11.3, which is based on the average results of the studies conducted by Fiedler and his associates. Task-oriented (low-LPC) leaders performed more effectively than high-LPC leaders in the most favorable situations (1, 2, and 3) and in the least favorable situation (8). In the most favorable situations—when the team supports the leader, the leader's power position is high, and the task is structured (situation 1)—an effective leader will strive to develop pleasant work relations in directing team members. Such leaders realize that conditions are very good and that successful task performance is likely. As a result, they can turn their attention to improving their relations with team members and often adopt a "hands-off" style. Employees value such treatment, and satisfaction and performance remain high.

Figure 11.3 also shows situations in which relationship-oriented (high-LPC) leaders will probably perform more effectively than low-LPC leaders. Relationship-oriented leaders get the best performance under conditions that are moderately favorable (situations 4 through 7). Situations 4 and 5 describe cases in which (1) the group has a structured task but dislikes the leader, who must demonstrate concern for employee feelings and emotions; or (2) the team likes the leader but has an unstructured task, and the leader must depend on the willingness and creativity of its members to accomplish the goals that have been set. As a result, high-LPC leaders may shift their attention to task performance. Recall Piero Di Matteo at the Los Angeles Air Force Base. Based on his subordinate's remarks, Di Matteo appears to be a high-LPC leader who delegates decision-making authority and supports subordinates in carrying out their assignments. He also gives them guidance when they get stuck on a problem.

Fiedler's contingency model has three other important implications for leaders. First, both relationship-motivated and task-motivated leaders perform well in certain situations but not in others. Outstanding people at one level who are promoted may fail at the higher level because their leadership style doesn't match the demands of the situation.[18] Second, leaders' effectiveness depends on the situation. Therefore an organization can affect a leader's effectiveness by changing the reward system or by modifying the situation itself. Third, leaders themselves can do something about their situations. Table 11.2 on page 337 presents some suggestions for modifying particular contingency variables, which fall into three main categories: group atmosphere, task structure, and position (legitimate and reward) power.

Fiedler's contingency model has several limitations.[19] Some have questioned the use of the least preferred coworker, suggesting that better measures of leader behaviors are needed. The LPC has been called a one-dimensional concept. It implies that individuals who are highly motivated to accomplish tasks are unconcerned about their relations with employees and vice versa. Three core assumptions in this model have been questioned: (1) a person's LPC score is constant over time, (2) the LPC score is not likely to change, and (3) the LPC score is a trait of a leader. Because a leader can change the task structure (as indicated in Table 11.2), it isn't a contingency variable in the model. However, the nature of a task can be influenced by the leader's style. For example, a leader can take a messy, ill-defined problem and structure it before presenting it to the team.

The following Managing Ethics Competency feature indicates another limitation of Fiedler's contingency model when the many facets of a leader's role are being considered. Stephen Hardis, chairman and CEO of Eaton Corporation, presents his perspectives on the fundamentals of business ethics expected and required throughout the company. It is a global manufacturer of highly engineered products, including hydraulic products and fluid connectors, electrical power distribution and control equipment, and truck drivetrain systems, among other products. Headquartered in Cleveland, Ohio, the company has 65,000 employees and 215 manufacturing sites in 25 countries. His leadership on core ethics and values are not a function of LPC scores nor are they based on Fiedler's situational factors. However, as chairman and CEO, he would clearly be rated as "strong" on position power in Fiedler's model.

COMPETENCY: MANAGING ETHICS

STEPHEN HARDIS'S LEADERSHIP IN ETHICS

In most cases, ethical questions answer themselves when they're discussed aloud. For example, if I were asked if Eaton would facilitate an under-the-table payment in a Third World country, simply saying the question aloud provides the answer: Of course, we wouldn't. By asking ourselves if we would be willing to do something dishonest, inconsistent with the laws either of our country or the local country with which we do business, or inconsistent with the way we want to be perceived by our customers and competitors, the question goes away. When it comes to integrity, there are no shades of gray. You're either honest or you're not.

People don't stay with a company unless they can feel good about it. And one of the ways they can feel good is to know they work for an ethical institution. The kinds of people who stay with a firm out of loyalty apply different criteria to their lives. They're not people who think it's ethical to move because you get a good opportunity, but it's a different mindset if you believe the only question you ask yourself is, "Will I be able to make more money in the next job?" as opposed to, "To what extent do I have a responsibility to help this organization accomplish its goals? To what extent do I have a responsibility to take care of the people who are working for me and are counting on me to be there? To what extent do I have a responsibility to help this company maintain its standing and reputation?" There's a link between the concept of loyalty and ethical behavior. People who are loyal to a company and who know that the company doesn't practice trade espionage, for instance, would never take away secrets themselves. There's a difference in the attitude of ethical people who leave. Those who have felt loyalty leave with a sense of reluctance. One of their most important objectives is that people don't think badly of them when they leave.

And that applies to all levels. It would be a major mistake to think there's a different concept of integrity at different levels of business. There's more of a burden on the people on top because they're more visible, but ethics run throughout a good organization. If the top people don't constantly practice ethical behavior, they'll never get it from their employees.

Ethical values are universal. Eaton operates worldwide and we do understand that within the law, different cultures may have different practices. We call on our local managers to figure out how they can best abide by our ethical standards, which are worldwide, but how they can make them work best in each country. For instance, in some Middle Eastern countries, there's something the law calls a "facilitating payment," or a tip to someone at a dock to make sure your goods get through. That's not considered unethical in that culture, although it is in ours, so we give our local managers some leeway as long as they don't violate basic ethical standards. Having said that, you simply cannot have a form of corruption somewhere in your business. Sooner or later, it will affect your stability. It's sometimes hard, though, to convince people they should compete on the basis of product quality, value, delivery, and price.[20]

For more information on the Eaton Corporation, visit the company's home page at ***www.eaton.com.***

Learning Objective:

4. Explain Hersey and Blanchard's situational model of leadership.

HERSEY AND BLANCHARD'S SITUATIONAL MODEL

Hersey and Blanchard's situational model is based on the amount of relationship (supportive) and task (directive) behavior that a leader provides to subordinates in a situation. In turn, the amount of either relationship or task behavior is based on the readiness of the followers to perform needed tasks.[21]

Table 11.2 **Leadership Actions to Change Contingency Variables**

Change Team Atmosphere

If you want to improve a situation, you can

1. spend more—or less—informal time with your employees (lunch, leisure activities, etc.);
2. request particular people to work in your team;
3. volunteer to direct difficult or troublesome employees;
4. suggest or effect transfers of particular employees into or out of your department; and
5. raise morale by obtaining positive outcomes for team members (e.g., special bonuses, time off, attractive jobs).

Change Task Structure

If you want to work with less structured tasks, you can

1. ask your leader, whenever possible, to give you the new or unusual problems and let you figure out how to get them done; and
2. bring the problems and tasks to your team members and invite them to work with you on the planning and decision-making phases of the tasks.

If you want to work with more highly structured tasks, you can

1. ask your leader to give you, whenever possible, the tasks that are more structured or to give you more detailed instructions; and
2. break the job down into subtasks that can be more highly structured.

Change Position Power

To raise your position power, you can

1. show others "who's boss" by exercising fully the powers that the organization provides;
2. make sure that information to others gets channeled through you; and
3. provide new rewards for good performance.

To lower your position power, you can

1. call on team members to participate in planning and decision-making functions; and
2. delegate decision making to others.

Source: Developed from Fiedler, F. E., and Garcia, J. E. *New Approaches to Effective Leadership.* New York: John Wiley & Sons, 1987, 49–93.

Task behavior is the extent to which a leader spells out to subordinates what to do, where to do it, and how to do it. Leaders who use precise directions and tight controls are engaged in close supervision of their subordinates. **Relationship behavior** is the extent to which a leader listens, provides support and encouragement, and involves subordinates in the decision-making process. **Follower readiness** is the subordinates' ability and willingness to perform the prescribed tasks. Followers have various degrees of readiness, as shown in Figure 11.4. In R1, the followers are either unable or unwilling to perform the task, whereas in R4, they are able, willing, and confident that they can. In R2, followers are unable but are willing to perform a task and are confident that they can. In R3, followers are able to do the task but aren't confident that they can. According to the situational leadership model, as the readiness level of individuals increases from R1 to R4, a leader should change his or her style from task to relationship behaviors to increase subordinates' commitment, competence, and performance.

Leadership Styles and Followers

Figure 11.4 also shows the linkages between task and relationship leader behaviors and follower readiness. The appropriate style of leadership is shown by the curve running through the four leadership quadrants, S1–S4.

A **telling style** provides clear and specific instruction. Because followers are either unable or unwilling to perform the task, specific direction and close supervision

Figure 11.4 **Hersey and Blanchard's Situational Leadership Model**

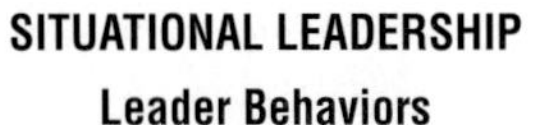

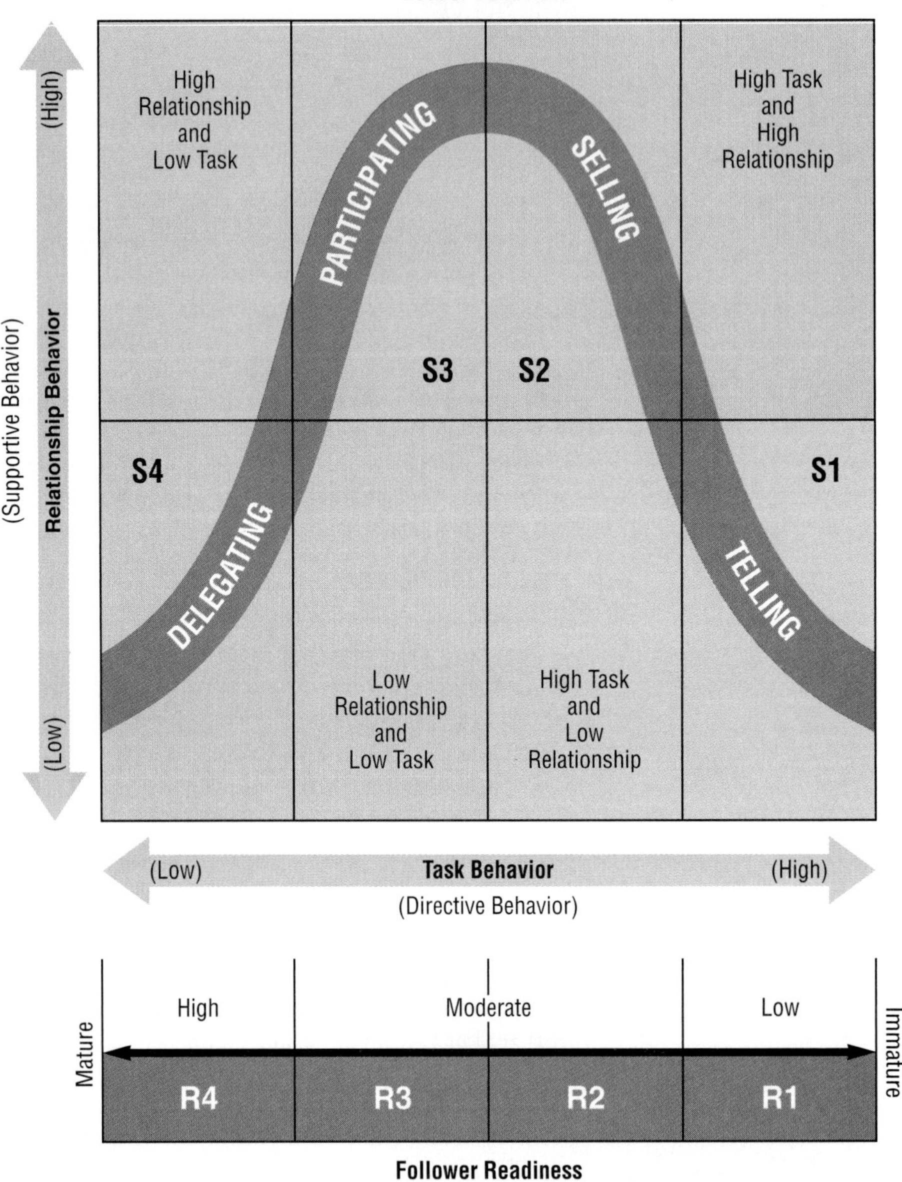

Source: Hersey, P., and Blanchard, K. H. *Management of Organizational Behavior: Utilizing Human Resource*, 5th ed. Englewood Cliffs, N.J.: Prentice-Hall, 1988. Used by permission from Ronald Campbell, President, Leadership Studies, Escondido, California.

are needed. That is, the leader tells subordinates what to do and how to perform various tasks.

A **selling style** is likely to be effective when followers are willing but still unable to carry out their tasks. The selling style provides both task and relationship leader behaviors. This style encourages two-way communication between the leader and followers and helps subordinates build confidence in their ability to perform the tasks.

A **participating style** seems to work best when the followers are able but not fully confident of their ability to perform their tasks. This level of follower readiness requires the leader to maintain two-way communication and to encourage and support followers in the use of the competencies they have developed.

When followers are able and willing to perform their tasks and confident that they can do so, a delegating style of leader behavior is most appropriate. A **delegating style** provides little task or relationship behaviors because subordinates are empowered to make decisions. They decide how and when to perform tasks and also know how to perform them.

Implications and Limitations

Hersey and Blanchard's situational leadership model is simple to understand, and its recommendations are straightforward. In practice, the readiness level of followers must be checked constantly in order for the leader to determine what combination of task and relationship behaviors would be most appropriate in the situation. An inexperienced employee (low readiness) may perform at as high a level as an experienced employee if given direction and close supervision. If the style is appropriate, it should also help followers increase their levels of readiness. Thus, as a leader develops a team and helps its members learn to manage themselves, the leadership style used should be changed to fit the changing situation.

The model has several limitations.[22] First, if each individual has a unique readiness level, how does a leader address those different readiness levels in a team situation? Does the leader assume the average level and choose a leadership style accordingly? Second, the model focuses on one contingency factor—follower readiness. In most situations, many other factors, such as time and work pressures, influence a leader's choice of behavior. A leader should take these other factors into account when choosing a leadership style. Third, the model assumes that a leader can easily adapt his or her leadership style to fit the situation, which is rarely the case. Fourth, although the model is widely used to help people improve their diagnostic abilities, it isn't strongly supported by scientific research. That is, some studies have supported the model, but others haven't been able to confirm the model's basic premises. For leaders of professionals and managers, we do not believe that the follower readiness dimension, ranging from "immature" to "mature," is very meaningful. Perhaps this concept has more meaning for leaders of nonprofessional employees.

The Managing Across Cultures Competency feature on page 340 illustrates how a combined selling–telling style of leadership may be used to introduce fundamental organizational change, but not without controversy. Featured is the leadership of Ferdinand Piëch, CEO of Volkswagen AG. His selling–telling style is clearly not based on or related to the degree of "immaturity" or "maturity" of his subordinates.

Learning Objective:

5. Discuss the Vroom–Jago time-driven leadership model.

VROOM–JAGO LEADERSHIP MODEL

Victor Vroom and Arthur Jago developed a model that focuses on the leadership role of managers in decision-making situations.[23] Victor Vroom has recently revised this model to (1) give greater consideration to ranges that may exist in situational (contingency) variables; (2) clarify the presentation of the five leadership styles in their earlier model; and (3) further emphasize the time-driven dimension to the choice of leadership style in relation to decision-making situations. The **Vroom–Jago time-driven leadership model** prescribes a leader's choice(s) among five leadership styles based on seven situational factors, recognizing the time requirements and other costs associated with each style.[24]

Leadership Styles

This model identifies five core leadership styles that vary in terms of the levels of empowerment and participation available to the leader's subordinates. These styles are summarized in increasing levels of empowerment and participation.

COMPETENCY: MANAGING ACROSS CULTURES

For more information on the Volkswagen Corporation, visit this firm's home page at ***www.volkswagen.com.***

FERDINAND PIËCH'S LEADERSHIP OF VW

The debate over Ferdinand Piëch has raged since he became chairman of Europe's biggest automaker in 1993. His turnaround of VW has been marked by controversy and innovation, including the conflict over ex-General Motors executive José Ignacio López and the introduction, in union-heavy Germany, of the 4-day workweek. His $1 billion purchase of the high-class Bentley, Bugatti, and Lamborghini brands earned him criticism from his competitors. Early in his tenure, his reduction of VW's 12-man management board to 5 got him a permanent group of hometown critics. His leadership style, which he calls democratic dictatorship, has won him few friends.

He is widely admired, however, for transforming what had become a sleepy carmaker that broke even financially only if its factories were fully utilized. He also focused employees' attention by creating expectations that VW was capable of taking on GM and Ford. The year he took the helm, VW lost $1.1 billion. In 1998, profits rose 63 percent, to $3.6 billion before taxes. "The breadth of his vision and his speed in pushing it through has been rather astounding," says John Lawson, Salomon Smith Barney's auto analyst in London. Sales of more than 4.7 million vehicles annually put VW neck and neck with Toyota as the world's third-largest carmaker. "VW has been on an incredible roll," says Jay Woodworth, a former Bankers Trust auto analyst who runs his own consulting company in Summit, New Jersey. "Piëch has turned the company around from a subpar performer that made a bunch of little Euroboxes to one that hits one home run after another." Piëch says, "For the moment, we are happy with the bronze medal. But we want to step up the stairway and into a permanent place as one of the world's three biggest car companies."

Using lessons he learned running Audi to focus on making great cars at low prices, Piëch has rapidly overhauled VW's culture and strategy. His first move, putting his own team in place, opened wounds that still haven't healed. The animosity reached its peak when GM sued VW over the hiring of purchasing chief López, alleging that López stole GM secrets and gave them to VW. Insiders say that many of the most damaging leaks to the press came from VW itself, where employees who had lost power themselves hoped that the López mess would tumble Piëch from power. Piëch hung on, settled with GM, fired his enemies, and today is surrounded by four loyalists.

The firings fueled Piëch's reputation as a manager who uses fear and brutality. "Do you really think we could be successful if this would be my management method?" retorts Piëch. "The culture at the time I came in was that nobody suffered if we lost money. My mother told me, 'Never borrow money and never make losses.' But my mother was quite different from me—she ran [Porsche Holding] like a woman. Women take care of the weak people. Fathers take care of the strong people. It took quite a while until I had the management I wanted."

He likes German accounting methods, which gives companies great flexibility to understate profits, because they keep competitors from seeing exactly how VW invests its money. They also keep suppliers, unions, and the tax collector from demanding more. "I don't say shareholders don't count for Volkswagen, but they count on the same level as our customers and our employees," says Piëch. "This is very European. If I would need a lot of capital, we would have to adapt. But as long as I can build up trust through the German system for our shareholders, what I try to do doesn't show up to our competitors."[25]

- **Decide style**—You make the decision and either announce or sell it to the team. You may use your expertise and collect information from the team or others who you believe can help solve the problem. The role of your employees is clearly one of providing specific information that you request, rather than generating or evaluating solutions.
- **Consult individually style**—You present the problem to team members individually, getting their ideas and suggestions without bringing them together as a group. Then you make the decision. This decision may or may not reflect their influence.
- **Consult team style**—You present the problem to team members in a meeting, get their suggestions, and then make the decision. It may or may not reflect their influence.
- **Facilitate style**—You present the problem to the team in a meeting. You act as facilitator, defining the problem to be solved and the boundaries within which the decision must be made. Your objective is to get concurrence on a decision. Above all, you take care to ensure that your ideas are not given any greater weight than those of others simply because of your position. Your role is much like that of chairperson, coordinating the discussion, keeping it focused on the problem, and being sure that the essential issues are discussed. You don't try to influence the team to adopt "your" solution. You are willing to accept and implement any solution that has the support of the entire team.
- **Delegate style**—You permit the team to make the decision within prescribed limits. The team undertakes the identification and diagnosis of the problem, developing alternative procedures for solving it and deciding on one or more alternative solutions. You don't enter into the team's deliberations unless explicitly asked, but behind the scenes you play an important role, providing needed resources and encouragement. This style represents the highest level of subordinate empowerment.

Situational Variables

The Vroom–Jago time-driven leadership model focuses on seven situational factors (contingency variables) that should be assessed by the leader to determine which leadership style to use.[26] Victor Vroom developed a Windows-based computer program called Expert System that enables the leader to record judgments on a five-point scale as to the extent to which a factor is present in a particular situation. Specifically, 5 = high presence, 3 = moderate presence, and 1 = low presence. We simplified the following presentation by using only a "high" or a "low" presence.

The seven situational factors (contingency variables) are as follows.

- *Decision significance*—the degree to which the problem is highly important and a quality decision is imperative. In brief, how important is the technical quality of the decision?
- *Importance of commitment*—the degree to which subordinates' personal willingness to support the decision has an impact on the effectiveness of implementation. In brief, how important is subordinate commitment to the decision? Employees are more likely to implement enthusiastically a decision that is consistent with their goals, values, and understanding of the problem.
- *Leader expertise*—the degree to which the leader has relevant information and competencies to fully understand the problem and select the best solution to it. In brief, does the leader believe that he or she has the ability and information to make a high-quality decision?
- *Likelihood of commitment*—the degree to which subordinates will support the leader's decision if it is made. Followers who have faith and trust in the judgments of their leaders are more likely to commit to a decision, even if the subordinates were not heavily involved in making it. In brief, if the leader were to make the decision, would subordinate(s) likely be committed to it?

- *Team support*—the degree to which subordinates relate to the interests of the organization as a whole or a specific unit in solving the problem. In brief, do subordinates share the goals to be achieved by solving this problem?
- *Team expertise*—the degree to which the subordinates have the relevant information and competencies to understand fully the problem and select the best solution to it. In brief, does the leader think that subordinates have the abilities and information to make a high-quality decision?
- *Team competence*—the degree to which team members have the abilities needed to resolve conflicts over preferred solutions and work together in reaching a high-quality decision. In brief, are team members capable of handling their own decision-making process? (See the discussion of the self-managing team model in Chapter 8 and Figure 8.4 in particular.)

Main Features of the Model

The matrix shown in Table 11.3 represents the main features of the Vroom–Jago time-driven leadership model. This matrix begins on the left where you evaluate the significance of the situation—high (H) or low (L). The column headings denote the

Table 11.3

Vroom–Jago Time-Driven Leadership Model

Problem Statement	Decision Significance	Importance of Commitment	Leader Expertise	Likelihood of Commitment	Team Support	Team Expertise	Team Competence	Note: Dashed line (—) means not a factor.
	H	H	H	H	—	—	—	*Decide*
				L	H	H	H	*Delegate*
							L	*Consult Group*
						L	—	
					L	—	—	
			L	H	H	H	H	*Facilitate*
							L	*Consult Individually*
						L	—	
					L	—	—	
				L	H	H	H	*Facilitate*
							L	*Consult Group*
						L	—	
					L	—	—	
		L	H	—	—	—	—	*Decide*
			L	—	H	H	H	*Facilitate*
							L	*Consult Individually*
						L	—	
					L	—	—	
	L	H	—	H	—	—	—	*Decide*
				L	—	—	H	*Delegate*
							L	*Facilitate*
		L	—	—	—	—	—	*Decide*

Source: Vroom, V. New developments in leadership and decision making. *OB News*, Briarcliff Manor, N.Y.: Organizational Behavior Division of the Academy of Management, headquartered at Pace University, Spring 1999, 5. Copyright © Victor Vroom, 1998. Used with permission.

situational factors that may or may not be present. You progress across the matrix by selecting high or low (H or L) for each relevant situation factor. After you determine the significance of the decision, you then evaluate the degree (high or low) to which employee commitment is important to implementation of the decision. As you proceed across the matrix, record a value (H or L) for only those situational factors that call for a judgment, until you reach the recommended leadership style.[27]

Decision Time. The *decision-time penalty* is the negative result of decisions not being made when needed. Leaders often must make decisions when time is of the essence. For example, air traffic control supervisors, emergency rescue squad leaders, and nuclear energy plant managers may have little time to get inputs from others before having to make a decision. The time penalty is low when there are no severe pressures on the leader to make a quick decision.

Negative effects on what Vroom and Jago call "human capital" occur because the delegate and consult styles (especially the consult-team version) use time and energy, which can be translated into costs even if there are no severe time constraints. Many managers spend almost 70 percent of their time in meetings and that time always has a value, although the precise costs of meetings vary with the reasons for them. For example, while Jonathan Wheeler, vice president of human resources at Centex Homes, is in a meeting, other decisions are being delayed. What's the cost to Centex for these delays? Some of the benefits from employees participating in meetings include being members of a team, strengthening their commitment to the organization's goals, and contributing to the development of their leadership capabilities (mainly as related to managing self and communication competencies). Thus the cost of holding a meeting must be compared to the cost of not holding a meeting. One cost therefore is the value of time lost through the use of participative decision making.

If participation has potential negative effects on human capital, it can also have positive effects, as discussed in Chapter 8. Participative leader behaviors help develop the technical and managerial competencies of employees, build teamwork, and foster loyalty and commitment to organizational goals. The Vroom–Jago model considers the trade-offs among four criteria by which a leader's decision-making style can be evaluated: decision quality, employee commitment to implementation, costs, and employee development. The consult and delegate styles are viewed as most supportive of employee development.

Expert System. As noted previously, Victor Vroom developed a Windows-based computer program called Expert System for leaders to use in applying this model to real problems. This program is simple and easy to use. An opening screen contains the names of the situational factors. Positioning the cursor over each factor elicits its description. Pull-down menus at the right enable the user to record judgments on a five-point scale of the degree—high to low—to which a factor is present and should be considered in making the decision. After the analysis is complete, the user then clicks *calculate* and the judgments are entered into equations predicting the consequences of the five processes for each of four outcomes: quality, implementation, cost, and development (as well as an overall assessment of their relative merit). These results are reflected in a series of bar graphs available to the user.[28]

We apply this model to a Starbucks Coffee Company manager in the following Managing Change Competency feature. Starbucks has a relatively short history. It began in Washington state in 1971 when three young entrepreneurs began to sell coffee at Pike Place Market in Seattle. The original Starbucks store was named after the first mate in *Moby-Dick*. Today, it is the largest specialty retail coffee roaster in the world with 2,000 coffee shops in a number of countries. It opens one or more stores each working day. As of a couple of years ago, Brooke McCurdy was in charge of each store's design team. In this feature we highlight some of the leadership challenges that she faced with the need to constantly select new sites and store designs. Following this account, we walk you through the Vroom–Jago model matrix solution.

COMPETENCY: MANAGING CHANGE

BROOKE MCCURDY'S LEADERSHIP

When she joined Starbucks in 1990, Brooke McCurdy found that employees working there had a passion for and believed in the product. She headed a 70-person team that included 5 regional project managers, 10 project captains, and 30 job captains who spent most of their time at construction sites. In addition, McCurdy oversaw the design and development group, which developed new store designs, and the remodel team, which remodeled existing stores.

As much as possible, Starbucks tries to stay away from cookie-cutter designs. Each restaurant is designed to fit into its neighborhood. McCurdy likened the stores to sisters or brothers: They share certain family characteristics, but maintain their own unique personality.

Her team consisted of diverse professionals who have lived all over the world. Each person brought a unique perspective to the job and drew heavily on his or her understanding of the mythology surrounding the coffee bean and coffee-making process. (To further this mythology, Starbucks financially assists people in the coffee-producing countries where it does business.) Getting the team to reach consensus on a store's design was no easy task because each team member had unique perspectives. The regional project managers wanted the new stores in their areas, whereas the job captains wanted locations where building codes were favorable for Starbucks and construction crews could easily work the site.[29]

If you were Brooke McCurdy—and armed with the solution matrix shown in Table 11.3—what leadership style should you choose when making a decision about which store to build? Start with *decision significance* on the left-hand side of the matrix. This first column requires that you make a decision about the importance of the issue. After you make that decision, go to the next column, *importance of commitment.* Again, you must make a decision about the importance of having staff members committed to the final design of a new store. After you make this decision, you face another decision and then another. As you make each decision, follow the columns across the matrix. Eventually, at the far right-hand side of the matrix, you will arrive at the recommended best style of leadership to use, which is based on your previous seven decisions. We used this method to determine the style of leadership that would have been recommended for Brooke McCurdy to use.

ANALYSIS	ANSWER
• Decision significance	High
• Importance of commitment	High
• Leader expertise	Low
• Likelihood of commitment	Low
• Team support	High
• Team expertise	High
• Team competence	High

Based on this analysis, Brooke McCurdy should use the facilitate style with the teams. A different answer to one or more of these situational factors would probably result in a different recommended leadership style.

For more information on Starbucks, visit this organization's home page at ***www.starbucks.com.***

IMPLICATIONS AND LIMITATIONS

The Vroom–Jago time-driven leadership model is consistent with earlier work on group and team behaviors (see Chapter 8). If leaders can diagnose situations correctly, choosing the best leadership style for those situations becomes easier.[30] These choices, in turn, will enable them to make high-quality, timely decisions. If the situation requires delegation, the leader must learn how to establish the desired goals and limitations and then let employees determine how best to achieve the goals within those limitations. If the situation calls for the leader alone to make the decision, the leader should be aware of potential positive and negative consequences of not asking others for their input.

The model does have some limitations. First, most subordinates have a strong desire to participate in decisions affecting their jobs, regardless of the model's recommendation of a style for the leader to use. If subordinates aren't involved in the decision, they are more likely to become frustrated and not be committed to the decision. Second, certain competencies of the leader play a key role in determining the relative effectiveness of the model. For example, in situations involving conflict, only leaders skilled in conflict resolution may be able to use the kind of participative decision-making strategy suggested by the model. A leader who hasn't developed these competencies may obtain better results with a more directive style, even though this style is different from the style that the model proposes. Third, the model is based on the assumption that decisions involve a single process. Often, decisions go through several cycles and are part of a solution to a bigger problem. In McCurdy's case, a design decision made for a store in west Los Angeles might affect a subsequent decision for another store in south Los Angeles.

Learning Objective:

6. State the differences in the three contingency models of leadership.

DIFFERENCES IN THE THREE CONTINGENCY MODELS

Choosing the most appropriate leadership style can be difficult. A theme of employee empowerment has begun to prevail in most leading business organizations. Evidence from Carly Fiorina, Steve Miller, Dee Hock, Lloyd Ward, and Douglas McKenna, among others, show that this leadership style can result in productive, healthy organizations. However, participative management is not appropriate for all situations, as contingency theorists note. Table 11.4 shows the differences in leader behaviors, situational variables, and outcomes for the three contingency models that we have discussed.

LEADER BEHAVIORS

Fiedler's model is based on the LPC style of a leader (high or low LPC) and the degree to which the situation is favorable for the leader. Leadership style is considered to be

Table 11.4

Differences in the Three Contingency Leadership Models

MODEL	LEADER BEHAVIORS	CONTINGENCY VARIABLES	LEADER EFFECTIVENESS CRITERIA
Fiedler's	• Task-oriented: low LPC • Relationship-oriented: high LPC	• Group atmosphere • Task structure • Leader position • Power	• Performance
Hersey and Blanchard's	• Task and Relationship	• Readiness level of team members	• Performance • Job satisfaction
Vroom–Jago	• Continuum of decide to delegate	• Seven situational variables	• Decision quality • Commitment to implementation • Cost • Employee development

relatively stable, and the model suggests that the leader choose a situation that matches his or her style. Hersey and Blanchard use the same two leadership dimensions that Fiedler identified: task and relationship behaviors. They went one step further by considering each as either high or low and then combining them into four specific leadership styles: directive, supportive, participating, and delegating. Vroom and Jago contend that leaders can choose from among a variety of leadership styles, ranging from highly directive to highly delegated. The leader's objective in choosing a style is to (1) improve the quality and acceptance of decisions; (2) increase the probability that employees will accept and implement decisions on a timely basis; and (3) develop effective leadership competencies in employees. Thus each of the four contingency models identifies different styles of leadership and views the leader's ability to choose among styles differently.

Contingency Variables

All three models emphasize somewhat different contingency variables. Fiedler's model suggests that the way the variables (team atmosphere, task structure, and leader position power) are arranged in a situation determines whether and to what extent the situation is favorable or unfavorable to the leader. As the combination of the three contingency variables changes, so do the leadership requirements. A leader who is effective in one situation may not be effective in another. He suggests that changing the situation is easier than changing the leader's style.

Hersey and Blanchard's contingency variable is the readiness of the employee. An employee having a low level of readiness is unable or unwilling to take responsibility or do something independently. An employee having a high readiness level is both willing to take responsibility and knows what to do, can work independently, and always meets deadlines. As the readiness levels of subordinates change, the leader's style should change accordingly. A directive style is most appropriate for employees having a low-readiness level, whereas a delegating style is most appropriate for employees having a high-readiness level.

The Vroom–Jago model identifies seven different contingencies for the leader to consider in deciding whether to use the decide style or a more participative style in a particular situation. Subordinate participation in a leader's decisions may increase quality, generate commitment, and develop employee competencies. However, it increases the amount of time required to make decisions and for the leader to develop subordinates' competencies.

Leadership Effectiveness

All three models use somewhat different criteria for evaluating leadership effectiveness. Fiedler emphasizes performance; Hersey and Blanchard use both employee job satisfaction and performance; and Vroom and Jago emphasize decision effectiveness on a timely basis. If a decision must be made with a team, the Vroom–Jago model may best assist leaders in choosing the appropriate leadership style. If improving individual performance is most important, perhaps Fiedler's or Hersey and Blanchard's model would be more useful.

CHAPTER SUMMARY

1. Outline the essentials of leadership.

Leadership includes the seven foundation competencies developed throughout this book and more. Leadership also includes developing ideas and a vision, expressing and living by values, influencing others, and making hard decisions. Leaders draw on five sources of power to influence the actions of followers: legitimate, reward, coercive, referent, and expert.

2. Explain two basic models of leadership—traits and behavioral.

The two most basic leadership models are the traits and behavioral models. The traits model emphasizes the personal qualities of leaders and attributes success to certain abilities, skills, and personality characteristics. However, this model fails to explain why certain people succeed and others fail as leaders. The primary reason is that it ignores how traits interact with other situational variables. The behavioral model emphasizes leaders' actions instead of their personal traits. We focused on two leader behaviors—initiating structure and consideration—and how they affect employee performance and job satisfaction. The behavioral model tends to ignore the situation in which the leader is operating. This omission is the focal point of the three contingency models of leadership that we reviewed. The contingency approach emphasizes the importance of various situations, factors, or contingencies to leaders and on their leadership styles.

3. Describe Fiedler's contingency model of leadership.

Fiedler's model focuses on effective diagnosis of the situation in which the leader will operate. It emphasizes understanding the nature of the situation and then matching the correct leadership style to that situation. Three contingency variables need to be diagnosed: group atmosphere, task structure, and the leader's position power. The model suggests that all leaders have a least-preferred coworker trait that is stable and determines the situations in which their particular leadership style will be effective.

4. Explain Hersey and Blanchard's situational model of leadership.

Hersey and Blanchard's model states that leaders should choose a style that matches the readiness of their subordinates to follow. If subordinates are not ready to perform a task, a directive leadership style will probably be more effective than a relationship style. As the readiness level of the subordinate increases, the leader's style should become more participative and less directive.

5. Discuss the Vroom–Jago time-driven leadership model.

The Vroom–Jago model presents a leader with choices among five leadership styles based on seven situational (contingency) factors. Time requirements and other costs associated with each style are recognized in the model. The leadership styles lie on a continuum from decide (leader makes the decision) to delegate (subordinate or team makes the decision). A solution matrix (Table 11.3) or Vroom's computer based Expert System is used to diagnose the situation and arrive at the favored leadership style.

6. State the differences in the three contingency models of leadership.

The three contingency models differ in terms of key leader behaviors, contingency variables employed, and criteria for evaluating leadership effectiveness. Table 11.4 provides a summary of these differences.

KEY TERMS AND CONCEPTS

Behavioral model of leadership
Consideration
Consult individually style
Consult team style
Decide style
Delegate style
Delegating style
Facilitate style
Fiedler's contingency model
Follower readiness
Group atmosphere
Hersey and Blanchard's situational model
Initiating structure
Leader
Leadership
Least preferred coworker (LPC)
Manager
Participating style
Position power
Relationship behavior
Selling style
Task behavior
Task structure
Telling style
Traits model of leadership
Vroom–Jago time-driven leadership model

DISCUSSION QUESTIONS

1. Think of a manager that you have worked for. Was this manager also a leader? Explain your response.
2. Max De Pree, CEO of Herman Miller, stated, "The first responsibility of a leader is to define reality. The last is to say thank you. In between the leader is a servant." What challenges and dilemmas might you experience in attempting to lead on the basis of this advice?
3. Describe a manager that you have worked for in terms of his or her use (or lack of use) of the five sources of power: legitimate, reward, coercive, referent, and expert.
4. In terms of your description in Question 3, how effective was this manager in using each of these sources of power?
5. How would you characterize Lloyd Ward, CEO of Maytag, in terms of the behavioral model of leadership? What specific indicators did you use to reach your conclusions from our description of Lloyd Ward in the Managing Self Competency feature?
6. Reread the Managing Communication Competency feature on Douglas McKenna. What aspects of McKenna's remarks appear to be consistent with Fiedler's contingency model of leadership? What aspects seem to differ from it?
7. When Norman Brinker, chairman of Brinker International, speaks on leadership, he says, "I don't send for people. For the most part, I go to other people's offices to see them instead of having them come see me." Which type of leadership style does this suggest? Under what conditions might it be most effective?
8. Make a list of the conditions under which you failed to exercise effective leadership in a situation. Make another list of the conditions under which you exercised successful leadership in a situation. What are the differences in the lists?
9. When someone asked Chris Kisko, regional manager for Celanese, what it took to be an effective restaurant store manager, his response was "great team members who are self-disciplined to serving the customer." Using Hersey and Blanchard's model, which style of leadership produces these results? What assumptions is Kisko making about his team members?
10. Susan Allen, field manager for Trammell Crow real estate, discovered that she could improve the performance of her subordinates through the decide style of leadership rather than the delegate style. According to the Vroom–Jago time-driven model of leadership, under what conditions would this style be effective? What are some drawbacks to this style that she should consider?

DEVELOPING COMPETENCIES

Competency: Managing Self—What's Your Leadership Style?

The following statements help to diagnose your self-perceptions of your leadership style according to the behavioral model of leadership. Read each item carefully. Think about how you usually behave when you are the leader. Then, using the following key, circle the letter that most closely describes your style. Circle only one choice per statement.[31]

A = Always O = Often ? = Sometimes S = Seldom N = Never

1. I take time to explain how a job should be carried out. A O ? S N
2. I explain the part that coworkers are to play in the group. A O ? S N
3. I make clear the rules and procedures for others to follow in detail. A O ? S N
4. I organize my own work activities. A O ? S N
5. I let people know how well they are doing. A O ? S N
6. I let people know what is expected of them. A O ? S N
7. I encourage the use of uniform procedures for others to follow in detail. A O ? S N
8. I make my attitude clear to others. A O ? S N
9. I assign others to particular tasks. A O ? S N
10. I make sure that others understand their part in the group. A O ? S N
11. I schedule the work that I want others to do. A O ? S N
12. I ask that others follow standard rules and regulations. A O ? S N
13. I make working on the job more pleasant. A O ? S N
14. I go out of my way to be helpful to others. A O ? S N
15. I respect others' feelings and opinions. A O ? S N
16. I am thoughtful and considerate of others. A O ? S N
17. I maintain a friendly atmosphere in the group. A O ? S N
18. I do little things to make it more pleasant for others to be a member of my group. A O ? S N
19. I treat others as equals. A O ? S N
20. I give others advance notice of change and explain how it will affect them. A O ? S N
21. I look out for others' personal welfare. A O ? S N
22. I am approachable and friendly toward others. A O ? S N

Scoring Form

The following boxes are numbered to correspond to the items in the survey instrument. In each box, circle the number next to the letter of the response alternative you picked. Add up the numbers you circled in each of the columns.

Interpretation

The items scored in Column 1 reflect an initiating structure or task leadership style. A score of greater than 47 would indicate that you describe your leadership style as high on initiating or task structure. You see yourself as planning, directing, organizing, and controlling the work of others. The items scored in Column 2 reflect a considerate or relationship style. A total score of greater than 40 indicates that you see yourself as a considerate leader. A considerate leader is one who is concerned with the comfort, well-being, and personal welfare of his or her subordinates. In general, managers rated high on initiating structure and moderate on consideration tended to be in charge of higher-producing teams than those whose leadership styles are the reverse.

Column 1

1	2
A = 5 O = 4 ? = 3 S = 2 N = 1	A = 5 O = 4 ? = 3 S = 2 N = 1
3 A = 5 O = 4 ? = 3 S = 2 N = 1	4 A = 5 O = 4 ? = 3 S = 2 N = 1
5 A = 5 O = 4 ? = 3 S = 2 N = 1	6 A = 5 O = 4 ? = 3 S = 2 N = 1
7 A = 5 O = 4 ? = 3 S = 2 N = 1	8 A = 5 O = 4 ? = 3 S = 2 N = 1
9 A = 5 O = 4 ? = 3 S = 2 N = 1	10 A = 5 O = 4 ? = 3 S = 2 N = 1
11 A = 5 O = 4 ? = 3 S = 2 N = 1	12 A = 5 O = 4 ? = 3 S = 2 N = 1

Total Column 1 = _____

Column 2

13	14
A = 5 O = 4 ? = 3 S = 2 N = 1	A = 5 O = 4 ? = 3 S = 2 N = 1
15 A = 5 O = 4 ? = 3 S = 2 N = 1	16 A = 5 O = 4 ? = 3 S = 2 N = 1
17 A = 5 O = 4 ? = 3 S = 2 N = 1	18 A = 5 O = 4 ? = 3 S = 2 N = 1
19 A = 5 O = 4 ? = 3 S = 2 N = 1	20 A = 5 O = 4 ? = 3 S = 2 N = 1
21 A = 5 O = 4 ? = 3 S = 2 N = 1	22 A = 5 O = 4 ? = 3 S = 2 N = 1

Total Column 2 = _____

Competency: Managing Communication—Richard Branson's Leadership

Richard Branson, founder and chairman of the London-based Virgin Group Ltd., has turned a lifelong disdain for conventional business wisdom into a multibillion dollar international conglomerate and one of the world's most recognizable brands. The Virgin Group has ventured into businesses ranging from retail stores to travel to financial services.

Branson loves challenge; he views the impossible as just another business opportunity. He put the vibrant Virgin label on the decaying British Rail with hopes of turning the railroad into a contemporary profitable business. Throughout his career, Branson has embraced the David role. He has taken on Goliaths such as British Airways, EMI Music, and Coca-Cola. His intent is to become the best rather than the biggest. He works on the premise that there are significant profits to be made in small pieces of big markets.

His personal trademark is doing outlandish publicity stunts. Branson will do almost anything to promote the Virgin brand: driving a tank down Fifth Avenue in New York to introduce Virgin Cola to the United States, engaging in high-profile hot-air balloon adventures, and portraying a drowning victim on television's *Baywatch*. Branson sets aside about 25 percent of his time for public relations activities. He has a staff member whose sole responsibility is devising headline-catching publicity stunts. Branson states, "Using yourself to get out and talk about it is a lot cheaper and more effective than a lot of advertising. In fact, if you do it correctly, it can beat advertising hands down and save tens of millions of dollars."

Creating a Culture

Branson has developed a set of business standards for the Virgin Group. Five standards are incorporated into every business he has started and every joint venture he has entered. A product or service that bears the Virgin label must have high quality, be innovative, provide good value for the money, be challenging to existing alternatives, and have a sense of fun.

When launching Virgin Atlantic Airways, Branson designed an airline to please himself, figuring that he symbolized the typical air traveler. Starting with a single 747-200 jet in 1984, Virgin Atlantic began flying the popular London-to-New York route with two things in mind: lower prices and better service. Because a passenger is in a plane for 7 hours, he set the goals of serving better meals, offering more entertainment, having enthusiastic flight crews, and creating fun. Virgin Atlantic's mission is to offer a first-class experience at business-class prices.

Branson flies frequently and usually spends the entire flight chatting with passengers and crew members, serving drinks, leading games over the public address system, and helping the flight crew with even the most menial tasks. In the early days, when there were far fewer than the current 22 aircraft in Virgin's fleet, Branson regularly appeared at Heathrow Airport to apologize personally to disembarking passengers if a flight was late. Though he is not physically on every flight, Branson's standards are felt through the enthusiasm expressed by his employees.

Indicators of Success

Branson's philosophy is centered on finding the best people to run the diverse businesses in the Virgin Group. He is not as much concerned about industry-specific expertise as he is with recruiting employees with strong communication and teamwork competencies that mesh with the Virgin culture. Branson states, "What makes somebody good is how good they are at dealing with people. If you can find people who are good at motivating others and getting the best out of people, they are the ones you want. There are plenty of so-called experts, but not as many great motivators of people." Virgin tends to promote from within. The desired profile, not surprisingly, is someone like Branson: someone who gets charged up when told that something cannot be done; someone who is unafraid of industry barriers and will not take no for an answer.

Employees First

Many chief executives focus on creating shareholder value and devote their attention primarily to customers. Branson thinks that the correct pecking order is employees first, customers next, and then shareholders. His logic is this: If your employees are happy, they will do a better job. If they do a better job, the customers will be happy, and thus business will be good and the shareholders will be rewarded. Branson regularly takes entire flight crews out to dinner and parties when he arrives on a Virgin Atlantic flight. He even stays at the crew's hotel rather than in expensive hotels downtown away from the crew. He gives every Virgin employee a Virgin card, which provides big discounts on the airline as well as at Virgin Megastores and other Virgin businesses.

Consider this recent example. While vacationing on his private Caribbean island, called Necker, he brought 20 employees from various Virgin companies to the island. These were not senior executives, but the rank and file—a housekeeper from Johannesburg, a switchboard operator, a reservations clerk, a pilot. They were invited because of excellent performance. This is a regular perk for Virgin employees, and Branson delights in the company. "The idea is to have fun, but by talking to employees, you learn a lot as well," he says. Reminded that it is the rare chief executive who takes employees along on vacation, Branson laughs and says, "I can assure you, it's no sacrifice." He attends as many orientations for new staff as possible in order to set the tone and send the message: "Get out there and have a good time. Really enjoy yourself, because most of your life is spent working, and you ought to have a great time doing it. It's much nicer paying the bills when everybody is having a good time."

He is frequently on the road to visit Virgin businesses, talking with employees and customers. He is known for his ever-present notebook and pen, which he pulls out whenever he chats with employees and customers. Branson insists that this is a crucial element in his role as chairman. By writing things down, he creates a regular list of items for immediate action. He reads mail from employees every morning before he does anything else. This habit, which he started in Virgin's early days, influences company–employee dynamics. Employees do not hesitate to air their grievances directly to him. Branson has proved with his actions that he actively listens. Although Virgin has more than 35,000 employees around the world, he gets only about 50 e-mails or letters each day from nonmanagerial employees. They vary from small ideas to frustrations with middle management to significant proposals. He addresses every one by answering personally or by initiating some action. Branson states, "Instead of needing a union when they have a problem, they come to me. I will give the employee the benefit of the doubt on most occasions."

For Branson, retaining the standards he has instilled as the company grows is his major task. He states, "You've got to treat people as human beings—even more so as the company gets bigger. The moment I start to think 'I've made lots of money, I'm comfortable. I don't need to bother with these things anymore,' that's when Virgin will be at real risk."[32]

For more information on the Virgin Group Ltd., visit this firm's home page at ***www.virgin.com.***

Questions

1. Review the seven core components of the managing communication competency presented in Chapter 1. How does Branson's communication competency as a leader stack up against each of these components?
2. Identify and assess Branson's use of the sources of power.
3. What examples of Branson's communication practices reflect initiating structure and consideration of the behavioral model of leadership?
4. Which of the contingency models of leadership appear to best reflect Branson's leadership? Explain.

REFERENCES

1. Adapted from Burrows, P., and Elstrom, P. The boss. *Business Week*, August 2, 1999, 76–84; Lubin, J., and Blumenstein, R. In this family, she's the CEO and he's home. *Wall Street Journal*, July 22, 1999, B1, B10; Vijayan, J. In first, Hewlett-Packard picks outsider as CEO. *Computerworld*, July 26, 1999, 29; Abelson, R. HP's glass ceiling cracks with help of one-time solo dad. *Houston Chronicle*, August 22, 1999, 24A–25A.
2. Adapted from Tichy, N. M. *The Leadership Engine: How Winning Companies Build Leaders at Every Level.* Glenview, Ill.: Harper Business, 1997.
3. The teachable point of view. *Journal of Business Strategy*, January/February 1998, 29–33.
4. McCauley, C. D., Moxley, R. S., and Van Velsor, E. (eds.). *The Center for Creative Leadership Handbook of Leadership Development.* San Francisco: Jossey-Bass, 1998.
5. *Make Yourself a Leader.* Boston: Fast Company, 1999; De Pree, L. *Leadership Is an Art.* East Lansing: University of Michigan Press, 1988.
6. Fryer, B. Bosses from heaven—and hell! *Computerworld*, August 9, 1999, 46–47.
7. Fryer, 46–47.
8. Fryer, 46–47.
9. Fryer, 46–47; also see VanDerWall, S. *The Courageous Follower: Standing Up To and For Our Leaders.* San Francisco: Berret-Koehler, 1998.
10. Fryer, 46–47.
11. Lord, R. G., Brown, D. J., and Freiberg, S. J. Understanding the dynamics of leadership: The role of follower self-concepts in the leader/follower relationship. *Organizational Behavior & Human Decision Sciences*, 1999, 78, 167–203.
12. Adapted from Leonhardt, D. The saga of Lloyd Ward. *Business Week*, August 9, 1999, 59–70; A watershed appointment. *Black Enterprise*, August 1999, 15.
13. Kouzes, J. M., and Posner, B. Z. *The Leadership Challenge: How to Keep Getting Extraordinary Things Done in Organizations.* San Francisco: Jossey-Bass, 1995; Judge, W. Q. *The Leader's Shadow: Exploring and Developing Executive Character.* Thousand Oaks, Calif.: Sage, 1999.
14. Bass, B. M. *Bass and Stogdill's Handbook of Leadership*, 3rd ed. New York: Free Press, 1990; Northouse, P. G. *Leadership: Theory and Practice.* Thousand Oaks, Calif.: Sage, 1997.
15. Fleishman, E. A., and Harris, E. E. Patterns of leadership behavior related to employee grievances and turnover: Some post HOC reflections. *Personnel Psychology*, 1998, 51, 825–834; Fleishman, E. A. Consideration and structure: Another look at their role in leadership research. F. Damserau and F.J. Yammarino (eds.), *Leadership: The Multi-Level Approaches.* Greenwich, Conn.: JAI press, 1998.
16. Adapted from Laaba, J. Taking a stand for leadership. *Workforce*, May 1999, 23–26.
17. Fiedler, F. E. *A Theory of Leadership.* New York: McGraw-Hill, 1967; Fiedler, F. E. Research on leadership selection and training: One view of the future. *Administrative Science Quarterly*, 1996, 41, 241–250.
18. Fiedler, F. E., and Chemers, M. M. *Improving Leadership Effectiveness: The Leader Match Concept*, 2nd ed. New York: John Wiley & Sons, 1982; Fiedler, F. E. Cognitive resources and leadership performance. *Applied Psychology—An International Review*, 1995, 44, 5–28.
19. Fiedler, F. E. *Leadership Experience and Leadership Performance.* Alexandria, Va.: U.S. Army Research Institute, 1994.
20. Adapted from Smiley, R. No shades of gray. *Financial Executive*, May/June 1998, 14–15; *Eaton Corporation 1998 Annual Report.* Cleveland: Eaton Corporation, 1999.
21. Hersey, P., and Blanchard, K. H. *Management of Organizational Behavior: Utilizing Human Resources.* Englewood Cliffs, N.J.: Prentice-Hall, 1993; Blanchard, K. H., and Hersey, P. Great ideas revisited. *Training & Development Journal*, January 1996, 42–48.
22. Yukl, G. A., and Van Fleet, D. D., Theory and research in organizations. In M. D. Dunnette and L. M. Hough

(eds.), *Handbook of Industrial and Organizational Psychology,* vol. 3. Palo Alto, Calif.: Consulting Psychologist Press, 1992, 147–198; Blanchard, K. H., Zigarmi, D., and Nelson, R. B. Situational leadership after 25 years: A retrospective. *Journal of Leadership Studies,* 1993, 1, 21–36.

23. Vroom, V. H., and Jago, A. G. *The New Leadership.* Englewood Cliffs, N.J.: Prentice-Hall, 1988.
24. The discussion of the revised model is based on Vroom, V. H. New developments in leadership and decision making. *OB News.* Briarcliff Manor, N.Y.: Organizational Behavior Division of the Academy of Management, headquartered at Pace University, Spring 1999, 4–5; Vroom, V. H. Leadership and the decision-making process. *Organizational Dynamics,* Spring 2000 (in press).
25. Adapted from Guyon, J. Getting the bugs out at VW. *Fortune,* March 29, 1999, 96–102; The scion steering VW. *Newsweek,* January 1, 1998, 42; Maling, N. Driving ambition. *Marketing Week,* March 4, 1999, 26–29; Einstein, P. What the doktor ordered. *Professional Engineering,* December 8, 1998, 25–26.
26. Vroom, 1999, 4–5; Vroom, Spring 2000 (in press); Vroom, V., and Jago, A. G. Situation effects and levels of analysis in the study of leader participation. *Leadership Quarterly,* 1995, 6, 45–52.
27. Vroom, 1999, 4–5; Vroom, Spring 2000 (in press); Vroom and Jago, 45–52.
28. Vroom, 1999, 4-5; Vroom, Spring 2000 (in press); Vroom and Jago, 45–52.
29. Adapted from McCurdy, B. Starbucks rides the caffeine wave. *Chain Store Age,* April 1996, 80–82; Simons, J. A case of the shakes: As Starbucks cafes multiply, so do the growing pains. *U.S. News Online.* www.usnews.com/usnews/issue/970714, July 14, 1997.
30. Field, R. H. G., and House, R. J. A test of the Vroom–Yetton model using manager and subordinate reports. *Journal of Applied Psychology,* 1990, 75, 362–366; Pasewark, W. E., and Strawser, J. R. Subordinate participation in audit budgeting decisions. *Decision Sciences,* 1994, 25, 281–299.
31. Schriesheim, C. *Leadership Instrument.* Used by permission, University of Miami, Miami, Florida, 1999.
32. Adapted from Rifkin, G. How Richard Branson works magic. *Strategy and Business,* 1998, 13(4), 44–52; Rifkin, G. *Radical Marketing.* New York: Harper Business, 1999; Buxton, P. Will Virgin reduce to a purer form? *Marketing Week,* April 22, 1999, 19–20; Hamilton, K. Branson to sell mobile phones at Our Price. *Sunday Times: Business,* August 8, 1999, 1; Virgin Group Ltd. *Hoovers' Online UK.* www.hoovers.co.uk/, August 28, 1999; Kets de Vries, M. F. R. Charisma in action: The transformational abilities of Virgin's Richard Branson and ABB's Percy Barnevik. *Organizational Dynamics,* Winter 1998, 7–21; Jackson, T. *Richard Branson: Virgin King.* London: HarperCollins, 1994; Hamel, G. Virgin's amazing business-making machine. *Harvard Business Review,* September–October 1999, 78–79.

CHAPTER

12 Leadership: Contemporary Developments

LEARNING OBJECTIVES

When you have finished studying this chapter, you should be able to:

1. Describe how a leader's attributions affect his or her leadership behaviors.
2. State the characteristics of and differences between the transactional and charismatic leadership models.
3. Explain the transformational leadership model.
4. Evaluate the limits of a leader's influence.

Preview Case: *Gordon Bethune on Teams and Leadership*

ATTRIBUTION MODEL OF LEADERSHIP

Attributions by Leaders

Attributions by Employees

Significance for Leaders

Competency: Managing Across Cultures*—Peter Job on International Managers*

TRANSACTIONAL AND CHARISMATIC LEADERSHIP MODELS

Transactional Leadership Model

Charismatic Leadership Model

Competency: Managing Change*—Robert Shapiro's Leadership of Monsanto*

Significance for Leaders

Competency: Managing Communication*—Herb Kelleher of Southwest Airlines*

TRANSFORMATIONAL LEADERSHIP MODEL

Inspirational Motivation

Intellectual Stimulation

Competency: Managing Self*—Alan Naumann of Calico Technologies*

Idealized Influence

Individualized Consideration

Competency: Managing Teams*—Laurie Tucker of FedEx*

Significance for Leaders

DO LEADERS MATTER?

Irrelevance of Leaders

Substitutes for Leaders

CHAPTER SUMMARY

Key Terms and Concepts

Discussion Questions

DEVELOPING COMPETENCIES

Competency: Managing Self*—Transformational Leadership*

Competency: Managing Communication*—Managing for the Future*

PREVIEW CASE

GORDON BETHUNE ON TEAMS AND LEADERSHIP

Gordon Bethune joined Continental Airlines in 1994 and became its CEO and chairman of the board in 1996. In recent years, he has been named one of the top 25 global managers by *Business Week* and ranked sixth among the 50 best CEOs by *Worth* magazine. The following comments are excerpts from an in-depth interview with Bethune that focuses on his views of teams and leadership.

Running an airline is the biggest team sport there is. It's not an approach, it's not reorganization, and it's not a daily team plan. We are like a wristwatch—lots of different parts, but the whole has value only when we all work together. It has no value when any part fails. So we are not a cross-functional team, we're a company of multi-functions that has value when we all work cooperatively—pilots, flight attendants, gate agents, airport agents, mechanics, reservation agents. And not to understand that means you're going to fail. Lots of people failed because they don't get it.

It's like basic human nature: if you take someone for granted or treat them like they have less value than someone else, they'll go to extraordinary lengths to show you that you're wrong. People who try to manage our business and ascribe various values to different functions and treat some with disdain because they are easy to replace might some day find the watch doesn't work—it might be the smallest part that's broken, but the whole watch doesn't work.

Before I became CEO, Continental's strategy was: We are going to be the lowest cost airline. So we had a mantra that low cost is everything, it's the Holy Grail. It's like having only one instrument, like an air speed indicator, on an airplane—air speed is important but it isn't the only thing. So, you're doing pretty well when you hit the mountain, right? When that happens, you say, wait a minute, cost isn't everything. Let's say we're in the pizza business. If I'm rewarded by making the product cost less, I'll take the cheese off the pizza and get paid. That's not what you wanted.

Our Working Together program stresses that you've got to have people work as a team, and every person on the team has to know what's going on. So we started telling all our employees what's going on every day—how our stock did, our on-time performance, baggage handling, and so on. Everybody knows these every day. Every Friday evening, I put out a voice mail that's also e-mailed all around the company. It's from the CEO's perspective—what happened and where we're going. Every month in Houston we have an open house, and every month we send employees a newsletter to their home. Every six months the president and I go to seven major domestic cities and give a formal presentation. It is also available on videotape for employees to take home. At Continental, we spend 100 percent of our time working together as a team, trying to figure out how to beat our competitors.

*For more information on Continental Airlines, visit this company's home page at **www.continental.com.***

Hispanic magazine rates us as one of the best companies to work for in its latest survey. Why? It's our collegial atmosphere where people are included in the decision making and made to feel appreciated. I don't know anybody—Mexican American, or anyone else—who doesn't appreciate that. It's not just rewards, it's how you are treated. If you recognize people's contribution and their value and treat them as part of the team—that's the real secret to being a good place to work.[1]

Continental Airlines is one of the largest airlines in the United States, operating more than 2,200 flights daily to some 200 destinations worldwide. The company has made a dramatic turnaround from bankruptcy in 1994 to become one of America's most admired corporations. Many individuals attribute this turnaround to Gordon Bethune and the other leaders he recruited to join Continental. The models of leadership you studied in Chapter 11 provide important insights into Bethune's success as a leader, but they do not provide a complete profile of his leadership or that of other leaders. These models did not address the full range of questions about what makes an effective leader.

Recall our comment from Chapter 11: *The topic of leadership is like that of a prism—there is something new and different each time you look at it from a new angle.* In this chapter we present additional lenses for understanding and addressing the range of questions about effective leadership and leaders in particular situations. These questions include: What impact do leaders' beliefs about their employees have on their choices of leadership style? What role does a leader's charisma play in getting followers to achieve the leader's goals? What are the most contemporary views on leadership? Is leadership always necessary? In this chapter, we focus on contemporary developments in leadership that address these questions.

Learning Objective:

1. Describe how a leader's attributions affect his or her leadership behaviors.

ATTRIBUTION MODEL OF LEADERSHIP

We presented the role of attribution theory as it relates to perception in Chapter 3. Recall that attribution theory focuses on understanding what causes various behaviors by individuals. In other words, when individuals behave in certain ways, why do they do so?

The **attribution model of leadership** contends that a leader's judgment about employees is influenced by the leader's interpretation of the causes of the employees' performance.[2] The leader's attributions, as much as the employees' behaviors, influence how the leader responds to their performance. A leader obtains information about employees and their behaviors through daily observations of their work. Based on this information, the leader interprets the reasons for employees' behaviors and takes actions to deal with them when necessary. Gordon Bethune's attributions about employees are illustrated in the Preview Case through remarks such as:

> It's like basic human nature: if you take someone for granted or treat them like they have less value than someone else, they'll go to extraordinary lengths to show you that you're wrong.
>
> It's not just rewards, it's how you are treated. If you recognize people's contribution and their value, and treat them as part of the team—that's the real secret to being a good place to work.

ATTRIBUTIONS BY LEADERS

Figure 12.1 provides an example of the attribution model of leadership. A leader observes poor quality and makes attributions about subordinates and situational factors. The course of action selected by the leader will differ substantially if the interpretation of the cause(s) of poor quality is based on the personal attributes of employees (low effort, low commitment, or lack of ability) versus situational factors (improper equipment, unreasonable deadlines, or poorly designed workflow).

As we explained in Chapter 3, the leader's attributions are influenced by how information is processed based on three dimensions of behavior:

- *Distinctiveness*—the degree to which the performance-related behaviors occurred on this task (issue) but not on others. That is, was the outcome for this particular task (issue) unusual?
- *Consistency*—the degree to which the performance-related behaviors are similar to other actions of the subordinate(s). Is the level of poor quality for this employee or team typical or something new?

Figure 12.1 **Application of Attribution Model of Leadership**

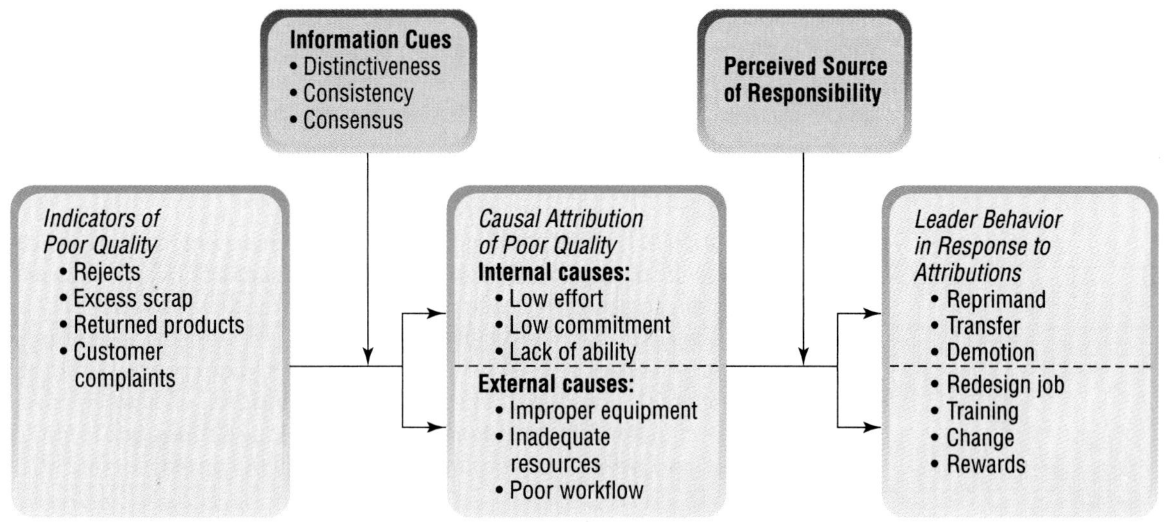

- *Consensus*—the degree to which other individuals or teams behave in similar ways in a like situation. Is this type of performance usual for other employees or teams?

The answers to these three questions identify for the leader either internal (personal) or external (situational) causes for employee performance. This distinction is crucial to good leader–employee relations.[3] An employee whose successes or failures are attributed to personal competencies is likely to have different interpersonal relations with the leader than an employee whose successes or failures are attributed to factors over which the employee has little, if any, control. Leaders should attempt to change the behavior of an employee or team only after attributing poor performance to an internal cause. Bethune and his fellow leaders at Continental focused on *external causes* as the main sources of poor service in undertaking the company's turnaround. He commented: "Employee satisfaction stems from feeling included, having the respect and dignity that you deserve, and management recognizing that, and appreciating you and letting you help formulate some of the strategies and the rules."[4]

Attributions by Employees

Employees may attribute causes of their performance to the leader, developing either positive or negative attitudes about their leader as a result. Thinking that their leader affects their performance can influence their perception of the leader's effectiveness. When employees succeed at a task, they tend to rate their leader as successful. When employees don't succeed, they are more likely to perceive their leader as ineffective. Their failure is attributed to the leader's actions, rather than to their own. (Recall our discussion of the self-serving bias in Chapter 3.) In sports, it is often the manager, not the players, who gets fired; in organizations, it's the CEO. The firing of the leader symbolizes top management's or the board of director's conviction that steps must be taken to improve effectiveness, and letting the leader go is a lot easier than letting a large number of players or employees go.[5]

Significance for Leaders

Leaders sometimes make internal attributions about poor subordinate performance that may lead to punitive actions. Subordinates, who often do not feel responsible for whatever problems exist, often resent such actions. Once the leader has attributed performance problems to subordinates, the leader is less likely to give them support, coaching, and resources. Moreover, when they make mistakes or have difficulty performing tasks, the leader is more likely to blame them rather than recognize situational causes or the leader's own contribution to the problems. Therefore leaders must learn to be careful, fair, and systematic about evaluating subordinates. They need to be aware of the many options available to them for dealing with different causes of performance problems and the importance of selecting an appropriate remedy.[6]

One of the greatest challenges to managers (and others) when they accept assignments to work abroad is to avoid making false or misleading attributions about the people they work with in that country. Recall that the managing across cultures competency involves the ability to recognize and embrace similarities and differences nation-to-nation and culture-to-culture and then approach key organizational and strategic issues with an open and curious mind. In the following Managing Across Cultures Competency feature, Peter Job, the CEO of Reuters, shares some of his views for reducing false or misleading attributions and stereotypes when conducting business in a foreign country. Headquartered in London, Reuters is a leading financial information and news organization with about 17,000 employees in 212 cities in 95 countries.

COMPETENCY: MANAGING ACROSS CULTURES

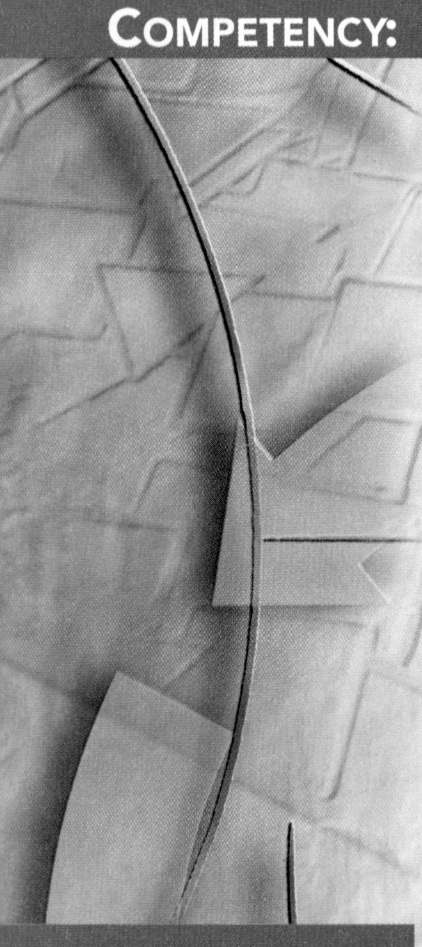

PETER JOB ON INTERNATIONAL MANAGERS

Everybody starts off thinking their own national culture is best, and therefore, as an international manager, you can never rest until you have discovered the positive characteristics of the new culture. Optimism is one of the major characteristics of a good international manager and this also includes optimism about the capabilities of others. It is extremely dangerous to underestimate the capability of others, but this is unfortunately what often happens in international business. I therefore see optimism as one of the major criteria of effective managers.

Other prime characteristics are curiosity and a celebration of "vive les differences." You need enthusiasm and interest in looking at the way things are done in an unfamiliar environment. There is a propensity for cultures to think badly of one another. This was certainly the case when Westerners tried to understand Japanese business. Because of differences in manners and business attitudes, Westerners thought negatively of Japanese managers and obviously did not understand them or make an attempt to understand them. If you threw away these bags of stereotypes and prejudices, the foreign managers would likely be seen as interesting and would explain their way of doing business and culture to you. For example, there was a common attitude among Westerners to not even attempt to learn the Japanese language because of potential mistakes one could make, thereby offending one's negotiation partners. This is a complete stereotype and does not correspond to reality. It is always advantageous to speak the foreign language—not necessarily to conduct the whole business negotiation in that language but to show an interest and respect to others.

The international manager is no longer seen as "God's gift to the world." There is also a demystification in terms of understanding other cultures. Today, there is less interest in manners and more in attitudes. Whereas it is important to comply with some basic manners in cross-cultural meetings, it is more important to have a positive attitude, trust and commitment to the business partner than to observe the rules of when to use "tu" or "vous" in France.[7]

*For more information on Reuters, visit this organization's home page at **www.reuters.com**.*

Learning Objective:

2. State the characteristics of and differences between the transactional and charismatic leadership models.

TRANSACTIONAL AND CHARISMATIC LEADERSHIP MODELS

Leadership is inherently future-oriented. It involves influencing people to move from where they are (here) to some new place (there). However, different leaders define or perceive *here* and *there* differently. For some, the journey between here and there is relatively routine, like driving a car on a familiar road. Others see the need to chart a new course through unexplored territory. Such leaders perceive fundamental differences between the way things are and the way things can or should be. They recognize the shortcomings of the present situation and offer a sense of passion and excitement to overcome them. In this section, we emphasize the characteristics and differences between two patterns of leadership in the workplace—transactional versus charismatic.

TRANSACTIONAL LEADERSHIP MODEL

Transactional leadership involves motivating and directing followers primarily through contingent reward–based exchanges. The transactional leader tends to focus on a carrot (but sometimes a stick) approach, set performance expectations and goals, and provide task-related feedback to followers.[8]

The three primary components of transactional leadership that are usually viewed as helping followers achieve their performance goals are:

- *Contingent rewards*—leader identifies a path that links the achievement of goals to rewards, clarifies expectations, exchanges promises and resources for support, arranges mutually satisfactory agreements, negotiates for resources, exchanges assistance for effort, and provides commendations for successful performance.
- *Active management by exception*—leader monitors followers' performance, takes corrective action if deviations from standards occur, and enforces rules to prevent mistakes.
- *Passive management by exception*—leader intervenes when problems become serious but may wait to take action until mistakes are brought to his or her attention.[9]

Transactional leadership is best viewed as insufficient, but not bad, in developing maximum leadership potential. One leadership expert makes the point that:

> Without the transactional base, expectations are often unclear, direction is ill-defined, and the goals you are working toward are too ambiguous. . . . Transactions clearly in place form the base for more mature interactions.[10]

The Managing Change Competency feature on the next page reflects how Robert Shapiro, the CEO of Monsanto, applies various transactional leadership behaviors. He has led Monsanto's transformation from a traditional chemical company to mainly a biotechnology company. Shapiro believes that the market will determine whether Monsanto is a pioneer of change or a company that went too far, too fast. His actions demonstrate one of the basics of the systems model of change—namely, *conceptualization.* Recall from Chapter 1 that this is the ability to identify key issues and diagnose them by examining the basic questions of *who, what, why, when, where,* and *how.* This feature draws on an extensive interview with Shapiro.

CHARISMATIC LEADERSHIP MODEL

Charismatic leadership involves motivating and directing followers primarily by developing their strong emotional commitment to a vision and set of shared values.[11]

COMPETENCY: MANAGING CHANGE

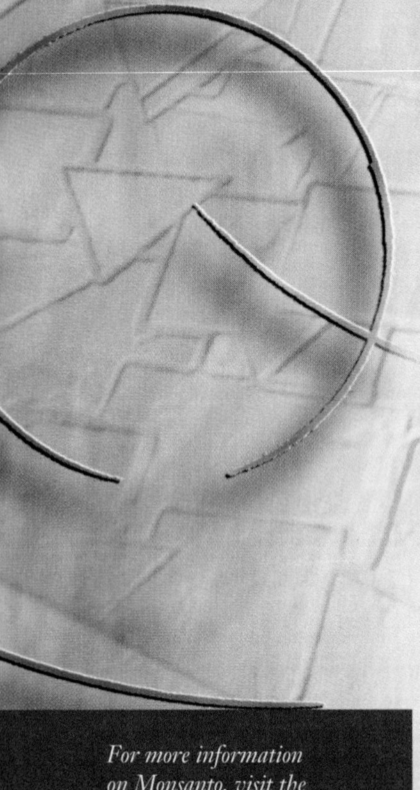

For more information on Monsanto, visit the company's home page at ***www.monsanto.com.***

ROBERT SHAPIRO'S LEADERSHIP OF MONSANTO

Large sectors of the economy are being dramatically affected by a major shift taking place as a result of technology. There aren't a lot of protected patches in markets anymore. You try to balance the benefits of changing early and massively and the risks associated with waiting. When do you make the definitive decision? When do you put the big bet on the table? Those are questions I'm always asking myself. There is no textbook answer. It isn't as though you're safe staying where you are. Even in biology, species that don't adapt risk extinction.

No CEO runs the business in a big company. We try to keep an eye on the people who do run the business and from time to time intervene. Leadership is not identical with hierarchy. Leadership is an individual choice that people take. You can ask people to follow orders. That's not an irrational system, and one that transformed the world in the Industrial Revolution. But it is not a system that most people find congenial or fun. If you want innovation, you're asking people to do things that you just can't command them to do and punish them if they don't. If you create an environment that people feel good about, the number of resisters will be smaller.

You can't get to good morale by lying. You can get to illusion that way. If I was faced with a decision that might hurt morale at a crucial time, I might delay the decision. In companies there is an exchange relationship. If you manipulate workers, they're going to manipulate you. The old Marxist class model was the people on top tried to manipulate the people on the bottom and the people on the bottom tried to manipulate the people on the top. You can't get innovation that way. You find an enormous amount of time and effort is dealing with the lack of trust of others. Look at all the inefficiencies of lack of trust. It tells you that an honest organization is going to be much more efficient. It just makes good business sense.[12]

Broad Concept. The broad concept of charismatic leadership suggests that it represents attributes such as the following:

- *Emphasizes shared vision and values*—leader focuses on creating mental image of a highly desirable future and shareholder values, linking these values to the organization's mission, goals, and expected behaviors.
- *Promotes shared identity*—leader focuses on creating common bonds among followers and shared sense of "who we are" and "what we stand for" as an organization.
- *Models desired behaviors*—leader displays personal commitment to the values, identity, and goals that he or she is promoting, engaging in self-sacrifice to show commitment to those values and goals.
- *Reflects strength*—leader displays and creates the impression of self-confidence, social and physical courage, determination, optimism, and innovation.[13]

Charismatic leaders obtain power through their followers' identification with them. Followers identify with and are inspired by charismatic leaders in the hope (and with the leaders' promises) that they will succeed. Charismatic leaders, such as Orit Gadiesh of Bain & Company, have the ability to distill complex ideas into simple messages, communicating with symbols, metaphors, and stories. They relish risk and emotionally put themselves on the line, working on followers' hearts as well as minds.[14]

Restricted Concept. Some leadership experts hold a more restricted concept of charismatic leadership. They contend that *charisma* exists only when the following five elements are present and operate in combination with each other:

- there is a person with extraordinary gifts and qualities,
- there is a social or organizational crisis or situation of desperation,
- there is a radical vision or set of ideas promising a solution to the crisis as proposed by the person (potential charismatic leader),
- there is a set of followers who are attracted to the gifted person (leader) and come to believe in the leader's exceptional powers and radical vision, and
- there is the realization (validation) of the person's (leader's) extraordinary gifts and the radical vision by repeated successes in dealing with the perceived crisis.[15]

This restricted concept of charismatic leadership has been summed up in this way:

> Charismatic leadership involves more than a set of extraordinary characteristics of a person—it involves a social process that is the product of the complex interactions of all of these elements. Especially important are the triggers provided by a perceived crisis and the radical vision promising a solution to the crisis. Without a crisis, the radical vision is unlikely to be attractive to followers. Without a radical vision, a person of exceptional qualities may be an inspirational or cultural leader who attracts people, but is unlikely to achieve the kinds of dramatic social change that charisma can produce. . . . Because of the highly emotional . . . basis of the followers' attraction to the leader and to the radical vision, charisma is inherently unstable. It must be transformed into institutional patterns in order to achieve permanence over time.[16]

Martin Luther King's leadership illustrates this concept of charisma. The crisis in civil rights, King's extraordinary personal characteristics, his ability to inspire commitment to a radical vision (at the time), followers who were attracted to him and his expressed vision, and a series of successes (breaking down the walls of segregation through nonviolent protest) all came together and resulted in a growing social movement. Recall the vision and values as dramatically expressed in Martin Luther King's "I Have a Dream" speech:

> I say to you today, my friends, that in spite of the difficulties and frustrations of the moment, I still have a dream . . . it is a dream deeply rooted in the American dream.
>
> I have a dream that one day this nation will rise up and live out the true meaning of its creed: "We hold these truths to be self-evident: that all men are created equal."
>
> When we let freedom ring, when we let it ring from every village and every hamlet, from every state and every city, we will be able to speed up that day when all of God's children, black men and white men, Jews and Gentiles, Protestants and Catholics, will be able to join hands and sing in the words of the old Negro spiritual, "Free at last! Free at last! Thank God Almighty, we are free at last!"[17]

The Managing Communication Competency feature on page 362 on Herb Kelleher, the CEO of Southwest Airlines, reflects several aspects of the broad concept of charismatic leadership. Although Southwest Airlines currently does not face a crisis and, accordingly, no radical vision or set of new ideas is being proposed, Kelleher's leadership can only be considered charismatic. The excerpts from interviews of Kelleher, who has served as CEO since 1978, reflect his strong communication competency and the importance he places on it for all employees. The communication skills emphasized include active listening, use of nonverbal communication, and empathy (detecting and understanding another person's values, motives, and emotions).

Significance for Leaders

Table 12.1 provides an overview of some of the contrasts between the transactional leadership and charismatic leadership models. These contrasts are presented in terms of seven dimensions, such as the primary sources of power used by the leader, the motivational basis for followers, and how performance goals are developed and framed for followers.

COMPETENCY: MANAGING COMMUNICATION

HERB KELLEHER OF SOUTHWEST AIRLINES

At a press conference following a Southwest Airlines annual meeting, Kelleher used his usual sense of humor when questions turned to succession. Asked about a shareholder complaint about "one-man rule," Kelleher joked: "Just the other day, I said to myself, 'Herb, as chairman, are you satisfied with the results of Southwest Airlines?' And the response I gave myself was, 'Well, Herb, as president, I think you ought to be complimented for the outstanding job you have done.' And then in my third capacity, I said, 'As CEO, Herb, I want you to know that both the president and chairman are proud of what you have accomplished.' "

In other interviews, he commented: "I've tried to create a culture of caring for people in the totality of their lives, not just at work. There's no magic formula. It's like building a giant mosaic—it takes thousands of little pieces. The intangibles are more important than the tangibles. Someone can go out and buy airplanes from Boeing and ticket counters, but they can't buy our culture, our esprit de corps. We want people with positive attitudes, who enjoy helping others.

"I give people license to be themselves and motivate others in that way. We give people the opportunity to be a maverick. You don't have to fit into a constraining mold at work—you can have a good time. People respond to that.

"We also try to show that what they do matters. That's why we share with employees the letters we get from passengers. We got one from a divorced dad who said that if it wasn't for our low fares, he wouldn't be able to visit his son as often as he does.

"One of the absolute keys to success these days is quickness. We've always had a flat structure so we could have a quick response capability. Take planning, for instance. We do it by scenario planning. Here are the five things that could happen. If No. 1 happens, we do this; if No. 2 happens, we do this; and so on. Then we go. Planning is necessary, but it can be done quickly. As you get larger, you have to get more systematized. But we fight bureaucracy and hierarchy all the time. People revile bureaucracy, because the process becomes the end.

"You have to recognize that people are still most important. How you treat them determines how they treat people on the outside. We have people going around the company all the time doing other people's jobs, but not for cross-utilization. We just want everybody to understand what everybody else's problems are."[18]

For more information on Southwest Airlines, visit the company's home page at www.southwest.com.

In practice, a person may incorporate components of both charismatic and transactional behaviors. Although Herb Kelleher is widely regarded as a charismatic leader, he also applies components of transactional leadership. For example, at Southwest, some financial rewards are tied to performance, commendations are given for successful follower performance, expectations are spelled out (e.g., having the right attitude and following safety regulations) and monitoring followers' performance (e.g., turning planes around according to schedule).

Learning Objective:

3. Explain the transformational leadership model.

TRANSFORMATIONAL LEADERSHIP MODEL

Transformational leadership involves anticipating future trends, inspiring followers to understand and embrace a new vision of possibilities, developing followers to be leaders or better leaders, and building the organization or group into a community of challenged and rewarded learners.[19] Transformational leadership may be found at all

Table 12.1 Contrasts between Transactional and Charismatic Leadership

DIMENSION	TRANSACTIONAL LEADERSHIP	CHARISMATIC LEADERSHIP
Primary sources of power	Reward, legitimate, expert	Referent and reward
Basis of follower motivation	Extrinsic/economic	Intrinsic/emotional
Performance goals for followers	Narrow, quantitative, specific to position	Broad, qualitative, specific to leader and vision
Emotional attachment to goals	Low	High
Expected followers' behaviors	Obey rules and regulations	Developed through norms and group pressures
Follower commitment to leader and vision	Low to moderate	High
Impression management tactics	Low use	High use

levels of the organization: teams, departments, divisions, and the organization as a whole.

As suggested in Figure 12.2, the transformational leadership model builds on and extends the features of the transactional, charismatic, and attribution models of leadership. For a leader this model clearly is the most comprehensive and challenging to implement. The following discussion of transformational leadership is based substantially on the work of Avolio and Bass.[20] The components of this model that primarily relate to followers include inspirational motivation, intellectual stimulation, idealized influence, and individualized consideration.

Figure 12.2 **Components of the Transformational Leadership Model**

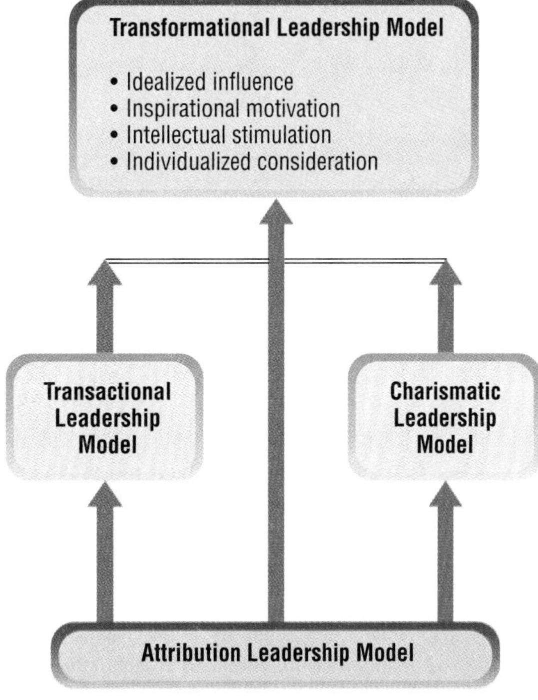

Inspirational Motivation

Inspirational motivation refers to the pattern of behaviors and communication that guide followers by providing them with a sense of meaning and challenge in their work. Transformational leaders display great enthusiasm and optimism, which carries over into the lives of followers and fosters a sense of team spirit. Such leaders get followers involved in, and eventually committed to, a vision of a new future state that may be significantly different from the present. Transformational leaders inspire others by what they say and do.

A **vision** is a view of a future desired state. Martin Luther King's vision was framed in his "I Have a Dream" speech in these words:

> I have a dream that one day this nation will rise up and live out the true meaning of its creed: "We hold these truths to be self-evident: that all men are created equal."

The framing and inspirational promotion of a consistent vision and set of values is the foundation of transformational leadership. One leadership expert sums it up this way:

> Transformational leaders are shapers of values, creators, interpreters of institutional purpose, exemplars, makers of meanings, pathfinders, and molders of organizational culture. They are persistent and consistent. Their vision is so compelling that they know what they want from every interaction. Their visions don't blind others, but empower them.[21]

Recall that the Preview Case presented Gordon Bethune's discussion of teams and leadership at Continental Airlines. Here is more of the story. When he joined Continental in 1994, it was on the verge of bankruptcy. Bethune and the other key executives engaged in transformational leadership. In 1994, the vision of Continental's key leaders was to become the lowest cost airline in the industry. After much discussion and in the midst of great gloom and despair among employees at all levels, a very simple transformation vision was formulated: "Go Forward." This elementary vision and theme was driven by the realization that the company's history was not going to be of help in avoiding bankruptcy. Nothing from the past could create inspiration for the future. The rallying cry of the turnaround was "Do it fast, do it right away, do it all at once."

Four cornerstones of change were encompassed in the "Go Forward" vision:

- *Fly to win*—change the markets served by emphasizing the Houston, Newark, and Cleveland hubs and change the customer mix by appealing to more business travelers.
- *Fund the future*—change the financing strategy to gain liquidity (cash) by selling nonstrategic assets and refinance the purchase of new planes.
- *Make reliability a reality*—change the customers' experiences regarding service, including better departure and arrival results relative to announced schedules.
- *Working together*—change the culture to one of fun and action while restoring employees' trust in higher management.

For 15 years, the way to get ahead at Continental was to torpedo someone and then get his or her job. As part of the company's transformation, in the span of several months, 50 of the 61 top managers were replaced with 20 individuals. Cutting the bureaucracy and costs facilitated the creation of the right culture. All new managers had to have three core qualities: They had to be bright; they had to be driven to get things done; and they had to be team players, willing to treat everyone with dignity, respect, and honesty so as to create a collaborative and fun work environment. When people were let go, the top leaders went out of their way to honor any contracts and let them resign with dignity. The transformational leadership of Bethune and his fellow executives was humane but not soft.[22]

Intellectual Stimulation

Intellectual stimulation is the encouragement given to followers to be innovative and creative. Transformational leaders urge followers to question assumptions, explore new ideas and methods, and approach old situations with new perspectives. In addition, such leaders actively seek out new ideas and creative solutions from followers. Followers' ideas are not criticized just because they may differ from those of the leader. Leaders have a relatively high tolerance for mistakes made by conscientious followers, who are not publicly criticized for those errors. Transformational leaders focus on the "what" in problems rather "who" to blame for them.

Under transformational leadership, followers feel free to encourage leaders to reevaluate their own perspectives and assumptions. Transformational leaders are willing to abandon systems and practices that are no longer useful even if they developed them in the first place. Nothing is too good, fixed, political, or bureaucratic that it can't be changed or discontinued. The prevailing view is that it is better to question ourselves than to leave all the questioning about us to our competitors. Transformational leaders view risk taking as necessary and desirable for the long-term development and success of the organization.

The following Managing Self Competency feature reflects how Alan Naumann, president and CEO of Calico Technologies, headquartered in San Jose, California, sees the importance of continuous learning and assessing your own strengths and limitations. Naumann emphasizes the importance of appraising and interpreting the immediate work environment.

Competency: Managing Self

Alan Naumann of Calico Technologies

There is no getting around it: we have to make decisions faster because our customers are making decisions faster, and the industry is changing faster than ever before. That means that, as an organization, we have to work with less top-down control. The only way to do that, without falling to pieces, is to build a company that's made up 100 percent of leaders. My number-one priority is to give everybody in the organization the tools and the confidence to make decisions faster.

We've created a three-day course—"Eight Calico Leadership Practices"—that everyone takes. These eight practices are behavioral principles that we integrate into performance reviews and use as a common vocabulary throughout the company. We've also instituted a lot of tactical mechanisms to make better decisions faster. For example, if anyone in the company has waited more than a week for an important decision to be made, that person has an open invitation to come find me, and I'll make the decision—on the spot. It turns out that I rarely have to "unstick" a situation, because people all over the organization have adopted this policy within their teams.

Despite all of our focus on speed, we consciously slow down for one thing: hiring people. That's tough to do when you're growing as fast as we are, but it's the one aspect of business today in which the cost of mistakes is greater than the advantage of acting in real time. Within the hiring process, we do spend a good deal of time defining a job's requirements and checking an applicant's references. That way, we can build a better partnership when an employee does come on board.[23]

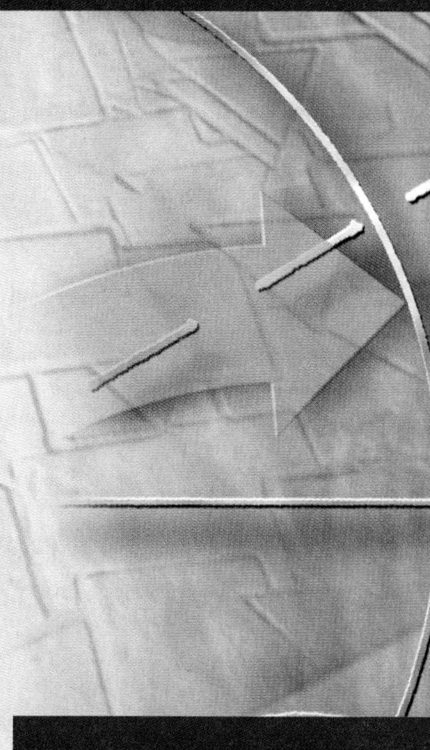

For more information on Calico Technologies, visit the company's home page at www.calicotech.com.

Idealized Influence

Idealized influence refers to the behaviors of transformational leaders that followers strive to emulate or mirror. Followers typically admire, respect, and trust such leaders. They identify with these leaders as people, as well as the vision and values that they are advocating. With positive idealized influence, followers feel free to question what is being advocated.

The goals of followers are often personally meaningful and consistent with their own self-concepts. They willingly give extra effort because of the intrinsic rewards obtained from performing well, not just because of the potential for receiving greater extrinsic rewards. Immediate short-term goals are viewed as a means to the followers' commitments to a greater vision.

To further earn such *idealized influence*, transformational leaders often consider the needs and interests of followers over their own needs. They may willingly sacrifice personal gain for the sake of others. Such leaders can be trusted and demonstrate high standards of ethical and moral conduct. Followers come to see these leaders as operating according to a pattern of principled leadership. Thus they can be very direct and challenging to some followers (e.g., poor performers) and highly empathetic and supportive of others (e.g., those with a seriously ill family member).

Although transformational leaders minimize the use of power for personal gain, they will use all of the sources of power—expert, legitimate, reward, referent, and coercive—at their disposal to move individuals and teams toward a vision and its related goals. As an example of referent power, followers often describe transformational leaders as individuals who have had a major impact on their own personal and professional development.

The Managing Teams Competency feature on page 367 reports on the team leadership of Laurie Tucker, senior vice president of electronic commerce and customer service at FedEx. It focuses on Tucker's ability to develop and lead teams to achieve major transformations at FedEx and clearly demonstrates her sense of mutual and personal accountability for the achievement of team goals. (See the Managing Communication Competency feature in Chapter 8 for a discussion of the use of electronic brainstorming at FedEx.)

Individualized Consideration

Individualized consideration is the special attention paid by a transformational leader to each follower's needs for achievement and growth. Transformational leaders may act as coach, mentor, teacher, facilitator, confidant, and counselor. Followers and colleagues are encouraged to develop to successively higher levels of their potential. Individual differences are embraced and rewarded to enhance creativity and innovation. An open dialogue with followers is encouraged and "management by continuous engagement" is standard practice. Listening skills are sharp and reflect this observation: It's not what you tell them, it's what they hear.

Transformational leaders empower followers to make decisions. At the same time, they monitor followers to determine whether they need additional support or direction and to assess progress. With trust in leaders' intentions, followers think: This person is trying to help me by noting mistakes, as opposed to pointing a finger at me in some accusatory way.

Kierstin Higgins is the founder of Accommodations by Apple, a small business in Lenexa, Kansas, that specializes in corporate relocations to the Kansas City area. She is a firm believer in individual consideration and applies it in working with the firm's customers and employees. Higgins says that, for example, when a client explodes in anger over a perceived shortcoming in the firm's services, "we try to round-table everybody together and discuss what happened to understand why the client reacted that way. The services we provide are very personal for our customers—ranging from airport pickups to the transfer of medical records. The focus on family issues for our

COMPETENCY: MANAGING TEAMS

LAURIE TUCKER OF FEDEX

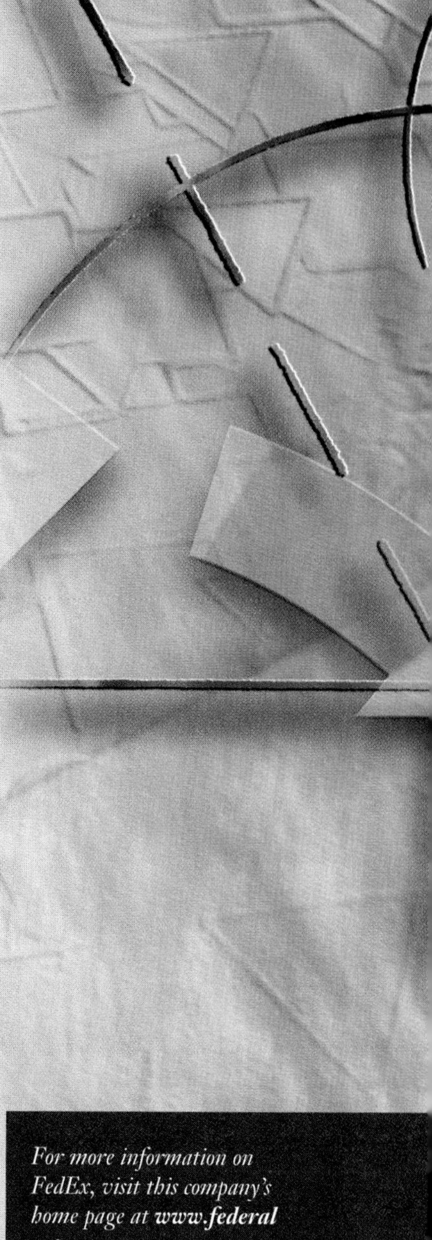

Making sense of radical change and strategic missteps is an unavoidable part of Laurie Tucker's job. "What Laurie demands of us is that we make an educated guess," says Dottie Berry, a FedEx vice president who has worked with Tucker for 20 of Tucker's 21 years at the company. "Nine times out of 10, you're wrong—but how are you supposed to find the one approach that's exactly right? The worst thing you can do, in her world, is not do anything. The thing about Laurie is that she is very genuine, very sincere, and very approachable. No one hesitates to talk to her—to tell her both good news and bad."

Tucker wrestles with two of the defining agenda items for every company these days: how to design a compelling customer experience and how to embrace the transforming power of the Web. She (along with the seven vice presidents and 6,000 employees in the units that she leads) is responsible for the FedEx customer experience on the Web, on the phone, and at the company's 1,400 World Service Centers. Tucker is responsible for challenging the status quo at FedEx. "It's my role to offer challenges to the existing way of doing business," she says. "This group is the future of the company."

Dennis Jones, executive vice president and chief information officer at FDX Corporation, FedEx's parent company comments: "Our paths first crossed about 20 years ago, in the finance department. Laurie has such charisma and enthusiasm—and incredible adaptability. She leads people to a conclusion that wouldn't be a natural path for them. She's able to get people to march in the same direction."

In the face of the changing technology landscape in 1994, Tucker organized a weekend meeting for her subordinates at her home. Her intention was to foster free-form thinking about new ways that FedEx might interact digitally with its customers. That first off-site meeting, says Berry, who was in attendance, "was the first time that we challenged ourselves to think strategically—to think beyond the next 90 days. It really broke through some cobwebs." One outcome of that first "learning journey," as Tucker refers to it, was that her team decided "that we had to shift to solutions that our customers could run on their own hardware or within their own systems." Tucker and Berry assembled a team of 100 employees to create a new version of the system that would run on any Windows or Macintosh computer. "She headed it, and listened every week," Berry remembers.

Tucker and her team of vice presidents still hold regular learning journeys, and the practice has begun to spread through the rest of the company. "This company has always listened to the customer," Tucker says. "Now it's about anticipating the customer. There's no time for incremental improvement."[24]

*For more information on FedEx, visit this company's home page at **www.federalexpress.com**.*

customers creates intense demands on our employees." Higgins states that, when problems occur, "It's important to shore up our employees. They are very young and energetic, but they're also very emotional, with major ups and major downs. Trying to help them learn from the challenges they've experienced, as opposed to getting burned out," is, she believes, the essence of being a good leader in her company.[25]

SIGNIFICANCE FOR LEADERS

Faced with increasing turbulence in their environments, organizations need transformational leadership more than ever—and at all levels, not just at the top. The need for leaders of vision, confidence, and determination, whether they are leading a small team or an entire organization, is increasing rapidly. Such leaders are needed to motivate others to assert themselves, to join enthusiastically in team efforts, and to have positive feelings about what they are doing. Top managers must come to understand, appreciate, and support as never before employees who are willing to make unpopular decisions, who know when to reject traditional ways of doing something, and who can accept reasonable risks. A "right to fail" must be nurtured and be an integral part of an organization's culture.

Transformational leadership fosters synergy. **Synergy** occurs when people together create new alternatives and solutions that are better than their individual efforts. The greatest chance for achieving synergy is when people don't see things the same way; that is, differences present opportunities. Relationships don't break down because of differences but because people fail to grasp the value of their differences and how to take advantage of them. Synergy is created by people who have learned to think win–win, and listen in order to understand the other person.[26] One of the messages of Martin Luther King's "I Have a Dream" speech was that of synergy. He challenged people to confront their differences and to learn from them. Stereotyping keeps people from appreciating and building on their differences because they limit listening for understanding.

Learning Objective:

4. Evaluate the limits of a leader's influence.

DO LEADERS MATTER?

The underlying assumption of all the models presented in Chapter 11 and this chapter is that leaders *can* and *do* make a difference. Although some of the models contain different conclusions about leadership style (e.g., use a consideration or an initiating structure or use an autocratic or a consultative approach), all are based on the assumption that leaders make a difference in their organizations. Some experts have questioned this assumption, believing that the varying nature of a situation or type of followers casts some doubt on the relative importance of leaders in organizations. They suggest that leaders sometimes have little impact on the attitudes and behaviors of their followers. In certain situations, no matter what a leader does, employees are satisfied or dissatisfied with their jobs, attain or fail to reach their goals, and perform well or poorly without a leader exerting much influence. The evidence for these assertions isn't conclusive, but they warrant your attention. As outlined in Table 12.2, these claims can be classified as (1) leader irrelevance and (2) substitutes for leadership.

Irrelevance of Leaders

One claim is that leaders are irrelevant for some organizational outcomes.[27] This view stresses a situation-based approach to understanding leadership, emphasizing

Table 12.2 Possible Limits on a Leader's Influence

LEADER IRRELEVANCE	SAMPLE LEADER SUBSTITUTES
• Key factors may be beyond leaders' control	• Group/team norms and cohesiveness
• Leaders have little control of needed resources	• Formal rewards beyond leaders' control
• Selection process limits leaders' individuality	• Organizational rules and regulations

that situations are more important determinants of organizational and follower effectiveness than leaders' behaviors. This perspective stresses three points.

First, *factors outside the leader's immediate control* affect profits and other factors of success more than anything a leader might do. Consider the situation facing Lockheed Martin, the largest defense contractor in the United States, several years ago. This giant corporation had been formed by the merger of Martin Marietta, Lockheed Corporation, and Loral Vought, and much of its revenues came from U.S. defense contracts. When the federal government announced that it was cutting defense contracts, Vance Coffman, CEO, found that he had to slash millions of dollars from the company's budget to keep the company operating. Second, *leaders may not unilaterally control the resources needed* to influence others. A leader's power to reward or punish people may be constrained by organizational policies, politics, and/or the power of external stakeholders. Lockheed Martin's shareholders and creditors exerted strong pressures on Coffman and the board to divest noncore businesses to raise cash and improve the firm's financial position.[28]

Third, *the selection process* through which the leaders pass may socialize them in such a way that they tend to act similarly. Therefore the impact of a leader on the organization may be reduced. For example, in presidential election campaigns, it is virtually impossible for some leaders—extremists of the right or left—to be elected. Candidates who eventually win elections are more alike than different.[29] Therefore selection processes generally reduce the impact of any change in high-level leadership. In some organizations, such as J.C. Penney, Allstate Insurance, and Alcoa, leaders tend to be longtime employees who have paid their dues while climbing the organizational ladder. In doing so, they have followed proven career paths that their predecessors used.

Substitutes for Leaders

A **leadership substitute** is something that acts in place of a formal leader and makes leadership unnecessary or less important.[30] According to this view, the success of a particular leader depends on the characteristics of the followers, team, situation, and/or organization. Each can act as a substitute for a particular leader behavior. Consider the case of Robert Kennedy, an ophthalmologist at the University of Texas Southwestern Medical Center. The tasks that his staff perform are intrinsically challenging and meaningful. Hence the leadership substitutes view suggests that leader consideration (see Chapter 11) would have little impact on his followers because the tasks that they are performing give them considerable intrinsic motivation and job satisfaction. Therefore Kennedy has little need generally to engage in considerate behaviors to influence his followers. The model further suggests, though, that Kennedy should direct his considerate behavior toward followers who perform routine tasks that provide little job challenge and satisfaction. In essence, substitutes can free up a leader's time to concentrate on other activities that need attention.

The research on leadership substitutes provides some support for this view.[31] Leadership substitutes, such as employee maturity, organizational rules, governmental regulations, group norms and cohesiveness, team performance, design of jobs, and professional recognition, affect subordinates' behaviors. Of course, leaders' actions still influence the substitutes through employee selection, task design, team assignments, and the design of reward systems. Part of being an effective leader is knowing when to use substitutes—indirect and more subtle means—to influence others. For example, a charismatic leader who is in charge of a highly effective team may need to provide less active leadership than a transactional leader in the same situation. Leadership substitutes may be important in some instances but do not eliminate the role of the leader. Still, we believe that leaders typically make a difference—or can make a difference—and a major difference in organizations.

CHAPTER SUMMARY

In this chapter we built on Chapter 11 by presenting several more complex and contemporary leadership developments.

1. Describe how a leader's attributions affect his or her leadership behaviors.

The attribution leadership model suggests that a leader's judgment about followers is influenced by the leader's interpretation of the causes of the employees' behaviors. These causes may either be external or internal. Effective leaders correctly identify the cause and then act accordingly. Attributions, in addition to actual followers' behaviors, influence how the leader responds to the followers' performance. These attributions are affected by three dimensions of behavior: distinctiveness, consistency, and consensus.

2. State the characteristics of and differences between the transactional and charismatic leadership models.

Transactional leadership involves influencing followers primarily through contingent reward–based exchanges. Leaders attempt to identify clear goals for followers, the specific paths for achieving the goals, and the rewards that will be forthcoming for achieving them. A follower's performance is monitored and corrective actions are taken if the subordinate strays from the expected path. The emphasis is on exchanging units of work for units of rewards (salary, bonuses, size of office, etc.). In contrast, charismatic leadership involves influencing followers primarily through developing their emotional commitment to a vision and set of shared values. The leader relies on referent and reward power in contrast to the transactional leader's reliance on reward, legitimate, and expert sources of power. There are two concepts of charismatic leadership: broad and restricted. The restricted concept suggests that charismatic leadership can occur only when there is a crisis, the leader proposes a radical vision or set of ideas, and the followers are emotionally attracted to the vision and leader.

3. Explain the transformational leadership model.

Transformational leadership involves influencing followers through a complex and interrelated set of behaviors and abilities. Some of these include: anticipating the future, inspiring relevant stakeholders (especially followers) to embrace a new vision or set of ideas, developing followers to be leaders or better leaders, and guiding the organization or group into a community of challenged and rewarded learners. This model extends and incorporates features of the attribution, transactional, and charismatic models of leadership. The components of transformational leadership that primarily relate to followers include inspirational motivation, intellectual stimulation, idealized influence, and individualized consideration. Transformational leaders are both challenging and empathetic—and are people of integrity.

4. Evaluate the limits of a leader's influence.

The question, Does leadership matter? focuses attention on situations in which leaders are constrained and their behaviors may have minimal impact on their followers. The issue of leader irrelevance relates to the characteristics of situations that make it difficult for the leader to influence followers effectively. Examples of leadership substitutes include rules and regulations and group or team peer pressure. Our position is clear: Leaders typically make a significant difference.

KEY TERMS AND CONCEPTS

Attribution model of leadership
Charismatic leadership
Idealized influence
Individualized consideration
Inspirational motivation
Intellectual stimulation
Leadership substitute
Synergy
Transactional leadership
Transformational leadership
Vision

DISCUSSION QUESTIONS

1. In the Preview Case, Gordon Bethune, CEO of Continental Airlines stated, "It's like basic human nature: if you take someone for granted or treat them like they have less value than someone else, they'll go to extraordinary lengths to show you that you're wrong." Think of a bad manager you may have worked for. Did that manager's subordinates reflect these attitudes? If so, in what ways?
2. As a follower, identify three of the attributions that you made about the last manager you worked for (or your current manager). Why did you make those attributions?
3. Assume that you are assigned temporarily (6 months) to a job in a large manufacturing facility that your company operates in Mexico. You will be working for a Mexican manager. What attributions about that manager come to mind before you leave on this assignment?
4. In what three ways did a manager you have worked for (preferably a different person than the manager you referred to in Question 2) follow the transactional leadership model?
5. Based on the manager identified in Question 4, in what ways did that person exhibit one or more characteristics of the charismatic leadership model? If none, explain your conclusion.
6. Think of a person that you know who exhibits or comes closest to exhibiting the broad concept of charismatic leadership. Describe three behaviors of this person that are consistent with being a charismatic leader.
7. Review the Managing Change Competency feature concerning Robert Shapiro's leadership. Identify three statements in the feature that appear to reflect transactional leadership.
8. Review the Managing Communication Competency feature about Herb Kelleher's leadership. Identify three statements in the feature that appear to reflect charismatic leadership.
9. What are the three competencies that you need to develop most in order to become a transformational leader?
10. Review the Managing Teams Competency feature describing Laurie Tucker. Identify three statements in the feature that reflect her transformational leadership.
11. Based on your work experiences to date, how would you answer the question, Does leadership matter? Explain.

DEVELOPING COMPETENCIES

Competency: Managing Self—Transformational Leadership[32]

Instructions: The following statements refer to the possible ways in which you might prefer to behave toward others when you are in a leadership role. Please read each statement carefully and decide to what extent it applies to your preferred or actual behaviors. Then circle the appropriate number.

To a Very Great Extent	5
To a Considerable Extent	4
To a Moderate Extent	3
To a Slight Extent	2
To Little or No Extent	1

Your preference is to . . .

1.	pay close attention to what others say when they are talking.	5	4	3	2	1
2.	communicate clearly.	5	4	3	2	1
3.	be trustworthy.	5	4	3	2	1
4.	care about other people.	5	4	3	2	1
5.	not put excessive energy into avoiding failure.	5	4	3	2	1
6.	make the work of others more meaningful.	5	4	3	2	1
7.	seem to focus on the key issues in a situation.	5	4	3	2	1
8.	get across your meaning effectively, often in unusual ways.	5	4	3	2	1
9.	be relied on to follow through on commitments.	5	4	3	2	1
10.	have a great deal of self-respect.	5	4	3	2	1
11.	enjoy taking carefully calculated risks.	5	4	3	2	1
12.	help others feel more competent in what they do.	5	4	3	2	1
13.	have a clear set of priorities.	5	4	3	2	1
14.	keep in touch with how others feel.	5	4	3	2	1
15.	rarely change once you have taken a clear position.	5	4	3	2	1
16.	focus on strengths, of yourself and of others.	5	4	3	2	1
17.	seem most alive when deeply involved in some project.	5	4	3	2	1
18.	show others that they are all part of the same group.	5	4	3	2	1
19.	get others to focus on the issues you see as important.	5	4	3	2	1
20.	communicate feelings as well as ideas.	5	4	3	2	1
21.	let others know where you stand.	5	4	3	2	1
22.	know just how you "fit" into a group.	5	4	3	2	1
23.	learn from mistakes, do not treat errors as disasters, but as learning.	5	4	3	2	1
24.	be fun to be around.	5	4	3	2	1

Interpretation

The survey measures your preferences on each of six basic leader behavior patterns, as well as a set of emotional responses, usually associated with transformational leaders. Your score can range from 4 to 20 on each leader behavior pattern. Each statement reflects the extent to which you prefer or actually engage in a particular behavior. The higher your score, the more you prefer or actually demonstrate transformational leader behaviors. Scores of 16 to 20 on a behavioral pattern are consistent with transformational leadership on that dimension.

Management of Attention (Add numbers for items 1, 7, 13, 19.) Your score ____

This dimension focuses on paying attention to people with whom you are communicating. You prefer to "focus in" on the key issues under discussion and help others to see clearly these key points. You have clear ideas about the relative importance or priorities of different issues under discussion.

Management of Meaning (Add numbers for items 2, 8, 14, 20.) Your score ____

This dimension centers on your communication competencies, specifically your ability to get the meaning of a message across, even if this means devising some quite innovative approach.

Management of Trust (Add numbers for items 3, 9, 15, 21.) Your score ____

This dimension focuses on your perceived trustworthiness as shown by your willingness to follow through on promises, avoidance of "flip-flop" shifts in position, and preference to take clear positions.

Management of Self (Add numbers for items 4, 10, 16, 22.) Your score ____

This dimension concerns your general attitudes toward yourself and others; that is, your overall concern for others and their feelings, as well as for "taking care of" feelings about yourself in a positive sense (e.g., self-regard).

Management of Risk (Add numbers for items 5, 11, 17, 23.) Your score ____

This dimension focuses on effective transformational leaders being deeply involved in what they do. They do not spend excessive amounts of time or energy on plans to "protect" themselves against failure or blame. These leaders are willing to take risks, not on a hit-or-miss basis, but after careful assessment of the odds of success or failure.

Management of Feelings (Add numbers for items 6, 12, 18, 24.) Your score ____

Transformational leaders seem to consistently generate a set of feelings in others. Others feel that their work becomes more meaningful and that they are the "masters" of their own behavior; that is, they feel competent. They feel a sense of community, a "we-ness" with their colleagues and coworkers.

Competency: Managing Communication—Managing for the Future[33]

Instructions: After reviewing the following list of behaviors and activities, check those items that you believe best describe what "managers of the future" need to do with their time. Don't overthink your responses; your initial reactions most accurately reflect your perceptions.

____ 1. Managers spend as much as 75 percent of their time being involved with other people.
____ 2. Managers go around the formal chain of command.
____ 3. Managers focus on building networks.
____ 4. Managers discuss anything and everything associated with their organization.
____ 5. Managers ask a lot of questions.
____ 6. Managers rarely make big decisions.
____ 7. Managers focus on developing agendas (goals, objectives, etc.).
____ 8. Managers joke, kid around, use humor, and talk about nonwork activities.
____ 9. Managers "waste" time discussing issues that appear to be nonsubstantive.
____ 10. Managers seldom tell people what to do.
____ 11. Managers frequently attempt to influence others.
____ 12. Managers frequently respond to others' initiatives.
____ 13. Managers focus on executing their agendas.
____ 14. Managers invest significant amounts of time in short and disjointed discussions.
____ 15. Managers work long hours (e.g., 60 hours per week).
____ 16. Managers rely on conversations with others for information, not on books, magazines, or reports.
____ 17. Managers realize that the size of their networks largely determines their degree of success.
____ 18. Managers seek out cooperative relationships with people who will have to help implement their agendas.
____ 19. Managers seek to maximize teamwork and minimize politics.
____ 20. Managers' network members are chosen for their ability to help accomplish the managers' agendas.

Interpretation

Give yourself five points for each item that you checked.

Your total score is _____.

90–100 = You have a strong grasp of the behaviors that characterize an effective manager in the future. Your main tasks for the future include patiently helping your organization and your colleagues learn more about these behaviors, being sure to model and reward these new behaviors and systematically coaching everyone around you to begin implementing appropriate leadership models.

80–89 = You have a moderately good understanding of what it takes to be an effective manager in the future. Your main tasks for the future include strengthening your familiarity with the behaviors, experimenting with the behaviors in low-to-moderate-risk situations, rewarding yourself when you are successful in using the behaviors, establishing goals for yourself that focus on increasing the frequency with which you use the behaviors, and letting others know about your efforts.

70–79 = You are aware of the management behaviors needed for the future but do not find them compelling, or you may work in a setting in which you cannot presently use the behaviors. Your main tasks for the future include continuing to learn about these new management behaviors, finding someone with whom you can talk about them, and identifying settings in which you can try out selected behaviors.

60–69 = You have a below-average understanding of what it takes to be a successful manager in the future. Your main tasks for the future include looking around to see what your organization's top competitors or peer organizations are doing as they prepare to meet the challenges ahead. You also should consider the long-term needs of your organization. How will your employer become steadily more competitive while utilizing fewer resources and responding to growing customer demands for higher levels of product and service quality? Armed with responses to questions such as these, you are then ready to examine the degree to which your current leadership or management style will help you and your employer to be successful in the future.

0–59 = You have little or no awareness of the management practices needed for the future. For a variety of reasons, you also may have little or no interest in altering that situation. Your main tasks for the future include taking time to reflect on where you want your career to lead, your effectiveness in working with other people, how you feel about yourself as a leader/manager, and how other people with whom you work seem to react to your present style of leadership.

REFERENCES

1. Adapted from Puffer, S. M. Continental Airlines' CEO Gordon Bethune on teams and new product development. *Academy of Management Executive,* August 1999, 29–35.
2. Gooding, R. Z., and Kinicki, A. J. Interpreting event causes: The complementary role of categorization and attribution process. *Journal of Management Studies,* 1995, 32, 1–23; Ashkanasy, N. M., and Gallois, C. Leader attributions and evaluations: Effects of locus of control, supervisory control, and task control. *Organizational Behavior & Human Decision Processes,* 1994, 59, 24–51; Daft, R. L. *Leadership: Theory and Practice.* Orlando: Harcourt Brace, 1999.
3. Vaill, P. B. *Spirited Leading and Learning: Process Wisdom for a New Age.* San Francisco: Jossey-Bass, 1998; Ashkanasy, N. M. Across-national comparison of Australian and Canadian supervisors' attributional and evaluative responses to subordinate responses. *Australian Psychologist,* March 1997, 29–36.
4. Puffer, 29–35.
5. Charin, R., and Colvin, G. Why CEOs fail. *Fortune,* June 21, 1999, 69–78.
6. Lucas, J. R. *Balance of Power: Authority or Empowerment.* New York: AMACOM, 1998.
7. Adapted from Mark, E. *Breaking Through Culture Shock: What You Need to Succeed in Business.* London: Nicholas Brealey, 1999, 162–170.
8. Jung, D. I,. and Avolio, B. J. Effects of leadership style and followers' cultural orientation on performance in group and individual task conditions. *Academy of Management Journal,* 1999, 42, 208–218.
9. Bass, B. M. Does the transactional–transformational leadership paradigm transcend organizational and national boundaries? *American Psychologist,* 1997, 52, 130–139.
10. Avolio, B. J. *Full Leadership Development: Building the Vital Forces in Organizations.* Thousand Oaks, Calif.: Sage, 1999, 15.
11. Conger, J. A., and Kanungo, R. N. *Charismatic Leadership in Organizations.* Thousand Oaks, Calif.: Sage, 1998; Waldman, D. A., and Yammarino, F. J. CEO charismatic leadership: Levels-of-management and levels-of-analysis effects. *Academy of Management Review,* 1999, 24, 266–285; Mitroff, I. I., and Denton, E. A. A study of spirituality in the workplace. *Sloan Management Review,* Summer 1999, 83–92.
12. Adapted from Jones, D. Driving change—Too fast?: Monsanto CEO talks about risk. *USA Today,* August 11, 1999, 6B.
13. Shamir, B., Zakay, E., Brenin, E., and Popper, M. Correlates of charismatic leader behavior in military units: Subordinates' attitudes, unit characteristics, and superiors' appraisals of leader performance. *Academy of Management Journal,* 1998, 41, 387–409; Gardner, W. L., and Avolio, B. J. The charismatic relationship: A dramaturgical perspective. *Academy of Management Review,* 1998, 23, 14–31; DuBrin, A. J. *Personal Magnetism: Discovering Your Own Charisma and Learn to Charm, Inspire, and Influence Others.* New York: AMACOM, 1997.
14. Sosik, J. J., and Dworakivsky, A. C. Self-concept based aspects of the charismatic leader—More than meets the eye. *Leadership Quarterly,* 1998, 9, 502–526; Conger, J. A.

Charismatic and transformational leadership in organizations: An insider's perspective on these developing streams of research. In J. A. Conger and J. G. Hunt (eds.), *Leadership Quarterly*, Special Issue: Part 1, 1999, 10, 145–180; Klein, K. J., and House, R. J. On fire: Charismatic leadership and levels of analysis. In F. Dansereau and F. J. Yammarino (eds.), *Leadership: The Multiple-Level Approaches.* Stamford, Conn.: JAI Press, 1998, 3–52.

15. Trice, H. M., and Beyer, J. M. Charisma and its routinization in two social movement organizations. In B. M. Staw and L. L. Cummings (eds.), *Research in Organizational Behavior*, 1986, 8, 113–164; also see Beyer, J. M. Taming and promoting charisma to change organizations. In J. A. Conger and J. G. Hunt (eds.), *Leadership Quarterly*, Special Issue: Part 1, 1999, 10, 307–330; Nur, Y. A. Charisma and managerial leadership: The gift that never was. *Business Horizons*, July–August 1998, 19–26; Steyrer, J. Charisma and the archetypes of leadership. *Organization Studies*, 1998, 19, 807–828.
16. Beyer, J. M., and Browning, L. D. Transforming an industry in crisis: Charisma, routinization, and supportive cultural leadership. Working paper, 2000, 8.
17. Washington, J. M. and King, M. L. Jr., (eds.). *A Testament of Hope: The Essential Speeches and Writings of Martin Luther King, Jr.* San Francisco: Harper, 1990; also see Daft, R. L., and Lengel, R. H. *Fusion Leadership: Unlocking the Subtle Forces That Change People & Organizations.* San Francisco: Berrett-Kohler, 1998.
18. Adapted from Lancaster, H. Herb Kelleher has one main strategy: Treat employees well. *Wall Street Journal*, August 31, 1999, B1; Zellner, W. Earth to Herb: Pick a co-pilot. *Business Week*, August 16, 1999, 70–71; Zellner, W. Southwest's new direction. *Business Week*, February 8, 1999, 58–59.
19. Anderson, T. D. *Transforming Leadership: Equipping Yourself and Challenging Others to Build the Leadership Organization*, 2nd ed. Boca Raton, Fla.: CRC Press, 1998; Kotter, J. P. *On What Leaders Really Do.* Boston: Harvard Business Review Book, 1999.
20. This section draws from Avolio, *Full Leadership Development*, 43–49; Bass, B. M. *Transformational Leadership: Industry, Military, and Educational Impact.* Mahwah, N.J.: Lawrence Erlbaum, 1998; Ackoff, R. L. Transformational Leadership. *Strategy & Leadership*, January–February 1999, 27, 20–26; Hinkin, T. R., and Tracey, J. B. The relevance of charisma for transformational leadership in stable organizations. *Journal of Organizational Change Management*, 1999, 12, 105–119; Sosik, J. J., Kahai, S. S., and Avolio, B. J. Transformational leadership and dimensions of creativity—Motivating idea generation in computer-mediated groups. *Creativity Research Journal*, 1998, 11, 111–121.
21. Egan, G. *Change Agent Skills.* Monterey, Calif.: Brooks/Cole, 1985, 204; also see Huseman, R. C., and Goodman, J. P. *Leading with Knowledge: The Nature of Competition in the 21st Century.* Thousand, Oaks, Calif.: Sage, 1999.
22. Adapted from Brenneman, G. Right away and all at once: How we saved Continental. *Harvard Business Review*, September–October 1999, 162–179; Kurtzman, J. Paying attention to what really counts: An exclusive conversation with Gordon Bethune. *Heidrick & Struggles Leadership Journal*, January 1998, 1–2.
23. Adapted from Labare, P. (ed.). Leaders.com. *Fast Company*, June 1999, 95–112.
24. Adapted from Kirsner, S. Laurie Tucker. *Fast Company*, December 1999, 166–172; also see Buckingham, M., and Coffman, C. *First, Break All the Rules: What the World's Greatest Managers Do Differently.* New York: Simon & Schuster, 1999.
25. Adapted from Barrier, M. Leadership skills employees respect. *Nation's Business*, January 1999, 28–30.
26. Covey, S. R. *The 7 Habits of Highly Effective People.* New York: Simon and Schuster, 1989; also see Ulrich, D., Zenger, J., and Smallwood, N. *Results-Based Leadership.* Boston: Harvard Business School Press, 1999; Black, J. S., Morrison, A. J., and Gregerson, H. B. *Global Explorers: The Next Generation of Leaders.* New York: Routledge, 1999.
27. Pfeffer, J. Why do smart organizations occasionally do dumb things? *Organizational Dynamics*, Summer 1996, 33–44; Pfeffer, J. The ambiguity of leadership. *Academy of Management Review*, 1977, 2, 100–112.
28. Zunitch, V. M. Lockheed Martin now concentrates on slashing debt. *Wall Street Journal*, April 26, 1996, A7; Wanted: Miracle worker. *Economist*, November 20, 1999, 77.
29. Barone, M. Great men need not apply: We are living in a time of lesser dangers and lesser leaders. *U.S. News & World Report*, February 19, 1996, 40–41.
30. Kerr, S., and Jermier, J. M. Substitutes for leadership: Their meaning and measurement. *Organizational Behavior and Human Performance*, 1978, 22, 374–403.
31. Podsakoff, P. M., MacKenzie, S. B., and Bommer, W. H. Meta-analysis of the relationships between Kerr and Jermier's substitutes for leadership and employee job attitudes, role perceptions, and performance. *Journal of Applied Psychology*, 1996, 81, 380–399.
32. Sashkin, M. *Visionary Leadership.* Washington, D.C.: George Washington University, 1997. Used with permission.
33. Adapted from Reagon, G. The managers of the 21st century inventory. In *The 1997 Annual: Volume 1—Training.* Copyright © 1997 by Pfeiffer, An Imprint of Jossey-Bass, Inc. Publishers, San Francisco, pp. 187–189. Used with permission.

CHAPTER

13 Interpersonal Communication

LEARNING OBJECTIVES

When you have finished studying this chapter, you should be able to:

1. State the essentials of interpersonal communication.
2. Discuss how interpersonal communication networks affect power and control relationships among employees.
3. Describe how information technologies affect communication.
4. Explain the skills and abilities that foster dialogue.
5. Describe how nonverbal communication supports dialogue.

Preview Case: *Karen Leary*

ESSENTIALS OF INTERPERSONAL COMMUNICATION

Sender and Receiver

Transmitters and Receptors

Messages and Channels

Meaning, Encoding, Decoding, and Feedback

Interpersonal Challenges

Competency: Managing Diversity—*Texaco's Discrimination Case*

Cultural Challenges

Competency: Managing Across Cultures—*Godiva Chocolates*

INTERPERSONAL NETWORKS

Types of Networks

Effects of Networks

Importance of Networks

Competency: Managing Teams—*Lisa Guedea Carreño's Team*

INFORMATION TECHNOLOGIES

Competency: Managing Ethics—*Putting Your Résumé Online*

FOSTERING DIALOGUE

Communication Openness

Constructive Feedback

Appropriate Self-Disclosure

Active Listening

Competency: Managing Self—*How Self-Aware Are You?*

NONVERBAL COMMUNICATION

Types of Nonverbal Cues

Cultural Differences

Status Differences

Gender Differences

CHAPTER SUMMARY

Key Terms and Concepts

Discussion Questions

DEVELOPING COMPETENCIES

Competency: Managing Self—*Interpersonal Communication Practices*

Competency: Managing Across Cultures—*Juan Perillo and Jean Moore*

PREVIEW CASE

KAREN LEARY

Karen Leary is a marketing manager at a medical diagnostics firm in Avalon, New Jersey. Her day begins at 6 A.M. with a phone call from another mother in her car pool. The mother is ill and wants Karen to pick up her children after school and take them for swimming lessons. She quickly remembers that Gina Wilcox, the division president, had invited her to attend an important meeting that afternoon on new product design. She turns to her husband and asks what his day is like and could he take over. Reluctantly, he says "Okay."

Karen Leary arrives at work at 8 A.M. for a meeting with a marketing group, which is designing an advertising campaign for the new product. She needs to get changes made in the ad, based on comments from a focus group. The marketing people are already behind schedule but agree that these changes will improve the campaign. Before she runs to the next meeting, she scans her e-mail for any up-to-the-minute news from the sales force about a competitor's new product. Scanning down her screen she notices that one of her friends has requested a brown-bag lunch to discuss some personal matters with her. She e-mails her agreement and runs off to her meeting with her boss to discuss her team's performance. Scheduled to last an hour, the discussion covers a variety of personnel issues from the firm's maternity leave policy to its retirement policies. She tries to focus on her team's performance and its objective criteria, but she finds that her boss is focusing on the need for compensation sacrifices.

Before lunch, her assistant brings her a fax from one of the company's Korean distributors complaining that the company must not value him as a strategic partner or it would have sent a more senior person, and not a woman, to work out an agreement. It was a standard contract, one that Karen had used all over the world. Leary couldn't understand his "getting all riled up" but knew that she had to handle this matter personally. She thought for a moment about her own experiences while living in Seoul when her husband was stationed there in the army. She knew that Koreans placed great importance on personal connections and that businesspeople spent considerable time developing and nurturing such relationships. In fact, maintaining harmonious relationships among business associates was more important than written contracts. Although Karen was aware of the changes in the status of women in Korea, the Confucian value system teaches that women must obey the male members of society. In many organizations, such as Hyundai, Samsung, and Sanyo, women are seen as temporary employees whose role is to serve the organization until marriage. Therefore women typically have lower job status then their male counterparts. Because maintaining this distributorship is vital to the firm and because she had violated Korean business practices by sending a woman, she now must spend time repairing this relationship. She would have to recall the woman and send an older man to represent the company.

Her friend joins her for a quick lunch. She has just returned from having her second child and realizes that she needs to drop back to part-time work. After small talk about her newborn, her friend wants Leary's advice on how to negotiate a part-time agreement that will not jeopardize her standing in the company. During lunch, she also takes a call from her husband saying that he's running late but will pick up the kids and get them to swimming lessons on time. He'll bring his work home.

After lunch, Leary needs some quiet time before going to the meeting to talk about new product design processes with Gina Wilcox. The meeting turns out to be an interesting one with lots of ideas that her advertising team can incorporate in its campaign. Wilcox asks Leary to head a task force for creating a new product. She's flattered and agrees but now has to find time to convince other managers to allow some of their people to join her team and find time and resources to do the work.

She looks at her watch and sees that it's 5:30 P.M. On the way home, she reflects on her new assignment. She'll have to develop a strategy to gain acceptance of the new product team and build support for it. She also knows that resistance to this team will be considerable because it will need resources that other project managers also want and need. What project manager would be willing to let her borrow people to work on a new project when most managers are strapped for resources? Finally, she reflects on her friend's situation. Although the firm values diversity and attempts to be sensitive to the needs of employees and their families, she knows that the boundaries are often cast in stone. It will be almost impossible for her to negotiate a part-time contract for her friend.

We identified communication as one of the seven foundation managerial competencies in Chapter 1. Effective interpersonal communication is the primary focus of this chapter. We begin by discussing the process, types, and patterns of verbal, nonverbal, and other forms of communication used by employees on the job. We then present ways to foster effective dialogue in organizations. Finally, we examine the nature and importance of nonverbal communication.

Interpersonal communication is the transmission and reception of thoughts, facts, beliefs, attitudes, and feelings—through one or more information media—that produce a response.[1] Through active listening, the messages intended by the sender are likely to be accurately understood and interpreted by the receiver. In the Preview Case, Karen Leary spent an entire day *communicating* with others.

Learning Objective:

1. State the essentials of interpersonal communication.

ESSENTIALS OF INTERPERSONAL COMMUNICATION

For accurate interpersonal communication to take place, the thoughts, facts, beliefs, attitudes, or feelings that the sender intended to transmit must be the same as those understood and interpreted by the receiver. Recently, the owners of National Basketball Association teams and the players' representatives were involved in lengthy negotiations over a new labor contract. As a result, the 1998–1999 NBA season had to be shortened by 32 games, but because the parties to the negotiations kept talking, an agreement was reached and the entire season did not have to be canceled. So long as opposing views are being transmitted, received, and understood with the intended meaning, accurate interpersonal communication is taking place and differences can be resolved. Figure 13.1 presents the essentials of interpersonal communication involving only two people; the process is not easy, and by looking at its components, you can easily see that it becomes increasingly complex as more people participate.

SENDER AND RECEIVER

Exchanges between people are an element of interpersonal communication. Thus labeling one person as the sender and the other as the receiver is arbitrary. These roles shift back and forth, depending on where the individuals are in the process. When the receiver responds to the sender, the original receiver becomes the sender and the initiating sender becomes the receiver.

Consider the comment of a manager at CIBC Oppenheimer about dealing with a stockbroker who made a mistake in a client's statement but failed to notify the client:

> I was facing a tough decision about whether to fire this broker or just reprimand him for knowingly violating our policy. I wrestled with it in my head for almost a week and pretty much made up my mind about what I was going to do. But I gave his former boss a call and talked it through with her. She was really sympathetic and knew that I was struggling. She made me talk out my decision and asked me hard questions along the way. We looked at the problem from several perspectives: mine, my boss's, the brokers' and the client's.[2]

The supervisor's statement suggests that the goals of the sender and receiver substantially influence the communication process. For example, the sender may have certain intentions in communicating, such as adding to or changing the thoughts, beliefs, attitudes, and/or behaviors of the receiver or changing the sender's relationship with the receiver. These intentions may be presented openly (the supervisor wanted a new broker) or developed deceptively. If the receiver doesn't agree with them, the probability of distortion and misunderstanding can be quite high (the manager concluded that the broker was immature and too embarrassed to call the client). The fewer the differences in goals, attitudes, and beliefs, the greater is the probability that accurate communication will occur.

Figure 13.1 **Elements of Interpersonal Communication**

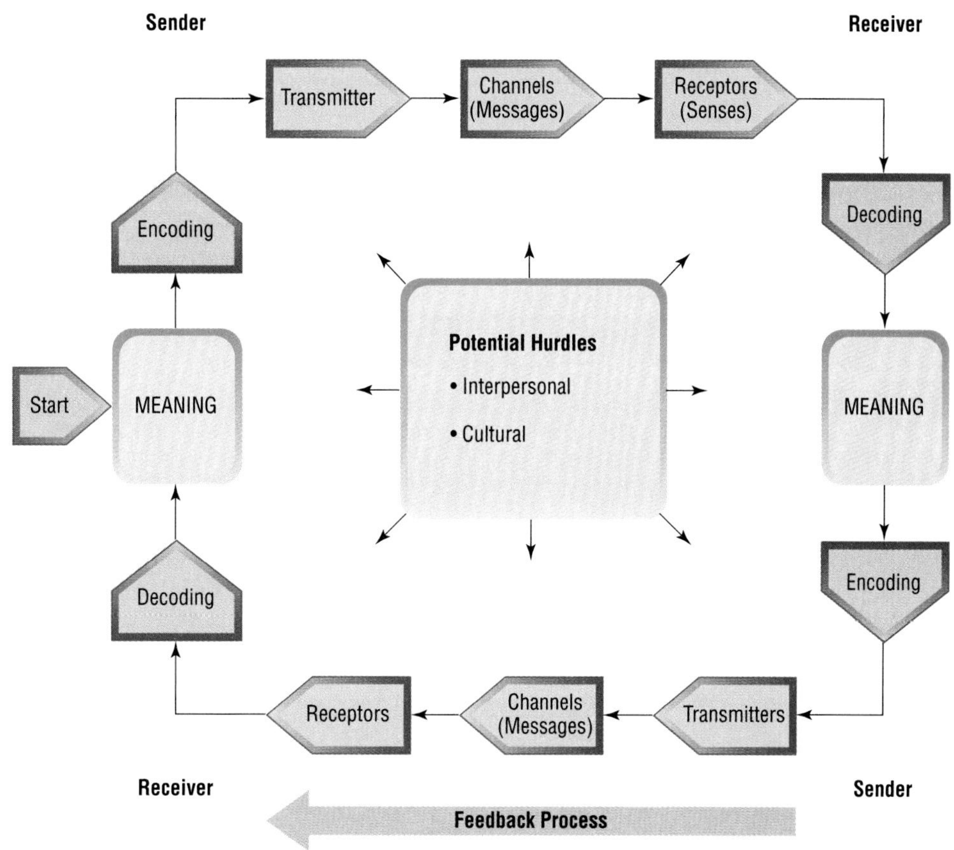

TRANSMITTERS AND RECEPTORS

Transmitters (used by the sender) and **receptors** (used by the receiver) are the means (media) available for sending and receiving messages. They usually involve one or more of the senses: seeing, hearing, touching, smelling, and tasting. Transmission can take place both verbally and nonverbally. Once transmission begins, the communication process moves beyond the direct control of the sender. A message that has been transmitted cannot be brought back. How many times have you thought to yourself: I wish I hadn't said that? In the Preview Case, Karen Leary's husband probably wished that he hadn't agreed to take the children to swimming class after thinking more clearly about his schedule for the day.

Several types of communication media are available for transmitting and receiving messages. They vary in terms of **media richness,** which are the media's capacities for carrying multiple cues and providing rapid feedback.[3] The richness of each medium involves a blend of four factors: (1) the use and rapidity (slow to rapid) of feedback to correct and/or confirm intended meanings; (2) the personalization (low to high) of messages to the circumstances of the receiver; (3) the ability to convey cues (single to multiple); and (4) language variety (standard to varied). Figure 13.2 relates nine different media to these four factors. Because these four factors are continual, a medium may vary somewhat in richness, depending on its use by sender and receiver. For example, electronic mail (e-mail) may be associated with slower or quicker feedback than indicated in Figure 13.2. The speed depends on accessibility to e-mail messages and the receiver's tendency to reply immediately or sometime in the future. Messages that require a long time to digest or that can't overcome biases are low in richness. During Karen Leary's day, she used multiple messages with varying degrees of media richness.

Figure 13.2 **Examples of Media Richness for Sending and Receiving Messages**

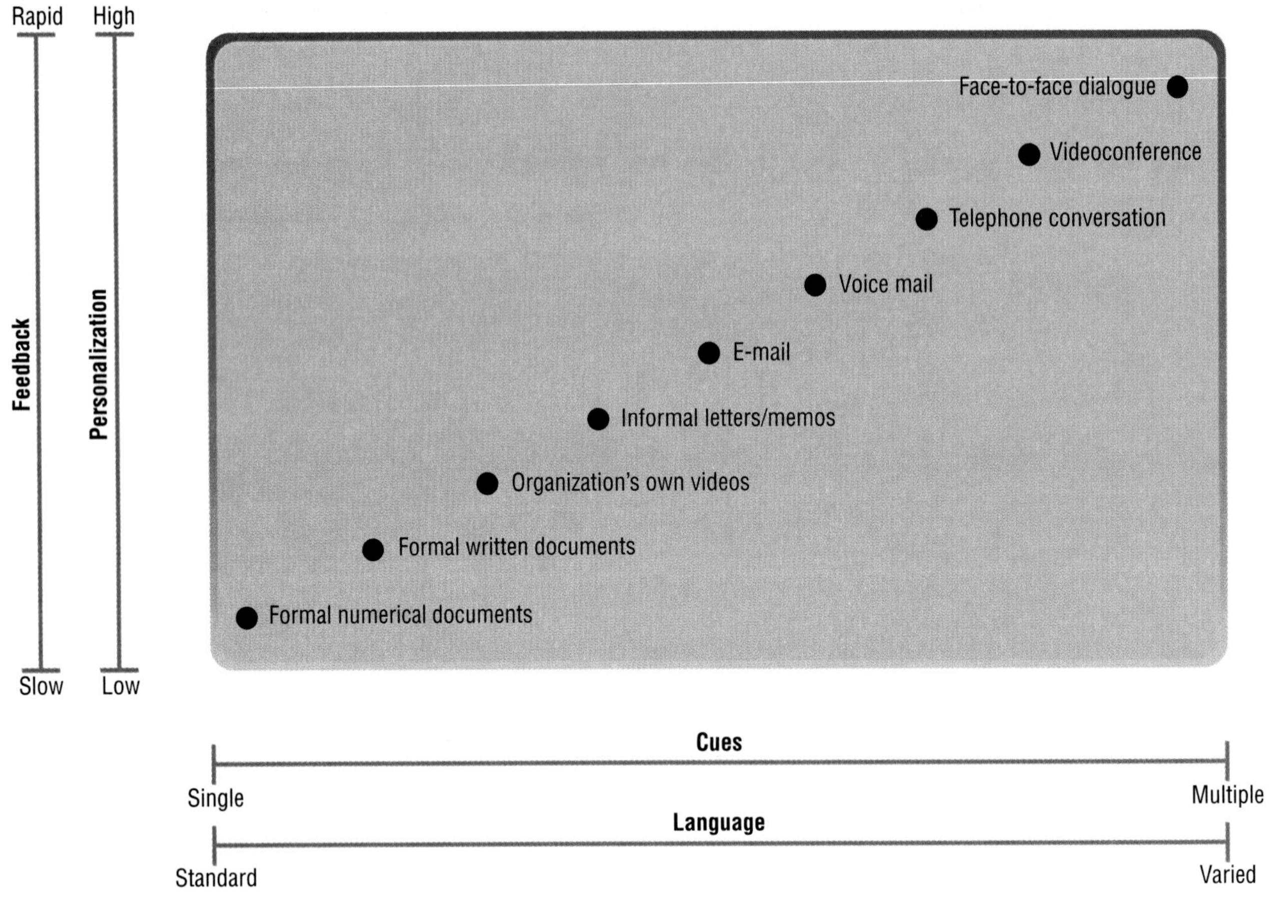

Source: Adapted from Daft, R. L., and Lengel, R. H. Organizational information requirements, media richness, and structural design. *Management Science*, 1986, 32, 554–571.

Data are the output of communication. The various forms of data include words spoken face to face, telephone calls, letters, memos, and computer printouts. They become information when they reinforce or change the receivers' understanding of their thoughts, feelings, attitudes, or beliefs. The use of groupware (various information technologies) may help such information exchange but can't always substitute for face-to-face dialogue. The reason is that, as suggested in Figure 13.2, face-to-face dialogue is the richest medium. It provides immediate feedback so that receivers can check the accuracy of their understanding and ask for clarification if they need to. It also allows sender and receiver simultaneously to observe body language, tone of voice, and facial expression. These observations add meaning to the spoken words. Finally, it enables sender and receiver quickly to identify symbols and use language that is natural and personal. Because of these characteristics, solving important and tough problems—especially those involving uncertainty and ambiguity—almost always requires face-to-face dialogue.

Messages and Channels

Messages include the transmitted data and the coded (verbal and nonverbal) symbols that give particular meaning to the data.[4] By using both verbal and nonverbal symbols, the sender tries to ensure that messages are interpreted by the receiver as the sender intended. To understand the difference between an original meaning and a received message, think about an occasion when you tried to convey inner thoughts and feelings of happiness, rage, or fear to another person. Did you find it difficult or impossible to transmit your true "inner meaning"? The greater the difference between the interpreted meaning and the original message, the poorer will be the interpersonal communication. Words and nonverbal symbols have no meaning by themselves. Their meaning is created by the sender, the receiver, and the situation or context. In our discussion of potential interpersonal and cultural hurdles, we explain why messages aren't always interpreted as they were meant to be. **Channels** are the means by which messages travel from sender to receiver. Examples of channels would be the "air" during face-to-face conversation, the Internet, and the telephone.

Meaning, Encoding, Decoding, and Feedback

The sender's message is transmitted through channels to the receiver's five senses. As Figure 13.1 suggests, received messages are changed from their symbolic form (e.g., spoken words) to a form that has meaning. Meaning represents a person's thoughts, feelings, beliefs (values), and attitudes.

Encoding gives personal meaning to messages that are to be sent. Vocabulary and knowledge play an important role in the sender's ability to encode. Unfortunately, some professionals have difficulty communicating with people in general. They often encode meaning in a form that only other professionals in the same field can understand. Lawyers often encode (write) contracts that directly affect consumers but use language that only other lawyers can decode. Consumer groups have pressed to have such contracts written in language that almost everyone can understand. As a result, many banks, credit card firms, and other organizations have simplified the language in their contracts.

Decoding gives personal interpreted meaning to messages that are received. Through a shared language, people can decode many messages so that the meanings received are reasonably close to the meanings transmitted. Decoding messages accurately is often a major challenge in communicating.[5] Figure 13.3 shows how some common symbols can be decoded around the world. Each of these symbols can present communication challenges for the receiver.

Interpersonal communication accuracy should be evaluated in relation to the ideal state, which occurs when the sender's intended meaning and the receiver's interpretation of it are the same. The transmission of factual information of a nonthreatening nature approximates the ideal state. For example, the sharing of the time, place, and procedures for high school or college commencement generally results in easy and accurate interpersonal communication. The communication between a manager and a subordinate during a performance feedback session is another matter.

The receiver's response to the message is **feedback.** It lets the sender know whether the message was received as intended. Interpersonal communication becomes a dynamic, two-way process, through feedback, rather than just an event. In the Preview Case, Karen Leary received feedback about her friend's situation.

Interpersonal Challenges

Numerous interpersonal communication hurdles exist, many of which we discussed in previous chapters. Let's review briefly the more important hurdles that stem from individual differences in personality and perceptions.[6]

Individual personality traits that serve as hurdles include low adjustment (nervous, self-doubting, moody), low sociability (shy, unassertive, withdrawn), low conscientiousness (impulsive, careless, irresponsible), low agreeableness (independent, cold, rude), and low intellectual openness (dull, unimaginative, literal-minded). Introverts are more likely to be quiet and emotionally unexpressive. Dogmatic individuals are rigid, closed-minded, and accept or reject other people on the basis of their agreement or disagreement with accepted authority or their own beliefs. (See Chapter 2.)

Figure 13.3

Hand Gestures: Different Meanings in Different Countries

The A-OK Sign

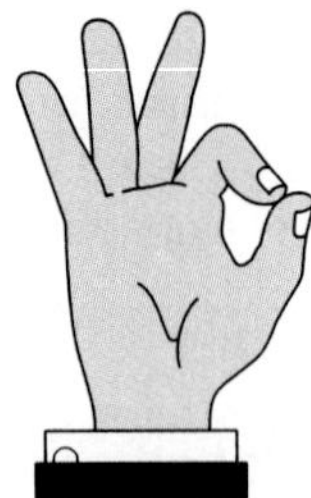

In the United States, this is just a friendly sign for "All right!" or "Good going." In Australia and Islamic countries, it is equivalent to what generations of high school students know as "flipping the bird."

The "Hook 'em Horns" Sign

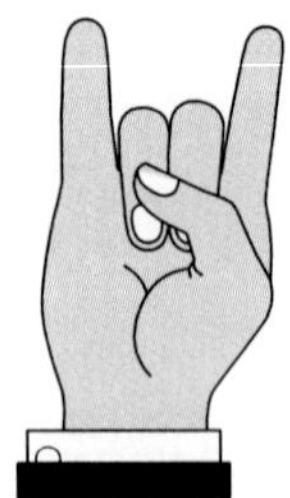

This sign encourages University of Texas athletes, and it's a good luck gesture in Brazil and Venezuela. In parts of Africa it is a curse. In Italy, it is signaling to another that "your spouse is being unfaithful."

"V" for Victory Sign

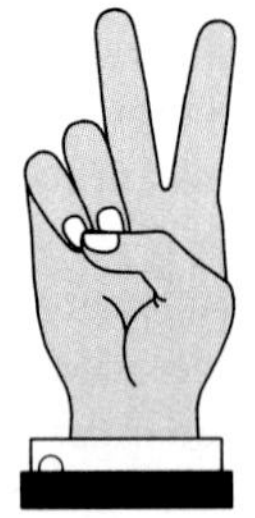

In many parts of the world, this means "victory" or "peace." In England, if the palm and fingers face inward, it means "Up yours!" especially if executed with an upward jerk of the fingers.

Finger-Beckoning Sign

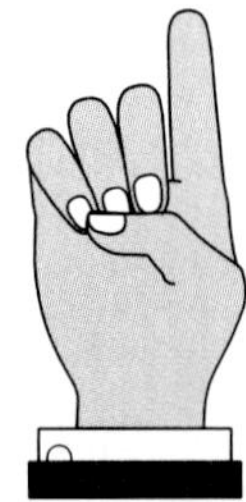

This sign means "come here" in the United States. In Malaysia, it is used only for calling animals. In Indonesia and Australia, it is used for beckoning "ladies of the night."

Source: What's A-O.K. in the U.S.A. is lewd and worthless beyond. *New York Times,* August 18, 1996, E7. From Axtell, R. E. *Gestures: The Do's and Taboos of Body Language Around the World.* New York: John Wiley & Sons. Copyright © 1991. This material is used by permission of John Wiley & Sons, Inc.

Individual perceptual errors include perceptual defense (protecting oneself against ideas, objects, or situations that are threatening), stereotyping (assigning attributes to someone solely on the basis of a category in which the person has been placed), halo effect (evaluating another person based solely on one impression, either favorable or unfavorable), projection (tendency for people to see their own traits in others), and high expectancy effect (prior expectations serving to bias how events, objects, and people are actually perceived).[7] Individuals who make the fundamental attribution error (underestimating the impact of situational or external causes of behavior and overestimating the impact of personal causes of behavior when they seek to understand why people behave the way they do) are less likely to communicate effectively. This error too readily results in communicating blame or credit to individuals for outcomes. A related attribution error is the self-serving bias (communicating personal responsibility for good performance but denying responsibility for poor performance). (See Chapter 3.)

In addition to these underlying interpersonal communication hurdles, there also are some direct hurdles. Most of them are caused, at least in part, by one or more of the underlying hurdles.

Noise. Any interference with the intended message in the channel represents **noise.**[8] A radio playing loud music while someone is trying to talk to someone else is an example of noise. Noise sometimes can be overcome by repeating the message or increasing the intensity (e.g., the volume) of the message.

Semantics. The special meaning assigned to words is called **semantics.** However, the same words may mean different things to different people. Consider this comment by a manager to a subordinate: How about the report for production planning? I think that they want it soon! The manager could have intended one of several meanings in her comment.

Directing: You should get the report to me now. That's an order.
Suggesting: I suggest that we consider getting the report out now.
Requesting: Can you do the report for me now? Let me know if you can't.
Informing: The report is needed soon by production planning.
Questioning: Does production planning want the report soon?

Consider the semantics for basic words such as sale, airport, and train in the following organizations. At Frito-Lay, a sale to the indirect marketing organization happens when a food distributor or grocery store orders chips from one of its warehouses. At Gateway Computers, Dell Computers, and other direct marketing (sells to the ultimate customer) organizations, a sale occurs only when the customer takes delivery. Even within direct marketing, there are differences of opinion: Salespeople record a sale when the order is placed, manufacturing when the product is assembled, distribution when the product is delivered, and finance when the product is paid for. At American Airlines, some managers argue that an airport is any location to which American has scheduled service; others count an airport as any facility granted that status by the international standards body.

Language Routines. A person's verbal and nonverbal communication patterns that have become habits are **language routines.** They can be observed by the ways that people greet one another. In many instances, language routines are quite useful because they reduce the amount of thinking time needed to produce common messages. They also provide predictability in terms of being able to anticipate what is going to be said and how it is going to be said. The unique culture of Ford Motor Company and its identity is reinforced through language routines, including slogans such as "Quality is Job 1."

Conversely, language routines sometimes cause discomfort, offend, and alienate when they put down or discriminate against others. Many demeaning stereotypes of individuals and groups are perpetuated through language routines. The following Managing Diversity Competency feature summarizes what happened several years ago when a manager at Texaco made tapes of conversations available to the public. These tapes contained demeaning comments made by board members and managers about minorities within the company, including blacks, Jews, other minorities, and women. Public outrage led to boycotts of Texaco, which ended up settling a racial discrimination case out of court for $176 million.

Lying and Distortion. The extreme form of deception in which the sender states what is believed to be false in order to seriously mislead one or more receivers is **lying.** The intention to deceive implies a belief that the receiver will accept the lie as a fact. In Texaco's case, the court believed that Ulrich was lying when he indicated that these racial slurs were not targeted at minority Texaco employees. In contrast, **honesty** means that the sender abides by consistent and rational ethical principles to respect the truth. Everyday social flattery in conversations may not be completely honest, but it is normally considered acceptable and rarely regarded as dishonest (lying). **Distortion** represents a wide range of messages that a sender may use between the

COMPETENCY: MANAGING DIVERSITY

TEXACO'S DISCRIMINATION CASE

At meetings several years ago when senior Texaco managers and board members mocked black employees, Jews, other minorities, and women, everyone present assumed that these remarks would remain behind closed doors. However, tapes of these meetings—secretly made by Richard Lundwall, a former Texaco personnel officer—came to light in federal court. Lundwall's tapes contained remarks by Robert Ulrich, former Texaco treasurer, that ultimately embarrassed Texaco into a very costly settlement, not only in dollars, but also in reputation. The racial comments Ulrich made during one of the meetings appeared to mock black employees, as well as employees of the Jewish faith. Ulrich was taped belittling blacks and their holiday, Kwanza. At one point on tape, Ulrich was heard saying, "I'm struggling with Hanukkah, and now we have Kwanza; I mean I lost Christmas, poor St. Nicholas, they [expletive] all over his beard."

The tapes further revealed Ulrich saying, "This diversity thing. You know how black jelly beans agree . . . ," followed by Lundwall's reply of, "That's funny. All black jelly beans seem to be glued to the bottom of the bag." Ulrich then replied, "You can't have just we and them. You can't just have black jelly beans and other jelly beans. It doesn't work." Lundwall followed with, "Yeah. But they're perpetuating the black jelly beans."

It was widely reported that other racial slurs and disparaging comments about blacks, Jews, other minorities, and women had been taped during these meetings. Ulrich and other Texaco executives said that they were misquoted and that a reference in the conversation to "black jelly beans" did not appear to have been intended as derogatory to African-American employees. Attorneys representing Texaco employees and the U.S. District Court in New York believed otherwise.

Texaco settled the racial discrimination lawsuit because Peter Bijur, chairman of Texaco, wanted to put it behind them. Bijur and Texaco's fundamental approach to the attacks of racism was: "We are a terrific company, we will not tolerate discrimination in the future, and we are sorry for the wrongdoing performed by a few bad apples." After the lawsuit was settled, boycotts were called off, criticism trickled off, and Texaco's sales rebounded.[9]

*For more information on Texaco, visit this company's home page at **www.texaco.com**.*

extremes of lying and complete honesty. Of course, the use of vague, ambiguous, or indirect language doesn't necessarily indicate the sender's intent to mislead. This form of language may be viewed as acceptable political behavior (see Chapter 9). Silence may also be a form of distortion, if not dishonesty. Not wanting to look incompetent or take on a manager in a departmental meeting, a subordinate may remain quiet instead of expressing an opinion or asking a question.

Personal distortion in interpersonal communications may occur through **impression management,** or the process by which a sender knowingly attempts to influence the perceptions that the receivers form (see Chapter 3).[10] Three impression management strategies—ingratiation, self-promotion, and face-saving—are commonly used.

- *Ingratiation* involves using flattery, supporting others' opinions, doing favors, laughing excessively at others' jokes, and so on.
- *Self-promotion* involves describing the sender's personal attributes to others in a highly positive and exaggerated way.
- *Face-saving* involves using various tactics, such as (1) apologizing in a way to convince others that the bad outcome isn't a fair indication of what the sender is really like as a person; (2) making excuses to others by admitting that the sender's

behavior in some way caused a negative outcome, but strongly suggesting that the person isn't really as much to blame as it seems (because the outcome wasn't intentional or there were extenuating circumstances); or (3) presenting justifications to others by appearing to accept responsibility for an outcome, but denying that the outcome actually led to problems.

Impression management strategies can range from relatively harmless and minor forms of distortion (being courteous to another person even if you don't like the individual) to messages that use extreme ingratiation and self-promotion to obtain a better raise or promotion than others. The personal ethics and self-awareness of the sender and the political nature of the individual's organization (see Chapter 9) combine to influence the degree to which distortion tactics are used. In brief, the greater the frequency of distortion tactics and the more they approach the lying end of the distortion continuum, the more they will serve as a hurdle to interpersonal communication.

Cultural Challenges

Culture refers to the distinctive ways that different populations, societies, or smaller groups organize their lives or activities. **Intercultural communication** occurs whenever a message sent by a member of one culture is received and understood by a member of another culture.[11] The effects of cultural differences on hurdles to interpersonal communication can be wide ranging. They depend on the degree of difference (or similarity) between people in terms of language, religious beliefs, economic beliefs, social values, physical characteristics, use of nonverbal cues, and the like. The greater the differences, the greater are the hurdles to achieving intercultural communication. Recall the cultural barriers that Karen Leary faced with her counterpart in South Korea when she sent a young woman to represent the firm in negotiations with a representative of its Korean distributor.

Cultural Context. The conditions that surround and influence the life of an individual, group, or organization is its **cultural context.**[12] Differences in cultural context may represent a hurdle to intercultural communication. Nations' cultures vary on a continuum from low context to high context. Figure 13.4 shows the approximate placement of various countries along this continuum.

In a **high-context culture,** interpersonal communication is characterized by (1) the establishment of social trust before engaging in work-related discussions, (2) the

Figure 13.4 **Examples of Cultures on the Cultural Context Continuum**

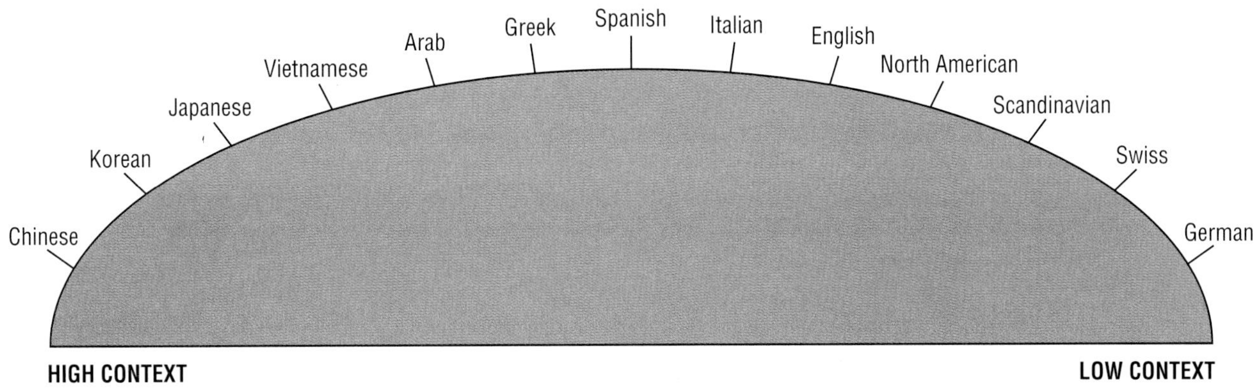

Source: Based on Hall, E. *Understanding Cultural Differences.* Yarmouth, Me.: Intercultural Press, 1989; Munter, M. *Guide to Managerial Communication: Effective Business Writing and Speaking,* 5th ed. Englewood Cliffs, N.J.: Prentice-Hall, 1999.

high value placed on personal relationships and goodwill, and (3) the importance of the surrounding circumstances during an interaction. In a high-context culture people rely on paraphrasing, tone of voice, gesture, posture, social status, history, and social setting to interpret spoken words, all of which requires time. Factors such as trust, relationships among friends and family members, personal needs and difficulties, weather, and holidays must be taken into consideration. For example, Japanese executives—when meeting foreign executives for the first time—do not immediately "get down to business." They engage in a period of building trust and getting to know each other that foreign executives often are impatient with but must conform to.

In contrast, a **low-context culture** is characterized by (1) directly and immediately addressing the tasks, issues, or problems at hand; (2) the high value placed on personal expertise and performance; and (3) the importance of clear, precise, and speedy interactions. The use of behavioral modification techniques and other reinforcement approaches discussed in Chapter 5 are based on low-context communication. There we described how a manager can motivate employees with statements focusing on positive or corrective feedback and goal setting. In a heterogeneous country, such as the United States, multiple subcultures have their own unique characteristics. In contrast, the cultural context of a homogeneous country, such as Japan, reflects the more uniform characteristics of its people.

Let's now consider three of the challenges in cross-cultural nonverbal communication—body language, personal space around an individual, and ethnocentrism. While considering them, we give some tips for successful nonverbal communication across cultures.

Body Language. Ideas of appropriate posture, gestures, eye contact, facial expression, touching, voice pitch and volume, and speaking rate differ from one culture to another (see Figure 13.3).[13] As a simple, but potentially disastrous example, nodding the head up and down in Bulgaria means "no," not "yes." In cross-cultural communication, you must avoid using any gestures considered rude or insulting. For instance, in Buddhist cultures, the head is considered sacred, so you must never touch anyone's head. In Muslim cultures, the left hand is considered unclean, so never touch, pass, or receive with the left hand. Pointing with the index finger is rude in cultures ranging from the Sudan to Venezuela to Sri Lanka. The American circular "A-OK" gesture carries a vulgar meaning in Brazil, Paraguay, Singapore, and Russia. Crossing your ankle over your knee is rude in Indonesia, Thailand, and Syria. Pointing your index finger toward yourself insults the other person in Germany, the Netherlands, and Switzerland. Avoid placing an open hand over a closed fist in France, saying "tsk tsk" in Kenya, and whistling in India.

Prepare yourself to recognize gestures that have meaning only in the other culture. Chinese stick out their tongues to show surprise and scratch their ears and cheeks to show happiness. Japanese suck in air, hissing through their teeth to indicate embarrassment or "no." Greeks puff air after they receive a compliment. Hondurans touch a finger to the face below the eyes to indicate caution or disbelief. Finally, resist applying your own culture's nonverbal meanings to other cultures. Vietnamese may look at the ground with their heads down to show respect, not to be "shifty." Russians may exhibit less facial expression and Scandinavians fewer gestures than Americans are accustomed to, but that doesn't mean that they aren't enthusiastic.

Personal Space. A second aspect of nonverbal communication has to do with norms regarding space.[14] North Americans generally feel comfortable in the following zones of space: 0–18 inches for intimacy only (comforting or greeting); 18 inches to 4 feet for personal space (conversing with friends); 4–12 feet for social space (conversing with strangers); and more than 12 feet for public space (standing in lobbies or reception areas). Different cultures define the acceptable extents of these zones differently. Venezuelans tend to prefer much closer personal and social space and might consider it rude if you back away. The British may prefer more distant personal and social space and might consider it rude if you move too close. Closely related is the concept of touch. Anglos usually avoid touching each other very much. In studies of touching behaviors, researchers observed people seated in outdoor cafes in each of four countries and counted the number of touches during an hour of conversation. The results were: San Juan, Puerto Rico, 180 touches per hour; Paris, 110 per hour; Gainesville, Florida, 1 per hour; and London, 0 per hour.

Ethnocentrism. The greatest barrier to intercultural communication occurs when a person believes: Only my culture makes sense, espouses the "right" values, and represents the "right" and logical way to behave.[15] This type of thinking is called **ethnocentrism.** When two ethnocentric people from different cultures interact, there is little chance that they will achieve understanding. Common ethnocentric reactions to strongly differing views are anger, shock, or even amusement.

The following Managing Across Cultures Competency feature illustrates a problem facing Godiva Chocolatiers, makers of prestige high-quality chocolate candy since 1926. Godiva's headquarters are in Brussels, Belgium. Its candies are sold all over the world in 150 Godiva specialty boutiques and in more than 1,000 additional

COMPETENCY: MANAGING ACROSS CULTURES

GODIVA CHOCOLATES

The marketing department at Godiva Chocolatiers was trying to make a decision about whether to standardize its advertisements in various countries. One group of employees argued that, because it is a global company, Godiva could use the same advertisements for all its markets. This approach would save on promotional costs and present a standardized message to consumers. Another group of employees argued that advertisements must always be individualized for each country, pointing to the many marketing blunders made by other firms when selling products globally.

To make a decision, Godiva designed some standardized advertisements (e.g., for Valentine's Day, Christmas, and birthdays) and others that were individualized to a specific country. They categorized cultures as either high-context or low-context. In a high-context culture (e.g., China, France, Japan, Spain, and Italy) most of the advertising was graphical or physical. The communicator is sensitive to situational data and describes the situation as accurately as possible. Tone of voice, timing, and facial expression are the primary means of expression. The situation requires very little encoding for the message to be received and understood. People rely on close personal relationships to gather information about the product. In a low-context culture (e.g., Australia, Canada, England, and the United States), use of words to convey meaning is critical. Receiving detailed information is important for a person to understand the message. Expressing complete, accurate meaning through appropriate word choice is important for the decoding process.

The company's researchers found that the effectiveness of the message depended on the context of the culture. Advertisements that were individualized to countries according to context were more effective than those that were standardized and used in various countries. In Japan, the individualized ads communicated warmth, trust, and family. Pictures of family members giving and receiving chocolates were emphasized. In the United States, these ads pictured executives giving chocolates to subordinates as a token of appreciation for their hard work and attention to detail.[16]

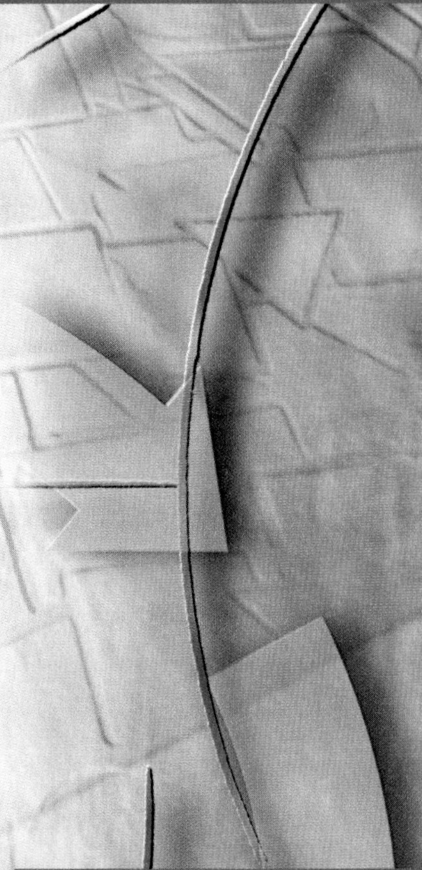

For more information on Godiva chocolates, visit this company's home page at ***www.godiva.com.***

fine department stores (e.g., Neiman Marcus and Nordstrom) and specialty shops. Godiva chocolates require special handling during display and storage. They have shell-molded designs, are beautifully packaged, and are sold at a premium because of the firm's innovative approaches to manufacturing, advertising, and packaging. Godiva chocolates are never sold in discount stores or at a discounted price.

Learning Objective:

2. Discuss how interpersonal communication networks affect power and control relationships among employees.

INTERPERSONAL NETWORKS

An **interpersonal communication network** is the pattern of communication flows over time among individuals.[17] The focus of this concept is on communication relationships among people over time, rather than on the individuals and whether a specific message was received as intended by the sender. Networks involve the ongoing flow of oral, written, and nonverbal messages (data) between two people or between one person and all other network members simultaneously. Communication networks can influence the likelihood of a match between messages as sent and as actually received and interpreted. The more accurately the message moves through the channel, the more clearly the receiver will understand it.

TYPES OF NETWORKS

Recall that the essentials of interpersonal communication shown in Figure 13.1 are based on the involvement of only two people. Obviously, communication often takes place among many individuals and larger groups. Claudia Gonzales, a telecommunications manager for Abaco Grupo Financiero in Mexico, normally has ongoing links with many people both inside and outside her organization. Her communication network extends laterally, vertically, and externally. Vertical networks typically include her immediate superior and subordinates and the superior's superiors and the subordinates' subordinates. Lateral networks include people in the same department at the same level (peers) and people in different departments at the same level. External networks include customers, suppliers, regulatory agencies, pressure groups, professional peers, and friends. Thus an employee's communication network can be quite involved.

When Zalee Harris was laid off, she built her own home page on the Web, with photograph, résumé, and statement of purpose. She registered her address in the Yahoo and WebCrawler search engines and bought contact-management software to keep track of her employment leads. She received more than 50 inquiries from headhunters and employers. Noting how easy it was to communicate, she formed a company to help others locate job openings. Jeff Taylor, CEO of Monster.com estimates that there are more than 2.5 million résumés online, more than 258,400 job openings, and 10 online job sites, such as www.hotjobs.com, www.careerpath.com, and www.jobsearch.org.[18]

Size limits the possible communication networks within a team. (As in Chapter 8, our use of the word *team* encompasses various types of formal and informal *groups*, unless we specifically use the word *group* for a particular reason.) In principle, as the size of a team increases arithmetically, the number of possible communication interrelationships increases exponentially. Accordingly, communication networks are much more varied and complex in a 12-person team than in a 5-person team. Although every team member (theoretically) may be able to communicate with all the others, the direction and number of communication channels often are somewhat limited. In committee meetings, for example, varying levels of formality influence who may speak, what may be discussed, and in what order. The relative status or ranking of group members also may differ. Members having higher status probably will dominate a communication network more than those with lower status. Even when an open network is encouraged, team members may actually use a limited network arrangement.

To provide a sense of the potential and powerful effects of communication networks, let's consider a single team of five members. In this example we don't address the complicating effects of multiple teams and different team sizes. A five-person team has about 60 possible communication networks but only 5 basic networks—the star (sometimes called the wheel), the Y, the chain, the circle, and the all-channel network—as shown in Figure 13.5. Each line between each pair of names represents two-way communication. The degree of restriction on members in communicating with each other differentiates the networks. At one extreme, the star network is the most restricted: All communication between members must flow through Jane. At the other extreme, the all-channel network is the least restricted and most open: Each member communicates with all other members directly.

Effects of Networks

Communication networks can affect the selection of team leaders, the ease and speed of team learning, the effectiveness and efficiency of the team, and member satisfaction with the team's progress.[19] Table 13.1 provides a brief comparison of the five basic communication networks in terms of four assessment criteria. The first criterion, *degree of centralization*, is the extent to which some team members have access to more

Figure 13.5 **Five Alternative Communication Networks for a Five-Person Group**

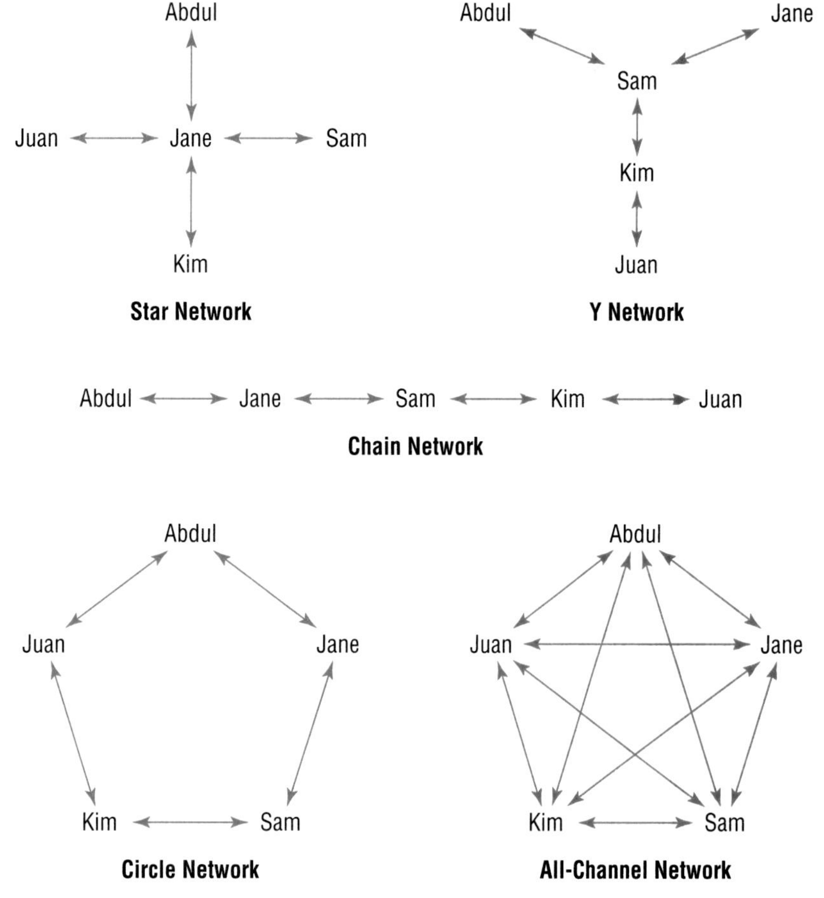

communication possibilities than do other members. The star network is the most centralized because all communication flows from and to only one member. The all-channel network is the least centralized because any member can communicate with all other members. The second criterion, *leadership predictability*, indicates the ability to anticipate which team member is likely to emerge as the leader. In Figure 13.5, the following individuals are likely to emerge as leaders: Jane in the star network, Sam in the Y network, and possibly Sam in the chain network. In each of these three networks, the anticipated leaders have more information and greater control over its dissemination than the other members.

The third and fourth assessment criteria in Table 13.1, *average group satisfaction* and *range in individual member satisfaction*, reflect the levels and range of satisfaction of team members. Several interesting relationships exist between these two criteria. In the star network, average member satisfaction is likely to be the lowest compared to the other networks. However, the range in individual member satisfaction is likely to be the highest relative to the other networks. Jane might find the star network highly satisfying because she is the center of attention and has considerable influence over the team. In contrast, the other members are highly dependent on Jane and may well play a small role in the decision-making process. Accordingly, the average satisfaction of the team as a whole is likely to be relatively low. The all-channel network creates the potential for greater participation by all members in terms of their interests and abilities to contribute to the team. Average satisfaction may be relatively high, and the range of satisfaction scores for individuals probably will be smaller than for the other networks.

Importance of Networks

Knowing the types of communication networks used is especially important in understanding power and control relationships among employees in organizations. Powerful individuals may limit access to information by others as one way of maintaining or increasing their power. (See Chapter 9.)

Problems may range from simple to complex. Simple problems (e.g., scheduling overtime work) make few demands on team members. Simple networks (e.g., superior to subordinate) often are effective for solving simple problems. However, complex issues and problems (e.g., British Petroleum deciding to buy Amoco and Atlantic Richfield) generate many decision-making demands throughout an organization. Plenty can go wrong in resolving complex issues and solving complex problems. For

Table 13.1 Effects of Five Communication Networks

	TYPE OF COMMUNICATION NETWORK				
FACTOR	Star	Y	Chain	Circle	All Channel
Degree of centralization	Very high	High	Moderate	Low	Very low
Leadership predictability	Very high	High	Moderate	Low	Very low
Average group satisfaction	Low	Low	Moderate	Moderate	High
Range in individual member satisfaction	High	High	Moderate	Low	Very low

example, some financial analysts say that British Petroleum didn't comprehend the truly global market for natural gas and how downsizing would affect employee morale. To tackle complex problems, an all-channel or open network often is the most effective approach.[20]

Another factor is the degree to which members must work together to accomplish a team's tasks. With problems requiring little member coordination, communication may be handled effectively through one of the more centralized networks. Think about various sports and the types of communication networks needed in them. In swimming, track, and golf, the coach coordinates and communicates with all team members. Team members can perform most of their tasks with minimal communication with other team members. With a high degree of member coordination—as in basketball, ice hockey, and soccer—the all-channel network is much more effective than a simple, centralized network. A complex communication network is required—both between coach and players and among players—as they perform their tasks.

Networks also are important for day-to-day communication in organizations. First, no single network is likely to prove effective in all situations for a team with a variety of tasks and goals. The apparently efficient, low-cost, and simple method of a superior instructing subordinates is likely to be ineffective if used exclusively. Dissatisfaction may become so great that members will leave the team or lose their motivation to contribute. Second, teams that face complex problems requiring high member interdependence may deal with them ineffectively because of inadequate sharing of information, consideration of alternatives, and the like. Third, a team must consider trade-offs or opportunity costs. A team committed to the exclusive use of the all-channel network may deal inefficiently with simple problems and tasks that require little member interdependence. In such cases, members also may become bored and dissatisfied with team meetings. They often simply come to feel that their time is being wasted. Another trade-off with the all-channel network is higher labor costs. That is, team members must spend more time on a problem and its solution in meetings with the all-channel network than with a star network. Hence a team should use the type of network that is most appropriate to its goals and tasks.

Informal networks in many organizations, such as Texaco, often create barriers for minorities and women as they seek opportunities and representation in white male-dominated roles and departments, especially in upper level managerial networks.[21] These informal managerial networks may value similarities among members in terms of gender, race, educational level, and the like. Xerox is one of the few organizations that support the use of caucus groups as a way to manage, value, and nurture diversity. These groups encourage networking to (1) link caucus members and upper management, (2) assist with personal and professional development, (3) provide support within the caucus, and (4) serve as role models to majority employees in managing diversity.

Once a week, Dungan Highsmith, president of Highsmith, Inc., closets himself for 2 hours in a small room near his office and tries to think deeply about global issues. He also sifts through stacks of articles on subjects ranging from juvenile crime to semiotics to the anatomy of dragonflies. Highsmith, Inc., is a $55 million mail-order business that sells more than 25,000 different products, including book displays, audio-video tools, and educational software for schools and libraries. Highsmith's overarching goal is for all the company's employees to shed their blinders and begin to think creatively—about customers, about the industry, and about life. He wants a flat, decentralized organization that excels at learning and employees who freely communicate with each other. Joining him in these sessions is his librarian, Lisa Guedea Carreño and her team. Their job is to maintain contact between the library staff and the firm's other employees. The following Managing Teams Competency feature describes how important networks are to this team's job.

COMPETENCY: MANAGING TEAMS

LISA GUEDEA CARREÑO'S TEAM

Carreño's team meeting room is small but brightly lighted and surrounded by things: things that team members are reading, things that they are putting aside for other people, and things that make them think. Immediately outside the meeting room is the library that includes more than 2,500 books, thousands of magazines (the library maintains more than 700 subscriptions), a PC for accessing CD-ROMs, electronic blackboards, scanners, groupware, and certain databases. Carreño and her team (two other librarians) are responsible for building an organization rich in human potential, but with few employees. The team provides employees with information and the context for making good decisions. She estimates that 15 percent of the team's time is spent finding answers to questions, some of which are straightforward, such as: What is the status of the Manufacturers Life Insurance class-action suit? Some 85 percent of the time the questions are more abstract, such as: Why does authenticity matter?

When the team can't immediately answer a question, it engages in an extensive network search process. Team members contact their friends in other educational organizations, scan electronic sources, and call employees who might help them. The team employs people outside the organization who read and scan materials for it all the time. These readers reduce the amount of external information that Carreño and her team must read by about 80 percent.

The team also knows the reading habits of the firm's employees. When a new employee joins the firm, team members spend about 45 minutes or longer with the person, during which they try to figure out how that person responds best to information. "People frame their requests in terms that they can understand," the team has learned. For John Kiley, director of marketing, a team provides an oral summary. "You can hand John this beautifully presented and annotated outline with tabs and everything, and he will call and say 'Could you come up here and tell me about it?'" The team has found that it must have the documentation but that Kiley prefers to talk about it. For another manager who wanted a report on evaluating and selecting employment tests, the team boiled down more information from a large number of sources into four pages of concrete steps, including questions to ask and things to avoid. The team also reads junk science material because Highsmith wants to understand how ideas and theories with no scientific basis become accepted as fact. That understanding could make the company more skeptical about emerging management fads. That skepticism could in turn affect how the company deals with the demand for materials supporting those approaches.

To make information available to all employees, Carreño's team uses the organization's intranet. It allows employees to search for information in a variety of ways and encourages people to list interests, areas of expertise, and experiences that they are willing to share with anyone who might contact them. The aim of the system is to make this information available to all employees so that they can work cooperatively on projects regardless of time or organizational boundaries.

Carreño's goal is to transform employees into sophisticated analysts of external information. Her team is there to help people integrate information into their jobs as seamlessly as possible.[22]

For more information on Highsmith, Inc., visit the organization's home page at ***www.highsmith.com.***

Learning Objective:

3. Describe how information technologies affect communication.

INFORMATION TECHNOLOGIES

The **Internet** is an integrated global network of computers that gives users access to information and documents. Anyone with a personal computer, modem, and proper software can access the Internet free and obtain and share information with others via e-mail, which are electronic messages transmitted to and from Internet host computers. More than 250 million people are projected to have access to the Internet in 2005, with 30 percent residing in the United States.[23]

Organizations are using the Internet to explain their benefits to newly hired employees. At Allegiance, a Dallas-based local telephone exchange carrier, all its policies and personnel benefits, covering anything from 401(k) plans to dental insurance, can be checked out on www.Online-benefits.com. This protected Web site allows Allegiance's employees to click an icon on their desktops to access the site, where they can calculate the impact of a particular health care plan on their paychecks or the cost of life insurance based on their ages.

The **World Wide Web** (www) is the part of the Internet that supports a retrieval system for a vast amount of information and documents on all manner of topics. Web sites, or home pages, are formatted (some elaborately) addresses that provide access to that material. Hypertext markup language (html) is used to format documents to be viewed by users accessing a Web site with a browser program, such as Netscape's Navigator or Microsoft's Internet Explorer. The hypertext transfer protocol (http) is the means by which documents are actually delivered from a Web site to a user's computer. The uniform resource locator (URL) identifies each site, a location in cyberspace akin to a traditional street address. For example, the Web site for this book is http://www.swcollege.com, the home page of the book's publisher.

Connections via modem to the Internet are available through local providers for a monthly fee. In addition to providing connections to the Internet, **commercial online services** offer many types of information to subscribers, also for a monthly fee. America Online, CompuServe, and Prodigy are well known commercial online services that operate nationally and even internationally. For example, America Online provides some 17 million customers globally with news, information, e-mail, Internet access, and online shopping opportunities. Subscribers can buy and sell investments through brokerage services and make airline, car-rental, hotel, and restaurant reservations. A popular Web site is www.priceline.com, which allows customers to bid on low-cost airfares and hotel rooms.

Many organizations have adapted Internet-based technology internally to support their external electronic commerce initiatives and many other functions. An **intranet** is an Internet/Web-based network used within an organization. An intranet is essentially a private electronic communication system that may or may not be connected to the Internet. Those that are connected are protected by *firewalls* from outside hackers.

Electronic mail (e-mail) is a computer-based system that enables individuals to exchange and store messages via their computers. Until several years ago, if an employee wanted to discuss an idea with Tom Cunningham, a vice president at Lockheed Martin, the employee had to convince a secretary that getting in to see him was important. Because the chance of bumping into Cunningham personally was slim, the employee had to submit the idea at a lower level; if it ever made its way up the hierarchy, it probably had been distorted, sanitized, or changed. Today, that same employee can simply send an e-mail to Cunningham, presenting the idea with minimal distortion, because e-mail doesn't follow the formal hierarchical structure. Quick and easy access to this communication medium has the potential to radically change internal coordination and integrating systems and communication with external suppliers and customers.

In sophisticated e-mail systems, the user gets a digest of all the incoming mail, with headings noting the name of the sender, the time and date the item was sent, and what it is about. The user can then choose which full messages to call up. In addition to transmitting messages between employees down the hall or overseas, e-mail technology even permits computer-to-computer exchanges of purchase orders, invoices, electronic payment of bills, and so on. For example, the authors, copy editor, and publisher of this book—all in widely separated locations—regularly transmitted manuscript, notes, and even drawings via e-mail messages and attachments during the book's preparation. Thus e-mail reduces barriers of time, distance, and cost to the creation and maintenance of effective communication networks. It also minimizes "phone tag," in which individuals trade numerous phone calls before catching up with each other. According to *U.S. News & World Report*, 200 million e-mail messages are sent each day and the number is continuing to increase.[24]

Along with easy access and efficiency in communication, e-mail creates challenges for organizations. For example, protecting confidentiality while using e-mail can create ethical problems for employees. The question is: Who owns the information? The following Managing Ethics Competency feature illustrates some of the new confidentiality problems facing employees.

COMPETENCY: MANAGING ETHICS

PUTTING YOUR RÉSUMÉ ONLINE

The director of human resources at Argus Technical Services was surfing an Internet job board and pulled Unmesh Laddha's résumé off the Net. Upon further review, he discovered that Laddha was one of the company's employees. Laddha's boss called him in and wanted to know what was going on. He explained that he had posted the résumé online before taking the job at Argus and thought that it had been taken off. He explained, "Once I put my résumé on the Internet, I couldn't do anything to control it." According to lawyers, "once you've posted it publicly, forget it." Many job boards don't let a candidate even remove outdated versions.

As a senior human resources consultant at Seer Technologies, Lori Laubach's job is to log onto résumé boards, such as www.JobOptions.com or www.hotjobs.com each day, type in the name of the company, and see if any of Seer's 700 employees pop up. If one does, Laubach notifies the employee's supervisor. They discuss whether the employee should be persuaded to stay or encouraged to leave and then arrange a meeting with the employee.

Donald Harries, chairman of the Privacy Committee of the International Association for Human Resource Information Management, says that such practices smack of guard towers and searchlights. This association argues that professionals who want to have their credentials out there while keeping their careers intact should have that right. Sensitive to mounting concerns, some job boards, such as www.hotjobs.com, are turning privacy into a selling point by offering candidates the option of "blocking" their résumés from scanning by certain employers. Unfortunately, employers can skirt some blocking mechanisms simply by registering under a noncorporate e-mail address. But at stake, Laubach insists, is a legitimate employer concern: protection of company secrets.

Before putting your résumé online, you should consider doing the following:

- Date your résumé in case it lands on your boss's desk 2 years from now.
- Include a legend that forbids its unauthorized transmission by headhunters.
- Call a job site's administrators before positing it and ask questions such as: Are résumés ever traded or sold to other databases? Who has access to the database?[25]

For more information on online résumés, visit ***www.robgalbraith.com.***

Voice mail is a computer-based message system that people access by telephone. They may use it as they would an answering machine to receive recorded messages or as they would memoranda to send recorded messages to others. Although more expensive to operate than an e-mail system, voice mail is a richer information medium than e-mail. Voice mail is an excellent medium for sending short, simple, and noncontroversial messages.

Telecommuting is the practice of working at home while being electronically linked to the office.[26] Employees who work out of a customer's office or communicate with the office or plant via a laptop computer or mobile phone would be classified as telecommuters. Telecommuting often involves the use of computer-based software, e-mail, voice mail, fax machines, and related technologies. Telecommuting jobs usually involve some combination of

- tasks that can be performed and transmitted electronically;
- regular telephone use;
- routine information handling;
- tasks that can be performed independently of others and, if necessary, be coordinated with others electronically; and/or
- project-oriented jobs with well-defined targets and schedules.

Telecommuting jobs include salesperson, real estate agent, computer systems analyst, data entry clerk, consultant, author, security broker, and copy editor. Millions of employees have already formed telecommuting arrangements with their employers, and the number is growing. Among the more well-known companies with successful telecommuting programs for some employees are IBM, Xerox, American Express, DuPont, Pacific Bell, J.C. Penney, and Apple Computer. However, telecommuting isn't for everyone. Some telecommuters experience a sense of isolation, stagnation, or compulsive overwork. Sandy Gustin, who works full-time from her home as a medical transcriber for a group of doctors at the Columbia Hospital System in Fort Myers, Florida, says: "Every day is the same. You put in your eight hours and there isn't anybody to talk to, and you miss what's going on in the outside world. You feel you're in your house constantly." Gustin clearly misses the social aspects of a job.

The potential advantages of information technologies are fairly obvious. They allow people to communicate with one another more easily, quickly, and less expensively. However, some problems need to be guarded against. First, these technologies haven't been effective for relationship building or complex team problem solving where face-to-face dialogue is needed. Bill Speer, facilities manager at Pier 1 Imports, comments, "E-mail doesn't have the nuances of real-time conversation. Senior-level managers lose track of the impact their mail may have on people. Because these people are busy, they forget that we have to implement the ideas they think are great. Often we simply need to find out what they were thinking when they dreamt up this idea."[27]

Second, information technologies can break down the boundaries between work time and nonwork time. For example, Gustin has a separate room in which she transcribes her tapes, but is faced with interruptions from her pets, the doorbell, husband, children (especially when they are out of school), and telephone. She gets up at 3:30 A.M. to start working because she knows that her day will be filled with interruptions. If not managed carefully, the use of these technologies can evolve into continuous distractions and invasion of privacy because they let managers and others contact the employee easily at any time.

Third, the Internet/intranet may erode the delegation of authority by creating too much and too frequent communication between superiors and subordinates. Robyn Youngjohn, a senior consultant for the Waters Consulting Group, comments: "I get 80 e-mails a day, and 60 of them are because I'm copied from multiple levels. I can put filters on my mailbox. But, I tell my people the best filter is to show self-restraint." These problems are not inevitable, and awareness is the first step in avoiding them. In addition, superiors may start to micromanage the work of subordinates because giving and getting constant feedback is too easy.

Fourth, e-mail opens the possibility of wasting time on increased volumes of meaningless data (junk) with the consequence of unnecessary work overload. Fifth, for most individuals, e-mail lacks confidentiality. Most e-mail messages can easily be read by others who have computers and access to the same intranet or to the Internet.

Learning Objective:

4. Explain the skills and abilities that foster dialogue.

FOSTERING DIALOGUE

The skills and behaviors that directly foster dialogue between individuals are the focus of this section because the lack of them hinders or prevents dialogue. **Dialogue** is a process whereby people suspend their defensive exchanges to enable a free flow of inquiry into their own and others' assumptions and beliefs.[28] As a result, dialogue can build mutual trust and common ground. A necessary condition for dialogue is assertive communication. **Assertive communication** means confidently expressing what you think, feel, and believe while respecting the right of the other to hold different views. True dialogue requires that interacting individuals demonstrate multiple skills and behaviors. Figure 13.6 illustrates the idea that dialogue is characterized by a specific group of skills and behaviors. They include communication openness, constructive feedback, appropriate self-disclosure, active listening, and supportive nonverbal cues.

COMMUNICATION OPENNESS

Communication openness may be viewed as a continuum ranging from closed, guarded, and defensive to open, candid, and nondefensive. Figure 13.7 shows that, at the extreme left-hand side of the continuum, every message (regardless of the medium of transmission) is weighed, analyzed, and scrutinized. Communication occurs on two levels: direct

Figure 13.6 **Network of Skills and Behaviors That Foster Dialogue**

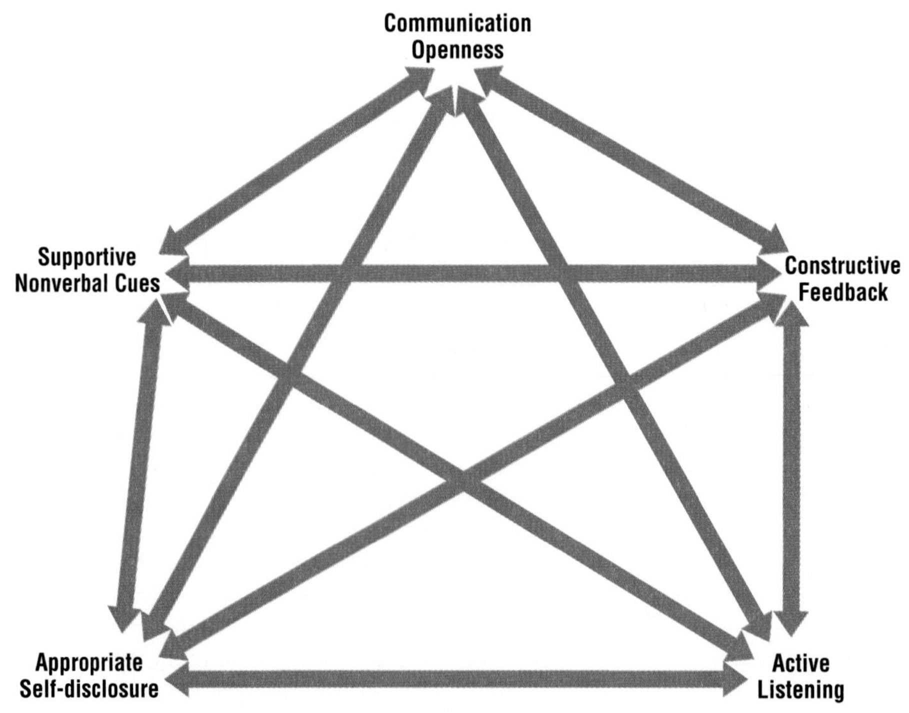

Figure 13.7 **The Communication Openness Continuum**

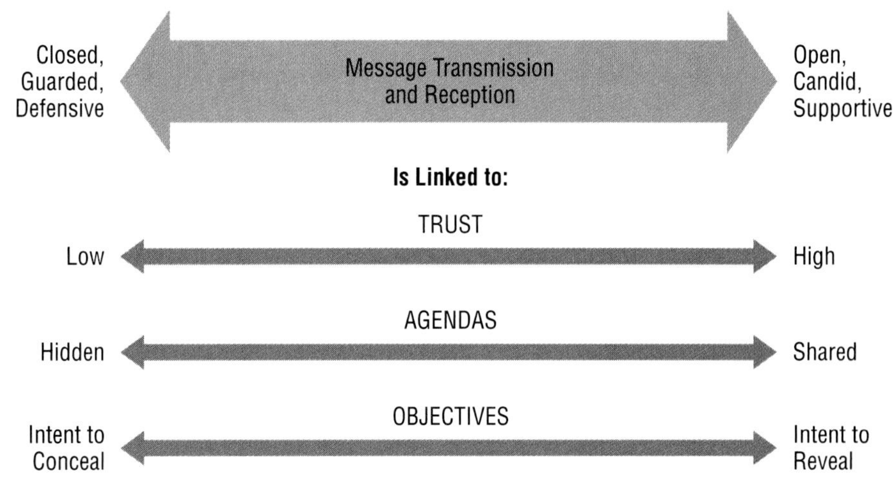

Source: Adapted from Sussman, L. Managers: On the defensive. *Business Horizons,* January–February 1991, 83; Munter, M. *Guide to Managerial Communication: Effective Business Writing and Speaking,* 5th ed. Englewood Cliffs, N.J.: Prentice-Hall, 1999.

and meta-communication. **Meta-communication** brings out the (hidden) assumptions, inferences, and interpretations of the parties that form the basis of open messages. In closed communication, senders and receivers consciously and purposely hide their real agendas and "messages," and game playing is rampant. Meta-communication focuses on inferences such as (1) what I think you think about what I said; (2) what I think you really mean; (3) what I really mean but hope you don't realize what I mean; (4) what you're saying but what I think you really mean; and (5) what I think you're trying to tell me but aren't directly telling me because . . . (you're afraid of hurting my feelings, you think being totally open could hurt your chances of promotion, and so on). At the extreme right-hand side of the continuum, the communication is totally open, candid, and supportive. The words and nonverbal cues sent convey an authentic message that the sender chose without a hidden agenda. The purpose of communication is to reveal intent, not conceal it. The individuals express what they mean and mean what they convey. Breakdowns in communication at this end of the continuum are due primarily to honest errors (e.g., the different meanings that people assign to words such as *soon* or *immediately*). Communication openness usually is a matter of degree rather than an absolute. The nature of language, linguistics, and different interpersonal relationships (coworker to coworker, subordinate to superior, friend to friend, or spouse to spouse) create the situational forces that allow for degrees of shading, coloring, amplification, and deflection in the use of words and nonverbal cues as symbols of meaning.

Contextual Factors. The degree of openness must be considered in relation to the context associated with such openness. (We address contextual factors at length in Chapter 9 in terms of power and political behavior, in Chapter 12 in terms of conflict and negotiation, and in Chapter 17 in terms of organizational culture.) We note just three of these factors here briefly. First, the history of the relationship is perhaps the most significant factor affecting trust and risk taking in interpersonal communication. Has the other person violated your or others' trust in the past? Has the other person provided cues (verbal and/or nonverbal) soliciting or reinforcing your attempts to be open and candid? Or has the other person provided cues to the contrary? Has the history of the relationship created a level of such comfort that both you and the other person can focus on direct communication, rather than meta-communication?

Second, if the communication is likely to be partly adversarial or the other person is committed to damaging or weakening your position or gaining at your expense, engaging in guarded communication is rational. Conversely, if the communication is likely to be friendly and the other person is trying to please you, strengthen your position, or enhance your esteem, guarded communication may be viewed as irrational.

Third, when you communicate with someone of higher status and power, you are communicating with someone who has some control over your future. That person may be responsible for appraising your performance, judging your promotability, and determining the amount of your merit pay increase. The tendency is to project a favorable image and to encode negative messages with qualifiers, which is understandable and certainly may be rational. This perception is especially valid if past encounters with that person reinforce your use of some distortion over completely honest disclosures.

Constructive Feedback

In giving feedback, people share their thoughts and feelings about others with them. Feedback may involve personal feelings or abstract thoughts, as when someone reacts to others' ideas or proposals. The emotional impact of feedback varies according to how personally it is focused. When you attempt to achieve dialogue, feedback should be supportive (reinforcing ongoing behavior) or corrective (indicating that a change in behavior is appropriate). The following are principles of constructive feedback that can foster dialogue.

- Constructive feedback is based on a foundation of trust between sender and receiver. When an organization is characterized by extreme personal competitiveness, the emphasis is on the use of power to punish and control, rigid superior–subordinate relationships, and a lack of trust for constructive feedback.
- Constructive feedback is specific rather than general. It uses clear and recent examples. Saying, "You are a dominating person," is not as useful as saying, "Just now when we were deciding the issue, you did not listen to what others said. I felt I had to accept your argument or face attack from you."
- Constructive feedback is given at a time when the receiver appears to be ready to accept it. When a person is angry, upset, or defensive, that probably isn't the time to bring up other issues.
- Constructive feedback is checked with the receiver to determine whether it seems valid. The sender can ask the receiver to rephrase and restate the feedback to test whether it matches what the sender intended.
- Constructive feedback covers behaviors that the receiver may be capable of doing something about.
- Constructive feedback doesn't include more than the receiver can handle at any particular time. For example, the receiver may become threatened and defensive if the feedback includes everything the receiver does that annoys the sender.[29]

In a recent study of why 37 CEOs failed, 17 (including Al Dunlap at Sunbeam, Les Alberthal at EDS, and Joseph Antonini at Kmart) failed because of people problems. These CEOs were unable to deal with a few key subordinates whose sustained poor performance hurt the organization. What's most striking is that they knew there was a problem, but their "inner" voices told them to suppress it. Constructive feedback is a vital process, but when indecisiveness takes over, fast-moving competitors gain the advantage. According to Elmer Johnson, a top GM executive who reported to Robert Stempel (CEO of GM from 1990–1992), "The meeting of many of our committees and policy groups had become little more than time-consuming formalities. The outcomes were almost never in doubt. . . . There was little discussion and almost nothing amounting to lively frank discussion. It was a system that resulted in lengthy delays and faulty decisions by paralyzing the operating of people."[30]

APPROPRIATE SELF-DISCLOSURE

Self-disclosure is any information that individuals communicate (verbally or nonverbally) about themselves to others. People often unconsciously disclose much about themselves by what they say and how they present themselves to others. The ability to express yourself to others usually is basic to personal growth and development. Nondisclosing individuals may repress their real feelings because to reveal them is threatening. Conversely, total-disclosure individuals, who expose a great deal about themselves to anyone they meet, actually may be unable to communicate with others because they are too preoccupied with themselves. The presence of appropriate self-disclosure, say, between superior and subordinate or team members and customers, can facilitate dialogue and sharing of work-related problems.

Before you read any further, please respond honestly to the statements in the Managing Self Competency feature on page 400. Your answers should reflect your attitudes and behavior as they are now, not as you would like them to be. This instrument is designed to help you discover how self-aware you are so that you can tailor your learning to your specific communication needs.

A person's level in an organization often complicates self-disclosure. Individuals are likely to dampen self-disclosure to those having higher formal power because of their ability to reward or punish. Even when a subordinate is able and willing to engage in "appropriate" forms of self-disclosure at work, a perception of the superior's trustworthiness in not using the revealed information to punish, intimidate, or ridicule is likely to influence the amount and form of self-disclosure.

ACTIVE LISTENING

Active listening is necessary to encourage maximum levels of feedback and openness. **Listening** is a process that integrates physical, emotional, and intellectual inputs in a search for meaning and understanding. Listening is effective when the receiver understands the sender's message as intended.

As much as 40 percent of an 8-hour workday for many employees is devoted to listening. However, tests of listening comprehension suggest that people often listen at only 25 percent efficiency. Listening skills influence the quality of peer, manager–subordinate, and employee–customer relationships. Employees who dislike a manager may find it extremely difficult to listen attentively to the manager's comments during performance review sessions. The following guidelines are suggested for increasing listening skills to foster dialogue.

- Active listening involves having a reason or purpose for listening. Good listeners tend to search for value and meaning in what is being said, even if they are not predisposed to be interested in the particular issue or topic. Poor listeners tend to rationalize any or all inattention on the basis of a lack of initial interest.
- Active listening involves suspending judgment, at least initially. Good listening requires concentrating on the sender's whole message, rather than forming evaluations on the basis of the first few ideas presented.
- Active listening involves resisting distractions, such as noises, sights, and other people, and focusing on the sender.
- Active listening involves pausing before responding to the sender.
- Active listening involves rephrasing in your own words the content and feeling of what the sender seems to be saying, especially when the message is emotional or unclear.
- Active listening seeks out the sender's important themes in terms of the overall content and feeling of the message.
- Active listening involves using the time differential between the rate of thought (400 or 500 words per minute) and the rate of speech (100 to 150 words per minute) to reflect on content and search for meaning.[31]

COMPETENCY: MANAGING SELF

HOW SELF-AWARE ARE YOU?

When answering these 11 questions, use the following rating scale.

1. Strongly disagree	4. Slightly agree
2. Disagree	5. Agree
3. Slightly disagree	6. Strongly agree

_____ 1. I seek information about my strengths and weaknesses from others as a basis for self-improvement.

_____ 2. When I receive negative feedback about myself from others, I do not get angry or defensive.

_____ 3. In order to improve, I am willing to be self-disclosing to others (i.e., share my feelings and beliefs).

_____ 4. I am very much aware of my personal style of gathering information and making decisions.

_____ 5. I am very much aware of my own interpersonal needs when it comes to forming relationships with other people.

_____ 6. I have a good sense of how I cope with situations that are ambiguous and uncertain.

_____ 7. I have a well-developed set of personal standards and principles that guide my behavior.

_____ 8. I feel very much in charge of what happens to me, good and bad.

_____ 9. I seldom, if ever, feel angry, depressed, or anxious without knowing why.

_____10. I am conscious of the areas in which conflict and friction most frequently arise in my interactions with others.

_____11. I have a close personal relationship with at least one other person with whom I can share personal information and personal feelings.

SCORING KEY

Skill Area	**Total**	**Grand Total**
Self-disclosure and openness to feedback from others (items 1, 2, 3, 9, 11)	_____	
Awareness of own values, cognitive style, change orientation, and interpersonal orientation (items 4, 5, 6, 7, 8, 10)	_____	
		_____

Comparison Data

Compare your scores to three standards: (1) the maximum possible (66); (2) the scores of other students in your class; and (3) the scores of a norm group consisting of more than 500 business students. In comparison to the norm group, if you scored

55 or above	You are in the top quartile.
52–54	You are in the second quartile.
48–51	You are in the third quartile.
47 or below	You are in the bottom quartile.[32]

Most of these active listening skills are interrelated. That is, you can't practice one without improving the others. Unfortunately, like the guidelines for improving feedback, the guidelines for improving active listening are much easier to understand than to develop and practice. The more you practice active listening skills, the more likely you will be able to enter into effective dialogue.

Learning Objective:

5. Describe how nonverbal communication supports dialogue.

NONVERBAL COMMUNICATION

Nonverbal communication includes nonlanguage human responses (e.g., body motions and personal physical attributes) and environmental effects (e.g., a large or small office).[33] Nonverbal cues may contain many hidden messages and can influence the process and outcome of face-to-face communication. Even a person who is silent or inactive in the presence of others may be sending a message, which may or may not be the intended message (including boredom, fear, anger, or depression).

Types of Nonverbal Cues

The basic types of nonverbal cues are presented in Table 13.2, along with the numerous ways people can and do communicate without saying or writing a word. Nonverbal communication is important to verbal communication in that neither is adequate by itself for effective dialogue. Verbal and nonverbal cues can be related by

- repeating, as when verbal directions to some location are accompanied by pointing;
- contradicting, as in the case of the person who says, "What, me nervous?" while fidgeting and perspiring anxiously before taking a test—a good example of how the nonverbal message might be more believable when verbal and nonverbal signals conflict;
- substituting nonverbal for verbal cues, as when an employee returns to the office with a stressful expression that says, "I've had a horrible meeting with my manager," without a word being spoken; and
- complementing the verbal cue through nonverbal "underlining," as when a person pounds the table, places a hand on the shoulder of a coworker, uses a tone of voice indicating the great importance attached to the message, or presents a gift as a way of reinforcing an expression of gratitude or respect.

Table 13.2 Basic Types of Nonverbal Cues

TYPE OF CUE	EXPLANATION AND EXAMPLES
Body motion	Gestures, facial expressions, eye behavior, touching, and any other movement of the limbs and body
Personal physical characteristics	Body shape, physique, posture, body or breath odors, height, weight, hair color, and skin color
Paralanguage	Voice qualities, volume, speech rate, pitch, nonfluencies (saying "ah," "um," or "uh"), laughing, yawning, and so on
Use of space	Ways people use and perceive space, including seating arrangements, conversational distance, and the "territorial" tendency of humans to stake out a personal space
Physical environment	Building and room design, furniture and other objects, interior decorating, cleanliness, lighting, and noise
Time	Being late or early, keeping others waiting, cultural differences in time perception, and the relationship between time and status

Nonverbal cues have been linked to a wide variety of concepts and issues. We briefly consider three: (1) cultural differences; (2) status, in terms of the relative ranking of individuals and groups; and (3) gender differences.

Cultural Differences

Throughout this chapter, we have mentioned the impact of culture on communication. Because of the many nonverbal differences in communication, people from different cultures often misunderstand each other, which is a significant barrier to cross-cultural understanding.[34] Earlier in this chapter, we examined how three forms of nonverbal communication—body language, personal space, and ethnocentrism—affect cross-cultural communication. Let's now examine two additional forms of nonverbal communication.

Chromatics. **Chromatics** is communication through the use of color. Colors of clothing, products, packaging, or gifts send intended or unintended messages when people communicate cross-culturally. For example, in Hong Kong red signifies happiness or good luck. The traditional bridal dress is red, and at Chinese New Year lucky money is distributed in *hong bao*, or red envelopes. Men in Hong Kong avoid green because of the Cantonese expression, "He's wearing a green hat," which means "His wife is cheating on him." In Chile, a gift of yellow roses conveys the message, "I don't like you," whereas in the Czech Republic giving red roses indicates a romantic interest.[35]

Chronemics. **Chronemics** reflect the use of time in a culture.[36] Before reading any further, please complete the instrument in Table 13.3 to determine how you use your personal time. In a culture with a **monochronic time schedule,** things are done linearly, or one activity at a time. Time is seen as something that can be controlled or

Table 13.3

The Polychronic Attitude Index

Please consider how you feel about the following statements. Circle your choice on the scale provided: strongly agree, agree, neutral, disagree, or strongly disagree.

	STRONGLY DISAGREE	DISAGREE	NEUTRAL	AGREE	STRONGLY AGREE
I do not like to juggle several activities at the same time.	5	4	3	2	1
People should not try to do many things at once.	5	4	3	2	1
When I sit down at my desk, I work on one project at a time.	5	4	3	2	1
I am comfortable doing several things at the same time.	1	2	3	4	5

Add up your points, and divide the total by 4. Then plot your score on the scale.

1.0 1.5 2.0 2.5 3.0 3.5 4.0 4.5 5.0

Monochronic Polychronic

The lower the score (below 3.0), the more monochronic your organization or department is; the higher the score (above 3.0), the more polychronic it is.

Source: Adapted from Bluedorn, A. C., Kaufman, C. F., and Lane, P. M. How many things do you like to do at once? An introduction to monochronic and polychronic time. *Academy of Management Executive*, 1992, 6(4), 17–26. Used with permission of Bluedorn, A. C., 1999.

wasted by people. This time schedule is followed in individualistic cultures, such as those in Northern Europe, Germany, and the United States. Being a few minutes late for a business appointment is an insult, so punctuality is extremely important. Keith Hughes, CEO of The Associates, locks the doors when a meeting is supposed to start and doesn't unlock them until the meeting is over.

With a **polychronic time schedule,** people tend to do several things at the same time. Many people may like to drive and conduct business at the same time (cars and cellular phones) or watch the news and a ball game at the same time (picture-in-picture TV). Schedules are less important than personal involvement and the completion of business. In Latin America and the Middle East, time schedules are less important than personal involvement. In Ecuador, businesspeople come to a meeting 15 or 20 minutes late and still consider that they're on time.

Status Differences

The following are only three of the many relationships between nonverbal cues and organizational status.

- Employees of higher status typically have better offices than do employees of lower status. For example, executive offices at EDS are more spacious, located on the top floors of the building, and have finer carpets and furniture than those of first-line managers. Most senior offices at EDS are at the corners, so they have windows on two sides.
- The offices of higher status employees are better "protected" than those of lower status employees. Here, *protected* means how much more difficult it would be for you to arrange to visit the governor of your state than for the governor to arrange to visit you. Top executive areas are typically least accessible and are often sealed off from others by several doors and assistants. Having an office with a door and a secretary who answers the telephone protects even lower level managers and many staff personnel.
- The higher the employee's status, the easier that employee finds it to invade the territory of lower status employees. A superior typically feels free to walk right in on subordinates, whereas subordinates are more careful to ask permission or make an appointment before visiting a superior.[37]

Carried to excess, these and other nonverbal status cues are likely to create barriers to dialogue, especially from the perspective of the employees with lower formal status. However, effective managers often use supportive nonverbal cues when meeting with subordinates, such as (1) lightly touching subordinates on the arm when they arrive and shaking hands, (2) smiling appropriately, (3) nodding to affirm what was said, (4) slightly pulling their chairs closer to subordinates and maintaining an open posture, and (5) engaging in eye contact to further demonstrate listening and interest.

Gender Differences

Gender differences contribute to nonverbal communication challenges. However, these differences are minor in comparison to the differences based on cultural influences. In addition to communicating gender, body language may communicate status and power. Many signs of dominance and submission are exchanged through nonverbal communication. Some nonverbal behaviors are associated with the subordinate position of either gender. But many of these same behaviors have been associated with women, regardless of status. In this section, we describe three nonverbal patterns and note how they may differ by gender. These patterns reflect generalities and certainly do not apply to all men and women. Moreover, we know that in some segments of the U.S. and Canadian societies, these patterns have changed or are changing.

Use of Space. Women's bodily behavior more often is restrained and restricted than men's. In fact, their femininity is gauged by how little space they occupy. Men's expansiveness and the strength of their gestures reflect masculinity. Men control greater territory and personal space, a property associated with dominance and status. Studies have found that people tend to approach women more closely than they do men, seat themselves closer to women, cut across women's paths in hallways, and so on.[38]

Eye Contact. Gender may influence eye contact. In personal interactions, women tend to look more at the other person than men do—and they maintain more woman-to-woman eye contact. Some research suggests that women are more skilled than men in accurately decoding nonverbal cues. People tend to maintain more eye contact with those from whom they want approval. Women are stared at and reciprocate by not looking back more than men. Men routinely stare at women in public. Our language even has specific words, *ogling* and *leering*, for this practice.

Touching. Touching may be another gesture of dominance. Cuddling in response to touch may be a corresponding gesture of submission. Just as a manager can put a hand on a worker, a master on a servant, and a teacher on a student, so men frequently put their hands on women.

Another side to touching is much better understood: Touching symbolizes friendship and intimacy. The power aspect of touching doesn't rule out its intimacy aspect. A particular touch may have both components and more, but it is the pattern of touching between individuals that tells us the most about their relationship. When touching is reciprocal—that is, when both people have equal touching privileges—we have information about the intimacy of the relationship. Much touching indicates closeness, whereas little touching indicates distance. The freedom of one person to touch the other but not vice versa provides information about status and power. The person with greater touching privileges probably has higher status or more power. Consider the experience of one information systems (IS) manager. He found himself the subject of a sexual harassment complaint. The IS manager, who wants to remain anonymous, says that he was training a female software engineer. While she sat at her workstation, he stood behind her and briefly put his hand on her shoulder. He says, "When I was called down to human resources and told about my inappropriate behavior I was stunned. Now, I keep my distance—literally. I stand three feet away with my hands in my pockets." Nonverbal communication can, indeed, have powerful consequences.[39]

Changing Patterns. Many women have been reversing these nonverbal interaction patterns. Women now feel freer to stop smiling when they are unhappy, stop lowering their eyes, stop getting out of men's way on the street, and stop letting themselves be interrupted. They can stare people in the eye, address someone by first name if that person addresses them by their first name, and touch when they feel that it is appropriate. Men need to become more aware of what they are signifying nonverbally. Men can restrain their invasions of personal space by avoiding staring, touching (if not by mutual consent), and interrupting.

CHAPTER SUMMARY

1. State the essentials of interpersonal communication.

The essential elements in the communication process—senders, receivers, transmitters, receptors, messages, channels, noise, meaning, encoding, decoding, and feedback—are interrelated.

Face-to-face interpersonal communication has the highest degree of information richness. An information-rich medium is especially important for performing complex tasks and resolving social and emotional issues that involve considerable uncertainty and ambiguity. Important issues usually contain significant amounts of uncertainty, ambiguity, and people-related (especially social and emotional) problems.

There are many potential challenges to effective interpersonal communication. We briefly reviewed the underlying interpersonal hurdles discussed in previous chapters. Direct hurdles include aggressive communication approaches, noise, semantics, demeaning language, and lying and distortion. The hurdles stemming from cultural differences always are present. They may be especially high when the interaction takes place between individuals from high-context and low-context cultures.

2. Discuss how interpersonal communication networks affect power and control relationships among employees.

Through their many communication networks, individuals may repeat the interpersonal communication process dozens of times each day. We identified five types of communication networks, including the star, Y, chain, circle, and all-channel. These networks operate both vertically and laterally in organizations. They can range from closed and centralized to open and decentralized and may hinder or support organizational diversity.

3. Describe how information technologies affect communication.

For employees, the increasing reliance on networks of people linked electronically means that they must develop their capabilities to use information technologies. Information technologies substitute e-mail, voice mail, teleconferencing, and telecommuting for face-to-face communication. Although these networks move information efficiently and quickly, they have some limitations, including social isolation, lack of privacy, supervising people whom the manager never sees, and information overload.

4. Explain the skills and abilities that foster dialogue.

The communication process involves a number of complex factors and barriers that require skill to overcome. The skills and behaviors that foster dialogue include communication openness, constructive feedback, active listening, and appropriate self-disclosure. They require both sender and receiver to play a dynamic role in the communication process. In open communication sender and receiver are able to discuss, disagree, and search for understanding without resorting to personal attacks or hidden agendas. Feedback received from others provides motivation for a person to learn and change his or her behavior. By being an active listener, the receiver hears the whole message without interpretation or judgment. How much someone is willing to share with others depends on the person's ability to disclose information.

5. Describe how nonverbal communication supports dialogue.

Nonverbal cues play a powerful role in supporting dialogue. Throughout this chapter, we described how cultural barriers can impede communication effectiveness. We examined specifically how certain nonverbal messages—the use of gestures, color, and time—can affect cross-cultural communication. Formal organizational position is often tied to status. Status symbols, such as office size, the floor on which the office is located, number of windows, location of a secretary, and access to senior-level employees, all influence communication patterns. Gender can also affect the use of nonverbal cues. Use of eye contact, space, and touching varies between men and women. If not used appropriately, these nonverbal cues will hinder dialogue.

KEY TERMS AND CONCEPTS

Assertive communication
Channels
Chromatics
Chronemics
Commercial online services
Cultural context
Data
Decoding
Dialogue
Distortion
Electronic mail (e-mail)
Encoding
Ethnocentrism
Feedback

High-context culture
Honesty
Impression management
Intercultural communication
Internet
Interpersonal communication
Interpersonal communication network
Intranet
Language routines
Listening
Low-context culture
Lying
Media richness
Messages
Meta-communication
Monochronic time schedule
Noise
Nonverbal communication
Polychronic time schedule
Receptors
Self-disclosure
Semantics
Telecommuting
Transmitters
Voice mail
World Wide Web

DISCUSSION QUESTIONS

1. What are the major essentials of the communication process?
2. Describe some problems that an individual from a low-context culture and an individual from a high-context culture could have in trying to communicate.
3. Describe your communication network at work or in school. Is it effective? Would you like to make any changes in it? Why or why not?
4. The Internet and e-mail are making it easier to communicate with people from different cultures. Do you agree or disagree? Explain.
5. What are three ethical concerns with e-mail?
6. Think of a team of which you are a member. How would you assess the members' self-awareness?
7. Why is media richness important when communicating?
8. According to Ken Blanchard, author of the *One Minute Manager*, feedback is the breakfast of champions. What are some of the barriers that managers need to overcome when giving others feedback?
9. Describe the common nonverbal cues used by someone you have worked for. Are these usually consistent or inconsistent with that person's verbal expressions? Explain.
10. If your job transfers you to a foreign culture, what nonverbal communication practices must you be sensitive to?
11. If a person of a different gender supervises you, what nonverbal problems might you encounter?

DEVELOPING COMPETENCIES

Competency: Managing Self—Interpersonal Communication Practices

Instructions: This survey is designed to assess your interpersonal communication practices.[40] For each item in the survey, indicate which of the alternative reactions best represents how you would handle the situation described. Some alternatives may be equally characteristic or equally uncharacteristic of your reaction. Although this is a possibility, choose the alternative that is relatively more characteristic of your reaction. For each item, distribute five points between the alternatives in any of the following combinations.

	A	B
1.	5	0
2.	4	1
3.	3	2
4.	2	3
5.	1	4
6.	0	5

Thus, there are six possible combinations for responding to the pair of alternatives presented to you with each survey item. Be sure that the numbers you assign to each pair sum to 5. To the extent possible, please relate each situation in the survey to your own personal experience. In this survey, we alternate the words he and she and him and her to balance use of the feminine and masculine genders.

1. If a friend of mine had a personality conflict with a mutual acquaintance of ours with whom it was important for her to get along, I would:
   _____A. Tell my friend that I felt she was partially responsible for any problems with this other person and try to let her know how the person was being affected by her.
   _____B. Not get involved because I would not be able to continue to get along with both of them once I had entered into the conflict.
2. If one of my friends and I had a heated argument in the past and I realized that he will be ill at ease around me from that time on, I would:
   _____A. Avoid making things worse by discussing his behavior and just let the whole thing drop.

______B. Bring up his behavior and ask him how he felt the argument had affected our relationship.

3. If a friend began to avoid me and act in an aloof and withdrawn manner, I would:
   ______A. Tell her about her behavior and suggest she tell me what was on her mind.
   ______B. Follow her lead and keep our contacts brief and aloof since that seems to be what she wants.
4. If two of my friends and I were talking and one of my friends slipped and brought up a personal problem of mine that involved the other friend, and of which he was not yet aware, I would:
   ______A. Change the subject and signal my friend to do the same.
   ______B. Fill in my uninformed friend on what the other friend was talking about and suggest that we go into it later.
5. If a friend were to tell me that, in her opinion, I was doing things that made me less effective than I might be in social situations, I would:
   ______A. Ask her to spell out or describe what she has observed and suggest changes I might make.
   ______B. Resent the criticism and let her know why I behave the way I do.
6. If one of my friends aspired to an office in our student organization for which I felt he was unqualified and if he had been tentatively assigned to that position by the president of the student society, I would:
   ______A. Not mention my misgivings to either my friend or the president and let them handle it in their own way.
   ______B. Tell my friend and the president of my misgivings and then leave the final decision up to them.
7. If I felt that one of my friends was being unfair to me and her other friends, but none of them had mentioned anything about it, I would:
   ______A. Ask several of those people how they perceived the situation to see if they felt she was being unfair.
   ______B. Not ask the others how they perceived our friend but wait for them to bring it up to me.
8. If I were preoccupied with some personal matters and a friend told me that I had become irritated with him and others and that I was jumping on him for unimportant things, I would:
   ______A. Tell him I was preoccupied and would probably be on edge a while and would prefer not to be bothered.
   ______B. Listen to his complaints but not try to explain my actions to him.
9. If I had heard some friends discussing an ugly rumor about a friend of mine that I knew could hurt her and she asked me what I knew about it, if anything, I would:
   ______A. Say I didn't know anything about it and tell her no one would believe a rumor like that anyway.
   ______B. Tell her exactly what I had heard, when I had heard it, and from whom I had heard it.
10. If a friend pointed out the fact that I had a personality conflict with another friend with whom it was important for me to get along, I would:
   ______A. Consider his comments out of line and tell him I didn't want to discuss the matter any further.
   ______B. Talk about it openly with him to find out how my behavior was being affected by this.
11. If my relationship with a friend has been damaged by repeated arguments on an issue of importance to us both, I would:
   ______A. Be cautious in my conversations with her so the issue would not come up again to worsen our relationship.
   ______B. Point to the problems the controversy was causing in our relationship and suggest that we discuss it until we get it resolved.
12. If in a personal discussion with a friend about his problems and behavior, he suddenly suggested we discuss my problems and behavior as well as his own, I would:
   ______A. Try to keep the discussion away from me by suggesting that other, closer friends often talked to me about such matters.
   ______B. Welcome the opportunity to hear what he felt about me and encourage his comments.
13. If a friend of mine began to tell me about her hostile feelings about another friend who she felt was being unkind to others (and I wholeheartedly agreed), I would:
   ______A. Listen and also express my own feelings to her so she would know where I stood.
   ______B. Listen but not express my own negative views and opinions because she might repeat what I said to her in confidence.
14. If I thought an ugly rumor was being spread about me and suspected that one of my friends had quite likely heard it, I would:
   ______A. Avoid mentioning the issue and leave it to him to tell me about it if he wanted to.
   ______B. Risk putting him on the spot by asking him directly what he knew about the whole thing.
15. If I had observed a friend in social situations and thought that she was doing a number of things that hurt her relationships, I would:
   ______A. Risk being seen as a busybody and tell her what I had observed and my reactions to it.
   ______B. Keep my opinions to myself, rather than be seen as interfering in things that are none of my business.
16. If two friends and I were talking and one of them inadvertently mentioned a personal problem that involved me but of which I knew nothing, I would:
   ______A. Press them for information about the problem and their opinions about it.
   ______B. Leave it up to my friends to tell me or not tell me, letting them change the subject if they wished.
17. If a friend seemed to be preoccupied and began to jump on me for seemingly unimportant things and to become irritated with me and others without real cause, I would:
   ______A. Treat him with kid gloves for a while on the assumption that he was having some temporary personal problems that were none of my business.
   ______B. Try to talk to him about it and point out to him how his behavior was affecting people.

18. If I had begun to dislike certain habits of a friend to the point that it was interfering with my enjoying her company, I would:
    _____A. Say nothing to her directly but let her know my feelings by ignoring her whenever her annoying habits were obvious.
    _____B. Get my feelings out in the open and clear the air so that we could continue our friendship comfortably and enjoyably.
19. In discussing social behavior with one of my more sensitive friends, I would:
    _____A. Avoid mentioning his flaws and weaknesses so as not to hurt his feelings.
    _____B. Focus on his flaws and weaknesses so he could improve his interpersonal skills.
20. If I knew I might be assigned to an important position in our group and my friends' attitudes toward me had become rather negative, I would:
    _____A. Discuss my shortcomings with my friends so I could see where to improve.
    _____B. Try to figure out my own shortcomings by myself so I could improve.

Scoring Key

In this survey 10 of the items deal with your receptivity to feedback and 10 are concerned with your willingness to disclose yourself. Transfer your scores from each item to this scoring key. Add the scores in each column. Now, transfer these scores to Figure 13.8 by drawing a vertical line through the feedback score and a horizontal line through the self-disclosure line.

Receptivity to Feedback	Willingness to Self-Disclose
2. B _____	1. A _____
3. A _____	4. B _____
5. A _____	6. B _____
7. A _____	9. B _____
8. B _____	11. B _____
10. B _____	13. A _____
12. B _____	15. A _____
14. B _____	17. B _____
16. A _____	18. B _____
20. A _____	19. B _____
Total: _____	Total: _____

As Figure 13.8 suggests, higher scores in receptivity to feedback and willingness to disclose yourself indicate a greater willingness to engage in open interpersonal communication. Of course, you need to be mindful of the situational factors that may influence your natural personal preference to be relatively more open or closed in interpersonal communication.

Figure 13.8 **Personal Openness in Interpersonal Communications**

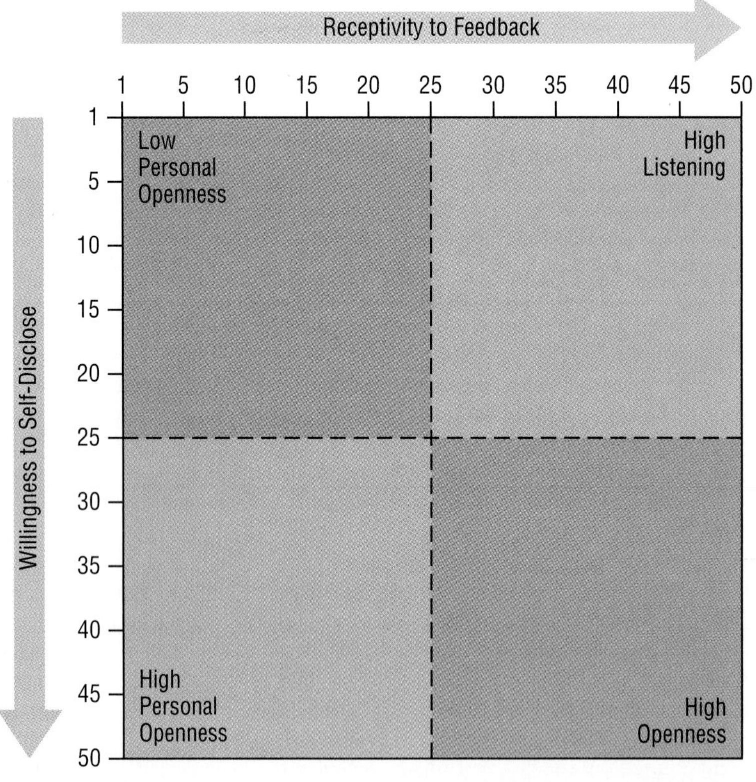

Competency: Managing Across Cultures—Juan Perillo and Jean Moore

Scene I: February 15, San Juan, Puerto Rico

Juan: Welcome back to Puerto Rico, Jean. It is good to have you here in San Juan again. I hope that your trip from Dayton was a smooth one.

Jean: Thank you, Juan. It's nice to be back here, where the sun shines. Fred sends his regards and also asked me to tell you how important it is that we work out a firm production schedule for the next three months. But first, how is your family? All doing well, I hope.

Juan: My wife is doing very well, but my daughter, Marianna, broke her arm and has to have surgery to repair the bone. We are very worried about that because the surgeon says she may have to have several operations. It is very difficult to think about my poor little daughter in the operating room. She was out playing with some other children when it happened. You know how rough children sometimes play with each other. It's really amazing that they don't have more injuries. Why, just last week, my son. . . .

Jean: Of course I'm very sorry to hear about little Marianna, but I'm sure everything will go well with the surgery. Now, shall we start work on the production schedule?

Juan: Oh, yes, of course, we must get started on the production schedule.

Jean: Fred and I thought that June 1 would be a good cutoff date for the first phase of the schedule. And we also thought that 100 A-type computers would be a reasonable goal for that phase. We know that you have some new assemblers whom you are training, and that you've had some problems getting parts from your suppliers in the past few months. But we're sure you have all of those problems worked out by now and that you are back to full production capability. So, what do you think? Is 100 A-type computers produced by June 1 a reasonable goal for your people?

Juan: (Hesitates a few seconds before replying) You want us to produce 100 of the newly designed A-type computers by June 1? Will we also be producing our usual number of Z-type computers, too?

Jean: Oh, yes. Your regular production schedule would remain the same as it's always been. The only difference is that you would be producing the new A-type computers, too. I mean, after all, you have a lot of new employees, and you have all of the new manufacturing and assembling equipment that we have in Dayton. So, you're as ready to make the new product as we are.

Juan: Yes, that's true. We have the new equipment and we've just hired a lot of new assemblers who will be working on the A-type computer. I guess there's no reason we can't meet the production schedule you and Fred have come up with.

Jean: Great, great. I'll tell Fred you agree with our decision and will meet the goal of 100 A-type computers by June 1. He'll be delighted to know that you can deliver what he was hoping for. And, of course, Juan, that means that you'll be doing just as well as the Dayton plant.

Juan: E-mail me the final decision after you talk to Fred.

Scene II: May 1, San Juan, Puerto Rico

Jean: Hello, Juan. How are things here in Puerto Rico? I'm glad to have the chance to come back and see how things are going.

Juan: Welcome, Jean. It's good to have you here. How was the weather last winter? How is your family?

Jean: The weather was bad—typical of Ohio. The family is fine, just fine. You know, Juan, Fred is really excited about that big order we just got from the Defense Department for 50 A-type computers. They want them by June 10, so we will ship them directly to Washington from San Juan as the computers come off your assembly line. Looks like it's a good thing we set your production goal at 100 A-type computers by June 1, isn't it?

Juan: Um, yes, that was certainly a good idea.

Jean: So, tell me. Have you had any problems with the new model? How are your new assemblers working out? Do you have any suggestions for changes in the manufacturing specs? How is the new quality control program working with this model? We're always looking for ways to improve, you know, and we appreciate any ideas you can give us.

Juan: Well, Jean, there is one thing. . . .

Jean: Yes? What is that?

Juan: Well, Jean, we have had a few problems with the new assemblers. Three of them have had serious illnesses in their families and have had to take off several days at a time to nurse a sick child or elderly parent. And another one was involved in a car accident and was in the hospital for several days. And you remember my daughter's surgery? Well, her arm didn't mend properly and we had to take her to Houston for additional consultations and therapy. But, of course, you and Fred knew about that. I e-mailed you in April about these.

Jean: Yes, we were aware that you had had some personnel problems and that you and your wife had to go to Houston with Marianna. But what does that have to do with the 50 A-type computers for the Defense Department?

Juan: Well, Jean, because of all these problems, we have had a few delays in the production schedule. Nothing serious, but we are a little bit behind our schedule.

Jean: How far behind is "a little bit"? What are you trying to tell me, Juan? Will you have 50 more A-type computers by June 1 to ship to Washington to fill the Defense Department order?

Juan: Well, I certainly hope we will have that number ready to ship. You know how difficult it can be to predict a precise number for manufacturing, Jean. You probably have many of these same problems in the Dayton plant, don't you? [41]

Questions

1. Based on the communication model (see Figure 13.1), what were some hurdles that prevented effective communication between Juan and Jean?
2. What are some cultural differences between the mainland and Puerto Rico that could have hindered communications?
3. What recommendations would you suggest to improve the communications between Juan and Jean?

REFERENCES

1. Axley, S. R. *Communication at Work: Management and the Communication Intensive Organization.* Westport, Conn.: Quorum Books, 1996.
2. Personal interview with D. Bitterman, director—investments, CIBC Oppenheimer, Dallas, Texas, 1999.
3. Russ, G. S., Daft, R. L., and Lengel, R. H. Media selection and managerial characteristics in organizational communications. *Management Communication Quarterly,* 1990, 4, 151–175; Ngwenyama, O. K., and Lee, A. S. Communication richness in electronic mail: Critical social theory and the contextuality of meaning. *MIS Quarterly,* 1997, 21, 145–167; Carlson, J. R., and Zmud, R. W. Channel expansion theory and the experiential nature of media richness perceptions. *Academy of Management Journal,* 1999, 42, 153–170.
4. Rothenbuhler, E. W. *Ritual Communication: From Everyday Conversation to Mediated Ceremony.* Thousand Oaks, Calif.: Sage, 1998.
5. Mortensen, C. D. *Miscommunication.* Thousand Oaks, Calif.: Sage, 1997.
6. Musgrave, J., and Anmis, M. *Relationship Dynamics: Theory and Analysis.* New York: Free Press, 1996.
7. Skarlicki, D. P., Folger, R., and Tesluk, P. Personality as a moderator in the relationship between fairness and retaliation. *Academy of Management Journal,* 1999, 42, 100–110.
8. Hall, D. T., Otazo, K. L., and Hollenbeck, G. P. Behind closed doors: What really happens in executive coaching. *Organizational Dynamics,* Winter 1999, 39–53.
9. Adapted from the Associated Press. Former Texaco executive seeks to suppress Kwanza remarks. *Dallas Morning News,* March 3, 1998, 10D; Associated Press. Texaco executives discussed shredding papers, tapes reveal. *Dallas Morning News,* March 29, 1998, 11D; Brinson, S. L., and Benoit, W. L. The tarnishing Star. *Management Communication Quarterly,* 1999, 12, 483–510; Labich, K. No more crude at Texaco. *Fortune,* September 6, 1999, 205–212; also see www.adl.org/presrele/asus.
10. Frink, D. D., and Ferris, G. R. Accountability, impression management and goal setting in the performance evaluation process. *Human Relations,* 1998, 51, 1259–1274; Ashford, S. J., Rothbard, N. P., Piderit, S. K., and Dutton, J. E. Out on the limb: The role of context impression management in selling gender-equity issues. *Administrative Science Quarterly,* 1998, 43, 23–58; Bolino, M. Citizenship and impression management: Good soldiers or good actors? *Academy of Management Review,* 1999, 24, 82–83.
11. Francesco, A. M., and Gold, B. A. *International Organizational Behavior.* Englewood Cliffs, N.J.: Prentice-Hall, Inc., 1998, 8.
12. Hofstede, G. The universal and the specific in 21st century management. *Organizational Dynamics,* Summer 1999, 34–44; Babcock, B. D., and Babcock, R. D. An analysis of language and cultural influences on international business communicators. Paper presented at the Pan-Pacific Conference, Fiji, June 1999.
13. Sussman, N. M., and Rosenfeld, H. M. Influence of culture, language, and sex on conversational distance. *Journal of Personality and Social Psychology,* 1982, 42, 66–74; Standifird, S. S., and Marshall, R. S. The transaction cost advantage of Guanxi-based business practices. *Journal of World Business,* 2000, 35 (in press).
14. Latane, B., Liu, J. H., Nowak, A., Bonevento, M., and Zheng, L. Distance matters: Physical space and social impact. *Personality and Social Psychology Bulletin,* 1995, 21, 795–805.
15. Taylor, L. I'm not insensitive to other cultures—As long as they don't keep bragging about it. *New Statesman,* January 29, 1999, 55–56; Varner, I., and Beamer, L. *Intercultural Business Communication in the Global Workplace.* Burr Ridge, Ill.: Irwin, 1995.
16. Adapted from Lynch, S. Ragu Pasta, Godiva Chocolate, Gatorade put interactive ads on Internet. *Orange County Register,* June 12, 1995, 6; Phalon, R. Beyond Godiva. *Forbes,* November 9, 1992, 310–312; also see Ryan, A. M., Chan, D., Ployhart, R. E., and Shade, L. A. Employee attitude surveys in a multinational organization: Considering language and culture in assessing measurement equivalence. *Personnel Psychology,* 1999, 52, 37–58.
17. Zaleznik, A. Real work. *Harvard Business Review,* 1997, 75(6), 53–60; Powell, W. W., Koput, K. W., and Smith-Doer, L. Interorganizational collaboration and the locus of innovation: Networks of learning in biotechnology. *Administrative Science Quarterly,* 1996, 41, 116–145.
18. Useem, J. For sales online: You. *Fortune,* July 5, 1999, 67–78; Dreman, D. Internet myth and reality. *Forbes,* July 5, 1999, 230; Caggiano, C. What's hot. *Inc.,* August 1998, 108.
19. Donnellon, A. *Team Talk: The Power of Language in Team Dynamics.* Boston: Harvard Business School Press, 1996; Ibarra, H. Race, opportunity, and diversity of social

circles in managerial networks. *Academy of Management Journal,* 1995, 38, 673–703.

20. Guyon, J. When John Browne talks, big oil listens. *Fortune,* July 5, 1999, 116–120.
21. Hubbard, A. S. Cultural and status differences in intergroup conflict resolution. *Human Relations,* 1999, 52, 303–305; Davidson, M., and Friedman, R. A. When excuses don't work: The persistent injustice effect among black managers. *Administrative Science Quarterly,* 1998, 43, 154–184; Chattopadhyay, P. J., Glick, W. H., Miller, C. C., and Huber, G. P. Determinants of executive beliefs: Comparing functional conditioning and social influence. *Strategic Management Journal,* 1999, 20, 763–789.
22. Adapted from Buchanan, L. The smartest little company in America. *Inc.,* January 1999, 43–54.
23. Reining in the e-mail beast. *Computer Weekly,* May 20, 1999, 10; Kunde, D. Monster.com to test auction for free-agent talent. *Dallas Morning News,* June 30, 1999, 1Dff.
24. Koerner, B. I. So that's why they call them users. *U.S. News & World Report,* March 22, 1999, 62–63.
25. Adapted from Useem, J. Read this before you put a résumé online. *Fortune,* May 24, 1999, 209–210.
26. Berner, J. *The Joy of Working from Home: Making a Life While Making a Living.* San Francisco: Berrett-Kolhler, 1994.
27. Personal communication from B. Speer, Pier 1 Imports, Dallas, Texas, 1999; also see Turk, H. What must employers consider before setting up a telecommuting program? *Employment Relations Today,* Spring 1999, 139–143; Hymowitz, C. More managers find ways to narrow the distance. *Wall Street Journal,* April 6, 1999, B1.
28. Isaacs, U. N. Taking flight: Dialogue, collective thinking, and organizational learning. *Organizational Dynamics,* Autumn 1993, 24–39; Pye, A. Strategy through dialogue and doing: A game of "Mornington Crescent"? *Management Learning,* 1995, 26, 445–462.
29. Pillutla, M. M., and Chen, X. Social norms and cooperation in social dilemmas: The effects of context and feedback. *Organizational Behavior & Human Decision Processes,* 1999, 78(2), 81–83; Bauer, T. N., Dolen, M. R., Maertz, C. P., and Champion, M. Longitudinal assessment of applicant reactions to employment testing and test outcome feedback. *Journal of Applied Psychology,* 1998, 83, 960–969; Goodman, J. S. The interactive effects of task and external feedback on practice performance and learning. *Organizational Behavior & Human Decision Processes,* 1998, 76(3), 223–226.
30. Charan, R., and Colvin, G. Why CEOs fail. *Fortune,* June 21, 1999, 69ff.
31. Nichols, M. P. *The Lost Art of Listening.* New York: Guilford, 1995.
32. Adapted from Whetten, D. A., and Cameron, K. S. *Developing Management Skills.* Reading, Mass.: Addison-Wesley, 1998, 36–37. Used with permission.
33. Bluedorn, A. C., Turban, D. B., and Love, M. S. The effects of stand-up and sit-down meeting formats on meeting outcomes. *Journal of Applied Psychology,* 1999, 84, 277–285; Mindell, P. The body language of power. *Executive Female,* May–June 1996, 48–52; Arthur, D. The importance of body language. *HR Focus,* June 1995, 27–40.
34. Kiritani, E. Body language. *Journal of Japanese Trade & Industry,* January–February 1999, 50–52; Walsh, J. P., Wang, E., and Xin, K. R. Same bed, different dreams: Working relationships in Sino–American joint ventures. *Journal of World Business,* Spring 1999, 69–93.
35. Bruhn, M. Business gifts: A form of non-verbal and symbolic communication. *European Management Journal,* 1996, 14, 61–68; Stroh, L. K., and Caligiuri, P. M. Increasing global competitiveness through effective people management. *Journal of World Business,* 1998, 33(1), 1–17.
36. Bluedorn, A. C., Kaufman, C. F., and Lane, P. M. How many things do you like to do at once? An introduction to monochronic and polychronic time. *Academy of Management Executive,* 1992, 6(4), 17–26.
37. Aquino, K., Brover, S. L., Bradfield, M., and Allen, D. G. The effects of negative affectivity, hierarchical status, and self-determination on workplace victimization. *Academy of Management Journal,* 1999, 42, 260–272; Belliveau, M. A., O'Reilly, C. A. III, and Wade, J. B. Social capital at the top: Effects of social similarity and status on CEO compensation. *Academy of Management Journal,* 1996, 39, 1568–1594.
38. Ashcraft, K. L. Managing maternity leave: A qualitative analysis of temporary executive succession. *Administrative Science Quarterly,* 1999, 44, 240–280; Briles, J. *Gendertraps.* New York: McGraw-Hill, 1997.
39. DiDio, L. This one's for the guys. *Computerworld,* January 6, 1997, 66.
40. Adapted from Douglas Roberts, formerly manager of training, LTV Missiles and Electronics Group, Grand Prairie, Texas. Used with permission.
41. Caltin, L., and White, T. *Cultural Sourcebook and Case Studies.* Cincinnati: South-Western, 1994, 40–41. Used with permission.

PART 3

Organizational Processes

Chapter 14 Decision Making in Organizations

Chapter 15 Job Design

Chapter 16 Organization Design

Chapter 17 Organizational Culture

Chapter 18 Organizational Change

CHAPTER

14 Decision Making in Organizations

LEARNING OBJECTIVES

When you have finished studying this chapter, you should be able to:

1. Explain the basic concepts of ethical decision making.
2. State the attributes of three basic models of managerial decision making.
3. Describe the stages and biases of managerial decision making.
4. Explain two methods for fostering organizational creativity.

Preview Case: *Cassandra Matthews's Tough Decision*

ETHICAL FOUNDATIONS
- Ethical Intensity
- ***Competency: Managing Ethics****—A Bottom-Line Issue*
- Ethical Principles and Rules
- Concern for Others
- Benefits and Costs
- Assessment of Rights
- ***Competency: Managing Across Cultures****—Business Ethics in Russia and the United States*

MODELS OF MANAGERIAL DECISION MAKING
- Rational Model
- Bounded Rationality Model
- ***Competency: Managing Self****—Ben Franklin on Making Trade-Offs*
- Political Model
- ***Competency: Managing Communication****—Knowledge Management at Renaissance, Inc.*

STAGES OF MANAGERIAL DECISION MAKING
- Recognition Stage
- Interpretation Stage
- Focus Stage
- ***Competency: Managing Diversity****—Barriers to Advancement*
- Choice Stage
- Consequences Stage

FOSTERING ORGANIZATIONAL CREATIVITY
- ***Competency: Managing Communication****—Decision Making at Alteon WebSystems*
- Lateral Thinking Method
- Devil's Advocate Method

CHAPTER SUMMARY
- Key Terms and Concepts
- Discussion Questions

DEVELOPING COMPETENCIES
- ***Competency: Managing Self****—Living Ethics*
- ***Competency: Managing Change****—Is Opportunity Knocking?*

PREVIEW CASE

CASSANDRA MATTHEWS'S TOUGH DECISION

Cassandra Matthews had a tough decision to make and she had to make it quickly. As chief information officer (CIO) of PECO Energy Company, a $4 billion public utility in Philadelphia, Matthews was preparing for utility deregulation—when consumers and businesses could choose their energy provider. She brought representatives from all the organization's business functions—electricity generation, gas storage, and power station management—as well as top technologists, together to work on a single floor of the PECO building. The project team was charged with replacing the current system that managed all billing and customer-service activities with one that could work under substantial deregulation—within the span of 9 months.

The effort was complicated greatly by continuing changes in governmental regulations for the energy industry. Even after PECO chose a leading software package to replace its in-house system, the regulations kept changing. Team members kept Matthews informed of how the fluctuating regulations affected their business functions so that she could track the project on both macro (enterprisewide) and micro (business unit) levels and then act quickly.

As energy deregulation continued at a furious pace, "gaps appeared between what the chosen software package could provide and what our various businesses needed," Matthews said. Within 4 months, Matthews's team had pushed the software package to its limits. The next month, plan B was put into motion—appointing a team to begin evaluating whether modification of the existing legacy system was an option. Two months later, Matthews made the decision: drop the new software package and devote all resources to revamping the current system.

For more information on PECO Energy, visit the company's home page at ***www.peco.com.***

The following month, the governmental regulations were finalized. The newly revitalized current system was able to accommodate all the last-minute changes and immediately began churning out bills by the project deadline. Matthews said: "We made the right decision: But it was made only through constant and effective communications."[1]

Key decisions in organizations often involve various pressures from the external environment, multiple participants in the decision process, and the need to modify or change the approach being taken along the way. Matthews concluded that a key to PECO's success was "constant and effective communications" among the many people involved throughout the change process.

We presented recommendations for improving organizational decision making in several previous chapters. In this chapter, we expand on them. First, we discuss several issues that are fundamental to ethical decision making.[2] Next, we review the features of three major decision-making models. Then, we relate those models to the stages of and biases in managerial decision making. We conclude with a presentation of two approaches for stimulating creativity in decision making.

Learning Objective:

1. Explain the basic concepts of ethical decision making.

ETHICAL FOUNDATIONS

Most decision making and behaviors in organizations have an underlying foundation of ethical concepts, principles, and rules. Because of the importance of ethics in management, we recognize it throughout this book in our Managing Ethics Competency features, as well as in relation to a number of topics, such as transformational leadership, organizational change, and power and political behaviors.

Ethics refers to the rightness or wrongness of the decisions and behaviors of individuals and the organizations of which they are a part. Ethical issues in organizations are more common and complex than generally recognized. In fact, ethical issues influence the decisions that employees make daily.[3] Some ethical issues involve factors that blur the distinction between "right" and "wrong." As a result, employees may experience ethical dilemmas. A recent survey of randomly selected employees in the United States, identified five main types of unethical behaviors that they had engaged in during the past year: (1) cutting corners on quality, (2) covering up errors, (3) abusing or lying about sick days, (4) lying to or deceiving customers, and (5) putting inappropriate pressure on others. Fifty-six percent of the respondents indicated that they felt some pressure to act unethically or illegally.[4]

There are no simple rules for making decisions that have important ethical content. Consistent with our earlier discussions of ethical issues, the goal here is to help you develop your competency in applying ethical concepts to decision making. Your assessment of alternatives will be improved by examining five key foundations of ethical decision making: ethical intensity, decision principles and rules, affected individuals, benefits and costs, and determination of rights.

ETHICAL INTENSITY

Ethical intensity is the degree of importance given to an issue-related moral imperative.[5] It is determined by the combined impact, as interpreted by the decision maker, of six factors. These factors are presented in the survey instrument shown in Table 14.1 and described as follows.

- **Magnitude of consequences** is the total of the harm or benefits accruing to individuals affected by a decision or behavior. An action that causes 1,000 people to suffer a particular injury has greater consequences than an action that causes 10 people to suffer the same injury. An action that causes the death of a human being is of greater consequence than an action that causes a sprained ankle.
- **Probability of effect** is the combined result of the likelihood that a decision will be implemented and that it will lead to the harm or benefit predicted. The production of an automobile that would be dangerous to occupants during normal driving has greater probability of harm than the production of a car that endangers occupants only when curves are taken at high speed. The sale of a gun to a known armed robber has a greater probability of harm than the sale of a gun to a law-abiding hunter.

Table 14.1 **Assessment of Ethical Intensity**

Instructions

Consider an issue or problem that is complex and difficult for you to resolve. Identify a possible course of action—choice—to resolve it. Then, evaluate this course of action in relation to the six factors of ethical intensity by marking a point on each scale. Then draw a line to connect the points marked for each factor. What does this result suggest in terms of the ethical intensity of the course of action you chose?

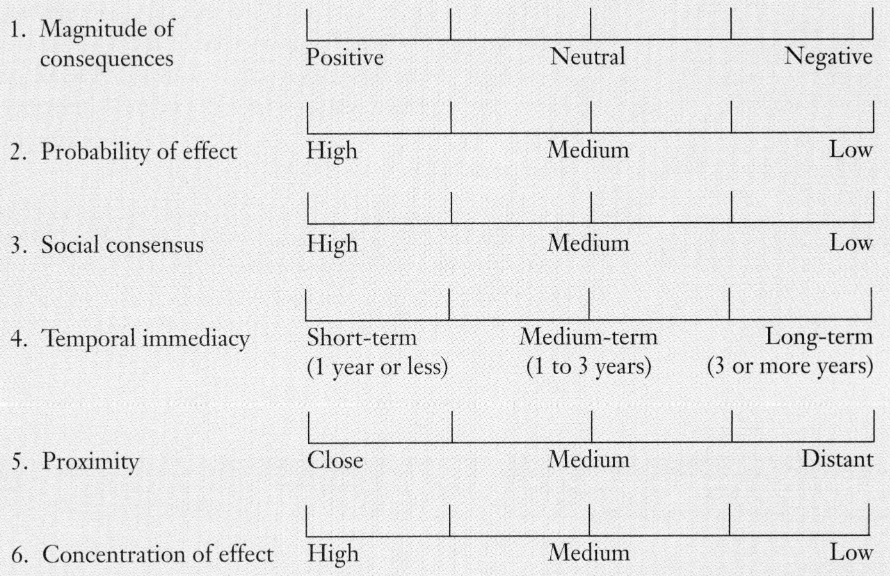

Factor			
1. Magnitude of consequences	Positive	Neutral	Negative
2. Probability of effect	High	Medium	Low
3. Social consensus	High	Medium	Low
4. Temporal immediacy	Short-term (1 year or less)	Medium-term (1 to 3 years)	Long-term (3 or more years)
5. Proximity	Close	Medium	Distant
6. Concentration of effect	High	Medium	Low

- **Social consensus** is the degree of public agreement that a proposed decision or action is bad or good. The consequences involved in actively discriminating against minority job candidates are worse than those involved in not actively seeking out minority job candidates. The bad behavior involved in bribing a customs official in Canada evokes greater public condemnation than that involved in bribing a customs official in a country where such behavior is generally accepted as a way of doing business, such as the Philippines. Managers and employees will have difficulty deciding what is and isn't ethical if they aren't guided by a high degree of social consensus, which reduces the likelihood of ambiguity.
- **Temporal immediacy** is the length of time that elapses from making a decision to the beginning of the consequences of that decision. A shorter length of time implies greater immediacy. Releasing a drug that will cause 1 percent of the people who take it to have acute nervous reactions within 1 month has greater temporal immediacy than releasing a drug that will cause 1 percent of those who take it to develop nervous disorders after 30 years of use. The reduction in the retirement benefits of current retirees has greater temporal immediacy than the reduction in the future retirement benefits of employees who are currently 22 years of age.
- **Proximity** is the sense of closeness (social, cultural, psychological, or physical) that the decision maker has for victims or beneficiaries of the decision. When Don Ritter at Mobil was laid off as a result of the Exxon/Mobil merger, it had a greater impact on his work team because of the ethical proximity (physical and psychological) of its perceived unfairness than did layoffs in another division of Mobil. For North Americans, the sale of dangerous pesticides in Canadian, U.S., and Mexican markets has greater ethical proximity (social, cultural, and physical) than does the sale of such pesticides in Russia.

- **Concentration of effect** is the inverse function of the number of people affected by a decision. A change in a warranty policy denying coverage to 20 people with claims of $20,000 each has a more concentrated effect than a change denying coverage to 2,000 people with claims of $200 each. Cheating an individual or small group of individuals out of $5,000 has a more concentrated effect than cheating an organization, such as the IRS, out of the same sum.

By working through the instrument in Table 14.1, you will see that the six factors of ethical intensity potentially are influenced by the characteristics of the issue itself. As a result, the factors and the specific issue have combined effects. Also, ethical intensity rises with increases in one or more of its factors and declines with reductions in one or more of its factors, assuming that all other conditions remain constant. However, individuals may rate the ethical intensity of the same decision differently, simply because they place different values on the principles and rules of ethics in decision making.

As suggested in the following Managing Ethics Competency feature, the individual's interpretation of the factors of ethical intensity and the importance assigned to them are likely to vary somewhat by the type of top leadership and formal processes in an organization. Stephen G. Butler, chairman and CEO of KPMG, a professional services firm with more than 150,000 employees, expresses his views on ethics in this feature. He makes clear the importance he places on assessing ethical issues in considering alternative courses of action.

COMPETENCY: MANAGING ETHICS

A BOTTOM-LINE ISSUE

Many major corporations have a high appreciation for the importance of ethics and a low tolerance for unethical behavior, and the tone is set at the very top. There are other organizations that pay lip service to ethics, but they don't conduct their business that way. They tolerate lapses.

I think ethics is a critical bottom-line issue for all businesses. And it becomes more important as we move into the information age, because there will be some real challenges from an ethical standpoint to businesses that deal in information. For one thing, people can do things today they couldn't do less than 10 years ago—before we had the Internet, for example. The use of technology is shrinking our world and dramatically aiding the global creation and sharing of information. There are weighty responsibilities that go with that. There's also an element of ethics that deals with how to treat human beings, and it's a real, fundamental business issue. I think ethics will become a critical success factor for businesses globally.

In the case of KPMG, accountability is critical—both within the firm and within the relationships we build with our clients and the communication by which we operate. The only way to institutionalize ethics in an organization is to start at the very top and give no free passes. You don't omit the first layer of management and say, "This is something we expect from you but not from someone higher up in the organization."

What drives most of the unethical behavior surfaces today are the two potentially conflicting messages organizations send out: "You've got to make your numbers" and "We want you to be ethical." A lot of people hear "make your numbers," more than they hear the second part; and that's why CEOs, boards of directors, and people at the top of organizations have to push the ethics button as hard as they push the numbers button.[6]

For more information on KPMG, visit the organization's home page at ***www.kpmg.com.***

Ethical Principles and Rules

There are no universally accepted principles and rules for resolving all the ethical issues in complex decision-making situations. In addition, individuals and groups differ over what influences both ethical and unethical behaviors and decisions.[7] Numerous principles and rules have been suggested to provide an *ethical justification* for a person's decisions and behaviors.[8] They range from those that justify self-serving decisions to those that require careful consideration of others' rights and costs.

Self-Serving Principles. The following three ethical principles attempt to justify self-serving decisions and behaviors.

- **Hedonist principle:** You do whatever is in your own self-interest, but not clearly illegal.
- **Might-equals-right principle:** You do whatever you are powerful enough to impose without respect to ordinary social conventions and widespread practices or customs, but not clearly illegal.
- **Organization interests principle:** You act on the basis of what is good for the organization and the achievement of its goals, but not clearly illegal.

All three of these self-serving principles appeared to be present in the following incident. The American Society of Composers, Authors and Publishers (ASCAP) sent a letter to summer camps warning them to pay up if they wanted to sing copyrighted songs such as *Edelweiss* and *This Land Is Your Land.* As a result, several cash-strapped camps stopped singing the songs. After television talk shows and newspapers reported the story, ASCAP took out full-page ads saying that it "never sought, nor was it ever its intention to license Girl Scouts singing around the campfire." The credibility of that denial wilted in light of ASCAP's admission that it would reimburse money to 16 Girl Scout councils that had already paid fees ranging from $77 to $257.[9]

Balancing Interests Principles. Many employees and organizations appear to use and apply ethical principles that tend to justify decisions and actions by attempting to balance multiple interests.[10] Three of these principles are as follows.

- **Means–end principle:** You act on the basis of whether some overall good justifies any moral transgression, but not clearly illegal.
- **Utilitarian principle:** You act on the basis of whether the harm inherent in the decision is outweighed by the good in it, but not clearly illegal.
- **Professional standards principle:** You act on the basis of whether the decision can be explained before a group of your peers, but not clearly illegal.

These principles provide the ethical foundation for much decision making in organizations. They create the basis for helping to resolve ethical dilemmas—for example, justifying employee layoffs but recognizing certain responsibilities for providing career counseling and severance packages for those employees.

As a result of the Internet and related information technologies, privacy issues have become major concerns in the attempt to balance the interests of individuals, organizations, and the public at large. A recent report, entitled *Nothing Sacred: The Politics of Privacy,* issued by the Center for Public Integrity concluded that the privacy of Americans is being compromised.[11] The growing perception among the public is that individuals in their roles as employees and consumers have lost too much of their privacy to employers, marketers, and governmental agencies. In a recent survey of adults, 82 percent complained that they had lost all control over how their personal information is used by companies. With regard to employees, an increasing number of firms are exercising their legal authority to monitor employee e-mail messages, use of the Internet, behaviors (by the use of security cameras), and conversations at work.[12]

Privacy issues have become ethical dilemmas in terms of (1) distribution and use of employee data from computer-based human resource information systems; (2) increasing use of paper-and-pencil honesty tests as a result of polygraph testing being declared illegal in most situations; (3) procedures and bases for substance abuse and AIDS testing; and (4) genetic testing. The ethical dilemmas in each of these areas revolve around balancing the rights of the individual, the needs and rights of the employer, and the interests of the community at large.

Concern for Others Principle. Three ethical principles that focus on the need to consider decisions and behaviors from the perspective of those affected and the public as a whole are as follows.

- **Disclosure principle:** You act on the basis of how the general public would likely respond to the disclosure of the rationale and facts related to the decision, but not clearly illegal.
- **Distributive justice principle:** You act on the basis of treating an individual or group equitably rather than on arbitrarily defined characteristics, but not clearly illegal.
- **Golden rule principle:** You act on the basis of placing yourself in the position of someone affected by the decision and try to determine how that person would feel.

These three ethical principles are often *imposed* on certain categories of decisions and behaviors through laws, regulations, and court rulings. In effect, governments impose ethical principles and rules that organizations are expected to comply with in certain situations. For example, Title VII of the 1964 U.S. Civil Rights Act forbids organizations from considering personal characteristics such as race, gender, religion, or national origin in decisions to recruit, hire, promote, or fire employees. This law is based on the ethical principle of distributive justice, which requires that the treatment of individuals differently not be based on arbitrarily defined characteristics such as age, race, or gender.[13] It states that (1) employees who are similar in relevant respects should be treated similarly and (2) employees who differ in relevant respects should be treated differently in proportion to the differences between them. On this basis, the U.S. Equal Pay Act of 1963 asserts that paying women and men different wages is illegal when their jobs in the same organization require equal skills, effort, responsibility, and working conditions.

Table 14.2 provides you with an opportunity to assess a major course of action that you have taken or are considering in relation to the nine ethical principles just described. You might apply these ethical principles to the same course of action that you used for the assessment of ethical intensity in Table 14.1.

As suggested previously, no single factor influences the degree to which decisions and behaviors by managers and employees are likely to be ethical or unethical. However, the following actions have been suggested for integrating ethical decision making into the day-to-day life of an organization.

- Top managers must demonstrate their commitment to ethical behaviors and decisions to other managers and employees.
- A clear code of ethics is needed, and it must be followed if it is to have meaning.
- A whistle-blowing and/or ethical concerns procedure should be established and followed.
- Employees should be involved in the identification of ethical problems to achieve a shared understanding and resolution of them.
- The performance appraisal process should include consideration of ethical issues.
- The organizational priorities and efforts related to ethical issues need to be publicized.[14]

Table 14.2

Ethical Assessment of a Decision

Instructions

Identify a possible or actual course of action that you might take or have taken to resolve a problem or issue that is complex and difficult for you. What is your assessment of the degree to which it is based on each of the ethical principles shown? Based on this assessment, how would you evaluate the ethics of your actual or proposed action?

ETHICAL PRINCIPLE	HIGH DEGREE 5	4	UNCERTAIN/ UNDECIDED 3	2	LOW DEGREE (NONE) 1
To what degree is the action based on this ethical principle:					
1. Hedonist	5	4	3	2	1
2. Might-equals-right	5	4	3	2	1
3. Organization interests	5	4	3	2	1
4. Means–end	5	4	3	2	1
5. Utilitarian	5	4	3	2	1
6. Professional standards	5	4	3	2	1
7. Disclosure	5	4	3	2	1
8. Distributive justice	5	4	3	2	1
9. Golden rule	5	4	3	2	1

Concern for Others

The highest form of ethical decision making involves a careful determination of who will receive benefits or incur costs as the consequence of a decision. For major decisions, this assessment may include a variety of stakeholders—shareholders, customers, lenders, suppliers, employees, and governmental agencies, among others. The more specific an individual or group can be about who may benefit and who may incur costs from a particular decision, the more likely it is that the ethical implications will be fully considered.

The ethical interpretation of the effects of decisions on specific individuals or groups can change over time. For example, **employment at will** means that the parties to an employment agreement have equal bargaining power and that, therefore, the right to fire is absolute and creates little cost to either party. The employer presumably can easily find another employee, and the employee presumably can easily find another job.

The employment-at-will doctrine increasingly has been challenged successfully in wrongful termination cases in the courts. These challenges are based on the distributive justice principle and the golden rule principle. Before 1980, companies in the United States were free to fire most nonunion employees "at will." That is, such employees could be fired for any reason without explanation. Employees rarely went to court to challenge a termination. The vast majority who did had their suits dismissed. However, the courts have increasingly ruled in favor of exceptions to the employment-at-will doctrine, especially if questionable termination procedures were followed.[15]

Benefits and Costs

An assessment of the benefits and costs of a decision requires a determination of the interests and values of those affected. When individuals value a situation, they want it to continue or to occur in the future. **Values** are the relatively permanent and deeply held desires of individuals. A recent global values survey by the Institute for Global

Ethics asked respondents to reply to the following: "Please look at the list of 15 values carefully and check the five values that are most important to you in your daily life." The most frequent choice was truth, followed by compassion, responsibility, freedom, and reverence for life. The five values chosen the least—starting with the very least—were respect for elders, devotion, honor, social harmony, and humility.[16]

However, care must be taken to guard against assuming that others attach the same importance to these values or that people in different cultures hold the same values. Conflicting values among stakeholders can lead to different interpretations of ethical responsibilities. For example, Greenpeace and other environmental groups have "preservation of nature" as one of their top values. In the survey just cited, it was ranked as eighth in importance and selected as most important by only 2 percent of the respondents. Active members of Greenpeace contend that most managers are irresponsible and unethical in not showing more concern about air and water pollution, land use, protection of endangered species, and the like.

The utilitarian principle is a common approach to the balancing or weighing of benefits and costs. Utilitarianism emphasizes the provision of the greatest good for the greatest number in judging the ethics of a decision. An individual who is guided by utilitarianism considers the potential effect of alternative actions on those who will be affected and then selects the alternative benefiting the greatest number of people. The individual accepts the fact that this alternative may harm others. However, so long as potentially positive results outweigh potentially negative results, the individual considers the decision to be both good and ethical.[17]

According to some critics, utilitarianism has been misused in North America. They suggest that there is too much short-run maximizing for personal advantage and too much discounting of the long-run costs of disregarding ethics. Those costs include rapidly widening gaps in income between rich and poor, creation of a permanent underclass with its hopelessness, and harm done to the environment. These critics believe that too many people and institutions are acquiring wealth for the purposes of personal consumption and power and that the end of acquiring wealth justifies any means of doing so. As a result, these critics suggest that trust of leaders and institutions, both public and private, has declined.[18]

Assessment of Rights

The notion of rights also is complex and continually changing. One dimension of rights focuses on who is entitled to benefits or to participation in decisions to change the allocation of benefits and costs.[19] Union–management negotiations frequently involve conflicts and dilemmas over management's rights to hire, promote, fire, and reassign union employees, as well as to move work to other countries or to outsource work. For example, a frequent issue in negotiations between American Airlines and its pilots' union has been the *right* of American to pay its American Eagle feeder airline's pilots and copilots substantially less than its regular, long-haul pilots and copilots. Slavery, racism, gender and age discrimination, and invasion of privacy often have been challenged by appeals to values based on concepts of fundamental rights.

As suggested previously, responsibilities and rights issues in the workplace are numerous and vary greatly. A few examples include unfair and reverse discrimination, sexual harassment, employee rights to continued employment, employer rights to terminate employment "at will," employee and corporate free speech, due process, and the right to test for substance abuse and acquired immune deficiency syndrome (AIDS). Some experts believe that workplace rights and the establishment of trust with employees is the most crucial internal issue facing organizations today.[20]

The assessment of ethical issues becomes even more complex when you consider how the culture of a country may influence, at least in part, behaviors and decisions that are viewed as ethical or unethical.[21] The following Managing Across Cultures Competency feature provides a sense of how cultural similarities and differences between the United States and Russia influence views of business ethics.

COMPETENCY: MANAGING ACROSS CULTURES

BUSINESS ETHICS IN RUSSIA AND THE UNITED STATES

Consider the situation faced by the senior American manager involved in Ben & Jerry's Homemade, Inc.'s, ice cream operations in the Karelia region of western Russia. When the senior Russian partner began to "borrow" company materials and equipment for use in his other businesses, the American was dismayed and viewed such behavior as unethical. However, the Russian manager felt that "borrowing" was a reasonable way to utilize the equipment because he was an owner of both companies.

As shown in Figure 14.1, some business activities are recognized as ethical by businesspeople in both countries (cell I), whereas other activities are considered to be unethical in both (cell II). Other behaviors, however, may be viewed as ethical by Russians but unethical to Americans (cell III), as well as the opposite situation (cell IV). We briefly comment on issues in cells III and IV—the situations of greatest contrast.

The behavior encountered most frequently in Russia that Americans consider unethical but that Russians view as largely ethical or acceptable would likely be the occurrence of *blat*. *Blat* involves excessive reliance on favors from people in influential positions, based on personal contacts. *Blat* is often accompanied by bribes or "grease payments" paid to a network of acquaintances and friends who facilitate the process of reaching the individual who can cause or allow the desired action to occur.

Whereas price gouging and keeping the excess is clearly considered unethical behavior in Russia, price fixing is not considered the same, so long as it doesn't result in overt gouging. Another set of Russian practices includes the manipulation of business data in reports to superiors, such as understating reserves of materials and labor, exaggerating the quality and quantity of goods produced, and covering up mistakes and operating deficiencies. The clear purpose, of course, is to meet externally imposed plans and goals and to receive the rewards for doing so. To Russian managers these practices are a logical extension of those under communism, when they had limited control over materials, labor, and equipment, and yet were required to meet unrealistic targets.

Russians do not condone some practices that Americans generally accept as ethical. For instance, American managers seldom question the capitalist view that supports the legitimacy of maximization of profits. Many Russians still do not accept capitalism as a way of doing business. Under communism, the only exposure to capitalist profit for most Russians was the "dirty" money made by black marketeers and the government's propaganda about the evils of Western capitalism. Recognizing the prevailing ambivalence, one young Russian entrepreneur, who formerly traded goods in the black market, later became engaged in a profitable legitimate real estate business. He explained, "Before they called me a speculator, now they call me a businessman. It's the same thing. The only difference is now I can register as a private company."

Let's return to how Ben & Jerry's manager handled the situation he faced. With patience, but firmness, he explained to the Russian partner that the equipment of the joint venture did not belong personally to the Russian manager, but to the joint venture. As such, it was not to be used in other businesses, but only in the business to which it belonged. Although the Russian manager might not have agreed with the conclusion, he complied with the decision. Ben & Jerry's manager stated his ethical and business beliefs and acted accordingly. Despite the vastly different business environments, he did not see a legitimate reason to change the company's standards. In other circumstances, he might well adapt to the Russian point of view.[22]

Figure 14.1 **Sample of Russian and U.S. Views of Business Ethics**

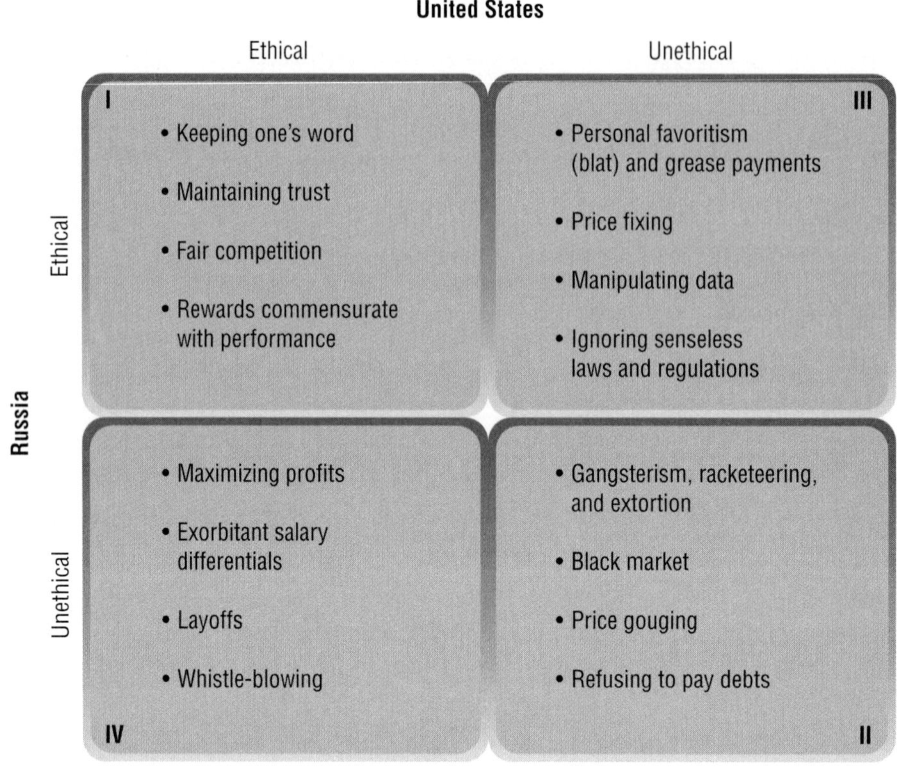

Source: Adapted from Puffer, S. M., and McCarthy, D. J. Finding the common ground in the Russian and American business ethics. Copyright © 1995, by The Regents of the University of California. Reprinted from the *California Management Review,* Winter 1995, 35. By permission of The Regents.

Learning Objective:

2. State the attributes of three basic models of managerial decision making.

MODELS OF MANAGERIAL DECISION MAKING

In this section, we describe the main features of three basic managerial decision-making models: rational, bounded rationality, and political. In doing so, we introduce you to the different ways in which managerial decision making is viewed. Each model is useful for gaining insights into the complex array of managerial decision-making situations in an organization.

RATIONAL MODEL

The **rational model** involves a process for choosing among alternatives to maximize benefits to an organization. It includes comprehensive problem definition, thorough data collection, analysis, and a careful assessment of alternatives. The criteria for evaluating alternatives are developed early in the process. The generation and exchange of information among the decision makers presumably is unbiased and accurate. Individual preferences and organizational choices are a function of the best alternative for the entire organization.[23] Thus the rational model of decision making is based on the explicit assumptions that (1) all available information concerning alternatives has been obtained, (2) these alternatives can be ranked according to explicit organizational criteria, and (3) the alternative selected will provide the maximum gain possible for the organization (or decision makers). An implicit assumption is that ethical dilemmas do not exist in the decision-making process and that the *means–end principle* and *utilitarian principle* will dominate the consideration of ethical issues.

Xerox's Six-Step Process. Xerox developed a companywide six-step rational process for making virtually all decisions of any importance. This process is presented in Table 14.3. Column 1 shows the six steps, column 2 identifies the key question to be answered in each step, and column 3 indicates what's needed to proceed to the next step. Managers and employees receive extensive training about various decision-making tools to help them work through these steps.[24] In terms of the individual, the rational model puts a premium on logical thinking.[25]

Trade-Offs. One of the most important and difficult challenges in decision making is making sound trade-offs. The more alternatives being considered and the more goals being pursued, the greater is the number of trade-offs needed by the decision maker. Benjamin Franklin proposed a basic way for individuals to use trade-offs in simplifying complexity while attempting to engage in rational decision making. As suggested in the Managing Self Competency feature on page 426, each time Franklin eliminated an item from the list of pros and cons, he replaced his original problem with an equivalent but simpler one, ultimately arriving at a more rational choice. This feature should help you perceive and appraise your immediate environment, interpret your own thoughts, and improve your ability to reason in decision-making situations. The letter from Ben Franklin used in this feature was sent to Joseph Priestley, a noted scientist, who was trying to choose between two alternatives.

Bounded Rationality Model

The **bounded rationality model** describes the limitations of rationality and emphasizes the decision-making processes actually used by individuals. This model helps explain why different individuals may make different decisions when they have exactly the same information. As outlined in Figure 14.2, the bounded rationality model reflects the individual's tendencies to (1) select less than the best goal or alternative solution (that is, to *satisfice*), (2) undertake a limited search for alternative solutions, and (3) possess inadequate information and control of external and internal environmental

Table 14.3 Portion of Xerox's Rational Decision-Making Process

STEP	QUESTION TO BE ANSWERED	WHAT'S NEEDED TO GO TO THE NEXT STEP
1. Identify and select problem	What do we want to change?	Identification of the gap; "desired state" described in observable terms
2. Analyze problem	What's preventing us from reaching the "desired state"?	Key cause(s) documented and ranked
3. Generate potential solutions	How could we make the change?	Solution list
4. Select and plan the solution	What's the best way to do it?	Plan for making and monitoring the change; measurement criteria to evaluate solution effectiveness
5. Implement the solution	Are we following the plan?	Solution in place
6. Evaluate the solution	How well did it work?	Verification that the problem is solved, or agreement to address continuing problems

Source: Adapted from Garvin, D. A. Building a learning organization. *Harvard Business Review,* July–August 1993, 78–91; Brown, J. S., and Walton, E. Reenacting the corporation: Organizational change and restructuring of Xerox. *Planning Review,* September/October 1993, 5–8.

BEN FRANKLIN ON MAKING TRADE-OFFS

London
Sept. 19, 1772

Dear Sir,

In the affair of so much importance to you, wherein you ask my advice, I cannot, for want of sufficient premises, advise you what to determine, but if you please I will tell you how.

When those difficult cases occur, they are difficult, chiefly because while we have them under consideration, all the reasons pro and con are not present to the mind at the same time; but sometimes one set present themselves, and at other times another, the first being out of sight. Hence the various purposes of inclinations alternatively prevail, and the uncertainty that perplexes us.

To get over this, my way is to divide half a sheet of paper by a line into two columns; writing over the one Pro, and over the other Con. Then, during three or four days consideration, I put down under the different heads short hints of the different motives, that at different times occur to me, for or against the measure.

When I have thus got them all together in one view, I endeavor to estimate their respective weights; and where I find two, one on each side, that seem equal, I strike them both out. If I find a reason pro equal to two reasons con, I strike out the three. If I judge some two reasons con, equal to some three reasons pro, I strike out the five, and thus proceeding I find at length where the balance lies; and if, after a day or two of further consideration, nothing new that is of importance occurs on either side, I come to a determination accordingly.

And, though the weight of reasons cannot be taken with the precision of algebraic quantities, yet when each is thus considered, separately and comparatively, and the whole lies before me, I think I can judge better, and am less liable to make a rash step; and in fact I have found great advantage from this kind of equation, in what may be called moral or prudential algebra.

Wishing sincerely that you may determine for the Best, I am ever, my dear friend, yours most affectionately,

B. Franklin[26]

Franklin's approach is based on the assumption that balancing pros and cons is generally possible. Unfortunately, that isn't always the case. Other approaches, beyond the scope of our presentation, have been developed to enable decision makers to list explicitly quantitative and qualitative goals and alternatives and to create equivalence for the purpose of comparing them.[27]

forces influencing the outcomes of decisions.[28] This model also recognizes the reality that complete information—concerning available alternatives or the outcome of some course of action—may be impossible for an individual to obtain, regardless of the amount of time and resources applied to the task.

Satisficing. **Satisficing** is the tendency to select an acceptable, rather than a maximum, goal or alternative solution. In this case, *acceptable* might mean easier to identify and achieve, less controversial, or otherwise safer than the best alternative. For

Figure 14.2 **Bounded Rationality Model**

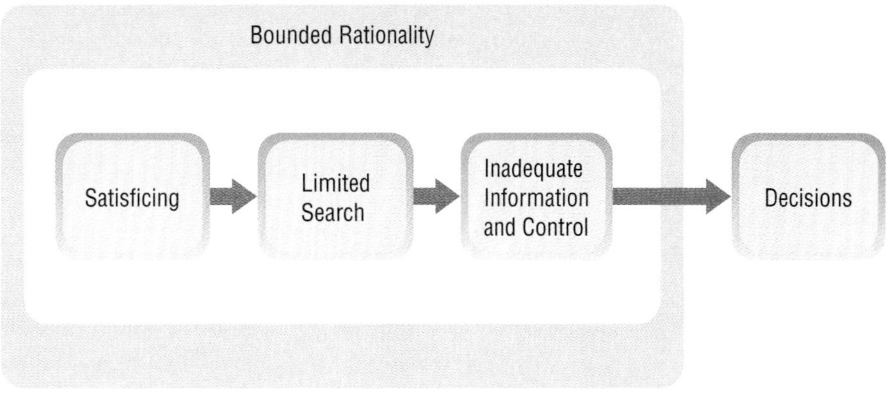

example, profit goals often are quantified, such as a 15 percent rate of return on investment or a 5 percent increase in profits over the previous year. These goals may not be the maximum attainable. They may, in fact, reflect little more than top management's view of reasonable goals, that is, challenging but not too difficult to achieve.

Herbert Simon, who introduced the bounded rationality model, described satisficing in these words before a management audience:

> Satisficing is intended to be used in contrast to the classical economist's idea that in making decisions in business or anywhere in real life, you somehow pick, or somebody gives you, a set of alternatives from which you select the best one—maximize. The satisficing idea is that first of all, you don't have the alternatives, you've got to go out and scratch for them—and that you might have shaky ways of evaluating them when you do find them. So you look for alternatives until you get one from which, in terms of your experience and in terms of what you have reason to expect, you will get a reasonable result.
>
> But satisficing doesn't necessarily mean that managers have to be satisfied with what alternative pops up first in their minds or in their computers and let it go at that. The level of satisficing can be raised—by personal determination, setting higher individual or organizational standards, and by the use of an increasing range of sophisticated management science and computer-based decision-making and problem-solving techniques.
>
> As time goes on, you obtain more information about what's feasible and what you can aim at. Not only do you get more information, but in many, if not most, companies there are procedures for setting targets, including procedures for trying to raise individuals' aspiration levels [goals]. This is a major responsibility of top management.[29]

Limited Search. Decision makers often make a limited search for possible goals or solutions to a problem, considering alternatives only until they find one that seems adequate. For example, in choosing the best job, college graduates can't evaluate every available job in a particular field. They might hit retirement age before obtaining all the information needed for a decision! Even the rational decision-making model recognizes that identifying and assessing alternatives cost time, energy, and money. In the bounded rationality model, individuals stop searching for alternatives as soon as they discover an acceptable goal or solution.

Inadequate Information and Control. Decision makers often have inadequate information about problems and face environmental forces that they can't control.

These conditions typically have an impact on the results of their decisions in unanticipated ways.

Decision rules are a part of the bounded rationality model. They provide quick and easy ways to reach a decision without a detailed analysis and search. They can be explicitly stated and easily applied. A general type of rule used by organizations—as well as by individuals—is the **dictionary rule.** It involves ranking items the same way a dictionary does: one criterion (analogous to one letter) at a time. The dictionary rule gives great importance to the first criterion. It is valid in decision making only if this first criterion is known to be of overriding importance.[30]

Consider what can happen when management too hastily uses the dictionary rule. The director and his staff at the Ohio Department of Claims experienced a growing backlog of social benefit appeals. They implemented a change in handling procedures. Their brief analysis led to a pooling idea that grouped similar claims for mass handling. However, the analysis failed to focus on the reason for the growing number of claims. After the backlog grew to the point that claims took a year to process, the director discovered a loophole in the legislation that had inadvertently eased eligibility requirements. The director made the legislature aware of the oversight and the loophole was closed. In the meantime, the agency was subjected to constant criticism and legal action for its slow, error-prone claims management. As the incident suggests, managers often want to find out quickly what is wrong and fix it immediately. The all too common result is poor problem definition and a choice of criteria that proves to be misleading. Symptoms are analyzed while more important concerns may be ignored.[31]

Recall one of the comments by Herbert Simon in the previous quote: "The level of satisficing can be raised—by personal determination, setting higher individual or organizational standards, and by the use of an increasing range of sophisticated management science and computer-based decision-making and problem-solving techniques." Knowledge management is an emerging focus for doing so.

Knowledge Management. **Knowledge management** is the art of adding or creating value by systematically leveraging the know-how, experience, and judgment found within and outside an organization.[32] Knowledge management is a means of raising the level of satisficing.[33] Knowledge is different than data and information. *Data* represent observations or facts having no context and are not immediately or directly useful. *Information* results from placing data within some meaningful context, often in the form of a message. **Knowledge** is that which a person comes to believe and value on the basis of the systematic organized accumulation of information through experience, communication, or inference. Knowledge can be viewed both as a *thing* to be stored and manipulated and as a *process* of applying expertise.

Knowledge can be either tacit or explicit. **Tacit knowledge** is personally understood and applied, sometimes difficult to express, developed from direct experience, and usually shared through conversation and storytelling. In contrast, **explicit knowledge** is more precise and formally expressed (e.g., a computer database and software program that creates information and analyses on customer purchasing habits or a training manual describing how to close a sale).

As suggested in the Managing Communication Competency feature on page 429, knowledge management is not just for giant organizations. This feature highlights how Renaissance, Inc., a 140-employee firm located in Carmel, Indiana, introduced and uses knowledge management.

Political Model

The **political model** describes decision making by individuals to satisfy their own interests. Preferences are established early, usually on the basis of personal self-interest goals, and seldom change as new information is acquired. Problem definition, data

Competency: Managing Communication

Knowledge Management at Renaissance, Inc.

According to President and CEO Paul Brooks, Renaissance began by helping financial advisers learn to use charitable-gift instruments with their clients. For years the company treated its employees (lawyers, tax professionals, and the like) as information "silos"—isolated individuals who would be forced to refer issues to others whenever matters strayed outside their areas of expertise. If a client called a lawyer with a difficult tax question about trust funds, the lawyer would research it the old-fashioned way. "He'd stick his head out the door and say, 'Hey, does anyone know the answer to this?' " says Brooks.

But Brooks recognized that wasn't the best way to serve customers, and it didn't take advantage of his employees' considerable talents. He stated: "We were clear that we generated income on the basis of what we knew, but what we knew was haphazardly held. We named the smartest guy in our company 'director of intellectual capital' when none of us knew what that meant."

With its newly designated intellectual-capital director leading the charge, Renaissance began a total review of what it does and how it operates. Instead of being a traditional support organization offering training and administrative help, the company is changing into what Brooks terms a "call center," a sort of clearinghouse that provides anyone involved in philanthropy with access to information on setting up and running charitable trusts.

To do that, Renaissance has had to become information-centric as opposed to consultant-centric. All its consultants' expertise has been harvested, mapped, and stored on a private Web site that clients can check for answers to many of their questions. Employees' roles and titles are also being adjusted. Instead of lawyers and receptionists, Renaissance now has "knowledge managers" (people who know or can find answers to questions), "client relationship managers" (people who ensure that clients get the answers), and members of an as-yet-unnamed group responsible for taxonomy (people who record questions and answers for easy retrieval in the company's database).[34]

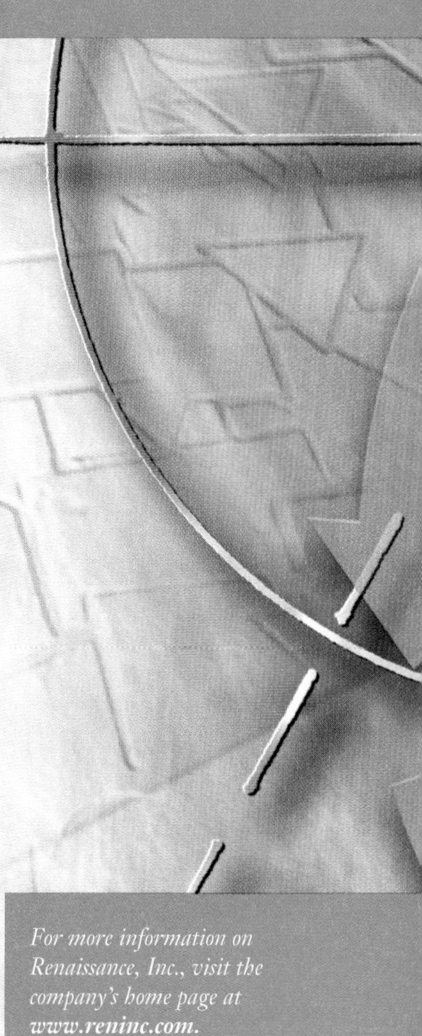

For more information on Renaissance, Inc., visit the company's home page at www.reninc.com.

search and collection, information exchange, and evaluation criteria are merely methods used to tilt (bias) the outcome in the decision maker's favor.[35]

The distribution of power in an organization and the effectiveness of the tactics used by the participants determine the impact of the decisions. The political model doesn't explicitly recognize ethical dilemmas. However, it often draws on two self-serving ethical principles discussed previously: (1) the *hedonistic principle*—do whatever you find to be in your own self-interest; and (2) the *might-equals-right principle*—you are strong enough to take advantage without respect to ordinary social conventions.

Deception is a common tactic of the political model. For example, to make top management look better to various stakeholders, some firms distort anticipated revenue flows and expenses. These doctored figures are even presented in documents such as venture capital business plans, real estate prospectuses, and corporate earnings forecast announcements.[36] In Chapter 9, we presented several other features of the political model.

The political model is prevalent in organizations throughout the world. For example, French culture values relatively high power distance. That is, relationships between superiors and subordinates are unequal, with the different levels of status and privilege seen as a normal state. The political model in French organizations is based on various underlying assumptions and expected behaviors. Three of them are as follows.

- Power, once attained, should not be shared except with the inside group of senior managers. Some are born to lead and others to follow; it is difficult for people to change. Secretaries are there to follow orders. Middle managers need to consult with their bosses as well as many others in the organization before making a decision.
- If individuals have been recognized as being top-management material, it does not matter if they are put in a job where they have no experience. Being of superior ability, they should be able to learn how to do their jobs with experience.
- It is harmful to reveal information unnecessarily, because then the decision-making process cannot be controlled. When, where, and how to communicate information is a delicate question that often only the upper echelons can decide.[37]

Learning Objective:

3. Describe the stages and biases of managerial decision making.

STAGES OF MANAGERIAL DECISION MAKING

Managerial decision making begins with the recognition of a problem and concludes with an assessment of the consequences of the action taken to solve it. Figure 14.3 depicts the essential stages of managerial decision making.[38] Although these stages appear to proceed in logical order, managerial decision making actually may be quite disorderly and complex as it unfolds. There seemingly is no beginning or end. Managers usually deal with unexpected crises and petty problems that require much more time than they're worth. A manager may go from a budget meeting involving millions of dollars to a discussion of what to do about a broken decorative water fountain. Thus managerial work is hectic and fragmented and requires the ability to shift continually from person to person, from subject to subject, and from problem to problem.

RECOGNITION STAGE

Managerial decision making rarely begins with a clean slate. Previous decisions and experiences and new information may determine whether a manager even recognizes a problem. Moreover, the characteristics of individual managers play an important role in problem recognition.

With **structured problems,** the problem recognition stage is straightforward. For example, a marketing manager at Cisco promises the delivery of an order within

Figure 14.3 **Stages of Managerial Decision Making**

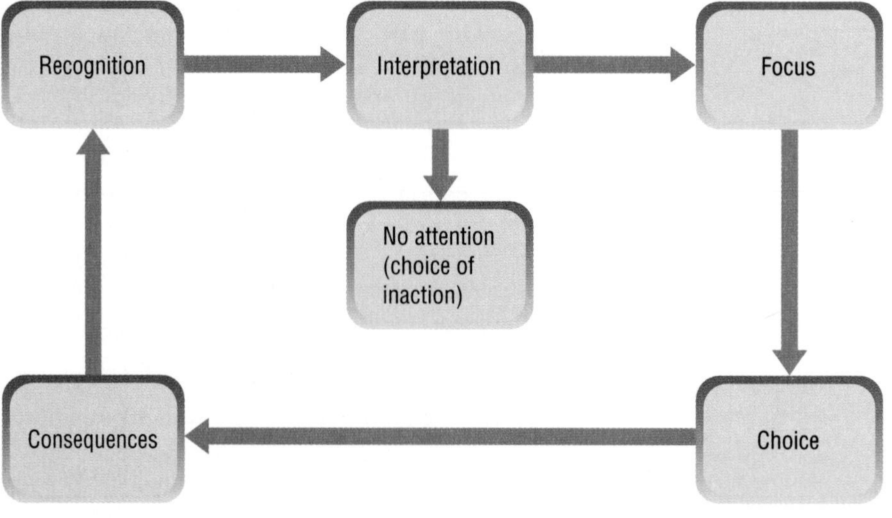

30 days. After 45 days, an Oracle manager calls and angrily complains: The order hasn't arrived. I need it pronto. The marketing manager is suddenly and forcefully made aware of a problem and the need to resolve it immediately. With **unstructured problems,** the problem recognition stage, itself, often is a problem. The "problem" of problem recognition can result from unclear or inadequate information about developments and trends in the environment. For example, Walt Disney, Hilton Hotels, and other organizations have market research departments to collect information about their customers to determine whether changing customer tastes and preferences are likely to create new problems. A challenge for successful organizations is to avoid the error of perceptual defense (see Chapter 3). In other words, people have a tendency to deny and protect themselves against threatening ideas or situations, especially when a successful outcome is at stake.

Recognition of a problem usually triggers activities that may either lead to a quick solution or be part of a long, drawn-out process. The amount of time required to solve a problem depends on its nature and complexity. For example, in the Preview Case, Cassandra Matthews and the members of her team engaged in a 9-month process to replace the existing system for managing all billing and customer-service activities. This problem was complex and unstructured, compounded by the uncertainties of utility deregulation facing PECO Energy. After about 6 months, Matthews terminated the proposed new system and revamped the existing system successfully.

A variety of conditions can increase the likelihood of incorrect problem recognition and formulation. The following are five such conditions.

- *You are given a problem.* When you are asked to help solve a problem that someone else has defined, you are likely to take that problem as a "given" and work within the constraints of the problem statement. The more authority or power that the other person wields, the more likely you are to accept, without question, the statement of the problem.
- *A quick solution is demanded.* If a decision is needed quickly, the amount of time spent in formulating or reformulating a problem is likely to be cut short.
- *Emotions are high.* Stressful or emotional situations often lead to an abbreviated search for a satisfactory statement of the problem.
- *There is little prior experience in defining problems.* For most people, questioning a problem statement requires training and practice. The habit of questioning is hard to get into (and easy to fall out of). Those unaccustomed to challenging or reformulating a problem statement are unlikely to do so.
- *The problem is complex.* When a situation involves many variables and the variables are hard to identify and measure, the problem is more difficult to formulate and solve.[39]

Interpretation Stage

The second stage in the decision-making process involves interpretation of the problem. A high voluntary turnover rate for sales representatives might be the result of looking for applicants in the wrong places, poor selection procedures and training, lack of supervision, a poor compensation system, an unacceptable level of work stress, or some combination of these inadequacies. Problem interpretation involves giving meaning and definition to the issues that have been recognized. Problem recognition doesn't mean that it will get attention. As suggested in Figure 14.3, one option for managers simply is not to give a recognized problem any attention—the choice of inaction. This choice may be a consequence of (1) demands on the manager to deal with too many high-priority problems, (2) a belief that the problem will go away with time, or (3) the judgment that an attempt to do something about the problem will fail or only worsen the situation.

There is no simple one-to-one relationship between the availability of "objective" information and how it is processed during problem interpretation. Various biases can affect decision making, including risk propensity, problem framing, availability bias, confirmation bias, selective perception bias, and law of small numbers bias.[40]

Risk Propensity. **Risk propensity** is the tendency of an individual or group to make or avoid decisions in which the anticipated outcomes are unknown. A risk-averse individual or team focuses on potentially negative outcomes. The probability of loss is overestimated relative to the probability of gain. Therefore the decision maker requires a high probability of gain to tolerate exposure to failure. Conversely, a risk-seeking decision maker focuses on potentially positive outcomes. Probability of gain is overestimated relative to the probability of loss. Thus risk seekers may be willing to tolerate exposure to failure with a low probability of gain. Some decisions can be understood in terms of a desire to avoid the unpleasant consequences of a decision that turns out poorly. A choice can be personally threatening because a poor result can undermine the decision maker's sense of professional competence, create problems for the organization, and even get the decision maker demoted or fired. Most individuals have a low propensity for risk. They purchase many types of insurance to avoid the risk of large but improbable losses. They invest in savings accounts, CDs, and money market funds to avoid the risk of extreme fluctuations in stocks and bonds. Generally, they prefer decisions that produce satisfactory results more than risky decisions that have the same or higher expected outcomes.[41]

Problem Framing. **Problem framing** is the tendency to interpret issues in either positive or negative terms. Individuals in favorable circumstances tend to be risk averse because they think that they have more to lose. In contrast, individuals in unfavorable situations tend to think that they have little to lose and therefore may be risk seeking. Focusing on potential losses increases the importance of risk. In contrast, focusing on potential gains lessens the importance of risk. Thus a positively framed situation fosters risk taking by drawing managerial attention to opportunities rather than the possibility of failure. An example of positive versus negative framing is that of the certainty of winning $6,000 or the 80 percent probability of winning $10,000. Most people prefer the certain gain to the uncertain chance of larger gain. Which would you choose? Although risk aversion commonly is assumed to hold for most decisions, many exceptions have been documented. People prefer to take risks when making a choice between a certain loss and a risky loss. For example, what happens when individuals are asked to choose between the certainty of losing $8,000 and the 80 percent probability of losing $10,000? In this case, most people prefer the risky alternative.[42] Which would you choose?

Availability Bias. The **availability bias** is the tendency to recall specific instances of an event and therefore to overestimate how often it occurs (and vice versa). If you have been in a serious automobile accident, you may overestimate the frequency of such accidents. This type of bias may be expressed as what's out of sight often is out of mind. In other words, personal experiences may carry more weight in interpreting the probability of an outcome than they should.[43] Bridge players provide a telling example. Experienced bidders take into account unusual events or ways to win hands by relying on various decision rules. Less experienced players believe that they can make hands they often cannot, precisely because they fail to consider uncommon occurrences.

Confirmation Bias. The **confirmation bias** is the tendency to seek out information that supports an initial interpretation of a situation while avoiding information that contradicts it. Unfortunately, the more uncertain and complex an issue, the more easily one-sided support can be found. This bias can be reduced by seeking negative, as well as positive, evidence. Interviewers tend to overstate the strength of evidence (how well a candidate did in an interview) relative to the credibility of that type of evidence (the limited insight gained from any single interview). Whenever source credibility is low and the strength of the evidence is highly suggestive, overconfidence is likely to occur (see Chapter 3). Thus interviewers may predict too readily that the interviewed candidate will be successful or unsuccessful as an employee, based on the fallible, limited evidence obtainable from a short interview.

Selective Perception Bias. The **selective perception bias** is the tendency to see what people expect to see. People seek information consistent with their own views and often downplay information that conflicts with their perceptions (see Chapter 3).[44] An example might be an interviewer of a job candidate who graduated from the same university with the same major as the interviewer.

Law of Small Numbers Bias. The **law of small numbers bias** is the tendency to consider a few cases or samples to be representative of a larger population (a few cases "prove the rule"), even when they aren't. An initial bad experience with the service in a restaurant may result in the individual concluding that the restaurant provides bad service, when in fact, it was the result of the action of a single waiter on one occasion.

Other biases emerge in various decision-making situations, including those discussed in other chapters throughout this book.[45] The likelihood that managers and employees can learn to recognize and interpret problems effectively is strongly influenced by an organization's culture (see Chapter 17), team processes (see Chapter 8), and approach to conflict management (see Chapter 10).

One of the continuing challenges for managers and organizations is to reduce and avoid decision-making biases in the selection, assignment, review, and promotion of employees on the basis of their personal characteristics (e.g., gender, race, ethnicity, and age). The Managing Diversity Competency feature on page 434 reports the views of human resource professionals presented in the recent *Barriers to Advancement Survey* by the Society for Human Resource Management (SHRM). Recall that the *managing diversity competency* involves the ability to value unique individual and group characteristics, embrace such characteristics as potential sources of organizational strength, and appreciate the uniqueness of each individual.

Focus Stage

After problems have been recognized and interpreted, judgments need to be made about which problems to focus on, how much focus they are to receive, and in what order they are to receive that focus. Managers must be aware of the relative focus they place, sometimes unconsciously, on the problems they deal with. The problems receiving the highest priority are likely to meet the following criteria.

- Focus on the problem is supported by strong external pressure (Cassandra Matthews, the CIO at PECO Energy insisted that the computer-based billing and customer-service support system be replaced within 9 months).
- Focus on the problem is supported by the resources necessary to take action (Matthews created a project team and brought together experts from every relevant department).
- Focus on the problem represents a major opportunity or threat (PECO Energy was facing both the opportunities and threats being created by utility deregulation, which would give residential, commercial, and industrial customers more choice in selecting their energy providers).

The number and variety of recognized problems needing focus almost always exceeds the manager's capacity for addressing and solving all of them within the desired time frame. In addition, pressures from the external environment can change the most carefully planned priorities for focusing on recognized problems.[46]

Competency: Managing Diversity

For more information on the Society for Human Resource Management, visit the organization's home page at ***www.shrm.org.***

Barriers to Advancement

Approximately 80 percent of human resource (HR) professionals believe that women and minorities will have more opportunities to advance their careers in the next 5 years than they've had in the past. But, at the same time, approximately three out of four respondents believe that women and minorities still face substantial barriers to corporate success and that the barriers are somewhat different for each group.

When asked to identify the main obstacles for women, the respondents most frequently cited the lack of females at the board level. That answer was closely followed by the perception that corporate cultures favor men. Other obstacles, in order of importance, included stereotypes or preconceptions about women, exclusion from informal networks, and lack of mentoring opportunities.

When asked about the barriers facing minorities, the respondents cited a lack of role models as the biggest obstacle. This perception was followed in order by limited mentoring opportunities, exclusion from informal networks, stereotypes or preconceptions based on race or ethnicity, and the perception that corporate cultures in general favors nonminorities.

The HR professionals were also asked to rank different practices that corporations could implement to lower the barriers for minorities and women. Four of the top five answers were the same for both groups. The respondents saw CEO support for women and minorities as the single most important factor to breaking down barriers; maintaining effective recruiting and retention programs came second; increasing the number of women and minorities on boards of directors was third; and providing career development programs targeted at women and minorities was listed as fifth.

The fourth most effective strategy selected by respondents was felt to be different for women and minorities. For women, the respondents cited the importance of flexible work schedules; for minorities, they cited mentoring programs.[47]

Choice Stage

The development and evaluation of courses of action (alternatives) and the implementation of the selected choice can range from a quick-action choice to a convoluted-action choice. A *quick-action choice* is appropriate when (1) the nature of the problem is well structured (two subordinates fail to show up for work, creating a problem in meeting a deadline for the next day); (2) a single manager (or at most, two managers) is clearly recognized as having the authority and responsibility to resolve the problem (the manager authorizes overtime for other employees to meet the deadline); and (3) the search for information about the problem and alternatives is quite limited (the manager might call the customer to determine the actual urgency of delivery to decide whether to schedule overtime, bring in help from a temporary employment service, or check with other managers to find out whether their departments are less busy and could loan some workers). A quick-action choice may be made within a matter of minutes or take as long as several days.

At the other extreme, the *convoluted-action choice* is drawn-out and mazelike. This process is often applied to problems and issues that have the following characteristics.

- The problem is unstructured.
- A long period of time is required to develop, evaluate, and implement the chosen alternative.

- Many vested interests and power relationships are involved in the choice selected.
- Many people are involved in an extensive search for the chosen solution.

Cassandra Matthews's ultimate decision to discontinue a new software package and system for billing and servicing PECO Energy's customers and to revamp the current system was a convoluted-action choice (see the Preview Case). Trade-offs, negotiations, conflict, and political processes usually are involved in making convoluted-action choices but much less often in making quick-action choices. Managers continuously face a variety of problems, many of which can be addressed through quick-action choice; far fewer require a convoluted-action choice. Quick-action choices with regard to complex problems may well lead to poor decisions.[48]

Consequences Stage

The consequences stage involves evaluation of the results obtained from the choices made. With structured problems, this evaluation usually is rather simple. The benefits and costs associated with alternative actions can easily be calculated. Consider the manager who schedules overtime to meet a deadline when two workers fail to show up. If the overtime worked results in meeting the deadline, the decision clearly led to the intended consequence.

The choice of a course of action and its implementation to deal with an unstructured problem may involve many individuals and subjective judgments, as in the situation facing Cassandra Matthews at PECO Energy (see the Preview Case). The full consequences of the choice made may not become apparent for months or even years. The ultimate decision to revamp the legacy system for billing and servicing customers may be effective in the short-run, but all the long-run consequences may not be. Unstructured problems thus require making choices in the face of risk and uncertainty.

Even the best managers and employees make mistakes. The challenge is to recognize and learn from these mistakes. Unfortunately, many managers and employees guard their reputations as capable people and go to extremes not to acknowledge their mistakes. Moreover, individuals and teams tend to overestimate the effectiveness of their judgments.[49] Sometimes the negative aftermath of a decision will result in an escalating commitment. **Escalating commitment** is a process of continuing or increasing the allocation of resources to a course of action even though a substantial amount of feedback indicates that the choice made is wrong.[50] One of the explanations for escalating commitment is that individuals feel responsible for negative consequences, which motivates them to justify previous choices. In addition, individuals may become committed to a choice simply because they believe that consistency in action is a desirable form of behavior. Our discussion of perception and attributions in Chapter 3 gives additional insights into the possible reasons for escalating commitment.

The Managing Communication Competency feature on page 436 reports on how the fast-paced stages of decision making—from recognition of a problem through choice to its consequences—are made possible through open and trusting communications at Alteon WebSystems, of San Jose, California. This account reports the views of Dominic Orr, president and CEO. With about 200 employees, Alteon WebSystems makes products to speed up the servers that feed data into networks and Web sites.

Learning Objective:

4. Explain two methods for fostering organizational creativity.

FOSTERING ORGANIZATIONAL CREATIVITY

Organizational creativity is the generation of unique and useful ideas by an individual or team in an organization. Innovation builds on unique and useful ideas. Accordingly, **organizational innovation** is the implementation of creative and useful ideas through unplanned or planned organizational change.[51]

Creativity assists employees in uncovering problems, identifying opportunities, and making novel choices to solve problems. In Chapter 8, we presented two

Competency: Managing Communication

Decision Making at Alteon WebSystems

Like a lot of young companies in new industries, we have to make choices every day about competitive strategy and product development. So how can we make decisions that we trust without wasting valuable time? Fast execution and fast delivery—that's easy. Fast decision making is harder. Young industries and startups are constantly changing—which means that even day-to-day decisions take on huge strategic importance. Deciding when to ship a product involves fundamental questions about how we develop products in the first place. Making high-stakes decisions as a team is important. But we don't have time for endless debate or for office politics.

We rely on brutal intellectual honesty. We've distilled that companywide philosophy into a few simple rules. We focus on collecting as many facts as quickly as we can, and then we decide on the best—but not necessarily the perfect—solution. There's no silent disagreement, and no getting personal, and definitely no "let's take it off-line" mentality. Our goal is to make each major decision in a single meeting. People arrive with a proposal or a solution—and with the facts to support it. After an idea is presented, we open the floor to objective, and often withering, critiques. And if the idea collapses under scrutiny, we move on to another: no hard feelings. We're judging the idea, not the person.

At the same time, we don't really try to regulate emotions. Passionate conflict means that we're getting somewhere, not that the discussion is out of control. But one person does act as referee—by asking basic questions like "Is this good for the customer?" or "Does it keep our time-to-market advantage intact?" By focusing relentlessly on the facts, we're able to see the strengths and weaknesses of an idea clearly and quickly.[52]

*For more information on Alteon WebSystems, Inc., visit the company's home page at **www.alteonwebsystems.com**.*

approaches for stimulating creativity in organizations—namely, the nominal group technique and brainstorming. In addition, we have repeatedly discussed ways for reducing barriers to creativity and innovation. Three broad categories of these barriers include perceptual blocks, cultural blocks, and emotional blocks. *Perceptual blocks* include such factors as the failure to use all the senses in observing, failure to investigate the obvious, difficulty in seeing remote relationships, and failure to distinguish between cause and effect. *Cultural blocks* include a desire to conform to established norms, overemphasis on competition or conflict avoidance and smoothing, the drive to be practical and narrowly economical above all else, and a belief that indulging in fantasy or other forms of open-ended exploration is a waste of time. Finally, *emotional blocks* include the fear of making a mistake, fear and distrust of others, grabbing the first idea that comes along, and the like.[53] For many organizations, fostering creativity and innovation are essential to their ability to offer high-quality products and services. The following two methods may be used to foster creativity with any individual, team, or group.

Lateral Thinking Method

The **lateral thinking method** is a deliberate process and set of techniques for generating new ideas by changing an individual's or team's way of perceiving and interpreting information. We can best explain this method by contrasting it with the **vertical thinking method**, which is a logical step-by-step process of developing ideas by proceeding continuously from one bit of information to the next. Table 14.4 presents the primary differences between lateral thinking and vertical thinking. Edward de Bono,

Table 14.4 Characteristics of Lateral Versus Vertical Thinking

LATERAL THINKING	VERTICAL THINKING
1. Tries to find new ways for looking at things; is concerned with change and movement.	1. Tries to find absolutes for judging relationships; is concerned with stability.
2. Avoids looking for what is "right" or "wrong." Tries to find what is different.	2. Seeks a "yes" or "no" justification for each step. Tries to find what is "right."
3. Analyzes ideas to determine how they might be used to generate new ideas.	3. Analyzes ideas to determine why they do not work and need to be rejected.
4. Attempts to introduce discontinuity by making "illogical" (free association) jumps from one step to another.	4. Seeks continuity by logically proceeding from one step to another.
5. Welcomes chance intrusions of information to use in generating new ideas; considers the irrelevant.	5. Selectively chooses what to consider for generating ideas; rejects information not considered to be relevant.
6. Progresses by avoiding the obvious.	6. Progresses using established patterns; considers the obvious.

Source: Based on de Bono, E. *Lateral Thinking: Creativity Step by Step.* New York: Harper & Row, 1970; de Bono, E. *Six Thinking Hats.* Boston: Little, Brown, 1985.

the British physician and psychologist who developed the lateral thinking method, stated that the two processes are complementary, not antagonistic.

Lateral thinking fosters the generation of unique ideas and approaches, and vertical thinking is useful for assessing them. Lateral thinking enhances the effectiveness of vertical thinking by offering it more to select from. Vertical thinking improves the impact of lateral thinking by making good use of the ideas generated. You probably use vertical thinking most of the time, but when you need to use lateral thinking, vertical thinking capabilities won't suffice.[54]

The lateral thinking method includes several techniques for (1) developing an awareness of current ideas and practices, (2) stimulating alternative ways of looking at a problem, and (3) aiding in the development of new ideas. Here, we consider only three of the techniques for fostering the development of new ideas: reversal, analogy, and cross-fertilization.[55]

Reversal. The **reversal technique** involves examining a problem and turning it completely around, inside out, or upside down. Engineers at Conoco asked, "What's good about toxic waste?" By so doing, they discovered a substance in refinery waste that they now are turning into both a synthetic lubricant and—they hope—a promising new market. Ronald Barbaro, president of Prudential Insurance, considered the idea, "You die before you die," and came up with "living benefit" life insurance. It pays death benefits to people suffering from terminal illnesses before they die. Prudential has sold more than a million such policies.[56]

Analogies. The **analogy technique** involves developing a statement about similarities between objects, persons, or situations. Some examples of analogies are: This organization operates like a beehive, or This organization operates like a fine Swiss watch. The technique involves translating the problem into an analogy, refining and developing the analogy, and then retranslating the problem to judge the suitability of the analogy. If an analogy is too similar to the problem, little will be gained. Concrete and specific analogies should be selected over more abstract ones. Analogies should describe a specific, well-known issue or process in the organization. For an organization that is ignoring increased environmental change, an analogy might be: We are like a flock of ostriches with our heads buried in the sand.

Cross-Fertilization. The **cross-fertilization technique** involves asking experts from other fields to view the problem and suggest methods for solving it from their own areas of expertise. For the technique to be effective, these outsiders should be from fields entirely removed from the problem. An attempt can then be made to apply these disparate methods to the problem. Hallmark Cards has its own variation of cross-fertilization. For example, staffers often go from Hallmark's midtown Kansas City headquarters to a downtown loft, where teams of writers and artists get away from phones to exchange ideas. They also may spend days in retreat at a farm in nearby Kearney, Missouri, taking part in fun exercises, such as building birdhouses.[57]

Devil's Advocate Method

In the devil's advocate method, a person or team—the devil's advocate—develops a systematic critique of a recommended course of action. This critique points out weaknesses in the assumptions underlying the proposal, internal inconsistencies in it, and problems that could lead to failure if it were followed. The devil's advocate acts like a good trial lawyer by presenting arguments against the majority position as convincingly as possible. Figure 14.4 illustrates the basic decision-making process when this method is utilized.

Individuals assigned to the devil's advocate role should be rotated to avoid any one person or team being identified as a critic on all issues. However, playing this role, even for a short time, may be advantageous for a person and the organization. Steve Huse, chairperson and CEO of Huse Food Group, indicates that the devil's advocate role is an opportunity for employees to demonstrate their presentation and debating skills. How well someone understands and researches issues is apparent when that person presents a critique. The organization avoids costly mistakes by hearing viewpoints that identify potential pitfalls. In addition, the use of the devil's advocate approach can increase the probability of creative solutions to problems and reduce the likelihood of groupthink.[58] Recall that groupthink in decision making is caused by excessive consensus and similarity of views in groups—a sure way to kill organizational creativity (see Chapter 8). The devil's advocate method is effective in helping bring to the surface and challenge assumptions on which a proposed course of action is based—an essential element in fostering creativity. The devil's advocate method shouldn't be overused, and it is best applied to especially important and complex issues.

Figure 14.4 **Decision Making with a Devil's Advocate**

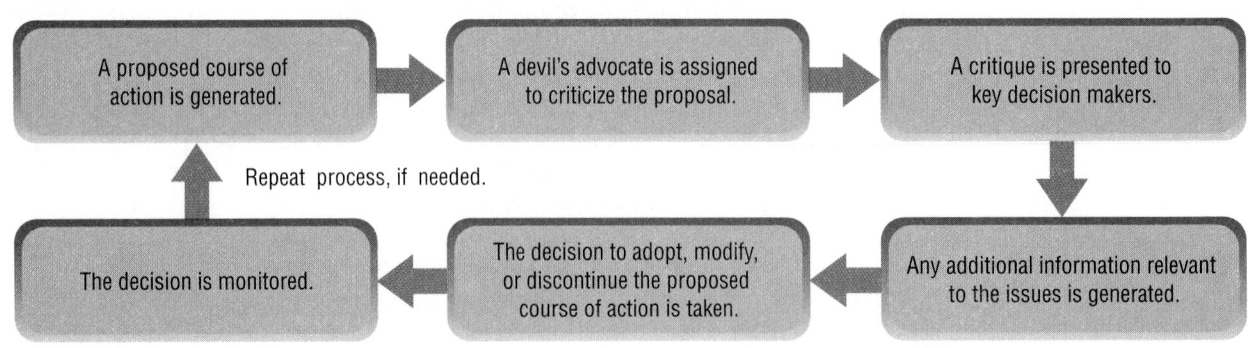

Source: Adapted from Cosier, R. A., and Schrivenk, C. R. Agreement and thinking alike: Ingredients for poor decisions. *Academy of Management*, February 1991, 71.

CHAPTER SUMMARY

1. Explain the basic concepts of ethical decision making.

Individuals experience ethical dilemmas when making some decisions. We addressed five important issues, which can be stated as questions, in ethical decision making: What is the ethical intensity? What are the principles and rules? Who is affected? What are the benefits and costs? Who has rights?

2. State the attributes of three basic models of managerial decision making.

The rational, bounded rationality, and political models are commonly used to explain managerial decision making. Each model captures some aspects of managerial decision-making situations and processes. All three models are needed to grasp the complexity and range of decision making.

3. Describe the stages and biases of managerial decision making.

The stages of managerial decision making include recognition, interpretation, focus, choice, and consequences. Although we discussed these phases separately, they don't unfold in a neat and orderly sequence. Several common decision-making biases were reviewed.

4. Explain two methods for fostering organizational creativity.

Creativity is needed in changing, complex, and uncertain environments. This situation often results in ambiguity and disagreement over both the goals to be achieved and the best course of action to pursue. Organizational creativity and innovation are crucial to the discovery and implementation of unique and useful ideas. Two approaches for stimulating organizational creativity are the lateral thinking method and the devil's advocate method.

KEY TERMS AND CONCEPTS

Analogy technique
Availability bias
Bounded rationality model
Concentration of effect
Confirmation bias
Cross-fertilization technique
Dictionary rule
Disclosure principle
Distributive justice principle
Employment at will
Escalating commitment
Ethical intensity
Ethics
Explicit knowledge
Golden rule principle
Hedonist principle
Knowledge
Knowledge management
Lateral thinking method
Law of small numbers bias
Magnitude of consequences
Managerial decision making
Means–end principle
Might-equals-right principle
Organization interests principle
Organizational creativity
Organizational innovation
Political model
Probability of effect
Problem framing
Professional standards principle
Proximity
Rational model
Reversal technique
Risk propensity
Satisficing
Selective perception bias
Social consensus
Structured problems
Tacit knowledge
Temporal immediacy
Unstructured problems
Utilitarian principle
Values
Vertical thinking method

DISCUSSION QUESTIONS

1. Evaluate the ethical intensity of the grading system and practices used by an instructor in a course that you have completed. Your evaluation should include an assessment of each of the six components of ethical intensity.
2. Review the comments by Stephen Butler, chairman and CEO of KPMG, in the Managing Ethics Competency feature. Use the components of ethical intensity to evaluate the merits of his perspective.
3. What are the differences between the organization interests principle and the utilitarian principle?
4. What are the differences between the professional standards principle and the distributive justice principle?
5. Arrange the ethical principles presented in this chapter in rank order from your most preferred to least preferred. What does this ranking tell you about how you are likely to interpret situations involving ethical dilemmas?
6. Review the Managing Self Competency feature on Ben Franklin's approach for making trade-offs. Why might some individuals not use this approach?
7. Think of an organization or group in which you are an active member. Describe a choice that seemed to be based on the political model. Why do you think the choice followed the political model?
8. Think of an important choice you have made within the past year. How did you come to recognize the problem that prompted the stages of decision making and your eventual choice? Was it a good or bad choice? Explain.
9. Review the Managing Communications Competency feature on decision making at Alteon WebSystems. Would this approach work at your current or last place of employment? Explain.
10. Describe your interpretation of a specific problem that you have experienced that was probably affected by the selective perception bias.
11. What are two differences between the lateral thinking method and the devil's advocate method?

DEVELOPING COMPETENCIES

Competency: Managing Self—Living Ethics[59]

Susan Johnson's Situation

Susan Johnson is a first-line manager. One of her employees, Meg O'Brien, has been in her department for 8 months. Despite Johnson's repeated efforts at training and coaching, O'Brien is performing below an acceptable level, but the supervisors of three other departments gave her "average" ratings. Johnson talked to these supervisors and discovered that they did so in order to avoid hassles resulting from the employee's likely reaction; they explained that O'Brien files grievances and Equal Employment Opportunity (EEO) complaints regularly. Johnson's supervisor, Barbara Lopez, has told Johnson to give O'Brien an excellent rating and a glowing recommendation for a vacant position in another division.

1. What ethical conflict(s) does Johnson face?
2. In addition to Johnson, O'Brien, and Lopez, who might be affected by Johnson's decision?
3. What actions are open to Johnson?
4. Which of these actions best meets ethical considerations while resolving the situation as positively as possible for the people involved/affected? What ethical principles serve as the basis for your actions?
5. How would you evaluate the ethical intensity of this situation?

Frank Epps's Situation

Frank Epps is a manager reviewing applications for an open position in his department. One of the company's standard procedures for the hiring process is a background check. Epps's friend, Michael Kee, is one of the applicants and is well qualified for the position. Kee recently told Frank that 12 years ago he embezzled $4,000 from his employer. The employer pressed charges, and Kee was ultimately sentenced to 1 year of probation. According to organizational policy, this incident would disqualify Kee as a candidate for the position. Kee has convinced Epps that the embezzlement was a one-time error in judgment that will never happen again. He has asked Epps not to do the formal background check.

1. What ethical conflict(s) does Epps face?
2. In addition to Epps and Kee, who might be affected by Epps's decision?
3. What actions are open to Epps?
4. Which of these actions best meets ethical considerations while resolving the situation as positively as possible for the people involved/affected? On what ethical principles did you base your response?
5. What level of ethical intensity would you assign to this situation?

Competency: Managing Change—Is Opportunity Knocking?[60]

I was excited just to meet the football legend in person. I never expected that a résumé sent to his corporate offices would produce a response, but it had. Now, I was responding to his telephone call and meeting him at his estate behind the high fence, which was a local landmark. The football stadium was named after him, as well as the expressway and the west wing of the hospital. And he wanted to talk to me, personally, about a job in his new restaurant. Me, a recent graduate of HRM at Tech!

The massive gates were ajar so I drove up the lengthy drive to the mansion on the hill. I couldn't help but notice that the lawn desperately needed attention and that the hedges needed trimming. The flower beds had more weeds than flowers. The fountain out front had stopped working a long time ago, judging from the debris rotting inside. But there was Hugh Aimsworth, on the great veranda, waiting for me. He greeted me with a firm handshake and said, "Glad you could make it." He gracefully led the way inside and told me to have a seat anywhere, pointing to a large dark room dominated by a stone fireplace. Every sofa and chair was cluttered with books, magazines, or newspapers. In one corner was a TV tray containing leftovers from earlier meals. Mr. Aimsworth came in and handed me a cup of coffee, "Way to start the day," he said. It was noon, and I was surprised by the remark. Then he surveyed the room and added, "Better we go sit a spell in another room."

I followed him into a large foyer and in passing the spiral staircase he yelled upstairs, "Bertha Mae, we have company, can you come down, darling?" "I'm not dressed," was the shrill response from somewhere on the second floor along with the loud sound of a slammed door. Into the kitchen area we walked. Dirty dishes were piled everywhere! Both sinks were full of greasy water that smelled like a marina. Then I saw the cat on the counter, licking from a cat food can. Explained the fishy smell!

We passed through the kitchen to the den, complete with a big-screen TV and an array of football trophies. Mr. Aimsworth threw the papers off the easy chairs and motioned for me to sit.

We spoke about his admittedly favorite subject, football; then he said, "Let's head out to the lake and look at the Victorian Manor—been in the family for years, great view. It would make a fine restaurant with a smart young whippersnapper like you running it." Had I been offered the job? I wondered! With that he handed me some worn plans of the Victorian Manor dating back to 1890. "You might need these," he added.

The day was brilliant and I was enjoying the 10-mile drive out of the city. At the next turn the concrete ended and gravel began. "Almost there now," said Mr. Aimsworth as he turned up a dirt road and sang loudly along with the CD playing from the Lincoln Town Car's dash, "I did it my way," trying to keep pace with Sinatra. I couldn't help thinking that Sinatra would cringe at the sound.

Five minutes later the Manor came into sight. What a beauty! It sat atop a hill, like out of a movie, but the closer we got the more apparent became its disrepair. First, I noticed that it badly needed paint, a new roof, and a full-time carpenter. A new veranda was a must. I made mental notes as we carefully stepped over missing floorboards. The wallpaper was peeling off and light fixtures were nonexistent. "Great hardwood floors under this paint some idiot covered it with," remarked Mr. Aimsworth. "Did I tell you this house is listed on the National Historic Register?" My mind focused on how the house needed new windows and how electric wire was running up the wall, askew, as if a giant spider had attempted to spin a web. But the biggest disappointment was the kitchen, or lack of one. Mr. Aimsworth continued, "Granddaddy used to have the cook-house going full blast all the time. Tore it down though. Put in this little kitchen in the '40s when we rented the place for a spell."

We made our way through some French doors onto a wide veranda that had the most spectacular view I had ever seen. I fell through a piece of banister while leaning a little too far for a better view. "Yep, own all the way down to the water; ever seen anything so splendid?" he asked "No, Mr. Aimsworth, I certainly haven't," I honestly replied.

Mr. Aimsworth slowly walked down to the water, and I followed. He was obviously deep in thought. At the water's edge he turned to me and said, "Well, what do you think, eh? I think this would make a fine French or maybe Italian restaurant. Think of the grand parties we could have here. Make me a list of things you would do if I were to make you the manager here. What do you think it would take to get it going?"

On the trip back to his home he offered, "Bring me some ideas on paper about how you would go about making my final dream come true. Bring along any questions you have. If I like your ideas, you have the job as manager." We agreed that our next meeting would be at noon, 2 weeks later. Mr. Aimsworth dropped me off at my car with "same time, same place."

Questions

You have just been offered an opportunity for your first job in quite an unorthodox manner by an eccentric gentleman. You are excited about the possibilities of the Victorian Manor becoming a popular dining destination. But, you realize that it would take a great deal of your time, hard work, and his money to make his dream of a restaurant a reality. You also realize that in 2 weeks you must come up with

1. a list of questions for Mr. Aimsworth (what will they be?);
2. a concept of how you would make the Victorian Manor into a restaurant (what do you have to do to form a concept?);
3. a rough idea of the amount of time and money that would be required to open and operate the restaurant (how will you go about putting together even a rough estimate?); and
4. further information about Mr. Aimsworth's background and his financial situation (how will you accomplish this?).

REFERENCES

1. Adapted from La Plante, A. Teaching an elephant to dance. *Computerworld*, November 16, 1998, 25–30.
2. Werhane, P., and Freeman, R. E. (eds.). *Blackwell Encyclopedic Dictionary of Business Ethics*. Cambridge, Mass.: Blackwell, 1999; DeGeorge, R. T., and DeGeorge, R. T. *Business Ethics*. Old Tappan, N.J.: Prentice-Hall, 1999.
3. Ciulla, J. B. (ed.). *Ethics, The Heart of Leadership*. Westport, Conn.: Quorum Books, 1998.
4. Jones, D. Doing the wrong thing. *USA Today*, April 4–6, 1997, 1A, 2A.
5. The framework for this section is based primarily on James, T. M. Ethical decision making by individuals in

organizations: An issue-contingent model. *Academy of Management Review,* 1991, 16, 366–395; also see Carroll, A. B., and Buchholtz, A. K. *Business and Society: Ethics and Stakeholder Management.* Cincinnati: South-Western, 1999.

6. Adapted from Ethics in the information age: An interview with Stephen G. Butler. *Leaders,* January–March 1998, 56–58.
7. Solomon, R. C. *A Better Way to Think About Business: How Personal Integrity Leads to Corporate Success.* New York: Oxford University Press, 1999.
8. Treviño, L. K., Weaver, G. P., Gibson, D. G., and Toffler, B. L. Managing ethics and legal compliance: What works and what hurts. *California Management Review,* Winter 1999, 131–151.
9. Adapted from Hassel, G. Memorable PR missteps of '96. *Houston Chronicle,* January 15, 1997, C1.
10. Wyburd, G. *Competitive and Ethical?: How Business Can Strike a Balance.* Dover, N.H.: Kogan Page, 1999.
11. Center for Public Integrity. *Nothing Sacred: The Politics of Privacy.* Washington, D.C.: Center for Public Integrity, 1998.
12. Pennenberg, A. L. The end of privacy. *Forbes,* November 29, 1999, 183–189; Serju-Harris, T. A question of privacy. *Houston Chronicle,* June 27, 1999, 1D, 5D.
13. Jennings, M. *Business: Its Legal, Ethical and Global Environment.* Cincinnati: South-Western, 1999.
14. Ferrell, O. C., Fraedrich, J., and Ferrell, L. *Business Ethics: Ethical Decision Making and Cases.* Boston: Houghton Mifflin College, 2000.
15. Solomon, R. C. *It's Good Business: Ethics and Free Enterprise for the New Millennium.* Lanham, Md.: Rowan & Littlefield, 1998.
16. Institute for Global Ethics. *Global Values, Moral Boundaries: A Pilot Survey.* Camden, Mass.: Institute for Global Ethics, 1997.
17. Barry, N. P. *Business Ethics.* Lafayette, Ind.: Purdue University Press, 2000.
18. Swanson, D. L. Toward an integrative theory of business and society: A research strategy for corporate social performance. *Academy of Management Review,* 1999, 24, 506–521.
19. Bowie, N. E. *Business Ethics: A Kantian Perspective.* Malden, Mass.: Blackwell, 1999.
20. Whitener, E. M., Brodt, S. E., Korsgaard, M. A., and Werner, J. M. Managers as initiators of trust: An exchange relationship framework for understanding managerial trustworthy behavior. *Academy of Management Review,* 1998, 23, 513–530.
21. Machan, T. R., Paul, E. F., and McGee, R. W. (eds.). *Business Ethics in the Global Market.* Stanford, Calif.: Hoover Institution Press, 1999.
22. Adapted from Puffer, S. M., and McCarthy, D. J. Finding the common ground in Russian and American business ethics. *California Management Review,* Winter 1995, 29–46; Puffer, S. M. and Associates. *Business and Management in Russia.* Chiltenham, U. K.: Edward Elger, 1996.
23. Hogart, R. M., and Reder, M. W. (eds.). *Rational Choice: The Contrasts Between Economics and Psychology.* Chicago: University of Chicago Press, 1986.
24. Garvin, D. A. Building a learning organization. *Harvard Business Review,* July–August 1993, 78–91.
25. Hammond, J. S., Keeney, R. L., and Raiffa, H. *Smart Choices: A Practical Guide to Making Better Decisions.* Boston: Harvard Business School Press, 1999.
26. Hammond, J. S., Keeney, R. L., and Raiffa, H. Even swaps: A rational method for making trade-offs. *Harvard Business Review,* March–April 1998, 148.
27. Hammond, Keeney, and Raiffa, 137–150.
28. Simon, H. A. *Administrative Behavior: A Study of Decision-Making Processes in Administrative Organizations,* 4th ed. New York: Free Press, 1997.
29. Roach, J. M. Simon says: Decision making is "satisficing" experience. *Management Review,* January 1979, 8–9; also see Simon, H. A. Bounded rationality and organizational learning. *Organization Science,* 1991, 2, 125–134.
30. Schoemaker, P. J. H., and Russo, J. E. A pyramid of decision approaches. *California Management Review,* Fall 1993, 9–31.
31. Adapted from Nutt, P. C. Surprising but true: Half the decisions in organizations fail. *Academy of Management Executive,* November 1999, 75–90.
32. Ruggles, R. The state of the notion: Knowledge management in practice. *California Management Review,* Winter 1998, 80–89.
33. Adapted from Mack, M. H. Managing codified knowledge. *Sloan Management Review,* Summer 1999, 45–58; Botkin, J. *Smart Business: How Knowledge Communities Can Revolutionize Your Company.* New York: Free Press, 1999.
34. Adapted from Fryer, B. Get smart. *Inc. Tech 1999,* 1999, 3, 61–69.
35. Pfeffer, J. *Managing with Power: Politics and Influence in Organizations.* Boston: Harvard Business School Press, 1992; Kramer, R. M., and Neale, M. A. (eds.) *Power and Influence in Organizations.* Thousand Oaks, Calif.: Sage, 1998.
36. Galbraith, C. S., and Merrill, G. B. The politics of forecasting: Managing the truth. *California Management Review,* Winter 1996, 29–43.
37. Adapted from Gouttefarde, C. American values in the French workplace. *Business Horizons,* March–April 1996, 60–69.
38. McCall, M. W., Jr., and Kaplan, R. E. *Whatever It Takes: The Realities of Managerial Decision Making,* 2nd ed. Englewood Cliffs, N.J.: Prentice-Hall, 1990; Harrison, E. F. *The Managerial Decision-Making Process,* 5th ed. Boston: Houghton Mifflin, 1999.
39. Adapted from Volkema, R. J. Factors which promote "solving the wrong problem." Unpublished statement. Fairfax, Va.: Institute for Advanced Study in the Integrative Sciences, George Mason University, 1988.
40. Beach, L. R. *The Psychology of Decision Making: People in Organizations.* Thousand Oaks, Calif.: Sage, 1997.
41. Bernstein, P. L. *Against the Gods: The Remarkable Story of Risk.* Somerset, N.J.: John Wiley & Sons, 1997.
42. Kahneman, D., and Tversky, A. Prospect theory: An analysis of decision under risk. *Econometricka,* 1987, 47, 263–291; Hodgkinson, G. P., Brown, N. J., Maule, A. J., Glaister, K. W., and Pearman, A. D. Breaking the frame: An analysis of strategic cognition and decision making under uncertainty. *Strategic Management Journal,* 1999, 20, 977–985.

43. Mitroff, I. *Smart Thinking for Crazy Times: The Art of Solving the Right Problems.* San Francisco: Berrett-Koehler, 1998.
44. Hammond, J. S., Keeney, R. L., and Raiffa, H. The hidden traps in decision making. *Harvard Business Review,* September–October 1998, 47–58; Bazerman, M. H., Moore, D. A., Tenbrunsel, A. E., Wade-Benzoni, K. A., and Blount, S. Explaining how preferences change across joint versus separate evaluation. *Journal of Economic Behavior & Organization,* 1999, 39, 41–58.
45. Bazerman, M. H. *Judgment in Managerial Decision Making.* New York: John Wiley & Sons, 1997; Simons, R. How risky is your company? *Harvard Business Review,* May–June 1999, 85–94.
46. Eisenhardt, K. M. Strategy as strategic decision making. *Sloan Management Review,* Spring 1999, 65–72; Beck, J. C., and Davenport, T. H. Learning to manage your organization's scarcest asset: Attention. *Inc. Outlook 1999,* 1999, 2, 44–51.
47. Adapted from Society for Human Resource Management. *1999 Barriers to Advancement Survey.* Alexandria, Va.: Society for Human Resource Management, 1999.
48. Sanders, R. *The Executive Decisionmaking Process.* Westport, Conn.: Quorum Books, 1999.
49. Weick, K. E. *Sensemaking in Organizations.* Thousand Oaks, Calif.: Sage, 1995.
50. Brockner, J. The escalation of commitment to a failing course of action: Toward theoretical progress. *Academy of Management Review,* 1992, 17, 39–61; Staw, B. M. The escalation of commitment: A review and analysis. *Academy of Management Review,* 1981, 6, 577–587.
51. Woodman, R. W., Sawyer, J. E., and Griffin, R. W. Toward a theory of organizational creativity. *Academy of Management Review,* 1993, 18, 293–321; Rubinstein, M. F., and Fersteinberg, I. R. *The Minding Organization: Bring the Future to the Present and Turn Creative Ideas into Business Solutions.* New York: John Wiley & Sons, 1999.
52. Adapted from Olofson, C. So many decisions, so little time. *Fast Company,* October 1999, 62–63.
53. Ford, C. M. A theory of individual creative action in multiple social domains. *Academy of Management Review,* 1996, 21, 1112–1142; Leonard, D. A., and Swap, W. C. *When Sparks Fly: Igniting Creativity in Groups.* Boston: Harvard Business School Press, 1999.
54. De Bono, E. *Serious Creativity: Using the Power of Lateral Thinking to Create New Ideas.* New York: HarperCollins, 1992.
55. This discussion is based on Van Gundy, A. B. *Techniques of Structured Problem Solving.* New York: Van Nostrand, 1981; Proctor, T. *Creative Problem Solving for Managers.* London: Routledge, 1999.
56. Farnham, A. How to nurture creative sparks. *Fortune,* January 10, 1994, 94–100; Amabile, T. M. How to kill creativity. *Harvard Business Review,* September–October 1998, 77–87.
57. Flynn, G. Hallmark cares. *Personnel Journal,* March 1996, 50–58; Dutton, G. Enhancing creativity. *Management Review,* November 1996, 44–46.
58. Cosier, R. A., and Schwenk, C. R. Agreement and thinking alike: Ingredients for poor decisions. *Academy of Management Executive,* February 1990, 69–74; Tierney, P., Farmer, S. M., Graen, G. B. An examination of leadership and employee creativity: The relevance of traits and relationships. *Personnel Psychology,* 1999, 52, 591–620.
59. Adapted from Duran, G. J., Gomar, E. E., Stiles, M., Vele, C. A., and Vogt, J. F. Living ethics: Meeting challenges in decision making. In *The 1997b Annual: Volume 1, Training.* Copyright © 1997 by Pfeiffer, An Imprint of Jossey-Bass, Inc., Publishers, San Francisco, Calif., 127–135. Used with permission.
60. Adapted from Is Opportunity Knocking? Copyright © 1995 by Cis Hawk, The Citizenship Foundation, Houston, Texas. Written as a basis for classroom discussion. Distributed by the International Case Clearinghouse. Used with permission.

CHAPTER

15 Job Design

LEARNING OBJECTIVES

When you have finished studying this chapter, you should be able to:

1. Describe and contrast the common approaches to job design.
2. Discuss the linkages between job design and technology.
3. Explain the job characteristics enrichment model and its relationship to work motivation.
4. Describe the sociotechnical systems model and its relationship to organizational effectiveness.

***Preview Case:** Texas Nameplate Company*

COMMON JOB DESIGN APPROACHES

Comparative Framework

Job Rotation

Job Engineering

Job Enlargement

***Competency: Managing Change**—Westinghouse Air Brake*

Job Enrichment

Sociotechnical Systems

Ergonomics

***Competency: Managing Diversity**—Benteler Automotive Corporation*

JOB DESIGN AND TECHNOLOGY

Role of Workflow Uncertainty

Role of Task Uncertainty

Combined Effects of Workflow and Task Uncertainty

Role of Task Interdependence

***Competency: Managing Communication**—David Berdish Fosters Dialogue*

Interrelationships among Job Design and Technology Concepts

JOB CHARACTERISTICS ENRICHMENT MODEL

Framework

Job Characteristics

Individual Differences

Job Diagnosis

Implementation Approaches

Job Characteristics and Technology

Social Information Processing

SOCIOTECHNICAL SYSTEMS MODEL

***Competency: Managing Across Cultures**—Job Design in the Malaysian Nursing Context*

Social Systems

Technological Systems

Moderators

Core Concepts

Implementation Issues

***Competency: Managing Teams**—Consolidated Diesel's Engine Plant*

CHAPTER SUMMARY

Key Terms and Concepts

Discussion Questions

DEVELOPING COMPETENCIES

***Competency: Managing Change**—Data Entry Operators*

***Competency: Managing Teams**—GE's Aircraft-Engine Assembly Facility*

PREVIEW CASE

TEXAS NAMEPLATE COMPANY

The Texas Nameplate Company (TNC) manufactures and sells identification and information labels that are put on refrigerators, oil field equipment, high-pressure valves, trucks, computer equipment, and other products made by its 1,000 customers. Located in Dallas, Texas, the family-owned business is the smallest company (with about 70 employees) ever to receive the Malcolm Baldrige National Quality Award.

Company president and CEO Dale Crownover and his seven top managers make up the Business Excellence Leadership Team. This team aligns the focus of all employees with the company's vision to "become the recognized supplier of commercial nameplates in the United States." Each senior leader acts as a champion for one or more of the company's seven key business drivers (KBDs): customer satisfaction, employee satisfaction, process optimization, environmental consciousness, controlled growth, fair profit, and external relations—including the quality and effectiveness of TNC's interactions with suppliers and the community.

The seven KBDs form the nucleus of the company's participatory strategic planning process. All employees are invited to submit proposals for new initiatives, which are evaluated for cost and their potential to contribute to company goals set for each KBD. The resulting strategic plan is depicted on a comprehensive, easy-to-scan grid that integrates goals, action plans, targeted outcomes, and indicators. For each action plan—currently totaling 96—initiatives, assigned leaders, and 3-year goals are displayed. All employees review progress monthly. Results of an employee survey provided the basis for the review process. Responses indicated that workers wanted regular updates to give them greater insight into production results and management activities.

Organization processes and jobs are designed to allow flexibility so that employees can respond quickly to customer requirements and changing business needs. Customer-contact employees are empowered to resolve customer complaints without consulting management. Production employees are responsible for tailoring processes to optimize contributions to company goals and to meet team-set standards. To help workers identify opportunities for improvements, each process is mapped in a flowchart, which includes requirements, metrics, and cause-and-effect diagrams. To foster continuous learning, TNC uses a variety of training methods, supplemented by tuition reimbursement and other "back-to-school" incentives.

Technology is key. A computer-aided design system enables electronic transfer of artwork for nameplates, helping reduce cycle time, and a local area network (LAN) provides workers with immediate access to process and business-related information, including profiles of all TNC customers. The capabilities for data interchange make it easy for customers to request quotes and transmit purchase orders electronically.

For more information on the Texas Nameplate Company, Inc., visit the company's home page at ***www.nameplate.com.***

To maintain its strong customer focus, TNC uses a wide range of listening and learning practices to capture information from former, current, and potential customers. For example, through its Customer Site Visit program, a team of TNC employees visits customer facilities to identify opportunities for improving products and services. The results of these visits are shared with everyone at TNC. In all customer contacts, workers and managers are instructed to ask, "What else could we be doing for you?" In addition, a "quick-response" survey card accompanies each TNC shipment, and an annual survey provides 70 different indicators of customer satisfaction.[1]

The underlying values, management principles, and strategic imperatives in the design or redesign of jobs are illustrated in the Preview Case. At Texas Nameplate Company, individual jobs are interwoven with a set of seven key business drivers, including customer satisfaction, employee satisfaction, and process optimization. Job design there is much more than defining tasks and responsibilities that are undertaken in isolation. Unfortunately, the comprehensive integrated approach to designing jobs utilized by TNC is not typical of most organizations.

In this chapter we first introduce job design by presenting a framework for describing and contrasting five job design approaches—two of which we discuss in greater detail in the last two sections of the chapter. Next, we outline several linkages between technology and job design. Then, we explain the job characteristics enrichment model. Finally, we describe the sociotechnical systems model, the most complex job design approach presented in this chapter. Job design at TNC draws on both the sociotechnical systems and the job characteristics enrichment models.

We've emphasized the importance of effectively designed jobs in previous chapters. For example, in Chapters 5 and 6 we presented the need to design jobs to give individuals challenging goals and a sense of meaning at work. In Chapter 8 we discussed job design in relation to the use of functional teams, problem-solving teams, cross-functional teams, and self-managed teams, which change and enrich the tasks performed by employees. In this chapter, we further develop and extend these and other job design concepts and issues.

Job design refers to the goals and tasks to be accomplished by managers and employees, including expected interpersonal and task relationships. Job design occurs each time individuals are assigned work, given instructions, or empowered to perform tasks and pursue goals. Formally or informally, customers, managers, teams, or individual employees may change the tasks to be undertaken and how they are to be done. Because both the tasks and the means for performing them can change, managers need to know how to design and redesign jobs to make them as motivating, meaningful, and productive as possible. Thus the needs and goals of both the employee and the organization should be considered in the design of jobs.[2]

Learning Objective:

1. Describe and contrast the common approaches to job design.

COMMON JOB DESIGN APPROACHES

The job design approach at TNC gives employees the tools they need and uses their competencies to provide high-quality products and efficient services to its customers—closely approaching the ideal. Although the ideal isn't always attainable, substantial improvements in job design that can benefit the customer, employee, and organization usually are possible with the use of one or more of the commonly used job design approaches.

COMPARATIVE FRAMEWORK

Five of the most common approaches to job design are shown in Figure 15.1. The *impact dimension*, on the vertical axis, is the degree to which a job design approach is linked to factors beyond the immediate job, such as reward systems, performance appraisal methods, leadership practices of managers, customer needs, organization structure, physical working conditions, and team composition and norms—as well as its likely effect on changes in effectiveness and quality. The *complexity dimension*, on the horizontal axis, is the degree to which a job design approach requires (1) changes in many factors, (2) the involvement of individuals with diverse competencies at various organizational levels; and (3) a high level of decision-making competency for successful implementation. In relation to Figure 15.1, the job design philosophy and practices at TNC reflect high impact and high complexity.

Figure 15.1 **Comparison of Five Job Design Approaches**

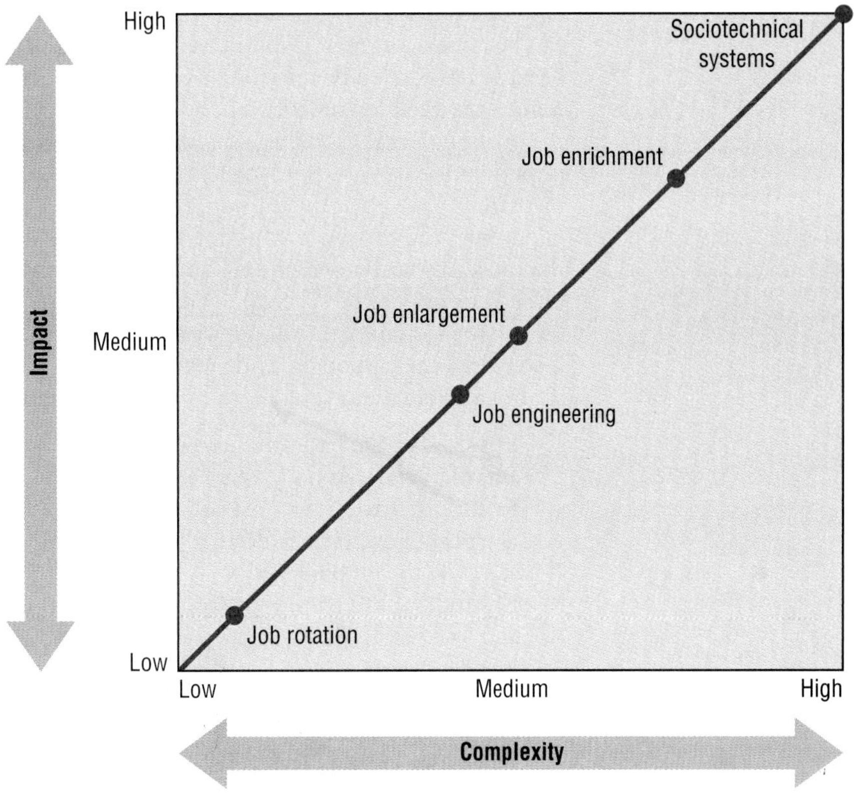

Job Rotation

Job rotation refers to moving employees from job to job to add variety and reduce boredom by allowing them to perform a variety of tasks. As traditionally used, job rotation is low in both impact and complexity because it typically moves employees from one routine job to another. Maids International, a housecleaning service franchise, uses job rotation with its four-person housecleaning teams by, for example, having a maid clean the kitchen in one house and the bedroom in another.[3] However, if all the tasks are similar and routine, job rotation may not have the desired effect of improving employee effectiveness and job satisfaction. For example, rotating automobile assembly-line workers from bolting bumpers on cars to bolting on tire rims isn't likely to reduce their boredom. However, job rotation may be of significant benefit if it is part of a larger redesign effort and/or it is used as a training and development approach to develop various employee competencies and prepare employees for advancement.[4] At times, it may be used to control the problem of repetitive stress injuries by moving people among jobs that require different physical movements.[5]

Job Engineering

Frederick W. Taylor established the foundation for modern industrial engineering late in the nineteenth century. He was concerned with product design, process design, tool design, plant layout, work measurement, and operator methods. **Job engineering** focuses on the tasks to be performed, methods to be used, workflows among employees, layout of the workplace, performance standards, and interdependencies between people and machines. Analysts often examine these job design factors by means of time-and-motion studies, determining the time required to do each task and the movements needed to perform it efficiently.[6]

A cornerstone of job engineering is specialization of labor with the goal of achieving greater efficiency. High levels of specialization are intended to (1) allow employees to learn a task rapidly, (2) permit short work cycles so that performance can be almost automatic and involve little or no mental effort, (3) make hiring easier because low-skilled people can be easily trained and paid relatively low wages, and (4) reduce the need for supervision, owing to simplified jobs and standardization.

Although traditional job engineering also can create boring jobs, it remains an important job design approach because the resulting cost savings can be measured immediately and easily. In addition, this approach is concerned with appropriate levels of automation, that is, looking for ways to replace workers with machines to perform the most physically demanding and repetitive tasks.[7] The job engineering approach often continues to be successfully used, especially when it is combined with a concern for the social context in which the jobs are performed. One expert who advocates the job engineering approach while involving employees in decisions about their jobs prescribes the following "golden rules of work design."

- Ensure that the end product/output of the work is clearly defined, unambiguous, and fully understood by the employees.
- Ensure that the steps/tasks to be performed to achieve the required end product/output are clearly defined in the appropriate sequence and are fully understood by the employees.
- Ensure that the employees know and understand where their responsibility starts and finishes in the work process.
- Ensure that the tools, facilities, and information needed to perform the work are readily available to and fully understood by the employees.
- Ensure that there is a process whereby the employees can suggest possible improvements in the work design and exercise initiative in implementing them.
- Ensure that the employees are involved in the work design process.[8]

The Managing Change Competency feature on page 449 focuses on the consequences of implementing a continuous improvement program for production workers at the Westinghouse Air Brake manufacturing facility in Chicago, Illinois. The program relied on the basic concepts of job engineering. Management claimed that the changes introduced, while demanding of the employees, were necessary for the plant to remain competitive.

Job Enlargement

Job enlargement is expansion of the number of different tasks performed by an employee in a single job. For example, one automobile assembly-line worker's job was enlarged from installing just one taillight to installing both taillights and the trunk. An auto mechanic switched from only changing oil to changing oil, greasing, and changing transmission fluid. Job enlargement attempts to add somewhat similar tasks to the job so that it will have more variety and be more interesting. As Figure 15.1 suggests, job enlargement is viewed as an extension of job engineering. However, it is more responsive to the higher level needs of employees by providing more variety in their jobs.[9] Jeffrey Byrom and the other production employees at Westinghouse Air Brake indicated that the fast pace made the day go by more quickly and that doing several tasks beat being stuck behind one machine all day.[10]

The job enlargement approach often has positive effects on employee effectiveness. However, some employees view job enlargement as just adding more routine, repetitive tasks to their already boring job. Other employees may view it as eliminating their ability to perform their jobs almost automatically. These employees may value the opportunity to daydream about a big date that night or think about the upcoming weekend. Others may simply prefer to spend their time socializing with

COMPETENCY: MANAGING CHANGE

WESTINGHOUSE AIR BRAKE

Every 2 minutes and 26 seconds, a buzzer sounds over the heads of workers inside Westinghouse Air Brake Company's small factory. It signals that the conveyor that carries parts down the line is about to move.

"If you don't hustle, you surely won't keep up," says Jeffrey Byrom. Moving between machines, Byrom is in continuous motion, lifting a finished part and putting it on the moving conveyor. If he doesn't feed the conveyor each time it moves, he risks hindering the next worker down the line. Speed is just part of it. In traditional factories, workers often are assigned to run single machines, producing many parts. Byrom's job requires him to juggle the operation of three different machines simultaneously while also checking regularly for defects in finished items. The idea is to fill every moment of his workday with only the most effective motions. The result is more efficiency.

By using the Japanese approach known as *kaizen*, which means "continuous improvement," Westinghouse Air Brake tries to get top performance from aging plants such as this one. Owing to the combination of radically streamlined processes and sheer speed, each worker on Byrom's line now produces 10 times more per day than in 1991.

From Byrom's perspective, it's no picnic. He works on a line that produces "slack adjusters," big pogo-stick-like devices used to keep the distance constant between the brakes and wheels on trains. His job is an elaborate juggling act. Operating in a tight U-shaped work area known as a "cell," he first uses a big blue metal-cutting device to shape both ends of a long bar, which he then puts into a second machine that threads one end. Then, he places the bar in a third machine that welds a metal ring onto it. He can't just walk one piece at a time through the operation and hope to keep up with the conveyor. Rather, he must zig and zag among the machines, which run at different speeds, working on several pieces at the same time.

Only if the line reaches its daily production quota do workers get a $1.50-an-hour bonus. To make the quota, everyone in the factory has to pull together because the extra pay is awarded for overall production, not just the output of each of the areas along the line. Management estimates that its goals are met about 5 out of every 7 workdays.

When Westinghouse Air Brake started making changes at the plant, production was spread out across a vast expanse of the factory floor. Workers produced parts at machines and then wheeled them into warehouses or to other machines far across the factory for further processing. The first improvement involved grouping machines so that workers no longer had to move parts as far or handle them as much. Later, the conveyor was installed. Before its installation, workers loaded parts on low carts, which they pushed up the line by hand. The conveyor was built so that parts can be laid in baskets that hang from overhead at waist height, thus minimizing bending and lifting.[11]

*To learn more about the Westinghouse Air Brake Company, visit the company's home page at **www.wabco-rail.com**.*

coworkers. If an enlarged job requires greater attention and concentration than the original job, most employees typically find it more interesting or challenging, but some may view the added demands negatively. The importance of individual differences in attempting to anticipate or understand the reactions of employees to redesigned jobs should not be underestimated.

Job Enrichment

Job enrichment refers to the empowerment of employees to assume more responsibility and accountability for planning, organizing, performing, controlling, and evaluating their own work.[12] The job enrichment approach originated in the 1940s at International Business Machines (IBM). In the 1950s, the number of companies interested in job enrichment grew slowly. However, successful and widely publicized experiments at AT&T, Texas Instruments (TI), and Imperial Chemicals eventually led to an increasing awareness of job enrichment and interest in this approach in the 1960s. The techniques used for enriching jobs often are specific to the job being redesigned. We discuss enrichment techniques when we present the job characteristics enrichment model later in this chapter.

Sociotechnical Systems

The **sociotechnical systems model** focuses on organizations as made up of people with various competencies (the *social system*) who use tools, machines, and techniques (the *technical system*) to create goods or services valued by customers and other stakeholders. Thus the social and technical systems need to be designed with respect to one another—and to the demands of customers, suppliers, and other stakeholders in the external environment. Because of its scope, sociotechnical systems are complex and have an impact on the way work is performed throughout the organization. Recall the relationship of this model to the other job design approaches, as shown in Figure 15.1. To a large extent, this model influences how effective an organization will be. All organizations are sociotechnical systems, but all don't necessarily reflect the principles underlying this approach.

The goal of sociotechnical systems analysis is to find the best possible match between the technology available, the people involved, and the organization's needs.[13] A crucial aspect of this approach is the recognition of task interdependence, which becomes the basis for forming teams. After teams have been formed, the specific tasks to be performed by team members are considered, along with the relationships among all these tasks. This approach has been applied most successfully—as has the job enrichment approach—to industrial organizations.

The sociotechnical systems approach emphasizes the diagnosis of demands by external stakeholders (customers, suppliers, shareholders, regulatory agencies, creditors, and others) and the internal adaptations needed to respond to those demands. From a job design perspective, passage of the Americans with Disabilities Act (ADA) in 1990 created one such demand for many U.S.-based organizations. The Managing Diversity Competency feature on page 451 reviews the accommodations that Benteler Automotive Corporation made on behalf of Brian Capshaw so that he could continue to work. Recall from Chapter 1 that one of the categories of diversity is *physical abilities and qualities*—the variety of characteristics, including body type, physical size, facial features, specific abilities or disabilities, and visible and invisible physical and mental talents or limitations.

Ergonomics

Figure 15.1 doesn't show all the job design approaches used by organizations. For example, **ergonomics** focuses on minimizing the physical demands and risks of work. This approach helps ensure that job demands are consistent with people's physical capabilities to perform them without undue risk. It involves the design of aids (ranging from hand tools to computer software to instruments) used to perform jobs.[14]

Consider the initiative by Dolby Laboratories at its Brisbane, California, manufacturing facility, which employs approximately 50 assembly workers. The plant produces digital cinema processors and sound equipment used in theaters. Although about 90 percent of the electronic assembly is automated, repetitive handwork is still

COMPETENCY: MANAGING DIVERSITY

BENTELER AUTOMOTIVE CORPORATION

On his way to work at one of Benteler Automotive Corporation's plants near South Bend, Indiana, Brian Capshaw was in a severe accident that paralyzed him from the waist down. Although he's in a wheelchair, Capshaw isn't confined. He coaches a kids' basketball team. He drives himself around in a hand-controlled van. And he still travels the familiar route to Benteler, where he works as an accountant.

Capshaw's injury was extraordinary and so were Benteler's efforts on his behalf. While he was still in rehabilitation, the company installed a wheelchair ramp, three electronic doors, and an eye-activated water fountain and redesigned a bathroom. The cost came to $30,000, all of it paid by CNA, the firm's insurance company. His manager drove him to and from work every day until he was able to drive himself.

Benteler's and CNA's willingness to go the extra mile was the humane thing to do, but it also made good business sense. In Capshaw's case, going back to work was a realistic possibility, enabling Benteler to keep a valuable, productive employee rather than spend money to recruit and train a replacement. CNA was able to keep its costs down, too. If Capshaw hadn't returned to work, he would have been eligible for long-term disability payments until he turned 65—money that CNA would have had to pay.

Benteler and CNA obviously more than met the standard of reasonable accommodation. The ADA says that reasonable accommodation may include (1) modifying existing employment facilities to make them readily accessible to individuals with disabilities; and (2) making modifications such as job restructuring, part-time or modified work schedules, reassignment to vacant positions, acquiring, adjusting, or modifying equipment or devices, adjusting or modifying examinations, developing new training materials or policies, providing qualified readers or interpreters, and other similar accommodations.[15]

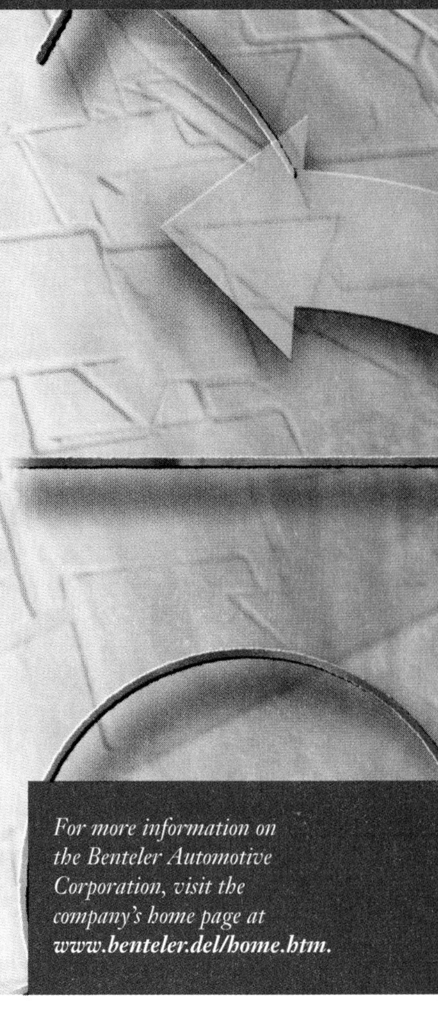

For more information on the Benteler Automotive Corporation, visit the company's home page at ***www.benteler.del/home.htm.***

essential for some operations. "There's some hand insertion of components and some mechanical assembly," production manager Marie Davies explained. In addition, technicians do test work and some repairs by hand. Even though Dolby Laboratories historically has had a low rate of reported carpal tunnel disabilities, Davies looked at ergonomic tools and ergonomic training as part of an overall safety and health plan. She assembled a tool team of assemblers who understood the requirement of using the right tool for the right job to look at tools in the workplace. She also set up ergonomic training and instituted tool audits.[16]

Learning Objective:

2. Discuss the linkages between job design and technology.

JOB DESIGN AND TECHNOLOGY

Technology refers to the techniques, tools, methods, procedures, and machines that are used to transform objects (materials, information, and people). Employees use technology to acquire inputs, transform inputs into outputs, and provide goods or services to clients and customers. Here, our discussion focuses on the concepts of workflow uncertainty, task uncertainty, and task interdependence as they relate to job design. We also present some examples of how various information technologies are being used to implement these concepts. Recall the various ways that the work of individuals and teams is being changed by information technologies, especially through groupware, the Internet, intranets, e-mail, mobile phones, and the like (see Chapters 8, 13, and 14).[17]

Role of Workflow Uncertainty

Workflow uncertainty is the degree of knowledge that an employee has about when inputs will be received and require processing. When there is little workflow uncertainty, an employee may have little discretion (autonomy) to decide which, when, or where tasks will be performed. For the most part, the production workers at an automobile assembly plant experience a low degree of workflow uncertainty. In fact, the application of the job engineering approach in automobile assembly plants is intended to minimize workflow uncertainty.

Recall our discussion of the Westinghouse Air Brake plant in the Managing Change Competency feature. Speed is crucial in this plant, but it isn't the only focus on the line. Rather, the emphasis is on what the managers call "single-piece flow," or the idea that they want to make products only at the speed necessary to meet customer demand. That's why the conveyor moves every 2 minutes and 26 seconds, which the managers have calculated is the rate needed to produce the right amount currently. That rate changes a couple of times a year to reflect shifts in customer demand. The ideal is for each cell to finish a single part just before it must be put on the conveyor.[18] There is little workflow uncertainty for Jeffrey Byrom and the other production workers in this plant.

Role of Task Uncertainty

Task uncertainty is the degree of knowledge that an employee has about how to perform the job and when it needs to be done. When there is little task uncertainty, an employee knows how to produce the desired results.[19] Through extensive training and the standardization of jobs, management typically attempts to minimize task uncertainty in assembly plants. Again, there is a minimum of task uncertainty for Jeffrey Byrom and the other production workers at the Westinghouse Air Brake plant. Paul Golden, the plant manager, comments: "To be true to these ideas, you're really supposed to dictate everything."[20] In a strict kaizen plant, that would include everything from which knee an employee is allowed to kneel on while doing a particular task to how far the employee should move his or her right arm to perform another task. Production workers in a plant experience somewhat more task uncertainty if they work as teams to study problems and refine procedures. At such a plant, teams often are asked to participate in proposing continuous improvements, one of the elements in total quality management.

With high task uncertainty, few (if any) prespecified ways exist for dealing with the job's tasks. This condition means that experience, judgment, intuition, and problem-solving ability usually are required of the employee. Recall the Preview Case about the Texas Nameplate Company. Virtually all its employees are engaged in some tasks that involve moderate to high levels of task and workflow uncertainty. For example, all employees are encouraged to submit proposals for new initiatives, and they review progress on initiatives and goals monthly. Employees are given the flexibility to respond quickly to unique customer requirements or complaints and changing business needs. Teams of employees visit customer facilities to identify opportunities for improving products and services.

Combined Effects of Workflow and Task Uncertainty

Figure 15.2 shows the main combinations of workflow uncertainty and task uncertainty. Each of the four cells contains examples of jobs that fall primarily into each category. However, be careful not to stereotype particular jobs by thinking of them only in terms of a single position on the grid. Job redesign often modifies them and changes their levels of workflow and task uncertainty. Managerial jobs—including some top-management jobs—could range from the extreme upper right corner in cell 3 to closer to the center of the grid. Also, some jobs don't fit neatly into a single cell. For example, an auditor's job at an accounting firm might generally be plotted somewhere in the middle of the grid.

Figure 15.2 **Technology Framework and Job Design**

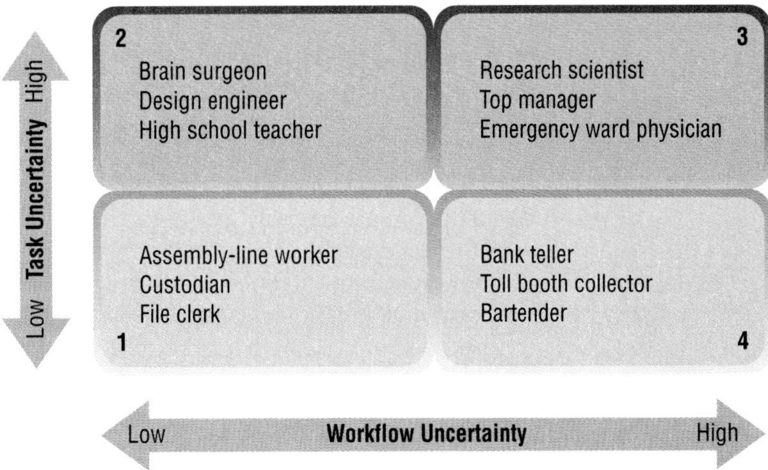

Source: Adapted from Slocum, J. W., Jr., and Sims, H. P., Jr. Typology for integrating technology, organization and job design. *Human Relations,* 1980, 33, 196; Susman, G. I. *Autonomy at Work—A Sociotechnical Analysis of Participative Management.* New York: Praeger, 1980, 132.

The sociotechnical system and job enrichment approaches generally increase workflow uncertainty and/or task uncertainty. However, the assembly-line job shown in cell 1 could be enriched but still be generally classified as a cell-1 type of job. Some people who occupy cell-3 types of jobs could experience stress from too much workflow and task uncertainty (see Chapter 7).

Role of Task Interdependence

Task interdependence is the degree to which decision making and cooperation between two or more employees is necessary for them to perform their jobs. The construction of the structural steel framework of a high-rise building involves a high degree of task interdependence between the crane operator, ground crew, and assembly crew in moving and joining the steel girders and beams.

The three basic types of interdependent task relations are pooled, sequential, and reciprocal.[21] **Pooled interdependence** is the ability of an employee (or team) to act independently of others in completing a task or tasks. Most real estate agents, who often act as independent contractors within a real estate firm, use pooled interdependence to coordinate their activities.

Sequential interdependence is the need for an employee (or team) to complete certain tasks before other employees (or teams) can perform their tasks. In other words, the outputs from some employees (teams) become the inputs for other employees (teams). The sequence of interdependencies can be a long chain in some mass-production activities. The Westinghouse Air Brake plant is an example of sequential interdependence.

Reciprocal interdependence means that the outputs from an individual (or team) become the inputs for others and vice versa. Reciprocal interdependencies are common in everyday life. Examples include (1) a family, (2) a basketball team, (3) a surgical team, (4) a decision-making team, and (5) a class project assigned to a small team of students. Reciprocal interdependence usually requires a high degree of collaboration, communication, and team decision making, as illustrated in the following Managing Communication Competency feature. It quotes David Berdish, an organizational-learning manager at Visteon Automotive Systems, a parts-manufacturing firm owned by the Ford Motor Company, on his experiences, approaches tried, and results obtained with the use of reciprocal interdependence.

COMPETENCY: MANAGING COMMUNICATION

DAVID BERDISH FOSTERS DIALOGUE

We had a program to encourage our suppliers to help us save money. If they came up with a design or process idea that cut our production costs, we applied 50 percent of the savings to their next bid. But we didn't get any suggestions, and we couldn't figure out why. So we got the suppliers together during a 3-day learning conference, and we asked them why they weren't contributing. And guess what? We were wrong—they had come up with plenty of ways to realize savings. But our engineers were ignoring them—our people thought the suppliers were trying to show them up. So we dug a little further.

We tracked the average time it took us to execute a change, once we'd made the decision to move on it. The answer just floored us. It took 89 weeks! We calculated that 39 of those weeks were a direct result of people sitting on information or refusing to share ideas. So the problem really wasn't the suppliers, or even the engineers. It was a whole chain of events in which people were driven by their own agendas and politics, instead of concern for the customer.

A large number of misunderstandings come from people who do not have an overall view of how their role—and other people's roles—fit within the organization. I've worked with engineers on getting them to do a better job of selling their projects to the finance group. We discuss how getting the go-ahead depends on showing how your effort will cut costs or deliver returns. But some engineers didn't even know what the word "returns" means. Out of that discussion, the engineers finally understood why the finance department asked for projections. Then they stopped thinking of the finance people as enemies—and started seeing them as critical allies.

From there, we were able to stop the cycle in which engineers submitted inflated project budgets because they feared finance was going to cut funds, and finance would automatically cut funds because they assumed the numbers were inflated. Now, project budgets come in and they're either approved or denied. But the numbers are real, and both groups realize that they're part of the same team.[22]

For more information on Visteon Automotive Systems, visit the company's home page at www.visteon.com.

INTERRELATIONSHIPS AMONG JOB DESIGN AND TECHNOLOGY CONCEPTS

Task interdependence, workflow uncertainty, and task uncertainty must all be considered in job design. An increase in the use of pooled interdependence decreases the amount of required coordination among jobs. Less coordination often means less sequential and/or workflow uncertainty for employees. New information technologies often change task interdependence, workflow uncertainty, and task uncertainty—either reducing or increasing them for the employee. The specific impacts will be influenced by how employees are expected to use the technology and whether higher management uses the technology to empower employees or more closely monitor and control them.

Learning Objective:

3. Explain the job characteristics enrichment model and its relationship to work motivation.

JOB CHARACTERISTICS ENRICHMENT MODEL

The job characteristics enrichment model is one of the best known approaches to job enrichment.[23] Before reading further, complete the questionnaire in Table 15.1.

FRAMEWORK

The **job characteristics enrichment model** involves increasing the amounts of skill variety, task identity, task significance, autonomy, and feedback in a job. The model

Table 15.1 Job Characteristics Inventory

Directions

The following list contains statements that could be used to describe a job. Please indicate the extent to which you agree or disagree with each statement as a description of a job you currently hold or have held, by writing the appropriate number next to the statement. Try to be as objective as you can in answering.

1	2	3	4	5
Strongly Disagree	Disagree	Uncertain	Agree	Strongly Agree

This job . . .

_____ 1. provides much variety.
_____ 2. permits me to be left on my own to do my work.
_____ 3. is arranged so that I often have the opportunity to see jobs or projects through to completion.
_____ 4. provides feedback on how well I am doing as I am working.
_____ 5. is relatively significant in my organization.
_____ 6. gives me considerable opportunity for independence and freedom in how I do the work.
_____ 7. provides different responsibilities.
_____ 8. enables me to find out how well I am doing.
_____ 9. is important in the broader scheme of things.
_____ 10. provides an opportunity for independent thought and action.
_____ 11. provides me with considerable variety of work.
_____ 12. is arranged so that I have the opportunity to complete the work I start.
_____ 13. provides me with the feeling that I know whether I am performing well or poorly.
_____ 14. is arranged so that I have the chance to do a job from the beginning to the end (i.e., a chance to do the whole job).
_____ 15. is one where a lot of other people can be affected by how well the work gets done.

Scoring

For each of the five scales, compute a score by summing the answers to the designated questions.

	Score
Skill variety: Sum the points for items 1, 7, and 11.	_____
Task identity: Sum the points for items 3, 12, and 14.	_____
Task significance: Sum the points for items 5, 9, and 15.	_____
Autonomy: Sum the points for items 2, 6, and 10.	_____
Job feedback: Sum the points for items 4, 8, and 13.	_____
Total Score	_____

Summary Interpretation

A total score of 60–75 suggests that the core job characteristics contribute to an overall positive psychological state for you and, in turn, leads to desirable personal and work outcomes. A total score of 15–30 suggests the opposite. We present additional interpretative comments later in this section of the chapter.

Source: Adapted from Sims, H. P., Jr., Szilagyi, A. D., and Keller, R. T. The measurement of job characteristics. *Academy of Management Journal*, 1976, 19, 195–212.

proposes that the levels of these job characteristics affect three critical psychological states: (1) experienced meaningfulness of the tasks performed; (2) experienced personal responsibility for task outcomes; and (3) knowledge of the results of task performance. If all three psychological states are positive, a reinforcing cycle of strong work motivation based on self-generated rewards is activated. A job without meaningfulness, responsibility, and feedback is incomplete and doesn't strongly motivate an employee. Because of our previous coverage of motivation (see Chapters 5 and 6), we focus here on the job characteristics and individual differences components of the model. Figure 15.3 illustrates the elements of the job characteristics enrichment model and their relationships.

Job Characteristics

Five job characteristics hold the key to job enrichment efforts in this model. They are defined as follows.

- **Skill variety**—the extent to which a job requires a variety of employee competencies to carry out the work.
- **Task identity**—the extent to which a job requires an employee to complete a whole and identifiable piece of work, that is, doing a task from beginning to end with a visible outcome.

Figure 15.3 **Job Characteristics Enrichment Model**

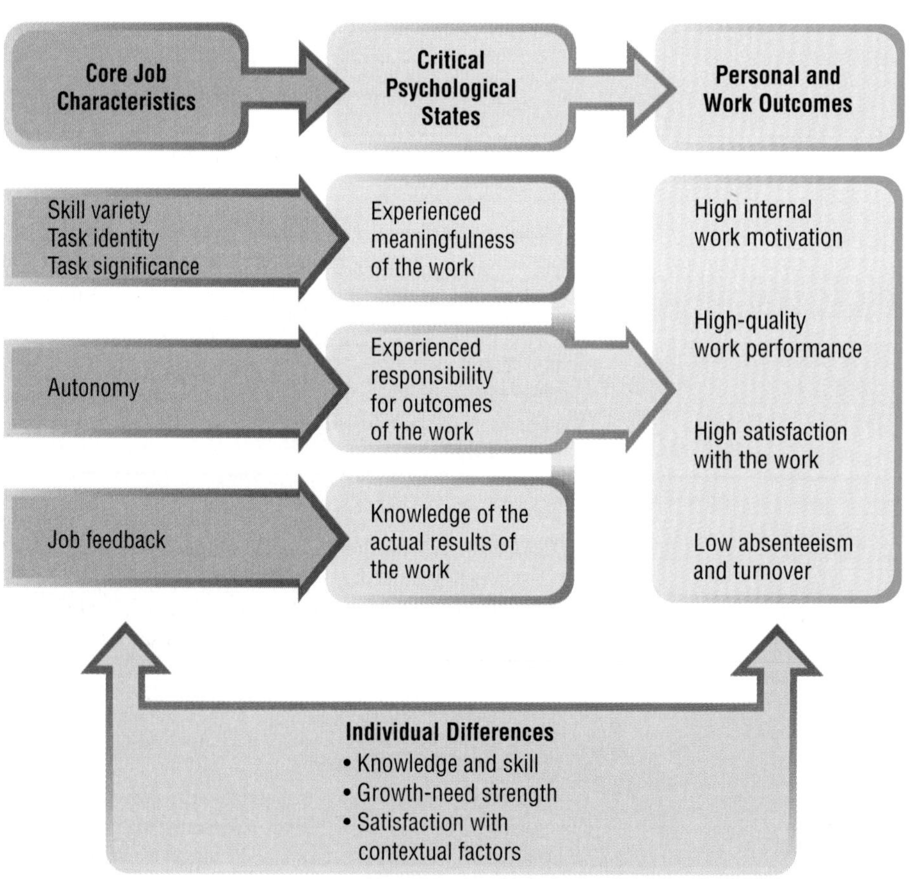

Source: Hackman, J. R., and Oldham, G. R. *Work Redesign*. Copyright © 1980. Addison-Wesley Publishing Co., Inc., Reading, Massachusetts (adapted from Fig. 4.6 on p. 90). Reprinted by permission of Addison Wesley Longman, Inc.

- **Task significance**—the extent to which an employee perceives the job as having a substantial impact on the lives of other people, whether those people are within or outside the organization.
- **Autonomy**—the extent to which the job provides empowerment and discretion to an employee in scheduling tasks and in determining procedures to be used in carrying out those tasks.
- **Job feedback**—the extent to which carrying out job-related tasks provides direct and clear information about the effectiveness of an employee's performance.[24]

Skill variety, task identity, and task significance strongly influence the experienced meaningfulness of work. Autonomy usually increases feelings and attitudes of personal responsibility and empowerment for work outcomes. Job feedback gives an employee knowledge about task results. This type of feedback comes from the work itself, not from a manager's performance appraisal. Refer back to Table 15.1 and your scores on each of the job characteristics. A score of 12–15 for a job characteristic is likely to contribute positively to one or more critical psychological states. A score of 3–6 for a job characteristic, in contrast, is likely to contribute negatively to one or more critical psychological states.

The job of surgeon can be used to further illustrate these points. This job seems to rate high on all the key job characteristics. It provides a constant opportunity for using highly varied skills, abilities, and talents in diagnosing and treating illnesses. Task identity is high because the surgeon normally diagnoses a problem, performs an operation, and monitors the patient's recovery. Task significance also is high because the surgeon's work can mean life or death to the patient. Autonomy is high because the surgeon often is the final authority on the procedures and techniques used. However, the growing prevalence and threat of malpractice suits may have lowered the surgeon's sense of autonomy in recent years. Finally, the surgeon receives direct feedback from the job, knowing in many cases almost immediately whether an operation is successful.

Individual Differences

The individual differences variable (see Figure 15.3) identified in this model influence how employees respond to enriched jobs. They include competencies, strength of growth needs, and satisfaction with contextual factors.[25] These individual differences have an impact on the relationship between job characteristics and personal or work outcomes in several important ways. Managers therefore should consider them when designing or redesigning jobs.

Competencies. Employees with the competencies needed to perform an enriched job effectively are likely to have positive feelings about the tasks they perform. Employees unable to perform an enriched job may experience frustration, stress, and job dissatisfaction. These feelings and attitudes may be especially intense for employees who desire to do a good job but realize that they are performing poorly because they lack the necessary skills and knowledge. Accordingly, assessing carefully the competencies of employees whose jobs are to be enriched is essential. A training and development program may be needed along with an enrichment program to help such employees attain the needed competencies.[26]

Recall from the Preview Case that the Texas Nameplate Company fosters continuous learning. The firm uses a variety of training methods, supplemented by tuition reimbursement and other "back-to-school" incentives. The average employee receives 75 hours of training during the first 2 years. Much of it is delivered on a "just-in-time" basis. About 1 in 10 workers is a "multipurpose employee," trained in three or more enriched jobs, allowing them to be moved to any area of the company that needs assistance to meet fluctuating customer demand.[27]

Growth-Need Strength. The extent to which an individual desires the opportunity for self-direction, learning, and personal accomplishment at work is called

growth-need strength. This concept is essentially the same as Alderfer's growth needs and Maslow's esteem needs and self-actualization needs concepts (see Chapter 5). Individuals with high growth needs tend to respond favorably to job enrichment programs. They experience greater satisfaction from work and are more highly motivated than people who have low growth needs. High growth-need individuals are generally absent less and produce better quality work when their jobs are enriched. Employee responses to enriched jobs usually range from indifferent to highly positive.[28]

Satisfaction with Contextual Factors. The extent to which employees are satisfied with contextual factors at work often influence their willingness or ability to respond positively to enriched jobs. **Contextual factors** include organizational policies and administration, technical supervision, salary and benefit programs, interpersonal relations, travel requirements, and work conditions (lighting, heat, safety hazards, and the like). Employees who are extremely dissatisfied with their superiors, salary levels, and safety measures are less likely to respond favorably to enriched jobs than are employees who are satisfied with these conditions. Other contextual factors (e.g., employee satisfaction with the organizational culture, power and the political process, travel requirements, and team norms) also can affect employee responses to their jobs.[29]

One controversial contextual factor is the growing use of electronic monitoring of work through the use of computers, video cameras, and telephone technologies to "listen in on" or "observe" employees as they perform their tasks. More than 15 million employees in the United States are electronically monitored each day. Such monitoring often occurs without employees being aware that it is taking place. Information technologies are being used to monitor attendance, tardiness, work speed (e.g., recording the number of computer keystrokes an employee performs per minute or hour), break length and frequency, types of messages being transmitted on computer networks, and the nature and quality of conversations with customers or others, among other activities. Such intrusiveness raises serious ethical concerns, which focus on the excessive invasion of privacy of employees while working, at or away from the normal place of business, and a growing concern that "Big Brother is watching."[30]

Job Diagnosis

Various methods are used to diagnose jobs, determine whether job design problems exist, and estimate the potential for job enrichment success. We limit our discussion to two of these methods: structural clues and surveys.

Structural Clues Method. The **structural clues method** is the process of examining contextual factors often associated with deficiencies in job design. The presence of five specific structural factors often suggests job design problems.

- *Inspectors or checkers.* Autonomy usually is reduced when inspectors or checkers, rather than employees or teams, examine outputs. Feedback is less direct because it doesn't come from the job itself.
- *Troubleshooters.* The existence of troubleshooters usually means that the exciting and challenging parts of a job have been taken away from employees or teams. Thus they have less sense of responsibility for work results. Task identity, autonomy, and feedback usually are lessened.
- *Communications and customer relations departments.* These departments usually cut the link between employees who do the job and customers or clients. They often dilute direct feedback and task identity for those creating the products or services. In contrast, recall the direct feedback from customers to the employees at the Texas Nameplate Company.

- *Labor pools.* On the surface, pools of word processors, computer programmers, and other employees are appealing because they seem to increase efficiency and the ability to meet workload fluctuations. However, such pools often destroy feelings of task ownership and identity.
- *Narrow span of control.* A manager with only a few subordinates (say, five to seven) is more likely to become involved in the details of their day-to-day tasks than a manager with a wider span of control. Centralization of decision making and overcontrol may result from too narrow a span of control and seriously reduce autonomy and a sense of empowerment.

Survey Method. Several types of questionnaires, one of which is the **job diagnostic survey** (JDS), make diagnosing jobs relatively easy and systematic.[31] The questionnaire presented in Table 15.1 measures the job characteristics shown in Figure 15.3. You can develop your own job profile by using the totals on the scales in Table 15.1, each of which has a score range of 3–15. You can calculate an overall measure of job enrichment, called the **motivating potential score** (MPS), as follows.

$$\text{MPS} = \frac{\text{Skill Variety} + \text{Task Identity} + \text{Task Significance}}{3} \times \text{Autonomy} \times \text{Feedback.}$$

The MPS formula sums the scores for skill variety, task identity, and task significance and divides the total by 3. Thus the combination of these three job characteristics has the same weight as autonomy and job feedback. The reason is that the job characteristics enrichment model requires that both *experienced responsibility* and *knowledge of results* be present for high internal job motivation. This outcome can be achieved only if reasonable degrees of autonomy and job feedback are present. The minimum MPS score is 1, and the maximum possible MPS score is 3,375. A clearly positive MPS score starts at 1,728, and a purely neutral MPS score is 729 (based on an average score of 9 per scale). What is your MPS score? Use the results from your completed questionnaire to calculate it.

Implementation Approaches

Any one of five approaches, or a combination of them, may be used to implement a job enrichment program. All need not be used in every job enrichment effort, nor are they mutually exclusive. The two main approaches are vertical loading and the formation of natural work teams. The other three—establishment of customer relationships, employee ownership of the product, and employee receipt of direct feedback—often are used within one of the two principal approaches.

Vertical Loading. **Vertical loading** is the delegation to employees of responsibilities and tasks that were formerly reserved for management or staff specialists. Vertical loading includes the empowerment of employees to

- set schedules, determine work methods, and decide when and how to check on the quality of the work produced;
- make their own decisions about when to start and stop work, when to take breaks, and how to assign priorities; and
- seek solutions to problems on their own, consulting with others only as necessary, rather than calling immediately for the manager when problems arise.

Employees often schedule their own work after vertical loading, although a manager may set deadlines or goals. Within these guidelines, employees are allowed some freedom in setting their own schedules and pace. **Flextime** allows employees, within certain limits, to vary their arrival and departure times to suit their individual needs and desires and helps in self-scheduling of work. With the new information technology capabilities (e.g., computer-based networks), an increasing number of jobs can be performed, at least part of the time, at the employee's residence, in hotels while traveling, and at customer locations.[32]

Natural Teams. The formation of natural teams combines individual jobs into a formally recognized unit (e.g., a section, team, or department). The criteria for the groupings are logical and meaningful to the employee and include the following.

- *Geographic:* Salespeople or information technology consultants might be given a particular region of the state or country as their territory.
- *Types of business:* Insurance claims adjusters might be assigned to teams that serve specific types of businesses, such as utilities, manufacturers, or retailers.
- *Organizational:* Word-processing operators might be given work that originates in a particular department.
- *Alphabetic or numeric:* File clerks could be made responsible for materials in specified alphabetical groups (A to D, E to H, and so on); library-shelf readers might check books in a certain range of the library's cataloging system.
- *Customer groups:* Employees of a public utility or consulting firm might be assigned to particular industrial or commercial accounts.

Customer Relationships. One of the most important concepts of job enrichment is putting employees in touch with the users of their output. The establishment of customer relationships often is a logical outcome if natural teams are formed. Employees too often end up working directly for their superiors rather than for customers or clients. Consider the approach used by Home Depot, a large retailer primarily for residential fixer-uppers. Home Depot encourages employees to build long-term relationships with customers. Employees are trained in home repair techniques and can spend as much time as necessary to help customers. There are no high-pressure sales tactics, and employees are on straight salary. In order to satisfy customers consistently, the leadership of Home Depot believes that employees must be committed. Instead of receiving discounts on merchandise, employees get shares in the company's stock. Salespeople are trained not to let customers overspend. "I love it when shoppers tell me they were prepared to spend $150 and our people have showed them how to do the job for four or five bucks," says CEO Bernard Marcus. He further states, "Every customer has to be treated like your mother, your father, your sister, or your brother."[33] Home Depot was ranked No. 1 in innovativeness and No. 2 in getting and keeping talent in *Fortune*'s rankings of most admired companies.[34]

Ownership of Product. Employees who assemble entire television sets or prepare entire reports identify more with the finished products than do employees who perform only parts of the job. Allowing employees to build or service entire products or complete entire tasks is likely to generate a sense of pride and achievement. The assignment of as much responsibility as possible in serving a certain geographic area also may create the feeling of ownership.

Before being promoted, Roger Liwer served as the manager of the Bureau of Motor Equipment in New York City's Department of Sanitation. His unit repaired garbage trucks and street sweepers in garages all over the city. When he became the manager, labor strife had gripped the operation for years, morale was bad, and half the vehicles were out of commission at one any time. Liwer began by breaking down the chain of command. He gave a labor committee the power to institute new methods and procedures. With no one looking over their shoulders, the mechanics' productivity surged. The workers, mostly trade-school graduates from New York City's schools, took new pride in their department. They initiated steps to prevent breakdowns, instead of merely responding to those that occurred. Ultimately, the workers were directly involved in choosing which equipment to purchase and helping their equipment vendors, such as GM and FMC, modify their designs.[35]

Direct Feedback. The job-enrichment approach stresses information to the employee directly from performance of the task. Reports or computer output may go directly to employees, instead of just to their managers. A common technique is to let people check their own work so that they can catch most of their own errors before others do. This technique also increases employee autonomy. Direct communication with customers or clients also may improve the timeliness and accuracy of feedback, thereby eliminating distortions and delays.

Job Characteristics and Technology

We now merge the concepts of job design and technology—and the technology framework (see Figure 15.2)—with that of the job characteristics enrichment model (see Figure 15.3). To change one or more of the five job characteristics usually means making changes in one or more of the three technological dimensions. To avoid excessive complexity, we consider only a basic job redesign situation wherein management decides to use a combination of vertical loading and the formation of natural work teams.

Vertical loading increases the amount of task and workflow uncertainty that employees must handle in redesigned jobs. Some of the changes caused by vertical loading tend to increase pooled interdependence and decrease sequential and reciprocal interdependence. For example, there is usually less need to obtain a quality control specialist's approval before proceeding with other tasks, which lessens sequential interdependence. The formation of natural work teams has the most direct impact on reducing task interdependence among departments or teams, with each team becoming self-managed. All the criteria for forming natural work teams tend to increase pooled interdependence and decrease sequential and reciprocal interdependence among departments, teams, and higher levels of the organization.

Figure 15.4 shows the technological changes that are likely to accompany a job redesign program involving vertical loading and the formation of natural work teams. These changes, in turn, can be expected to lead to changes in job characteristics. In brief, job characteristics and technological dimensions are closely and intricately linked.

Social Information Processing

The job characteristics enrichment model is based on the assumption that employees can respond reasonably, accurately, and objectively when asked about the characteristics of their jobs. However, their perceptions of job characteristics may be influenced by social information, which includes comments, observations, and similar cues provided by people whose view of the job an employee values. Social information may be provided by people directly associated with the job (e.g., coworkers, managers, and customers) and by people not employed by the organization (e.g., family members

Figure 15.4 **Sample Job Characteristic and Technological Links**

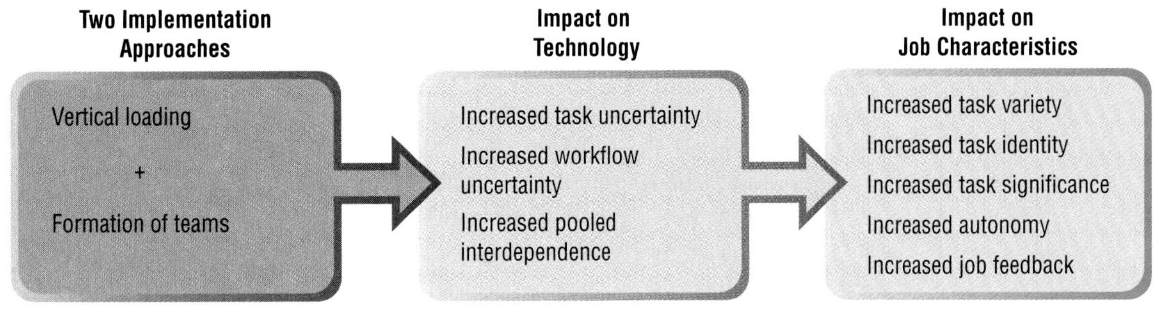

and friends). Some aspects of a job aren't likely to be influenced by cues from others (a hot work environment will be hot despite what anyone tells an employee). But most of an employee's perceptions of job characteristics are subject to the influence of others with whom the employee has contact.[36]

Based on this perspective, the **social information processing model** states that the individual's social context provides

- cues as to which dimensions might be used to characterize the work environment;
- information concerning how the individual should weigh the various dimensions—whether autonomy is more or less important than skill variety or whether pay is more or less important than social usefulness or worth;
- cues concerning how others have come to evaluate the work environment on each of the selected dimensions; and
- direct positive or negative evaluation of the work setting, leaving the individual to construct a rationale to make sense of the generally shared affective reactions.[37]

The importance of the social information processing model can be illustrated with a simple example. Two employees at Microsoft performing the same programming tasks with the same job characteristics under different managers could respond differently to the objective characteristics of their jobs on the JDS. The differences in perceived social information cues could account for some of the variation in the employees' responses. For example, one manager may praise subordinates a great deal, whereas the other manager may criticize subordinates repeatedly. The social information processing model suggests that receiving praise or criticism could affect how employees respond to the JDS. An integrated perspective is more accurate than one or the other points of view. The integrative perspective suggests that (1) job characteristics and social information (cues) combine to affect employees' reactions to their jobs and (2) introducing changes in the work environment can produce those reactions. However, the intricate and varied ways that social information in the workplace can affect the perceptions of job characteristics is beyond the scope of this discussion.[38] To reduce possible distortions caused by social information influences, the employees' managers, and possibly a trained job analyst, should also rate the characteristics of jobs being considered for redesign.

The Managing Across Cultures feature on page 463 provides additional caution about automatically generalizing all the features of the job characteristics enrichment model to other cultural settings. It provides a summary of several key findings from a study conducted in a Malaysian public health organization.

Learning Objective:

4. Describe the sociotechnical systems model and its relationship to organizational effectiveness.

SOCIOTECHNICAL SYSTEMS MODEL

The sociotechnical systems model views organizations as entities with complex relationships within their social systems. This model emphasizes grouping jobs by team when the reciprocal and/or sequential interdependence among jobs can't be reduced.[39] The use of pooled interdependence therefore tends to occur among teams rather than among individual jobs. Use of this model involves vertical job loading to a cluster of jobs within a team as a whole, rather than to each individual job. Management can use the sociotechnical systems model to design work that integrates people and technology and to optimize the relationships between the technological and social systems. When applied to manufacturing, the needed changes in technology sometimes are too difficult and costly to make in an existing plant. Thus the sociotechnical systems model more frequently works best in designing jobs for an entirely new plant. Numerous organizations in Western Europe and North America, including General Foods, GM, Weyerhauser, TRW, Rushton Mining, Volvo, and the

COMPETENCY: MANAGING ACROSS CULTURES

JOB DESIGN IN THE MALAYSIAN NURSING CONTEXT

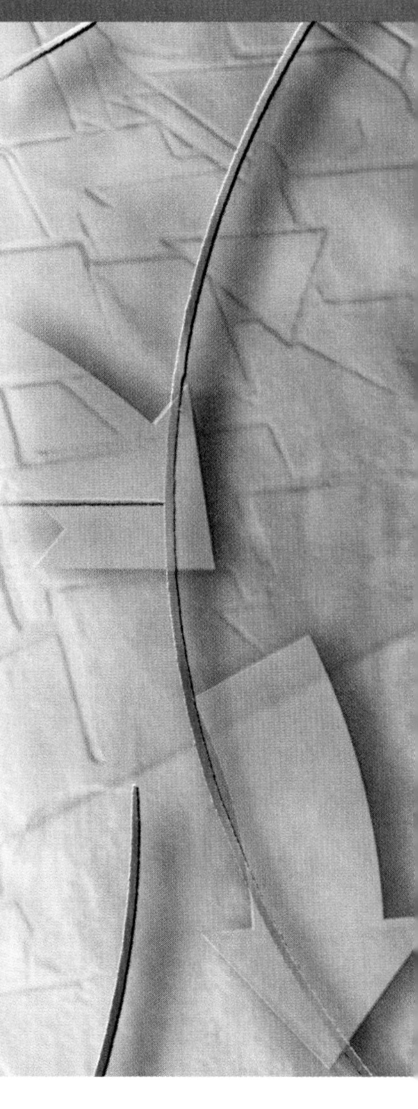

This study investigated the extent to which content task characteristics and information cues from colleagues and supervisors influenced the level of job satisfaction and organizational commitment of a Malaysian nursing staff. The study revealed that the job content task dimensions of nursing had a negligible impact on job satisfaction. However, feedback from others appeared to influence substantially the nurses' responses to their jobs. Most of the content and context task dimensions, except for job feedback, favorably contributed to organizational commitment. Moreover, the results suggest that societal values and attitudes affected the nurses' reactions to their jobs.

One important implication is directly related to the design of jobs for nurses in this culture. Implementation of strategies to achieve a quality health-care delivery system depends on the extent of employee innovation, accountability, self-management, and leadership. The findings of this study suggest that management training and education programs that lead to employee effectiveness are more likely to be successful if they are integrated with the prevailing beliefs, values, and attitudes of the workplace. The relative importance of a relationship-oriented job design for the job satisfaction of Malaysian nurses was clearly demonstrated. Yet Western literature has generally promoted the benefits of a task-oriented design to improve effectiveness and job satisfaction and has even reported the lack of contribution of the social dimensions to job satisfaction. In Western nursing studies, the importance of autonomy or control has frequently been identified as vital for the enhancement of job satisfaction.

In contrast, the work satisfaction for the Malaysian nurses was strongly linked to the social fabric of the culture. A strong inference of these findings is that the designers of training programs, and job redesign in particular, for Malaysian health-care workers would be advised to consider local cultural conditions rather than blindly applying the job design strategies and techniques that have been formulated and used in developed Western countries.[40]

Tennessee Valley Authority, have implemented sociotechnical systems projects. Although successes have been reported, so have failures.

Figure 15.5 presents the sociotechnical systems model. It has four main parts: environmental forces, the social system, the technological system, and moderators. We don't review environmental forces (e.g., customers, suppliers, and regulatory agencies) further in this model because of our detailed treatment of them elsewhere in the book.

SOCIAL SYSTEMS

The **social system** of an organization comprises those aspects of its "human side" that can influence how individuals and teams perform tasks and their attitudes toward work and the organization. The social system factors shown in Figure 15.5 are discussed in other chapters. (In Chapters 8, 11, and 17, in particular, we present the main elements and processes of work-related social systems.) For example, if employees characterize their organization as one marked by distrust, backstabbing, and infighting, the creation of self-managed work teams is likely to be counterproductive until some degree of trust and cooperation can be established.

Figure 15.5 **Sociotechnical Systems Model**

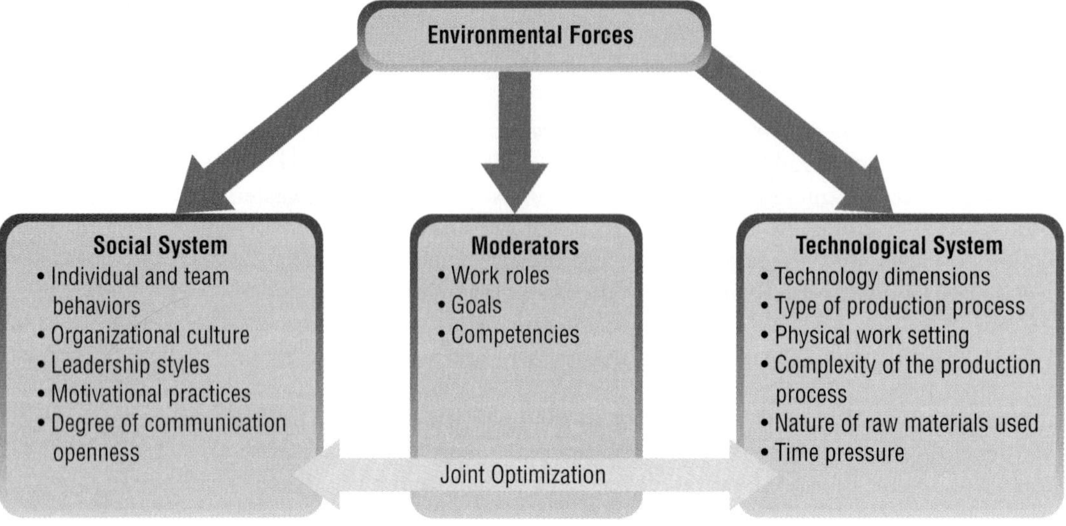

Technological Systems

Task uncertainty, workflow uncertainty, and task interdependence need to be diagnosed. These three technological dimensions are likely to vary with the type of production process being used or planned. For example, utilization of an assembly line or, alternatively, small units is an important technological characteristic. Different production processes require different approaches to job design. In a process-technology operation, such as an EXXON oil refinery, most work is automated. The relatively few workers spend much of their time monitoring dials and performing maintenance tasks. By contrast, small-unit technologies—plumbing, appliance repair, sales, and investment advice—involve relatively large amounts of labor to achieve the required outputs.

Another technological characteristic is the physical work setting (amount of light, temperature, noise, pollution, geographical isolation, and orderliness). For example, if the workplace is too hot or noisy, employees may have difficulty performing tasks that require intense thought and concentration.

Complexity of the production process also is an important technological characteristic. Someone at Black & Decker might easily learn how to build an entire toaster, but someone at GE's Propulsion Division may not be able to learn how to build an entire jet aircraft engine. The more complex the production process, the greater are the degrees of task and workflow uncertainty and the requirements for reciprocal task interdependence.

Other important technological characteristics are the nature of raw materials used in production and the time pressure inherent in the production process. For example, daily newspapers are published on a rigid time schedule. Bottlenecks must be dealt with quickly, and employees must speed up their pace if production falls behind schedule by even a few minutes.

Moderators

Work roles act as moderators in the sociotechnical systems model, establishing a set of expected employee behaviors. Work roles define the relationships between the people who perform tasks and the technological requirements of those tasks, binding the sociotechnical systems to each other. The vision, goals, and values of an organization also moderate the relationship between the social and technical systems. Recall in the Preview Case that the vision for the Texas Nameplate Company is to "become the recognized supplier of commercial nameplates in the United States." Seven key business drivers were noted, including customer satisfaction, employee satisfaction, process optimization, and environmental consciousness. A final moderator involves employee competencies. The sociotechnical systems model is most effective in an organization with a highly competent and educated workforce.

Core Concepts

The degree to which an organization operates according to the sociotechnical systems model can be assessed in terms of six core concepts, all of which are reflected in the Preview Case.

- *Innovation*—Organizational leaders and members maintain a futuristic versus historical orientation, including a propensity for risk taking and provision of rewards for innovation.
- *Human resource development*—The talents, knowledge, skills, and abilities of organizational members are developed and tapped through job design, supervisory roles, organizational design, and the workflow process.
- *Environmental agility*—The organization maintains awareness of the environment and responds appropriately to it by recognizing customer importance, proactivity versus reactivity, and product or service flexibility.
- *Cooperation*—Individuals, teams, and departments work together to accomplish common goals through openness, mutual support, shared values, and common rewards.
- *Commitment and energy*—Employees are dedicated to accomplishing organizational goals and are prepared to expend energy in doing so.
- *Joint optimization*—The organization uses both its social and technical resources effectively, including the design of technology to support teamwork and flexibility.[41]

The Managing Teams Competency feature on page 466 reports on the application of the sociotechnical systems model at the Consolidated Diesel Company factory, a joint venture of Cummins Engine Company and J.I. Case Corporation, in Whitaker, North Carolina. It is a 1.2 million-square-foot plant where 1,700 employees produce 650 engines per day in four different models, which can be configured in any of 3,500 different ways. Recall from Chapter 1 that the *managing teams competency* involves the ability to develop support, facilitate, and lead groups to achieve organizational goals. The use of self-managed teams is a core component in the sociotechnical system at this plant.

Implementation Issues

The factors to be diagnosed in designing jobs under the sociotechnical systems model are complex. The basic issues are the management philosophy and the values that define the organization's culture. Jim Lyons, the general manager at Consolidated Diesel's engine plant, reflected a philosophy of trust and values of openness in his comments. Managers interested in improving both the social system and organizational effectiveness may find either the job enrichment or sociotechnical systems models to be appropriate. Managers interested only in production and efficiency may concentrate on the job engineering, job enlargement, or job rotation approaches.

Technology is a primary variable in job design. Some jobs cannot be enriched without redesigning an entire operation. When changing a job is impossible, other

Competency: Managing Teams

Consolidated Diesel's Engine Plant

Most plants average 1 supervisor for every 25 employees, but Consolidated Diesel only has 1 for every 100 employees—a difference that yields a savings of about $1 million a year. Moreover, the plant's injury rate is about one-fifth the national average for the industry. Jim Lyons, the general manager, comments: "In the right environment, people at all levels of an organization can make contributions. The people who are closest to the work are the ones who typically understand that work best."

Consolidated Diesel has developed policies and practices in four key areas that are consistent with the sociotechnical systems model. First, the company plays fair. For example, when it comes to bonuses, everyone gets one or no one does. Fairness is also evident in the plant's schedule, which switches entire teams from a day shift to an evening shift every 2 weeks.

Second, the company uses extensive cross-training. One day, a team member might be doing quality inspection; the next day, that same person might be running a lathe. "When you do a job that somebody else has done, you have a lot more respect for what that job involves," says Richard Strawbridge, a veteran of the plant, who works in electrical and mechanical maintenance. "That understanding builds cooperation in a team."

Third, Consolidated Diesel listens to its employees and involves them in coming up with solutions to problems in the plant. For example, in a recent quarter, customer demand was so high that the assembly and process teams had to work huge amounts of overtime. Lyons comments: "We added a third-shift skeleton crew, but there was only incremental improvement. Then we got our team leaders involved, and they asked their teams, 'How should we handle this?'"

The teams designed new schedules that allowed more flexibility. Shifts suddenly decreased in length from 9 or 10 hours to 8 hours—and no one was working Saturdays anymore. Lyons states: "Sometimes the fact that it's the team's plan, and not a plan dictated by management, means everything. The teams will make it work."

Fourth, the teams have responsibility that matters. For example, they hire—and when necessary, fire—their own members. Strawbridge states: "The teams solve a lot of our problems. When I came here, I realized that in other places where I had worked, decisions had been made for me. Here I'm required to be involved in the decision-making process."

Lyons (like other managers at the company) takes an hour or two every day to walk around the shop floor, the offices, and the lab. He comments: "You want to remove all unnecessary barriers between management and the workforce." Lyons and other managers use other channels of communication as well. For example, Lyons divided the 1,400 production employees into 15 groups. He meets with each group each quarter over a 2-day period. The groups are small enough that he can elicit questions and comments from the production employees. When he is not able to give a response on the spot, he follows up in *CDC Wire*, the weekly in-house newsletter, or on *WCDC*, the plant's closed-circuit television network. Lyons comments: "We share the good, the bad, and the ugly. When good people are given good information, they typically make good decisions."[42]

*To learn more about the Consolidated Diesel Company, visit the home page of the primary parent company—Cummins Engine Company—at **www.cummins.com**.*

techniques (e.g., flextime) may soften the effects of a boring job. Moreover, new information technologies, especially those involving the Internet or robotics (in manufacturing), are being used increasingly to eliminate routine jobs and thus the need to redesign them. Perhaps the best approach is to understand fully the various job design approaches and to use the approach or combination of approaches that best fits the organization and employees. However, with an increasing segment of the workforce, fewer and fewer employees are subordinates in the traditional sense, even in fairly low level jobs. As Peter Drucker comments:

> Increasingly, they are knowledge workers. Knowledge workers cannot be managed as subordinates; they are associates. They are seniors or juniors but not superiors and subordinates. This difference is more than cosmetic. Once beyond the apprentice stage, knowledge workers must know more about their job than their boss does—or what good are they? The very definition of a knowledge worker is one who knows more about his or her job than anybody else in the organization.[43]

CHAPTER SUMMARY

1. Describe and contrast the common approaches to job design.

The most common job design approaches are job rotation, job engineering, job enlargement, job enrichment, ergonomics, and the sociotechnical systems model. The relative impact of these approaches on an organization varies significantly according to the complexity of the situation and the amount of implementation required. Job engineering includes traditional industrial engineering techniques that simplify a job in order to make it more efficient. Job enlargement and job rotation seek to make boring jobs interesting by adding variety. Ergonomics, one of several other approaches, was noted because of its importance in designing jobs to be consistent with the health and safety needs of employees.

2. Discuss the linkages between job design and technology.

Three important technological factors in job design are task uncertainty, workflow uncertainty, and task interdependence (pooled, sequential, and reciprocal). They must be diagnosed in addressing job design alternatives and often are modified by management in the redesign of jobs.

3. Explain the job characteristics enrichment model and its relationship to work motivation.

Job enrichment makes jobs more meaningful and challenging. The job characteristics enrichment model focuses on modifying five job characteristics: task variety, task identity, task significance, autonomy, and job feedback. Usually, technological factors that affect these job characteristics must be changed. The job enrichment approach is implemented through vertical loading, formation of natural work teams, establishment of client relationships, employee ownership of the product, and employee receipt of direct feedback. Properly designed jobs often result in more satisfied and higher performing employees. Individual differences must be considered in redesigning jobs because some people may not want enriched jobs or may not want to work in teams. Also, some organizational or technological situations may not permit job enrichment.

4. Describe the sociotechnical systems model and its relationship to organizational effectiveness.

The sociotechnical systems model focuses on integrating the organization's social and technical systems after careful diagnosis of the environmental forces acting on the organization. Three moderators—work roles, goals, and competencies—influence optimization of the social and technical systems. Relative to the other approaches to job design, it is the most complex and offers the greatest potential impact on organization effectiveness as a whole. The six core concepts in this model are innovation, human resource development, environmental agility, cooperation, commitment and energy, and joint optimization.

KEY TERMS AND CONCEPTS

Autonomy
Contextual factors
Ergonomics
Flextime
Growth-need strength
Job characteristics enrichment model
Job design
Job diagnostic survey
Job engineering
Job enlargement
Job enrichment
Job feedback
Job rotation
Motivating potential score
Pooled interdependence
Reciprocal interdependence
Sequential interdependence
Skill variety
Social information processing model
Social System
Sociotechnical systems model
Structural clues method
Task identity
Task interdependence
Task significance
Task uncertainty
Technology
Vertical loading
Workflow uncertainty

DISCUSSION QUESTIONS

1. Review the Preview Case on the Texas Nameplate Company. What examples of the five job characteristics in the job characteristics enrichment model can you identify?
2. Review the Managing Change Competency feature on Westinghouse Air Brake. Which of the "golden rules" of job design according to the job engineering approach are illustrated in this feature?
3. Describe a current (or previous) job that you have held in terms of workflow uncertainty and task uncertainty. Based on this diagnosis, should the job be redesigned? Explain.
4. Based on the job diagnosed in Question 3, describe it in terms of type and degree of task interdependency. Was the task interdependency optimal for effective performance? Explain.
5. Think of your typical classroom experiences over the period of a semester or term. What examples of pooled interdependence, sequential interdependence, and reciprocal interdependence can you identify?
6. Describe your "job" as a student in relation to the five approaches for implementing a job enrichment program. Which of these approaches do you use most often in your student "job?" Should you change any of them? Explain.
7. How did social information processing influence your perception of a recent job compared to the views expressed by a coworker holding the same or similar job?
8. Did the management of an organization you have worked for apply the sociotechnical systems model in its approach to job design for you and your coworkers? Explain.
9. Review the Managing Teams Competency feature on the Consolidated Diesel Engine Plant. What applications of the core concepts of the sociotechnical systems model can you identify in this description?
10. Why might some managers and employees welcome the sociotechnical systems approach to job design and others oppose it?

DEVELOPING COMPETENCIES

Competency: Managing Change—Data Entry Operators[44]

Instructions: This exercise may be undertaken individually in whole or part. For example, the "proposal" phase may be undertaken individually and the "analysis phase" be undertaken by a student team.

Current Situation

There are 25 data entry operators at the Associates First Financial Corporation Credit Card Division in Irving, Texas, who report to one supervisor. Each day these operators enter a wide variety of credit card data that is supplied by various customers, departments, and teams. Some jobs are small, some much larger, and some are more sensitive or critical than others. Credit cards come with a payment due date. A due date remainder is prescheduled on a routine basis to meet the customer's requirements.

The work is supplied to the data entry operators by an assignment clerk. The assignment clerk looks at the work before giving it to the data entry operators to make sure that it is legible. If it is not, this person gives it to the supervisor who returns the work to the originating department. The assignment clerk attempts to see that each operator gets exactly one-twenty-fifth of the work even if this requires assigning parts of the same job to different operators. Because of the exactness of the work, each job is entered twice by different operators and then verified through the computer to help keep errors to a minimum. However, some errors are not discovered until the finished job is turned out by the computer. Turnover is more than 38 percent a year.

Proposal Phase

Some proposals listed below might result in improving work performance. Read over the list and decide whether you would or would not implement the proposal. Put an X in the appropriate space next to each of the items in the list. Next, rank order the action you would take first and number it 1. Then pick 2, etc., and continue to do the same for the changes that you think are necessary.

Possible Changes	Would	Would Not	Rank Order
1. Make sure the forms from which the operators get their information are arranged in the best way	_____	_____	_____
2. Let some data entry operators decide whether or not their work should be double entered and verified.	_____	_____	_____
3. Do the work that has specific due dates first.	_____	_____	_____
4. Train the assignment clerks on the PCs so they can help out when the workload is heavy.	_____	_____	_____
5. Add another supervisor and split the group into two teams.	_____	_____	_____
6. Have the data entry operators inspect the media they receive for legibility.	_____	_____	_____
7. When errors are discovered, feed back the details to the data entry operator who made the error(s).	_____	_____	_____
8. Have the data entry operators verify their own work.	_____	_____	_____
9. Assign responsibility for entering a whole job to an individual.	_____	_____	_____
10. Arrange for departmental contacts for certain operators.	_____	_____	_____
11. Let some data entry operators schedule their own day.	_____	_____	_____
12. Make sure that jobs for a particular team or account always go to the same data entry operator.	_____	_____	_____

Analysis Phase

For each of the changes that you would make, identify the concept in the job characteristics enrichment model that would be enhanced by the specific change. For each of the changes that you did not make, justify each decision through the use of one or more concepts in the job characteristics enrichment model.

Competency: Managing Teams—GE's Aircraft-Engine Assembly Facility

General Electric's aircraft-engine assembly facility in Durham, North Carolina, has 170 employees, but just one plant manager. Paula Sims had been the manager until recently. Sims has moved on and was replaced by Colleen Athans. Three teams of employees were involved in interviewing Athans and the other candidates.

The jet engines are produced by nine teams of people—teams that are given just one basic directive: the day that their next engine must be loaded onto a truck. All other decisions—who does what work; how to balance training, vacations, overtime against workflow; how to make the manufacturing process more efficient; how to handle teammates who slack off—are made by team members.

Everyone knows how much money everyone else makes. Employees are paid according to their skills. There are three grades of jet-assembly technician at this plant—tech-1, tech-2, and tech-3—and there is one wage rate for each grade. There is no conventional assembly line. One team "owns" an engine from beginning to end—from the point when parts are uncrated and staged to the moment a team member climbs on a forklift to place the finished engine on a truck for shipment. The members of the team do the jobs that interest them. No one ever does the same job shift after shift, day after day. There is usually choice—and there is always variety.

The plant has no time clock. Workers leave to go to their kids' band concerts and Little League games. Every technician has an e-mail address and Internet access, voice mail, business cards, and a desk shared with one teammate. The plant manager sits in an open cubicle on the factory floor: Engines move by, just 20 feet away. In an engine that weighs 8.5 tons and has 10,000 parts, even a nut that weighs less than an ounce must be installed to a very specific tightness. Every part is tightened with a torque wrench. Some parts are so vital, and so sensitive, that a computer is used to tighten the nuts that attach them to the engine. And after each step, a technician takes responsibility by entering his or her initials on a computer terminal.

The employees who work at this plant try to make perfect jet engines. And they come close. On average, one-quarter of the engines that GE/Durham sends to Boeing have just a single defect—something cosmetic, such as a cable not lined up right or a scratch on a fan case. The other three-quarters are, in fact, perfect. That is one big reason why Boeing, in a vote of confidence, recently chose a new version of the GE_{90} as the exclusive engine for its new, long-range 777 jetliner. For the new 777s, which will be able to fly 10,000 miles without refueling, the GE_{90} will be the only engine—and only GE/Durham makes the GE_{90}.

AT GE/Durham, there is no cynicism about the drive for perfection. "It matters," says Bill Lane, a tech-2. "I've got a 3-year old daughter, and I figure that every plane we build engines for has someone with a 3-year-old daughter riding on it."

At GE/Durham, virtually every team decision is made by consensus. Consensus is another of the founding principles of GE/Durham. It is so ingrained that technicians have turned consensus into a verb. The people at the plant routinely talk about "consensing" on something. Duane Williams, a tech-3, comments: "Everybody doesn't see things in the same way. But we've had training on how to reach consensus. We've had training on how to live with ideas that we might not necessarily agree with. All the things you normally fuss and moan about to yourself and your buddies—well, we have a chance to do something about them. I can't say, 'They' don't know what's going on, or, 'They' made a bad decision. I am 'they.'"

Everyone learns to assemble different parts of the engine. "Multiskilling is how the place is kept together," says Derrick McCoy, a tech-3 and a friend of Duane Williams on Team Raven. (The teams came up with names for themselves.) "You don't hoard your skills. That way, when I'm on vacation, the low-pressure turbine can still be built without me."

In addition to building engines, everyone serves at one time or another on one of several work councils that cut across team lines. The councils handle HR issues, supplier problems, engineering challenges, computer systems, discipline, and rewards. And everyone participates in training—from sessions on how to give and receive feedback to advanced classes on cost accounting.

GE/Durham has a continuous-feedback culture. "We call this the feedback capital of the world," says Paula Sims—meaning that although in one sense it's true that no one here has a boss, the opposite is also true. "I have 15 bosses," says Keith McKee. "All of my teammates are my bosses." No one is exempt. "Not long after I started here," says Sims, "an employee came to me and said, 'Paula, you realize that you don't need to follow up with us to make sure we're doing what we agreed to do. If we say we'll do something, we'll do it. You don't need to micromanage us.' I sat back and thought, 'Wow. That's so simple. I'm sending the message that I don't trust people, because I always follow up.' I took that to heart. This was a technician, and I had been at the plant less than 30 days. I appreciated that he felt comfortable enough to tell me this. And I thought, 'This really is a different place.'"

At GE/Durham, job candidates are rated in 11 areas. "Only one of those involves technical competence or experience," says Keith McKee, 27, a tech-3 on Team Raven. "You have to be above the bar in all 11 of the areas: helping skills, team skills, communication skills, diversity, flexibility, coaching ability, work ethic, and so forth. Even if just one thing out of the 11 knocks you down, you don't come to work here." To see how candidates cooperate, they are interviewed in groups and given group tasks. Each team includes technicians who have been trained as "assessors," and they do the interviewing. Both the team and the plant manager have to agree—to "consense"—on the hiring of a new team member.[45]

Questions

1. For the GE/Durham facility, identify examples of the five job characteristics that are key to the job enrichment model.
2. What examples of the implementation approaches to job enrichment are evident in the GE/Durham facility?
3. Use Figure 15.5 to describe the GE/Durham facility as an application of the sociotechnical systems model.
4. What are three of limitations on using the GE/Durham version of the sociotechnical systems model in all organizations?

REFERENCES

1. Adapted from 1998 Winner—Texas Nameplate Company, Inc. www.quality.nist.gov/docs/winners/98win/texas–2q.htm. July 12, 1999.
2. Parker, S., and Wall, T. *Job and Work Design: Organizing Work to Promote Well-Being and Effectiveness.* Thousand Oaks, Calif.: Sage, 1998.
3. Denton, D. K. I hate this job. *Business Horizons,* January–February 1994, 46–52.
4. Cheraskin, L., and Campion, M. A. Study clarifies job-rotation benefits. *Personnel Journal,* November 1996, 31–38.
5. Ellis, T. Implementing job rotation. *Occupational Health & Safety,* January 1999, 82–84.
6. Niebel, B. W., and Freivalds, A. *Methods, Standards, and Work Design,* 10th ed. New York: McGraw-Hill, 1998; White, J. B. The line starts here. *Wall Street Journal,* January 11, 1999, R25, R28.
7. Pruijt, H. D. *Job Design and Technology: Taylorism vs. Anti-Taylorism.* New York: Routledge, 1998.
8. Adapted from Bentley, T. Computer talk: Workflow systems. *Management Accounting—London,* January 1999, 54–55.
9. Wright, B. M., and Cordery, J. L. Production uncertainty as a contextual moderator of employee reactions to job design. *Journal of Applied Psychology,* 1999, 84, 456–463.
10. Adapted from Aeppel, T. Rust-belt factory lifts productivity, and staff finds no picnic. *Wall Street Journal,* May 18, 1999, A1, A10.
11. Aeppel, A10.

12. Orsburn, J. D., and Moran, L. *The New-Self Directed Work Teams: Mastering the Challenge.* New York: McGraw-Hill, 2000.
13. Miller, E. J. *The Tavistock Institute Contribution to Job and Organizational Design.* Brookfield, Vt.: Ashgate, 2000.
14. Karwowski, W., and Marras, W. S. *The Occupational Ergonomics Handbook.* Boca Raton, Fla.: CRC Press, 1999.
15. Adapted from Roha, R. R. The long road to recovery. *Kiplinger's Personal Finance Magazine,* March 1997, 163; West, J. *Implementing the Americans with Disabilities Act.* Cambridge, Mass.: Blackwell, 1996.
16. Adapted from Weigel, M. Beefing up the toolbox. *Occupational Health & Safety,* July 1999, 71–72.
17. Kempis, R.D., and Ringbeck, J. *Do It Smart: Seven Rules for Superior Information Technology Performance.* New York: Free Press, 1998.
18. Aeppel, A10.
19. Slocum, J. W., Jr., and Sims, H. P., Jr. A typology for integrating technology, organization, and job design. *Human Relations,* 1980, 33, 193–212.
20. Aeppel, A10.
21. Thompson, J. D. *Organizations in Action.* New York: McGraw-Hill, 1967.
22. Adapted from Breen, B., and Dahle, C. Field guide for change. *Fast Company,* December 1999, 384–404.
23. Hackman, J. R., and Oldham, G. R. *Work Redesign.* Reading, Mass.: Addison-Wesley, 1980.
24. Hackman and Oldham, 77–80.
25. Hackman and Oldham, 82–88.
26. Lucia, A. D., and Lepsinger, R. *The Art and Science of Competency Models: Pinpointing Critical Success Factors in Organizations.* San Francisco: Jossey-Bass, 1999.
27. 1998 Winner—Texas Nameplate Company, Inc.
28. Parker, S. K. Enhancing role breadth self-efficacy: The roles of job enrichment and other organizational interventions. *Journal of Applied Psychology,* 1998, 83, 835–852.
29. Joyce, W. F. *Mega Change: How Today's Leading Companies Have Transformed Their Workforces.* New York: Free Press, 1999.
30. Fairweather, N. B. Surveillance in employment: The case of teleworking. *Journal of Business Ethics,* 1999, 22, 39–49.
31. Sanchez, J. I., Zamora, A., and Viswesvaran, C. Moderators of agreement between incumbent and non-incumbent ratings of job characteristics. *Journal of Occupational and Organizational Psychology,* 1997, 70, 209–219.
32. Jackson, P. J., and van der Wielen, J. M. *Teleworking: International: Perspectives.* New York: Routledge, 1998.
33. Lieber, R. B. Storytelling: A new way to get closer to your customer. *Fortune,* February 3, 1997, 102–110.
34. Kahn, J. The world's most admired companies. *Fortune,* October 11, 1999, 267–280.
35. Adapted from Petzinger, T., Jr. A city executive learns to adapt to his workers' style. *Wall Street Journal,* May 1, 1998, B1.
36. Edwards, J. R., Scully, J. A., and Brtek, M. D. The measurement of work: Hierarchical representation of the multimethod job design questionnaire. *Personnel Psychology,* 1999, 52, 305–334.
37. Thomas, J. G., and Griffin, R. W. The power of social information in the workplace. *Organizational Dynamics,* Winter 1989, 63–75.
38. Ramamoorthy, N., and Carroll, S. J. Individualism/collectivism orientations and reactions toward alternative human resource management practices. *Human Relations,* 1998, 51, 571–588.
39. Trist, E., and Murray, H. (eds.). *The Social Engagement of Social Science: An Anthology, Vol. II: The Socio-Technical Perspective.* Philadelphia: University of Pennsylvania Press, 1993.
40. Adapted from Pearson, C. A., and Chong, J. Contributions of job content and social information and job satisfaction: An exploration in a Malaysian nursing context. *Journal of Occupational and Organizational Psychology,* 1997, 70, 357–375.
41. Pasmore, W. A. *Creating Strategic Change: Designing the Flexible, High-Performing Organization.* New York: John Wiley & Sons, 1994.
42. Adapted from Sittenfeld, C. Power by the people. *Fast Company,* July–August 1999, 178–189.
43. Drucker, P. F. Management's new paradigm. *Forbes,* October 5, 1998, 164; also see Horibe, F. *Managing Knowledge Workers: New Skills and Attitudes to Unite Intellectual Capital in Your Organization.* New York: John Wiley & Sons, 1999.
44. Halsey Jones, Professor of Management, Department of Management, University of Central Florida, 1994. Used with permission.
45. Adapted from Fishman, C. Engines of democracy. *Fast Company,* October 1999, 174–202.

CHAPTER

16 Organization Design

LEARNING OBJECTIVES

When you have finished studying this chapter, you should be able to:

1. Explain how environmental factors, strategic choices, and technological factors affect the design of organizations.
2. State the differences between mechanistic and organic systems.
3. Describe four traditional organization designs—functional, place, product, and multidivisional—and the requirements for their integration.
4. Explain four newer organization designs—matrix, multinational, network, and virtual.

Preview Case: *Procter & Gamble*

KEY FACTORS IN ORGANIZATION DESIGN
- Environmental Factors
- Strategic Choices
- Technological Factors
- ***Competency: Managing Communication—****U.S. West*
- Comparative Framework

MECHANISTIC AND ORGANIC SYSTEMS
- Hierarchy of Authority
- Division of Labor
- Rules and Procedures
- Impersonality
- Chain of Command
- Span of Control

TYPES OF ORGANIZATION DESIGNS
- Functional Design
- ***Competency: Managing Change—****Cisco Systems, Inc.*
- Place Design
- Product Design
- Multidivisional Design
- ***Competency: Managing Communication—****Johnson & Johnson's Multidivisional Design*
- Integration Issues

ORGANIZATIONS OF THE FUTURE
- Matrix Design
- Multinational Design
- Network Design
- ***Competency: Managing Across Cultures—****Electrolux*
- Virtual Organization
- ***Competency: Managing Teams—****British Petroleum's Virtual Organization*

CHAPTER SUMMARY
- Key Terms and Concepts
- Discussion Questions

DEVELOPING COMPETENCIES
- ***Competency: Managing Self—****Inventory of Effective Design*
- ***Competency: Managing Change—****Salomon*

PREVIEW CASE

PROCTER & GAMBLE

When Durk Jager took over as CEO of Procter & Gamble (P&G) in 1999, he replaced John Pepper as the head of this 160-year-old company. Pepper had assumed this position 3 years earlier and had downsized P&G in the hope that the smaller company would be more responsive to customers. This restructuring forced P&G to lay off more than 13,000 workers and close 30 plants, but it saved the firm more than $600 million. During Pepper's tenure, P&G grew 4 percent a year. To achieve its goal as the world's largest consumer goods company, P&G needs to grow at a rate of 9 percent each year. The sales goal for P&G in 2005 is $70 billion, or almost double what it is today. P&G, which sells more than 300 brands to 5 billion consumers in 140 countries, needed to change its structure to accelerate its growth.

Jager's charge was to restructure P&G so that it can achieve its growth potential in sales and revenues. He has proposed restructuring the company around seven global product groups—baby care, beauty care, fabric and home care, feminine protection, food and beverage, health care and corporate new ventures, and tissues and towels—instead of four geographical regions (North America, Europe, Asia, and Latin America). Under the geographical structure, a laundry product in Europe might compete for marketing funds against P&G diaper or tissue products. Under the new global product design, managers in each product line will make decisions based on P&G's global strategy for each product line rather than decisions based on a particular region. These seven global product group managers will have the responsibility for the profitability of existing and new brands and have the resources to quickly respond to competitors and customers. P&G also established a single global business service organization whose mission is to provide essential business services such as accounting, employee benefits and payroll, purchasing, and information and technology services to the entire company. By establishing this unit, P&G hopes to achieve significant economies of scale while improving overall quality and speed of these services. Jager chose this design because of P&G's inability to establish brands quickly around the world. Moreover, many of P&G's products increasingly share key technologies and innovations that require global scale to be economical. For example, when Febreze, a clothes freshener, was introduced in the United States, the product was slowly rolled out around the world. As a result, instead of reaching its sales goal of $500 million, Febreze sales were only $200 million.

Jager also believes that P&G needs greater innovation. Its strategy over the past 50 years has been to develop brands that are distinct from those of its competitors, such as Colgate–Palmolive, Lever Brothers, and Heinz. As markets have matured, new product development has become more difficult because many consumer needs have been largely satisfied. At the same time, many of P&G's innovations in emulsifiers and blending are laying the foundation for future products.

*For more information on Procter & Gamble, visit this company's home page at **www.pg.com**.*

P&G needs to change the way it develops products. According to Jager, P&G has been very good at inventing new products, such as Olestra, a reengineered fat, but slow to bring them to the market. For example, it spent more than 25 years developing Olestra. Traditionally, only when products are launched in a market and given a major advertising campaign are they able to build market share. However, P&G's competitors have been able to remove this "first mover advantage" by bringing their products to the market faster. For example, Lever Brothers launched Persil Tablets in the spring of 1998 in the U.K. and three other European markets without undertaking exhaustive testing while P&G was still testing the performance of Ariel Discs. Almost 1 year later, P&G managers were still trying to decide whether these new laundry detergent tablets were a superior product.[1]

Organization design is the process of assessing and selecting the structure and formal system of communication, division of labor, coordination, control, authority, and responsibility necessary to achieve an organization's goals.[2] The Preview Case noted that for years Procter & Gamble used a geographical design. Increased competitive pressures and changing customer preferences triggered a reevaluation of P&G's organization design.

Organization design decisions often involve the diagnosis of multiple factors, including the organization's culture, power and political behaviors, and job design. Organization design represents the outcomes of a decision-making process that includes environmental factors, strategic choices, and technological factors. Specifically, organization design should

1. ease the flow of information and decision making in meeting the demands of customers, suppliers, and regulatory agencies;
2. clearly define the authority and responsibility for jobs, teams, departments, and divisions; and
3. create the desired balance of integration (coordination) among jobs, teams, departments, and divisions, with fast response to changes in the environment.

One cornerstone of organization design is the design of individual jobs (see Chapter 15). A second cornerstone is the formation and use of teams—such as problem-solving teams, special-purpose teams, and self-managed teams (see Chapter 8). A third cornerstone includes organizational power, political behavior, and organizational culture (see Chapters 9 and 17). **Organizational culture** is a set of shared philosophies, values, assumptions, and norms that influence organizational decisions and actions. An organization's culture is likely to influence organization design decisions about the delegation of authority or the use of teams. Culture is important because it shapes how managers view their jobs and influences their behavior. Power and political behavior usually come into play when major changes in organization design are being considered. With P&G's new design, the locus of power will shift from regional presidents to the seven global brand managers.

In this chapter, we frequently refer to departments and divisions as we discuss organization design. The term *department* typically is used to identify a specialized function within an organization, such as human resources, production, accounting, and purchasing. In contrast, the term *division* typically is used to identify a broader, often autonomous part of an organization that performs many, if not all, the functions of the parent organization with respect to a product or large geographic area. At P&G, for example, under its new organization design, one division is responsible for all the functions involved in developing, producing, and marketing baby care products, and another is responsible for those functions with regard to beauty care products.

In this chapter, we first note how environmental factors, strategic choices, and technological factors can influence the design of an organization.[3] We present a broad framework to suggest how particular patterns of these influences tend to fit different organization designs and briefly discuss how they are related. Then, we introduce and compare mechanistic and organic systems and show how each type reflects a basic design decision. Strategic choice by top managers influences the structure of the organization. Next, we describe the functional, place, product, and multidivisional bases of design and the requirements for their integration. Then, we explain how to use matrix designs to improve integration across units. Next, we present multinational design options as ways to respond to multiple demands, primarily owing to diversity in customers, cultures, and geographic markets served. Finally, we describe the newest approaches to organization design—network and virtual organizations. These designs are intended to overcome the limitations of the others in the face of complex, diverse, and changing environments, technologies, and strategic choices.

Learning Objective:

1. Explain how environmental factors, strategic choices, and technological factors affect the design of organizations.

KEY FACTORS IN ORGANIZATION DESIGN

Organization design decisions (e.g., greater decentralization and empowerment of employees) may solve one set of problems but create others. Because every organization design has some drawbacks, the key is to select one that minimizes them. Table 16.1 identifies several variables for each of the three primary factors—environment, business strategy, and technology—that affect organization design decisions.

ENVIRONMENTAL FACTORS

The environmental forces that managers and employees need to assess are (1) the characteristics of the present and possible future environments and (2) how these demands affect the organization's ability to process information, cope with changes in markets and technologies, and achieve desired levels of differentiation (division of labor) and integration (coordination). Hypercompetition in some industries, including consumer electronics, airlines, and personal computers, is requiring managers to adopt new ways of thinking about their environments. As government regulation increases and markets become global, the quest for productivity, quality, and speed has spawned a remarkable number of new organization designs. Yet, many organizations have been frustrated by their inability to redesign themselves quickly enough to stay ahead of their rivals.

Environmental Characteristics. The **environment** includes those external stakeholders and forces that directly affect the organization's survival. Major stakeholders include customers, suppliers, regulatory agencies, shareholders, and creditors. After identifying the relevant stakeholders and forces in the environment, management should assess their characteristics and relative importance to the organization. Environmental characteristics basically vary in terms of complexity and dynamism.

Complexity refers to whether characteristics are few and similar (uniform) or many and different (varied). Carmike Cinemas of Columbus, Georgia, for example, operates in a uniform environment. It owns 400 movie theaters in southern U.S. cities and towns with populations of less than 200,000. Its revenues exceed $16 million. It serves its customers through standardized low-cost theater complexes requiring few screens and unsophisticated standard projection technology. A single manager can run the entire theater. The manager typically hires family members to help operate the theater for two reasons: Family members don't quit on each other, and family members don't steal from each other. All employees, including the manager, are paid a straight salary. Top management, using databanks in Dallas and Atlanta, does the

Table 16.1

Factors in Organization Design Decisions

FACTORS	INDICATORS
Environment	Degree of complexity Degree of dynamism
Business strategy	Low cost Differentiation Focused
Technology	Task interdependence

booking and buying of movies for all the theaters. Once a movie has been selected, the theater manager is required to show it. Operating in small towns allows Carmike to use a highly personal form of marketing in which the theater manager knows patrons and promotes attendance through personal contacts, such as sponsoring Little League teams. By being the dominant theater in the market, its main competition is often the local high school football and basketball teams.[4] It is also able to negotiate better rental terms from landlords than if it were in competition for sites. In contrast, Tinsletown, a firm that builds large theaters that show as many as 20 movies simultaneously in major metropolitan areas, faces a much more competitive environment. Each theater has a manager and three assistant managers, six ticket takers, five concession stations, several pizzerias, seating for 5,200 patrons, and shows movies 18 hours a day. The theaters often face typical urban problems such as crime and lack of parking space. Intense competition from other movie theaters, including SONY and AMC, and other forms of entertainment—opera, symphony, legitimate theater, and professional sports teams, among others—add to the complexity of operating in this environment.

Rating an environment as uniform or varied depends on the number of factors involved. As suggested by the Preview Case, organizing Procter & Gamble by four regions proved too complex and did not enable the company to bring products to the market quickly. Customers in different regions of the world were demanding products that called for specific and varied technologies. Procter & Gamble needed an organization design that could integrate these technologies or lose customers to competitors that were able to bring new products to the market more quickly. The need for this capability became especially urgent for P&G because its increasingly global environment made it susceptible to competitors' moves and choices in meeting customer demands in many different markets.

Dynamism relates to whether environmental characteristics remain basically the same (are stable) or change (are unstable). Procter & Gamble identified a changing environment and decided to make its organization design more responsive to those changes. Dynamism also relates to the need for speed in responding to customers' and other stakeholders' demands. Organizations increasingly must be able to respond quickly and flexibly.

Types of Environments. Figure 16.1 illustrates the basic classification of task environments. The four "pure" types of task environments are uniform–stable, varied–stable, uniform–unstable, and varied–unstable. You can use this grid to classify the environment for any organization.

The simplest organization design can be effective in a *uniform–stable environment* (box 1). The environment holds few surprises, and the manager's role is to ensure that employees consistently follow established routines and procedures. Managers and employees need relatively fewer competencies and less formal training and job experience to operate successfully in this environment than in the others. Organizations that primarily operate in this environment include lawn care firms, local delivery service firms, car wash firms, mail service firms, and self-service storage firms. Although the environment is relatively stable, these firms do face some uncertainties because of competitors' actions, customers' changing preferences, and potential substitutes for their products and services.

The *varied–stable environment* (box 2) poses some risks for managers and employees, but the environment and the alternatives are fairly well understood. The environment is relatively stable, but employees may need considerable training and experience to understand it and make it work. For example, at Ritz-Carlton hotels, employees are trained to observe the preferences that individual guests show during each stay—preferences for hypoallergenic pillows, classical radio stations, or chocolate chip cookies. Ritz-Carlton management then stores this information in a database and uses it to tailor the service that each guest receives during his or her next visit. The more someone stays in Ritz-Carlton hotels, the more the company learns and the more customized goods and services it fits into the standard Ritz-Carlton service.

Figure 16.1 **Basic Types of Task Environments**

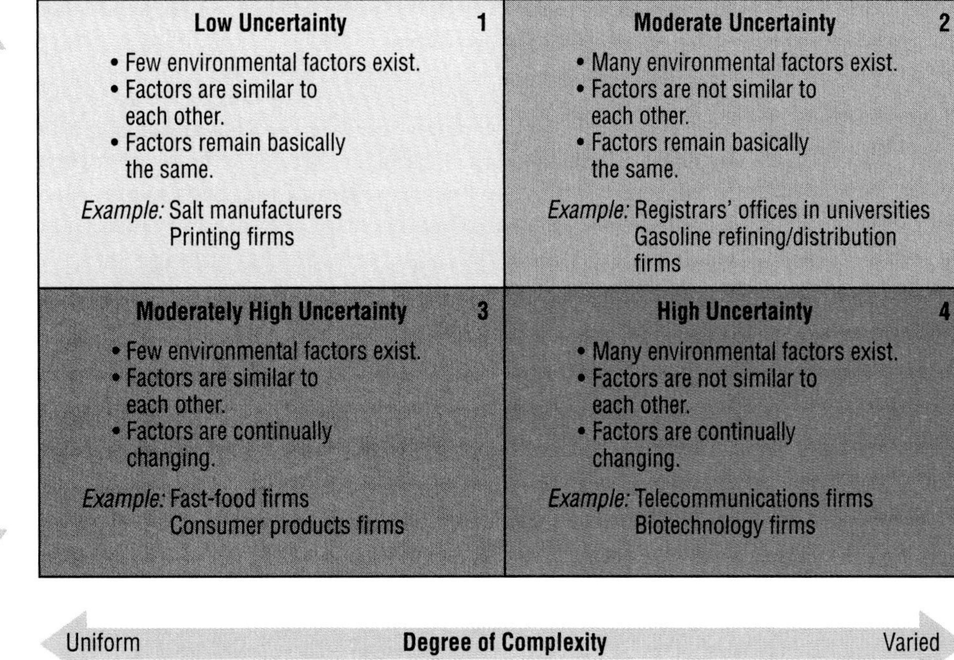

Source: Adapted from Rasheed, A., and Prescott, J. E. Dimensions of organizational task environments: Revisited. Paper presented at 1987 Academy of Management meeting, New Orleans; Duncan, R. What is the right organization structure? Decision tree analysis provides the answer. *Organizational Dynamics,* Winter 1979, 60–64.

The *uniform–unstable environment* (box 3) requires managers, employees, and organization designs to be flexible. Computer-based information systems often help keep track of the changes. Rapid response to sudden changes in market demand or technologies means that companies need organization designs that allow for considerable flexibility and speed in allocating resources to new products. Procter & Gamble, Kraft Foods, Lever Brothers, and Colgate–Palmolive, among other consumer product firms, frequently create new products to attract and retain customers. Procter & Gamble, for example, has aggressively redesigned its organization around product lines. Its foods division accounts for 12 percent of corporate sales, and its beauty care division 80 percent, but its newly formed pharmaceutical division contributes only 8 percent. Durk Jager, P&G's CEO, believes that, with the growth of managed care, gross margins for pharmaceuticals will be higher than for food and beauty products. Therefore P&G plans to spend more than $1.2 billion on pharmaceutical research and development and has charged that division with developing medicines that attack bacterial infections, bone diseases, and cardiovascular ailments. According to Jager, the growth of P&G will be linked to the success of the new products created and sold by its pharmaceutical division. New plants and distribution centers around the world will be built to help P&G aggressively enter this global market.

The *varied–unstable environment* (box 4) represents the most challenging situation for an organization because the environment presents numerous uncertainties. This environment requires the most managerial and employee sophistication, insight, and problem-solving abilities. Managers can't solve the problems confronting them merely by using standard procedures. In this environment, standard operating procedures become much less important than individual initiative and the ability to work with other people quickly.

New computer networks, such as the Internet and intranets, enable organizations to satisfy quickly the changing and complex demands of customers. Through America Online, CompuServe, and other service providers and with browsers such as Netscape and Microsoft's Internet Explorer, suppliers and customers can even access certain data stored in an organization's computer system. For example, a FedEx customer can track packages by logging onto FedEx's home page on the World Wide Web, which is linked to the company's internal databases. The Web has also become an important means of tying together various organizations to accelerate many business processes.

Once found only at "techie" organizations such as Sun Microsystems or Digital Equipment, intranets are driving entire organizations and even entire industries. Internal computer networks create webs for organizations that allow employees to call up data such as customer profiles and product inventory. Previously such information was hidden in databases and was accessible only to technicians. The intranet at Morgan Stanley Dean Witter, a global brokerage firm, links all 37 of its offices and 9,600 employees around the world. With money markets open somewhere in the world 24 hours a day, the Web permits money managers to move money from New York to Tokyo to London continually. Moreover, brokers can continually update customers' portfolios, based on the latest financial information.

Each type of task environment requires different approaches to designing and managing an organization. As we go through this chapter, we relate different organization designs to the general types of environment in which they are most likely to be effective.

Strategic Choices

Many of top management's strategic choices affect organization design decisions. **Strategic choices** enable an organization to capitalize on its unique capabilities. According to Michael Porter, companies need to distinguish and position themselves differently from their competitors in order build and sustain a competitive advantage.[5] Organizations have attempted to build competitive advantages in various ways, but three underlying strategies appear to be essential in doing so: low cost, differentiation, and focused. These strategies are shown in Figure 16.2. Let's examine how each affects the design of an organization.

Figure 16.2 **Strategies Model**

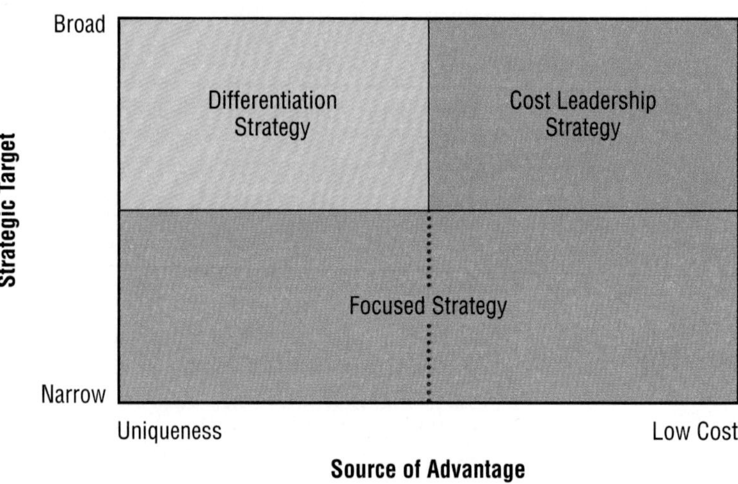

Source: Adapted with the permission of The Free Press, a division of Simon & Schuster, from *Competitive Strategy: Techniques for Analyzing Industries and Competitors* (p. 39) by Michael E. Porter. Copyright © 1980 by The Free Press.

Low cost. A **low-cost strategy** is based on an organization's ability to provide a product or service at a lower cost than its rivals. An organization that chooses a low-cost strategy seeks to gain a significant cost advantage over other competitors and pass the savings on to consumers in order to gain a large market share. Such a strategy aims at selling a standardized product that appeals to an "average" customer in a broad market. The organization must attain significant economies of scale in key business activities (e.g., purchasing and logistics). Because the environment is uniform and stable, few product modifications are needed to satisfy customers. The organization's design is functional, with accountability and responsibility clearly assigned to various departments (see pages 487–489 to learn more about this design).

Organizations that have successfully used a low-cost strategy include Carmike Cinemas in movie theaters, Whirlpool in washers and dryers, Black & Decker in power tools, BIC in ballpoint pens, Wal-Mart in discount stores, PetSmart in pet stores, and Procter-Silex in coffeemakers. The risks involved in following this strategy are (1) getting "locked in" to a technology and organization design that is expensive to change, (2) the ability of competitors to copy the strategy (e.g., Target copying Wal-Mart), or most important, (3) management not paying attention to shifts in the environment (e.g., customer demand for different types of products and/or services).

Differentiation. A **differentiation strategy** is based on providing customers with something that is unique and makes the organization's product or service distinctive from its competition. An organization that chooses a differentiation strategy typically uses a product organization design whereby each product has its own manufacturing, marketing, and research and development (R&D) departments (see pages 490–491 to learn more about this design). The key managerial assumption behind this strategy is that customers are willing to pay a higher price for a product that is distinctive in some way.[6] Superior value is achieved through higher quality, technical superiority, or some special appeal. Toyota's strategy with Lexus is based on exceptional manufacturing quality, the use of genuine wood paneling, advanced sound systems, high engine performance, and comparatively high fuel economy (for luxury cars).

Organizations that have successfully used a differentiation strategy include Procter & Gamble in a variety of product lines, American Express in credit cards, Nordstrom in department stores, Krups in coffeemakers and espresso makers, and 3M in coatings and adhesives are some of the organizations that have successfully used this strategy. The biggest disadvantage that these organizations face is maintaining a price premium as the product becomes more familiar to customers. Price is especially an issue when a product or service becomes mature. Organizations may also overdo product differentiation, which places a burden on their R&D departments, as well as a drain on their financial and human resources. Nissan faced this issue during the 1990s. The carmaker had created so many different types of automobiles that they confused customers and caused production costs to soar. Nissan scaled back the number of different models, but it still lags behind its competitors in styling.

Focused. A **focused strategy** is designed to help an organization target a specific niche within an industry, unlike both the low-cost and the differentiation strategies, which are designed to target industrywide markets. An organization that chooses a focused strategy may utilize any of a variety of organization designs, ranging from functional to product to matrix to network, to satisfy their customers' preferences (see pages 495–496 for descriptions of these designs). The choice of organization design reflects the niches of a particular buyer group, a regional market, or customers that have special tastes, preferences, or requirements. The basic idea is to specialize in ways that other organizations can't match effectively. These organizations generally operate in either varied–stable or uniform–unstable environments.

Organizations that have successfully used a focused strategy include Karsten Manufacturing, Southwest Airlines, Nucor, and Chaparral Steel. Karsten Manufacturing has implemented its focused strategy by designing and producing a line of golf clubs under the Ping label. It was able to carve out a defensible niche in the hotly contested golf equipment business. Karsten uses ultrasophisticated manufacturing equipment and composite materials to make golf clubs almost on a customized basis. Southwest Airlines is among the most profitable airlines in the industry. It achieved its success by focusing on short-haul routes, flying into airports located close to or within cities, not serving meals, not transferring baggage, and offering no reserved seating.

The greatest disadvantage that an organization faces in using a focused strategy is the risk that its underlying market niche may gradually shift toward a broader market. Distinctive customer tastes may "blur" over time, thus reducing the defensibility of the niche. For example, American Airlines has started service to Austin, Texas, from Love Field in Dallas, one of Southwest Airlines' main hubs. It offers a full complement of services for its passengers, including meals, reserve seating, use of its lounge, and baggage transfer service. It remains to be determined if Southwest Airlines can profitably maintain its customer base in this market.

Technological Factors

In Chapter 15, we noted how technology affected employee job design. Technology also influences organization design in terms of the creation of teams and departments, the delegation of authority and responsibility, and the need for formal integrating mechanisms. In P&G's new design, each global product division is self-contained and responsible for its own manufacturing, R&D, human resources, and marketing. When the company used a geographic organization design, responsibility for coordinating products was in the hands of regional managers, not product managers. Therefore one of the primary differences between the geographic design and the product design is the degree to which managers responsible for various products share information and resources.

Task Interdependence. Recall that task interdependence may be pooled, sequential, or reciprocal.[7] In terms of organization design, we can characterize them in the following manner.

- *Pooled interdependence* occurs when departments or teams are relatively autonomous and make an identifiable contribution to the organization. For example, the many sales and services offices of State Farm Insurance don't engage in day-to-day decision making, coordination, and communication with each other. The local State Farm agents operate their offices without much interaction with other agents. Managers in regional offices coordinate, set policies, and solve problems for agents in their territories. The performance of each agent and regional office is readily identifiable. Pooled interdependence exits when the performance of one person has no direct impact on that of another.
- *Sequential interdependence* occurs when one department or team must complete certain tasks before one or more other departments or teams can perform their tasks. For example, British Petroleum uses sequential interdependence to deliver gasoline and other products to a variety of consumers. This process starts with exploration (the search for crude oil and natural gas), production (drilling of wells for retrieval of gas and oil), supply (transport of the raw material via ship or pipeline to refineries), refining (the breakdown of hydrocarbons into various by-products), distribution (transportation of product by pipeline or truck), and marketing (the sale of products to the customer). The flow of material is always the same. A predetermined order or flow of activities defines sequential interdependence.[8]

- *Reciprocal interdependence* occurs when the outputs from one department or team become the inputs for another department or team and vice versa. Essentially, reciprocal interdependence exists when all units within an organization depend on one another to produce an output. As pointed out in the Preview Case, one of P&G's problems was that customers were demanding quick introduction of new and/or improved products. Until the establishment of centralized manufacturing, engineering, and R&D departments for each product, introduction of a new or improved product had to wait until a regional manager decided whether to market it. Now each global product manager has complete authority and responsibility for the division's products.

Figure 16.3 shows that reciprocal interdependence is the most complex type and that pooled interdependence is the simplest type of technological interdependence. As P&G learned, greater interdependence among its geographic divisions required more integration. Placing reciprocally interdependent departments or teams under one executive often improves integration and minimizes information processing costs within a unit. For example, in P&G's baby care division, the marketing research, advertising, and sales departments all report to the vice president of marketing for that product line. Employees in these departments must communicate and coordinate more with each other than, for example, with employees in the foods division.

In previous chapters, we discussed how new information technologies are changing the flow of communication in organizations. These information technologies also affect the design of organizations and the flows of information through them.[9] The following Managing Communication Competency feature illustrates how U.S. West uses its communications system to enhance productivity.

Figure 16.3 **Types of Task Interdependence in Organization Design**

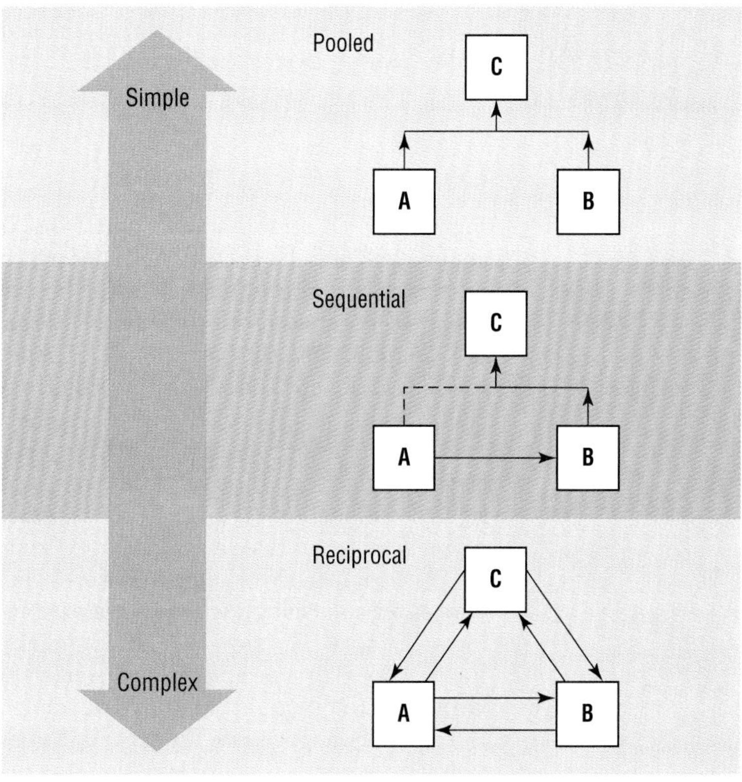

Competency: Managing Communication

U.S. West

Margaret Turney, a top financial executive at U.S. West, was looking for a way to show employees how fast-changing technologies would affect the telephone services that the company offered. She asked Sherman Woo, the company's director of information tools and technologies, to help her. Little did she realize that her request would result in the Global Village, an intranet that now connects 15,000 employees at U.S. West and has changed the way the company operates.

Woo believed that the best way to interest employees in new technology was to have them experience it for themselves. He created a basic intranet in a conference room by linking some computers to communications lines and a video screen. He gave browser software to any computer users who wanted it and connected their machines to his newly constructed web. In exchange, Woo requested that the users show at least two other employees how the web worked. Almost everyone who saw it wanted to be connected, too.

Today, employees in 14 states work together on the intranet. Some meet in online chat rooms to exchange documents and discuss ongoing projects. Salespeople use the web to keep in touch with managers in Denver, U.S. West's headquarters. The intranet also functions as an electronic suggestion box. Employees in different departments create their own home pages and keep their own documents current.

Customers also have benefited from U.S. West's internal web. Service representatives now use the intranet to fill orders (e.g., for call waiting) while the customer is on the phone. The service representative simply enters the order on the web browser, which sends it to the phone-switching network. Within a few minutes, the customer's call waiting is activated. Under the old system, that process took days. This new technology has enabled U.S. West to become more sensitive and responsive to its customers' needs.[10]

For more information on U.S. West, visit this organization's home page at www.uswest.com.

Comparative Framework

Figure 16.4 illustrates seven approaches to common organization design. These approaches, and the conditions under which they are most likely to be effective, are contrasted in terms of the key factors in organization design. Environmental forces comprise a continuum on the vertical axis, ranging from a simple, stable environment to a complex, dynamic environment. Technological interdependence comprises a continuum on the horizontal axis, ranging from pooled to reciprocal. At one end of the continuum is a cluster of choices that reflect uniformity in customers, technologies, and geographic markets, represented by firms such as Avis Rent-a-Car, Allstate Insurance Company, and Motel 6. At the other end of the continuum are organization design choices that reflect diversity in customers, technologies, and geographic markets, represented by firms such as Procter & Gamble, DuPont, Kao, and General Electric.

The comparative framework broadly portrays how the design of an organization may differ and change as a result of various patterns of environmental and technological factors. The simplest environment (lower left) implies that some version of the functional organization design is likely to be appropriate. The most complex environment (upper right) implies that some form of the network organization design is likely to be appropriate. In general, designs become more complex as an organization moves from a functional design to a network design. Moreover, the designs require more coordination among people and activities as they become increasingly complex.

Figure 16.4 **Options of Organizational Designs**

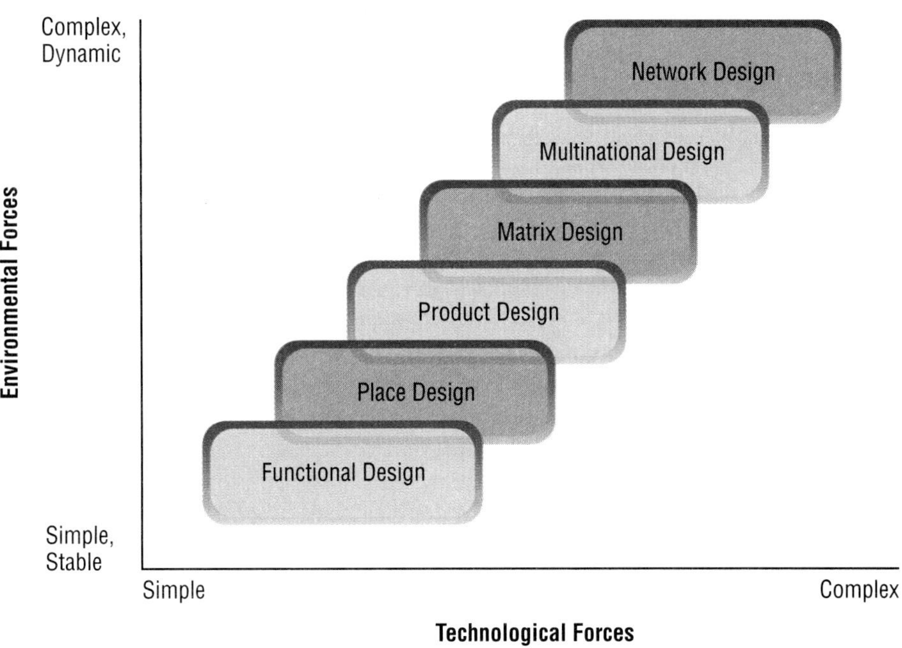

Learning Objective:

2. State the differences between mechanistic and organic systems.

MECHANISTIC AND ORGANIC SYSTEMS

A **mechanistic system** is characterized by reliance on formal rules and regulations, centralization of decision making, narrowly defined job responsibilities, and a rigid hierarchy of authority. The emphasis is on following procedures and rules. In contrast, an **organic system** is characterized by low to moderate use of formal rules and regulations, decentralized and shared decision making, broadly defined job responsibilities, and a flexible authority structure with fewer levels in the hierarchy.[11]

Top management typically makes decisions that determine the extent to which an organization will operate as a mechanistic system or an organic system. At P&G, the four regions of the world operated relatively autonomously (pooled interdependence) until top management decided to coordinate all manufacturing, engineering, R&D, marketing, and other functions for each product line. This move created the need for vastly more coordination of its operations throughout the world. Although mechanistic and organic systems are organization design choices, environmental forces (e.g., a dynamic, complex environment versus a stable, simple environment), strategic choices (low cost, differentiation, or focused), and technology (task interdependence) also influence whether the design is mechanistic or organic.

A mechanistic system is essentially a bureaucracy. Max Weber, a German sociologist and economist in the early 1900s, defined a bureaucracy as an organization having the following characteristics.[12]

- The organization operates according to a body of rules or laws that are intended to tightly control the behavior of employees.
- All employees must carefully follow extensive impersonal rules and procedures in making decisions.
- Each employee's job involves a specified area of expertise, with strictly defined obligations, authority, and powers to compel obedience.
- The organization follows the principle of hierarchy; that is, each lower position is under the tight control and direction of a higher one.

- Candidates for jobs are selected on the basis of "technical" qualifications. They are appointed, not elected.
- The organization has a career ladder. Promotion is by seniority or achievement and depends on the judgment of superiors.

The word **bureaucracy** often brings to mind rigidity, incompetence, red tape, inefficiency, and ridiculous rules. In principle, though, the basic characteristics of a mechanistic system may make a bureaucratic organization design feasible or even desirable in some situations. Any discussion of a mechanistic system must distinguish between the way it should ideally function and the way some large-scale organizations actually operate.

The degrees to which an organization emphasizes a mechanistic or an organic system can vary substantially, as suggested in Figure 16.5. Radio Shack, McDonald's, and Target are organizations that have relatively mechanistic systems in terms of the selected dimensions. They are represented by organization B. Cisco Systems, Solectron Corporation, Apple, and Microsoft are organizations that place more emphasis on the dimensions that represent an organic system. They are represented by organization A. The organic system emphasizes employee competence, rather than the employee's formal position in the hierarchy, as a basis for rewards, including promotion. This system has a flexible hierarchy and empowers employees to deal with uncertainties in the environment.

Hierarchy of Authority

Hierarchy of authority represents the extent to which decision-making processes are prescribed and where formal power resides. In a mechanistic system, higher level departments set or approve goals and detailed budgets for lower level departments and issue directives to them. A mechanistic system has as many levels in its hierarchy as

Figure 16.5 **Organic and Mechanistic Design Features**

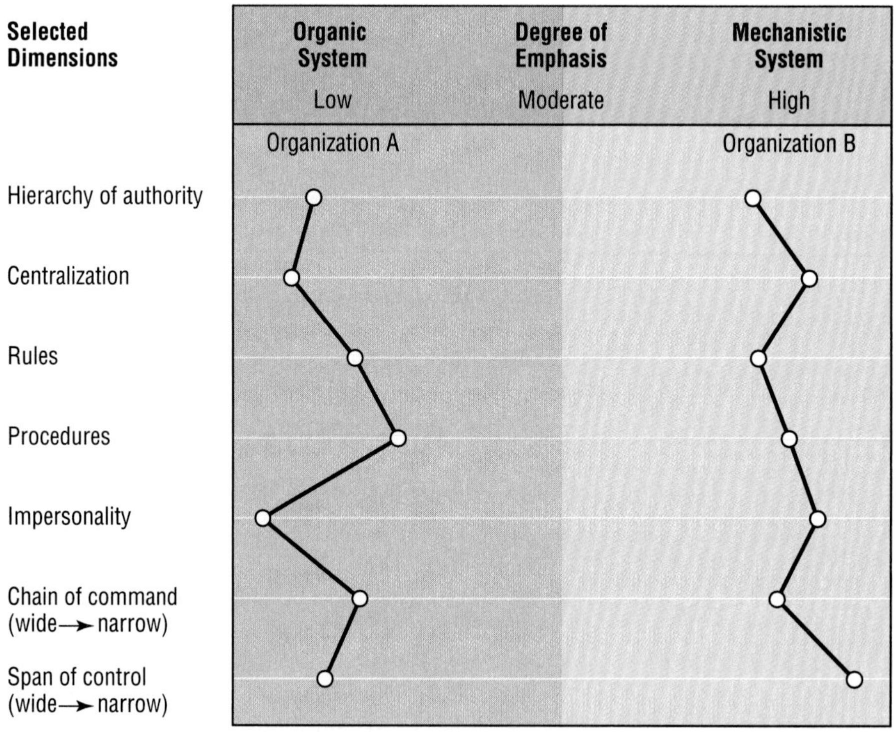

necessary to achieve tight control. An organic system has few levels in its hierarchy, which makes coordination and communication easier and fosters innovation.

The hierarchy of authority is closely related to centralization. **Centralization** means that all major, and oftentimes many minor, decisions are made only at the top levels of the organization. Centralization is common in mechanistic systems, whereas decentralization and shared decision making between and across levels are common in an organic system. At Jiffy Lube, McDonald's, and Pier I Imports, top executives make nearly all decisions affecting store operations. Rules and regulations are sent from headquarters to each store, and reports from the stores are sent up the hierarchy.

Division of Labor

Division of labor refers to the various ways of dividing up tasks and labor to achieve goals. Adam Smith, the father of capitalism, recognized the importance of this concept in his book *An Inquiry into the Nature and Cause of the Wealth of Nations*, first published in 1776.[13] Smith suggested that, in general, the greater the division of labor in organizations, the greater would be the efficiency of organizations and the amount of wealth created.

The mechanistic system typically follows Smith's views. However, a continued increase in the division of labor may eventually become counterproductive. Employees who perform only very routine and simple jobs that require few skills may become bored and frustrated. The results may be low quality and low productivity, high turnover, and high absenteeism. This situation occurred in numerous U.S. industries (e.g., automobile, consumer electronics, and steel) during the 1970s and 1980s. Excessive division of labor was compounded by rigid union work rules, which eventually compromised these companies' ability to respond to new technologies and customer needs. In addition, the managerial costs (volume of reports, more managers, and more controls to administer) of integrating highly specialized functions usually are high. Many companies in the fast-food industry, including McDonald's, Wendy's, Burger King, and Taco Bell, report that employee turnover exceeds 300 percent a year. To cope with such high turnover, most processes are automated and can be quickly learned. In contrast, the organic system tends to reduce the costs of high turnover by delegating decision making to lower levels in the organization. Delegation also encourages employees and teams to take on responsibility for achieving their tasks and linking them to those of others in the organization. The organic system takes advantage of the benefits from the division of labor, but it is sensitive to the negative results of carrying the division of labor too far.

Rules and Procedures

Rules are formal statements specifying acceptable and unacceptable behaviors and decisions by employees. One of the paradoxes of rules that attempt to reduce individual autonomy is that someone must still decide which rules apply to specific situations. Rules are an integral part of both mechanistic and organic systems. In a mechanistic system, the tendency is to create detailed uniform rules to cover tasks and decisions whenever possible. United Parcel Service (UPS) has rules that cover all aspects of delivering a package to a customer, including which arm to carry the clipboard under (right arm) for the person to sign and which arm to carry the package with (left arm). In an organic system, the tendency is to create rules only when necessary (e.g., safety rules to protect life and property). Managers and employees alike tend to question the need for new rules, as well as existing rules that no longer seem to have any validity. In a mechanistic system, the tendency is to accept the need for extensive rules and to formulate new rules in response to new situations.

Procedures refer to preset sequences of steps that managers and employees must follow in performing tasks and dealing with problems. Procedures often comprise rules that are to be used in a particular sequence. For example, in order to obtain reimbursement for travel expenses in most organizations, employees must follow specific reporting procedures, including submission of receipts. Procedures have many of the same positive and negative features that characterize rules, and they often proliferate in a mechanistic system. Managers in organic systems usually know that rules and procedures can make the organization too rigid and thus dampen employee motivation, stymie innovation, and inhibit creativity. In a mechanistic system, rules and procedures tend to be developed at the top and issued via memoranda. Such memos may convey the expectation of strict compliance and the adverse consequences of not complying. In an organic system, employee input is likely to be sought on changes in current rules and procedures or on proposed rules and procedures when they are absolutely necessary. In an organic system employees at all levels are expected to question, evaluate, and make suggestions about such proposals, with an emphasis on collaboration and interdependence.

Impersonality

Impersonality is the extent to which organizations treat their employees, customers, and others according to objective, detached, and rigid characteristics. Managers in a highly mechanistic system are likely to emphasize matter-of-fact indicators (college degrees, certificates earned, test scores, training programs completed, length of service, and the like) when making hiring, salary, and promotion decisions. Although managers may consider these factors in an organic system, the emphasis is likely to be on the actual achievements and professional judgments of individuals rather than on rigid quantitative indicators. Andersen Consulting is a leading business consulting company that operates as an organic system. A college graduate applying for a job at Andersen Consulting goes through an extensive interview process. This process may involve several managers, many (if not all) of the employees with whom the applicant would work, and even a casual and informal "interview" by a team of employees. The person responsible for filling the open position solicits opinions and reactions from these employees before making a decision. In most instances, the manager calls a meeting of the employees and other managers who participated in the interview process to discuss a candidate.

Chain of Command

Early writers on organization design stressed two basic ideas about the chain of command.[14] First, in a scalar **chain of command,** authority and responsibility are arranged hierarchically. They flow in a clear, unbroken vertical line from the highest executive to the lowest employee. Clarity of direction is the basis for the chain. Second, these writers emphasized **unity of command,** which holds that no subordinate should receive direction from more than one superior. Although some organizations don't rigidly follow unity of command in their designs, overlapping lines of authority and responsibility can make both managing and production tasks more difficult than they should be. Without unity of command, who may direct whom to do what may become cloudy and confusing. As you read in the Preview Case, P&G's product-line managers have the authority to make decisions about their brands. Managers in various countries now report to these global brand managers. Of course, the issues of chain of command and unity of control don't just apply to mechanistic design. They must be addressed in all organization designs.

Span of Control

Span of control refers to the number of employees reporting directly to one manager. When the span of control is broad, relatively few levels exist between the top and bottom of the organization. Conversely, when the span of control is narrow, more levels are required for the same number of employees. Although there is no "correct" number of subordinates that a manager can supervise effectively, the competencies of both the manager and employees, the similarity of tasks being supervised, and the extent of rules and operating standards all influence a manager's span of control. A manager at Carmike Cinemas faces a relatively uniform environment and asks employees to perform simple and repetitive operations (taking tickets, operating the concession stands, and performing housekeeping duties). At higher organizational levels, however, a regional manager might effectively supervise as many as 15 theater managers who are geographically spread over a wide area. These regional managers report to managers at headquarters in Columbus, Georgia.

In both mechanistic and organic systems, well-defined rules and procedures may have to be developed and applied through a relatively impersonal process in certain instances. For example, laws, court rulings, and regulatory agency decisions may even mandate impersonality, extensive rules, and rigid procedures.

In tomorrow's global environment many firms will find that, in order to stay competitive, they must change how they manage. Management blunders by AT&T, Eastman Kodak, and General Motors have occurred because of their inability to adapt to the speed and turbulence of a changing environment. In some cases, even after massive high-tech investments, management is only beginning to make the organizational changes needed to transform their organizations. One company that has changed from a mechanistic to an organic system is Cisco Systems, Inc. The Managing Change Competency feature on page 488 illustrates how Cisco embraces many of the concepts of the organic organization.

Learning Objective:

3. Describe four traditional organization designs—functional, place, product, and multi-divisional—and the requirements for their integration.

TYPES OF ORGANIZATION DESIGNS

Now that we have examined the various factors that affect managers' choice of an organization design, let's consider some of the design choices available. As we discuss them, we refer to the factors that influence a particular choice of design.

FUNCTIONAL DESIGN

Functional design involves the creation of positions and departments on the basis of specialized activities. Functional grouping of employees is the most widely used and accepted form of departmentalization. Although the functions vary widely, depending on the organization (e.g., Presbyterian Hospitals do not have production departments, nor does Bank of America), grouping tasks and employees by function can be both efficient and economical.

Key Characteristics. Departments of a typical manufacturing firm with a single product line often are grouped by function—engineering, human resources, manufacturing, shipping, purchasing, sales, and finance. Tasks also are usually divided functionally by the process used—receiving, stamping, plating, assembly, painting, and inspection (sequential interdependence). Figure 16.6 shows how Callaway Golf Corporation, the largest golf club manufacturer in the United States, uses both managerial functions and processes in its design.[15] A common theme of functional design proponents was the desirability of standardizing repetitive tasks and making them routine whenever possible. This approach helped reduce errors and lowered costs. Management could then concentrate on exceptions to eliminate any gaps or overlaps.

Significance in Practice. A functional design has both advantages and disadvantages. On the positive side, it permits clear identification and assignment of responsibilities, and employees easily understand it. People doing similar tasks and facing similar problems work together, thus increasing the opportunities for interaction and mutual support. A disadvantage is that a functional design fosters a limited point of

COMPETENCY: MANAGING CHANGE

CISCO SYSTEMS, INC.

Cisco Systems, Inc., is a global leader in data-networking equipment for the Internet. It is located in San Jose, California, has annual sales of more than $8 billion, and employs more than 13,000 people. It makes tools (bridges and switches) for building powerful electronic networks that link businesses to their customers and suppliers. Part of Cisco's business strategy is to connect users with standard Internet protocols. John Chambers, who led the company throughout the 1990s, had seen firsthand how mechanistic management practices at IBM and Wang lead to poor morale and productivity. As a result, Chambers based Cisco's organization design on organic principles.

He believes that tomorrow's successful organization will be built on change, not on a rigid hierarchy; based on interdependencies of partners, not on self-sufficiency; and require that employees be able to continuously learn and adapt, not simply follow orders and "check their brains at the door." Cisco relies on networks to achieve integration throughout the company. These networks connect Cisco with its web of suppliers and manufacturers, making Cisco look like one company. Via the company's intranet, outside vendors directly monitor orders from Cisco customers and ship the assembled hardware to buyers later in the day, often without Cisco even touching the order.

To achieve Cisco's goals, Chambers emphasizes five management concepts.

- Personal touch. Technology goes only so far. Managers must spend time mentoring, coaching, and communicating with people. No one can be fired unless Chambers gives his consent. "Never ask your team to do something that you wouldn't do yourself," is one of Chambers's mottos. He holds quarterly meetings with all employees to update them on the latest business developments and has "birthday breakfasts" with all employees who had a birthday that month.
- Focus on the customer. Let your core customers, such as Boeing, Ford Motor Company, and Dell Computer, determine your strategy. Customers know more about what they need than Cisco does.
- Team up for success. Create alliances with partners based on trust and the potential for long-term wins for both. Using Cisco's networks, Dell Computer connects to its suppliers who bring them inventory only when it is needed, eliminating the need for Dell to carry inventories of parts, screens, and the like. Working together, GTE, U.S. West, Cisco, and Dell are able to get new technology and services out quicker than any of them could acting alone.
- Share the wealth. Cisco uses stock plans to reward and retain employees. One share of Cisco stock purchased in 1990 is now worth 72 shares. Chambers and his senior managers use stock options to reward their people for outstanding performance. Many secretaries at Cisco are now millionaires. All employees, including Chambers, fly coach and there are no reserved parking spaces at headquarters. When employees want information about Cisco, they have more than 1.7 million pages of data available to them.
- Buy smart. Pursue acquisitions not to grow per se, but to capture the acquired company's human capital and its next-generation products. People are the only true asset that Cisco wants to acquire. Cisco has been able to integrate successfully the people and operations of more than 20 acquisitions over the past 10 years because it empowers acquired managers to pursue their interests at the company and rewards them according to their success.[16]

For more information on Cisco Systems, visit this organization's home page at ***www.cisco.com.***

Figure 16.6 **Callaway Golf's Design by Function and Process**

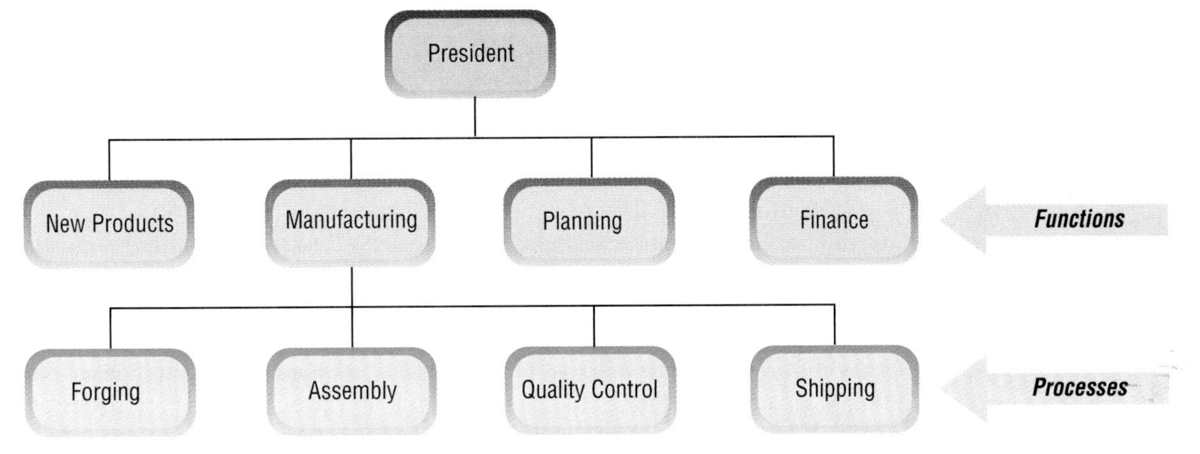

Source: Adapted from *Callaway Golf 1996 Annual Report.* Carlsbad, California, 1997.

view that focuses on a narrow set of tasks. Employees may lose sight of the organization as a whole. Horizontal integration across functional departments often becomes difficult as the organization increases the number of geographic areas served and the range of goods or services provided. With the exception of marketing, most employees in a functionally designed organization have no direct contact with customers and may lose touch with the need to meet or exceed customer expectations.

A functional design may be effective when an organization has a narrow product line, competes in a uniform environment, pursues a low-cost or focused business strategy, and doesn't have to respond to the pressures of serving different types of customers. The addition of specialized staff departments to a functional design may enable an organization to deal effectively with some degree of environmental complexity and dynamism. Staff departments may provide line departments with expert advice, such as dealing with certain technologies. As shown previously in Figure 16.4, functional design is the most elementary type of organization design and often represents a base from which other types of designs evolve. It is the organization design that Carmike Cinemas uses to implement its low-cost business strategy.

Place Design

Place design involves establishing an organization's primary units geographically while retaining significant aspects of functional design. All functional groups for one geographic area are in one location. Before P&G adopted its new product-line structure, it was organized by place, focusing on four regions of the world because top management believed that each region faced unique challenges. Companies that are marketing-intensive and need to respond to local market conditions or customer needs typically use place designs.

Key Characteristics. Many of the tasks required to serve a geographic territory are placed under one manager, rather than grouping functions under different managers or all tasks in one central office. Large companies such as American Airlines, FedEx, and Allstate Insurance Company use place design in the form of regional and district offices. Similarly, many governmental agencies such as the Federal Reserve Board, the federal courts, and the U.S. Postal Service use place design in providing their services.

Link to Internationalization. Many international firms use place design to address cultural and legal differences in various countries and the lack of uniformity among customers in different geographic markets.[17] For example, Kendall Healthcare Products Company established a German subsidiary to manufacture locally and market a broad line of products developed in the United States for German consumption. In this case, localized manufacturing makes sense because health-care product standards vary considerably from country to country. Moreover, the German health-care system has long been a major consumer of Kendall's products.[18]

Significance in Practice. Place design has several potential advantages. Each department or division is in direct contact with customers in its locale and can adapt more readily to their demands. Fast response is a major asset for organizations using place designs. For Hoechst Celanese Chemical Corporation, it means locating plants near raw materials or suppliers. Potential gains may include lower costs for materials, freight rates, and (perhaps) labor costs. In 1998, Hoechst opened a new plant in Singapore to serve the growing demand for its products in the Far East. It saved millions of dollars in shipping costs (from the United States) and was able to deliver products to customers in Hong Kong, Malaysia, and Laos much faster than before. For marketing, locating near customers might mean lower costs and/or better service. Salespeople can spend more time selling and less time traveling. Being closer to the customer may help them pinpoint the marketing tactic most likely to succeed in that particular region.

Organizing by place clearly increases control and coordination problems. If regional units have different personnel, purchasing, and distribution procedures, management may have difficulty achieving integration. Further, regional and district managers may want to control their own internal activities to satisfy local customers. Employees may begin to emphasize their own geographically based unit's goals and needs more than those of the organization as a whole. To help ensure uniformity and coordination, organizations such as the IRS, Southland (7-Eleven stores), Maytag, Sanyo, and Hilton Hotels make extensive use of rules that apply in all locations.

Product Design

Product design involves the establishment of self-contained units, each capable of developing, producing, marketing, and distributing its own goods or services. The Preview Case related how P&G used this type of design and emphasized pooled interdependence among its seven product lines. Figure 16.7 shows the product organizational structure of United Technologies, an organization that provides high-tech products to the aerospace, building systems, and automotive industries throughout the world.

Elisha Graves Otis, who invented the elevator in 1853, provided the foundation for what we know today as United Technologies.[19] Throughout its existence, various companies having widely different product lines, as illustrated in Figure 16.7, were added and deleted. Today, it is a $25 billion company organized around five distinct product lines. Note that, although these five product lines are all involved in technology, there is little overlap among them in terms of customers, distribution channels, and technology. That is, customers such as Boeing buy Pratt & Whitney jet engines but do no business with UT Automotive products. Each product line faces a different set of competitors and has crafted its business strategy to compete in its particular business environment. Pratt & Whitney's major competitor for jet engines is General Electric and it has developed a focused business strategy to compete in this market. In its Flight Systems product lines, customers for its Sikorsky helicopters include the major oil companies that use helicopters to shuttle crews to and from oil platforms in the ocean, hospitals that use them to move accident patients and the critically ill to their facilities, and the armed forces of the United States for troop movements. Managers handling this product line have little need to communicate with those manufacturing elevators as part of the Otis product line.

Significance in Practice. Most organizations that produce multiple goods or services, such as Morgan Stanley Dean Witter, United Technologies, and American

Figure 16.7 **United Technologies**

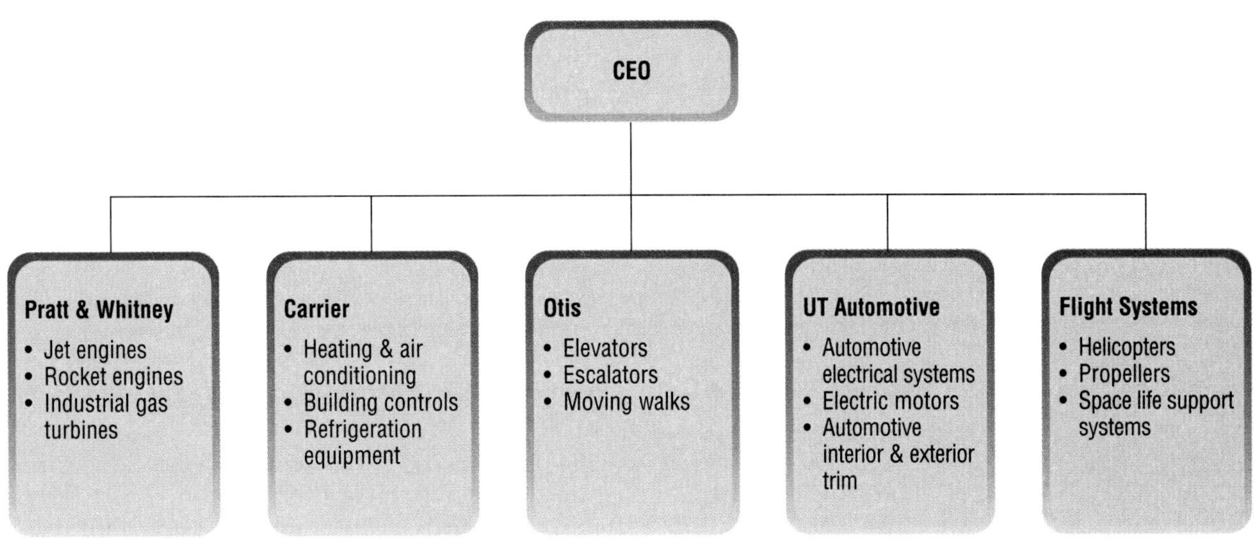

Source: http/www.utc.com

Brands, utilize a product design. It reduces the information overload that managers face in a purely functional organization design. Under a purely functional design, the vice president of marketing at United Technologies would have to be able to market a wide variety of products, understand the competitive forces in many industries, and focus on crafting a business strategy to compete in each industry. When the diversity of goods or services and types of customers reach a certain point, the creation of multiple marketing vice presidents (one vice president for each product line) to handle the complexity of the business can be more effective. Each division is then evaluated for its own performance. Moreover, a product design is an attractive alternative to a functional design when environmental and technological factors for each product line are different. Organizations with a product design usually begin with a functional design and then add some place design features as they begin to serve new geographic markets. Eventually, serving multiple customers creates management problems that can't be effectively dealt with by a functional or place design alone. The addition of new product lines, diverse customers, and technological advances also increases the complexity and uncertainty of the organization's business environment. When changing to a product design, however, companies usually don't completely discard functional or place designs. Instead, the product design may incorporate features of functional and place designs into the organization of each product division. For example, Otis Elevator has functional departments of advertising, finance, manufacturing, and distribution at each of its international plant locations in Russia, Japan, and Korea.

Multidivisional Design

A variation of the product design is the multidivisional design, sometimes referred to as the M-form.[20] In **multidivisional design,** tasks are organized by division on the basis of the product or geographic markets in which the goods or services are sold. Divisional managers are primarily responsible for day-to-day operating decisions within their units. Freed from these day-to-day operating responsibilities, top-level corporate managers concentrate on strategic issues, such as allocating resources to the various divisions, assessing new businesses to acquire and divisions to sell off, and communicating with shareholders and others. These top-level managers often are supported by elaborate accounting and control systems and specialized staff. Top-level corporate management may also delegate to product divisions the authority to develop their own strategic plans.

The following Managing Communication Competency feature describes Johnson & Johnson Corporation's multidivisional design. The company manufactures and markets a wide range of products, including anesthetics, Band-Aids, baby powder, and contact lenses. This account also reveals some of the company's efforts to overcome the limitations of this type of design.

COMPETENCY: MANAGING COMMUNICATION

JOHNSON & JOHNSON'S MULTIDIVISIONAL DESIGN

At Johnson & Johnson (J&J), the presidents of its 166 multidivisional companies aren't just encouraged to act independently—they're expected to do so. They travel at will and decide who will work for them, what products to produce, and which customers to sell to. They prepare budgets and marketing plans, and many oversee their own R&D operations. Although they are accountable ultimately to executives at corporate headquarters, some of the presidents see headquarters executives rarely and as rarely communicate with each other. The J&J approach "provides a sense of ownership and responsibility for a business that you simply cannot get any other way," says CEO Ralph S. Larsen.

However, this multidivisional design caused problems with some large customers. Dozens of J&J representatives called on the same customers (e.g., Wal-Mart and Kmart). But big retailers increasingly want to simplify their dealings with their suppliers by reducing the number of different representatives they have to deal with. Another concern for a multidivisional company is overhead expenses. Overhead at J&J was 41 percent of sales, compared with 30 percent for its more integrated rival, Merck & Company, and 28 percent for Bristol-Myers Squibb Company. At J&J, divisions perform their own purchasing, billing, and distribution functions. Duplication of these functions is part of the reason that J&J's overhead is relatively high.

The J&J organization design isn't static. Since taking over as CEO, Larsen has pushed the J&J companies to achieve more integration among common functions, such as payroll processing, computer services, purchasing, distribution, accounts payable, and employee fringe benefits. This push is intended to share the provision of more services efficiently among divisions to cut down on duplication of effort and improve communication with J&J's largest customers. Also, it helps streamline key activities (e.g., logistics and purchasing) among its businesses in serving key customers. To keep large retailers happy, J&J established "customer-support centers." The centers' employees work on-site with major retailers to ease distribution and ordering problems. Giant customers, such as Kmart, still get sales calls from dozens of different J&J units. But the goods from most of J&J's divisions are now delivered to retailers' warehouses in large single shipments. "We're very excited about it," says James A. Glime, manager of business development at Kmart. "This makes sense, and it certainly supports our business."

Larsen also launched an effort to unite customer service and credit functions. Code named Pathfinder, it replaced four separate departments that used to do credit reviews, sometimes on the same customers. "If a customer has a question about a delivery, they don't have to call the baby company, then our consumer-products organization, and so on," says Larsen. "They make one phone call to one person who specializes in them, and no matter where the problem is, that person takes care of it."[21]

For more information on Johnson & Johnson, visit this company's home page at ***www.johnsonandjohnson.com****.*

Significance in Practice. A multidivisional design eases problems of integration by focusing expertise and knowledge on specific goods or services. For example, the sales efforts of a single marketing department at a firm such as Johnson & Johnson would likely be ineffective in marketing products ranging from anesthetics to contact lenses to baby powder. Each product line is best handled by a department or division thoroughly familiar with it and its set of customers. Such a design clearly meets the needs of a company such as J&J, which provides diverse products to diverse customers (ranging from family-run pharmacies to global retailers to hospitals to government agencies) in geographic locations throughout the world.

One disadvantage of the multidivisional design is that a firm must have a large number of managerial personnel to oversee all the product lines.[22] Another disadvantage is the higher cost that results from the duplication of various functions by the divisions. Johnson & Johnson addressed it by combining some processes and introducing horizontal mechanisms to link its independent units in dealing with common issues.

Adoption of a multidivisional design often reduces the environmental complexity facing any one team, department, or division. Employees in a product-based unit can focus on one product line, rather than be overextended across multiple product lines. As with a functional design, an organization with a multidivisional design can deal with complex environments by adding horizontal mechanisms, such as linking roles, task forces, integrating roles, and cross-functional teams. Johnson & Johnson did so with its payroll, computer services, purchasing, distribution, accounts payable, and benefits functions. These activities are now shared by the product divisions, resulting in lower costs for Johnson & Johnson.

INTEGRATION ISSUES

Integration is the degree of collaboration and mutual understanding required among departments to achieve their goals. Integration may be either vertical or horizontal; here, we focus on horizontal integration. Integration is greatest between departments that are reciprocally interdependent and least when they are in a pooled interdependent relationship. Integration decisions are affected primarily by three interrelated variables:

Figure 16.8 **Variables That Affect Horizontal Relations between Units**

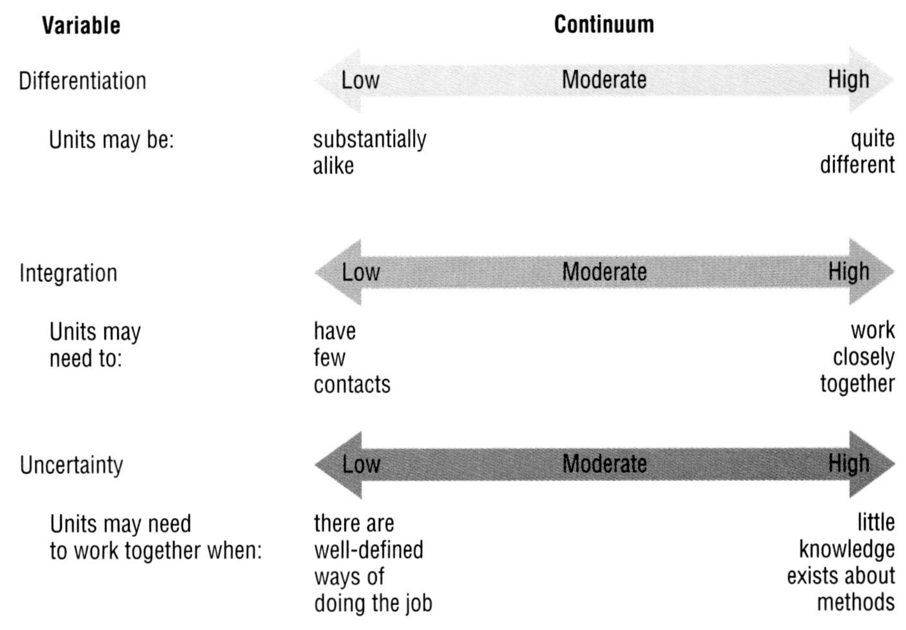

Variable	Continuum: Low	Moderate	High
Differentiation	Low	Moderate	High
Units may be:	substantially alike		quite different
Integration	Low	Moderate	High
Units may need to:	have few contacts		work closely together
Uncertainty	Low	Moderate	High
Units may need to work together when:	there are well-defined ways of doing the job		little knowledge exists about methods

(1) the level of horizontal departmental integration indicated; (2) the level of departmental differentiation desirable; and (3) the level of uncertainty (including task, workflow, and environmental) confronting each department. As Figure 16.8 shows, each variable has a range from low to high. The diagnosis of these variables and their impact on operations is a necessary step in designing an effective organization.

Horizontal Integration. **Horizontal integration** refers to the processes and mechanisms for linking dissimilar functions (teams and departments) laterally—for example, marketing and manufacturing.[23] An essential part of organization design is to determine the optimal amount of horizontal integration among individuals, teams, departments, and divisions. Management must be careful not to establish too much or too little horizontal integration. Too little probably will lead to lower quality decisions and the misuse of resources because each unit will "do its own thing." The costs associated with too much integration are likely to far exceed any possible benefits. With excessive horizontal integration, departments often get in the way of each other, rather than help each other perform their tasks and achieve their goals.

In Chapter 8, we discussed several approaches to fostering effective dynamics and outcomes between horizontally integrated and reciprocally interdependent teams. Achieving horizontal integration between products also is important. Recall that P&G achieved horizontal integration among its seven product divisions by merging various common functions at corporate headquarters. Many of the dynamics between teams apply to horizontal relations. From a design perspective, horizontal integration enables managers to cultivate and implement reciprocal interdependence on activities that span the organization. Horizontal integration processes and mechanisms include team goals and rewards, plans, linking roles, cross-functional teams, integrating roles and teams, and various groupware aids.

Differentiation. **Differentiation** is the degree to which departments differ in structure (low to high), members' orientation to a time horizon (short to long), managers' orientation to other people (permissive to authoritarian), and members' views of the task environment (certain to uncertain).[24] Production departments often have a high degree of formal structure with many rules and procedures, tight supervisory control, frequent and specific reviews of individual and departmental performance, and structured relationships among coworkers (mechanistic system). Research departments and planning departments often are just the opposite with their personnel needing open and close working relationships (organic system). Production workers have short time horizons (minutes, hours, and days) and think about immediate problems. Research and planning employees think in terms of months and even years into the future. In general, the greater the differences among departments, the greater is management's challenge to get them to work together (e.g., marketing with production).

Uncertainty. **Uncertainty** is the gap between what is known and what needs to be known to make decisions and perform tasks effectively. Factors that should be evaluated in determining the degree of uncertainty that a department faces include

- the completeness of information and guidelines available to help employees perform their tasks;
- the frequency with which departments can be expected to face problems that they have to solve jointly; and
- the probability that departments can be reasonably certain of the results of their independent and mutual efforts.

Significance in Practice. The combination of the three variables—horizontal integration, differentiation, and uncertainty—have several significant implications for organization design. The simplest situation involves low uncertainty, low differentiation, and low integration among departments. Such organizations produce standardized goods or services and are practically independent of each other. State Farm Insurance has designed regional offices that illustrate the effective use of such design.

Higher degrees of integration, differentiation, and uncertainty are more costly. They require greater expenditures of resources (e.g., time, personnel, and communications networks), an increase in the number of formal horizontal mechanisms (e.g., cross-functional teams), and the use of behavioral processes (e.g., reward systems and leadership and communication styles) to obtain integration. For example, extensive collaboration among manufacturing, marketing, planning, design, and engineering at General Motors and its Oldsmobile Division was required to create the new Aurora automobile.

The most difficult interdepartmental situation involves high differentiation, high integration, and high uncertainty. Organizations must expend even more resources and use a variety of horizontal mechanisms and behavioral processes to manage interdepartmental relations under such conditions.

Learning Objective:

4. Explain four newer organization designs—matrix, multinational, network, and virtual.

ORGANIZATIONS OF THE FUTURE

Four types of organization design—matrix, multinational, network, and virtual—have emerged in response to certain deficiencies in traditional organization designs and to rapid advances in technology.

MATRIX DESIGN

A **matrix design** is based on multiple support systems and authority relationships whereby some employees report to two superiors rather than one.[25] As Figure 16.9 illustrates, a matrix design usually involves a combination of functional and product

Figure 16.9 **Partial Illustration of Basic Matrix Design**

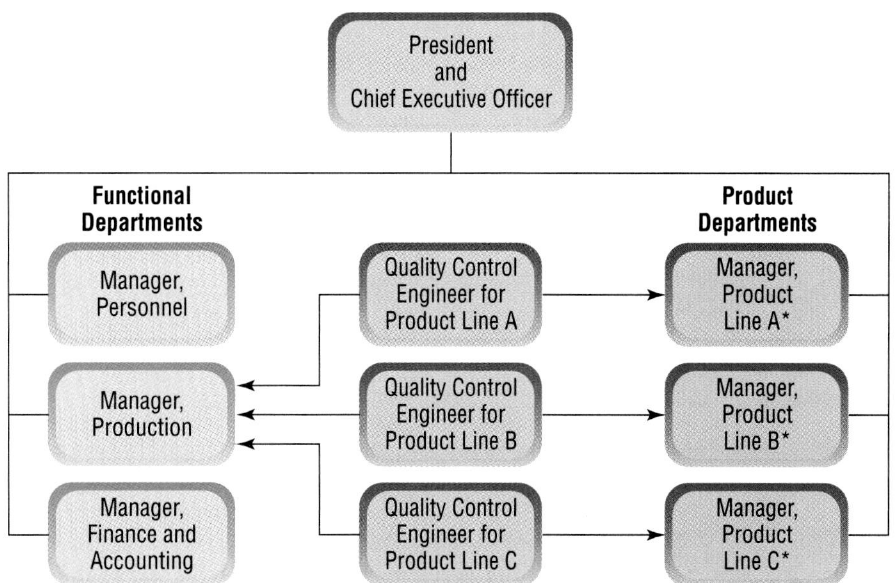

designs through the use of dual authority, information, and reporting relationships and networks. Every matrix contains three unique sets of role relationships: (1) the top manager, who heads up and balances the dual chains of command; (2) the managers of functional and product departments, who share subordinates; and (3) the managers (or specialists) who report to both a functional manager and a product manager. In an organization that has major operations throughout the world, matrix managers could be designated for each of the firm's main geographic areas (e.g., Europe, South America, North America, the Pacific Rim, and the Middle East).

Boeing, Lockheed Martin, and other aerospace companies were the first to use matrix design. Today, organizations in many industries (including chemical, banking, insurance, packaged goods, electronics, and computer) and fields (including hospitals, governmental agencies, and professional organizations) use various matrix design adaptations.

Typical Evolution. A matrix design typically evolves in stages.[26] The first stage may be the use of a temporary task force. Let's say that a task force composed of representatives from different departments or divisions of an organization is created to study a problem and make recommendations for its solution. Task force members retain their usual departmental affiliations (an engineer continues to report to the head of engineering and a market analyst to the head of marketing). However, these temporary members also are accountable to the task force's leader.

The second stage usually involves the creation of a permanent team or committee to address a specified issue or problem. Again, representatives from the various functional and product departments comprise the team, each representing individual departmental viewpoints.

The third stage may occur when a project manager is appointed and given the responsibility and authority for integrating the team's activities and inputs for its final output. Project managers often must negotiate or "buy" the human resources necessary to carry out the tasks from the managers of functional departments. With the appointment of project managers, an organization is well on the way to a matrix design and faces all the difficulties and benefits of multiple-authority relationships. These new relationships replace the simple, straightforward, single chain of command and are the distinguishing characteristic of the matrix design. Whereas the traditional hierarchical design rests on formal reward or position power, the matrix design demands negotiations by peers with a high tolerance for ambiguous power relationships. Managing these power relationships is one of the most challenging aspects of matrix design.

Significance in Practice. A matrix design may be appropriate when (1) employees must be highly responsive to both functional or product line (or place) concerns; (2) organizations face complex, dynamic environments coupled with unproved technologies that require employees to process lots of data and information; and (3) organizations have multiple products and limited resources. This type of design makes specialized, functional employees' knowledge available to all projects.[27] Also, it uses people flexibly, as employees are assigned to functional and product departments simultaneously.

A matrix design demands substantial managerial support while employees learn how to operate in the new organization. Learning may require two or three years because significant changes in attitudes and behaviors are required. Employees used to unity of command, a clear authority structure, and top-down directives may be uncomfortable with the dual-authority structure required under a matrix design. Special training programs often are needed to implement the new design. In order to work properly, a matrix design must maintain a continuing tension between multiple orientations (e.g., functional specialty and product line). This tension, in turn, requires effective interpersonal skills in communication, conflict resolution, and negotiation.

MULTINATIONAL DESIGN

Large multibusiness firms, such as General Motors, Toyota, Sanyo, and British Petroleum, operate in various countries, each of which has its own set of stakeholders. On the one hand, managers face pressures from their local environment to be "local insiders"; that is, design organizations that follow rules and regulations accepted as legitimate by local stakeholders. The saying "In Rome, do as the Romans do" applies. On the other hand, managers face pressures to be "company insiders"; that is, to design their organization to minimize coordination problems with company units in other countries, to manage a diverse set of company stakeholders, and to adhere to rules and regulations seen as appropriate by the company. The problem of operating companies in many countries presents enormous challenges for top managers. These multibusiness firms are called **multinational organizations** because they produce and sell products and/or services in two or more countries. According to a report released by the United Nations, recently there were more than 45,000 multinational organizations. The largest 500 accounted for 80 percent of the world's direct foreign investment. Of these 500, 443 were headquartered in the United States, the European Union, and Japan. Collectively, they have annual revenues in excess of $11 trillion and employ more than 35 million people. Additionally, these organizations produce a wide range of products such as autumobiles, chemicals, computers, industrial equipment, and steel. Clearly, these organizations have a significant impact on the global business world, and being employed by one of them will present ever greater challenges in the coming decades.[28]

A company can be global without necessarily being multinational. Boeing, for example, produces planes in the United States only, but works with a worldwide network of suppliers and subcontractors and sells planes all over the world. Companies can become multinational by setting up their own subsidiaries in other countries, by establishing joint ventures in other countries with local partners, or by acquiring companies. IBM, for example, has built up its worldwide network of subsidiaries by setting up wholly owned companies in a large number of countries. To become fully established in the U.S. auto market, Toyota entered into a joint venture with General Motors in California and then set up a wholly owned subsidiary 3 years later in the United States. It now produces cars and trucks at several U.S. locations.

A **multinational design** attempts to maintain coordination among products, functions, and geographic areas.[29] Meeting the need for extensive three-way cooperation is especially difficult because operating divisions are separated by distance and time. A further complication is that managers often are separated by culture and language. A "perfect" balance, if such were possible, would require a very complex matrix design. Hence most multinational designs focus on the relative emphasis that should be given to place and product organization design.

Basic Options. Figure 16.10 suggests the various combinations that might be selected in arriving at a multinational design. It also shows the likely effects of choosing a design based primarily on place or product. At Campbell Soup, strong delegation of authority by place gives country or regional managers the ability to respond and adapt to local food preferences. In contrast, product-line managers with worldwide authority may focus on achieving global efficiencies (integration) in production and universal (standard) products.

Significance in Practice. The forces generating more global integration in many industries include (1) the growing presence and importance of global competitors and customers, (2) the global rise in market demand for products, (3) new information technologies, and (4) efficient factories that can manufacture goods for customers throughout the world.[30] Worldwide product divisions in firms dealing with such forces are likely to dominate decisions, overpowering the interests of geographically based divisions. Pressures from national governments and local markets also may be

Figure 16.10 **Basic Options in Multinational Design**

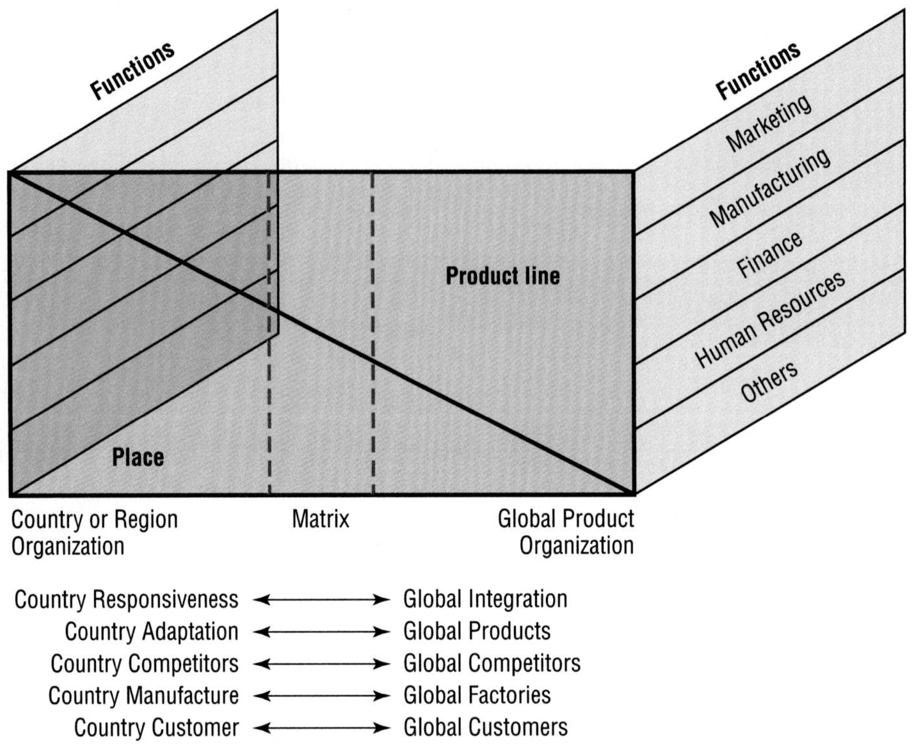

strong, often requiring multinational corporations to market full product lines in all the principal countries they serve. Marketing opportunities, however, may not be open to companies unless they negotiate terms with the host government. Therefore a worldwide product-line division may not be as effective at opening new markets as a geographically organized division because local managers can respond more effectively to local governments' concerns. A division operating under a place design often can establish relations with host governments, invest in distribution channels, develop brand recognition, and build competencies that no single product-line division could afford. Thus valid reasons still exist for country or regional (Europe, North America, Latin America, the Pacific Rim, and the Middle East) organization.

The Managing Across Cultures Competency feature on page 499 illustrates how Electrolux uses a multinational design that emphasizes global operations. It also reveals some of the tensions inherent in multinational design when top management tries to balance place, function, and product-line considerations. Originally founded in 1912, this Swedish company is best known for its vacuum cleaners. By the early 1960s, Electrolux was in serious financial difficulty primarily because of its limited product line, dated technology, and its product organization design. In the mid-1960s, Electrolux was bought by the Wallenbergs, a Swedish family that also had major holdings in other businesses, including Ericsson (telecommunications), Saab (automobiles), and Astra (pharmaceuticals). The Wallenbergs infused capital into Electrolux, but a slowdown in the European economy during the 1970s, forced it to sell off Electrolux's North American vacuum cleaner business. Since then, Electrolux has acquired more than 40 different companies throughout Europe.

Network Design

All the organization designs discussed so far have limitations that often hinder organizations in coping with turbulent environments and technologies. Tomorrow's organizations face two important trends. First, is the shift from traditional mechanistic systems

COMPETENCY: MANAGING ACROSS CULTURES

ELECTROLUX

Until the 1970s, the appliance industry in Europe had been segmented by national markets: differences in customer tastes and income levels, distribution channels, high transportation costs and governmental regulations and tariffs all played a part in ensuring that local markets were served by local producers. By the late 1970s, several European countries had formed a Common Market and the appliance industry started to go multinational. In response, Electrolux decided to redesign itself to become a multinational corporation, which required several significant changes.

First, the company needed to centralize its planning process so that products could be produced and introduced in several countries simultaneously. Local plants needed to be coordinated and share resources to achieve a common goal. Second, integration of management philosophy was needed. For example, when Electrolux acquired Zanussi, an Italian appliance maker, it needed to change Zanussi's hierarchical top-down mechanistic system to be more consistent with Electrolux's team-based, organic system. At Electrolux, managers were known by their first names throughout the organization, whereas at Zanussi, managers were addressed by their titles. Third, inefficiencies were rampant. Because of tailor-made specifications for different markets (e.g., Spain, Italy, and France), product development centers in Europe weren't being used efficiently. At one point, these centers were producing hundreds of different motors for vacuum cleaners and refrigerators, even though market research had revealed that the firm needed fewer than 10. Plant utilization was quite low, employment levels were high, and output per employee was unacceptably low. Similarly, Zanussi had too many staff people for its production level, and staff reductions were needed.

To gain some efficiency from being a multinational corporation, Electrolux tried to match staffing requirements with sales and limited the number of motors it was going to market around the world. Standardizing motors allowed Electrolux to develop a global product strategy, letting it change certain features for local market tastes but retaining a product's essential features. For example, when Electrolux introduced its new "Jet-System" washing machine that allowed people to use less detergent and reduced water consumption by one-third, it was able to introduce that product throughout Europe. Because nearly 70 percent of the company's production costs are in raw materials and components from external suppliers, Electrolux began to negotiate rates with a few suppliers for all product lines, thus achieving considerable standardization from its suppliers and lowering its costs by 17 percent. It also required all suppliers to make a commitment to quality and to use just-in-time (JIT) delivery systems for inventory. Currently, Electrolux organizes its businesses around product lines. These product lines (e.g., vacuum cleaners) have common distribution channels, technologies, customers, competitors, and geographic markets. Managers are responsible for all functions, including manufacturing, advertising, and sales, for their product lines.[31]

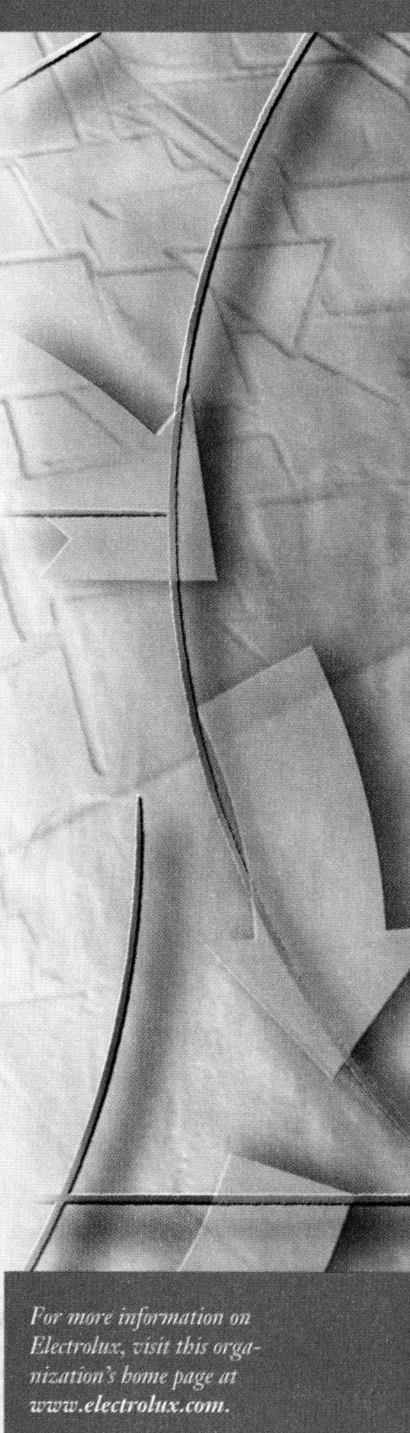

For more information on Electrolux, visit this organization's home page at www.electrolux.com.

to more organic systems. This shift is accompanied by the realization that an organization's competitive advantage lies in its ability to manage its knowledge assets, or human capital, more effectively. Doing so requires sharing and shifting power and decision making away from top management toward employees at all levels. Second, as multinational organizations become larger, subsidiaries within these are becoming geographically dispersed. There is a need to take into account and act on ideas of managers in foreign lands. General Electric sees itself as a "boundaryless" organization, noting that it wants people to behave entrepreneurially and share ideas across organizational lines.

A network design is intended to overcome those limitations and facilitate the management of highly diverse and complex organizations involving multiple departments and many people. A primary concern in all the other organization designs is how to allocate authority and resources among positions, teams, departments, and divisions. A **network design** focuses on sharing authority, responsibility, and resources among people and departments that must cooperate and communicate frequently to achieve common goals.[32] Various designs (functional, product, or place) must be applied in a network organization as the tasks to be performed and the goals to be achieved change.

Key Characteristics. A network design is sometimes called a spiderweb or cluster organization (as at Eastman Chemical). It resembles a mosaic of mutually interdependent departments and managerial processes. This mosaic can't be woven from typical organization charts that show vertical authority and reporting relationships. A network organization exists only when most of the following factors operate in support of one another.

- *Distinctive competence.* The organization maintains superiority through innovation and adaptation by combining resources in novel ways. Often these resources come from different parts of the organization.
- *Responsibility.* People who must collaborate to perform their tasks share responsibility. The organization's design includes extensive use of cross-functional, special-purpose, and self-managed teams.
- *Goal setting.* Common goals linked to satisfying the needs of one or more important external stakeholders (e.g., customers or clients, suppliers, shareholders, lenders, and governments) are formulated. Performance is less internally driven and more dependent on satisfying customers' needs or speeding up product development.
- *Communication.* The primary focus is on lateral rather than vertical communication. The information necessary to make decisions is widely shared and distributed, and open communication is the norm.
- *Information technology.* Many information technologies (including groupware) assist employees in networking internally (with others in the organization who may even be separated geographically by great distances) or externally (with customers, suppliers, regulatory agencies, and others). Typical information technologies and related groupware include e-mail, special PC software decision aids, voice mail, mobile phones, fax, telecommuting, teleconferencing, local and wide-area computer networks, and the like.
- *Organizational culture.* The culture has a bias toward the organic system and as few organizational levels as possible. The culture supports individual initiative and collaboration among individuals in teams.
- *Balanced view.* Individuals, teams, departments, and divisions do not view themselves as isolated islands having only their unique goals and ways of doing things. They view themselves in relation to others with common goals and rewards. Forms of cooperation and trust evolve over time, based on a history of past performance. The basic assumption of trust is that each person or department depends on resources controlled by others and that mutual gains are obtained by pooling resources and finding win–win solutions for all.

Significance in Practice. A network design is particularly effective in creating alliances of flexible partnerships.[33] Partners in an alliance could be customers, suppliers, and firms that would be defined as competitors under different circumstances. Corning, Inc., uses its 23 joint ventures with foreign partners such as Siemens (Germany), Samsung (South Korea), Asahi Chemical (Japan), and CIBA-GEIGY (Switzerland), to compete in a growing number of related high-tech markets. The flexibility with which Corning approaches its partnerships—letting the form be determined by the goals and letting the ventures evolve over time—is one reason for its success. But even more important is the time and effort expended by Corning executives to create the conditions for long-lasting, mutually beneficial relationships.

A network design is intended to create successful external relationships by having "six I's" in place: importance, investment, interdependence, integration, information, and institutionalization. Because the relationships are important, they get adequate resources, management attention, and sponsorship. Agreement to provide long-term investment tends to help equalize benefits and costs over time. The participants are interdependent, which helps maintain a balance of power. The participants are integrated in order to maintain essential points of contact and communication. Each partner is informed about the plans and directions of the other. Finally, when a network design is institutionalized, it is bolstered by a framework of supporting mechanisms from legal requirements to social ties to shared values. These mechanisms solidify trust.

Figure 16.11 shows a schematic representation of Eastman Chemical's new network design.[34] "Our organization chart is now called the pizza chart because it looks like a pizza with a lot of pepperoni sitting on it," says Ernest W. Davenport Jr., who as president is the "pepperoni" at the center of the pie. "We did it in circular form to show that everyone is equal in the organization. No one dominates the other. The space inside the circles is more important than the lines."[35]

The "pepperoni" in the individual "slices" represent the main cross-functional teams responsible for managing a key product line, a geographic area, a function, or a "core competence" in a specific technology or area such as innovation. The space around the "pepperoni" is where collaborative interaction is supposed to occur. The small pepperoni typically represent support teams (e.g., human resources) or special project teams that will be discontinued after their goals are accomplished.

Self-managed teams replaced several of the senior vice presidents who had been responsible for key functions. Instead of having a head of manufacturing, for example, the company now uses a team consisting of all its plant managers. This change was the most dramatic in the company's history according to Davenport. He further indicated that the teams have given managers and employees alike a much broader perspective and has brought decision making down at least one level in the organization.

In creating the new organization, the company's senior managers agreed that the primary role of the functions was to support Eastman's businesses in chemicals, plastics, fibers, and polymers. In other words, a function shouldn't have its own separate mission. But over the years, the functional departments had grown strong and powerful, often at the expense of the company overall as they fought to protect their own turf and build their own empires. The company's managers now work on at least one cross-functional team, and most work on two or more. Tom O. Nethery, a group vice president,

Figure 16.11 **Eastman Chemical's Network (Pizza) Design**

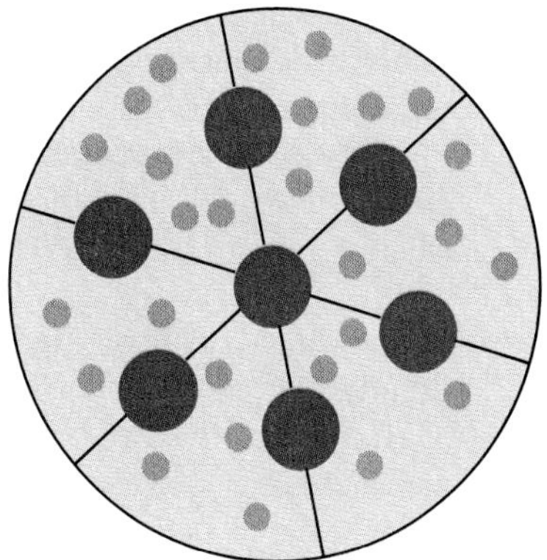

leads an industrial-business group. He also serves on three teams that deal with diverse issues such as human resources, cellulose technology, and product-support services.

Virtual Organization

The principal developments in information technologies over the past 10 years have both pushed and enabled organizations to move toward a virtual organization. A **virtual organization** is one whereby people use a computer network to work cooperatively and share knowledge quickly and easily regardless of time, distance, and organizational boundaries.[36] In a virtual organization users of sophisticated personal computers can easily tap company databases and work together as if they were in the same room. The PCs have videoconferencing capability, electronic blackboards, scanners, faxes, and groupware. These PCs are also connected to the company's intranet, which contains home pages for various functions and sources of information.

Four of the information technology advances that have enabled organizations to utilize a virtual form of organization design and fostered internal and external networking are open systems, distributed computing, real time, and global networking.

Open Systems. Portable software and compatible technology now exist and are widely used. These capabilities extend to the external network of suppliers, consumers, regulatory agencies, and even competitors. The shift is away from departments or divisions with their own unique computing capability to a network of linked business processes. In addition, organizations can be in closer touch with their customers, suppliers, and others, enabling people to act not only in their own self-interests, but with a shared vision and commitment. Open systems also mean that teams are free to work with other teams to pursue a common task. Often these other teams represent suppliers and customers.

Distributed Computing. Access and use have shifted from centralized computing where access was limited to a few people or departments to network computing whereby information is available to the primary users of that information. Centralized and limited access computing systems are typical of a mechanistic system. In contrast, planning, information processing, and the application of knowledge to business problems are being worked on and distributed throughout organic organizations by empowered individuals and teams.

Real Time. The new information technologies now capture information online and update databanks in real time. These capabilities provide an instantaneous, accurate picture of many processes, such as sales, production, and cash flow. At Frito-Lay, a real-time network allows the company's manufacturing plants to adjust continuously to changing market conditions. Just-in-time receipt of raw materials from suppliers and delivery of products to customers minimizes the need for warehousing and has permitted Frito-Lay to shift from mass production to custom online production. Customer orders arriving electronically can be processed instantly. Corresponding invoices are sent electronically and databases automatically updated.[37]

New software by Oracle and Siebel Systems enable organizations to gather and distribute up-to-the-minute sales forecasts and results from salespeople in the field who interact with each other through their companies' intranets.

Global Networking. Information networks are the backbone of virtual organization design.[38] Global networking permits both real-time communication and access of electronically stored information at will from anywhere in the world. For global organizations such as British Petroleum, Texas Instruments, Ford, Samsung, and NEC, a virtual organization design redefines time and space for employees, suppliers, customers, and competitors alike. At Ford, for example, the company is using the Web as a way for suppliers to work more closely with designers in the lab or on test sites. In a virtual design, any individual, team, or department can quickly communicate and share information with any other individual, team, or department. Work can be performed at a variety of locations, including employees' homes, with the office becoming part of a network rather than a place.

The following Managing Teams Competency feature illustrates how British Petroleum (BP) has used a virtual design to create problem-solving teams. British Petroleum employs more than 53,000 people, operates in 60 countries around the world, and has annual sales that exceed $70 billion. It explores for gas and oil reserves in the Gulf of Mexico, South America, western Africa, the Caspian Sea, the Middle East, and the Atlantic Ocean west of the Shetland Islands. Its exploration and development costs are among the lowest in the industry.

COMPETENCY: MANAGING TEAMS

BRITISH PETROLEUM'S VIRTUAL ORGANIZATION

When John Browne, BP's CEO, took over from David Simon in 1995, he knew that for BP to be successful, he had to develop an organization that learns and gets all employees involved in solving problems. He believed that the people closest to BP's assets and customers should make decisions.

To implement his strategy, he created virtual teams. These teams enable people separated by time, distance, and geography to share their knowledge. If it is easy for people to communicate, connect, and share knowledge, Browne believes that they will. To make doing so easier, BP produces videos that can be viewed on its intranet, has created electronic yellow pages that can be searched in a variety of ways, and encourages people to list interests, expertise, and experiences that they are willing to share with anyone who wants to contact them. BP's virtual organization relies on a growing system of sophisticated PCs that permit users to tap into BP's databases. All its PCs are connected to BP's intranet, which contains more than 40,000 home pages. These home pages are sites where functional experts describe the experience they have to offer. There are sites for sharing technical data on the muds used as drilling lubricants and for sharing information about processes that are available to reduce the amount of pipe that gets stuck in wells. There was a site where people concerned about how to get computers to handle the transition to the year 2000 (Y2K) could raise questions and exchange information. Brown's idea was to create an organization that would enable the best minds to solve a problem, even if it meant scouring the world for these people.

British Petroleum used the virtual team design to pass on lessons from its development of the Andrew oil field in the North Sea to contractors and suppliers. Using virtual teams, BP and its suppliers were able to figure out radical ways to cut the project's cost and time. People who had encountered similar exploration problems in the Gulf of Mexico shared information quickly with those in the Andrew field. BP also worked closely with contractors and shared cost concerns with them. By fully utilizing the expertise of its own people and working closely with contractors, BP saved an estimated $30 million or more in the Andrew field's first year of operation. But this estimate, according to Browne, doesn't take into account harder to measure benefits, such as the ability to see the expression in someone's eyes during a videoconference when that person makes a commitment. Each member of Browne's staff and each general manager of a business unit is a member of at least one virtual team. These teams allow people to share information with each other continuously. Browne recently participated in a management conference that connected people in Johannesburg with others in Singapore.[39]

For more information on British Petroleum, visit this company's home page at ***www.britishpetroleum.com.***

Significance in Practice. Virtual design is the latest type of organization design that managers are using to satisfy customer demands. A virtual design permits managers to change an organization's structure quickly to meet changing conditions and situations. Internal departments, job responsibilities, and lines of authority are shifted as needed. Boundaries between an organization and its customers and suppliers are blurred; indeed, some customers and suppliers begin to spend more time in the organization than some of its own employees. General Electric's thrust during the 1990s was to become ever more boundaryless, both internally and externally with customers and suppliers.

In addition to constantly re-creating organizational structures, a virtual organization has several other charactertistics.

- Its employees continually master new manufacturing and information technologies, speeding the production process and the flow of information through the organization.
- Its employees respond quickly to changing customer demands with customized products and services available at any time and place.
- Its employees are reciprocally interdependent. The entire workforce must be capable of mastering all the competencies needed to serve clients effectively.
- Its managers delegate authority and responsibility to employees while providing them with a clear vision of the organization's purpose and goals.

CHAPTER SUMMARY

1. Explain how environmental factors, strategic choices, and technological factors affect the design of organizations.

The environment facing an organization consists of all those stakeholders that are external to the organization, including customers, suppliers, competitors, and regulators, among others. A useful way to think about the environment is to characterize it along two dimensions: simple to complex and stable to dynamic. Combinations of these dimensions present various challenges. The choice of business strategy—low cost, focused, differentiation—has a direct impact on an organization's design. Organizations pursuing a low-cost strategy usually seek designs that emphasize functional departments (e.g., accounting, finance, marketing) and operate in simple–stable environments. Focused strategies are intended to help an organization target a specific niche within an industry. Organizations pursuing this strategy are typically organized by product and operate in complex–stable environments. Differentiation strategies are based on the organization's ability to provide customers with a unique product or service. Organized along product lines, these organizations operate in complex–unstable environments. Technological interdependence reflects the degree of coordination needed among departments to reach the organization's goals. We identified three types of interdependence: pooled, sequential, and reciprocal.

2. State the differences between mechanistic and organic systems.

If top management supports tight, centralized control of day-to-day decisions, a mechanistic system is more likely to be used than an organic one. Mechanistic systems are effective in stable environments, whereas organic systems are more effective in unstable environments.

3. Describe four traditional organization designs—functional, place, product, and multidivisional—and the requirements for their integration.

An organization facing a somewhat simple and stable environment can utilize a functional design effectively. Separated along various departmental lines, such as marketing, finance, human resources, top managers may integrate departments as needed. In place departmentalization, different geographical areas served by the organization face different environmental conditions. All functions are usually duplicated at each place. A product design emphasizes the nature of the organization's products and/or services. Each product is unique and requires special attention by top management. A multidivisonal form (M-form) is a product design that is useful to organizations that offer a wide array of products in geographically dispersed markets. Integration decisions are strongly influenced by three variables: the amount of horizontal integration desired, the amount of differentiation needed, and the amount of uncertainty facing the organization. The stronger the need for these three variables, the greater is the need for integration by top management. Integration can be achieved by task forces, ad-hoc project teams, formal planning activities, and cross-functional teams.

4. Explain four newer organization designs—matrix, multinational, network, and virtual.

A matrix design is based on multiple support systems and authority relationships whereby some employees report to two superiors rather than one. It usually involves some combination of functional and product designs. Employees come together to solve problems and then return to their own department or team. A multinational design attempts to maintain three-way organizational capabilities among products, functions, and geographic areas. Production in several countries presents enormous coordinating problems for managers who must adhere to headquarters policies and local customs at the same time. A network design emphasizes horizontal coordination for managing complex task interdependencies. This type of design also features the use of various information technologies that enable the organization to process vast amounts of data. A virtual design is based on the concept that people do not need to work face-to-face but may function well when connected electronically. Mainly used in high-tech organizations, this type of design cannot be effectively implemented without adequate electronic capabilities.

KEY TERMS AND CONCEPTS

Bureaucracy
Centralization
Chain of command
Complexity
Differentiation
Differentiation strategy
Division of labor
Dynamism
Environment
Focused strategy
Functional design
Hierarchy of authority
Horizontal integration
Impersonality
Integration
Low-cost strategy
Matrix design
Mechanistic system
Multidivisional design
Multinational design
Multinational organizations
Network design
Organic system
Organization design
Organizational culture
Place design
Procedures
Product design
Rules
Span of control
Strategic choices
Uncertainty
Unity of command
Virtual organization

DISCUSSION QUESTIONS

1. Do the changes in Procter & Gamble's organization design fit the demands of its environment?
2. What are the managerial competencies that Procter & Gamble's managers need to develop with its new design for the organization to reach its goals by 2005?
3. What is the basic strategy of a business organization with which you are familiar? What impact does this choice of strategy have on the design of this organization?
4. How does technological interdependence affect the design of Johnson & Johnson?
5. What do you see as the major strengths of Cisco's organization design? Its major weaknesses? What managerial competencies would you need to develop to work at Cisco?

6. The following are some reasons for organizational ineffectiveness.
   - Lack of goal clarity—strategic goals are not clear or linked to particular aspects of the organization's design.
   - Lack of internal alignment—the design of the organization is internally inconsistent.
   - Ineffective links to customers—the design does not effectively integrate the demands of customers.
   - Lack of external fit—the design does not fit the needs of the environment.

   Identify and describe briefly some organizations that you believe to be ineffective to illustrate these reasons.
7. Global managers must be capable of balancing the often-contradictory pulls of being locally responsive and globally efficient. How did Electrolux address these contradictory pulls? Should Electrolux adopt a virtual design? Support the rationale for your answer.
8. ARAMARK Corporation, a global provider of managed services, is organized by product line, including campus dining, business dining, uniform rentals, corrections (feeding prisoners), and sports and recreation (managing concessions at various sports arenas). The sports and recreation division, for example, in 1996 served more than 60,000 meals each day for 17 days at the Olympic Village in Atlanta, Georgia. What are some likely organization design problems that Joe Neubauer, ARAMARK's CEO, faces?
9. Does the choice of a mechanistic system fit well with the conditions facing McDonald's? British Petroleum? Cisco?
10. What practices typically found in mechanistic systems have to be changed when top management chooses a network design?

DEVELOPING COMPETENCIES

Competency: Managing Self—Inventory of Effective Design

Instructions: Listed are statements describing an effective organization design. Indicate the extent to which you agree or disagree with each statement as a description of an organization you currently work for or have worked for in the past. Write the appropriate number next to the statement.[40]

1. Strongly disagree
2. Disagree
3. Somewhat disagree
4. Uncertain
5. Somewhat agree
6. Agree
7. Strongly agree

_____ 1. Employees who try to change things are usually recognized and supported.
_____ 2. The organization makes it easy to get the skills needed to progress.
_____ 3. Employees almost always know how their work turns out, whether it is good or bad.
_____ 4. Employees have flexibility over the pace of their work.
_____ 5. Managers facilitate discussion at meetings to encourage participation by subordinates.
_____ 6. Few policies, rules, and regulations restrict innovation in this organization.
_____ 7. Boundaries between teams, departments, and divisions rarely interfere with solving joint problems.
_____ 8. There are few hierarchical levels in this organization.
_____ 9. Everyone knows how their work will affect the work of the next person or team and the quality of the final product or service.
_____10. The organization is well informed about technological developments relevant to its processes, goods, or services.
_____11. The organization is constantly trying to determine what the customer wants and how to meet customer needs better.
_____12. The organization can adapt to most changes because its policies, organization design, and employees are flexible.
_____13. Different parts of the organization work together; when conflict arises, it often leads to constructive outcomes.
_____14. Everyone can state the values of the organization and how they are used to make decisions.
_____15. A great deal of information is shared openly, as appropriate.

Scoring and Interpretation

Sum the points given to statements 1–15. A score of 75–105 suggests an effective organization design. A score of 70–89 suggests a mediocre design that probably varies greatly in terms of how specific aspects of the organization work for or against the design's effectiveness. A score of 50–69 suggests a great deal of ambiguity about the organization and how it operates. A score of 15–49 suggests that the design is contributing to serious problems.

Questions

1. What specific structures or processes in your organization led you to rate it as you did?
2. What competencies were most important for you in that organization?
3. What competencies do you think were most important for your manager?

Competency: Managing Change—Salomon

Salomon is a French manufacturer of outdoor sports equipment. Its revenues for 1998 exceeded FF5 billion ($US 840 million). The firm is global, with balanced sales in Asia, North America, and Europe. It is the world leader in winter sports gear, with a market share of 24 percent. In volume, Salomon is number one in downhill ski bindings (43 percent market share) and in cross-country skiing equipment (59 percent market share), and number two in downhill skis (21 percent market share) and downhill boots (23 percent market share). Salomon also serves the golf (Taylor Made), cycling (Mavic), and hiking boots markets. Each of its product lines has achieved a large market share through radical product technological innovation. For Salomon, technology is a means for achieving market share. It does not conduct basic research; rather it builds on its

Figure 16.12 **Salomon Organization Chart**

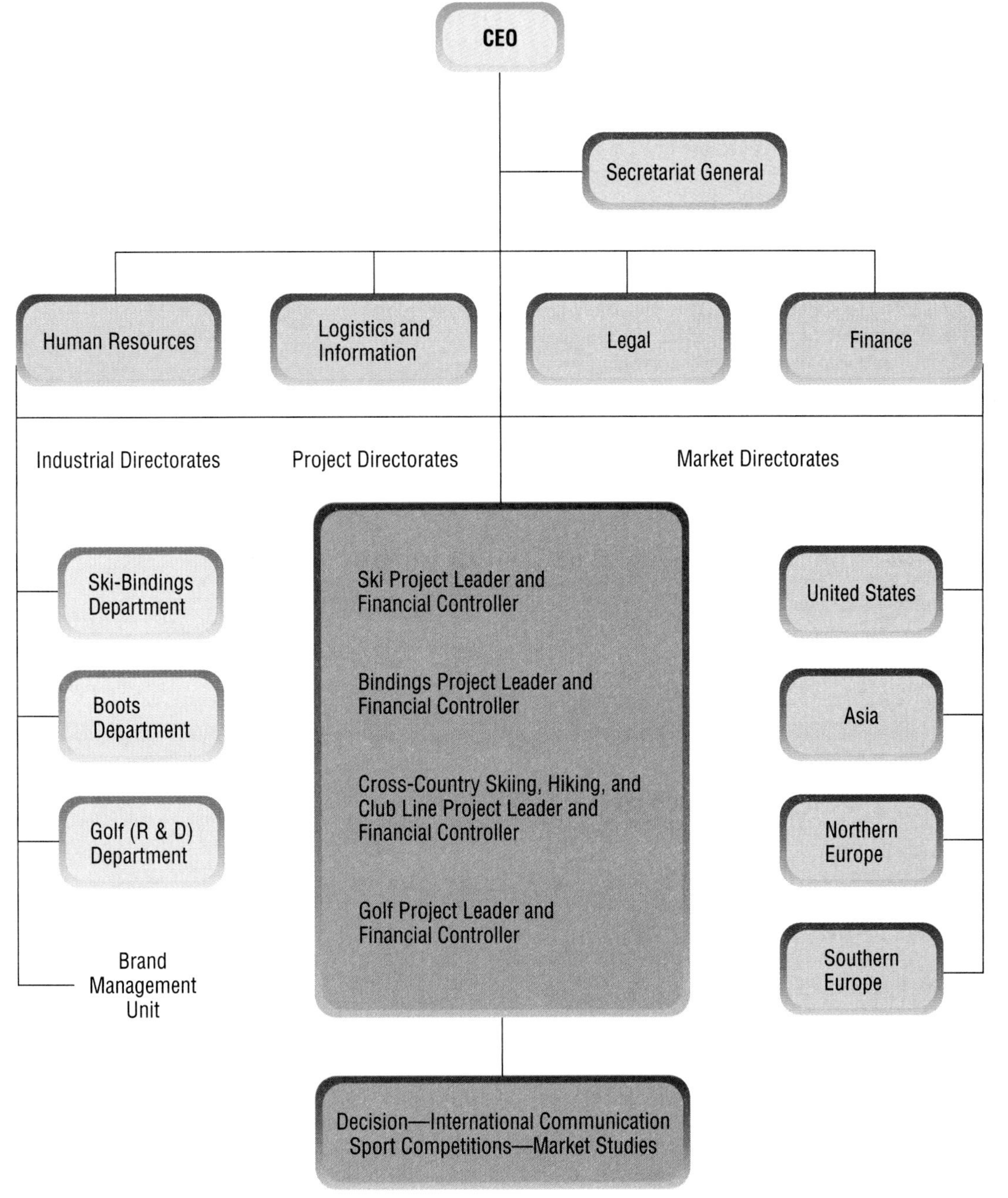

knowledge of advanced materials to develop new products. Its mastery of mechanical skills is essential for production of its ski bindings and cycles; its mastery of composite materials is essential for its production of skis and golf equipment for which gluing and decoration are essential.

Salomon's roots go back to 1947 when the Salomon family opened a workshop to manufacture saws and ski edges in Annecy, in the Haute Savoie region of France. In 1967, Salomon created a revolutionary technology by designing and selling the first ski bindings having a cable. In 1979, it entered the ski boot market by providing a rear-entry boot. By having a limited number of products, Salomon was able to become one of the world's principal manufacturers of ski boots in less than 3 years. In 1980, a Salomon team working in Scandinavia with a large customer developed a new boot and binding system for cross-country skiing. In 1984, Salomon purchased Taylor Made, a manufacturer of golf equipment, primarily in order to compensate for the seasonality of its winter sports lines. In 1994, with the purchase of Mavic, Salomon entered the cycling market (touring and mountain bikes). As had been the case with the purchase of Taylor Made, Mavic had a strong reputation for technological sophistication and innovation. During its history, Salomon has gone through several organization designs. To facilitate diversification into other products, it has moved from a functional structure to a divisional structure, as shown in Figure 16.12. The structure consists of the CEO, various staff functions, three functional directorates, three operational departments (i.e., ski bindings, boots, and golf), and a unit to manage the Salomon brand name. The industrial directorates have three missions: support technological innovation and advance the firm's industrial skills; create, develop, and produce products; and take responsibility for prices, total investment, and the cost structure. The project directorates have seven missions: facilitate relationships between the industrial directorates and the market directorates, formulate and implement product strategies, lead the projects, launch new products, guarantee the overall profitability of the product line, manage long-term planning, and support the creation of "cult products," or those that change the industry structure through its innovative technology. The market directorates have four missions: manage the leaders of subsidiaries, maintain margins and ensure profitability of the subsidiaries, develop sales and distribution channels, and forecast future growth in sales.

As shown in Salomon's organizational chart, the project directorates have been placed in a central position. These directorates play a fundamental interface role between the market directorates and industrial directorates, which often have different goals. They rely heavily on marketing development specialists in the industrial departments, on marketing distribution specialists in the market directorates, and on the brand management group (which has the responsibility for testing prototype products). This role requires the project directorates to gather large amounts of information during product development. All project leaders are located in headquarters to encourage face-to-face communication. They are also in constant communication with the financial controller to ensure compliance with a project's financial goals. The firm's innovation and development activities, which are crucial to the firm's success, encourage people to take on projects. Thus the project directorates play an essential role in the formulation and implementation of ideas, following the general direction set by the firm's top-management team.[41]

Questions

1. How would you characterize the environment in which Salomon operates?
2. What business strategy have Salomon's top managers chosen?
3. What are two potential strengths and limitations of Salomon's organization design?
4. What managerial competencies would you need in order to succeed at Salomon?

REFERENCES

1. Adapted from Parker-Pope, T. New CEO preaches rebellion for P&G cult. *Wall Street Journal*, December 11, 1998, B1ff; Benady, D. Procter and Gamble. *Marketing Week*, September 17, 1998, 16–17; Parker-Pope, T. P&G's new chief, never Procterized, loves a gamble. *Wall Street Journal*, December 15, 1998, B4; Address by Peper, J. Challenges for P&G. Amos Tuck School, Dartmouth College, January 28, 1999, Hanover, N.H.
2. Hamel, G., and Prahalad, C. K. *Competing for the Future.* Cambridge, Mass.: Harvard Business School Press, 1994.
3. Joyce, W. F. *Megachange.* New York: Free Press, 1999; also see Nadler, D. A., and Tushman, M. L. The organization of the future: Principles of design for the 21st century. *Organizational Dynamics*, Summer 1999, 45–60.
4. Pfeffer, J. *New Directions for Organization Theory: Problems and Prospects.* New York: Oxford University Press, 1997; also see www.carmike.com.
5. Porter, M. E. *Competitive Strategy.* New York: Free Press, 1980; Surowiecki, J. The return of Michael Porter. *Fortune*, February 1, 1999, 135–136.
6. Reichheld, F. F. *The Loyalty Effect.* Cambridge, Mass.: Harvard Business School Press, 1996.
7. Thompson, J. D. *Organizations in Action.* New York: McGraw-Hill, 1967.
8. Florent-Treacy, E., de Vries, M. K., and d'Avaucourt, R. *British Petroleum: Transformational Leadership in a Transnational Organization.* Foutainebleau, France: INSEAD, 1997.
9. Si, S. X. Knowledge transfer in international joint ventures in transitional economies: The China experience. *Academy of Management Executive*, 1999, 13(1), 83–90.
10. Sprout, A. L. The Internet inside your company. *Fortune*, November 27, 1995, 164.
11. Burns, T., and Stalker, G. *The Management of Innovation.* London: Social Science Paperbacks, 1961, 96–125.

12. Adapted from Weber, M. *The Theory of Social and Economic Organization* (trans., Parsons, T.). New York: Oxford University Press, 1947, 329–334.
13. Smith, A. *An Inquiry into the Nature and Causes of the Wealth of Nations* (1776). *New York:* Modern Library, reprint 1937, 48.
14. Hellriegel, D., Jackson, S. E., and Slocum, J. W., Jr. *Management*, 8th ed. Cincinnati: South-Western, 1999, 40–58.
15. See www.callawaygolf.com/99site.
16. Adapted from Mardesich, J. Cisco's plan to pop up in your home. *Fortune*, February 1, 1999, 119–120; Byrne, J. A. The corporation of the future. *Business Week*, August 31, 1998, 104–106.
17. Kostova, K., and Zaheer, S. Organizational legitimacy under conditions of complexity: The case of the multinational enterprise. *Academy of Management Review*, 1999, 24, 64–81; Ireland, R. D., and Hitt, M. A. Achieving and maintaining strategic competitiveness in the 21st century: The role of strategic leadership. *Academy of Management Executive*, 1999, 13(1), 43–57.
18. Morrison, A. J., Ricks, D. A., and Roth, K. Globalization versus regionalization: Which way for the multinational? *Organizational Dynamics*, Winter 1991, 17–29.
19. See www.utc.com.
20. Jones, G., and Hill, C. Transaction cost analysis of strategy structure choice. *Strategic Management Journal*, 1988, 19, 159–172.
21. Adapted from Ettore, B. James Burke: The fine art of leadership. *Management Review*, 1996, 85(10), 13–17; also see www.jnj.com.
22. McGrath, R. G., Jer-Chen, M., and MacMillan, I. C. Multimarket maneuvering in uncertain spheres of influence: Resource diversion strategies. *Academy of Management Review*, 1998, 23, 724–740.
23. Galbraith, J. R. *Competing with Flexible Lateral Organizations.* Reading, Mass.: Addison-Wesley, 1996.
24. Lawrence, P. R. Organization and environment perspective: The Harvard research program. In A. H. Van de Ven and W. F. Joyce (eds.), *Perspectives on Organization Design and Behavior.* New York: John Wiley & Sons, 1981, 311–337.
25. Joyce, W. F., McGee, V. E., and Slocum, J. W., Jr. Designing lateral organizations: An analysis of the benefits, costs, and enablers of nonhierarchical organizational forms. *Decision Sciences*, 1997, 28, 1–26.
26. Ford, R. C., and Randolph, W. A. Cross-functional structures: A review and integration of matrix organization and project organization. *Journal of Management*, 1992, 18, 267–294.
27. Lei, D., Slocum, J. W., Jr., and Pitts, R. A. Designing organizations for competitive advantage: The power of unlearning and learning. *Organizational Dynamics*, Winter 1999, 24–38.
28. Chandler, A. The functions of the HQ unit in the multibusiness firm. In R. Rumelt, D. Schendel, and D. Teece (eds.), *Fundamental Issues in Strategy.* Boston: Harvard Business School Press, 1994, 323–360; Larsson, R., and Finkelstein, S. Integrating strategic, organizational and human resource perspectives on mergers and acquisitions. *Organization Science*, 1999, 10, 1–26.
29. Zahra, S. A. The changing rules of global competitiveness in the 21st century. *Academy of Management Executive*, 1999, 13(1), 36–42; Sanders, W. G., and Carpenter, M. A. Internationalization and firm governance: The roles of CEO compensation, top team composition and the board structure. *Academy of Management Journal*, 1998, 41, 158–178.
30. Moingeon, B., Ramanantsoa, B., Metais, E., and Orton, J. D. Another look at the strategy–structure relationships: The resource-based view. *European Management Journal*, 1998, 16, 297–305
31. Ancona, D., Kochan, T. A., Scully, M., Van Maanen, J., and Westney, D. E. *Organizational Behavior & Processes.* Cincinnati: South-Western, 1999, 9–20.
32. Miles, R. E., and Snow, C. C. The new network firm. *Organizational Dynamics*, Spring 1995, 5–18.
33. Kraatz, M. S. Learning by association? Interorganizational networks and adaptation to environmental change. *Academy of Management Journal*, 1998, 41, 621–643.
34. Adapted from Birchard, B. Closing the strategy gap. *CFO:The Magazine for Senior Financial Executives*, October 1996, 26–34; also see www.eastman.com.
35. Hansen, M. T. Combining network centrality and related knowledge: Explaining effective knowledge sharing in multiunit firms. Unpublished manuscript, Harvard Business School, 1999; Birkinshaw, J. Corporate entrepreneurship in network organizations: How subsidiary initiative drives internal market efficiency. *European Management Journal*, 1998, 16(3), 355–364.
36. Thomas, H., Pollock, T., and Gorman, P. Global strategic analyses: Frameworks and approaches. *Academy of Management Executive*, 1999, 13(1), 70–82; Boudreau, M. C., Loch, K. D., Robey, D., and Straud, D. Going global: Using information technology to advance the competitiveness of the virtual transnational organization. *Academy of Management Executive*, 1998, 12(4), 120–128.
37. Personal conversation with R. Sorrentino, senior manager, Deloitte & Touche LLP, Dallas, Texas, August 1999; also see Townsend, A. M., DeMarie, S., and Hendrickson, A. R. Virtual teams: Technology and the workplace of the future. *Academy of Management Executive*, 1998, 12(3), 17–29.
38. Hitt, M. A., Keats, B. W., and DeMarie, S. M. Navigating in the new competitive landscape: Building strategic flexibility and competitive advantage in the 21st century. *Academy of Management Executive*, 1998, 12(4), 22–42.
39. Adapted from Prokeach, S. E. Unleashing the power of learning: An interview with British Petroleum's John Browne. *Harvard Business Review*, September–October, 1997, 147–168.
40. Adapted from Pasmore, W. A. *Designing Effective Organizations: The Sociotechnical Systems Perspective.* New York: John Wiley & Sons, 1988, 157–186.
41. Adapted from Moingeon, B., et al., 297–305.

CHAPTER

17

Organizational Culture

LEARNING OBJECTIVES

When you have finished studying this chapter, you should be able to:

1. Explain how organizational cultures are developed, maintained, and changed.
2. Describe four types of organizational culture.
3. Identify the potential relationships between organizational culture and performance.
4. Discuss how organizational culture can influence the ethical behavior of employees.
5. Explain the importance of effectively managing cultural diversity.
6. Describe the process of organizational socialization and its relationship to organizational culture.

Preview Case: *DaimlerChrysler's Diverse Cultures*

DYNAMICS OF ORGANIZATIONAL CULTURE

Competency: Managing Self—*Gene Veno Finds a Cultural Fit*

Developing Organizational Culture

Competency: Managing Across Cultures—*Pharmacia & Upjohn*

Maintaining Organizational Culture

Changing Organizational Culture

Competency: Managing Change—*Harley-Davidson: Learning Organization*

TYPES OF CORPORATE CULTURES

Bureaucratic Culture

Clan Culture

Entrepreneurial Culture

Market Culture

Competency: Managing Teams—*Conflict at Andersen Worldwide*

Organizational Implications

PERFORMANCE AND ORGANIZATIONAL CULTURE

Strong Cultures

Cautionary Notes

ETHICAL BEHAVIOR AND ORGANIZATIONAL CULTURE

Impact of Culture

Whistle-Blowing

MANAGING CULTURAL DIVERSITY

Significant Challenges

Competency: Managing Communication—*Marriott Marquis*

Some Guidelines

ORGANIZATIONAL SOCIALIZATION

Socialization Process

Socialization Outcomes

CHAPTER SUMMARY

Key Terms and Concepts

Discussion Questions

DEVELOPING COMPETENCIES

Competency: Managing Ethics—*Assessing a Culture's Ethical Behaviors*

Competency: Managing Teams—*Southwest Airlines' Team Culture*

PREVIEW CASE

DAIMLERCHRYSLER'S DIVERSE CULTURES

In a windowless conference room 15 stories below the executive suite, seven German and American employees of DaimlerChrysler are in a deep debate over the newly merged automaker's future. At the heart of the debate is the fact that, after the formal merger of the two organizations, the new corporation remains essentially two separate companies, one German and one American. Why?

If DaimlerChrysler is to become a global organization, it must convince employees at all levels that moving around the world is important. Dozens of teams are now shuttling between the company's dual headquarters in Stuttgart, Germany, and Auburn Hills, Michigan. In 1999, the company wanted to move 60 employees between Germany and the United States on jobs lasting between 2 and 5 years. There were few takers. Part of the problem has to do with personal concerns: Most American don't speak German and don't want to leave their spacious U.S. homes for apartments or smaller houses in Stuttgart, where real estate is far more expensive. However, DaimlerChrysler is providing **expats** (those who live in a foreign country while maintaining residence in another) 3 months' salary to cover miscellaneous expenses for setting up housing arrangements; all moving expenses, including hotels and meals, and a salary bonus if the cost of living in the new country was higher than in the United States.

The crux of the problem lies in the differences in the corporate cultures of the two companies. Chrysler managers want to operate by using a low-cost business strategy. They want advertisements for new cars to be placed on the Internet, reducing the need for elaborate four-color brochures that focus on reliability, efficiency, and an easygoing lifestyle. Daimler managers want glossy four-color brochures that emphasize distinctiveness, wealth, and demanding engineering. While both groups debated the brochure, they agreed upon the brochure's colors of blue and yellow. Ms. Vahdiek, the Daimler lawyer, noted that those were also the colors of Lufthansa, the German airline. Mr. Wilhelm, Chrysler's human resource representative, noted that these were the colors of the University of Michigan.

In Germany, meetings would last all day and then all the managers would go out to dinner. In Stuttgart, the group usually dined at Dopo, an Italian restaurant with a good wine list. Over dinner, the real issues surfaced. The Americans wanted to use video-conferencing or conference calls in an effort to reduce the 14 hours of travel time between their locations in the United States and Stuttgart and the expense involved. The Americans pictured their German counterparts as "running around with steel helmets and always saying 'Yes, General.'" The Germans pictured the Americans as "cowboys—always shooting from the hip."

Another difference is that the American and German managers had different notions of what is valued. In the old Chrysler organization, "empowerment" was practiced. Employees had access to senior managers and addressed them by first name. At Daimler, employees focused on social justice. Titles, office location, and other perks were important status symbols that dictated power and authority relationships among employees. The differences in these corporate values created stumbling blocks for the development of effective cross-cultural teams. The Daimler managers perceived that the Chrysler managers only wanted to see results and were not detail-oriented. Conversely, the Americans believed that the Daimler managers were more process-oriented, too slow in accomplishing their goals, and very detail-oriented. Finally, Chrysler was a much less global company than Daimler, so it placed less value on international assignments as stepping-stones for its managers. Most Daimler managers, however, had lived outside of Germany at some point in their careers. Taking an international assignment was a necessary step in their professional development to broaden their managing across cultures and managing self competencies.[1]

The competencies and values of employees and managers do not fully determine the effectiveness and success of an organization. As illustrated by the Preview Case, both Chrysler and Daimler had invisible qualities—certain styles, character, and ways of doing things—that were more powerful than the dictates of any one person or any formal system. To understand the soul of an organization requires that we plunge below the charts, rule books, machines, and buildings into the deeper world of organizational culture.[2]

In this chapter, we examine the concept of organizational culture and how such cultures are formed, maintained, and changed. We also explore some possible relationships between organizational culture and performance; the relationship between organizational culture and ethical behavior; the challenge of managing a culturally diverse workforce; and, finally, how organizations socialize individuals into their particular cultures. We begin with a brief overview of what organizational culture is and how organizational cultures are developed, maintained, and changed.

Learning Objective:

1. Explain how organizational cultures are developed, maintained, and changed.

DYNAMICS OF ORGANIZATIONAL CULTURE

Organizational culture represents a complex pattern of beliefs, expectations, ideas, values, attitudes, and behaviors shared by the members of an organization.[3] More specifically, organizational culture includes

- routine behaviors when people interact, such as organizational rituals and ceremonies and the language commonly used;
- the norms that are shared by teams throughout the organization, such as "a fair day's work for a fair day's pay";
- the dominant values held by an organization, such as "product quality" or "price leadership";
- the philosophy that guides an organization's policies toward its employees and customers;
- the rules of the game for getting along in the organization or the "ropes" that a newcomer must learn in order to become an accepted member; and
- the feeling or climate conveyed in an organization by the physical layout and the way in which managers and employees interact with customers and other outsiders.[4]

None of these components individually represents the culture of the organization. Taken together, however, they reflect and give meaning to the concept of organizational culture. Using these six attributes, how would you describe Chrysler's culture? Daimler's? These descriptions should give you some insight into why the merger has not gone as smoothly as each company would have liked.

As indicated by Figure 17.1, organizational culture exists on several levels, which differ in terms of visibility and resistance to change. The least visible or deepest level is that of basic **shared assumptions,** which represent beliefs about reality and human nature that are taken for granted. For example, a basic assumption that still guides some organizations in the development of reward systems, rules, and procedures is that employees are naturally not highly motivated and must be tightly controlled in order to enhance their performance.

The next level of culture is that of **cultural values,** which represent collective beliefs, assumptions, and feelings about what things are good, normal, rational, valuable, and so on.[5] Cultural values might be very different in different organizations; in some, employees may care deeply about money, but in others, they may care more about technological innovation or employee well-being. These values tend to persist over time even when organizational membership changes.

The next level is that of **shared behaviors,** including norms (see Chapter 8), which are more visible and somewhat easier to change than values. The reason, at least in part, is that people may be unaware of the values that bind them together.

Figure 17.1 **Levels of Organizational Culture**

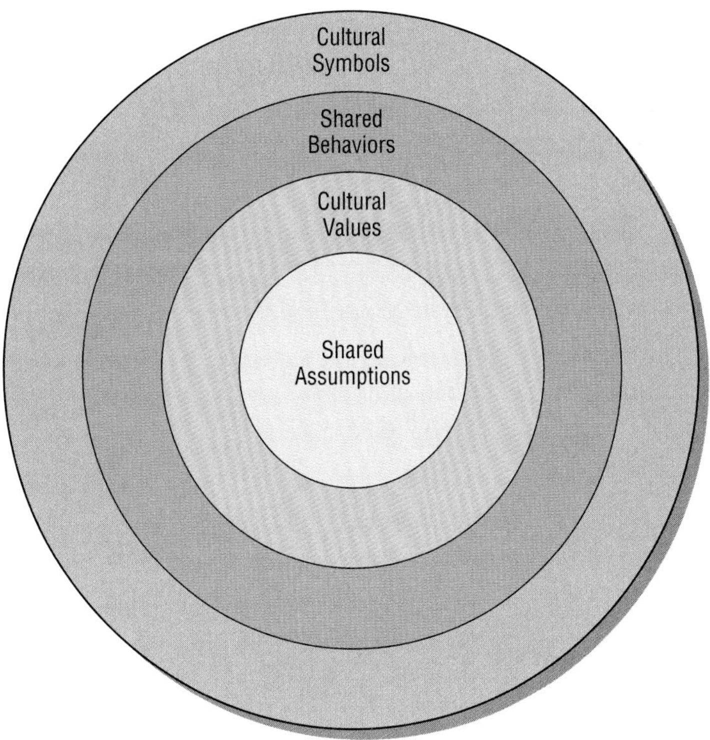

Source: Adapted from Cummings, T. G., and Worley, C. G. *Organization Development and Change*, 6th ed. Cincinnati: South-Western, 1997.

The Managing Self Competency feature on page 514 highlights what happens when a person and the culture of an organization clash. Gene Veno's story reveals the perils of cultural conflict.

The most superficial level of organizational culture consists of symbols. **Cultural symbols** are words (jargon or slang), gestures, and pictures or other physical objects that carry a particular meaning within a culture.[6] Someone entering the Dallas Police Department encounters symbols of authority and spartan surroundings, including physical barriers between employees and clients; the attire of receptionist; emblems of authority, such as the American flag, seals, certificates, photos of various city leaders, and signs prohibiting certain behaviors; and hard straight chairs, vending machines, and instructions. In contrast, someone entering the lobby of OxyChem encounters warmth, including comfortable chairs and soft couches, decorative pictures, plants and flowers, reading materials, and a badge giving the receptionist's name.

The cultural symbols of McDonald's also convey a uniform meaning. McDonald's restaurants are typically located in rectangular buildings with large windows to let the sun in and with neatly kept surroundings. Parking lots are large and paved; there is rarely any visible litter. A drive-in window means that speedy service is available. The most prominent symbol is the golden arch sign that towers over the building, where zoning laws permit. Inside, bright colors and plants create a homey atmosphere. Glistening stainless steel appliances behind the counter provide an up-to-date, efficient, and sanitary appearance. Above all, everything is clean. Cleanliness is achieved by endless sweeping and mopping of floors, rapid removal of garbage, instant collecting of dirty trays and cleaning of spills, washing of windows to remove fingerprints, cleaning of unoccupied tables, and constant wiping of the counter. Both the interior and exterior convey cultural symbols of predictability, efficiency, speed, courtesy, friendliness, and cleanliness.

COMPETENCY: MANAGING SELF

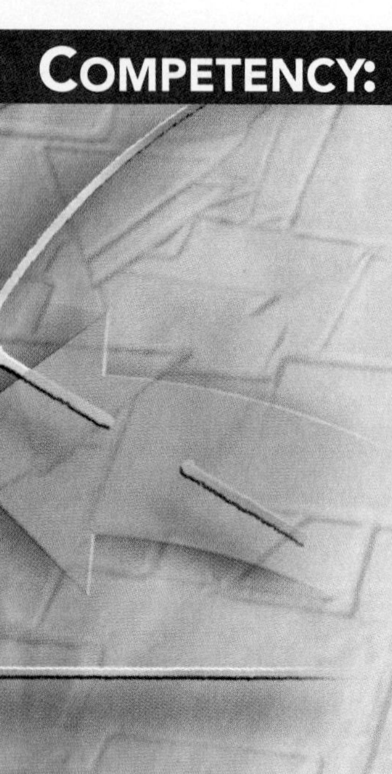

GENE VENO FINDS A CULTURAL FIT

Gene Veno finally relented after 2 years of recruiting efforts and made the leap from his health-care consulting practice to executive vice president for a large, managed care company. He stated, "I knew the day I got there the culture was wrong for me. Everything was computer-driven, not relationship-driven."

Five years later, the experience prompted him to dig deeper before moving to his next job. Veno took a job as executive vice president of the Pennsylvania Chiropractic Association, a group he used to represent as a consultant. He looked at the organization's charitable efforts—something that's important to him. He also asked himself, Does the organization demonstrate commitment to its people? Does it show appreciation to its people?

He remembered when he was a consultant and yet the organization gave him a plaque for service. He also liked the organization's willingness to discuss its problems without political infighting.

According to Dennis Kreiger, an executive recruiter, "When something isn't working out, it's almost always cultural fit. People should not be seduced by the job or money, but rather should look for telltale clues about a culture mismatch."[7]

Organizational culture is at least as important for employees as it is for managers. As managers and employees at DaimlerChrysler discovered, achieving a good match between the values of the organization and employee is a two-part task. First, potential employees must figure out what the organization values. Second, potential employees must identify organizations that share their personal values. You can address the first task by making a list of the eight values that are most characteristic of your ideal workplace and the eight that are least characteristic from the 54 values in Table 17.1. Then return to the Preview Case: What are Daimler's values? Chrysler's?

DEVELOPING ORGANIZATIONAL CULTURE

An organizational culture forms in response to two major challenges that confront every organization: (1) external adaptation and survival and (2) internal integration.[8]

External adaptation and survival has to do with how the organization will find a niche in and cope with its constantly changing external environment. External adaptation and survival involves addressing the following issues.

- *Mission and strategy:* Identifying the primary purpose of the organization; selecting strategies to pursue this mission.
- *Goals:* Setting specific targets to achieve.
- *Means:* Determining how to pursue the goals, including selecting an organizational structure and reward system.
- *Measurement:* Establishing criteria to determine how well individuals and teams are accomplishing their goals.

Internal integration has to do with the establishment and maintenance of effective working relationships among the members of an organization. Internal integration involves addressing the following issues.

- *Language and concepts:* Identifying methods of communication and developing a shared meaning for important concepts.

Table 17.1

What Do You Value at Work?

The 54 items listed below cover the full range of values you'd likely encounter at an organization. Please divide it into two groups—the 27 that would be most characteristic of your ideal workplace and the 27 that would be the least characteristic. Keep halving the group until you have a rank ordering, then fill in your top and bottom eight choices. Please be sure that you choose four values from the **YOU ARE** list and four values from **YOUR COMPANY OFFERS** list. Test your fit at a firm by seeing whether the company's values match your top and bottom eight.

Top Eight Choices

Bottom Eight Choices

The Choice Menu

YOU ARE: 1. Flexible 2. Adaptable 3. Innovative 4. Able to seize opportunities 5. Willing to experiment 6. Risk-taking 7. Careful 8. Autonomy-seeking 9. Comfortable with rules 10. Analytical 11. Attentive to detail 12. Precise 13. Team-oriented 14. Ready to share information 15. People-oriented 16. Easygoing 17. Calm 18. Supportive 19. Aggressive 20. Decisive 21. Action-oriented 22. Eager to take initiative 23. Reflective 24. Achievement-oriented 25. Demanding 26. Comfortable with individual responsibility 27. Comfortable with conflict 28. Competitive 29. Highly organized 30. Results-oriented 31. Interested in making friends at work 32. Collaborative 33. Eager to fit in with colleagues 34. Enthusiastic about the job

YOUR COMPANY OFFERS: 35. Stability 36. Predictability 37. High expectations of performance 38. Opportunities for professional growth 39. High pay for good performance 40. Job security 41. Praise for good performance 42. A clear guiding philosophy 43. A low level of conflict 44. An emphasis on quality 45. A good reputation 46. Respect for the individual's rights 47. Tolerance 48. Informality 49. Fairness 50. A unitary culture throughout the organization 51. A sense of social responsibility 52. Long hours 53. Relative freedom from rules 54. The opportunity to be distinctive, or different from others

Source: Adapted from Siegel, M. The perils of culture conflict. *Fortune*, November 9, 1998, 259; Chatman, J. A. and Jehn, K. A. Assessing the relationship between industry characteristics and organizational culture: How different can they be? *Academy of Management Journal*, 1994, 37, 522–553.

- *Group and team boundaries:* Establishing criteria for membership in groups and teams.
- *Power and status:* Determining rules for acquiring, maintaining, and losing power and status.
- *Rewards and punishments:* Developing systems for encouraging desirable behaviors and discouraging undesirable behaviors.[9]

An organizational culture emerges when members share knowledge and assumptions as they discover or develop ways of coping with issues of external adaptation and internal integration. Figure 17.2 shows a common pattern in the emergence of organizational cultures. In new companies, such as Dell Computers, Intel, and Microsoft, the founder or a few key individuals may largely influence the organization's culture. Later in the life of the organization, its culture will reflect a complex mixture of the assumptions, values, and ideas of the founder or other early top managers and the subsequent experiences of managers and employees.

The national culture, customs, and societal norms of a country also shape the cultures of organizations operating in it. The dominant values of a national culture may be reflected in the constraints imposed on organizations by others. For example, a country's form of government may have a dramatic impact on how an organization does business. In addition, the members of the organization have been raised in a particular society and thus bring the dominant values of the society into the firm. For example, in the United States individuals learn values such as freedom of speech and respect for individual privacy from the nation's cultural values. Thus the presence or absence of these and other values within the larger society has implications for organizational behavior. Finally, increased global operations have forced awareness that differences in national cultures may have a significant impact on organizational effectiveness. Multinational corporations have discovered that organizational structures and cultures that might be effective in one part of the world may be ineffective in another. The following Managing Across Cultures Competency feature illustrates the impact of both the Swedish and U.S. culture on Pharmacia & Upjohn, a company created through a merger. Because they were in the same industry, the two firms shared some common values, but these commonalties seemed small in light of the differences between them.

Figure 17.2 **One Common Pattern in the Emergence of Corporate Cultures**

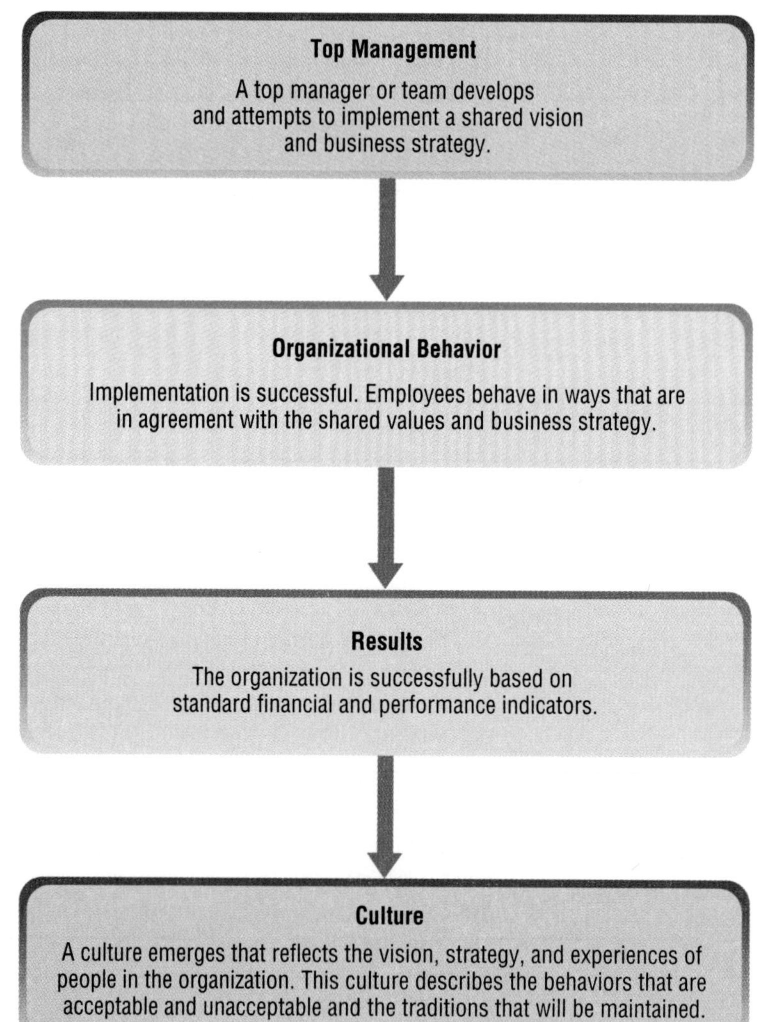

Source: Adapted from Kotter, J. P., and Heskett, J. L. *Corporate Culture and Performance*. New York: Free Press, 1992, 8.

malized a guaranteed continuous employment policy in 1958. Every worker with more than 2 years' service with the company has been guaranteed at least 30 hours per week, 49 weeks per year. The company responded to declining demand for its arc welding products and electrical motors during the recession of the 1980s by cutting back all employee hours from 40 to 30. Many employees were reassigned and the total workforce was reduced slightly through normal retirement and restricted hiring. Year-end incentive bonuses were paid.[12]

Role Modeling, Teaching, and Coaching. Aspects of an organization's culture are communicated to employees by the way managers fulfill their roles. In addition, managers and teams may specifically incorporate important cultural messages into training programs and day-to-day coaching on the job. For example, training films shown to new employees at the Four Seasons Hotels and Resorts emphasize customer service. Managers also demonstrate good customer or client service practices in their interactions with customers. The repeated emphasis on good customer relations in both training and day-to-day behavior helps create and maintain a customer-oriented culture throughout Four Seasons. Arthur Andersen, the large public accounting firm, sends all newly hired accountants to an extensive training program, not only to learn accounting procedures used by the firm, but also to become steeped in the organization's culture.[13]

Allocation of Rewards and Status. Employees also learn about an organization's culture through its reward system. The rewards and punishments attached to various behaviors convey to employees the priorities and values of both individual managers and the organization. When Richard Teerlink became president of Harley-Davidson, for example, he instituted a pay-for-performance system whereby all employees are paid on the basis of their individual performance, team member performance, and the entire organization's performance. Similarly, an organization's status system maintains certain aspects of its culture. The distribution of perks (a corner office on an upper floor, executive dining room, carpeting, a private secretary, or a private parking space) demonstrates which roles and behaviors are most valued by the organization. At Chase Manhattan Bank in New York City, a manager was promoted to a new job. His new office was well furnished with most of the symbols of relatively high status. But before he was allowed to move in, his superiors ordered the maintenance department to cut a 12-inch strip from the entire perimeter of the carpet. At Chase Manhattan, wall-to-wall carpeting is a status symbol given to senior vice presidents and above. However, an organization may use rewards and status symbols ineffectively and inconsistently. If it does, it misses a great opportunity to influence its culture because an organization's reward practices and its culture appear to be strongly linked in the minds of its members. In fact, some authorities believe that the most effective method of influencing organizational culture may be through the reward system.

Recruitment, Selection, Promotion, and Removal. As Figure 17.3 suggests, one of the fundamental ways that organizations maintain a culture is through the recruitment process. In addition, the criteria used to determine who is assigned to specific jobs or positions, who gets raises and promotions and why, who is removed from the organization by firing or early retirement, and so on, reinforce and demonstrate basic aspects of an organization's culture. These criteria become known throughout the organization and can maintain or change an existing culture.

Rites and Ceremonies. **Organizational rites and ceremonies** are planned activities or rituals that have important cultural meaning. Certain managerial or employee activities can become rituals that are interpreted as part of the organizational culture. Rites and ceremonies that sustain organizational culture include rites of passage, degradation, enhancement, and integration. Table 17.2 contains examples of each of these four types of rites and identifies some of their desirable consequences.

Table 17.2

Organizational Rites and Ceremonies

TYPE	EXAMPLE	POSSIBLE CONSEQUENCES
Rites of passage	Basic training, U.S. Army	Facilitate transition into new roles; minimize differences in way roles are carried out
Rites of degradation	Firing a manager	Reduce power and identity; reaffirm proper behavior
Rites of enhancement	Mary Kay Cosmetics Company ceremonies	Enhance power and identity; emphasize value of proper behavior
Rites of integration	Office party	Encourage common feelings that bind members together

Source: Adapted from Trice, H. M., and Beyer, J. M. *The Cultures of Work Organizations*. Englewood Cliffs, N.J.: Prentice-Hall, 1993, 111.

A ceremony used at Mary Kay Cosmetics Company provides a good example of rites of enhancement. During elaborate awards ceremonies, gold and diamond pins, fur stoles, and the use of pink Cadillacs are presented to salespeople who achieve their sales quotas. Music tends to arouse and express emotions, and all the participants know the Mary Kay song: "I've Got That Mary Kay Enthusiasm," which was written by a member of the organization to the tune of the hymn "I've Got That Old Time Religion." This song is a direct expression of the Mary Kay culture and is fervently sung during the awards ceremonies. The ceremonies are reminiscent of a Miss America pageant, with all the participants dressed in glamorous evening clothes. The setting is typically an auditorium with a stage in front of a large, cheering audience. The ceremonies clearly are intended to increase the identity and status of high-performing employees and emphasize the company's rewards for excellence.[14]

Organization Stories. Many of the underlying beliefs and values of an organization's culture are expressed as stories that become part of its folklore. These stories transmit the existing culture from old to new employees and emphasize important aspects of that culture—and some may persist for a long time. Southwest Airlines has a unique culture. Herb Kelleher, its CEO, has made the development and maintenance of culture one of his primary duties. Kelleher's style can be described as a combination of Sam Walton's thriftiness (e.g., no company cars or club memberships, and executives stay in the same hotels as flight crews) and Robin Williams's wackiness. He has shown up at Southwest parties as Elvis, a drag queen, and in other "fun uniforms." He arm-wrestled the president of a North Carolina aviation firm over the right to use the slogan "Just Plane Smart." (Kelleher lost, saying he had suffered a wrist fracture diving in front of a bus to save a small child.) He also lost a H-O-R-S-E game at Hobby Airport to Houston Rockets Coach Rudy Thomjanovich. He writes a column for the company's newsletter entitled "So, What Was Herb Doing All This Time?" In one column, he recalls the time when a customer service representative volunteered to stay with an elderly passenger who was afraid to stay alone when her flight was grounded due to fog. The agent "knew" that was what Herb would have done. He also remembers when five out-of-state medical students complained that their regularly scheduled flight got them to class 15 minutes late and Southwest moved its departure time forward to get them to class on time. Another story recounts how an agent babysat a passenger's dog for 2 weeks so that the customer could take a flight on which no pets were allowed. Kelleher regularly works at cleaning planes and helps passengers onto planes during peak seasons and holidays. Southwest employees and passengers love to tell stories about Kelleher and others who go out of their way to demonstrate superior customer service. All these stories help perpetuate the culture of Southwest Airlines that no other airline has been able to duplicate.[15]

Changing Organizational Culture

The same basic methods used to maintain an organization's culture may be used to modify it. Culture might be modified by changing (1) what managers and teams pay attention to, (2) how crises are handled, (3) criteria for recruiting new members, (4) criteria for promotion within the organization, (5) criteria for allocating rewards, and (6) organizational rites and ceremonies.[16]

Changing organizational culture can be tricky, and at least two concerns suggest caution. First, some people question whether the deeply held, core values of organizational culture are amenable to change. In their view, focusing managerial efforts on changing ineffective behaviors and procedures is more meaningful than attempting to change organizational culture. Some managers further argue that changing behavior will work only if it can be based on the existing culture.

Second, accurately assessing organizational culture in itself is difficult. Most large, complex organizations actually have more than one culture. General Electric, for example, has distinctly different cultures in different parts of its multidivisional, worldwide operations. Sometimes these multiple cultures are called **subcultures.** Every organization may have at least three cultures—an operating culture (line employees), an engineering culture (technical and professional people), and an executive culture (top management)—stemming from the very different world views typically held by these different groups of individuals.[17] Faced with a variety of subcultures, management may have difficulty (1) accurately assessing them and (2) effecting needed changes.

Despite these concerns, we believe that changing organizational cultures is both feasible and, in the case of failing organizations, sometimes essential. Successfully changing organizational culture requires

- understanding the old culture first because a new culture can't be developed unless managers and employees understand where they're starting from;
- providing support for employees and teams who have ideas for a better culture and are willing to act on those ideas;
- finding the most effective subculture in the organization and using it as an example from which employees can learn;
- not attacking culture head-on but finding ways to help employees and teams do their jobs more effectively;
- treating the vision of a new culture as a guiding principle for change, not as a miracle cure;
- recognizing that significant organizationwide cultural change takes 5 to 10 years; and,
- living the new culture because actions speak louder than words.

The transformation of Harley-Davidson is one example of how a company changed its culture. The following Managing Change Competency feature highlights how this organization changed and has come back from the brink of bankruptcy in the 1970s to regain its status as producer of the number one bike in the motorcycle business. In the 1970s, the demand for motorcycles grew rapidly, and Honda, Yamaha, Suzuki, and Kawasaki quickly entered the U.S. market with bikes that required little maintenance, were easy to handle, and were of high quality. Soon these Japanese firms accounted for more than 85 percent of all bikes sold in the United States. Despite declining sales, older models with poor quality, and poor dealer relations, Harley-Davidson believed that customer loyalty would enable the organization to survive. After the company almost failed twice, Richard Teerlink became president in 1989 and began a cultural revolution. Currently, Harley-Davidson has over 70 percent of the heavyweight motorcycle segment in the United States, a one-year production backlog, and a revitalized Harley mystique—rugged individualism, living on the edge, and frontier spirit.

COMPETENCY: MANAGING CHANGE

HARLEY-DAVIDSON: LEARNING ORGANIZATION

When Richard Teerlink became president, the differences between Harley-Davidson and its competitors were striking. For example, only 5 percent of Honda's motorcycles failed to pass inspection; over 50 percent of Harleys failed the same test. Honda's value added per employee was three times that of Harley's. Harley's relations with its dealers were poor because they were forced to provide customers with free service because of factory defects. So what did Teerlink do? He set out to create a learning organization.

First, he began emphasizing organizational and individual learning at all levels through a Leadership Institute. The institute was designed to introduce new workers to Harley's goals and culture while providing current workers with a better understanding of the organization's design and effects of competition on Harley's performance. Table 17.3 illustrates some of the values of this new learning organization. Managers prepared a series of nontechnical explanations of how cash flows and flexible production affect financial success. Line workers were taught how products, sales, and productivity affect profitability. Substantial changes in employee job descriptions, responsibilities, and production processes were undertaken in an effort to increase job enrichment and worker empowerment. These efforts were implemented through cross-training and expansion of job responsibility. Teerlink eliminated the positions of vice president in marketing and operations because these jobs didn't add value to the product. Teams of employees, such as a "create-demand team" that is in charge of producing products and a "product-support team," now make these decisions. Employees formed quality circles that became a source of bottom–up ideas for improving quality. Employees created a peer review system to evaluate each other's performance instead of relying solely on first-line supervisors' evaluations. These evaluations help determine an employee's pay.

Second, to recapture the Harley mystique, Teerlink revitalized the Harley Hogs, a customer group formed to get people more actively involved in motorcycling. To attract women riders, "The Ladies of Harley" group was formed to increase ridership and interest among young women motorcyclists. Teerlink and his staff regularly attend road rallies and help clubs sponsor various charitable events. Harley also issued a credit card to its more than 60,000 riders and encourages them to use the card for the purchase of a motorcycle, service, and accessories. The sale of merchandise, including T-shirts, clothing, jewelry, small-leather goods, and numerous other products, permits customers to identify with the company. As Teerlink noted, "There are very few products that are so exciting that people will tattoo your logo on their body."[18]

*For more information on Harley-Davidson, visit this company's home page at **www.harley-davidson.com.***

We cover planned organizational change extensively in Chapter 18. Many of the specific techniques and methods for changing organizational behaviors presented in that chapter also may be used to change organizational culture. Indeed, any comprehensive program of organizational change, in some sense, is an attempt to change the culture of the organization.

We can't overemphasize how difficult deliberately changing organizational cultures may be. In fact, the incompatibility of organizational cultures and their resistance to change has been one of the most significant barriers to successful corporate

Clan Culture

Tradition, loyalty, personal commitment, extensive socialization, teamwork, self-management, and social influence are attributes of a **clan culture.**[20] Its members recognize an obligation beyond the simple exchange of labor for a salary. They understand that contributions to the organization (e.g., hours worked per week) may exceed any contractual agreements. The individual's long-term commitment to the organization (loyalty) is exchanged for the organization's long-term commitment to the individual (security). Because individuals believe that the organization will treat them fairly in terms of salary increases, promotions, and other forms of recognition, they hold themselves accountable to the organization for their actions.

A clan culture achieves unity with a long and thorough socialization process. Longtime clan members serve as mentors and role models for newer members. These relationships perpetuate the organization's values and norms over successive generations of employees. The clan is aware of its unique history and often documents its origins and celebrates its traditions in various rites. Members have a shared image of the organization's style and manner of conduct. Public statements reinforce its values.

In a clan culture, members share feelings of pride in membership. They have a strong sense of identification and recognize their interdependence. The up-through-the-ranks career pattern results in an extensive network of colleagues whose paths have crossed and who have shared similar experiences. Shared goals, perceptions, and behavioral tendencies foster communication, coordination, and integration. A clan culture generates feelings of personal ownership of a business, a product, or an idea. In addition, peer pressure to adhere to important norms is strong. The richness of the culture creates an environment in which few areas are left totally free from normative pressures. Depending on the types of its norms, the culture may or may not generate risk-taking behavior or innovation. Success is assumed to depend substantially on sensitivity to customers and concern for people. Teamwork, participation, and consensus decision making are believed to lead to this success.

Fel-Pro, an auto-parts maker in Skokie, Illinois, has a clan culture, which valued the family atmosphere that had evolved over time. The firm operated a summer camp for children of its employees, always sent parents a Treasury Bond upon the arrival of a new child, and funded scholarships for employees and their children. Teamwork among employees was promoted, and turnover was unusually low. The family programs cost the company 57 cents per worker-hour, and company data indicated that employees who took advantage of the programs were more likely to participate in team problem solving and offer suggestions for operational improvements. When chairman Richard Snell of Federal-Mogul approached Fel-Pro about buying the company, he was told that a deal could be worked out only if Fel-Pro's culture was maintained and protected. Although he worried about how Federal-Mogul's employees might react, Snell agreed to continue operating Fel-Pro's summer camp for at least 2 years and to continue the scholarship fund for at least 5 years.[21]

Entrepreneurial Culture

High levels of risk taking, dynamism, and creativity characterize an **entrepreneurial culture.** There is a commitment to experimentation, innovation, and being on the leading edge. This culture doesn't just quickly react to changes in the environment—it creates change. Effectiveness means providing new and unique products and rapid growth. Individual initiative, flexibility, and freedom foster growth and are encouraged and well rewarded.

Entrepreneurial cultures usually are associated with small to mid-sized companies that are still run by a founder, such as Microsoft, Intel, e-Bay, and many Silicon Valley start-ups. The Man.com venture is one such Silicon Valley company (www.man.com).

Started by two students, Man.com is an e-commerce organization that has an entrepreneurial culture. Calvin Lui and Steve Lombardi, its founders, believe that if one person has an idea, it's safe to assume that four or five other people will have the same idea. It's not the person with the best idea who wins, but the team that can execute it quickly. People have to take initiative and risks. A new hire is affectionately referred to as the FNG (f . . . . . . new guy) and forced to carry a Rugrat doll and order take-out Chinese food, the nightly company meal. "How do you indoctrinate people into your culture? You baptize them, by making them drink out of the same vat of Kool-Aid," says Lui. For example, before employees leave on Fridays, they have to rate themselves publicly, from one to four stars, on their week's performance. Employees who don't like it and can't take the 17-hour days, leave. Lui and Lombardi want people who have a passion for the business. Besides these tasks, all employees use foldout desks and are paid minimal salaries to keep them hungry for the eventual initial public offering (IPO). If and when the organization goes public, both Lui and Lombardi have promised to have "Man.com" tattooed on their bodies. Magic marker scrawlings are on whiteboards all over the room, along with motivational quotes from Steve Young, Jerry Garcia, and Hannibal. When Lombardi's meetings end, he typically says, "All right, dudes, let's rock and roll."[22]

Market Culture

The achievement of measurable and demanding goals, especially those that are financial and market-based (e.g., sales growth, profitability, and market share) characterize a **market culture.** Hard-driving competitiveness and a profit orientation prevail throughout the organization. Frito-Lay, Aramark, and Gulf & Western, among others, are organizations that have created market cultures.

In a market culture, the relationship between individual and organization is contractual. That is, the obligations of each party are agreed upon in advance. In this sense, the formal control orientation is quite stable. The individual is responsible for some level of performance, and the organization promises a specified level of rewards in return. Increased levels of performance are exchanged for increased rewards, as outlined in an agreed upon schedule. Neither party recognizes the right of the other to demand more than was originally specified. The organization doesn't promise (or imply) security, and the individual doesn't promise (or imply) loyalty. The contract, renewed annually if each party adequately performs its obligations, is utilitarian because each party uses the other to further its own goals. Rather than promoting a feeling of membership in a social system, the market culture values independence and individuality and encourages members to pursue their own financial goals. For example, the store manager at Pizza Hut who increases sales will make more money, and the firm will earn more profits through the greater sales volume generated.

A market culture doesn't exert much informal, social pressure on an organization's members. They don't share a common set of expectations regarding management style or philosophy. Superiors' interactions with subordinates largely consist of negotiating performance-reward agreements and/or evaluating requests for resource allocations. Superiors aren't formally judged on their effectiveness as role models or mentors. The absence of a long-term commitment by both parties results in a weak socialization process. Social relations among coworkers aren't officially emphasized, and few economic incentives are tied directly to cooperating with peers. Managers are expected to cooperate with managers in other departments only to the extent necessary to achieve their performance goals. As a result, they may not develop an extensive network of colleagues within the organization. The market culture often is tied to monthly, quarterly, and annual performance goals based on profits.

The following Managing Teams Competency feature about Andersen Worldwide highlights how divisions pursuing different goals in a market culture can impede an organization's desire to build effective cross-functional teams. When Arthur Andersen,

COMPETENCY: MANAGING TEAMS

CONFLICT AT ANDERSEN WORLDWIDE

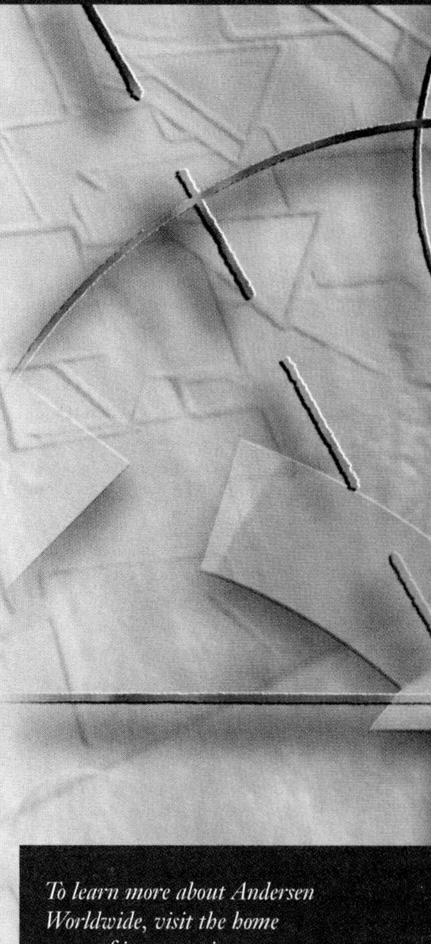

Andersen Worldwide has experienced debilitating internal conflicts between its accounting and consulting units. Since its founding in 1913, the accounting firm of Arthur Andersen had built a reputation for being so internally cohesive that employees were sometimes referred to as "Androids." Its consulting activities, which focus on information technology, didn't begin until 1954. During the first years of its existence, the mature accounting business helped smooth out the ups and downs of the entrepreneurial consulting business. For years, people who specialized in accounting and consulting coexisted in relative peace, relying on give-and-take to resolve conflicts. New recruits were hired straight out of college and socialized through rigorous training and mentorship programs. They were taught to believe that the firm as a whole was greater than the sum of its parts. Consultants, who didn't need in-depth knowledge of accounting, were expected to pass the CPA exam nevertheless. Most of the people who became partners had been with the firm their entire careers.

By the 1980s, the culture had become fragmented. Some partners had come to the firm later in their careers and weren't CPAs. The consultants began to question the assumption that the two businesses were better off combined than they would be as separate firms. According to a former board member, "They began to think, 'well, we'd rather not be in one pot.'" In 1989, after several key partners from the consulting business left, the remaining partners negotiated a compromise that established Andersen Consulting as a separate business unit.

Since then, the two business units have continued to grow apart, each with its own culture and vision of the future. News stories have chronicled the infighting in detail, and some competitors have tried to use the feud to their own advantage. Deloitte & Touche Consulting Group, for example, ran full-page advertisements that read, "Andersen Consulting: Distracted by infighting. Deloitte Consulting: Focused on our clients. When you hire a consulting firm, you can't afford for them to be more concerned with their own problems than they are with your well-being . . . since we're not wasting time fighting with each other, we give every client our undivided attention."[23]

To learn more about Andersen Worldwide, visit the home pages of its two units: Arthur Andersen at ***www.arthurandersen.com*** *and* ***Andersen Consulting*** *at* ***www.ac.com.***

the accounting arm of Andersen Worldwide, was first established, it focused on providing accounting expertise to organizations and performing audits. Its competition was other major accounting firms, including Deloitte & Touche, Ernst & Young, and Price Waterhouse Coopers. In an attempt to grow, it started Arthur Andersen Consulting. This division competed not with traditional accounting firms, but with Bain and Company, McKenzie, and other full-service consulting firms. Historically, consulting firms have had market cultures and accounting firms have developed clan cultures.

ORGANIZATIONAL IMPLICATIONS

Organizational culture has the potential to enhance organizational performance, individual satisfaction, the sense of certainty about how problems are to be handled, and so on. However, if an organizational culture gets out of step with the changing expectations of internal and/or external stakeholders, the organization's effectiveness can be hindered.

The need to determine which attributes of an organization's culture should be preserved and which should be modified is constant. In the United States during the 1980s, many companies began changing their cultures to be more responsive to customers' expectations of product quality and service. During the late 1990s, many organizations began to reassess how well their organizational cultures fit the expectations of the workforce. Since World War II, the U.S. workforce has changed demographically, becoming more diverse. More and more employees have begun to feel that organizational cultures established decades ago are out of step with contemporary values. We address the challenge of adjusting established organizational cultures to meet the expectations of a demographically diverse workforce in the remainder of this chapter.

Learning Objective:

3. Identify the potential relationships between organizational culture and performance.

PERFORMANCE AND ORGANIZATIONAL CULTURE

An underlying assumption is that an organization's culture and its performance or effectiveness are directly related. Thus the rationale for attempting cultural change is to create a more effective organization.

The common theme of several popular books about management and organizations is that strong, well-developed cultures are an important characteristic of organizations that have outstanding performance records. The term **strong culture** implies that most managers and employees share a set of consistent values and methods of doing business. Strong cultures can be found in many organizations, including Wal-Mart, Southwest Airlines, Mary Kay, Hewlett-Packard, and Pier 1.

STRONG CULTURES

Strong cultures may be associated with strong performance for three reasons. First, a strong culture often provides for a good fit between strategy and culture. This fit is considered essential for successfully implementing corporate strategy. Vignette Corporation, an Austin, Texas-based software firm, has developed a strong culture by attracting a diverse group of employees.[24] The motto of the organization is: "funky and intense." Funky because most behaviors are tolerated, including people with rings in every possible part of their bodies and people who wear suits. Vignette also encourages its employee to spend evenings at home, even if some of those hours are in front of a home computer. Mike Strong notes that he tends to work 10- to 14-hour days, but confesses that some of this time is spent hugging his kids and giving them noogies. Vignette believes that for the organization to win, its employees must win also.

Vignette's employees say that being able to telecommute really appeals to them. But, so do other aspects of its work environment. Office space, for example, was designed to invite smiles, with spacey-looking furniture and brightly colored walls that thrust out at angles. Spouses are sent flowers to thank them for being understanding during particularly frantic periods. And every Friday, Vignette hosts beer busts and yoga classes, providing a weird array of techniques that employees can participate in to help them unwind.

Vignette treats people with respect. Unlike other organizations, there are no "haves" and "have-nots," with engineers putting themselves above everyone else. The organization's official culture document contains headings such as "impeccable character," "tolerance and forgiveness," and "office politics." Under the last heading, for example, it states that "backbiting, manipulating, and other divisive activities are causes for termination." Like all strong cultures, people have to buy the vision to fit in. Who doesn't fit in? Anyone with a large ego.

CAUTIONARY NOTES

Organizational culture and performance clearly are related, although the evidence regarding the exact nature of this relationship is mixed. For example, strong cultures may not always be superior to weak cultures. Some studies indicate that the type of culture may, in fact, be somewhat more important than its strength. A comparison of the cultures of 334 colleges and universities revealed no differences in organizational effectiveness between those with strong cultures and those with weak cultures. However, the type of culture possessed by these institutions *was* related to their effectiveness. Colleges and universities that possessed a type of culture that matched their market niche and strategy were more effective than institutions whose cultures lacked such a match.[25]

Another cautionary note comes from studies showing that the relationship between many cultural attributes (featured in the popular press as being important for performance) and high performance hasn't been consistent over time. Based on what we know about culture–performance relationships, a contingency approach seems to be a good one for managers and organizations to take. Further investigations of this issue are unlikely to discover one "best" organizational culture (either in terms of strength or type).

A 4-year study of a large number of organizations resulted in the following conclusions about the relationships between culture and performance.

- Organizational culture can have a significant impact on a firm's long-term economic performance.
- Organizational culture will probably be an even more important factor in determining the success or failure of firms in the next decade.
- Organizational cultures that inhibit strong long-term financial performance are not rare; they develop easily, even in firms that are filled with reasonable and intelligent people.
- Although tough to change, organizational cultures can be made more performance enhancing if managers understand what sustains a culture.[26]

High degrees of participative management and an emphasis on teamwork often are cited as characteristics of successful, effective organizational cultures. In **participative management,** managers share decision-making, goal-setting, and problem-solving activities with employees. However, high levels of participation don't fit all settings and tasks. Further, changing an organization from a more traditional management approach to greater collaboration with employees may be extremely difficult. A type of organizational culture designed to foster high performance with high levels of employee involvement is called a **high performance–high commitment work culture.**[27] As with participative management, cultures that foster high involvement and commitment on the part of employees often exist in organizations that have a record of high performance. We examine high performance–high commitment work cultures and systems in greater detail in Chapter 18.

We can summarize the effects of organizational culture on employee behavior and performance with four key ideas. First, knowing the culture of an organization allows employees to understand both the firm's history and current approach. This knowledge provides guidance about expected behaviors for the future. Second, organizational culture can foster commitment to corporate philosophy and values. This commitment generates shared feelings of working toward common goals. Third, organizational culture, through its norms, serves as a control mechanism to channel behaviors toward desired behaviors and away from undesired behaviors. Finally, certain types of organizational cultures may be related directly to greater effectiveness and productivity than others.

Learning Objective:

4. Discuss how organizational culture can influence the ethical behavior of employees.

ETHICAL BEHAVIOR AND ORGANIZATIONAL CULTURE

Ethical problems in organizations continue to concern managers and employees greatly. As an example of this concern, KPMG Peat Marwick, a Big Four accounting firm, recently formed a new unit designed to help its clients create a "moral organization." The firm maintains that the process of auditing ethics can promote good business practices and benefit its corporate culture.

Impact of Culture

Managers and researchers are beginning to explore the potential impact that organizational culture can have on ethical behavior. The ethics component of organizational culture is a complex interplay of formal and informal systems that may support either ethical or unethical organizational behavior. The formal systems include leadership, structure, policies, reward systems, orientation and training programs, and decision-making processes. Informal systems include norms, heroes, rituals, language, myths, sagas, and stories.

Organizational culture appears to affect ethical behavior in several ways. For example, a culture emphasizing ethical norms provides support for ethical behavior. In addition, top management plays a key role in fostering ethical behavior by exhibiting the correct behavior. If lower level managers observe top level managers sexually harassing others, falsifying expense reports, diverting shipments to preferred customers, and other forms of unethical behavior, they assume that these behaviors are acceptable and will be rewarded in the future. Thus the presence or absence of ethical behavior in managerial actions both influences and reflects the prevailing culture. The organizational culture may promote taking responsibility for the consequences of actions, thereby increasing the probability that individuals will behave ethically. Alternatively, the culture may diffuse responsibility for the consequences of unethical behavior, thereby making such behavior more likely. In short, ethical business practices stem from ethical organizational cultures.

An important concept linking organizational culture to ethical behavior is **principled organizational dissent,** by which individuals in an organization protest, on ethical grounds, some practice or policy. Some cultures permit and even encourage principled organizational dissent; other cultures punish such behavior.

An employee might use various strategies in attempting to change unethical behavior, including

- secretly or publicly reporting unethical actions to a higher level within the organization;
- secretly or publicly reporting unethical actions to someone outside the organization;
- secretly or publicly threatening an offender or a responsible manager with reporting unethical actions; or
- quietly or publicly refusing to implement an unethical order or policy.

Whistle-Blowing

As a form of principled organizational dissent, **whistle-blowing** is the disclosure by current or former employees of illegal, immoral, or illegitimate organizational practices to people or organizations that may be able to change the practice.[28] As discussed in Chapter 16, the whistle-blower lacks the power to change the undesirable practice directly and so appeals to others either inside or outside the organization.

"Are you sitting down?" was the question posed by Michael Monaco, Cendant Corporation's chief financial officer to Cendant's CEO Henry Silverman.[29] Cendant had recently purchased HFS and CUC International and Monaco had discovered a problem. In sworn affidavits taken by Cendant investigators, managers at CUC admitted that they were told to record millions of dollars in phony orders and adjust expenses accordingly. Financial officers at CUC took money from cash reserves to cover revenue shortfalls. These managers also ordered CUC's divisional controllers to do the same by increasing revenues a few hundred thousand dollars at a time. To cover up these transactions, the term *consolidation entries* had been used. The top executives at CUC International had "cooked" the books to make its financial situation look better than it actually was. According to Arthur Andersen and other auditors, about \$500 million of reported revenue was simply invented. The whistle was blown by two former CUC International employees who went with Cendant after the merger. The presidents of HFS and CUC International have been found guilty and have paid a fine. The whistle-blowers are still working at Cendant.

These types of whistle-blowing activities aren't without risk. The individual engaging in principled organizational dissent risks dismissal, demotion, isolation, ostracism, and threats of harm and even death to self and family. Often millions or even billions of dollars are at stake. Moreover, the whistle-blower could be wrong about individual or organizational actions. Thus misguided attempts to stop apparently unethical behavior might unnecessarily harm employees or organizations.

Much remains to be learned about creating organizational cultures that encourage ethical behavior. The following suggestions are a beginning.

- Be realistic in setting values and goals regarding employment relationships. Do not promise what the organization cannot deliver.
- Encourage input from throughout the organization regarding appropriate values and practices for implementing the culture. Choose values that represent the views of both employees and managers.
- Do not automatically opt for a "strong" culture. Explore methods of providing for diversity and dissent, such as grievance or complaint mechanisms or other internal review procedures.
- Provide training programs for managers and teams on adopting and implementing the organization's values. These programs should stress the underlying ethical and legal principles and present the practical aspects of carrying out procedural guidelines.[30]

An effective organizational culture should encourage ethical behavior and discourage unethical behavior. Admittedly, ethical behavior may "cost" the organization and individuals. A global firm that refuses to pay a bribe to secure business in a particular country may lose sales. An individual may lose financially by not accepting a kickback. Similarly, an organization or individual might seem to gain from unethical actions. An organization may flout U.S. law by quietly paying bribes to officials in order to gain entry to a new market. A purchasing agent for a large corporation might take kickbacks for purchasing all needed office supplies from a particular supplier. However, such gains are often short term. The Sears experience provides a clear example of short-term gain, but long-term loss, for an organization. Sears spent $60 million to settle lawsuits and give customers refunds after being accused of selling unnecessary auto parts and repair services in more than 40 states. Auto repairmen reported pressure from their managers to achieve sales quotas. Those who didn't achieve their quotas were fired. To avoid being fired, repairmen often performed extra work on customers' cars that wasn't required, but by doing so they could reach their quotas and keep their jobs.

In the long run, an organization can't successfully operate if its prevailing culture and values aren't congruent with those of society. That is as true as the observation that, in the long run, an organization cannot survive unless it provides goods and services that society wants and needs. An organizational culture that promotes ethical behavior is not only more compatible with prevailing cultural values, but it also makes good business sense.

Learning Objective:

5. Explain the importance of effectively managing cultural diversity.

MANAGING CULTURAL DIVERSITY

In Chapter 1, we emphasized that organizations are becoming increasingly diverse in terms of gender, race, ethnicity, and nationality. More than half the U.S. workforce consists of women, minorities, and recent immigrants. The growing diversity of employees in many organizations can bring substantial benefits, such as more successful marketing strategies for different types of customers, improved decision making, and greater creativity and innovation. At DuPont, a group of African-American workers recently opened promising new markets for the firm by focusing on black farmers. A multicultural team gained the company about $45 million in new business by changing the way DuPont designs and markets decorating materials (e.g., countertops) in order to appeal more to overseas customers.

SIGNIFICANT CHALLENGES

Along with its benefits, cultural diversity brings costs and concerns, including communication difficulties, intraorganizational conflict, and turnover. Effectively managing cultural diversity promises to continue to be a significant challenge for organizations for a long time. To succeed, organizations have to work hard at acculturation. **Acculturation** refers to methods by which cultural differences between a dominant culture and minority or subcultures are resolved.[31] Both the benefits and the challenges stemming from a multicultural workforce are described in the following Managing Communication Competency feature that highlights how employees at the Marriott Marquis communicate with each other.

COMPETENCY: MANAGING COMMUNICATION

MARRIOTT MARQUIS

The staff of the Marriott Marquis in New York's Times Square is highly diverse. The hotel's 1,700 employees represent every race, hail from 70 countries, and speak 47 languages. As a hotel catering to multinational guests, such diversity can ease communication problems. According to Human Resources Director Ray Falcone, "We have a diverse clientele, and we need a diverse workforce to effectively communicate with them." But managing both employees and guests from such a wide range of backgrounds also presents a communications problem.

Prickly racial, ethnic, and gender concerns are an undercurrent in virtually all communication at the Marriott. Some workers are quick to charge discrimination when they can't communicate effectively with their manager. Just maintaining a basic level of civility can be a daily struggle. In required diversity training classes, employees and managers are taught that the best communication strategy is to focus on performance issues and never define the problem in terms of race, gender, and age. Marriott managers have been accused of overcommunicating with workers and attempting to bend over backward to be fair about issues, such as scheduling assignments, vacation days, and observance of national holidays. Room Director Susan Gonzalez keeps track of her department's nearly 400 housekeeping employees' requests for time off to observe national holidays. Her records tracking holiday requests go back 4 years, and she relies on these data to demonstrate how holiday requests have been honored.

It is important that guests be able to communicate with a hotel employee in their native tongue. Guests make reservations to arrive at all hours of the day because of their travel arrangements. For example, a Japanese manager arriving on a 14-hour flight from Tokyo to New York City loses a day. Monday in Tokyo is now Sunday in New York City. The manager's eating schedule in still on Japanese time. At 6:00 P.M. on Monday evening in New York City it is 8:00 A.M. Tuesday in Tokyo. The guest wants an Asian breakfast, not an American dinner. Menus need to be translated into a guest's native language and strict dietary laws of many different cultures observed.[32]

*To learn more about the Marriott's communication competencies, visit this organization's home page at **www.marriott.com**.*

Some Guidelines

There are no easy answers to the challenges of managing a culturally diverse workforce. However, research has revealed some common characteristics of employee values, managerial philosophy, and organizational culture that are present in organizations having effective diversity management programs. These characteristics have been distilled into the following helpful guidelines.

- Managers and employees must understand that a diverse workforce will embody different perspectives and approaches to work and must truly value variety of opinion and insight.
- The leadership of the organization must recognize both the learning opportunities and the challenges that the expression of different perspectives presents for an organization.
- The organizational culture must create an expectation of high standards of performance from everyone.
- The organizational culture must stimulate personal development.
- The organizational culture must encourage openness.
- The organizational culture must make workers feel valued.
- The organization must have a well-articulated and widely understood mission.
- The organization must have a relatively nonbureaucratic structure.[33]

Table 17.4 contains a questionnaire that you can use to examine your awareness of diversity issues.

Table 17.4

Diversity Questionnaire

Directions

Indicate your views by placing a T (true) or F (false) next to each of these nine statements.

1. I know about the rules and customs of several different cultures. ____
2. I know that I hold stereotypes about other groups. ____
3. I feel comfortable with people of different backgrounds from my own. ____
4. I associate with people who are different from me. ____
5. I find working on a multicultural team satisfying. ____
6. I find change stimulating and exciting. ____
7. I enjoy learning about other cultures. ____
8. When dealing with someone whose English is limited, I show patience and understanding. ____
9. I find that spending time building relationships with others is useful because more gets done. ____

Interpretation

The more true responses you have, the more adaptable and open you are to diversity. If you have five or more true responses, you probably are someone who finds value in cross-cultural experiences.

If you have less than five true responses, you may be resistant to interacting with people who are different from you. If that is the case, you may find that your interactions with others are sometimes blocked.

Source: Adapted from Gardenswartz, L., and Rowe, A. What's your diversity quotient? *Managing Diversity Newsletter,* Jamestown, New York (undated).

Learning Objective:

6. Describe the process of organizational socialization and its relationship to organizational culture.

ORGANIZATIONAL SOCIALIZATION

The general meaning of the term **socialization** is the process by which older members of a society transmit to younger members the social skills and knowledge needed to function effectively in that society. Similarly, **organizational socialization** is the systematic process by which an organization brings new employees into its culture.[34] In other words, it involves the transmission of organizational culture from senior to new employees, providing the social knowledge and skills needed to perform organizational roles and tasks successfully.

Organizational socialization provides the means by which new employees learn the ropes. It includes learning work group, departmental, and organizational values, rules, procedures, and norms; developing social and working relationships; and developing the competencies needed to perform a job. Interestingly, the stages that an employee goes through during organizational socialization resemble, in many respects, the stages in group development discussed in Chapter 8.

SOCIALIZATION PROCESS

Figure 17.5 presents an example of an organizational socialization process. It isn't intended to depict the socialization process of every organization. However, many firms with strong cultures—such as Disney, Procter & Gamble, Southwest Airlines, and Wal-Mart—frequently follow these steps for socializing new employees.

Step One. Entry-level candidates are selected carefully. Trained recruiters use standardized procedures and seek specific traits that tie to success in the business.

Step Two. Humility-inducing experiences in the first months on the job cause employees to question their prior behaviors, beliefs, and values. Such experiences might include giving a new employee more work to do than can reasonably be done. Self-questioning promotes openness to accepting the organization's norms and values.

Step Three. Tough on-the-job training leads to mastery of one of the core disciplines of the business. Promotion is then tied to a proven track record.

Step Four. Careful attention is given to measuring operational results and rewarding individual performance. Reward systems are comprehensive and consistent and focus on those aspects of the organization that are tied to success and organizational culture.

Step Five. Adherence to the organization's values is emphasized. Identification with common values allows employees to justify personal sacrifices caused by their membership in the organization.

Step Six. Reinforcing folklore provides legends and interpretations of important events in the organization's history that validate its culture and goals. Folklore reinforces a code of conduct for "how we do things around here."

Step Seven. Consistent role models and consistent traits are associated with those recognized as being on the fast track to promotion and success.[35]

SOCIALIZATION OUTCOMES

All organizations and groups socialize new members in some way, but the process can vary greatly in terms of how explicit, comprehensive, and lengthy it is. Generally, rapid socialization is advantageous. For the individual, it quickly reduces the uncertainty and anxiety surrounding a new job. For the organization, it helps the new employee become productive quickly. Organizations with strong cultures may be particularly skillful at socializing individuals. If the culture is effective, the socialization process will contribute to organizational success. However, if the culture needs changing, a strong socialization process reduces the prospects for making the needed changes.

Figure 17.5 **An Example of an Organizational Socialization Process**

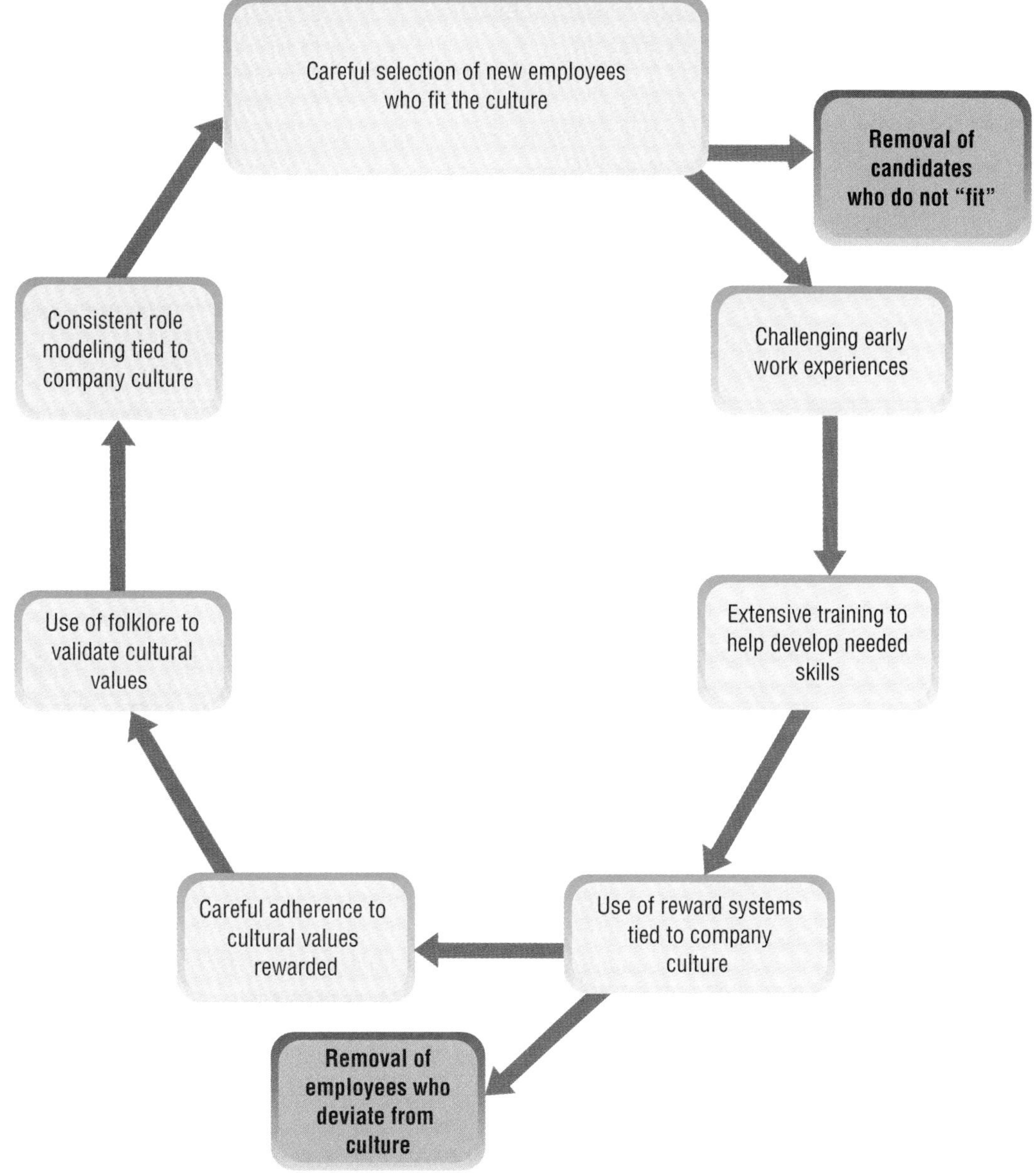

Some additional dilemmas are created by strong socialization processes. For example, a business school is concerned with issues surrounding the socialization of its students. How strong should the socialization be? Does the business school want students to think alike, at least in terms of a certain level of logic and intelligent analysis? To have the same appropriate values and sense of professionalism? In some sense, the answer to these questions has to be "yes." Yet, oversocialization runs the risk of creating rigid, narrow-minded corporate men and women. The ideal goal of business school socialization, then, may be to develop independent thinkers committed to what they believe to be right, while at the same time educating students to be collaborative team players who have good interpersonal skills and are able to relate well to others. These goals pose a challenge for the socialization process, which, in order to be effective, must balance these demands. Although this example applies to a business school, to a certain extent the same need for balance exists for all organizations.

Table 17.5 Possible Outcomes of Socialization Process

SUCCESSFUL SOCIALIZATION IS REFLECTED IN	UNSUCCESSFUL SOCIALIZATION IS REFLECTED IN
• Job satisfaction	• Job dissatisfaction
• Role clarity	• Role ambiguity and conflict
• High work motivation	• Low work motivation
• Understanding of culture, perceived control	• Misunderstanding, tension, perceived lack of control
• High job involvement	• Low job involvement
• Commitment to organization	• Lack of commitment to organization
• Tenure	• Absenteeism, turnover
• High performance	• Low performance
• Internalized values	• Rejection of values

The socialization process may affect employee and organizational success in a variety of ways.[36] Table 17.5 lists some possible socialization outcomes. We don't claim that these outcomes are determined solely by an organization's socialization process. For example, job satisfaction is a function of many things, including the nature of the task, the individual's personality and needs, the nature of supervision, opportunities to succeed and be rewarded, and the like (see Chapter 2). Rather, the point here is that successful socialization may contribute to job satisfaction, whereas unsuccessful socialization may contribute to job dissatisfaction.

CHAPTER SUMMARY

1. Explain how organizational cultures are developed, maintained, and changed.

Organizational culture is the pattern of beliefs and expectations shared by members of an organization. It includes norms, common values, company philosophy, the "rules of the game" for getting along and getting things done, and ways of interacting with outsiders, such as customers. Some aspects of organizational culture are indicated by cultural symbols, heroes, rites, and ceremonies. Organizational culture develops as a response to the challenges of external adaptation and survival and of internal integration. The formation of an organization's culture also is influenced by the culture of the larger society within which the organization must function.

The primary methods for both maintaining and changing organizational culture include (1) what managers and teams pay attention to, measure, and control; (2) the ways managers and employees react to crises; (3) role modeling, teaching, and coaching; (4) criteria for allocating rewards; (5) criteria for recruitment to, selection and promotion within, and removal from the organization; and (6) organizational rites, ceremonies, and stories.

2. Describe four types of organizational culture.

Although all organizational cultures are unique, four general types were identified and discussed: bureaucratic, clan, entrepreneurial, and market organizational cultures. They are characterized by differences in the extent of formal control (ranging from stable to flexible) and focus of attention (ranging from internal to external).

3. Identify the potential relationships between organizational culture and performance.

Culture may be related to effective organizational performance, although no "best" organizational culture exists. Organizations with strong cultures find that these cultures bolster performance because they align employees with the organizational goals and the means that employees should follow to reach these goals. Effective organizational cultures are usually found in organizations that practice participative decision making. Such cultures foster employee commitment and high involvement.

4. Discuss how organizational culture can influence the ethical behavior of employees.

Organizational culture also can have a strong effect on ethical behavior by managers and employees alike. One concept linking culture to ethical behavior is principled organizational dissent. Cultures that permit dissent encourage whistle-blowing and other behaviors that provide guidelines for ethical behaviors.

5. Explain the importance of effectively managing cultural diversity.

Managing cultural diversity is expected to be one of the principal managerial challenges facing organizations for years to come. How organizations respond to this challenge will determine the effectiveness of culturally diverse teams, an organization's communication process, and employees' personal development.

6. Describe the process of organizational socialization and its relationship to organizational culture.

Socialization is the process by which new members are brought into an organization's culture. At firms having a strong culture, the socialization process is well developed and the focus of careful attention. All organizations socialize new members, but depending on how it is done, the outcomes could be either positive or negative in terms of job performance, satisfaction, and commitment to the organization. We presented a seven-step process that is often followed for socializing new employees.

KEY TERMS AND CONCEPTS

Acculturation
Bureaucratic culture
Clan culture
Cultural symbols
Cultural values
Entrepreneurial culture
Expats
External adaptation and survival
High performance–high commitment work culture
Internal integration
Market culture
Organizational culture
Organizational rites and ceremonies
Organizational socialization
Participative management
Principled organizational dissent
Shared assumptions
Shared behaviors
Socialization
Strong culture
Subcultures
Whistle-blowing

DISCUSSION QUESTIONS

1. Provide three examples of how organizational culture is expressed in your college or university.
2. Describe how that culture affects your behavior.
3. How did your college or university develop its culture?
4. What are the primary methods that Richard Teerlink used to change the culture of Harley-Davidson?
5. Can Teerlink's methods be used in other organizations? Explain your answer.
6. Using the words in Table 17.1, describe the culture of Starbucks (visit its Web site at www.starbucks.com), Dell Computer (visit its Web site at www.dell.com), or another organization with which you are familiar. How does its organizational culture affect the type of employee who chooses to work there?
7. What role do reward systems play in maintaining the cultures at Pharmacia & Upjohn?
8. How do organizational culture and performance seem to be related? What competencies do managers need in order to transmit culture throughout their organization? Explain.
9. How might an organization use its culture to increase the probability of ethical behavior and decrease the probability of unethical behavior by its managers and employees?
10. Consult Ben & Jerry's Web site at www.benjerry.com to discover why managing cultural diversity is crucial to the firm's success. How does it achieve such success?
11. What type of organizational culture would you prefer to work in? Why? You might refer to Table 17.1 to help you understand your own values.
12. Describe the socialization process used by an organization with which you are familiar. What were the results of this socialization process?

DEVELOPING COMPETENCIES

Competency: Managing Ethics—Assessing a Culture's Ethical Behaviors

Instructions: Think of a job you currently hold or used to have. Indicate how you feel about each behavior. Use the following scale and place one number after each behavior to indicate your response. There are no right or wrong answers.

1. Very acceptable
2. Acceptable
3. Somewhat acceptable
4. Uncertain
5. Somewhat unacceptable
6. Unacceptable
7. Very unacceptable

_____ 1. Taking home a few supplies (e.g., paper clips, pencils, and pens).

_____ 2. Calling in sick when some personal time (e.g., play golf or take in a movie) is needed.

_____ 3. Using a company telephone, fax, or computer for personal business.

_____ 4. Making personal copies on a company copy machine.

_____ 5. Using a company car to make a personal trip.

_____ 6. Eating at a very expensive restaurant on a company business trip.

_____ 7. Charging wine and cocktails as well as food on a company business trip.

_____ 8. Taking a significant other along on a company business trip at the company's expense.

_____ 9. Staying at an expensive hotel on a company business trip.

_____10. On a company business trip, charging a $7 cab ride to your expense account when you actually walked.

Interpretation of Results

More than 200 managers responded to this survey. Compare your responses to theirs.

1. 50 percent thought that taking home a few office supplies was acceptable.
2. 70 percent reported that calling in sick to take personal time was unacceptable.
3. 74.7 percent reported that making personal calls on the telephone, using a fax, or computer was unacceptable.
4. 54.6 percent indicated that making personal copies on a copy machine was acceptable.
5. 70.6 percent thought that using a company car for a personal trip was unacceptable.
6. 59.1 percent reported that eating at a very expensive restaurant was acceptable.
7. 50 percent believed that charging wine and cocktails was acceptable.
8. 85 percent thought that taking a significant other along on a business trip at the company's expense was unacceptable.
9. 55 percent indicated that staying at an expensive hotel on a company business trip was acceptable.
10. 41 percent indicated that charging $7 for a cab ride when they walked was very unacceptable.[37]

Questions

1. Would you expect these results to vary by type of culture (e.g., bureaucratic, clan, entrepreneurial, or market)?
2. Choose several items that you and the managerial respondents are in disagreement over. What steps would you recommend to change these behaviors? How do your recommendations reflect your own values (see Table 17.1).

Competency: Managing Teams—Southwest Airlines' Team Culture

Few industries have experienced the turmoil faced by the U.S. domestic airlines since 1980. Once characterized by high wages, stable prices, and government regulation, the industry changed swiftly and dramatically when deregulation took effect in 1978. Pan Am, Eastern, Reno, and other airlines disappeared through mergers or bankruptcies. New competitors, such as Southwest, Air Tran, and Vanguard, aggressively came into the marketplace. Despite the volatile economic conditions facing competitors in this industry, Southwest has emerged as one of its most profitable.

Southwest Airlines is pursuing a business strategy of cost leadership. It is a low fare/no frills airline. It has implemented this strategy by serving smaller, less-congested secondary airports in and near larger cities (e.g., Manchester, New Hampshire, not Boston; Midway in Chicago, not O'Hare; Islip on Long Island, not LaGuardia or JFK in New York City), that tend to have lower gate costs and landing fees. This strategy also helps Southwest maintain schedules easily and cheaply because it need not coordinate flight schedules into connecting hubs such as Dallas–Fort Worth, Atlanta, and Los Angeles, reducing scheduling complexity and costs. Landing at less congested airports also permits more rapid turnaround than the industry average (15–20 minutes versus 55 minutes). In essence, Southwest's business strategy is to be the cheapest and most efficient airline in specific domestic regional markets while providing its customers with a high level of convenience and its exceptional LUV culture. (LUV is Southwest's symbol on the New York Stock Exchange.) In keeping with its customer orientation, Southwest uses frequent fliers to help select new flight attendants.

According to CEO Herb Kelleher, people are the airline's most important asset. Southwest is in the business of providing legendary service. He believes that people want to work for a "winner." As a result, Southwest can hire and hold the very best people. At Southwest Airlines the human resource function is called the People Department, which is crucial to Southwest's success. According to the department's mission statement, "recognizing that our people are the competitive advantage, we deliver resources and services to prepare our people to be winners, to support the growth and profitability of the company, while preserving the values and special culture of Southwest Airlines." Elizabeth Sartain, executive vice president of the People Department, comments that Southwest can change a person's competency levels through training, but it cannot change attitudes, so people are hired for their attitude, not for their technical skills. In fact, the airline rejects about 100,000 applicants a year and the turnover rate is less than half (e.g., about 7 percent) that of most other airlines. Because its organizational culture is crucial for developing dedication to excellence, a new hire's first 6 months at Southwest are a period of indoctrination and mentoring. These 6 months are also used to weed out anyone who does not mesh with the culture.

All new hires attend Southwest's University for People. During classes, everyone at Southwest is told that they have a responsibility for self-improvement and training. Once a year, all employees, including senior management, are required to participate in a program designed to reinforce shared values. Except for flight training, which is regulated by the FAA, all training is done on the employee's own time. The university operates at full capacity, 7 days a week. The fun and spirit of Southwest emerges in graduates very early. Humor and service are significant aspects of the culture. Employees are taught that, if they want customers to have fun, they must create a fun-loving environment. That means that employees must be self-confident enough to reach out and share their sense of humor and fun. They must be willing to play and expend the extra energy it takes to create a fun experience for their customers. For example, positively outrageous service stresses friendliness, caring, warmth, and company spirit. Gate attendants are taught how to play games with customers, such as guess the weight of the gate agent, name three things to do in Tulsa, who has the most holes in his or her sock, if a plane is delayed. The games are never in poor taste and provide the winners with free dinner or a Southwest "fun" hat.

Another characteristic of the strong culture is employee commitment and motivation, which leads to cooperative relationships among employee teams. That is, the majority of employees share the same goals and basically agree on how to pursue them. For example, gate agents and flight crews clean planes along with members of the maintenance department. All share the goal of a 17-minute turnaround, about one-third of the time needed by competitors. Because of these team-oriented values, the company has few of the rigid work rules that characterize most of its competitors. Thus at Southwest everybody pitches in regardless of the task. Although 85 percent of Southwest's pilots are unionized, they identify more with the airline than with their union. As a result, there have been few strikes since Southwest was formed in 1971.[38]

Questions

1. Using the words in Table 17.1, describe the organizational culture of Southwest Airlines.
2. Why haven't other airlines and/or organizations been able to copy Southwest's culture?
3. Why is an organization's socialization process so important? What role does the socialization process play at Southwest Airlines?
4. Consult the Southwest Airlines Web site at www.iflyswa.com. What symbols does Southwest use on its Web site to convey its culture?

REFERENCES

1. Adapted from Ball, J. Your career matters: DaimlerChrysler's transfer woes. *Wall Street Journal*, August 24, 1999, B1; Bradsher, K. Management by 2 cultures may be a growing source of strain for DaimlerChrysler. *New York Times*, March 24, 1999, C2.
2. Hendry, J. Cultural theory and contemporary management organization. *Human Relations*, 1999, 52, 557–559.
3. Trice, H. M., and Beyer, J. M. *The Cultures of Work Organizations*. Englewood Cliffs, N.J.: Prentice-Hall, 1993, 1–8.
4. Martin, J. *Cultures in Organizations*. New York: Oxford University Press, 1992.
5. Silvester, J., Anderson, N., and Patterson, F. Organizational culture change: An inter-group attributional analysis. *Journal of Occupational and Organizational Psychology*, 1999, 72, 1–3; Schein, E. H. Culture: The missing concept in organization studies. *Administrative Science Quarterly*, 1996, 41, 229–240; Trice, H. M., and Beyer, J. M. *The Cultures of Work Organizations*. Englewood Cliffs, N.J.: Prentice-Hall, 1993.
6. Gamble, P. R., and Gibson, D. A. Executive values and decision-making: The relationship of culture and information flows. *Journal of Management Studies*, 1999, 36, 217–227.
7. Adapted from Lancaster, H. Managing your career. *Wall Street Journal*, July 14, 1998, B1 ff.
8. Schein, E. H. *Organizational Culture and Leadership*. San Francisco: Jossey-Bass, 1985.
9. Schein, E. H. How culture forms, develops, and changes. In R. H. Kilmann, M. I. Saxton, and R. Serpa (eds.), *Gaining Control of the Corporate Culture*. San Francisco: Jossey-Bass, 1985, 17–43; Schein, E. H. *Organizational Culture and Leadership*, 49–84; Schein, E. H. Organizational culture. *American Psychologist*, 1990, 45, 109–119.
10. Adapted from Friedman, A. A case of corporate culture shock in a global arena. *International Herald Tribune*, April 23, 1997, 1, 11; Calori, R., and Dufour, B. Management European style. *Academy of Management Executive*, 1995, 9(3), 61–73.
11. Chatman, J. A., Polzer, J. T., Barsade, S. G., Neale, M. A. Being different yet feeling similar: The influence of demographic composition and organizational culture on

work process and outcomes. *Administrative Science Quarterly*, 1998, 43, 749–779.

12. Buller, P. F., and Schuler, R. S. *Managing Organizations and People.* Cincinnati: South-Western, 2000, 280–302.
13. Conversation with M. Welsh, partner, Arthur Andersen, Dallas, Texas, February 2000.
14. Trice and Beyer, *The Cultures of Work Organizations*, 115–116.
15. Freiberg, J., and Freiberg, K. *NUTS! Southwest Airlines' Crazy Recipe for Business and Personal Success.* Austin, Tex.: Bard Books, 1996.
16. Trice, H. M., and Beyer, J. M. Using six organizational rites to change culture. In R. H. Kilmann, M. I. Saxton, and R. Serpa (eds.), *Gaining Control of the Corporate Culture.* San Francisco: Jossey-Bass, 1985, 372.
17. Schein, *American Psychologist*, 109–119.
18. Adapted from Schellenbarger, S. From Harley factories to gold mines, more bosses get it. *Wall Street Journal*, July 21, 1999, B1ff; Gallun, A. Manufacturers let the good times roll for another quarter. *Business Journal-Milwaukee*, May 14, 1999, 8–9; Buller and Schuler, *Managing Organizations and People*, 327–345.
19. Hellriegel, D., Jackson, S. E., and Slocum, J. W., Jr. *Management*, 8th ed. Cincinnati: South-Western, 1999, 624–628.
20. Kerr, J., and Slocum, J. W., Jr. Managing corporate cultures through reward systems. *Academy of Management Executive*, 1987, 1(2), 99–108.
21. Melcher, R. A. Warm and fuzzy, meet rough and tumble. *Business Week*, January 26, 1998, 38.
22. Ratnesar, R., and Stein, J. This week's model. *Time*, September 27, 1999, 71–77.
23. Adapted from MacDonald, E. Andersen Consulting breakup battle with Arthur Andersen nears showdown. *Wall Street Journal*, July 28, 1999, A2; MacDonald, E. Andersen Consulting tried to thwart Arthur Andersen's attempt to buy firm. *Wall Street Journal*, June 14, 1999, B12.
24. Garner, R. Vendor ventures. *Computerworld*, July 26, 1999, 50–52; also see Kotter, J. P., and Heskett, J. L. *Corporate Culture and Performance.* New York: Free Press, 1992.
25. Cameron, K. S., and Freeman, S. J. Cultural congruence, strength, and type: Relationships to effectiveness. In R. W. Woodman and W. A. Pasmore (eds.), *Research in Organizational Change and Development*, vol. 5. Greenwich, Conn.: JAI Press, 1991, 23–58; Berry, L. L. *Discovering the Soul of Service.* New York: Free Press, 1999.
26. Kotter, and Heskett, *Corporate Culture and Performance*, 11–12.
27. De Vries, M. F. R. High-performance teams: Lessons from the Pygmies. *Organizational Dynamics*, Winter 1999, 66–77.
28. Near, J. P. Responses to legislative changes: Corporate whistleblowing policies. *Journal of Business Ethics*, 1998, 1551–1561; Sims, R. L., and Keenan, J. P. Predictors of external whistleblowing: Organizational and intrapersonal variables. *Journal of Business Ethics*, 1998, 17, 411–422.; Jubb, P. B. Whistleblowing: A restrictive definition and interpretation. *Journal of Business Ethics*, 1999, 21, 77–94.
29. Nelson, E., and Lublin, J. S. How whistle-blowers set off a fraud probe that crushed Cendant. *Wall Street Journal*, August 13, 1998, A1ff; Cendant repaid by ex-chairman. *New York Times*, February 24, 2000, C10.
30. Key, S. Organizational ethical culture: Real or imagined? *Journal of Business Ethics*, 1999, 20, 217–226; Buskirk, W. V., and McGrath, D. Organizational cultures as holding environments: A psychodynamic look at organizational symbolism. *Human Relations*, 1999, 52, 805–820.
31. Jung, D. I., and Avolio, B. J. Effects of leadership style and followers' cultural orientation on performance in group and individual task conditions. *Academy of Management Journal*, 1999, 42, 208–218.
32. Adapted from Markels, A. How one hotel manages staff's diversity. *Wall Street Journal*, November 20, 1996, B1ff.
33. Powell, G. N. The simultaneous pursuit of person–organization fit and diversity. *Organizational Dynamics*, Winter 1998, 50–61; Gilbert, J. A., Stead, B. A., and Ivancevich, J. M. Diversity management: A new management paradigm. *Journal of Business Ethics*, 1999, 21, 61–76.
34. Robinson, S. L., and O'Leary-Kelly, A. M. Monkey see, monkey do: The influence of work groups on the antisocial behavior of employees. *Academy of Management Journal*, 1998, 41, 658–672; Phillips, J. M. Effects of realistic job previews on multiple organizational outcomes: A meta-analysis. *Academy of Management Journal*, 1998, 41, 673–691.
35. O'Reilly, C. A., and Chatman, J. A. Culture as social control: Corporations, cults, and commitment. In B. M. Staw and L. L. Cummings (eds.), *Research in Organizational Behavior*, vol. 18. Greenwich, Conn: JAI Press, 1996, 157–200.
36. Taormina, R. J. Employee attitudes toward organizational socialization in the People's Republic of China, Hong Kong, and Singapore. *Journal of Applied Behavioral Science*, 1998, 34, 468–481; Ashforth, B. E., Saks, A. M., and Lee, R. T. Socialization and newcomer adjustment: The role of organizational context. *Human Relations*, 1998, 51, 897–927.
37. Adapted from Reiss, M. C., and Mitra, K. The effects of individual difference factors on the acceptability of ethical or unethical workplace behaviors. *Journal of Business Ethics*, 1998, 17, 1581–1593.
38. Adapted from Freiberg and Freiberg. *NUTS! Southwest Airlines' Crazy Recipe . . .*, 1996; Whiteley, R. and Hessan, D. *Customer Centered Growth.* Reading, Mass.: Addison-Wesley, 1996; Buller and Schuler, *Managing Organizations and People*, 261–279; Branch, S. The 100 best companies to work for in America. *Fortune*, January 11, 1999, 118–142; also see www.southwest.com/about_swa/press/factsheet.html.

CHAPTER

18 Organizational Change

LEARNING OBJECTIVES

When you have finished studying this chapter, you should be able to:

1. Identify characteristics of effective change programs and explain the importance of an accurate diagnosis of organizational functioning and problems.
2. Diagnose sources of individual and organizational resistance to change and describe methods for overcoming that resistance.
3. Explain the main features of organization development (OD) approaches to change.
4. Give examples of behavioral, cultural, task, technology, design, and strategy change approaches.
5. Describe the role and importance of ethical issues in organizational change.

***Preview Case:** What Horse's Rear Designed That?*

THE CHALLENGE OF CHANGE

- Pressures for Change
- Characteristics of Effective Change Programs
- ***Competency: Managing Change**—The Challenge for J.C. Penney*
- Organizational Diagnosis
- ***Competency: Managing Communication**—The Chairman's Rice Pudding*

RESISTANCE TO CHANGE

- Individual Resistance
- ***Competency: Managing Change**—St. Louis Mall Declares War on E-Commerce*
- Organizational Resistance
- Overcoming Resistance

ORGANIZATION DEVELOPMENT

- ***Competency: Managing Teams**—Overcoming Resistance at Nucor*
- Action Research
- Appreciative Inquiry

CHANGE MANAGEMENT

- Changing Behavior
- Changing Culture
- Changing Task and Technology
- ***Competency: Managing Across Cultures**—An Interview with Ford's Jacques Nasser*
- Changing Organization Design
- ***Competency: Managing Change**—Dumbsizing*
- Changing Strategy

ETHICAL ISSUES IN ORGANIZATIONAL CHANGE

CHAPTER SUMMARY

- Key Terms and Concepts
- Discussion Questions

DEVELOPING COMPETENCIES

- ***Competency: Managing Self**—Measuring Support for Change*
- ***Competency: Managing Ethics**—Kindred Todd and the Ethics of OD*

PREVIEW CASE

WHAT HORSE'S REAR DESIGNED THAT?

The standard railroad gauge (distance between the rails) in the United States is 4 feet, 8.5 inches. That's an odd number. Why is that gauge used? Because that's the way they built them in England, and English expatriates built the first U.S. railroads.

So, why did the English build their railroads to that size? Because the first rail lines were built by the same people who built the prerailroad tramways, and that's the gauge they used at that time.

So, why did the folks who built the tramways use that gauge? Because the people who built the tramways used the same jigs and tools that they used for building wagons. And they used 4 feet, 8.5 inches for the wheel spacing on wagons.

Okay! Why did the wagons have that particular wheel spacing? Well, if the wagon makers tried to use any other spacing, the wagon wheels would break on some of the roads then in use in England, as that was the spacing of the wheel ruts in the roads.

So, who built those old rutted roads? The first long-distance roads in England (and elsewhere in Europe) were built by Imperial Rome for their legions. The same roads have been in use ever since.

So, what caused the ruts? Roman war chariots first made the initial ruts, which everyone else had to match for fear of destroying their wagon wheels and wagons. And the wheel spacing for all the chariots made by and for Imperial Rome was uniform.

So, here's the final answer to the original question. The U.S. standard railroad gauge of 4 feet, 8.5 inches derives from the original specifications for an Imperial Roman war chariot. And the Imperial Roman war chariots were made just wide enough to accommodate the back ends of two warhorses.[1]

The Preview Case appeared on an organization's computer bulletin board. It reminds us, in a humorous fashion, about the "connections" that often exist in human affairs, even in the midst of change. It also reminds us of the interesting tension between stability and change. In spite of constant changes in transportation, a certain stability (in terms of gauge) has existed for more than 2,000 years. At the same time, this stability is somewhat illusory. We certainly wouldn't argue, for example, that simply because the gauge is identical, Roman war chariots and modern trains are basically identical forms of transportation. So it is with organizations. Stability is crucial for effectiveness and efficiency, yet much of perceived organizational stability is illusory. Rather, the reality of organizations is change, constant change.

Understanding and managing organizational change presents complex challenges.[2] Planned change may not work, or it may have consequences far different from those intended. In many sectors of the economy, organizations must have the capacity to adapt quickly and effectively in order to survive. Often the speed and complexity of change severely test the capabilities of managers and employees to adapt rapidly enough. However, when organizations fail to change, the costs of that failure may be quite high. Hence managers and employees must understand the nature of the change needed and the likely effects of alternative approaches to bring about that change.

Because organizations exist in a changing environment and are themselves constantly changing, organizations that emphasize bureaucratic or mechanistic systems are increasingly ineffective. Organizations with rigid hierarchies, high degrees of functional specialization, narrow and limited job descriptions, inflexible rules and procedures, and impersonal, autocratic management can't respond adequately to demands for change. As we pointed out in Chapter 16, organizations need designs that are flexible and adaptive. They also need systems that both require and allow greater commitment and use of talent on the part of employees and managers alike.

In this chapter, we examine the pressures on organizations that create the need for change, identify characteristics of effective change programs, and emphasize the importance of accurate organizational diagnosis. We explore the difficult issue of resistance to change at both the individual and organizational level and examine ways to cope with that inevitable resistance. We examine the field of organization development as a major approach to managing organizational change. In addition, we identify some specific approaches and techniques for making organizational and behavioral changes. Finally, we explore some ethical issues associated with programs of organizational change.

Learning Objective:

1. Identify characteristics of effective change programs and explain the importance of an accurate diagnosis of organizational functioning and problems.

THE CHALLENGE OF CHANGE

Organizational change can be difficult and costly. Despite the challenges, many organizations successfully make needed changes, but at the same time, failure also is common. There is considerable evidence that adaptive, flexible organizations have a competitive advantage over rigid, static organizations.[3] As a result, managing change has become a central focus of effective organizations, and this focus is even creating its own vocabulary. Table 18.1 presents some of the concepts made popular by the increasing emphasis on effective organizational change. These ideas have appeared in various forms throughout the book, and we examine them further in this chapter. In many respects, then, managing change effectively requires an understanding and use of many of the important principles and concepts of organizational behavior that we have explored in this book.

PRESSURES FOR CHANGE

Both advanced industrialized and developing countries are changing in important ways that have significant impacts on organizations. Many organizations have had to undergo a radical reorientation with regard to the way they do business. As reported in *Fortune* magazine, the following trends are expected to have profound effects on organizations in the years ahead.

Table 18.1

The Language of Organizational Change

CONCEPT	EXPLANATION
The learning organization	The notion that learning is central to success and effectiveness. Management must learn to see the "big picture" and understand subtle relationships among parts of the system.
Reengineering	A fundamental rethinking and redesign of systems and processes. Work should be organized around outcomes, not tasks or functions.
Core competencies	The notion that companies need to identify and organize around what they do best. Strategy should be based on these core competencies rather than products or markets.
Organizational architecture	The idea that managers need to think broadly about the organization in terms of how work, people, and designs fit together.
Time-based competition	The notion that time is money. Time is manageable and can be a source of competitive advantage affecting productivity, quality, and innovation.
Growth strategies	Methods to lift profits by expanding revenues, not just cutting costs.
Mission and vision statements	Description of what the company will become and how it will get there.
Strategic alliances	Ways to create business partnerships among customers, suppliers, and even competitors.

Source: Adapted from Byrne, J. A. Management's new gurus. *Business Week*, August 31, 1992, 45; Rigby, D. K. What's today's special at the consultant's café? *Fortune*, September 7, 1998, 162–163.

- Government will get out of the way.
- E-business outlays will boom.
- Biotechnology will arrive.
- Net connections will get faster.
- Gadgets will get even cooler.[4]

According to this analysis, companies that are well positioned to take advantage of these trends will prosper, but those that ignore them will founder. For example, Sycamore Networks, a maker of hardware and software for optical networks that interface with existing Internet and computer systems, is in a position to exploit some of the trends mentioned. Genentech and other large biotechnology firms should thrive in the emerging global economy. AES, which owns power generation facilities in 16 countries, is well positioned to take advantage of the trend toward deregulation in the electrical power industry as governments around the world seek to reduce government regulation and red tape.

An almost infinite variety of **pressures for change** impinge on organizations. Here, we examine three of the most significant such pressures: (1) the globalization of markets, (2) the spread of information technology and computer networks, and (3) changes in the nature of the workforce employed by organizations.

Globalization. Organizations face global competition on an unprecedented scale. **Globalization** means that the main players in the world's economy are now international or multinational corporations.[5] Their emergence creates pressures on domestic corporations to internationalize and redesign their operations. Global markets now exist for most products, but in order to compete effectively in them, firms often must transform their cultures, structures, and operations.

Historically, the primary forces at work in globalization have included

- the economic recoveries of Germany and Japan after their defeat in World War II;
- the emergence of new "industrial" countries, such as Korea, Taiwan, Singapore, and Spain;
- the dramatic shift from planned economies to market economies that has occurred in Eastern Europe, Russia and other republics of the former Soviet Union, and to a certain extent in the People's Republic of China; and
- the emergence of new "power blocks" of international traders, stemming from the economic unification of Europe that is underway and the "yen block" of Japan and its Pacific Rim trading partners.[6]

These and other powerful globalization forces are pushing domestic firms around the world to abandon "business as usual" in order to remain competitive. In many industries, global strategies are replacing country-by-country approaches. For example, consider Gillette's shift to world products. As was typical for consumer goods companies, Gillette traditionally developed new products one market at a time, with gradual roll-outs around the world. Starting with its Sensor razor, however, Gillette created a global product with a global launch—the same improved product was advertised and available everywhere in the world at roughly the same time. Although globalization strategies aren't easy to implement, many organizations have effectively moved outside their domestic markets. Ford, Merck & Company, IBM, and Hewlett-Packard have strong, profitable operations in Europe. McDonald's, Walt Disney, DuPont, and Amway have highly successful Asian operations. Amway sells more than $500 million worth of housewares door to door in Japan each year. Procter & Gamble has recently reorganized in order to ensure that its marketing efforts proceed simultaneously worldwide. The company has eliminated regional business units and put profit responsibility in the hands of seven executives who are responsible for global product units (see the Preview Case in Chapter 16).[7]

Information Technology and Computers. Coping with international competition requires a flexibility that traditional organizations often do not possess. Fortunately, the revolution in information technology permits many organizations to develop the needed flexibility. A second major category of change facing organizations stems from the proliferation of sophisticated information technology. **Information technology** comprises networks of computers (many of them complex), telecommunications systems, and remote-controlled devices.[8] As discussed throughout this book, information technology (IT) is having a profound impact on individual employees, teams, and organizations. For example, experts who have studied its impact on organizations have observed that IT

- changes almost everything about a company—its structure, its products, its markets, and its processes;
- increases the value of invisible assets, such as knowledge, competencies, and training;
- democratizes a company because employees have more information and can talk to anyone in the company;
- increases the flexibility of work by allowing more people to work at home, on the road, or at hours that suit them; and
- allows companies to unify their global operations and to work a 24-hour day throughout the world.[9]

However, the potential effects of IT are not uniformly positive. Organizations that rely on sophisticated information technologies are more vulnerable to sabotage, espionage, and vandalism. Moreover, IT can create new social divisions (e.g., the computer literate versus the nonuser and the educated versus the uneducated) even as it brings people together. If the full potential of IT is to be realized, employees must be better educated, better trained, and better motivated than at any time in history.

However, wisdom and intuition remain essential for good management, and having more information, faster, cannot replace good judgment and common sense.

Still, despite these cautions, the impact of IT is dramatic. For example, Adaptec is a Silicon Valley producer of computer hardware. Just a short time ago, Adaptec had to wait 105 days after placing an order to receive computer boards from its Singapore assembly plant. By using more sophisticated computer software and the Internet, Adaptec has reduced its production cycle to 55 days. Not only do its customers now get their orders filled in half the time, but the company also has cut its work-in-process inventory by half, with a positive impact on profits.[10] The Internet makes it possible for a design, a fashion, or an idea to be known instantaneously around the world. A New York apparel manufacturer put his spring line on the Internet and had five orders from Beijing in the People's Republic of China within hours. Information technology permits an IBM engineer to ask colleagues in virtually any country for help when confronted with a difficult problem. General Electric operates its own private global phone network, allowing employees to communicate directly with each other from anywhere in the world by using just seven digits. Information technology allows CRSS, a large architectural firm, to exchange drawings with 3M, one of its largest clients, almost instantaneously.[11]

The globalization phenomenon and information technologies are linked in interesting ways. Highly decentralized organizations, with operating units scattered throughout the world, face some significant challenges in terms of coordination and cooperation. However, advanced computer and telecommunication technologies provide mechanisms to link employees in ways only imagined in the past. For example, many multinational corporations rely on the use of virtual teams to accomplish their work. **Virtual teams** are groups of geographically and/or organizationally dispersed coworkers who are assembled via a combination of telecommunications and information technologies to accomplish an organizational task.[12] Such teams rarely meet or work together face-to-face. Virtual teams may be set up on a temporary basis and used to accomplish a specific task, or they may be relatively permanent and used to address ongoing strategic planning issues. The membership of virtual teams may be quite fluid, with members changing according to task demands even for those teams with an ongoing assignment.

Changing Nature of the Workforce. In addition to coping with the challenges presented by globalization and rapid changes in information technology, organizations must attract employees from a changing labor market. For this reason among others, we have explored the challenges of managing cultural diversity throughout this book.

As discussed in Chapter 1, the labor market continues to grow more diverse in terms of gender and ethnicity. Thus equal opportunity pressures on hiring practices and promotion decisions will persist for some time to come. Other trends add to the challenge for organizations. For example, the dual-career family has become the norm, rather than the exception, in most industrialized societies. Further, the number of temporary workers continues to grow as a percentage of all workers. The **contingency workforce** includes part-time employees, freelancers, subcontractors, and independent professionals hired by companies to cope with unexpected or temporary challenges. By some accounts, about 25 percent of U.S. workers now fall into these categories. This percentage is expected to continue to grow as companies find that they can operate efficiently and effectively with a smaller core of permanent employees supplemented by a changing cast of temporary help—and save money by not having to provide employee benefits. The U.S. Bureau of Labor Statistics expects the number of temporary workers to increase by another 50 percent by 2006.[13] Temporary-employment agencies, such as Manpower and Kelly Services, are among the fastest growing organizations in the United States. The largest of the agencies—Manpower, Inc.—has more employees than General Motors or IBM. Among the challenges facing organizations are those of motivating and rewarding temporary and part-time employees whose morale and loyalties may be quite different from those of permanent employees.

The workforce is increasingly better educated, less unionized, and characterized by changing values and aspirations. Although these changes won't lessen the motivation to work, they continue to affect the rewards that people seek from work and the balance that they seek between work and other aspects of their lives. The **quality of work life** (QWL) represents the degree to which people are able to satisfy important personal needs through their work. Achieving a high QWL is an important goal for many working women and men. Typically, employees desire pleasant working conditions, more participation in decisions that affect their jobs, and valuable support facilities such as day-care centers for their children. These and other employee expectations put additional pressures on organizations and affect their ability to compete effectively in the labor market.

Of course, changes in globalization, information technology, and the workforce represent only some of the challenges facing organizations. The following Managing Change Competency feature identifies additional pressures for change that challenge J.C. Penney as it struggles to survive and prosper in a rapidly evolving retailing environment.

CHARACTERISTICS OF EFFECTIVE CHANGE PROGRAMS

Distinguishing between change that inevitably happens to all organizations and change that is planned by members of an organization is important. Our focus is primarily on

COMPETENCY: MANAGING CHANGE

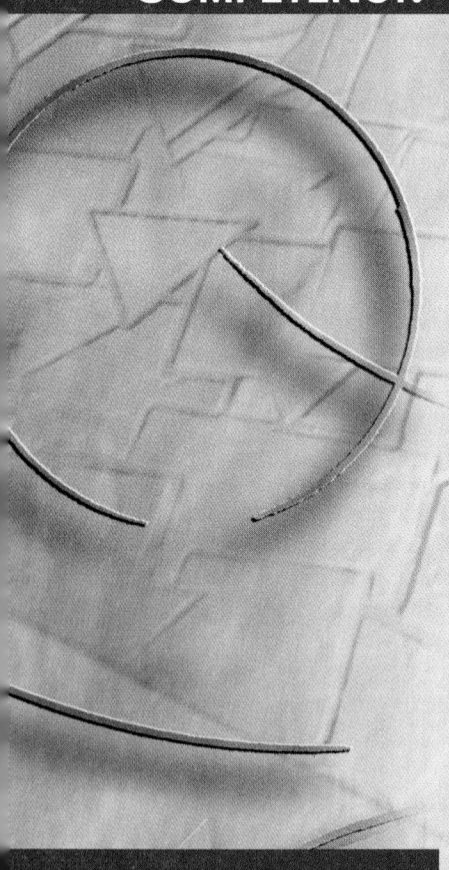

For more information on J.C. Penney, visit the company's home page at ***www.jcpenney.com.***

THE CHALLENGE FOR J.C. PENNEY

In January 2000, managers from J.C. Penney stores nationwide gathered for a meeting in Plano, Texas. Surprisingly, the last time that all Penney store managers had gathered in one place was in 1927! However, executives of the 98-year-old firm felt the need to take stock and one way of doing so was to ask managers what needed to be changed.

The company is largely missing out on the biggest consumer-spending boom in years. It carries much of the same merchandise—basic casual and business clothing, including essentially the same brands—as its competitors (e.g., Kohl's, Dillard's, and Sears), but it is being badly outperformed by them. Penney and its direct competition target the same customers, primarily women who buy for themselves and their families. Penney executives have blamed slumping sales on changes in the retail marketplace. The company continues to be a traditional, moderately priced department store in an era of specialty stores, discount chains, and Internet shopping. However, critics point out that other moderately priced department store chains, such as Kohl's, are actually doing quite well. These critics argue that Penney's failures are largely failures of execution—how well the stores keep what people want in stock, how easily customers can find what they want, how effectively sales and promotions are advertised, and so on.

J.C. Penney is considering some major changes and promises to be more aggressive in addressing its problems. In addition, it has some strengths to build on. Drawing on its long experience with catalog sales, the company's Web site is doing well, with more than $100 million in sales in 1999. The firm has begun to share information with suppliers via the Internet in an attempt to keep stores better stocked with more popular items. And, in a break with its tradition of promoting from within, the company recruited Vanessa Castagna from Wal-Mart as the firm's new executive in charge of department store operations. In her first press conference after joining J.C. Penney, Castagna stated simply, "I am the agent of change."[14]

intentional, goal-oriented organizational change. **Planned organizational change** represents a purposeful attempt by managers and employees to improve the functioning of teams, departments, divisions, or an entire organization in some important way.[15]

Effective planned change efforts are often characterized by some common characteristics. For example, effective change programs may involve

- motivating change by creating a readiness for the change among employees and attempting to overcome resistance to change (which we discuss in detail shortly);
- creating a shared vision of the desired future state of the organization;
- developing political support for the needed changes;
- managing the transition from the current state to the desired future state; and
- sustaining momentum for change so that it will be carried to completion.[16]

The initiatives required to address each of these aspects of a change program are summarized in Figure 18.1.

Figure 18.1 **Initiatives Contributing to Effective Change Management**

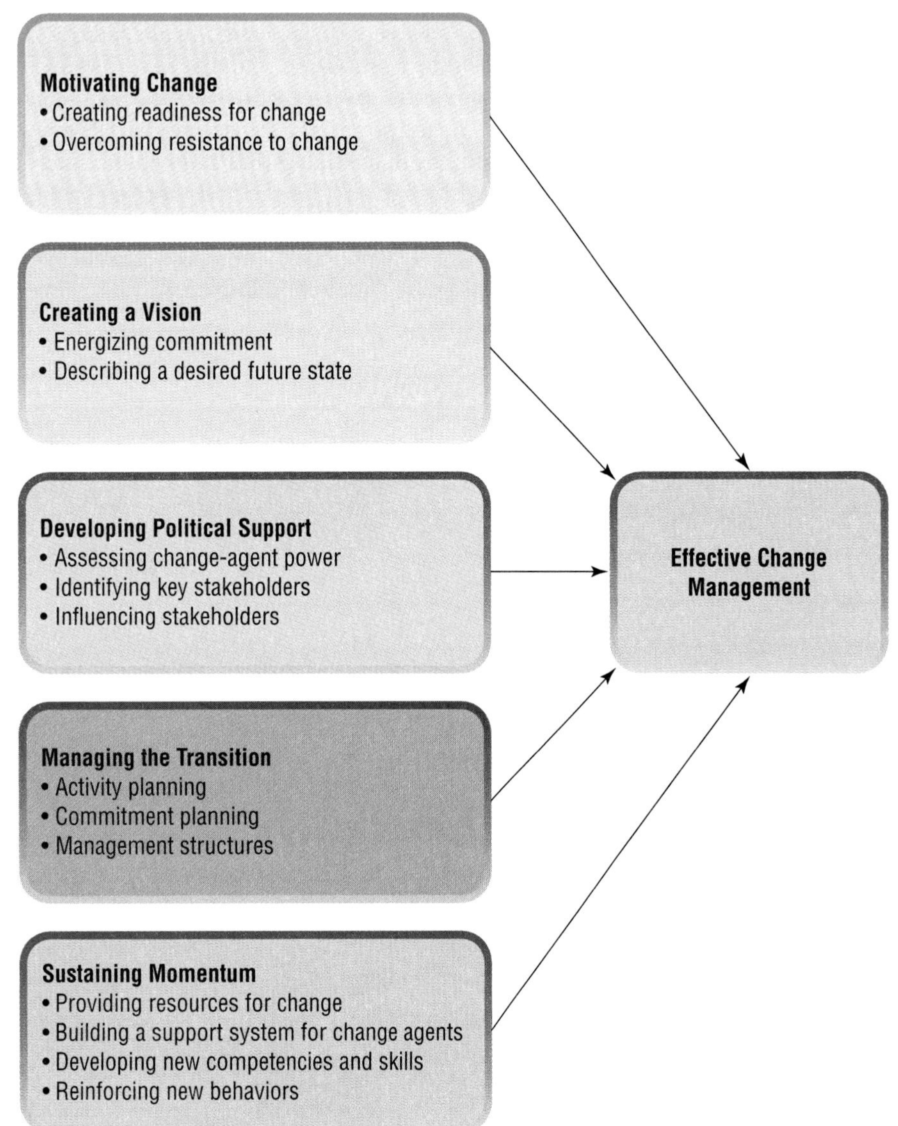

Source: Reprinted with permission from Cummings, J. G., and Worley, C. G. *Organization Development and Change*, 6th ed. Cincinnati: South-Western, 1997, 154.

Similarly, the conditions necessary for successfully carrying out effective change programs include the following.

- The organization's members must be the key source of energy for change, not some party external to the team or organization.
- Key members of the organization must recognize the need for change and be attracted by the potentially positive outcomes of the change program.
- A willingness to change norms and procedures must exist.[17]

These two lists are similar in certain respects. Change must come from within the organization. People must be aware of the need for change, believe in the potential value of the changes proposed, and be willing to change their behaviors in order to make the team, department, or organization more effective. Absent these beliefs and behaviors, effective organizational change is problematic. In addition, effective change must rely on a contingency perspective that is open to trying different things at different times.

Organizationwide Change. Meeting the challenge posed by organizational change often means not doing things piecemeal. To be successful, change usually must be organizationwide.[18] The systems model shown in Figure 18.2 provides a useful way to think about organizationwide change.

The **systems model of change** describes the organization as six interacting variables that could serve as the focus of planned change: people, culture, task, technology, design, and strategy. The **people variable** applies to the individuals working for the organization, including their individual differences—personalities, attitudes, perceptions, attributions, needs, and motives (see Chapters 2, 3, and 5). The **culture variable** reflects the shared beliefs, values, expectations, and norms of organizational members (see Chapter 17). The **task variable** involves the nature of the work itself—whether jobs are simple or complex, novel or repetitive, standardized or unique. The

Figure 18.2 **A Systems Model of Change**

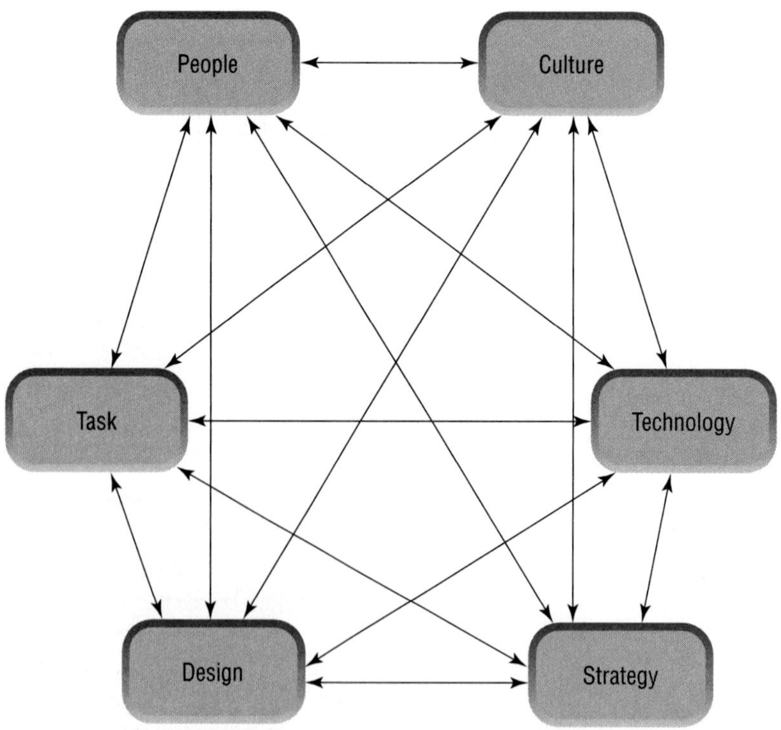

technology variable encompasses the problem-solving methods and techniques used and the application of knowledge to various organizational processes. It includes such things as the use of information technology, robots and other automation, manufacturing processes, tools, and techniques (see Chapter 15 for a discussion of both task and technology in job design). The **design variable** is the formal organizational structure and its systems of communication, control, authority, and responsibility (see Chapter 16). Finally, the **strategy variable** comprises the organization's planning process and includes decisions about how the organization chooses to compete. It typically consists of activities undertaken to identify organizational goals and prepare specific plans to acquire, allocate, and use resources in order to accomplish those goals (see Chapter 16).

As Figure 18.2 indicates, these six variables are interdependent. A change in any one usually results in a change in one or more of the others. For example, a change in the organization's strategic plan might dictate a change in organization design to an adaptive or network form. This change, in turn, could result in the reassignment of people. At the same time, the redesign may also lead to a change in the technology used by the organization, which affects the attitudes and behaviors of the employees involved, and so on. All these changes would occur within a particular organizational culture, which might either support or resist them. Moreover, change itself may either modify or reinforce the prevailing culture. An advantage of a systems approach to organizational change is that it helps managers and employees understand and think through such interrelationships. The systems approach reminds management that it cannot change part of the organization without, in some sense, changing the whole.

Contingency Perspective. Disagreement exists about the best ways to achieve organizational change. Many different approaches to organizational change have been used successfully, but what works in one organization under a particular set of circumstances may not necessarily work in another. We favor a contingency perspective, which recognizes that no single best approach to change exists—no approach is likely to be effective under all conditions and circumstances. The contingency perspective leads directly to the need for an accurate diagnosis of organizational functioning and problems. Before you can change something effectively, you must understand it.

Organizational Diagnosis

An accurate diagnosis of organizational problems and functioning is absolutely essential as a starting point for planned organizational change. In a humorous way, the Managing Communication Competency feature on page 552 suggests the importance of organizational diagnosis.

All organizations have "rice puddings"—patterns of behavior and procedures that, at one time and place, made perfect sense but no longer do. Diagnosing needed change, in part, means uncovering the organization's "rice puddings." Four basic steps are undertaken in effective **organizational diagnosis**:

- recognize and interpret the problem and assess the need for change;
- determine the organization's readiness and capability for change;
- identify managerial and employee resources and motivations for change; and
- determine change goals and a change strategy.[19]

Information needed to diagnose organizational problems may be gathered by questionnaires, interviews, or observation—and from the organization's records. Typically, some combination of these data gathering methods is used. An advantage of the information collecting process is that it increases awareness of the need for change. Even when widespread agreement exists concerning the need for change, people may have different ideas about the approach to be used and when, where, and how it

COMPETENCY: MANAGING COMMUNICATION

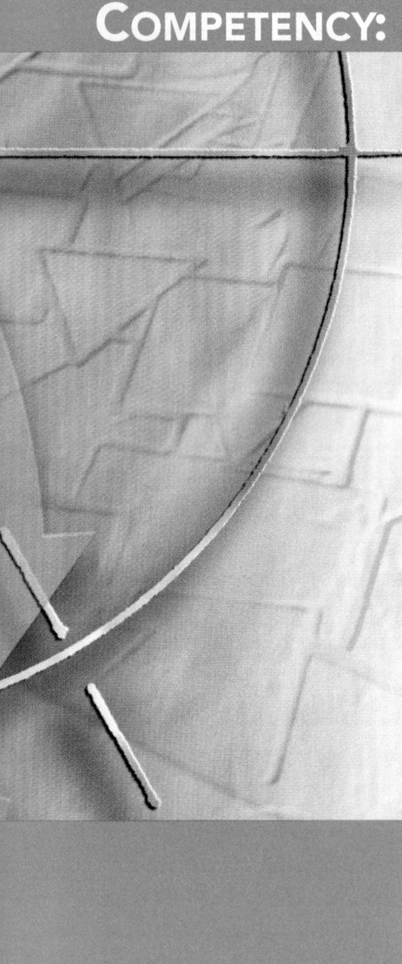

THE CHAIRMAN'S RICE PUDDING

A senior manager was given the responsibility for examining all operations and procedures at corporate headquarters. She formed a task force to help with this review. The top executives of the organization had their own private kitchen and dining room facilities. Although this perk wasn't high on its list of priorities, the task force eventually got around to taking a look at the operations of this kitchen and executive dining room.

The task force discovered that two rice puddings were made every day at 12:15 P.M. and thrown away at 2:45 P.M. Mysteriously, the rice puddings were not listed on the dining room's menu. When the chef was questioned about this practice, he admitted that, to the best of his knowledge, no patron of the dining room had ever eaten one of these puddings. Nor did he know why they were being made. The practice was in place when he had joined the organization 8 years before, and he had simply continued it.

Intrigued, the task force decided to investigate further the origin of this odd ritual. They discovered that, 17 years before, the individual who was chairman of the organization at that time had strolled through the kitchen one day. In a conversation with the chef, he had mentioned how much he liked rice pudding. The chef then instructed his kitchen staff to prepare two rice puddings each day but not to include them on the menu. When the chairman came to lunch, his waiter could then offer him a rice pudding. The second rice pudding was made in case anyone else in the chairman's luncheon party should also request one.

The chairman, who apparently had a rice pudding occasionally, retired 4 years later. Thirteen years after his retirement, the kitchen staff was still making rice puddings. By now, however, none of them knew why they were doing so, nor did any of the patrons of the dining room know that the pudding was available.[20]

should be implemented. Thus some systematic attempt should be made to determine the focus and goals of a change effort, which is precisely what Vanessa Castagna of J.C. Penney spent her first 6 months doing.

Any planned change program also requires a careful assessment of individual and organizational capacity for change. Two important aspects of individual readiness for change are the degree of employee satisfaction with the status quo and the perceived personal risk involved in changing it. Figure 18.3 shows the possible combinations of these concerns. When employees are dissatisfied with the current situation and perceive little personal risk from change, their readiness for change probably would be high. In contrast, when employees are satisfied with the status quo and perceive high personal risk in change, their readiness for change probably would be low.

With regard to individual readiness for change, another important variable is employee expectations regarding the change effort.[21] Expectations play a crucial role in behavior. If people expect that nothing of significance will change, regardless of the amount of time and effort they might devote to making it happen, this belief can become a self-fulfilling prophecy. And when employee expectations for improvement are unrealistically high, unfulfilled expectations can make matters worse. Ideally, expectations regarding change should be positive yet realistic.

In addition, the organization's capacity for change must be accurately assessed. Approaches that require a massive commitment of personal energy and organizational resources probably will fail if the organization has few resources and its members do not have the time or opportunity to implement the needed changes. Under such cir-

Figure 18.3 **Employee Readiness for Change**

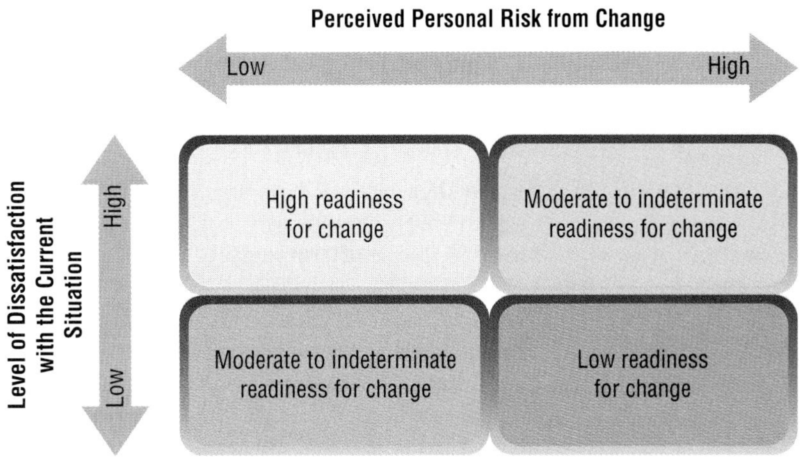

Source: Adapted from Zeira, Y., and Avedisian, J. Organizational planned change: Assessing the chances for success. *Organizational Dynamics,* Spring 1989, 37.

cumstances, the organization may benefit most from starting with a modest effort. Then, as the organization develops the necessary resources and employee commitment, it can increase the depth and breadth of the change.

When managers and employees conduct an organizational diagnosis, they should recognize two additional important factors. First, organizational behavior is the product of many interacting forces. Therefore, what is observed or diagnosed—employee behaviors, problems, and the current state of the organization—has multiple causes. Trying to isolate single causes for complex problems can lead to simplistic and ineffective change strategies. Second, much of the information gathered about an organization during a diagnosis will represent symptoms rather than causes of problems. Obviously, change strategies that focus on symptoms won't solve underlying problems. For example, in one organization, an awards program that recognized perfect attendance failed to reduce absenteeism because it didn't deal with the causes of the problem. Careful diagnosis revealed that employees were absent from work because of pressures created by excessive workloads and an inefficient, frustrating set of procedures for doing their jobs. The awards offered weren't sufficient to change employee behaviors and, more important, didn't address the real problems of work overload and poor job design.[22]

Potential resistance to change represents another important aspect of readiness and motivation for change. Both individual and organizational resistance to change must be diagnosed.

Learning Objective:

2. Diagnose sources of individual and organizational resistance to change and describe methods for overcoming that resistance.

RESISTANCE TO CHANGE

Inevitably, at least to some extent, both individuals and groups in organizations resist change. **Resistance to change** often is baffling because it can take so many forms. Overt resistance may be expressed through strikes, reduced productivity, shoddy work, and even sabotage. Covert resistance may be expressed by increased tardiness and absenteeism, requests for transfers, resignations, loss of motivation, lower morale, and higher accident or error rates. One of the most damaging forms of resistance is passive resistance by employees—a lack of participation in formulating change proposals and ultimately a lack of commitment to the proposals, even when they have had an opportunity to participate in making such decisions.

As Figure 18.4 shows, resistance to change stems from a variety of sources. Some are traceable to individuals, but others involve the nature and structure of organizations.[23] Managers and employees need to understand the reasons for resistance to change and its sources. A dramatic example of such resistance is presented in the Managing Change Competency feature on the next page.

Individual Resistance

Figure 18.4 shows six important sources of individual resistance to change. These aren't the only reasons why individuals might resist change at work, but they are common and frequently important.

Perceptions. In Chapter 3, we discussed the notion of perceptual defense—a perceptual error whereby people tend to perceive selectively those things that fit most comfortably into their current view of the world. Once individuals have established an understanding of reality, they may resist changing it. Among other things, people may resist the possible impact of change on their lives by (1) reading or listening only to what they agree with, (2) conveniently forgetting any knowledge that could lead to other viewpoints, and (3) misunderstanding communication that, if correctly understood, wouldn't fit their existing attitudes and values. For example, managers enrolled in management training programs are exposed to different managerial philosophies and techniques. In the classroom, they may competently discuss and answer questions about these new ideas, yet carefully segregate in their minds the approaches that they believe wouldn't work from those that they already practice.

Personality. Some aspects of an individual's personality (e.g., dogmatism or dependency) may predispose that person to resist change.[24] In Chapter 2, we defined *dogmatism* as the rigidity of a person's beliefs. The highly dogmatic individual is close-minded and more likely to resist change than is a less dogmatic person. Another example is dependency. If carried to extremes, dependency on others can lead to resistance to change. People who are highly dependent on others often lack self-esteem. They may resist change until those that they depend on endorse it. Employees who are highly dependent on their supervisors for performance feedback probably will not accept any new techniques or methods for doing their jobs unless their supervisors

Figure 18.4 **Sources of Resistance to Change**

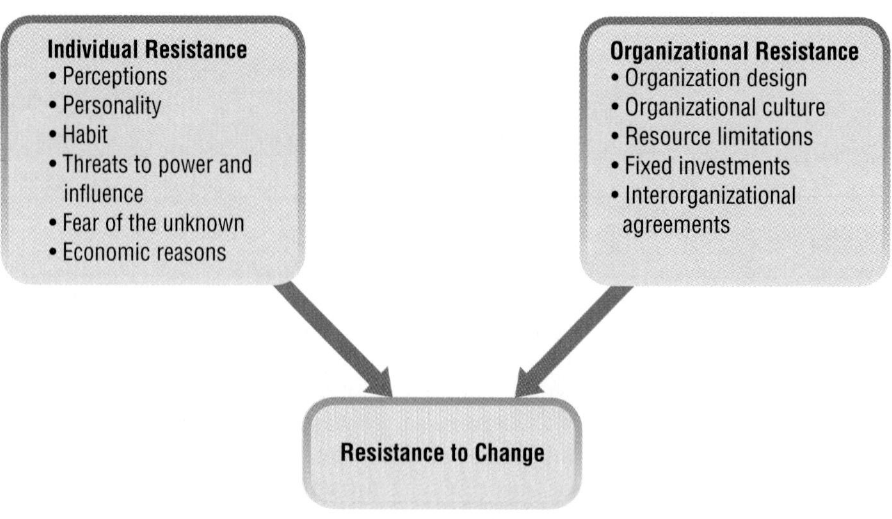

COMPETENCY: MANAGING CHANGE

ST. LOUIS MALL DECLARES WAR ON E-COMMERCE

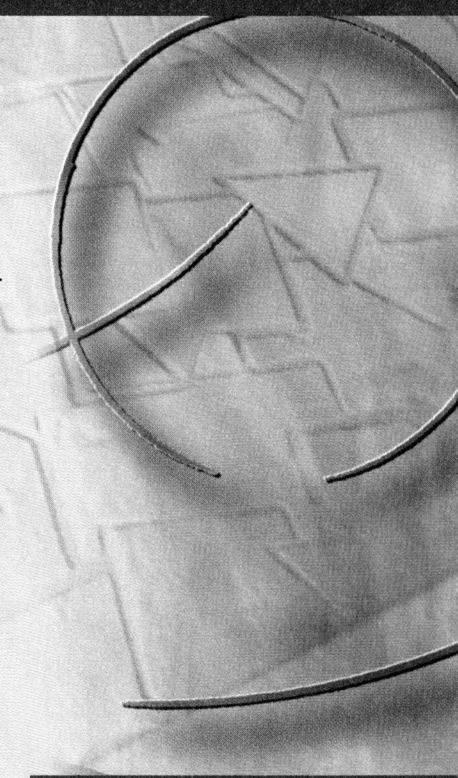

In suburban St. Louis, Missouri, an upscale mall briefly attempted to wage war against the Internet. The Saint Louis Galleria informed its 170 retail tenants of a new policy that prohibited any in-store "signs, insignias, decals or other advertising or display devices which promote and encourage the purchase of merchandise via e-commerce." The policy shocked some store owners and prompted threats of litigation from Right Start, an educational toys retailer. A spokesperson for Right Start suggests that it is foolish to attempt to fight the "evolution of retailing." The new policy was described as going over like a "lead balloon" at the Bombay Company, headquartered in Fort Worth. Bombay Company president Carmie Mehrlander remarked that, "No one has ever improved business by making it more difficult for the consumer."

Initially, mall management was unfazed by this resistance to its resistance to e-commerce. Mark Zorensky, president of the company that owns Saint Louis Galleria, defended its approach. "We recognize that there is no way to stop the Internet, but what we're trying to stop is the retailer blatantly redirecting sales from the mall to their Web page." However, one week after the new policy was established, there was little evidence of compliance on the part of store owners. Walking about the mall, *Wall Street Journal* reporters observed that most stores still had numerous posted references to online catalog sales, company Web sites, and the like.

At this point, Zorensky stated, "Some have removed the (Internet) signs. Some have not. We're trying to deal with each of these on an individual basis." Most major national firms represented in the mall apparently advised their stores to ignore the policy. About 2 weeks after the mall policy was announced, it was quietly withdrawn.[25]

*For more information on Right Start and Bombay Company, visit these companies' home pages at **www.rightstart.com**.*

personally support the changes and indicate how these changes will improve performance and/or otherwise benefit the employees.

Managers must be careful to avoid overemphasizing the role played by personality in resistance to change because they can easily make the fundamental attribution error (see Chapter 3). There is a tendency to "blame" resistance to change in the workplace on individual personalities. Although personality may play a role (as we have just discussed), it seldom is the most important factor in a situation involving change.

Habit. Unless a situation changes dramatically, individuals may continue to respond to stimuli in their usual ways.[26] A habit can be a source of comfort, security, and satisfaction for individuals because it allows them to adjust to the world and cope with it. Whether a habit becomes a primary source of resistance to change depends, to a certain extent, on whether individuals perceive advantages from changing their behaviors. For example, if an organization suddenly announced that all employees would immediately receive a 20 percent pay raise, few would object even though the pay raise might result in changes in behavior as employees could enjoy a more expensive lifestyle. However, if the organization announced that all employees could receive a 20 percent pay raise only if they switched from working during the normal workday to working evenings and nights, many might object. Employees would have to change many deeply ingrained habits about when they slept, ate, interacted with their families, and so on.

Threats to Power and Influence. Some people in organizations may view change as a threat to their power or influence. The control of something needed by others, such as information or resources, is a source of power in organizations (see Chapter 9). Once a power position has been established, individuals or teams often resist changes that they perceive as reducing their ability to influence others. For example, programs to improve the quality of work life (QWL programs) tend to focus on nonmanagerial employees and are often perceived as increasing their power. As a result, managers and supervisors may resist such programs. Novel ideas or a new use for resources also can disrupt the power relationships among individuals and departments in an organization and therefore are often resisted.

Fear of the Unknown. Confronting the unknown makes most people anxious. Each major change in a work situation carries with it an element of uncertainty. People starting a new job may be concerned about their ability to perform adequately. Women starting a second career after raising a family may be anxious about how they will fit in with other employees after a long absence from the workplace. An employee may wonder what might happen if he or she relocates to company headquarters in another state. Will my family like it? Will I be able to find friends? What will top managers think of me if I refuse to relocate? Consequences of these types of decisions cannot be known in advance, so people are typically anxious about making them. Individuals may be so anxious and threatened by change that they refuse promotions that require moving to a new location or significant shifts in job duties and responsibilities.

Economic Reasons. Money weighs heavily in people's considerations, and they certainly can be expected to resist changes that might lower their incomes. In a very real sense, employees have invested in the status quo in their jobs. That is, they have learned how to perform their work well, how to get good performance evaluations, and how to interact effectively with others. Changes in established work routines or job duties may threaten their economic security. Employees may fear that, after changes are made, they won't be able to perform as well and thus may not be as valuable to the organization, their supervisors, or their coworkers.

Organizational Resistance

To a certain extent, the nature of organizations is to resist change. Organizations often are most efficient at doing routine tasks and tend to perform more poorly, at least initially, at doing something for the first time. Thus, to ensure operational efficiency and effectiveness, organizations may create strong defenses against change. Moreover, change often opposes vested interests and violates certain territorial rights or decision-making prerogatives that departments, teams, and informal groups have established and accepted over time. Figure 18.4 shows several of the more significant sources of organizational resistance to change.

Organization Design. Organizations need stability and continuity in order to function effectively. Indeed, the term *organization* implies that individual, team, and informal group activities have a certain structure. Individuals have assigned roles, established procedures for getting the job done, consistent ways of getting needed information, and the like. However, this legitimate need for structure also may lead to resistance to change. Organizations may have narrowly defined jobs, clearly identified lines of authority and responsibility, and limited flows of information from top to bottom. The use of a rigid design and an emphasis on the authority hierarchy may cause employees to use only certain specific channels of communication and to focus narrowly on their own duties and responsibilities. Typically, the more mechanistic the organization, the more numerous are the levels through which an idea must travel (see Chapter 16). This type of design, then, increases the probability that any new idea will be screened out because it threatens the status quo. More adaptive and flexible organizations are designed to reduce the resistance to change created by rigid organizational structures.

Organizational Culture. Organizational culture plays a key role in change. Cultures are not easy to modify and may become a major source of resistance to needed changes (see Chapter 17).[27] One aspect of an effective organizational culture is whether it has the flexibility to take advantage of opportunities to change. An ineffective organizational culture (in terms of organizational change) is one that rigidly socializes employees into the old culture even in the face of evidence that it no longer works.

IBM and General Motors dominated their industries by creating organizations with cultures that were excellent at producing very large products—mainframe computers and large, powerful cars. When demand for their products dropped off dramatically, both IBM and GM were forced to undertake drastic cultural changes in order to remain profitable. Among other things, the sheer size of these organizations made it difficult for them to change their cultures quickly.

Resource Limitations. Some organizations want to maintain the status quo, but others would change if they had the resources to do so. Change requires capital, time, and individuals with a lot of competencies. At any particular time, an organization's managers and employees may have identified changes that could or should be made, but they may have to defer or abandon some of the desired changes because of resource limitations. Continental Lite, formerly a division of Continental Airlines, quickly learned that it didn't have the resources (planes, ground crews, and terminals) to compete effectively against Southwest Airlines for the budget-conscious traveler. Without these resources, Continental was unable to change quickly and had to abandon its attempt to compete directly with Southwest in certain air commuter markets.

Fixed Investments. Resource limitations aren't confined to organizations with insufficient assets. Capital intensive organizations, such as Exxon/Mobil, Lockheed Martin, or Oxychem, may be unable to change because of fixed capital investments in assets that they can't easily alter (equipment, buildings, and land). The plight of the central business districts in many cities illustrates this resistance to change. Most large cities developed before the automobile and can't begin to accommodate today's traffic volumes and parking demands. The fixed investments in buildings, streets, transit systems, and utilities are enormous and usually prevent rapid and substantial change. Therefore, many older central urban areas are unable to meet the competition of suburban shopping centers.

Fixed investments aren't limited to physical assets; they also may be expressed in terms of people. For example, consider employees who no longer are making a significant contribution to an organization but have enough seniority to maintain their jobs. Unless they can be motivated to perform better or retrained for other positions, their salaries and fringe benefits represent, from the organization's perspective, fixed investments that can't easily be changed.

Interorganizational Agreements. Agreements between organizations usually impose obligations on them that can restrain their actions. Labor negotiations and contracts provide some examples. Ways of doing things that once were considered the prerogatives of management (the right to hire and fire, assign tasks, promote and demote, and the like) may become subject to negotiation and fixed in a negotiated contract. Other types of contracts also may constrain organizations. For example, proponents of change may face delay because of arrangements with competitors, commitments to suppliers and other contractors, and pledges to public officials in return for licenses, permits, financing, or tax abatement.

Overcoming Resistance

Realistically, resistance to change will never cease completely. Managers and employees, however, can learn to identify and minimize resistance and thus become more effective change agents.

People often have difficulty with clearly understanding situations that involve change. Part of the reason is that even analyzing a change problem may be quite complex when a large number of variables must be considered. Kurt Lewin, a pioneering social psychologist, developed a way of looking at change that has been highly useful for managers and employees when faced with the challenge of change.[28] Lewin viewed change not as an event, but as a dynamic balance of forces working in opposite directions. His approach, called **force field analysis,** suggests that any situation can be considered to be in a state of equilibrium resulting from a balance of forces constantly pushing against each other. Certain forces in the situation—various types of resistance to change—tend to maintain the status quo. At the same time, various pressures for change are acting opposite to these forces and are pushing for change. The combined effect of these two sets of forces is illustrated in Figure 18.5 in terms of their impact on a planned improvement in group performance.

To initiate change, the current equilibrium of forces must be modified by one or more of three actions:

- increasing the strength of pressure for change;
- reducing the strength of the resisting forces or removing them completely from the situation; and/or
- changing the direction of a force—for example, by changing a resistance into a pressure for change.

Using force field analysis to understand the processes of change has two primary benefits. First, managers and employees are required to analyze the current situation. By becoming competent at diagnosing the forces pressing for and resisting change, individuals should be able to understand better the relevant aspects of a change situation. Second, force field analysis highlights the factors that can be changed and those

Figure 18.5 **Force Field Analysis**

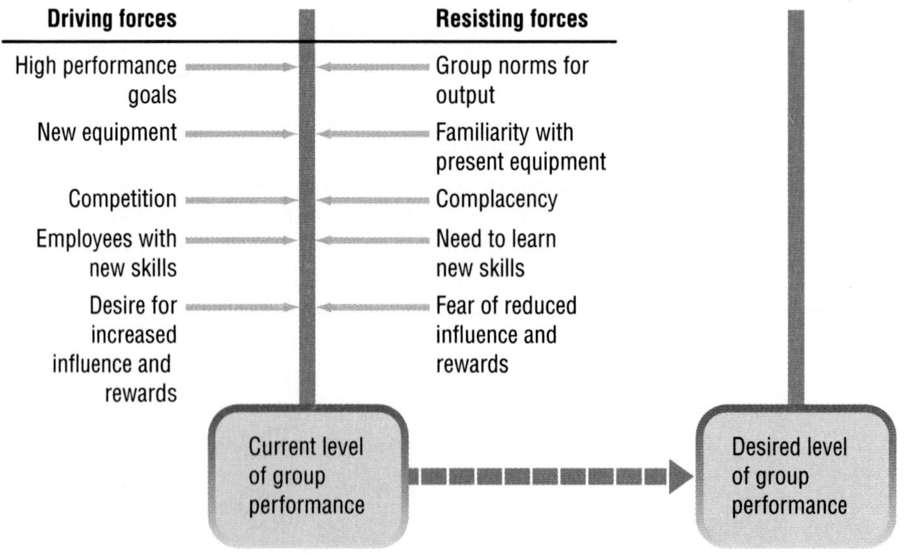

Source: Adapted from Zand, D. E. Force field analysis. In N. Nicholson (ed.), *Blackwell Encyclopedic Dictionary of Organizational Behavior*. Oxford, England: Blackwell, 1995, 181.

that can't be changed. People typically waste time considering actions related to forces over which they have little, if any, control. When individuals and teams focus on the forces over which they do have some control, they increase the likelihood of being able to change the situation.

Of course, careful analysis of a situation doesn't guarantee successful change. For example, people in control have a natural tendency to increase the pressure for change in a situation in order to produce the change they desire. Increasing such pressure may result in short-run changes, but it also may have a high cost: Strong pressure on individuals and teams may create conflicts that disrupt the organization. Often the most effective way to make needed changes is to identify existing resistance to change and focus efforts on removing resistance or reducing it as much as possible.

An important part of Lewin's approach to changing behaviors consists of carefully managing and guiding change through a three-step process.

1. *Unfreezing.* This step usually involves reducing those forces maintaining the organization's behavior at its present level. Unfreezing is sometimes accomplished by introducing information to show discrepancies between behaviors desired by employees and behaviors they currently exhibit.
2. *Moving.* This step shifts the organization's behavior to a new level. It involves developing new behaviors, values, and attitudes through changes in organizational structures and processes.
3. *Refreezing.* This step stabilizes the organization's behavior at a new state of equilibrium. It is frequently accomplished through the use of supporting mechanisms that reinforce the new organizational state, such as organizational culture, norms, policies, and structures.[29]

In addition to completing the three-step process successfully, other important factors play a role in overcoming resistance to change in the workplace. For example, studies have shown that methods for dealing with resistance to change often include the following components when they are successful.

- *Empathy and support.* Understanding how employees are experiencing change is useful. It helps identify those who are troubled by the change and understand the nature of their concerns. When employees feel that those managing change are open to their concerns, they are more willing to provide information. This openness, in turn, helps establish collaborative problem solving, which may overcome barriers to change.
- *Communication.* People are more likely to resist change when they are uncertain about its consequences. Effective communication can reduce gossip and unfounded fears. Adequate information helps employees prepare for change.
- *Participation and involvement.* Perhaps the single most effective strategy for overcoming resistance to change is to involve employees directly in planning and implementing change. Involved employees are more committed to implementing the planned changes and more likely to ensure that they work than are employees who have not been involved.

The Managing Teams Competency feature on page 560 demonstrates the effects of participation and involvement in overcoming resistance to change at Nucor.

Learning Objective:

3. Explain the main features of organization development (OD) approaches to change.

ORGANIZATION DEVELOPMENT

Organization development (OD) is a planned, systematic process of organizational change based on behavioral science research and theory. The goal of OD is to create adaptive organizations capable of repeatedly transforming and reinventing themselves, as needed to remain effective.[30] As a field of behavioral science, OD draws heavily from psychology, sociology, and anthropology. Organization development relies on

COMPETENCY: MANAGING TEAMS

For more information on Nucor, visit the company's home page at www.nucor.com.

OVERCOMING RESISTANCE AT NUCOR

Ken Iverson, chairman of Nucor, a multibillion-dollar steel company discovered something very profound and powerful about involving employees and teams in learning and changing. Early in his career, Iverson was working in a unit of the firm that produced parts for airplanes. They were having a difficult time with their parts being rejected. Owing to the critical nature of specifications in aircraft, parts must be machined to extremely close tolerances, with no margin for error. The approach taken prior to Iverson's involvement was traditionally straightforward. Supervisors would bring defects to workers' attention and tell them how to improve the quality of their work. However, this approach was failing, as the output of many employees just didn't seem to improve following such instruction. In addition, social support for change was lacking, as teams on the shop floor were resistant to changing production processes, procedures, and training.

Iverson and one of his foreman decided to try a different approach. They hauled a bright red bench to the center of the foundry floor. They piled all the rejects for the day on the bench and walked away. They didn't say a word. Eventually, some employees walked over to the bench to see what was going on. Individuals began to examine the rejects and to discuss why these parts hadn't met specifications. They concluded that most of the errors were due to preventable mistakes and identified ways to correct the problems. After about 6 weeks, with employees working on the problems and learning how to fix them, few rejected parts appeared on the red bench on a typical day. On many days there were none. All of this happened without the foreman or Iverson ever saying a word directly to the employees about correcting mistakes.[31]

information from personality theory, learning theory, and motivation theory (see Chapters 2, 4, 5, and 6) and on research about group dynamics, power, leadership, and organization design (see Chapters 8, 9, 11, 12, and 16). It is based on many well-established principles regarding the behaviors of individuals and groups in organizations. In sum, OD rests on many of the facets of organizational behavior presented in this book.

Organization development isn't a single technique but a collection of techniques that have a certain philosophy and body of knowledge in common. The basic tenets that set OD approaches apart from other approaches to organizational change include the following.

- OD seeks to create self-directed change to which people are committed. The problems and issues to be solved are those identified by the organization's members who are directly concerned with and affected by them.
- OD is an organizationwide change effort. Making lasting changes that create a more effective organization requires an understanding of the entire organization. Changing part of the organization isn't possible without changing the entire organization in some sense.
- OD typically places equal emphasis on solving immediate problems and the long-term development of an adaptive organization. The most effective change program isn't one that just solves present problems but one that also prepares individuals to solve future problems.
- OD places more emphasis than do other approaches on a collaborative process of data collection, diagnosis, and action for arriving at solutions to problems.
- OD has a dual emphasis on organizational effectiveness and human fulfillment through the work experience.[32]

A survey of 110 of the Fortune 500 industrial corporations revealed that all but 3 of these organizations had viable OD change programs underway. Some 82 percent of these organizations considered their OD change programs to be effective.[33]

Action Research

A primary change process used in most OD programs is action research. **Action research** is a data-based, problem-solving process of organizational change that closely follows the scientific method.[34] It represents a powerful approach to organizational change consisting of three essential steps:

1. gathering information about problems, concerns, and needed changes from the members of an organization;
2. organizing this information in some meaningful way and sharing it with those involved in the change effort; and
3. planning and carrying out specific actions to correct identified problems.

An organizational change program may go through repeated cycles of data gathering, information sharing, and action planning and implementation. The action research sequence often concludes with a follow-up evaluation of the implemented actions.

The strength of the action research approach to change lies in (1) its careful diagnosis of the current situation and (2) its involvement of employees in the change process. In other words, effective team, department, or organizational change can occur only if those involved understand the current situation, including what tasks are done well and what tasks need to be improved. Moreover, employee involvement can spur change for at least two reasons. First, people are more likely to implement and support a change that they have helped create. Second, once managers and employees have identified the need for change and have widely shared this information, the need becomes difficult for people to ignore. The pressure for change thus comes from within the team, department, or organization, rather than from outside. Such internal pressure is a particularly powerful force for change.[35]

Appreciative Inquiry

A variety of action research that is gaining in popularity is known as appreciative inquiry. **Appreciative inquiry** is an approach to organizational change in which change agents and employees identify what the organization does well and analyze how to re-create the conditions that foster peak performance.[36] This approach is similar to action research in terms of discovering and sharing information widely among organizational members; however, it departs philosophically from traditional action research. From the perspective of appreciative inquiry, the major limitation of action research is the emphasis on problem solving. A focus on problem solving creates defensive behavior about what the organization is doing badly—and needs to stop doing—without identifying what the organization currently is doing well. Table18.2 contrasts some of the differences between problem solving and appreciative inquiry.

Table 18.2 The Contrast between Traditional Problem Solving and Appreciative Inquiry

PROBLEM SOLVING	APPRECIATIVE INQUIRY
• Identify problem	• Appreciate "what is"
• Conduct search for cause	• Imagine "what might be"
• Develop solutions	• Determine "what should be"
• Develop action plans	• Create "what will be"

Source: Adapted from Zemke, R. Don't fix that company. *Training*, June 1999, 32.

Appreciative inquiry begins with research on the organization that is

- aimed at identifying and fostering an appreciation of what works;
- applicable and useful for organizational members;
- provocative—that is, it should create a vision of "what might be"; and
- a collaborative large-scale change effort involving all levels of the organization.[37]

GTE utilized appreciative inquiry as its central change process during an organizationwide effort to change the firm's culture. GTE trained several hundred change agents in appreciative inquiry and then sent them out with instructions simply to "change the culture."

Although appreciative inquiry has received a great deal of favorable publicity, not surprisingly the approach has its critics. Among other things, the imprecision of appreciative inquiry troubles some, as does the lack of strong evidence with regard to its specific applicability. Some experts caution against its use except in a relatively narrow range of situations.[38] For example, when trust is low among managers and employees, appreciative inquiry may be relatively ineffective. In addition, when no tradition of collaboration and participation exists in the organizational culture, appreciative inquiry may not be effective. Efforts may need to be made to increase levels of participation before appreciative inquiry can be utilized as an approach to organizational change.

Learning Objective:

4. Give examples of behavioral, cultural, task, technology, design, and strategy change approaches.

CHANGE MANAGEMENT

The main objective of planned organizational change is to alter the behavior of individuals within the organization. In the final analysis, organizations survive, grow, prosper, decline, or fail because of employee behaviors—the things that employees do or fail to do. Behavior therefore should be a primary target of planned organizational change. In other words, to be successful, change programs must have an impact on employee roles, responsibilities, and working relationships.

At some fundamental level all organizational change depends on changes in behavior, but managing effective change also depends on identifying specific aspects of the organization that will be the initial target of change efforts. We use Figure 18.2 as an organizing framework to explore specific approaches to change that focus on people, culture, task, technology, design, and strategy.

CHANGING BEHAVIOR

Change programs focused on behavior (the people variable in Figure 18.2) tend to rely on active involvement and participation by many employees. Successfully changing behaviors can improve individual and team processes in decision making, problem identification, problem solving, communication, working relationships, and the like. Four approaches to organizational change that initially focus on people are survey feedback, team building, process consultation, and quality of work life programs.

Survey Feedback. In **survey feedback** information is (1) collected (usually by questionnaire) from members of an organization, department, or team, (2) organized into an understandable and useful form, and (3) fed back to the employees who provided it.[39] Some or all of these employees then use this information as a basis for planning actions to deal with specific issues and problems. Survey feedback typically follows the action research process. The primary objective of survey feedback is to improve the relationships among team members or between departments through the discussion of common problems, rather than to introduce a specific change, such as a new computer system. Survey feedback also is frequently used as a diagnostic tool to identify team, department, and organizational problems. Because of its value in organizational diagnosis, survey feedback often is utilized as part of large-scale, long-term change programs in combination with other approaches and techniques.

Team Building. In **team building** team members diagnose how they work together and plan changes to improve their effectiveness. Many different teams comprise an organization, and much of its success depends on how effectively those teams and the people in them can work together.[40]

Effective team building often involves use of the action research process. Team building begins when members recognize a problem in group functioning and that this approach might be an appropriate way to attack it. An effective team can recognize barriers to its own effectiveness and design and take actions to remove them. During team building, members of the team contribute information concerning their perceptions of issues, problems, and working relationships. They may gather information informally during team meetings or prior to meetings, using interviews or questionnaires. They then analyze the information and diagnose work-related problems. Using problem diagnosis as the starting point, members of the team plan specific actions and assign individuals to implement them. At some later stage, team members evaluate their plans and progress to determine whether their actions solved the problems identified. As team effectiveness grows, the potential impact on organizational performance increases. Another good way to define team building is that it consists of the activities designed to move the team up the performance curve shown in Figure 18.6.

Figure 18.6 **The Team Performance Curve**

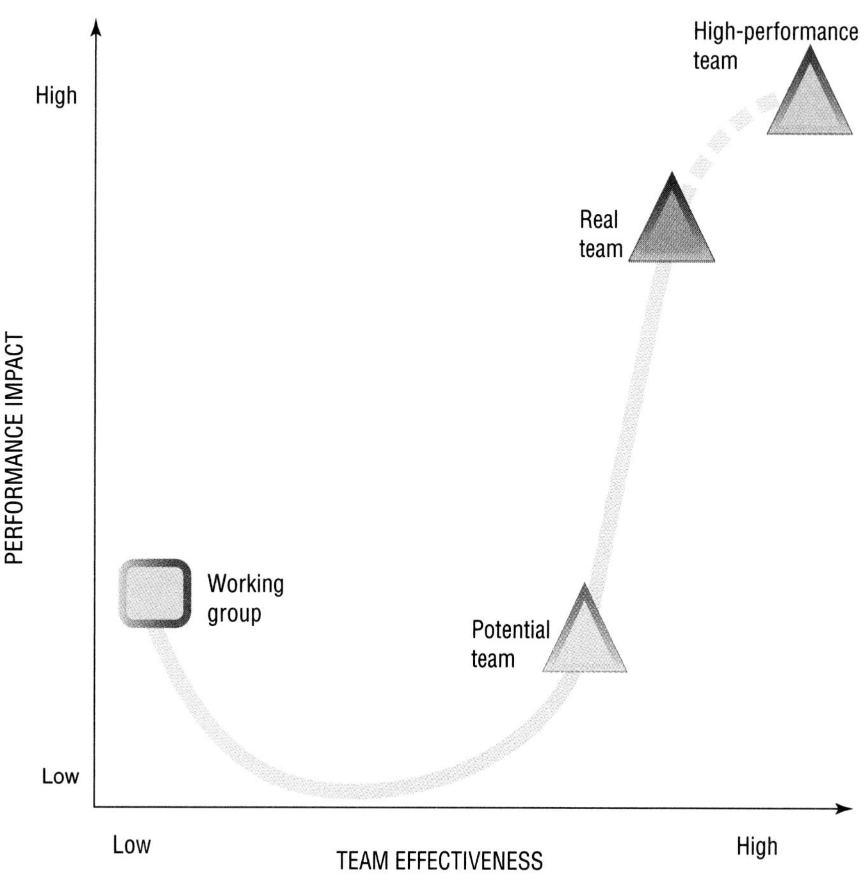

Source: Adapted from Katzenbach, J. R., and Smith, D. K. *The Wisdom of Teams.* Boston: Harvard Business School Press, 1993, 84.

Process Consultation. In **process consultation** guidance is provided by a consultant to help members of an organization perceive, understand, and act on process events that occur in the work environment.[41] *Process events* are the ways in which employees do their work, including the behavior of people at meetings; formal and informal encounters among employees at work; and, in general, any of the behaviors involved in performing a task.

Process consultation involves the use of a skilled third party, or facilitator, who may be an outsider to the organization (e.g., an external behavioral science consultant) or a member of the organization (e.g., a human resource professional or a manager competent in process activities). Process consultation is typically used to address communication issues, leadership problems, decision-making processes, role problems, and conflict resolution. Process consultation is seldom the sole component of an organizational change program; rather, it usually is used in combination with other approaches.

Quality of Work Life Programs. In **quality of work life programs** activities are undertaken to improve conditions that affect an employee's experience with an organization. Many QWL programs focus on security, safety and health, participation in decision making, opportunities to use and develop competencies, creating meaningful work, control over work time or place, protection from arbitrary or unfair treatment, and opportunities to satisfy social needs. Such programs became popular in response to demands from employees for better working conditions. In addition, QWL programs have been undertaken to increase productivity and quality of output through greater involvement and participation by employees in decisions that affect their jobs.

Organizations increasingly are attempting to improve employee quality of work life through the use of alternative work schedules.[42] **Alternative work schedules** might include flextime (giving employees some control over their own work schedules), part-time employment, job sharing (where two individuals share the same job, each working part of the day or week), or work at home (telecommuting). A survey of companies affiliated with the Conference Board found that 92 percent used flextime, 69 percent allowed compressed work schedules, 95 percent utilized part-time employees, 67 percent allowed some job sharing, and 76 percent had some employees who were allowed to do at least part of their jobs at home.

Changing Culture

Earlier we explored changing organizational culture and pointed out just how difficult such changes can be (Chapter 17). Among other issues and problems, just assessing accurately the organization's culture before any plans for change can be developed may be a daunting task. In addition, some aspects of culture (e.g., the deepest core values shared by employees) may be almost impossible to change. Despite these challenges, some organizations have successfully changed their culture. How did they do it?

A detailed examination of cultural change suggests that the odds for success can be increased by giving attention to seven main issues.[43] First, *capitalize on dramatic opportunities.* The organization needs to take advantage of the moment when obvious problems or challenges that are not being met "open the door" to needed change. When Ford acquired Jaguar, obvious quality problems with the Jaguar automobile made justifying needed changes easier.

Second, *combine caution with optimism.* Managers and employees need to be optimistic with regard to the advantages of cultural change; otherwise they will be unwilling to make the attempt. Yet, because cultural change can have negative impacts, the organization needs to proceed with caution. Expectations for improvement must be positive, yet realistic.

Third, *understand resistance to cultural change.* Resistance to change needs to be diagnosed. Identifying and reducing sources of resistance is valuable in cultural change as well as in other change programs.

Fourth, *change many elements but maintain some continuity.* "Don't throw the baby out with the bathwater" is a common saying that sums up the importance of recognizing what is of value and retaining it. Hewlett-Packard, a firm that we have examined in several places in this book, successfully changed its culture as it grew and prospered, yet it managed to retain a core of cultural ideas and beliefs from its founders that have served it well.

Fifth, *recognize the importance of implementation.* A survey indicated that over 90 percent of planned changes in strategy and culture were never fully implemented. A large percentage of failed change programs are failures of implementation rather than failures of ideas. Management needs to recognize that having a vision and a plan, although important, is only part of the battle. Planned changes must be carried through.

Sixth, *modify socialization tactics.* Socialization is the primary way that people learn about a culture (see Chapter 17). Thus changing socialization processes can be an effective approach to cultural change.

Finally, *find and cultivate innovative leadership.* Cultural change must begin at the top of the organization, and good leadership is crucial. When Lockheed got into serious trouble with its L-1011 jet airliner, an ineffective culture at its primary manufacturing facility was identified as a major part of the problem. The turnaround at Lockheed began with the appointment of Dale Daniels as Vice President of manufacturing at the L-1011 plant. Daniels brought a change in managerial philosophy that effectively changed the culture of the firm.

High Performance–High Commitment Work Systems. The goal of many cultural change efforts is to produce a "high-involvement" type of work culture. One example of this type of culture is known as a **high performance–high commitment** (HP–HC) **work system.**[44] These work systems blend technology and teamwork to create a sense of ownership among employees while utilizing the most sophisticated work practices and technologies.

High performance–high commitment work systems have the following characteristics.

- *Delegation.* People who have the most relevant and timely information or the most appropriate competencies for a task are given responsibility for decisions and actions.
- *Teamwork across boundaries.* All employees in the organization are focused on the product and serving customers for the product, rather than their functions or departments.
- *Empowerment.* Everybody is expected to accept and exercise the responsibility necessary to do their jobs and help others accomplish theirs. Providing opportunities to be responsible empowers people—the opposite of limiting roles and contributions. No one feels free to say, "It's not my job."
- *Integration of people and technology.* People are in charge of the technology, instead of technology being in charge of the people.
- *A shared sense of purpose.* People in the work culture share a vision of the organization's purpose and the methods for accomplishing this purpose.[45]

An assumption underlying the HP–HC work system is that superior technology, efficient task design, matching organizational design and processes, good planning, and the like are necessary, but not sufficient, for high performance. Individuals and teams must be committed to make the technology, task design, structure, and strategy work. The HP–HC work system is designed to manage human, technological, and financial resources efficiently and to engage the competencies of employees more fully.

Learning Organizations. A second popular goal of cultural change programs is to create an organization capable of adapting to changes in the external business environment through continual renewal of processes and practices.[46] The **learning**

organization has a culture based on the notion that learning is central to success and effectiveness (see Table 18.1). This notion is similar to our earlier description of the goals of organization development (OD): creating adaptive organizations capable of repeatedly transforming and reinventing themselves as needed to remain effective.

What does having an organization with a learning culture actually mean? The Ford Motor Company under the direction of its new CEO, Jacques Nasser, provides an excellent example of a learning organization. Ford has 340,000 employees in some 200 countries. Under Nasser, Ford's change program is based on teaching, but not of the traditional classroom variety. Teaching and learning at Ford are achieved through small group discussions devoted to strategy and understanding markets and competition, coupled with stints of community service on the part of participants in the change program. The heart of Ford's learning culture is a 3-day workshop that culminates in an assignment whereby "students" (Ford managers) have 100 days to deliver a significant new cost saving or revenue source. The teaching and learning initiative has been so successful that Nasser intends to present it to hourly workers in 2001. Nasser stated, "You can't change a company like Ford overnight, but there is no question that we have to change our fundamental approach to work. And, our teaching and learning approach does that better than any other way I know."[47] The Managing Across Cultures feature on the next page reports a *Fortune* magazine interview with Nasser. (We have edited this interview in order to focus on topics relevant to our discussion here.)

Changing Task and Technology

Approaches to change focusing on the task emphasize modifying the work of individuals and teams. Approaches focusing on technology concentrate on the technological processes and tools used to perform the work. We examine task and technology together because several change approaches—including job redesign, sociotechnical systems, quality circles, reengineering, and total quality management—often affect these areas simultaneously.

Job Redesign. As an approach to change, **job redesign** represents a deliberate, planned restructuring of the way work is performed in order to increase employee motivation, involvement, and efficiency—and ultimately to improve performance. Recall that job design encompasses a group of specific organizational change techniques, including job engineering, job rotation, job enlargement, job enrichment, and the redesign of core task characteristics (see Chapter 15).

Each technique is an effective approach to organizational change under certain conditions. However, managers sometimes use specific job design approaches inappropriately. For example, job enrichment programs may fail if managers wrongly assume that all employees want enriched work and do not allow for differences in employee needs and values. Job redesign techniques are most successful in the context of a comprehensive organizational change program that examines the complex fit among the tasks to be performed, the types of technology used, the design and culture of the organization or team, and the nature and characteristics of the people doing the work.

Sociotechnical Systems. Analysis of **sociotechnical systems** (STS) simultaneously focuses on changing both the technical and social aspects of the organization to optimize their relationship and thus increase organizational effectiveness.[48] In this approach the organization is viewed as more than just a technical system for making products and providing services. Ultimately, the organization is a collection of human beings—a social system. Changes made in the technical system affect the social fabric of the organization. Thus managing organizational change effectively means dealing with both the social and technical aspects of that change.

COMPETENCY: MANAGING ACROSS CULTURES

AN INTERVIEW WITH FORD'S JACQUES NASSER

Ford has been making cars for nearly a century. Why change the company's mind-set now?
Because Ford as we know it won't be around in 5 years. That's the most compelling answer I can give. We can't survive in a world of rapidly changing consumer demand without having leaders and employees capable of rapid decision making. If we move slowly or operate inefficiently, we won't survive.

As a related point, the markets value a global approach to business. All of our teams, divisions, functions, and regions must be tightly integrated and synchronized across borders. We must increase our capacity to learn and respond so that we have people thinking in these terms. People need to ask, "What can I do to make this company work better and smarter and faster?"

At this moment, how close is Ford to being a global company?
We have a strong international presence. We operate in 200 countries. But having assembly plants in Brazil, product development teams in Europe, and dealerships in Mexico doesn't make us a global company. What makes a global company is the right mind-set. Our new compact, Focus, is a great example of our new mind-set. Focus was engineered by one set of people, not multiple design groups scattered around. The vehicle was introduced to the world at a single show in Paris. We brought in 1,500 journalists from all over the world and they all got to drive the Focus. The Focus is an exciting vehicle that provides enormous value to the consumer. It has a real flair to the design, great fuel efficiency, solid safety engineering, and tremendous spaciousness. We are using one advertising agency—one—to handle the roll-out, so we can tell a consistent story about the car everywhere. When we attempted to sell the Escort worldwide, we engineered it in multiple locations, introduced it country by country and told different stories in different locations. That didn't work.

Getting from the Escort to the Focus must have required a major cultural shift. How were you able to make that change?
Change has to be understood on the individual level. Every manager, every designer, every engineer, every person in the plants has to change her or his way of thinking. We believe that the only way to change at the individual level is through teaching. Teaching is an amazingly effective way to change an organization. Over the past 3 years, our employees have delivered two billion dollars to the bottom line, either in reduced costs or increased revenue, as a result of our teaching and learning philosophy. This has happened because people's mind-sets have changed.

Consider what typically happens in change programs in large companies. Consultants come in with their PowerPoint presentations. They lecture people about why change is important. And, after they leave, nothing happens. But once you create a learning culture and begin to teach in-house with your own people, the teachers themselves have no choice but to behave differently. Teaching enforces the discipline of change.[49]

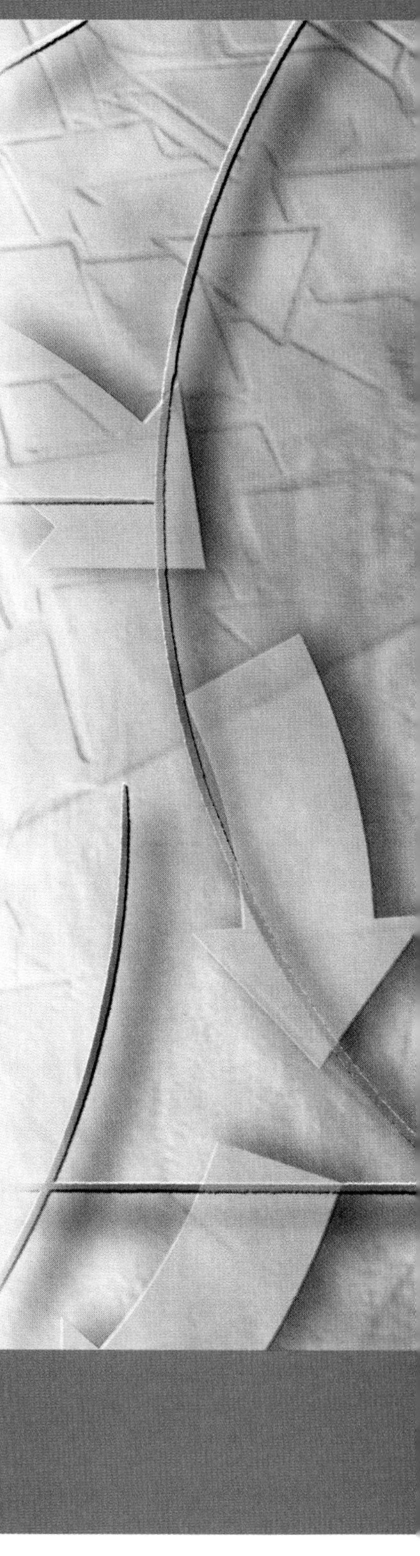

The STS approach to organizational change usually incorporates a major redesign of the way work is done (the task variable), in addition to emphasizing technological and social issues (the technology and people variables). We described the STS approach to job design in detail in Chapter 15.

We have discussed self-managed teams throughout this book. From the perspective of organizational change, the idea of autonomous, or self-managed, teams is a major contribution of sociotechnical systems theory. **Autonomous groups** are self-managed teams that plan their work, control its pace and quality, and make many of the decisions traditionally reserved to management. The STS approach involves redesigning teams to give them as much control as possible over the resources and competencies needed to manufacture a specific product or deliver a specific service to a customer. The role of management in STS is to ensure that teams have sufficient resources to accomplish their objectives.

Quality Circles. **Quality circles** are work groups, generally containing less than a dozen volunteers from the same work area, who meet regularly to monitor and solve job-related quality or production problems.[50] Quality circles also may be utilized to improve working conditions, increase the level of employee involvement and commitment, and encourage employee self-development. In these instances, they frequently are an important component of QWL programs. Adapted initially from Japanese quality control practices, their use has spread rapidly in the United States.

Quality circles typically have a narrower focus than many of the other change techniques described. They also differ from other approaches in that management retains more control over the activities of the employees than is possible, or desirable, in most of the other approaches. Although quality circles may make a contribution relatively quickly, sustaining an initial success over a period of time requires considerable energy and creating new challenges to maintain employee interest. Quality circles may not fit well into an organization's culture and are not likely to move the organization toward a highly participative culture if other changes aren't made at the same time. Quality circles appear to cope successfully with only a limited range of problems; accurate diagnosis is essential to ensure that the problems facing an organization can be best addressed by this approach.

Reengineering. Reengineering is another term that has appeared frequently throughout this book. It also represents a major change approach currently popular with organizations. **Reengineering**, sometimes called process redesign, is a fundamental rethinking and radical redesign of business processes to reduce costs and improve quality, service, and speed.[51] Reengineering represents a more radical approach to change than do most of the other methods discussed. During reengineering, the most fundamental ideas and assumptions of the organization are challenged. Recall that reengineering begins with no assumptions and asks fundamental questions such as: Why does the organization do what it does? Why does it do it the way that it does?

At GE, Chairman Jack Welch compared his company to a 100-year-old attic that collected a lot of useless junk over the years. Welch views reengineering as the process of cleaning all the junk out of the attic, and GE calls its reengineering activities "workout."

When an organization reengineers its business processes, the following changes typically occur.

- Work groups change from functional departments to process teams.
- Individual jobs change from simple to multidimensional tasks.
- People's roles change from being controlled to being empowered to make decisions.
- Performance appraisal changes from measuring activities (attending meetings or arriving at work on time) to measuring results (customer satisfaction, costs, and performance).

- Managers change from supervisors to coaches.
- Organization designs change from tall to flat hierarchies.[52]

Reengineering shares many of the objectives of other change approaches. Despite these similarities, reengineering programs (if they truly are reengineering) represent a dramatic and revolutionary, rather than an evolutionary or gradually transformational, approach to organizational change.

Total Quality Management. **Total quality management** (TQM) focuses on meeting or exceeding customer expectations. Quality ultimately is defined by the customer. When an organization achieves "total quality," all activities and processes are designed and carried out to meet all customer requirements while reducing both the time and cost required to provide them.[53]

Total quality management is partly technical. Just-in-time (JIT) inventory systems, for example, frequently are utilized by TQM organizations. It also is partly cultural—the shared values must emphasize quality, and employees must be empowered to carry out needed changes. The concept of continuous improvement is central to TQM. One-time programs or "quick-fix" solutions for productivity or quality problems are unacceptable. The cultural value of **continuous improvement** means having a set of principles and behaviors designed to achieve positive and continuous change in deliverables (goods or services), operating procedures, and systems by the people who actually perform these procedures and work under these systems.[54]

Changing Organization Design

Organizationwide change programs frequently are aimed at changing the organization's design. Approaches to change that focus on the design variable involve redefining positions or roles and relationships among positions and redesigning departmental, division, and/or organizational structure. Unfortunately, implementing design or structural change has sometimes been used as an excuse for organizations simply to downsize their workforces without identifying and exploring the reasons for inefficiency and poor performance. Some of the negative consequences of poorly thought out organizational changes are presented in the Managing Change Competency feature on page 570.

As organizations grow increasingly complex and face the challenge of managing constant change, they often need new ways of organizing their activities. They particularly need more flexibility and adaptive capabilities than allowed in the traditional mechanistic system, with its rigid hierarchy and standardized procedures. Here, we explore three forms of organizational design that characterize flexible, adaptive organizations: collateral organization, matrix organization, and network organization.

Collateral Organization. A **collateral organization** is a parallel, coexisting organization that can be used to supplement an existing formal organization.[55] The collateral organization utilizes teams of people outside normal channels of communication and authority to identify and solve difficult problems that the formal organization may be unwilling or unable to solve. A collateral organization has norms—ways of working together, making decisions, and solving problems—that are different from those of the rest of the organization. However, the collateral organization requires no new people, is carefully linked to the formal organization, and coexists with it. Collateral organizations have the following characteristics.

- All communication channels are open and connected. Managers and employees freely communicate without being restricted to the formal channels of the organizational hierarchy.

COMPETENCY: MANAGING CHANGE

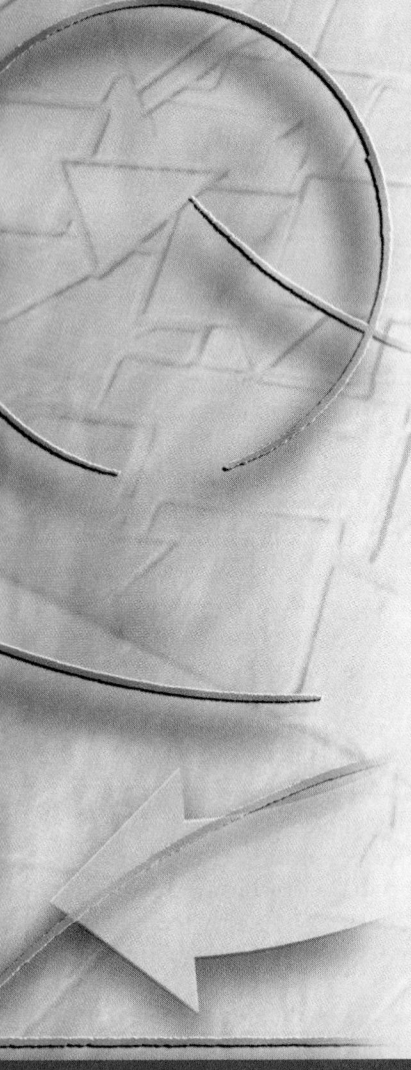

*For more information on AT&T, Eastman Kodak, and Nynex, visit these companies' home pages at **www.att.com**, **www.kodak.com**, and **www.nynex.com**.*

DUMBSIZING

Corporate America loves to talk about the nimbleness and efficiency gained by restructuring. Pressured by low-cost foreign competitors that threaten to snare their customers and by Wall Street's demands for quick returns, executives have taken to cutting costs by reducing the number of employees with fervor. Despite warnings about downsizing becoming dumbsizing, many companies continue to make flawed decisions—hasty across-the-board cuts—that come back to haunt them in less profitability, in negative public relations, in strained relationships with customers and suppliers, and in demoralized employees.

At AT&T, CEO Robert Allen had long been one of America's most admired executives. He guided the world's most powerful telecommunications company through wrenching changes, transforming a staid monopoly into a competitive powerhouse. However, in the twilight of his career, Allen came under attack when he announced the layoff of an additional 50,000 employees—layoffs that presumably would not be necessary if previous reorganizations had been successful. To critics Allen now appears to be an uncaring and unaccountable chief executive whose numerous restructurings wiped out $15 billion in earnings during the past decade.

Eastman Kodak Company expected to save thousands of dollars a year when it laid off Maryellen Ford in a companywide downsizing. But within weeks, Kodak was paying more for the same work. Ford, a computer-aided designer, was snapped up by a local contractor that gets much of its work from Kodak. Ford says, "I took the project I was working on at Kodak and finished it here." But instead of paying her $15 an hour, Kodak now pays the contractor $65 an hour.

Cutbacks that result in poor customer service can also lead to problems. Nynex Corporation was recently ordered by New York's Public Service Commission to rebate $50 million to customers because its reduced staff fell behind in responding to problems. Nynex has hired back hundreds of employees, including managers already receiving pensions. Even greater than the rehiring expense is the blight on Nynex's reputation for customer service. "Their past reputation for customer service is their key competitive advantage," says Joe Kraemer, a management consultant at A.T. Kearney. "They've put all that at risk, just to gain a few cents per share in a given quarter. It's just plain dumb."

Even reengineering guru Michael Hammer has been humbled by the negative results of some restructuring and downsizing stemming from reengineering. He states that he and other leaders in the reengineering movement sometimes forgot about people. "I wasn't smart enough about that," he says, "I was reflecting my engineering background and was insufficiently appreciative of the human dimension. I've learned that's critical."[56]

- Relevant information about problems and issues is exchanged rapidly and completely. The outputs of the collateral structure are ideas, solutions to problems, and innovation.
- The norms in use encourage critical questioning and careful analysis of goals, assumptions, methods, alternatives, and evaluation criteria.
- Managers can approach and enlist others in the organization to help solve a problem; they are not restricted to using their subordinates in the formal organizational hierarchy.
- Mechanisms are developed to link the collateral and formal organizations.[57]

Matrix Organization. Many organizations have turned to a matrix design to address the limitations of mechanistic or bureaucratic structures. Recall that a **matrix organization** represents a balance between organizing resources by product or by function (see Chapter 16).

A mutually beneficial relationship often exists between the matrix form of organization and the capacity to change. For example, many features of OD programs, such as an emphasis on collaborative behavior and the effective use of teams, also are important for implementing a matrix structure with its decentralized decision making and extensive use of temporary task forces and teams. In general, the matrix form helps create a culture receptive to organizational improvement efforts.

Changing an organization to a matrix form is never easy. Often, managers need a change strategy focusing on people to facilitate the transition. For example, team building has helped organizations introduce matrix designs successfully. One senior executive put it this way: "The challenge is not so much to build a matrix structure as it is to create a matrix in the minds of our managers."

Network Organization. The **network organization**, as described in Chapter 16, is a complex mosaic of lateral communication, decision-making, and control processes. Although a network organization might have an organization chart showing typical hierarchical authority and communication relationships, such a chart cannot begin to describe the reality of this complex organizational form. Figure 18.7 shows three basic types of network organizations.

The components business of General Motors represents an *internal network*. Corporate headquarters serves a "brokerage function" that coordinates activities of the

Figure 18.7 **Examples of Network Designs**

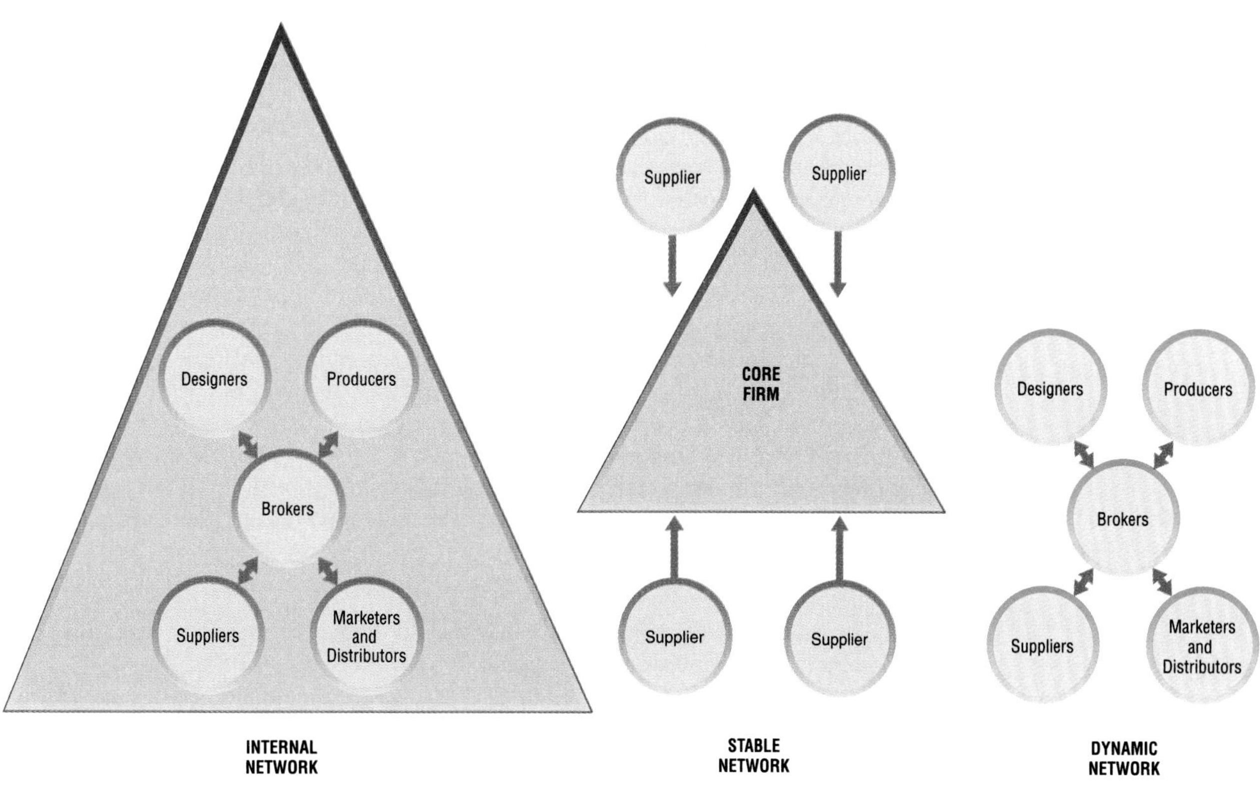

Source: Snow, C. C., Miles, R. E., and Coleman, H. J. Managing 21st century network organizations. *Organizational Dynamics*, Winter 1992, 12. Reprinted by permission of the publisher, from *Organizational Dynamics*, Winter/1992 © 1992. American Management Association, New York. All rights reserved.

divisions producing components. The separate divisions sell some of their products on the open market. In contrast, the Bavarian Motor Works (BMW) is a *stable network*. Every part of the BMW automobile is a candidate for outsourcing and some 55 to 75 percent of the total cost of the car is in outside parts. Even more decentralized is Lewis Galoob Toys, which operates as a *dynamic network*. It has only about 100 permanent employees, who run the core business. Most of its products are invented, designed, and engineered outside the firm. Galoob also contracts with other organizations for manufacturing and packaging products. Thus it operates as a "broker," coordinating the activities of independent specialty firms.[58]

The dynamic network design shown in Figure 18.7 is also called a virtual organization. A **virtual organization** is a temporary network of independent companies linked by information technology to share competencies, costs, and access to customers.[59] Galoob Toys clearly fits the definition of a virtual organization.

Network organizations share some features with both matrix and collateral organizations, yet place more emphasis on sophisticated information technologies to coordinate activities and perform work. Managers in a network organization function much like switchboard operators in terms of coordination and control. They can pull together temporary teams of employees to bring expertise to bear on projects and concerns as needed. The collaborative behaviors and attitudes characterizing the network organization are similar to those typical of the high performance–high commitment work systems described earlier. Many adaptive organizations—especially global organizations that need the flexibility to function effectively in many countries and different cultures—use some version of network design.

Changing Strategy

Issues of strategic change need to be addressed in comprehensive organizational change programs. At its most basic level, a strategy is a *plan*—an intended course of action to attain organizational goals. **Strategic change** is planned organizational change designed to alter the organization's intended courses of action to attain its goals. Strategic change may include assessment and redefinition of the goals themselves.

Dick Clark Productions provides a good example of a firm that has constantly reassessed its options and developed new strategies and lines of business over the years. The company is a diverse entertainment enterprise that operates three core businesses: television productions, corporate productions (trade shows, special event marketing, etc.), and theme restaurants that draw on the names of Dick Clark and American Bandstand. The corporate production and theme restaurants segments of the business represent successful new strategic reorientations that the firm has undertaken. Dick Clark Productions maintains an active, effective planning and strategy formulation process that constantly assesses performance and looks for new opportunities.[60]

A good example of a strategic change program is the process of open systems planning. **Open systems planning** is designed to help an organization systematically assess its environment and develop a strategic response to it. It consists of the following steps.

- Assess the external environment in terms of its expectations and demands on the organization's behavior.
- Assess the organization's current response to these environmental demands.
- Identify the organization's core mission.
- Create a realistic scenario of future environmental demands and organizational responses.
- Create an ideal scenario of future environmental demands and organizational responses.
- Compare the present with the ideal future and prepare an action plan for reducing the discrepancy.[61]

Learning Objective:

5. Describe the role and importance of ethical issues in organizational change.

ETHICAL ISSUES IN ORGANIZATIONAL CHANGE

Serious ethical issues may arise in any organizational change program, no matter how carefully thought out and well managed it might be. Managers and employees need to be aware of potential ethical issues in four main areas: change approach selection, change target selection, managerial responsibilities, and manipulation.[62]

When choosing the change approach or combination of approaches deemed best for the situation, managers and employees should recognize the ethical issues involved in selecting the criteria to be used. Does the manager or change agent have a vested interest in using a particular technique so that other alternatives might not receive a fair hearing? Do individuals involved in the organizational diagnosis have biases that might predetermine the problems identified and thus influence the change approach chosen?

Selection of the change target raises ethical concerns about participation in the change program. What is to be the target of change? Which individuals, teams, or departments of the organization will the change effort focus on? Which members of the organization will participate in diagnosing, planning, and implementing the change and to what degree? Who will make this determination? Issues of power and political behavior raise serious ethical concerns when managers attempt to make inappropriate changes or choices concerning what is to be changed that overstep the boundaries of their legitimate roles. To what extent can managers make choices about changing the behaviors of employees, and where should the line be drawn in this regard?

A major ethical concern in the area of managerial responsibility involves whose goals and values are to guide the change effort. The reason is that organizational change is never value-free. The value systems of managers and employees always underlie assumptions about what the organization should be doing. Ethical concerns arise if managers involved in the change process fail to recognize the potential problems associated with incompatible goals and values held by the organization's members. Whose vision guides the change? Whose values influence the adoption of goals and methods chosen to accomplish them?

Finally, the reality of power differences raises the possibility of manipulation in the change process. Making changes in organizations without some employees feeling manipulated in some way is difficult. Often the organization needs to make changes that do, in fact, result in some individuals or groups being worse off after the change than they were before. Ethical issues concern the degree of openness surrounding planned changes. To what extent should the organization disclose all aspects of the change in advance? To what degree do employees have the right to participate in, or at least be aware of, changes that affect them, even indirectly?

These questions are not easily addressed and we have no simple answers to them. As a starting point, managers and employees need some basis for recognizing the potential ethical concerns involved in organizational change so that fair and informed choices can be made. Organizations must be sensitive to the probability that ethical problems will emerge during planned change programs. One of the features at the end of this chapter is a case description that will help you think further about ethical issues in organizational change.

CHAPTER SUMMARY

1. Identify characteristics of effective change programs and explain the importance of an accurate diagnosis of organizational functioning and problems.

A rapidly changing environment places many demands on managers and employees, including the need to plan for and manage organizational change effectively. Pressures for change stem from globalization, the increasingly heavy use of computers and other sophisticated information technology, and the changing nature of the workforce.

Planned organizational change attempts to alter the design and processes of an organization to make it more effective and efficient. For planned change programs to be effective, employees must be aware of the need for change, believe in the potential value of the changes, and be willing to change their behaviors. Typically, change is also more effective when it is organizationwide. The systems model of change—focusing on the variables of people, culture, task, technology, design, and strategy—provides a useful way to conceptualize organizationwide change. An accurate, valid diagnosis of current organizational functioning, activities, and problems is an essential foundation for effective organizational change. The readiness for change, availability of resources for change, and possible resistance to change are among the factors that should be accurately diagnosed.

2. Diagnose sources of individual and organizational resistance to change and describe methods for overcoming that resistance.

Individuals may resist change because of their perceptions or personalities. In addition, habitual behaviors, fear of the unknown, economic insecurities, and threats to established power and influence relationships may generate further resistance to change. Organizational resistance to change may be caused by organizational structure and culture, resource limitations, fixed investments not easily altered, and interorganizational agreements. Force field analysis can help managers and employees diagnose and overcome resistance to change. Resistance can also be reduced through good communications and high levels of employee participation in the change process.

3. Explain the main features of organization development (OD) approaches to change.

Organization development (OD) is a field of applied behavioral science that focuses on understanding and managing organizational change. The OD change approaches are characterized by a focus on self-directed change, the development of both short-range and long-range solutions to issues and concerns, and a relatively high level of collaborative effort involving many individuals in the organization among other characteristics. Successful change programs often utilize an action research sequence of information gathering, feedback, and action planning. A new version of action research known as appreciative inquiry is becoming increasingly popular.

4. Give examples of behavioral, cultural, task, technology, design, and strategy change approaches.

Managers and employees must understand the likely effects of various change approaches and carefully match change programs to the problems that they are intended to solve. When the initial focus of the change effort is on people, managers might choose to use survey feedback, team building, process consultation, or quality of work life programs. Comprehensive change often means that the culture of the organization must be considered. Although cultural change is difficult, the probability of success can be increased by careful attention to some key issues. Creating a high performance–high commitment work system or a learning organization often are goals of cultural change efforts. When the initial focus is on task or technology, managers typically utilize job redesign, sociotechnical systems, quality circles, reengineering, or total quality management. The last two may involve significant changes in organizational culture. Approaches to change that focus on organization design might include creating more adaptive organizational structures, such as collateral, matrix, or network designs. Strategic change often is the focus of organizationwide change efforts. Open systems planning is one method of achieving strategic change. Comprehensive organizational change programs, regardless of their initial focus, often make simultaneous changes in several aspects of the organization. In practice, the approaches presented in this chapter are commonly used in combination to manage organizational change.

5. Describe the role and importance of ethical issues in organizational change.

Managers and employees need to be aware of and knowledgeable about potential ethical issues that can arise during organizational change. Ethical issues may emerge during selection of the change approach, selection of the change targets, determination of managerial responsibilities for the goals selected, and potential manipulation of employees.

KEY TERMS AND CONCEPTS

Action research
Alternative work schedules
Appreciative inquiry
Autonomous groups
Collateral organization
Contingency workforce
Continuous improvement
Culture variable
Design variable
Force field analysis
Globalization
High performance–high commitment work system
Information technology
Job redesign
Learning organization
Matrix organization
Network organization
Open systems planning
Organization development
Organizational diagnosis
People variable
Planned organizational change
Pressures for change
Process consultation
Quality circles
Quality of work life
Quality of work life programs
Reengineering
Resistance to change
Sociotechnical systems
Strategic change
Strategy variable
Systems model of change
Survey feedback
Task variable
Team building
Technology variable
Total quality management
Virtual organization
Virtual teams

DISCUSSION QUESTIONS

1. Identify and explain some of the pressures for change and resistance to change facing Vanessa Castagna at J.C. Penney.
2. Use Figure 18.4 to identify and explain the primary types of resistance to change that exist in the college or university that you are attending.
3. Use force field analysis to diagnose and describe the pressures for and resistance to change facing an organization or group with which you are familiar. If you were going to change that organization or group, which pressures and types of resistance would be the most crucial to deal with?
4. Based on your own work experience and using Figure 18.3, analyze a change situation. In addition to assessing overall readiness for change, also analyze employee expectations and the resources available for change.
5. Use the three-step process of unfreezing, moving, and refreezing to describe some significant behavioral change in your life.
6. Use the three-step process of unfreezing, moving, and refreezing to describe some significant behavioral change in the life of someone you know well.
7. Have you ever been involved with an organization that had a flexible, adaptive design (e.g., collateral, matrix, or network)? If so, describe it. If not, go to the Cisco Systems Web site (www.cisco.com) and analyze its design.
8. Based on your own experience, describe a team, department, or organization that needed to change. Which of the change approaches presented would you have used? Why?
9. Identify and describe an ethical dilemma or issue that was created by some organizational change effort with which you are familiar. How was the ethical problem handled? What, if anything, would you do differently?

DEVELOPING COMPETENCIES

Competency: Managing Self—Measuring Support for Change

Instructions

This questionnaire is designed to help you understand the inherent level of support or opposition to change within an organization. Please respond to each item according to how true it is in terms of an organization for which you are currently working or used to work. Circle the appropriate number on the scale that follows the item.

Not True	Usually Not True	Somewhat Untrue	Neutral	Somewhat True	Usually True	True
1	2	3	4	5	6	7

Values and Visions

1. Do people throughout the organization share values or visions?

   1 2 3 4 5 6 7

History of Change

2. Does the organization have a good track record in implementing change smoothly?

   1 2 3 4 5 6 7

Cooperation and Trust

3. Is there a lot of cooperation and trust throughout the organization (as opposed to animosity)?

   1 2 3 4 5 6 7

Culture

4. Does the organization's culture support risk taking (as opposed to being highly bureaucratic and rule bound)?

   1 2 3 4 5 6 7

Resilience

5. Are people able to handle change (as opposed to being worn out from recent, unsettling changes)?

   1 2 3 4 5 6 7

Punishments and Rewards

6. Does the organization reward people who take part in change efforts (as opposed to subtly punishing those who take time off from other work to get involved)?

   1 2 3 4 5 6 7

Respect and Status

7. Will people be able to maintain respect and status when the change is implemented (as opposed to losing these as a result of the change)?

   1 2 3 4 5 6 7

Status Quo

8. Will the change be mild (and not cause a major disruption of the status quo)?

   1 2 3 4 5 6 7

Interpretation

Scores 1, 2, and 3 are low; 4 and 5 are mid-range; and 6 and 7 are high. However, these are just numbers, and one person's 5 may be another person's 3. The value of the scores lies in understanding the meanings that people attach to them.

Generally, low to mid-range scores should be cause for concern. Lower scores indicate possible areas of resistance to change.

Values and Visions

Low scores may indicate that values may be in conflict and that individuals and groups may not perceive any common ground. This situation is serious and almost guarantees that any major change will be resisted unless people learn how to build a shared set of values. In contrast, low scores may indicate a communication problem. In some organizations, values and visions remain secret, with people not knowing where the organization is headed. Although this communication problem needs to be solved, it may not indicate deeper potential resistance.

History of Change

Low scores indicate a strong likelihood that a change will be resisted forcefully. Those who want the change will need to demonstrate repeatedly that they are serious this time. People are likely to be very skeptical, so persistence will be crucial.

Cooperation and Trust

Low scores should be taken seriously. Building support for any major change without some degree of trust is difficult, if not impossible. The opposite of trust is fear, so a low score indicates not just the absence of trust but the presence of fear.

Culture

Mid-range to low scores indicate that people may have difficulty carrying out changes even though they support the changes. They are saying that the systems and procedures in the organization hinder change. The change agents must be willing to examine these deeper systemic issues.

Resilience

Low scores probably indicate that people are burned out. Even though they may see the need for change, they may have little strength to give to the effort. Two important questions should be asked:

- Is this change really necessary at this time?
- If it is, how can the organizations support people so that the change causes minimal disruption?

Punishments and Rewards

Low scores indicate strong potential resistance. Who in their right minds would support something that they knew would harm them? If the respondents' perceptions are accurate, the change agents must find a way to move forward with the change *and find ways to make it rewarding for others*. If the low scores indicate a misperception, the change agents must let people know why they are misinformed. This message will likely need to be communicated repeatedly (especially if trust also is low).

Respect and Status

Low scores indicate that change agents must find ways to make this a win–win situation.

Status Quo

Low scores indicate that people regard the potential change as very disruptive and stressful. The more involved people are in the change process, the less resistance they are likely to experience. Most often, people resist change when they feel out of control.[63]

Competency: Managing Ethics—Kindred Todd and the Ethics of OD

Kindred Todd had just finished her master's degree in organization development and had landed her first consulting position with a small consulting company in Edmonton, Alberta, Canada. The president, Larry Stepchuck, convinced Todd that his organization was growing and that it offered her a great opportunity to learn the consulting business. He had a large number of contacts, an impressive executive career, and several years of consulting experience behind him.

In fact, the firm was growing, adding new clients and projects as fast as Stepchuck could hire consultants. A few weeks after Stepchuck hired Todd, he assigned her to a new client, a small oil and gas company. "I've met with the client for several hours. They are an important and potentially large opportunity for our firm. They are looking to us to help them address some long-range planning issues. From the way they talk, they could also use some continuous quality improvement work as well."

As Todd prepared for her initial meeting with the client, she reviewed financial data from the firm's annual report, examined trends in the client's industry, and thought about the issues that young firms face. Stepchuck indicated that Todd would first meet with the president of the firm to discuss initial issues and next steps.

When Todd walked into the president's office, she was greeted by the firm's entire senior management team. Team members expressed eagerness to get to work on the important issues of how to improve the organization's key business processes. They believed that an expert in continuous quality improvement (CQI), such as Todd, was exactly the kind of help they needed to increase efficiency and to cut costs in the core business. Members began to question Todd directly about technical details of CQI, the likely time frame within which they might expect results, how to map key processes, and how to form quality improvement teams to identify and implement process improvements.

Todd was stunned and overwhelmed. Nothing that Stepchuck had said about the issues facing this company was being discussed, and worse, it was clear that he had sold Todd to the client as an "expert" in CQI. Her immediate response was to suggest that all of their questions were good ones, but that they needed to be answered in the context of the long-range goals and strategies of the firm. Todd proposed that the best way to begin was for team members to provide her with some history about the organization. In doing so, she was able to avert disaster and embarrassment for herself and her company and to appear to be doing all the things necessary to begin a CQI project. The meeting ended with Todd and the management team agreeing to meet again the following week.

The next day, Todd sought out Stepchuck. She reported on the results of the meeting and her surprise at being sold as an expert on CQI to this client. Todd suggested that her competencies didn't fit with the needs of the client and requested that another consultant, with expertise in CQI, be assigned to the project.

Stepchuck responded to her concerns: "I have known these people for over 10 years. They don't know exactly what they need. CQI is an important buzzword. It's the flavor of the month, and if that's what they want, that's what we'll give them." He also told Todd that there were no other consultants available for this project. "Besides," he said, "the president of the client firm had just called to say how much he had enjoyed meeting with you and was looking forward to getting started on the project right away."

Todd felt that Stepchuck's response to her concerns included a strong, inferred ultimatum: If you want to stay with this company, you'd better take this job. "I knew I had to sink or swim with this job and this client," Todd later reported.

As Todd reflected on her options, she pondered the following questions:

- How can I be honest with this client and thus not jeopardize my values of openness and honesty?
- How can I be helpful to this client?
- How much do I know about quality improvement processes?
- How do I satisfy the requirements of my employer?
- What obligations do I have?
- Who's going to know if I do or don't have the credentials to perform this work?
- What if I fail?

After thinking about these issues, Todd summarized her position in terms of three dilemmas: a dilemma of self (who is Kindred Todd?), a dilemma of competence (what can she do?), and a dilemma of confidence (do I like who I work for?). Based on these issues, Todd made the following tactical decisions. She spent 2 days at the library reading about and studying total quality management and continuous improvement. She also contacted several of her friends and former classmates who had experience with quality improvement efforts. Eventually, she contracted with one of them to be her "shadow" consultant—to work with her behind the scenes on formulating and implementing an intervention for the client.

Based on her preparation in the library and the discussions with her shadow consultant, Todd was able to facilitate an appropriate and effective intervention for the client. Shortly after completing her assignment, she resigned from the consulting organization.[64]

Questions:

1. Discuss the course of action followed by Kindred Todd in terms of its strengths and weaknesses. What, if anything, would you have done differently if you were Todd?
2. Based on the material in this chapter, describe an effective, and ethical, alternative way to approach helping this organization.

REFERENCES

1. Adapted from a story posted on a computer bulletin board and reprinted on the Internet. Author unknown.
2. Greve, H. R. Performance, aspirations, and risky organizational change. *Administrative Science Quarterly*, 1998, 43, 58–86; Pasmore, W. A., and Woodman, R. W. (eds.). *Research in Organizational Change and Development*, vol. 12. Stamford, Conn.: JAI Press, 1999; Van de Ven, A. H., and Poole, M. S. Explaining development and change in organizations. *Academy of Management Review*, 1995, 20, 510–540; Weick, K. E., and Quinn, R. E. Organizational change and development. *Annual Review of Psychology*, 1999, 50, 361–386.
3. Burke, W. W., and Trahant, W. *Business Climate Shifts: Profiles of Change Makers.* Boston: Butterworth/Heinemann, 2000; Hammer, M., and Champy, J. *Reengineering the Corporation.* New York: HarperBusiness, 1993; Kanter, R. M., Stein, B. A., and Jick, T. D. *The Challenge of Organizational Change.* New York: Free Press, 1992; Pfeffer, J. Seven practices of successful organizations. *California Management Review*, Winter 1998, 96–124; Wind, J. Y., and Main, J. *Driving Change.* New York: Free Press, 1998.
4. Creswell, J., Mclean, B., and Koudsi, S. The next big things. *Fortune*, December 20, 1999, 86–100.
5. Griffin, R. W., and Pustay, M. W. *International Business: A Managerial Perspective*, 2nd ed. Reading, Mass.: Addison-Wesley, 1999; Hellriegel, D., Jackson, S. E., and Slocum, J. W. Global Considerations. In *Management*, 8th ed. Cincinnati: South-Western, 1999, 110–141.
6. Griffin and Pustay, 26–30; Peters, T. Prometheus barely unbound. *Academy of Management Executive*, November 1990, 70–84.
7. Kanter, R. M. Managing the extended enterprise in a globally connected world. *Organizational Dynamics*, Summer 1999, 7–23; Norton, E. Global makeover. *Wall Street Journal Reports: World Business*, September 26, 1996, R14.
8. DeSanctis, G. Information technology. In Nickolson, N. (ed.), *Blackwell Encyclopedic Dictionary of Organizational Behavior.* Oxford, England: Blackwell, 1995, 232–233; Thach, L., and Woodman, R. W. Organizational change and information technology: Managing on the edge of cyberspace. *Organizational Dynamics*, Summer 1994, 30–46.
9. Wind and Main, 30–31.
10. Siehman, P. How a tighter supply chain extends the enterprise. *Fortune*, November 8, 1999, 272A–272B.
11. Kanter, 10; Peters, 72–73.
12. Townsend, A. M., DeMarie, S. M., and Hendrickson, A. R. Virtual teams: Technology and the workplace of the future. *Academy of Management Executive*, August 1998, 17–29.
13. Aley, J. The temp biz boom: Why it's good. *Fortune*, October 16, 1995, 53, 55; Conlin, M., and Coy, P. The wild new workforce. *Business Week*, December 6, 1999, 39–44; Fierman, J. The contingency work force. *Fortune*, January 24, 1994, 30–36.
14. Adapted from Nelson, E., and Coleman, C. Y. America is shopping with abandon—Just not at J.C. Penney. *Wall Street Journal*, January 14, 2000, A1, A7.
15. Cummings, T. G., and Worley, C. G. *Organization Development and Change*, 6th ed. Cincinnati: South-Western, 1997, 26–45; Woodman, R. W. Change methods. In C. L. Cooper and C. Argyris (eds.), *The Concise Blackwell Encyclopedia of Management.* Oxford, England: Blackwell, 1998, 75–77.
16. Cummings and Worley, 153–154.
17. Porras, J. I., and Robertson, P. J. Organizational development: Theory, practice, and research. In M. D. Dunnette and L. M. Hough (eds.), *Handbook of Industrial and Organizational Psychology*, 2nd ed., vol. 3. Palo Alto, Calif.: Consulting Psychologists Press, 1992, 719–822.
18. Armenakis, A. A., Harris, S. G., and Field, H. S. Making change permanent: A model for institutionalizing change interventions. In W. A. Pasmore and R. W. Woodman (eds.), *Research in Organizational Change and Development*, vol. 12. Stamford, Conn.: JAI Press, 1999, 97–128; Robertson, P. J., Roberts, D. R., and Porras, J. I. An evaluation of a model of planned organizational change: Evidence from a meta-analysis. In R. W. Woodman and W. A. Pasmore (eds.), *Research in Organizational Change and Development*, vol. 7. Greenwich, Conn.: JAI Press, 1993, 1–39.
19. Beckhard, R. Strategies for large system change. *Sloan Management Review*, 1975, 16, 43–55; Beckhard, R., and Harris, R. T. *Organizational Transitions: Managing Complex Change.* Reading, Mass.: Addison-Wesley, 1987, 29–44;

Woodman, R. W. Issues and concerns in organizational diagnosis. In C. N. Jackson and M. R. Manning (eds.), *Organization Development Annual Volume III: Diagnosing Client Organizations.* Alexandria, Va.: American Society for Training and Development, 1990, 5–10.

20. Adapted from Carnall, C. A. *Managing Change in Organizations.* London: Prentice-Hall, 1990, 68–69.
21. Eden, D. Creating expectation effects in OD: Applying self-fulfilling prophecy. In W. A. Pasmore and R. W. Woodman (eds.), *Research in Organizational Change and Development*, vol. 2. Greenwich, Conn.: JAI Press, 1988, 235–267; Woodman, R. W. Organizational change and development: New arenas for inquiry and action. *Journal of Management*, 1989, 15, 209–210; Woodman, R. W., and Tolchinsky, P. D. Expectation effects: Implications for organization development interventions. In D. D. Warrick (ed.), *Contemporary Organization Development: Current Thinking and Applications.* Glenview, Ill.: Scott, Foresman, 1985, 477–487.
22. Beard, J. W., Woodman, R. W., and Moesel, D. Using behavioral modification to change attendance patterns in the high performance–high commitment environment. In R. W. Woodman and W. A. Pasmore (eds.), *Research in Organizational Change and Development*, vol. 11. Stamford, Conn.: JAI Press, 1998, 183–224.
23. Dent, E. B., and Goldberg, S. G. Challenging "resistance to change." *Journal of Applied Behavioral Science*, 1999, 35, 25–41; Dirks, K. T., Cummings, L. L., and Pierce, J. L. Psychological ownership in organizations: Conditions under which individuals promote and resist change. In R. W. Woodman and W. A. Pasmore (eds.), *Research in Organizational Change and Development*, vol. 9. Greenwich, Conn.: JAI Press, 1996, 1–23; Hollander, E. P. Resistance to change. In C. L. Cooper and C. Argyris (eds.), *The Concise Blackwell Encyclopedia of Management.* Oxford, England: Blackwell, 1998, 560–561; Strebel, P. Why do employees resist change? *Harvard Business Review*, May–June 1996, 86–92.
24. Judge, T. A., Thoresen, C. J., Pucik, V., and Welbourne, T. M. Managerial coping with organizational change: A dispositional perspective. *Journal of Applied Psychology*, 1999, 84, 107–122.
25. Adapted from Coleman, C. Y., and Gumbel, P. St. Louis mall declares war on e-retailing. *Wall Street Journal*, November 24, 1999, B1, B4.
26. Ouellette, J. A., and Wood, W. Habit and intention in everyday life: The multiple processes by which past behavior predicts future behavior. *Psychological Bulletin*, 1998, 124, 54–74.
27. Cameron, K. S., and Quinn, R. E. *Diagnosing and Changing Organizational Culture.* Reading, Mass.: Addison-Wesley, 1999.
28. Lewin, K. *Field Theory in Social Science.* New York: Harper & Row, 1951; Lewin, K. Frontiers in group dynamics. *Human Relations*, 1947, 1, 5–41; Zand, D. E. Force field analysis. In N. Nicholson (ed.), *Blackwell Encyclopedic Dictionary of Organizational Behavior.* Oxford, England: Blackwell, 1995, 180–181.
29. Cummings and Worley, 27.
30. Woodman, R. W. Observations on the field of organizational change and development from the lunatic fringe. *Organization Development Journal*, 1993, 11, 71–74; Woodman, R. W. Organization development and change. In C. L. Cooper and C. Argyris (eds.), *The Concise Blackwell Encyclopedia of Management.* Oxford, England: Blackwell, 1998, 444–445.
31. Adapted from Make employees engines of progress. *Managers Edge.* Alexandria, Va.: Pryor Reports, 1999; also see, Iverson, K. *Plain Talk: Lessons from a Business Maverick.* New York: John Wiley & Sons, 1999.
32. Beer, M. *Organization Change and Development: A Systems View.* Santa Monica, Calif.: Goodyear, 1980, 10; Woodman, R. W. Organization development. In N. Nicholson (ed.), *Blackwell Encyclopedic Dictionary of Organizational Behavior.* Oxford, England: Blackwell, 1995, 359–361.
33. McMahan, G. C., and Woodman, R. W. The current practice of organization development within the firm: A survey of large industrial corporations. *Group & Organization Management*, 1992, 17, 117–134.
34. French, W. L., and Bell, C. H. *Organization Development: Behavioral Science Interventions for Organization Improvement*, 6th ed. Upper Saddle River, N. J.: Prentice-Hall, 1999, 130–144.
35. See, for example, the classic statement by Cartwright, D. Achieving change in people: Some applications of group dynamics theory. *Human Relations*, 1951, 4, 381–392.
36. Cooperrider, D. L., and Srivastva, S. Appreciative inquiry in organizational life. In R. W. Woodman and W. A. Pasmore (eds.), *Research in Organizational Change and Development*, vol. 1. Greenwich, Conn.: JAI Press, 1987, 129–169; Hammond, S. A. *The Thin Book of Appreciative Inquiry*, 2nd ed. Plano, Texas: Thin Book, 1998; Zemke, R. Don't fix that company. *Training*, June 1999, 26–33.
37. Cooperrider and Srivastva, 160–161; French and Bell, 138–139; Whitney, D., and Schau, C. Appreciative inquiry: An innovative process for organization change. *Employment Relations Today*, Summer 1998, 17–29.
38. Golembiewski, R. T. Appreciating appreciative inquiry: Diagnosis and perspectives on how to do better. In R. W. Woodman and W. A. Pasmore (eds.), *Research in Organizational Change and Development*, vol. 11. Stamford, Conn.: JAI Press, 1998, 1–45.
39. Cummings and Worley, 133–139; French and Bell, 202–205.
40. Forrester, R., and Drexler, A. G. A model for team-based organization performance. *Academy of Management Executive*, August 1999, 36–49; Guzzo, R. A., and Dickson, M. W. Teams in organizations: Recent research on performance and effectiveness. *Annual Review of Psychology*, 1996, 47, 307–338; Katzenbach, J. R., and Smith, D. K. *The Wisdom of Teams: Creating the High-Performance Organization.* Boston: Harvard Business School Press, 1993.
41. Schein, E. H. *Process Consultation Revisited: Building the Helping Relationship.* Reading, Mass.: Addison-Wesley, 1999.
42. Boltes, B. B., Briggs, T. C., Huff, J. W., Wright, J. A., and Neuman, G. A. Flexible and compressed workweek schedules: A meta-analysis of their effects on work-related criteria. *Journal of Applied Psychology*, 1999, 84, 496–513;

Dunham, R. B., and Pierce, J. L. Flexible workplace/telecommuting. In C. L. Cooper and C. Argyris (eds.), *The Concise Blackwell Encyclopedia of Management.* Oxford, England: Blackwell, 1998, 228.

43. Trice, H. M., and Beyer, J. M. *The Cultures of Work Organizations.* Englewood Cliffs, N.J.: Prentice-Hall, 1993, 393–428.
44. French and Bell, 233–234; Woodman, R. W. Organizational change and development: New arenas for inquiry and action. *Journal of Management*, 1989, 15, 218–219.
45. Sherwood, J. J. Creating work cultures with competitive advantage. *Organizational Dynamics*, Winter 1988, 5–26.
46. Burgoyne, J. Learning organization. In C. L. Cooper and C. Argyris (eds.), *The Concise Blackwell Encyclopedia of Management.* Oxford, England: Blackwell, 1998, 359; Fulmer, R. M., Gibbs, P., and Keys, J. B. The second generation learning organizations: New tools for sustaining competitive advantage. *Organizational Dynamics*, Autumn 1998, 7–20; Fulmer, R. M., and Keys, J. B. A conversation with Peter Senge: New developments in organizational learning. *Organizational Dynamics*, Autumn 1998, 33–42.
47. Wetlaufer, S. Driving change: An interview with Ford Motor Company's Jacques Nasser. *Harvard Business Review*, March–April 1999, 78.
48. Pasmore, W. A. *Designing Effective Organizations: The Sociotechnical Systems Perspective.* New York: John Wiley & Sons, 1988; Vansina, L. S., and Taillieu, T. Business process reengineering or socio-technical design in new clothes? In R. W. Woodman and W. A. Pasmore (eds.), *Research in Organizational Change and Development*, vol. 9. Greenwich, Conn.: JAI Press, 1996, 81–100.
49. Adapted from Wetlaufer, 77–88.
50. Cole, R. E. Learning from the quality movement: What did and didn't happen and why. *California Management Review*, Fall 1998, 43–73; Steel, R. P., and Jennings, K. R. Quality improvement technologies for the '90s: New directions for research and theory. In W. A. Pasmore and R. W. Woodman (eds.), *Research in Organizational Change and Development*, vol. 6. Greenwich, Conn.: JAI Press, 1992, 1–36.
51. Hammer and Champy; Jaffe, D. T., and Scott, C. D. Reengineering in practice: Where are the people? Where is the learning? *Journal of Applied Behavioral Science*, 1998, 34, 250–267; Moosbruker, J. B., and Loftin, R. D. Business process redesign and organization development: Enhancing success by removing the barriers. *Journal of Applied Behavioral Science*, 1998, 34, 286–304.
52. Hammer and Champy, 65–82.
53. Coyle-Shapiro, J.A-M. TQM and organizational change: A longitudinal study of the impact of a TQM intervention on work attitudes. In W. A. Pasmore and R. W. Woodman (eds.), *Research in Organizational Change and Development*, vol. 12. Stamford, Conn.: JAI Press, 1999, 129–169; Thompson, K. R. Confronting the paradoxes in a total quality environment. *Organizational Dynamics*, Winter 1998, 62–72; Zbaracki, M. J. The rhetoric and reality of total quality management. *Administrative Science Quarterly*, 1998, 43, 602–636.
54. Lillrank, P., Shani, A. B., Kolodny, H., Stymne, B., Figuera, J. R., and Liu, M. Learning from the success of continuous improvement change programs: An international comparative study. In R. W. Woodman and W. A. Pasmore (eds.), *Research in Organizational Change and Development*, vol. 11. Stamford, Conn.: JAI Press, 1998, 47–71.
55. Bushe, G. R., and Shani, A. B. *Parallel Learning Structures: Increasing Innovation in Bureaucracies.* Reading, Mass.: Addison-Wesley, 1991; French and Bell, 94–95; Woodman, R. W. Collateral organization. In N. Nicholson (ed.), *Blackwell Encyclopedic Dictionary of Organizational Behavior.* Oxford, England: Blackwell, 1995, 70–71.
56. Keller, J. J. AT&T's Robert Allen gets sharp criticism over layoff, losses. *Wall Street Journal*, February 22, 1996, A1, A6; Markels, A., and Murray, M. Call it dumbsizing: Why some companies regret cost-cutting. *Wall Street Journal*, March 14, 1996, A1, A6; Stewart, T. A. Watch what we did, not what we said. *Fortune*, April 15, 1996, 140–141; White, J. B. Re-engineering gurus take steps to remodel their stalling vehicles. *Wall Street Journal*, November 26, 1996, A1, A13.
57. Bushe, G. R., and Shani, A. B. Parallel learning structure interventions in bureaucratic organizations. In W. A. Pasmore and R. W. Woodman (eds.), *Research in Organizational Change and Development*, vol. 4. Greenwich, Conn.: JAI Press, 1990, 167–194; Zand, D. E. Collateral organization: A new change strategy. *Journal of Applied Behavioral Science*, 1974, 10, 63–89.
58. Miles, R. E., and Snow, C. C. The new network firm: A spherical structure built on a human investment philosophy. *Organizational Dynamics*, Spring 1995, 5–18; Snow, C. C., Miles, R. E., and Coleman, H. J. Managing 21st century network organizations. *Organizational Dynamics*, Winter 1992, 5–20.
59. Boudreau, M. C., Lock, K. D., Robey, D., and Straud, D. Going global: Using information technology to advance the competitiveness of the virtual transnational organization. *Academy of Management Executive*, November 1998, 120–128; Handy, C. Trust and the virtual organization. *Harvard Business Review*, May–June 1995, 40–50; Upton, D. M., and McAfee, A. The real virtual factory. *Harvard Business Review*, July–August 1996, 123–133.
60. Hellriegel, Jackson, and Slocum, 218.
61. Cummings and Worley, 458–459.
62. Connor, P. E., and Lake, L. K. *Managing Organizational Change.* New York: Praeger, 1988, 171–175; Lowman, R. L. (ed.). *The Ethical Practice of Psychology in Organizations.* Washington, R. L.: American Psychological Association, 1998.
63. Adapted from Maurer, R. Working with resistance to change: The support for change questionnaire. In J. W. Pfeiffer (ed.), *The 1996 Annual—Volume 2 Consulting.* San Diego: Pfeiffer & Company, 1996, 161–174.
64. Adapted from *Organization Development and Change*, 6th ed., by T. G. Cummings and C. G. Worley. Copyright © 1997. By permission of South-Western College Publishing, a division of International Thomson Publishing, Inc., Cincinnati, Ohio 45227.

APPENDIX

Tools and Techniques for Studying Organizational Behavior

This appendix introduces you to the tools and techniques used to assess problems in organizational behavior. Ways to think about issues and apply sound research methods to solve them are presented. Examples that illustrate how research has been used to answer specific questions that puzzle organizations' management are highlighted.*

THE SCIENTIFIC APPROACH

Effective management involves the ability to understand job-related problems and to make valid predictions about employee behavior. The key to such understanding is the **scientific approach,** a method for systematically collecting and analyzing information in an unbiased manner. Figure A.1 illustrates the three basic steps of the scientific approach: observation, measurement, and prediction. These steps are so basic that, without even realizing it, most people use them every day.

One use of the scientific approach is to study the effect of an organization's employee benefit programs on health-care costs and employee attendance.[1] Monfort, Inc., a meatpacking subsidiary of ConAgra Foods, discovered that annual medical costs for employees had topped $5 million, largely because of premature and low birth-weight babies. The director of human resources showed top management that medical claim costs and lost earnings owing to parental leave surrounding pregnancy and childbirth could be reduced if the company established a neonatal program for employees reluctant to seek prenatal care. Management provided incentives, including $50 up front and a car seat when the baby was born to jumpstart the program. As a result of the program, Monfort, Inc.'s medical costs dropped from $5.5 million to $2.3 million in 1 year, and the average hospital stay for premature and low-weight babies following birth dropped from 17 to 11 days in just 3 years.

Figure A.1 **The Scientific Approach**

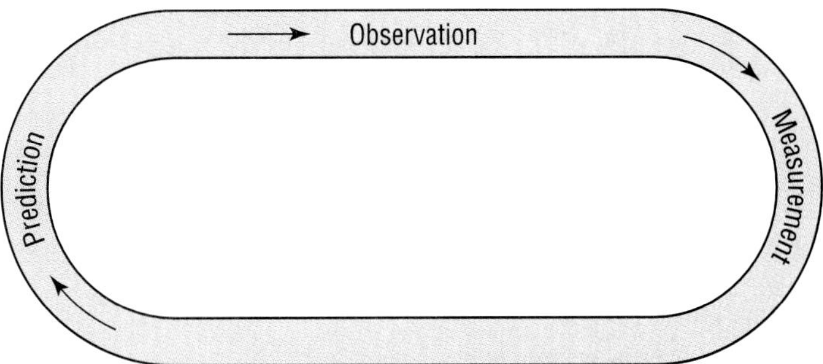

* This appendix was revised by Lucinda Lawson, Department of Management, Lowry Mays College and Graduate School of Business, Texas A&M University, College Station, Texas.

Another example involves Wilmington, Delaware-based DuPont. DuPont observed that absenteeism increased to 20 percent when snowstorms shut down local schools and day-care centers. In response, the company created an emergency child-care program called Just in Time. The service was used by employees a total of 2,300 times in a recent year. The company estimated that this program saved more than 1,800 employee workdays.

A recent survey released by Families & Work Institute reported that, although many company executives are aware of the advantages of employee benefits, only a small portion of the 1,057 companies surveyed provide them.[2] However, one CEO explained that his company had observed that at least one-half to a full day's work before a national holiday was lost because employees left early. The company initiated a new performance-based policy that allows employees to earn an extra day off before the holiday if the entire company meets specific goals.

The scientific approach requires a systematic test of assumptions. Such testing may reveal that a problem does not exist or is less or more serious than initially assumed. The scientific approach helps management guard against preconceptions or personal bias by requiring as complete an assessment of the problem or issue as resources allow.

PREPARATION OF RESEARCH DESIGNS

A **research design** is a plan, structure, and strategy of investigation intended to obtain answers to one or more questions.[3] The research design includes everything the researcher will do during the project from data collection through data analysis to report preparation and submission. The plan should identify the types of data to be collected, the target population and sample(s) to be drawn, research instruments to be used, methods of analysis to be used, and tentative completion dates to be met. The structure is an outline of the specific variables to be measured. Diagrams may be used to illustrate how the variables—and their assumed relationships—are to be examined. The strategy presents the methods to be used to validate the data, achieve research objectives, and resolve problems encountered during the research.

PURPOSES OF RESEARCH DESIGNS

A research design has two major purposes: to provide answers to questions and to provide control for nuisance variables.[4] A **nuisance variable** is anything that the researcher has little control over but could affect research results. In the Monfort, Inc. example, a decrease in the number of employees requiring maternity benefits is a nuisance variable, whereas in the DuPont example, unreliable and hazardous transportation associated with snow and ice are nuisance variables. Researchers devise research designs to obtain answers to questions as objectively, accurately, and economically as possible. The design determines the observations to be made and how they are to be obtained and analyzed.

Rarely does a research design satisfy all the criteria associated with the scientific approach, but researchers should try to satisfy as many as possible when choosing a design. The ultimate findings of a poorly conceived research design may be invalid or have limited applicability. The ultimate product of a well-conceived design is more likely to be valid and receive serious attention.

HYPOTHESIS

The design of a research project typically involves stating a hypothesis so that inferences of a causal relationship between an **independent** (causal) **variable** and a **dependent** (effect) **variable** can legitimately be drawn or discarded. A hypothesis is a statement about the relationship between two or more variables. More specifically, a

hypothesis asserts that a particular characteristic or occurrence of one of the factors (the independent variable) determines a characteristic or occurrence of another factor (the dependent variable). A researcher might state the following hypotheses with regard to employee commitment, satisfaction, and performance.

- Employees whose employers provide benefits will be more committed to their organization than employees whose employers do not offer such benefits.
- Spending money to institute employee benefit programs will be more than offset by the reduction in costs associated with health care and absenteeism.
- The quality of employee output will be higher when individuals work in an environment that is free from smoke than when smoking is permitted.

After researchers state a hypothesis, they collect facts and analyze them (usually statistically) to determine whether the facts support or fail to support the hypothesis. A cause-and-effect relationship often isn't easy to establish. With all this in mind, let's examine the basic parts of an experimental design.

Experimental Design

The concept of causality in relation to experimental designs is complex, and a thorough analysis is beyond the scope of this appendix. However, some types of research designs provide more valid grounds for drawing causal inferences than others.[5] Here, we limit the discussion to points that are essential to an understanding of adequate research design requirements.

An experimental design incorporates random assignment of participants into experimental and control groups to provide researchers control over the research environment. Random assignment ensures that an experimenter's preconceptions or biases do not influence the choice of participants or their assignment to either the experimental or control group. Members of the **experimental group** are exposed to the treatment, or the independent variable. Members of the **control group** are not exposed to the treatment or the independent variable.

One way to obtain a random assignment is to give each person a number and then use a table of random numbers to make the selection. A second way is to flip a coin for each person; heads are members of the experimental group; tails are members of the control group. Another way of selecting participants is by matching people who are alike in all aspects relevant to the experiment.

An experimental design that incorporated the matching technique investigated the causes of lower back injuries at work.[6] Lower back injuries cause more absence from work than any other injury or disease.[7] Compensation for back injuries costs organizations approximately $36 billion annually and accounts for 31 percent of all work-related injury compensation.[8] Researchers at Johns Hopkins University investigated the factors associated with lower back injuries in a sample of Baltimore city workers. The experimental group contained municipal workers who suffered a lower back injury during the study period. Two control groups contained matched noninjured municipal workers. The first control group consisted of noninjured workers matched by department, job, gender, and presence at work on the day of the injury. A second control group consisted of noninjured workers matched only on job, gender, and presence at work on the day of injury. To be eligible for the study, neither experimental group members nor control group members could have had a back injury or back pain during the preceding 12 months. In total, 200 injured workers and 400 workers in the control groups completed questionnaires. Participants were interviewed about work injuries and characteristics of their specific work and work environment. Anthropometric data, including weight and circumference of the worker's wrist, upper arm, and waist were also obtained. The results indicated that high job stress (measured as, among other things, low amounts of social support from supervisors and peers and low amounts of control) was the most important factor affecting lower back injury. Employees with high levels of job stress were more likely to sustain a lower back injury than those with low levels of job stress. Body mass index (a good measure of obesity and a crude measure of physical fitness) and work movement index (twisting, extended reaching, and stooping) were also significant factors affecting lower back injuries. The larger the body mass and the greater the work movement index, the greater was the chance of a worker sustaining a lower back injury.

An experimental design is used to rule out other causes for the experimental results and reduce threats to validity. Other factors affecting lower back injury that had to be controlled for in the study by the researchers at Johns Hopkins included the following significant possibilities.

- *Natural maturing or development.* If the maturing process was assumed to be the same for members of both the experimental and control groups, the effects of maturation could be ruled out when comparing the results achieved by the different groups.
- *Influence of the measurement process itself.* Because the participants knew that they were being studied, they might have responded differently than if they hadn't known. And, if they felt that they were expected to answer a certain way, their responses and thus the measurements obtained could have distorted the results. Complex variations in experimental designs can be used to account for the effects of the measuring process.[9]
- *Contemporaneous events other than the exposure of the employees to the condition.* Events that occurred during the research period that the researcher couldn't control might have affected the factors associated with lower back injury. For example, if the organization introduced extremely strenuous physical requirements on two new jobs but allowed workers to rotate among jobs requiring different levels of physical activity, both the experimental and control groups may have altered their perceptions of the work environment despite becoming more susceptible to lower back injury. Like maturational effects, however, if such a perception had affected members of the experimental and control groups the same way, it wouldn't have affected the comparisons between groups.

TYPES OF RESEARCH DESIGN

Many different types of research design exist, and numerous books have been written on the subject.[10] There is growing recognition that managers and others need a basic knowledge of certain research methods in order to understand the contributions and limitations of research in organizational behavior. An understanding of these methods should rein in the tendency to rush into often erroneous cause-and-effect analyses and solutions to problems.

Managers should familiarize themselves with several research designs so that they can select the most appropriate design for the problem at hand. They should select the design that will do the most complete job, which depends on

- the types of information each design provides;
- the validity of the data, that is, how confident the researchers can be about inferences based on the findings; and
- the amount of time, money, and other resources required and available to perform the research.

Instead of properly evaluating these and other considerations, managers often approve a research design, become comfortable with it, and then apply it inappropriately to situations. Unfortunately, prior habits, experiences, and biases often determine the choice of a research design. Instead of becoming solely interested in, say, laboratory experiments or field surveys, managers should understand and appreciate the usefulness and limitations of various types of research design.

The four most common types of research design are the case study, the field survey, the laboratory experiment, and the field experiment. They may be interrelated in many ways; Figure A.2 suggests one logical sequence of research.

Case Study

A **case study** is an intensive investigation of a situation and the behaviors of the people involved in it. Case studies arise out of a need to understand and explain complex actions and events for which little experience or theory is available to serve as a guide. A case study allows a researcher to present a broader perspective than can be achieved through other research designs. It can also be used to establish valid and reliable evidence or as a vehicle for creating a story or narrative description.[11]

Three distinctive features of the case study make it an important tool for stimulating new insights. First, the researcher can let the factors being studied guide the research as it progresses and not be limited to testing preformulated hypotheses. Second, the case study is intense because the researcher attempts to obtain sufficient information to characterize and explain the unique aspects of the situation being studied. Third, the case study tests the researcher's ability to assemble many diverse bits of information and base a unified interpretation on them.

If the researcher is comfortable with these three key features, the case study can be an effective way to analyze organizational behavior. It is highly adaptable to many organizational situations, such as uncovering the power relationships in an organization, which can be quite different from those presented in the formal organizational chart. A researcher can view organizational records, conduct interviews, distribute questionnaires, and make personal observations of interactions among employees to uncover the true power relationships that exist.

The researcher must also consider the limitations of the case study. This method's main disadvantage is that generalizing the results of one case study to other cases usually isn't valid. That is, only rarely can two cases be compared directly in terms of their essential characteristics (e.g., number of employees, location, number and type of products manufactured, levels of hierarchy, and the technology used to produce goods and services). Therefore results of a case study usually cannot be applied specifically to other settings. A second disadvantage is that a case study usually does not lend itself to a systematic investigation of cause-and-effect relationships. Although a case study extending over time can help identify changes that have occurred, the range of variations observed may be too limited for practical cause-and-effect analysis. Case studies therefore may not allow the researcher to accept or reject a hypothesis. However, case studies frequently provide many clues and insights for further investigation.

Field Survey

A **field survey** involves collecting data through interviews or a questionnaire from a sample of people selected to represent the group being studied. The use of a sample avoids an expensive and time-consuming census (contacting every person in the group being studied).[12] One of the best known practitioners of the field survey is the Gallup

Figure A.2 **One Possible Sequence of Research Designs**

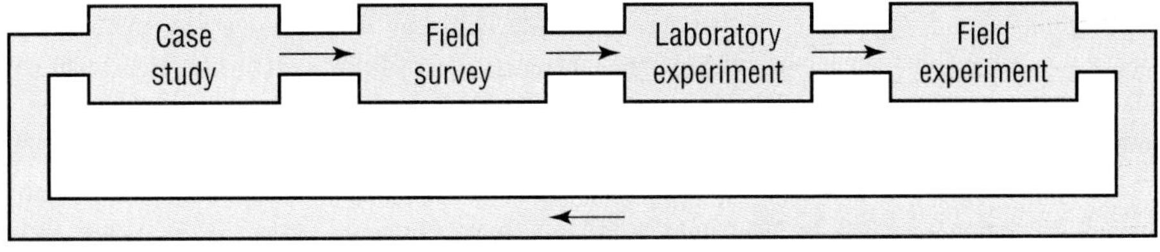

Organization. Since 1935, its telephone and door-to-door interviewers have collected data on everything from the economy to views on bilingual education and has issued special reports on public opinion regarding those topics.[13]

The intent of a field survey is to gather information—to discover how people feel and think—and not to change or influence the respondents. A field survey generally requires a large sample for valid conclusions to be drawn from the responses. Of those initially selected, many fail to respond. Typically, only about 20 to 30 percent of the people who receive a questionnaire return a completed survey. Researchers tabulate the responses, analyze them, draw conclusions, and state the results.

Kimberly Clark's Away from Home sector was interested in determining the problems that office workers would like to see eliminated in the future. Management employed Opinion Research Corporation International to conduct a national survey of full- and part-time white-collar office workers. The results indicated that the top three problems that office workers would like to see eliminated were gossip, difficult bosses, and dirty rest rooms.[14]

The field survey is not the best research design for obtaining some types of data; its use is limited to data about things of which the respondents are consciously aware. If unconscious motivations were important, an in-depth personal interview would be more productive and valid. Problems with inferring cause-and-effect relationships also arise with field surveys. Consider an analysis of the relationships among job satisfaction, organizational commitment, and performance. Does job satisfaction lead to higher performance, causing higher levels of organizational commitment? Or is organizational commitment related to job satisfaction, causing high performance? Because of the large number of unmeasured variables usually involved in a field survey, such questions concerning causal relations among the variables cannot be answered.

Laboratory Experiment

Compared to the case study and the field survey, the laboratory experiment increases the researcher's ability to establish cause-and-effect relationships among the variables. The laboratory setting permits the researcher to control the conditions under which the experiment is carried out.

The essence of the **laboratory experiment** is the manipulation of one or more independent variables and observation of the effect on one or more dependent variables. For example, a researcher tells one group of participants that it performed poorly on a previously administered difficult task and tells another group of participants that it performed well when, in truth, performance on the difficult task wasn't even evaluated. The researcher then instructs both groups to perform the task again and predicts actual performance on the task. The independent variable is positive or negative performance feedback and the dependent variable is the second performance of the task.

Laboratory experiments are most useful when the conditions required to test a hypothesis are not practical or readily obtainable in natural situations and when the situations can be replicated under laboratory conditions. For example, Chili's restaurant has built a challenge course to demonstrate how teamwork can improve managerial effectiveness. The challenge course comprises 15 events performed close to the ground. These events include having members of a group exchange places while standing on a horizontal telephone pole suspended 6 inches off the ground. Another 8 events are performed high off the ground. These events include climbing and then rappelling down a 60-foot-high tower. By manipulating the types of challenges facing the group, Wade Bibbee, the course's director, can observe the changes in team effectiveness, cooperation, and commitment and draw some conclusions about ways to increase teamwork in a restaurant.[15]

The use of the laboratory research design has several disadvantages. For practical reasons, college students are the most common source of participants in laboratory research. However, it is difficult to claim that college students represent employees actually involved in behaviors at work, such as making managerial decisions.

Unlike employees at work, many students are young, transient, and have not yet occupied positions of responsibility. Furthermore, their livelihood doesn't depend on the successful accomplishment of the task being completed in the laboratory. To what populations and treatment variables, then, can the results of laboratory experiments involving students be generalized? The fact is that most laboratory results aren't valid when broadly interpreted because the experiments are usually limited in scope—to narrowly defined behaviors of narrowly defined groups.

In addition, simulating many of the properties of organizational structure and processes in the laboratory can be extremely difficult. For example, many behavioral problems in organizations, such as turnover and poor performance, cannot be isolated to permit their simulation and examination under laboratory conditions. Conversely, much of the work undertaken in the laboratory deals with matters that cannot be reproduced in or applied to real-life situations. For example, an organization could not readily redesign its hierarchy to fit an ideal model. Even if it could find and hire "perfect" personnel, the changeover would likely result in serious morale and productivity problems. Researchers thus tend to focus narrowly on problems that can be addressed in the laboratory. These experiments should be derived from studies of real-life situations, and results should continually be checked against them.

Field Experiment

A **field experiment** involves the application of the laboratory method to ongoing real-life situations.[16] A field experiment permits the manipulation of one or more independent variables. The researcher can study the changes in the dependent variables and infer the direction of causality with some degree of confidence.

The participants in a field experiment usually know that they are being observed. Thus the researcher must use procedures that minimize the possibility of participants changing their behavior simply because they are being observed. Compared to the laboratory experiment, the field experiment provides the researcher with fewer controls.

Researchers at the Dana-Farber Cancer Institute conducted a field experiment with 22 worksites in Boston and surrounding cities in Massachusetts.[17] This field experiment featured the random assignment of people to one of three interventions that promoted increased consumption of fruits and vegetables. The control groups received the "basic" intervention. It included (1) periodic exposure to a national 5-a-Day media campaign; (2) promotions of the Cancer Information Service HotLine; and (3) a 1-hour general nutrition presentation and taste test. The first experimental groups received the "worksite" intervention. It included the "basic" intervention and other interventions aimed at individual behavior change. These interventions included (1) a kickoff event; (2) the Eatwell 5-a-Day discussion series; (3) an educational campaign that lasted for 3 to 5 weeks; and (4) posters, videos, and brochures about fruits and vegetables placed in areas where employees gathered to eat. The second experimental groups received the "worksite-plus" intervention, which included both the "basic" and "worksite" interventions plus (1) a written learn-at-home program, "Fit in 5"; (2) family newsletters; (3) family festivals; and (4) periodic mailings of program material. This intervention was designed to create a home environment supportive of the workers' attempts to change eating patterns and encourage other family members to do so. Results indicated that the "worksite-plus" intervention was more successful in increasing fruit and vegetable consumption than either the "basic" or "worksite" interventions.

COMPARISON OF RESEARCH DESIGNS

Each of the four types of research design has both strengths and weaknesses. By selecting one type of design, the researcher must often forgo some of the advantages of the others but, at the same time, can avoid their disadvantages.

Realism

A primary advantage of doing research in a natural setting, such as a field experiment within an organization, is the ability to increase the level of realism. The researcher can be confident that the participants are generally behaving under natural and ongoing conditions. This approach offers an advantage over the laboratory setting, which typically involves artificial conditions. However, the researcher in the field loses the ability to manipulate independent (causal) variables as freely as in the laboratory.

Scope

Case studies and field surveys usually are broad in scope and contain many variables of interest to the investigator. Laboratory experiments, by their nature, are the most limited in scope, and field experiments often are simply extensions of laboratory experiments.

Precision

Laboratory research usually is more precise than field research. In the laboratory, the use of multiple measures of the same variable or variables under controlled conditions allows the researcher to obtain more accurate information about the variables than with the other methods. The use of videotape, for example, permits the researcher to record an entire experiment and then study it later, examining behavior, expressions, gestures, and the like.

Control

Researchers try to control an experiment so that events being observed will be related to hypothesized causes, not to some unknown, unrelated events. The laboratory experiment allows researchers to reproduce a situation repeatedly so that they don't have to rely on a single observation for their conclusions. By replicating a study, predictions about cause-and-effect relationships can be refined from "sometimes" to, say, "95 times in 100." The laboratory experiment also avoids many factors present in the field over which the investigator has little control (e.g., personnel changes or employees forgetting to fill out questionnaires). However, the results obtained from ideal circumstances may not fit the real situation.

Cost

Research designs differ in terms of relative costs and resources required. Designs vary in initial setup costs, including the time and resources needed to plan and initiate them. They also vary in the cost per additional sample. For example, a laboratory experiment has relatively low setup costs, requires few other resources, and costs little for additional subjects—and the resources required can be found in most colleges and universities. Because of high costs, field experiments tend to be carried out by large research organizations rather than by a researcher and a few assistants. These experiments require a large number of subjects and computer facilities to analyze the data.

DATA COLLECTION METHODS

Managers observe events and gather data all day, every day. Some data they reject, some they store away, and some they act on. The problem with this ordinary method of data gathering, as opposed to scientific data gathering, is that day-to-day observations of behavior frequently are unreliable or are biased by personal attitudes or values. Also, the sample of behaviors observed is often limited and doesn't truly represent typical behavior, making it a poor basis for generalizations. Hence erroneous conclusions frequently are drawn from observations of human behavior.

The quality of research depends on the adequacy of the research design as well as the adequacy of the data-collection methods used. The researcher can collect data in various ways: by interviews, questionnaires, observations, nonreactive measures, or qualitative methods.[18] The rules for using these data-collection methods to make statements about the relevant subject matter may be built into the data-collection technique, or they may be developed during the researcher's study.

Interviews

An **interview** refers to a face-to-face verbal exchange in which one person, the interviewer, attempts to acquire information, opinions, or beliefs from another person, the interviewee. Interviews are one of the oldest and most often used methods for obtaining information. Asking someone a direct question allows greater flexibility of responses and follow-up questions not available with formal questionnaires and can save considerable time and money if the person is willing to talk and responds honestly. However, the success of an interview relies on the willingness of people to communicate and the skill of the interviewer.

An interview's quality depends heavily on the mutual trust and goodwill established between interviewer and respondent. A trained interviewer builds these relationships early in the interview so that the greatest number of responses will be useful. One way to build trust is to assure the respondent that all answers are confidential. In addition, an interviewer must be a good listener in order to draw information from the respondent.

The interview method has several shortcomings. First, people may be unwilling to provide certain types of information readily to an interviewer, face-to-face. Employees, for example, may be unwilling to express negative attitudes about a superior when the interviewer is from the organization's human resources department. Getting employees to talk openly—even to a skilled outsider—and answer questions about their jobs, other individuals, and their organization is a difficult task. Thus the importance of establishing trust cannot be overstated. The second shortcoming of this method is that interviews take considerable time, which costs money. Skilled interviewers charge more than $25 per hour plus transportation costs. Third, to achieve reliability interviewers must be well trained, present questions in a way that ensures validity, and eliminate personal biases. Their questions must be tested in advance of the actual interviews for hidden biases. Fourth, the questions asked by the interviewer limit the answers that respondents may freely give.

America @ Work, a study conducted annually for the American Management Association, uses interviews to investigate employee commitment and loyalty.[19] The 1999 results suggested that commitment and loyalty toward employers had increased since 1998. One finding indicated that commitment and loyalty are positively associated with employee benefit programs. Moreover, employers who help employees balance the demands of work and family by allowing them a moderate amount of time each week to attend to personal matters at work had significantly more committed employees than employers who did not do so.

Questionnaires

Questionnaires are sets of written questions that respondents are asked to answer. They are the most popular data collection method in business studies.[20] Questionnaires are used to measure the respondent's attitudes, opinions, or demographic characteristics. They are used to measure numerous variables, such as personality, needs fulfillment, power, job stress, teamwork and competencies, which have been discussed throughout this book.

The purpose of the study, the nature of the population to be sampled, and the research budget must be addressed before a sound decision can be made about the use of a questionnaire. After thinking through the reasons for using a questionnaire, a researcher must then decide either to purchase a previously developed and validated questionnaire or to develop a specific questionnaire for the situation. Sound survey development and construction can have a profound and long-lasting impact on the success or failure of any survey effort.[21] When developing a questionnaire, a researcher must determine the depth of the information desired from the responses, which can be simply *yes* or *no* or more detailed. A Likert-type response scale is useful in determining the strength of agreement or the frequency of an action identified by the response to a question. Responses may also be totally unstructured. In this situation, a question is followed by sufficient blank space for the respondent to explain the answer. For example, an item about a respondent's engagement in extra-role behavior at work can be phrased differently with provision for correspondingly different responses.

1. Do you engage in behaviors at work that are beneficial to the organization but not part of your required job responsibilities? (a) yes (b) no.
2. I engage in behaviors at work that are beneficial to the organization but not part of my required job responsibilities. (a) strongly agree (b) agree (c) neither agree nor disagree (d) disagree (e) strongly disagree; or (a) never (b) sometimes (c) frequently (d) very often.
3. Please explain the behaviors you engage in at work that are beneficial to your employer but not part of your required job responsibilities. ________________

   ____

   ____

Saja Software, Inc. markets Survey Select Expert, an advanced survey computer software tool intended to simplify developing and administering employee surveys.[22] This software allows users to build surveys from customized question libraries and conduct surveys through corporate intranets, local area networks, e-mail, or the Internet.

The use of questionnaires to collect data has both advantages and disadvantages. Advantages of questionnaires include the following.

- They provide a relatively inexpensive way to collect data.
- They can be administered by relatively unskilled people.
- They can be administered through several types of media (e.g., e-mail, Internet, and hard copy).
- They provide the same stimulus to everyone surveyed.
- They often can be answered anonymously, which may lead to more open and truthful responses than might be obtained, for example, during an interview.

Questionnaires may have one or more of the following disadvantages.

- Missing data may be a problem if people do not answer all the questions.
- A low response rate (less than 20 percent) may invalidate the results.
- Questionnaires cannot be used with individuals who have severe reading problems or are unfamiliar with the English language. When individuals cannot read English, questionnaires must be translated for them, but translations aren't always precise.
- The respondent has no flexibility in answering, which limits the amount of information that can be obtained.

Simcom, a small privately held company that builds flight simulators and trains pilots, recently asked its employees to evaluate the need for an incentive pay program.[23] In phase 1, management developed a survey to address the research question. In phase 2, management developed and implemented an incentive pay system. In phase 3, management assessed the effectiveness of the incentive pay plan by comparing survey results prior to the incentive pay system with survey results after implementation.

Observation

Managers observe the actions of others and, based on these observations, infer others' motivations, feelings, and intentions. A principal advantage of **observation** is that the observer can actually see the behavior of individuals rather than rely on verbal or written descriptions of it, which may be inaccurate or biased. One problem with observation is that observers must absorb the information seen and then draw inferences from what they have observed—and inferences are often incorrect. Suppose, for example, that an observer is unfamiliar with the standard operating procedures of a Safeway grocery store's meat department. While observing several employees at work, the observer notices that a new employee is performing a task differently than several longer tenured employees. This observation may lead the observer to infer that the new employee is incorrectly performing the task. In fact, the new employee is performing the task correctly while the longer tenured employees are using shortcuts that are both incorrect and unsafe.

Nonreactive Measures

A manager who wants to know something about an employee also might turn to nonreactive sources of information. A **nonreactive measure** is one that provides information about an individual without that person's knowledge. In some cases, nonreactive measures may yield more accurate data than those obtained by directly questioning the employee. Company records provide researchers with valuable data on demographics, absenteeism, turnover, grievances, and performance ratings. Customers' specific buying histories, which are obtained and updated with each transaction, provide Safeway Foods with information about customer preferences that they use to stock their stores accurately.[24] A computerized reservation system at Seattle's Palisade restaurant keeps personal information, including birthdays, anniversaries, and past reservation information, about patrons.[25] The management and wait staff use this information to provide more personalized service to guests. A recent study published in the *New England Journal of Medicine* used car phone billing records of individuals involved in car accidents to investigate the relationship between using a car phone and having an accident.[26] The results indicated that individuals talking on the phone are four times more likely to have an accident than those not doing so, a rate equal to that of people driving while mildly intoxicated but beyond the legal limit.

Qualitative Methods

Qualitative methods encompass a variety of approaches used by researchers to describe and clarify the meaning of naturally occurring events in organizations. These approaches are open-ended and interpretative and often involve the use of nonstatistical means to analyze and interpret the data. Because qualitative data are rarely quantifiable, the researcher's interpretation and description are highly significant. Qualitative methods rely on the investigator's experience and intuition to describe the organizational processes and behaviors being studied.

The type of data collected with qualitative methods requires the researcher to become involved in the situation or problem being studied. For example, a qualitative method used for years by anthropologists is ethnography. As applied to organizational behavior, ethnography requires the researcher studying an organization to become a participant observer for long periods of time. That is, the investigator takes part in the situation being studied to understand what it is like for the subjects. One researcher studying a big-city police department accompanied police officers as they performed their duties. This person informally interviewed police officers, read important police documents, and used nonreactive measures (e.g., police records) to gather other data, and, as a result, provided vivid descriptions of what police work was really like.[27]

CRITERIA FOR DATA COLLECTION

Any data-collection method used to measure attitudes or behaviors must meet three important requirements: reliability, validity, and practicality.[28]

RELIABILITY

Reliability reflects the accuracy and consistency of measurement. It is one of the most important characteristics of any good data-collection method. A bathroom scale would be worthless if you stepped on it three times in 60 seconds and got a different reading each time. Similarly, a questionnaire would be useless if the scores obtained on successive administrations of it were inconsistent. Different scores obtained for the same individual at different times reflect low reliability, unless something happened (experimental change) between each measurement to warrant the differences.

Control is normally the only prerequisite for reliability. So long as the directions for a data-collection method are clear, the environment is comfortable, and ample time is given for the subject to respond, the method should give reliable results. All data-collection methods, except those utilizing nonreactive measures, are affected to some degree by random changes in the subject (e.g., fatigue, distraction, mood, or emotional strain). These conditions also can affect the researcher's reliability, especially in making observations. Finally, changes in the setting, such as unexpected noises or sudden changes in the weather, can also affect data reliability.

An observed relationship is weakened by unreliability in the independent and/or dependent variable. If the reliability of the measures is known, the relationship can be corrected for attenuation. This correction provides an estimate of the relationship to be expected if both measures had perfect reliability.

VALIDITY

A reliable data-collection method is not necessarily valid. **Validity** is the degree to which a method actually measures what it claims to measure. Validity is an evaluation, not a fact, and usually is expressed in broad terms, such as high, moderate, or low, instead of precise quantities. However, a method can reliably measure the wrong variables. For example, a low score on a verbal ability test may be used to screen out a potential forklift driver. The test may have reliably measured the applicant's verbal ability, but it may not be a valid measure of the applicant's actual ability to drive a forklift. A job knowledge test on the safe operational procedures used when driving a forklift would most likely be a more valid measure of the applicant's forklift driving ability.

The validity of some psychological tests used by organizations in employee selection is being questioned. The U.S. Equal Employment Opportunity Commission (EEOC) insists that the use of tests that cannot be validated be discontinued. Tests that are not valid are worse than useless: They are misleading and dangerous. At times, such tests have been used—either consciously or unwittingly—to discriminate against members of minority groups. Those who challenge the use of verbal ability tests in the hiring process question their validity, not their reliability.

PRACTICALITY

Practicality is the ability of the method to save time and money and minimize disruption of operations for both the participants and researchers. Questionnaires, interviews, and other methods should be acceptable to both management and the employees who are asked to participate in the study. Where employees are unionized, the union typically must approve the data-collection method. The use of a planning committee composed of representatives from each management level and the union(s) can help gain widespread acceptance of the method to be used.

ETHICS IN RESEARCH

Researchers who obtain data from the general public, students, or employees must recognize the ethical and legal obligations they have to the participants. Generally, managers and researchers face three types of ethical issues:

- misrepresentation and misuse of data;
- manipulation of the participant; and
- value and goal conflict.

MISREPRESENTATION AND MISUSE OF DATA

Misrepresentation and misuse of data are widespread problems. The issue for the researcher is to decide between fully disclosing all the information obtained or sharing just some of it. For example, a manager may easily gather data about a department's performance under the guise of asking about a competitor's. People might talk freely and give the manager essential information about the department. What happens, however, if a higher level manager asks for that information? The dilemma for the manager is whether to reveal data gathered confidentially, breaking the trust of the employees, or to refuse to furnish the data, incurring the wrath of the boss.

General Electric recently mailed thousands of surveys, which appeared to be anonymous, to GE Investments-managed mutual fund shareholders (many of whom were GE employees). Unbeknownst to the respondents, the surveys had been secretly coded to learn the respondents' identity. When he learned of it, CEO John F. Welch, Jr, sent a message electronically to several hundred thousand employees, stating that the action was clearly wrong, should never have happened, and should never be repeated. He further assured them that employee attitude surveys regularly administered by GE were absolutely essential and totally anonymous and confidential.[29]

Electronic surveillance involves the collection of detailed, second-by-second or minute-by-minute information on employee performance by means of electronic devices for use by management.[30] Sixty-seven percent of organizations engage in some type of electronic monitoring and surveillance. An estimated 30 million workers are currently being monitored, often without their knowledge.[31] New technology allows employers to monitor many aspects of their employees' jobs, especially those who work on telephones and computer terminals or use voice mail. According to the American Management Association, the share of major U.S. organizations that check employee e-mail messages jumped to 27 percent in 1999 from 15 percent in 1997. Overall monitoring of communications and performance has increased to 45 percent from 35 percent in the same period. Employers eavesdrop on an estimated 400 million telephone conversations every year, or more than 750 calls every minute. Often electronic surveillance techniques are introduced to employees as ways to help them improve their performance and gain valuable rewards. However, many managers collect such data to discipline employees who talk too long on the phone with customers, make personal calls, and the like.

In laboratory experiments, researchers sometimes present false statements or attribute true statements to false sources. The code of ethics of the American Psychological Association states that "only when a problem is significant and can be investigated in no other way is the psychologist justified in giving misinformation to research subjects." Many researchers feel an ethical obligation to inform subjects of any false information presented as soon as possible after terminating the research.

Several years ago the U.S. Department of Health, Education, and Welfare issued an extensive report recommending research requirements to protect human subjects.

One recommendation was that a committee conduct objective and independent reviews of research projects and activities involving the use of human subjects when federal funds are involved. Most universities have an independent review committee composed of directors of research from the colleges within the university. Each member uses professional judgment to determine whether the proposed research will place the participants at risk. If a majority of the review committee members believe that the procedure employed will not put the participants at risk, the committee will approve the proposal. After this approval, each research participant must sign an agreement of informed consent. The basic elements of an informed consent agreement include

- a fair explanation of the procedures to be followed, including those that are experimental;
- a description of the study;
- an offer to answer any inquiries concerning the procedures;
- an announcement that the subject is free to withdraw consent and discontinue participation in the activity at any time; and
- an offer to make available an abstract of the report to all participants upon completion of the research.

Manipulation

Manipulation involves tampering with a person's exercise of free will. Basically, manipulation occurs when the researcher requires participants to do something opposed to their personal values. College students participating in laboratory experiments are sometimes asked to lie to others about the results of the experiment. This practice is inappropriate unless the experimenter, immediately after the experiment, tells all the subjects the reasons for such manipulation.

Value and Goal Conflicts

The third major issue is that of value and goal conflicts. The American Civil Liberties Union and other organizations protest the use of employee alcohol and drug testing unless the organization can show probable cause. However, the American Management Association reported that 81 percent of major U.S. companies surveyed use drug tests to detect substance abusers and estimated that drug testing cost businesses nearly $250 million annually.[32] No single symptom is indicative of substance abuse, although behavioral changes (including increased absenteeism, disappearance from the work area, failure to complete tasks, accidents, and changes in work quality) may suggest substance abuse. General Motors and Pennzoil, among others, have set up sting operations to uncover substance abusers in their organizations. These sting operations are extremely controversial because they entail surveillance, search, and detection to identify employees involved in the sale and abuse of illegal drugs. One type of drug test, urinalysis, can detect beer and alcohol consumed during the previous 6–12 hours, barbiturates taken during the previous 2–12 days, and marijuana used during the previous 12 weeks. However, organizations must be careful not to violate federal, state, and local laws, especially a constitutionally protected right to privacy, when conducting drug tests.

SUMMARY

All research designs have both strengths and weaknesses. Too much has been written about the reasons that one strategy is weak or one strategy is better than others. No one strategy is best in every case. More important is the ability to determine how each type of research design differs from and complements the others. Rather than search for the ideal, effective investigators select the research design that is best for their purposes and circumstances at the time, use all the strengths of that design, and limit or offset its weaknesses whenever possible.

Data collection may involve the use of interviews, questionnaires, observation, nonreactive measures, and qualitative methods. Each method has advantages and disadvantages and may be appropriate in some cases but not in others. Data-collection methods used to measure attitudes or behaviors must meet three conditions: They must be reliable, valid, and practical. Researchers have certain ethical obligations when analyzing and reporting data collected from people. They should not misrepresent or misuse the data or manipulate the participants without later disclosure. And, researchers should resolve any value and goal conflicts involved in the research.

KEY TERMS AND CONCEPTS

Case study
Control group
Dependent variable
Electronic surveillance
Experimental group
Field experiment
Field survey
Hypothesis
Independent variable
Interview
Laboratory experiment
Nonreactive measure
Nuisance variable
Observation
Practicality
Research design
Qualitative methods
Questionnaires
Reliability
Scientific approach
Validity

REFERENCES

1. Duff, S. Work-life benefits shedding fuzzy image in favor of hard numbers. *Employee Benefit News*, http://www.benefitnews.com/, November 15, 1999.
2. Duff, S. Work-life benefits can be healthy for the bottom line, too. *Employee Benefit News*, http://www.benefitnews.com/, November 15, 1999.
3. Creswell, J. W. *Research Design.* Thousand Oaks, Calif.: Sage, 1996.
4. Schwab, D. P. *Research Methods for Organizational Studies.* Mahwah, N.J.: Lawrence Erlbaum Associates, 1999.
5. Schwab.
6. Myers, A. H., Baker, S. P., Li, G., Smith, G. S., Wiker, S., Liang, K. Y., and Johnson, J. V. Back injury in municipal workers: A case-control study. *American Journal of Public Health*, 1999, 89, 1036–1041.
7. Klein, B. P., Jensen, R. C., and Sanderson, L. M. Assessment of workers' compensation claims for back strains/sprains. *Journal of Occupational Medicine*, 1984, 26, 443–448.
8. *Accident Facts.* Chicago, Ill.: National Safety Council, 1993, 42.
9. Sackett, P. R., and Larson, J. R., Jr. Research strategies and tactics in industrial and organizational psychology. In M. D. Dunnette and L. M. Hough (eds.). *Handbook of Industrial & Organizational Psychology*, 2nd ed., vol. 1. Palo Alto, Calif.: Consulting Psychologists Press, 1990, 419–490.
10. Harrison, M. J. *Diagnosing Organizations.* Thousand Oaks, Calif.: Sage, 1994.
11. Remenyi, D., Williams, B., Money, A., and Swartz, E. *Doing Research in Business and Management.* Thousand Oaks, Calif.: Sage, 1998.
12. Weisberg, H. F., Krosnick, J. A., and Bowen, B. D. *An Introduction to Survey Research.* Thousand Oaks, Calif.: Sage, 1996.
13. *Hoovers Company Capsules.* Austin, Texas: Hoovers, Inc.; August 1, 1999.
14. What do office workers want? Less gossip, easy going bosses and clean rest rooms; Survey asks employees about the office of the future. *PR Newswire*, July 15, 1999.
15. Personal communications with W. Bibbee, Director, Challenge Course, Brinker International, Dallas, September 1999.
16. Cook, T. D., Campbell, D. T., and Peracchio, L. Quasi experimentation. In M. D. Dunnette and L. M. Hough (eds.). *Handbook of Industrial & Organizational Psychology*, 2nd ed., vol. 1. Palo Alto, Calif.: Consulting Psychologists Press, 1990, 491–576.
17. Sorenson, G., Stoddard, A., Peterson, K., Cohen, N., Hunt, M. K., Stein, E., Palombo, R., and Lederman, R. Increasing fruit and vegetable consumption through worksites and families in the Treatwell 5-a-Day study. *American Journal of Public Health*, 1999, 89, 54–60.
18. Sapsford, R., and Jupp, V. *Data Collection and Analysis.* Thousand Oaks, Calif.: Sage, 1996.
19. Employee Loyalty surprisingly strong despite tight job market, according to 1999 America @ Work Study. *PR Newswire*, April 20, 1999.
20. Ghauri, P. N., Grønhaug, K., and Krisianslund, I. *Research Methods in Business Studies.* London: Prentice-Hall, 1995.
21. Church, A. H., and Waclawski, J. *Designing and Using Organizational Surveys.* Hampshire, England: Gower. 1998.

22. Survey select expert enables advanced online, networking, database and reporting functions for conducting intricate intranet and Internet surveys. *Business Wire,* June 28, 1999.
23. Heneman, R. L., Eskew, D. E., and Fox, J. A. Using employee attitude surveys to evaluate a new incentive pay program. *Compensation and Benefits Review,* 30, January 19, 1998.
24. Miller, R. A holistic approach to keeping clients. *Marketing,* July 29, 1999, 22–23.
25. LeVecchia, G. Guest tracking. *Restaurant Hospitality,* 1998, 82(4), 73–74.
26. Barlow, J. A safer way to use cell phone, drive. *Houston Chronicle,* August 29, 1999, 1D.
27. Jermier, J., Slocum, J. W., Jr., Fry, L. W., and Gaines, J. Organizational subcultures in a soft bureaucracy: Resistance behind the myth and façade of an official culture. *Organization Science,* 1991, 2, 170–194.
28. Wright, D. *Understanding Statistics.* Thousand Oaks, Calif.: Sage, 1996.
29. O'Harrow, R., Jr. Welch calls survey 'clearly wrong'; GE tracked identity of respondents. *Washington Post,* June 11, 1999, E3.
30. *Employee Monitoring in the Workplace.* San Diego: University of San Diego, Center for Public Interest Law, 1996.
31. More U.S. firms checking e-mail, computer files, and phone calls, says American Management Association Survey, http://www.amanet.org/research/specials/monit/, November 15, 1999.
32. May, D. Testing by necessity. *Occupational Health and Safety,* 1999, 68(4), 48–51.

Integrating Cases

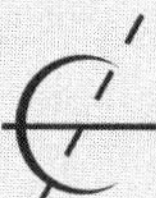

ROBERT PRINCETON AT FALLS VIDEO

In May 1987, Robert Princeton, 24, graduated from Middlebury College with a bachelor's degree in theater. In October 1987, he accepted a job as the assistant manager of Falls Video, a rapidly growing chain of video rental outlets located in northeastern New York State.

BACKGROUND ON FALLS VIDEO

Falls Video had been founded by "Momma and Poppa" Valencia in 1983. The operation began as a video rental business in a corner of their Glens Falls grocery store. The Valencias's business was an immediate success, and they had expanded it to include four new video rental outlets by 1985. As they were expanding the video business, they were also expanding the grocery business, establishing three new stores in surrounding towns. Momma Valencia was the mastermind behind this growth. Poppa Valencia was content to remain in the Glens Falls office and keep the books for the growing businesses. One of the decisions that Momma Valencia had made was to separate the grocery and video stores. As she expanded the number of grocery and video outlets, it became apparent that she needed management assistance. In June 1985, she split the management duties of the organization. Momma Valencia continued to manage the grocery stores, and she brought in her son, Mario, to run the video business.

Mario Valencia, who was 28 in 1987, had been working in the grocery stores since he was 18. In May 1985, after several years of part-time study and evening classes, he had graduated with his associate's degree in accounting from a nearby community college. He was eager to take charge of the rapidly growing video business. Momma Valencia put him in charge of hiring, firing, loss prevention, video buying, and the day-to-day management of all video stores, including supervision of personnel.

By the summer of 1987, Falls Video had eight rental outlets within a 25-mile radius of Glens Falls. However, problems had begun to arise. Losses due to stolen or misplaced videotapes were up. Supplies of newly released films were inadequate to satisfy customer demand. Turnover, absenteeism, and tardiness were way up among the 35 full- and part-time employees of the chain. Momma Valencia was particularly puzzled by the personnel problems. She was experiencing no such difficulties with her grocery staff. When she asked her son about it, he replied that she had only four stores to manage, and he had eight! Besides, he insisted, it was hard to attract competent workers at the low wages that they had to pay to remain profitable.

PRINCETON JOINS THE TEAM

In the early fall of 1987, Momma Valencia decided to hire Robert Princeton as the assistant manager of Falls Video to help her son. The average starting salary for a liberal arts graduate in 1987 was about $16,000, but Momma Valencia hired Princeton at an annual salary of $21,500 because she believed that he had a lot of potential. Princeton had convinced Momma Valencia that he was very interested in working in business. He had taken a course in organizational behavior, as well as several courses in industrial psychology, while in college.

Princeton began his work with enthusiasm. He made it a point to visit each store at least twice a week, and, over time, got to know every staff member personally. He found that by taking individual staff members out to lunch or dinner he could get them to open up about their perceptions of the business. Princeton found this contact with the staff very gratifying. However, he quickly encountered some misunderstandings with his boss. On one occasion, he allowed a part-time employee to take the weekend off in order to attend an out-of-state funeral. When Mario Valencia found out, he was furious that the store was understaffed during the critical weekend period. He informed Princeton that all future schedule changes would have to have his personal approval. Feeling somewhat embarrassed, Princeton sheepishly agreed. On another occasion, Princeton offered to train the staff in the basics of film appreciation because he felt that this knowledge would help them assess and satisfy customer needs better. Valencia said that it was a foolish idea and told Princeton not to waste any company time on it. Although Princeton felt that this was indeed a good idea, he did not pursue it. At one point, Princeton mentioned that many of the full-time employees wanted the company to institute an employee health insurance program. Valencia's casual response was that they could not afford the expense and that Princeton should be channeling his efforts into saving money rather than spending it. Even though Princeton was convinced that such a program would boost morale and reduce turnover, he let the matter drop.

In spite of all of these frustrations, Princeton kept at it. Although he was troubled by the lack of guidance that he received from Valencia, he felt that he could demonstrate his value to the organization. After all, when he had approached Momma Valencia with his concerns about his working relationship with her son, she had said: "Mario is a good and capable boy, and so are you. Work hard and you will be successful." This discussion motivated Princeton to take a more strategic perspective in his efforts.

Princeton initiated a survey of customer preferences in movies to develop recommendations for new titles to purchase. He began exit interviews with employees who quit and informally surveyed staff members to obtain their perceptions of Falls Video management. Finally, he developed a proposal to track video rentals and customer creditworthiness via microcomputer.

THE FINAL DAYS

In early January 1988, Princeton scheduled a meeting with Valencia to discuss his accomplishments during the previous 3 months. Valencia was silent and looked sullen as Princeton presented the results of his work. Princeton provided detailed recommendations for the purchase and resale of new titles. He suggested a variety of changes in personnel policy and management practices designed to boost morale and reduce absenteeism and turnover. He explained how the computer tracking system could reduce losses of videos and improve customer service. Princeton was taken aback by Valencia's sudden response:

> **Valencia:** Who the * * * * * do you think you are?" (followed by a long pause . . .) Strategic management is *my* job! *Your* job is to supervise the workers. I tell *you* what to do, and you tell *them* what to do! It's as simple as that. Any questions?
>
> **Princeton:** Well, yes . . . but . . . I thought. . . .
>
> **Valencia:** You're not paid to think—you're paid to do what you're told. Poppa showed me your expense account yesterday. The poor old guy almost had a coronary when he tallied it. It's off the wall! Your travel and entertainment expenses in one week are more than mine in a whole month! We give you an office and a telephone here in Glens Falls. I expect you to use them! We hardly ever see you around this office. We're not rich like your family and that snobby private school they sent you to. We have to run this operation on a shoestring. *As I've told you before, that's* where I need your help. Now get to work on making a *real* contribution to this organization's bottom line.

Princeton was flabbergasted! He was proud of his accomplishments and thought that they proved his value to the business. Rather than get into a heated argument on the spot, Princeton felt that he had better sleep on it.

The next morning when Princeton arrived for work he found a sealed envelope on his desk with his name on it, marked "Personal and Confidential." At first he assumed that it must be an apology from Valencia. He was surprised to find that it was a letter of reprimand for abuse of his expense account and insubordination, signed by both Poppa and Mario Valencia. It concluded with the statement: "If you wish to continue your employment with Falls Video, you must learn to become more cost conscious!"

Princeton spent the rest of the morning in his office with the door closed, thinking.

At 11:30, he asked Momma Valencia to have lunch with him. After some hesitation, she agreed. During lunch, Princeton complained that he was not being allowed to have a strategic impact on the organization. Momma's response had been: "Roberto, I hired you as an assistant manager to Mario. Your job is to work for Mario. Mario's job is strategic planning. I still believe that you have a lot of potential. But you must understand the ways of the family. Poppa and Mario run the business. You must cooperate with them. Without cooperation, we cannot run a successful family business."

At 1:30 that afternoon Princeton submitted his resignation. He had no job prospects and wasn't sure what his next move would be. His parents had offered to pay for him to enroll in an MBA program. His immediate plan was to explore this possibility.

Questions

1. Which of the core competencies does Mario Valencia possess? Robert Princeton? Which core competencies does each not possess? Explain.
2. Describe the sources of personality differences between Princeton and Valencia.
3. How could Valencia have used the guidelines for applying the expectancy model of motivation to manage Princeton better?
4. How might Falls Video have benefited from implementation of the self-managing team model of decision making?
5. Identify the sources of power possessed by Princeton and Valencia.
6. Use the characteristics of leaders and managers to compare and contrast Valencia and Princeton.
7. Characterize the interpersonal conflict handling styles used by Valencia and Princeton.

Source: Case prepared by David M. Leuser, Ph.D., of Plymouth State College of the University System of New Hampshire. It was edited for *Organizational Behavior*, 9th edition, and used with permission.

He tended to take the first alternative presented, making decisions himself, viewing decisions as single events, and not having an overall concept of how to approach decision making. He based decisions on his own personal and organizational values and tended not to evaluate outcomes with reference to a plan of any type.

Although relatively unconcerned about the reactions of others, the chief acknowledged that allowing time for dealing with objections to his approaches or to build consensus and commitment in order to move things forward might be useful. Additionally, he tended to consult with people informally, using key people he trusted as sounding boards and, at times, bypassing certain formal organizational structures and procedures. The chief's penchant for making decisions unilaterally was influenced, perhaps, by the quasi-military, hierarchical structure of the department. At the same time, he was deeply committed to creating a department in which individuals could take responsibility for their actions, assume risks, and become self-initiating in their behaviors.

Questions

1. Why did Chief Shake's plan to change the department encounter widespread resistance?
2. What actions should he initiate to counter the resistance? Should he abandon his desire to reorganize the department? Explain.
3. Should the chief adopt a different decision-making (leadership) style? Explain.
4. Should the mayor take any action? If yes, what actions? If no, why not?

Source: This case was prepared by David W. Frantz, Associate Professor of Organizational Leadership and Supervision at Purdue University, and is intended to be used as the basis for class discussion. The views represented here are those of the case author and do not necessarily reflect the views of the Society for Case Research. The author's views are based on his own professional judgments. It was edited for *Organizational Behavior*, 9th edition, and used with permission.

IT'S MY BIKE

Debbie Martin was overjoyed when she was selected the new supplier quality manager for the commercial product division of Cold Air Corporation. In this role, she was responsible for monitoring the quality of component parts for 12 production lines scattered throughout the large manufacturing plant. When she started the new position, Martin knew that she would face many opportunities and conflicts. Her immediate supervisor, the manager of shipping and receiving, was not known as an easy person to work for. He expected his subordinates to have a take-charge attitude and to avoid bothering him with trivial issues. What Martin hadn't envisioned was just how trivial and nonproductive some of the conflicts would be. She certainly had not expected to be on the verge of a fistfight.

Martin was just starting her shift when she received a telephone call from Ronnie Best, one of her subordinates. Best was a purchasing parts inspector, responsible for inspecting certain incoming parts for all production lines in the plant. He was complaining that the Airhandler Quality team had borrowed "the bike" for a special project and would not return it. He reminded Martin of his current project and how covering the entire 15-acre plant on foot would only delay completion of the project. She rolled her eyes as she thought about the logistics of inspecting component parts in the plant's three separate buildings. She also realized that Best had a tendency to get excited over little things. He was a conscientious, detail-oriented worker but was easily upset when things didn't go according to his plans. Martin asked him to work on another project while she checked into the bike problem.

The bike, actually an adult-sized tricycle with a basket, had a colorful history at Cold Air. The bike had been acquired by Martin's predecessor to aid in transporting testing materials and small samples from one end of the plant to another. Given the size of the plant, it was often necessary to travel a quarter of a mile or more to test parts delivered to some of the more distant lines. Martin knew of three other bikes in use in the plant, but in the 6 months that she had been supervisor, she had experienced far more problems with her bike than the other supervisors had.

First, it had been taken and painted by people in the metal works department. The bike had been missing for more than 2 weeks when Best spied a bike with a new paint job. Since he had had previously etched "Receiving Inspection" on the bottom of the bike's frame, they were able to identify and retrieve it. After getting the bike back, Martin had assumed that the problems were over. Being a new manager, she also did not want to raise a stink over the bike being taken. Also, the ill will would not be worth the inconvenience and the possibility of creating an enemy in another department.

The second episode began more innocently than the first. The Airhandler quality group was being pushed to expedite the transfer of new production processes from a plant in Illinois. The Illinois plant was being closed and operations transferred to the local plant. The new equipment had to be installed and begin operating quickly. Because portions of the new production lines were at one end of the main plant and the Airhandler office was at the other, a lot of walking was involved. Steve Gregg, Airhandler quality engineer, approached Martin about borrowing the bike to expedite the Airhandler project. She agreed to accommodate him on the condition that the bike be returned when her department needed it. Gregg agreed to the arrangement.

Approximately a week later the company changed suppliers for one of its components. A few problems were encountered in integrating the slightly different components into production, which required Best to make more frequent inspections. He needed the bike to complete his assignment efficiently. He called Frank Jones, Gregg's assistant, and told him that he needed the bike and that he would be by later that morning to pick it up. That afternoon Gregg called Martin to find out why Best had come and taken the bike. She promptly reminded him of their agreement. Gregg said he understood the arrangement and asked to borrow the bike again once Best had finished with it. Wanting to be cooperative, Martin agreed to loan the bike one more time.

The second time that the Airhandler quality team borrowed the bike brings us to the situation at hand. Martin couldn't believe what Best was telling her. How could Gregg refuse to return something that he had just recently borrowed? She was heading out the door to see Gregg when the phone rang again. It was Best. He had just met Gregg and had requested that he return the bike immediately. Gregg stated that he wouldn't return the bike without an official request from Martin.

Best was angry. He told Martin that if she wanted the bike he would be happy to get it. He wasn't afraid to confront Gregg and take the bike by force if necessary. He just wanted her approval. Martin told him again to be patient while she talked to Gregg. She hung up the phone and marveled at the amount of time and energy being consumed by the $250 tricycle!

After taking two "productive" telephone calls, Martin was again headed out the door to find Gregg when the phone rang. It was Best again, but this time he had Jones with him. He asked Martin to tell Jones to give him the bike. She told him to put Jones on the telephone and she would talk to him. After talking with Martin, Jones agreed to return the bike. Even though the situation was resolved for the moment, Martin knew that she still needed to speak to Gregg.

Gregg was headed out of his office when Martin first saw him. She stopped and asked him if he had a minute to discuss the bike. He said he didn't at the moment as he was late for a meeting. Plus, he didn't see what the big deal was about the bike. His group needed it more than her department, so she could just give him the bike and buy a new one. As he was heading down the hall, he reminded her that the product transition was the most important project in the plant and that she should not mind helping his department succeed.

His comments struck a nerve. Was this the type of thanks she got for helping someone? She realized that the product transition was an important project. That was why she let the Airhandler quality group borrow the bike in the first place. She knew that she could no longer tolerate the situation. She could talk to her superior and get him to talk to Gregg's superior or go to their common manager, the production manager. But, she wondered, were there other options that she did not see? What would be the consequences of taking any of those actions?

Questions

1. Are conflicts such as this unusual in organizations? Explain.
2. Why is the $250 bike a source of conflict?
3. What are the causes of the conflict?
4. What environmental factors served to increase the intensity of the conflict?
5. How did Debbie Martin's inexperience contribute to escalation of the conflict?
6. What options are available to Martin to resolve the conflict? What conflict management style is represented by each option?

Source: This case was prepared by Joe Thomas and Bill Gash, Middle Tennessee State University, and is intended to be used as a basis for class discussion. The views represented are those of the case authors and do not necessarily reflect the views of the Society for Case Research. The authors' views are based on their own professional judgments. The names of the organization and individuals have been disguised to preserve the identity of individuals for purpose of anonymity. Presented to and accepted by the Society for Case Research. It was edited for *Organizational Behavior*, 9th edition, and used with permission.

IS TECHNICAL COMPETENCE ENOUGH?

With a slight frown on his face, Ken Barton eased back into his chair. His boss, Bob Arnold, vice president of research and systems at A&J Bank, had just left Barton's office. Arnold had asked Barton's opinion of James Spinner, the programmer–analyst who worked for them. Arnold indicated that the bank president John Kingston thought that Spinner should be fired. Arnold asked Barton to think about the situation and give him some ideas.

BACKGROUND

At the time Ken Barton was completing his doctoral program in finance, a member of the graduate faculty encouraged him to interview for the economist position at A&J Bank. He took the advice and applied for the position. As part of the selection process, Barton traveled to the bank and interviewed with Bob Arnold, vice president of research and systems, and John Kingston, president and CEO. Barton felt very positive after the interviews and was excited by the prospect of working with both men on some new projects. A few weeks after the interview trip, A&J Bank offered Barton the position and he accepted.

His title was bank economist. The bank was in the process of developing a planning program. Arnold wanted Barton on board and working as soon as possible because the bank needed a system for gathering and analyzing market information. Arnold worked with Barton to outline the project. Barton expended substantial effort on the market analysis system even before finishing his degree and working full-time at the bank.

SETTLING IN ON THE JOB

In the course of their working together, Arnold informed Barton that James Spinner, the bank's programmer–analyst, would be available to help with the computer implementation of Barton's work. When he arrived at the bank, Barton was introduced to Spinner and scheduled some time with him. Barton wanted to assess the type of help Spinner could provide in using the computer to implement both the information gathering and analysis systems.

Barton's initial assessment of Spinner wasn't particularly favorable. During their early conversations, Spinner made several snide remarks about economists. He also made some off-hand comments about Barton's appearance. Barton didn't mind a little give-and-take in the office among good friends, but he felt that Spinner's comments were inappropriate in dealing with someone he had just met. However, Barton soon became aware that Spinner had the technical ability to get the output Barton needed out of an overtaxed computer system.

After being on the job for a short time, Barton found that the bank had no internal graphics capability. Because substantial amounts of graphics were needed to illustrate the bank's market analyses, Barton asked for permission to hire someone to provide them. Kingston approved the request, and Barton called the local university to get the names of the two top illustrators in the current class of design students. Barton telephoned one of the students, Jan Lavensky, about doing the illustration work; he indicated that he was very interested. Barton was favorably impressed during the telephone interview and asked Lavensky to come to the bank with some samples of his work.

The next day Barton had just entered his office and sat down to work when Arnold came in. He said, "John wants to know what that thing is that is sitting in the bank waiting area." Barton replied, "What do you mean?" Arnold answered, "John stuck his head in my office and made that statement. I called the secretary, and she said the person was waiting to meet with you." Barton then said, "Oh, that must be Jan Lavensky. What's the problem?" Arnold replied, "The person has on frayed cutoffs and a ripped T-shirt." Arnold then left, and Barton asked the secretary to show Lavensky into his office. Lavensky showed Barton his work. Barton liked it and told Lavensky that he would contact him in the near future.

Barton then visited with Kingston and indicated that he would like to hire Jan Lavensky. Kingston reluctantly agreed but indicated that Lavensky was "not to work at the bank." Barton would have to go to the university to work with him. Barton indicated that this would be acceptable to him. As he had already spent large amounts of time at the university library gathering information, it would work out fine. Lavensky was hired and started working the next week.

Barton's working relationship with Lavensky was excellent. The illustrator had great ideas, and Barton used them to illustrate his market analyses. At one point, in response to a few basic ideas from Barton, Lavensky designed an impressive cover for a publication to be sent out by the bank. Kingston suggested that Barton submit the publication to an interbank publication design competition that Kingston thought it "would have a good chance of winning." After Barton pointed out that the design was Lavensky's work and that he would have to go to the trade meeting to accept any award, Kingston decided not to submit the publication.

As Barton settled into his daily work routine, he soon learned what commuting in a large metropolitan area was all about. His drive to work the first morning had been pure frustration. He had spent 20 minutes stopped on the freeway, had difficulty finding a parking place, and had arrived at the bank at 9:30 A.M. instead of the 9:00 A.M. starting time.

After fighting traffic for the first few weeks, Barton worked out an informal flextime arrangement with Arnold and Kingston. Barton had arrived at the bank at 7:00 A.M. one morning and noticed that the drive was much more pleasant at that time of day. Arnold and Kingston agreed that there was no reason he couldn't come to work early every morning and then leave earlier in the afternoon. Barton was an early morning person, so he jumped at the chance and began coming in at 7:00 A.M. and leaving at 3:00 P.M., which eliminated his frustration with the traffic congestion.

WORKING WITH SPINNER

The flextime arrangement worked out beautifully for Barton. It had removed one frustration from his life, and he was now trying to decide how to remove another. James Spinner's overbearing behavior toward him hadn't improved. Spinner had even taken a few jabs at projects that Barton and Arnold completed. Some of the jabs were somewhat painful because Barton recognized that they had some merit. Overall, his assessment of Spinner was that he was technically well qualified and could be very helpful. Barton did feel, however, that working with Spinner directly could be challenging. His attitude toward Barton was one of superiority. He did not hesitate to attack Barton on either personal or professional grounds at nearly every opportunity.

Barton recognized the situation as both a challenge and an opportunity. He viewed Spinner as a potentially positive resource, but one who lacked interpersonal skills. Barton didn't mention his concerns to either Arnold or Kingston, but he had real concerns about a long-term working relationship with Spinner. After several negative exchanges, Barton wanted to establish some less confrontational way to interact with him.

Following several weeks of relaxed and productive mornings, Barton realized that not being around Spinner for the first 2 hours of each day was pleasant. Then one morning Barton wrote a detailed memo concerning the work he wanted Spinner to complete and left it in Spinner's mailbox. Spinner reacted positively to the memo, so Barton began communicating with Spinner through detailed memos. These memos took more time than face-to-face oral communication, but they forced Barton to think through what he wanted accomplished. He had inadvertently found a way to accomplish his goals and to use Spinner and his excellent computer skills effectively. The situation evolved into a comfortable working relationship. Early each morning, Barton arrived at the office before the others, wrote his memos, and left them in Spinner's mailbox before he arrived. Barton felt good about the new working arrangement. Spinner was quite productive, and Barton didn't have his day ruined by negative encounters with him. Barton's projects were proceeding well, and Spinner became an important link in the information gathering system.

DISCUSSION ABOUT SPINNER

Bob Arnold walked into Barton's office, closed the door, and asked: "What is your evaluation of James Spinner?" Barton answered, "He does a lot of work for me." Arnold then said, "He does a lot of work for me, too. How do you like working with him?" Barton responded, "I've developed a comfortable way of interacting with him to do my work." Arnold then said, "John thinks he has to go. John says that James has everyone upset, everyone from those of us at the top on through to the secretaries." Barton thought for a moment and then responded, "Letting him go would be a mistake. He is technically very competent and would be difficult to replace."

Barton then suggested that Spinner be put on the night shift where he could work at his leisure with the computer and interact less directly with the people for whom he performed services. Barton pointed out that this move would have the added advantage of employing Spinner when the overtaxed computer was less busy. Bank personnel could communicate with Spinner in writing, just as he had been doing successfully for some time. This move would also free up additional computer time for Arnold and Barton during the day when they sometimes needed the computer for work that didn't require Spinner's services. Arnold thought that Barton's suggestion was excellent and said that he would pass it on to Kingston.

Later, Arnold returned to Barton's office with a dejected look on his face. He announced, "John says he feels the bank can't afford the luxury of employing James if he is not available for work while the other employees are around." As he turned to leave, Arnold ended the conversation by saying, "John may be open to other suggestions. Think about this and give me some ideas." And with that he walked out the door.

Questions

1. How would you characterize the management style and culture at A&J Bank?
2. Should the bank managers have attempted to change James Spinner's behavior? Explain.
3. What do you think of the way Jan Lavensky was treated by the bank? Should he have been managed differently? Explain.
4. What should Ken Barton do now?

Source: This case was prepared by Gary R. Wells and William E. Stratton of Idaho State University and is intended to be used as a basis for class discussion. The views represented here are those of the case authors and do not necessarily reflect the views of the Society for Case Research. The authors' views are based on their own professional judgments. The names of the organization and individuals and the location have been disguised to preserve requests for anonymity. Presented and accepted by the Society for Case Research. It was edited for *Organizational Behavior*, 9th edition, and used with permission.

FRIENDS OR FOES?

As Mike Russo left James Blair's office, he was totally dumfounded. First his secretary and friend, Linda Slotki, had turned on him. Then the firm's managing partner, Jerome Harris, had reprimanded him. Now this—how could Blair be so unfair?

Linda Slotki was a legal secretary at Harris, Tessler, and Brock (HTB), a fast-paced, competitive law firm in Chicago. Slotki had worked for the same attorney, Mike Russo, an associate of the firm, for more than 5 years. Russo often worked under a great deal of pressure (which sometimes set off his temper), and he relied greatly on his secretary. HTB had about 80 full-time employees, including 40 attorneys (25 associates and 15 partners), and roughly the same number of staff (including secretaries, paralegals, accountants, and other clerical employees). The atmosphere at HTB was socially relaxed though professionally intense. The structure of HTB (see Figure 1) was such that the name partners (Jerome Harris, Frank Tessler, and Sam Brock) had the most authority, though they shared their powers with the other partners in the firm. The associates and staff managers were next on the organizational ladder, followed by the staff (including secretaries and paralegals). Regardless of this formal hierarchy, the partners liked to refer to the firm as "a family" and claimed that each employee was valued as a person. The secretaries and attorneys often ate lunch together, shared stories, and even told off-color jokes. Although Linda Slotki didn't commonly use profanity, other employees at the firm did swear occasionally.

In the past, Slotki had been a highly competent secretary when the pressure was on, which seemed to be most of the time with Russo, but her performance had been somewhat inconsistent lately. He discussed problems with her as they arose but chose not to enter any official complaints in her employee file because he viewed her as a friend. He also knew that her annual raises were based almost solely on the written evaluation he placed in her file each year. After all, he knew that there had been times during his first few years when, as Russo told Slotki, "you really pulled me out of the fire."

He was especially patient when she went through a divorce. She explained the problems with her work as temporary by-products of her marital problems during several emotional sessions in Russo's office, during which she vented her anger and depression about the breakup of her marriage. Russo provided free legal advice, tried to help the couple negotiate their divorce settlement, and finally referred the couple to a competent divorce lawyer. He did all this informally and without charge. Throughout this time, Russo often felt that Slotki's work was unsatisfactory. He frequently sought additional help from the secretarial pool, which usually provided fill-in secretaries when the regular legal secretaries took vacations and sick leave and handled the overload of secretarial work for attorneys involved in trials. In an effort to explain why he seemed to be continually requesting additional help from the secretarial pool, he let the other secretaries know of his frustrations with Slotki's behavior and attitude (which he described as "lackadaisical at best").

Knowing that he could be a demanding boss, Russo was lenient in his written evaluation. Yet, he made it perfectly clear to Slotki in person what his carefully worded written evaluations meant. He had rated her "average" or "above average" in every category. He was a bit more critical of her work when discussing the ratings in person with her. The firm's policy for evaluating the secretaries required that the evaluating attorney discuss each evaluation with the secretary being evaluated, who then signed the evaluation to indicate that the person understood the comments and had discussed them with the evaluator. Slotki had signed each of the evaluations.

Russo's ratings of Slotki during her first 4 years had helped her earn a substantial Tier I raise every year. Staff raises at HTB were given in three tiers, based on the performance record, with Tier I being the highest. Russo's most recent evaluation of Slotki, though still "average" or above overall, was a factor in her most recent Tier II raise. He felt that his evaluation had to be honest, though he believed that he was still a bit lenient, given what he perceived to be a recent downslide in her work.

THE INCIDENT

On one particularly harrowing day, Russo returned from court enraged. He called Slotki into his office and shouted that she had typed the wrong courtroom number as well as the wrong address for the federal court building (an address that she had typed at least a hundred times before) on the official documents that he needed to file that day. The judge had been lenient and agreed to consider the documents but had pointed out the mistake in a crowded courtroom in a sarcastic manner, severely embarrassing Russo. Slotki considered it to be a small and simple mistake and was offended at Russo's tone. She responded by reminding him that it was his responsibility to proofread anything he signed. She then turned to leave his office and return to her desk outside. Russo didn't consider their conversation finished and was so angry at her flippant response that he followed after her and threatened, "Next mistake like that and I am going to write you up." (This action involves putting a note in the employee's file, indicating some problem with his or her work.) He then flipped the document into her IN box to be retyped and refiled. "Don't throw things at me!" she retorted defiantly. "Just get it **** right this time!" he yelled back. Then he returned to his office to cool down and get back to work, while she sat at her desk fuming.

As far as Russo was concerned, the whole thing was past and forgotten. His relationship with Slotki seemed back to normal by the end of the day, and the next day it was business as usual. But the coordinator of the secretaries, James Blair, had reported to Jerome Harris, the managing partner of the firm, that Slotki had complained about Russo's "verbal abuse and public humiliation" of the day before.

Figure 1 **Organization Chart**

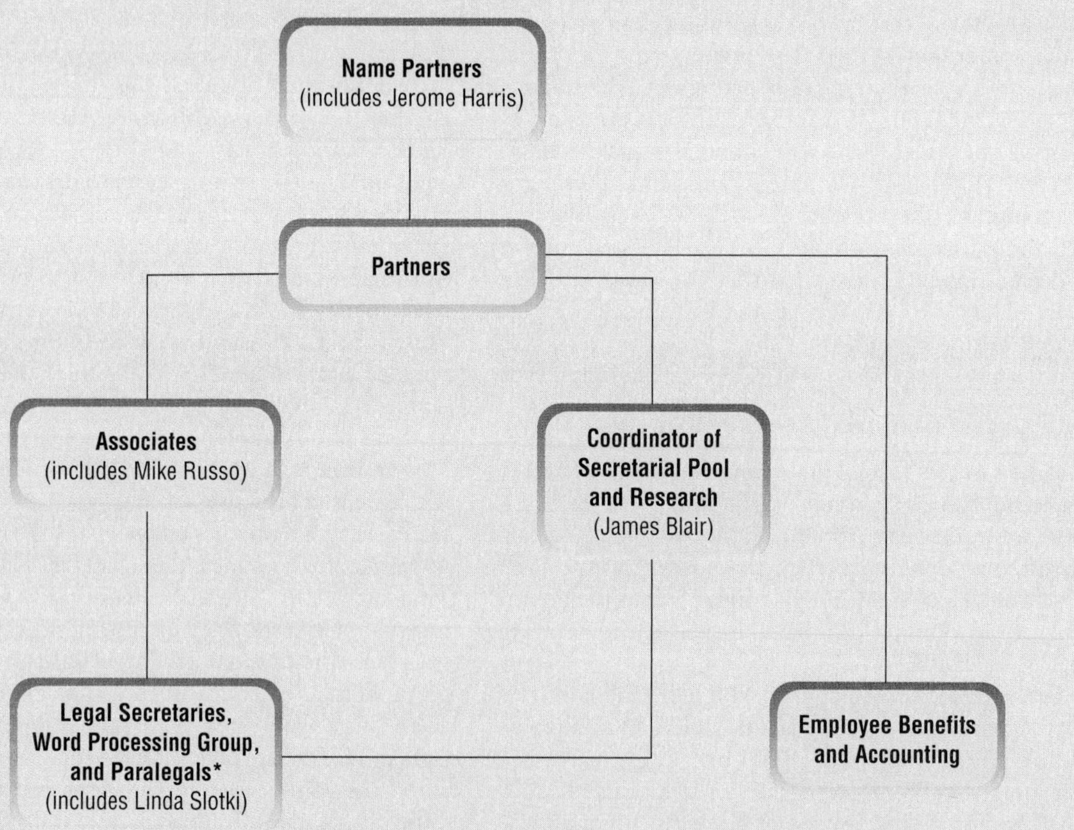

* This firm has a word processing department that does overflow work as part of the secretarial pool. These secretaries do not work for any single lawyer on a long-term basis, as legal secretaries do. All secretaries are theoretically accountable to the secretarial pool coordinator, as well as to the lawyer for whom they are working. The paralegal staff is also accountable to both the coordinator and the attorney in charge of the cases on which they are working.

MIKE RUSSO'S REPRIMAND

The following week, Russo was called into Jerome Harris's office. He had no idea why. Then, Harris explained that the meeting was a formal reprimand for Russo's "unprofessional conduct" and, in particular, for his "use of profanity." A written reprimand would be included in his personnel file, which was used annually by the partners to evaluate the associates in order to determine raises and promotions. Harris demanded that Russo formally apologize, refrain from ever using profanity in the office again, and address any further concerns he had with Linda Slotki through the secretarial coordinator, James Blair.

Russo felt humiliated and extremely angry. Practically everyone at the firm used the kind of language he had used, and he had heard more than a few choice words come out of Slotki's mouth when she was talking with him about her husband. Nevertheless, he apologized to her. But he still felt unsettled about the whole situation. He felt betrayed and a little nervous about how to speak with her after this episode. He made up his mind to speak to her no more than was absolutely necessary to get his work done.

CONTINUING PERFORMANCE PROBLEMS

Linda Slotki felt vindicated, but her work continued to slide. She still regarded Mike Russo as a close friend and even sought to confide in him about the problems she was facing as a newly divorced, single parent. He was unsympathetic but tried hard to maintain a purely professional relationship and resisted all leads into a personal conversation. Still, she continued to talk about her child-care problems as an explanation for why she was continually leaving early or taking days off. She assured him that she would regain her focus once things settled down at home.

This situation was not only personally uncomfortable but also professionally crippling for Russo because his productivity was hampered by his lack of a competent secretary. The problems that he had overlooked in the past were much more annoying to him now. However, after his reprimand, he was skittish about confronting Linda over her absenteeism, excessive time on the phone, disregard for proper filing procedures, or any other work-related problem. He feared that anything he said would be regarded as a form of revenge for the letter of reprimand in his file. He followed Jerome Harris's instructions by calling these problems to the attention of James Blair, the secretarial coordinator, but Blair was unresponsive. Finally, exasperated, Russo requested a new secretary. Blair told him curtly, "There are no other secretaries. You'll either have to learn to work with Linda Slotki or write up the appropriate documentation to have her fired. That's the only way we can give you a new secretary."

Mike was at a loss as to what to do.

Questions

1. What formal and informal communication networks at HTB can you identify? How do these networks affect what is said to whom?
2. How do upward, downward, and horizontal communications operate or fail to operate in this case?
3. What are Mike Russo's options? Which would you choose? Explain.
4. What ethical issues exist between Russo and Slotki?

Source: This case was prepared by Diana W. Kincaid, Gerald D. Hamsmith, and Thomas D. Cavenagh, all of North Central College, and is intended to be a basis for class discussion rather than to illustrate either effective or ineffective handling of the situation. The names of the organization, individuals, and location have been disguised to preserve the organization's desire for anonymity. Presented to and accepted by the Society for Case Research. It was edited for *Organizational Behavior*, 9th edition, and used with permission.

BUD THORNTON'S BRUSH WITH DEATH

Bud Thornton stood trembling and exhausted in front of his dead, jammed ripsaw, his mind flitting across the events of the past 30 seconds that almost resulted in his being the fatal victim of the saw. His emotions were mixed as weakness and nausea swept over him. He was angry at himself for not being more cautious. He was angry that his coworkers did not try to help him. He was thankful that a friend had happened by and stopped his saw in the nick of time. He was puzzled by the whole situation. He stood, thinking, How could this happen? What is wrong with me? What is wrong with them? How could everyone stand and watch and not try to help me?

BUD THORNTON, THE PERSON

Bud Thornton, 32, the only child of a financially poor mother and father, was reputedly an honest, hard-working lumberman. His parents were "lumber people." His wife's family also were "lumber people." Bud and his wife had two sons, ages 7 and 5. His pay as a skilled worker enabled him to obtain a mortgage on a small, five-room, wood-frame house. Home ownership was important to him for two reasons: Though it strapped the family budget, the space was necessary for his family; and it afforded an element of independence from the company. He and his family previously had rented and lived in smaller company housing.

Though reasonably friendly, Thornton didn't initiate friendships or mix easily with others. He was a member of the local lumber workers union, but he had joined simply because it was the thing to do; all plant workers were union members. He was an excellent skilled worker—a variable ripsaw operator—having the ability to become absorbed in his work, losing consciousness of time and the rate at which he was working. In sum, he took his work very seriously, which put him in good stead with company management.

THE COMPANY AND THE UNION

Perry Lumber Company (PLC) was a family-owned, hierarchically managed manufacturer of varied wood building products—hardwood and softwood flooring, composition (or particle) board, plywood, planed structural lumber, and treated fence posts and utility poles—all marketed both nationally and internationally. The company operated three plants in the South. The installation at which Thornton's incident occurred was the largest of the three. The plant employed about a thousand people and was located in Mableville, Alabama, population, 2,500. About one-third of the plant's employees lived in low-rent, wood-frame, company-owned housing. The company owned either the timberland or the logging rights to the timberland in every direction within 10 to 25 miles of the plant. In addition to its lumber business, the company operated the largest retail merchandise store in town—a general store, selling groceries, clothing, appliances, automobile and home accessories, and hardware. This company store offered bargains and credit arrangements to patrons having a PLC "employee privilege" card that other stores in town couldn't match. In short, the company was powerful, influencing people's lives both outside and inside the plant. And the plant's managers didn't miss any opportunity to remind the workers of that fact with high-handed, authoritarian behavior, which always rankled the workers. However, management seemed not to fear a strike. The union had called a strike a few years earlier, but the company was able to "starve" the union out and break the strike in just over 2 weeks.

By contrast, the union, Perry Loggers and Lumberworkers, a nonaffiliated company union, dealt from a position of weakness in its relations with management. Although all the plant's blue-collar workers were union members, verbal expressions of feelings of powerlessness and of being "locked in" were common among them. The union strike fund was very limited: Reliable estimates indicated that a strike lasting 2 weeks would exhaust the fund. Many members openly voiced fear of objecting too loudly to management offenses, fearing that they might lose their jobs or, at least, their company privilege card, the discounts from which reduced their cost of living, helping them to make ends meet. As a result, most of the time only about 10 percent of the union membership attended its regular, biweekly meetings. Moreover, there were no other employment opportunities in town, aside from a few small stores, shops, and service-type businesses. So, if a strike were to be called and lasted more than 2 weeks, some families would be forced to move elsewhere in search of employment. For many workers, such a move was unthinkable. Mableville, Alabama, and Perry Lumber Company had been their families' home and their source of livelihood, respectively, for up to three generations. For these "lumber people" lumber work was not a job, but a way of life.

Because of the common feeling of powerlessness among union members, some hotheads tended to compensate by overreacting when plant management behaved in a particularly offensive manner. Bitterness over their inability to redress these offenses sometimes led these members to commit a rash of transparent acts of industrial sabotage and/or vandalism. Although most of these acts were relatively minor, one recent incident was serious enough to indicate that somebody was disgruntled enough to stop at nothing. On that occasion, one unseasonably warm February night, a small section of company woods was set on fire in more than one place simultaneously—supposedly to show that it was no accident. When some other property owners began fighting the fire to keep it off their property, they received warning gunfire from the cover of the woods. Luckily, nobody was hurt and the fire was brought under control in less than 24 hours, with an assist from rainy weather.

Conditions were ripe for an ugly incident. Relations were so bad between the union and management that any type of incident could easily develop into a life-threatening situation. One such situation did develop.

THE SITUATION

Relations between Bud Thornton and his coworkers were going downhill—and had been for several months. The union's unwritten but widely understood policy for its members was always to slow down the work. No love was lost between the union and management because management's harsh, unjust treatment of blue-collar workers was regarded by the workers as exploitative. This treatment included the managers' harshly "chewing out" workers for any small error and unjustly reprimanding one person for another's mistake. Ordinarily, the work itself was unpleasant enough, including long hours of bone-aching work for low pay; unclean, noisy, and dangerous working conditions; and not enough break time for meals (30 minutes). An overlay of arrogant, harsh management made the workers' plight almost intolerable.

Thornton worked faithfully, even though he personally was displeased with the company's treatment of the workers, as he admitted to his few close friends. His diligence at work was an important source of his trouble with his coworkers for several reasons. First, because he was not slowing down his work, his coworkers blamed him for acting in direct violation of union policy. Second, he was causing the work of others affected by his work to appear to be inferior—in other words, too slow. Third, because of his apparent "goodwill" with management, his coworkers accused him of being no friend of the worker. For example, the rough shed manager, who generally was arrogant and disrespectful to other workers, was always friendly with Thornton and never chewed him out. As a result, some of Bud's coworkers now communicated with him only when absolutely necessary. Some were shunning him completely.

In addition, his coworkers were giving him not-so-subtle clues (and had been for 2 months) that he should slow down his work or suffer the consequences. At times Thornton did slow down for a while. When lumber would begin to stack up at his workstation, he would speed up—and not without some justification. His workstation was one of the first in the rough shed section of the planing mill to receive lumber from the sawmill. Thus the speed of his work was dictated largely by the speed at which lumber came to his workstation from the sawmill, that speed being machine dictated. If he slowed his work for a short time, a large, unstable stack of heavy, jagged-edged lumber accumulated at his workstation, making his job much more dangerous than it ordinarily was.

On this sunny July morning, about an hour after starting time (about 8:30 A.M.), lumber from the sawmill deluged Thornton's workstation. He was working faster than usual to reduce the size of the stack. The planing mill was constructed of corrugated sheet metal and had no air conditioning, only a system of large fans for air circulation. By 8:00 A.M. each day, the plant became very hot. As was the case with most of the workers, Thornton had removed his shirt. He was working in denim overalls, covered in front by a thick, leather, body apron, which extended from his chest to his knees. The apron had a leather cord that looped around his neck. Another thick leather cord tied about his waist. He wore the apron to protect his body from the large splinters that covered the unfinished lumber.

Thornton's ripsaw had a single, 36-inch, circular blade. His work consisted of ripping unfinished lumber 10 to 20 feet long, 2 inches thick, and 14 to 24 inches wide into various widths of 2-inch, high-grade lumber. The ripsaw was a high-speed saw that could rip the full length of a 2-inch, 20-foot board in about 10 seconds. As he worked this morning, for some reason, he momentarily became careless. Just as he introduced the end of a 20-foot board into his ripsaw, a long hook on the edge of the board—created by a long knothole on the board's edge—caught his overalls and the thick apron where they were open at his side, just above the waist. He was jerked off balance, and by the time he regained his balance, he did not have time to get himself unhooked from the board, which now had pulled him up against the abutment of the saw platform. Only about 3 feet separated him from the whining saw blade. He braced himself against the pull of the saw with both arms and both legs against the front of the saw platform. There was no way for him to turn the saw off; the power button was out of reach behind him, and the saw was slowly winning. He began to weaken. All he could do was yell for help, and that he was doing.

Thornton saw two coworkers who had stopped their work and were standing a few feet away, just watching him. They made no move to help him, which almost caused him to panic. He held on a few seconds more, mentally reliving his life, and just as he was about to turn loose and accept his fate, for no reason apparent to him, the saw stopped. He weakly unhooked himself from the board and slumped on the saw platform for a few seconds. When he regained his composure and a little strength, he stood up unsteadily and turned to see a friend from another part of the plant, not one of his coworkers, standing with his thumb still near the power button for his saw. The friend had just happened to be walking past, on his way to another part of the plant. Thornton could see his astonishment reflected on his friend's face as the friend stood staring back at him.

Thornton stood trembling, trying to make sense of the whole confusing situation. He knew that there must be an explanation of why all the work-related difficulties and pressure had beset him in recent months, almost costing him his life. He wondered about what caused his coworkers to callously fail to help him and what he could do about it.

Questions

1. In terms of group dynamics, why did Bud Thornton's coworkers not help him?
2. Briefly apply/relate each of the following concepts to Thornton's work situation: role, norm, intrarole conflict, interrole conflict, deviate, and sanctions.
3. How would you describe the ethics of Thornton's coworkers?

4. What did Thornton do to contribute to this situation?
5. What did PLC management do to contribute to this situation?
6. What did the union do to contribute to this situation?
7. Should Thornton confront PLC management about the incident? If so, how?

Source: This case was prepared by R. B. Barton, Jr., Murray State University, and is intended to be used as a basis for class discussion. The views represented here are those of the case author and do not necessarily reflect the views of the Society for Case Research. The author's views are based on his own professional judgments. The names of the organizations, location, and the individual have been disguised to preserve the organization's and individual's anonymity. Presented to and accepted by the Society for Case Research. It was edited for *Organizational Behavior*, 9th edition, and used with permission.

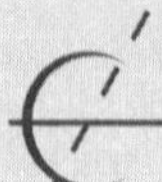

BOB KNOWLTON

Bob Knowlton was sitting in the conference room of the laboratory. The rest of the group had gone. One of the secretaries had stopped and talked for a while about her husband's coming induction into the Army and had finally left. Knowlton, now alone in the laboratory, slid a little farther down in his chair, looking with satisfaction at the results of the first test run of the new photon unit.

He liked to stay after the others had gone. His appointment as project head was still new enough to give him a deep sense of pleasure. His eyes were on the graphs before him, but in his mind he could hear Dr. Jerrold, the head of the laboratory, saying again. "There's one thing about this place that you can bank on. The sky is the limit for a person who can produce." Knowlton felt again the tingle of happiness and embarrassment. Well, damn it, he said to himself, he had produced. He had come to Simmons Laboratories 2 years ago. During a routine testing of some rejected Clanson components he had stumbled on the idea of the photon correlator, and the rest had just happened. Jerrold had been enthusiastic; a separate project had been set up for further research and development of the device, and Knowlton had gotten the job of running it. The whole sequence of events still seemed a little miraculous to him.

He had shrugged off his reverie and bent determinedly over the sheets when he heard someone come into the room behind him. He looked up expectantly. Jerrold often stayed late himself, and now and then dropped in for a chat. This always made his day's end especially pleasant. But it wasn't Jerrold. The man who had come in was a stranger. He was tall, thin, and rather dark. He wore steel-rimmed glasses and had on a very wide leather belt with a large brass buckle. The stranger smiled and introduced himself. "I'm Simon Fester. Are you Bob Knowlton? Knowlton said, "yes," and they shook hands. "Doctor Jerrold said I might find you in. We were talking about your work, and I'm very much interested in what you're doing." Knowlton waved him to a chair. Fester didn't seem to belong in any of the standard categories of visitors: customer, visiting fireman, or shareholder. Knowlton pointed to the sheets on the table. "These are the preliminary results of a test we're running. We've got a new gadget by the tail and we're trying to understand it. It's not finished, but I can show you the section that we're testing." He stood up, but Fester was deeply engrossed in the graphs. After a moment he looked up with an odd grin. "These look like plots of a Jennings surface. I've been playing around with some autocorrelation functions of surfaces—you know that stuff." Knowlton, who had no idea what Fester was referring to, grinned back and nodded, and immediately felt uncomfortable. "Let me show you the monster," he said, and led the way to the workroom.

After Fester left, Knowlton slowly put the graphs away, feeling vaguely annoyed. Then, as if he had made a decision, he quickly locked up and took the long way out so that he would pass Jerrold's office. But the office was locked. Knowlton wondered whether Jerrold and Fester had left together.

The next morning Knowlton dropped into Jerrold's office, mentioned that he had talked with Fester, and asked who he was. "Sit down for a minute," Jerrold said. "I want to talk to you about him. What do you think of him?" Knowlton replied truthfully that he thought Fester was very bright and probably very competent.

Jerrold looked pleased. "We're taking him on," he said. "He has a very good background at a number of laboratories, and he seems to have ideas about the problems we're tackling here." Knowlton nodded in agreement, instantly hoping that Fester would not be placed with him.

"I don't know yet where he will finally land," Jerrold continued, "but he seems interested in what you're doing. I thought he might spend a little time with you by way of getting started." Knowlton nodded thoughtfully. "If his interest in your work continues, you can add him to your group."

"Well, he seemed to have some good ideas even without knowing exactly what we are doing." Knowlton answered. "I hope he stays; I'd be glad to have him."

Knowlton walked back to the lab with mixed feelings. He told himself that Fester would be good for the group. He was no dunce; he'd produce. Knowlton thought again of Jerrold's promise when he had promoted him: "The person who produces gets ahead in this outfit." The words now seemed to him to carry the overtones of a threat.

The next day, Fester didn't appear until midafternoon. He explained that he had had a long lunch with Jerrold, discussing his place in the lab. "Yes," said Knowlton. "I talked with him this morning about it, and we both thought that you might work with my group for a while."

Fester smiled in the same knowing way that he had smiled when he mentioned the Jennings surfaces. "I'd like to," he said.

Knowlton introduced Fester to the other members of the lab. Fester and John Link, the mathematician of the group, hit it off well together. They spent the rest of the afternoon discussing a method of analysis of patterns that Link had been worrying over for the last month.

It was 6:30 when Knowlton finally left the lab that night. He had waited almost eagerly for the end of the day to come—when all the lab personnel would all be gone and he could sit in the quiet room, relax, and think it over. Think what over? he asked himself. He didn't know. Shortly after 5:00 they had all gone except Fester, and what followed was almost a duel. Knowlton was annoyed that he was being cheated out of his quiet period, and finally resentful, determined that Fester should leave first.

Fester was sitting at the conference table reading, and Knowlton was sitting at his desk in the little glass-enclosed office that he used during the day when he needed to be undisturbed. Fester had gotten last year's progress reports out and was studying them carefully. Time dragged. Knowlton doodled on a pad, the tension growing inside him. What the hell did Fester think he was going to find in the reports?

Knowlton finally gave up, and they left the lab together. Fester took several of the reports with him to study that evening. Knowlton asked him if he thought the reports gave a clear picture of the lab's activities.

They're excellent," Fester answered with obvious sincerity. "They're not only good reports; what they report is damn good too!" Knowlton was surprised at the relief he felt, and grew almost jovial as he said goodnight.

Driving home, Knowlton felt more optimistic about Fester's presence in the lab. He had never fully understood the analysis that Link was attempting. If there was anything wrong with Link's approach Fester would probably spot it.

And if I'm any judge, he thought, he won't be especially diplomatic about it.

He described Fester to his wife, Lucy, who was amused by the broad leather belt and the brass buckle.

"It's the kind of belt the Pilgrims must have worn," she laughed.

"I'm not worried about how he holds his pants up," Knowlton laughed with her. "I'm afraid that he's the kind that just has to make like a genius twice each day. And that can be pretty rough on the group."

Knowlton had been asleep for several hours when he was jarred awake by the telephone. He realized it had rung several times. He swung off the bed, muttering about damn fools and telephones. It was Fester. Without any excuses, apparently oblivious of the time, he plunged into an excited recital of how Link's patterning problem could be solved.

Knowlton covered the mouthpiece to answer his wife's stage whisper, "Who is it?"

"It's the genius."

Fester, completely ignoring the fact that it was 2:00 in the morning, proceeded excitedly to explain a completely new approach to certain of the photon lab problems that he had stumbled onto while analyzing some past experiments. Knowlton managed to put some enthusiasm in his own voice and stood there, still half-dazed and very uncomfortable, listening to Fester talk endlessly, it seemed, about what he had discovered. He said that he not only had a new approach but also an analysis that showed how inherently weak the previous experiment had been. He finally concluded by saying that further experimentation along that earlier line certainly would have been inconclusive.

Later that morning, Knowlton spent several hours with Fester and Link, calling off the usual morning group meeting so that the three of them could go over Fester's work of the previous night intensively. Fester was very anxious that this be done, and Knowlton wasn't too unhappy to call the meeting off for reasons of his own.

For the next several days Fester sat in the back office that had been turned over to him and did nothing but read the progress reports of the work that had been done during the past 6 months. Knowlton caught himself feeling apprehensive about the reaction that Fester might have to some of his work. He was a little surprised at his own feelings. He had always been proud—although he had put on a convincingly modest face—of the way his team had broken new ground in the study of photon measuring devices. Now he wasn't sure. It seemed to him that Fester might easily show that the line of research they had been following was unsound or even unimaginative.

The next morning, as was customary, the members of Knowlton's group, including the secretaries, sat around the table in the conference room. He had always prided himself on the fact that the team as a whole guided and evaluated its work. He was fond of repeating that it was not a waste of time to include secretaries in such meetings. He would point out that often what started out as a boring recital of fundamental assumptions to a naïve listener uncovered new ways of regarding these assumptions that wouldn't have occurred to the lab member who had long ago accepted them as a necessary basis for the research he was doing. These group meetings also served another purpose. He admitted to himself that he would have felt far less secure if he had had to direct the work completely on his own. Team meetings, as a principle of leadership, justified the exploration of blind alleys because of the general educative effect of the team. Fester and Link were there, as were Lucy Martin and Martha Ybarra. Link sat next to Fester, the two of them continuing their conversation concerning Link's mathematical study from yesterday. The other group members, Bob Davenport, George Thurlow, and Arthur Oliver, sat there waiting quietly.

Knowlton, for reasons that he didn't quite understand, brought up a problem that all of them had previously spent a great deal of time discussing. The team had come to an implicit conclusion that a solution was impossible and that there was no feasible way of treating it experimentally. Davenport remarked that there was hardly any use of going over it again. He was satisfied that there was no way of approaching the problem with the equipment and the physical capacities of the lab.

This statement had the effect of a shot of adrenaline on Fester. He said he would like to know in detail what the problem was, and walking to the blackboard, began both discussing the problem and simultaneously listing the reasons why it had been abandoned. Very early in the description of the problem it became evident that Fester was going to disagree about the impossibility of solving it. The group realized this and finally the descriptive materials and their recounting of the reasoning that had led to its abandonment dwindled away. Fester began his analysis, which as it proceeded might have well been prepared the previous night although Knowlton knew that to be impossible. He couldn't help being impressed with the organized and logical way that Fester was presenting ideas that must have occurred to him only a few minutes before.

However, Fester said some things that left Knowlton with a mixture of annoyance, irritation, and, at the same time, a rather smug feeling of superiority in at least one area. Fester was of the opinion that the way that the problem had been analyzed was typical of what happened when a team attempted such thinking. With an air of sophistication that made it difficult for a listener to dissent, he proceeded to make general comments on the American emphasis on team ideas, satirically describing the ways in which they led to a "high level of mediocrity."

Knowlton observed that Link stared studiously at the floor and was conscious of George Thurlow's and Bob Davenport's glances at him at several points of Fester's little speech. Inwardly, Knowlton couldn't help feeling that this was one point at least in which Fester was off on the wrong foot. The whole lab, following Dr. Jerrold's lead, talked, if not actually practiced, the theory of small research teams as the basic organization for effective research. Fester insisted that the problem could be solved and that he would like to study it for a while himself.

Knowlton ended the session by remarking that the meetings would continue and that the very fact that a supposedly insoluble experimental problem was now going to get another look was yet another indication of the value of such meetings. Fester immediately remarked that he was not at all averse to meetings for the purpose of informing the group of the progress of its members. He went on to say that the point he wanted to make was that creative advances were seldom accomplished in such meetings, that they were made by the individual "living with" the problem closely and continuously, forming a sort of personal relationship with it. Knowlton responded by saying that he was glad Fester had raised these points and that he was sure the team would profit by reexamining the basis on which they had been operating. Knowlton agreed that individual effort was probably the basis for making major advances but that he considered the group meetings useful primarily because of the effect they had on keeping the team together and on helping the weaker members of the team keep up with the advances of the ones who were able to move more easily and quickly when analyzing problems.

As days went by and the meetings continued, Fester came to enjoy them because of the direction the meetings soon took. Typically, Fester would hold forth on some subject, and it became clear that he was, without question, more brilliant and better prepared on the topics germane to the problems being studied. He probably was more capable of going ahead on his own than anyone there, and Knowlton grew increasingly disturbed as he realized that his leadership of the team had been, in fact, taken over. In Knowlton's occasional meetings with Jerrold, whenever Fester was mentioned, he would comment only on Fester's ability and obvious capacity for work, somehow never quite feeling that he could mention his own discomforts. He felt that they revealed a weakness on his own part. Moreover, Dr. Jerrold was greatly impressed with Fester's work and with the contacts he had with Fester outside the photon laboratory.

Knowlton began to feel that the intellectual advantages that Fester had brought to the team might not quite compensate for evidences of a breakdown in the cooperative spirit that had been evident in the group before Fester's coming. More and more of the morning meetings were skipped. Fester's opinion concerning the abilities of others of the team, with the exception of Link's, was obviously low. At times during morning meetings or in smaller discussions he had been rude, refusing at certain times to pursue an argument when he claimed that it was based on the other person's ignorance of the facts involved. His impatience with the others also led him to make remarks of this kind to Jerrold in private conversations. This Knowlton inferred from a conversation he later had with Jerrold. The head of the lab had asked whether Davenport and Oliver were going to be retained, but he hadn't mentioned Link.

Knowlton had little difficulty making a convincing case regarding whether Fester's brilliance actually was sufficient recompense for the beginning of his team's breaking up. He spoke privately with Davenport and Oliver. Both clearly were uncomfortable with Fester's presence. Knowlton didn't press the discussion beyond hearing them in one way or another say that they sometimes felt awkward around Fester. They said that sometimes they had difficulty understanding the arguments he advanced. In fact, they often felt too embarrassed to ask Fester to state the grounds on which he based such arguments. Knowlton didn't talk to Link in this manner.

About 6 months after Fester's coming to the photon lab, meetings were scheduled to which the sponsors of much of the ongoing research were coming to get some idea of its progress. At special meetings, project heads customarily presented the research being conducted by their groups. The other members of the laboratory groups were invited to other, more general meetings later in the day that were open to all. The special meetings usually were restricted to project heads, the head of the laboratory, and the sponsors. As the time for his special meeting approached, Knowlton felt that he must avoid the presentation at all costs. He felt that he couldn't present the ideas that Fester had advanced—and on which some work had been done—in sufficient detail and answer questions about them. However, he didn't feel that he could ignore these newer lines of work and present only the work that had been started or completed before Fester's arrival (which he felt perfectly competent to do). It seemed clear that keeping Fester from attending the meeting wouldn't be easy in spite of the fact that he wasn't on the administrative level that had been invited. Knowlton also felt that it wouldn't be beyond Fester, in his blunt and undiplomatic way, if he was present at the meeting, to comment on Knowlton's presentation and reveal the inadequacy that he felt.

Knowlton found an opportunity to speak to Jerrold and raised the question. He remarked to Jerrold that, of course, with the interest in the work and Fester's contributions he probably would like to come to these meetings. Knowlton said that he was concerned about the feelings of the others in the group if Fester were invited. Jerrold brushed this concern aside by saying that he felt the group would understand Fester's rather different position. He thought that, by all means, Fester should be invited. Knowlton then immediately said that he had thought so too and further that Fester should make the presentation because much of it was work that he had done. As Knowlton put it, this would be a nice way to recognize Fester's contributions and to reward him because he was eager to be recognized as a productive member of the lab. Jerrold agreed, and so the matter was decided.

Fester's presentation was very successful and in some ways, dominated the meeting. He held the interest and attention of those attending, and following his presentation the questions persisted for a long period. Later that evening at the banquet, to which the entire laboratory was invited, a circle of people formed about Fester during the cocktail period before the dinner. Jerrold was part of the circle and discussion concerning the application of the theory Fester was proposing. Although this attention disturbed Knowlton, he reacted and behaved characteristically. He joined the circle, praised Fester to Jerrold and the others, and remarked how able and brilliant some of his work was.

Knowlton, without consulting anyone, began to consider the possibility of a job elsewhere. After a few weeks he found that a new laboratory of considerable size was being organized in a nearby city. His training and experience would enable him to get a project-head job equivalent to the one he had at the lab, with slightly more money.

He immediately accepted it and notified Jerrold by letter, which he mailed on a Friday night to Jerrold's home. The letter was brief, and Jerrold was stunned. The letter merely said that Knowlton had found a better position; that there were personal reasons why he didn't want to appear at the lab anymore; that he would be glad to come back later (he would be only 40 miles away), to assist if there were any problems with past work; that he felt sure that Fester could, however, supply any leadership that was required for the group; and that his decision to leave so suddenly was based on some personal problems (he hinted at family health problems involving his mother and father, which was fictitious). Dr. Jerrold took it at face value but still felt that Knowlton's behavior was very strange and quite unaccountable. Jerrold had always felt that his relationship with Knowlton had been warm; that Knowlton was satisfied and, as a matter of fact, quite happy and productive.

Jerrold was considerably disturbed because he had already decided to place Fester in charge of another project that was going to be set up soon. He had been wondering how to explain this decision to Knowlton in view of the obvious help, assistance, and value Knowlton had been getting from Fester and the high regard in which Knowlton held him. In fact, Jerrold had considered letting Knowlton add to his staff another person with Fester's background and training, which apparently had proved so valuable.

Jerrold did not make any attempt to contact Knowlton. In a way he felt aggrieved about the whole thing. Fester, too, was surprised at the suddenness of Knowlton's departure and when Jerrold, in talking to him, asked him whether he preferred to stay with the photon group rather than to head the Air Force project that was being organized, he chose the Air Force project and moved into that job the following week. The photon lab was hard hit. The leadership of the group was given to Link, with the understanding that it would be temporary until someone else could be brought in to take over.

Questions

1. What attributions did Bob Knowlton make?
2. What team norms seemed to be operating in Knowlton's team?
3. What leadership style did Knowlton *need* from Dr. Jerrold after Fester arrived? Explain.
4. What leadership style did Knowlton seem to get from Dr. Jerrold *before* and *after* Fester arrived?
5. What leadership style did Knowlton use with his subordinates?
6. What leadership style did Knowlton use with Fester? Was it effective? Explain.
7. What would you have done with Fester if you were Knowlton?
8. What would you have done to influence Dr. Jerrold if you were Knowlton?

Source: This case was developed by Dr. Alex Bavelas. It was edited for *Organizational Behavior*, 9th edition, and used with permission.

NORDSTROM, INC.

Nordstrom, Inc., based in Seattle, Washington, is a fashion specialty retailer that operates 61 full-time stores in 14 states. In 1996, sales were more than $4 billion. The company has been named by *Hispanic* magazine as one of the best workplaces for Hispanics. Nordstrom demonstrates its concern with diversity in its catalogs, not just in terms of age, but also in terms of race and disabilities. Since 1989, Nordstrom has had a Supplier Diversity Program that purchases goods and services from women- and minority-owned businesses. In 1994, Nordstrom introduced The Nordstrom Partnership, a set of guidelines for its foreign and domestic partners. The guidelines focus on five areas: legal requirements, health and safety standards, employment practices, environmental standards, and documentation and inspection. For example, the guidelines prohibit the use of child or forced labor to produce goods for Nordstrom. Labor Secretary Reich praised Nordstrom for its efforts to prevent abusive working conditions by its partners.

Throughout the industry, Nordstrom is well known for its superb customer service. The level of customer service and amount of sales per square foot represent the most valuable measures of success in a retail environment. Nordstrom is consistently a leader in the retail industry in both categories. The Nordstrom corporate philosophy places the responsibility for achieving this superiority in the hands of the people who deal with Nordstrom customers daily—the sales force. Because the company's prosperity depends on the efficacy of its sales associates, their motivation is crucial. Nordstrom explicitly defines its job expectations for employees and corresponding rewards in the form of promotion, salary increases, liberal merchandise discounts, and other benefits.

Nordstrom has identified three performance categories in which it expects sales associates to excel: customer service, team play, and productivity. An equilateral triangle, with each side of the triangle representing one of the categories, illustrates the importance of meeting stated expectations in order to achieve desired results (see Figure 1). That is,

Customer service + Team play + Productivity = Results.

Each new Nordstrom sales associate must attend an orientation session before beginning his or her first assignment with the company. At that time, employees receive a list of qualities, known as the Expectation List, representative of each performance category. Demonstration of product knowledge and always putting the customer first indicates exemplary customer service; the notion of a customer being "our" customer rather than "my" customer illustrates teamwork; and prompt and satisfactory completion of assignments and projects demonstrates an employee's productivity. (Figure 1 contains the complete Expectation List.)

Through actively practicing the attributes on the list, associates display their commitment to the values that Nordstrom promotes. Department managers evaluate the overall performance of sales associates in terms of the qualities identified in the Expectation List. An employee's success in meeting the teamwork, customer service, and productivity goals manifests itself in the "ranking of the schedule." Sales associates receive a new work schedule bimonthly. Each new schedule lists all the employees in

Figure 1

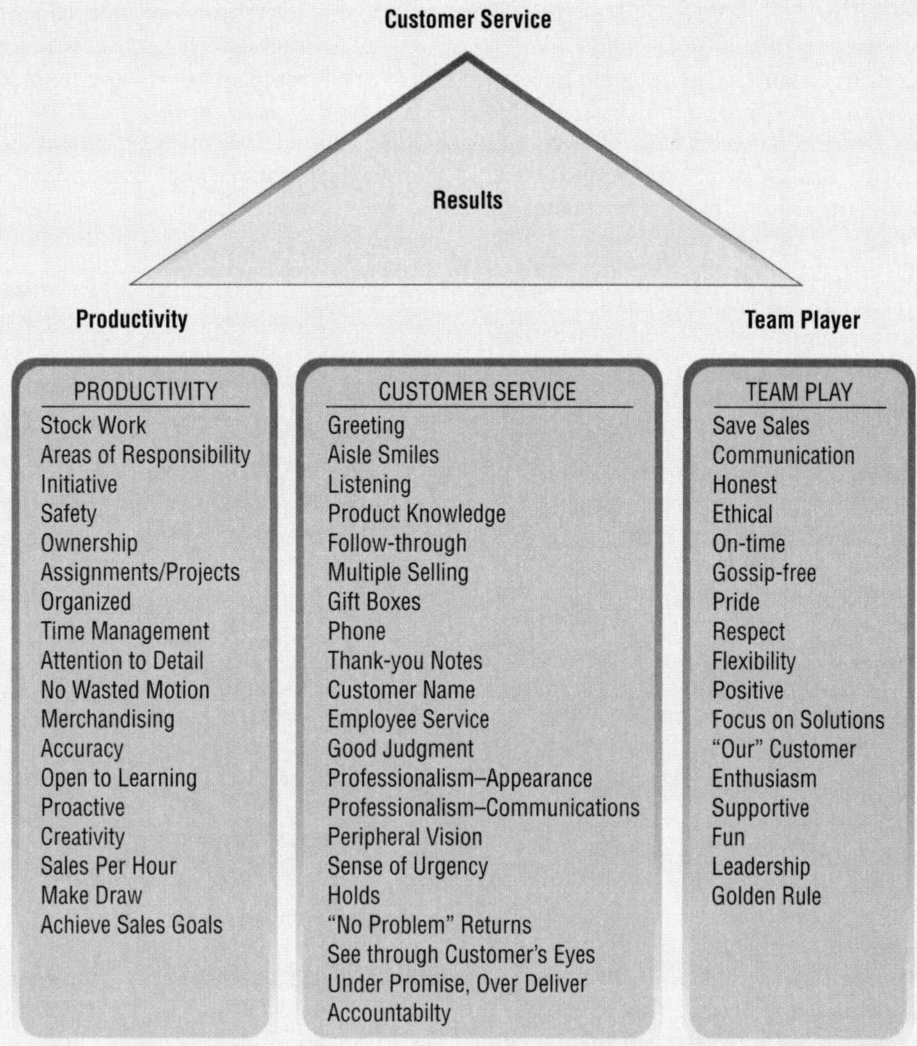

the department in the order in which they have succeeded in accomplishing those goals. The schedules are posted for everyone to see and are frequently used as the main source of information for assessing employee performance. A common question that Nordstrom managers ask their sales associates is: "Where are you on the schedule?" In other words, "How well are you performing within the framework of our expectations?"

Employees' ranks on the schedule indicate their status/power positions in the department's hierarchy. Sales associates ranked among the top 25 percent of employees in their departments gain additional responsibilities and serve in a managerial capacity in the department manager's absence. These top-ranked employees typically receive the first chance at filling vacated managerial positions.

Sales associates determine the level of compensation they want to receive, which is based on their productivity. Through a program called Write Your Own Paycheck, employees state the amount of commission they want to earn during a particular pay period. Once the associate has settled on a dollar figure, the productivity level needed to attain it can be calculated. Thus the sales associates can determine in advance the effort required to reach a desired financial outcome.

Nordstrom sets an annual sales goal within each department, which is known as the Pacesetter mark. All employees have a fair chance of meeting the goal and attaining Pacesetter status—an elite group of top salespeople. Associates receive a calendar page to chart their progress in meeting this goal. Bulletin boards in each stockroom serve as a constant reminder of everybody's status. The Customer Service All-Star Award has a less tangible goal than a sales figure; progress toward achieving it is measured by the volume of favorable customer service letters and other feedback.

The recognition associated with reaching either of these achievement levels is significant. Pacesetters and

All-Stars receive a 33 percent house discount (as opposed to the standard 20 percent), an awards dinner-dance in their honor sponsored by the Nordstrom family, recognition in the local papers and the Nordstrom newsletter, special business cards reflecting the award, and mounted photographs in the stores. The required level of performance to achieve these rewards is known to everyone in the organization and is calculated in a straightforward manner. Sales associates know the requirements for becoming a Pacesetter or All-Star and can adjust their efforts accordingly.

However, Nordstrom has encountered some difficulties in following these practices. The most prevalent discrepancy lies in the area of productivity, measured in sales per hour (SPH). The SPH defines each associate's sales performance by dividing total sales by the number of hours worked. The logical step for an employee wanting to appear to maximize productivity in order to receive a reward is to reduce the number of hours worked without reducing sales volume. The problem of employees "clocking out" but continuing to work on the sales floor has arisen. The employees most likely to clock out but continuing to work often have been those nearest the top of the ranking schedule, leaving employees working fairly on the clock at a great disadvantage.

Despite the controversy over SPH, it does provide a tangible measurement of a sales associate's productivity. Customer service and teamwork present an entirely different type of problem because their less concretely defined expectations are more difficult to measure performance against. The department manager's best judgment, in the end, represents the only appraisal of performance in these categories.

Questions

1. What motivational principles does Nordstrom use to reward its employees?
2. What attributions might managers make about sales associates who don't achieve their sales targets?
3. What are some of the potential barriers that sales associates would face if they wanted to form effective teams?

Source: This case was prepared by Susan Summers under the direction of Professor John W. Slocum, Cox School of Business, Southern Methodist University, Dallas, Texas, 1997. It was edited for *Organizational Behavior*, 9th edition, and used with permission.

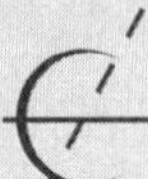

WHAT DO WE DO WITH HOWARD?

Agrigreen, Inc., manufactures various agricultural fertilizers in several plants in the western United States and Canada. Tad Pierson, appointed 3 months ago as a project engineer at one of the Agrigreen plants, had been told last week by Burt Jacobs, the new manager of engineering to whom he reports, that he was to take on the added responsibility of supervising the plant surveying group. Having worked with members of this group in the past, Pierson was aware of some performance problems and conflicts that existed within the group. Contemplating what action, if any, he should take as their new supervisor, he reviewed the history of the surveying group with others in the company (see Figure 1) and then talked with each group member individually to arrive at the following picture of the situation.

HOWARD LINEBERRY, LEAD SURVEYOR

After receiving his surveyor's certificate from the local civil technologies college, Howard Lineberry had gone to work for the State Highway Department as a chainman. The job hadn't paid very well, and he always felt that the lead surveyor didn't like him and often had him doing work that was better suited for a rodman, a position of lower status than chainman on a survey crew.

So, when a job for a lead surveyor had opened up at Agrigreen 18 years ago, Lineberry had been glad to get it. He told Pierson how excited he had been to be hired into the newly created position. Previously, survey work at Agrigreen had been handled on a part-time basis by drafting personnel or project engineers, mainly Frank Silverton (see Figure 2). Because of significant growth during the preceding 3 years, survey work had begun to eat up nearly all of Silverton's working hours. As a project engineer, his salary was too high to justify using him for surveying, so management had decided to hire someone with an education in surveying and some experience to support the work of Silverton and the five other project engineers.

Jerry Givens, manager of the engineering staff at the time, and since retired, was the man who had hired and first supervised Howard Lineberry. Since being hired, Lineberry has worked for four different supervisors. He remembered Givens as a "cantankerous, hardheaded boss who had very specific things that he wanted done and definite ideas on how they should be accomplished." He often lost his temper and openly criticized Lineberry or anyone else doing something he

Figure 1

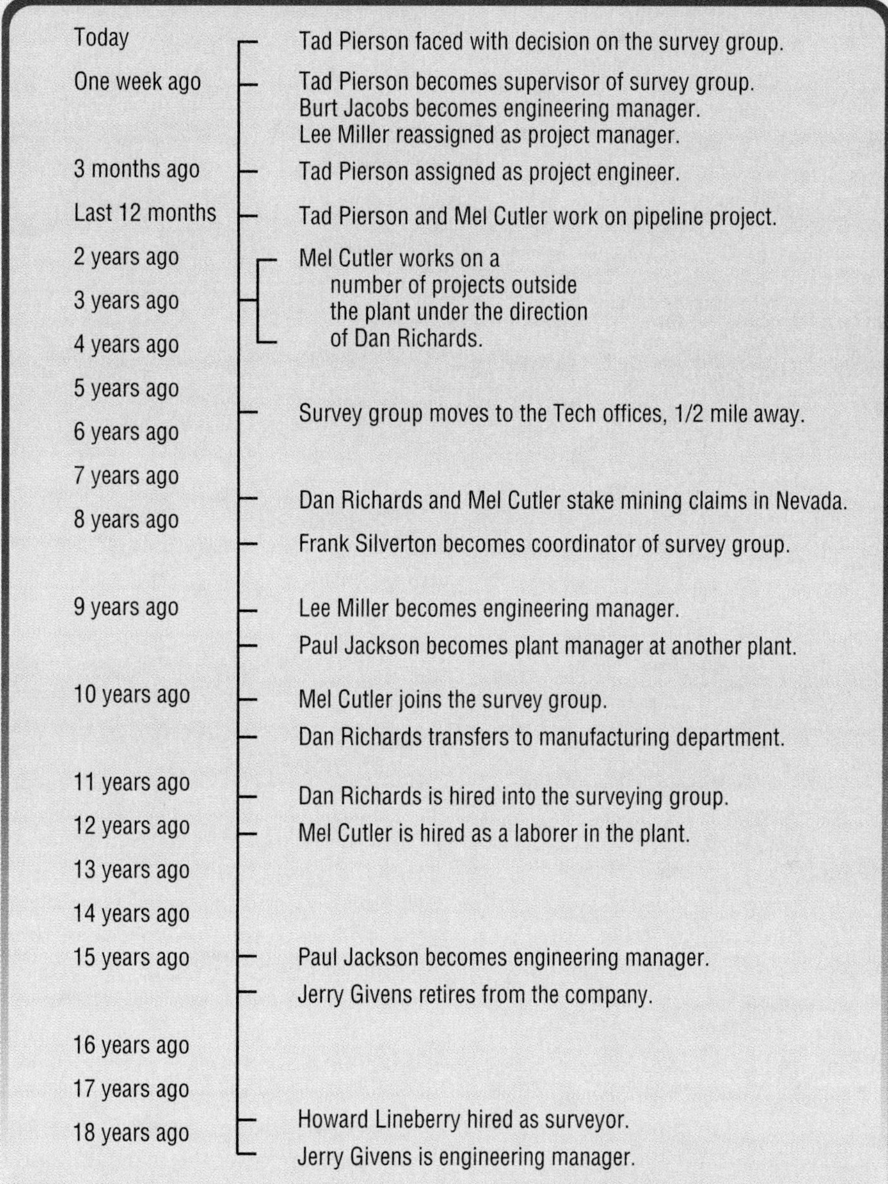

didn't like. Nevertheless, Lineberry felt that he got along well with Givens. He usually had Lineberry's daily work scheduled by the time Lineberry arrived in the morning and explained what needed to be done and how it should be done. Only occasionally would Givens have to stop by during the day to change the focus of activities.

After Givens retired, Lineberry reported to Paul Jackson, the new manager of engineering. Unlike Givens, Jackson expected Lineberry to plan his day based on the work that needed to be done and to go ahead and do it. About that time, Lineberry had been thinking that he could do a better job supporting the project engineers, who were increasingly busy on more and larger projects, if he worked with them more directly. The increased pace of work often resulted in last minute requests for Lineberry to provide information and fieldwork. He felt that he had handled fairly well what had become frequent daily changes in his work schedule.

Then one day Jackson accused Lineberry, in front of a couple of the engineers, of being "disorganized and possibly lazy." Later, maybe as a result of thinking about what Paul had said, or maybe as a result of just bad luck, according to Lineberry, he made an error fixing the location of a building foundation. The error wasn't noticed until it was time to erect the new mill. What followed,

Figure 2

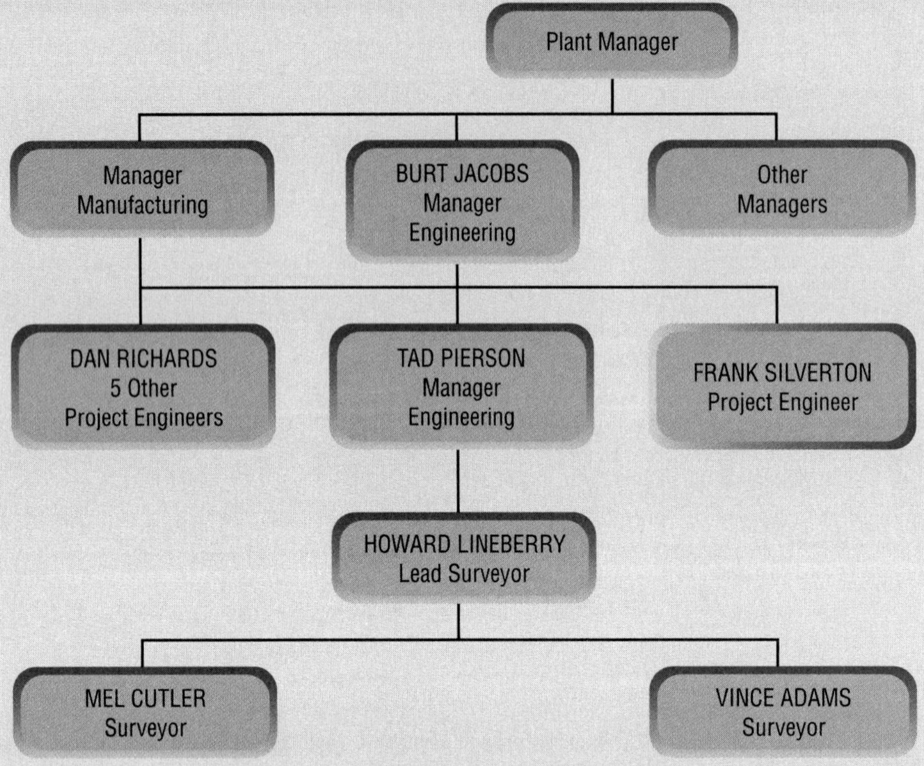

Lineberry remembered, was "pure hell as the foundation was demolished and replaced at considerable cost in time and money." After that, people stopped talking when he walked up, and he often overheard "little biting comments" about him. Lineberry had "considered quitting, but good jobs were hard to get."

After the foundation incident, Jackson became increasingly critical and finally decided that Lineberry needed someone to assist him and double check his "error-prone" work. At the same time, Agrigreen was planning to build a new wastewater holding pond, and the project would require extra surveying help. Jackson hired Dan Richards to assist Lineberry. Richards was a bright, hard-working young man who had had the same training as Lineberry and who was also pursuing a degree in engineering. As the project proceeded, Richards had openly expressed his feelings that his leader, Howard Lineberry, was slow and stupid. Lineberry felt relieved a year and half later when Richards was transferred to the manufacturing department.

Mel Cutler, who had been employed in the plant for 2 years as a laborer, replaced Richards. He had previously worked for another employer as a draftsman and had also gained considerable experience in surveying. Lineberry immediately liked Cutler, something he had never felt for Dan Richards. Cutler was willing to work with Linebery on how to do the jobs and often caught small errors before they became problems.

Ten years have passed since Cutler first joined Lineberry, who now felt a "slight pang" as he wished things were still the same between them. But, during the past 5 years, relations between them had become increasingly tense. Recently, the only verbal exchanges between them had been terse and directly concerned with the job. Much of the enjoyment of his job is gone, and Lineberry often dreaded coming to work.

A few months after Cutler had been hired, another supervisory change occurred. Lee Miller, a former project engineer, took the manager's job when Paul Jackson was promoted to plant manager at another Agrigreen plant. Miller had been very successful as an engineer but as a supervisor was somewhat indecisive.

Meanwhile, increasing workloads had resulted in the hiring of additional draftsmen, and office space was getting tight. Miller corrected the situation by remodeling some space in the basement of the Tech offices located about half a mile from the plant, and Lineberry and Cutler moved there. Nobody bothered either of them much in the new location. Lineberry felt good about the change because he now had space for the surveying equipment and he was away from the mainstream of the operation. He needed to see the engineers only when he felt like it and wasn't bothered as often by hearing their derogatory comments.

Four years ago, Miller had told Lineberry and the other surveyors that he would like them to coordinate their job assignments and schedules through Frank Silverton, indicating that Silverton had much more surveying experience than he did and would know better what the needs were. Lineberry remembered feeling uncomfortable about this arrangement because Silverton wasn't really his boss, and he still had to have Miller sign his time cards and approve his vacation.

During the past 4 years, Cutler had occasionally worked on small projects outside the plant, most frequently for Dan Richards, who always specified which individual he wanted when requesting help.

Recently, the company had constructed a 50-mile pipeline to deliver raw materials to the plant, and Cutler was chosen to work under Tad Pierson on that project. Pierson was a recent engineering graduate charged with overseeing the pipeline survey and construction, which had lasted from April through December the previous year. Lineberry still felt angry about Cutler's assignment to the project because he has had "more experience than Mel at surveying and could have used the overtime money." The only benefit to Lineberry resulting from Cutler's outside work was that Miller had hired Vince Adams to help Lineberry during the summer months. Lineberry and Adams thought much the same way about many things, and Lineberry had a genuine affection for this "just-out-of-high-school" young man.

Following completion of the pipeline project, Tad Pierson had been made a project engineer, and because of the lack of space in the plant offices, was given space in the Tech offices near Lineberry, Adams, and Cutler. Pierson was openly friendly with Cutler, but Lineberry felt that Pierson "acted coolly" toward him and Adams. They seemed to have nothing in common, and each time Lineberry had tried to talk to Pierson, Pierson seemed to cut the discussion short and make an excuse to leave.

A week ago, Lee Miller had stepped down as manager of engineering and resumed duties as one of the project engineers. Burt Jacobs, a big, loud, direct person (in Lineberry's opinion), who had been the manager of purchasing and stores (plant supplies) replaced him as manager. Jacobs was an engineer about half Miller's age and several years younger than Lineberry. Only this morning, Jacobs had called the engineering department together to say that change was needed because of the friction between engineering and the other departments in the plant. He also said that the surveyors were now to report to Pierson (which made Lineberry very uneasy) and that anyone needing surveying services must now schedule them through Pierson.

MEL CUTLER, SURVEYOR'S HELPER

Mel Cutler arrived in town without a job and was a "happy man" when he got the call from Agrigreen. The company needed a plant laborer, and he needed a job. He remembered the job for the next 2 years as "the most exhausting and filthy job I have ever worked." Finally, 10 years ago a surveyor's helper position had opened up, and with his background in surveying and drafting he was able to get the job.

Cutler was assigned to Howard Lineberry. For the first few years, they worked well together. Both men had young families, and they shared many of the same outside interests. Cutler had been willing to go along with the way Lineberry had always done things until about 5 years ago when he noticed that they "experienced continual problems because of the way Howard kept his notes." Cutler tried to show Lineberry the way he had been trained to keep notes, but "Howard would have nothing to do with it." The debate continued for several weeks.

Soon, Lineberry started keeping the work schedule to himself, and Cutler often had no idea what they were going to do next until Lineberry stopped the truck and started unloading equipment. In addition, Lineberry's frequent snack breaks were starting to bother Cutler. He began losing respect for Lineberry and thought that Lineberry was "growing less concerned about his job." No amount of criticism from Frank Silverton, their boss, seemed to have any effect on Lineberry or the number of errors he committed.

Moving the surveyors out of the plant had been wrong in Cutler's opinion. He said, "Howard started taking advantage of the situation almost immediately by coming in late and leaving early a couple of times each week." Lately, Lineberry had been taking naps after lunch, justifying it by saying that he often worked late and was just making up the time. For the past year or so, he had been far more likely to be late for work than to be on time. Whenever Silverton mentioned it, Lineberry always had an excuse. Silverton gave up trying to get him to work on time and settled for just getting some good work done.

Years ago, Dan Richards had first called to see if Cutler wanted to help him stake Agrigreen mining claims in Nevada, and Cutler had jumped at the chance. This turned out to be the first of many surveying expeditions that the two men made together. Looking back, Cutler could see how they had developed a "lot of respect and trust in each other's work." They often joked about Lineberry's laziness and what an idiot they thought he was.

Cutler had been extremely happy when he became part of the pipeline survey crew. He had met Tad Pierson, the pipeline field engineer, at a party that Richards had given and had immediately liked him. Shortly into the project, Pierson, on Richard's recommendation, put Cutler in charge of the pipeline survey crew and made him responsible for inspections for the eastern half of the pipeline.

Cutler felt good about the assignment and vowed that he would be "the best worker Tad had ever seen." The hours were long—he had averaged more than 35 hours overtime a week for 15 weeks straight and had never once complained. Pierson also was working long days, and Cutler felt that they had developed an unspoken respect for each other as solid, hard workers. Pierson had backed him without question when Cutler had ordered the contractor to dig up a quarter mile of pipeline that had been buried rather hastily while he had been gone from the work site. Cutler had felt, and later proved, that the contractor buried the pipe to prevent proper inspection.

Cutler had talked with Pierson about Lineberry, indicating he "didn't look forward to working for him again when the pipeline is completed." Later, after Pierson had been reassigned to the plant, Cutler regularly stopped by to talk with him, often pointing out some of the things that Lineberry and Adams were doing; Cutler and Pierson laughed and shook their heads.

Cutler had been excited to hear at this morning's meeting that Tad Pierson was now in charge of the surveyors. He wondered how long it would take Pierson to fire Howard.

TAD PIERSON, PROJECT ENGINEER

In reviewing his own career with Agrigreen, Tad Pierson had the following thoughts.

> I don't know; I guess I've known Dan Richards since I was about 14 or so. We used to pal around in high school and have always been close. Dan told me he had wanted out of this area so badly because of Howard. He really hates the guy, and I guess I don't have much respect for him either. It's really ironic that now I'm Howard's boss.
>
> Yeah, it was Dan that talked me into going back to school. When I was ready to give up as I'd done before, he told me, "You can always quit." He knew it'd make me mad enough to stay. I guess I owe him for that. That, and his pulling the strings that got me on here. When I called him yesterday, to let him know about the change, he almost fell off his chair laughing. Then he stopped and said that he wished he was me so he could fire Howard. He was serious; he really hates him.
>
> I don't know what I'm going to do. I think the company would be money ahead to fire Howard. But, I went through the firing thing with a guy on the pipeline crew last summer. With all the letters and documentation and stuff you have to go through, it'd take 2 years to get rid of him. When I think of how long he's been here and his family and all, I get kind of squeamish. I guess I just don't know what to do. I'm going to think on it some.
>
> When Burt asked me if I'd take the surveyors I told him I would, but not like Frank had. If I wanted to fire Howard, I wanted to be able to do it. He told me, "They'll be yours; just document it. I'm going to have my hands full trying to fix other messes without trying to handle that problem too." I almost get the feeling that both of us are in up to our ears.
>
> With regard to Howard, about a month ago I went over to see Mel for a minute. There was Howard, with his head down on the drafting table, sound asleep. He didn't even hear me come or go. Vince wasn't any better, he was sitting there holding his hard hat and staring into it, dazed. I don't know if he knew I was there or not either. What a pair!
>
> The pipeline was different. You knew it was just a summer thing, so we could put up with a lot of stuff. Mel's a good man. He's pretty sour on the company though. He doesn't think Howard should get paid more than he does and "still get away with the crap he does." He's already told me I should fire both Howard and Vince.
>
> I just don't know what to do. I talked with some of the engineers. Half of them don't trust the work they get from Howard—they'd rather go out and do it themselves, and they do. I sometimes wonder what the heck we even have the surveyors for. I wonder what I should do.

Questions

1. What is the problem in this case?
2. What is your view of Howard Lineberry's performance? Discuss how motivational models can be applied to explain his behavior.
3. How would you describe the behaviors of Dan Richards and Mel Cutler? What was the nature of their relationships with Lineberry?
4. What part do informal relationships play in the case? What do they indicate about the culture of the organization?
5. What problems, if any, were created with the placement of the surveying group within the structure of the organization?
6. What responsibility, if any, should management bear for the problems that developed?
7. What else can you discern about the culture of the organization? What factors in the culture help or hinder performance, or account for the behaviors observed? What should Pierson do to resolve the situation involving Lineberry?

Source: This case was prepared by William E. Stratton of Idaho State University, Pocatello, Idaho, and J. Dale Reavis. It was presented to and accepted by the refereed Society for Case Research. It was edited for *Organizational Behavior*, 9th edition, and used with permission.

Author Index

A

Abelson, R., 323
Ackoff, R. L., 363
Ackroyd, S., 225
Adams, J. S., 150
Adhearne, M., 169
Adler, J., 202, 217
Adler, N. J., 136
Aeppel, T., 448, 452
Affleck, G., 88
Agunis, H., 296
Ajzen, I., 50, 51
Albanese, R., 22
Alderfer, C. P., 136
Aley, J., 547
Allen, D. G., 403
Allen, R. E., 149, 199
Allen, R. W., 279
Allen, T. D., 155
Alleven, M., 296
Allison, M. A., 238
Allvesson, M., 300
Amabile, T. M., 437
Ambady, N., 81
Ambrose, M. L., 133
Ancona, D., 499
Anderson, N., 512
Anderson, T., 309
Anderson, T. D., 362
Andrews, S. B., 274
Anfuso, D., 108
Ang, S., 156
Anmis, M., 381
Anonyus, C., 87
Applebaum, S. H., 104
Aquino, K., 403
Arbose, J., 195
Archambault, A., 75
Argyris, C., 266, 280, 285, 294, 298, 299, 300, 308, 549, 554, 564, 565
Armenakis, A. A., 550
Arnold, J. A., 313
Arthur, D., 401
Ashcraft, K. L., 404
Ashford, S. J., 384
Ashforth, B. E., 76, 205, 536
Ashkanasy, N. M., 356
Ashkenas, R., 13
Atwater, L. E., 271
Austin, J. T., 171
Avedisian, J., 553
Avolio, B. J., 359, 360, 363, 532
Axley, S. R., 378
Axtel, R. E., 382
Azar, B., 85

B

Babcock, B. D., 385
Babcock, R. D., 385
Babladelis, G., 88
Bacharach, S. B., 279
Badaracco, J. L., Jr., 16
Badham, R., 280
Baker, S. P., 583
Bales, R. E., 239
Balkin, D. B., 180
Ball, G. A., 113
Ball, J., 511
Bandura, A., 102, 105, 106, 116
Barksdale, K., 153
Barlow, J., 591
Barnard, C. I., 269
Barnes, F. C., 258
Baron, R. M., 77, 84, 192, 209
Baron, R. A., 201, 209, 284, 295
Barone, M., 369
Barrick, M. R., 38, 42
Barrier, M., 367
Barry, B., 241
Barry, N. P., 422
Barsade, S. G., 518
Barsoux, J. L., 87
Bartlett, C. A., 9
Barton, R. B., Jr., C-14
Baruch, Y., 54
Baskerville, D. M., 316
Bass, B. M., 329, 359
Bateman, T. S., 241
Bates, E., 230
Bauer, T. N., 398
Baum, A. S., 192, 209
Baumeister, R. F., 49
Bavelas, Alex, C-18
Bazerman, M. H., 433
Beach, L. R., 432
Beamer, L., 387
Beard, J. W., 126, 553
Beatty, S., 120
Beck, J. C., 434
Becker, T. E., 54, 170
Becker, W. S., 137
Beckhard, R., 551
Beckstead, S. M., 238
Beemon, D. R., 281
Beer, M., 560
Bell, C. H., 561, 562, 565
Bell, M. P., 243
Belliveau, M. A., 403
Benady, D., 473
Ben-Avi, L., 196
Bennett, N., 156
Bennis, W., 325
Benoit, W. L., 384
Benson, J. A., 173
Bentley, T., 448
Berelson, B., 238
Bernstein, P. L., 432
Berry, L. L., 166, 223, 224, 529
Bersticker, A. C., 19
Bertenthal, B. I., 68
Besser, T. L., 110, 181, 243
Beyer, J. M., 361, 512, 520, 521, 564
Bhawak, D. P. S., 279
Bibbee, W., 586
Biech, E., 200, 266, 304
Biles, R. J., 250
Billings, R. S., 54, 170
Birchard, B., 501
Birkenshaw, J., 501
Bishof, W. F., 75
Bitterman, D., 378
Black, J. S., 45, 313, 368
Blake, R., 68, 314
Blakeley, G. L., 153
Blanchard, K. H., 306, 336, 338
Bliese, P. D., 105, 194
Blitt, B., 254, 255
Bluedorn, A. C., 323, 401, 402
Blumenstein, R., 323
Bobko, P., 125
Bodham, R., 266
Boehme, D. M., 146
Boeker, W., 271
Bok, D., 10
Bolino, M. C., 78, 155, 384
Boltes, B. B., 564
Bolton, B., 325
Bommer, W. H., 369
Bond, M. H., 78
Bonevento, M., 386
Booth, P., 272
Booth-Kewley, S., 209
Bouchard, T. J., 39
Boudreau, M. C., 232, 502, 572
Bowen, B. D., 585
Bowen, W. G., 10
Bowie, N. E., 422
Bradfield, M., 403
Bradford, D. L., 278
Bradford, S., 12
Bradsher, K., 511
Brass, D. J., 17, 226, 242, 271
Braverman, M., 299
Breckler, S. J., 49
Breen, B., 454
Brehm, B. A., 210

Brenin, E., 360
Brenneman, G., 364
Brenner, S. N., 17
Brett, J. F., 308
Brett, J. M., 308, 313
Bretz, R. D., 277
Breznitz, S., 193
Briggs, T. C., 564
Briles, J., 404
Brinson, S. L., 384
Brockner, J., 154, 435
Brodt, S. E., 121, 422
Brover, S. L., 403
Brown, D. J., 327
Brown, L. D., 294
Brown, N. J., 432
Brown, S. P., 47, 54, 125, 133, 169, 171
Brown, S. W., 166
Browning, L. D., 361
Brtek, M. D., 462
Bruhn, M., 402
Buchanan, D., 266, 280
Buchanan, L., 392
Buchholtz, A. K., 416
Buck, T., 165
Buckingham, M., 367
Buckley, S., 228
Buller, P. F., 519, 522, 523, 539
Burgoyne, J., 565
Burke, W. W., 544
Burkhardt, M. E., 271
Burkhart, G., 10
Burnham, D., 140
Burns, T., 483
Burrows, P., 323
Bush, R. A., 314
Bushe, G. R., 569, 570
Buskirk, W. V., 531
Buss, D. D., 24
Butler, J., 13
Butler, S. G., 418
Butterfield, K. D., 17, 113, 242
Button, S. B., 46
Buunk, B. P., 154, 205
Byosiere, P., 192
Byrne, D., 84, 201, 209
Byrne, J. A., 488, 544
Byrum-Robinson, B., 210

C

Cabana, S., 229
Cable, D. M., 81
Caduette, M., 234
Caggiano, C., 388
Calder, N., 228
Caligiuri, P. M., 78, 143, 402
Calori, R., 517
Caltin, L., 410
Cameron, K. S., 400, 529, 557
Caminti, S., 48
Campbell, D. T., 587
Campbell, R. J., 227
Campion, M. A., 447
Canney Davidson, S., 143
Cannon-Bowers, J. A., 235
Carlson, J. R., 379
Carmel, E., 231
Carnall, C. A., 552
Carpenter, M. A., 497
Carpi, J., 192, 211
Carroll, A. B., 56, 416
Carroll, S. J., 462
Cartwright, D., 267, 561
Cascio, W. F., 78, 205
Caspi, A., 38, 39
Catlin, L. B., 19
Caudron, S., 16
Cavanagh, G. F., 19
Cavenagh, D., C-11
Chah, D., 297
Chaiken, S. 49
Champion, M., 398
Champy, J., 544, 568, 569
Chan, D., 387
Chandler, A., 497
Chandrashekaran, M., 166
Chapman, R. J., 253
Charin, R., 357, 398
Chatman, J. A., 515, 518, 534
Chattopadhyay, P. J., 73, 155, 391
Chaudhry, A. M., 251
Chemers, M. M., 335
Chen, C. C., 150
Chen, X., 398
Cheraskin, L., 447
Chhokar, J., 186
Chiltenham, U. K., 423
Chong, J., 463
Christie, R., 285
Church, A. H., 590
Cialdini, R. B., 277
Cirka, C. C., 155
Clarke, L., 174
Clarkson, A. E., 294
Coffman, C., 367
Cohen, A., 54, 174, 278
Cohen, L., 6
Cohen, N., 587
Cohen, S., 202
Cole, R. E., 568
Colella, A., 81
Coleman, C. Y., 548, 555
Coleman, H. J., 572
Collings, V. B., 72
Colvin, G., 266, 268, 357, 398
Conger, J. A., 10, 289, 359, 360
Conlin, M., 301, 547
Conlon, D. E., 295
Connor, P. E., 573
Contrada, R., 192, 209
Cook, T. D., 587
Cooper, C. R., 40
Cooper, C. L., 195, 266, 280, 285, 294, 298, 299, 300, 308, 549, 554, 564, 565
Cooperrider, D. L., 561, 562
Cordery, J. L., 448
Cortina, J. M., 169
Cosier, R. A., 438
Costa, P. T., 41
Costantino, C. A., 296
Cote, S., 50, 52
Covey, S. R., 368
Coy, P., 547
Coyle-Shapiro, J. A-M., 569
Crant, J. M., 42
Cray, D., 19
Creswell, J., 545, 582
Cron, W. L., 47, 125, 133, 148, 169, 171
Cropanzano, R., 49, 205, 296
Cross, S. E., 40
Crosson, C., 279
Crump, C. E., 213
Cuilla, J. B., 416
Cummings, L. L., 49, 76, 171, 279, 361, 534, 554, 559, 562, 572, 578
Cummings, T. G., 218, 513, 549
Cusak, L., 167
Czander, W. H., 298

D

d'Avaucourt, R., 480
Daft, R. L., 356, 361, 379, 380
Dahl, J. G., 146
Dahles, C., 454
Dana, D., 304
Danserau, F., 330, 360
Davenport, T. H., 232, 434
Davidson, M., 391
Davis, S., 25
De Bono, E., 437
De Diemar, L., 211
De George, R. T., 416
de Gilder, D., 54
De Marie, S., 502
De Pree, L., 326
Dearborn, D., 73
Deckrop, J. R., 155
DeFrank, R. S., 191
Delbecq, A. L., 211, 252
DeMarie, S. M., 231, 547
Denham, D. L., 296
DeNisi, A. S., 81
Denner, J., 40
Dennis, A. R., 254
Dent, E. B., 554

Denton, D. K., 236, 447
Denton, E. A., 359
Deogun, N., 120
DePaulo, B. M., 80
DeSanctis, G., 546
Dess, G. G., 176, 181
Dessler, G., 54
Dickson, M. W., 563
Dickson, W. J., 242
DiDio, L., 404
Dipboye, R. L., 279
Dolen, M. R., 398
Donahue, R. T., 19
Donaldson, T., 16
Donnellon, A., 389
Donovan, J. J., 169
Dorfman, P. W., 73
Doucet, M. S., 303
Douglas, P. C., 228
Drago, M., 57
Drain, M., 72
Drexler, A. G., 563
Drexler, A. B., 22
Drucker, P. F., 7, 467
Du Brin, A. J., 360
Duarte, D. L., 229
Duff, S., 581, 582
Duffy, M. K., 53
Dufour, B., 517
Dulebohn, J. H., 277, 283
Dunegan, K. J., 113
Dunham, R. B., 564
Dunnette, M. D., 41, 50, 72, 100, 192, 241, 243, 302, 339, 550, 594, 587
Duran, G. J., 440
Durham, C. C., 51, 169
Dutton, J. E., 384
Dweck, C. S., 45
Dworakivsky, A., 360

E

Eagly, A. H., 49
Earley, P. C., 19, 209
Eden, D., 206, 552
Edmondson, A., 243
Edward, E., 423
Edwards, J. R., 6, 462
Egan, G., 364
Eisenhardt, K. M., 434
Elangovan, A. R., 318
Elenkov, D. S., 267
Elizur, D., 140
Elkins, T. J., 87
Ellemers, N., 54
Ellerbee, S. B., 200
Ellingson, J. E., 38
Ellinor, L., 6
Ellis, R. A., 42
Ellis, T., 447
Ellison, K., 195
Elstrom, P., 323
Engle, R. W., 100
Engler, B., 47
Ensloe, B., 167
Erez, M., 19, 297
Ergi, C. P., 279
Eskew, D. E., 590
Ettore, B., 492
Etzion, D., 206
Eveleth, D. M., 54, 170
Evers, F. T., 6
Eysenck, H. J., 38, 47
Ezzamel, M., 242

F

Fabrigar, L. R., 49, 51
Fadil, P., 102
Faircloth, A., 89
Fairweather, N. B., 458
Falbe, C. M., 277
Fang, T., 311
Fankel, L. P., 247
Farah, M. J., 72
Farid, E., 19
Farmer, S. M., 277, 438
Farnham, A., 437
Farrell, C., 82
Faure, G. O., 313
Fedor, D. B., 277, 279
Feldman, D. C., 242
Fenn, D., 178
Fenton-O'Creevey, M., 176
Ferrell, L., 420
Ferrell, O. C., 420
Ferris, G. R., 78, 177, 277, 279, 281, 283, 384
Festinger, L. A., 298
Fiedler, F. E., 333, 335, 337
Field, D., 301
Field, H. S., 550
Field, R. H. G., 344
Fierman, J., 547
Figuera, J. R., 569
Filatotchev, I., 165
Finkelstein, S., 497
Fishbein, M., 50
Fisher, A., 63
Fisher, B., 179
Fisher, C. D., 81
Fisher, C. T., 19
Fisher, M., 252
Fisher, R., 309
Fishman, C., 230, 470
Fiske, S. T., 76
Fleishman, E. A., 330
Florent-Treacy, D., 480
Flynn, G., 438
Folger, J. P., 314
Folger, R., 382
Ford, C. M., 436
Ford, R. C., 496
Forrester, R., 22, 563
Fox, J. A., 179, 590
Fox, M. L., 194
Fraedrich, J., 420
Francesco, A. M., 385
Frantz, D. W., C-5
Freedman, S. M., 211
Freeman, R. E., 16, 416
Freeman, S. J., 529
Freiberg, J., 521, 539
Freivalds, A., 447
French, J. R. P., 267
French, W. L., 561, 562, 565, 569
Frieberg, K., 521, 539
Friedlander, F., 211
Friedman, A. A., 517
Friedman, H. S., 209
Friedman, M., 209
Friedman, R. A., 311, 391
Friend, R., 192, 209
Frink, D. D., 78, 177, 279, 384
Fritsch, P., 276
Frost, P. J., 279
Fry, L. W., 592
Fryer, B., 326, 327, 429
Fudge, R. S., 149
Fulmer, R. M., 565
Funder, D. C., 80
Fung, S., 285
Fuquay, J., 125
Fusilier, M. R., 193

G

Gaines, J., 592
Galbraith, C. S., 429
Galbraith, J. R., 494
Galleen, A., 522
Gallois, C., 356
Gallos, J. V., 10, 15
Gamble, P. R., 513
Ganster, D. C., 53, 194
Ganzach, Y., 51
Garcia, J. E., 337
Gardenswartz, L., 15, 533
Gardner, D. G., 44
Gardner, W. L., 360
Garner, R., 528
Garvin, D. A., 425
Gash, B., C-6
Gebhardt, D. L., 213
Geis, F. L., 285
Gelfand, M. J., 241, 314
George, J. M., 38, 236

Gerard, G., 6
Gerhart, B., 181
Gershenfeld, M. K., 225
Ghauri, P. N., 311, 589
Ghoshal, S., 9
Giacalone, R. A., 70
Gibbs, P., 565
Gibson, C. B., 237
Gibson, D. A., 513
Gibson, D. G., 17, 419
Giersick, C. J., 233
Gilbert, J. A., 533
Gilbert, N. L., 54, 170
Gilmore, D. C., 279
Gilovich, T., 81
Gioia, D. A., 283, 284
Glaister, K. W., 432
Glass, D., 192, 209
Glew, D. J., 199, 299
Glick, W. H., 73, 391
Goddard, R. W., 58
Gold, B. A., 385
Goldberg, S. G., 554
Goldberger, L., 193
Goldsmith, J., 325
Goldstone, R. L., 68
Golembiewski, R. T., 562
Gomar, E. F., 440
Gomez-Mejia, L. R., 179, 180
Gooding, R. Z., 356
Goodman, J. S., 398
Goodman, J. P., 364
Goodstein, L. D., 91
Gorman, P., 502
Gouttefarde, C., 430
Graen, G. B., 438
Graham, S., 72
Graziano, W. G., 77, 193, 209
Greco, S., 223
Green, M. S., 196
Greenberg, J., 154, 284
Greenberger, D. B., 87
Greene, C. N., 271
Greenhalgh, L., 294
Greenwood, R. G., 175
Greer, C. R., 144
Gregerson, H. B., 368
Greve, H. R., 115, 544
Griffin, R. W., 199, 299, 435, 462, 545, 546
Gronhaug, K., 589
Grote, D., 115
Gruys, M. L., 38
Guiney, P., 234
Gully, S. M., 142
Gumbel, P., 555
Gustafson, D. H., 252
Gustin, J., 109
Guyon, J., 340, 391
Guzzo, R. A., 227, 563

H

Hackman, J. R., 243, 454, 456, 457
Hall, C., 99
Hall, D. T., 7, 16, 383
Hall, E., 385
Hamblin, D., 177
Hambrick, D. C., 143, 245
Hamel, G., 351, 474
Hamilton, D. L., 76
Hamilton, K., 351
Hammer, M. 544, 568, 569
Hammond, J. S., 425, 426, 433
Hammond, R., 156
Hammond, S. A., 561
Hammonds, K. H., 14
Hamsmith, G. D., C-11
Handy, C., 572
Hanisch, K. A., 52
Hanks, S. H., 238
Hanna, B. A., 277
Hansemark, O. C., 142
Hansen, M. T., 501
Hanson, J. R., 274
Hare, A. P., 225
Harris, E. E., 330
Harris, P. R., 18, 19
Harris, R. T., 551
Harris, S. G., 550
Harris, T. J., 214
Harrison, D. A., 243
Harrison, E. F., 430
Harrison, M. J., 584
Harvey, J. H., 84
Hassel, G., 419
Hatfield, J. D., 304
Hawkins, K., 303
Hayes, C., 228
Haynes, S., 254
Hayward, M. L. A., 271
Hellriegel, D., 149, 386, 523, 545, 572
Henderson, J. M., 71
Hendrickson, A. R., 231, 502, 547
Hendry, C., 117, 512
Heneman, R. L., 87, 590
Heninger, W. G., 254
Henry, J. E., 226
Herbelin, S., 234
Herbert, T. T., 91
Hersey, P., 336, 338
Herzberg, F. 142, 143
Heskett, J. L., 516, 528, 529
Hessan, D., 539
Hiebeler, R., 151
Hilb, M., 43
Hill, C., 491
Hills-Storks, H., 31
Hilton, J. L., 81
Hinkin, T. R., 363
Hinton, P. R., 78, 86
Hitt, M. A., 490, 502
Hodgkinson, G. P., 432
Hofstede, G., 19, 385
Hogan, R. T., 41, 72
Hogart, R. M., 424
Hollander, E. P., 266, 554
Hollenbeck, G. P., 383
Hollenbeck, J. R., 169, 171, 183
Hollingworth, A., 71
Hollway, W., 199
Holmes, T. H., 201
Holt-Lunstad, J., 193
Homans, G. C., 224
Hooijberg, R., 524
Hooks, K. L., 303
Horibe, F., 467
Hough, L. M., 41, 50, 100, 192, 241, 243, 302, 339, 550, 584, 587
House, R. J., 139, 360
Howard, J. M., 60
Howard, P. J., 60
Hubbard, A. S., 391
Huber, G. P., 73, 391
Huber, V. L., 108, 116
Huff, J. W., 564
Huffcutt, A. I., 81
Hui, H., 150
Hulin, C. L., 50, 52
Hultin, M., 271
Humphrey, R. H., 76
Hunt, J. G., 360
Hunt, M. K., 587
Huseman, R. C., 364
Hymowitz, C., 3, 395

I

Iaffaldano, M. T., 52
Ibarra, H., 274, 389
Ireland, R. D., 490
Isaacs, U. N., 396
Ivancevich, J. M., 191, 192, 211, 533
Iverson, K., 560

J

Jackofsky, E. F., 143
Jackson, C. N., 193, 551
Jackson, P. J., 460
Jackson, S. E., 14, 143, 179, 486, 523, 545, 572
Jackson, S. L., 279
Jackson, T., 351
Jaffe, D. T., 568
Jago, A. G., 248, 339, 342, 343
James, T. M., 416
Jamieson, L. F., 209
Janis, L. L., 245

Jankowski, M., 310
Jefferson, T., 199
Jeffrey, N. A., 214
Jehn, K. A., 302, 515
Jennings, K. R., 568
Jennings, M. 420
Jensen, M. A., 232, 233
Jensen, R. C., 583
Jer-Chen, M., 493
Jermier, J., 592
Jermier, J. M., 369
Jex, S. M., 105, 192, 194, 195, 203, 206
Jick, T. D., 13, 544
John, O. P., 38, 39, 40, 41, 49, 72
Johns, G., 203
Johnson, C., 253
Johnson, J. V., 583
Johnson, R. S., 15
Jones, D., 360, 416
Jones, G. R., 236, 491
Jones, H., 468
Jones-Yang, D., 129
Joordens, S., 71
Joyce, J., 179
Joyce, W. F., 458, 474, 494, 495
Jubb, P. B., 530
Judge, T. A, 51, 277, 306, 554
Judge, W. Q., 329
Jung, D. I., 459, 532
Jupp, V., 589

K

Kacmar, D. M., 281
Kahai, S. G., 363
Kahan, R. L., 299
Kahn, A., 300
Kahn, J., 460
Kahn, R. L., 192
Kahneman, D., 432
Kaltzenbach, J. R., 563
Kanfer, R. 100, 274, 544, 546, 547
Kanungo, R. N., 359
Kaplan, A. R., 136
Kaplan, M., 247
Kaplan, R. E., 430
Kaptein, M., 172
Karwowski, W., 450
Kasof, J., 86
Kaufman, C. F., 402
Kaydo, C., 163
Keats, B. W., 502
Keenan, J. P., 530
Keeney, R. L., 425, 426, 433
Keleman, R. S., 242
Keller, J. J., 570
Keller, R. T., 455
Kelley, H. H., 86
Kelly, S., 238
Kelly, T. B., 151
Kempis, R. D., 451
Kendall, L. M., 52
Kenny, D. A., 80
Kerr, J., 525
Kerr, S., 13, 115, 369
Kets, de Vries, M. F. R., 351, 480, 529
Ketteman, C., 151
Key, S., 531
Keys, J. B., 565
Kidwell, R. E., 156
Kilbourne, L. M., 81
Kilduff, M., 226
Kilmann, R. H., 316, 515, 521
Kim, D., 180
Kim, H., 277
Kim, J. S., 169
Kim, Y. Y., 88
Kimar, K., 165
Kincaid, D. W., C-11
Kinchla, R. A., 71
King, D. G., 229
King, M. L., Jr., 361
King, R. T., Jr., 234
Kingstone, A., 75
Kinicki, A. J., 356
Kinni, T. B., 104
Kipnis, D., 277
Kiritani, E., 402
Kirkman, B. I., 227
Kirks, K. T., 554
Kirsner, S., 159, 367
Klein, B. P., 583
Klein, H. J., 169, 171
Klein, K. J., 360
Kluger, A. N., 51
Knight, D., 169
Knowlton, B., 75
Kochan, T. A., 499
Koerner, B. I., 394
Kolodny, H., 569
Komaski, J. L., 108
Koput, K. W., 388
Korine, H., 21
Kormanski, C., 233
Korsgaard, M. A., 121, 150, 422
Korshak, S. R., 309
Kossek, E. E., 10, 51, 143, 200
Kostova, K., 490
Kotter, J. P., 278, 362, 516, 528, 529
Kottler, J., 294
Koudsi, S., 545
Kouzes, J. M., 329
Kowalski, R. M., 78
Kraatz, M. S., 500
Krackhardt, D., 274
Kraft, R., 246,
Kraimer, M. L., 42
Kramer, M. W., 7
Kramer, R. M., 266, 267, 270, 277, 278, 279, 294, 429
Kray, L., 150
Krembs, P., 6
Krisianslund, I., 589
Kriska, P., 138
Kristof, A. L., 78, 164
Krosnick, J. A., 585
Kruglanski, A. W., 80
Kulik, C. T., 133
Kunde, D., 393
Kurowski, L. L., 241
Kurtzman, J., 364

L

Laaba, J., 332
Labich, K., 229, 384
Labig, C. E., 295
Lake, L. K., 573
Lancaster, H., 79, 82, 226, 235, 305, 362, 514
Landy, F. L., 137
Lane, P. M., 402
Lapidot, Y., 206
Lardner, J., 129
Larson, J. R., Jr., 584
Larsson, R., 497
Latane, B., 386
Latham, G. P., 108, 116, 133, 164, 167, 168, 178, 186
Lau, D. C., 14, 240
LaVecchia, G. H., 591
Lawler, E. E., 178
Lawler, E. J., 279
Lawrence, P. R., 494
Lawson, B., 179
Lazarus, R. S., 194
Leary, M. R., 44, 78
Leavitt, H. J., 243
Lebare, P., 365
Lederman, R., 587
Lee, A. S., 379
Lee, C., 125, 209
Lee, R. T., 205, 536
Lefcourt, H. M., 44
Leggett, E. L., 45
Lei, D., 165, 496
Leigh, J. H., 197
Lengel, R. H., 361, 379, 380
Lengnick-Hall, M. L., 199
Lenzner, R., 300
Leonard, D. A., 436
Leonhardt, D., 328
Lepsinger, R., 457
Leuser, D. M., C-2
Levine, R. V., 74
Levinson, H., 206
Levy, P. E., 88

Lewicki, F. J., 294
Lewicki, R. J., 250, 308, 318
Lewin, K., 558
Lewis, B., 298
Lewis, M., 38
Li, G., 583
Liang, K. Y., 583
Liden, R. C., 78
Lieber, R. B., 460
Lillrank, P., 569
Lin, R. Y., 20
Lind, E. A., 150
Linowes, R. G., 78
Lipman-Blumen, J., 243
Lipnack, J., 231, 232
Liu, J. H., 386
Liu, M., 569
Lobel, S. A., 10
Loch, K. D., 232, 502, 572
Locke, E. A., 51, 133, 164, 167, 168, 169, 186, 297
Loden, M., 13
Loftin, R. D., 568
Longenecker, C. O., 283, 284
Lopez, S., 120
Lord, R. G., 327
Love, M. S., 401
Lowman, R. L., 573
Lubin, J., 323, 530
Lublin, J. A., 205
Lubove, S., 229
Lucas, G. H., 197
Lucas, J. R., 358
Lucero, M. A., 149, 199
Lucia, A. D., 457
Lustig, M. W., 239
Luthans, B. C., 122
Luthans, F., 103, 104, 118, 121, 122, 169
Luthans, K. W., 122
Luz, J., 196
Lykken, D. T., 39
Lynch, S., 387
Lynd-Stevenson, R. M., 149
Lytle, A. L., 308

M

Maccoby, M., 298
MacDonald, E., 527
Machan, T. R., 422
Mack, M. H., 428
MacKenzie, S. B., 169, 369
MacMillan, I. C., 493
Macy, H., 159
Maddi, S. R., 38
Madison, D. L., 279
Maertz, C. P., 398
Mahway, N. J., 582
Main, J., 24, 544, 546
Mallory, G. R., 19
Mangel, R., 155
Manning, M. R., 193, 551
Mannix, E. A., 278
Manzoni, J. F., 87
March, S., 302
Marchetti, M., 164, 175
Mardesich, J., 488
Markels, A., 532, 570
Markis, H. R., 40
Marras, W. S., 450
Marschan, R., 19
Marshall, R. S., 386
Marten, J., 512
Martin, C. L., 154
Martin, J., 270, 284
Martinko, M. J., 102, 134, 136
Martocchio, J. J., 306
Maslyn, J. M., 277, 279
Mathieu, J. E., 46, 54
Matteson, M. T., 192, 211
Maule, N. J., 432
Maurer, R., 577
Maurer, T. J., 125
Mausner, B., 142
May, D., 594
Mayer, R., 308
Mayes, B. T., 279
McAfee, A., 572
McAllister, D. J., 250
McBain, R., 180
McBurney, D. H., 72
McCall, M. W., Jr., 430
McCarthy, D. J., 19, 143, 423
McCartney, S., 180
McCauley, C. D., 325
McClelland, D. C., 139, 140, 284
McCrae, R. R., 41
McCurdy, B., 344
McFadyen, R. G., 149
McGee, R. W., 422
McGee, V. E., 495
McGill, M. E., 177, 180, 182
McGrath, D., 531
McGrath, R. G., 493
McGue, M., 39
McGuigan, F. J., 193
McIntyre, M. G., 21
McKearnan, S., 307
McKersie, R. B., 308
McLagan, P., 6
Mclean, B., 545
McMahan, G. C., 561
McManus, K., 253
McMorris, F. A., 202
Medina, P. L., 60
Mehra, A., 226
Meindl, J. R., 150
Melamed, S., 196
Melcher, R. A., 525
Mendenhall, M., 43, 313
Merchant, C. S., 296
Merikle, P. M., 71
Merrill, G. B., 429
Metais, E., 497
Meyer, C., 25
Meyerson, D., 270, 284
Michalski, W. J., 228
Milbank, D., 198
Miles, R. E., 500, 572
Milkovich, G. T., 237
Miller, C. C., 73, 391
Miller, E. J., 450
Miller, J., 224
Miller, J. G., 40, 87
Miller, K. I., 88
Miller, R. A., 591
Miller, R. R., 285
Milliken, B., 71
Mindell, P., 401
Miner, J. B., 53, 54, 197
Minton, J. W., 294, 308, 318
Mintzberg, H., 9, 274
Mischel, W., 38
Mitra, K., 538
Mitroff, I. I., 56, 359, 442
Moesel, D., 126, 553
Mohrman, A. M., Jr., 21
Mohrman, A. S., 21
Moingeon, B., 497, 508
Mollander, E. A., 17
Mone, M. A., 104
Money, A., 585
Montebello, A. R., 233
Montuori, A., 81
Moore, C. W., 314
Moore, D. A., 433
Moorman, R. H., 153
Moosbrucker, J. B., 568
Moran, L., 450
Moran, R. T., 18
Morgan, G., 4
Morris, W. C., 248
Morrison, A. J., 368, 490
Morrison, M. A., 15
Mortensen, C. D., 381
Moss, J. E., 16
Mossholder, K. W., 156
Mount, M. K., 38, 42
Mouton, J. S., 314
Mowday, R. T., 54
Moxley, R. S., 325
Muchinsky, P. M., 52, 53
Muczyk, J. P., 23
Mullen, B., 253
Munk, N., 23, 228
Munter, M., 385, 397
Murakin, R., 111
Murninghan, J. K., 14, 240
Murphey, K. R., 240

Murray, B., 181
Murray, H., 462
Murray, M., 570
Musen, G., 75
Musgrave, J., 381
Musson, G., 6
Myers, A. H., 583
Myers, D. G., 49, 84
Myers, R. M., 143

N

Nadler, D. A., 474
Napier, R. W., 225
Narum, B., 99
Naumov, A. I., 143
Neale, M. A., 266, 267, 270, 277, 278, 279, 302, 429, 518
Near, D., 285
Near, J. P., 530
Nelson, D. L., 211
Nelson, E., 530, 548
Nelson, R. B., 339
Neubert, M. J., 38
Neufeld, R. W. J., 210
Neuman, G. A., 564
Newman, J. M., 237
Ngwenyama, O. K., 379
Nichols, M. P., 399
Nicholson, N., 546, 558, 560, 569
Niebel, B. W., 447
Niehoff, B. P., 153
Niehouse, O. I., 206
Northcraft, G. B., 302, 308, 314
Norton, E., 546
Norwood, D., 156, 180
Nowak, A., 386
Nur, Y. A., 361
Nutt, P. C., 428

O

O'Connor, B., 234
O'Connor, K. M., 313
O'Connor, M., 306
O'Donnell, C., 75
O'Harrow, R., Jr., 593
O'Leary-Kelly A. M., 169, 199, 299, 534
O'Neill, B. S., 104
O'Reilly, C. A., III, 403, 534
Obert, S. L., 232
Oddou, G., 43
Oldham, G. R., 454, 456, 457
Oliver, J. E., 200
Olofson, C., 436
Organ, D. W., 155
Ornstein, C., 125
Ornstein, S., 70
Orsburn, J. D., 450
Orton, J. D., 497
Osborn, A. F., 253
Ostapski, S. A., 200
Ostroff, C., 53
Otazo, K. L., 383
Ouellette, J. A., 555
Ozeki, C., 51, 143, 200

P

Pablo, A. L., 286
Padilla, C., 106
Palma-Rivas, N., 16
Palombo, R., 587
Parachin, V. M., 325
Park, P., 120
Parker, C. P., 279
Parker, S., 105, 446, 458
Parker-Pope, T., 473
Parks, C. D., 225
Parra, L. F., 51
Pascarella, P., 236
Pasewark, W. E., 344
Pasmore, W. A., 58, 126, 465, 506, 529, 544, 550, 553, 554, 562, 566, 568, 569, 570
Patterson, F., 512
Paul, A. M., 81
Paul, E. F., 422
Payne, D. K., 140
Pearlson, K., 232
Pearman, A. D., 432
Pearson, C. A., 463
Pedone, R., 153
Pelled, L. H., 302
Pendergast, M., 254
Pennenberg, A. L., 419
Penrod, S., 50
Peper, J., 473
Peracchio, L., 587
Pervin, L. A., 38, 39, 40, 41, 49, 72, 194
Peters, T., 546, 547
Peterson, K., 587
Peterson, M. F., 195, 197, 300
Petrock, F., 524
Petty, R. E., 49, 51
Petzinger, T., Jr., 460
Pfeffer, J., 266, 267, 277, 544
Pfeiffer, J. W., 60, 91, 210, 289, 368, 372, 429, 476, 577
Phalon, R., 387
Pham, C., 174
Phillips, J. M., 142, 534
Phillips, J. S., 87, 211
Picken, J. C., 176, 181
Piderit, S. K., 384
Pierce, H. R., 125
Pierce, J. L., 44, 554, 564
Pillutla, M. M., 398
Pinkley, R. L., 308, 314
Pittinsky, T. L., 81
Pitts, R. A., 165, 496
Plomin, R., 39
Ployhart, R. E., 387
Podsakoff, P. M., 169, 267, 271, 369
Pollock, T., 502
Polzer, J. T., 299, 300, 308, 518
Poole, M. S., 544
Pooley, E., 305
Popper, M., 360
Porras, J. I., 550
Porras, J. L., 550
Porter, L. W, 54, 279
Porter, M. E., 478
Posner, B. Z., 329
Powell, G. N., 11, 533
Powell, M., 177
Powell, W. W., 388
Prahalad, C. K., 474
Prescott, J. E., 477
Price, K. H., 243
Prien, K. O., 44
Pritzker, S. R., 86
Proctor, T., 437
Prokeach, S. E., 503
Pruitt, H. D., 448
Pucik, V., 554
Puffer, S. M., 19, 32, 143, 355, 357, 423
Purser, R., 81, 229
Pustay, M. W., 545, 546

Q

Quick, J. C., 211
Quick, J. D., 211
Quinn, R. E., 525, 544, 557
Quinn, R. P., 299

R

Rafaeli, A., 199
Ragins, B. R., 284
Rahe, R. H., 201
Rahim, M. A., 307, 316
Raiffa, H., 425, 426, 433
Raiford, R., 70
Ramamoorthy, N., 462
Ramanantsoa, B., 497
Ramsey, V. J., 10, 15
Randolph, W. A., 496
Rasheed, A., 477
Ratcliff, R. L., 238
Ratnesar, R., 526
Raven, B., 267
Ravlin, E. C., 78
Reagon, G., 372

Realo, A., 314
Reavis, D. J., C-24
Reber, R. A., 186
Reddy, W. B., 289
Reder, M. W., 424
Reich, R. B., 131
Reiss, M. C., 538
Remenyi, D., 585
Renn, R. W., 44
Renwick, P. A., 279
Revelle, W., 38
Richheld, F. F., 479
Ricks, D. A., 490
Rifkin, G., 351
Rigano, D., 6
Rigby, D. K., 544
Ringbeck, J., 451
Ritti, R. R., 94
Roach, J. M., 427
Roberson, L., 150
Roberts-Lallister, R., 7
Roberts, B. W., 38
Roberts, D., 406
Roberts, D. R., 550
Roberts, K., 143
Roberts, M., 214
Robertson, P. J., 550
Robey, D., 232, 502, 572
Robie, C., 51
Robinson, B., 211
Robinson, G., 325
Robinson, S. L., 534
Rodosevich, D. J., 169
Roethlisberger, F. J., 242
Rogers, D., 280
Rogovsky, N., 183
Roha, R. R., 451
Roitblat, H. L., 75
Rose, E., 228
Rose, R. J., 39
Rosen, R. H., 18, 227
Rosener, J., 13
Rosenfeld, H. M., 386
Rosenfeld, T., 70
Rosenman, R., 209
Rosenthal, R. A., 299
Rosenzweig, P., 10
Ross, D. L., 173
Roth, D., 296
Roth, K., 490
Roth, P. L., 81
Rothbard, N. P., 384
Rothenbukler, E. W., 380
Routh, D., 141
Rowe, A., 15, 533
Rubinstein, D., 285
Rubinstein, M. F., 435
Ruderman, M. N., 14
Ruggles, R., 428
Rumelt, R., 497
Runco, M. A., 86
Rush, J. C., 6
Rush, M. C., 155
Russ, G. S., 379
Russo, J. E., 428
Ryan, A. M., 51, 387
Ryan, K., 155
Rymph, R. D., 150

S

Sackett, P. R., 38, 584
Sagie, A., 140
Saks, A. M., 536
Salacuse, J. W., 311
Salas, E., 235, 253
Salter, C., 170
Sanchez, J. I., 459
Sanders, R., 435
Sanders, W. G., 497
Sanderson, L. M., 583
Sankowsky, D., 284
Sanna, L. J., 225
Sapsford, R., 589
Sashkin, M., 248, 371
Saunders, D. M., 294, 308, 318
Sawyer, J. E., 435
Saxton, M. I., 515, 521
Scarborough, J., 21
Schaeffer, A., 297
Schau, C., 562
Schaubroeck, J., 194
Schaufeli, W. B., 154, 205
Schein, E. H., 512, 514, 515, 521, 564
Schein, J. H., 7
Schendel, D., 497
Schifrin, M., 172
Schiminke, M., 250
Schlacter, J. L., 149
Schlenker, B. R., 78
Schmidt, S. M., 277
Schmieder, R. A., 51
Schminke, M., 296
Schnake, M. E., 22
Schoemaker, P. J. H., 428
Schoenfeldt, L. F., 81
Schrage, M., 82
Schrieshiem, C. A., 267, 348
Schuler, R. S., 143, 179, 183, 519, 522, 523, 539
Schultz, H., 129
Schwab, D. P., 582, 583
Schwenk, C. R., 438
Schyns, P. G., 75
Scott, C. D., 568
Scully, J. A., 462
Scully, M., 499
Seglin, J. L., 158
Seibert, S. E., 42
Seiders, K., 166
Seiffert, A. E., 71
Seijts, G. H., 167
Sekular, R., 68
Seligman, S. D., 21
Selye, H., 193
Serpa, R., 515, 521
Shade, L. A. 387
Shalley, C. A., 178
Shamir, B., 360
Shani, A. B., 569, 570
Shapiro, D. L., 308
Shapiro, R., 310
Sharkey, T. W., 281
Shaw, J. B., 81
Shaw, J. D., 53
Shea, G. P., 227
Shellenbarger, S., 53, 55, 194, 197, 198, 207, 213, 522
Shepard, H. A., 314
Sherman, E., 265
Sherman, S. J., 76
Sherriton, J. C., 22
Sherwood, J. J., 565
Shih, M., 81
Shimp, T. A., 100
Shoda, Y., 38
Shore, L. M., 153
Shore, T. H., 153
Si, S. X., 481
Siegel, M., 515
Siehman, P., 547
Silvester, J., 512
Simon, H. A., 73, 302, 426, 427
Simons, J. A., 344
Simons, R., 433
Simons, T., 302
Sims, H. P.,283, 284, 452, 453, 455
Sims, R. L., 530
Sims, R. R., 245
Sitkin, S. B., 286
Sittenfeld, C., 466
Skaggs, B. C., 17, 242
Skarlicki, D. P., 382
Skinner, B. F., 102
Slaikeu, K. L., 313
Slocum, J. W., Jr., 47, 125, 133, 143, 148, 149, 169, 171, 182, 452, 453, 486, 495, 496, 523, 525, 545, 572, 592, C-20
Smallwood, N., 368
Smiley, R., 336
Smith, A., 485
Smith, D. K., 563
Smith, E. A., 266
Smith, E. D., Jr., 174
Smith, G. S., 583
Smith, K. A., 302
Smith, K. G., 297
Smith, P. B., 78

Smith, P. C., 51, 52
Smith-Doer, L., 388
Snell, S. A., 143
Snoek, J. D., 299
Snow, C. C., 143, 500, 572
Snyder, M., 83
Snyder, T. N., 229
Snyderman, B. B., 142
Solomon, R. C., 16, 419, 421
Somerset, N. J., 432
Sommer, S. M., 122
Sorenson, G., 587
Sorenson, P. W., 303
Sorenson, R. L., 303
Sorrentino, R., 502
Sosik, J. J., 360-363
Sotile, M., 209
Sotile, W., 290
Spangler, W. D., 139
Spector, P. E., 285
Speer, B., 395
Spich, R. S., 242
Spreitzer, G. M., 104
Sprout, A. L., 482
Squire, L. R., 75
Srivastva, S., 41, 561, 562
Stajkovic, A. D., 103, 104, 118, 121, 122, 169
Stalker, G., 483
Stamps, J., 231, 232
Standifird, S. S., 386
Stangor, C., 77, 192, 209
Staw, B. M., 49, 76, 279, 534
Stead, B. A., 533
Steel, R. P., 23, 568
Steers, R. M., 54
Stein, B. A., 544
Stein, E., 587
Stein, J., 526
Steinberg, L., 310
Steiner, G. A., 238
Stephens, G. K., 144
Stern, J. L., 22
Stevens, C. K., 78
Stewart, G. L., 38
Stewart, T. A., 570
Steyrer, J., 361
Stiles, M., 440
Stoddard, A., 587
Stone, D. L., 81
Stratton, W. E., C-9, C-24
Straud, D., 232, 502, 572
Strawser, J. R., 344
Strebel, P., 554
Stroh, L. K., 143, 402
Stuart, E. W., 100
Stukas, A. A., 83
Stymne, B., 569
Subramanian, R., 165
Sullivan, D. P., 295
Summer, S., 104, C-20
Sundstrom, E., 284
Surowiecki, J., 458
Susman, G., 453
Susskind, L., 307
Sussman, L., 397
Sussman, N. M., 386
Sutton, R. I., 199
Swanson, D. L., 17, 422
Swap, W. C., 436
Swartz, E., 585
Syer, J., 226
Szilagyi, A. D., 455
Szulkin, R., 271

T

Taillieu, T., 566
Tanaka, J. N., 72
Tannen, D., 270
Taormina, R. J., 536
Tax, S. S., 166
Taylor, J. R., 6
Taylor, L., 387
Taylor, M. S., 42
Teece, D., 497
Tellegen, A., 39
Tenbrunsel, A. E., 433
Tennen, H., 88
Tesluk, P., 382
Tesser, A., 49
Thach, L., 546
Thacker, R. A., 277
Thomas, D. C., 78
Thomas, H., 502
Thomas, J., 149, C-6
Thomas, J. G., 462
Thomas, K. W., 227, 302, 316
Thomas-Larmer, J., 307
Thompson, J. D., 453, 480
Thompson, K. R., 569
Thompson, L., 150
Thompson, P., 225
Thomson, L., 293
Thoresen, C. J., 554
Tichy, N. M., 324
Tierney, P., 438
Tietjen, M. A., 143
Tinsley, C., 311
Tobin, D. R., 273
Toffer, B. L., 17, 419
Tolchinsky, P. D., 552
Tomer, J. F., 153
Townsend, A. M., 502, 547
Townsend, D. M., 231
Tracey, J. B., 363
Trahant, W., 544
Trevino, L. K., 17, 54, 58, 113, 419
Triandis, H. C., 19, 241
Trice, H. M., 361, 512, 520, 521, 564
Trist, E., 462
Trost, C., 211
Tsang, E. N., 21
Tubbs, M. E., 146
Tuckman, B. W., 232, 233
Turban, D. B., 7, 401
Turk, W., 395
Turkheimer, E., 39
Turniansky, B., 225
Turnley, W. H., 78
Tushman, M. L., 474
Tversky, A., 432
Tyler, L. S., 179
Tyler, T. R., 267
Tymon, W. G., Jr., 227

U

Uchino, B. N., 193
Ukumura, T., 313
Ulrich, D., 13, 368
Uno, D., 193
Upbin, B., 300
Upton, D. M., 572
Ury, W., 309
Useem, J., 388
Usunier, J., 22, 311

V

Vaill, P. B., 357
Van de Ven, A. H., 252, 544
van den Heuvel, H., 54
Van der Heyden, L., 274
Van Der Wall, S., 327
Van der Wielen, J. M., 460
Van deVen, A. H., 494
Van Dierendonck, D., 154, 205
Van Dyne, L., 156
Van Every, E. J., 6
Van Fleet, D. D., 22, 339
Van Gundy, A. B., 437
Van Maanen, J., 499
Van Norman, K. L., 149
VandeWalle, D., 47, 169, 171
Vansina, L. S., 566
Varma, A., 81
Varner, I., 387
Vele, C. A., 440
Velsor, V., 325
Vijayan, J., 323
Villanova, P., 144
Viswesvaran, C., 459
Vogt, J. F., 440
Volkema, R. J., 431
von Fersen, L., 75
Von Glinow, M. A., 174

von Hippel, W., 81
Voos, P. B., 180
Vrania, S., 120
Vroom, V. H., 146, 248, 339, 342, 343

W

Waclowski, J., 590
Wade, J. B., 403
Wageman, R., 278
Wagner, J. A., 183
Wahn, J., 154
Waldman, D. A., 359
Waldroop, J., 13
Walker, E. D., 254
Wall, T., 446
Waller, M. J., 73
Wallin, J. A., 186
Walls, J. A., Jr., 294
Walsh, J. P., 402
Walton, R. E., 308
Wang, E., 402
Warrick, D. D., 552
Washington, J. M., 361
Washington, R. L., 573
Watkins, M., 294
Waxler, C., 168
Wayne, S. J., 78, 277, 285
Weaver, G. R., 17, 419
Weber, C. E., 305
Weber, M., 483
Wegener, D. T., 49, 51
Weick, K. E., 435, 544
Weider-Hatfield, D., 304
Weigel, M., 451
Weigold, M. F., 78
Weiner, B., 72
Weisberg, H. F., 585
Weisenger, H., 6
Weiss, D. S., 313
Weiss, H. M., 49, 100
Weiss, N., 129
Welbourne, T. M., 179, 554
Welch, D., 19
Welch, L., 19
Wells, G., 84
Wells, G. R., C-9
Wells, J. T., 153
Wells, O., 250
Welsh, D. H. B., 122
Welsh, M., 519
Wempe, J., 172
Wentling, R. M., 16
Werhane, P., 16, 416
Werner, J. M., 121, 257, 422
West, J., 451
Westney, D. E., 499
Wetlaufer, S., 227, 301, 566, 567
Wheeler, M. L., 11, 13
Whetten, D. A, 400
White, J. B., 447, 570
White, T., 410
White, T. F., 19
Whiteley, R., 539
Whitener, F. M., 121, 422
Whitney, D., 562
Whyte, G., 245
Widmaier, E. P., 192
Wiesenfeld, B. M. 154
Wiker, S., 583
Wilke, J. R., 272
Williams, B., 585
Williams, G., 289
Williamson, G. M., 202
Willmott, H., 242
Wilson, D. S., 285
Wilson, K. D., 72
Wind, J. Y., 24, 544, 546
Winer, B., 137
Wiredu, V., 119
Witt, L. A., 281
Wolfe, D. M., 299
Wolfe, E., 74
Wood, J. T., 6
Wood, R., 4
Wood, W., 555
Woodman, R. W., 58, 81, 126, 149, 197, 252, 285, 435, 529, 544, 546, 549, 550, 551, 552, 553, 554, 559, 560, 561, 562, 565, 566, 568, 569, 570
Worley, C. G., 218, 513, 549, 559, 562, 572, 578
Worton, B., 15
Woyke, J., 139
Wright, B. M., 448
Wright, D., 592
Wright, J. A., 564
Wright, M., 165
Wright, P. M., 169
Wright, T. A., 205
Wyburd, G., 419

X

Xie, J. L., 203
Xin, K. R., 402

Y

Yamauchi, H., 140
Yammarino, F. J., 330, 359, 360
Yankelovich, D., 6
Yost, E. B., 91
Youngblood, S. A., 54
Yukl, G., 277, 339

Z

Zaheer, S., 490
Zahra, S. A., 497
Zajac, D. M., 46, 54
Zakay, E., 360
Zaleznik, A., 388
Zamora, A., 459
Zand, D. E., 558, 570
Zbaracki, M. J., 569
Zeira, Y., 553
Zellner, W., 362
Zemke, R., 561
Zenger, J., 368
Zheng, L., 386
Zhou, J., 279
Zhuplev, A. V., 19
Zigarmi, D., 339
Zmud, R. W., 379
Zunitch, V. M., 369

Subject and Organizational Index

A

ARCO Alaska, 247
Abaco Grupo Financiero, 388
Ability, 132
Accommodating style, 306
Acculturation, 532
Achievement motivation model
  defined, 139
  financial incentives, 141
  high achiever profile, 140
  practices, 142
  Thematic Apperception Test, 139
  U.S. Presidents, 139
AC-Nielsen, 53
Active listening, 8
Adjustment, 41
Aetna, 15
Affective conflict, 294
Affiliation needs, 135
Affirmative action programs, 176
Africa, 273
Agreeableness, 41
Alamco, 177
Alteon WebSystems, 436
Amazon.com, 166
American Airlines, 489
American Express, 395
Amoral management, 56
Amway, 111
Analogy technique, 437
Andersen Consulting, 486
Andersen Worldwide, 526
Antecedent, 106
Approach–approach conflict, 298
Approach–avoidance conflict, 298
Aramark, 133, 506, 526
Argus Technical Services, 394
Assertive communication, 396
Associates First Capital, 176, 518
AT&T, 115, 214
Attitudes
  affective component, 49
  behavior, 50
  behavior component, 49
  behavioral intentions model, 50
  cognitive component, 49
  cognitive moral development, 54
  conflict, 295
  defined, 49
  ethics, 54-58
  job satisfaction, 51
  groupthink, 244
  negotiation, 309
  norms, 50
  organizational commitment, 54
  women, 15
  work attitudes, 51–54
Attitudinal structuring, 309
Attribution model of leadership
  defined, 356
  dimensions, 357–358
  international managers, 358
  significance, 357
  see Leadership
Attribution process
  antecedents, 85
  components, 85
  consensus, 86
  consequences, 85
  consistency, 86
  defined, 84
  distinctiveness, 86
  external attributions, 86
  failure attributions, 88
  fundamental attribution error, 87
  internal attributions, 86
  job dismissal, 89
  Kelley's theory of causal attributions, 86
  self-serving bias, 88
  success attributions, 88
  employees, 357
  leadership, 356
  performance, 357
Authoritarianism, 48
Authority, 267
AutoNation, 176
Autonomy, 457
Availability bias, 432
Avoidance-avoidance conflict, 298
Avoidance learning, 111
Avoiding style, 303
Aversive events, 107

B

Bally's, 117
Baxter Pharmaceutical, 149
Behavioral intentions model, 50
Behavioral model of leadership, 330
Behavioral modification
  charting, 119
  defined, 118
  ethical considerations, 122
  ethics, 122
  group norms, 121
  model, 118
  Russia, 122
Ben & Jerry's, 423
Benteler Automotive, 451
"Big Five" personality factors
  defined, 41
  measure of, 60–62
Black & Decker, 479
Blacks
  informal groups, 226
  Ward, Lloyd, 327
  see Diversity
Blank, Arthur, 89
Blur, 24
Boeing, 496
Bounded rationality model
  defined, 426
  dictionary rule, 428
  information, 427
  knowledge management, 428
  satisficing, 426
  Simon, Herbert, 427
Bristol-Myers Squibb, 174
British Petroleum, 391, 480, 502
Bureaucracy, 484
Bureaucratic culture, 524

C

Cafeteria-style benefit plans, 156
Calico Technologies, 365
Callaway Golf, 487
Calvert Inc., 108
Career, 7
Career development, 8, 198
Career management
  career, 7
  dimensions, 7
  glass ceiling, 15
Carmike Cinemas, 475
Celanese Chemical, 72, 130
Cendant Corporation, 530
Centralization, 485
Chain of Command, 486
Change
  see Managing change competency
  see Organizational change
Channels, 381
Charismatic leadership model
  broad concept, 359
  defined, 359
  dimensions, 360
  Kelleher, Herb, 362
  King, Martin Luther, 361
  restricted concept, 361
  significance, 361
Charting, 119

Chase Manhattan Bank, 519
Chili's restaurants, 105
China, 286, 313
Chinese culture, 21
Chromatics, 402
Chroenemics, 402
Chrysler, 289
Cisco Systems, 484, 487
Citicorp, 58
Clan culture, 525
Classical conditioning
 defined, 100
 figure, 101
 reflexive behavior, 101
Closure, 75
Code of ethics, 172, 420
Coercive power, 268
Cognitive conflict, 294
Cognitive dissonance, 298
Cognitive moral development, 54
Cohesiveness, 243
Colgate-Palmolive, 477
Collaborating style, 306
Collectivism, 20
Columbia Medical Center of Plano, 109
Commercial on-line services, 393
Communication
 Berdish, David, 454
 feedback, 177, 461
 job feedback, 457
 network analysis, 274
 performance appraisal, 177
 social information processing model, 462
 see Interpersonal communication
 see Managing communication competency,
Compensation, 153
Competencies
 individual differences, 457
 job design, 457
 managerial roles, 9
Competency, 4
Complexity, 475
Compliance conformity, 243
Compromising style, 307
Comp USA, 32
Computex Corp., 43
Conceptualization, 23
Confirmation bias, 432
Conflict
 accommodating style, 306
 affective conflict, 294
 Anderson Worldwide, 527
 approach–approach conflict, 298
 approach–avoidance conflict, 298
 attitudes, 295
 avoidance–avoidance conflict, 298
 avoidance styles, 303
 cognitive conflict, 294
 cognitive dissonance, 298
 collaborating style, 306
 compromising style, 307
 conflict styles questionnaire, 316
 culture, 311
 defined, 294
 dimensions of, 297
 diversity, 303
 family business, 300
 forcing style, 304
 goal conflict, 294
 goal incompatibility, 294
 horizontal conflict, 302
 intergroup conflict, 301
 interorganizational, 517
 interpersonal conflict, 299
 interrole conflict, 300
 intersender role conflict, 299
 intragroup conflict, 300
 intrapersonal conflict, 297
 intrasender role conflict, 299
 levels of, 297
 line-staff conflict, 302
 mediation, 313
 negotiation, 308–314
 neurotic tendencies, 298
 organizational culture, 517
 person-role conflict, 300
 procedural conflict, 295
 punishment, 112
 role ambiguity, 300
 vertical conflict, 302
 work-life balance, 303
 workplace violence, 199, 299
Conflict management
 defined, 297
 negotiation, 308–314
 stress, 196
 see Conflict
Connectivity, 24
Conscientiousness, 41
Consequence, 106
Consideration, 330
Consolidated Diesel, 466
Consult individually style, 341
Consult team style, 341
Content models of motivation
 achievement motivation model, 139–142
 compared, 145
 ERG model, 136–139
 motivator-hygiene model, 142–145
 needs hierarchy, 134–136
Context, 236
Contextual factors, 458
Continental Airlines, 355
Contingencies of reinforcement
 defined, 106
 guidelines, 115
 model, 107
 negative reinforcement, 111
 omission, 112
 positive reinforcement, 107–111
 punishment, 112–115
Continuity, 75
Continuous reinforcement, 116
Coolidge, Calvin, 57
Corning, Inc., 500
Creativity
 cross-fertilization technique, 438
 cultural blocks, 436
 de Bono, Edward, 437
 devil's advocate method, 438
 electronic brainstorming, 253
 emotional blocks, 436
 intellectual openness, 41
 lateral thinking method, 436
 nominal group technique, 525
 organizational creativity, 435
 organizational innovation, 435
 perceptual blocks, 436
 reversal technique, 437
 teams, 252
 traditional brainstorming, 253
 Ventana Corp., 254
 vertical thinking method, 436
Cross-fertilization technique, 438
Cross-functional teams, 233, 229
Cultural context, 385
Cultural symbols, 513
Cultural values, 512
Culture
 attributions, 358
 China, 20
 Chinese negotiation, 313
 chroenemics, 402
 chromatics, 402
 communication style, 312
 defined, 18
 ethnocentrism, 387
 expats, 511
 France, 429
 high-context culture, 385
 Hungary, 111
 intercultural communication, 385
 Japanese, 18
 job design, 462
 low-context culture, 386
 Malaysia, 463
 monchronic time schedule, 402
 motivation, 143
 negotiating attitude, 312
 negotiation, 311
 nonverbal communication, 402
 perception, 73
 personality, 40
 polychronic time schedule, 403

rewards, 183
risk preferences, 286
Sweden, 517
United States, 517
values, 19
Western culture, 20
see Managing across cultures competency
Custom Research, Inc., 223
Customers
goals, 166
job design, 460
satisfaction, 53
Customer service, 166

D

Daimler-Chrysler, 511
Dallas Police Department, 513
Data, 380
Deciding style, 341
Decision making
action planning, 249
Alteon WebSystems, 436
analogy technique, 437
availability bias, 432
bounded rationality model, 425
Butler, Stephen, 418
choice stage, 434
cognitive conflict, 294
cognitive dissonance, 298
confirmation bias, 432
consequences stage, 435
convoluted-action, 434
cross-fertilization technique, 438
devil's advocate method, 438
dictionary rule, 428
disclosure principle, 420
escalating commitment, 435
ethical foundations, 416–424
ethical intensity, 416
ethics, 416
evaluation learning, 249
expectancy model, 146
expert system, 343
focus stage, 433
Ford Motor Co., 7, 251
Franklin, Benjamin, 425
goal conflict, 294
golden rule principle, 420
groupthink, 244
hedonist principle, 419
idea evaluation, 249
idea generation, 248
interpretation stage, 431
knowledge, 428
knowledge management, 428
lateral thinking method, 436
law of small numbers bias, 433
magnitude of consequences, 416
Matthews, Cassandra, 415
means-end principle, 419
might-equals-right principle, 419
organizational creativity, 435
organization interests principle, 419
political model, 428
power, 273
probability of effect, 416
problem definition, 248
problem framing, 432
professional standards principle, 419
project teams, 415
proximity, 417
rational model, 424
recognition stage, 430
Renaissance, Inc., 429
reversal technique, 437
risk, 7
risk propensity, 432
risk-seeking propensity, 285
risk taking, 23
satisficing, 426
selective perception bias, 433
self-managing teams, 248–251
social consensus, 417
structured problems, 430
task uncertainty, 452
temporal immediacy, 417
trade-offs, 425
uncertainty, 494
unstructured problems, 431
utilitarian principle, 410, 422
values, 421
vertical thinking method, 436
Vroom-Jago Leadership Model, 339
workflow uncertainty, 452
Decision making as power, 273
Deficiency needs, 136
Delegate style, 341
Depersonalization, 205
Describing skill, 8
Devil's advocate method, 438
Dictionary rule, 428
Dialogue
communication openness, 396–398
constructive feedback, 398
contextual factors, 397
defined, 396
listening, 399
meta-communication, 397
self-disclosure, 399
Diet industry, 120
Differentiation, 494
Differentiation strategy, 479
Disclosure principle, 420
Disney, 534
Disseminator role, 9
Distortion, 383
Distributive justice principle, 420
Distributive negotiations, 308
Diversity
acculturation, 532
age, 16
attitudes, 31
barriers, 433
Benteler Automotive, 451
bilingual employees, 276
boundaryless behavior, 13
customers, 14
diversity questionnaire, 533
ethnicity, 15
gender, 14
gender conflicts, 303
gender differences, 403
goal setting, 176
Marriott Marquis, 532
motivation, 131
organizational culture, 531
power, 276
primary categories, 12
questionnaire, 31
race, 15
secondary categories, 12
sexual harassment, 199
stereotyping, 81
U.S. Civil Rights Act, 420
Ward, Lloyd, 328
workforce, 14
see Managing diversity competency
Diversity Questionnaire, 533
Division of labor, 485
Dogmatism, 47
Dolby Laboratories, 450
DuPont, 531
Dynamism, 476

E

Eastman Chemical, 501
Eastman Kodak, 232
Eaton Corp., 335
EDS, 155, 398
Effectiveness
conflict styles, 307
groupthink, 244
groups, 225
leadership, 345
productivity, 245
teams, 236
Texas Nameplate Co., 445
Electrolux, 498
Electronic mail (e-mail), 393
Emotional intelligence, 62
Empowerment, 104, 457
England, 74

Entrepreneurial culture, 525
Environment
  agility, 465
  complexity, 475
  defined, 475
  dynamism, 476
  organizational behavior, 25
Equity model of motivation
  defined, 150
  general model, 150–152
  inequity, 152
  inputs, 150
  organizational citizenship, 155
  outcomes, 150
  procedural justice, 153
Equity theory of motivation, 155
ERG model
  defined, 137
  existence needs, 136
  fulfillment–progression process, 137
  growth needs, 136
  relatedness needs, 136
Ergonomics, 450
Ernst & Young, 156
Escalating commitment, 435
Escape learning, 111
Esteem needs, 135
Ethical behavior, 54–58, 529
Ethical dilemmas, 17
Ethical intensity, 416
Ethics
  affirmative action programs, 176
  amoral management, 56
  assessment questionnaire, 421
  attitudes, 57
  behavioral modification, 122
  Ben & Jerry's, 423
  Cendant Corp., 530
  Citicorp, 58
  code of ethics, 172, 420
  cognitive moral development, 54
  cultural diversity, 531
  cultural impact, 530
  cultural influences, 423
  decision making, 421
  defined, 416
  disclosure principle, 420
  discrimination, 384
  distortion, 383
  distributive justice principle, 420
  diversity, 433
  employment at will, 421
  equity model, 150
  ethical intensity, 416
  ethical intensity questionnaire, 417
  forcing style, 305
  golden rule principle, 420
  hedonist principle, 419
  honesty, 383, 436
  immoral management, 56
  impression management, 384
  inequity, 152
  Internet, 419
  KPMG, 418
  living ethics, 440
  lying, 383
  magnitude of consequences, 416
  McCulloch Corp., 56
  means-end principle, 419
  might-equals-right principle, 419
  moral management, 56
  Nestlé, 56
  Northeast Utilities, 305
  organizational citizenship behavior, 155
  organizational culture, 529
  organization interests principle, 419
  probability of effect, 416
  procedural justice, 153
  professional standards principle, 419
  profits, 423
  proximity, 417
  principled organizational dissent, 530
  privacy, 419
  rights, 422
  Russia, 423
  social consensus, 417
  temporal immediacy, 417
  Texaco, 384
  theft, 154
  United States, 423
  U.S. Civil Rights Act, 420
  U.S. Equal Pay Act, 420
  utilitarian principle, 419, 422
  values, 336, 421
  whistle-blowing, 172, 305, 530
Ethics competency
  see Managing ethics competency
Ethnocentrism, 387
Exchange process, 278
Existence needs, 136
Expats, 511
Expectancy, 147
Expectancy effects, 83
Expectancy model
  defined, 146
  diagram, 148
  expectancy, 147
  first-level outcomes, 146
  practice, 149
  instrumentality, 147
  research, 148
  second-level outcomes, 146
  valence, 147
Expert power, 270
Explicit knowledge, 428
External adaptation and survival, 514
External locus of control, 44
Extrinsic factors, 142
Extroversion, 47

F

Facilitate style, 341
Federal National Mortgage Assoc., 16
FedEx, 367, 478, 489
Feedback
  constructive, 398
  goal setting, 171
  interpersonal, 381
  performance appraisal, 177
Fel-Pro, 525
Feng shui, 72
Field dependence/independence, 72
Fight-or-flight response, 192
First-level outcomes, 146
Fixed internal schedule, 116
Fixed ratio schedule, 117
Fiedler's contingency model, 333–336
Fleet Financial Group, 179
Flexible benefit plans, 180
Flextime, 459
Focused strategy, 479
Follower readiness, 337
Followers, 326
Forcing style, 304
Ford Motor Co., 7, 251, 502
Four Seasons Hotels, 519
Free rider, 22
Friendship group, 224
Frigitemp Corp., 56
Frito-Lay, 383, 502, 526
Fruit of the Loom, 166
Fundamental attribution error, 87
Functional design, 487
Functional teams, 228

G

Gain-sharing plans, 179
Gateway Computers, 383
General Electric, 13, 181, 469
General Motors, 398
General theory of behavior, 38
Glass ceiling, 15
Global mindset, 19
Goal, 133
Goal commitment, 169
Goal commitment questionnaire, 171
Goal conflict, 294
Goal incompatibility, 294
Goal orientation, 45–47
Goal setting
  affirmative action programs, 176
  challenge, 168
  concept, 175
  customer service goals, 166
  defined, 164
  diversity programs, 176
  Fruit of the Loom, 167

gain-sharing plans, 179
goal clarity, 168
goal commitment, 169
goal commitment questionnaire, 171
goal difficulty, 168
IBM, 164
importance, 164
management by objectives, 174–178
Marriott Hotels, 163
mediators, 171
model, 168
moderators, 169
NASCAR, 169
performance, 172
questionnaire, 185
rewards, 172–174
satisfaction, 174
stakeholders, 165
Texas Industries, 168
Goals
academic goal orientation, 46
achievement motivation, 140
customer service, 166
ethics, 172
job design, 446
learning goal orientation, 45
Marshall Industries, 175
motivation, 133
NASCAR, 170
norms, 242
performance, 172
rewards, 172
superordinate goals, 237
team goals, 237
Godiva Chocolates, 387
Golden rule principle, 420
Collectivism, 20
Great North American, 99
Greece, 38
Group, 224, 287
Group atmosphere, 334
Groups
clan culture, 525
collectivism, 22
compliance conformity, 243
defined, 224
effective, 225
enforcement, 242
free rider, 22
friendship group, 224
informal group, 224
importance of, 22
intragroup conflict, 300
personal acceptance conformity, 243
personality, 40
norms, 50, 235, 242
social system, 463
socialization outcomes, 535
socialization process, 534
stress, 193
task group, 224
types, 224
see teams, 22
Groupthink, 244
Growth-need strength, 457
Growth & Leadership Center, 301
Growth needs, 136
Gulf & Western, 526

H

Hallmark Cards, 181
Halo effect, 83
Hardiness, 209
Harley-Davidson, 519, 521
Harrah's, 117
Harris Methodist Health Plan, 125
Health, 202
Hedonist principle, 419
Heidrick & Struggles, 53
Heredity, 39
Hersey and Blanchard's Situational Model, 336
Hewlett-Packard, 3, 48, 323, 578
Hierarchy of authority, 484
High-context culture, 385
High performance–high commitment work culture, 529
High-performance work system, 178
Highsmith, Inc., 391
Hispanics
see Diversity
Hoechst Celanese Chemical Co., 490
Home Depot, 89
Honeywell, 181
Horizontal conflict, 302
Horizontal integration, 494
Hot group, 243
Hungary, 111
Hygiene factors, 142

I

IBM, 164, 241, 395
Idealized influence, 366
Immoral management, 56
Impersonality, 486
Implicit personality theories, 77
Impression construction, 78
Impression management, 78, 384
Impression motivation, 78
India, 87
Individual differences
defined, 38, 68
ethical behavior, 54–56
intrapersonal conflict, 297, 300
stress, 194
Individualized consideration, 366
Individualism, 20
Indonesia, 74
Inequity, 152
Informal group, 224
Informal leader, 245
Information technologies
electronic mail (e-mail), 393
Internet, 398
résumés, 394
telecommuting, 395
virtual organization, 502
voice mail, 395
World Wide Web, 393
Initiating structure, 330
Inspirational motivation, 364
Instrumentality, 147
Intangibles, 24
Integration, 493
Integrative negotiations, 308
Intel, 174, 232
Intellectual capital, 272
Intellectual openness, 41
Intellectual stimulation, 365
Interactionist perspective, 49
Internal locus of control, 44
Internal integration, 514
Internet, 9, 393, 419
Intergroup conflict, 301
see Conflict
Intergroup dialogue technique, 314
Intermittent reinforcement, 116
International management
attributions, 358
Ben & Jerry's, 423
expats, 511
job design, 463
multinational organizations, 497
Russia, 423
see Managing across cultures competency
Interpersonal communication
assertive communication, 396
body language, 386
channels, 381
chromatics, 402
chronemics, 402
communication openness, 396
cultural challenges, 385
cultural context, 385
data, 380
decoding, 381
defined, 378
dialogue, 396–401
distortion, 383
encoding, 381
ethnocentrism, 387
eye contact, 404
feedback, 381, 397
gender differences, 403

hand gestures, 382
high-context cultures, 385
honesty, 383
impression management, 384
information technologies, 393–396
intercultural, 358
interpersonal challenges, 381–385
interpersonal networks, 388–393
language routines, 383
listening, 399
low-context culture, 386
lying, 383
media richness, 379
messages, 380
meta-communication, 397
model, 379
noise, 383
nonverbal communication, 401–404
personal space, 386
receptors, 379
self-awareness questionnaire, 400
self-assessment questionnaire, 406–408
self-disclosure, 399
semantics, 383
sender and receiver, 378
status differences, 403
touching, 404
transmitters, 379
trust, 397
Interpersonal communication networks
defined, 388
effect of, 389
importance, 390–393
types of, 388
Interpersonal conflict, 299
Interrole conflict, 300
Intersender role conflict, 299
Intragroup conflict, 300
Intranet, 393
Intraorganizational negotiations, 310
Intrapersonal conflict, 297, 299
Intrasender role conflict, 299
Intrinsic factors, 142
Introversion, 47
Italy, 74

J

Japan, 73, 74, 78
Japanese culture, 18
Jenny Craig Diet Centers, 120
Jiffy Lube, 485
Job burnout
defined, 205
see Stress
Job characteristics enrichment model
autonomy, 457
contextual factors, 458
culture, 463
customers, 460
defined, 454
feedback, 461
growth-need strength, 458
individual differences, 457
job diagnosis, 458
job diagnostic survey, 459
job feedback, 457
Malaysia, 463
motivating potential score, 459
skill variety, 456
social information processing model, 462
structural clues method, 458
task identity, 456
task significance, 457
teams, 460
technology, 461
vertical loading, 459
Job characteristics inventory, 455
Job Descriptive Index (JDI), 51
Job Design
aircraft-engine assembly, 469
autonomy, 457
comparative framework, 447
complexity, 446
Consolidated Diesel Co., 466
contextual factors, 458
culture, 463
customers, 460
defined, 446
Dolby Laboratories, 450
environment, 465
ergonomics, 450
feedback, 461
flextime, 459
General Electric, 469
growth-need strength, 457
impact, 446
individual differences, 457
job characteristics enrichment model, 454
job characteristics inventory, 455
job diagnosis, 458, 459
job engineering, 447
job enlargement, 448
job enrichment, 450
job feedback, 457
job rotation, 447
moderators, 465
motivating potential score, 459
pooled interdependence, 453
reciprocal interdependence, 453
rewards, 110
self-managed teams, 229
self-managing teams, 469
sequential interdependence, 453
skill variety, 456
social information processing model, 462
social system, 463
sociotechnical systems model, 450
structural clues method, 458
task complexity, 171
task identity, 456
task interdependence, 453
task significance, 457
task uncertainty, 452
Taylor, Frederick, 447
teams, 227, 460
technological systems, 464
technology, 450, 461
Texas Nameplate Co., 445
vertical loading, 459
Visteon Automotive Systems, 454
Westinghouse Air Brake Co., 449
workflow uncertainty, 452
Job diagnostic survey, 459
Job engineering, 447
Job enlargement, 448
Job enrichment, 450
Job feedback, 457
JoAnn Stores, 172
Johnson & Johnson, 182, 492
Job rotation, 447
Job satisfaction
behavior, 52
defined, 51
sources, 51

K

Kaizen, 110
Karsten Manufacturing, 480
Kendall Healthcare, 490
Kelley, Harold, 86
Kendall-Futuro, Inc., 236
Kmart, 398
Knowledge, 428
Knowledge as power, 272
Knowledge management
defined, 428
explicit knowledge, 428
Renaissance, Inc., 429
tacit knowledge, 428
Knowledge workers, 272
KPMG, 418
Kraft Foods, 477
KTNT Communications, 57

L

Law of small numbers bias, 433
Lateral thinking method, 436
Language routines, 383
Leader, 324

Leadership
- Aetna, 15
- attribution model of leadership, 356
- behavioral model of leadership, 330
- Bethune, Gordon, 355
- Branson, Richard, 350
- charismatic leadership model, 359–361
- communication behaviors questionnaire, 372
- coercive power, 327
- consideration, 330
- consult individually style, 341
- consult team style, 341
- contingencies, 331
- contingent rewards, 359
- contingency variables, 337, 341, 345
- Crownover, Dale, 445
- Danaher, Cynthia, 3
- deciding style, 341
- defined, 324
- delegate style, 341
- employee attributions, 357
- expert power, 327
- expert system, 343
- facilitate style, 341
- Fiedler's contingency model, 333
- Fiorina, Carly, 323
- follower readiness, 337
- followers, 326
- group atmosphere, 334
- Growth & Leadership Center, 301
- Haas, Robert, 22
- Hersey & Blanchard's Situational Model, 336
- Holland, Jean, 301
- idealized influence, 366
- individualized consideration, 366
- informal leader, 245
- initiating structure, 330
- inspirational motivation, 364
- intellectual stimulation, 365
- irrelevance, 368
- Job, Peter, 358
- Kelleher, Herb, 520
- King, Martin Luther, 361
- leadership questionnaire, 348
- leadership substitute, 369
- Leary, Karen, 377
- least preferred coworker (LPC), 334
- legitimate power, 326
- Lyons, Jim, 466
- Mackey, John, 230
- management by exception, 359
- McCoy, Joan, 247
- McCurdy, Brooke, 344
- McKenna, Douglas, 332
- nature of, 325
- Naumann, Alan, 365
- participating style, 338
- Piëch, Ferdinand, 340
- position power, 334
- power, 326
- referent power, 327
- relationship behavior, 337
- reward power, 326
- Roth, Michael, 17
- Schnatter, John, 141
- Schultz, Howard, 130
- selling style, 338
- Sims, Paula, 469
- substitutes, 369
- task behavior, 337
- task structure, 334
- teams, 245
- telling style, 337
- time, 343
- traits model of leadership, 329
- transactional leadership model, 359, 362–368
- transformational leadership questionnaire, 371
- Tucker, Laurie, 367
- vision, 324, 364
- Vroom-Jago Leadership Model, 339
- Ward, Lloyd, 328
- Welch, Jack, 13, 23

Leadership substitute, 369

Learning
- aversive events, 107
- avoidance learning, 111
- behavioral modification, 118
- challenge course, 106
- change, 109
- charting, 119
- classical conditioning, 100
- consequence, 106
- contingency of reinforcement, 106, 115, 116
- decision making, 249
- defined, 100
- escape learning, 111
- fixed interval schedule, 116
- fixed ratio schedule, 117
- framework, 25
- goals, 169
- individual differences, 121
- intermittent reinforcement, 116
- interval schedule, 116
- learning goal orientation, 45
- negative reinforcement, 111
- omission, 112
- operant conditioning, 102
- Pavlov, Ian, 101
- perceptual set, 72
- positive events, 107
- primary reinforcer, 108
- principle of contingent reinforcement, 108
- principle of immediate reinforcement, 109
- principle of reinforcement size, 109
- punishment, 112
- ratio schedule, 116
- reflexive behavior, 100
- reinforcement, 107
- reward, 107, 110
- secondary reinforcer, 108
- self-control theory, 103
- self-efficacy, 104
- social cognitive theory, 102
- teams, 104
- variable interval schedule, 116
- variable ratio schedule, 117
- vicarious learning, 103

Learning goal orientation, 45

Learning and reinforcement
- behavioral modification, 118–123
- classical conditioning, 100–102
- contingencies of reinforcement, 106–116
- operant conditioning, 102
- schedules of reinforcement, 116
- social cognitive theory, 102–106

Least preferred coworker (LPC), 334
Legitimate power, 269
Lever Brothers, 447
Levi Strauss, 22, 234
Lexus, 166, 479
Liaison role, 9
Life stressors, 201
Lincoln Electric, 518
Line-staff conflict, 302
Listening, 399
L.L. Bean, 214
Lockheed Martin, 136, 393, 496
Locus of control, 44, 285
Low-context culture, 386
Low-cost strategy, 479
Lucent Technologies, 76
Lying, 383

M

Machiavellians, 284
Maddi, Salvatore, 38
Magnitude of consequences, 416
Malaysia, 463
Management by exception, 359

Management by objectives
- defined, 174
- implementation, 177
- model, 175
- performance appraisal, 177

Management ethics, 56
Managerial effectiveness, 5
Managerial roles, 9

Managing across cultures competency
- Africa, 273
- Amway, 111
- Ben & Jerry's, 423
- China, 20
- Chinese culture, 286
- collectivism, 20
- components, 18
- Computex Corp., 43
- culture, 18
- DaimlerChrysler, 511
- defined, 5
- democracy, 273
- Electrolux, 499
- ethics, 423
- global mindset, 19
- Hungary, 111
- individualism, 20, 22
- international managers, 358
- Japanese culture, 18
- job design, 463
- Malaysia, 463
- Mexico, 195
- motivation, 138
- personality, 43
- Pharmacia &Upjohn, 517
- Piëch, Ferdinand, 340
- reward practices, 183
- risk preferences, 286
- Russia, 423
- teams, 22
- time perception, 74
- values, 19
- virtual teams, 232
- Volkswagen AG, 340
- western cultures, 20
- work stress, 195

Managing change competency
- blur, 24
- Chrysler, 289
- Cisco Systems, Inc., 488
- Columbia Medical Center, 109
- components, 6, 23
- conceptualization, 23
- conflict management, 296
- connectivity, 24
- data entry operators, 468
- defined, 5
- Ford Motor, 7
- Godiva Chocolates, 387
- Harley-Davidson, 522
- innovation, 280
- intangibles, 24
- learning organization, 522
- McCurdy, Brooke, 344
- middle managers, 268
- Monsanto, 360
- Motorola, 296
- opportunities, 440
- persuasion, 289
- politics, 280
- power, 268
- reinforcement, 109
- risk taking, 23
- safety, 186
- Santin Engineering, 25
- speed, 24
- Shapiro, Robert, 360
- stress management, 197
- technological forces, 24
- transformational leadership questionnaire, 371
- Welch, Jack, 23
- Westinghouse Air Brake Co., 449

Managing communication competency
- active listening, 8
- Alteon WebSystems, 436
- behavioral modification, 122
- Branson, Richard, 350
- brainstorming, 253
- Brooks, Paul, 429
- communication behaviors questionnaire, 372
- components, 8
- Comp USA, 32
- customer goals, 167
- customer satisfaction, 53
- defined, 4
- describing skill, 8
- disseminator role, 9
- diversity, 532
- emotion, 10
- FedEx, 254
- Fruit of the Loom, 167
- honesty, 436
- Internet, 9
- job burnout, 207
- job satisfaction, 53
- Johnson & Johnson, 492
- Kelleher, Herb, 362
- liaison role, 9
- managerial roles, 9
- Marriott Marquis, 532
- McKanna, Douglas, 332
- monitor role, 9
- motivation, 151
- questioning skill, 8
- nonverbal communication, 9
- office design, 70
- Renaissance, Inc., 429
- Southwest Airlines, 362
- spokesperson role, 10
- Texas Nameplate Co., 445
- Trinity Communications, 70
- Turney, Margaret, 482
- U.S. West, 482
- verbal communication, 9
- Visteon Automotive Systems, 453
- Walt Disney Co., 151
- written communication, 9

Managing diversity competency
- Aetna, 15
- age, 16
- attitudes, 31
- Benteler Automotive Corp., 450
- bilingual employees, 276
- blacks, 226
- boundaryless behavior, 13
- components, 11
- conflict management 303
- Danaher, Cynthia, 4
- diversity questionnaire, 31
- defined, 4
- ethnicity, 15
- Federal National Mortgage Association, 16
- gender, 14
- gender issues, 303
- General Electric, 13
- glass ceiling, 15
- IBM, 241
- informal groups, 226
- motivation, 131
- National Multicultural Institute, 11
- power, 276
- practices, 433
- racism, 15
- Salett, Elizabeth Pathy, 11
- stereotypes, 82
- teams, 238, 240
- women, 82
- women as managers survey, 91
- workforce, 14
- see Diversity

Managing ethics competency
- amoral management, 57
- Butler, Stephen, 418
- components, 16
- defined, 4
- discrimination, 384
- Eaton Corp., 336
- e-mail, 394
- employee appraisal, 283
- ethical dilemmas, 17
- ethics behaviors questionnaire, 538
- forcing style, 305
- goals, 173
- Hardis, Stephen, 336
- impression management, 93
- KPMG, 418
- leadership, 329
- living ethics, 440
- medical incentives, 125
- MONY Group, 18
- politics, 283
- résumé, 394
- Sundstrand, 173

Texaco, 384
theft, 154
values, 336
whistle-blowers, 305
see Ethics
Managing self competency
Big Five locator questionnaire, 60
Calico Technologies, 365
career development, 8
career management, 7
challenge course, 106
communication practices survey, 406
conflict interventions, 318
conflict styles questionnaire, 316
Danaher, Cynthia, 3
defined, 4
effective design inventory, 506
Emotional IQ scale, 62
Franklin, Benjamin, 425
gender, 15
glass ceiling, 15
goal setting questionnaire, 185
impression management, 79
individual difference, 301
integrity, 310
job characteristics preferences, 158
job dismissal, 89
leadership, 332
leadership questionnaire, 348
McCoy, Joan, 247
Merck-Medco, 55
Mott's Inc., 79
Naumann, Alan, 365
negotiation, 310
office conflicts, 301
organizational commitment, 55
organizational culture, 514
Papa John's, 141
power in group questionnaire, 287
self-awareness questionnaire, 400
self-efficacy questionnaire, 125
stress assessment questionnaire, 217
stress management, 198, 204
technology workers, 198
time management, 213
trade-offs, 425
Ward, Lloyd, 327
work values questionnaire, 515
Managing teams competency
aircraft engine facility, 469
assessment questionnaire, 257
brainstorming, 253
British Petroleum, 503
Carreño, Lisa Guedea, 392
Carson, Judy, 223
cohesiveness, 243
communication networks, 392
components, 21
conformity, 243
Consolidated Diesel Co., 466
Custom Research, Inc., 223
defined, 5
diversity, 240
FedEx, 254, 367
Ford Motor Co., 251
free rider, 22
goal setting, 170
groupthink, 244
Hewlett-Packard, 48
hot group, 243
IBM, 241
individualism, 22
informal groups, 225
informal leader, 245
leadership, 245
Levi Strauss, 22
Mazza, Merrily, 228
nominal group technique, 252
norms, 242
personality, 48
positive multiculturalism, 241
questionnaire, 240
relations-oriented role, 239
SEI Investments, 159
self-managing teams, 248
self-oriented role, 239
Sims, Paula, 469
Southwest Airlines, 538
Steelcase Incorporated, 104
superordinate goals, 237
task-oriented role, 239
team empowerment, 226
team goals, 237
Tucker, Laurie, 367
virtual organizations, 503
Vroom-Jago Leadership Model, 339–345
Whole Foods Markets, 230, 246
see Teams
Man.com, 526
Market culture, 526
Marriott Hotels, 163
Marriott Marquis, 532
Mary Kay Cosmetics, 116, 520, 528
Marcus, Bernard, 89
Marshall Industries, 175
Matrix design, 495
Maytag, 328
McCulloch Corp., 56
McDonald's, 485, 513
McGraw Hill, 228
Means-end principle, 419
Mechanistic system, 438
Media richness, 379
Mediation, 313
Merck, 166
Merck-Medco, 55
Messages, 380
Meta-communication, 397
Mexico, 73, 195
Microsoft Corp., 332
Might-equals-right principle, 419
Monitor role, 9
Monochronic time schedule, 402
Monsanto, 53, 360
Moral management, 56
Motivating potential score, 459
Motivation
ability, 132
achievement motivation model, 239
affiliation motivation, 139
affiliation needs, 135
banking time off, 181
Basic Process, 130–134
behavioral intentions model, 50
behavioral modification, 118
cafeteria-style benefit plans, 156
challenges, 133
charismatic leadership, 359
compensation, 153
content models, 134–146
contingency of reinforcement, 106
continuous reinforcement, 116
core phases, 132
culture, 138, 143
deficiency needs, 136
defined, 130
diversity, 131
equity model, 150
ERG model, 136
esteem needs, 135
existence needs, 136
expectancy, 147
expectancy model, 146
extrinsic factors, 142
first-level outcomes, 146
fixed interval schedule, 116
fixed ratio schedule, 117
flexible benefit plans, 180
fulfillment–progression process, 137
gain-sharing plans, 179
goals, 133
goal setting, 175
growth needs, 136
growth-need strength, 457
hygiene factors, 142
idealized influence, 366
impression motivation, 78
individualized consideration, 366
inequity, 152
informal groups, 225
instrumentality, 147
intellectual stimulation, 365
intermittent reinforcement, 116
intrinsic factors, 142
job characteristics preferences, 158

job satisfaction, 51
management by objectives, 174
Marriott Hotels, 163
motivating potential score, 459
motivator factors, 142
motivator-hygiene model, 142
needs hierarchy model, 134
negative reinforcement, 111
norms, 121
omission, 112
organizational citizenship behavior, 155
Papa John's, 141
participation, 177
perception, 74
performance appraisal, 177
performance goal orientation, 45
personality, 42
physiological needs, 134
power motivation, 139
primary reinforcer, 108
principle of contingent reinforcement, 108
procedural justice, 153
process models, 146–156
profit-sharing plans, 180
punishment, 112
reinforcement, 107
relatedness needs, 136
reward power, 326
rewards, 107, 110, 172
reward systems, 178
Romania, 138
secondary reinforcer, 108
second-level outcomes, 146
security needs, 134
SEI Investments, 159
self-actualization needs, 135
self-esteem, 42
skill-based pay, 181
Starbucks, 129
teams, 159
Thematic Apperception Test, 139
transactional leadership, 359
transformational leadership, 362–368
valence, 147
variable interval schedule, 116
variable ratio schedule, 117
Walt Disney Co., 151

Motivator factors, 142
Motivator-hygiene model
controversy, 144
cultural influences, 143
defined, 142
extrinsic factors, 142
hygiene factors, 142
intrinsic factors, 142
motivator factors, 142

Motorola, 296
Mott's Inc., 79
Multidivisional design, 491, 497
Multinational organizations, 497

N

NASCAR, 169
Nature-nurture controversy, 39
National Multicultural Institute, 11
NBA Players, 165
NEC, 502
Need for power, 284
Needs, 132
Needs hierarchy model
affiliation needs, 135
defined, 134
diagram, 135
esteem needs, 135
physiological needs, 134
security needs, 134
self-actualization needs, 135

Negative reinforcement, 111
Negotiation
attitudinal structuring, 309
China, 313
compromising style, 307
culture, 311
defined, 308
distributive negotiations, 308
integrative negotiations, 308
intraorganizational negotiations, 310
intergroup dialogue technique, 314
mediation, 313
negotiator's dilemma, 310

Negotiators' dilemma, 310
Network analysis, 274
Network design, 500
Networks as power, 273
New England General Electric, 115
Nike, 71
Nissan, 479
Noise, 383
Nonverbal communication
cultural differences, 402
defined, 401
gender differences, 403
importance, 9
status differences, 403
types of, 401
see Interpersonal communication

Nordstrom, 149, 479
Norms,
behavioral modification, 121
defined, 242
deviates, 100
goals, 242
teams, 235

Northeast Utilities, 305

O

Omission, 112
Operant conditioning, 102
Organic system, 438
Organization design
basic environments, 477
British Petroleum, 503
bureaucratic culture, 524
bureaucracy, 484
chain of command, 486
Cisco Systems, Inc., 488
comparative framework, 482
complexity, 475
defined, 474
differentiation, 494
differentiation strategy, 479
division of labor, 485
dynamism, 476
effectiveness questionnaire, 506
effective design inventory, 506
Electrolux, 499
environments, 475–578
focused strategy, 479
functional design, 487
global networking, 502
hierarchy of authority, 484
horizontal integration, 494
impersonality, 486
integration, 493
Johnson & Johnson, 492
key factors, 475–483
low-cost strategy, 479
matrix design, 495
mechanistic system, 483–487
multidivisional design, 491
multinational design, 491, 497
network design, 198–502
open systems, 502
organic system, 483–487
organizational culture, 474
place design, 489
pooled interdependence, 480
power, 271
procedures, 485
Procter & Gamble, 473
product design, 490
reciprocal interdependence, 481
rules, 485
sequential interdependence, 480
sociotechnical systems model, 450, 462–467
span of control, 486
strategic choices, 478–480
task interdependence, 453, 480
task uncertainty, 452
technological factors, 480–482
uncertainty, 494
U.S. West, 482

virtual organization, 502–504
workflow uncertainty, 452
Organization interests principle, 419
Organizational behavior
competencies, 4–6
defined, 6
environmental forces, 25
individual processes, 25
learning, 26
organizational processes, 28
team and interpersonal processes, 27
Organizational change
see Managing change competency
Organizational citizenship, 155
Organizational commitment. 54
Organizational creativity, 435
see Creativity
Organizational culture
acculturation, 532
Andersen Worldwide, 527
Ben & Jerry's, 423
bureaucratic culture, 524
ceremonies, 519
changing, 521–523
clan culture, 525
conflict, 527
Continental Airlines, 355, 364
crises, 518
cultural symbols, 513
cultural values, 514
DaimlerChrysler, 511
defined, 474
development of, 514–517
diversity, 531
diversity questionnaire, 533
dynamics, 512–523
emergence, 516
entrepreneurial culture, 525
ethic behavior questionnaire, 538
ethical behavior, 529–531
external adaptation and survival, 514
Fel-Pro, 525
framework of, 524
Harley-Davidson, 522
high performance–high commitment work culture, 529
learning organization, 522
levels, 513
internal integration, 514
Kelleher, Herb, 520
learning organization, 522
maintaining, 517–521
Man.com, 526
Mary Kay Cosmetics, 520
market culture, 526
McDonald's, 513
model, 535
organizational socialization, 534–536
participative management, 529
Pennsylvania Chiropractic Assoc., 514
performance, 528
Pharmacia & Upjohn, 517
principled organizational dissent, 530
rewards, 519
rites, 519
shared assumptions, 512
shared behaviors, 512
socialization outcomes, 534
socialization process, 534
Southwest Airlines, 520, 538
status symbols, 519
strong cultures, 528
stories, 520
teams, 518
top management, 516
types of, 523–528
Virgin Group Ltd., 350
whistle-blowing, 530
Whole Foods Markets, 230
work values questionnaire, 515
Organizational politics, 279
Organizational rewards, 110
Organizational socialization
defined, 534
outcomes, 534
process, 534
OxyChem, 513

P

Papa John's Pizza, 141, 167
Participation, 529
Participating style, 338
Participative management, 529
PECO Energy Co., 415
Pennsylvania Chiropractic Assoc. 514
Perception
closure, 75
continuity, 75
creativity, 436
defined, 68
external factors, 71
field dependence/independence, 72
environmental stimuli, 69
halo effect, 83
implicit personality theories, 77
impression construction, 78
impression management, 79
impression motivation, 79
internal factors, 72
interpretation, 69
motivation, 74
perceiver, 77
perceptual defense, 81
perceptual errors, 80
perceptual grouping, 75
perceptual organization, 69, 75
perceptual selection, 71
perceptual set, 72
person perception, 76
primary effect, 77
Pollyanna principle, 75
projection, 83
privacy, 419
projection effects, 83
proximity, 76
response, 69
similarity, 76
stereotyping, 81
stress, 193
time perception, 74
Perceptual defense, 81
Perceptual errors
expectancy effects, 83
halo effect, 83
judgment, 80
perceptual defense, 81
projection, 83
stereotyping, 81
Perceptual grouping, 75
Perceptual organization, 75
Perceptual selection
defined, 71
external factors, 71
internal factors, 72–75
learning, 72
motivation, 74
perceptual set, 72
personality, 72
Perceptual set, 72
Performance
achievement motivation, 139
expectancy model, 148
flexible benefit plans, 180
goal setting, 164, 167
goals, 172
high-performance work system, 178
organizational culture, 528
performance goal orientation, 45
profit-sharing plans, 180
Scanlon plan, 179
skill-based pay, 181
stress, 202–205
Performance appraisal, 177, 283
Performance goal orientation, 45
Perla Hargita, 138
Person perception
defined, 76
errors, 80
influences, 77
Person-role conflict, 300
Personal acceptance conformity, 243
Personality
adjustment, 41
agreeableness, 41
authoritarianism, 48
behavior, 42–48
"Big Five" personality factors, 41
conscientiousness, 41

culture, 40
defined, 38
differences, 38–40
dogmatism, 47
emotional intelligence, 62
environment, 39
external locus of control, 44
extroversion, 47
family, 40
field dependence/independence, 72
general theory of behavior, 38
goal orientation, 45
groups, 40
heredity, 39
intellectual openness, 41
interactionist perspective, 49
internal locus of control, 44
interpersonal conflict, 300
introversion, 47
life experiences, 40
locus of control, 44, 285
Machiavellians, 284
nature-nurture controversy, 39
need for power, 284
neurotic tendencies, 298
perception, 72
performance goal orientation, 45
personality trait, 41
political behavior, 284
risk-seeking propensity, 285
self-esteem, 42
sociability, 41
stress, 206
structure of, 41
Type A inventory, 208
Type A personality, 209
Type B personality, 209
Personality trait, 41
PetSmart, 479
Pharmacia & Upjohn, 516
Physiological needs, 134
Pizza Hut, 141
Place design, 489
Political behavior
avoiding, 282
culture, 286
defined, 279
employee appraisal, 283
forces for, 281
locus of control, 285
Machiavellianism, 285
Machiavellians, 284
organizational politics, 279
personality, 284
political tactics, 281
probability of, 282
risk-seeking propensity, 285
Political model, 429
Pollyanna principle, 75
Polychronic time schedule, 403
Pooled interdependence, 453
Position power, 334
Positive discipline, 114
Positive events, 107
Positive multiculturalism, 241
Positive reinforcement, 107–111
Post-traumatic stress disorder, 202
Power
authority, 267
bilingual employees, 276
coercive power, 268, 327
decision making, 273
defined, 266
effective use, 277
employee appraisal, 283
employees, 275
exchange process, 278
expert power, 270, 327
group norms, 121
influence strategies, 277
intellectual capital, 272
interpersonal sources, 267
knowledge as power, 272
leadership, 326
legitimate power, 269, 326
Machiavellianism, 285
Machiavellians, 284
motivation, 139
need for power, 284
network analysis, 274
networks, 274
organizational currencies, 278
organizational politics, 279
personality, 284
political behavior, 279–287
political model, 428
position characteristics, 272
position power, 334
power in group questionnaire, 287
power relationships, 266
powerlessness, 275
referent power, 270, 327
resources as power, 273
reward power, 268, 326
Ruesch International, 265, 326
stakeholders, 165
structural sources, 271
zone of indifference, 269
Presbyterian Hospital, 101
Primacy effect, 77
Primary reinforcer, 108
Principle of contingent reinforcement, 108
Principle of immediate reinforcement, 109
Principle of reinforcement deprivation, 109
Principle of reinforcement size, 109
Principled organizational dissent, 530
Procter & Gamble, 473, 476, 477, 479, 481, 482, 486, 490, 494, 534
Privacy, 419
Probability of effect, 416
Problem framing, 432
Problem-solving teams, 228
Procedural conflict, 295
Procedures, 485
Procedural justice, 153
Process models of motivation
compared, 156
defined, 146
equity model, 150–156
expectancy model, 146–150
Procter & Gamble, 473
Product design, 490
Productivity, 245
Professional standards principle, 419
Profit sharing, 180
Profits, 423
Projection, 83
Proximity, 76, 417
Punishment
defined, 112
effective use, 114
effects, 113
model, 113
negative effects, 113
positive discipline, 114
undesirable behavior, 112

Q

Quality management, 445
Questioning skill, 8

R

Racism, 15
Radio Shack, 484
Rational model
defined, 424
Franklin, Benjamin, 425
process, 425
trade-offs, 425
Xerox six-step process, 425
Receptors, 379
Reciprocal interdependence, 453
Referent power, 270
Reinforcement, 107–116
Relatedness needs, 136
Relationship behavior, 337
Renaissance, Inc., 429
Resources as power, 273
Reuters, 358

Reversal technique, 437
Reward, 107
Reward power, 268
Reward systems
  alternatives, 183
  banking time off, 181
  flexible benefit plans, 180
  gain-sharing plans, 179
  global issues, 183
  high-performance work systems, 178
  profit-sharing, 180
  skill-based pay, 181
  types of, 179–184
Rewards
  contingent rewards, 359
  culture, 183
  flexible benefit plans, 180
  gain-sharing plans, 179
  goal setting, 163
  IBM, 164
  interpersonal, 110
  Marshall Industries, 175
  material, 110
  organizational, 110
  organizational culture, 519
  profit-sharing plans, 180
  Scanlon plan, 179
  self-administered, 110
  status symbols, 110
Risk propensity, 432
Risk-seeking propensity, 285
Ritz Carlton Hotels, 166, 476
Role, 299
Role ambiguity, 197, 300
Role conflict, 197, 299
Role overload, 195
Romania, 138
Routh Street Brewery, 133
Ruesch International, 265
Rules, 485

S

Salomon, 507
Samsung, 502
Santin Engineering, 25
Satisficing, 426
Scanlon Plan, 179
Schedules of reinforcement, 116
Sears, 531
Second-level outcomes, 146
Secondary reinforcer, 108
Security needs, 134
Self-actualization needs, 135
Self competency
  see Managing self competency
Self-control learning, 103
Self-disclosure, 399
Self-efficacy, 104, 125
Self-esteem, 42
Self-fulfilling prophecy, 84
Self-managed teams, 229, 248–251
Self-serving bias, 88
SEI Investments, 159
Selective perception bias, 433
Selling style, 338
Semantics, 383
Sequential interdependence, 453
Shakespeare, 83
Shared assumptions, 512
Shared behaviors, 512
Siemens, 500
Similarity, 76
Singapore, 72
Skill-based pay, 181
Skill variety, 456
Sociability, 41
Social cognitive theory
  defined, 102
  guidelines, 105
  model, 103
  self-efficacy, 103
Social consensus, 417
Social information processing model, 462
Social system, 463
Socialization, 534
Sociotechnical systems model
  Consolidated Diesel Co., 466
  core concepts, 465
  defined, 450
  implementation, 465
  moderators, 464
  social system, 463
  technological systems, 464
Southwest Airlines, 166, 360, 480, 520, 528, 534, 538, 539
Span of control, 486
Speed, 24
Spokesperson role, 10
Stakeholders, 165
Starbucks, 129, 180, 340
State Farm Insurance Co., 166, 480
Status symbols, 110
Steelcase Inc., 104
Stereotyping
  defined, 81
  gender role, 82, 91
  measure of, 91–93
Stonebriar Country Club, 101
Strong culture, 528
Strategic choices
  defined, 478
  differentiation, 479
  focused 479
  low-cost, 479
  model, 478
Stress
  behavioral effects, 202
  career development, 198
  college students, 201
  defined, 192
  depersonalization, 205
  effects, 201–206
  emotional effects, 202
  fight-or-flight response, 192
  hardy personality, 209
  health, 202
  incidence, 195
  individual differences, 194
  interpersonal relations, 199
  job burnout, 205–207
  job conditions, 196
  life stressors, 200
  past experience, 193
  perception, 193
  performance, 202–205
  personality, 206
  physiological effects, 202
  post-traumatic stress disorder, 202
  role ambiguity, 197
  role conflict, 197
  role overload, 195
  sexual harassment, 199
  social support, 193
  sources, 194
  stress management, 210–216
  technology workers, 198
  Type A inventory, 208,
  Type A personality, 209
  Type B personality, 209
  workplace violence, 199
  work stressors, 194
Stress management
  health care programs, 215
  individual methods, 210
  organizational methods, 211
  perception, 210
  personal vision, 210
  programs, 212
  stress assessment questionnaire, 217
  stress response, 210
  time management, 213
  wellness programs, 213
  work stressors, 212
Structural clues method, 458
Structured problems, 430
Subcultures, 521
Sun Microsystems, 53
Sunbeam, 398
Sundstrand Corporation, 172
Superordinate goals, 237
Sweden, 43, 517
Synergy, 368

T

Tacit knowledge, 428
Taco Bell, 101
Taiwan, 73, 74
Tandem Computers, 232
Task behavior, 337
Task group, 224
Task identity, 456
Task interdependence, 453
Task significance, 457
Task structure, 334
Task uncertainty, 452
Team empowerment, 48, 226
Team goals, 237
Teams
  adjourning stage, 235
  assessment questionnaire, 257
  autonomy, 227
  traditional brainstorming, 253
  clan culture, 525
  cohesiveness, 243
  collaborative software, 230
  collectivism, 236
  conformity, 243
  Consolidated Diesel Co., 466
  context, 236
  Continental Airlines, 355
  creativity, 252
  cross-functional teams, 223, 229, 454
  Custom Research, Inc., 223
  decision making, 246–251
  development stages, 233
  diversity, 238, 240
  effectiveness, 236
  electronic brainstorming, 253
  empowerment questionnaire, 227
  FedEx, 254
  Ford Motor, 251
  forming stage, 233
  free rider, 22
  functional teams, 228
  groupthink, 244
  hot group, 243
  impact, 227
  individualism, 236
  job design, 460
  Kendall-Futuro, Inc., 236
  leaders, 246
  leadership, 245, 355
  Levi Strauss, 22, 234
  managing teams competency, 5
  meaningfulness, 227
  member roles, 239
  nominal group technique, 252
  norming stage, 235
  norms, 242
  organizational culture, 518
  performing stage, 235
  positive multiculturalism, 241
  potency, 227
  problem-solving teams, 228
  productivity, 245
  project team, 415
  relations-oriented role, 239
  self-managed teams, 229, 469
  self-oriented role, 239
  size, 238
  storming stage, 234
  superordinate goals, 237
  task-oriented role, 239
  team empowerment, 226
  team goals, 237
  Texas Nameplate Co., 445
  types, 226
  virtual team, 230
  Whole Foods Markets, 230, 246
Technological factors
  task interdependence, 480
  model, 481
Technology
  defined, 451
  forces, 24
  job characteristics, 461
  job design, 451
  task interdependence, 453
  task uncertainty, 452
  technological systems, 464
  workflow uncertainty, 452
Telecommuting, 395
Telstra, 133
Temporal immediacy, 417
Texaco, 383
Texas Industries, 168
Theft, 154
The Associates, 9, 76
Thematic Apperception Test, 139
Theophrastus, 38
Tinsletown, 476
Towers Perrin, 180
Traditional brainstorming, 253
Traits model of leadership, 329
Transformational leadership, 362
Transformational leadership model
  Bethune, Gordon, 364
  Calico Technologies, 365
  components, 363
  defined, 359
  dimensions, 359
  Higgins, Kierstin, 366
  idealized influence, 366
  inspirational motivation, 364
  intellectual stimulation, 356
  King, Martin Luther, 364
  Naumann, Alan, 365
  questionnaire, 371
  significance, 361, 367
  Shapiro, Robert, 360
  synergy, 368
  Tucker, Laurie, 367
  vision, 359
Transmitters, 379
Traveler's Insurance, 180
Trinity Communications, 70
TRW, 181
Tupperware, 116
Type A inventory, 208
Type A personality, 209
Type B personality, 209

U

Uncertainty, 494
Union Carbide, 115
United Technologies, 490
Unity of command, 486
Unstructured problems, 431
UPS, 485
U.S. Equal Pay Act, 420
U.S. Peace Corps, 74
U.S. West, 482
Utilitarian principle, 419

V

Valence, 147
Values
  Branson, Richard, 350
  China, 21
  cultural values, 512
  culture, 19
  defined, 421
  ethics, 336
  France, 429
  individualism, 20
  work values questionnaire, 515
Vantive Corp., 175
Variable interval schedule, 116
Variable ratio schedule, 117
Verbal communication, 9
Vertical conflict, 302
Vertical loading, 459
Vertical thinking method, 436
Vicarious learning, 103
Vignette Corp., 528
Virgin Group Ltd., 350
Virtual organization, 502
Virtual teams
  defined, 229
  Eastman Kodak, 232
  features, 231
  global, 232
  Tandem Computers, 232
  technology, 231
Vision, 364
Voice mail, 395

Volkswagen AG, 340
Vroom-Jago Leadership Model, 339

W

Wall Street Journal, 89
Wal-Mart, 479, 528
Walt Disney, 150
Waters Consulting Group, 395
Wellness programs
  AT&T, 214
  defined, 213
  importance, 177
  L.L. Bean, 214
Westinghouse, 125, 181
Whistleblowers, 172, 530
Whistle-blowing, 305
Whole Foods Markets, 230
Women in management
  Carreño, Lisa Guedea, 392
  Carson, Judy, 223
  Danaher, Cynthia, 3
  Fiorina, Carly, 323
  glass ceiling, 15
  Higgins, Kierstin, 366
  Holland, Jean, 301
  Leary, Karen, 377
  Matthews, Cassandra, 415
  Mazza, Merrily, 228
  Moffat, Joan, 129
  Sims, Paula, 469
  Tucker, Laurie, 367
Workflow uncertainty, 452
Workplace violence
  defined, 199
  implications, 199
  intrapersonal conflict, 299
Work stress
  see Stress
World Wide Web, 393
Written communication, 9

X

Xerox, 395, 426

Z

Zone of indifference, 269

Internet Organization Index

A
AC-Nielsen
http://www.acnielsen.com/
Advanced Micro Devices, Inc.
http://www.amd.com/
Aetna
http://www.aetna.com/aindex.htm
Alteon Web Systems, Inc.
http://www.alteonwebsystems.com/
American Airlines
http://www.americanair.com/
Amway
http://www.amway.com/
Arthur Andersen
http://www.arthurandersen.com/
Andersen Consulting
http://www.ac.com/
Aon Consulting
http://www.hrservices.aon.com/
Apple Computer
http://www.apple.com/
ARCO Alaska
http://www.ARCOalaska.com/
AT&T
http://www.att.com/

B
Ben & Jerry's Ice Cream
http://www.benjerry.com/
Benteler Automotive Corporation
http://www.benteler.del/home.htm/
Bombay Company
http://www.bombayco.com/
British Petroleum
http://www.britishpetroleum.com/

C
Calico Technologies
http://www.calicotech.com/
Carmike Cinemas
http://www.carmike.com/
Chinese Culture Online Library
http://www.librarycatalog.com/ccol/index/
Chrysler
http://www.chryslercars.com/
Cisco Systems, Inc.
http://www.cisco.com/
Columbia Medical Center of Plano
http://www.columbia-hca.com/
CompUSA
http://www.compusastores.com
Computex Corporation
http://www.computexas.com/
Consolidated Diesel Company
http://www.cdc.com/
Continental Airlines
http://www.continental.com/
Cummins Engine Company
http://www.cummins.com/
Custom Research, Inc. (CRI)
http://www.cresearch.com/

D
DaimlerChrysler
http://www.daimlerchrysler.dc/
Dallas Morning News
http://www.dallasnews.com/
Dell Computer
http://www.dell.com/
Deloitte & Touche
http://www.deloitte.com/
Dolby Laboratories
http://www.dolby.com/

E
Eastman Kodak
http://www.kodak.com/
http://www.eastman.com/
Eaton Corporation
http://www.eaton.com/
Electrolux
http://www.electrolux.com/
Ernst & Young
http://www.ey.com/
Eskom
http://www.eskom.co.za/

F
Fannie Mae
http://www.fanniemae.com/
Federal Express
http://www.federalexpress.com/
Ford Motor Company
http://www.ford.com/
Fruit of the Loom
http://www.fruit.com/

G
General Electric
http://www.ge.com/
Godiva Chocolates
http://www.godiva.com/
Growth and Leadership Center
http://www.glc-corp.com/

H
Harley-Davidson
http://www.harley-davidson.com/
Hewlett-Packard
http://www.hp.com/
http://www.healthcare.agilent.com/mpg/
Highsmith, Inc.
http://www.highsmith.com/
Hoechst-Celanese
http://www.hoechst.com/
Home Depot
http://www.homedepot.com/
Hoovers' Online UK
http://www.hoovers.co.uk/

I
IBM
http://www.ibm.com/
Intel
http://www.intel.com/
International Food Policy Institute
http://www.ifpri.org/
Inc.
http://www.inc.com/incmagazine/archives/

J
J. C. Penney Company
http://www.jcpenney.com/
Johnson & Johnson
http://www.johnsonandjohnson.com/

K
KPMG
http://www.kpmg.com/

M

Man.com
http://www.man.com/
Management Recruiters International
http://www.brilliantpeople.com/
Marriott
http://www.marriott.com/
Marshall Industries
http://www.marshall.com/
Maytag
http://www.maytag.com/
McKinley Marketing Partners
http://www.mckinleyinc.com/
Merck-Medco
http://www.merck-medco.com/
Microsoft Corporation
http://www.microsoft.com/
Monsanto
http://www.monsanto.com/
MONY
http://www.mony.com/
Motorola
http://www.mot.com/
Mott's Inc.
http://www.motts.com.htm/

N

NASCAR
http://www.nascar.com/
Northeast Utilities
http://www.nu.com/
Nuclear Regulatory Commission
http://www.nrc.gov/
Nucor
http://www.nucor.com/
Nynex Corporation
http://www.nynex.com/

P

Papa John's Pizza
http://www.papajohns.com/
PECO Energy Company
http://www.peco.com/
Pharmacia & Upjohn
http://www.pharmacia.se/
Pratt & Whitney
http://www.pratt-whitney.com/
Procter & Gamble
http://www.pg.com/

R

Renaissance, Inc.
http://www.reninc.com/
Reuters
http://www.reuters.com/
Right Start
http://www.rightstart.com/
Ritz Carlton Hotels
http://www.ritzcarlton.com/
Ruesch International, Inc.
http://www.ruesch.com/

S

Santin Engineering, Inc.
http://www.santineng.com/
SEI Investments
http://www.seic.com/
Society for Human Resource Management
http://www.shrm.org/
Southwest Airlines
http://www.southwest.com/
http://www.iflyswa.com/
Southwestern Bell
http://www.swbell.com/
Starbucks
http://www.starbucks.com/
Steelcase
http://www.steelcase.com/
Steinberg & Moorad
http://www.steinbergandmoorad.com/
Sun Microsystems
http://www.sun.com/
Sundstrand
http://www.sundstrand.com/

T

Tandem Division of Compaq
http://www.tandem.com/
Texaco
http://www.texaco.com/
Texas Nameplate Company
http://www.nameplate.com/
Trinity Communications
http://www.trinitycommunications.com/

U

United Technologies
http://www.utc.com/
U. S. News Online
http://www.usnews.com/usnews/issue/970714
U. S. West
http://www.uswest.com/

V

Ventana Corporation
http://www.ventana.com/
Virgin Group Ltd.
http://www.virgin.com/
Visteon Automotive Systems
http://www.visteon.com/
Volkswagen Corporation
http://www.volkswagen.com/

W

Wall Street Journal
http://www.wsj.com/
Walt Disney Company
http://www.disney.com/
Westinghouse Air Brake Company
http://www.wabco-rail.com/
Westinghouse Electric Corporation
http://www.westinghouse.com/
Whole Foods Markets
http://www.wholefoods.com/